AUTHORITARIAN GOVERNMENT v. THE RULE OF LAW

LECTURES AND ESSAYS (1999-2014) ON THE VENEZUELAN AUTHORITARI-
AN REGIME ESTABLISHED IN CONTEMPT OF THE CONSTITUTION

Allan R. BREWER–CARÍAS

Professor of Law, Central University of Venezuela

Fellow, Trinity College, and Simón Bolívar Professor, University of Cambridge, UK (1985–1986).

Professeur Associé, Université de Paris II (1989–1990)

Adjunct Professor of Law, Columbia University, New York, (2006–2008).

Vice President, International Academy of Comparative Law (1982–2010).

AUTHORITARIAN GOVERNMENT

v.

THE RULE OF LAW

LECTURES AND ESSAYS (1999-2014) ON THE VENEZUELAN AUTHORITARIAN REGIME ESTABLISHED IN CONTEMPT OF THE CONSTITUTION

FUNDACIÓN DE DERECHO PÚBLICO

EDITORIAL JURÍDICA VENEZOLANA

Caracas

2014

Hecho el Depósito de Ley
ISBN: 978-980-365-227-2
Depósito Legal: lf54020133402852

Edited by: Editorial Jurídica Venezolana
Avda. Francisco Solano López, Torre Oasis, P.B., Local 4, Sabana Grande,
Apartado 17.598 - Caracas, 1015, Venezuela
Teléfono 762-25-53 / 762-38-42/ Fax. 763-52-39
Email: fejv@cantv.net
http://www.editorialjuridicavenezolana.com.ve

Printed by: Lightning Source, an INGRAM Content company
Distributed by: Editorial Jurídica Venezolana International Inc.
Panamá, República de Panamá.
Email: editorialjuridicainternational@gmail.com

Formatting, Composition and Editing by: Francis Gil,
Letter: Times New Roman, 10.5. Line Spacing: 11.
Dimension text: 19 x 12.5. Dimension book: 22.9 x 15.2

CONTENT

PART FIFTH

THE 2007 CONSTITUTIONAL REFORM ATTEMPT, THE 2009 CONSTITUTIONAL AMENDMENT AND THE ILLEGITIMATE MUTATION OF THE CONSTITUTIONAL

PART SIXTH

REFLECTIONS ON THE ORIGINS OF CONSTITUTIONALISM IN VENEZUELA AT THE BEGINING OF THE 19TH CENTURY

AUTHOR'S NOTE

Since the election of the late Hugo Chávez Frías as President of the Republic of Venezuela in December 1998, this Latin American formerly envied country because of its democratic tradition and accomplishment during the second half of the 20th century, suffered a tragic setback regarding democratic standards, experiencing a continuous, persistent and deliberated institution demolishing process and destruction of democracy, never before occurred in the constitutional history of the country.

The process of subverting democratic principles and values began in 1999, by means of a constitutional-making process developed through a Constituent Assembly that was convened without being established in the then in force 1961 Constitution, that is, against its provisions. Its purpose was to impose the supposedly people's sovereignty over the principle of constitutional supremacy, resulting in the intervention and takeover of all branches of government by the elected Constituent Assembly.

This assault of power allowed the imposition in the country of an authoritarian, centralistic and militaristic government, eliminating, against the Constitution, any sort of check and balance framework, and consequently, the rule of law. It was the same "formula" that leaving aside the Constitution then in force, a few years later was also applied in Ecuador (2007), and ten years later was tried to be imposed in Honduras (2009), in a failed presidential attempt that in that case, the Supreme Court declared unconstitutional. The idea, in any case, continues to be a recurrent one that in many countries has been proposed.

In the initial case of the Constituent Assembly of Venezuela, the former Supreme Court of Justice, in January 1999, instead of imposing the rule of the Constitution, renounced to rule on the unconstitutionality of the proposed unconstitutional formula, being the result of the constitutional constituent process effectively developed, the approval of the new 1999 Constitution discussed by the Constituent Assembly that in the name of the popular will took over and intervened all branches of government except the Executive.

Although considered by many of its drafters as one of the best constitutional texts in contemporary Latin America, for the purpose of the said institutional destruction it has been constantly violated, unfortunately with the acceptance by the new Supreme Tribunal of Justice completely controlled by the Government, particularly its Constitutional Chamber (Constitutional Jurisdiction), that has molded and accepted as legitimate all the constitutional violations that have occurred. And worst of all, that process has been conducted by the Government in contempt of the same Constitution.

In effect, since the sanctioning of the 1999 Constitution and despite all its florid language establishing global values and principles of a Social and Democratic Rule of Law State of Justice, the main provisions of the Constitution regarding for instance the decentralized form of government, the principle of separation of powers, the independence of the judiciary and the representative democratic government, were suspended in their effective enforcement due to an endless transitional constitutional regime that have endured for years, which was illegitimately adopted without the vote of the people. In other cases, the provisions of the Constitution have been in practice distorted and manipulated in an illegitimate way by the same organs of the State, changing their sense or mutating their content.

The result has been the complete lack of the essential elements of democracy as were defined by the 2001 Inter American Democratic Charter, namely the access to power and its exercise subject to the rule of law; the performing of periodic, free and fair elections based on universal and secret vote as an expression of the sovereignty of the people; the plural regime of political parties and organizations; the separation and independence of all branches of government, and the respect for human rights and fundamental freedoms.

This book is a collection of all the essays I have written in English during the past fourteen years, analyzing not only the most important aspects of constitutional law in Venezuela according to the provisions of the 1999 Constitution, but also how an authoritarian government has ruled against the rule of the Constitution, subverting the democratic regime from within, using its institutions and tools. In these essays I have also analyzed how the provisions of the Constitution have been progressively deformed and distorted as a consequence of the authoritarian regime and government the country has suffered since the very moment of the installment of the National Constituent Assembly that sanctioned the Constitution, itself, as mentioned, the product of a violation of the previous Constitution of 1961.

For the purpose of this book, I have preserved the original text of the essays that they had when they were written,* being conscious of the fact that in some cases, some of the same ideas and references are repeated. Nonetheless, I have preferred no to re-write them, in order to serve to understand the testimony I expressed at the time when they were written, on the course of the different events that lead to the complete destruction of the constitutional rule and of the democratic principle in the country.

I have organized all the Essays in Thirty Chapters, within the following Six Parts:

PART ONE *contains the text of the following essays devoted to the study of the* **1999 Constitution Making-Process and the Rule of the Constitution***:*

---

*   Many of the ideas expressed in some of these essays, were the inspiration of some chapters of my book: *Dismantling Democracy. The Chávez Authoritarian Experiment*, Cambridge University Press, New York, 2010, 418 pp.

Chapter I is the essay written in order to analyze, in general terms, the 1999 Constitution Making Process and the development in Venezuela during the past years of an Authoritarian Government in contempt of the Constitution. The origin of this Paper, titled the **"Constitution Making Process in Defraudation of the Constitution and Authoritarian Government in Defraudation of Democracy. The Recent Venezuelan Experience**," was the text written for the initial remarks that I was to deliver at the *1ˢᵗ* **Plenary session of the VII International Congress of Constitutional Law**, held in Athens, on 10-17 June 2007 on **"The Constitution between conflict and stability.**" Unfortunately, following advice based on personal security concerns due to circumstantial attempts of political persecution by the Venezuelan Government, I could not attend the Congress as planned. The text was intended to analyze how the 1999 election of a Constituent Assembly in Venezuela not provided nor authorized in the then in force 1961 Constitution, prevented the establishment of a stable democratic government and, conversely, how it was the main tool used for the consolidation of authoritarianism in contempt of the Constitution and of democracy. A revised version of that paper was published with the title: "Constitution Making in Defraudation of the Constitution and Authoritarian Government in Defraudation of Democracy. The Recent Venezuelan Experience," in Lateinamerika Analysen, 19, 1/2008, GIGA, German Institute of Global and Area Studies, Institute of Latin American Studies, Hamburg 2008, pp. 119-142.

Chapter II is the text of the essay titled "Constitutional Review Models (Reform and Amendments) in Latin America. A Comparative Law Approach," that was the paper written for my presentation on the subject at the **VI International Congress of Constitutional Law**, organized by the International Association of Comparative Law, in Santiago de Chile, January 15, 2014. It was only published in Spanish with the title: "Modelos de revisión constitucional en América Latina," in the book: Walter Carnota y Patricio Marianello (Directores), Derechos Fundamentales, Derecho Constitucional y Procesal Constitucional, Editorial San Marcos, Lima 2008, pp. 210-251; and in Boletín de la Academia de Ciencias Políticas y Sociales, enero-diciembre 2003, Nº 141, Caracas 2004. pp. 115-156.

Chapter III is the text of the Essay on "The 1999 Venezuelan Constitution-Making Process as an Instrument for framing the Development of an Authoritarian Political Regime," in which I specifically deal in detail with the Constitution-Making Process developed in Venezuela in 1999, which precisely resulted in an instrument for framing the authoritarian political regime in the country. It was written for my participation in the **"Project on Constitution-Making, Peace Building and National Reconciliation,**" directed by the United States Institute of Peace, Washington, D.C., and my Presentation at the Conference organized by the Institute in Washington, D.C., in October, 11, 2002. The final version of the paper was published in the book: Laura E. Miller (Editor), Framing the State in Times of Transition. Case Studies in Constitution Making, United States Institute of Peace Press, Washington 2010, pp. 505-531.

Chapter IV is the text of a paper containing my first "Critical reflections on the 1999 Constitution," that I wrote immediately after my work as en Elected Member of the National Constituent Assembly of 1999, a few weeks after the approval of the Constitution. It was the Paper I submitted for my presentation in the **Conference on**

Challenges to Fragile Democracies in the Americas: Legitimacy and accountability, *organized by the* Faculty of Law of the University of Texas, *held in Austin, Texas, on February 25, 2000. An abstract of my oral presentation in the Symposium was published in the* Texas International Law Journal, *University of Texas at Austin, Volume 36, Austin 2001, pp. 333-338. The essay was extensively published in Spanish, specifically in Diego Valadés, Miguel Carbonell (Coordinadores),* Constitucionalismo Iberoamericano del Siglo XXI, *Cámara de Diputados. LVII Legislatura, Universidad Nacional Autónoma de México, México 2000, pp. 171-193; in* Revista Facultad de Derecho, Derechos y Valores, *Volumen III Nº 5, Universidad Militar Nueva Granada, Santafé de Bogotá, D.C., Colombia, Julio 2000, pp. 9-26; and in the book published by the Venezuelan Academy of Political and Social Sciences,* La Constitución de 1999, *Caracas 2000, pp. 63-88.*

Chapter V *is an essay on the contrast between the formal provisions of the constitution and the reality of political facts, titled "Global Values in the Venezuelan Constitution: Some Prioritizations and several In congruencies," which was written as my presentation at the* **Conference en the existence of Global Values explored through National Constitutional Jurisprudence**, *organized by Dennis Davis, Alan Richter and Cheryl Saunders, and held at the* Rockefeller Foundation Bellagio Center, *Bellagio, Italy, on September 22-26, 2008.*

PART TWO *contains the text of following essays devoted to study* **The 1999 Constitution and the Authoritarian Government:**

Chapter VI *on the "Endless Transitory Constitutional Regime that without being approved by the people, suspended in many aspects the enforceability of the Constitution, preventing its complete application," is the text of an essay written between 2001 and 2002, analyzing the "Illegitimate constitutional Transitory Regime adopted by the National Constituent Assembly after the popular approval of the new Constitution." That regime provoked arbitrary decisions that violated the Constitution that were endorsed by the Supreme Tribunal of Justice, who's Magistrates were precisely appointed by such Transitory Regime. The initial version of these reflections was published in Spanish in my book:* Golpe de Estado y Proceso Constituyente, *Universidad Nacional Autónoma de México, México 2002, pp. 341-405; and also in my book* La Constitución de 1999, Derecho Constitucional Venezolano, *Vol. II, Caracas 2004, pp. 1.017-1.115.*

Chapter VII *on "The Impact of the Authoritarian Government Upon Democracy," is the text of an essay on the Inter American Democratic Charter and the situation of the Venezuelan Democratic Regime, written between December 2001 and January 2002 denouncing all the violations to the democratic principles committed already at that time by the Venezuelan Government. The text was initially diffused by Internet and was later published in Spanish in my book:* La crisis de la democracia en Venezuela. La Carta Democrática Interamericana y los sucesos de abril de 2002, *Libros El Nacional, Caracas 2002, pp. 137-218.*

Chapter VIII *on the "The Centralization of Power in a "Centralized Federation", is an essay devoted to study the situation of the Federation in Venezuela, as a highly "Centralized Federation," based on a Paper written for the* **Seminar on Federalism in the Americas... and Beyond**, *organized by Prof. Robert Barker, Duquesne University,* Duquesne School of Law, *Pittsburgh, on November 13, 2004. It* *was published as "Centralized Federalism in Venezuela," in* Duquesne Law Review, *Volume 43, Number 4, Summer 2005, Duquesne University, Pittsburgh, Pennsylvania, 2005, pp. 629-643. Some of the reflections contained in this essay were initially written in the paper on "The Centralized Federation in Venezuela and Subnational Constitutions," for the Conference on* **Federalism and Sub-National Constitutions, Design and Reform,** *organized by the* Center for State Constitutional Studies, Rutgers University, *New Jersey, held at the Rockefeller Foundation Study and Conference Center, in Bellagio, Italy, on May 23-26.*

Chapter IX *on "Venezuela: the End of Federalism?" is the paper written with the collaboration of* Jan Kleinheisterkamp, *as the Venezuelan National Report on the Subject of "Unification of Laws in Federal Systems," for the* **Congress of the International Academy of Comparative Law,** *held in México 2008. The text was initially published as "Unification of Laws in Federal Systems. National Report on Venezuela," in Daniel Halberstam, Mathias Reimann and Jorge A. Sánchez Cordero (Editors),* Federalism and Legal Unification: A Comparative Empirical Investigation of Twenty Systems, *International Academy of Comparative law, Instituto de Investigaciones Jurídicas, Universidad Nacional Autónoma de México, México 2012, pp. 378-391; and a revised version was published as "Venezuela: The End of Federalism?," in Daniel Halberstam and Mathias Reimann (Editors),* Federalism and Legal Unification: A Comparative Empirical Investigation of Twenty Systems, *Springer, London 2014, pp. 523-543.*

Chapter X *on "The Concentration of Powers and Authoritarian Government," is the text of an essay on the principle of separation of powers and Authoritarian Government in Venezuela, written for the* **Seminar on Separation of Powers in the Americas... and Beyond,** *also organized by Prof. Robert Barker,* Duquesne University, School of Law, *Pittsburgh, November 7 and 8, 2008. A first version of these reflections were initially written as "Separation of Powers and Authoritarianism in Venezuela," for the lecture I gave in the* **Constitutional Comparative Law Course** *of Prof. Ruti G. Teitel,* Fordham Law School, *New York City, on February 11, 2008. A further development of this essay was written for the lecture on "Venezuela under Chávez: Blurring between Democracy and Dictatorship?, which I gave at the* University of Pennsylvania Law School, *Philadelphia, April 16, 2009. The text was published as "The Principle of Separation of Powers and Authoritarian Government in Venezuela," in* Duquesne Law Review, *Vol. 47, Number 4, Pittsburgh, Fall 2009, pp. 813-838.*

Chapter XI *on " The Consolidation of Authoritarianism in Defraudation of Democracy," is the text of essay on the Authoritarism in Venezuela built in defraudation of the Constitution initially written for the* **IX Congresso Ibero-Americano de Direito Constitucional e VII Simposio Nacional de Direito Constitucional,** *organized by the Associação Brasileira dos Constitucionalistas Demócratas, Seção Brasileira do Instituto Ibero-Americano de Direito Constitucional, Academia Brasileira de Direito Constitucional, held on November 11-15, 2006, in Curitiba, Parana, Brasil. It was rewritten in 2007 and published in Spanish in* Temas constitucionales. Planteamientos ante una Reforma, *Fundación de Estudios de Derecho Administrativo, Caracas 2007, pp. 13-74.*

Chapter XII is an essay written to analyze the grave *"Restrictions to Freedom of Expression, imposed by the Supreme Tribunal in Venezuela, in 2007, after the shout-down of a TV Station (RCTV)," that the government considered was opposing it, achieving the judicial confiscation of its assets, possession and private property. It was submitted as a paper to the* **Notre Dame Law Review Symposium on Freedom of Expression in Latin America**, *Centre for Civil and Human Rights, University of Notre Dame, The Law, School, March 29, 2010.*

Chapter XIII is the text of the essay on *"Global Administrative Law on International Police Cooperation: A Case of Global Administrative Law Procedure," written between 2007 and 2009, in order to study the procedure in order to stop the international political persecution attempts made by the authoritarian government of Venezuela against dissidents, improperly using the channels of Interpol. It was first discussed in the* **Seminar on Global Security Challenges. Anticipating Answers before New Threats**, *organized by the* **Universidad Internacional Menéndez Pelayo**, *and sponsored by* Fundación Alfonso Martín Escudero, *held in La Línea de la Concepción, Campo de Gibraltar, Cádiz (Spain), on October 20, 2008. It was published as: "Global Administrative Law on International Police Cooperation: A Case of Global Administrative Law Procedure," in Javier Robalino-Orellana and Jaime Rodríguez-Arana Muñoz (Editors),* Global Administrative Law Towards a Lex Administrativa, *Cameron May International Law & Policy, London 2010, pp. 343-395.*

PART THREE, on the **Lack of Judicial Independence and Judicial Review**, *contains the text of following essays:*

Chapter XIV is the text of the Presentation I gave on *"The Process of Dismantling the Rule of Law, and the political submission of the Judiciary," before the* **New York City Bar Committee on Inter-American Law**, *at the New York City Bar, New York, October 5th, 2010.*

Chapter XV is an essay containing an *"Overview of the Judiciary and the lack of judicial independence," written for the purpose of up-dating the text of the previous Chapter, in order to prepare different* **Legal Opinions** *I gave in 2010 and 2011 on the situation of the Judiciary in Venezuela under the Authoritarian Government. Its content was included in my article "Sobre la ausencia de independencia y autonomía judicial en Venezuela, a los doce años de vigencia de la constitución de 1999 (O sobre la interminable transitoriedad que en fraude continuado a la voluntad popular y a las normas de la Constitución, ha impedido la vigencia de la garantía de la estabilidad de los jueces y el funcionamiento efectivo de una "jurisdicción disciplinaria judicial"), published in Spanish in the book:* Independencia Judicial, *Colección Estado de Derecho, Tomo I, Academia de Ciencias Políticas y Sociales, Acceso a la Justicia org., Fundación de Estudios de Derecho Administrativo, Universidad Metropolitana, Caracas 2012, pp. 9-103.*

Chapter XVI on *"The Citizen's Access to Constitutional Jurisdiction: Special Reference to the Venezuelan System of Judicial Review," is the modified text of the essay written for my presentation at the* **Round-Table Conference of the International Association of Constitutional Law, IACL** *on* "Challenges to the consolidation of the Rule of Law and of Democracy in Latin America – compared experiences", *held in Porto de Galinhas, State of Pernambuco, Brazil, 23-25 August, 2009.*

The original text was published in Cuadernos de Soluções Constitucionais, N° 4, *Associaçào Brasileira de Constitutionalistas Democratas, ABCD, Malheiros Editores, São Paulo 2012, pp. 13-29.*

Chapter XVII *on "The Illegitimate Judicial Mutation of the Constitution," is an essay written for the Lecture I gave on the Constitutional Judge and the Destruction of the Rule of Law, at the* **Administrative Law Seminar of Professor Eduardo García de Enterría, in the Complutense University of Madrid,** *on April 1ˢᵗ, 2009. The text was devoted to specifically analyzed the deviations of judicial review when the Constitutional Court is controlled by the Government, as happens in Venezuela; and was published as "El juez constitucional al servicio del autoritarismo y la ilegítima mutación de la Constitución: el caso de la Sala Constitucional del Tribunal Supremo de Justicia de Venezuela (1999-2009)," in* Revista General de Derecho Administrativo, N° 21, *Ed. Iustel, Madrid 2009, ISSN-1696-9650; and in* Revista de Administración Pública, *N° 180, Madrid 2009, pp. 383-418; and with the title: "La ilegítima mutación de la Constitución por el juez constitucional y la demolición del Estado de derecho en Venezuela," in* Revista de Derecho Político, *N° 75-76, Homenaje a Manuel García Pelayo, Universidad Nacional de Educación a Distancia, Madrid, 2009, pp. 291-325.*

Chapter XVIII *on* **"***Constitutional Litigation in Venezuela: General Trends of the Amparo Proceeding and the Effects of the Lack of Judicial Independence," is a Paper written for my Presentation at the* **Seminar on Constitutional Litigation: Procedural Protections of Constitutional Guarantees in the Americas ... and Beyond,** *organized by Professor Robert S. Baker, Duquesne University School of Law, Pittsburgh, November 5, 2010. The complete text was published as "The Amparo Proceeding in Venezuela: Constitutional Litigation and Procedural Protection of Constitutional Rights and Guarantees," in* Duquesne Law Review, *Vol. 49, Number 2, Pittsburgh, Spring 2011, pp. 161-241.*

Chapter XIX *on "The Situation of the Judiciary in Venezuela as an Instrument for Political Persecution," is the text prepared for the Presentation I made at the Forum on Political Use of the Judicial System, The State of Justice in Latin America, organized by the* **American Forum for Freedom and Prosperity and the Inter American Institute for Democracy,** *at the United States Capitol, Rayburn House Office Building, Room B340, Washington, October 8ᵗʰ, 2013.*

PART FOUR *contains the text of following essays devoted to study of* **The Mixed Economic System established in the Constitution, and its Distortions by the policy of the Authoritarian Government:**

Chapter XX *on the processes of "The destruction of the Economy: Statizaton, Nationalization, Expropriation and Confiscation of Private assets and Enterprises," has its origin in an essay I wrote analyzing the "Recent Compulsory Take Over Process of Private Economic Activities in Venezuela," that followed, in contemporary times, the paths of the nationalization of the oil industry in 1975, but with the main difference that not always compensation were satisfied. One initial part of the essay, as: "The 'Statization' of the Pre 2001 Primary Hydrocarbons Joint Venture Exploitations: Their Unilateral termination and the Assets' Confiscation of Some of the Former Private parties," was published in* **Oil, Gas & Energy Law Intelligence,** *www.gasandoil.com/ogel/ ISSN: 1875-418X, Issue Vol. 6, Issue 2, (OGEL/TDM*

Special Issue on Venezuela: The battle of Contract Sanctity vs. Resource Sovereignty, edited By Elizabeth Eljuri), April 2008; and in Spanish in Víctor Hernández Mendible (Coordinador), Nacionalización, Libertad de Empresa y Asociaciones Mixtas, *Editorial Jurídica Venezolana, Caracas 2008, pp. 123-188.*

Chapter XXI *on "The Pro-Arbitration Trend of the 1999 Constitution and the Anti-Arbitration Policy of the Authoritarian Government: Venezuela Before ICSID," is an* **essay** *based on different* **Legal Opinions** *I gave, as an Expert Witness, in various Arbitration Cases before* **ICSID Arbitral Tribunals.**

Chapter XXII *on "The Imposition of a Socialist (Communist) Economic System by Statute, without Reforming the Constitution," is a Paper prepared for the Panel on Doing Business in Hostile Environments: The case of Venezuela, Ecuador and Bolivia, organized by Columbia International Arbitration Association (CIAA); and Columbia Latin-American Business Law Association (CLABLA), and held at* **Columbia Latin-American Week**, **Columbia Law School** */ New York, April 11 2011.*

PART FIFTH *contains the text of following essays devoted to study* **The 2007 Constitutional Reform Attempt, the 2009 Constitutional Amendment and the Illegitimate Mutation of the Constitution:**

Chapter XXIII *is the text of an essay written in order to analyze the* Constitutional Reform Draft *submitted by the late President Chávez to the National Assembly in 2007, which was rejected by the people in the Referendum held on December 2007, and that was designed for the consolidation of an Authoritarian, Socialist, Centralized, Repressive and Militarist State and Government. The reflections contained in this essay were incorporated in my book published in Spanish:* Hacia la consolidación de un Estado socialista, centralizado, policial y militarista. Comentarios sobre el sentido y alcance de las propuestas de reforma constitucional 2007, *Editorial Jurídica Venezolana, Caracas 2007, 157 pp. The text also oriented the essay written after the popular rejection of the Reform Draft, ans published in my book:* La reforma constitucional de 2007 (Comentarios al proyecto inconstitucionalmente sancionado por la asamblea nacional el 2 de noviembre de 2007), *Editorial Jurídica Venezolana, Caracas 2007, 224 pp.; and in the following articles: "La reforma constitucional en Venezuela de 2007 y su rechazo por el poder constituyente originario," in* Revista Peruana de Derecho Público, *Año 8, N° 15, Lima, Julio-Diciembre 2007, pp. 13-53; and "La proyectada reforma constitucional de 2007, rechazada por el poder constituyente originario," in* Anuario de Derecho Público 2007, *Año 1, Instituto de Estudios de derecho Público de la Universidad Monteávila, Caracas 2008, pp. 17-65.*

Chapter XXIV *on "The Alternate Principle of Government and the 2009 Constitutional Amendment on Continuous Re-Election," is the text of a paper written in 2009 dealing with the 2009* Constitutional *Amendment that was approved after the rejection of the same constitutional review proposal in 2007, by a referendum held on February 2009. Through this Amendment, the alternate character of government was changed, establishing in the Constitution the possibility for the continuous and indefinite reelection of the President of the Republic that was previously restricted. It was initially written with the title "Venezuela 2009 Referendum on Continuous Reelection: Constitutional implications" for the Panel Discussion on* Venezuela Referendum: Public Opinion, Economic Impact and Constitutional Implications,

Moderated by Christopher Sabatini, **Americas Society/Council of the Americas**, *held in New York, February 9, 2009. The text was published in Spanish as "El Juez Constitucional vs. La alternabilidad republicana (La reelección continua e indefinida), in* Revista de Derecho Público, *Nº 117, (enero-marzo 2009), Caracas 2009, pp. 205-211.*

Chapter XXV *on "The "Bolivarian Revolution" and Venezuelan Constitutional Law," is the text of the essay written for my Presentation at the* **33d. Conference of the German Society of Comparative Law**, **Legal Limits of Liberty and Legal Protection**, *held in Trier, Germany, September 16, 2011. It was published in Uwe Kischel und Christian Kirchner (Coord.),* Ideologie und Weltanschauung im Recht, *Gesellschaft für Rechtsvergleichtung e.V., Rechtsvergleichung und Rechtsvereinheitlichung, Mohr Siebeck, Tübingen 2012, pp. 121-148*

Chapter XXVI *is the text of the paper on "The "Bolivarian Revolution" in Venezuela and the Regime's Contempt for Constitutional Law. The Popular Power and the Communal State, or the Creation of a XXI Century Neo-Communist State by-passing the Constitution," based on the ideas expressed in the essay included in the previous Chapter, and that was used for my Presentations on "The "Deconstitucionalization" of the Venezuelan State and the Creation of a Communal State By-Passing The Constitution," delivered at the* Inter-American Bar Association, *Washington, September 21, 2012; at the* **Venezuelan Democracy Caucus, Western Hemisphere Subcommittee**, *Washington, DC, November 8, 2011; ant at the Seminar on* **Venezuela 2012. The Next Generation Hosts a Roundtable Discussion on Challenges to and Prospects for Growth and Stability**, *Liechtenstein Institute on Self-Determination at Princeton University, Princeton NJ, November 18th, 2011. The ideas expressed in such Papers were later followed in the paper written for my Presentation at the Seminar on* **Current Constitutional issues in the Americas ... and Beyond, Duquesne University School of Law**, *Pittsburgh, 9/10 November 2012, which was published as "The Process of "Deconstitutionalization" of the Venezuelan Constitutional State, as the Most Important Current Constitutional Issue in Venezuela," in* Duquesne Law Review, *Volume 51, Number 2, Spring 2013, Pittsburgh 2013, pp. 349-386.*

Chapter XXVII *is the text of the essay "About the Popular Power and the Communal State in Venezuela (Or how a Socialist State is imposed on the Venezuelan People, Violating the Constitution and Defrauding the Will of the People," written in December 2010, once the* Popular Power Organic Laws *were sanctioned. Reflections on such legislation were latter published with the title: "La Ley Orgánica del Poder Popular y la desconstitucionalización del Estado de derecho en Venezuela," in* Revista de Derecho Público, *Nº 124, (octubre-diciembre 2010), Editorial Jurídica Venezolana, Caracas 2010, pp. 81-101; and with the title:* **"Las leyes del Poder Popular dictadas en Venezuela en diciembre de 2010, para transformar el Estado Democrático y Social de Derecho en un Estado Comunal Socialista, sin reformar la Constitución," in Cuadernos Manuel Giménez Abad, Fundación Manuel Giménez Abad de Estudios Parlamentarios y del Estado Autonómico, Nº 1, Madrid, Junio 2011, pp. 127-131. A complete analysis of the statutes was latter published as** *"Introducción General al Régimen del Poder Popular y del Estado Comunal (O de cómo en el siglo XXI, en Venezuela se decreta, al margen de la Consti-*

*tución, un Estado de Comunas y de Consejos Comunales, y se establece una socie-
dad socialista y un sistema económico comunista, por los cuales nadie ha votado),"
in the book: Allan R. Brewer-Carías, Claudia Nikken, Luis A. Herrera Orellana,
Jesús María Alvarado Andrade, José Ignacio Hernández y Adriana Vigilanza,* **Leyes Orgánicas sobre el Poder Popular y el Estado Comunal (Los consejos comunales, las comunas, la sociedad socialista y el sistema económico comunal)**
*Colección Textos Legislativos N° 50, Editorial Jurídica Venezolana, Caracas 2011,
pp. 9-182*

Chapter XXVIII *is the text of the Paper written for the Presentation I made on
"The situation of the Venezuelan state after the April 2013 Presidential Elections:
The Chávez's Institutional Legacy," at the Program on "Presidential election and
beyond," organized by the* **Venezuelan American Association of the United States**,
New York, April 9, 2013.

PART SIXTH, *with* **Reflections on the Origins of Constitutionalism in Venezuela at the Beginning of the 19th Century**, *contains the following essays:*

Chapter XXIX on **"Reflections On The Interesting Official Documents Relating to the United Provinces of Venezuela,** *published in London in 1812 (2012), is
an essay originally written for the Lecture I gave on the* **"The** *Connection Between
the United States Independence and the Hispanic American Independence Movement, and the* **Role Played by** *some Key Books Published at the beginning of the Xix
Century," in the* **Law Library of Congress**, *Mumford Room, on November 22nd,
2011, on the occasion of the Bicentenary of the publication of the book:* Interesting
Official Documents Relating to the United Provinces of Venezuela, London 1812.
The text was later extended and published as the General Introduction of the book
Constitutional Documents of the Independence, with the facsimile edition of the
book Interesting Official Documents Relating to the United Provinces of Venezuela,
London 1812, Editorial Jurídica Venezolana, Bilingual Edition, Caracas 2012, pp.
59-299 of Venezuela, London 1812, Editorial Jurídica Venezolana, By lingual Edi-
tion, Caracas 2012, pp. 59-299.

Chapter XXXX *on "Alexis De Tocqueville and Simon Bolívar. Two Approaches
on the Principles of Modern Constitutionalism," is the text of an essay I wrote confronting their ideas on principles like Participation, Representation, Sovereignty of
the People, Republicanism, Limited Government, Federalism and the Constitution,
at the beginning of the nineteen century, on the occasion of the Bicentennial of the
collapse of the First Republic in Venezuela after the Spanish Army invasion in 1812,
as a consequence of the declaration of Independence and the establishment of the
Venezuelan State. The text was written for a Lecture that was to be delivered in
2012.*

Almost all these essays were written in New York, where since 2005 I have been
living due to the political persecution I have suffered from the Venezuelan Government. They all follow the same line of thoughts that have oriented my analysis of the
authoritarian government developed by the late Hugo Chávez since his election as
President of the Republic in 1998, after having failed in his 1992 military coup
d'État attempt he promoted against the democratic government. That authoritarian
government, without doubts, has been the main political legacy that he left after his

death, and that after 2013, his designated political heirs have been erratically trying to manage, although in the most incompetent, felonious and corrupt way.

Since the presidential campaign of 1998, being myself at that time President of the Venezuelan National Academy of Political and Social Sciences, I strongly opposed not only the Chávez's candidacy because lacking of any democratic values, having enter into the Venezuelan political arena after his failure in the 1992 military coup; but also, his main political electoral offer and proposal of convening a Constituent Assembly not provided in the Constitution, through a simple "consultative referendum." My first reflections on these matters were published that same year 1998, as "Reflexiones sobre la crisis del sistema político, sus salidas democráticas y la convocatoria a una Constituyente," that was the Introduction to the book: Los Candidatos Presidenciales ante la Academia. Ciclo de Exposiciones 1998, *Academia de Ciencias Políticas y Sociales, Caracas 1998, pp. 9-66, in which all the main proposals of all the 1998 presidential candidates, including Chávez, were analyzed.*

In particular, my opposition to his political project of beginning a constitution-making process in contempt of the rule of the 1961 Constitution continued during 1999 when I personally challenged before the former Supreme Court of Justice, on grounds of unconstitutionality, the Chávez's Decree convening the National Constituent Assembly as a mean for constitutional reform. Although a correction of the Decree was forced through some judicial decisions, my opposition to his political project persisted during the months of functioning of the Constituent Assembly, to which I was elected as an independent candidate. Together with other three distinguish Venezuelans politicians and thinkers; we formed the very tiny but substantive minority opposition group of an Assembly that resulted to be completely dominated by Chávez, confronting his authoritarian project.

Once the new Constitution was drafted, I continued my opposition by promoting the negative vote to its approval through referendum, because considering that its authoritarian, centralistic and militaristic trends serve to allow the unlimited concentration and centralization of State powers, as unfortunately occurred. Once the Constitution was approved by the vote of the people, since 2000 and in the following years, I continued denouncing all the successive antidemocratic, centralistic and militaristic decisions and measures taken by the Government, writing books, essays, lectures and speeches, many of them already published in Spanish and some in English.

The fact is that the authoritarian government that the country has suffered during these past fourteen years, has limited and restricted all rights and freedom, particularly, personal freedom and property rights, and freedom of expression, and has criminalized all dissidence, using for such purpose as instruments for persecuting, not only the Public Prosecutor Office that has been at the service of the Executive, but basically, the judicial system, which has been packed up with temporal and provisional judges, completely subjected to political control. Other public powers with functions of control simply appear to be inexistent, like the People's Defendant, an institution embedded in the Constitution, but about which almost nobody have heard, particularly in moments of grave violations of human rights like those that were precisely occurring in the country when I am was finishing to write this Note.

In February 2014, in effect, serious incidents of violence took place in the most important cities of the country in the context of student's protest demonstrations, particularly after the protesters were attacked by pro-government armed civilian groups, and the State security agents used disproportionate force against the un-harmed students. All these facts, were accompanied by State's acts of censorship against media outlet and news blackout imposed on them; signal cutting of foreign news channel transmitting in Venezuela via cable television and expulsion of jour-nalist of major TV international channels; attacks on organizations that defend hu-man rights; and acts of political persecution against opposition leaders and their families. In the events, some unarmed students were assassinated by military, para-military and security forces; students were arrested and taken into custody at mili-tary and State's Intelligence Service facilities; where some were tortured, held in-communicado, and were not allowed to have initial contact with their lawyers or relatives. In addition, during those incidents, some governmental officials made public statements stigmatizing and disparaging civil society groups identified with the opposition, evidencing unacceptable governmental political intolerance in a way contrary to the full possibility of exercising human rights, placing civil society groups in a position of greater vulnerability and risk. The consequence was that despite the florid words of the 1999 Constitution, the authoritarian government de-nied in Venezuela any effective guarantee regarding the right to life, humane dignity and security, as well as political rights, the right of assembly, the rights of freedom of association and the right of freedom of expression.

That is why I want to offer the publication of this collection of Essays to all those that even facing persecution, continue to publicly express their opinion against an authoritarian regime that has dismantled the institutions, the values, the social net-work and the economy of the country, using the uncontrolled oil revenue as a weap-on to create a system in which all activities are controlled and depends on the State; a State that is conducted by an incompetent, corrupt and uncontrolled bureaucracy that has used the extended system of social subsidies, not for socially developing the country, but as a mean to produce an unjust and extensive misery, only explained by the destruction of almost all private mean of production.

With that same economic weapon, the same authoritarian government has also distributed and disposed abroad, in an un controlled way, national revenues, unfor-tunately buying and neutralizing many consciences in the international community, only interested in the economic profits that could derived from having in the country a "stable authoritarianism," which has prevented any kind of international reac-tion. This has eventually place Venezuelans, who in the Independence two hundred years ago gave their life seeking freedom in so many other Latin American coun-tries, and who more recently, protected and sheltered so many Latin Americans from dictatorship persecutions; in an extraordinary international situation of soli-tude and isolation, witnessing the inhibition of other countries to even trying to en-force the most elemental principles of the Inter-American Democratic Charter of 2001, which seems to be no more than a death letter in the Continent.

New York, February 2014

PART ONE

THE 1999 CONSTITUTION MAKING-PROCESS AND THE RULE OF THE CONSTITUTION

CHAPTER I

CONSTITUTION MAKING-PROCESS IN CONTEMPT OF THE CONSTITUTION AND AUTHORITARIAN GOVERNMENT IN DEFRAUDATION OF DEMOCRACY

(2007)

This Chapter is the text of the Paper on "Constitution Making Process in Defraudation of the Constitution, and Authoritarian Government in Defraudation of Democracy. The Recent Venezuelan Experience," written for the purpose of being the initial remarks on "The Constitution between conflict and stability," that I was asked to deliver at the 1st *Plenary session of the VII International Congress of Constitutional Law*, which was held in Athens, on June 10-17, 2007. A revised version of that paper was published with the title: "Constitution Making in Defraudation of the Constitution and Authoritarian Government in Defraudation of Democracy. The Recent Venezuelan Experience," in *Lateinamerika Analysen*, 19, 1/2008, GIGA, German Institute of Global and Area Studies, Institute of Latin American Studies, Hamburg 2008, pp. 119-142.

I

In modern constitutionalism, the Constitution, as a political pact sanctioned by the representative of the people, has always been the result of political conflicts, whether for their prevention or their conclusion, and consequently, has always tended to create democratic institutions in order to achieve political stability. This, of course, is the situation in democratic regimes, because in authoritarian ones, the Constitution, even covered by democratic veils when approved by voters, always remains as the sole expression of a ruler's will.

The question, of course in democratic regimes imposes the need to determine to what extent Constitutions can contribute to resolve conflict and to create stable democratic governments; or in other words, how Constitutions must be adopted in order to effectively prevent conflicts and build stable democratic institutions.

The fact is, as constitutional history shows, that those goals have not always been achieved; Constitutions not being the magical instrument many think they are to guarantee the ending of political conflicts or the founding of a permanent stability. The real possibility for a Constitution to contribute to both resolve and prevent conflicts and assure stability basically depends on the way constitution making processes are conceived and developed and how Constitutions are drafted and adopted.

During the past two hundred years, all kind of constitutional review proceedings have been experienced, and still the ideal path of a constitution making process in order for a Constitution to contribute to resolve conflict and create stable democratic government has yet to be designed. However, one thing is clear and definitive: no constitution making process in a given country implemented by one political or social faction to impose a way of life or a specific political and economic system endures. In such cases, conflicts are not definitively resolved and constitution making processes restart, sometimes over and over in an endless process.

II

Latin American countries have had a long history of constitution making processes by means of Constituent Assemblies many times convened and elected without being regulated in the Constitutions.

This has generally occurred after a factual rupture of the legal constitutional order produced by a *coup d'Etat*, a revolution, or a civil war. In such cases, the Constituent Assembly has always been convened by the winners and later, the sanctioned Constitution is legitimized by the new leadership. In these matters, without doubts and historically, Latin American countries have a recognized expertise constructed during almost two hundred years of political turmoil.

In such cases, the elected Constituent Assemblies normally have exercised unlimited constitution making power, pretending to represent the will of the people without being subject to the provisions of the previous Constitution. Nonetheless, some stony principles or clauses imposed by the republican form of government have always been preserved.

However, in the past decades a new constitution making process has taken shape in Latin America also by mean of the election of Constituent Assemblies, in some cases regulated in the Constitutions as was the case in Bolivia where in 2008 a Constitutional Assembly was convened according to the provisions of the 2004 Constitution; but in many cases, not regulated in the Constitutions, although without previous rupture of the constitutional order. In these latter cases, the convening of the Constituent Assembly has been made by means of judicial interpretation of the Constitution and through democratic elections, as was the case in Colombia in 1991, in

Venezuela in 1999 and in Ecuador in 2007.[1] Among this new modality, the case of Venezuela must be highlighted because in 1999 a rupture of the constitutional order effectively occurred but in an *ex post facto* manner, made by the same Constituent Assembly once elected. In such case, the *coup d'Etat* was given by the Constituent Assembly itself.[2]

That is why this new constitution making process can be characterized as being done in defraudation to the Constitution, because the latter has been deliberately used and interpreted in order to elect a body with the final purpose of violating the same Constitution used to give birth to the Assembly, and, as has also happened in Venezuela since 1999, to set forth the foundations for the enthroning of an authoritarian regime and an institution demolishing process, in this case done in defraudation to democracy. That is, using relatively free but manipulated elections leading to a democracy destruction process, and the consolidation of an authoritarian government.

III

The first fraudulent event committed against the Venezuelan Constitution occurred in January 1999, when the then newly elected President, Hugo Chávez Frías, following the Colombian experience in 1991, convened a referendum without constitutional authorization in order to ask the opinion of the people regarding the installment of a National Constituent Assembly.[3] The referendum took place in April 1999; the convening of a Constituent Assembly was approved, and it was elected on

---

1   It was not the case in Honduras where after the proposal made in such sense by President Manuel Zelaya following foreign influences, trying to implement in June 2009 a popular referendum regarding the convening of a Constituent Assembly, the Supreme Court of Justice of the country ruled declaring such proposal contrary to the Constitution. In the case of Honduras, not only the Constituent Assembly is not a valid procedure for constitutional review, not being provided in the Constitution, but its express provisions prohibits any public official, including the President, to even propose reforms to the Constitution in order to alter the principle of alternate government and to change the prohibition established for presidential reelection, which is conceived as a "rocklike" principle. The Constitution even establishes that any public official that proposes such reform will immediately ceased in his functions (Article 239). The actions of the President provoked the functioning of the democratic check and balance system of his country (the Supreme Electoral Tribunal, the Supreme Court, the Attorney General, the Human Rights Commissioner and the Congress declared the President intention unlawful), but unfortunately the Military intervened expelling the President from the country, in what the international community considered as a *coup d'État*.

2   See Allan R. Brewer-Carías, *Golpe de Estado y proceso constituyente en Venezuela*, Universidad Nacional Autónoma de México, México 2002, pp. 181 ff.

3   See the political discussion regarding the constitution making process proposed in Allan R. Brewer-Carías, *Asamblea Constituyente y ordenamiento constitucional*, Biblioteca de la Academia de Ciencias Políticas y Sociales, Caracas 1999, pp. 38 ff.

June 1999, in a process where the principle of popular sovereignty was forced to prevail over the principle of constitutional supremacy.[4]

Although with a different phraseology, but with the exact sense and content, in January 2007, the then newly elected President of Ecuador, Rafael Correa, also convened a referendum in order to ask the people about the convening and election of a National Constituent Assembly not established nor regulated in the 1998 Constitution still in force. After three months of bitter political and institutional conflicts, the referendum took place last April 15th, approving the presidential proposal.

In the three cases: the 1991 Colombian, which evolved democratically, the 1999 Venezuelan, which has produced eight subsequent years of endless political conflicts, and the 2007 Ecuadorian, which produced the 2008 Constitution, the common trend is that the constitution making process was initiated without any constitutional foundation, but also without any previous *de facto* rupture of the Constitution, being the interpretation of the existing Constitution which allowed the election of the Constituent Assemblies. So in Colombia, Venezuela and Ecuador, no *coup d'Etat* preceded the election of the Constituent Assembly, as was the Latin American tradition.

In the case of Venezuela, as aforementioned, such Constituent Assembly was the one that gave a "constituent" *coup d'Etat* against the then in force 1961 Constitution and against all the existing constituted powers accordingly elected. In this case, the existing Constitution (1961) and all democratic tools were fraudulently used to violate the Constitution, setting forth the basis for the progressive undermining of the democratic form of government, and allowing the authoritarian seizure of all the State branches of government by the new political forces supporting the President, crushing the traditional political parties.

Such purposes, of course, were not previously announced, explained nor proposed to the people when the President convened in 1999 the Constituent Assembly by forcing the provisions of the then existing 1961 Constitution. The main motives publicly proposed were ones that hardly anybody could possibly challenge and that everybody was willing to support, particularly in situations of political crisis of the State institutions and of the party system: to achieve the process of reform of the State institutions and to improve democracy.

The Venezuelan people in January 1999, like the Ecuadorian people in 2007, needed to know in advance and before the voting and election of the Constituent Assembly what kind of institution were being proposed to conduct the constitution making process.

From the text of the January 2007 Presidential Ecuadorian decree, the Constituent Assembly proposed to be elected was not only one for the drafting "of a new

---

4   See Allan R. Brewer-Carías, "El desequilibrio entre soberanía popular y supremacía constitucional y la salida constituyente en Venezuela en 1999," in *Revista Anuario Iberoamericano de Justicia Constitucional,* N° 3, 1999, Centro de Estudios Políticos y Constitucionales, Madrid 2000, pp. 31-56. See also Allan R. Brewer-Carías, *Asamblea Constituyente y Ordenamiento Constitucional,* Academia de Ciencias Políticas y Sociales, Caracas 1999, pp. 152 ff.

Constitution," but in addition, one with "full powers in order to transform the institutional frame of the State." Nonetheless, according to the by-laws of the Assembly, all those possible decisions could only have effects after the approval of the new Constitution through referendum. Nonetheless, this provision approved in the April 2007 referendum, unless the Constitutional Tribunal would had clarify its contents and meaning before the election of the Constituent Assembly on September 2007 - which did not happen-, lead, as happened in Venezuela in 1999, to a Constituent Assembly with two different and basic missions: first, to transform the institutional framework of the State; and second, to write the draft of a new Constitution. The first mission -as was the case in Venezuela- could signify a Constituent Assembly with full and unlimited powers to transform the institutional framework of the State during its functioning with the possibility to interfere in all the constituted branches of government, for example, removing or limiting the government; dissolving the Congress, assuming the legislative function; intervening in the provincial and municipal powers; removing the Justices of the Supreme Court, the Supreme Electoral Tribunal and the Constitutional Tribunal; the General Comptroller of the State, and in general, intervening in the Judiciary and the Public Prosecutors' Office.

That is why, precisely, the main subject on the constitutional discussion that took place in Ecuador during the first month of 2007 referred to the establishment of limits to the "full powers" attributed to the Constituent Assembly in order to assure the respect of the terms of the constituted powers that had just been elected in December 2006. To realize the intensity of the bitter political conflicts derived from that discussion during the first months of 2007, for instance, it is enough only to bear in mind the subsequent institutional decisions that were adopted in only three month, from January to April 2007.[5] Once the Supreme Electoral Council received the Presidential decree in January 16th, according to the Constitution but with the manifest opposition of the President, the Tribunal decided to submit the Decree to the Congress for its approval. The Congress then issued a decision considering urgent the convening of the Assembly, but introducing modifications to the original presidential Decree. The Supreme Electoral Tribunal ignored the Congress' decision, and on March 1st convened the referendum only according to the original Presidential Decree with some modifications proposed by the President himself. The Congress, by a vote of 57 of its members, decided to dismiss the President of the Supreme Electoral Tribunal because he ignored the Congress' decision, and the Congress also decided to challenge the Supreme Electoral Tribunal's decision before the Constitutional Tribunal because they considered it unconstitutional. In response to these actions, the Supreme Electoral Tribunal dismissed the 57 Congressional representatives who adopted such decision because they interfered with a voting process, even though the current Constitution only establishes the possibility for a recall referendum for

---

5   See Allan R. Brewer-Carías, "El inicio del proceso constituyente en Ecuador en 2007 y las lecciones de la experiencia venezolana de 1999. Videoconference, University San Francisco de Quito, April 19, 2007. See in www.allanbrewercarias.com, Section I, 1 (Conferencias), 942 (2007).

such purposes. Before the referendum took place on April 15th a few "amparo" actions were filed not only before the Constitutional Tribunal, but also before various lower courts arguing that the representatives were unconstitutionally dismissed. Some of the amparo judges granted constitutional protection to the dismissed representatives, ordering their reincorporation to Congress, a decision that was accepted by the President of the Congress, notwithstanding that the previous week, he had sworn their substitutes. Then, the Supreme Electoral Tribunal decided to dismiss the lower courts judges that had granted the amparo protection, ignoring their judicial adjudication that protected the dismissed representatives, considering them invalid. The President also considered those amparo decisions invalid, even though the Constitutional Tribunal considered them obligatory as any constitutional judicial decision. Members of the Supreme Electoral Tribunal threatened to dismiss the members of the Constitutional Tribunal because they admittedly considered some of the amparo actions filed against the convening of the referendum. Once the referendum took place on April 15[th,] the Constitutional Tribunal after reviewing one of the lower courts' amparo decisions ruled granting constitutional protection to fifty of the dismissed representatives to Congress, ordering their reincorporation. The Congress, this time integrated by a new and different majority because of the substitutes already sworn in, on April 23rd considered exhausted the term of the Magistrates of the Constitutional Tribunal from January 2007 which has given rise to endless discussions regarding the validity of all the Constitutional decisions adopted by the Tribunal since January 2007.

Thus, as can be deduced from this intense three months institutional quarrel, the constitutional discussion regarding the powers of the Constituent Assembly were not ended, and on the contrary, because before the election of the Assembly on September 2007 the matter was not resolved, the bitter political conflict that occurred after the installment of the Assembly continued aggravated, due to the natural tendency of such bodies to assume global powers.

IV

In general terms, this was precisely what happened in Venezuela in 1999 through the convening and election of the Constituent Assembly which resulted in the sanctioning of the 1999 Constitution.

It was not the first Constituent Assembly convened in Venezuelan constitutional history,[6] but in contrast with all the other historical Constituent Assemblies, the 1999 one, as was the 1991 Colombian Constituent process and the 2007 Ecuadorian one, as aforementioned, had the peculiarity of not being the result of a factual rupture of the constitutional order because of a revolution, a war or a *coup d'Etat*, but

---

6   See the text of all the previous Venezuelan Constitutions (1811-1961) in Allan R. Brewer-Carías, *Las Constituciones de Venezuela*, Biblioteca de la Academia de Ciencias Políticas y Sociales, Caracas 1997. Regarding the constitutional history behind those texts, see this author's "Estudio Preliminar" in the same book, pp. 11-256.

the result of a process developed under a democratic rule although in the middle of the most severe political crisis of the democratic system.[7]

As mentioned, what characterized such process in Venezuela was that the *coup d'Etat* was given by the same Constituent Assembly after being elected in July 1999, which brushed aside the then in force 1961 Constitution whose interpretation had served to allow its birth.

It is important to highlight the Venezuelan process not only because it marks a new trend to constitution making processes in Latin America done in defraudation of the Constitution, but because of the lessons that can be learned from it in order to avoid its repetition, or if repeated, to be aware of their meaning; in particular, those implying the fraudulent use of the Constitution and democratic elective tools for the establishment of a system founded in the violation of the former and in the demolition of the latter. All of which has exploited the peoples' legitimate hopes and expectations for the need of a political recompose of the State as a consequence of the decline of the party system.

In the middle of the terminal crisis of the Venezuelan political centralized democratic multiparty system that had functioned since 1958, its necessary redesign in order to assure its governance imposed the need to search for new political instruments to assure democratic conciliation between the political forces by means of political pacts or consensus among all the political actors and factions of society, for which purpose the convening of a Constituent Assembly could be justified and needed.[8] Accordingly, in the decree convening a Constituent Assembly issued by President Chávez on February 1999, the question submitted to popular vote referred to the election of a Constituent Assembly "with the purpose to transform the State and to create a new juridical order allowing the effective functioning of a social and participative democracy." Such was the formal *raison d'étre* of the 1999 Venezuelan Constituent process, a purpose that was difficult for anybody to contradict.

---

7   See Allan R. Brewer-Carías, *La crisis de las instituciones: responsables y salidas,* Cátedra Pío Tamayo, Centro de Estudios de Historia Actual (mimeo) Facultad de Economía y Ciencias Sociales, Universidad Central de Venezuela, Caracas 1985; also published in *Revista del Centro de Estudios Superiores de las Fuerzas Armadas de Cooperación,* N° 11, Caracas 1985, pp. 57-83; and in *Revista de la Facultad de Ciencias Jurídicas y Políticas,* N° 64, Universidad Central de Venezuela, Caracas 1985, pp. 129-155. Also see Allan R. Brewer-Carías, *Instituciones Políticas y Constitucionales,* Vol. I (*Evolución histórica del Estado),* Universidad Católica del Táchira, Editorial Jurídica Venezolana, San Cristóbal-Caracas, 1996, pp. 523-541.

8   See Allan R. Brewer-Carías, "Reflexiones sobre la crisis del sistema político, sus salidas democráticas y la convocatoria a una Constituyente," in *Los Candidatos Presidenciales ante la Academia.* Ciclo de Exposiciones 10-18 Agosto 1998, Biblioteca de la Academia de Ciencias Políticas y Sociales, Caracas 1998, pp. 9-66; also published in *Ciencias de Gobierno* N° 4, Julio-Diciembre 1998, Gobernación del Estado Zulia, Instituto Zuliano de Estudios Políticos Económicos y Sociales (IZEPES), Maracaibo, Edo. Zulia, 1998, pp. 49-88; and in Allan R. Brewer-Carías, *Asamblea Constituyente y ordenamiento constitucional,* Biblioteca de la Academia de Ciencias Políticas y Sociales, Caracas 1999, pp. 13-77.

But what the country expected at that moment was a constitution making process based on political conciliation for which the participation of all society sectors needed to be assured. Nonetheless, this was not achieved, and those were not the intentions of the convening actors. What in fact resulted, due to the aggressive anti-party and anti-representative democracy presidential campaign and to the lack of effective popular participation, were the accentuation of the differences among political sectors and the reinforcement of the fractioning of the country. So, far from being a mechanism for dialogue and peace consolidation, the constitution making process served to aggravate the existing political crisis.

V

Nowadays, ten years after the 1999 constitution making process, in spite of the political verbalism and the exuberant spending and waist of an immense fiscal income of a rich State in a poor country, the result has been that no effective reform of the State was achieved in order to improve the social and participatory democracy, the process resulting in the configuration of a centralized and concentrated authoritarian regime that seeks to impose a Socialist model of society, covered with a democratic-elective veil in which the destruction of the direct representative democracy has been almost completed through centralized populist programs and institutions pretending to be participatory.

In this sense, it is possible to consider that from the democratic point of view, the 1999 Constitution making process was a failure, and if it is true that the country has experienced important political changes, what they have provoked is the accentuation of the crisis of the democratic system through the concentration of all power in the President's hands and through the centralization of all the former territorial and local governments which have limited representation. This process has, of course, caused great changes in the political actors of the country due to the seizure of all political power by new groups that with extreme hate and resentment insufflated by the President's well orchestrated speeches, diffused by the controlled State media, have crushed the traditional parties and has accentuated the differences among Venezuelans in a context of extreme political polarization, making conciliation even more difficult.[9]

But from the authoritarian and antidemocratic point of view, the 1999 Constitution making process conversely can be considered a success, because it allowed the complete takeover of all political power by only one faction or person and party which has been used to crush all the others, opening wounds and social and political rivalries which for decades were unknown in the country, reinforcing social and

---

9   See Allan R. Brewer-Carías, "El proceso constituyente y la fallida reforma del Estado en Venezuela" in *Estrategias y propuestas para la reforma del Estado,* Universidad Nacional Autónoma de México, México 2001, pp. 25-48; also published in Allan R. Brewer-Carías, *Reflexiones sobre el constitucionalismo en América,* Editorial Jurídica Venezolana, Caracas 2001, pp. 243-253.

political conflicts and destroying the democratic institutions that during half a century took so many efforts to build.

The 1999 crisis of the democratic and representative party system, in fact, imposed upon the Venezuelan leadership to seek for its transformation, but not for its destruction and demolition. What was needed for the democratic system was its improvement in order to give way to a more participative democracy which, of course, can only take place at local government levels with autonomy. Such was the main objective the people wanted to achieve through the constitution making process in 1999, drafting the effective decentralization of the Federal State, and transforming the Centralized Federation the country has had for decades into a decentralized democracy for participation.

In the modern world, consolidated democracies have always been the result and at the same time the cause of political decentralization, that is, decentralization has been a consequence of the democratization process and at the same time, it has been a condition for democracy's survival and improvement. Thus, decentralization is the political instrument designed in a democracy to articulate all the intermediate political powers within the territory, allowing the accomplishment of government actions close to the regions, communities and the people. That is why decentralized autocracies have never existed, being the decentralization a matter of democracies.

The convening of a Constituent Assembly in Venezuela in 1999, after more than 40 years of democratic regime, was supposed to have had that purpose of accentuating the democratic principle through the decentralization of power, but not to destroy it, as has been happening during the past decade with the transformation of the Federal form of government into a simple constitutional label stamped over a completely centralized State ruled by one person who at the same time, is the Head of the State, the Head of the Executive, the Head of Public Administration, Head of the military, the Head of the ruling single socialist party, and who has pretended to be called "the Leader."

Another aspect that needed the most important reforms in Venezuela referred to the equilibrium, or checks and balances, between the branches of government. This was another objective that everybody sought to achieve through the constitution making process of 1999, particularly regarding the system of government, that is, the relations between the executive and legislative power. Paradoxically, the crisis of the democratic governance in the nineties was not due to the excess of presidentialism, but to the excess of party parliamentarism, particularly due to the tight political control the parties exercised over the Congress. In particular, for instance, regarding the classical problem of the exclusively partisan nomination and appointment of the non elected high public officials of State, like the Justices of the Supreme Court, the head of the General Comptroller Office, the Public Prosecutors Office, the Peoples Defendant Office and the Supreme Electoral Council, nasty criticisms were made due to the excessive partisan character of such appointments which were always made without any possibility of civil society organizations' participation. The need for reform in such matters was directed to assure more balance between the independent powers and more effective checks among them, limiting their partisan's conformation; and in particular to build a complete independent and autonomous Judiciary. But none of these reforms have been applied because of the absolute concentration of State powers that has developed during the past seven years.

VI

The mechanism adopted in order to achieve all these reforms in Venezuela in 1999 was the convening of a Constituent Assembly which as mentioned, at the time had great support as an instrument for the introduction of reforms to reframe democracy and to allow the effective participation in the political process of all sectors, many of which were excluded from the democratic practice due to the monopoly that the traditional political parties exercised over political representation and participation.

Notwithstanding all its benefits, the proposal was not supported by the traditional political parties which ignored it and rejected it. Their ignorance about the magnitude of the political crisis was pathetic, so the convening of the Constituent Assembly turned out to be the only and exclusive political project of Chávez, initially as presidential candidate, and later, in the beginning of his term in December 1998, as President elected.

But the election of the Constituent Assembly in 1999 faced the already mentioned basic constitutional obstacle derived from the fact that such institution was not established in the text of the in force 1961 Constitution as a system for constitutional review which only provided for two systems for such revision, the amendment process for partial reforms and the general reform of the Constitution. In this regard, as mentioned, the constitutional situations in Colombia in 1991 and in Ecuador in 2007 were very similar.

That is why, after the December 1998 presidential election, the political discussion ceased to be about the need for the convening of a Constituent Assembly and turned to be about the way to do it, and particularly, about if it was necessary or not to previously amend or reform the 1961 Constitution in order to create the institution and establish its regime before its election. The discussion, or course, refers to the already mentioned dilemma that always exists in moments of political crisis and constitutional revision between constitutional supremacy and popular sovereignty and about the weight that one or the other principle must have in modern constitutional States.

But since the matter of constitutional reform is more political than legal, before the Supreme Court could issue any ruling as was requested by civil society organizations, the elected President publicly announced his intention, as his first act of government to be issued on his inauguration day (February 2, 1999), to convene the Constituent Assembly by decree based only in the provision of the 1961 Constitution which referred to the principle of popular sovereignty, giving prevalence to that principle over constitutional supremacy.

For such purpose, the previous week (January 19th 1999) the Supreme Court, after being the target of direct and open political pressure from the elected President, unfortunately ruled in a very ambiguous way without resolving the main question of the need for a previous reform of the Constitution before the Assembly could be convened. On this matter, the Court, in its decision, just referred in theoretical ways to the traditional constitutional doctrine on the constituent power, including quotations from the 1789 writings of the Abate Sieyès; quotations that were subsequently used by those that were defending the argument of the possibility of convening a Constituent Assembly even if it was not established in the Constitution.[10]

The result of this ambiguous ruling was the presidential decree convening the consultative referendum proposing not only the election of a Constituent Assembly, but to allow the President itself to define its composition, duration, mission and limits. The President pretended to convene a "blind" referendum on a Constituent Assembly without previously defining and submitting to popular vote its composition, the number of representatives to be elected, the electoral system to be applied, and its mission, duration and limits.

The Presidential decree, of course, was challenged multiple times before the Supreme Court on the grounds of being unconstitutional[11] and after a few rulings, one issued on March 18th 1999, imposed the National Electoral Council to submit to the popular vote not only the question about the convening of the Assembly, but also the complete text of its bylaws that the President was forced to produce.[12] This was the

10   See comments on the decisions in Allan R. Brewer-Carías, "La configuración judicial del proceso constituyente o de cómo el guardián de la Constitución abrió el camino para su violación y para su propia extinción," *in Revista de Derecho Público,* N° 77-80, Editorial Jurídica Venezolana, Caracas 1999, pp. 453-514.; Allan R. Brewer-Carías, *Asamblea Constituyente y Ordenamiento Constitucional,* Academia de Ciencias Políticas y Sociales, Caracas 1999, pp. 152-228; .Allan R. Brewer-Carías, *Golpe de Estado y proceso constituyente en Venezuela,* Universidad Nacional Autónoma de México, México 2002, pp. 65 ff.; Lolymar Hernández Camargo, *La Teoría del Poder Constituyente. Un caso de estudio: el proceso constituyente venezolano de 1999,* Universidad Católica del Táchira, San Cristóbal 2000, pp. 53 ff.; Claudia Nikken, *La Cour Suprême de Justice et la Constitution vénézuélienne du 23 Janvier 1961,* Thèse Docteur de l'Université Panthéon Assas, (Paris II), Paris 2001, pp. 366 ff.

11   See the text of the challenging action this author brought before the Supreme Court in Allan R. Brewer-Carías, *Asamblea Constituyente y Ordenación Constitucional,* Academia de Ciencias Políticas y Sociales, Caracas 1999, pp. 255-321. Regarding the other challenging actions brought before the Supreme Court, see Carlos M. Escarrá Malavé, *Proceso Político y Constituyente,* Caracas 1999, Exhibit 4. See Allan R. Brewer-Carías, "Comentarios sobre la inconstitucional de la convocatoria a Referéndum sobre una Asamblea Nacional Constituyente, efectuada por el Consejo Nacional Electoral en febrero de 1999" in *Revista Política y Gobierno,* Vol. 1, N° 1, enero-junio 1999, Fundación de Estudios de Derecho Administrativo, Caracas 1999, pp. 29-92.

12   See the text of the March 18, 1999, March 23, 1999, April 13, 1999, June 3, 1999, June 17, 1999, and July 21, 1999, Supreme Court decisions in *Revista de Derecho Público,* N° 77-80, Editorial Jurídica Venezolana, Caracas 1999, pp. 73-110.; and in Allan R. Brewer-Carías, *Poder Constituyente Originario y Asamblea Nacional Constituyente,* Editorial Jurídica Venezolana, Caracas 1999, pp. 169-198 and 223-251. See comments in Allan R. Brewer-Carías, "Comentarios sobre la inconstitucional convocatoria a referendo sobre una Asamblea Nacional Constituyente efectuada por el Consejo Nacional Electoral en febrero de 1999," *Revista*

path followed in January 2007 in Ecuador by President Correa, without a doubt, learning from the Venezuelan experience. Nonetheless, like in Ecuador, even with this judicial correction, the content of the bylaws of the Constituent Assembly was unilaterally imposed by the President, and was not the result of any kind of agreement or negotiation between the various interested political sectors.

Regarding the by-laws of the Constituent Assembly, the Venezuelan Supreme Court, in April 13, 1999 expressly ruled that the Assembly, had to be elected within the framework of the judicial interpretation of the 1961 Constitution, and could not have "original constituent powers" as was proposed by the President, expressly ordering the National Electoral Council to eliminate from the by-laws to be submitted to the April 25th referendum those pretended full and unlimited powers.[13]

The consultative referendum took place on April 25th 1999, approving the convening of a Constituent Assembly, which gave way for the election on July 1999 of the 141 members of the Assembly. All but four[14] of these members were proposed by the President, which caused the Assembly to lack any sense of pluralistic character. The constitution making process was, on the contrary, conducted with a total exclusion of the traditional political parties of the country, the Assembly being oriented and conducted personally by the President through his followers.

An Assembly conformed in such way, of course was not a valid instrument for dialogue, political conciliation, negotiation and consensus; on the contrary, it was the exclusive political tool used by the group supporting the President to impose their own ideas upon the rest of society and the political spectrum with total exclusion of other groups and of any political participation. It was the main political tool used by the newly elected officials to complete the seizure of all political power and to control all the branches of government, even eliminating the political parties from the scene.

VII

One thing was initially clear, the 1999 Venezuelan Constituent Assembly was not elected in order to govern the country or to substitute all the elected branches of government; it had neither "full powers" or "original constituent powers," as was expressly decided by the Supreme Court when ruling on the challenged bylaws proposed by the President for the Assembly's election. In principle it had the particular

---

Política y Gobierno, Vol. I, N° 1, Fundación de Estudios de Derecho Administrativo, Caracas, Enero-Junio 1999, pp. 29-92; and in Allan R. Brewer-Carías, *Golpe de Estado y proceso constituyente en Venezuela,* Universidad Nacional Autónoma de México, Mexico 2002, pp. 160 ff

13   In particular, see the Supreme Court decisions of April 13, 1999, June 17, 1999 and July 21,1999, in *Revista de Derecho Público,* N° 77-80, Editorial Jurídica Venezolana, Caracas 1999, pp. 85 ff.; and in Allan R. Brewer-Carías, *Poder Constituyente Originario y Asamblea Nacional Constituyente,* Editorial Jurídica Venezolana, Caracas 1999, pp. 169-198, 223-251.

14   This author was one of the four "opposition" elected members of the 1999 National Constituent Assembly.

mission of drafting a new Constitution and was due to function in parallel with the constituted branches of government that were elected in November 1998, particularly, the National Congress, the States' Legislatures and Governors and the Municipal Councils and Mayors.

Nonetheless, in its first installment session, through the vote of the overwhelming majority of its members and without any constitutional support, the Assembly proclaimed itself as having "original constituent power," and in particular, the powers to "limit or to decide to cease the activities of the authorities conforming the branches of government," setting forth in its internal by-laws that "all the State entities are subordinated to the National Constituent Assembly and are obliged to execute and to provide for the execution of the public acts issued by the Assembly."[15]

In this way, by proclaiming itself as a super State power, the Assembly set forth the provisions in order to give a *coup d'Etat* by usurping and intervening in all branches of government in violation of the 1961 Constitution, provoking the rupture of the constitutional order. Accordingly, during its first month of its functioning (August-September 1999), the Assembly intervened in all the constitute branches of government that had been elected a few months earlier by declaring their reorganization,[16] in particular, intervening in the Judiciary and creating a "Judicial Emergency Commission" (still acting in 2009) which substituted the existing Judiciary Council harming the autonomy and independence of the courts;[17] ruling on the functioning of the Legislative Power by abolishing both the Senate and the Chamber of representatives and dismissing the elected senators and representatives, as well as the

---

15   See in *Gaceta Constituyente (Diario de Debates), Agosto-Septiembre 1999,* Session of August 3d, 1999, N° 1, p. 4. See the author's dissenting vote in *Gaceta Constituyente (Diario de Debates), Agosto-Septiembre 1999*, Session August 7th, 1999, N° 4, pp. 6-13; and in Allan R. Brewer-Carías, *Debate Constituyente, (Aportes a la Asamblea Nacional Constituyente)* Vol. I *(8 agosto-8 septiembre 1999)*, Fundación de Derecho Público, Caracas 1999, pp. 15-39.

16   Decree of August 12, 1999. See the text in *Gaceta Constituyente (Diario de Debates), Agosto-Septiembre de 1999,* Session August 12, N° 8, pp. 2-4, and in *Gaceta Oficial* N° 36.764 de 13-08-99. See this author's dissenting vote in Allan R. Brewer-Carías, *Debate Constituyente (Aportes a la Asamblea Nacional Constituyente),* Vol. I *(8 agosto-8 septiembre 1999)*, Fundación de Derecho Público, Caracas 1999, pp. 43-56.

17   Decree of August 19, 1999. See the text in *Gaceta Constituyente (Diario de Debates), Agosto-Septiembre de 1999,* Session de August 18, 1999, N° 10, pp. 17 a 22, and in *Gaceta Oficial* N° 36.782 de 08-September-1999. See this author's dissenting vote in Allan R. Brewer-Carías, *Debate Constituyente (Aportes a la Asamblea Nacional Constituyente),* Vol. I *(8 agosto-8 septiembre 1999)*, Fundación de Derecho Público, Caracas 1999, p. 57-73. See the comments in Allan R. Brewer-Carías, *Golpe de Estado y Proceso constituyente en Venezuela,* Universidad Nacional Autónoma de México, México 2002, pp. 184 ff.; and in Allan R. Brewer-Carías, "La progresiva y sistemática demolición institucional de la autonomía e independencia del Poder Judicial en Venezuela 1999-2004" in *XXX Jornadas J.M Domínguez Escovar, Estado de derecho, Administración de justicia y derechos humanos*, Instituto de Estudios Jurídicos del Estado Lara, Barquisimeto 2005, pp. 33-174.

State Legislative Assemblies representatives.[18] The Assembly also intervened in the local government autonomous entities (Municipalities) and suspended the local elections that were scheduled for that same year, 1999.[19]

No doubt, that first period of the Constituent Assembly's rule was a time of confrontation and political conflict among all branches of government and the country's various political factions since the Assembly was in no way a means for dialogue and peace consolidation nor an instrument to avoid conflict. On the contrary, the Assembly was the elected instrument for confrontation, conflict and crushing all opposition or dissidence, allowing a new political faction to seize control of all powers, conducted by the direct instructions of the President of the Republic.

VIII

Once all the branches of government were intervened in violation to the 1961 in force Constitution, the Assembly's second period (September - October 1999) was devoted to draft a new Constitution, for which purpose the Assembly did not dispose of any integral draft to be followed in the discussions which could allow public and popular participation. On the contrary, the Assembly, in its second month of functioning began to draft the new Constitution in a collective way, abandoning the orthodox way characterized by the previous drafting of a constitutional project generally by a plural Constitutional Commission in order for its subsequent discussion.

The adopted model, turned out to be the less adequate, characterized by the appointment within the Assembly of twenty different, and isolated Commissions with the mission of drafting twenty different chapters of the Constitution. To such purpose the Assembly only devoted one month in which only scattered requests for advice from other institutions were made. No open participation by interest groups in each Commission was possible. By the end of September 1999, the twenty Commissions submitted to a Constitutional Commission, also appointed within the Assembly, the drafts of the twenty chapters of a Constitution they had prepared, comprising of more than 800 articles. A "Constitutional Commission" had the task of integrating such number of provisions into a reasonable text that could serve as a Constitution draft that the Commission accomplished in the very brief term of two weeks, preventing any possible public discussions and any possible popular participation.

---

18   Decree of August 28, 1999. See the text in *Gaceta Constituyente (Diario de Debates), Agosto-Septiembre 1999,* Session of August 25, 1999, N° 13. See this author's dissenting vote in Allan R. Brewer-Carías, *Debate Constituyente (Aportes a la Asamblea Nacional Constituyente),* Vol. I *(8 agosto-8 septiembre 1999),* Fundación de Derecho Público, Caracas 1999, pp. 75-113.

19   Decree of August 26, 1999. See the text in *Gaceta Constituyente (Diario de Debates), Agosto-Septiembre 1999,* Session of August 26, 1999, N° 14, pp. 7-8, 11, 13 and 14; and in *Gaceta Oficial* N° 36.776 de 31-08-99. See the author's dissenting vote in Allan R. Brewer-Carías, *Debate Constituyente (Aportes a la Asamblea Nacional Constituyente),* Vol. I *(8 agosto-8 septiembre 1999),* Fundación de Derecho Público, Caracas 1999, pp. 115-122.

The result was that in October 1999 the Constitutional Commission handed over to the Assembly a very deficient draft of 350 constitutional articles, conforming a conglomerate or catalogue of wishes, petitions, grievances and good intentions, without any substantive consideration to the basic aspects of the organization of the State.[20]

The haste imposed by the government in order to have the new Constitution sanctioned as soon as possible, forced the Assembly to discuss and approve those 350 articles of the Constitution after only 22 days of discussions which were held between October and November 1999: 19 plenary sessions devoted to the first discussion, and only 3 sessions to the second discussion.[21]

Within this short period of time subjected to an irrational and hastily pressure imposed by the President, no political participation or public debate on the basic constitutional issues was possible, so popular participation was reduced to watching television broadcasts of the Assembly sessions. The basic principles of the Constitution, such as the presidential system of government, the separation of powers, the decentralization process, federalism, local government, military status, or the basic principles of the political system such as democracy, representation, participation, rule of law, human rights or economic system, were not a matter of public discussion nor of any debate in the Assembly. In addition, no public educational program was designed in order to allow the incorporation of civil society groups or non-governmental organizations to the debate with exception made to the indigenous peoples who were directly represented in the Assembly.

Those who controlled the work of the Assembly were conscious that participation required time and instead they have chosen the fast track without participatory procedure. The result was that political participation eventually was reduced just to voting, first, in the consultative referendum on the convening of the Constituent Assembly in which only a turnout of 37% of the registered voters occurred; second, in July 1999, in the election of the members of the Assembly, which had only a turnout of 46% of the registered voters; and third, in December 1999, in the approval referendum of the new Constitution, with only a turnout of 44% of registered voters.

IX

The 1999 Constitution, in any event and from the democratic point of view, did not result to be the promised document according to the question submitted to the people in the April 25th consultative referendum seeking to assure the transformation of the State and the democratic system; in the sense that it did not conform to the

---

20   This author was also member of the Constitutional Commission. See the difficulties of its participation in the drafting process in Allan R. Brewer-Carías, *Debate Constituyente (Aportes a la Asamblea Nacional Constituyente)*, Vol. II (9 Septiembre-17 Octubre), Fundación de Derecho Público, Caracas 1999, pp. 255-286.

21   See the text of all of this author's 127 dissenting or negative votes in Allan R. Brewer-Carías, *Debate Constituyente (Aportes a la Asamblea Nacional Constituyente)*, Vol. III (18 Octubre-30 Noviembre), Fundación de Derecho Público, Caracas 1999, pp. 107-308.

new vision that was needed to consolidate the democratic principles and to achieve the political reorganization of the country substituting the centralized party and State system for a decentralized one.[22]

On the contrary, the result was the consolidation in the Constitution of an author-itarian system of centralized government based in the State intervention in the econ-omy, helped by the disposal of the uncontrolled public oil income, with a reinforced presidentialism that has concentrated and controlled all State powers with a sharp anti-party tendency and a military power framework never before incorporated in the Constitution, nowadays fueled by a single party system which is being embodied within the State.

It has been within this constitutional framework that during the past eight years an authoritarian government has been consolidated in Venezuela with a President that after ten years in office has succeed in his persistent effort to amend the Consti-tution in order to assure the possibility of his indefinite reelection, which was ap-proved by referendum in 2009, and contrary to the will of the people rejecting his constitutional reform proposals in 2007, in defraudation of the Constitution has been erasing the federation and has been building a Socialist State above the debris of the demolished democratic institutions.

All these trends found their origin in the 1999 constitution making process, which far from being a mean for political conciliation of the country, accentuated the fundamental differences within social classes, multiplied and increased the polit-ical fractionation of the country, and provoked the extreme polarization which now

---

22   See this author's critical comments regarding the new Constitution expressed immediately after its approval, in his papers on "Reflexiones Críticas y Visión General de la Constitución de 1999," Inaugural Lecture on the *Curso de Actualización en Derecho Constitucional*, Aula Magna de la Universidad Católica Andrés Bello, Caracas, February 2, 2000; on *"La Consti-tución de 1999 y la reforma política, Colegio de Abogados del Distrito Federal*, Caracas, February 9, 2000; on "The constitutional reform in Venezuela and the 1999 Constitution," Seminar on *Challenges to Fragile Democracies in the Americas: Legitimacy and accounta-bility*, organized by the Faculty of Law, University of Texas, Austin, February 25, 2000; on "Reflexiones Críticas sobre la Constitución de 1999," *Seminario Internacional: El Constitu-cionalismo Latinoamericano del Siglo XXI en el marco del LXXXIII Aniversario de la Pro-mulgación de la Constitución Política de los Estados Unidos Mexicanos*, Cámara de Diputa-dos e Instituto de Investigaciones Jurídicas UNAM, México, January 31, 2000; on *"La nueva Constitución de Venezuela del 2000,"* Centro Internationale per lo Studio del Diritto Compa-rato, Facoltà di Giurisprudenza, Facoltà di Scienze Politiche, Universita'degli Studi di Urbi-no, Urbino, Italia, March 3, 2000; and on "Apreciación General sobre la Constitución de 1999," *Ciclo de Conferencias sobre la Constitución de 1999, Academia de Ciencias Políticas y Sociales*, Caracas, May 11, 2000. The text of these papers were published in Diego Va-ladés, Miguel Carbonell (Coordinadores), *Constitucionalismo Iberoamericano del Siglo XXI*, Cámara de Diputados. LVII Legislatura, Universidad Nacional Autónoma de México, Méxi-co 2000, pp. 171-193; in *Revista de Derecho Público*, N° 81, Editorial Jurídica Venezolana, Caracas, enero-marzo 2000, pp. 7-21; in *Revista Facultad de Derecho, Derechos y Valores*, Volumen III N° 5, Universidad Militar Nueva Granada, Santafé de Bogotá, D.C., Colombia, Julio 2000, pp. 9-26; and in *La Constitución de 1999*, Biblioteca de la Academia de Ciencias Políticas y Sociales, Caracas 2000, pp. 63-88.

exists. That process also served as the main instrument in order to assure that one and only one political group supporting the President could seize all powers of the State and take absolute control of all the institutions; all fueled by the extraordinary increase of public funds to be disposed without control. That is, the 1999 constitution making process, far from being an instrument for conciliation and inclusion, has been the instrument for exclusion of the political parties and all of those dissenting the President's will and for the establishment of an hegemonic control of power.

X

But the assault, seizure and takeover of all power by the political group that controlled the Constituent Assembly did not finish with the drafting of the Constitution, on the contrary it continued after its approval in the December 15th referendum. This time the *coup d'Etat* given by the Constituent Assembly in open violation of the new Constitution, imposed new "constitutional" provisions never approved of by the people that allowed the complete seizure of all branches of government and the final assault of power.

For such purpose, on December 22, 1999, one week after the popular approval of the Constitution, in parallel to the provisions of the Constitution and not submitted to popular approval, the Assembly adopted a "Decree for a Transitory Regime," through which, as expected, only the President of the Republic was ratified in his office and conversely, all the other elected and non elected high officials of the State were definitively dismissed.[23]

To fill the institutional gap and vacuum deliberately created by the same Constituent Assembly without popular approval, the Assembly directly and without fulfilling the new conditions established in the provisions of the new Constitution, appointed the members of the Supreme Tribunal and of the National Electoral Council, the Public Prosecutor, the Comptroller General and the Peoples' Defendant. In addition, also without any constitutional support, the Assembly created and appointed the members of a National Legislative Commission to act as a non elected Legislative body in substitution of the dismissed Congress until the election of the new National Assembly. The Constituent Assembly, in addition, without any constitutional authorization, directly assumed legislative functions and sanctioned some statutes, among them, the Electoral Law.

All these unconstitutional decisions, of course and unfortunately, were covered up and endorsed by the new Supreme Tribunal of Justice whose members were precisely appointed by the same Assembly with the basic task of giving judicial support to the unconstitutional transitory regime in judicial proceedings where the Tribunal acted as judge in its own cause. Consequently, the new Tribunal appointed by the

---

23   See the Decree of December 22, 1999, on the "Transitory Constitutional Regime," in *Gaceta Oficial* N° 36.859 of December 29, 1999. See the comments regarding this decree in Allan R. Brewer-Carías, *Golpe de Estado y Proceso Constituyente en Venezuela*, Universidad Nacional Autónoma de México, México, pp. 354 ff.; and in *La Constitución de 1999. Derecho Constitucional Venezolano*, Editorial Jurídica Venezolana, Vol. II, Caracas 2004.

Assembly recognized the supposedly "original character" of the Constituent Assembly with "supra constitutional" power, justifying all the transitory political decisions adopted many of which have subsisted to the present, justifying and covering up the unconstitutional and endless intervention of the Judiciary.[24]

XI

The result of this 1999 Venezuelan constitution making process which was made fraudulently to the Constitution, in spite of the political changes that have taken place in Venezuela, has been the complete takeover of all levels of power and branches of government by the supporters of President Hugo Chávez, imposing on the Venezuelan people a centralized form of government and a political socialist project whose meaning can easily be understood by decoding the sense of the newly favorite presidential phrase of "motherland, socialism or death" recurrently pronounced since taking the oath in his second presidential term in January 2007, for which nobody has voted nor approved, and now even imposed as a duty for the military to express in any salute.[25]

The 1961 Constitution was fraudulently used in order to provoke the 1999 constitution making process by means of the election of a Constituent Assembly not established in the Constitution, which after being democratically elected, staged a *coup d'Etat*. Since 2000, based on the authoritarian Constitution that resulted, it is now representative democracy's turn to be used, also fraudulently, in order to demolish democracy itself. That is, from the defraudation of the Constitution, Venezuela went to the defraudation of democracy. During the constitution making process of 1999, using the judicial interpretation of the Constitution, the result was its violation (Constitutional fraud); and in the same way, the regime that began with said fraud in 1999, during the succeeding years up to the present, has used representative democracy to eliminate it progressively, and supposedly substitute it for a "participative democracy" of the Popular Power; which only by name is participative and democratic (democratic fraud).

In this way, the democratic rule of law, due to this fraud committed against the popular will by means of use of electoral mechanisms, has been and is being progressively substituted by a "State of the Popular Power," which pretends to establish the "democratic system" in a supposedly direct relation between a leader and the people, basically through popular mobilization, populism and the organization of "Communal Councils of the Popular Power." Its members are non elected and directly appointed by open Citizens Assemblies, which are, of course, controlled by

---

24   See for instance the January 26, 2000, decision N° 4 (*Caso: Eduardo García*), and the March 28, 2000, Decision N° 180 (*Case: Allan R. Brewer-Carías and others*) in *Revista de Derecho Público*, N° 81, Editorial Jurídica Venezolana, Caracas 2000, pp 93 ff. and 86 ff. See the comments in Allan R. Brewer-Carías, *Golpe de Estado y proceso constituyente en Venezuela*, Universidad Nacional Autónoma de México, México, 2002, pp. 354 ff.

25   See what was expressed by Alberto Muller Rojas, Military Presidential Chief of Staff, in *El Universal*, Caracas May 11, 2007; and by Hugo Chávez Frías, *El Nacional*, Caracas April 13, 2007, Política p. 4.

the governmental single party, maintaining the populist system that has been developed based on the uncontrolled disposal of oil wealth.[26]

The main trend of such system is that all the power is concentrated in the Head of State, who in the near future may become "President of the Popular Power," being neither democratic, nor representative or participative, and on the contrary, being severely controlled and directed through the governing socialist single party.

All these proposals and reforms announced since January 2007 tend to consolidate what the then Vice President of the Republic called the "the dictatorship of democracy."[27] Nonetheless, in democracy no dictatorship is acceptable or possible, not even an alleged "dictatorship of democracy," which in a different context and time is similar to the never accepted and failed "dictatorship of the proletariat" which emerged from the Russian revolution in 1918, based on the Soviets of soldiers, workers and peasants.

Unfortunately, and astonishingly out of date with a ninety year delay, something similar is currently being proposed and constituted in Venezuela, but with the creation of the aforementioned Communal Councils dependant on the President of the Republic in order to channel the Popular Power, with the supposed participation of the organized people, to install the "dictatorship of democracy."

History has shown that these supposed popular dictatorships have always been fraudulent instruments used by circumstantial leaders to gain control of power, and in the name of the popular power, to demolish every trace of democracy and to impose by force a socialist regime to a country without the people voting for it.

This prove that in some countries, nothing has been learned from what the recently deceased first ever elected President of the Russian Federation, Boris Yelstin, said in 1998, on the occasion of the burial of the remains of the Romanov family, expressing what can be considered as one of the most bitter lessons of human history when putting an end to the time of what was believed to be the most definite Revolution of all known to modern history; simply, he said that: "The attempts to change life by means of violence are doomed to fail"[28].

---

26   See Allan R. Brewer-Carías, "El autoritarismo en Venezuela construido en fraude a la Constitución (De cómo en un país democrático se ha utilizado el sistema eleccionario para eliminar la democracia y establecer un régimen autoritario de supuesta "dictadura de la democracia")," Ponencia para las *VIII Jornadas de Derecho Constitucional y Administrativo* y el *VI Foro Iberoamericano de Derecho Administrativo*, Universidad Externado de Colombia, Bogotá, 25-27 de julio de 2007. See in www.allanbrewercarias.com, Scetion I, 1 (Conferencias), N° 956 (2007).

27   Jorge Rodríguez, Vice-President of the Republic, in January 2007, expressed: "Of course we want to install a dictatorship, the **dictatorship of the true democracy** and the democracy is the dictatorship of everyone, you and us together, building a different country. Of course we want this **dictarorship of democracy** to be installed forever," in *El Nacional*, Caracas 02-01-2007, p. A-2.

28   See in *The Daily Telegraph*, London, 08-08-98, p. 1.

But even without taking into account this lesson, what is true is that any dictatorship, whatever its origin and kind, being inevitably the result of the exercise of violence, physical or institutional, sooner or later is condemned to fail and collapse.

XII

Going back to the constitution making processes, all the experiences developed in Modern constitutionalism of durable democratic Constitutions when being the outcome of conflicts show that they have always been the product of a constitution making process characterized by political agreements and consensus among conflicting parties with extended public participation and consultation. On the contrary, when being the result of the imposition to the country by a political leader, a faction or a dominant party, of their own particular conception of the State and of society, without any inclusive dialogue or political participation, eventually they implode within the system imposed.

When being the result of an agreement and consensus, precisely of a constitution making process in which parties effectively talk to each other and where peace is the key opening all doors to all, constitutions can be, on the one hand, at the eve of a war, the final product of a political pact of different forces, parties or factions of a society that are in conflict, in order to avoid a civil war; or on the other hand, at the end of a war, the result of some kind of political armistice achieved by the conflicting parties. In both cases, Constitutions are the result of a conflict, and as political pacts, they tend to create the conditions for stability and stable democratic government.

Constitutions can also often be the result of an imposition made by one political force of society upon the others, for instance by means of a revolution, in those cases they are also the result of conflict but not the result of the agreement of the political forces in conflict, but in a deeply divided society, the expression of the sole will of one predominant faction of society that imposes itself upon the others. In these cases, eventually, in the post conflict transition no stability can be achieved, and of course, stability can never be identified with the silence of the graves.

The fact is that the impositions by force to a country of a specific political system of government, of a specific economic or social system, of a territorial artificial organization or of the predominance of an ethnic group or religion over the others, has never attained long life. Eventually, the State and political institutions resulting from violence, in one way or the other always finish by being demolished or imploding. In other words, in any constitution making processes, any attempt to impose to a society, through violence -including institutional violence- a political system of government, a territorial division or a territorial integration of the State, a religion or an ethnic prevalence, even enshrining them in a Constitution, sooner or later are condemned to failure.

CHAPTER II

CONSTITUTIONAL REVIEW MODELS (CONSTITUTIONAL RE-
FORM AND AMENDMENTS) IN LATIN AMERICA.
A COMPARATIVE LAW APPROACH

(2004)

This essay deals with the various models for constitutional review in Latin America, evidencing that their express regulation in the Constitutions is the main characteristic of the principle of constitutional rigidity. In particular, a Constitutional Assembly, as a mean to reform a Constitution has to be provided in its text, and cannot be convened without constitutional provisions as occurred in Venezuela in 1999. The essay was written in 2003 for my Presentation at the *VI International Congress of Constitutional Law*, **organized by the International Association of Comparative Law, Santiago de Chile, January 15, 2014. It was published as: "Modelos de revisión constitucional en América Latina," in the book: Walter Carnota y Patricio Marianello (Directors),** *Derechos Fundamentales, Derecho Constitucional y Procesal Constitucional,* **Editorial San Marcos, Lima 2008, pp. 210-251; and in** *Boletín de la Academia de Ciencias Políticas y Sociales*, **enero-diciembre 2003, Nº 141, Caracas 2004. pp. 115-156.**

All the Latin American Constitutions were adopted at the beginning of the 19th century on the occasion of gaining their independence from Spain, by popular will expressed through elected Congresses, Conventions or Constituent Assemblies. They assumed the original constituent power for the organization of the State with a republican form.

As rigid constitutions, the means for their amendment or review were set forth as derived constituent power, being the convening of a Convention or Constituent Assembly an exceptional constitutional review procedure, as it was established in the 1853 Argentinean Constitution, following the North American model.

The Latin American Constitutions of the 19th century, during the almost two hundred years that have elapsed since independence, have been reformed or amended several times, but not necessarily following the procedures set forth (derived constituent power) in the Constitutions. Instead, almost all the Constitutions now in force in Latin America have been the result of Constituent Assemblies or Conventions, which in their moment assumed the constituent power without being ruled in an express way in the former constitutions, such as happened in recent years in Colombia (1991) and in Venezuela (1999).

In any case, as all rigid Constitutions of the current world, the Constitutions in force of the Latin American countries expressly set forth the constitutional review procedures, different from those established to reform the legislation; assuring in them not only the participation of the popular representation organs of the State (Congresses or Parliaments) , but also assuring in most of the cases, a direct people's participation through a vote or for the election of a Constituent Assembly or Convention or for the approval through a referendum on the constitutional reform or amendment.

Thus, in general terms, in the Constitutions of Latin American countries is possible to distinguish three general constitutional review procedures regulating the derived constituent power, depending on who exercises the constituent power: a procedure hereby the constituent power is exercised directly by the people, or whereby it is exercised by the popular representation organs of the State (Congresses or parliaments) on behalf of the people, or whereby it is exercised by a Constituent Assembly or Convention called for that purpose.

Some countries have ruled the three constitutional amendment procedures at the same time, as in Colombia, where article 374 of the Constitution set forth that:

> "The Political Constitution shall be reformed by the Congress, by a Constituent Assembly or by the people through a referendum."

All these constitutional review procedures ruled in the Latin American Constitutions are of course obligatory. Therefore, their own texts do not acknowledge a constitutional reform carried out through procedures not foreseen in the Constitution. Thus, for example, article 120 of the Dominican Republic Constitution set forth:

> "Article 120. A Constitutional amendment shall be make only in the manner set forth in itself, and shall never be suspended or revoked by any power or authority or by popular acclaim either."

In a similar sense, the Venezuelan Constitution set forth in article 333 the following:

> "Article 333. This Constitution shall not lost its validity if it is ignored by an act of force or if it is repelled by any other mean different from that foreseen in it.
>
> In such a case, every citizen empowered or not with authority shall be obliged to help in restoring its effective validity."

On the other hand, being a derived constituent power the one ruled in the constitutional texts, the same has limits not only as to the powers that the constituent organ might assume regarding the constituted Powers of the State, but also as to the matters to be amended or reformed, wherefore many constitutions through very rigid provisions, exclude from revision certain principles and provisions declared immutable and, therefore, not reviewable and not amendable.

For the purpose of studying the constitutional review procedures in Latin America, from a comparative constitutional law approach, this study is divided in two parts, devoting the first part, to analyze the procedures set forth for a constitutional review (amendment and reform); and the second part, to study the limits imposed upon the constituent power.

In general terms, we can outline three constitutional review procedures in the Latin American Constitutions, whereby the derived constituent power is shown:

In the *first place,* several constitutions grant the constituent power directly to the sovereign people, who express it by ratifying the reform or amendment through a referendum or a popular consultation. In some cases, (i) the people's participation as constituent power is set forth in an exclusive way, as the only constitutional review procedure (Uruguay); and in other cases, (ii) it is set forth as one of the alternatives of constitutional review procedures together with others. That is the case, for example, of Venezuela, Colombia, Paraguay, Guatemala and Costa Rica, where it is also regulated a Constituent Assembly; and of Peru, Cuba, Chile, Ecuador and Panama, where additionally, the legislative organ is granted the power of approving the constitutional amendment. In Colombia, as it has been said, in addition to the constitutional review procedure through referendum, it is also regulated a Constituent Assembly and the constitutional reform through Legislative Acts sanctioned by the Congress.

In the *second place,* many other Constitutions grant the derived constituent power to a Constituent Assembly or Convention, (i) as an exclusive constitutional reform process, such as in Argentina; (ii) as an exclusive process for total constitutional reforms, different from the amendments, such as in Costa Rica, Paraguay and Nicaragua; (iii) as an exclusive process for the reform just of certain provisions of the Constitution, such as in Guatemala; or (iv) together with other constitutional review procedures as the popular referendum, such as in Colombia and Venezuela.

In the *third place,* other Constitutions grant the derived constituent power to the Legislative Branch of government (Congresses or Parliaments), (i) sometimes in an exclusive way, such as in Bolivia and El Salvador; (ii) in other cases also in an exclusive way but combining the work of the national (federal) Legislative organ with the participation of the States legislatures; (iii) in other cases, as an alternative mean of reform other than the procedure of referendum, such as in Panama, Colombia, Cuba, Chile and Ecuador; or (iv) also as an alternative reform mean other than the Constituent Assembly, such as in Colombia, Costa Rica and Nicaragua.

I.   CONSTITUTIONAL REVIEW POWER EXERCISED DIRECTLY BY THE PEOPLE

As it has been said, in several Latin American Constitutions, the power to review the Constitution is directly granted to the people.

In some cases, this popular participation is set forth to review the Constitution in an exclusive way, and in other cases, it is ruled as one of the constitutional review procedures, combined with others such as the call for a National Constituent Assembly.

1. *Constitutional Review Exercised Exclusively by the People: The Case of Uruguay*

In Latin America, only the Constitution of Uruguay grants the people in an exclusive way, the ultimate power of approving all total or partial constitutional reforms through referendum (Article 331).

Constitutional reform procedures, therefore, only vary according to the initiative for the same, which might correspond (i) to popular initiative, (ii) to the Legislative Branch (General Assembly); (iii) to the Senate, Representatives and the Executive Power, by calling a Constituent Assembly.

A.   *The Popular Initiative*

In the *first place,* there is the possibility that by the initiative of a ten per cent of the citizens, registered in the National Civic Registry, a proposal for constitutional review can be raised before the President of the General Assembly, which shall be submitted to popular approval, in the closest election. In this case, the General Assembly, deciding in joint session of both Chambers (Senate and Deputies), can also submit alternative proposals that shall be presented for ratification in a plebiscite together with the popular proposal.

For the ratification by plebiscite it is required that the absolute majority of the citizens attending the election voted "yes", which must represent at least thirty five per cent of the total registered in the National Civic Registry.

In this case, only can be submitted to popular ratification by referendum simultaneously with the closest elections, the proposals submitted six months –at least- prior to those elections or three months prior to them, for the alternative proposals approved by the General Assembly. Those rose after such time shall be submitted to plebiscite in the following elections.

In the *second place,* the constitutional review might be proposed by the General Assembly, in that case, article 331 set forth two constitutional reform procedures : through the ratification of reform drafts or through the approval of constitutional laws.

B.   *General Assembly initiative through Constitutional Reform Drafts*

Article 331, Paragraph B of the Constitution set forth that the General Assembly might also propose constitutional reforms that shall be supported by two fifth out of the total General Assembly members, which shall be submitted to the President of the same, and they shall be submitted to plebiscite in the first coming election.

For the approval in the plebiscite, it is required as well that the absolute majority of the citizens attending the election voted "yes", which shall represent as well at least thirty five per cent of the total registered in the National Civic Registry.

In this case, only the drafts submitted six months –at least- prior to the closest elections shall be submitted to popular approval by plebiscite simultaneously with such election. Those rose after such time shall be submitted to referendum in the following elections.

C. *General Assembly initiative through Constitutional Laws*

Article 331, Paragraph D of the Constitution set forth that it can also be reformed through Constitutional Laws, approved by two thirds out of the total members of both Chambers in the same Legislature. Constitutional Laws shall not be vetoed by the Executive Power and they will in force, after an election, specially called at the date determined by the same laws, ratified them by the absolute majority of the votes and shall be enacted by the President of the General Assembly.

D. *The initiative to convene a Constituent Assembly*

In the *third place,* the Executive Power, the Senate or representatives before the General Assembly are also entitled to propose constitutional reforms through calling a National Constituent Assembly. In such a case, article 331, paragraph C of the Constitution set forth that the Senate, the Representatives and the Executive Power are entitled as well to propose reforms, which shall be ratified by the absolute majority out of the total General Assembly members. Should the proposed reform is not ratified the same shall not be proposed once again until the next legislative period, and shall comply with the same requirements.

Now, once the proposal is ratified and enacted by the President of the General Assembly, the Executive Power shall call, within the ninety following days, an election of a National Constituent Assembly that shall deliberate and decide upon the proposed reforms, as well as upon the other proposals that might be submitted to the Convention.

With the purpose of electing the National Constituent Assembly members, article 331 of the Constitution establishes forth that the number of convention members shall be double the number of Congress members, electing also alternates double the number of Convention members, being the requirements to be elected, immunities and incompatibilities the same for the Representatives. The election shall be made for department lists, using the system of integral proportional representation and pursuant to the legislation in force for the election of the Representatives.

The Convention shall meet within a year counted from the date of the enactment of the proposed reform. Its decisions shall be made by absolute majority of the total number of Convention members, and its duties shall be terminated within a year counted from the date of its installation. The draft proposed by the Convention shall be communicated to the Executive Power for its immediate and wide publication.

The draft or drafts proposed by the Convention shall be ratified by the voters called with that purpose by the Executive Power, at the date fixed by the National Constituent Assembly.

In this case, voters shall also vote "Yes" or "No" and in the case of several proposed amendments, they shall vote each one of them separately. With that purpose, the Constituent Assembly shall gather the proposed reforms that require to be voted together by their nature. Nevertheless, a third of the Convention members might request that one or several proposed amendments be voted separately.

The reform or reforms shall be ratified by the majority of the votes, not less than thirty five per cent of the citizens registered in the National Civic Registry.

Finally, it is noteworthy that in all the constitutional reform procedures afore-mentioned, if the call of the voters for the ratification coincides with any election of State organs members, citizens shall vote the constitutional reforms in a separate ballot and independently from the election lists. When the reforms are referred to the election of State elective officials, when submitted to plebiscite, the vote for those positions shall also be make simultaneously by the proposed system and by the fore-going, prevailing the decision of the plebiscite.

2.   Constitutional Review Exercised by the People (in a non Exclusive Way) as Alternative among Other Procedures

Except for Uruguay, where popular participation is always required to ratify con-stitutional reforms, in other Latin American countries, the people's participation in the constitutional review process is set forth with exceptions or together with other review procedures which are developed without popular ratification. That is the case, for example, of Venezuela, Colombia, Paraguay, Guatemala and Costa Rica, where also the functioning of a Constituent Assembly is established; and of Peru, Cuba, Chile, Ecuador and Panama, where the ordinary Legislature is granted the power of ratifying constitutional reforms. In Colombia, in addition to the constitu-tional review procedure through referendum, reforms can by adopted through a Con-stituent Assembly and by Legislative Acts of constitutional reform ratified by the Congress.

A.   Referendum Ratifying Constitutional Reforms and its Exception in Peru

Pursuant to the Peruvian Constitution, constitutional reforms may be proposed by (i) the President of the Republic, with the approval of the Cabinet; (ii) members of the Congress and (iii) a number of citizen equal to zero point three per cent (0.3%) of the voters, whose signatures have been checked by the Electoral Authority.

Pursuant to article 206 of the Constitution of Peru, all constitutional reform shall be submitted to the consideration of the Congress, which shall ratify them with the absolute majority of its members, and shall be ratified by referendum.

However, the same article set forth that the referendum can be omitted when the agreement of the Congress is obtained in two successive ordinary legislatures with a favorable vote, in each case, superior to the two thirds of its congressmen.

In any case, the constitutional reform law shall not be vetoed by the President of the Republic.

B.   Referendum Ratifying Constitutional Reforms in Colombia

In the Colombian case, as it was said, article 337 of the Constitution set forth that the same shall be reformed through three procedures: (i) by the Congress, through the enactment of legislative acts; (i) by a Constituent Assembly convened for that purpose or (iii) by the people through referendum.

Constitutional reform needed to be ratified by the people through referendum, (i), in some cases of reforms ratified by the Congress through Legislative acts referred to certain matters; and (ii) in the event of a governmental or popular initiative.

Indeed, in the first place, article 377 of the Constitution establishes that the constitutional reforms ratified by the Congress through Legislative acts shall be submitted to referendum, when referred to: 1) rights declared in Chapter 1 of Title II of the Constitution and their guarantees; 2) procedures of popular participation, or 3) the Congress; and furthermore, if within six months following the enactment of the Legislative act it is requested by a five per cent of the citizens registered in the Voters Registry. In all these cases, the reform shall be deemed repealed when a negative vote is casted by the majority of the voters, provided that in the voting at least the fourth part of the voters participated.

In the second place, pursuant to article 378 of the Constitution, when a constitutional reform project is proposed at the initiative of the Government or of the citizens complying the requirements set forth in article 155 of the Constitution, the Congress, through a law ratified by the majority of the members of both Chambers, can submit to referendum the proposed constitutional reform it includes in the law. In this case, the referendum shall be designed so that the voters can freely choose within the proposed matters or articles what are they voting affirmatively and what are they voting negatively.

For the approval of the constitutional reform draft, it is required in the referendum the affirmative vote of more than a half of the voters and they must exceed the fourth part of the total citizens registered in the Voters Registry.

C. *Approbatory Referendum for Constitutional Amendments and Reforms in Venezuela*

In the case of Venezuela, a constitutional review can be carried out through amendments and reforms of the Constitution requiring popular ratification through referendum, or through the convening of a National Constituent Assembly.

In the first place, article 340 and 341 of the Constitution set forth the *Constitutional Amendments,* for the purpose of adding or modifying one or several articles of the Constitution, without altering its fundamental structure. The procedure for constitutional amendments according to article 341 is as follows:

1. An initiative may be raised by fifteen per cent of the voters registered in the Civil and Electoral Registry, or by a thirty per cent of the members of the National Assembly or by the President of the Republic in Cabinet.

2. When the initiative is raised by the National Assembly, the amendment draft requires the ratification of the latter by the majority of its members and must be discussed according to the ordinary law-making procedure set forth in the Constitution.

3. The Electoral Power shall submit the amendments to referendum thirty days after its formal reception.

4. The amendments shall be deemed approved as per the provisions of the Constitution and the law referring to approval referenda.

5. The approved amendments shall be listed in a consecutive way and shall be published after the text of the Constitution without altering it, but placing at the end of the amended article or articles a note with a reference of the number and date of the amendment that modified it.

The President of the Republic is obliged to enact the amendments within ten days after their approval. If he did not do it, then according to articles 346 and 216 of the President and Vice-presidents of the National Assembly must enact the law.

In the second place, the Constitution also regulates the *Constitutional Reforms*, which pursuant to article 342 of the Constitution aim at a partial review of the same and at changing of one or several articles that do not alter the fundamental structure and principles of the Constitution.

In this case, the initiative may be raised (i) by the National Assembly through a decision approved by the vote of the majority of its members; (ii) by the President of the Republic in Cabinet, or (iii) by a number of at least fifteen per cent of the voters registered in the Civic and Electoral Registry.

Article 343 of the Constitution set forth the procedure of constitutional reform in case of initiative by the National Assembly, in the following way:

1. The proposed constitutional reform shall have its first discussion in the session periods corresponding to its rising.

2. A second discussion for Title or Chapter, according to the case.

3. A third and last discussion article by article.

4. The National Assembly shall approve the proposed constitutional reform within two years counted from the date of approval of the request of reform.

5. The proposed reform shall be deemed approved by the vote of the two thirds of the National Assembly members.

The proposed constitutional reform approved by the National Assembly, pursuant to article 344 of the Constitution, shall be submitted to referendum within thirty days after its approval. The vote in the referendum shall be given as a whole, but up to one third of the proposal can be voted separately if it is decided by at least one third part of the members of the National Assembly or if in the initiative of the reform it was requested by the President of the Republic or by a number not least than five per cent of the voters registered in the Civic and Electoral Registry. .

The constitutional reform shall be deemed approved if the number of affirmative votes is superior to the number of negative vote. A constitutional reform initiative that is not approved shall not be raised again in the same constitutional period to the National Assembly (Art. 345).

The President of the Republic is obliged to enact the reforms within ten days after their approval. If he did not do it, then according to articles 346 and 216 of the President and Vice-presidents of the National Assembly must enact the law.

D. *Approbatory Referendum for Constitutional Amendments in Paraguay*

In addition to the process to reform the Constitution through a National Constituent Assembly, the Constitution of Paraguay also establishes the amendment procedure, which shall be approved by a referendum.

With that purpose, article 290 of the Constitution set forth that after three years of its enactment; amendments might be made by an initiative of the fourth part of the members of any of the Chambers of the Congress, of the President of the Republic or of thirty thousand voters, in a written request.

The full text of the amendment shall be approved by an absolute majority both in the Chamber proposing it and in the Chamber ratifying it as well. If in any of the Chambers the majority is not obtained for its approval, the amendment shall be deemed rejected, and it shall not be raised within a year period.

Once the amendment is approved in both Chambers of the Congress, it shall be submitted to the Superior Court of Electoral Justice, which within one hundred and eighty days shall call a referendum. If the result is affirmative, the amendment shall be sanctioned and enacted, incorporating it to the Constitution. If the amendment is not approved, another on the same subject shall not be raised before three years.

Instead of the aforementioned amendment procedure, the reform procedure must be followed if it is referred to the provisions involving the election method, composition, duration of mandates or attributions of any of the State powers, or the provisions of Chapters I, II, III, and IV of Title II, Part I, referred to constitutional rights and guarantees, specially, right to live, right to a safe environment, the right to protection of the personal freedom and security, right to equal treatment, and finally, family rights.

E. *Ratifying Referendum for Constitutional Reforms on Fundamental Issues in Cuba*

As per article 137 of the Cuban Constitution, the Popular Power's National Assembly has the authority to approve constitutional reforms; however, if the reform referrers to the composition and attributions of the Popular Power's National Assembly, or to its State Council, or to the constitutional rights and duties declared in the Constitution, it requires a ratification by the favorable vote of the majority of the citizens with vote right, in a referendum called by the Assembly.

F. *The Popular Approval of Constitutional Reforms on Certain Constitutional Issues in Guatemala*

The Constitution of Guatemala establishes two constitutional reform procedures according to the part of the Constitution to be reformed: first, if the reform is about article 278 (which regulates the same constitutional reform) or any other article included in Chapter I of Title II (which declares individual rights), it shall be carried out through a National Constituent Assembly; second, if it is about any other constitutional reform, according to article 280 of the Constitution it is required that the reforms be approved by the Congress, by the affirmative vote of two thirds out of the total Deputies , but they shall only become effective once ratified through the popular consultation referred to in article 173 of the Constitution, which regulates the consultation procedure regarding specially important political decisions.

Same article 280 set forth that if the result of the popular consultation is the ratification of the reform, the latter shall become effective sixty days after the Electoral Supreme Court announces the result of the consultation.

G. *Approbatory Referendum of Constitutional Reforms in the Event of a Disagreement between the State Powers in Chile*

In Chile, articles 112 and following of the Constitution in general terms empowered the Congress to approve constitutional reforms. Now, once the proposed reform is approved, the same shall be sent to the President of the Republic for its enactment, who might reject it, in which case, if the Congress insisted on it, the President shall enact it, unless he consulted the citizens through a referendum. Likewise, in the event that the President makes partial observations to a proposed constitutional reform approved by the Congress, if both Chambers insisted on the part of the proposal approved by them, the insisted part of the proposal shall be returned to the President for its enactment, except in the case that he consulted the citizens through a plebiscite as to the points in disagreement.

As per article 119 of the Constitution, the call to a plebiscite shall be make within thirty days after the insistence of the Chambers on the proposal approved by them, and it shall be call through a Supreme presidential decree in which shall be fixed the date of the plebiscite, which shall not be held before thirty days or after sixty, counted from the publication of the decree. Once that period passed without the call by the President of a plebiscite, the proposed reform approved by the Congress shall be enacted.

The decree calling a plebiscite shall contain (i) the proposed reform approved by the Congress and fully vetoed by the President of the Republic, or (ii) the matters in which the Congress insisted on. In this case, each of said matters in disagreement shall be voted separately.

A Qualifying Court shall communicate the President the result of the plebiscite, and shall specify the draft text approved by the voters, which shall be enacted as constitutional reform within five days after said notice. Once the proposal is enacted and from the date of its validity, its provisions shall be a part of the Constitution and shall be deemed incorporated to it.

H.   *The Popular Consultation to Approve Constitutional Reforms in the Event of an Urgency or Refusal of the Congress in Ecuador*

According to article 280 of the Political Constitution of Ecuador, it shall be reformed through the Congress or through popular consultation.

Regarding the latter, and according to article 283 of the Constitution, the President of the Republic, in the event of urgency, previously qualified by the Congress with a majority of their members, shall submit to popular consultation the approval of constitutional reforms.

Also, en the event that the proposed reforms are submitted to the Congress and it had not decided , approved or rejected them in a period of one hundred and twenty days counted from the term of a year, set forth in article 282 to commence the second debate to approve reforms, a popular consultation proceeds as well.

In both cases, the specific text of the proposed reforms shall be submitted to the voters, which, if approved, shall be immediately incorporated to the Constitution.

I.   *Popular Approval of Constitutional Reforms in the Event of a Disagreement between Two Legislatures in Panama*

According to Article 308 of the Constitution of Panama, the constitutional reform procedure might be initiated by the Legislative Assembly, the Cabinet or the Supreme Court of Justice, and always implies the submission of the draft to the Legislative Assembly and its approval by a Legislative Act, adopted with qualified majorities in two subsequent Legislatures. If in the second Legislature there are no modifications, the reform is deemed approved. However, if in the second Legislature there are new modifications, then a popular approval of the constitutional reform through referendum is required.

This popular consultation in the procedure of constitutional reform is regulated in the same article 308 of the Constitution, as follows: the constitutional reform must be sanctioned by a Legislative Act approved in three debates by the absolute majority of the members of the Legislative Assembly in one legislature, and then sanctioned approved as well in three debates by the absolute majority of the members of the aforementioned Legislative Assembly in the subsequent legislature. If in the latter, the text approved is modified, the second Legislative Act shall be published in the Official Gazette and submitted to direct popular consultation through referendum, which shall be held in a date fixed by the Legislative Assembly, within a period not minor than three months or larger than six months, counted from the approval of the Legislative Act in the second legislature.

A Legislative Act approved pursuant the forgoing process shall become effective from its publication in the Official Gazette, which shall be made by the Executive Organ within thirty working days after its approval through referendum, according to the case, not being a cause of unconstitutionality the publication made after those terms.

J.   *Approbatory Referendum for Partial Reform when agreed by the Legislative Assembly in Costa Rica*

In Costa Rica, there are two constitutional reform procedures, one for general reforms, by a National Constituent Assembly, and the other for partial reforms, by the Legislative Power with discussions and approval in two Legislatures. In the latter case, article 8 of the Constitution set forth that pursuant to article 105 of the same, constitutional reforms might be submitted to referendum after their approval in one legislature and before the other, if agreed by two thirds out of the total Legislative Assembly members.

II.   CONSTITUTIONAL REVIEW POWER EXERCISED BY A CONSTITUTIONAL ASSEMBLY

In several Latin American Countries, as it has been said, a derived constituent power is constitutionally granted to a Constituent Convention or Assembly, (i) as the exclusive constitutional reform procedure , as in Argentina; (ii) as an exclusive constitutional reform procedure only for total reforms (different from the amendments or partial reforms), as in Costa Rica, Paraguay and Nicaragua; (iii) as an exclusive procedure for reforming certain provisions of the Constitution, as in Guatemala; or (iv) together with other constitutional review procedures as the popular referendum, as in Colombia and Venezuela.

1. *Constituent Assembly with Exclusive power to reform the Constitution: The Argentinean Constituent Convention*

In Argentina, the Constitution can be totally or partially reformed in any of its parts. For this purpose, Article 30 of the same set forth two steps to take for that: first, a Congress statement on the necessity of reforming it approved with the vote of at least two thirds of its members; and second, once such a statement has been made, the reform must be approved by a Constitutional Convention called for that purpose.

2. *Constituent Assembly with Exclusive power to make Constitutional Reforms or total Constitutional Reforms (Different from Amendments or partial reforms)*

A. *Constituent Assembly of Costa Rica for General Reforms*

In Costa Rica, article 196 of the Constitution expressly set forth that a general reform (different from partial reforms) of the Constitution shall only be made by a Constituent Assembly called for that purpose. Such a call shall be made through a law approved by at least two thirds out of the total Legislative Assembly members, requiring no enactment of the Executive Power.

B. *National Constituent Convention of Paraguay to Make Constitutional Reforms*

The Paraguayan Constitution makes a difference between a reform and an amendment as constitutional review procedures, granting the former to a National Constituent Assembly, and submitting the latter to the approval of a referendum.

As to the reform procedure through a National Constituent Assembly, it shall be used for reforming those provisions affecting the election mode, the composition, lasting of term and attributions of any of the State Power, or the provisions of Chapter I, II, III and IV of Title II, Part I, referred to constitutional rights and guarantees, specially, right to live, right to a safe environment, the right to protection of the personal freedom and security, right to equal treatment, and finally, family rights.

Now, article 289 of the Constitution set forth that a reform can be made only ten years after its promulgation , and it shall be requested by (i) a twenty five per cent of the members of any of the Chambers of the Congress, (i) the President of the Republic or (iii) thirty thousand voters, in a signed request. However, a statement on the necessity of the reform must be approved by an absolute majority of two thirds of the members of each Chambers of the Congress.

Once the necessity of the reform is decided, the Superior Electoral Tribunal must call the election of a National Constituent Convention within a term of one hundred and eighty days, in a general election that do not collide with any other election.

The number of members in the National Constituent Assembly cannot exceed the total members of the Congress; and the conditions to be elected and the determination of their incompatibilities shall be set forth by a law. The Convention members shall have the same immunities of the Congress members.

Once the new Constitution is enacted by the National Constituent Assembly it shall be deemed promulgated as a matter of law.

C. *National Constituent Assembly for a Total Reform of the Constitution in Nicaragua*

The Constitution of Nicaragua also distinguishes two constitutional reform procedures for total or partial reforms. Partial reforms are granted to the National Assembly as well as the power to discuss and decide on the initiative of a total constitutional reform with the vote of a half plus one of the members of the National Assembly (Art 191).

Article 193 set forth that the initiative of total reform is granted to a half plus one of the members of the National Assembly (Art 191) and the approval requires the vote of two thirds out of the total members (Art. 192).

Once the total reform initiative is approved, the National Assembly shall fix a term to call the election of the National Constituent Assembly. The National Assembly will keep its mandate until the installation of the new elected National Constituent Assembly.

In any case, article 194 expressly set forth that "while the new Constitution is approved by the National Constituent Assembly, this Constitution shall remain in force".

3. *The Constituent Assembly with Exclusive Power to reform Certain Constitutional Matters: The National Constituent Assembly of Guatemala*

As per article 277 of the Constitution the initiative to propose constitutional reforms correspond to (i) the President of the Republic in Cabinet; (ii) ten or more Congressmen, (iii) the Constitutionality Court, and (iv) the people through a petition addressed to the Congress by at least five thousand citizens duly registered in the Citizen Registry.

The power to decide upon the constitutional reforms, depending on the article to be reformed, is granted both to the Congress with popular approval and to a National Constituent Assembly.

When reforming article 278 (ruling the National Constituent Assembly) as well as any other article in Chapter I of Title II of the Constitution (referring to individual rights), it is necessary that the Congress, with the affirmative vote of two thirds of its members, call a National Constituent Assembly.

In the decree calling it, the Congress shall point out the article or articles to be reviewed, and shall notify the Supreme Electoral Court in order to fix a date in which the election shall be made within a maximum term of one hundred and twenty days, as per the Constitutional Electoral Law.

Article 279 of the Constitution establishes the qualities required to be a National Constituent Assembly member, which is the same as to be a congressman; the Constituent Assembly members shall have the same immunities and prerogatives as the congressmen. Nevertheless, the same person shall not be a National Constituent Assembly member and a Congress member at the same time. The elections of the National Constituent Assembly members, the number of members to be elected and other matters related to the electoral process shall be ruled in the same way as the elections of the Congress.

As to the functioning of the National Constituent Assembly, article 279 of the Constitution set forth that "the National Constituent Assembly and the Congress shall work at the same time."

4. Constituent Assembly with (non Exclusive) Alternative Power among other Constitutional Review Procedures

A. Constituent Assembly in Colombia

The 1991 Colombian Constitution, product of a Constituent Assembly called in that moment without being expressly ruled in the Constitution, set forth expressly and as alternative for a constitutional review, in addition to the approving referendum and the Legislative acts issued by the Congress, the review procedure through a Constituent Assembly.

Accordingly, article 376 of the Constitution set forth that through a law approved by the majority of the members of both Chambers of the Congress, it can call the people in a popular vote to decide the calling of a Constituent Assembly, with the powers, the term and integration that the same law set forth.

It shall be understood that the people call the Assembly, if the law is approved by at least a third part of those in the electoral registry. In that case, the Assembly shall be elected by the direct vote of the citizen, in an election that does not coincide with another one.

In this case of a calling of a Constituent Assembly for a constitutional review, the Assembly exclusively assumes the derived constituent power, wherefore from its election the ordinary power of the Congress to reform the Constitution is suspended during the term fixed for the Assembly to comply its functions.

Once elected and installed, the Assembly shall adopt its own rules.

B. National Constituent Assembly in Venezuela

In Venezuela and with the same orientation of the 1991 Colombian experience, in 1999 the calling of a National Constituent Assembly was submitted to consultation through a referendum, as an instrument for constitutional review, without being established said process of constitutional review in the 1961 Constitution. As in Colombia, after an intense political and constitutional debate on the issue, and after various judicial review decisions issued by the Supreme Court, the National Constituent Assembly was eventually elected, and in the constitutional text it sanctioned (1999) and submitted to approving referendum it was expressly set forth this procedure, in parallel to those of amendment and reform both with approving referenda.

According to article 347 of the Constitution, "the Venezuelan people are the depositary of the original constituent power," and by "exercising that power," the people "might call a National Constituent Assembly aiming at transforming the State, creating a new legal order and writing a new constitution." With this express statement, the 1999 Constitution eliminated all discussion on whether the National Constituent Assembly, once elected, could assume or not the original constituent power or just a derived constituent power. Such a discussion presided the functioning of the National Constituent Assembly of 1999, who arrogated such original constituent power, carrying out a coup d'Etat. On the contrary, the 1999 constitutional text it sanctioned eliminated all possibility for a National Constituent Assembly of usurping the original constituent power that only belongs to the people.

Now, as per article 348 of the Constitution, the initiative to call a National Constituent Assembly is attributed to (i) the President of the Republic in Cabinet; (ii) the National Assembly, through a decision adopted by two thirds of its members, (iii) Municipal Councils, through the vote of two thirds of the same, or (iv) fifteen percent of the voters registered in the Civil and Electoral Registry. This initiative must be submitted to popular approval trough a referendum altogether with the statute governing the Constituent Assembly.

Once its members elected, according to such statute approved by the people, during its functioning as a mechanism of constitutional review aiming at "transforming the State, creating a new legal order and writing a new constitution" (Art. 347), the organs of the "constituted power shall not impede in any way the decisions of the National Constituent Assembly" (Art. 349).

On the other hand, article 349 of the Constitution set forth that the President shall not veto the new Constitution adopted by the Constituent Assembly, which, once enacted, must be published in the *Official Gazette* of the Republic or in the National Constituent Assembly Gazette.

III. CONSTITUTIONAL REVIEW POWER EXERCISED BY THE LEGISLATIVE POWER

Finally, other constitutions grant the derived constituent power to the organ exercising the Legislative Power, in some cases in an exclusive way, as in Bolivia and El Salvador, and as in Mexico, but combining the participation of the federal legislative organs and those of the federal States; and in other cases, as an reform alternative as to other procedures as a referendum, as in Panama, Colombia, Cuba, Chile and Ecuador; or as the Constituent Assembly, as in Colombia, Costa Rica and Nicaragua.

1. *The Legislative Power Organ with Exclusive Powers in Matters of Constitutional Reform*

A. *Constitutional Amendment by the Chambers in Bolivia*

The Bolivian Constitution only permits its partial reform or amendment by granting the Senate and Representatives Chambers the constituent power pursuant to the procedure established in articles 230 to 233 of the fundamental text, which is as follows:

The initiative for a partial reform (article 230) corresponds to the Chambers, through a prior statement on the need of the reform, embodied in an ordinary law approved by two thirds of the members in both Chambers. This law might be initiated in any of the Chambers, in the manner set forth in the Constitution to sanction laws (Art. 71 and following). Once the law stating the necessity of the reform is sanctioned, it shall be sent to the Executive for its promulgation, who shall not veto it.

The law stating the necessity of the reform, containing its draft, as per article 231 of the Constitution, shall be discussed in the first sessions of the legislature of a new constitutional term by the Chamber that proposed the reform, and if it is approved by two thirds of the votes, it shall be submitted to the other Chamber for its review, which shall require two thirds as well; fulfilling the constitutional requirements regarding the relations between both Chambers.

In any case, the Chambers shall discuss and vote the reform adapting it to provisions set forth in the law declaring the need of the reform. The sanctioned reform shall be submitted to the Executive for its promulgation, and the President shall make no observations.

The amendment will be valid since its publication, except if it is regarding the constitutional term of the President, in whose case it shall only apply from the following term (Art. 233).

B. *Constitutional Reform by the Legislative Assembly in El Salvador*

Pursuant to article 248 of the Constitution of El Salvador, all constitutional reform shall be decided by the Legislative Assembly, only if proposed by at least ten Deputies and with the vote of a half plus one of the elected Deputies. However, in order to decree the reform, it shall be ratified by the next Legislative Assembly with the vote of two thirds of the elected Deputies. Ratified in this way, the corresponding decree shall be issued and published in the Official Newspaper.

C. *Constitutional Reform by the Congress in Dominican Republic*

The Constitution of Dominican Republic expressly set forth its reform procedure, making it clear that:

> "Article 120. The Reform of the Constitution shall only be made in the manner set forth in itself, and shall never be suspended or annulled by any power or authority or by popular acclamations either."

In this way, article 116 establishes the constitutional reform procedure, indicating that the proposal of the same shall be submitted to the Congress by a third party of the members of one or the other Chamber, or by the Executive Power.

Once the proposed reform is submitted, as per article 117, the Congress shall make a statement on the necessity of the reform through a law, through which a meeting of the National Assembly shall be ordered, the object of the reform shall be determined and the articles of the Constitution involved in the reform shall be indicated. This law shall not be observed by the Executive Power.

In order to decide the proposed reforms, article 118 set forth that the National Assembly shall meet within fifteen days after the publication of the law stating the necessity of the reform, being present more than a half of the members of each one of the Chambers. As an exception to the provision set forth in article 27 of the Constitution, in this case decisions shall be made by a majority of two thirds of the votes.

Once the reforms are voted and declared by the National Assembly, the Constitution shall be fully published with the reformed texts.

D. *The Constitutional Amendment by the Congress in Brazil*

In Brazil, the Constitution shall only be amended by the Congress, as a part of the "legislative process" (Art. 59); but no amendment shall be approved under federal intervention, state of defense or siege (Art. 60, § 1°).

The proposed amendment shall be submitted pursuant to the provision of article 60 of the Constitution: (i) By at least a third of the members of the Chamber of Deputies or the Federal Senate; (ii) .by the President of the Republic; or (iii) by more than a half of the Legislative Assemblies of the States of the Federation, each one of them deciding by relative majority of their members.

The proposal must be discussed and voted twice in each Chamber of the Congress, and it shall be deemed approved if three fifths of the votes from the respective members of both Chambers are obtained (Art. 60 § 2°).

The Constitutional amendment must be promulgated by the boards of the Chamber of Deputies and the Federal Senate, with its order number. (Art. 60 § 3°).

A proposed amendment rejected or deemed ineffective shall not be proposed again in the same legislative session. (Art. 60 § 5°).

2.   *The Organs of the Federal or State Legislative Power with Exclusive Competency in Matters of Constitutional Reform*

The Mexican Constitution is the only Federal Latin America country that set forth that constitutional reforms need to be approved not only by the Federal Congress but also by the Legislative Assemblies of the Federal States.

Article 135 of the 1917 Constitution establishes in this respect that the Constitution can be changed or reformed, being necessary for that purpose that the Union Congress, by the vote of two thirds of those present, agreed on the reforms or additions, and that they be approved by the majority of the legislatures of the States. The Union Congress or a Permanent Commission shall make the calculations regarding the State Legislature votes as well as the statement on the approval of the reforms or additions.

3.   *The Legislative Power Organ with (non Exclusive) Power in Matters of Constitutional Reform as an Alternative to its Approval by Referendum*

A.   *Constitutional Reform by the Legislative Assembly in Panama as an Alternative to the Referendum Procedure*

As it was said, in Panama there are two constitutional reform procedures: one of them carries popular participation through approving referendum when in the discussion of the reform in two legislatures of the Legislative Assembly, modifications are made in the second; the other procedure allows a constitutional reform to be made with the single participation of the legislative organ as per the following procedure set forth in article 308 of the Constitution:

The initiative to propose constitutional reforms correspond to the Legislative Assembly, to the Cabinet or to the Supreme Court, and the reforms must be approved by a Legislative Act approved in three debates by the absolute majority of the members of the Legislative Assembly, which shall be published in *Official Gazette*. This text must be transferred by the Executive Organ to said Assembly, within the first five days of the ordinary session after the elections to renew the Legislative organ, where it must be debated once again and be approved without modifications, in one single debate, by the absolute majority of its members.

The legislative act approved likewise will be in force since its publication in the Official Gazette, by the Executive Organ, which must occur within ten working days after its ratification by the Legislative Assembly. Nevertheless, the publication after said term will not be a cause of unconstitutionality.

B.   *Constitutional Reform by a Legislative Act in Colombia as an Alternative to the Referendum or Constituent Assembly Procedures*

As it has been said, in Colombia three alternative constitutional reform procedures are ruled: through referendum, through a Constituent Assembly or through Legislative Act issued by the Congress.

Regarding the latter, article 375 of the Constitution establishes that (i) the Government, (ii) ten members of the Congress, (iii) twenty per cent of the municipal council members or of the Deputies, and (iv) a number of citizens equal to at least five percent of the current voters, might submit before the Congress Legislative Act drafts for constitutional reforms.

The discussions of the draft must take place in two ordinary and consecutive legislative periods. Once approved in the first of them by the majority of those present, the draft shall be published by the Government. In the second term, the approval shall require the vote of the majority of the members of each Chamber. In this second term, only initiatives proposed in the first term shall be discussed.

C.   *Partial Constitutional Reforms by the Legislative Assembly in Costa Rica*

In Costa Rica, as it has been said, there are two constitutional reform procedures: one for general reforms and the other for partial reforms. In the former, a Constituent Assembly shall be called; and in the latter, the constituent power is granted to the Legislative Assembly.

In effect, according to article 195 of the Constitution, the Legislative Assembly can partially reform the Constitution, complying with the following provisions:

1. The proposal to reform one or several articles shall be submitted to the Legislative Assembly in ordinary session, subscribed by at least five per cent (5%) of the citizen registered to vote.

2. This proposal shall be read three times with a six-day interval to decide whether it is admitted or not for a discussion.

3. If admitted, the proposal shall be submitted to a commission appointed by absolute majority of the Assembly, for a decision in a term up to twenty working days.

4. Once the decision is made, it shall be discussed as per the provisions to make laws, but said reform shall be approved by the votes of at least two thirds out of the total members of the Assembly.

5. Once the reform is approved, the Assembly must prepare the corresponding draft, through a Commission, being sufficient the absolute majority to approve it.

6. Said draft shall be afterwards submitted to the Executive Power, who shall send it to the Assembly with a presidential message at the beginning of the next ordinary legislature, with his observations, or recommending it.

7. The Legislative Assembly, in its first decisions, shall discuss the draft in three debates, if approved by the vote of at least two thirds out of the total Assembly members, and then it shall become a part of the Constitution, and shall be communicated to the Executive Power for its publication and compliance

D. Constitutional Reforms by the Popular Power Assembly in Cuba

According to article 137 of the Cuban Constitution, the general principle is that the Constitution shall only be reformed by the Popular Power's National Assembly through a decision adopted, in a nominal vote, by a majority not inferior than two thirds out of its total members.

As it has been said, only if the reform refers to the composition and faculties of the Popular Power's National Assembly or of the State Council or to rights and duties set forth in the Constitution, it is further required a ratification by the favorable vote of the majority of the citizen with electoral right, in a referendum called for that purpose by the Assembly.

E. The Constitutional Reforms by the National Congress in Chile

Article 116 of the Chilean Constitution set forth that the proposed reforms to the Constitution shall be initiated by a message of the President of the Republic or by any of the members of the National Congress, with the limitations set forth in the first paragraph of article 62 (depending on the matter, the debate shall arise in the Deputies Chamber or in the Senate).

The proposed reform needs the approval of three fifths of the congressmen of each Chamber. However, if the reform is about Chapters I, III, VII, X, XI or XIV (ruling the basis of institutions, constitutional rights, Constitutional Court, Armed Forces, Public Security and Order, National Security Council and the constitutional reform process), it shall need in both Chambers, the approval of two thirds of the congressmen. The urgency system shall be applied to constitutional reform drafts.

As per article 117, both Chambers fully gathered shall be called by the President of the Senate to a public session, which shall be held not before thirty days or after sixty days counted from the approval of a draft in the manner described hereinbefore, being present the majority of its members, and shall study and vote it without a debate.

If at the time fixed for the session, a majority of the total Congress members is not attending it, the session shall be held the same day, at a later time fixed by the President of the Senate in the calling, with the congressmen attending it.

The draft approved by the majority of the Congress shall be submitted to the President of the Republic. If he rejected the complete draft approved by the Congress and the Congress insisted on it as a whole, by the two thirds of the members of both chambers, the President then must promulgate said draft, unless he decide to consult the people by a plebiscite.

If the President makes partial observations on a reform draft approved by the Congress, the observations shall be deemed approved by the affirmative vote of three fifths or two thirds of the members of each Chambers, as per article 116 and it shall be returned to the President for its promulgation.

In the event that the Chambers do not approve all or some presidential observation, no constitutional reform shall be made on the matters in disagreement, unless both Chambers insisted on them by two thirds of its members. In this case, the part of the draft in which they are insisted on, shall be returned to the President for its promulgation, except if he decides to consult the citizen by a plebiscite regarding the matters in disagreement.

F.   Constitutional Reforms by the National Congress in Ecuador

According to the Ecuadorian Constitution (Art. 280), the Political Constitution can be reformed by the National Congress or by popular consultation.

As to the reforms that can be approved by the National Congress, article 281 set forth that the constitutional reform drafts shall be submitted before the National Congress by: (i) a number of deputies equal to twenty per cent of its members or a legislative block; (ii) the President of the Republic; (iii) the Supreme Court; (iv) the Constitutional Court, or (v) a number equal to one per cent of people with political rights, whose names are listed in the Electoral Registry.

The National Congress shall judge and discuss the constitutional reform drafts, through the same proceeding set forth to approve laws (Art. 282). Nevertheless, the second debate, in which it is required the favorable vote of two thirds out of the total members of the Congress, shall be held once a year from the first debate has passed. Once the draft is approved, the Congress shall submit it to the President of the Republic for its sanction or objection, as per the provisions of the Constitution.

G.   The Partial Constitutional Reforms by the National Assembly in Nicaragua

The National Assembly of Nicaragua is also empowered to partially reform the Political Constitution (Art. 191) and to consider and decide on the initiative of total reform of the same. The following procedure is set forth (which also must be applicable to the reforms of constitutional laws (Electoral, on Emergency and on Amparo as per article 195, with the exception of the requirement of two legislatures) (Art. 195):

The partial reform initiative correspond to the President of the Republic, or to a third of the congressmen to the National Assembly, and as per article 192, it shall contain the article or articles to be reformed, stating the motifs. Such initiative shall be sent to a special commission that shall decide in a term not longer than sixty days. The reform draft shall be submitted to the procedure set forth to make laws, and shall be discussed in two legislatures.

The approval of a partial reform requires the favorable vote of sixty per cent of the congressmen. The President of the Republic must promulgate the partial reform and in this case he cannot exercise the right to veto (Art. 194).

IV. THE CONSTITUTIONAL LIMITS IMPOSED UPON THE DERIVED CONSTITUENT POWER

As it has been pointed out, constitutional review procedures in Latin America are set forth in the Constitutions, wherefore the derived constituent power is subject to constitutional limits. These limits are, in the first place, those derived from the constitutional provisions themselves as to the constitutional review procedures; in the second place, those derived from the so-called unchangeable clauses; and in the third place, those derived from the functioning of the constituted State organs during the constitutional reform or amendment procedures.

1.   *Limits Set Forth in the Constitution*

Every constitutional review procedure, being set forth in the Constitution, is subjected to follow the constitutional provisions ruling it. Constitutional supremacy is applied even to exercising the constituent power set forth in the Constitution itself.

The consequence is that the compliance of such procedures is subject to judicial constitutional review by the Constitutional Jurisdiction.

In many Latin American Constitutions that is expressly established. That's the case, for example of the Colombian Constitution, whose article 241 established that the Constitutional Court is the guardian of the Constitution's integrity and supremacy, granting it in particular power to:

1. Decide the unconstitutionality claims raised by the citizens challenging the acts reforming the Constitution, whatever their origin is, only due to procedural mistakes in their formation.

2. Decide, prior to the popular decision, on the constitutionality of the call to a referendum or to a Constituent Assembly to reform the Constitution, only due to procedural mistakes in its formation.

3. Decide upon the constitutionality of referenda on laws and national popular consultations and plebiscite.

Additionally, Article 379 of the Colombian Constitution, set forth that in all constitutional review procedures whereas by legislative acts, the calling to a referendum for popular consultation or the covenant of a Constituent Assembly, the same shall be declared unconstitutional by the Constitutional Court when breaking the requirements set forth in Title XIII of the Constitution whereby the constitutional reform is ruled. The public action challenging those acts shall only be raised within a year after their promulgation, complying the provisions of article 241, paragraph 2 of the Constitution (power of the Constitutional Court to decide, prior to the popular decision, on the constitutionality of the calling of a referendum of a Constituent Assembly to reform the Constitution, only due to procedural mistakes).

On the other hand, pursuant to the Bolivian Constitution, the Constitutional Court is empowered to (Art. 119, VII, 10) judge and decides the claims regarding procedures in the reform of the Constitution.

In Costa Rica, article 10, b) of the Constitution granted the Constitutional Chamber of the Supreme Court the faculty to decide consultations on the constitutional reform drafts.

In the Chilean Constitution, pursuant to article 82, 2 the Constitutional Court is empowered the faculty to decide constitutional issues rose during the constitutional reform procedures. In this case, the Court shall only decide the issue at a request of the President of the Republic, of any of the Chambers or of a fourth part of its members, provided that it is raised before the promulgation of the reform.

The Court shall decide within a ten–day term counted from the reception of the request unless it decided to extend it p to other ten days due to serious and qualified motifs

The request shall not suspend the draft procedure, but its challenged part cannot be promulgated until the said term passed.

In any event, it can be said that during all the constitutional review procedures, the organs exercising the constituent power are subjected to the Constitution, which, as is stated in the Constitution of Nicaragua, must be considered in force "while the National Constituent Assembly approves the new Constitution" (Article 194).

2.   *Limits Derived from Unchangeable Clauses*

Other limit established to the constituent power is the one derived from the unchangeable clauses set forth in the Constitutions, which established principles or rules stated as non review able. In several cases, they are express clauses, in other they are clauses derived from the interpretation of the constitutional text.

Among the former, it is outstanding article 248 of the Constitution of El Salvador, which set forth:

> Art. 248: "...In no case the articles of this Constitution ruling the governmental form and system, the territory of the Republic and the alterability exercising the Presidency shall be reformed."

In the same sense, article 119 of the Constitution of Dominican Republic is outstanding, which set forth that:

> Art. 119. No reform can refer to the government form, which shall always be civil, republican, democratic and representative."

The Brazilian Constitution, in article 60 § 4 set forth:

> "It shall not be discussed the proposed amendment tending to abolish: I. The Federal form of the State; II. The direct, secret, universal and periodical vote; III: Separation of Powers; IV. Individual rights and guarantees."

Article 137 of the Cuban Constitution set forth as well an unchangeable clause, by excluding from constitutional reforms everything "referring to the political, economic and social system, whose unchangeable character is set forth in article 3, Chapter I, and the prohibition of making business under aggression, threaten or coercion from a foreign power." Furthermore, in the reform of June, 2002, the Popular Power's National Assembly added to the Constitution other unchangeable clause which reads:

> "*Special Provision.* The Cuban people, almost entirely, expressed between the days June 15 and 18, 2002, its decided support to the constitutional reform draft proposed by the mass organizations in special meetings of all their national authorities held on June 10th, ratifying in

all its parts the Constitution of the Republic, and proposing that the socialist character and the political and social system contained in it be declared irrevocable, as a honorable and categorical answer to exigencies and threatens from the imperialist government of the United States on May 20th, 2002."

But besides the unchangeable clauses expressly set forth in the Constitutions, from their provisions many other clauses that would fit in the non reviewable character by the constituent power can derived.

That is the case, for example, of the constitutions setting forth in some articles the "eternal" character of a principle or provision, as is stated in article 1 of the Venezuelan Constitution when saying that the Republic "is irrevocably free and independent..."; or article 5 when stating that "sovereignty resides untransferable in the people"; or article 6 when setting forth that the government of the republic "and of the political entities composing it, is and shall always be democratic, participative, elective, decentralized, alternative, responsible, plural and of revocable mandates."

3.   Limits Derived from the Functioning of the State Constituted Powers

Constitutional review procedures established in the Constitutions are intended to reform or amend the Constitutions but without altering during its development, the State constituted organs.

This is the general principle resulting from all the Latin American Constitutions, notwithstanding the constitutional review process set forth.

In effect, in the cases in which the derived constituent power is granted to the people for the reform or amendment approval, during the procedure of making the reform or amendment draft and popular approval of the same through referendum, plebiscite or popular consultation, State constituted organs continue performing their activities with no interruption or interference of any kind. Only exceptionally certain s State organ powers might be affected during the constitutional review procedures, but they shall be set forth in an express way, as the limitations to the presidential veto as to the acts of the legislative organs concerning constitutional reforms or amendments, established for instance in the Constitution of Bolivia, Costa Rica, Chile, Peru, Nicaragua, Dominican Republic, Uruguay and Venezuela.

In the cases in which the constituent power is granted to a National Constituent Assembly and except for express provisions otherwise, the functioning of the National Constituent Assembly does not affect or impede the simultaneous functioning of the constituted state organs. This principle is expressly set forth in the Constitution of Paraguay, whose article 291 set forth the following:

> Art. 291. *Power of the National Constituent Convention.* The National Constituent Convention is independent from the constituted power. During the term of its discussions, it shall only carry out reform duties, excluding any other work. It shall not arrogate attributions of the State Powers, it shall not substitute those exercising them or shorten or extend its mandate.

In the same sense, but regarding the Congress functioning during the performance of the National Constituent Assembly, in the Constitution of Guatemala, article 279 set forth that "the National Constituent Assembly and the Congress shall function simultaneously." The exception to the rule, in an express way as well, is set forth in the Constitution of Nicaragua, whose article 193 set forth that once approved a total reform initiative by the National Assembly, it shall fix a term to call the election of the National Constituent Assembly, maintaining "its mandate until the installation of the National Constituent Assembly."

In other Constitutions, as the Colombian one, once installed the National Constituent Assembly, the powers of the State constituted organs are limited only regarding the constitutional review procedures. Thus, pursuant to article 376, from the election of the Constituent Assembly for a constitutional review "the ordinary faculty of the Congress to reform the Constitution is suspended during the term fixed for the Assembly to perform its duties."

Finally, it shall be mentioned that the Venezuelan Constitution established that during the functioning of the National Constituent Assembly, whose single purpose is "transforming the State, creating a new legal order and writing a new Constitution" (Art. 347), "the constituted power shall impede in no way the decisions of the National Constituent Assembly" (Art. 349). This has to be interpreted, of course, according to the terms of the Constitutions, in the sense that the Constituent Assembly has no power to alter the rules of the Constitution, particularly regarding the functioning of the constituted powers, while in force and before it is not substituted by the new one.

4.   *Limits Derived from the Existence of Extraordinary Circumstances*

Another limit to constitutional review derives from the existence of extraordinary constitutional circumstances, as exceptional state or siege, which once decreed, impede the development of reform procedures.

It is the case of the Brazilian Constitution, which established (article 60, § 1°) that "no constitutional amendment shall be approved under a federal intervention, defense state or siege." These exceptional circumstances shall be decreed by the President of the Republic (Art. 84, IX and X) with the varied participation of other Union Powers (Arts. 34 and ff. and 136 and ff.)

In Venezuela, a similar limitation was set forth in the 1997 Organic Law on Suffrage and Political Participation, reformed in 1998 (*Official Gazette* N° 5233 Extraordinary of 05-28-98), in which Article 186 established that "Referenda shall not take place during emergency states, during suspension or restriction of constitutional guarantees or serious public disorders foreseen in articles 240, 241 and 244 of the Constitution." In that moment, the referendum was established only legally as a mean of political participation, since the Constitution of 1961 ruled anything on that; thus it was possible that the same law ruling it set forth limitations of this type. However, being the referenda now established in the 1999 Constitution, including those needed to approve constitutional reforms and amendments and to convene a National Constituent Assembly for a constitutional review, being set forth no limit to carry out referenda, a law cannot establish any limit. Therefore, article 186 of the Organic Law on Suffrage and Political Participation shall be deemed tacitly repealed by the 1999 Constitution, existing therefore, no limits to carry out a constitutional review process due to the decree of an exceptional state.

5. *Temporary Limits*

Certain Constitutions established temporary limits for the constitutional review, meaning that the constitutional text established a non reviewable minimum term. That's the case, for example, of Paraguay, whose Constitution (Art. 289) set forth that constitutional reform "shall only proceed after ten year from its promulgation"; and amendments "shall only proceed after three years from its promulgation" (Art. 290).

FINAL COMMENTS

Constitutional review means are the core of the constitutional process. There are not and cannot exist unchangeable or eternal Constitutions; on the contrary, constitutional texts require permanent change to rule the society according to social and political changes. One of those constitutional review means is the review or formal reform of the Constitution.

However, it is not the only one. Constitutional adaptation can occur through other means that the Constitution itself established to assure the constitutional change, without starting the formal instruments of constitutional review (amendments, reforms, constituent assemblies), as it happens when the constitutional text ruled the sanctioning of special and specific laws to develop certain subject of constitutional order, such as political decentralization. Those laws have then constitutional rank as well as the constitutional rigidity, producing a modification in the Constitution authorized in the text itself.

Of course, other mean to assure the constitutional change is the development of Constitutional Jurisdictions in Latin America, through Constitutional Courts or Constitutional Chambers of the Supreme Courts, with constitutional power to make biding interpretations of the constitution according to its principles. Through constitutional interpretation, without formally amending or reforming the Constitution, it can be accomplished the adaptation of the formal constitutional provisions to the new political and social requirements of a society in a given moment. Therefore, the constitutional judge can be certainly considered a great adaptation instrument of the Constitution, but he can also be a diabolic instrument of constitutional dictatorship, not subjected to controls, when justifying all constitutional violations produced in authoritarian regimes or where the separation of powers is not really accomplished.

Apart from these constitutional adaptation means, constitutional review means formally established in the Constitutions, as amendment, reform or call of Constituent Assemblies or Convention procedures, allow constitutional modifications with the direct people's participation (through referendum or plebiscite) or its representatives elected in Parliaments or in Constituent Assemblies. In any case, they are constitutional review models whereby the derived constituent power is shown, subjected to the limits and procedures expressly ruled in the Constitutions. On the contrary, the original constituent power is only shown in the *de facto* constitutional review procedures, aside from the constitutional line.

Now, from the comparative analysis of the constitutional review procedures ruled in Latin American Constitutions, the following general comments can be made:

1. In almost all the Constitutions, the popular participation is ruled in the constitutional review procedures, being exceptional the countries that do not foreseen some referendum or popular consultation that allow the people's participation as original constituent power. That's the case of Argentina and Nicaragua that only ruled as constitutional review means a Constituent Assembly or Convention; and Bolivia, El Salvador and Mexico that grant the derived constituent power only to the Legislative organs, of course, through special procedures with qualified majorities. In Uruguay, Colombia, Venezuela, Paraguay, Guatemala, Costa Rica, Peru, Cuba, Chile, Ecuador and Panama it is ruled the people's participation in the constitutional review, and even in Uruguay, as the only mean of constitutional reform.

2. In all Latin American Constitutions, it is ruled the participation of the national legislative organ (Congresses, Assemblies) in constitutional review procedures, wherefore in the same popular representation always participates. Only exceptionally the legislative organs are the only ones exercising the derived constituent power, through special qualified majorities, as in Bolivia, El Salvador and Mexico. In the latter, in addition to the Union Congress, the Legislative Assemblies of the Federal States also participates in the constitutional review procedure. In no other federal Constitution (Argentina, Brazil or Venezuela) is ruled the participation of the Legislative Assemblies of the States in the constitutional review procedure. In Argentina and Brazil, however, States would participate through the representation in the Senate.

3. In all the Constitutions it is ruled the participation of the President of the Republic in the constitutional review procedure, by means of the reform initiative or by means of the promulgation of the same, being limited in the latter, in many Constitutions, the presidential veto power (Bolivia, Peru, Nicaragua, Uruguay and Venezuela).

4. In all Latin American Constitutions, constitutional review procedures are expressly ruled, wherefore the same, having constitutional rank, shall be complied by all the State organs. Therefore, it is not possible to make a constitutional reform through a procedure different from the one ruled in the Constitution. Consequently, constitutional reform or amendment procedures developed not complying constitutional rules governing them, or about issues or matters prohibited by the Constitution are unconstitutional and are able to be controlled by the Constitutional Jurisdiction.[29] That is foreseen even in an express way in certain constitutions that grant the

---

29   In Venezuela, nonetheless, the Supreme Tribunal of Justice avoided to exercise judicial review upon the 2007 Constitutional Review procedure. See Allan R. Brewer-Carías, "El juez constitucional vs. la supremacía constitucional O de cómo la jurisdicción constitucional en Venezuela renunció a controlar la constitucionalidad del procedimiento seguido para la 'reforma constitucional' sancionada por la Asamblea Nacional el 2 de noviembre de 2007, antes de que fuera rechazada por el pueblo en el referendo del 2 de diciembre de 2007," en Eduardo Ferrer Mac Gregor y César de Jesús Molina Suárez (Coordinadores), *El juez constitucio-*

Constitutional Courts or Constitutional Chambers of the Supreme Courts the control of constitutionality of the acts regarding constitutional reforms or amendments, as the Constitutions of Bolivia, Colombia, Costa Rica and Chile.[30]

nal en el Siglo XXI, Universidad nacional Autónoma de México, Suprema Corte de Justicia de la Nación, México 2009, Tomo I, pp. 385-435; and in *Revista de Derecho Público,* N° 112, Editorial Jurídica Venezolana, Caracas 2007, pp. 661-694

30   On this particular aspects see Allan R. Brewer-Carías, "La reforma constitucional en América Latina y el control de constitucionalidad," in *Reforma de la Constitución y control de constitucionalidad.* Congreso Internacional, Pontificia Universidad Javeriana, Bogotá Colombia, junio 14 al 17 de 2005, Bogotá, 2005, pp. 108-159.

CHAPTER III

THE 1999 VENEZUELAN CONSTITUTION-MAKING PROCESS AND THE FRAMING OF AN AUTHORITARIAN POLITICAL REGIME

(2002)

This essay was written for my participation in the "Project on Constitution-Making, Peace Building and National Reconciliation," directed by the United States Institute of Peace, Washington, D.C. The first version of the work was used for my Presentation at the Conference on Constitution-Making Processes, organized by the Institute of Peace in Washington, D.C., in October 11, 2002. The final version of the paper was published in the book: Laura E. Miller (Editor), *Framing the State in Times of Transition. Case Studies in Constitution Making*, United States Institute of Peace Press, Washington 2010, pp. 505-531

I.   THE 1999 NATIONAL CONSTITUENT ASSEMBLY

In December 1999, as a result of a constitution making process developed during that year a new Constitution was approved in Venezuela. A National Constituent Assembly elected that same year sanctioned the new Constitution, which was submitted to an approval referendum held on December 15, 1999.

As a member of the National Constituent Assembly, that participated in all its sessions and in all the constitutional discussions held, I opposed the sanctioning of the Constitution, and lead the political campaign for a "No" vote in the Constitution approval referendum. This position was based on my multiple dissenting and negative votes in the Constituent Assembly and on my publicly express fear that new the Constitution[31], in spite of its advanced civil and political rights regulations,[32] was an

---

31   See the text of all this author's dissenting and negative votes in Allan R. Brewer-Carías, *Debate Constituyente (Aportes a la Asamblea Nacional Constituyente)*, Vol. III (18 Octubre-30 Noviembre 1999), Fundación de Derecho Público, Caracas 1999, pp. 107-308 ff.

instrument framed for the development of an authoritarian regime. This fear was due to the Constitution's provisions allowing the possibility of the concentration of State power, State centralization, extreme presidentialism, extensive State participation in the economy, and general marginalization of civil society in public activities, exaggerated State social obligations reflecting State oil income populism, and extreme militarism[33].

Unfortunately, the warning signs of 1999-2000[34] have become reality, and the political system which resulted from the 1999 constitution making process has turned out to be the current authoritarian regime, led by former Lieutenant-Colonel Hugo Chávez Frías, one of the leaders of the failed 1992 military *coup d'Etat.*[35] Chavez was elected President of the Republic in the general elections of December

---

32   See the proposal of this author in this matter in Allan R. Brewer-Carías, *Debate Constituyente (Aportes a la Asamblea Nacional Constituyente)*, Vol. II (9 Septiembre-17 Octubre), Fundación de Derecho Público, Caracas 1999, pp. 76-155 ff.

33   See "Razones para 'No' firmar el proyecto" and "Razones para el voto 'No' en el Referéndum sobre la Constitución" in Allan R. Brewer-Carías, *Debate Constituyente (Aportes a la Asamblea Nacional Constituyente)*, Vol. III (*18 Octubre-30 Noviembre 1999*), Fundación de Derecho Público, Caracas 1999, pp. 311 ff.

34   See this author's critical comments regarding the new Constitution expressed immediately after its approval, in his papers on "Reflexiones Críticas y Visión General de la Constitución de 1999," Inaugural Lecture on the *Curso de Actualización en Derecho Constitucional*, Aula Magna de la Universidad Católica Andrés Bello, Caracas, February 2, 2000; on "*La Constitución de 1999 y la reforma política, Colegio de Abogados del Distrito Federal*, Caracas, February 9, 2000; on "The constitutional reform in Venezuela and the 1999 Constitution," Seminar on *Challenges to Fragile Democracies in the Americas: Legitimacy and accountability*, organized by the Faculty of Law, University of Texas, Austin, February 25, 2000; on "Reflexiones Críticas sobre la Constitución de 1999," *Seminario Internacional: El Constitucionalismo Latinoamericano del Siglo XXI en el marco del LXXXIII Aniversario de la Promulgación de la Constitución Política de los Estados Unidos Mexicanos,* Cámara de Diputados e Instituto de Investigaciones Jurídicas UNAM, México, January 31, 2000; on "*La nueva Constitución de Venezuela del 2000,"* Centro Internationale per lo Studio del Diritto Comparato, Facoltà di Giurisprudenza, Facoltà de Scienze Politiche, Universita'degli Studi di Urbino, Urbino, Italia, March 3, 2000; and on "Apreciación General sobre la Constitución de 1999," *Ciclo de Conferencias sobre la Constitución de 1999, Academia de Ciencias Políticas y Sociales*, Caracas, May 11, 2000. These papers were published in Diego Valadés, Miguel Carbonell (Coordinadores), *Constitucionalismo Iberoamericano del Siglo XXI*, Cámara de Diputados. LVII Legislatura, Universidad Nacional Autónoma de México, México 2000, pp. 171-193; in *Revista de Derecho Público*, N° 81, Editorial Jurídica Venezolana, Caracas, enero-marzo 2000, pp. 7-21; in *Revista Facultad de Derecho, Derechos y Valores*, Volumen III N° 5, Universidad Militar Nueva Granada, Santafé de Bogotá, D.C., Colombia, Julio 2000, pp. 9-26; and in *La Constitución de 1999*, Biblioteca de la Academia de Ciencias Políticas y Sociales, Caracas 2000, pp. 63-88.

35   See regarding the February 4th 1992 *coup d'Etat* attempt, in H. Sonntag y T. Maingón, *Venezuela: 4F1992. Un análisis socio-político,* Caracas 1992; and Gustavo Tarre Briceño, *4 de febrero-El espejo roto,* Caracas 1994.

1998,[36] elected in 2000 after the approval of the new 1999 Constitution, and was reelected in December 2006.[37] After nine years of consolidating the existing authoritarian regime, in August 2007 he proposed before the National Assembly a radical reform to the constitution in order to formally consolidate a socialist, centralized, and militaristic police state.[38] The reform was sanctioned by the Assembly on November 2, 2007, but was rejected by the people in a referendum held on December 2, 2007.[39] In any event, these sorts of fundamental transformations of the State could only be sanctioned by a National Constituent Assembly, as it is expressly set forth in the 1999 Constitution (Article 347), and cannot be approved by a "constitutional reform" procedure (Article 342), as was proposed by the President in contravention of the Constitution.[40]

The 1999 Constitution replaced the previous 1961 Constitution[41], becoming the 26th in the constitutional history of the country[42]. As mentioned, it was discussed and

---

36   In the 1998 presidential election, Hugo Chávez Frías obtained the 56.20% of the cast votes, followed by Henrique Salas Römer, who obtained 39.99% of the votes. Approximately, 35% of the eligible voters did not turn out to vote. See the references in *El Universal,* Caracas December 11th, 1998, p. 1-1.

37   In the 2006 presidential election, Hugo Chávez Frías obtained 62.84% of the cast votes, and the opposition candidate, Manuel Rosales, obtained 36.9% of the votes. Approximately 25.3% of the eligible voters did not turn to vote.

38   See *Proyecto de Reforma Constitucional. Elaborado por el ciudadano Presidente de la República Bolivariana de Venezuela, Hugo Chávez Frías,* Editorial Atenea, Caracas agosto 2007, 58 pp. See the comments on the draft in Allan R. Brewer-Carías, *Hacia la consolidación de un Estado socialista, centralizado, policial y militarista. Comentarios sobre el alcance y sentido de la Reforma Constitucional 2007,* Editorial Jurídica Venezolana, Caracas 2007, 157 pp; and in *La Reforma Constitucional de 2007 (Sancionada inconstitucionalmente por la Asamblea Nacional el 2 de Noviembre de 2007),* Editorial Jurídica venezolana, Caracas 2007, 225 pp.

39   The reform was submitted to referendum held on December 2, 2007, where a majority of the people rejected it. The "No" votes comprised 51% (4.5 million) of the cast votes (9.2 million); approximately 44.11% of the eligible voters did not turn to vote.

40   See Allan R. Brewer-Carías, "El autoritarismo establecido en fraude a la Constitución y a la democracia y su formalización en Venezuela mediante la reforma constitucional. (De cómo en un país democrático se ha utilizado el sistema eleccionario para minar la democracia y establecer un régimen autoritario de supuesta "dictadura de la democracia" que se pretende regularizar mediante la reforma constitucional)," in *Temas constitucionales. Planteamientos ante una Reforma,* Fundación de Estudios de Derecho Administrativo, FUNEDA, Caracas 2007, pp. 13-74; and in Allan R. Brewer-Carías, *Estudios sobre el Estado Constitucional 2005-2006,* Editorial Jurídica Venezolana, Caracas 2007, pp. 79 ff.

41   See, Allan R. Brewer-Carías, *La Constitución y sus Enmiendas,* Editorial Jurídica Venezolana, Caracas, 1991; and *Instituciones Políticas y Constitucionales,* Vol. I *(Evolución histórica del Estado),* Universidad Católica del Táchira, Editorial Jurídica Venezolana, San Cristóbal-Caracas, 1996, pp. 455 ff.

42   See the text of all the Constitutions (1811-1999) in Allan R. Brewer-Carías, *Las Constituciones de Venezuela,* Biblioteca de la Academia de Ciencias Políticas y Sociales, Caracas 2008. Regarding the constitutional history behind those texts, see this author's "Estudio Preliminar" in the same book, Vol. I, pp. 23-526.

drafted by a National Constituent Assembly called and elected for that purpose, and was approved by referendum held on December 15 1999[43].

The 1999 constitution making process was not the first of its kind in Venezuelan constitutional history. Originally, the independent and autonomous State of Venezuela was created through two initial constitution making processes. The first one took place in 1811, after the Declaration of Independence (July 5th, 1811) of the Spanish Colonies that were integrated in 1777 in the General Captaincy of Venezuela, creating the Confederation of States of Venezuela (1811 Constitution). The second one took place in 1830, after the separation of the Provinces of Venezuela from the Republic of Colombia that had been created nine years earlier, in 1821, by Simon Bolivar, when he managed to integrate the ancient Spanish Colonies established in what is today the territories of Ecuador, Colombia and Venezuela (1830 Constitution).

After those two original constitution making processes, seven other constitution making processes were carried out in 1858, 1863, 1893, 1901, 1914, 1946 and 1953 through Constituent Assemblies or Congresses with as many resulting constitutions. In each case, the constitution-making process was the consequence of a *de facto* rejection of the existing constitution, through a *coup d'Etat*, a revolution, or a civil war.[44]

The constitution making process of 1999, in contrast, had a peculiarity that made it different from all the previous ones in Venezuelan history, and even from many similar processes which have occurred in other countries in the last decades: It was not the result of a *de facto* rejection of the 1961 constitution, through a revolution, a war, or a *coup d'Etat*. With some similarities to the 1991 Colombian, the 2008 Bolivian, and the 2007 Ecuadorian[45] constitutional processes, it can be said, that the Venezuelan constitutional process of 1999 began as a democratic process that in its origins did not involve a rupture of the previous political regime.[46]

---

43   See Allan R. Brewer-Carías, *La Constitución de 1999*, Editorial Jurídica Venezolana, Caracas 2000; and *La Constitución de 1999. Derecho Constitucional Venezolano*, 2 vols. Caracas, 2004. Also see, Hildegard Rondón de Sansó, *Análisis de la Constitución venezolana de 1999*, Editorial Ex Libris, Caracas 2001; Ricardo Combellas, *Derecho Constitucional: una introducción al estudio de la Constitución de la República Bolivariana de Venezuela*, Mc Graw Hill, Caracas, 2001; and Alfonso Rivas Quintero, *Derecho Constitucional*, Paredes Editores, Valencia, 2002.

44   See Elena Plaza and Ricardo Combillas (coordinators), *Procesos constituyentes y reformas constitucionales en la historia de Venezuela; 1811-1999*, 2 Vols. Universidad central de Venezuela, Caracas 2005; and Allan R. Brewer-Carías, "Las Asambleas Constituyentes en la historia de Venezuela," *El Universal*, Caracas September 8th, 1998, p. 1-5.

45   See Allan R. Brewer-Carías, "El inicio del proceso constituyente en Ecuador en 2007 y las lecciones de la experiencia venezolana de 1999," in *Estudios sobre el Estado Constitucional 2005-2006*, Editorial Jurídica Venezolana, Caracas 2007, pp. 766 ff.

46   See Allan R. Brewer-Carías, "Reflexiones sobre la crisis del sistema político, sus salidas democráticas y la convocatoria a una Constituyente," in *Los Candidatos Presidenciales ante la Academia*. Ciclo de Exposiciones 10-18 Agosto 1998, Biblioteca de la Academia de Cien-

However, it took place in the context of a severe political crisis[47], which was affecting the functioning of the democratic regime that had been established in 1958[48]. The crisis had arisen as a result of the lack of evolution from a system of overly centralized political parties[49], which existed then and still exists to this day. In fact, the call for the referendum consulting the people on the establishment of the Constituent National Assembly, made by the then newly elected President of the Republic, Hugo Chavez, through a Decree issued on February 2, 1999, intended to ask the people their opinion on a Constituent National Assembly "aimed at transforming the State and creating a new legal order that allows the effective functioning of a social and participative democracy[50]." That was the formal *raison d'etre* of the constitutional process of 1999, and that is why, with few exceptions, it would have been difficult to find anyone in the country who could have disagreed with those stated purposes: transforming the State, on the one hand, and on the other, putting into practice a form of democracy that would be social, participative, and effective. For that purpose, undoubtedly, a political conciliation and participative process was necessary.

But unfortunately, Chavez did not formally conceive the constitutional process as an instrument of conciliation aimed at reconstructing the democratic system and assuring good governance. That would have required the political commitment of all

---

cias Políticas y Sociales, Caracas 1998, pp. 9-66; also published in *Ciencias de Gobierno N°* *4*, Julio-Diciembre 1998, Gobernación del Estado Zulia, Instituto Zuliano de Estudios Políticos Económicos y Sociales (IZEPES), Maracaibo, Edo. Zulia, 1998, pp. 49-88; and in Allan R. Brewer-Carías, *Asamblea Constituyente y ordenamiento constitucional*, Biblioteca de la Academia de Ciencias Políticas y Sociales, Caracas 1999, pp. 13-77.

47   See Allan R. Brewer-Carías, *La crisis de las instituciones: responsables y salidas,* Cátedra Pío Tamayo, Centro de Estudios de Historia Actual (mimeo) Facultad de Economía y Ciencias Sociales, Universidad Central de Venezuela, Caracas 1985; also published in *Revista del Centro de Estudios Superiores de las Fuerzas Armadas de Cooperación*, N° 11, Caracas 1985, pp. 57-83; and in *Revista de la Facultad de Ciencias Jurídicas y Políticas*, N° 64, Universidad Central de Venezuela, Caracas 1985, pp. 129-155. Also see Allan R. Brewer-Carías, *Instituciones Políticas y Constitucionales,* Vol. I (*Evolución histórica del Estado)*, Universidad Católica del Táchira, Editorial Jurídica Venezolana, San Cristóbal-Caracas, 1996, pp. 523-541.

48   Regarding the democratic political process after 1958, see Allan R. Brewer-Carías. *Cambio político y reforma del Estado en Venezuela. Contribución al estudio sobre el Estado democrático y social de derecho*, Ed. Tecnos, Madrid 1975.

49   See Allan R. Brewer-Carías, *El Estado. Crisis y Reforma*, Biblioteca de la Academia de Ciencias Políticas y Sociales, Caracas 1982; *Problemas del Estado de partidos*, Editorial Jurídica Venezolana, Caracas 1988.

50   See the text of the Decree in *Gaceta Oficial* N° 36.634 of February 2d, -1999, and its modification in *Gaceta Oficial* N° 36.658 of March, 10th, 1999. See the criticisms of the Decree as a "constitutional fraud" in Allan R. Brewer-Carías, *Asamblea Constituyente y ordenamiento constitucional*, Biblioteca de la Academia de Ciencias Políticas y Sociales, Caracas 1999, pp .229 ff.

components of society and the participation of all sectors of society in the design of a new, functioning democracy, which did not occur[51].

The constitutional process of 1999, in fact, served to facilitate the total takeover of State power by a new political group which crushed all the others, including the then existing political parties. As a result, almost all of the opportunities for inclusion and public participation were squandered. Moreover, the constitution making process became an endless *coup d'Etat*[52] when the Constituent Assembly, elected in July of 1999, began violating the existing Constitution of 1961 by assuming powers it lacked under that text and under the terms of the April referendum that created it. As an independent non-partisan candidate, I was elected to the 1999 Constituent Assembly, thus being able to participate in all its discussions, dissenting orally and in writing on all those unconstitutional and undemocratic decisions[53]. Therefore I was a witness of this seizure of power from the consultative referendum on the calling of a Constituent Assembly held in April 1999; through the election of the Constituent Assembly in July 1999; through the period from August 1999 to January 2000, during which time the Constituent Assembly exercised supra constitutional power, and finally through the drafting, discussion and approval of a new Constitution by referendum in December 1999.

The result of this process was that the 1999 constitution making process was a failure as an instrument for political reconciliation and democratization[54]. With the benefit of hindsight, it is now clear that the stated democratic purposes of the process have not been accomplished. There has not been an effective reform of the State, except for the purpose of authoritarian institution building, or the creation of a social and participative democracy, unless one can consider as democratic the election of a populist government that has concentrated all branches of government and crushed political pluralism. Thus, if it is true that political changes of great importance have been made, some of them have contributed to the aggravation of the factors that provoked the crisis in the first place. New political actors have assumed power, but far from implementing a democratic conciliation policy, they have accen-

---

51   See the 1998 political discussion regarding the necessary inclusive character of the constitutional-making process proposed, in Allan R. Brewer-Carías, *Asamblea Constituyente y ordenamiento constitucional*, Biblioteca de la Academia de Ciencias Políticas y Sociales, Caracas 1999, pp. 38 ff.

52   See Allan R. Brewer-Carías, *Golpe de Estado y proceso constituyente en Venezuela*, Universidad Nacional Autónoma de México, México 2002, pp. 181 ff.

53   See the author's dissenting votes in Allan R. Brewer-Carías, *Debate Constituyente*, (Aportes a la Asamblea Nacional Constituyente), vols. I (8 Agosto-8 Septiembre) and III (18 Octubre-30 Noviembre), Fundación de Derecho Público, Editorial Jurídica Venezolana, Caracas 1999, pp. 17 ff. and 109 ff.

54   See Allan R. Brewer-Carías, "El proceso constituyente y la fallida reforma del Estado en Venezuela" in *Estrategias y propuestas para la reforma del Estado*, Universidad Nacional Autónoma de México, México 2001, pp. 25-48; also published in Allan R. Brewer-Carías, *Reflexiones sobre el constitucionalismo en América*, Editorial Jurídica Venezolana, Caracas 2001, pp. 243-253.

tuated the differences among Venezuelans, worsening political polarization, and making conciliation increasingly difficult. The seizure of power which characterized the process has opened new wounds, making social and political rivalries worse than they have been for more than a century. Despite Venezuela's extraordinary oil wealth during the first years of the 21st century, the social problems of the country have increased.

II. THE 1998 CRISIS OF THE POLITICAL SYSTEM AND THE NEED FOR DEMOCRATIC RECONSTRUCTION

In order to understand the failure of this constitution making process as an instrument aimed at reinforcing democracy, it is essential to analyze its political background. As previously mentioned, the process began in the midst of a crisis facing the political system that was established in Venezuela at the end of the 1950's. That system was established as a consequence of the democratic (civil-military) revolution of 1958, during which then President of the Republic General Marcos Perez Jimenez, who had led a military government for almost a decade, fled the country.

Three political parties, whose consolidation began in the forties, mainly led this democratic revolution: the social democratic (*Acción Democrática AD*), the Christian democratic (*COPEI*), and the liberal (*Unión Republicana Democrática URD*) parties. The parties agreed to establish democracy in Venezuela through a series of written agreements, the most famous of which was the so called "*Pacto de Punto Fijo*" (1958). That document constitutes an exceptional example in the political history of Latin America of an agreement among political elites to assure the democratic governance of a country[55].

The democratic political system consolidated during the decades of the sixties and seventies, precisely under that agreement, featured the following elements: a democracy of parties, centralism of the State, and a system of presidential government subject to parliamentary control.

1. *Party Domination and the Demand for Participation*

The political parties increasingly monopolized the political regime established from the sixties as a representative and pluralist democracy. They were the ones who established the democracy, but they did not understand, after establishing it, that the

---

55   Regarding the Punto Fijo Pact, the origins of the 1961 Constitution and the political party system, see Juan Carlos Rey, "El sistema de partidos venezolano" in J.C. Rey, *Problemas socio políticos de América Latina,* Caracas 1980, pp. 255 a 338; Allan R. Brewer-Carías, *Instituciones Políticas y Constitucionales,* vol. I (*Evolución histórica del Estado),* Universidad Católica del Táchira, Editorial Jurídica venezolana, San Cristóbal-Caracas, 1996, pp. 394 ff.; Allan R. Brewer-Carías, *Las Constituciones de Venezuela,* Caracas 1997, pp. 201 ff.; and Allan R. Brewer-Carías, *La Constitución y sus Enmiendas,* Editorial Jurídica Venezolana, Caracas 1991, pp. 13 ff. The text of the Pact was published in *El Nacional,* Caracas 27-01-98, p. D-2.

effects of the democratization process required the system of governance to become more representative and participatory.[56]

Democratic representation ended up being an issue exclusively for parties themselves. The d'Hondt method of electing party representatives constituted a system of proportional representation in which party representatives felt more and more accountable to their party rather than to their constituents or to their community. In addition, public participation became a monopoly of the political parties, and they progressively penetrated all of civil society from trade unions and professional associations to neighborhood organizations.

It must be noted that the proportional representation system was established directly in the 1961 Constitution and it applied to all representative elections at the national, state and municipal levels, allowing only the possible establishment by statute of a different system at the local level, which partially occurred in the eighties and the nineties[57]. The absolute dominance of Congress by representatives of two or three political parties with no direct relationships to their supposed constituencies provoked the progressive popular rejection of the parties and of Congress which was seen as an exclusive, partisan body and not as the house of representatives of the people. The consequence was that the electoral support for the two main traditional parties (*AD* and *COPEI*) varied from 92.83% in 1988; to 45.9% in 1993; to 36.1% in November 1998; and to 11.3% in December 1998, when Chavez was elected President of the Republic.[58]

Thus, at the beginning of the eighties, the public began to make new and diverse demands for representation and political participation, but those demands were not met. Among other things, they called for a reform of the electoral system. In general, they wanted to make democracy more participative. There was thus an urgent need for local government reform since this was the only effective way of assuring democratic participation. However, this was not generally understood.

Municipalities in Venezuela were and still are so disconnected from the citizens as to be of no benefit to them. They are not the primary political unit, the center of political participation, or an effective instrument to manage local interests. They are

---

56   See Allan R. Brewer-Carías, *El Estado. Crisis y Reforma,* Academia de Ciencias Políticas y Sociales, Caracas, 1982, pp. 7 a 89; and Allan R. Brewer-Carías, *El Estado Incomprendido. Reflexiones sobre el sistema político y su reforma,* Editorial Jurídica Venezolana, Caracas, 1985.

57   See Allan R. Brewer-Carías, "La reforma del sistema electoral" in *Revista Venezolana de Ciencias Políticas,* CEPSAL-Postgrado en Ciencias Políticas, Universidad de Los Andes, N° 1, Mérida, diciembre 1987, pp. 55-75; Allan R. Brewer-Carías, *Ley Orgánica del Sufragio,* Caracas 1993; J.G. Molina y C. Pérez Baralt, "Venezuela ¿un nuevo sistema de partidos? Las elecciones de 1993, en *Cuestiones Políticas,* N° 13, 1994, pp. 63-99.

58   See the references in *El Universal,* Caracas, December, 11th, 1998, p. 1-1.

accountable to no one; no one is interested in them except the political parties, and they have become a mechanism of political activism and unpunished corruption[59].

Thus, while not eliminating political representation, the reforms should have created mechanisms that would have allowed people to participate on a daily basis in their local affairs. That should have been one of the purposes of the constitutional process of 1999[60].

2.   State Centralism and the Crisis of Decentralization

At the outset, it should be noted that Venezuela has been a federal State since the "Constitution of the Confederation of the States of Venezuela," dated December 21, 1811. Just as federalism was the only constitutional force uniting the previously independent thirteen colonies of the United States, in 1811 in Venezuela, it constituted the only constitutional means of bringing together the dispersed and isolated seven provinces that comprised the General Captaincy of Venezuela. Subsequently, Venezuelan political history has been marked by the swing of the pendulum between centralization and decentralization[61]: In the early stages of the Republic, in spite of the centralist orientations of Simon Bolivar (1819-1821),[62] regionalist pressure led in 1830 to the formation of a mixed central-federal form of State, which became definitively consolidated as a federal system in 1864 when the United States of Venezuela was established.

However, the federation as it existed in the 19th century was abandoned in 1901, and throughout the 20th century, the country experienced a process of political centralization[63]. Centralized governance was autocratic in its first phase, but beginning in 1935 it evolved to the more democratic form of the past decades.

---

59   See Allan R. Brewer-Carías, "Municipio, democracia y participación. Aspectos de la crisis," *Revista Venezolana de Estudios Municipales,* N° 11, Caracas, 1988, pp. 13-30; and "Democracia municipal, descentralización y desarrollo local, *Revista Iberoamericana de Administración Pública,* N° 11, Ministerio de Administraciones Públicas. Julio-Diciembre 2003, Madrid 2004, pp. 11-34.

60   See in this regard, one of the author's proposals to the 1999 Constituent Assembly in Allan R. Brewer-Carías, *Debate Constituyente (Aportes a la Asamblea Nacional Constituyente),* Vol. I (8 Agosto-8 Septiembre), Fundación de Derecho Público, Caracas 1999, pp. 156 ff.

61   See regarding the Venezuelan Federation evolution, Allan R. Brewer-Carías, *Instituciones Políticas y Constitucionales,* Vol. I (*Evolución histórica del Estado), Universidad Católica del Táchira, Editorial Jurídica Venezolana, San Cristóbal-Caracas 1996, pp. 351 ff.; and Vol. II (El Poder Público Nacional, Estadal y Municipal), Universidad Católica del Táchira, Editorial Jurídica Venezolana, San Cristóbal-Caracas, 1996, pp. 394 ff.

62   See Allan R. Brewer-Carías, "Ideas centrales sobre la organización el Estado en la Obra del Libertador y sus Proyecciones Contemporáneas" in *Boletín de la Academia de Ciencias Políticas y Sociales,* N° 95-96, Caracas 1984, pp. 137-151.

63   See Allan R. Brewer-Carías, "El desarrollo institucional del Estado Centralizado en Venezuela (1899-1935) y sus proyecciones contemporáneas" en *Revista de Estudios de la Vida Local y Autonómica,* N° 227 and 228, Madrid 1985, pp. 487-514 and 695-726; *Instituciones Políticas y Constitucionales,* Vol. I (*Evolución histórica del Estado), Universidad Católica del Táchira, Editorial Jurídica Venezolana, Caracas-San Cristóbal 1996, pp. 351 ff.; and "La

As of the end of the 20th century, Venezuela remained a centralized federation, with power concentrated at the national level and in which delegations of power to the federal States were illusory. At the same time, the centralism of the State led to the centralization of the political system, since the political parties became dominated by party leaders and party organizations that were governed from the center (i.e., from Caracas).

After the regional and local leadership of the 19th century (*caudillos*) had long since come to an end and the 20th century consolidation of the national State had been accomplished, the call for increased democratization and decentralization in the modern era faced formidable challenges. It not only was difficult to enhance the autonomy of local authorities, but there was resistance also to admit the need to devolve power even to intermediate levels of government.

This state of affairs constituted an impediment to the democratization of the country. Decentralization is a consequence of democracy and, at the same time, a condition necessary to its survival and improvement. It is an instrument for the exercise of power on the intermediate level in the territory, which should, in turn, link the activities of the center to the communities and regions. There are no decentralized autocracies[64]; decentralization of power is only possible in a democracy. Consequently, the public outcry of 1989 called for the parties to accelerate State reforms related to political decentralization on the basis of provisions in the 1961 Constitution. As a result of these demands, in 1989 state governors were directly elected for the first time in 100 years, and the introduction of direct election of mayors superseded exclusive government by council on the local level[65].

These democratic "remedies," without doubt, breathed life into the system and allowed democracy to survive in the nineties. Nevertheless, the decentralizing advances made as of 1993[66] were abandoned, and the political system entered into a terminal crisis in the last years of that decade.[67] That crisis, as mentioned above,

---

Reforma Política del Estado: la Descentralización Política" in Allan R. Brewer-Carías, *Estudios de Derecho Público (Labor en el Senado 1982)*, Vol. I, Ediciones del Congreso Nacional, Caracas 1983, pp. 15-39.

64   See Allan R. Brewer-Carías, *Reflexiones sobre la Organización Territorial del Estado en Venezuela y en la América Colonial*, Editorial Jurídica Venezolana, Caracas 1997, pp. 108 ff.

65   See Allan R. Brewer-Carías, "Los problemas de la federación centralizada en Venezuela," *Revista Ius et Praxis*, Universidad de Lima, Nº 12, Lima 1988, pp. 49-96; and "Bases Legislativas para la descentralización política de la Federación Centralizada, (1990: el inicio de una reforma)," in Allan R. Brewer-Carías et al., *Leyes y Reglamentos para la Descentralización política de la Federación*, Caracas 1994, pp. 7 a 53. Also see Allan R. Brewer-Carías, *Instituciones Políticas y Constitucionales*, Vol. II (*El Poder Público Nacional, Estadal y Municipal*), Universidad Católica del Táchira, Editorial Jurídica Venezolana, San Cristóbal-Caracas, 1996, pp. 394 ff.

66   See discussion of the 1993 last efforts to reinforce the decentralization process in Venezuela, in *Informe sobre la descentralización en Venezuela 1994. Memoria del Dr. Allan R. Brewer-Carías, Ministro de Estado para la Descentralización*, Caracas 1994.

67   See Pedro Guevara, *Estado vs. Democracia*, Caracas 1997; Miriam Kornblith, *Venezuela en los 90. Crisis de la Democracia*, Caracas, 1998; Allan R. Brewer-Carías, *Cinco siglos de*

provoked the calling of a Constituent Assembly, whose main objectives should have been the realization of the decentralization of power and the consolidation of democracy.

3.   *The Demand for Reform*

Latin American constitutionalism in recent decades has experienced an expansion of the traditional horizontal concept of separation of powers beyond the classic legislative, executive and judicial powers. Many Latin American states have introduced a series of constitutional and autonomous institutions outside of the three classical branches of government, such as "General Controllerships," "Defenders of the People or of Human Rights," Judiciary Councils, and "Public Ministries" (Public Prosecutor). In addition, in order to increase the participation of citizens in the democratic order, they have introduced new remedies for the protection of their rights. These measures have included judicial review of the constitutionality of legislation and judicial guarantees of constitutional rights, together with improvement in the ability of citizens to use the action of *amparo* (a specific judicial remedy for the protection of constitutional rights),[68] all of which have required more independence and autonomy of the judiciary. These reforms have brought about a significant transformation of the system of checks and balances regulating the traditional powers in those states. There were demands for instituting similar reforms in Venezuela in the last years of the nineties, which would have required a transformation of the balance and counterbalance among the traditional powers of the State. The accomplishment of those reforms should have been, without doubt, the purpose of the constitution making process of 1999.

Historia y un Puls en Crisis, Academia de Ciencias Políticas y Sociales y Comisión Presidencial del V Centenario de Venezuela, Caracas 1998, pp. 95-117; Allan R. Brewer-Carías, "La crisis terminal del sistema político," in *Una evaluación a estos cuarenta años de democracia, El Globo,* Caracas, November 24, 1997, pp. 12-13; Allan R. Brewer-Carías, "La crisis terminal del sistema político venezolano y el reto democrático de la descentralización" (paper submmited to the *IV Congreso Venezolano de Derecho Constitucional,* Caracas, noviembre 1995), published in Allan R. Brewer-Carías, *Instituciones Políticas y Constitucionales,* Vol. III, (*El Poder Nacional y el Sistema democrático de gobierno),* Universidad Católica del Táchira, Editorial Jurídica Venezolana, Caracas-San Cristóbal, 1996, pp. 655-678. See also Allan R. Brewer-Carías, "Presentación," in *Los Candidatos Presidenciales ante la Academia,* Academia de Ciencias Políticas y Sociales, Caracas, 1998, pp. 9-66, and Allan R. Brewer-Carías *Asamblea Constituyente y Ordenamiento Constitucional,* Academia de Ciencias Políticas y Sociales, Caracas 1999, pp. 15-85.

68   See Allan R. Brewer-Carías, *Judicial Protection of Human Rights in Latin America. A Comparative Constitutional Law study on the Latin American Injunction for the Protection of Constitutional rights ("Amparo" Proceeding),* Privately Printed for the Exclusive Use of Students at the Columbia University School of Law, New York, 2007, 383 pp.; *El amparo a los derechos y garantías constitucionales (Una aproximación comparativa),* Editorial Jurídica Venezolana, Caracas 1993; and in *Instituciones Políticas y Constitucionales,* Vol. V, *Derecho y acción de amparo,* Universidad Católica del Táchira, Editorial Jurídica Venezolana, San Cristóbal-Caracas 1998.

There was a particular need for reform in Venezuela. Although the Venezuelan system, like other Latin American systems has been characterized by presidentialism, it was a moderated one due to a series of parliamentary controls on the executive. Paradoxically, the crisis of the Venezuelan system, therefore, stemmed not from an excess of presidentialism, but from an excessive parliamentarism, which took the form of a monopolistic control of power by the political parties[69].

The criticisms of this monopolistic control in the late nineties focused, in particular, on the appointment by the Congress of the heads of the non-elected organs of public power (Supreme Court, Judicial Council, General Controller of the Republic, General Prosecutor of the Republic, Electoral Supreme Council). Serious criticism arose because of the excessive partisanship that had been shown in these appointments, and because of the lack of transparency or participation of civil society associated with them[70].

Therefore, the demands for reform called for increased checks and balances so as to break the monopoly of the political parties and reduce partisanship, on the one hand, and for an increase in the judicial guarantees of constitutional rights so as to guarantee greater citizen participation in the democratic order, on the other.

Consequently, the calling of a Constituent Assembly in 1999 should have been used as a vehicle for including and reconciling all political stakeholders beyond traditional political parties[71] in the redesign of the democratic system. The Constituent Assembly should have focused on establishing a system that would guarantee not only elections, but also all the other essential elements of democracy, as were later set forth in the Inter American Democratic Charter enacted by the General Assembly of the Organization of American States on September, 11th 2001. These elements include "the respect for human rights and fundamental freedoms, the access to power and its exercise subject to the rule of law, the making of periodic, free and fair elections based on universal and secret vote as an expression of the sovereignty of the people, the plural regime of parties and political organizations and the separation and independence of the public powers" (Article 3).

III. THE CONSTITUTION-MAKING PROCESS AND ITS DEFORMATION

1. The Choice of a National Constituent Assembly

Although the call for a Constituent Assembly materialized in 1999, the demand for such a body as a vehicle of conciliation or political reconstruction had actually arisen earlier. It had been proposed before and in the aftermath of the two attempted

---

69   See Allan R. Brewer-Carías, *Problemas del Estado de Partidos,* Editorial Jurídica Venezolana, Caracas, 1988, pp. 92 ff.
70   *Idem.*
71   See the author's proposal regarding the convening off the 1999 Constituent Assembly in Allan R. Brewer-Carías, *Asamblea Constituyente y ordenamiento constitucional*, Biblioteca de la Academia de Ciencias Políticas y Sociales, Caracas 1999, pp. 56-60.

military coups of 1992[72], which had been carried out, among others, by then Lieutenant Colonel Hugo Chávez Frías, currently President of the Republic.

The subject, in fact, was publicly discussed from 1992 on[73], but the leaders of the main political parties failed to appreciate the magnitude of the political crisis and instead of attempting to democratize institutions, they tried to maintain the status quo. This response served to discredit the leaders and their political parties, leading to a leadership vacuum in a regime that had been previously characterized by the hegemony of the political parties and their leaders.

In the middle of this political crisis, in 1998, Hugo Chávez Frías as presidential candidate raised the issue of calling a Constituent Assembly, only a few years after criminal charges against him stemming from his 1992 attempted military coup were withdrawn. The proposal was disputed by some of the traditional political parties and rejected by others; and all political elements rejected the idea that the Congress elected in December of 1998 could take the lead in the constitution making process[74].

Consequently, the calling of the Constituent Assembly became the exclusive project of candidate Chávez,[75] and remained such after he was elected President in December of 1998, with an overwhelming majority of 60% of the cast votes. However, the call for a Constituent Assembly posed a seemingly insurmountable constitutional problem: the text of the 1961 Constitution did not provide for the institution of a Constituent Assembly as a mechanism of constitutional reform. That text set out only two procedures for the revision of the constitution, one that would apply in the case of a simple amendment and another that would apply in the case of a larger

---

72   See, for example, Frente Patriótico, *Por una Asamblea Constituyente para una nueva Venezuela*, Caracas 1991.

73   See regarding the initial 1992 proposals: Allan R. Brewer-Carías, *El Nacional*, Caracas March, 1st., 1992, p. D-2, also published in Allan R. Brewer-Carías, *Asamblea Constituyente y Ordenamiento Constitucional*, Academia de Ciencias Políticas y Sociales, Caracas 1999, pp. 30-34; Consejo Consultivo de la Presidencia de la República, *Recomendaciones del Consejo Consultivo al Presidente de la República*, Caracas 1992, p. 15; Oswaldo Álvarez Paz, *El Camino Constituyente*, Gobernación del Estado Zulia, Maracaibo, Junio 1992; Ricardo Combellas, "Asamblea Constituyente. Estudio jurídico-político" and Ángel Álvarez, "Análisis de la naturaleza de la crisis actual y la viabilidad política de la Asamblea Constituyente," in COPRE, *Asamblea Constituyente: Salida democrática a la crisis*, Folletos para la Discusión N° 18, Caracas 1992; R. Escovar Salom, "Necesidad de una Asamblea Nacional Constituyente" en *Cuadernos Nuevo Sur*, N° 2-3, julio-diciembre, Caracas 1992, pp. 156 a 160; Frente Amplio Proconstituyente *¿Qué es la Constituyente?*, El Nacional, Caracas, June 30, 1994; Hermánn Escarrá Malavé, *Democracia, Reforma Constitucional y Asamblea Constituyente*, Caracas 1995.

74   See this author's comments on November 1998 in Allan R. Brewer-Carías, *Asamblea Constituyente y Ordenamiento Constitucional*, Academia de Ciencias Políticas y Sociales, Caracas 1999, pp. 78-85.

75   See his "Propuestas para transformar Venezuela" in Hugo Chávez Frías, *Una Revolución Democrática*, Caracas 1998, p. 7.

"general reform[76]." Both procedures required the vote of both houses of Congress, with additional approval by popular referendum or by the majority of the States Assemblies, without any provision for the creation of a separate Constituent Assembly.

2. *The constitutional debate regarding the election of the Constituent Assembly*

Consequently, in December 1998 and January 1999, after the election of President Chavez, and due to his commitment to the Constituent Assembly process, the political debate was not about whether or not to call a Constituent Assembly, but about the way to do it[77]. The question was whether the election of the Constituent Assembly required a previous constitutional amendment or whether the concept of popular sovereignty justified the election of a Constituent Assembly in the absence of pre-existing constitutional authority. In short, this was a conflict between constitutional supremacy and popular sovereignty[78].

In hindsight, considerations of rule of law should have resolved the debate. Viewed from this perspective, there is no doubt that a constitutional amendment was required. This was the only way in which the issue could have been resolved without violating the text of the existing Constitution[79]. On the contrary, the violation of the Constitution for the purpose of a constitution making process, giving preference to the supposed will of the people (popular sovereignty) over the rule of law (constitutional supremacy), always leaves an indelible imprint of political legitimacy doubts, which eventually can serve as an excuse to revert the situation.[80]

---

76 See Allan R. Brewer-Carías, "Los procedimientos de revisión constitucional en Venezuela" in *I Procedimenti di revisione costituzionale nel Diritto Comparato,* Atti del Convegno Internazionale organizzato dalla Facoltà di Giurisprudenza di Urbino, 23-24 aprile 1997, Università Degli Studi di Urbino, pubblicazioni della Facoltà di Giurisprudenza e della Facoltá di Scienze Politiche, Urbino, Italia, 1999, pp. 137-181; and in *Boletín de la Academia de Ciencias Políticas y Sociales,* Nº 134, Caracas 1997, pp. 169-222. See also Allan R. Brewer-Carías, *Asamblea Constituyente y Ordenamiento Constitucional,* Academia de Ciencias Políticas y Sociales, Caracas 1999, pp. 84-149.

77 See the author's 1998 proposal in Allan R. Brewer-Carías, *Asamblea Nacional Constituyente y Ordenamiento Constitucional,* Academia de Ciencias Políticas y Sociales, Caracas 1999, pp. 56-69; see the position in contrary sense of Carlos M. Escarrá Malavé, *Proceso Político y Constituyente. Papeles Constituyentes,* Maracaibo 1999, pp. 33 ff.

78 See Allan R. Brewer-Carías, "El desequilibrio entre soberanía popular y supremacía constitucional y la salida constituyente en Venezuela en 1999," in *Revista Anuario Iberoamericano de Justicia Constitucional,* Nº 3, 1999, Centro de Estudios Políticos y Constitucionales, Madrid 2000, pp. 31-56. See also Allan R. Brewer-Carías, *Asamblea Constituyente y Ordenamiento Constitucional,* Academia de Ciencias Políticas y Sociales, Caracas 1999, pp. 152 ff.

79 See Allan R. Brewer-Carías, "Comentarios sobre la inconstitucional de la convocatoria a Referéndum sobre una Asamblea Nacional Constituyente, efectuada por el Consejo Nacional Electoral en febrero de 1999" in *Revista Política y Gobierno,* Vol. 1, Nº 1, enero-junio 1999, Fundación de Estudios de Derecho Administrativo, Caracas 1999, pp. 29-92. See also Allan R. Brewer-Carías, *Asamblea Constituyente y Ordenamiento Constitucional,* Academia de Ciencias Políticas y Sociales, Caracas 1999, pp. 229 ff.

80 Among the authors that considered that the convening of the Constituent Assembly needed a prior constitutional provision establishing it was Ricardo Combellas, who in 1998 was head

However, buoyed by his popularity of the moment, the President-elect publicly pressured the Supreme Court to decide the question. Members of civil society had brought the issue before the Court through a request for interpretation, which was available under the statute governing the Supreme Court. On January 19, 1999, almost two weeks before the President took office; the Court issued two decisions which failed to resolve the issue in an express manner[81]. The decisions acknowledged the possibility of calling for a consultative referendum in order to seek popular opinion regarding the election of a Constituent Assembly, and presented a theoretical summary of the constitutional doctrine of constituent power. However, they said nothing about whether a constitutional amendment was required[82], which was the main purpose of the request for interpretation.

That decision emboldened the President, without constitutional authorization, in his first official act after assuming office on February 2, 1999,[83] to issue a decree ordering a "consultative referendum" in which he proposed to ask the people to authorize him, and him alone, not only to call the Constituent Assembly, but also to define its composition, procedure, mission and duration. Thus, he purported to hold a referendum on a Constituent Assembly in which people would vote blindly with-

---

of the Presidential Commission on State Reforms. See Ricardo Combellas, *¿Qué es la Constituyente?. Voz para el futuro de Venezuela,* Caracas 1998, p. 38. The next year, after been appointed by President Chávez as member of the Presidential Commission for the Constitutional Reform, he changed his opinion, admitting the possibility to elect the Assembly even without constitutional support. See Ricardo Combellas, *Poder Constituyente,* Presentación, Hugo Chávez Frías, Caracas 1999, pp. 189 ff. In 1999, Combellas was elected a member of the Constituent Assembly from the lists supported by Chávez, but a few years later, he withdrew his support for the President, becoming a critic of his antidemocratic government.

81 See the texts in *Revista de Derecho Público,* N° 77-80, Editorial Jurídica Venezolana, Caracas 1999, pp. 56-73; and in Allan R. Brewer-Carías, *Poder Constituyente Originario y Asamblea Nacional Constituyente,* Editorial Jurídica Venezolana, Caracas 1999, pp. 25 ff.

82 See comments on the decisions in Allan R. Brewer-Carías, "La configuración judicial del proceso constituyente o de cómo el guardián de la Constitución abrió el camino para su violación y para su propia extinción," *in Revista de Derecho Público,* N° 77-80, Editorial Jurídica Venezolana, Caracas 1999, pp. 453-514.; Allan R. Brewer-Carías, *Asamblea Constituyente y Ordenamiento Constitucional,* Academia de Ciencias Políticas y Sociales, Caracas 1999, pp. 152-228; .Allan R. Brewer-Carías, *Golpe de Estado y proceso constituyente en Venezuela,* Universidad Nacional Autónoma de México, México 2002, pp. 65 ff.; Lolymar Hernández Camargo, *La Teoría del Poder Constituyente. Un caso de estudio: el proceso constituyente venezolano de 1999,* Universidad Católica del Táchira, San Cristóbal 2000, pp. 53 ff.; Claudia Nikken, *La Cour Suprême de Justice et la Constitution vénézuélienne du 23 Janvier 1961,* Thèse Docteur de l'Université Panthéon Assas, (Paris II), Paris 2001, pp. 366 ff.

83 See the text in *Gaceta Oficial* N° 36.634 de February 2d, 1999, and its modification in *Gaceta Oficial* N° 36.658 de 10-March-1999. See the comments regarding the Decree in Allan R. Brewer-Carías, *Golpe de Estado y proceso constituyente en Venezuela,* Universidad Nacional Autónoma de México, México 2002, pp. 113 ff; and in Allan R. Brewer-Carías, *Asamblea Constituyente y Ordenamiento Constitucional,* Academia de Ciencias Políticas y Sociales, Caracas 1999, pp. 229 ff.

out knowing the procedure for its election, its composition, or the nature or duration of its mission.

It is thus hardly surprising that the constitutionality of President Chavez' decree was challenged before the Supreme Court[84], which ruled in a series of judicial review decisions that the manner in which the President had acted in calling for the consultative referendum on the Constituent Assembly was unconstitutional[85]. It also declared that the composition, procedure, mission, and duration of the Constituent Assembly would have to be submitted to the people. It further ruled that there was no authority under the Constitution of 1961 to endow an assembly with "original"[86] constituent power as the President's proposal had purported to do.

The members of the Supreme Court had been elected years before by the party-controlled Congress, and it was that same Court which under tremendous political pressure from President-elect Chavez issued the aforementioned ambiguous decision of January 1999, by which it allowed, without expressly deciding it, the possibility of the election of a Constituent Assembly. After having freed the political "constituent forces" of society as a means for participation, when the Supreme Court tried to control them by ruling that the Constituent Assembly to be elected had to observe and act according to the 1961 Constitution[87], it was too late to achieve that goal. After its election in July 1999, the Constituent Assembly crushed all the constituted

---

84   See the text of the challenging action this author brought before the Supreme Court in Allan R. Brewer-Carías, *Asamblea Constituyente y Ordenación Constitucional*, Academia de Ciencias Políticas y Sociales, Caracas 1999, pp. 255-321. Regarding the other challenging actions brought before the Supreme Court, see Carlos M. Escarrá Malavé, *Proceso Político y Constituyente*, Caracas 1999, Exhibit 4.

85   See the text of the March 18, 1999, March 23, 1999, April 13, 1999, June 3, 1999, June 17, 1999, and July 21,1999, Supreme Court decisions in *Revista de Derecho Público*, N° 77-80, Editorial Jurídica Venezolana, Caracas 1999, pp. 73-110.; and in Allan R. Brewer-Carías, *Poder Constituyente Originario y Asamblea Nacional Constituyente,* Editorial Jurídica Venezolana, Caracas 1999, pp. 169-198 and 223-251. See comments in Allan R. Brewer-Carías, "Comentarios sobre la inconstitucional convocatoria a referendo sobre una Asamblea Nacional Constituyente efectuada por el Consejo Nacional Electoral en febrero de 1999," *Revista Política y Gobierno*, Vol. I, N° 1, Fundación de Estudios de Derecho Administrativo, Caracas, Enero-Junio 1999, pp. 29-92; and in Allan R. Brewer-Carías, *Golpe de Estado y proceso constituyente en Venezuela*, Universidad Nacional Autónoma de México, Mexico 2002, pp. 160 ff.

86   Venezuelan constitutional law distinguishes between "derivative constituent authority" and "original constituent authority," the latter being the kind of non-limited authority such an institution would have at the very moment of conception of a new state. The Constitutional Convention of the United States would be an example of the kind of institution which would be considered "original" in this sense.

87   In particular, see the Supreme Court decisions of April 13, 1999, June 17, 1999 and July 21, 1999, in *Revista de Derecho Público*, N° 77-80, Editorial Jurídica Venezolana, Caracas 1999, pp. 85 ff.

powers, including the Supreme Court itself, violating the then in force 1961 Constitution[88].

3.   The Electoral Rule for the election of the Assembly

In spite of the Supreme Court's rulings and in the absence of any political negotiations among the various sectors of society, the President proceeded unilaterally with the consultative referendum on the calling of a Constituent Assembly on April 25, 1999. In a voting process in which only the 38.7% of eligible voters cast their ballots (62.2 % of eligible voters did not turn out to vote), the "yes" votes obtained 81.9 % and the "no" votes 18.1 %.[89] The approved proposal provided for the election of a 131-member Constituent Assembly: 104 members to be elected in 24 regional constituencies corresponding to the political subdivisions of the territory (States and the Federal District); 24 members to be elected in a national constituency; and three members representing the Indian peoples, who comprise a very small portion of the Venezuelan population.

The referendum set up an electoral system in which candidates were to run individually. The 104 regional constituency seats were allotted according to the population of each State and the Federal District. A list of all of the candidates in each regional constituency was placed on the ballot in each constituency, and the voters had the right to vote for the number of candidates on their constituency's list corresponding to the number of seats allotted to their constituency. The elected candidates corresponding to the number of seats allotted were those receiving the highest number of votes. Voting proceeded in the same way on the national level for the 24 seats allotted, except that the voters were only allowed to choose 10 candidates from the list of those who were running. This electoral system was without any precedent in previous elections in Venezuela.

This electoral system really amounted to a ruse by the President of the Republic and his followers to assure their absolute control of the Constituent Assembly. In a campaign financed, among others, as it was later known, by Venezuelan insurance companies and foreign banks,[90] the President appeared personally in every State of the country proposing his list of candidates to be elected in each constituency. On the national level, he proposed only 20 candidates for the 24 seats allotted; dividing the country in two, he proposed a list of 10 candidates to the voters of the eastern States of the country, and a separate list of 10 to the voters of the western States. This was rather unusual in Venezuelan political tradition. After more than a hundred

---

88   See the references to all those decisions in Allan R. Brewer-Carías, *Debate Constituyente (Aportes a la Asamblea Nacional Constituyente)*, Vol. I (8 Agosto-8 Septiembre), Fundación de Derecho Público, Caracas 1999, pp. 11-124.

89   See José E. Molina V. y Carmen Pérez Baralt, "Procesos Electorales. Venezuela, abril, julio y diciembre de 1999" en *Boletín Electoral Latinoamericano*, CAPEL-IIDH, N° XXII, Julio-Diciembre 1999, San José, 2000, pp. 61 ff.

90   For which a few high former officials of the *Banco Bilbao Vizcaya* of Spain were criminally indicted on Feb. 8th, 2006, by the *Juzgado Central de Instrucción N° 5, Audiencia Nacional*, Madrid (Procedure N° 251/02-N).

years of a non-reelection constitutional rule, Venezuelans were not used to having Presidents of the Republic directly involved in electoral campaigns, and any governmental involvement in elections had been considered illegitimate.

The election was carried out on July 25, 1999; only 46.3% of eligible voters cast their ballots (53.7% of eligible voters did not turn out to vote)[91]. The candidates supported by the President obtained 65.8% of the cast votes, but the election resulted in control by his followers of 94% of the seats in the Constituent Assembly. It can be said that all of the President's supported candidates except one were elected, for a total of 123: of the 104 candidates elected at the regional (State) level, only one belonged to the traditional parties (*Acción Democrática*), and of the 24 candidates elected at the national constituency, only 4 independent candidates who opposed the President were elected without his support, and perhaps because the President only proposed 20 candidates at the national level out of the 24 to be elected. The three Indian representatives elected were all followers of the President and his party.

The result of this electoral scheme was that instead of contributing to democratic pluralism, the election established a Constituent Assembly totally controlled by the very newly established government party and by the President's followers, and in which all of the traditional political parties were excluded. As mentioned, only one of the members out of 131 belonged to the traditional parties (one regional member), and four others were elected independently opposing the President[92]. Together, they instinctively became the "opposition" group in the Assembly.

A Constituent Assembly formed by a majority of that nature was not a valid instrument for dialogue or for political conciliation and negotiation. It really was a political instrument to impose the ideas of a dominating group on the rest of the society, totally excluding the other groups.

4.   *The Seizure of the Constituted Powers*

In the meanwhile, and before the election of the Constituent Assembly, not only President Chavez but all the representatives to the National Congress had been elected in December 1998, as per the provisions of the 1961 Constitution. The Governors of the 23 States, the representatives of the State Legislative Assemblies, and the Mayors and members of the Municipal Councils of the 338 Municipalities had also been elected in November 1998. That is to say, all the heads of the public powers set forth in the Constitution had been popularly elected before the constitution making process of 1999 had begun. In addition, the non-elected heads of the organs of state, such as the Judges of the Supreme Court of Justice, the General Prosecutor of the Republic, the General Controller of the Republic, and the members of the Supreme Electoral Council, had been appointed by the National Congress, again in accordance with the 1961 Constitution.

---

91   José E. Molina V. y Carmen Pérez Baralt, "Procesos Electorales. Venezuela, abril, julio y diciembre de 1999" en *Boletín Electoral Latinoamericano*, CAPEL-IIDH, N° XXII, Julio-Diciembre 1999, San José, 2000, pp. 61 ff

92   Allan R. Brewer-Carías, Claudio Fermín, Alberto Franchesqui and Jorge Olavarría

Therefore, by the time the Constituent Assembly was elected on July 25, 1999, the constituted public powers elected and appointed only months before were functioning in parallel, with different missions. The Constituent Assembly was elected, according to the consultative referendum of April 1999 and to the Supreme Court's interpretation, to design the reform of the State and to establish a new legal framework institutionalizing a social and participative democracy, which was to be submitted to popular approval in a final referendum. It was not elected to govern, substitute it for or interfere with the constituted powers. Moreover, as the Supreme Court of Justice had declared, it had no "original" constituent authority[93].

However, in its first decision, which was the adoption of its own statute governing its functioning, the Constituent Assembly declared itself as "an original constituent power," granting itself the authority to "limit or abolish the power of the organs of state" and setting forth that "all the organs of the Public Power are subjected to the Constituent National Assembly" and are "obliged to comply with its the juridical acts[94]."

With this act, the Constituent Assembly declared itself as a state superpower, assuming powers that even the referendum of April 1999 had failed to grant. It was in this way that the Constituent Assembly, which functioned between July 1999 and January 2000, usurped public power, violated the Constitution of 1961, and, in sum, accomplished a *coup d'Etat*[95].

It was during the first months of its functioning, from August to September 1999, that the Assembly, instead of conciliating and forming a new political pact for society, usurped the role of the constituted powers elected in December 1998, which were functioning according to the 1961 Constitution still in force. In August 1999, the Constituent Assembly decreed the reorganization of all the public powers (that is, the three branches of government):[96] It encroached upon the judicial branch by creating a Commission of Judicial Emergency for the purpose of intervening in judicial

---

93   See the decision of April 13th, 1999, in *Revista de Derecho Público*, N° 77-80, Editorial Jurídica Venezolana, Caracas 1999, pp. 85 ff.; and in Allan R. Brewer-Carías, *Poder Constituyente Originario y Asamblea Nacional Constituyente*, Editorial Jurídica Venezolana, Caracas 1999, pp. 169-198, 223-251.

94   See in *Gaceta Constituyente (Diario de Debates), Agosto-Septiembre 1999*, Session of August 3d, 1999, N° 1, p. 4. See the author's dissenting vote in *Gaceta Constituyente (Diario de Debates), Agosto-Septiembre 1999*, Session August 7th, 1999, N° 4, pp. 6-13; and in Allan R. Brewer-Carías, *Debate Constituyente, (Aportes a la Asamblea Nacional Constituyente)* Vol. I *(8 agosto-8 septiembre 1999)*, Fundación de Derecho Público, Caracas 1999, pp. 15-39.

95   See Allan R. Brewer-Carías, *Golpe de Estado y Proceso constituyente en Venezuela*, Universidad Nacional Autónoma de México, México 2002, pp. 181 ff.

96   Decree of August, 12, 1999. See the text in *Gaceta Constituyente (Diario de Debates), Agosto-Septiembre de 1999*, Session August 12, N° 8, pp. 2-4, and in *Gaceta Oficial* N° 36.764 de 13-08-99. See this author's dissenting vote in Allan R. Brewer-Carías, *Debate Constituyente (Aportes a la Asamblea Nacional Constituyente)*, Vol. I *(8 agosto-8 septiembre 1999)*, Fundación de Derecho Público, Caracas 1999, pp. 43-56.

matters to the detriment of the autonomy and independence of the existing judges;[97] it dissolved both the Senate and the Chamber of Representatives of the National Congress and the Legislative Assemblies of the States;[98] and it suspended municipal elections.[99]

All these actions were challenged before the Supreme Court, but the Court, in a decision of October 14, 1999, in contrast with its ruling in its earlier decision, upheld their constitutionality, recognizing the Constitutional Assembly as a "supra constitutional" power.[100] This implied the attribution to the Assembly of "sovereign power," which it does not have, because the only sovereign power in a Constitutional State is the people. It was the only way to justify the otherwise unconstitutional intervention of the constituted branches of governments, a confusion that was expressly pointed out by various magistrates' dissenting votes.[101] In issuing this decision, the Court actually decided its own death sentence[102].

It must be noted that the Supreme Court did not rule consistently with its previous decisions relating to the Constituent Assembly, even with the ambiguous one.

---

97   Decree of August 19, 1999. See the text in *Gaceta Constituyente (Diario de Debates), Agosto-Septiembre de 1999,* Session of August 18, 1999, N° 10, pp. 17 a 22, and in *Gaceta Oficial* N° 36.782 de 08-September-1999. See this author's dissenting vote in Allan R. Brewer-Carías, *Debate Constituyente (Aportes a la Asamblea Nacional Constituyente),* Vol. I *(8 agosto-8 septiembre 1999),* Fundación de Derecho Público, Caracas 1999, p. 57-73. See the comments in Allan R. Brewer-Carías, *Golpe de Estado y Proceso constituyente en Venezuela,* Universidad Nacional Autónoma de México, México 2002, pp. 184 ff.; and in Allan R. Brewer-Carías, "La progresiva y sistemática demolición institucional de la autonomía e independencia del Poder Judicial en Venezuela 1999-2004" in *XXX Jornadas J.M Dominguez Escovar, Estado de derecho, Administración de justicia y derechos humanos,* Instituto de Estudios Jurídicos del Estado Lara, Barquisimeto 2005, pp. 33-174.

98   Decree of August 28, 1999. See the text in *Gaceta Constituyente (Diario de Debates), Agosto-Septiembre 1999,* Session of August 25, 1999, N° 13. See this author's dissenting vote in Allan R. Brewer-Carías, *Debate Constituyente (Aportes a la Asamblea Nacional Constituyente),* Vol. I *(8 agosto-8 septiembre 1999),* Fundación de Derecho Público, Caracas 1999, pp. 75-113.

99   Decree of August, 26, 1999. See the text in *Gaceta Constituyente (Diario de Debates), Agosto-Septiembre 1999,* Session of August 26, 1999, N° 14, pp. 7-8, 11, 13 and 14; and in *Gaceta Oficial* N° 36.776 de 31-08-99. See the author's dissenting vote in Allan R. Brewer-Carías, *Debate Constituyente (Aportes a la Asamblea Nacional Constituyente),* Vol. I *(8 agosto-8 septiembre 1999),* Fundación de Derecho Público, Caracas 1999, pp. 115-122.

100 See the decisión of October 14, 1999 in *Revista de Derecho Público,* N° 77-80, Editorial Jurídica Venezolana, Caracas 1999, pp. 111-132. See the comments in Allan R. Brewer-Carías, "La configuración judicial del proceso constituyente o de cómo el guardián de la Constitución abrió el camino para su violación y para su propia extinción," in *Revista de Derecho Público,* N° 77-80, Editorial Jurídica Venezolana, Caracas 1999, pp. 453 ff.

101 Particularly by Magistrate Humberto J. La Roche, who was the one who rendered the opinion of the Court in its initial decision of January 19, 1999. See supra note 45.

102 As predicted by the resigning President of the Supreme Court. See the comments in Allan R. Brewer-Carías, *Golpe de Estado y Proceso constituyente en Venezuela,* Universidad Nacional Autónoma de México, México 2002, pp. 218 ff.

The political pressure exercised upon it provoked this change, and the Supreme Court not only adopted a ruling in support of the Constituent Assembly's intervention in the Judiciary, but also appointed one of its magistrates as a member of the Commission of Judicial Emergency. In this situation only the President of the Supreme Court resigned[103]. The others, by action or omission, submitted themselves to the new power, but only for two months, until almost all were sacked by the same Constituent Assembly, using its "supra constitutional" power to replace the Court[104] (see below).

As a result, the initial period of the functioning of the Constituent Assembly was a period of confrontation and political conflict between the public power and the various political sectors of the country. The constituent process, in this initial phase, was not a vehicle for dialogue and for consolidating peace or an instrument for avoiding conflict. On the contrary, it was a mechanism for confrontation, crushing all opposition or dissidence. The Constituent Assembly was thus subject to the exclusive domination by one new political party (*Movimiento V República MVR*), that of the government, which answered to the President of the Republic. It was in this way that the constitution making process was used to abolish the political class and parties that had dominated the scene in former decades.

5. *The Drafting Phase: Haste and Exclusion*

After the constituted powers had thus been either encroached upon or entirely usurped, the Constituent Assembly entered its second phase of work (September-October 1999), which involved the elaboration of the text of a draft constitution. The extreme brevity of this phase did not allow for any real public discussion or popular participation. The Constituent Assembly rejected the method adopted in other constitutional processes whereby a broadly representative Constitutional Commission elaborates a draft that is later presented in plenary session[105].

It is true that the President of the Republic, in the period just before he took office, had informally created a Constitutional Council composed of independent political figures, but that Council had actually devoted it's time to the issues surround-

---

103 See the Decree of Judicial Emergency in *Gaceta Oficial* N° 36.772 of August 25, 1999, and in *Gaceta Oficial* N° 36.782 of September 9, 1999. The Supreme Court issued a formal act accepting the Assembly's intervention of the Judiciary, and later the new Supreme Tribunal upheld the Decree in decision of March 24, 2000, N° 659 (*Caso: Rosario Nouel*), in *Revista de Derecho Público* N° 81, Editorial Jurídica Venezolana, Caracas 2000, pp. 102-105. See the comments regarding the Supreme Court submission to the Assembly's will and its consequences, in Allan R. Brewer-Carías, *Debate Constituyente (Aportes a la Asamblea Nacional Constituyente)*, Vol. I (8 Agosto-8 Septiembre), Fundación de Derecho Público, Caracas 1999, pp. 141-152.

104 See the Decree of December 22, 1999, on the "Transitory Constitutional Regime," in *Gaceta Oficial* N° 36.859 of December 29, 1999.

105 Such a method was used, for instance, for the development of the 1947 Constitution. See the *Anteproyecto de Constitución de 1947. Elección directa de Gobernadores y eliminación de Asambleas Legislativas,* Papeles de Archivo, N° 8, Ediciones Centauro, Caracas 1987.

ing the election of the Constituent Assembly. It never worked to develop a coherent constitutional draft, nor were its proceedings public or participative. It held no public meetings, and met only with the President during the weeks prior and subsequent to the installation of his government.

Thus, the Constituent Assembly began to work collectively without an initial draft. The President did submit to the Constituent Assembly a document prepared with the assistance of the Constitutional Council he had appointed. Its intention was to propose ideas for the new Constitution, but its contents were not completely coherent.[106] Even though this document was not adopted by the Constituent Assembly as the draft constitution, parts of it were used by the drafting commissions, particularly because their members in general had no constitutional studies expertise. Also, two constitution drafts were submitted to the Constituent Assembly, one by a tiny left wing party and another by a non-governmental organization named *Primero Justicia*, which in 2002 became a center-right political party. Neither of these was adopted as drafts for the discussions and due to their origins they had no particular influence in the drafting commissions.

The Constituent Assembly after two months of functioning began the process of elaborating a draft by appointing 20 commissions, which dealt with the essential subjects of any constitution. Each commission was charged with coming up with a proposed draft for its respective subject area. This all occurred during only a few days, between September 2 and 28, 1999. During this very short period each commission acted in an isolated manner, consulting only briefly with groups the commission considered appropriate[107].

The President of the Republic, once all public power had been usurped by the Constituent Assembly, urged it to quickly complete the constitution drafting in order to end the political instability provoked by the constituent process and use the new constitutional framework to "re-legitimate" the public powers through new elections. The timetable to finish the drafting of the constitution was not established by the referendum of April 1999, nor by the Constituent Assembly, but by its Board of Directors in response to the presidential pressure.

As of September 1999, the 20 commissions sent their drafts to an additional Constitutional Commission of the Constituent Assembly, in charge of integrating the texts received. Collectively, the commissions' submissions included almost 800 articles. The Constitutional Commission was charged with forming a single draft. Unfortunately, the Board of Directors of the Constituent Assembly gave to the Constitutional Commission a period of just two weeks to integrate all those isolated drafts. The hasty process of elaboration of the draft left no room for public discus-

---

106 See Hugo Chávez Frías, *Ideas Fundamentales para la Constitución Bolivariana de la V República,* Caracas, agosto 1999.

107 This author was President of the Commission on Nationality and Citizenship. See the Report of the Comission in Allan R. Brewer-Carías, *Debate Constituyente (Aportes a la Asamblea Nacional Constituyente),* Vol. II *(9 Septiembre-17 Octubre),* Fundación de Derecho Público, Caracas 1999, pp. 45- 74.

sion or for the participation of civil society whose input could have been incorporated into the discussions in plenary session[108].

The draft that the Constitutional Commission submitted to the Constituent Assembly on October 18 turned out to be very unsatisfactory, since it was an aggregate or catalogue of wishes, petitions and good intentions integrated into an excessively large text[109]. The draft followed many of the provisions of the 1961 Constitution, with the addition of some portions of the President's proposed document. Some foreign constitutional provisions, particularly copied from the Colombian and Spanish Constitutions,[110] were included in the draft constitutional text, and part of the text of the American Convention on Human Rights enriched the draft as well. Nevertheless, it can be said that in the Constituent Assembly process in general no particular publicly known role was played by foreign experts[111] or governments, or by international or regional organizations. There was no time left for that possibility.

The urgency in finishing the constitutional draft was imposed by the government, which required the Constituent Assembly to discuss and approve the draft in just one month, from October 19 to November 17, 2000, in order to submit the constitution for approval by referendum in December 1999. This schedule explains why only 19 days were devoted to the first round of discussion sessions (October 20 to November 9) and three days devoted to the second round (November 12 to 14), for a total of 22 days, in which I intervened, proposing drafts and expressing my dissenting votes.[112] Together with the other "opposition" members of the Constituent Assembly, I par-

---

108   This author was also member of the Constitutional Commission. See the difficulties of its participation in the drafting process in Allan R. Brewer-Carías, *Debate Constituyente (Aportes a la Asamblea Nacional Constituyente)*, Vol. II (9 Septiembre-17 Octubre), Fundación de Derecho Público, Caracas 1999, pp. 255-286.

109   See *in Gaceta Constituyente* (Diario de Debates), Octubre-Noviembre 1999, N° 23, Sesión de 19-10-99.

110   See for instance Allan R. Brewer-Carías, "La Constitución Española de 1978 y la Constitución de la República Bolivariana de Venezuela de 1999: algunas influencias y otras coincidencias," in Francisco Fernández Segado (Coordinador), *La Constitución de 1978 y el Constitucionalismo Iberoamericano*, Ministerio de la Presidencia. Secretaría General Técnica, Centro de Estudios Políticos y Constitucionales, Madrid 2003, pp. 765-786.

111   All the multiple suggestions made by this author to the Board of Directors of the Constituent Assembly to invite the most distinguished constitutional lawyers of Latin America and Spain to advise the constitution making process were systematically denied. Nonetheless, after the Constitution was approved it was known that some teaching members of the University of Valencia, Spain helped the Vice President of the Assembly in the Technical Committee of the Assembly. See Roberto Viciano Pastor y Rubén Martínez Dalmau, *Cambio político y proceso constituyente en Venezuela (1998-2000)*, Valencia, 2001.

112   See the text of all this author's 127 dissenting or negative votes in Allan R. Brewer-Carías, *Debate Constituyente (Aportes a la Asamblea Nacional Constituyente)*, Vol. III (*18 Octubre-30 Noviembre*), Fundación de Derecho Público, Caracas 1999, pp. 107-308.

ticipated in the political campaign for the vote "No" in the referendum on the Constitution, because it's authoritarian content.[113]

After one month of campaigning the Constitution was approved in the December 15, 1999, referendum. Turnout was low: only 44.3% of eligible voters cast their votes (57.7% of eligible voters did not turn out to vote), with 71.8% for the "Yes" votes and 28.2% for the "No" votes.[114]

However, the text approved did not conform to the operational language of the consultative referendum of April 1999. It failed to provide the new democratic and pluralistic vision the society required, or to define the fundamental principles required to reorganize the country politically, or to create a decentralized state based on participative democracy.

In spite of some good intentions and some brief attempts at public education, the hastiness of the process rendered any effective public and political participation impossible. It must be noted that one of the 20 commissions of the Constituent Assembly was a "Participatory Commission" totally controlled by the President's followers, which developed some "divulging" activity related to the drafting process and to the content of the other commissions' drafts, including television programs. The sessions of the Constituent Assembly were also directly broadcast on television, allowing the public to follow the daily discussions. But the great debate that should have taken place in the Constituent Assembly, on such issues as the monopoly of the political parties, decentralization and the power of local government, the expansion of institutional protection of human rights, or the basic mission of the constitution, never took place. There was no program of public education to encourage the submission of proposals from civil society groups and non-governmental organizations. The only minority group that can be said to have been offered an opportunity to participate was that of the indigenous peoples who were allowed three seats in the Assembly. In the end, public participation was reduced to the vote cast by the public in the two referenda, where the majority of eligible voters did not vote.

IV. THE PARALLEL TRANSITORY REGIME

The ramifications of the departure from the rule of law entailed in the deformation of the constitutional process, described above, can be perceived not only in the events that immediately followed, but also in the crisis that continues to plague the political system.

In the week following the adoption of the Constitution by popular referendum, the Constituent Assembly, without questioning the duration of its authority, on December 20, 1999, adopted a new decree establishing a "Transitory Constitutional

---

113 See the arguments in Allan R. Brewer-Carías, *Debate Constituyente (Aportes a la Asamblea Nacional Constituyente)*, Vol. III (*18 Octubre-30 Noviembre*), Fundación de Derecho Público, Fundación de Derecho Público, Caracas 1999, pp. 309-340.

114 See José E. Molina V. y Carmen Pérez Baralt, "Procesos Electorales. Venezuela, abril, julio y diciembre de 1999" in *Boletín Electoral Latinoamericano*, CAPEL-IIDH, N° XXII, Julio-Diciembre 1999, San José, 2000, pp. 67-68.

Regime,"[115] which was not approved by popular referendum and which violated the newly adopted Constitution, including its transitional provisions.[116] The 1999 Constitution provides, for instance, a very important participatory role to "the diverse sectors of the civil society" in the appointment of the heads of the branches of government not elected by universal vote, i.e., the Judges of the Supreme Tribunal of Justice, the General Prosecutor of the Republic, the General Controller of the Republic, the Defender of the People, and the members of the National Electoral Council (Arts. 264, 279, 295). The proposal for the appointments of such officials by the legislative body was due to be submitted by various Nominating Committees whose membership would include representatives of civil society. Under the terms of the new Constitution, the National Assembly ought to appoint persons to these posts only on the basis of proposals submitted by the Nominating Committees. This innovation in the Constitution was an attempt to reduce the power of political parties in the National Assembly, which, as described above, had been making those appointments on the basis of patronage in the absence of transparency.

As part of the unconstitutional transition set forth in the "Transitory Constitutional Regime" decree, the Constituent Assembly ratified the President of the Republic in his post, and acting in violation of the new Constitution and in the absence of any participation by civil society, directly appointed the members of the new Supreme Tribunal of Justice, the members of the new National Electoral Council, the General Prosecutor of the Republic, the Defender of the People, and the General Controller of the Republic, ending the tenure of those previously appointed. The Constituent Assembly, moreover, eliminated definitively the Congress and created and appointed a new Legislative National Commission that had not been provided for in the 1999 Constitution; the new Commission assumed legislative power until the new National Assembly (supplanting the dissolved Congress) was elected. This unconstitutional transitional regime was challenged on judicial review before the new Supreme Judicial Tribunal created as part of the very same regime; deciding in its own cause, the Supreme Tribunal upheld the transitional regime's constitutionality, justifying it on the basis of the Constituent Assembly's supra constitutional powers.[117]

---

115 See in *Gaceta Oficial* N° 36.859 of December 29, 1999.

116 See the comments regarding this decree in Allan R. Brewer-Carías, *Golpe de Estado y Proceso Constituyente en Venezuela*, Universidad Nacional Autónoma de México, México, pp. 354 ff.; and in *La Constitución de 1999. Derecho Constitucional Venezolano*, Editorial Jurídica Venezolana, Vol. II, Caracas 2004.

117 See the January 26, 2000, decision N° 4 (*Case: Eduardo García*), and the March 28, 2000, Decision N° 180 (*Case: Allan R. Brewer-Carías and others*) in *Revista de Derecho Público*, N° 81, Editorial Jurídica Venezolana, Caracas 2000, pp. 93 ff. and 86 ff. See the comments in Allan R. Brewer-Carías, *Golpe de Estado y proceso constituyente en Venezuela*, Universidad Nacional Autónoma de México, México, 2002, pp. 354 ff.

Once the new National Assembly was elected in August 2000, it adopted a "special statute,"[118] which granted to it almost the same appointment powers that the dissolved Congress had and that had been unconstitutionally exercised by the Constituent Assembly during the "transitional" period: the power to appoint the Judges of the Supreme Tribunal of Justice, the General Prosecutor of the Republic, the General Controller of the Republic, the Defender of the People, and the National Electoral Council. Before the newly elected Assembly had a chance to make appointments under that special statute, an action challenging it was brought before the transitional Supreme Tribunal by the People's Defender. Several other judicial actions were brought before the Supreme Tribunal against other actions taken by the transitional authorities, but all of them were upheld as constitutional.[119]

Of all of the decisions taken by the Supreme Tribunal, the one in response to the challenge of the People's Defender was perhaps the most startling since it called upon the Tribunal to be a judge and party in its own cause. (It was a ruling on the constitutionality of its own appointment.) Even though the Supreme Tribunal did not finally decide the action regarding the constitutionality of the 2000 special statute, in a preliminary decision it accepted that the newly elected National Assembly was also exercising "transitional constitutional" authority.[120]

The subsequent statutes regulating the other constitutional branches of government also failed to respect the new Constitution. Instead of forming the constitutionally required Nominating Committees integrating representatives of the various sectors of civil society, the new National Assembly established as vehicles for making appointments only Parliamentary Commissions, which included scattered participation by some members of civil society.[121]

---

118 Special Statute for the ratification or appointment of the public officials of the Citizen's Power and of the Justices of the Supreme Tribunal of Justice for the first constitutional term, November 14, 2000," in *Gaceta Oficial* N° 37.077 of November 14, 2000.

119 See for instance decisión of March 28, 2000, N° 179 (*Case: Gonzalo Pérez M.*), in *Revista de Derecho Público*, N° 81, Editorial Jurídica Venezolana, Caracas 2000, pp 81 ff.

120 Decisión of December 12, 2000 (*Case: People's Defender*), in *Revista de Derecho Público*, N° 84, Editorial Jurídica Venezolana, Caracas 2000, pp. 108 ff.

121 Allan R. Brewer-Carías, "La progresiva y sistemática demolición institucional de la autonomía e independencia del Poder Judicial en Venezuela 1999-2004," in *XXX Jornadas J.M Domínguez Escovar, Estado de derecho, Administración de justicia y derechos humanos*, Instituto de Estudios Jurídicos del Estado Lara, Barquisimeto 2005, pp.33-174; *La Sala Constitucional versus el Estado democrático de derecho. El secuestro del poder electoral y de la Sala Electoral del Tribunal Supremo y la confiscación del derecho a la participación política*, Los Libros de El Nacional, Colección Ares, Caracas 2004; and "El secuestro del Poder Electoral y de la Sala Electoral del Tribunal Supremo y la confiscación del derecho a la participación política mediante el referendo revocatorio presidencial: Venezuela: 2000-2004" in *Revista Costarricense de Derecho Constitucional*, Tomo V, Instituto Costarricense de Derecho Constitucional, Editorial Investigaciones Jurídicas S.A. San José, Costa Rica 2004. pp. 167-312; and in *Revista Jurídica del Perú*, Año LIV, N° 55, marzo-abril. Lima 2004. pp. 353-396.

It was the "Transitional Constitutional Regime" set forth in 1999 by the Constituent Assembly without popular approval that fixed the general framework for the subsequent process of concentration of powers and the consequent development of the current authoritarian political regime. This regime, which unfortunately has enjoyed the support of the Constitutional Chamber of the Supreme Judicial Tribunal, has taken shape in Venezuela as envisaged when President Chavez came to power in 1998, and characterized by the complete control of all branches of government by the President of the Republic. In particular, the control of the Supreme Tribunal has lead to a Judiciary composed of more than 90% provisional or temporary judges[122], thus without no autonomy or independence whatsoever.[123]

V. THE AUTHORITARIAN SEEDS IN THE CONSTITUTION

One of the main aspects regarding constitution making processes, which is also relevant to the 1999 Constitution of 1999, relates to the so-called "immutable principles" that are found in many of the modern constitutions of the world. It should be noted in this regard that the 1961 Constitution, in its Title I, Articles 1 and 3, established the independence of the state and the republican and democratic form of government as immutable. That feature has been retained in Title I, Articles 1 and 6 of the 1999 Constitution. Apart from those very fundamental principles, there are no other immutable principles to be found *expressis verbis* in either text.

But regarding the concept of the democratic form of government, it must be noted that the 1999 Constitution, notwithstanding the immutable provision, breaks the essential democratic principles of separation of powers and of vertical distribution of State powers,[124] allowing the development of a centralized and plebiscitary system

---

122 Almost two years after the Constituent Assembly's intervention in the judiciary, some Justices of the Supreme Tribunal acknowledged that more than the 90% of the judges of the Republic were provisional ones. See in *El Universal*, Caracas, August 15, 2001. In May 2001, other Justices recognized that the so-called "judicial emergency" was a failure. See *El Universal*, Caracas May 30, 2001, p. 1-4. See also, *Informe sobre la Situación de los Derechos Humanos en Venezuela*; OAS/Ser.L/V/ II.118. d.C. 4rev. 2; December 29, 2003; paragraph 11; p. 3. It reads: "The Commission has been informed that only 250 judges have been appointed by opposition concurrence according to the constitutional text. From a total of 1772 positions of judges in Venezuela, the Supreme Court of Justice reports that only 183 are holders, 1331 are provisional and 258 are temporary."

123 See Allan R. Brewer-Carías, "La progresiva y sistemática demolición institucional de la autonomía e independencia del Poder Judicial en Venezuela 1999-2004," in *XXX Jornadas J.M Dominguez Escovar, Estado de derecho, Administración de justicia y derechos humanos*, Instituto de Estudios Jurídicos del Estado Lara, Barquisimeto 2005, pp.33-174; and Rogelio Pérez Perdomo, "Judicialization in Venezuela" in Rachel Sieder, Line Schjolden and Alan Angell, *The Judicialization of Politics in Latin America*, Palgrave Macmillan, 2005, pp. 145 ff.

124 See Allan R. Brewer-Carías, "La opción entre democracia y autoritarismo," in Allan R. Brewer-Carías, *Reflexiones sobre el constitucionalismo en América*, Editorial Jurídica Venezolana, Caracas 2001, pp. 41-59; Allan R. Brewer-Carías, *Constitución, Democracia y control del Poder*, Centro Iberoamericano de Estudios Provinciales y Locales (CIEPROL), Universidad de Los Andes, Editorial Jurídica Venezolana, Mérida 2004.

of government that is crushing democracy. This inconsistency within the text is a direct consequence of the successful effort by the President and his followers to use the constitution making process to consolidate their power while at the same time maintaining a surface appearance of adherence to democratic norms.

The centralized and plebiscitary system established by the 1999 Constitution is characterized, first, by the marginalization of the concept of political parties. In the constitutional text itself, even the expression "political parties" has disappeared. The 1999 Constitution forbids public (State) financing of political organizations, as well as the existence of party parliamentarian groups. It requires "conscience voting" by the members of the Legislative Assembly, forbidding any kind of voting instructions. Moreover, the Constitution in principle limits the possibility of parties reaching agreement on the appointment of the non-elected high public officials (Justices of the Supreme Tribunal, General Comptroller, Public Prosecutor, members of the Electoral Council), by requiring the previously mentioned Nominating Committees to be formed only on the basis of representation of the various sectors of civic society .

However, not one of these prescriptions is really in force: the President of the Republic is the acting head of his own party, which completely controls the National Assembly. He is in fact the director of his party parliamentary group, in which he has imposed a rigid party discipline. Through these mechanisms, he has intervened in the designation of the Justices of the Supreme Tribunal and of the members of the National Electoral Council, as well as the other non-elected high officials, disregarding the constitutional conception of the Nominating Committees which have effectively been converted into extended "Parliamentary Commissions" firmly controlled by the government's party.[125]

Another aspect of such plebiscitary democracy that has been built under the new Constitution is the progressive concentration of State powers, abrogating the principle of separation of powers among the branches of government. This has happened even though the 1999 Constitution explicitly set forth a *penta* separation of powers among the executive, legislative, judicial, citizens[126] and electoral branches of government. The Constitution repeatedly specifies the independence of such branches of

---

125 See Allan R. Brewer-Carías, "La progresiva y sistemática demolición institucional de la autonomía e independencia del Poder Judicial en Venezuela 1999-2004," in *XXX Jornadas J.M Domínguez Escovar, Estado de derecho, Administración de justicia y derechos humanos*, Instituto de Estudios Jurídicos del Estado Lara, Barquisimeto 2005, pp.33-174; Allan R. Brewer-Carías, *La Sala Constitucional versus el Estado democrático de derecho. El secuestro del poder electoral y de la Sala Electoral del Tribunal Supremo y la confiscación del derecho a la participación política*, Los Libros de El Nacional, Colección Ares, Caracas 2004; Allan R. Brewer-Carías et al, *Leyes Orgánicas del Poder Ciudadano*, Editorial Jurídica Venezolana, Caracas 2004; and Allan R. Brewer-Carías, *La crisis de la democracia en Venezuela (La Carta Democrática Interamericana y los sucesos de abril se 2002)*, Ediciones Libros El Nacional, Caracas 2002.

126 The "citizens" branch is composed of the General Comptroller, the Public Prosecutor and the People's Defender.

government, but in practice, such independence has been undermined by the same constitutional text when providing the National Assembly (legislative branch) not only the power to appoint but to remove the Justices of the Supreme Judicial Tribunal, the members of the National Electoral Council, the General Comptroller, the Public Prosecutor and the Peoples Defender, in some cases by an simple majority vote.[127] The sole fact that it is constitutionally provided that the head of the non-elected branches of government can be removed from their offices by means of a parliamentary political vote (with no requirement of proof of misconduct or other objective grounds for removal, and no procedural safeguards) is contrary to their independence, which has been corroborated in recent political practice.[128]

With these provisions, the *penta* separation of powers framework in fact has developed into a system of concentration of powers, totally controlled by the President of the Republic by means of the above-mentioned control he exercises over the National Assembly. In particular, the judiciary has lost its independence, which is confirmed by the fact that 90% of the judges are provisional or temporary judges, thus, by definition, political dependents. Unfortunately, the mastermind of this system of concentration of powers in the end has been the Supreme Tribunal itself, and particularly it's Constitutional Chamber, which by means of successive constitutional interpretation has cleared all the violations of the Constitution committed by the other branches of government.[129]

Within this framework of concentration of powers, even more alarming is the unprecedented exaggeration of the power of the President that appears in the new Constitution. As noted above, the excessive presidentialism that has characterized other Latin American systems has been traditionally checked in Venezuela by the powers of parliament. Nonetheless, several provisions of the new Constitution represent a reversal of that tradition. First, the President continues to be elected by a relative majority, even though an absolute majority had long been recommended (Article 228).[130] Second, the President's term was increased by 5 to 6 years (Article

---

127 This is also the case for the Justices of the Supreme Tribunal. Article 23.4 of the Supreme Tribunal Organic Law refers to "simple majority," in the sense of more than 50% of those present and voting. See the comments in Allan R. Brewer-Carías, *Ley Orgánica del Tribunal Supremo de Justicia. Procesos y procedimientos constitucionales y contencioso administrativos*, Editorial Jurídica Venezolana, Caracas 2004.

128 See the comments in Allan R. Brewer-Carías, *Constitución, Democracia y control del Poder*, Centro Iberoamericano de Estudios Provinciales y Locales (CIEPROL), Universidad de Los Andes, Editorial Jurídica Venezolana. Mérida 2004.

129 See Allan R. Brewer-Carías, *Crónica sobre la "In"Justicia Constitucioal. La Sala Constitucional y el Autoritarismo*, Editorial Jurídica Venezolana, Caracas, 2007; in particular, "*Quis custodiet ipsos custodes: de la interpretación constitucional a la inconstitucionalidad de la interpretación*," Paper submitted to the VIII Congreso Peruano de Derecho Constitucional. Colegio de Abogados de Arequipa, 22/24 septiembre 2005, pp. 47 ff.

130 See this author's dissenting vote in this regard in Allan R. Brewer-Carías, *Debate Constituyente (Aportes a la Asamblea Nacional Constituyente)*, Vol. III (18 Octubre-30 Noviembre), Fundación de Derecho Público, Caracas 1999, pp. 288 ff.

230).[131] Third, for the first time in a century, the President could be elected for a consecutive additional term (Article 230),[132] a provision that was amended in 2009 in order to allow the continuous election of all elected officials. Fourth, the National Assembly may delegate law-making power to the President, and there is no limit on the powers that can be the subject of such a delegation (Articles 203 and 236.8).[133] Fifth, the President has the power to dissolve the National Assembly after three votes of censure against the Vice President (Article 236, section 21), who nonetheless is conceived as an Executive branch official (appointed by the President) with no parliamentary role. The parliamentary censure vote has a long tradition in Venezuela regarding Cabinet Ministers, but the provision concerning the Vice President was an invention of the 1999 Constitution.

Finally, and perhaps most significantly, the unprecedented increase in Presidential power under this text has been accompanied by an equally unprecedented increase in the power of the military. It is important to note in this connection that the new Constitution, for the first time in the history of Venezuelan constitutionalism, exempts the military from all civilian control apart from that of the President himself.[134] The consequence has been the progressive intervention in the Armed Forces by the Executive, as well as the creation of a "Militia" (reserve force),[135] tending toward the creation effectively of a "military party."

The other main aspect of a constitution making power refers to certain fundamental issues, such as the power and status to be accorded to territorial subdivisions, and the centralization or devolution of power, as aspects that could help the construction of a stable peace. This aspect is particularly poignant in the Venezuelan case, since this is another area where the deformation of the constitutional process

---

131 In the 2007 Constitutional Reform draft proposals, the term is extended up to seven years. See *Proyecto de Reforma Constitucional. Elaborado por el ciudadano Presidente de la República Bolivariana de Venezuela, Hugo Chávez Frías,* Editorial Atenea, Caracas agosto 2007, 58 pp.

132 See this author's dissenting vote in this regard in Allan R. Brewer-Carías, *Debate Constituyente (Aportes a la Asamblea Nacional Constituyente),* Vol. III (18 Octubre-30 Noviembre), Fundación de Derecho Público, Caracas 1999, pp. 289 ff. In the 2007 Constitutional Reform draft proposals, the indefinite possible reelection of the President is established. See *Proyecto de Reforma Constitucional. Elaborado por el ciudadano Presidente de la República Bolivariana de Venezuela, Hugo Chávez Frías,* Editorial Atenea, Caracas agosto 2007, 58 pp.

133 See the comments regarding this provision in Allan R. Brewer-Carías, "Régimen Constitucional de la delegación legislativa e inconstitucionalidad de los Decretos Leyes habilitados dictados en 2001" in *Revista Primicia,* Informe Especial, Caracas, Diciembre 2001.

134 See this author's dissenting vote in this regard in Allan R. Brewer-Carías, *Debate Constituyente (Aportes a la Asamblea Nacional Constituyente),* Vol. III (18 Octubre-30 Noviembre), Fundación de Derecho Público, Caracas 1999, pp. 303 ff.

135 In the 2007 Constitutional Reform draft proposals, a new component of the Armed Forces is proposed: *The Popular Bolivarian Militia.* See *Proyecto de Reforma Constitucional. Elaborado por el ciudadano Presidente de la República Bolivariana de Venezuela, Hugo Chávez Frías,* Editorial Atenea, Caracas agosto 2007, 58 pp.

previously described has resulted in an alarming incongruity between different portions of the Constitution's text.

While Article 4 of the 1999 Constitution defines the State as a "Federal Decentralized State," and Article 158 defines decentralization as a national policy, other sections of the Constitution make possible an entirely different reality. Those sections allow the centralization of powers at the national level, progressively drowning any real possibility of political participation by the States of the federation and by the Municipalities (local governments).[136]

Some historical analysis will help to underscore the incongruity. As noted above, prior to the establishment of the Constituent Assembly, there had been great public demand for reforms that would bring about the decentralization of the federal state. These reforms were to build upon those initiated in 1989, which resulted in the direct election of State Governors and in the transfer of national powers to the states.

However, in contrast to the general declaration of policy found in the text of Article 158, the new Constitution has resulted in major setbacks to the prior reforms. First, the Senate, and the bicameral nature of the legislature, has been eliminated in Art. 159. This removes all possibility of equality among the federal states as a result of the unequal number of votes in the new single legislative chamber.[137] Second, the national government has been given authority in all tax matters not expressly delegated to the states and municipalities (Art. 156, section 12). Third, no tax power has been given to the states, and even their power over sales tax has been eliminated (Art. 156, section 12). Fourth, Article 167, section 5 provides that the states shall only have tax powers in the matters expressly assigned by national law. Fifth, with the new text, powers that had previously been designated as exclusive to states have been subjected to the regulations of national legislation (Art. 164). Sixth, even the exercise of concurrent powers has been made subject to the dictates of national law. Seventh, the autonomy of the States has been seriously limited by the constitutional provisions that allow the National Assembly to regulate by means of statute applicable throughout the federation the designation of the States' general comptrollers, as well as the organization and functioning of the States' legislative councils or assemblies (Art. 162).[138]

---

136 See Allan R. Brewer-Carías, *Federalismo y Municipalismo en la Constitución de 1999 (Alcance de una reforma insuficiente y regresiva)*, Editorial Jurídica Venezolana, Caracas-San Cristóbal 2001.

137 See this author's dissenting vote in this regard in Allan R. Brewer-Carías, *Debate Constituyente (Aportes a la Asamblea Nacional Constituyente)*, Vol. III (18 Octubre-30 Noviembre), Fundación de Derecho Público, Caracas 1999, pp. 286 ff.

138 Allan R. Brewer-Carías, "La 'Federación Descentralizada' en el marco de la centralización de la Federación en Venezuela. Situación y perspectivas de una contradicción constitucional," in Allan R. Brewer-Carías, *Constitución, Democracia y Control el Poder*, Centro Iberoamericano de Estudios Provinciales y Locales, Universidad de los Andes, Editorial Jurídica venezolana, Mérida 2004, pp. 111-143. See the author's proposals to the Constituent Assembly regarding the political decentralization of the Federation in Allan R. Brewer-Carías, *Debate Constituyente*, Vol. I (8 Agosto- 8 Septiembre), Fundación de Derecho Público, Caracas

It is clear from the foregoing that, in spite of the language of Article 158, the Constitution of 1999 has actually effected a reversal of the previous decentralizing reforms instead of building upon them.[139] This critical substantive development is a direct consequence of the manipulation of the constitution making process by the President and his followers.

In particular, regarding the local governments (Municipalities), in practice and in the constitutional text they continue to be very far from the citizens' reach, impeding any kind of real political participation.[140] In fact, what has been created under the 1999 Constitution is a centralized and anti-participatory democratic system, in which the instruments for direct democracy have been deliberately confused with effective political participation. That is why local governments are gradually being replaced by newly created communal councils (2006) and citizens assemblies, all directed from the center, and without any electoral origin, creating the idea that the people are "participating."[141]

In fact, to participate is to be part of, is to appertain to, is to be associated with, and that is only possible for the citizen when the political power is decentralized and close to them. Thus, participative democracy, beside elections, is only possible when effective decentralization of power exists. That is why only democracies can be de-

---

1999, pp. 155-170; and Vol. II (9 Septiembre-17 Octubre), Fundación de Derecho Público, Caracas 1999, pp. 227-233.

139   In the 2007 Constitutional Reform draft proposals, article 158 of the Constitution and all the constitutional provisions referring to political decentralization are eliminated and changed to consolidate a centralized state. See *Proyecto de Reforma Constitucional. Elaborado por el ciudadano Presidente de la República Bolivariana de Venezuela, Hugo Chávez Frías*, Editorial Atenea, Caracas agosto 2007, 58 pp.

140   See Allan R. Brewer-Carías et al, *Ley Orgánica del Poder Público Municipal*, Editorial Jurídica Venezolana, Caracas 2005; and "El inicio de la desmunicipalización en Venezuela: La organización del Poder Popular para eliminar la descentralización, la democracia representativa y la participación a nivel local," en *AIDA, Opera Prima de Derecho Administrativo. Revista de la Asociación Internacional de Derecho Administrativo*, Asociación Internacional de Derecho Administrativo, UNAM, México, 2007, pp. 49 to 67.

141   In the 2007 Constitutional Reform draft proposals, a new branch of government was proposed to be created, the "Popular Power," seeking to consolidate the power of communal councils, with members who are not elected by popular vote and are dependent on the Office of the Head of State. See the comments in Allan R. Brewer-Carías, *Hacia la consolidación de un Estado Socialista, centralizado, policial y Militarista. Comentarios sobre el alcance y sentido de la Reforma Constitucional 2007*, Editorial Jurídica Venezolana, Caracas 2007, 157 pp; and in *La Reforma Constitucional de 2007 (Sancionada inconstitucionalmente por la Asamblea Nacional el 2 de Noviembre de 2007)*, Editorial Jurídica venezolana, Caracas 2007, 225 pp.

centralized.[142] Only with local governments established throughout the territory of a country can democracy be part of everyday life.[143]

In any event, what is certain is that the goal of participation cannot be achieved only by inserting instruments of direct democracy in a representative democratic framework, as has occurred in modern constitutionalism. Referendums can be useful instruments in order to perfect democracy, but by themselves cannot satisfy the aim of participation. This can be understood by studying the 2002-2004 process concerning the Venezuelan presidential recall referendum, which was illegitimately converted into a "ratification" referendum of a plebiscitary nature.[144] A recall referendum is a vote asking the people if the mandate of an elected official must be revoked or not; it is not a vote asking if the elected official must remain or not in office. But in the 2004 recall referendum, the National Electoral Council, when giving the voting results, converted it into a plebiscite ratifying the President.

The result of the implementation of the 1999 Constitution is that the Venezuelan democracy, from being a centralized representative democracy of more or less competitive and pluralist parties which alternated in government, has been transformed into a centralized plebiscite democracy, in which effectively all power is in only one hand, that of the President of the Republic, supported by the military and by what amounts to a one-party system. The plebiscite democracy system has created a popular participation illusion, particularly by means of the uncontrolled distribution of state oil income among the poor through governmental social programs that are not precisely tailored to the promotion of investment and to employment generation.

This plebiscite democracy, without doubt, is less representative and less participatory than the traditional representative party democracy, which, notwithstanding all the warnings that were raised,[145] the traditional parties failed to preserve. All this is unfortunately contributing to the disappearance of democracy itself as a political system (which is much more than only elections and referenda, as has been made clear by the 2001 Inter American Democratic Charter), a development that was in-

---

142 See Allan R. Brewer-Carías, "Democracia municipal, descentralización y desarrollo local," en *Revista Iberoamericana de Administración Pública*, N° 11, Ministerio de Administraciones Públicas. Madrid Julio Diciembre (2003) 2004 pp.11-34.

143 See Allan R. Brewer-Carías, "Democratización, descentralización política y reforma del Estado" and "El Municipio, la descentralización política y la democracia," in Allan R. Brewer-Carías, *Reflexiones sobre el constitucionalismo en América*, Editorial Jurídica Venezolana, Caracas 2001, pp. 105-141-243-253.

144 Allan R. Brewer-Carías, "El secuestro del Poder Electoral y de la Sala Electoral del Tribunal Supremo y la confiscación del derecho a la participación política mediante el referendo revocatorio presidencial: Venezuela: 2000-2004" in *Revista Costarricense de Derecho Constitucional*, Tomo V, Instituto Costarricense de Derecho Constitucional, Editorial Investigaciones Jurídicas S.A. San José, Costa Rica 2004. pp. 167-312; and in *Revista Jurídica del Perú*, Año LIV, N° 55, marzo-abril. Lima 2004. pp. 353-396.

145 See regarding this author's wittings, Allan R. Brewer-Carías, *El Estado. Crisis y reforma*, Academia de Ciencias Políticas y Sociales, Caracas 1982; and *Problemas del Estado de partidos*, Editorial Jurídica Venezolana, Caracas 1988.

tended to be furthered by the November 2, 2007, constitutional reforms sanctioned by the National Assembly but nonetheless rejected by popular vote in the December 2, 2007, referendum.

*

From all that has been stated above, it is clear that the Venezuelan constitution making process of 1999 failed to achieve its stated mission regarding political conciliation and improvement of democracy. Contrary to the democratic principle, instead of offering the participation sought by so many, the process resulted in the imposition of the will of one political group upon the others and upon the rest of the population.

That is why, in contrast, as an instrument for the development of a constitutional authoritarian government, it can be considered a success. Undoubtedly, the democratically elected Constituent Assembly was the institution that conducted the *coup d'Etat* against the 1961 constitutional regime, facilitated the complete takeover of all the branches of government by one political group crushing the other political parties, and drafted and approved a Constitution with an authoritarian framework that has allowed the installment of a government that has concentrated and centralized all State powers.

Not being the result of a political pact among all the main political factions of the country, but rather of one group's imposition upon all the others, the durability of the new Constitution can be predicted to be the same as the durability of the power of those who imposed it and remain in control. That is why it can be considered that reforms of the political system, founded in the democratization and political decentralization of the country, remain as pending tasks that the Constituent Assembly of 1999 was unable to accomplish.

In the mean time, on August 15, 2007, the President of the Republic presented to the National Assembly a constitutional reform proposal intending to consolidate a socialist, centralized, and militaristic police state, minimizing democracy and limiting freedoms and liberties.[146] The main purpose of the proposals can be understood from the President's speech at the presentation of the draft constitutional reforms,[147] in which he said that the reforms' main objective is "the construction of a Bolivarian

---

146 See *Proyecto de Reforma Constitucional. Elaborado por el ciudadano Presidente de la República Bolivariana de Venezuela, Hugo Chávez Frías,* Editorial Atenea, Caracas agosto 2007, 58 pp. See the comments on the draft in Allan R. Brewer-Carías, *Hacia la consolidación de un Estado Socialista, centralizado, policial y Militarista. Comentarios sobre el alcance y sentido de la Reforma Constitucional 2007,* Editorial Jurídica Venezolana, Caracas 2007, 157 pp.

147 "Discurso de Orden pronunciado por el ciudadano Comandante Hugo Chávez Frías, Presidente Constitucional de la República Bolivariana de Venezuela en la conmemoración del Ducentésimo Segundo Aniversario del Juramento del Libertador Simón Bolívar en el Monte Sacro y el Tercer Aniversario del Referendo Aprobatorio de su mandato constitucional," Sesión especial del día Miércoles 15 de agosto de 2007, Asamblea Nacional, División de Servicio y Atención legislativa, Sección de Edición, Caracas 2007.

and Socialist Venezuela."[148] This is intended, as he explained, to sow "socialism in the political and economic realms."[149] This is something that the Constitution of 1999 did not do. When the Constitution of 1999 was sanctioned, said the President, "We were not projecting the road of socialism." "Just as candidate Hugo Chávez repeated a million times in 1998, 'Let us go to a Constituent [Assembly]', so candidate President Hugo Chávez said [in 2006]: 'Let us go to Socialism' and, thus, everyone who voted for candidate Chávez then, voted to go to socialism."[150]

Thus, the draft constitutional reforms presented by the President on this basis, according to what he said in his speech, propose the construction of "Bolivarian Socialism, Venezuelan Socialism, our Socialism, and our socialist model."[151] It is a socialism whose "basic and indivisible nucleus" is "the community" ("*la comunidad*"), one "where common citizens shall have the power to construct their own geography and their own history."[152] This is all based on the premise that, "real democracy is only possible in socialism."[153] However, the supposed "democracy" referred to is one which, as the President suggests in his proposed reform to article 136, "is not born of suffrage or from any election, but rather is born from the condition of organized human groups as the base of the population." Of course, this is a "democracy" that is not democracy, as there can be no democracy without the election of representatives.

The President in his speech summarized all of the proposed reforms in this manner: "on the political ground, deepen popular Bolivarian democracy; on the economic ground, create better conditions to sow and construct a socialist productive economic model, our model; the same in the political field: socialist democracy; on the economic, the productive socialist model; in the field of Public Administration: incorporate new forms in order to lighten the load, to leave behind bureaucracy, corruption, and administrative inefficiency, which are heavy burdens of the past still upon us like weights, in the political, economic and social areas."[154]

All these 2007 constitutional reform proposals were sanctioned by the National Assembly on November 2, 2007, and rejected in the December 2, 2007, popular referendum, increasing the extreme polarization the country has experienced since 1999. That is why no one should discard the possibility that in the future there will be a new demand for a new Constituent Assembly -a mechanism that the President and his supporters discarded in 2007- faced with the same challenge of serving as an agent of political conciliation and democratic reform. When the time comes, in order to succeed where the 1999 Constituent Assembly failed and reverse the tendency

---

148 Id., p. 4
149 Id., p. 33.
150 Id., p. 4.
151 See "Discurso de Orden pronunciado por el ciudadano Comandante Hugo Chávez Frías,....," *cit.*, p. 34
152 Id., p. 32.
153 Id., p. 35.
154 Id., p. 74

toward which the 2007 constitutional reforms headed, in conceiving and electing such a body, Venezuela must bear in mind that it is always better to conciliate and achieve agreements before passing through the pain of civil strife than to arrive at the same agreements but by means of some kind of post-confrontation "armistice," which never eliminates the wounds of civil conflict.

CHAPTER IV

CRITICAL REFLECTIONS ON
THE 1999 CONSTITUTION
(2000)

This essay was written during the month following the approval of the Constitution, for my participation in the *Conference on Challenges to Fragile Democracies in the Americas: Legitimacy and accountability,* organized by the *Faculty of Law of the University of Texas*, held in Austin, on February 25, 2000. An abstract of my oral presentation in the Symposium was published in the *Texas International Law Journal*, University of Texas at Austin, Volume 36, Austin 2001, pp. 333-338. The text of this essay was extensively published in Spanish, in Diego Valadés, Miguel Carbonell (Coord.), *Constitucionalismo Iberoamericano del Siglo XXI*, Cámara de Diputados. LVII Legislatura, Universidad Nacional Autónoma de México, México 2000, pp. 171-193; in *Revista Facultad de Derecho, Derechos y Valores*, Volumen III N° 5, Universidad Militar Nueva Granada, Santafé de Bogotá, D.C., Colombia, Julio 2000, pp. 9-26; and in the book published by the Venezuelan Academy of Political and Social Sciences, *La Constitución de 1999*, Caracas 2000, pp. 63-88.

As Member of the National Constituent Assembly in Venezuela in 1999, I not only participate in the discussion of all the content of the 1999 Constitution that was sanctioned by it, and later approved by the people in the referendum of December 15th 1999, but also expressed many dissenting votes in many aspects of the new text.

A few weeks after the approval of the new Constitution, to which I strongly opposed,[155] I wrote the following reflections on its content, in which I summarize my general appreciation of the Constitution.

---

155 These reflections were latter developed in Allan R. Brewer-Carías, *La Constitución de 1999*, Editorial Jurídica Venezolana, Caracas 2000; and *La Constitución de 1999. Derecho Constitucional Venezolano*, 2 vols., Editorial Jurídica Venezolana, Caracas 2004.

I.   THE CONSTITUTION OF 1999 OR THE FRUSTRATION OF THE NECESSARY POLITICAL CHANGE

According to the referendum of April 25, 1999, which created a National Constituent Assembly, this institution had as its mission to elaborate a new Constitution in order to transform the state and create a new legal order, which would permit the effective functioning of a social and participatory democracy. For that purpose, the members of the assembly were elected on July 25, 1999.

The creation of the assembly and the election of its members responded to the requirements of the constituent moment existing in the country, provoked by the terminal crisis of the political system of centralized government of parties.

This system of centralized state of parties has been based first on the state centralism and second on the democracy of parties, in which they exercised the monopoly of the participation and representation. It was established from the forties and restored in 1958, and needed to be changed in order to allow the improvement and survival of democracy itself.

This implied the transformation of said centralized government of parties into a system of decentralized and participatory state, based on the political decentralization of the State in the territory and on people's participation.

The mission of the Assembly was then to introduce these changes: On one hand, the transformation of the State to make it more democratic, demolishing the centralism and constructing a decentralized State. On the other hand, the creation of a new legal order that permits the effective functioning of a social and participatory democracy, which would incorporate individuals and private institutions to the social, economic and political process and ensure political participation in the conduction of the State.

The Assembly sessions ended in December 1999 and the Constitution Project was approved through referendum on December 15, 1999 receiving 71% of affirmative votes and 29% of negative ones. But there was a 55% abstention, which means the Constitution was approved by just 30% of the Venezuelans with right to vote.

The new Constitution was published and is in force since December 30, 1999. It is time then to establish if said text responds to the demands of political transformation determined in the referendum of April 25, 1999, and if the *"transformation of the State"* and *"new legal order"* it contains contribute not only to overcome the crisis of the system of centralized government of parties, but to structure, in its place, that system of decentralized and participatory State that would allow the preservation of democracy.

In our opinion and as conclusion of said evaluation, the new Constitution neither ensures nor establishes a basis for said transformation of the political system. On the contrary, it consolidates both the prevailing state centralism, which moves backwards the decentralization process initiated in 1989, and the partisanship since it reiterates the electoral system of proportional representation as the only one with constitutional rank. Said system ensures the monopoly of the representation by the political parties and their agents and the tendency towards democratic illegitimacy when it maintains, for example, the relative majority for the election of the executive authorities.

Then, the essential tasks of the 1999 Assembly were the transformation of the State from centralized State into decentralized State, and from a Government of parties into State of participation. These tasks were not achieved in the new Constitution and therefore, a unique historical opportunity to introduce them in democracy was lost: to convoke a National Constituent Assembly in democracy is not a common political fact in our history; it is rather a very exceptional one.

We have had constituent moments like this in our constitutional history, particularly when similar situations like the breakdown of the political process arose because of its exhaustion and the necessity of its radical change. In those moments, Constituent Assemblies have always played a decisive role, but they have always been established as a consequence of a revolution or war, and have never been elected peacefully in democracy.

In effect, the first period of our constitutional history began in 1811 with the Constituent Congress that declared our Independence from Spain. After the Independence wars and the disappearance of Venezuela as an independent republic due to its union with the Republic of Colombia, a new Constitutional Assembly was elected in 1830 to restore the Republic. This period of formation of the new state ended abruptly with the Federal Wars and again, a Constituent Assembly was elected in 1863 to establish the constitutional basis of a new state system, the one of the Federal State.

This initiated the second political period, which once again ended abruptly after its terminal crisis with the Restoring Liberal Revolution in 1899, which provoked the election of the Constituent Assembly of 1901. This Assembly also designed a radical change in the political-state system, giving birth, contrary to the Federal State, to a centralized and autocratic State, which consolidated during the first half of the last century.

Once again, this third political period of our constitutional history ended abruptly with the Revolution of October 1945 and a new Constituent Assembly on 1946 assumed the task of designating the democratic political system of centralized State we have had during the last decades, which consolidated after a military interregnum (1948-1958). It has been this system of State centralism and democracy of parties the one that during the last two decades has demanded a radical change. That change should have been designed by the Constituent Assembly of 1999, but in this case, as never before, in democracy and without constitutional break. That is why if the Constitution of 1999 is, indeed, the first one of a fifth period of our political history or the last one of the fourth period mentioned, cannot be known; it is only going to be said by history. What we can evaluate now is the greatness of the political change expected with the new Constitution.

The truth is that the new Constitution does not solve the central problem and the core of the political crisis to improve the democracy and does not establish the basis of the democratic political change. Its approval does not contribute to overcome the crisis of the State centralism and the government of parties: As a matter of fact, it aggravates the crisis because its approval establishes the constitutional basis for the development of a political authoritarianism based on regulations that reinforce the centralism, presidentialism, statism, State paternalism, partisanship and militarism, with the danger of the collapse of the democracy itself.

This is the political frame that the new Constitution gives us, which we want to analyze with the main regulations it contains, referring the three central elements that make up any constitution: the political constitution, the social constitution and the economic constitution.

II. THE PROBLEM OF A POLITICAL CONSTITUTION CONCEIVED FOR AUTHORITARIANISM

The object of every political constitution is the organization of the State, the constitutional authority of the State and, in consequence, the organization of the State itself.

This organization, in any constitution, is determined by different options: the first one derived from the distribution of the State power, which originates Unitary States or Decentralized Sates; second: the one that provokes the separation of powers, which originates the uniqueness or separation of powers. The latter is the feature of democratic systems, based on the separation, balance and counterweight of the powers of the State and giving rise to the system of presidential or parliamentarian government.

Moreover, the political constitution designs the political system with option between autocracy and democracy, depending on whether sovereignty lies in an autocrat or in the people effectively, giving rise to the electoral and party system.

Now, in relation to the Constitution of 1999 and from the point of view of the political constitution, we would like to point out the regulations that, in our opinion, contain the negative aspects of the Constitution, particularly in relation to the improvement of democracy. Said negative aspects in our opinion count more than the reforms that could deserve our approval, which refer to the formal consolidation of the principles of the rule of law and justice with excellent mechanisms of judicial review and of judicial reform. Sadly, these mechanisms run the risk of being put out of action, given the elements of authoritarianism and concentration of powers derived from other aspects of the approved text, to which we are going to refer next.

1.   The New Name of "República Bolivariana de Venezuela" ("Bolivarian Republic of Venezuela") and its Partisan Character

The new Constitution, in its first article, changes the name of the "República de Venezuela" ("Republic of Venezuela") and replaces it with the name "República Bolivariana de Venezuela" ("Bolivarian Republic of Venezuela"), referring to the ideas and conduct of Simón Bolívar, Liberator of Venezuela, and other "Bolivarian" Republics of Latin America.

Now, the name Republic of Venezuela has accompanied us all along our constitutional political history since 1811, when, after the Independence from Spain, the Confederation of States of Venezuela was constituted. The sole exception was the constitutional period that followed the Congress of Angostura, 1819, up to the reconstitution of the Republic of Venezuela by the Convention of Valencia of 1830. In effect, in 1819, Bolívar made the Congress of the Republic of Venezuela sanction the Laws of the Union of the Peoples of Colombia, which decree the disappearance of the Republic of Venezuela. A new law similar to the former was approved in 1821, and in the same year, the Constitution of Cucuta consolidated that situation when it established the "Republic of Colombia," with a territory made up by both the one of the former Captaincy General of Venezuela (where the Republic of Venezuela was established in 1811) and the former Viceroyalty of Nueva Granada. With this Constitution of 1821, part of what had been the dream of the Liberator regarding the union of the peoples of America came true.

Thus, the idea of the Bolivarian Republic historically points to a political organization that implied the disappearance of Venezuela as State. That is why the change of the name of the Republic is totally unacceptable and contrary to the idea of independence of our country itself. In any case, to name Venezuela, only, as a Bolivarian Republic does not correspond to the thoughts of Bolívar, who followed the idea of the disappearance of the Republic of Venezuela.

So the change of the name of the Republic cannot respond to a romantic desire of evoking the thought and action of the Liberator in the formation of our Republic. To that, it would be enough to make that indication both in the Preamble and in the Article 1°, as was approved in the first discussion of the project of Constitution.

The change of name, therefore, has to have another explanation far away from the ideas of Bolívar and it is no other than an actual political or partisan motivation, derived from the initial denomination of the political movement established and presided by the President of the Republic, Hugo Chávez Frías as a political party, initially named Bolivarian Movement 2000. The party of the President of the Republic is, in fact, the "Bolivarian party," and this is why his adherents pretend to impose it as the name of the Republic; like it happened in Nicaragua, with the Sandinista Party. That, in our opinion, should be rejected, not only because it is anti-Bolivarian (we should remember that the last cry of the Liberator, on the eve of his death, was for the ceasing of the parties but it should be rejected also because it pretends to consolidate, from the first article of the Constitution, the division of the country between "Bolivarian" and those who are not; patriots and realists; good and bad people; pure and corrupt people, revolutionary and anti-revolutionary ones, all that by manipulating history and popular feelings through the control of Power.

2. *The Mockery of the Process of Decentralization: The Decentralized Federal State with a Centralist Frame and the Elimination of the Senate*

One of the great political changes that should make the new Constitution was to transform in a definitive way the "Centralized Federation" we have had during the last hundred years into a Decentralized Federation, with an effective territorial distribution of the power towards the States and Municipalities. The constitutional reform should have pointed to that direction, conceiving the state as a Decentralized Federal State (Art. 4), and it should have foreseen the political decentralization of the Federation as a national policy of strategic character (Art. 158).

However, the final result of the approved constitutional scheme of territorial distribution of power hasn't mean any substantial advance regarding the previous process of decentralization initiated in 1989 according to the Constitution of 1961 through the Organic Law of Decentralization. Moreover, in many aspects, the new Constitution has meant an institutional step backwards, being the denomination of "Decentralized Federal State" only nominal, and decentralization continues being a "desideratum" to be achieved, as in the Constitution of 1961.

On the other hand, in this case, the constitutional regime is conceived in a contradictory way, since institutionally, the autonomy of the States and Municipalities (consequence of decentralization) could be limited by national laws, which is contrary to what should be a constitutional guarantee of said autonomy. It is also contradictory because the equality of the States is damaged as the Senate is eliminated, and replaced by a Unicameral National Assembly. With that, the possibility of an equal political participation of the States in the conduction of the national policies is eliminated.

This unicameral organization of the National Assembly (Art.186) not only breaks a tradition that goes back to 1811, but it also is contradictory to the federal form of State, which requires a Legislative Chamber with equal representation of the States, whichever their population is, that serves as political counterweight to the chamber of people's representation, depending on the population of the states. The "elimination" of the Senate or Federal Chamber is an attack on the effective political decentralization, since it extinguishes the instrument to make States equal in the treatment of the national affairs. It is also a step backwards both in the process of forming national laws and in exercising powers of parliamentary control over the Executive.

On the other hand, the autonomy of territorial entities (States and Municipalities) requires its constitutional guarantee, which means that it could not be limited by a subsequent national law. That is why a constitutional distribution of the political power in the territory is established.

However, in the new Constitution, the regulation on the functioning and organization of the State Legislative Councils is referred to a national law (Art. 162), which is contradictory to the attribution given to the States of dictating their own Constitution to organize their sovereign powers. This regulation is an unacceptable interference of the National Power into the regime of the States.

Regarding the Municipalities, their autonomy, traditionally guaranteed in the Constitution itself, is also interfered, because it is granted "within the boundaries" established not only in the Constitution, but within the ones established in national laws (Art. 168). Therefore, the basic decentralizing principle, which is the autonomy, is minimized.

On the other hand, regarding the distribution of powers between territorial entities, the decentralization process required, above all, the effective allocation of taxation powers to States, specifically regarding sale taxes, as it happens in almost all Federations. The advances that the project of Constitution had in this subject in the first discussion were abandoned, and in the second discussion, all taxation powers assigned to States were removed, which did a step backwards to the same stage that existed in the 1961 Constitution. In this way, States still depend on the national financial contribution, called "Situado Constitutional," which has a maximum top of 20% of the national public income and which can be diminished. Said top did not exist in the Constitution of 1961, which only established a minimum. And even though a Federal Council of Government is created in the new Constitution (Art. 185) as an inter-governmental organ, its organization by national law can lead to its control by national organs.

According to what has been said, broadly speaking, the scheme of centralized Federation of the Constitution of 1961 couldn't be overcome in the new Constitution, and although it talks about decentralization, it is still being a desideratum to be achieved.

The great reform of the political system, necessary and essential to improve the democracy, was to demolish the centralism of the State and to distribute the political power in the territory. It was the only way to make political participation come true. Only this justified the constituent process; this, however, was postponed and with it, the great opportunity of substituting the Centralized State into a Decentralized State was lost.

The Constituent Assembly, in order to overcome the political crisis, should have designed the transformation of the State, decentralizing the power and establishing the basis to effectively approach it to the citizen. As the Assembly didn't do that, it neither transformed the State nor arranged the necessary elements to make participation effective.

3   *The Proportional Representation and the Survival of Democracy of Parties*

The new Constitution did not tackle the other aspect of the political system that required a radical reform: political representation and participation, in order to avoid the monopoly that, in this subject, political parties have had.

As part of the political system, the centralism of State has been accompanied by the State of Parties in which the political parties have been the sole mechanism of political participation and the only ones who have obtained representatives seats in state organs. This is assured through the method of plural-nominal scrutiny based on the proportional representation, which hasn't been changed; moreover, it is the only one established in the Constitution (Art. 63). Although the guarantee of "personalizing" the vote is pointed out in the Constitution, it does not change the representation if the method of proportional representation is followed, because it leads to the representation of parties. Sadly, the proposal of establishing the uninominal election for the representatives to Parochial Council, Municipal Councils and State Legislative Councils, in order to obtain a territorial representation of the respective communities wasn't accepted.

In any case, in our opinion, to maintain, in general, the system of proportional representation guarantees that the democracy of the parties continues and nothing has change, except the representation of one party for another.

4.   *The Exaggerated Presidentialism*

In the horizontal organization of the Sovereign Power, in the new Constitution the presidential system of government continues existing, even though it introduced some parliamentary elements, as happened in the Constitution of 1961.

However, in the new Constitution, it can be said that presidentialism has been exaggerated because of the extension of the constitutional period of the President of the Republic with an immediate reelection and the lost of balance or counterweight of powers because of the elimination of the bicameral system for the Legislative Power.

In the chosen presidential model, the following four factors are combined: In first place, the extension of the presidential period to six years; in second place, the immediate reelection of the President of the Republic (Art. 230). These elements threaten the principle of republican alternation, because it allows for a government period of twelve years. But the former two elements are combined with other two. The third one is the complex referendum established in order to revoke the mandate (Art. 72), which makes it almost inapplicable; and fourth, the elimination of the principle of the election of the President by absolute majority and double ballot, which was established in the Project approved in the first discussion, and was eliminated in the second discussion, keeping the election by relative majority (Art. 228), as the Constitution of 1961 foresaw, and, therefore, keeping the idea of governments elected by a minority of votes, which has affected governance.

With this presidential model, to which the possibility of dissolution of the Assembly by the President of the Republic is added (in exceptional cases of three parliamentary votes of no confidence in the Executive Vice-president -Art. 240-); presidentialism is exaggerated since it hasn't counterweight in the bicameral system. Moreover, it is reinforced in other reforms, as the admission of enabling laws or the legislative delegation to the President of the Republic by the National Assembly in order to enact Decrees-Laws, not limited only to economic and financial subjects (Art. 203), but in any subject whatsoever.

5.   The Unbalance in the Separation of Powers Because of the Concentration of Power in the National Assembly

The Constitution adopts a scheme of separation of powers not only between the Legislative and the Executive with the shaping of the presidential system of government, but also between the Judicial Power, whose autonomy is repeatedly established, and other two new powers of constitutional rank: the Citizen Power, which involves the Public Ministry (General Prosecutor of the Republic), the People's Defender, General Controllership of the Republic and the Electoral Power, exercised by the National Electoral Council.

But an effective separation of powers is based on the independence among them, so the origin of their tenure by election or appointment is not at the mercy of any of the powers of the State. The guarantee of the counterweight consists in that.

In the new Constitution, on the contrary, an unbalance among the State Powers is established. The National Assembly is authorized to remove the General Prosecutor of the Republic, the People's Defender, the General Controller of the Republic, the members of the National Electoral Council and worst, the Magistrates of the Supreme Court of Justice (Arts. 265 and 296). That constitutes the antithesis of the independence and counterweight between the Powers of the State and makes up a model of concentration of Power in the National Assembly, which is totally incompatible with a democratic-political society.

6.   *The Constitutional Base for Militarism*

In the new Constitution, a marked militarist scheme is added to the presidentialism as a government form and to the concentration of Power in the National Assembly, whose combination can easily lead to authoritarianism.

In effect, in the constitutional text the whole idea of subjection or subordination of the military authority to the civil authority was eliminated. On the contrary, a great autonomy of the military authority and of the National Armed Forces was established. Also the Constitution established the unification of the four forces, with the possibility of intervening without any limits in civil functions.

That is shown in the following regulations: first, the elimination of the traditional prohibition of exercising simultaneously the military and civil authority established in the article 131 of the Constitution of 1961. Second, the control exercised by the National Assembly regarding the promotion of the high-ranked military is eliminated. In the new Constitution, on the contrary: this is an exclusive attribution of the Armed Forces (Art. 331). Third, the apolitical character of the military institution and its condition of non-deliberator established in the article 132 of the Constitution of 1961 are eliminated. This opens a path for the Armed Forces to deliberate and intervene on the affairs being resolved by the State organs. Fourth, the obligation of the Armed Forces of looking after the stability of the democratic institutions, foreseen in the article 132 of the Constitution of 1961, was also eliminated. Even more serious is, fifth, the elimination of the obligation the Armed Forces had of obeying the Constitution and laws "whose observance is always over any other obligation," as the article 132 of the Constitution of 1961 said. Sixth, the military are granted the right to vote in an express way (Art. 330), which could be politically incompatible with the principle of obedience. Seventh, the Constitution established the necessity of a decision from the Supreme Court judging on the merit of prosecuting high-ranked military of the Armed Forces, which has always been a procedural privilege kept for high State civilian officials (Art. 266.3). Eighth, war weapons and everything regarding the use of any kind of arms is subjected to the authority of the Armed Forces, which used to be subjected to the civil administration of the State (Art. 324). Ninth, the Armed Forces can be granted all competencies on administrative police (Art. 329). Tenth, the concept of the national security doctrine, defined in a global, total and omni-comprehensive way, is adopted, according to which almost everything that happens in the State and nation concerns the State security, even the economic and social development (Art. 326).

All this gives rise to a militarist scheme, which is constitutionally a novelty, and which can lead to a situation in which the Armed Forces could constitutionally seize the civil administration of the State. The new Constitution additionally granted the latter "active participation in the national development" (Art. 328).

All that shows a constitutional picture of militarism really unique in our constitutional history, which isn't ever found in the constitutions of former military regimes.

III. THE PROBLEM OF A SOCIAL CONSTITUTION CONCEIVED FOR PATERNALISM AND POPULISM

The second part of every constitution, as a supreme law, is the social Constitution or the one that establishes the status of the citizen, and the relation between the State and the society. Therefore, the social constitution regulates the human rights and the rights of citizens, and also establishes the correlative duties of the State regarding its protection and satisfaction. The truth is that it couldn't exist a constitutionally established right that doesn't have a correlative duty or obligation to the State.

In this subject, the new Constitution has signs of advances as the enumeration of the individual rights and the incorporation of the International treaties on human rights into the constitution; with preferential application when more favorable. But in spite of these advances of the Constitution, the negative aspects of the text are heavier than the reasons we might have to approve it.

1. *The Serious Damage to the Constitutional Guarantee of Limitations only Through Statutes*

The true effectiveness of enunciating the constitutional rights in a Constitution is the foresight of their guarantees. In this aspect, the new Venezuelan Constitution has an excellent and an extensive enumeration of constitutional rights. The same line was followed in Latin America by the Constitution of Brazil and Colombia. Additionally, the new Constitution expressly granted the International treaties on human rights constitutional rank and foresaw their immediate application by judges and their preferential application in everything that benefits people (Article 31).

However, this mention can be ineffective because of the prevision, in the Constitution itself, of rules, which mean an antithesis of the constitutional guarantee of human rights. Among those guarantees, the most important is the one that required a formal statute in order to limit or restrict human rights. It means that the limitations to constitutional rights can only be established by a statute, which is the act emanated from the legislative organ (National Assembly) integrated by representatives elected in a democratic way. However, in the new Venezuelan Constitution, a system of delegated legislation by enabling laws is foreseen, which hasn't comparison with any other Latin American Constitution. Said system confers the President of the Republic the authority of ruling in any subject. With it, the constitutional guarantee of reserve required by statute is totally minimized and with that, the exhaustive list of the constitutional rights can be ruined.

2. *The Lack of Constitutional Establishment of Rights of Protection of Children from Conception*

On the other hand, in spite of the advance of the constitutional text regarding individual rights and in spite of the repetition of the rules of the Constitution of 1961 on the inviolable character of the right of life (Art. 43), in the new Constitution, the right of integral protection of children "from conception" wasn't established. But it was established in the Article 74 of the Constitution of 1961.

The Constituent Assembly, regarding this point, violated the rules established in the referendum of April, 25 1999 that gave rise to it, which imposed it as limit the progress on protecting human rights. On the contrary, in this sensitive field, we can consider that a step backward in the constitutional regulation took place; all conditioned by the discussion between abortionists and not abortionists and between feminist movements and the Catholic Church itself.

The National Constituent Assembly didn't want to mark the boundaries of the regulation area. It expected to satisfy the requirements of the Church, which wished the establishment of the right of protection of children from conception, but pretended to lie the Church by only foreseeing the protection of maternity "from conception" (Art. 76), which has no sense, because no other moment exists from which maternity could start.

In the new Constitution, the necessary balance between the rights of children and the rights of the mother does not exist. In this matter, the general balance of the protection and the mutual rights should have been kept, since the boundary of the exercise of every human right is "the right of others and the public and social order."

A Constitution that doesn't guarantee specifically the right of children to be protected from conception doesn't deserve our approval, since it is regressive regarding protection of individual rights.

3. *The Constitutional Sowing of the Principle to Control the Freedom of Information*

The Constitution establishes everyone's right to express freely his or her ideas, thoughts, opinions and to use for that any means of communication, without censorship. The person who makes use of said right is responsible for what had expressed (Art. 57).

Additionally, the Constitution establishes everyone's right to information, that is to say, to be informed, incorporating to the word information the adjectives "impartial, opportune and reliable" (Art. 58). In fact, this is a desideratum that should be derived from the general principle that the limit of one's rights is other's right and public and social order (Art. 20). But expressed in that way, in the new Constitution, it could give origin to a development of a political or public control that could lead to the definition of an "official" true and, therefore, the rejection of any other true in the information. In a Constitution determined by the principle of progress in the regulation of the individual rights, this step backwards is unacceptable, since it could open a path to authoritarianism.

4. *The Confusion between Good Intentions and Constitutional Rights and the Lie Derived from the Impossibility of Satisfying Some Social Rights*

One essential principle of constitutional rank in the establishment of human rights is the one called principle of altering. It implies that every right carries an obligation and that everyone entitling a right has to have relation to an obligated character, on the contrary there is no constitutional right.

Therefore, there are no rights without obligations and obligated ones. So the establishment of alleged rights that couldn't originate obligations or obligated ones is nothing, but a lie due to its conceptual impossibility.

This happens with several "social rights" and guarantees established in the Constitution, whose satisfaction is simply impossible. They are declarations of principles and of intention of indubitably teleological character, but they hardly can be considered as constitutional "rights," because a character obliged to satisfy them does not exist.

The "right to health" is, for example, one case. It is established as a fundamental social right; the State is obligated by it and guarantees it as "part of the right to life" (Art. 83). It is impossible that someone guarantees somebody's health and that the right to health can be constitutionally established. That equals to establish in the Constitution the "right to not get sick," which is impossible, since nobody is able to guarantee to another person that he or she is not going to get sick.

Actually, the right that can be established as a constitutional right regarding health is the right to health care which carries the obligation of the State of looking after said protection by establishing public services of preventive and curative medicine.

The same can be said regarding the right established in the Constitution in favor of "every person" "to a adequate, secure, comfortable, hygienic house with essential basic services that include a habitat that makes more human the familiar, neighboring and community relations" (Art. 82). The way it is established, this right is a declaration of principle or intention beautifully structured that doesn't lead to identify a person obliged to satisfy it because it is impossible to satisfy.

It is also a lie to establish in the Constitution, pure and simple, that "every person has the right to social security as non lucrative public service that guarantees health and ensure protection in contingencies... of social prevision." It is also impossible to foresee that "The State has the obligation of ensuring the effectiveness of this right, creating a system of social security..." (Article 86).

Once again, the intention is beautiful, but not to pretend to regulate it as a constitutional "right" with a correlative constitutionally ranked State obligation, whose satisfaction is impossible. In this matter, good intentions and social declarations were mistaken with constitutional rights and obligations that originate another type of legal relations, even with right of being constitutionally protected.

5. The Excessive State Paternalism and the Minimization of Private Initiatives Regarding Health, Education and Social Security

In regulating social rights, the new Constitution puts in State's hands excessive burdens, obligations and guarantees of impossible compliance and execution. In many cases, it also minimizes, and even excludes, private initiatives. In this way, public services, essentially and traditionally concurrent between the State and individuals, as education, health and social security are regulated with a marked State and mutually exclusive accent.

For example, regarding health, "to guarantee it, State will create, exercise the ruling and arrange a national public health system, ...integrated to the social security system, ruled by principles of free health, universality, comprehensiveness, equity, social integration and solidarity" (art. 84). Therefore, it is about a public health system, ruled as a free public service that is part of the social security system. Nothing is said in the article about private health services, even though in another article it is indicated that the State "will regulate public and private health institutions" (Art. 85).

As regards as social security, the state feature is even greater: social security is declared a free public service. The State is obliged "to ensure the effectiveness of this right, creating a universal, comprehensive, unitary, efficient and participatory social security system of joint financing and of direct or indirect contributions." It is specified that the obligatory contributions just "can be administrated with social purposes under the ruling of the state" (Art. 86). Thus, all private enterprise is excluded regarding social security and the private participation in the administration of pension funds is minimized.

Regarding education, the tendency is similar. Education is regulated, generally, as a human right and a fundamental social duty. It is declared "democratic, free and obligatory" and is defined as "a public service," which should be assumed by the state as "a function that cannot be declined" (art. 102). As regard as private education, nothing is said. It is just in another article that the people's right to "found and maintain private educational institutions under the strict inspection and surveillance of the State, previous its acceptance" is declared (Art 106). The possibility of turning education into a state one hasn't limits in the Constitution; and an article regarding this subject in the Constitution of 1961 that established that "the State will stimulate and protect private education given according to the principles established in this Constitution and laws" (Art. 79) was eliminated.

In this subject, the Assembly once again violated the electoral basis of the referendum of April 25, 1999 when it ignored the progressive character of the protection of human rights, eliminating this right of protection corresponding to private education.

6.   The regime regarding Indigenous Peoples and the Possibility of Affecting the Territorial Integrity of the State

One novelty of the new Constitution is the inclusion of a chapter on the rights of the Indigenous peoples very rich in content if compared to the rule of the Constitution of 1961, which referred to a statute to rule on the protection of the Indian communities and their progressive incorporation to Nation's life" (Art. 77).

From the idea of a special protection, the new Constitution passed to an excessive discriminatory regime as regards the rest of the population of our territory; giving rise to a regime of a State within a State, in which the integrity of the territory and of the Nation could be on future risk.

The State is defined in Constitutional law as a people settled in a territory with its own government. These three elements: people, territory and political organization define a State and it can be just one. Several States cannot coexist in the same territory.

However, the first article of the new Constitution related to the rights of the Indian peoples establishes that "the State recognizes the existence of *peoples* and Indian Communities, *their own* social, *political* and economic *organization*, their cultures, uses and customs, languages and religions as well as their habitat and original rights *over the lands* they traditionally occupy since ancient times and which are necessary to develop and guarantee their forms of life" (Art. 119).

Once again, this declaration of principles is a human desideratum. But its establishment in a constitutional text as a constitutional right is something different. It generates rights and duties and, in a certain way, constitutes the recognition of a State within a State, with serious risk of generating conflict affecting the territorial integrity of the nation.

IV. THE PROBLEM OF AN ECONOMIC CONSTITUTION CONCEIVED FOR INSOLVENT STATISM

The third part of the Constitution, as any contemporary Constitution, is destined to regulate the economic Constitution. In it the rules of the game of the economic system of the country are established. The system is still conceived as a mixed economy system, based on recognizing the private enterprise and the right of property and economic freedom, but basing it on principles of social justice, which allows the state to intervene in the economy, in some cases in a huge way. Additionally, The State paternalism in the social area leads to conceive an economic Constitution with a great state burden.

In this area, even though in the discussions in the Assembly, some important balances between economic freedom and State intervention were established, a marked state accent remained in the Constitution. This together with the tax consequences of social paternalism and populism it had makes the role of the State financially non-viable and originates a scheme of tax terrorism that informs the constitutional text.

1.   *The Almost Unlimited Possibility of State Intervention in the Economy*

In the economic area, the Constitution is marked by statism, since it attributes the State the fundamental responsibility in the arrangement and provision of basic public services in health, education and social security areas and the ones of home character: distribution of water, gas and electricity. It is also derived from the regulation of state power to control and planning economic activities.

The articles of the Constitution regarding economy are basically those destined to foresee the intervention of the State. Only succinct rules are devoted to regulate economic freedom (Art. 112) and private property (Art. 115), the necessary balance between public and private sectors is absent. In the latter, only activities non fundamental in the generation of wealth and employment are privileged, such as agricultural (Art. 305), crafts (Art. 309), small and medium enterprise (Art. 308) and tourism (Art. 310).

Control and prosecution rules are added to that, such as those regarding monopoly and economic crime, (Arts. 113 and 114), and the declaration of the subsoil, maritime shores and waters as state public properties (Art. 112 and 304), which opens an unlimited field regarding the State control of the use and exploitation of said goods.

The Constitution has also established the reserve to the State of the oil industry and the possibility of reserving other activities, services or exploitation of strategic character (Article 302) and the rules that foresee the State's planning authority, both at national and local level (Article 178).

Thus, State is, in the Constitution, responsible for almost everything and is able to regulate everything. The private enterprise appears fringe and shunned. The experience of the regulating, control, planning and Entrepreneur State's failure of the last decades wasn't assimilated. The necessity of granting privileges to private enterprises and stimulating the generation of wealth and employment to society wasn't understood.

Globally, the result of the constitutional text regarding economy is a Constitution done for State's intervention in economy and not for the development of the economy by private sectors under the principle of subsidiary State intervention.

2. The State's Financial Incapacity to Attend the Tasks and Responsibilities Assigned to It

The State conceived in the new Constitution is financially unable to attend the huge amount of responsibilities attributed to it in the social, educational, labor and social security fields. There was not any calculation of costs in foreseeing the regulations of the Paternalist State established in the Constitution. From the beginning, it puts the State, if it pretends to assume those responsibilities, in bankruptcy, since it is obliged to pay more than it is able to and more than it is able to collect in taxes, especially in a country in which there exist no habit of tax-payer citizens.

The constitutionally-ranked prevision that the tax management should be balanced in a pluri-annual frame of the budget "so the ordinary income should be sufficient to cover ordinary expenses" (Art. 311) is added to that situation. We cannot understand how the State is going to attend all the obligations imposed to it.

3. The Establishment of Tax Terrorism as Illusion to Solve the State Insolvency and the Abandonment of Tax-Payers

The huge social responsibility imposed to the state and the financial costs that carries its attention will imply, of course, the exaggeration of the exercise of the State's tax authority in its different territorial levels and, immediately, at national and municipality levels. This required the establishment of an adequate balance between the public authority and the individual rights, so the exercise of the first won't affect the economic capacity of taxpayers or their constitutional guarantees, which require special protection.

Nevertheless nothing specific was regulated in the new Constitution about the necessary respect of the tax capacity of persons according to the taxation powers granted to National, State and Municipal entities or about the principle of reversion on the taxpayers-citizens of the tax in adequate public services. Moreover, nothing was regulated about the taxpayer's constitutional guarantee opposite to the tax authority, since it is precisely on the occasion of said exercise that all the power of the State can fall over individuals.

On the contrary, the new rules foreseen in the Constitution about this subject are destined to regularize tax terrorism and tend to penalize the tax evasion with deprivation of personal freedom (art. 317). (Fifth Transitory Disposition), and were made as if only big enterprises were taxpayers, and who must be persecuted. They ignore that in a system with state financial incapacity, everyone is or should be potentially taxpayer, and, therefore, subject of tax persecution.

The Constitution, in this subject, forgot the citizen and the protection and security it should bring him.

4.   *The Damage to the Autonomy of the Central Bank of Venezuela*

The new Constitution attributes the Central Bank of Venezuela the exclusive and obligatory exercise of monetary authority, attributing the Central Bank the necessary autonomy to that, in coordination with the general economic policy (Art. 318).

Nevertheless, that autonomy is limited in the Constitution to the point that it can be totally neutralized, making the management of the institution political. That derived from the following provisions: *first*, the possibility of regulating legally the removal of the Bank's Directory because of the failure to accomplish goals and aims of the monetary policy; *second*, the compulsory rendering accounts before the National Assembly of its performance, goals and results regarding its policies; t*hird* the prevision of inspection and surveillance of the Bank by the Superintendence of Banks; *fourth*, the approval by the National Assembly of the Bank's budget of operating and investment expenses (Art. 319). Finally, according to the Fourth Transitory Disposition, there is the intervention of the National Assembly in the appointment and ratification of the members of the Bank's Directory (paragraph 8).

With this constitutional scheme, the established autonomy of the Central Bank of Venezuela can be minimized, opening a path to politicize the Institution.

*

From the aforementioned results, regarding the 1999 *political Constitution* that, when analyzed globally, highlights an institutional framework conceived for authoritarianism. It is derived from combining the State centralism, the exaggerated presidentialism, the democracy of parties, the concentration of power in the Assembly and the militarism that constitute the central elements designed for the organization of the Power of the State.

In my opinion, that is not the political Constitution required to improve democracy. On the contrary, it should be based on decentralization of power, a controlled presidentialism, politic participation to balance the powers of the state and the subjection of the military authority to the civil one.

Regarding the 1999 *social Constitution*, when enumerating the human rights and guarantees and State obligations, the new Constitution, unfortunately, opens the door to their limitation by the Executive through delegated legislation. Moreover, analyzed globally, it shows a marginalization of society and private enterprises, falling on the State all the imaginable obligations, impossible to comply with. It is a Constitution conceived for paternalism, which leads to populism.

That is not the social Constitution needed to found a social and participating democracy. To that, it should re-value the participation of all private enterprises in educational, health and social security process, as activities in which a mutual responsibility between the state and Society must exist.

Finally, the new Constitution, in its component *economic Constitution*, completes the paternalist picture of social Constitution. It inclines the constitutional regime towards the state instead of the private enterprise, which originates an exaggerated statism. It creates the risk of increasing tax voracity that cannot be controlled, conceived to squash taxpayers, who aren't constitutionally protected.

That is not the economic Constitution needed to found the policy of economic development the country requires, which has to point to the creation of wealth and employment that the State is unable to accomplish without the decisive participation of private enterprises, which should be protected and stimulated.

Due to the aforementioned, in our opinion the Constitution of 1999 hasn't introduce the changes the country needed, on the occasion of the constituent moment that originated the crisis of the political model of Centralized State of Parties established from 1945 and restored in 1958. The country needed a radical change to improve the democracy, make it more representative and to structure a democratic decentralized and participating State. Nothing of this was accomplished, so only history will say if this Constitution is the last of the four politic historical periods of Venezuela or the first of the fifth.

CHAPTER V

GLOBAL VALUES IN THE VENEZUELAN CONSTITUTION: SOME PRIORITIZATIONS AND SEVERAL INCONGRUENCES
(2009)

This essay on "Global Values in the Venezuelan Constitution: Some Prioritizations and several Incongruence" was written for my Presentation at the *Conference on The Existence of Global values Explored through National Constitutional Jurisprudence*, held at The Rockefeller Foundation Bellagio Center, Bellagio, Italy, on September 22-26, 2008; and was due to be published in a Collective Study and Book coordinated by Dennis Davis, Alan Richter And Cheryl Saunders, on *The Existence of Global Values Explored Through National Constitutional Jurisprudence*, 2009, as discussed in the Bellagio Conference.

I. INTRODUCTION AND CONSTITUTIONAL BACKGROUND

Venezuela was the first Latin American country to gain independence from the Spanish Crown in 1810. A general congress of representatives of the former colonial provinces of the *Capitanía General de Venezuela* enacted on 21 December 1811 the Federal Constitution for the States of Venezuela, the first constitution on the South American continent, and the third in Modern Constitutional history.[156] This Constitution followed the general principles of modern constitutionalism derived from the North American and French Revolutions, organizing the State according to the prin-

---

156 See on the consttiucional texts of the Venezuelan independence: Allan R. Brewer-Carías, *Documentos Constitucionales de la Independencia/ Constitucional Documents of the Independence 1811*, Colección Textos Legislativos N° 52, Editorial Jurídica Venezolana, Caracas 2012. This book contains the facsimilar text of the book: *"Interesting Documents relating to Caracas/ Documenbtos Interesantes relativos a Caracas; Interesting Official Documents relating to the United Provinces of Caracas, viz. Preliminary Remarks, The Act of Independence. Proclamation, Manifesto to the World of the Causes which have impelled the said provinieses to separate from the Mother Country; together with the Constitution framed for the Administration of their Government. In Spanish and English,"* published in a bilingual format in London, 1812 (pp. 301-637)

ciples of constitutional supremacy; sovereignty of the people, republicanism and political representation, separation of power, presidential system, check and balance and superiority of the law as expression of the general will; territorial distribution of power with the federal system of government and the municipal organization; an extended declaration of fundamental rights of Man and Society; and a Judiciary integrated by judges imparting justice in the name of the nation with judicial review powers.

The constitutional history of the two hundred years of republicanism shows the persistent attempts to consolidate such principles, concluding for instance with the adoption of a comprehensive system of judicial review, now common in almost all the Latin American countries, that combines the concentrated method (European Model) attributed to the Constitutional Chamber of the Supreme Tribunal, with powers to annul statutes on the grounds of unconstitutionality when reached by means of popular actions; with the diffuse method (American Model) empowering all courts to declare the inapplicability of statutes in cases or controversies when considered unconstitutional.[157] In addition, as in all the Latin American countries, in Venezuela there also exists the amparo action as a specific judicial mean that can be exercised before any court for the protection of constitutional rights.[158]

Since 1811 the Constitution has been modified (reformed or amended) on 26 occasions, having really being substantially reformed in 1830, 1864, 1901, 1947, and 1999.[159] The XX century democratic system of government effectively began in 1958 after the main political parties signed a political pact known as "*Pacto de Punto Fijo*" which conditioned the drafting of the 1961 Constitution which governed the democratic system for the four last decades of the twentieth century. At the end of that period, the political parties entered into a profound political crisis that affected their leadership, provoking a political vacuum that was filled by an authoritarian, centralized and militaristic government lead by Hugo Chávez Frías, who was elected in 1998 and reelected in 2006. In 1999, a new Constitution[160] was sanctioned by a

157 See Allan R. Brewer-Carías, "Judicial Review in Venezuela", in *Duquesne Law Review*, Volume 45, Number 3, Spring 2007, pp. 439-465

158 See Allan R. Brewer-Carías, "The Amparo Proceeding in Venezuela: Constitutional Litigation and Procedural Protection of Constitutional Rights and Guarantees," en *Duquesne Law Review*, Volume 49, Spring 2011, Pittsburgh, pp. 161-241

159 For a detailed study of the historical constitutional periods in Venezuelan constitutionalism, see Allan R. Brewer-Carías, *Instituciones Políticas y Constitucionales*, Vol I. Evolución Histórica del Estado, Caracas-San Cristóbal, 1996, pp. 257 - 389; Allan R. Brewer-Carías, "Estudio Preliminar", *Las Constituciones de Venezuela*, Academia de Ciencias Políticas y Sociales, Caracas 2008, vol. I. pp. 25-526; and Allan R. Brewer-Carías, Historia Constitucional de Venezuela, Editorial Alfa, caracas 2008, 2 vols.

160 See Allan R. Brewer-Carías, *La Constitución de 1999. Derecho Constitucional Venezolano*, 2 Vols., Editorial Jurídica Venezolana, Caracas 2004; Hildegard Rondón de Sansó, *Análisis de la Constitución Venezolana de 1999*, Editorial Ex Libris, Caracas 2001; Ricardo Combellas, *Derecho Constitucional: una introducción al estudio de la Constitución de la República Bolivariana de Venezuela*, Mc Graw Hill, Caracas, 2001; and Alfonso Rivas Quintero, *Derecho Constitucional*, Paredes Editores, Valencia, 2002.

Constituent Assembly,[161] and subsequently approved by referendum in the midst of the most severe political crisis of the country affecting the democratic parties and democracy itself.

This Constitution formally establishes the general trends of a democratic regime and of the rule of law, which in political practice has been distorted; and in addition, in spite of the extensive declaration of global values and human rights it contains, following its provisions during the past decade an Authoritarian and Centralized State has taken shape, and based in populist policies of socialist trends, it has demolished the rule of law principles, the separation of powers and the federation (decentralization); weakening the effectiveness of the protection of constitutional rights by subjecting the judicial review system and others check and balance institutions to the Executive, and by progressively destroying representative democracy itself in the name of a supposedly "participatory democracy".[162]

Nonetheless, as for the text of the Constitution, it defines Venezuela as a Democratic and Social rule of Law and Justice State (*Estado democratico y social de derecho y de justicia*) (Article 2), declaring that the Rule of Law (*Estado de Derecho*) is the State submitted to the "empire of the Law" as stated in the *Preamble*, that is, the State submitted to legality. The Constitution also includes the principle of "supremacy of the Constitution" (article 7) submitting all State entities to the Constitution and the laws (article 137). It also establishes a complete judicial review system in order to assure the control of the constitutionality (articles 334 and 336) and legality of all State acts and actions (article 259) (Constitutional Jurisdiction and Administrative Jurisdiction).

In spite of its authoritarianism framework,[163] on matters of principles and values, the 1999 Venezuelan Constitution is one of the recent Constitutions in the contemporary world containing not only an extensive amount of articles devoted to enumerate human rights (120), but also a very rich text full of values, principles and

---

161 This author was elected member of the Constituent Assembly, being one of the four Members (of 131 members) that opposed the project proposed by President Hugo Chávez. See Allan R. Brewer-Carías, *Debate Constituyente (Aportes a la Asamblea Nacional Constituyente),* Tomo I (8 agosto-8 septiembre 1999); Tomo II (9 septiembre-17 octubre 1999), Tomo III (18 octubre-30 noviembre 1999), Fundación de Derecho Público-Editorial Jurídica Venezolana, Caracas 1999. On the 1999 constitution making process see: Allan R. Brewer-Carías, "The 1999 Venezuelan Constitution-Making Process as an Instrument for Framing the development of an Authoritarian Political Regime," in Laura E. Miller (Editor), *Framing the State in Times of Transition. Case Studies in Constitution Making*, United States Institute of Peace Press, Washington 2010, pp. 505-531

162 See on this process Allan R. Brewer-Carías, *Dismantling Democracy. The Chávez Authoritarian Experiment*, Cambridge University Press, New York 2010,

163 This was denounced by this author in the electoral campaign for the approval referendum of the Constitution in 1999, in order to justify the vote N° See Allan R. Brewer-Carías, *Debate Constituyente (Aportes a la Asamblea Nacional Constituyente),* Tomo III (18 octubre-30 noviembre 1999), Fundación de Derecho Público-Editorial Jurídica Venezolana, Caracas 1999. Nonetheless, the Constitution was approved in the referendum held on December 15th, 1999.

global declarations. It has, perhaps, one of the most florid constitutional wordings that can be found in constitutional texts,[164] establishing its axiological foundations, which in principle are set forth to be followed by the National Assembly and all branches of government, and particularly by the courts. For such purposes, the Constitutional Chamber of the Supreme Tribunal of Justice has said that the Constitution is "an instrument with legal spirit that connects, according to the nature of the applicable precept, both the bodies of the State and the individuals;" and that imposes constitutional juridical situations "with reference to indispensable values for the assurance of human freedom, equality and dignity;" guaranteed by the Judiciary.[165]

These global values that in the Venezuelan case are declared in the Constitution, have been as those "values generally shared by the society" as "declarations of intent" that "have an indubitable value, both for the bodies of the State that must be guided by them, and for the judges."[166] For such purposes, as ruled by the same Constitutional Chamber, "Constitutions are, among other things, texts in which "legally organized societies regulate their structures and functioning, and determine the scope of the citizen rights and the public authorities' powers;" and also, texts "in which the wishes of this same society are exposed –sometimes difficult to satisfy– and the means that have been created to satisfy them... The diverse duties that the State assumes are orders that must be executed. A text lacking of compulsory character for its addressees (public authorities and individuals) would be of little use".[167]

Constitutional values in the Venezuelan Constitution are expressed not only in its Preamble but in many of its articles, in a very enumerative and formal way, as goals intending to guide the State, the Society and the individuals' general conduct[168]. Consequently, in Venezuela, global values and principles do not derive from the sole interpretation and application of the Constitution by the courts, but from what is set forth in a precise and express way in the Constitution itself.[169] Nonetheless, by

---

164 See Allan R. Brewer-Carías, *La Constitución de 1999. Derecho Constitucional Venezolano*, 2 Vols., Editorial Jurídica Venezolana, Caracas 2004; Hildegard Rondón de Sansó, *Análisis de la Constitución Venezolana de 1999*, Editorial Ex Libris, Caracas 2001; Ricardo Combellas, *Derecho Constitucional: una introducción al estudio de la Constitución de la República Bolivariana de Venezuela*, Mc Graw Hill, Caracas, 2001; and Alfonso Rivas Quintero, *Derecho Constitucional*, Paredes Editores, Valencia, 2002.

165 See decision N° 963 dated June 5, 2001. Case: *José A. Guía y otros vs. Ministerio de Infraestructura*, in *Revista de Derecho Público*, N° 85-88, Editorial Jurídica Venezolana, Caracas, 2001, p. 447.

166 See Constitutional Chamber decision, N° 1278 dated June 17, 2005. Case: *Aclaratoria de la sentencia de interpretación de los artículos 156, 180 y 302 de la Constitución*, in *Revista de Derecho Público*, N° 102, Editorial Jurídica Venezolana, Caracas, 2005, pp. 56 ff.

167 See Case: *Aclaratoria de la sentencia de interpretación de los artículos 156, 180 y 302 de la Constitución*, decision N° 1278 dated June 17, 2005, in *Revista de Derecho Público*, N°102, Editorial Jurídica Venezolana, Caracas 2005, pp. 56 ff.

168 See Allan R. Brewer-Carías, "La constitucionalización del derecho administrativo", in *Derecho Administrativo*, Vol. I, Universidad Externado de Colombia, Bogotá 2005, pp. 215 ff.

169 See Allan R. Brewer-Carías, *Principios fundamentales del derecho público*, Editorial Jurídica Venezolana, Caracas, 2005.

means of constitutional judicial decisions, the sense, the scope and the priority character of many of these constitutional principles and values have been defined and enriched; and also, unfortunately, in many cases, some constitutional incongruence have been established between the constitutional text and the political practice of government.

II. CONSTITUTIONAL VALUES AND THEIR PRIORITIZATION

The values expressed in the 1999 Constitution, in many cases, are referred to the State (the Republic, the Nation), its organization (distribution of State powers and branches of government) and functioning (government and Public Administration), and also to the legal system.

In this sense, the Preamble of the Constitution began by declaring that it was adopted by the representatives of the Venezuelan people, having in mind the achievement of a series of goals "guided by social, economical, political and judicial values"[170], in order to inspire the action of the State, "which must respond to equalitarian, international, democratic, moral and historical principles."

In this context, the State is defined itself as a "State of justice, federal and decentralized", that must develop its action to enforce the values of "freedom, independence, peace, solidarity, common good, territorial integrity, cohabitation and the empire of the law for these and all future generations", in a society that is qualified as "democratic, participatory, multiethnic and pluri-cultural", which is confirmed, for instance, by the express recognition in the Constitution of the indigenous populations' status (Articles 119 ff.).

These goals, objectives or purposes constitute, without a doubt, the fundamental principles and constitutional values that inspire the constitutional text as a whole, and as such, they have the same imperative, binding, and constitutional rigidity as constitutional provisions, and consequently are also enforceable. As affirmed by the Constitutional Chamber of the Supreme Tribunal, "the statutes must have those values as their north, so those that do not follow them or that are contrary to those objectives become unconstitutional"[171].

But besides the values guiding the configuration of the State declared in the Preamble, the Constitution also enumerates as superior values of the legal system and of the whole State activity: "life, freedom, justice, equality, solidarity, democracy, social responsibility and, in general, the preeminence of the human rights, the ethics and the political pluralism" (Article 2).

Additionally, the Constitution identifies "the defense and the development of the individual and the respect of his/her dignity, the democratic exercise of the popular

---

170 Regarding the nature of the Preamble and its constitutional value, see the decision of the former Supreme Court of Justice in its Political-Administrative Chamber, dated August 8, 1989, in *Revista de Derecho Público* N° 39, Editorial Jurídica Venezolana, Caracas, 1989, p. 102.

171 See Case: *Deudores hipotecarios vs. Superintendencia de Bancos*, in *Revista de Derecho Público*, N° 89-92, Editorial Jurídica Venezolana, Caracas, 2002, pp. 94 ff.

will, the construction of a fair and peace loving society, the promotion of the prosperity and wellbeing of the people and the guaranty of the fulfillment of all principles, rights and duties recognized and enshrined in the Constitution" as essential
goals of the State; considering "education and work" as fundamental processes to
reach said ends (Articles 3).

On the other hand, the "re-foundation of the Republic" intended in the constitutional text also responded to a series of social ends specified in the Preamble with
the object of ensuring "the right to a life, work, culture, education, social justice and
equality without discrimination nor subordination of any kind". In the Constitution,
reference is also made regarding the social goals of society and of the State in order
to achieve "social justice." It is also mentioned as a fundamental social goal, the
assurance of "equality without discrimination or subordination of any kind."

Referring to the Republic, a few fundamental values are expressly emphasized in
the Constitution, and in addition to the already mentioned values (freedom, equality,
justice and international peace); there is the principle that the Nation's rights ("independence, freedom, sovereignty, immunity, territorial integrity and the national self-
determination") cannot be renounced or abandoned (Article 1).

In the scope of international relations, the Preamble also mentions as one of the
goals of the State, the "peaceful cooperation between nations", which implies the
commitment to look for the peaceful solution of controversies, and the rejection of
war. This peaceful cooperation must be executed in accordance to the "principle of
the nonintervention" in the affairs of other countries, and to the principle of "self-
determination of the people". Also, it is said that international cooperation must be
carried out "according to the universal and indivisible guaranty of human rights and
the democratization of the international society".

References are also made in the Constitution to other values that must guide the
international relations of the Republic, like the "nuclear disarmament, the ecological
balance and the environment considered as a common and non renounceable patrimony of humanity". In particular, always according to the Preamble, another fundamental goal that must serve as guidance of the State's actions is referred to "the
impulse and consolidation of the Latin-American integration" (art. 153).

Some of the values declared in the Constitution have been prioritized in political
practice and through judicial decisions, in the sense that they have been considered
as having some kind of superior hierarchy regarding other principles that are governed by the former. This is the case for 1) Human Dignity; 2) Fairness/Justice/Rule
of Law-State of Justice; 3) Equality/ Respect/ Tolerance/ Diversity/ Multicultural-
ism; 4) Democracy/ Participation/ Decentralization /Inclusion; 5) Compassion/ Car-
ing/ Solidarity/ Social Justice /Social State; 6) Community/Civil Society; 7) Family;
8) Life; 9) Honesty/Integrity; 10) Learning/ Education; 11) Freedom/ Liberty
/Independence; 12) Security; 13) Responsibility /Accountability/Transparency; 14)
Environment.

1.   *Human Dignity*

One of these values that have been prioritized, particularly on matters of the human rights, is the value of "human dignity," considered by the courts "as inherent to

the human condition" that exists "before the State" and imposes on all branches of government the need to be "at the service of the human being." [172] This implies not only the existence of constitutional rights considered "inherent to human beings" but the emergence of the "principle of progressiveness" in their interpretation and enforcement. According to the criteria of the Constitutional Chamber of the Supreme Tribunal, in this regard, the courts have an obligation "to interpret the entire legal system in the light of the Right of the Constitution ... which also means, that they have to interpret the system congruently with the fundamental rights or human rights, that must be respected above all, making a progressive and complete interpretation"[173].

The Constitution refers to this value in many articles, when guarantying to anybody deprived of liberty the right to be "treated with respect due to the inherent dignity of the human being" (article 46); when guarantying that the judicial seizure of a person's home must be made "always respecting human dignity" (art. 47); when imposing the obligation on the State's security offices to always "respect the human dignity and rights of all persons" (article 55); when establishing the duty of the State to protect senior citizens and disabled persons always respecting their "human dignity," (articles 80, 81); and when guarantying that the salary of every worker must be "sufficient to enable him or her to live with dignity"(article 91).

In this regard, the Constitutional Chamber of the Supreme Tribunal has considered human dignity as "one of the values on which the Social rule of law and Justice State is based, and around which all the legal system and all the actions of the branches of government (public powers) must turn." Based on this approach, the Chamber defined human dignity as "the supremacy that persons have as an inherent attribute of its rational being, which imposes on public authorities the duty to watch for the protection and safe-conduct of the life, freedom and autonomy of men and women for the sole fact of their existence, independently of any other consideration." That is why, "the sole existence of man grants him the right to exist and to obtain all the guarantees needed to assure him a dignified life, that is, his own existence, proportional and rational to the recognition of his essence as a rational being." This concept of human dignity implies the imposition "upon the State of the duty to adopt the necessary protective measures to safeguard the legal assets that define man as a person, that is, life, integrity, freedom, autonomy."[174]

---

172 See decision of the First Court of the Administrative Jurisdiction dated June 1, 2000. Case: *Julio Rocco A.*, in *Revista de Derecho Público*, N° 82, Editorial Jurídica Venezolana, Caracas 2000, pp. 287 ff.

173 See First Court of the Administrative Jurisdiction in a decision dated June 1, 2000 . Case: *Julio Rocco A.*, in *Revista de Derecho Público*, N° 82, Editorial Jurídica Venezolana, Caracas 2000, pp. 287 ff.

174 With this purpose, the Constitution, in its article 3, "establishes that the recognition of the human dignity constitutes a structural principle of the Social rule of law State and for that, it forbids, in its Title III, Chapter III, the forced disappearances, the degrading treatments, the tortures or cruel treatments that could harm the life as an inviolable right, the degrading punishments and all other inherent rights of the human person (articles 43 ff.)" See decision N°

In this same sense, the Political-Administrative Chamber of the same Supreme Tribunal of Justice has made special emphasis in the preeminent character of the dignity, considering it the "axiological" element representing "the ideological base that supports the dogmatic order of the current Constitution," limiting the exercise of public power and establishing an effective judicial guarantee system." That is why this "prevalent position of human dignity" considered as a "superior value of the legal system" implies "the obligation of the State and of all its bodies to protect and guarantee human rights as the main purpose and objective of its public action." Consequently, the defense and the development of human dignity is considered by the Supreme Tribunal as "one of the superior values of the legal system," being its "defense and development one of the essential objectives of the State (Articles 2 and 3)."[175]

Human dignity, on the other hand, implies the idea of the "preeminence of human rights" (Preamble); which according to the "principle of progressiveness" (art. 19), imposes the need for the interpretation of statutes in the most favorable way for their enjoyment. In this regard, Article 19 of the 1999 Constitution begins the Title on "Duties, Rights and Constitutional Guarantees "by setting forth that the State must guarantee every person, "according to the progressiveness principle and without discrimination whatsoever, the enjoyment and non renounceable, indivisible and interdependent exercise of human rights". The provision adds that "the respect and the guarantee of the rights are mandatory to all State bodies in accordance with the Constitution, the treaties on human rights signed and ratified by the Republic and the statutes."[176] That is, as affirmed by the courts, "the interpretation of the corresponding constitutional provisions and any future constitutional revision must be performed in the most favorable way for the exercise and enjoyment of the rights;" adding that "this principle is so important that its application obliges the State to update legislation in favor of the defense of the human rights and in view to dignify the human condition, adapting the interpretation of the norms 'to the sensibility, thought and needs of the new times in order to adapt them to the new established order and to reject any anachronic precept that opposes their effective force.'" [177]

2442, dated September 1, 2003. Case: *Alejandro Serrano López*, in *Revista de Derecho Público*, N° 83-96, Editorial Jurídica Venezolana, Caracas 2003, pp. 183 ff.

175 See in decision N° 224 dated February 24, 2000, in *Revista de Derecho Público*, N° 81, Editorial Jurídica Venezolana, Caracas, 2000, pg. 131 ff. See also, decision of the Constitutional Chamber of the Supreme Tribunal N° 3215 dated June 15, 2004, in *Revista de Derecho Público*, N° 97-98, Editorial Jurídica Venezolana, Caracas, 2004, p. 428.

176 About this principle, the Constitutional Chamber of the Supreme Tribunal of Justice, quoting article 2 of the American Convention on Human Rights, in a decision N° 1154, dated June 29, 2001, based on the same principle, has ruled that it is necessary "to adapt the legal system in order to ensure the efficiency of said rights, being unacceptable the excuse of the inexistence or unsuitability of the means provided in the internal order for their protection and application." See in *Revista de Derecho Público*, N° 85-88, Editorial Jurídica Venezolana, Caracas 2001, pp. 111 ff.

177 In this sense the First Court of the Administrative Jurisdiction has considered as its obligation "to interpret the entire legal system in the light of the Right of the Constitution, even

In order to give human dignity its complete shape, article 23 of the 1999 Constitution granted to international treaties on human rights signed and ratified by Venezuela, constitutional rank, adding that they "prevail in the internal order when containing more favorable provisions regarding their enjoyment than those contained in the Constitution and the laws of the Republic." The same article provides for the immediate and direct application of these treaties by the State bodies, particularly by the courts[178].

On the other hand, in order to reinforce the constitutional value of human dignity, the human rights that are guaranteed and protected are not only the ones enumerated in the Constitution, but also those that although not being enumerated are considered "inherent to the human person" (Article 22)[179]. That is why the last phrase of article 22 of the Constitution established that "the lack of regulatory statutes regarding human rights do not diminish their exercise"; that is, their application "cannot be conditioned by the existence of a statute developing it; and on the contrary, the lack of legal instruments regulating them does not diminish their exercise, being such

---

more, when acting in exercise of the constitutional power for protection, which also means, that we have to interpret the system congruently with the fundamental rights or human rights, that must be respected above all, making a progressive and complete interpretation." See decision dated June 1, 2000. Case: *Julio Rocco A.*, in *Revista de Derecho Público*, N° 82, Editorial Jurídica Venezolana, Caracas 2000, pp. 287 ff.

178   The Constitutional Court of the Supreme Tribunal has for instance applied this provision regarding due process rights, applying preferentially article 8 of the American Convention on Human Rights. See decision dated March 14, 2000 (Case: *C.A. Electricidad del Centro and C.A. Electricidad de los Andes*), in *Revista de Derecho Publico*, N° 81, Editorial Jurídica Venezolana, Caracas 2000, pp. 157-158; quoted also in decison N° 328 dated March 9, 2001, of the same Chamber, in *Revista de Derecho Publico*, N° 85-88, Editorial Juridica Venezolana, Caracas 2001, p. 108. The Political-Administrative Chamber of the Supreme Tribunal interpreted and developed the criteria established by the Constitutional Chamber regarding the lack of applications of Article 185 of the Organic Law of the Supreme Court of Justice in decision N° 802 dated April 13, 2000 (Case: *Elecentro vs. Superintendencia Procompetencia*), in *Revista de Derecho Publico* N° 82, Editorial Jurídica Venezolana, Caracas 2000, p. 270. On a similar matter, see also, the decision N° 449 dated March 27, 2001 (Case: *Dayco de Construcciones vs. INOS*) in *Revista de Derecho Publico*, N° 85-88, Editorial Jurídica Venezolana, Caracas 2001. Nonetheless, the Political-Administrative Chamber has denied giving prevalence to Article 8 of the American Convention regarding the requests made by corporate persons, understanding that the Convention only refers to the "human" rights of individuals. See decision N° 278 dated March 1, 2001, in *Revista de Derecho Publico*, N° 85-88, Editorial Juridica Venezolana, Caracas 2001, p. 104.

179   This open clause is more extensive in comparison with the original wording of the North American constitutionalism (Amendment IX), in the sense that it refers not only to the rights and guarantees not enumerated in the Constitution but also in the international instruments on human rights, which conforms a truly unlimited cast of unstated, but protected rights that are inherent to the human person

rights "of immediate and direct application by the courts and all other bodies of the State" (Articles 22, 23 Constitution).[180]

2. *Fairness/Justice/Rule of law-State of Justice*

"Justice" (Preamble) has also been considered as a global and "fundamental value" that must contribute to "the construction of a just and peace loving society resulting from the democratic exercise of popular will (Article 3)". For such purpose, the Constitutional Chamber has considered that "the power to administer justice must be exercised in the name of the Republic and come from the citizens (Article 253);"which "must be executed with independence and impartiality" by judges "free from subordinations and inadequate pressures" (Articles 254 and 256 of the Constitution). This has been considered as "a new paradigm about values and constitutional principles connected to the justice," which has led to the conception of the "State of Justice," considering the Judiciary not just one more branch of government but "the integrating and stabilizing State power with authority to control and even dissolve the rest of the branches of government" (Judicialist State).[181]

This conception of the "State of Justice" (*Estado de Justicia*) not only results from the provisions of the Preamble and of article 1 that declares justice as a constitutional value, but from the constitutional provisions establishing "the prevalence of the notion of material justice over formalities and technicalities;"[182] and providing for the "effective judicial protection" of human rights by means of a system of justice that must be "free, available, impartial, apt, transparent, autonomous, independent, responsible, fair and expeditious, without improper delays, formalisms or useless repositions" (article 26).[183] To that effect, the procedural laws must establish the "simplification, uniformity and efficiency of the proceedings and adopt a brief, oral and public procedure, without sacrificing justice because of omission of non essential formalities" (Article 257).

On the other hand, article 253 provides that the system of justice is composed not only by the organs of the Judicial Branch, comprising the Supreme Tribunal of Justice and all the other courts established by law, but also by the Public Ministry (Public Prosecutor), the Peoples' Defendant, the criminal investigatory organs, judicial

---

180 See decision N° 723, dated May 15, 2201, in *Revista de Derecho Público*, N° 85-88, Editorial Jurídica Venezolana, Caracas 2001, p. 111.

181 See decision N° 659 of the Political-Administrative Chamber dated March 24, 2000. Case: *Rosario Nouel vs. Consejo de la Judicatura y Comisión de Emergencia Judicial*, in *Revista de Derecho Público* N° 81, Editorial Jurídica Venezolana, Caracas, 2000, pp. 103-104.

182 See Supreme Tribunal of Justice, in a decision N° 949 of the Political-Administrative Chamber dated April 26, 2000, in *Revista de Derecho Público*, N° 82, Editorial Jurídica Venezolana, Caracas, 2000, pp. 163 ff.

183 This conception of the "State of Justice" has also been analyzed by the Constitutional Chamber of the Supreme Tribunal of Justice, particularly in a decision N° 389 dated March 7, 2002, in which the principle of the informality of the process was repeated, also asserting the principle of *pro actione* as another principle of the State of Justice. See in *Revista de Derecho Público*, N° 89-92, Editorial Jurídica Venezolana, Caracas, 2002, 175 ff.

staff and assistants, the penitentiary system, the alternative means of adjudication, the citizens who according to the law participate in the administration of justice, and the attorneys authorized to practice law. Article 258 imposes on the Legislator the duty to promote arbitration, conciliation, mediation, and other alternative means of conflict resolution.

Article 254 of the Constitution declares the principle of the independence of the Judicial Branch and establishes that the Supreme Tribunal is to have "functional, financial, and administrative autonomy." In order to guarantee the independence and autonomy of courts and judges, Article 255 provides for a specific mechanism to ensure the independent appointment of judges and to guaranty their stability. In this regard, the judicial office is considered as a career, in which the admission, as well as the promotion of judges within it, must be the result of a public competition or examinations to ensure that the candidates are adequately qualified. The candidates are to be chosen by panels from the judicial circuits, and the judges are to be designated by the Supreme Tribunal of Justice. The Constitution also creates a Judicial Nominations Committee (article 270) to assist the Judicial Branch in selecting the Magistrates for the Supreme Tribunal of Justice (article 264) and to assist judicial colleges in selecting judges for the lower courts. This Judicial Nominations Committee is to be composed of representatives from different sectors of society as determined by law. The Constitution also guarantees the stability of all judges, prescribing that they can only be removed or suspended from office through judicial disciplinary procedures on trials led by Judicial Disciplinary Judges (art. 255).

3. *Equality/ Respect/Tolerance/Diversity/Multiculturalism*

The Preamble of the Constitution also declares as a fundamental social value, the assurance of "equality without discrimination or subordination of any kind," which results from the traditional and historical equalitarian character of the Venezuelan society, which rejects any kind of discrimination and servility (Articles 19, 21). This has also been considered "as a fundamental principle of democracy."[184]

Regarding the principle of equality, it has been defined in a very explicit way in Article 21 of the Constitution, stating that all persons are equal before the law, and consequently, no discrimination could be allowed based on race, sex, religion, social condition, or any other cause having the purpose or consequence of annulling or harming the recognition, enjoyment and exercise of rights and liberties in conditions of equality. For such purpose, the Constitution provides for the juridical and administrative conditions in order to really and effectively guaranties that equality before the law, for instance providing for positive measures in favor of persons or groups that could be discriminated, marginalized or vulnerable; specially protecting persons located in circumstance of manifest weakness and sanctioning abuses and harms inflicted against them.

---

184 See decision N° 439 of the Political-Administrative Chamber dated October 6, 1992, in *Revista de Derecho Público*, N° 52, Editorial Jurídica Venezolana, Caracas, 1992, pp. 91-92.

On matters of religion and cult, the Constitution expressly declares that the State must guarantee the freedom of cult and religion (article 50); everybody having the right to profess religious faith and cults, and to express their beliefs in private or in public by teaching and other practices, provided that such beliefs are not contrary to moral, good customs and public order. No one shall invoke religious beliefs or discipline as a means for evading the compliance with the laws or preventing another person from the exercising of his rights. The autonomy and independence of religious confessions and churches is likewise guaranteed in the Constitution, subject only to such limitations as may derive from this Constitution and the law. The Constitution also entitles parents to determine the religious education to be given to their children in accordance with their convictions.

The Constitution also guaranties the freedom of conscience, although conscientious objections cannot be invoked in order to evade the compliance of laws or prevent others from complying with it or exercising their rights (article 60).

Finally, the Preamble of the Constitution expressly declares the Venezuelan Society as multiethnic and pluri-cultural.

4. *Democracy/Participation/Decentralization/Inclusion*

Another fundamental value also established in the Constitution is "democracy" (Preamble), not only as a political regime and as a condition of government, but also as a way of life, founded in the ideas of the political pluralism and equal "participation" of everyone in the political processes. In this sense, the concept of the "democratic State" (*Estado democrático*) is also identified as a constitutional principle that gives roots to the political organization of the Nation, as it derives from the Preamble ("democratic society") and from articles 2, 3, 5 and 6 of the Constitution. Democracy is also established in article 6 of the Constitution as an immutable regime of the government of the Republic and of its political entities (States and municipalities), by declaring that it is and always will be "democratic, participative, elective, decentralized, alternative, responsible, pluralist, and of revocable mandates."

In this respect, the Constitutional Chamber of the Supreme Tribunal of Justice, in a decision N° 23 dated January 22, 2003 points out that the intention of the 1999 Constitution was to "establish a democratic, participative and protagonist society, which implies that it is not just the State who has to adopt and submit its institutions to the ways and principles of democracy, but it is also the society (formed by the Venezuelan citizens) who must play a decisive and responsible role in the conduction of the Nation"[185].

On the other hand, the 1999 Constitution by establishing the concept of participation as a fundamental principle of democracy, also regulated it as a political constitutional right "considering individuals as member of a determined political community, in order to take part in the formation of public decisions or of the will of the public institutions"; a right that is related to other political rights established in the

---

185 See Case: *Interpretación del artículo 71 de la Constitución* in *Revista de Derecho Público*, N° 93-96, Editorial Jurídica Venezolana, Caracas 2003, pp. 530 ff.

Constitution, like the right to vote (article 63), to petition (article 51), to have access to public offices (article 62), to political association (article 67), to demonstration (article 68), and to be informed in due time and truthfully by Public Administration (article 143). It is also related to the social rights, like the right to health (article 84), educational rights (article 102) and environmental rights (article 127)[186].

"Participative democracy," in addition to "representative" and "direct" democracy, is also materialized in other constitutional instruments established for the direct intervention of citizens in the decision making process of public affairs, and in particular, "in political matter: the election of public office, the referendum, the revocation of the term of office, the initiative for legislation, for constitutional reforms and for the constituent process, the open municipal council and the citizens' assembly whose decisions will be of binding force" (article 70).

The Constitution also has directly regulated some mechanisms in order to guarantee direct participation of the representatives of the different sectors of the society in the adoption of some public decisions, particularly through the integration of "Nominating Committees" for the appointment by the National Assembly of high public officials not popularly elected, namely, the Prosecutor General, the General Comptroller, the Magistrates of the Supreme Court, and the members of the Electoral National Council, seeking to avoid the traditional agreements between political parties[187]. This was considered by the Constitutional Chamber of the Supreme Tribunal of Justice, in a decision N° 23 dated January 23, 2003, as the result of the "struggles to change the negative political culture generated by decades of a centralized State of political parties (Cfr. Allan R. Brewer-Carías, *Problemas del Estado de Partidos*, Caracas, 1988, pp. 39 ff.) that interfered with the development of democratic values, through the participation of the people which is no longer limited to electoral processes," recognizing their "intervention in the formation, formulation and execution of public politics as a mean to overcome the deficits of governability that have affected our political system due to the lack of harmony between the State and the society;" and radically changing "from the root, the relations between State and society in which the latter receives back its legitimate and undeniable protagonist role by means of the exercise of its fundamental political rights."[188]

According to this doctrine, one of the first values of political constitutionalism, as we have mentioned before, is democracy, being the Democratic State enshrined in the fundamental principles of the constitutional text, beginning with the way the sovereignty of the people is exercised, whether through representative methods or as direct democracy (article 70).

---

186 See Case: *Interpretación del artículo 71 de la Constitución* in *Revista de Derecho Público*, N° 93-96, Editorial Jurídica Venezolana, Caracas 2003, pp. 530 ff.

187 See for example, Allan R. Brewer-Carías, *Los problemas del Estado de Partidos*, Editorial Jurídica Venezolana, Caracas 1988.

188 See Case: *Interpretación del artículo 71 de la Constitución* in *Revista de Derecho Público*, N° 93-96, Editorial Jurídica Venezolana, Caracas 2003, pp. 530 ff.

In order to assure the enforcement of the citizens' right to political participation, regarding the organization of the State, it has been conformed as a Federation, which above all, is a form of government in which public power is territorially distributed among various levels of government each of them with autonomous, democratic political institutions. That is why in principle, federalism and political decentralization are intimately related concepts. Specifically, decentralization is the most effective instrument not only for the guarantying of civil and social rights, but to allow effective participation of the citizens in the political process. In this context, the relationship between local government and the population is essential. That is why all consolidated democracies in the world today are embodied in clearly decentralized forms of governments, such as Federations, or like the new Regional States, as is the case of countries like Spain, Italy and France. That is why it can be said that the strong centralizing tendencies developing in Venezuela in recent years are contrary to democratic governance and political participation.

According to Article 4 of the 1999 Constitution, the Republic of Venezuela is formally defined "as a decentralized Federal State under the terms set out in the Constitution" governed by the principles of "territorial integrity, solidarity, concurrence and co-responsibility." Nonetheless, "the terms set out in the Constitution," are without a doubt centralizing, and Venezuela continues to be a contradictory "Centralized Federation."[189]

Article 136 of the 1999 Constitution states that "public power is distributed among the municipal, state and national entities," establishing a Federation with three levels of political governments and autonomy: *a national level* exercised by the Republic (federal level); the *States level*, exercised by the 23 States and a Capital District; and the *municipal level,* exercised by the 338 existing Municipalities. On each of these three levels, the Constitution requires "democratic, participatory, elected, decentralized, alternative, responsible, plural and with revocable mandates" governments (Article 6). Regarding the Capital District, it has substituted the former Federal District which was established in 1863, with the elimination of traditional federal interventions that existed regarding the authorities of the latter.

5.   Compassion/Caring/Solidarity/ Social Justice /Social State

Article 2 of the 1999 Constitution defines the Venezuelan State as a Social and Democratic rule of law State, in which the principle of "social responsibility" (Preamble) prevails in guiding public policies, configuring the State as a "Social State," with specific social duties regarding Society. In particular, the Constitution refers to the social goal of society and of the State in order to ensure "social justice," guarantying the equitable participation of all in the enjoyment of wealth, preventing its concentration only in a few hands, avoiding unfair income differences, and seeking

---

189 See Allan R. Brewer-Carías, *Federalismo y Municipalismo en la Constitución de 1999,* Universidad Católica del Táchira-Editorial Jurídica Venezolana, Caracas, 2001; "Centralized Federalism in Venezuela", in *Duquesne Law Review*, Volume 43, Number 4, Summer 2005. Duquesne University, Pittsburgh, Pennsylvania, 2005, pp. 629-643.

the guaranty of a dignified and prosperous existence for the collectivity (Articles 112, 299).

This idea of "Social State" (*Estado Social*) refers to a State with social obligations that strives for social justice, which allows its intervention in social and economic activities, as a welfare State. Such social character mainly derives from the fundamental constitutional value of "equality and non discrimination" that comes from the Preamble, and from article 1° of the Constitution which, besides declaring it as a fundamental right (article 21), is the milestone of the performance of the State (article 2), and of the principle of "social justice" as the base of the economic system (article 299).

Regarding this concept of "Social State", it has been defined by the Constitutional Chamber of the Supreme Court in a decision N° 85 dated January, 24, 2002, in the sense that, "it searches for the harmony between classes, avoiding that the dominant class, having the economic, political or cultural power, abuses and subjugates the other classes or social groups, preventing their development and submitting them to poverty and ignorance; as naturally exploited without the possibility to redeem their situation". The same Chamber continued its analysis stating that:

> "The Social State must protect people or groups that regarding others are in a situation of legal weakness, regardless of the principle of equality before the law, which in practice does not resolve anything, because unequal situations cannot be treated with similar solutions. In order to achieve the balance, the Social State not only intervenes in the labor and social security factor, protecting the salaried workers not related to the economical or political power, but it also protects their health, housing, education and economical relations. That is why the Economic Constitution must be seen from an essentially social perspective.
>
> ... The State is obligated to protect the weak, defend their interests protected by the Constitution, particularly through the courts; and regarding the strong, its duty is to watch that their freedom is not a load for everybody. As a juridical value, there cannot be constitutional protection at the expense of the fundamental rights of others...
>
> The Social State tries to harmonize the antagonistic interests of society, without allowing unlimited actions from social forces based on the silence of the statutes or their ambiguities, because otherwise that would lead to the establishment of an hegemony over the weak by those economically and socially stronger, in which the private power positions become an excessive diminution of the real freedom of the weak, in a subjugation that constantly encourages the social crisis"[190].

Regarding the "solidarity" goal within the Social State, it tends to reaffirm that people have, besides rights, social and community duties; so that the right of each individual, necessarily, finds its limits and boundary in the rights of others (Article 20). Regarding the principle of "common good", it has the purpose of ensuring the satisfaction of all the individual and collective needs, being the latter of priority regarding the former, which also implies that the individual rights can always be limited by reasons of public and social order (Article 20).

---

190 See Case: *Deudores hipotecarios vs. Superintendencia de Bancos*, in *Revista de Derecho Público*, N° 89-92, Editorial Jurídica Venezolana, Caracas, 2002, pp. 94 ff.

6. *Community/Civil Society*

Being the participation of citizens in public matters a constitutional value, in order to sustain the participatory democracy the Constitution contains specific provisions that refer to the community, the family and civil society, implying the existence, in addition to personal and individual rights, of collective rights. These have been analyzed by the Constitutional Chamber of the Supreme Tribunal in a decision N° 1395 dated November 21, 2000, as corresponding to the organized community (article 84), like the right to participate in the decision making process of the public health institutions; to the Venezuelan people (articles 99 and 347), like the right to cultural values; to the community (article 118), like the right to develop associations of social and participative character; to the indigenous people (articles 121, 123, and 125), like the right to maintain their ethnic and cultural identity, and to maintain their own economic practices and to the political participation. These are, according to the Chamber's doctrine, differentiated entities that are considered as holders of collective rights by express order of the Constitution[191].

On the other hand, the Constitution grants certain guarantees to some of those entities, as is the case established in article 59, in favor of the "organized community"; in article 124, in favor of the "indigenous people"; in article 21.2 and in articles 75 and 111, in favor of groups, families and sportsmen and women; and also in article 102, in favor of society.

Likewise, the Constitution also seeks for the aforementioned entities and others to give advice, to be represented or to participate, just as it occurs, for instance, in the following articles when referring to the organized society (articles 182, 185, 211); to the Venezuelan people (articles 62, 70, 347); to the community (articles 184,2, 4,7; 264); to the people and indigenous communities (articles 119, 120,166); to the civil society (articles 206, 296, 326); to the society in general (articles 79, 80, 81, 102, 127, 270, 279, 295); to the families (articles 78, 79, 80, 81, 102), and to the organized communities (articles 166, 184)[192].

From these constitutional provisions comes the need for the State to grant guaranties and participation, as well to makes consultations to the different collective entities, in answer to moral demands for justice, giving origin to what the Constitutional Chamber considers as "non enunciated moral rights"[193].

The Constitutional Chamber of the Supreme Tribunal has defined the "collective entities", and among them, "civil society", adopting the principles that "civil society is different from the State and the entities that form it" in the sense that "under any direct or indirect form, the State cannot be part of the civil society". Consequently,

---

191 See in *Revista de Derecho Público*, N° 84, Editorial Jurídica Venezolana, Caracas 2000, p. 331 ff.

192 See in *Revista de Derecho Público*, N° 84, Editorial Jurídica Venezolana, Caracas 2000, p. 331 ff.

193 See in *Revista de Derecho Público*, N° 84, Editorial Jurídica Venezolana, Caracas 2000, p. 331 ff.

the "foundations, associations, societies or groups, completely financed by the State, even those of private character, can not represent society, unless they can demonstrate that the State has no influence on their direction and activities". Therefore, civil society has to be different from the political forces "whose exponents are the political parties or groups. Consequently, the political organizations are not part of the civil society, but of the political society, whose spaces are delimited by the Constitution and the laws." On the other hand, the Chamber considered that being civil society, the "Venezuelan civil society", "those who represent it cannot be aliens, nor organs directed, affiliated, helped, financed or supported directly or indirectly by foreign States or movements or groups influenced by those States; nor by associations, groups or global or transnational movements that follow political or economical ends for their own benefit." In addition, "The social actors that form the civil society are non-governmental organizations whatever their diverse nature and their spokespersons cannot be active military or religious". 6) "The civil society... is an intermediary between the citizen and the State" formed by "institutions or organizations with legal personality, which will be regulated according to the requirements imposed by the law"[194].

As for the concept of "community"(articles. 84, 120, 166, 184, 264 and 326 of the Constitution), according to the same Constitutional Chamber decision, it identifies "restricted groups of persons occupying sectors of the territory, that at the same time can be considered as element of the society in general, or coincide occasionally with the civil society in particular."[195]

Finally, the provisions in the Constitution giving a direct role to the representatives of Civil Society in the nomination of the non elected high officials of the State (Magistrates of the Supreme Tribunal, members of the National Electoral Council, General Prosecutor, Comptroller General, Peoples' Defendant) must be highlighted, limiting the discretional power of the National Assembly in the process of their appointment. In this matter, the principle of participation prevailed over the principle of representation, regulating a precise way for the *active participation of the society* by assigning the *exclusive power* to make the nomination of candidates to occupy said high positions before the National Assembly to several "Nominating Committees" formed by the "representatives of the various sectors of society" (articles 270, 279, 295).[196]

---

194 See in *Revista de Derecho Público*, N° 84, Editorial Jurídica Venezolana, Caracas 2000, p. 331 ff.

195 See in *Revista de Derecho Público*, N° 84, Editorial Jurídica Venezolana, Caracas 2000, p. 331 ff.

196 See Allan R. Brewer-Carías, "La participación ciudadana en la designación de los titulares de los órganos no electos de los Poderes Públicos en Venezuela y sus vicisitudes políticas", in *Revista Iberoamericana de Derecho Público y Administrativo*, Año 5, N° 5-2005, San José, Costa Rica 2005, pp. 76-95

7.   *Family*

On matters of social rights, the Constitution has established several personal rights to be protected by the State, beginning with the protection of the family and of families. In this regard, Article 75 imposes on the State the obligation to protect families as a natural association in society, and as the fundamental space for the overall development of human beings. According to the same constitutional provision, family relationships must be based on equality of rights and duties, solidarity, common effort, mutual understanding and reciprocal respect among family members. In order to protect families, the State must guarantee protection to the mother, father or other person acting as head of a household.

Children and adolescents specifically have the right to live, be raised and develop in the bosom of their original family. When this is impossible or contrary to their best interests, they shall have the right to have a substitute family, in accordance with law. Adoption has effects similar to those of parenthood, and is established in all cases for the benefit of the adoptee, in accordance with law. International adoption shall be subordinated to domestic adoption.

Article 76 of the Constitution provides for the full protection of motherhood and fatherhood, whatever the marital status of the mother or father. Couples have the right to decide freely and responsibly how many children they wish to conceive, and are entitled access to the information and means necessary to guarantee the exercise of this right. The State guarantees overall assistance and protection for motherhood, in general, from the moment of conception, throughout pregnancy, delivery and the puerperal period, and guarantees full family planning services based on ethical and scientific values. This provision, particularly when protecting maternity from the moment of conception, implies limits to abortion for being configured as a right.

Article 77 of the Constitution also expressly "protects marriage between a man and a woman, based on free consent and absolute equality of rights and obligations of the spouses;" consequently, same sex "marriages" are not protected in the Constitution, and only a stable de facto union between a man and a woman that meets the requirements established by law shall have the same effects as marriage.

Children and adolescents are considered as full legal persons that shall be protected by specialized courts, organs and legislation, which shall respect, guarantee and develop the contents of the Constitution, the law, the Convention on Children's Rights and any other international treaty that may have been executed and ratified by the Republic in this field. The State, families and society shall guarantee their full protection as an absolute priority, taking into account their best interest in actions and decisions concerning them. The State shall promote their progressive incorporation into active citizenship, and shall create a national guidance system for the overall protection of children and adolescents (article 78).

On the other hand, Article 79 of the Constitution guaranties the right and duty of young people to actively participate in the development process. For such purpose, the State, with the joint participation of families and society, shall create opportunities to stimulate their productive transition into adult life, including in particular training for and access to their first employment, in accordance with law.

Regarding senior citizens, Article 80 of the Constitution imposes on the State the duty to guarantee the full exercise of their rights and guarantees; providing that the State, with the participation of families and society, is obligated to respect their human dignity, autonomy and to guarantee them full care and social security benefits to improve and guarantee their quality of life. Pension and retirement benefits granted through the social security system shall not be less than the urban minimum salary. Senior citizens shall be guaranteed to have the right to a proper work if they indicate a desire to work and are capable to.

8. Life

The first and most important civil right according to the Venezuelan Constitution is the right to life, which is set forth in Article 43, as "inviolable." Therefore, the Constitution prohibits the death penalty, providing that "no law shall provide for the death penalty and no authority shall apply the same." In addition, the same Article obliges the State to "protect the life of persons who are deprived of liberty, are in military or civil services, or are subject to its authority in any other manner." The right to life, therefore, is an absolute right that cannot be "suspended" or restricted in cases of States of Exception decreed by the President of the Republic.

9. Learning/Education

One very important chapter in the 1999 Constitution is the one devoted to the educational rights. In this respect, its Article 102 establishes in a general way that "education is a human right and a fundamental social duty that is democratic, cost-free, and mandatory." The consequence of this declaration is the provision in the same article of the irrevocable State obligation to assume education as a function of greatest interest, at all levels and in all modes, as an instrument of scientific, humanistic and technical knowledge at the service of society. Accordingly, every person has the right to a full, high-quality, ongoing education under conditions and circumstances of equality, subject only to personal aptitude, vocation or aspiration limitations. According to the Constitution, education is obligatory at all levels from maternal to the diversified secondary level.

On the other hand, education is also constitutionally declared to be a public service (Article 102), although it states that, "the State will stimulate and protect private education imparted according with the principles established in this Constitution and the Laws." As a public service, education is grounded on the respect for all currents of thought in order to develop the creative potential of every human being and the full exercise of his or her personality in a democratic society based on ethical value and on active, conscious and joint participation in the processes of social transformation embodied in the values which are part of the national identity, and with a Latin American and universal vision. The State, with the participation of families and society, must promote the process of civic education in accordance with the principles contained in the Constitution and in the laws.

In addition, the Constitution establishes that education offered in State institutions is free of charge up to the undergraduate university level. To this end, the State shall make priority investment in accordance with United Nations recommendations. The State shall create and sustain institutions and services sufficiently equipped to ensure the admission process, ongoing education and program completion in the education system (Article 103). The communications media, public and private, shall contribute to civil education. The State guarantees public radio and television services and library and computer networks, with a view to allowing universal access to information (Article 108).

Regarding the right to educate, article 106 of the Constitution guaranties every natural or juridical person, subject to demonstration of its ability and provided it meets at all times the ethical, academic, scientific, financial, infrastructure and any other requirements that may be established by law, to be permitted to fund and maintain private educational institutions under the strict inspection and vigilance of the State, with the prior approval of the latter. For such purposes, only persons of recognized good moral character and proven academic qualifications shall be placed in charge of education (Article 104). The State shall encourage them to remain continuously up to date, and shall guarantee stability in the practice of the teaching profession, whether in public or private institutions, in accordance with this Constitution and the law, with working conditions and a standard of living commensurate with the importance of their mission. Admissions, promotion and continued enrollment in the education system shall be provided for by law, and shall be responsive to evaluation criteria based on merit, to the exclusion of any partisan or other nonacademic interference.

10. *Honesty/Integrity*

The Preamble of the Constitution refers to the values of "ethics," and ethical values are mentioned in the provisions regarding education. Consequently, beyond the legal provisions referred to public ethics in Public Administration, there is a set of ethical norms that must guide society and State officials in the task of transforming the State and creating a new legal system. As for Public Administration, which must be "at the service of the people", the Constitution also enumerates the principles and values on which it must be based: "honesty, participation, celerity, efficiency, effectiveness, transparency, the accounting and responsibility in the execution of the public function, with complete subjection to the statutes and to the Law" (Article 141).

As for the bodies of the Electoral power, the Constitution enumerates the following principles that must be guaranteed regarding the electoral processes: "equality, reliability, impartiality, transparency and efficiency"; besides the "personalization of the vote and the proportional representation" principles (Article 293);

Regarding the public services corresponding to the State, the Constitution also enumerates a series of governing principles: For instance, regarding the national public health system, it states that it must be "inter-sectorial, decentralized and participative, and managed by the principles of gratuitousness, universality, integrality, impartiality, social integration and solidarity" (Article 84); in matter of the social security system, it indicates that the system must be "universal, integral, unified (*solidario*), unitary, efficient and participative financing, from direct or indirect contributions" (Article 86); and as for the education, the Constitution expresses that it must be "democratic, free and mandatory, based on the respect to all thought tendencies, in order to develop the creative potential of every human being and the complete exercise of his/her personality inside a democratic society based on the ethical valuation of the labor and the active, conscientious and unified (*solidario*) participation in the processes of social transformation related with the values of the national identity and with a Latin-American and universal vision" (Article 102).

Regarding the socioeconomic regime of the Republic, the Constitution enumerates the following principles on which the system must be based: "social justice, democracy, efficiency, free competition, environmental protection, productivity and solidarity, in order to guarantee the integral human development, a dignified and prosperous existence for the collectivity, the generation of labor sources, high national added value, elevation of the standard of living of the people and to strengthen the economical supremacy of the country, guarantying juridical security, stability, dynamism, supportability, permanence and equity of the economic growth, in order to achieve a fair distribution of the wealth by means of a democratic, participative and of open consultation strategic planning" (Article 299).

11. *Freedom/Liberty/Independence*

The Constitution establishes some rights of the Nation that cannot be renounced or abandoned, those rights being, the "independence, freedom, sovereignty, immunity, territorial integrity and the national self-determination" (Article 1).

Regarding Independence, in the provisions referred to the territorial organization of the State, particularly regarding the "decentralized federal State" (art. 4), it is established that it must be configured following the principles of "territorial integrity, cooperation, solidarity, concurrence and co-responsibility" (Article 4). Also, as for the national statutes that can be sanctioned by the National Assembly regarding concurrent competences between the national, the states and the municipal levels, the Constitution prescribes that they must be oriented by "the principles of independence, coordination, cooperation, co-responsibility and subsidiary" (Article 165).

"Independence" is also reaffirmed in the Preamble, in the sense of reaffirming the existence of the Republic itself, which obtained its independence from the Spanish monarchy in 1810, not subjected to any nature of foreign domination. Consequently, the "territorial integrity" of the Nation is also conceived as another fundamental value of the country, which impedes the modification of its borders in any way. Regarding the aims of "peace", as a fundamental value, it implies the existential rejection to war.

On the other hand, "Freedom," according to the Preamble is also one of the most fundamental values, understood in its most classical expression as the right of every individual to do anything that does not harm others; to not be obliged to do what the Law does not order nor to be impeded to execute what it does not forbid; that is, the right to the "free development of the personality", which is also expressly regulated (Article 20) without any other limitation than those derived from the rights of others and the public and social order".

12. *Security*

According to Article 55 of the Constitution, every person has the right to be protected by the State, through the entities established by law for the protection of citizens, from situations that constitute a threat, vulnerability or risk to the physical integrity of individuals, their properties, and the enjoyment of their rights or the fulfillment of their duties. The citizens' participation in programs for purposes of prevention, citizen safety and emergency management shall be regulated by a special law.

The Constitution guaranties that the State's security entities shall respect the human dignity and rights of all persons; and sets forth in an express way that the use of weapons or toxic substances by police and security officers shall be limited by the principles of necessity, convenience, opportunity and proportionality in accordance with law.

Also, the Constitution enumerates the following principles regarding the Nation's security: "independence, democracy, equality, peace, freedom, justice, solidarity, promotion and conservation of the environment, the affirmation of the human rights and the progressive satisfaction of all individual and collective needs of the Venezuelan people" (Article 326).

13. *Responsibility /Accountability/Transparency*

The 1999 Constitution establishes the general principle of State liability, incorporated in an express way in its Article 140, setting forth that "The State is liable for the damages suffered by individuals in their goods and rights, provided that the injury be imputable to the functioning of Public Administration," being possible to comprise in the expression "functioning of Public Administration", its normal or abnormal functioning. Although doubts can result from the wording of the Article regarding the liability of the State caused by legislative actions that nonetheless are derived from the general principles of public law, regarding the liability caused by judicial acts, it is clarified by the express provisions of Articles 49.8 and 255 of the Constitution, in which it is established, in addition, the State liability caused because of "judicial errors or delay."

On the other hand, Article 139 of the Constitution also establishes the general principle of liability of public officials in the exercise of public functions, based on the "abuse or deviation of powers or on the violation of the Constitution or of the law." In addition, Article 25 of the Constitution, following a long constitutional tradition, expressly establishes the specific civil, criminal and administrative liability of any public officials when issuing or executing acts violating human rights guaranties in the Constitution and the statutes, not being acceptable any excuse due to superior orders.

From the political point of view, the Constitution also provides for the elected public officials to be subject to accountability (*rendición de cuentas*), specifically establishing the possibility for all of them to be subjected to repeal referendums for the revocation of mandates (Article 6), which according to Article 72 can only take place at the mid-point of the term in office. The corresponding petition for a repeal referendum can only be one of popular initiative that must be signed by at least twenty percent (20%) of the registered voters in the corresponding jurisdiction. In order for a mandate to be repealed or revoked, the concurrence of a number of voters equal to or greater than the number that originally elected the official is needed, and the voters must total at least twenty-five percent (25%) of the registered voters in the corresponding jurisdiction. If the repeal petition is approved, the substitute officer must be elected immediately according to the electoral procedures established in the Constitution and laws. This repeal referendum has been distorted in 2004 regarding its application to the President of the Republic, and was transformed against the constitutional provision into a "ratifying" referendum.[197]

Finally, regarding transparency, Article 143 of the Constitution guaranties the Citizens Rights to be informed and to have access to administrative information. In the first place, it provides for the right of Citizens to be promptly and truly informed by Public Administration regarding the situation of the procedures in which they have direct interest, and to know about the definitive resolutions therein adopted, to be notified of administrative acts and to be informed on the courses of the administrative procedure.

The constitutional Article also establishes for the individual right everybody has to have access to administrative archives and registries, without prejudice of the acceptable limits imposed in a democratic society related to the national or foreign security, to criminal investigation, to the intimacy of private life, all according to the statutes regulating the matter of secret or confidential documents classification. The same Article provides for the principle of prohibition of any previous censorship referring to public officials regarding the information they could give referring to matters under their responsibility.

On this matter, regarding the public economy, the Constitution also states the following principles that must rule the fiscal management: "efficiency, solvency, transparency, responsibility and fiscal balance" (Article 311); and regarding the taxation system, it must be ruled by the following principles: "progressiveness, protection of the national economy and the elevation of the standard of living of the population" (Article 316).

14. *Environment*

The Constitution of 1999 is also innovative with respect to its regulation of constitutional rights concerning the environment, declaring that each generation has the right and duty to protect and maintain the environment for its own benefit and that of the world of the future; and that everyone has the right, individually and collectively, to enjoy a safe, healthful and ecologically balanced life and environment.

The State shall protect the environment, biological and genetic diversity, ecological processes, national parks and natural monuments, and other areas of particular ecological importance. The genome of a living being shall not be patentable, and the field shall be regulated by the law relating to the principles of bioethics.

It is a fundamental duty of the State, with the active participation of society, to ensure to people their development in a pollution-free environment in which air,

---

197 See Allan R. Brewer-Carías, "El secuestro del Poder Electoral y la confiscación del derecho a la participación política mediante el referendo revocatorio presidencial: Venezuela 2000-2004", in *Boletín Mexicano de Derecho Comparado*, Instituto de Investigaciones Jurídicas, Universidad Nacional Autónoma de México, N° 112. México, enero-abril 2005 pp. 11-73

water, soil, coasts, climate, the ozone layer and living species receive special protection, in accordance with law (Article 127).

In order to guaranty the protection of environment, Article 129 of the Constitution prescribes that any activities capable of generating damage to ecosystems must be preceded by environmental and socio-cultural impact studies. The State shall prevent toxic and hazardous waste from entering the country, as well as preventing the manufacture and use of nuclear, chemical and biological weapons. A special law shall regulate the use, handling, transportation and storage of toxic and hazardous substances.

As a matter of public policy, Article 128 of the Constitution imposes on the State the duty to develop a land use policy taking into account ecological, geographic, demographic, social, cultural, economic and political realities, in accordance with the premises of sustainable development, including information, consultation and male/female participation by citizens. An organic law shall develop the principles and criteria for this zoning.

Regarding the content of education, Article 106 of the Constitution sets forth that environmental education is obligatory in the various levels and modes of the education system, as well as in informal civil education. Spanish, Venezuelan geography and history and the principles of the Bolivarian thought shall be compulsory courses at public and private institutions up to the education diversified level.

III. THE INCONGRUENCES BETWEEN DECLARED VALUES AND POLITICAL AND JUDICIAL PRACTICE

The constitutional process in Venezuela developed during the past decade has not remained in the paths set forth within the values and principles inserted in the Constitution in order to guide the performance of both, the government and the governed; and not always has resulted in giving the needed prioritization or prevalence to some rights over others by means of judicial decisions. Unfortunately, in some cases some incongruence can be identified, originated in the political and legislative practice and in court decisions.

Some examples can be identified regarding the exact rank of the constitutional values and principles, as superior or global values above the Constitution itself; the exact hierarchy of international treaties on human rights regarding internal law, and particularly the Constitution; and the exact scope of citizens participation allowed by the State; and the exact role of civil society in the process of participation and its State control.

1.   *The subjection of the superior values of the Constitution to its "political project" and the rejection of the supra-constitutional rank of international instruments on human rights*

In effect, in a completely incongruent way regarding the superior character of the values enshrined in the Constitution, recognized by the Supreme Tribunal of Justice, its Constitutional Chamber in decision N° 23 of January 22, 2003 when arguing about constitutional interpretation, has transformed the values incorporated in the Constitution into sub constitutional provisions, subjecting them to the interpretation that the politically controlled constitutional judge can make of the Constitution. That is, the universal meaning of the values has been put aside, considering that "to interpret the legal system according to the Constitution, means to protect the Constitution itself from every diversion of principles and from every separation from the political project that it embodies by will of the people;" adding that:

> "[A] system of principles, assumed to be absolute and supra historical, cannot be placed above the Constitution, nor that its interpretation could eventually contradict the political theory that supports it. From this perspective, any theory that proposes absolute rights or goals must be rejected and, ... the interpretation or integration [of the Constitution] must be done according to the living cultural tradition whose sense and scope depends on the specific and historical analysis of the values shared by the Venezuelan people. Part of the protection and guarantee of the Constitution is established then, in an *in fieri* politic perspective, reluctant to the ideological connection with theories that can limit, under pretext of universal validities, the supremacy and the national self-determination, as demanded in article 1° *eiusdem*"[198].

This doctrine of subjection of the global constitutional values to the political project as interpreted of the Constitution by the constitutional judge has been ratified in decision N° 1.939 of December 18, 2009 (Case *Gustavo Álvarez Arias y otros*) in which the Constitutional Chamber has declared a decision of the Inter American Court of Human Rights as non enforceable in Venezuela, rejecting the existence of superior values out of the reach of the government. The Chamber argued that the legal order "is a normative theory at the service of politic defined in the axiological project of the Constitution;" that the standard in order to resolve conflicts between principles and provisions must be "compatible with the political project of the Constitution," and such provisions "cannot be affected with interpretations that could give prevalence to individual rights or that could give prevalence to the international order regarding the national one affecting the State sovereignty;" that no system of principles "supposedly absolute and supra-historic can be placed above the Constitution," and "theories based on universal values that pretend to limit the sovereignty and national auto-determination are unacceptable."[199]

This rejection of superior and universal values and principles above the Constitution has been followed by the rejection of the supra constitutional rank that the Constitution has given to international instruments of human rights and to their direct and immediate application by all courts.

In effect, as aforementioned, Article 23 of the 1999 Constitution, without doubts one of the most important ones in matters of human rights, sets forth the constitutional rank of international treaties on human rights and their prevalence when containing provisions more favorable to their enjoyment than those established in the internal legal order. Its inclusion in the new Constitution was a significant advancement in the completion of the protection framework of human rights.

---

198 Case: *Interpretación del article 71 de la Constitución*, in *Revista de Derecho Público*, N° 93-96, Editorial Jurídica Venezolana, Caracas 2003, pp. 530 ff.

199 Véase en http://www.tsj.gov.ve/decisiones/scon/Diciembre/1939-181208-2008-08-1572.html

Nonetheless, in the judicial practice and particularly regarding the provisions of the American Convention of Human Rights, the doctrine of the Supreme Tribunal in this case has also been progressively restrictive, eventually rejecting the supra constitutional rank to the international instruments of human rights. This restrictive approach by the Constitutional Chamber that has affected the role of the Inter American institutions for the protection human rights, began with a decision dated May 5th, 2000, in which the Constitutional Chamber objected the "quasi-jurisdictional" powers of the Inter American Commission when issuing provisional protective measures regarding a State, qualifying it as "unacceptable", stating that they "imply a gross intrusion in the country Judiciary, like the suspension of the judicial proceeding against the plaintiff, measures that can only be adopted by the judges exercising their judicial attributions and independence, according to what is stated in the Constitution and the statutes of the Republic"[200].

This unfortunate ruling directed to question the superior role of the international institutions on matters of human rights, in addition can be considered contrary to article 31 of the Constitution that establishes the rights of everybody to bring before the international institutions on human rights, precisely like the Inter American Commission on Human Rights, petitions or complaints to seek protection (amparo) of their harmed constitutional rights.

The restrictive approach regarding the role and value of international institutions for the protection of human rights was also applied in decision N° 1.942 of July 15, 2003 (Case: *Impugnación de artículos del Código Penal, Leyes de desacato*),[201] in which the Constitutional Chamber, when referring to International courts, stated that "in Venezuela, in general, in relation to article 7 of the Constitution, no jurisdictional organ could exist above the Supreme Tribunal of Justice, and even in such case, its decisions when contradicting constitutional provisions are inapplicable in the country." The restrictive approach on the matter was finished with the decision of the Constitutional Chamber No 1.939 of December 18, 2008 (Case *Abogados Gustavo Álvarez Arias y otros*), in which it declared a decision of the Inter American Court on Human Rights as non enforceable in Venezuela. The decision of the former of August 5, 2008 (Case *Apitz Barbera y otros ("Corte Primera de lo Contencioso Administrativo") vs. Venezuela*,)[202] condemned the Venezuelan State for the violation of the judicial guaranties of three former judges of a First Contentious Administrative Court that were dismissed by a Special Commission of the Supreme Tribunal. The Constitutional Chamber in its decision rejected the supra- constitutional character of the provisions of the American Convention, considering that in case of contra-

---

200 See Case: *Faitha M.Nahmens L. y Ben Ami Fihman Z.* (*Revista Exceso*), Exp. n° 00-0216, decisión n° 386 dated May 17, 2000. See the reference in Carlos Ayala Corao, "Recepción de la jurisprudencia internacional sobre derechos humanos por la jurisprudencia constitucional" en *Revista del Tribunal Constitucional*, n° 6, Sucre, Bolivia, Nov. 2004, pp. 275 ff.

201 Véase en *Revista de Derecho Público*, N° 93-96, Editorial Jurídica Venezolana, Caracas 2003, pp. 136 ss.

202 See in www.corteidh.or.cr . Excepción Preliminar, Fondo, Reparaciones y Costas, Serie C N° 182.

diction of a provision of the Constitution and a provision of an international treaty, the Judiciary is the one that has the attribution to determine the applicable provisions.[203] The non enforceability in Venezuela of the decisions of the Inter American Court of Human Rights was ratified by the Supreme Tribunal of Venezuela in decision N° 1547 of October 17, 2011 (Case *Estado Venezolano vs. Corte Interamericana de Derechos Humanos*),[204] in which the Constitutional Chamber decided on the "unconstitutionality" of the decision of the Inter American Court on Human Rights of September 1, 2011 (case *Leopoldo López vs. Estado de Venezuela).* [205]

The result has been that based on sovereignty principles, the decisions adopted by international courts cannot be enforceable in Venezuela, except if they are according to what is stated in the Constitution but in the opinion of the Constitutional Chamber. Thus, the supra constitutional rank of treaties when establishing more favorable regulations regarding human rights has been suddenly eliminated by the Constitutional Chamber, assuming an absolute monopoly of Constitutional interpretation in order to determine when a treaty provision prevails in the internal order; a power that according to the Constitution the Constitutional Chamber does not have.

This political-positivistic conception of the Constitution unfortunately leaves the interpretation of the very rich constitutional values and principles extensively enumerated in the Constitution, and of the Constitution itself, at the mercy of the Constitutional Chamber, that is unfortunately controlled by the Executive.[206] This conception has implied the rejection of the power of all courts established in the same article 23 of the Constitution to apply in a direct and immediate way, international instruments on human rights for the resolution of judicial cases. On the contrary, the Constitutional Chamber has established, contrary to what was the intention of the Constituent Assembly,[207] its own monopoly to interpret when a constitutional provi-

---

203 Available   at   http://www.tsj.gov.ve/decisiones/scon/Diciembre/1939-181208-2008-08-1572.html

204 Availavle   at   http://www.tsj.gov.ve/decisiones/scon/Octubre/1547-171011-2011-11-1130.htmll

205 Available at http://www.corteidh.or.cr/docs/casos/articulos/resumen_233_esp.pdf . See the comments in Allan R. Brewer-Carías, "El ilegítimo "control de constitucionalidad" de las sentencias de la Corte Interamericana de Derechos Humanos por parte la Sala Constitucional del Tribunal Supremo de Justicia de Venezuela: el caso *Leopoldo López vs. Venezuela, septiembre 2011*," in *Revista de Derecho Público*, N° 128 (octubre-diciembre 2011), Editorial Jurídica Venezolana, Caracas 2011, pp. 227-250

206 See Allan R. Brewer-Carías, "El juez constitucional al servicio del autoritarismo y la ilegítima mutación de la constitución: el caso de la Sala Constitucional del Tribunal Supremo de Justicia de Venezuela (1999-2009)", in *Revista de Administración Pública*, N° 180, Madrid 2009, pp. 383-418.

207 Allan R. Brewer-Carías, "Quis Custodiet ipsos Custodes: De la interpretación constitucional a la inconstitucionalidad de la interpretación", in *VIII Congreso Nacional de derecho Constitucional, Perú,* Fondo Editorial 2005, Colegio de Abogados de Arequipa, Arequipa, septiembre 2005, pp. 463-489.

sion is of immediate application and, particularly, when its content is justiciable.[208]
In decision N° 1942 of July 7th, 2003,[209] the Chamber ruled that once the provisions
of the international instruments have been incorporated into the constitutional hierarchy, "the maximum and last interpreter of them [including international instru-
ments] regarding internal law, is the Constitutional Chamber, which must determine
the content and scope of the constitutional norms and principles (Article 335)."
From this proposition, the Constitutional Chamber concluded that "the Constitutional Chamber is the only one that determines which norms on human rights contained
in treaties, covenants and conventions, prevails in the internal legal order; as well as
which human rights non incorporated in such international instruments have effect
in Venezuela"; concluding that:

> "This power of the Constitutional Chamber on the matter, derived from the Constitution,
> cannot be diminished by adjective norms contained in the treaties or in other international
> texts on human rights subscribed by the country, which allows the States' parties to ask inter-
> national institutions for the interpretation of rights referred to in the Convention or covenant,
> as it is established in article 64 of the Approbatory statute of the American Convention of
> Human Rights, San José Covenant, because otherwise the situation would be of a constitu-
> tional amendment, without following the constitutional procedures, diminishing the powers of
> the Constitutional Chamber, transferring it to international or transnational bodies with the
> power to dictate obligatory interpretations"[210].

The final result of this incongruence between the provisions of the Constitution
and the political reality has been the formal decision adopted by the Executive in
September 2012, at the request of the Supreme Tribunal of Justice, to withdraw the
Venezuelan Stat from the American Convention of Human Rights, a decision without precedent in the democratic history of Latin America.[211]

**2.   *The illusion of the rule of law- State of Justice, the concentration of State
powers, and the subjection of the Judiciary to the political power***

As aforementioned, one of the most fundamental principles regarding the organization of the State established in the 1999 Constitution is the principle of separation

---

208   See Case: *Aclaratoria de la sentencia de interpretación de los artículos 156, 180 y 302 de la
      Constitución*, decision N°. 1278 dated June 17, 2005, in *Revista de Derecho Público*, N° 102,
      Editorial Jurídica Venezolana, Caracas, 2005, pp. 56 ff. The Constitutional Chamber ruled in
      decision N° 332 dated March 14, 2001, that "it is the constitutional jurisdiction represented
      by this Constitutional Chamber, who will resolve the controversies that might arise as the re-
      sult of the legislatively undeveloped constitutional provisions, until the laws that regulate the
      constitutional jurisdiction decide otherwise." See Case: INSACA vs. Ministerio de Sanidad y
      Asistencia Social, in *Revista de Derecho Público*, N° 85-88, Editorial Jurídica Venezolana,
      Caracas, 2001, p. 492.

209   See the text in *Revista de Derecho Público*, N°93-96, Editorial Jurídica Venezolana, Caracas
      2003, pp. 136 ff.

210   See the text in *Revista de Derecho Público*, N°93-96, Editorial Jurídica Venezolana, Caracas
      2003, pp. 136 ff.

211   See in http://www.ejiltalk.org/venezuela-denounces-american-convention-on-human-rights/

of powers, particularly at the national (federal) level of government, giving way to a penta division of branches of government. This division is established as a democratic tool for limiting the exercise of State powers, in order to preserve freedom, by means of the balance that must exist between the different branches of government.

But unfortunately, this division of branches of government in five independent and autonomous ones (Legislative, Executive, Judicial, Citizens and Electoral), seeking to avoid the concentration of the same, has resulted in an illusion, being distorted in the same Constitution which has provided the germ for the "disequilibrium" of those branches, allowing a concentrated system of powers giving way to the installment of an authoritarian regime.

The origin for the power concentration system was expressly established in the Constitution by assigning the National Assembly (the Legislative branch of government) a superior position regarding the other branches, with the authority not only to appoint the Magistrates of the Supreme Tribunal of Justice and the Head of the Electoral Power (National Electoral Council) and Citizens Power (Prosecutor General, Comptroller General Peoples' Defendant), but to *dismiss* them from office, according to provisions that eventually have been applied only based on political motives.

Regarding the appointment of such High public officials, even though the Constitution tried to limit the political discretional power of the Assembly to make the appointments by means of creating "Nominating Committees" integrated by representatives of sectors of civil society, they have not worked as envisaged because the legislation enacted for such purpose has deliberately distorted the effective civil society participation, and on the contrary, the National Assembly has retained the exclusive discretional political power to nominate and elect the candidates; and through it, assuring the Executive control of the Judiciary. This has been particularly grave regarding the Judicial Power.[212]

---

212 The nomination and appointment of the magistrates of the Supreme Tribunal by means of the new "Nominating Committee" was completely controlled by the political organs of the government. This was publicly acknowledged by the President of the Parliamentary Nominating Commission in charge of selecting the candidates for Magistrates of the Supreme Tribunal (who a few months later was appointed Ministry of the Interior and Justice). In December 2004, he stated to the press: "Although we, the representatives, have the authority for this selection, the President of the Republic was consulted and his opinion was very much taken into consideration." He added: "Let's be clear, we are not going to score own-goals. On the list, there were people from the opposition who comply with all the requirements. The opposition could have used them in order to reach an agreement during the last sessions, but they did not want to. We are not going to do it for them. There is no one in the group of candidates that could act against us..." See in *El Nacional*, Caracas 12-13-2004. The Inter-American Commission on Human Rights suggested in its Report to the General Assembly of the OAS for 2004 that "these regulations of the Organic Law of the Supreme Court of Justice would have made possible the manipulation, by the Executive Power, of the election process of judges that took place during 2004". See Inter-American Commission on Human Rights, 2004 *Report on Venezuela*; paragraph 180

Regarding the political dismissal from office of the Magistrates of the Supreme Tribunal of Justice and of the heads of the Electoral (National Electoral Council) and Citizens (General Prosecutor, General Comptroller and Peoples' Defendant) branches of government, the Constitution itself has established a contradiction regarding the autonomy and independence between them, by allowing their almost unrestrained dismissal from office by the National Assembly (Articles 265, 279, 296). For such purposes, in general terms, a two third of the votes of the Assembly is required, based on vaguely defined grave motives. Nonetheless, in some cases, and contrary to this vote restriction, in the case of the magistrates of the Supreme Tribunal the National Assembly has bypassed it, and through a statute has set forth a simple absolute majority for their dismissal, transforming in fact the autonomy and independence of the Judiciary in a simple illusion[213]. The sole fact that this power to dismiss exists in the hands of the most political of all the branches of government impedes the development of real independent and autonomous bodies.

The fact is that with these attributions, an inconvenient supremacy of the Legislative Power (National Assembly) over the Judiciary and the Citizens and Electoral powers has been developed during the past decade, following the provisions set forth in the Constitution itself, which has provoked that the members of said bodies have become mostly dependent regarding the political will of the Legislator, without any check and balance whatsoever. This regulation, through the partisan political control of the National Assembly, has eventually derived in the supremacy of the Executive, converting it into a power controlling all the others, and effectively concentrating State powers.

So in Venezuela, the separation of powers, even in a penta division framework, is no more than a constitutional illusion, and the consequence is that the Judicial Power has been completely controlled by the Executive.[214] For such purpose, none of the constitutional provisions regarding the appointment and stability of judges in

---

213 See the comments in Allan R. Brewer-Carías, "La progresiva y sistemática demolición institucional de la autonomía e independencia del Poder Judicial en Venezuela 1999-2004", in *XXX Jornadas J.M Dominguez Escovar, Estado de derecho, Administración de justicia y derechos humanos*, Instituto de Estudios Jurídicos del Estado Lara, Barquisimeto 2005, pp.33-174; "Sobre la ausencia de independencia y autonomía judicial en Venezuela, a los doce años de vigencia de la constitución de 1999 (O sobre la interminable transitoriedad que en fraude continuado a la voluntad popular y a las normas de la Constitución, ha impedido la vigencia de la garantía de la estabilidad de los jueces y el funcionamiento efectivo de una "jurisdicción disciplinaria judicial"), en *Independencia Judicial*, Colección Estado de Derecho, Tomo I, Academia de Ciencias Políticas y Sociales, Acceso a la Justicia org., Fundación de Estudios de Derecho Administrativo (Funeda), Universidad Metropolitana (Unimet), Caracas 2012, pp. 9-103.

214 See Allan R. Brewer-Carías, "El principio de la separación de poderes como elemento esencial de la democracia y de la libertad, y su demolición en Venezuela mediante la sujeción política del Tribunal Supremo de Justicia,"en *Revista Iberoamericana de Derecho Administrativo, Homenaje a Luciano Parejo Alfonso*, Año 12, N° 12, Asociación e Instituto Iberoamericano de Derecho Administrativo Prof. Jesús González Pérez, San José, Costa Rica 2012, pp. 31-43.

order to assure their independence and autonomy have been implemented. On the contrary, since 1999, the Venezuelan Judiciary has been almost exclusively made up of temporary and provisional judges,[215] and the public competition processes for the appointment of judges with citizens' participation has not been implemented. Consequently, in general, judges lack stability, and since until 2011 the constitutional provisions creating the Judicial Disciplinary jurisdiction had not been implemented by legislation, matters of judicial discipline were in the hands of the "Functioning and Restructuring Commission of the Judiciary"[216] (not established in the Constitution but created by the National Constituent Assembly in 1999) which had the power to remove temporary judges without due process guarantees,[217] and in those of a Judicial Commission of the Supreme Tribunal, which also had discretionary powers to remove all temporary judges.[218] Since 2011 a Disciplinary Jurisdiction has been created, replacing the aforementioned "Commissions" but unfortunately, organized in a way that its members are appointed by the National Assembly and not by the Supreme Tribunal, implying a possibility of greater political control over such "Jurisdiction."[219]

On the other hand, the President's influence on the Supreme Tribunal was admitted by himself when he publicly complained that the Supreme Tribunal had issued an important ruling[220] in which it "modified" the Income Tax Law, without previ-

---

215 In 2003, the Inter-American Commission on Human Rights said: "The Commission has been informed that only 250 judges have been appointed by public competition according to the constitutional text. From a total of 1772 positions of judges in Venezuela, the Supreme Court of Justice reports that only 183 are holders, 1331 are provisional and 258 are temporary," *Informe sobre la Situación de los Derechos Humanos en Venezuela*; OAS/Ser.L/V/II.118. d.C. 4rev. 2; December 29, 2003; paragraph 11. The same Commission also said that "an aspect linked to the autonomy and independence of the Judicial Power is that of the provisional character of the judges in the judicial system of Venezuela. Today, the information provided by the different sources indicates that more than 80% of Venezuelan judges are "provisional." *Idem.*, Paragraph 161.

216 The Politico-Administrative Chamber of the Supreme Tribunal has ruled that the dismissal of temporary judges is a discretional power of the Functioning and Restructuring Commission of the Judiciary. This Commission, created after 1999, adopts its decisions without following any administrative procedure. See decision N° 00463-2007. The same doctrine has been established by the Constitutional Chamber in decisions N° 2414 of December 20, 2007; decision N° 280 of February 23, 2007; and decision 00673-2008.

217 See Allan R. Brewer-Carías, "La justicia sometida al poder y la interminable emergencia del poder judicial (1999-2006)", en *Derecho y democracia. Cuadernos Universitarios*, Órgano de Divulgación Académica, Vicerrectorado Académico, Universidad Metropolitana, Año II, N° 11, Caracas, septiembre 2007, pp. 122-138

218 See the decision of the Constitutional Chamber of the Supreme Tribunal N° 1.939 of December 18, 2008 (Case *Gustavo Álvarez Arias y otros*).

219 See Allan R. Brewer-Carías, "La Ley del Código de Ética del Juez Venezolano de 2010 y la interminable transitoriedad del régimen disciplinario judicial," en *Revista de Derecho Público*, N°128 (octubre-diciembre 2011), Editorial Jurídica Venezolana, Caracas 2011, pp. 83-93

220 That was a very controversial case, decided by the Constitutional Chamber of the Supreme Tribunal in decision N°301 of February 27, 2007. Case: *Adriana Vigilanza y Carlos A. Vec-*

ously consulting the "leader of the Revolution," and warning courts against decisions that would be "treason to the People" and "the Revolution.[221]

Another important aspect of the new Organic Law of the Supreme Tribunal concerned dismissal of the Magistrates of the Supreme Tribunal. According to article 265 of the 1999 Constitution, a Magistrate can be dismissed only by the vote of a qualified majority of two-thirds of the National Assembly, following a hearing, in cases of "grave faults" committed by the accused, following a prior qualification by the Citizens Power. The Organic Law defines "grave faults" very broadly, leaving open the possibility of dismissal based exclusively on political motives.[222] Furthermore, the qualified two-thirds majority was required by the Constitution in order to avoid leaving the tenure of the Magistrates in the hands of a simple majority of Legislators. The 2004 Organic Law circumvented this requirement by authorizing the dismissal of Magistrates by a simple majority vote by revoking the "administrative act of their appointment" (article 23.4).[223] Accordingly, the National Assembly used its power to dismiss Magistrates who ruled on sensitive issues against the government's wishes.[224]

---

chio, Expediente n° 01-2862. Véase *en Gaceta Oficial* n° 38.635 de fecha 01-03-2007. See the comments in Allan R. Brewer-Carías, "El juez constitucional en Venezuela como legislador positivo de oficio en materia tributaria", in *Revista de Derecho Público*, N° 109 (enero – marzo 2007), Editorial Jurídica Venezolana, Caracas 2007, pp. 193-212; and "De cómo la Jurisdicción constitucional en Venezuela, no sólo legisla de oficio, sino subrepticiamente modifica las reformas legales que "sanciona", a espaldas de las partes en el proceso: el caso de la aclaratoria de la sentencia de Reforma de la Ley de Impuesto sobre la Renta de 2007, in *Revista de Derecho Público*, N° 114, Editorial Jurídica Venezolana, Caracas 2008, pp. 267-276.

221 (Emphasis added.) The Spanish text is as follows: "Muchas veces llegan, viene el Gobierno Nacional Revolucionario y quiere tomar una decisión contra algo por ejemplo que tiene que ver o que tiene que pasar por decisiones judiciales y ellos empiezan a moverse en contrario a la sombra, y muchas veces logran neutralizar decisiones de la Revolución a través de un juez, o de un tribunal, o hasta en el mismísimo Tribunal Supremo de Justicia, *a espaldas del líder de la Revolución*, actuando por dentro contra la Revolución. Eso es, repito, traición al pueblo, traición a la Revolución." (emphasis added). *Discurso en el Primer Evento con propulsores del Partido Socialista Unido de Venezuela desde el teatro Teresa Carreño, 24 marzo 2007.*

222 See the comments in this regard in Allan R. Brewer-Carías, *Ley Orgánica del Tribunal Supremo de Justicia*, Editorial Jurídica venezolana, Caracas 2010, pp. 41 ff.

223 See the comments on this reform in Allan R. Brewer-Carías, *Ley Orgánica del Tribunal Supremo de Justicia*, Editorial Jurídica Venezolana, Caracas 2004, Third Editon, Caracas 2006, 41 ff. The provision was eliminated in the 2010 reform of the Supreme Tribunal Organic Law.

224 That was the fate of Franklin Arrieche, Vice-President of the Supreme Tribunal of Justice, who delivered the decision of the Supreme Tribunal of 08-14-2002 regarding the criminal process against the generals who acted on April 12, 2002, declaring that there were no grounds to prosecute them because no military coup had taken place. It was also the fate of Alberto Martini Urdaneta, President of the Electoral Court, and Rafael Hernandez and Orlando Gravina, Judges of the same Court who signed decision N° 24 of 03-15-2004 (Case:

As described above, the constitutional principles tending to assure the autonomy and independence of judges at all levels of the Judiciary are yet to be applied, particularly regarding the admission of candidates to the judicial career through "public competition" processes, with citizen participation in the procedure of selection and appointment, and regarding the prohibition of removal or suspension of judges except through disciplinary trials before disciplinary courts and judges (articles 254 and 267). In reality, since 1999 the Venezuelan Judiciary has been composed primarily of temporary and provisional judges, without career or stability, appointed without the public competition process of selection established in the Constitution, and dismissed without due process of law for political reasons.[225]

This reality amounts to political control of the Judiciary, as demonstrated by the dismissal of judges who have adopted decisions contrary to the policies of the governing political authorities. It was the case in 2003 when a contentious-administrative court ruled[226] against the government in a politically charged case.[227] In response, the government intervened (took over) the court and dismissed its judges,[228] and, after the Inter-American Court of Human Rights ruled in 2008 that the dismissal had violated the American Convention of Human Rights and Venezuela's international obligations,[229] as aforementioned, the Constitutional Chamber upheld the government's argument that the decision of the Inter-American Court cannot be enforced in Venezuela.[230] This is one of the leading cases showing clearly the pre-

---

Julio Borges, Cesar Perez Vivas, Henry Ramos Allup, Jorge Sucre Castillo, Ramón Jose Medina and Gerardo Blyde vs. the National Electoral Council), which suspended the effects of Resolution N° 040302-131, dated 03-02-2004, of the National Electoral Council which, at that time, stopped the realization of the presidential recall referendum.

225 See Inter-American Commission on Human Rights, *Informe sobre la Situación de los Derechos Humanos en Venezuela*, OEA/Ser.L/V/II.118, d.C. 4 rev. 2, December 29, 2003, Paragraph 11, p. 3.

226 See Decision of August 21 2003, in *Revista de Derecho Público*, n° 93-96, Editorial Jurídica Venezolana, Caracas, 2003, pp. 445 ff.

227 See Claudia Nikken, "El caso "Barrio Adentro": La Corte Primera de lo Contencioso Administrativo ante la Sala Constitucional del Tribunal Supremo de Justicia o el avocamiento como medio de amparo de derechos e intereses colectivos y difusos," in *Revista de Derecho Público*, n° 93-96, Editorial Jurídica Venezolana, Caracas, 2003, pp. 5 ff.

228 See Allan R. Brewer-Carías, "La progresiva y sistemática demolición institucional de la autonomía e independencia del Poder Judicial en Venezuela 1999–2004, " in *XXX Jornadas J.M Domínguez Escovar, Estado de derecho, Administración de justicia y derechos humanos,* Instituto de Estudios Jurídicos del Estado Lara, Barquisimeto, 2005, pp. 33–174; "La justicia sometida al poder (La ausencia de independencia y autonomía de los jueces en Venezuela por la interminable emergencia del Poder Judicial (1999-2006))", in *Cuestiones Internacionales. Anuario Jurídico Villanueva 2007,* Centro Universitario Villanueva, Marcial Pons, Madrid, 2007, pp. 25–57.

229 See decision of August 5, 2008, Case *Apitz Barbera y otros ("Corte Primera de lo Contencioso Administrativo") vs. Venezuela,* in www.corteidh.or.cr . Excepción Preliminar, Fondo, Reparaciones y Costas, Serie C N° 182.

230 See the Constitutional Chamber decision N° 1939 of December 12, 2008.

sent subordination of the Venezuelan Judiciary to the policies, wishes and dictates of the President of the Republic.[231] The Constitutional Chamber, by refusing to decide judicial review actions against executive acts, has in fact become a most effective tool for the existing consolidation of power in the person of President of the Republic.[232]

3. The distortion of the citizens' right to political participation and of the participation of representatives of civil society in the appointment of High State officials.

The 1999 Constitution in a very repetitive way is full of provisions establishing the "participatory democracy" and the citizens right to participate; and in some cases it has even directly regulated one of such means, as is the case of the right assigned to civil society to participate in a public decision making process for the appointment of High State non elected officials. For such purpose, as aforementioned, the Constitution established the existence of a few "Nominating Committees" that must be exclusively conformed by "representatives of the different sectors of the society," with the attribution to propose candidates before the National Assembly for the appointment of the Magistrates of the Supreme Court of Justice, the Prosecutor General of the Republic, the General Comptroller of the Republic, the Peoples' Defendant, and the members of the National Electoral Council. That is, according to the constitutional provisions, the National Assembly can only appoint candidates nominated by such Committees, which must only be integrated by representatives of the various sectors of society. Nonetheless, in the political and legislative practice, said participation has not been assured, because the National Assembly has practically kept the same discretional power that the old National Congress had.

---

231 This situation has been recently summarized by Teodoro Petkoff, editor and founder of *Tal Cual*, one of the important newspapers in Caracas, as follows: "Chavez controls all the political powers. More than 90% of the Parliament obeys his commands; the Venezuelan Supreme Court, whose numbers were raised from 20 to 32 by the parliament to ensure an overwhelming officialist majority, has become an extension of the legal office of the Presidency... The Prosecutor General's Office, the Comptroller's Office and the Public Defender are all offices held by "yes persons", absolutely obedient to the orders of the autocrat. In the National Electoral Council, four of five members are identified with the government. The Venezuelan Armed Forces are tightly controlled by Chávez. Therefore, from a conceptual point of view, the Venezuelan political system is autocratic. All political power is concentrated in the hands of the President. There is no real separation of Powers. See Teodoro Petkoff, "Election and Political Power. Challenges for the Opposition", in *ReVista. Harvard Review of Latin America*, David Rockefeller Center for Latin American Studies, Harvard University, Fall 2008, pp. 12. See Allan R. Brewer-Carías, "Los problemas de la gobernabilidad democrática en Venezuela: el autoritarismo constitucional y la concentración y centralización del poder", in Diego Valadés (Coord.), *Gobernabilidad y constitucionalismo en América Latina*, Universidad Nacional Autónoma de México, México 2005, pp. 73-96.

232 To the point that in 2001, when he approved more than 48 Decree laws, via delegate legislation, which the Supreme Tribunal refused to scrutinize, the President of the Republic said: "The law is me. The State is me." "*La ley soy yo. El Estado soy yo*". See in *El Universal*, Caracas 4–12–01, pp. 1,1 and 2,1.

The Constitution conceives the "Judicial Nominating Committee" (article 270), as a counseling organization of the Judiciary for the selection of candidates to be appointed Magistrates of the Supreme Tribunal of Justice (article 264), which must be "formed by representatives of the different sectors of the society, in accordance to what is established by the law," providing for the direct participation of the "diverse sectors of the society" in a public decision-making process. However, after enacting a Special Law in 2002 without complying with the constitutional provision, in the 2004 Organic Law of the Supreme Tribunal of Justice of 2004[233], the Judicial Nominating Committee, instead of being formed solely and exclusively "by representatives of the diverse sectors of the society" as demanded by the Constitution, was formed by "eleven (11) principal members, five (5) of them to be elected from within the representatives of the National Assembly, and the other six (6) members, from sectors of the society, elected by the Assembly in a public proceeding" (Article 13,2). In fact, the result has been the creation of an "amplified" Parliamentary Commission of the National Assembly (Article 13), half integrated by its members (representatives), even though by essence, representatives cannot be considered representatives of the "civil society."

Also, in the case of the Electoral Power, in order to guarantee the autonomy of the National Electoral Council, the Constitution limited the discretional power that the previous Congress has had for the appointment of its holders, regulating also an "Electoral Nominating Committee" formed by representatives of the different sectors of the society. However, in the 2002 Organic Law of the Electoral Power[234], regardless of the constitutional provisions, the integration of the Electoral Nominating Committee with representatives from the different sectors of the society was not respected; establishing instead another "amplified" Parliamentary Commission with that same name, integrated by twenty one (21) members, from which eleven (11) arc representatives before the National Assembly, and ten (10) from sectors of society" appointed by the same Assembly. With this regulation, the right to political participation of the different sectors of the civil society that have the exclusive right to conform the Nominating Committee has also been confiscated[235].

The same has occurred regarding the nomination and appointment of the High officials of the Citizens Power, by means of the Organic Law of the Citizens Power

---

233 See in *Official Gazette* N° 37.942 de 05-20-2004. See the comments on the matter in Allan R. Brewer-Carías, *Ley Orgánica del Tribunal Supremo de Justicia. Procesos y procedimientos constitucionales y contencioso-administrativos*, Editorial Jurídica Venezolana, Caracas, 2004. The Organic Law was reformed in 2010, without changing these provisions. See in *Official Gazette* N° 5.991 Extra. of 07-29-2010, and N° 39.483 de 08-09-2010. See the comments in Allan R. Brewer-Carías y Víctor Hernández Mendible, *Ley Orgánica del Tribunal Supremo de Justicia*, Editorial Jurídica Venezolana, Caracas 2010.

234 See *Official Gazette* N° 37.573 dated 11-19-2002.

235 See the comments on the matter in Allan R. Brewer-Carías, *La Sala Constitucional versus el Estado democrático de derecho. El secuestro del poder electoral y de la Sala Electoral del Tribunal Supremo y la confiscación del derecho a la participación política*, Los Libros de El Nacional, Colección Ares, Caracas 2004.

of 2004, resulting also in the conformation of the Nominating Committee as a parliamentary Commission bypassing the exclusive right of the sectors of society to conform them. [236]

In this way, the constitutional mechanism created to guarantee the possibility of a direct participation of citizens, through representatives of the various sectors of society, in the process of selection and nomination of high non elected public officers of the State, was completely distorted by the National Assembly.

With the distortion of the Nominating Committees in a way contrary to the Constituent, the diverse branches of government have become more dependant regarding the political power, giving way in the constitutional order to a concentrated system of powers that is contrary to the proclaimed principles of autonomy and independence which were derived to form the penta division of the branches of government. Through legislative practice and the omission of the Supreme Tribunal to exercise judicial review over the unconstitutional statutes, a very important constitutional innovation, unique in the world, has been left on paper. With this, unfortunately, the constitutionally guaranteed political participation of the citizens has also been left on paper and has been deceived by those who control power from Parliament.

4. The contradictory centralized federal State, the abandonment of the decentralization policies and the illusion of political participation

But regarding the other constitutional principle established in order to limit State power by its vertical or territorial distribution, tending to frame a "decentralized Federal State" as it is defined in article 4 of the Constitution, and to convert decentralization into a national policy in order to allow political participation as is also defined in article 158, again, it has been in the Constitution itself, that some contradictory provisions were inserted, originating, in a contrary sense, a "Centralized federation"[237].

Federalism, as aforementioned, is a decentralized form of government based on an effective distribution of powers within the various territorial levels of the State. It is true that the Constitution enumerates the competencies attributed in an exclusive way to the national (Article 156), state (Article 154), and municipal (Article 178) levels of government, but reserving almost all to the national and municipal levels, with just a very few attributed to the States. On the other hand, State Legislative Councils can enact legislation on matters that are in the States' scope of powers

---

236 See Allan R. Brewer-Carías, "Sobre el nombramiento irregular por la Asamblea Nacional de los titulares de los órganos del poder ciudadano en 2007", in Revista de Derecho Público, N° 113, Editorial Jurídica Venezolana, Caracas 2008, pp. 85-88

237 See Allan R. Brewer-Carías, Federalismo y Municipalismo en la Constitución de 1999 (Alcance de una reforma insuficiente y regresiva), Editorial Jurídica Venezolana, Caracas-San Cristóbal 2001; Allan R. Brewer-Carías, "La 'Federación Descentralizada' en el marco de la centralización de la Federación en Venezuela. Situación y perspectivas de una contradicción constitucional", in Allan R. Brewer-Carías, Constitución, Democracia y Control el Poder, Centro Iberoamericano de Estudios Provinciales y Locales, Universidad de los Andes, Mérida 2004, pp. 111-143.

(Article 162), but being almost all of them concurrent matters, according to the same Constitution their exercise depends on the previous enactment of national general statutes, being the possibility for states to regulate them very small.

In terms of residual powers, the principle of favoring the states as in all federations, that was a constitutional tradition in Venezuela, has also been limited in the 1999 Constitution by expressly assigning the national level of government a parallel and prevalent residual taxation power in matters not expressly attributed to the states or municipalities (Article 156.12).

In the Venezuelan federation, the Senate, and the bicameral nature of the legislature, was eliminated (article 159), resulting in a rare federal state without a federal chamber or Senate, where the States, through its representatives, have no way to be equals in the sense of equal vote. In the National Assembly there are no representatives of the States, and its members are global representatives of the citizens and of all the States collectively.

On the other hand, except on matters of official stationery and revenue stamps (Article 164.7), no taxation power has been given to the states, and virtually everything in the 1999 Constitution concerning the taxation system is more centralized. Lacking their own resources from taxation, state financing is accomplished by the transfer of national financial resources through three different channels, which are all politically controlled by the national government.

The States, according to the federal Constitution, have the power to enact their own sub nationals Constitution, mainly for the organization of their branches of government (article 162); but this power has been seriously limited by the 1999 Constitution, which empowers the National Assembly to enact national statutes on the matter, in a manifestation of centralism never before envisioned. In particular, the National Assembly had sanctioned an Organic Law for the State Legislative Councils (2001) in which detailed regulations have been established on their organization and functioning, provoking the voiding of the State's Constitutions on the matter. Additionally, the possibility of organizing the Executive branch of each state's government is also being limited by the 1999 Constitution, which has established the basic rules concerning the Governors as head of the executive branch, as well as for all public administration. And even the National Assembly has sanctioned a Law on the appointment of the States' Controller (2001), limiting the powers of the State Legislative Councils without constitutional authorization.[238]

On the other hand, the scarce exclusive attributions of powers to the States have been "nationalized" by means of constitutional interpretation, as has happened with their exclusive power to administer national highways, ports and airports that the Constitutional Chamber in 2008 has changed into a concurrent attribution subjected to federal rule.[239]

---

238 See Allan R. Brewer-Carías, *Derecho administrativo*, Vol II, Universidad Externado de Colombia, Bogotá 2005, pp. 197 ff.

239 See decision of the Constitutional Chamber N° 565 of April 15, 2008 (Case *Procuradora General de la República, recurso de interpretación del artículo 164.10 de la Constitución de*

This contradictory process of State centralization[240] has made participatory democracy an illusion, particularly because it cannot be reduced to direct democracy mechanisms. To participate means to be part of, to appertain to, to be associated with, which in fact, is only possible for the citizen when political power is decentralized and thus, close to them. So participative democracy, beside elections, is only possible when effective decentralization of power exists, which explains why only democracies can be decentralized[241], and why authoritarian regimes can never be installed in effective decentralized States. Only with local governments established throughout the territory of a country can democracy be part of everyday life.[242]

In particular, regarding the local governments (Municipalities), even though considered in the Constitution as the primary political unit (article 168), in practice and in the constitutional text they continue to be very far from the citizens' reach, impeding any kind of real political participation. In fact, what has been created under the 1999 Constitution is a centralized and anti-participatory democratic system, in which the instruments for direct democracy have been deliberately confused with effective political participation. That is why local governments are gradually being bypassed by newly created councils and citizens assembly, within a statutory framework of "popular power" all directed from the center by means of a Presidential Commission for the Popular Power, creating the idea that the people are "participating".

For this purpose, the project to transform the Constitutional State into a "Communal State based on the "Popular Power" was the object of a constitutional review proposal[243] which after being approved by the national Assembly was eventually

---

1999) in http://www.tsj.gov.ve/decisiones/scon/Abril/565-150408-07-1108.htm. See Allan R. Brewer-Carías, "La Sala Constitucional como poder constituyente: la modificación de la forma federal del estado y del sistema constitucional de división territorial del poder público, en *Revista de Derecho Público*, N° 114, (abril-junio 2008), Editorial Jurídica Venezolana, Caracas 2008, pp. 247-262

240   See in general on this process, Allan R. Brewer-Carías and Jan Kleinheisterkamp, "Unification of Laws in Federal Systems. National Report on Venezuela," in Daniel Halberstam, Mathias Reimann AND Jorge A. Sánchez Cordero (Editors), *Federalism and Legal Unification: A Comparative Empirical Investigation of Twenty Systems*, International Academy of Comparative law, Instituto de Investigaciones Jurídicas, Universidad Nacional Autónoma de México, México 2012, pp. 378-391.

241   See Allan R. Brewer-Carías, "Democracia municipal, descentralización y desarrollo local", en *Revista Iberoamericana de Administración Pública*, N° 11, Ministerio de Administraciones Públicas. Madrid, Julio Diciembre 2003, pp.11-34.

242   See Allan R. Brewer-Carías, "Democratización, descentralización política y reforma del Estado" and "El Municipio, la descentralización política y la democracia", in Allan R. Brewer-Carías, *Reflexiones sobre el constitucionalismo en América*, Editorial Jurídica Venezolana, Caracas 2001, pp. 105-141 and 243-253.

243   See on the 2007 constitutional reforms proposals, Allan R. Brewer-Carías, *Hacia la consolidación de un Estado socialista, centralizado, policial y militarista. Comentarios sobre el sentido y alcance de las propuestas de reforma constitucional 2007*, Editorial Jurídica Venezolana, Caracas 2007; *La reforma constitucional de 2007 (Comentarios al proyecto inconsti-*

rejected by the people in a referendum held in December of 2007. The draft was intended to radically transform the most essential and fundamental aspects of the state,[244] being one of the most important reforms proposals in all of Venezuelan constitutional history. With it, the decentralized, democratic, pluralistic, and social state built and consolidated since the Second World War, would have been radically changed to create instead a socialist, centralized, repressive, and militaristic state grounded in the so-called "Bolivarian doctrine," identified with "21st century socialism" and a socialist economic system of State Capitalism. As mentioned, the constitutional reform draft was rejected by the people in December 2012,[245] which did not prevent the President of the Republic and the National Assembly to implement the draft through ordinary and delegate legislation, violating the Constitution.

Thus in disdain of the popular will the National Assembly to proceed in 2010 to sanction a set of organic laws through which it finished defining the legislative framework for a new State, different to the Constitutional State,[246] regulating a socialist, centralized, military and police State, called the "Communal State" or the State of "Popular Power." The organic laws that were approved on December 21, 2010 are the laws on the Popular Power; the Communes; the Communal Economic System; the Public and Communal Planning; and the Social Comptrollership.[247] Furthermore, in the same framework of organizing the Communal State[248] based on

tucionalmente sancionado por la Asamblea Nacional el 2 de noviembre de 2007), Editorial Jurídica Venezolana, Caracas 2007

244 See Rogelio Pérez Perdomo, "La Constitución de papel y su reforma," in *Revista de Derecho Público* 112 *(Estudios sobre la reforma constitucional)*, Editorial Jurídica Venezolana, Caracas 2007, p. 14; G. Fernández, "Aspectos esenciales de la modificación constitucional propuesta por el Presidente de la República. La modificación constitucional como un fraude a la democracia," *Id*, p. 22; Alfredo Arismendi, "Utopía Constitucional," in *id.*, p. 31; Manuel Rachadell, "El personalismo político en el Siglo XXI," in *id.*, p. 66; Allan R. Brewer-Carías, "El sello socialista que se pretendía imponer al Estado," in *id.*, p. 71-75; Alfredo Morles Hernández, "El nuevo modelo económico para el Socialismo del Siglo XXI," in *id.*, p. 233-36.

245 See Allan R. Brewer-Carías, "La proyectada reforma constitucional de 2007, rechazada por el poder constituyente originario", in *Anuario de Derecho Público 2007,* Año 1, Instituto de Estudios de Derecho Público de la Universidad Monteávila, Caracas 2008, pp. 17-65.

246 See Allan R. Brewer-Carías, "The Process of De-Constitutionalization of the Venezuelan State." Presentation at the Inter-American Bar Association, D.C. Chapter's Luncheon Series, held at Georgetown University Law Center . Washington, D.C. September 21, 2012, available   at   http://www.allanbrewercarias.com/Content/449725d9-f1cb-474b-8ab2-41efb849fea2/Content/I,%201,%201053,%20THE%20DECONSTITUCIONALIZATION%20OF%20THE%20VENEZUELAN%20STATE.%20FIA,%20Washington,%20September%202012.doc.pdf

247 See *Gaceta Oficial* N° 6.011 Extra. 12-21-2010.The Constitutional chamber through decision N° 1329 12-16-2009, among others, declared the constitutionality of the organic character of these Laws. See http://www.tsj.gov.ve/decisiones/scon/Diciembre/%201328-161210-2010-10-1437.html

248 See on all these organic laws, Allan R. Brewer-Carías *et al.*, *Leyes Orgánicas sobre el Poder Popular y el Estado Comunal*, Editorial Jurídica Venezolana, Caracas 2011, pp. 361 ff.

the Popular Power, the reform of the Organic Law of Municipal Public Power, the Public Policy Planning and Coordination of the State Councils[249] and of the Local Council Public Planning Laws stand out.

The main purpose of these laws is the organization of the "Communal State" which has the commune as its fundamental unit, supplanting in an unconstitutional way the municipalities as the "primary political units of the national organization" (Art. 168 of the Constitution) The exercise of Popular Power is made through the Communes, as expression of the exercise of popular sovereignty although not through representatives. It is therefore a political system in which representative democracy is ignored, openly violating the Constitution,[250] based on the functioning of Communal Councils with non elected "spokespersons", appointed by "Citizens Assemblies" directly controlled by the National Executive.

In any event, what is certain is that the goal of participation cannot be achieved without decentralization and elected political entities at the local level, and only by inserting instruments of direct democracy in a representative democratic framework, or by financing community actions controlled by the national Executive power.

Referendums can be useful instruments in order to perfect democracy, but by themselves cannot satisfy the aim of participation. This can be understood by studying the 2002-2004 process concerning the Venezuelan presidential recall referendum, which was converted into a presidential "ratification" referendum of a plebiscitary nature[251]. A recall referendum is a vote asking the people if the mandate of an elected official must be revoked or not; it is not a vote asking if the elected official must remain or not in office. But in the 2004 recall referendum, the National Electoral Council, when giving the voting results, converted it into a plebiscite ratifying the President.

The result of the implementation of the 1999 Constitution is that the Venezuelan democracy, from being a centralized representative democracy of more or less competitive and pluralist parties which alternated in government (1958-1998), since 2000 has been transformed into a centralized plebiscite democracy, in which effectively all power is in only one hand, that of the President of the Republic, supported by politically partisan votes of the National Assembly and the military, very close to a one-party system.

---

249 See *Gaceta Oficial* N° 6.015 Extra. 12-28-2010.

250 See Allan R. Brewer-Carías, "El inicio de la desmunicipalización en Venezuela: La organización del poder popular para eliminar la descentralización, la democracia representativa y la participación a nivel local," in *AIDA, Revista de la Asociación Internacional de Derecho Administrativo,* Universidad Nacional Autónoma de México, Asociación Internacional de Derecho Administrativo, Mexico City 2007, 49-67

251 See Allan R. Brewer-Carías, "El secuestro del Poder Electoral y de la Sala Electoral del Tribunal Supremo y la confiscación del derecho a la participación política mediante el referendo revocatorio presidencial: Venezuela: 2000-2004" in *Revista Costarricense de Derecho Constitucional,* Tomo V, Instituto Costarricense de Derecho Constitucional, Editorial Investigaciones Jurídicas S.A. San José, Costa Rica 2004. pp. 167-312; and in *Revista Jurídica del Perú,* Año LIV, n° 55, marzo-abril. Lima 2004. pp. 353-396

This plebiscite democracy system has created a popular participation illusion, particularly by means of the uncontrolled distribution of state oil income among the poor through governmental social programs that are not precisely tailored to the promotion of investment and to create employment. This plebiscite democracy, without doubt, is less representative and less participatory than the traditional representative party democracy, which, notwithstanding all the warnings[252] that were raised, the traditional parties failed to preserve. All this is unfortunately contributing to the disappearance of democracy itself as a political regime, which is much more than only elections and referenda, as has been made clear by the 2001 Inter American Democratic Charter.

5.   The contradictory State intervention in the internal life of civil society entities

But in some cases, the incongruence between constitutional provisions is not the product of judicial rulings or of political application of the Constitution, but of some norms of the Constitution. In this sense, the 1999 Constitution, contrary to all the participative phraseology it contains, can be considered as an interventionist and limiting text regarding the organizations of civil society itself by establishing the jurisdiction of the National Electoral Council for "the organization of the elections of trade unions, professional associations and organizations with political objectives" and in general, to guarantee "the equality, reliability, impartiality, transparency and efficiency of the electoral processes..." (Article 293.6).

According to this provision, it is the Constitution that sets forth that the internal elections that can take place within the political parties, the trade union and professionals associations of any kind, in a compulsory way must be organized by the State through one of the branches of governments (Electoral power), which constitutes an open contradiction with the participatory feature attributed to the Constitution and with its declared goal to promote citizens participation.

Consequently, all the internal electoral processes within the political parties in Venezuela from 2000 on must have been organized by the National Electoral Council; which in fact has not always occurred due to the progressive configuration of the political arena in the country as a one party prevalent one.

On the other hand, the State intervention has been active regarding civil society organizations. For instance, even though the trade unions are considered as not being

---

252   See regarding this author's wittings, Allan R. Brewer-Carías, *El Estado. Crisis y reforma*, Academia de Ciencias Políticas y Sociales, Caracas 1982; and *Problemas del Estado de partidos*, Editorial Jurídica Venezolana, Caracas 1988; Allan R. Brewer-Carías, "La crisis de las instituciones: responsables y salidas" (Cátedra Pío Tamayo, Centro de Estudios de Historia Actual, Facultad de Economía y Ciencias Sociales, Universidad Central de Venezuela, Caracas 1985), published in *Revista del Centro de Estudios Superiores de las Fuerzas Armadas de Cooperación*, N° 11, Caracas 1985, pp. 57-83; and in *Revista de la Facultad de Ciencias Jurídicas y Políticas*, N° 64, Universidad Central de Venezuela, Caracas 1985, pp. 129-155. Also see Allan R. Brewer-Carías, *Instituciones Políticas y Constitucionales*, Vol I, *Evolución histórica del Estado*, Universidad Católica del Táchira, Editorial Jurídica Venezolana, San Cristóbal-Caracas, 1996, pp. 523-541.

"inside the structure of the Venezuelan public organization"[253], the Electoral Chamber of the Supreme Court, in a decision N° 46 dated March 11, 2002, has justified such anomalous State intervention and supervision regarding social organizations, arguing that it tends:

> "To guarantee [internal] democracy in said organizations through the transparency and celerity of their electoral processes and the selection of the legitimate authorities that are called to represent the interests and rights of those affiliated in the negotiations and collective conflicts of labor; in the procedures of conciliation and arbitrage; in the promotion, negotiation, celebration, revision and modification of collective labor conventions, and in everything necessary for the guarantee of the patrimony and the interests of the trade union organization"[254].

On the other hand, regarding other civil associations of individuals or corporations, based on the same constitutional provision, the Electoral Chamber of the Supreme Tribunal of Justice has decided in many cases to participate in their internal functioning, as has happened for instance regarding neighborhood associations. In a decision N° 61 dated May 29, 2001, the Constitutional Chamber considered that the matter was about organizations "that the constitutional text, itself, refers to as 'civil society', being able to request, from the National Electoral Council, its intervention in order to organize their internal elections."[255] It has also happened even regarding social clubs or recreational associations, as it has been determined in a decision dated November 1, 2000, in which the Electoral Chamber, once it was informed about the filing of an action for protection (*amparo*), ruled against the electoral regulations issued by the Electoral Commission of a social club, considering that the club even though being an association "that the constitutional text itself refers to as forming part of "civil society", with authority to be freely constituted by its members, providing for their own organization, being nonetheless able to "request the intervention of the National Electoral Council for the organization of their internal elections"[256].

As for other civil associations, like those referred to businesses and businessmen of industrial or commercial character, constituted as Boards (*Cámaras*), the Electoral Chamber of the Supreme Tribunal, in decision N° 18, dated February 15, 2001, considered that a civil association called *"Cámara de Comercios e Industrias del Estado Aragua"* in virtue of its objectives to "encourage for the economical development and the social progress of the region, providing the collective effort of the sectors that form it", as well as "the defense and the strengthening of the free initia-

---

253 See in *Revista de Derecho Público*, N° 84, Editorial Jurídica Venezolana, Caracas, 2000, pp. 132 ff.

254 See in *Revista de Derecho Público*, N° 89-92, Editorial Jurídica Venezolana, Caracas, 2000, pp. 148-149.

255 See Exp. 000064, Case: *Asociación de Residentes de la Urbanización La Trinidad*. See the reference in Allan R. Brewer-Carías, *Derecho Administrativo*, Vol. I, Universidad Externado de Colombia, Bogotá 2005, pp. 413 ff.

256 See Exp. 0115, Case: *Asociación Civil Club Campestre Paracotos*. See the reference in Allan R. Brewer-Carías, *Derecho Administrativo*, Vol. I, Universidad Externado de Colombia, Bogotá 2005, pp. 413 ff.

tive and the freedom of the enterprise", constitutes an indirect participative mechanism – both economically and socially – of a sector of the people (industrials and commercials) in the national society life; thus " even if the referred civil association is of a private character, its objectives transcend to the core particular interest". For that reason, the Chamber considered that it was "justified to include it as one of the organizations of the "civil society" implicitly stated in article 293.6 of the Constitution", a reason for which it declared its jurisdiction to resolve on the challenging of the election held in the association "independently of the nature of the entity from which these proceed"[257].

But in other more emblematic cases, the Electoral Chamber has admitted the obligatory intervention of the National Electoral Council in the electoral processes of civil associations like those of university professors, as it has occurred regarding internal elections in the professors' association of the Universidad Central de Venezuela. Regarding these associations, the Electoral Chamber ruled in a decision N° 51 dated May 19, 2000, that article 293.6 refers to those "groups of people that in their condition of professionals, unite to defend their common interests and to achieve improvements also of common character, independently from the fact that their conformation is not done by expressed disposition of a statute, but by common agreement from its members, under a form of private right". Within these, the Electoral Chamber precisely included the associations established inside the Universities, formed by the professionals of diverse disciplines or knowledge areas that are part of the institution in their condition of professors, teachers or instructors, imposing on them the intervention of the State to organize their internal electoral processes[258].

6.   *The dangerous expansion of the Security and defense values*

The 1999 Constitution made substantial departures from the provisions of the 1961 Constitution regarding the National Security and Defense system and the Military. The latter Constitution contained only three provisions on the subject: Article 133, establishing restrictions regarding the possession of arms; Article 131, prohibiting the simultaneous exercise of civilian and military authority by any public official other than the President of the Republic as Commander in Chief of the Armed Forces; and, Article 132, referring to the general regulation of the Armed Forces.

In the 1999 Constitution, on the contrary, a marked militarist shape was given to the State with board provisions regarding not only the Military but the security and defense system, without precedent in Venezuelan constitutionalism.

---

257 See Exp. 000017, Case: *Cámara de Comercios e Industrias del Estado Aragua*. This jurisprudence was ratified by the same Chamber according to verdict N° 162, Exp. 2002-000077 dated 10-17-02 (Case: Cámara de Comercio e Industrias del Estado Bolívar). See the reference in Allan R. Brewer-Carías, *Derecho Administrativo*, Vol. I, Universidad Externado de Colombia, Bogotá 2005, pp. 413 ff.

258 See Case: *Asociación de Profesores de la Universidad Central de Venezuela*, in *Revista de Derecho Público*, N° 82, Editorial Jurídica Venezolana, Caracas, 2000, pp. 92 ff.

Article 322 of the Constitution of 1999 begins by stating that the security of the Nation falls within the essential competence and responsibility of the State, founded upon the State's "integral development;" the defense of the State being the responsibility of Venezuelans, and of all natural and legal persons, whether of public or private law, founded within the geographic territory of the State.

In addition, Article 326 sets forth the general principles of National Security declaring that its preservation in "economic, social, political, cultural, geographic, environmental and military areas," mutually corresponds ("co-responsibility") *to* the State and to Civil Society, in order to fulfill the principles of "independence, democracy, equality, peace, liberty, justice, solidarity, promotion and conservation of the environment, the affirmation of human rights, and, the progressive satisfaction of the individual and collective needs of Venezuelans on the basis of sustainable and productive development fully covering the national community." All of these principles are also those enumerated in the opening Articles 1, 2, and 3 of the Constitution of 1999. For the purposes of implementing these principles of National security in the country's territorial border regions, Article 327 provides for the establishment of a special regime.

Also for such purposes, the Constitution created a new council, the "National Council of Defense" (Article 323), as the nation's highest authority for defense planning, advice, and consultation to the State (Public Powers) on all matters related to the defense and security of the Nation's sovereignty, territorial integrity, and strategic thinking. This Council is presided over by the President of the Republic, and integrated by the Executive Vice President, the President of the National Assembly, the President of Supreme Tribunal of Justice, the President of the Moral Republican Council (Citizen Branch of government, Article 237), the Ministers of the defense sectors: interior security, foreign relations, and planning, and others whose participation is considered pertinent.

According to the Constitution, the traditional National Armed Forces (which is comprised of the Army, the Navy, the Air Force, and the National Guard) have become integrated into a single institution, named the "National Armed Force," which nonetheless, according to Article 328, is comprised of the Army, the Navy, the Air Force, and the National Guard, each working within its area of competence to fulfill its mission, and with its own system of social security, as established by its respective organic legislation.

It must be mentioned that the 2007 constitutional reform project that was rejected by popular referendum, the proposal of the President of the Republic was to change the name of the National Armed Force to the "Bolivarian Armed Force," to create a "Bolivarian Military Doctrine," to create the "Bolivarian Popular Militia," as a new component of the Armed Force, and to eliminate the character of the Armed Force as an "essential professional institution, without political militancy", converting it into "an essentially patriotic, popular and anti-imperialist corp." As mentioned, the people, through referendum rejected all such Constitutional Reforms, but nonetheless, the President of the Republic approved them all, six months after the popular rejection, in July 2008, through delegate legislation.[259]

According to Article 329, the Army, Navy, Air Force, and National Guard each has essential responsibilities for planning, execution and control of military operations necessary to ensure the defense of the Nation. The National Guard, however, only has a cooperative role in these functions and basic responsibility to carry out operations necessary for the maintenance of internal order in the country. The Constitution also establishes that the National Armed Forces can carry out police administrative activities and criminal investigation as authorized by law.

Article 328 defines the character of the Armed Forces as an essentially professional institution, without a militant political function, organized by the State to guarantee the independence and sovereignty of the Nation, and to ensure the integrity of the Nation's geographic space by means of military defense and cooperation in the maintenance of internal order, as well as active participation in national development. According to the wording of this Article, in order to fulfill these functions, the Armed Force is at the exclusive service of the Nation and in no case may be at the service of any particular person or political partiality. The foundations of the Armed Forces are discipline, obedience and subordination.

Nonetheless, the 1999 Constitution failed to provide for the "apolitical and nondeliberative" character of the Armed Force that was established in Article 132 of the Constitution of 1961; and it has no provision establishing the essential obligation of the Armed Force to ensure "the stability of the democratic institutions" and to "respect the Constitution and laws, the adherence of which is above any other obligation," as was declared in Article 132 of the 1961 Constitution. What the 1999 Constitution was innovative on these matters was in giving the military the right to vote (Article 325).

In addition, the Constitution established the general regime applicable to military promotions, providing that they are to be based on merit, seniority and the availability of vacancies, and are the exclusively competence of the National Armed Forces (Article 331). Consequently, the traditional intervention of the Legislature to approve the promotions of high ranking military officials (Article 150.5, 1961 Constitution) was eliminated.

All these constitutional provisions configure a normative framework of a militarist structure, which when combined with the centralization tendency of State Power and the concentration of State power in the President of the Republic by his control over the National Assembly, the result is a system that unfortunately has led to authoritarianism. In particular, in the 1999 Constitution's provisions on military matters, the idea of the subjection or subordination of military authority to civilian authority has disappeared; and instead what has been consecrated is a greater autonomy of the National Armed Forces, whose four branches (and since 2008, five branches) have been unified into one institution with the possibility of intervention

---

259 See Organic Law on the Bolivarian Armed Force, *Gaceta Oficial* N° 5.891 Extra. of July 31, 2008.

in civilian functions. This militaristic tendency is evidenced by the following constitutional rules, as already indicated: *first,* the elimination of the traditional prohibition that military and civilian authority be exercised simultaneously, as was established by Article 131 of the 1961 Constitution; *second*, the elimination of control by the National Assembly of military promotions in the top brass, as provided in Article 331 of the 1961 Constitution and throughout the country's traditional constitutionalism; *third,* the elimination of the constitutionally "non-deliberative and apolitical" character of the military institution, as established in Article 132 of the 1961 Constitution, which has opened the way for the Armed Force, as a military institution, to deliberate politically, intervene, and give its opinion on matters under resolution within the civil organs of the State; *fourth,* the elimination of the obligation of the Armed Force to ensure the stability of democratic institutions required by Article 132 of the 1961 Constitution; *fifth,* the elimination of the obligation of the Armed Force to respect the Constitution and laws "the adherence to which will always be above any other obligation" as was set forth in Article 132 of the 1961 Constitution; *sixth,* the express right of suffrage granted to members of the military in Article 330 of the 1999 Constitution, which in many cases has been politically incompatible with the principle of obedience; *seventh,* the submission of authority over the use of all weapons, for war or otherwise, to the Armed Force, while removing this authority from the civil Administration of the State (Article 324); *eighth,* the general attribution of police administrative functions to the Armed Force (Article 329); *ninth,* the establishment of procedural privilege for generals and admirals in the sense that in order for them to be tried, the Supreme Tribunal of Justice must declare in advance of trial whether or not the proceeding has merit (Article 266,3); and *tenth*, the adoption in the Constitution of the concept of the "doctrine of national security," as a global, totalistic, and Omni-comprehensive doctrine in the sense that everything that happens in the State and in the Nation concerns the security of the State, including economic and social development (Article 326); with the duty for the Armed Force to have an "active participation in national development" (Article 328). All these provisions set forth a picture of militarism, unique in Venezuelan constitutional history, not even found in former military regimes.

FINAL REMARKS

As aforementioned, the Venezuelan 1999 Constitution is one of those that in the contemporary world have incorporated in its text a very enumerative, express and extensive list of constitutional values and principles defined as goals intending to guide the conduct and activities of the State, the Society and the individuals.

Thus, those global values and principles do not derive from the process of interpretation and application of the Constitution particularly by the courts, but from what it is expressly established in the text of the Constitution.

Undoubtedly, by means of constitutional interpretation mainly through the Constitutional Chamber of the Supreme Tribunal Court decisions issued as Constitutional Jurisdiction, the sense, the scope and the priority character of many of the constitutional principles and values have been defined and enriched, even by giving some of them a prioritization regarding others; but unfortunately, in other cases, they have been distorted by political legislative practice and even by court decisions,[260] originating some constitutional incongruence between what is said in the Constitution and what has been decided in the political practice of government.

---

260 See Allan R. Brewer-Carías, *La patología de la justicia constitucional*, Investigaciones Jurídicas, San José, Costa Rica 2012.

PART TWO
THE 1999 CONSTITUTION AND THE AUTHORITARIAN GOVERNMENT

CHAPTER VI

THE ENDLESS TRANSITIONAL CONSTITUTIONAL
REGIME, NOT APPROVED BY THE PEOPLE, PREVENTING
THE INTEGRAL APPLICATION OF THE 1999 CONSTITUTION

(2002)

This essay was written between 2001 and 2002, analyzing the "Illegitimate Constitutional Transitory Regime adopted by the National Constituent Assembly after the popular approval of the new Constitution," provoking arbitrary decisions that violated the Constitution that were endorsed by the Supreme Tribunal of Justice, whose Magistrates were precisely appointed by such Transitory Regime. The initial version of these reflections were published in Spanish in my book *Golpe de Estado y Proceso Constituyente*, Universidad Nacional Autónoma de México, México 2002, pp. 341- 405; and also in my book *La Constitución de 1999, Derecho Constitucional Venezolano*, Vol. II, Caracas 2004, pp. 1.017-1.115.

I. FAILED EFFORTS TO CREATE A CONSTITUTIONAL FRAMEWORK FOR THE TRANSITION OF PUBLIC POWERS THROUGH AN APPROBATORY REFERENDUM

The 1999 Constitution was sanctioned by the National Constituent Assembly elected for such purpose in July 1999, containing just few transitory provisions as were sanctioned by the Assembly and approved by the people in the referendum held on December 15, 1999. The Constitution does not contain any provision regarding the then existing constituent powers, and the situation of the head officials of the branches of government, so the applicable principle was the continuation of the elected officials in 1998 up to the election of the new ones according to the provisions of the new Constitution.

The Constitution Draft sanctioned on November 1999, did not contain any such provision. That is why, on November 19, 1999, the same day that the Constitution draft was signed in order to be submitted to the approbatory referendum, the National Constituent Assembly approved a Decree also convening a parallel "consultative referendum" that was to take place on the very day set for the aforementioned, that is, December 15, 1999. The purpose of the proposed "consultative referendum" was for "the Venezuelan people to decide on the permanence (or not) of the President of the Republic, and of the governments of each of the 23 states, subject to popular election, in exercise of their functions"[1].

The underlying intention of this proposal was to convert the approbatory referendum of the Constitution into a sort of plebiscite on the permanence of the President of the Republic, Hugo Chávez Frías, distorting the significance of the popular approval of the Constitution. Nonetheless, in a very confusing way, a few days later, in its session of December 12, 1999, three days before the approbatory referendum was to be held, the Assembly revoked without any motives the proposed consultative plebiscite, basing the decision only in a supposed prior one of revocation adopted in "plenary session," which never took place[2]. The result was that a first effort to change the Transitory Provisions of the 1999 Constitution draft, which contained no clause whatsoever that addressed the termination of the terms of office of the elected heads of the branches of government, was frustrated. But this would be only for a short time[3].

After the new 1999 Constitution was approved in the referendum of December 15th, in the next ordinary session of the Assembly, held on December 20, 1999, the Constitution was formally proclaimed, technically meaning that the Assembly had accomplished its functions according to the basic rules (bases comiciales) adopted in the consultative referendum of April 25, 1999 that allowed the Assembly to function for six month (July-December 1999). But instead of ending its mission, the Constituent Assembly decided to extend its tenure and convened for its session of closure to be held on January 30 of 2000.[4] With the decree, the Assembly provided clear signs of its intention to continue exercising the "original" constituent power which it

---

1   *Gaceta Constituyente (Diario de Debates, Noviembre 1999-Enero 2000, cit.*, Sesión 19-11-99, N° 46, p. 3.

2   *Gaceta Constituyente (Diario de Debates) Noviembre 1999 -Enero 2000, cit.*, Sesión 09-12-99, N° 48, p. 5.

3   It should be emphasized that the constituent representative Hermán Escarrá Malavé, in the Assembly's session of November 15, 1999, distinguished the Transitory Provisions (*Disposiciones Transitorias*) from a supposed "Transitory Regimen" ("*Régimen Transitorio*"), which ought to have been approved by referendum and about which he asked not to be questioned. See, *Gaceta Constituyente (Diario de Debates), Noviembre 1999-Enero 2000, cit.*, Sesión de 15-11-99, N° 45, p. 9

4   *Gaceta Constituyente, Diario de Debates, Noviembre 1999-Enero 2000, cit.*, Sesión 20-12-99, N° 49, p. 6.

had bestowed upon itself, well beyond the terms of the new Constitution[5]. In order to set its Session of Closure, the Assembly departed from the consideration that supposedly the powers given to it "had been recognized by the Supreme Court of Justice, in a formal decision, as *original and supra-constitutional,*"[6] that is, even above the very new Constitution; and concluded announcing, ignoring the new Constitution, that it was "necessary to decree constitutional acts required for the transition to the new State foreseen in the Constitution approved by the people of Venezuela." The fact was that the latter was the only text that could establish a regimen for a "transition to the new State," but in its Transitional Provisions that the same National Constituent Assembly had itself drafted, nothing was addressed on this matter

The Assembly has, in a certain way, tricked the people: it sanctioned a Constitution and submitted it to popular approval without any provision for the termination of the term of the 1998 elected officials, and after the Constitution was approved and proclaimed, it decreed its violation announcing that it was going to remain, exercising "supra-constitutional powers" in order to dictate "constitutional acts" that were not authorized by the Transitional Provisions of the Constitution.

II. THE ILLEGITIMATE "REGIMEN FOR THE TRANSITION OF PUBLIC POWERS" DECREED AFTER THE POPULAR APPROVAL OF THE NEW CONSTITUTION

The first violation of the Constitution took place by the National Constituent Assembly, itself, in the days after December 15, 1999, precisely during the national commotion caused by massive flooding in the Central Coast of the country in the state of Vargas that occurred on that day, by means of sanctioning a Decree on the Regimen for the Transition of Public Powers ("Decree on Transition Regime") issued on December 22, 1999.[7] This occurred, just two days after the proclamation of the new Constitution, but before the Constitution's entry into effect with its publication, which was deliberately delayed until December 30, 1999.[8]

Through this Decree, given the absence of clauses in the Transitory Provisions of the new Constitution providing for the termination of the terms of the holders of titular offices of the State, or allowing the provisional appointment of new officials

---

5 See Lolymar Hernández Camargo, *La Teoría del Poder Constituyente. Un caso de estudio: el proceso constituyente venezolano de 1999,* UCAT, San Cristóbal, 2000, p. 76.

6 Decision of October 6, 1999, published on October 14, 1999 (*Case: Henrique Capriles, Decreto de regulación de funcionamiento del Poder Legislativo),* in which the Supreme Court of Justice ruled in an action filed by the President of the Representative Chamber of Congress, seeking to nullify the National Constituent Assembly Decree Regulating the Legislative Power, by attributing supra-constitutional rank to the provisions contained in the text approved in the referendum on April 25, 1999, for the election of the National Constituent Assembly, but not to its acts.

7 See the *Gaceta Oficial* N° 36.859 de 29-12-99.

8 See the *Gaceta Constituyente (Diario de Debates), Noviembre 1999-Enero 2000, cit.* Sesión de 22-12-9, N° 51, pp. 2 ff., Session of 22 December 1999, N° 51, p. 2 et seq.]; See *Gaceta Oficial* N° 36.859 de 29-12-99; and, *Gaceta Oficial* N° 36.860 de 30-12-99.

to replace them, in the context of sudden political eagerness to name new titular offices without waiting for the election of the new Legislature (National Assembly), on December 22, 1999 the National Constituent Assembly, without any constitutional authority sanctioned the aforementioned Decree. In it, and in order to "make the process of transition to the regimen established in the Constitution of 1999 effective" through the termination of the titular officers of the State, the Constitutional Assembly once again relied upon its supposed self-attributed powers as "original constituent," which it assumed in Article 1 of its Statute of Functioning, considering them with "supra-constitutional character."

This Decree, as was set forth in its Chapter I, had the objective of establishing a "regimen of transition" supposedly "allow the immediate going into effect of the Constitution" (article 1), which was not yet published. In fact nothing impeded the immediate effectiveness of the Constitution, as it was provided in its Transitory Provisions approved by the people. Nonetheless, the Constituent Assembly decided to "develop and complement the Transitory Provisions of the new Constitution" (art. 2), for which it had no authority. This was not authorized in the new Constitution that it had drafted and sanctioned, and even formally proclaimed two days before, on December 20, 1999.

This new Transitory Regime Decree, nonetheless, was in fact devoted to fill the vacuum that the Constituent Assembly had created itself, when failing to incorporate in the Transitory Provisions of the Constitution draft submitted to referendum approval, the regime for the transfer of power. The principle that then needed to be applied was the one assuring the continuity of government mentioned in Article 16 of the Decree. But instead, the Constituent Assembly simply usurped the authority of the original (the people) AND against to what was approved in the referendum of December 15, 1999, one week later, on December 22, 1999, through the aforementioned Decree, violated the basic text for its election approved by referendum on April 25, 1999, and gave a new coup d'Etat, this time against the new Constitution.

1. *The elimination of the Congress and the creation of a "National Legislative Commission" not provided for in the new Constitution approved by the people*

The National Constituent Assembly in its Transitory Regime Decree, decided first of all to definitively dissolve the former Congress (Article 4) and dismiss its elected (in 1989) senators and representatives. This decision adopted after the popular approval of the new Constitution violated the democratic principle, and created a constitutional vacuum which implied that until the election of a new Legislature (National Assembly), the Republic would had remained without a national legislative organ. For this reason, in order to "fill" the self-created vacuum, the Constituent Assembly made another decision, also without constitutional basis or authority, creating a new "National Legislative Commission" (or *"Congresillo"*) not provided for in the new Constitution as was approved by the people. By doing so, it attributed to this Commission, in an illegitimate way, the exercise of the Legislative Power, "until the representatives to the new National Assembly are elected and in office" (art.

5). The members of such *Congresillo,* were appointed by the National Constituent Assembly (art. 5), among partisans of the new power and members of the political parties that supported the government.[9] The National Legislative Commission functioned "in a permanent form" from the date of its installation on February 1, 2000 (art. 7), until the date of the effective installment of the new elected National Assembly" (art. 8), assuming all of "the rights and obligations" of the former Congress of the Republic (art. 9).

These decisions of the National Constituent Assembly violated the basic text adopted in the referendum of April 25, 1999 for its election. The decision to terminate the popular mandates of elected representatives in democratic elections, in order to constitute a new legislative organ, even temporarily, and moreover to assign legislative functions to not elected persons, violated the principle of representative democracy, the principle of the progressiveness of the political right to democratically participate and to have elections, and furthermore, violated international treaties requiring the Republic to ensure the effective exercise of representative democracy.[10] The result of all these decisions was the installment of a "National Legislative Commission," created by the Constituent Assembly, composed of non elected members, in open violation of the new Constitution.

One month later, on January 30, 2000, the National Constituent Assembly issued another Decree "Amplifying the Powers of the National Legislative Commission,"[11] assigning it a series of special powers to legislate upon various matters. The Assembly issued this Decree, again "in the exercise of the sovereign original constituent power," which later the new Constitutional Chamber of the Supreme Tribunal of Justice, considered as having "constitutional hierarchy."[12]

All these unconstitutional acts of the Constituent Assembly, violated the new Constitution, and were successively and unfortunately "laundered" by the new Supreme Tribunal, whose Magistrates had also been appointed by the same Constituent Assembly precisely in the same Transitory Regime. For such purpose, on the occasion of deciding the judicial review actions challenging an act of the Legislative Commission ("Resolution recommending the reincorporation to their jobs of labor leaders and workers unjustly and unconstitutionally dismissed in different regions of the country") of May 19, 2000 [13] in exercise of the powers conferred on it by the National Constituent Assembly through the above mentioned Amplifying Decree,

---

9   The Assembly, in January 28, 2000, again "in exercise of the original constituent power" that it had conferred upon itself, named additional members of the new National Legislative Commission. See *Gaceta Oficial* N° 36.903 of March 1, 2000.

10   Charter of the Organization of American States, OAS, and the American Convention on Human Rights, art. 23. See Allan R. Brewer-Carías, *Debate Constituyente,* Vol. I, *op. cit.,* p. 76 a 81.

11   *Gaceta Oficial* N° 36.884 of February 3, 2000

12   See Decision *N° 1454* of February 18, 2001 (*Case: C.A. Good Year de Venezuela).*

13   *Gaceta Oficial* N° 36.965 of June 5, 2000

the Constitutional Chamber of the Supreme Tribunal of Justice considered that such Resolution had constitutional rank."[14]

2. The dissolution of the Legislative Assemblies of the States and the creation of State Legislative Commissions not provided for in the new Constitution approved by the people

The National Constituent Assembly, in its Decree of December 22, 1999 also violated the new Constitution when it ordered the "dissolution of the Legislative Assemblies of the States" and the dismissal of the elected representatives (elected on 1989) who composed them (art. 11), for which it had no constitutional authority, due to the fact that this was not provided for in the Transitory Provisions of the Constitution approved by the people.

The National Constituent Assembly, in the same sense to what it decided regarding the National Legislative Power, on the states level it also created in each State a "State Legislative Commission," empowering the "Coordinating Commission of the National Constituent Assembly" and not to the Assembly itself for the appointment of their members (art. 12). This decision, not authorized in any constitutional or legal norm, also violated the abovementioned democratic guarantee, which was one of the limits established upon the Constituent Assembly.

On January 4, 2000, the Coordinating Commission of the National Constituent Assembly, supposedly "in accordance with powers conferred to it by the Assembly in its session of December 22, 1999" (powers that were not identified), resolved to institute a "Regimen for the Creation of Legislative Commissions of the States," [15] for which purpose it created a "National Nominating Commission" in order to select candidates for the Legislative Commissions, and also conferred powers upon the "Legislative Commissions of the States." This was not even authorized by the "Regimen of Transition of the Public Powers," so the Coordinating Commission of the National Constituent Assembly in this case, "usurped" the powers of constitutional regulation that the National Assembly had self-attributed.

---

14   The Constitutional Chamber ruled the following: "Because the then Supreme Court of Justice, in plenary session, on the 14th of October of 1999, ruled that the basic text (*bases comiciales*) submitted to the Consultative Referendum on April 25, of that year, were of *supra-constitutional rank* with respect to the Constitution of 1961, it has been concluded that the normative and organizational acts of the National Constituent Assembly in execution of the *bases comiciales* have *constitutional rank*. Due to the fact that the National Constituent Assembly implicitly referred the *bases comiciales* in the 'Decree Amplifying the Powers of the National Legislative Commission" founding its authority on the "*referendum democratically approved on the twenty-fifth of April of nineteen hundred and ninety-nine*," the Decree amplifying the powers of the Commission would also effectively have *constitutional rank.*" See Decision *N° 1454* of February 18, 2001 (*Caso: C.A. Good Year de Venezuela),* in *Revista de Derecho Público,* N° 85-88, Editorial Jurídica Venezolana, Caracas 2001.

15   *Gaceta Oficial* N° 36.865 of January 7, 2000.

3. The control upon the Municipalities

With respect to the organs of the Municipal level of government, Article 15 of the Decree on Transition regime[16] set forth that the existing Municipal Councils were to exercise their functions "under the supervision and control of the National Constituent Assembly or the National Legislative Commission" until new popularly elected representatives were in office. The decree furthermore, authorized the Coordinating Commission of the National Assembly or the National Legislative Commission the power to partially or completely substitute the members of the Municipal Councils, and Mayors, in cases of serious administrative irregularities.

These provisions were also contrary to the new Constitution that guarantee municipal autonomy, as well as to the democratic principle with respect to municipal authorities, who needed to be popularly elected.

4. The intervention of the Judiciary

Article 17 of the Transitory Regime Decree also provided for the termination of the Supreme Court of Justice in order to give way to the new Supreme Tribunal of Justice. For such purpose, the three Chambers of the former Supreme Court of Justice (Politico Administrative Chamber and Criminal and Civil Cassation Chambers), were extinguished, and its Magistrates dismissed. In substitution, the Constituent Assembly without any constitutional authority created the new Chambers of the new Supreme Tribunal (Constitutional, Politico Administrative, and Electoral Chambers and Social, Civil and Criminal cassation Chambers), although the Constitution of 1999 was not yet in effect.

The Assembly also designated the new Magistrates of the new Supreme Tribunal of Justice (Article 19), but for such purpose did not hold itself to the conditions for those appointments established in the new Constitution (article 263), neither to the citizens participation provisions established in article 270 of the Constitution. Among the Magistrates selected was the former President of the Supreme Court of Justice, who had an occupied that position for the previous two months. His services were acknowledged.

In the text of the new Constitution, there was a glaring absence of Transitory Provisions regarding the functioning of the Judicial Power; containing only one reference to a "Commission on the Functioning and Re-structuring of the Judicial System" (Fourth Transitory Provision) regarding the transitional "system for public defense" until relevant legislation had been passed. Moreover, the Commission mentioned in that Transitory Provision did not yet exist when the Constitution was drafted and submitted to referendum. It came into existence only later through the aforementioned Decree of Transition Regime of December 22, 1999 (Article 27). In the new Constitution, however, this organ had competence only to develop a system for the public defense as stated in the Fourth Transitory Provision.

---

16   See *Gaceta Constituyente (Diario de Debates), Noviembre 1999-Enero 2000, cit.,* Sesión de 22-12-99, N° 51, p. 5.

The Transitory Regime Decree, in any case, was completely incongruous. As aforementioned, before the new Constitution came into effect (December 31, 1999), on December 22, 1999, the Decree appointed the Magistrates to the Supreme Tribunal of Justice (articles 17, 19), although provisionally (art. 20), even though at that point in time the Chambers had no legal existence, since the new Constitution did not provided for the number of its members and also was not in effect. Thus, the Assembly "created" the Chambers of the Tribunal as well (art. 17), something for which it had no constitutional authority.

On the other hand, the Assembly adopted a variety of transitory norms not provided for in the new 1999 Constitution in order to ensure the new Constitution's "immediate effect," although as stated, the new Constitution was not yet operative. These included a provision that transformed the former Council for the Judiciary into an "Executive Office of the Judiciary of the Supreme Tribunal of Justice" established in Article 267 of the new Constitution, not yet effective, and dismissed the members of the Council for the Judicature (art. 26).

Immediately following this, the Assembly provided for another transitional regimen without any authority to do so, providing that until the Supreme Tribunal had organized the aforementioned Executive Office, the government, administration, inspection, and vigilance over the Courts, as well as all the powers which up to that time had been legislatively lodged in the Council for Judicature, be now exercised by the Commission on the Functioning and the Re-structuring of the Judicial System" (art. 21). The National Constituent Assembly in this way, confiscated from the Supreme Tribunal of Justice, (whose members it had, itself, selected) one of the Tribunal's new functions, and attributed it to a "Commission," also created, whose members were appointed by the Constituent Assembly itself, and not even by the new Supreme Tribunal of Justice. The Constituent Assembly accepted this situation to persist, even after the new Constitution went into effect, an irregular situation that the new Supreme Tribunal resignedly has accepted for the past decade (1999-2009).

Another unconstitutional provision adopted by the National Constituent Assembly in the Decree on Transitory Regime of December 22, 1999, was to attribute to the Commission on the Functioning and the Re-structuring of the Judicial System, the judicial disciplinary Jurisdiction that article 267 of the Constitution assigns to judicial courts or tribunals. This transitory provision was to be in effect *"until* the National Assembly *approves legislation* that determines the disciplinary *procedures and tribunals,* which up to 2009 has never occurred. In this way, during the past decade, no stability of judges had existed, being in general appointed on a temporal base, and being dismissed in a discretionary way by the aforementioned Commission, without any due process of law guaranties.

According to the new Constitution, only judges can exercise judicial functions (art. 253), being totally illegitimate and contrary to the guarantee of due process (art. 49) to confer judicial functions to a Commission such as this one, not a Court. If the intention was to establish, even arbitrarily, a transitory regimen of judicial discipline, the judicial disciplinary jurisdiction should have been vested in pre-existing courts or judges, not in an *ad hoc* "Commission." The latter violated both the guarantee of due process and the right to a natural judge expressly regulated in the new Constitution (art. 49).

On January 18, 2000, also "in exercise of the sovereign original constituent power," the National Constituent Assembly issued two other Decrees relating to the Judicial Power. These concerned the designation of the Inspector of Courts[17] and the members of the Commission on the Functioning and the Re-structuring of the Judicial System[18].

5. Dismissal and appointment of the titular officials of the organs of the Citizens' Power

The National Constituent Assembly, through the Decree on the Regimen for the Transition of Public Powers,[19] dismissed the former General Comptroller and General Prosecutor, and appointed its substitutes (articles 35, 36). It also appointed the People's Defendant (art. 34), which in fact was the only titular head it was constitutionally authorized to designate under the Transitory Provisions of the new 1999 Constitution. They were appointed until the new National Assembly, after being elected, named new officials to those posts. Nonetheless, the appointments were made without any sort of citizen's participation as established in article 279 of the Constitution.

In addition, however, the Decree assigned powers to the Comptroller General that were not authorized by any constitutional or legal provision, as was the power to *intervene* into the functions of the State and Municipal Comptrollers and to provisionally designate the titular officials of these entities (art. 37). This was in violation of State and Municipal autonomy as guaranteed in the new Constitution.

6. Dismissal and appointment of the members of the National Electoral Council

Finally, with respect to the Electoral Power, the National Constituent Assembly, being wholly without competence or authority, and in an illegitimate way, also by means of the Decree on Transition Regime of December 22, 1999, conferred unto itself the power to appoint the members of the new National Electoral Council (art. 40), and, consequently, a few days later, dismissed the members of the former Supreme Electoral Council and provisionally also appointed to the Council persons all tied to the new power and to the political parties that supported the government, without any citizens participation. This act, additionally failed to guarantee electoral impartiality, violating Articles 295 and 296 of the new Constitution.

The Constituent Assembly also conferred upon itself the power to set the dates for the first elections to fill representative offices established in the new Constitution (art. 39). It also self-attributed to its body the power to issue the Electoral Statute (*Estatuto Electoral*) intended to govern the first elections for all representative legislative bodies and executive organs within the Public Powers.

---

17   *Gaceta Oficial* N° 36.878 of January 26, 2000

18   *Idem*

19   See the *Gaceta Oficial* N° 36.859 of December 29, 1999.

III. THE JUDICIAL ACCEPTANCE OF A DOUBLE CONSTITUTIONAL REGIME

The Decree on the Regimen for the Transition of the Public Powers, was challenged on the grounds of its unconstitutionality before the then still existing Supreme Court of Justice on the 29th of December of 1999, with respect to its provisions for the appointments of the Prosecutor General of the Republic, the Comptroller General of the Republic, the Magistrates in the new Supreme Tribunal of Justice, the Peoples Defender, the members of the new National Electoral Council, and the members of the National Legislative Commission or *"Congresillo."*

> After January 1st 2000, the files of the action for judicial review were transferred to the new Constitutional Chamber of the Supreme Tribunal of Justice, who decided the case on Decision N° 4 of January 26th, 2000 (*Case: Eduardo García*), base on the opinion written by the same Magistrate who although being President of the former Supreme Court was appointed President of the new Supreme Tribunal. The decision precisely recognized that the transition Decree through which all the Magistrates were appointed, was "of constitutional rank and nature," and "of an organizational nature, producing the appointment of high officials in the National Public Powers, based upon the intent to re-organize the State, which purpose had been assigned to the National Constituent Assembly."[20]

Based on the latter, the Chamber concluded its decision determining "that given the original character of the power conferred by the people of Venezuela upon the National Constituent Assembly by means of Question N° 1 and the Eighth *Base Comicial* approved in the April 25th, 1999 national consultative referendum, *this power is not subject to the constitution then in effect* [1961 Constitution], and the judicial challenge now proposed based on presumptive transgressions of the referenced constitution but not of the standards determined in the [April 25, 1999] referendum, is considered without merit to proceed."[21]

The new Constitutional Chamber of the Supreme Tribunal of Justice ruled in similar way regarding the challenge on January 17 of 2000, of the same Decree on the Regimen for the Transition of Public Powers. In its decision N° 6 of January 27, 2000, the action for judicial review unconstitutionally filed against the decree was also rejected because considered without grounds, based upon the following arguments:

> ... This Chamber understands that until the date of publication of the new Constitution [December 31, 1999], the Constitution that preceded it (of 1961) was in force. This derives from the Single Derogatory Clause [of the 1999 Constitution]; and as the acts of the National Constituent Assembly *were not subject to the derogated Constitution (1961),* those acts were subject to supra-constitutional norms only, as was ruled by the Plenary Supreme Court of Justice as quoted above. Thus, by obverse argument, only those acts issued by the National Constituent Assembly *after the publication of the new Constitution were subject to it.*

---

20   See in *Revista de Derecho Público*, N° 81, Editorial Jurídica Venezolana, Caracas 2000, pp. 91 ff.

21   *Idem.*

It arises from all the aforementioned that the act of the National Constituent Assembly that is challenged here, published in the Official Gazette on the 29th of December of 1999 [N° 36.859], before the Constitution of the Bolivarian Republic of Venezuela of 1999 entered into force, *it is not subject to it, nor to the Constitution of 1961.*[22]

The Supreme Tribunal of Justice, created by the challenged Decree and the magistrates appointed for it, thus recognized the constitutional rank of the transitional regimen invented by the National Constituent Assembly and contained in the Decree, declaring that such decree was neither subjected to the Constitution of 1961 nor to the Constitution of 1999, but to supra constitutional norms. Being an act on which all the magistrates had personal and direct interest because they were appointed by it, the least the Magistrates could have done would have been to recuse themselves, but they didn't. This as well as other decisions in which they judged the Transition Regimen were violations of the most elemental principles of the Rule of law, that no one can be a judge in his own case.

The Supreme Tribunal of Justice ratified the criteria of the Para constitutional character of the Decree on the Transition Regime (not subjected to any Constitution) in another decision N° 186 of March 28, 2000 (*case: Allan R. Brewer-Carías and others*), issued to resolve the challenge for judicial review of the Electoral Statute of the Public Powers[23] approved by the National Constituent Assembly on its last session, on January 30 of 2000. The Supreme Tribunal rejected the action of unconstitutionality filed by former members of the Constituent Assembly, basing its decision on the argument that the Constituent Assembly, according to the basic rules approved in the referendum of April 25, 1999, in order to fulfill its mission of transforming the State, create a new legal order, and draft a new Constitution to replace that of 1961, had several supposed alternatives with respect to regulating a constitutional transition regime: First, to draft Transitory Provisions within the text of the Constitution approved by the people in the December 15th, 1999 referendum; and Second, to pass separate constituent acts, giving origin to a parallel transitory regimen of constitutional nature and rank, approved by the people. The Supreme Tribunal, in effect, ruled as follows:

"The National Constituent Assembly, with the purpose of fulfilling the mandate conferred to it by the people, had several alternatives: one to draft a constitution with a set of transitory provisions in order to regulate as possible the juridical implementation of the transition regime between the institutions provided for in the Constitution of the Republic of Venezuela of 1961, and those provided for in the Constitution of the Bolivarian Republic of Venezuela of 1999.

Another alternative was not to include such implementation in the transitory provisions of the Constitution, and instead to effectuate it through a separate body of legislation (sic), complemented by acts aimed at filling the institutional vacuum that would be created when the

---

22   See in *Revista de Derecho Público*, N° 81, Editorial Jurídica Venezolana, Caracas 2000, pp. 81 ff.

23   *Gaceta Oficial* N° 36.884 of February 3, 2000.

new Constitution went into effect. This was the route chosen by the National Constituent Assembly, when it enacted the Decree on the Regime for the Transition of the Public Powers."[24]

This assertion had no constitutional or logical basis, and violated the constitutional principle of the need for popular approval regarding the Constitution, set forth
in the referendum of April 25, 1999, and particularly in its Ninth basic rule (*Base
Comicial*), which the former Supreme Court considered as having supra-
constitutional rank. According to this provision that was not considered by the new
Supreme Tribunal, any constitutional provision resulting from the constitution making process of 1999 required popular approval through a referendum. This was the
will of the people as expressed on April 25, 1999: that the National Constituent Assembly was not to place constitutional acts into force, but rather only the people, by
means of referendum could place a new Constitution into force. It was for this purpose that the Venezuelan people were convened to vote in referendum on December
15th, 1999: to approve the new Constitution. Because, in conformity with the people's will established on April 25th, 1999, only the people themselves were authorized to approve the Constitution through an approbatory referendum. Thus no other
norm of constitutional rank, not approved by the people, could legitimately exist.

Therefore, the Supreme Tribunal of Justice, by deciding that the Electoral Statute
sanctioned by the National Constituent Assembly was of constitutional rank, enacted
for the purpose of filling supposed gaps or vacuums in the Transitory Provisions of
the 1999 Constitution -vacuums that had been both invented and caused by the National Constituent Assembly, itself, before publishing the 1999 Constitution- violated the people's sovereign will as expressed on April 25th, 1999. The truth is that
there was no point for Venezuelans to approve a Constitution on the referendum
held on December 15th, 1999, if the National Constituent Assembly could pass other parallel constitutional texts not approved by the people.[25].

The most important feature of the aforementioned Supreme Tribunal's decision
is that it laid down the principle that the National Constituent Assembly could enact
norms of constitutional hierarchy, not approved through popular referendum. This,
beyond a doubt, was a principle in violation of the Ninth basic rule (*Base Comicial*)
approved by referendum on April 25th, 1999, which the former Supreme Court of
Justice considered "supra-constitutional" in the decision of October 14th, 1999
(*Case: Henrique Capriles Radonski vs. Decreto de Regulación de funciones del
Poder Legislativo*).

The Ninth *Base Comicial*, which, it must again be emphasized, was considered to
have a "supra-constitutional" rank, meaning that the acts of the National Constituent
Assembly were subject to it, established that the new Constitution to be written
would enter into force only if approved in a referendum. From this it could be deduced that the popular will in Venezuela as expressed on April 25th, 1999, was that

---

24   See in *Revista de Derecho Público*, N° 81, Editorial Jurídica Venezolana, Caracas 2000, pp.
     86 ff

25   See Allan R. Brewer-Carías, *La Constitución de 1999*, 3ª Edición, Caracas 2001, pp. 270 et
     seq.

the National Constituent Assembly could not give effect to the new constitution or to any constitutional provision of act, not approved by the people by means of referendum.

However, that was not the criteria employed by the Supreme Tribunal in its decision, opening the door to arbitrariness and to and endless transitory constitutional situation that in some cases has endured a decade, as it has been the case of the intervention of the Judicial Power.

The Supreme Tribunal, in effect, in the aforementioned decision, deduced the constitutional absurdity that a constitutional transitional regimen could exist even if not foreseen in the 1999 Constitution approved by the people, but dictated by the National Constituent Assembly, without mentioning the Ninth *Base Comicial* (its decision made reference only to the First and the Eighth) of the April 25th Referendum that imposed with supra-constitutional status, the requirement that every provision of constitutional rank produced by the National Constituent Assembly in order to have effects must be approved by the people, by means of referendum. This was what took place regarding the Transitory provisions of the 1999 Constitution approved in the referendum of December 15, 1999, but which never occurred with the "Regimen for the Transition of the Public Powers" enacted by the Constituent Assembly afterwards. The Supreme Tribunal nonetheless, ignoring the will of the people, assigned to such Regimen "rank analogous to the Constitution," and a juridical status "parallel to the current [1999] Constitution."

From the aforementioned decision of the Supreme Tribunal N° 186 of March 28, 2003 (*Case: Allan R. Brewer-Carías et al.*),[26] the following irregular situation resulted:

1. On November 17, 1999, the National Constituent Assembly approved a Constitution with a transition regimen established in its Transitory Provisions, which implied the permanence of the organs of the Public Powers until new titular officials were elected. In the expression of public will (in the referendum of December 15th, 1999) and the will of the same National Constituent Assembly that approved and proclaimed the Constitution, therefore, there was no legal vacuum whatsoever with respect to the constitutional transition.

2. The Constitution of 1999, with the stated Transitory Provisions was submitted to an approbatory referendum on December 15th, 1999, was approved by the people, and was formally proclaimed by the National Constituent Assembly on December 20th, 1999.

3. Two days later, the National Constituent Assembly changed its opinion and resolved to alter the transitory provisions foreseen in the 1999 Constitution already approved by the people, and before publishing it in the Official Gazette, on December 22, 1999 the same National Constituent Assembly enacted the "Regimen for the Transition of the Public Powers," substituting all titular officials of government

---

branches and modifying the structure of the State. This Transition Regimen originated, therefore, a supposed vacuum that the Constituent Assembly sought to fill
with provisions of constitutional rank not approved by the people.

4. The Supreme Tribunal of Justice, in its decision of March 28, 2000 attributed
constitutional rank and value to that Transition Regimen enacted by the National
Constituent Assembly without the approval of the people, in contravention of the
Ninth basic rule (*Base Comicial*) of the referendum of April 25, 1999, which allowed the election of the Constituent Assembly and had supra-constitutional rank,
containing limits upon the activity of the Assembly.

5. In the country, then, and as a consequence of the Supreme Tribunal's decision, two parallel constitutional regimes existed at once: one contained in the Transitory Provisions of the 1999 Constitution, approved by the people; the other, passed
after this approval, by the National Constituent Assembly, without constitutional
support. The latter was both not approved by the people and of imprecise duration,
since it was deemed to have legal effect until the passage of all implementing legislation foreseen by the Constitution of 1999, which could be a period of decades.

The Supreme Tribunal of Justice, unfortunately, instead of fulfilling its duty as
guardian of the Constitution, wishing to resolve the supposedly vacuum created by
the same National Constituent Assembly after the popular approval of the 1999
Constitution, accepted the dual constitutional transitory regime in many aspects up
to 2009, for instance, it still prevails on judicial matters with the continuous interference of the Commission on the Functioning and the Re-structuring of the Judicial
Power.

IV. THE CONSTITUTION KIDNAPPED, AND THE SUBJECTION OF THE JUDICIAL BRANCH OF GOVERNMENT

Transitory constitutional regimes defined by the Supreme Tribunal, had different
durations. The Transitory Provisions of the 1999 Constitution mainly devoted to
define a legislative program that the new National Assembly was to develop, had a
sunset clause within a precise number of years. But the Decree of the Transition
Regime's duration was imprecise and on that matter, the Constitutional Chamber of
the Supreme Tribunal issued contradictory rulings. For instance in decision N° 179
of March 28, 2000 (Case: *Gonzalo Pérez Hernández*), it was decided that the constitutional Transition Regimen created by the National Constituent Assembly was to
last "until the constituted powers were designated or elected" (in 2000)[27]; however
in the aforementioned decision N° 180 (*Case: Allan R. Brewer-Carías et al)* issued
that same day (March 28th, 2000), it was stated that "The regimen for the transition
of the Public Powers projects into the future, not just until the National Assembly
[Legislature] is formed, but even beyond that," until the new legislation is approved.
Consequently "the norms and acts of the National Constituent Assembly remain in
full effect, and will remain so until the legal regimen that derogates the provisional

---

27   See in *Revista de Derecho Público*, N° 81, Editorial Jurídica Venezolana, Caracas 2000, pp.
      83

regimen is established in conformity with the Constitution, leaving without effects the norms and acts sanctioned by the Constituent Assembly.[28]

This situation implied that the 1999 Constitution has never being completely in force due to the fact that in some aspects, after a decade of application, no legislation has been sanctioned by the Legislature (National Assembly), and thus an imprecise Transition Regime remains into effects, applied according to the variable interpretations of the government and the controlled Supreme Tribunal; and this has been particularly shocking regarding the Judicial Branch of Government, and in particular regarding the constitutional provisions on the conditions and procedures for the appointment of Magistrates of the Supreme Tribunal, and on the stability of judges, by means of implementing the judicial carrier and the disciplinary judicial Jurisdiction, which up to 2009 are still inapplicable.

1. *The confiscation of the constitutional right of civil society to participate in the appointment of the Magistrates of the Supreme Tribunal in 2000*

One of the principal purposes of the constitution making process of 1999 was to reform the procedure for the appointment of the non elected high officials of the State, in a way out of the reach of the political parties' control, and with citizen's participation in such appointments, removing the absolute discretion the former Congress had on the matter. Consequently, the 1999 Constitution regulated a precise system of *active participation of society* in those appointments creating various Nominating Committees, integrated by representatives of the different sectors of society, with the exclusive authority to make the nominations of candidates before the National Assembly. In a Constitution with more than 50 articles referring to citizens participation, the only mean for such participation directly provided in the constitutional text is the one that ensures the participation of the "different sectors of society" in the Nominating Committees. In this case, it is not a mean for consultation, much less for dialogue, but rather a mechanism for active participation. The consequence of this system of rules is that, under the Constitution, nominations for the high non elected official positions discussed cannot be made directly by the National Assembly, but are required to be formulated before it by the Committees; the National Assembly has no constitutional authority to appoint persons not presented by the Committees.

Following these principles, article 270 of the Constitution of 1999 provides that nominations for Magistrates of the Supreme Tribunal of Justice may only be made by the Judicial Nominating Committee integrated by representatives of the different sectors of society, and candidates may file their proposals on their own initiative, or through organizations with activities in legal and judicial matters. In order to send to the national Assembly the candidates, the Committee must follow a complex procedure of selection, with citizens' participation, and the participation of the Citizen Power.

---

28   See in *Revista de Derecho Público*, N° 81, Editorial Jurídica Venezolana, Caracas 2000, pp. 87-88.

Nonetheless, the National Constituent Assembly, when issuing the Decree on the Transition Regimen of December 22, 1999, provisionally appointed Magistrates to the Supreme Tribunal that were to remain in office until the new National Assembly could make permanent appointments "according to the requirements of the Constitution" (art. 20), without following the strict constitutional procedure, and without guarantying the citizen's right to participation. Thus the new National Assembly elected on August 2000 had a constitutional obligation to make the permanent Magistrates' appointments in accord with the Constitutional procedure. The same was to be done regarding the appointments by the new National Assembly of the Prosecutor General of the Republic, the Comptroller General of the Republic, the Peoples' Defender and the members of the National Electoral Council (articles 279, 295). However, this was never done.

In effect, in order to integrate the Nominating Committees according to the provisions of the Constitution, the new National Assembly elected in August 2000 was obligated to enact the respective organic laws for the different entities, and in particular, the Organic law of the Supreme Tribunal of Justice. The Assembly could not "legislate" in order to not legislate," it did when sanctioning in November 14, 2000, a "Special Law for the Ratification or Appointment of Officials of the Citizens' Power and Magistrates of the Supreme Tribunal of Justice,"[29] providing for the appointment of the non elected high officials of the State without following the constitutional provisions, and thus, violating Articles 264, 270 and 279 of the Constitution, as well as articles 20 and 33 of the National Constituent Assembly's Decree on the Transitory Regimen. This Special Law, in effect, organized the Nominating Committees as a Parliamentary Commission integrated of 15 representatives and six other persons elected by the Assembly (articles 3, 4), and not as provided in the Constitution, exclusively with representatives of the different sectors of society. This Special Law, in fact constituted an "extension" of the transition regime in the matter, instead of ending it, confiscating the right to political participation guaranteed in express form in the Constitution. In this context, the Special Law lead to the appointment of the Prosecutor General of the Republic, the Peoples' Defender, the Comptroller General of the Republic, and the Magistrates of the Supreme Tribunal of Justice by the national Assembly, without the guaranties established in Articles 264, 270 and 279 of the Constitution.[30]

This motivated the Peoples' Defender[31] to file an action of unconstitutionality against the Special Law, seeking its judicial review and annulment by the Supreme Tribunal. Even though the Supreme Tribunal never decided the case, in a preliminary decision N° 1.562 of December 12, 2000, (deciding to ask the Peoples Defender to clarify the amparo petition conjunctly filed with the nullity action), the Tribunal recognized that "the full normalization of new institutions such as the Citizens'

---

29   *Gaceta Oficial* N° 37.077 of November 14, 2000. See Carlos Luis Carrillo Artiles, "El desplazamiento del principio de supremacía constitucional," *loc. cit.*, pp. 86 ff.

30   *Gaceta Oficial,* N° 37.105 of December 22, 2000.

31   See, *El Universal,* Caracas December 13, 2000, p. 1-2.

Power and the Supreme Tribunal of Justice requires Organic Laws developed in the constitutional context," and affirmed that "as long as these are not enacted, these institutions are governed by two co-existent formative bodies of law, the Decree for the Transition of the Public Powers and the Constitution of the Bolivarian Republic of Venezuela," which form a single "constitutional block," just as this Chamber has indicated in its decisions of the 14th and 28th of March of 2000.[32] The consequence of this assertion was that the Transitory Provisions of the Constitution and the Transition Regimen enacted by the Constituent Assembly were to remain in effect until National Assembly enacted the said Organic Laws. But instead of exhorting the National Assembly to enact the needed organic laws, annulling the Special Law that failed to apply the Constitution, what the Chamber did was to "legitimize" the contents of the above mentioned Special Law.[33]

Is important to point out that the Justification Report of the Special Law Draft referred to the "absence of express provisions regulating the appointment of the members of the Citizens' Power and of the Magistrates of the Supreme Tribunal" (which only the national Assembly could enact), and to the fact that the Nominating Committees for the appointments "do not yet exist" (which only the National Assembly could regulate); and instead of enacting the required organic law, the Special Law was draft for the "the National Assembly to fill the legal vacuum," without ending the provisional regimen, and forfeiting its obligation to legislate.

2.   The appointment of the Magistrates of the Supreme Tribunal of Justice in 2000 without fulfilling the personal conditions required in the Constitution

The systematic violation of the 1999 Constitution on this matter of appointment of the magistrates of the Supreme Tribunal in 2000, reached its zenith when the Constitutional Chamber of the Supreme Tribunal of Justice held that eligibility requirements for Magistrates of the Tribunal set forth in very precisely way in Article 263 of the Constitution, were inapplicable to Magistrates, particularly those sitting in the Supreme Tribunal in 2000 who were issuing the provisional ruling in the aforementioned case filed by the peoples' Defender.

The Magistrates decided that they could be "ratified" in their positions by the National Assembly, although not complying with the conditions set forth in the Constitution to be appointed. The Constitution, as supreme norm, was deemed to be mandatory for all people and institutions (Article 7) except for the Magistrates of the Supreme Tribunal of Justice, whose signatures appeared at the foot of the decision. For such purpose, the Constitutional Chamber invented the argument that "ratification" was a concept not foreseen in the Constitution, and therefore, Article 263 applied only to *ex novo* appointments of Magistrates but not to the tenure of those provisionally appointed. This concept of "ratification," instead, was incorporated in the

---

32   See in *Revista de Derecho Público*, N° 84, Editorial Jurídica Venezolana, Caracas 2000, pp. 108 ff.

33   The Director General of the Office of the Defender of the People, Juan Navarrete, characterized the decision of the Supreme Tribunal of Justice, as an abuse of power. See, *El Universal*, Caracas December 14, 2000, p. 1-2.

Decree for the Transition Regimen enacted by the Constituent Assembly, and only applicable to the Magistrates of the Supreme Tribunal, and since such Decree only provided the need to appoint new Magistrates "according to the Constitution," the Tribunal concluded that the ratification of the Magistrates did not need to respect the Constitution.

Accordingly, in a single pen stroke, the Constitutional Chamber, the institution established to guarantee the supremacy of the Constitution, decided that it was inapplicable precisely with respect to its own Magistrates that were the deciding judges in this case. Justice was handed down by those who stood to benefit from the decision[34].

The result was that the Magistrates of the Constitutional Chamber created and defined a "special regimen" concerning the conditions of eligibility for their own offices, applicable only to them, considering that to require other conditions than the effective accomplishment of their functions, would be to discriminatory against those whose positions were to be ratified, in relation to those who have not been Magistrates but aspire to sit in the chambers of the Supreme Tribunal of Justice.

The consequence of this decision was the decision of the National Assembly in December 2000 ratifying or appointing the Magistrates of the Supreme Tribunal of Justice, many of whom did not fill the conditions set forth in the Constitution to be Magistrates, almost all close allies of the Government. With this, the political control of the Supreme Tribunal was consolidated in the country, and consequently the endless intervention of the Judiciary by the Commission on the Functioning and Re-structuring of the Judicial System, began.

3. The consolidation of the Commission on the Functioning and Re-structuring of the Judicial System and the complete political control of the judiciary

Since 2001-2002, when this essay was written, the Commission on the Functioning and Re-structuring of the Judicial System has continue to exist in parallel to the Supreme Tribunal of Justice and with its recognition; consolidating the political intervention of the judiciary, due to the inapplicability of the 1999 constitutional provisions that guarantees the independence and autonomy of judges.

In effect, according to the 1999 Constitution judges can only enter into the judicial career, and benefit of stability, by means of public competitions with citizens participation (article 255); and judges can only be dismiss from the their tenure through disciplinary processes, conducted by disciplinary courts and judges conforming a disciplinary judicial jurisdiction (article 253). Consequently, according to the Constitutional provisions is completely illegitimate and contrary to due process guaranty (article 49), to assign disciplinary judicial functions regarding judges to an "ad hoc" Commission as the aforementioned. If the original purpose was to provisionally assign, in a transitory way the disciplinary jurisdiction to specific entities before the formal creation of the Disciplinary Jurisdiction, that function must have

---

34   Because of this situation the Peoples' Defender asked the Magistrales to recuse themselves in the case. See *El Universal,* Caracas December 16-, 2000, p. 1-4.

been attributed to preexisting courts or judges, and not to an "ad hoc" Commission not integrated by judges, in violation to the due process guaranteed and to the right of everybody to be judged by their "natural judge" (article 49).

The fact has been that the "ad hoc" Commission has continued to exist. In effect, after its creation in the December 22, 1999 Transitory Regime Decree of the National Constituent Assembly, it enacted two more Decrees on the matter on January 18, 2000, also in exercise of a supposedly "original constituent power," appointing a Tribunal Inspector and the members of the Commission on the Functioning and Re-structuring of the Judicial System.[35].

The situation of completely transitory regime and inapplicability of the Constitution has indefinitively being prolonged because the omission of the Legislature and of the Supreme Tribunal as head of the Judiciary, in spite of the Regulations the same Supreme Tribunal enacted on August 2, 2000, containing the "Rules on the Direction, Government and Administration of the Judiciary," by which supposedly the provision of article 267 would be satisfied in order to "end the effects of the transitory regime issued by the Constituent Assembly," a fact that did not occur.

In effect, article 1 of the Rules issued by the Supreme Tribunal had the purpose of creating the Executive Office of the Judiciary in order to exercise by delegation the functions of direction, government and administration of the Judiciary assigned to the Supreme Tribunal. Nonetheless, in matters of disciplinary jurisdiction, through article 30 of the Rules, the Supreme Tribunal without any authority, and defrauding the Constitution, extended the existence of the Commission on the Functioning and Re-structuring of the Judicial System, which it was to continue in its transitory functions according to the organization rules to be established by the Supreme Tribunal, assigning it "disciplinary functions while the corresponding legislation is enacted and the Disciplinary Judicial Courts are created."

With these Rules, the Supreme Tribunal renounced to exercise its own normative attributions on judicial organization matters, and it was the Commission on the Functioning and Re-structuring of the Judicial System the one that enacted in November 2000, without any constitutional or legal basis, the new Rules in order to punish and dismiss judges contained in its own Regulation.[36]

It has been according to these new Rules, that the Commission has "cleansed"[37] the Judiciary from judges not adept to the new political authoritarian regime. The extraordinary of this Rules is that they were not even issued by the Supreme Tribu-

---

35   *Gaceta Oficial* N° 36.878 of January 26, 2000.

36   Véase en *Gaceta Oficial* N° 37.080 of November 17, 2000.

37   The Word used by the Constitutional Chamber to describe the functions of the Commission has been "*depurar*" which means to "cleanse." See decision N° 1.939 of December 18, 2008 (*Case: Abogados Gustavo Álvarez Arias et al.*), on the non execution in Venezuela of the decision of the Inter American Court on Human Rights, issued on August 8th, 2008 in the case of the former magistrates of the First Court on Contentious Administrative matters (*Case: (Apitz Barbera y otros ("Corte Primera de lo Contencioso Administrativo") vs. Venezuela*). See in *Revista de Derecho Público*, N° 116, Editorial Jurídica Venezolana, Caracas 2008.

nal, which according to the Constitution is the branch of government in charge precisely of the government and administration of the Judiciary; and that the submissive Supreme Tribunal accepted them, endorsing the functioning of an unconstitutional entity, admitting not only that it could enact its own functioning rules, but as well the disciplinary regime for judges, that is, to establish the rules for sanctioning and the causes for judges dismissal.

Accordingly, the "ad hoc" Commission continued to exist with the endorsement of the Supreme Tribunal exercising in a transitory way disciplinary functions that according to the Constitution ought to be "judicial" functions; and its existence was again extended, this time by the Legislature in the Organic Law of the Supreme Tribunal of May 2004,[38] in which a Transitory Disposition (Paragraph 2.e) was included setting forth that:

> "e) The Commission on the Functioning and Re-structuring of the Judicial System will only have disciplinary functions while legislation is enacted, and the disciplinary jurisdiction and the corresponding disciplinary courts are created."

Consequently, the constitutional provision imposing that "the disciplinary jurisdiction will be in charge of disciplinary courts determined by law" (article 267), Turing all the years of enforcement of the 1999 Constitution has never been applied; and up to 2009, judges have not had any guaranty regarding their stability, and their permanence in the Judiciary has been at the mercy of a non "judicial" "ad hoc" Commission that has cleansed the Judiciary, particularly removing judges that have issued decisions not within the complacency of the government.

Unfortunately, on these judicial matters, the judicial activism of the Constitutional Chamber deployed in other fields that, for instance, has lead it to decide ex officio cases of unconstitutional legislative omissions like the one referred to the Organic Municipal Power Law,[39] has not been seen in its own judicial matters compelling the Legislature to enact the Laws that are required in order to precisely guarantee the independence and autonomy of the Judicial Power by means of guarantying the judges' stability. On the contrary, the Politico Administrative Chamber of the Supreme Tribunal affirmed in decision N° 673 of 2008 that "the exercise of disciplinary functions in all its extension, that is, regarding titular judges that have attained stability by means of public competition, and regarding provisional judges, is today attributed in an exclusive way to the Commission on the Functioning and Re-structuring of the Judicial System, as an organ created with transitory character while the disciplinary jurisdiction is created."[40]

---

38   Véase en *Gaceta Oficial* N° 37942 of May 20, 2004.

39   See decision N° 3118 of October 6, 2003 in *Revista de Derecho Público*, N° 93-96, Editorial Jurídica Venezolana, Caracas 2003. Véanse los comentarios en Allan R. Brewer-Carías, *La Constitución de 1999. Derecho Constitucional Venezolano*, Tomo II, *cit.*, pp. 970 ff.

40   Quoted in decision N° 1.939 of December 18, 2008 (Case: *Abogados Gustavo Álvarez Arias et al.*), in *Revista de Derecho Público*, N° 116, Editorial Jurídica Venezolana, Caracas 2008.

Two essential pieces were established in the Constitution in order to guarantee judges' autonomy and independence: first, the procedure to appoint judges within the judicial carrier, by means of public competition with popular participation set forth in order to choose the most competent persons; and second, the judicial disciplinary jurisdiction, in charge of judicial courts in order to guarantee their possible punishment and dismissal according to the due process of law rules. Nonetheless, none of these constitutional guaranties have been applied in the country.

The same Constitutional Chamber of the Supreme Tribunal of Justice has summarized this situation in decision N° 1.939 of December 18, 2008, issued in order to declare and justify that a decision of the Inter American Court on Human Rights of August 2008 condemning the Venezuelan State for violating the due process of law rights of the First Court on Administrative Contentious matters judges, that were dismiss in 2004, was non executable in Venezuela. The Court, in this decision, in addition to recognizing the powers on disciplinary matters of the Commission on the Functioning and Re-structuring of the Judicial System, confirmed that the Supreme Tribunal itself through its "Judicial Commission" has had and have the power to dismiss, in any case, in a discretionary way, without any due process of law guaranties, any provisional or temporal appointed judge. Therefore, being the First Court judges dismissed by the Supreme Tribunal the Constitutional Chamber rejected the Inter American Court on Human Rights decision, considering it as contrary to the sovereignty of the Venezuelan State and non-executable, because such Court cannot impose its decisions upon the Venezuelan Judicial Power.[41]

---

41   *Idem*

CHAPTER VII

THE IMPACT OF THE AUTHORITARIAN GOVERNMENT
UPON DEMOCRACY

(2002)

This essay on the Inter-American Democratic Charter and the precarious situation of Venezuelan Democracy in 2002, is the text of a paper on "The Inter American Democratic Charter and the situation of the Venezuelan Democratic Regime," written between December 2001 and January 2002 denouncing all the violations to the democratic principles committed by the Venezuelan Government. The text was initially diffused by Internet and was later published in Spanish in my book *La crisis de la democracia en Venezuela. La Carta Democrá-tica Interamericana y los sucesos de abril de 2002*, Libros El Nacional, Caracas 2002, pp. 137-218

One of the most important international instruments adopted in contemporary world regarding democracy and democratic principles, has been the Inter-American Democratic Charter *(Carta Democratica Interamericana),* signed in Lima on September 11, 2001 (the same day of the terrorists attacks in the United States), by the Organization of American States in its Twenty-eighth Extraordinary period of sessions. After so many antidemocratic and militarist regimes that have existed in Latin American history, and so many authoritarian regimes disguised as democratic that have been developed, the need to adopt a continental doctrine about democracy was an imperious necessity.

In the following month after its adoption, I began to confront the provisions of the Charter with the achievements of the government installed in Venezuela since 1999, and the results were the following reflections that were written between December 2001 and January 2002.

I.   THE 2001 INTER-AMERICAN DEMOCRATIC CHARTER

The General Assembly of the Organization of American States, for the purpose of adopting the Charter, departed from the fact that the Charter of the Organization of American States recognizes that representative democracy is indispensable for the stability, peace, and development of the region, and that one of the purposes of the

OAS is to promote and consolidate representative democracy, with due respect for the principle of nonintervention; that solidarity among and cooperation between American states require the political organization of those states based on the effective exercise of representative democracy, and that economic growth and social development based on justice and equity, and democracy are interdependent and mutually reinforcing.

The General Assembly, furthermore, recognized the contributions of the OAS and other regional and sub-regional mechanisms to the promotion and consolidation of democracy in the Americas; that a safe environment is essential to the integral development of the human being, which contributes to democracy and political stability; that the right of workers to associate themselves freely for the defense and promotion of their interests is fundamental for the fulfillment of democratic ideas; and that all the rights and obligations of member states under OAS Charter represent the foundation on which democratic principles in the Hemisphere are built.

Among the backgrounds of the Charter in the international ambit there is the adoption by the Heads of State and Government of the Americas, gathered at the Third Summit of the Americas, held from April 20 to 22, 2001 in Quebec City, adopted a democracy clause which establishes that any unconstitutional alteration or interruption of the democratic order in a state of the Hemisphere constitutes an insurmountable obstacle to the participation of that state's government in the Summits of the Americas process. Moreover, the American Declaration on the Rights and Duties of Man and the American Convention on Human Rights contain the values and principles of liberty, equality, and social justice that are intrinsic to democracy; and the Protocol of San Salvador on Economic, Social, and Cultural Rights emphasizes the great importance of the reaffirmation, development, improvement, and protection of those rights in order to consolidate the system of representative democratic government.

Aimed at adopting the Charter, the General Assembly reaffirmed that the participatory nature of democracy in our countries in different aspects of public life contributes to the consolidation of democratic values and to freedom and solidarity in the Hemisphere; that the fight against poverty, and especially the elimination of extreme poverty, is essential to the promotion and consolidation of democracy and constitutes a common and shared responsibility of the American states; and that the promotion and protection of human rights is a basic prerequisite for the existence of a democratic society, and recognizing the importance of the continuous development and strengthening of the inter-American human rights system for the consolidation of democracy.

Furthermore, in the Santiago Commitment to Democracy and the Renewal of the Inter-American System, the ministers of foreign affairs expressed their determination to adopt a series of effective, timely, and expeditious procedures to ensure the promotion and defense of representative democracy, with due respect for the principle of nonintervention; and that resolution AG/RES. 1080 (XXI-O/91) therefore established a mechanism for collective action in the case of a sudden or irregular interruption of the democratic political institutional process or of the legitimate exercise of power by the democratically-elected government in any of the Organization's member states, thereby fulfilling a long-standing aspiration of the Hemisphere to be able to respond rapidly and collectively in defense of democracy.

Additionally, in the Declaration of Nassau [AG/DEC. 1 (XXII-O/92)], it was agreed to develop mechanisms to provide assistance, when requested by a member state, to promote, preserve, and strengthen representative democracy, in order to complement and give effect to the provisions of resolution AG/RES. 1080 (XXI-O/91).

On the other hand, in the Declaration of Managua for the Promotion of Democracy and Development [AG/DEC. 4 (XXIII-O/93)], the member states expressed their firm belief that democracy, peace, and development are inseparable and indivisible parts of a renewed and integral vision of solidarity in the Americas; and that the ability of the Organization to help preserve and strengthen democratic structures in the region will depend on the implementation of a strategy based on the interdependence and complementarities of those values. Finally, in the Declaration of Managua for the Promotion of Democracy and Development, the member states expressed their conviction that the Organization's mission is not limited to the defense of democracy wherever its fundamental values and principles have collapsed, but also calls for ongoing and creative work to consolidate democracy as well as a continuing effort to prevent and anticipate the very causes of the problems that affect the democratic system of government.

Based on all those these backgrounds, the Ministers of Foreign Affairs of the Americas, at the thirty-first regular session of the General Assembly, held in San Jose, Costa Rica, in keeping with express instructions from the Heads of State and Government gathered at the Third Summit of the Americas, in Quebec City, accepted the base document of the Inter-American Democratic Charter and entrusted the Permanent Council of the Organization with strengthening and expanding the document, in accordance with the OAS Charter, for final adoption at a special session of the General Assembly in Lima, Peru, from September 11, 2001.

II. GENERAL SCOPE OT THE INTERAMERICAN DEMOCRATIC CHARTER ON THE CONTENT OF "DEMOCRACY"

The Charter is divided in six chapters, in which the following aspects are developed: democracy and the Inter-American system; democracy and human rights; democracy, integral development and combating poverty; strengthening and preservation of democratic institutions; democracy and electoral observation missions, and promotion of a democratic culture.

1. *Democracy and the Inter-American System: The Right to Democracy*

The Article 1 of the Charter recognizes and declares that the peoples of the Americas have a right to democracy and their governments have an obligation to promote and defend it, considering that democracy is essential for the social, political, and economic development of the peoples of the Americas.

A. *The Reaffirmation of Representative Democracy and Political Participation*

The effective exercise of representative democracy as per Article 2 of the Charter is the basis for the rule of law and for the constitutional regimes of the member states of the Organization of American States.

Representative democracy, on the other hand, is strengthened and deepened by permanent, ethical, and responsible participation of the citizenry within a legal framework conforming to the respective constitutional order.

B. *Essential Elements of Representative Democracy*

Article 3 of the Charter lists as essential elements of representative democracy among others, the following: 1) respect for human rights and fundamental freedoms, 2) access to and the exercise of power in accordance with the rule of law, 3) the holding of periodic, free, and fair elections based on secret balloting and universal suffrage as an expression of the sovereignty of the people, 4) the pluralistic system of political parties and organizations, 5)and the separation of powers and independence of the branches of government.

C. *Essential Components of the Exercise of Democracy*

The following are essential components of the exercise of democracy, as listed in Article 4° of the Charter: 1) transparency in government activities, 2) probity, 3) responsible public administration on the part of governments, 4) respect for social rights, and 5) freedom of expression and of the press.

Furthermore, it is stated that are equally essential to democracy, 1) The constitutional subordination of all state institutions to the legally constituted civilian authority and 2) respect for the rule of law on the part of all institutions and sectors of society.

D. *Political Parties and their Financing*

Article 5 of the Charter considers that the strengthening of political parties and other political organizations is a priority for democracy. Moreover, it adds that special attention will be paid to the problems associated with the high cost of election campaigns and the establishment of a balanced and transparent system for their financing.

E. *Political Participation*

Article 6 of the Charter declares that it is the right and responsibility of all citizens to participate in decisions relating to their own development. This is also a necessary condition for the full and effective exercise of democracy. Promoting and fostering diverse forms of participation strengthens democracy.

2. Democracy and Human Rights

A. *Democracy and the Exercise of Rights and Freedoms*

Democracy, as defined in Article 7 of the Charter, is indispensable for the effective exercise of fundamental freedoms and human rights in their universality, indivisibility and interdependence, embodied in the respective constitutions of states and in inter-American and international human rights instruments.

B.   *The Right of Persons to Report Violations of Human Rights before International Organizations*

Article 8 of the Charter establishes the right of any person or group of persons who consider that their human rights have been violated may present claims or petitions to the inter-American system for the promotion and protection of human rights in accordance with its established procedures.

For that purpose, the Charter is a reaffirmation of the intention of the member states to strengthen the inter-American system for the protection of human rights for the consolidation of democracy in the Hemisphere.

C.   *The Elimination of Discrimination*

In particular, Article 9 of the Charter considers that the elimination of all forms of discrimination, especially gender, ethnic and race discrimination, as well as diverse forms of intolerance, the promotion and protection of human rights of indigenous peoples and migrants, and respect for ethnic, cultural and religious diversity in the Americas contribute to strengthening democracy and citizen participation.

D.   *Democracy and Workers Rights*

In addition, The Charter sets forth that the promotion and strengthening of democracy requires the full and effective exercise of workers' rights and the application of core labor standards, as recognized in the International Labor Organization (ILO) Declaration on Fundamental Principles and Rights at Work, and its Follow-up, adopted in 1998, as well as other related fundamental ILO conventions (Art. 10), which is completed with the statement that democracy is strengthened by improving standards in the workplace and enhancing the quality of life for workers in the Hemisphere.

3.   *Democracy, Integral Development and Combating Poverty*

Article 11 of the Charter considers and declares that democracy and social and economic development are interdependent and are mutually reinforcing.

A.   *Democracy and Social Problems*

Poverty, illiteracy, and low levels of human development are considered by Article 12 of the Charter as factors that adversely affect the consolidation of democracy. Consequently, the OAS member states are committed to adopt and implement all those actions required to generate productive employment, reduce poverty, and eradicate extreme poverty, taking into account the different economic realities and conditions of the countries of the Hemisphere.

This shared commitment regarding the problems associated with development and poverty also underscores the importance of maintaining macroeconomic equilibrium and the obligation to strengthen social cohesion and democracy.

B.   *Democracy and Economic Development*

Article 13 of the Charter declares that the promotion and observance of economic, social, and cultural rights are inherently linked to integral development, equitable economic growth, and to the consolidation of democracy in the states of the Hemisphere.

C.   *OAS Roll in Matters of Development*

In Article 14 of the Charter, member states agree to review periodically the actions adopted and carried out by the Organization to promote dialogue, cooperation for integral development, and the fight against poverty in the Hemisphere, and to take the appropriate measures to further these objectives.

D.   *Democracy and Environment*

Article 15 of the Charter provides for the exercise of democracy in order to promote and preserve environment, imposing the need for the states of the Hemisphere to implement policies and strategies to protect the environment, including the application of various treaties and conventions, and to achieve sustainable development for the benefit of future generations.

E.   *Democracy and Education*

Article 16 of the Charter, on the other hand, considers that education is a key to strengthening democratic institutions, promoting the development of human potential, and alleviating poverty and fostering greater understanding among our peoples. To achieve these ends, it is essential that a quality education be available to all, including girls and women, rural inhabitants, and minorities.

4.   *Strengthening and Preservation of Democratic Institutions*

A.   *The Request of OAS Assistance*

Article 17 of the Charter sets forth that when the government of a member state considers that its democratic political institutional process or its legitimate exercise of power is at risk, it may request assistance from the Secretary General or the Permanent Council for the strengthening and preservation of its democratic system.

B.   *OAS Visits*

When situations arise in a member state that may affect the development of its democratic political institutional process or the legitimate exercise of power, as per Article 18 of the Charter, the Secretary General or the Permanent Council may, with prior consent of the government concerned, arrange for visits or other actions in order to analyze the situation. The Secretary General will submit a report to the Permanent Council, which will undertake a collective assessment of the situation and, where necessary, may adopt decisions for the preservation of the democratic system and its strengthening.

C. *Effects of the Interruption of the Democratic Order or the Alteration of the Constitutional Order in a Member State*

Article 19 of the Charter sets forth that based on the principles of the Charter of the OAS and subject to its norms, and in accordance with the democracy clause contained in the Declaration of Quebec City, an unconstitutional interruption of the democratic order or an unconstitutional alteration of the constitutional regime that seriously impairs the democratic order in a member state, constitutes, while it persists, an insurmountable obstacle to its government's participation in sessions of the General Assembly, the Meeting of Consultation, the Councils of the Organization, the specialized conferences, the commissions, working groups, and other bodies of the Organization.

D. *Initiatives in the Event of Alteration of the Constitutional Order in a State*

Pursuant to Article 20 of the Charter, in the event of an unconstitutional alteration of the constitutional regime that seriously impairs the democratic order in a member state, any member state or the Secretary General may request the immediate convocation of the Permanent Council to undertake a collective assessment of the situation and to make such decisions as it deems appropriate.

The Permanent Council, depending on the situation, may undertake the necessary diplomatic initiatives, including good offices, to foster the restoration of democracy.

If such diplomatic initiatives prove unsuccessful, or if the urgency of the situation so warrants, the Permanent Council shall immediately convene a special session of the General Assembly. The General Assembly will adopt the decisions it deems appropriate, including the undertaking of diplomatic initiatives, in accordance with the Charter of the Organization, international law, and the provisions of this Democratic Charter.

The necessary diplomatic initiatives, including good offices, to foster the restoration of democracy, will continue during the process.

E. *The Consequence of the Interruption of the Democratic Order Determined by the General Assembly: The Suspension of the Right to Participate in OAS*

Article 21 of the Charter sets forth that when the special session of the General Assembly determines that there has been an unconstitutional interruption of the democratic order of a member state, and that diplomatic initiatives have failed, in accordance with the Charter of the OAS, the special session shall make the decision to suspend said member state from the exercise of its right to participate in the OAS by an affirmative vote of two thirds of the member states. In such event, the suspension shall take effect immediately. Notwithstanding the suspension of the member state, the Organization will maintain diplomatic initiatives to restore democracy in that member state.

Nevertheless, the suspended member state shall continue to fulfill its obligations to the Organization, in particular its human rights obligations.

F. *Lifting of the Suspension*

Once the situation that led to suspension has been resolved, pursuant to Article 22 of the Charter, any member state or the Secretary General may propose to the General Assembly that suspension be lifted. This decision shall require the vote of two thirds of the member states in accordance with the OAS Charter.

5. *Democracy and Electoral Observation Missions*

A. *Electoral Processes and International Assistance*

The Article 23 of the Charter declares that member states are responsible for organizing, conducting, and ensuring free and fair electoral processes. The provision specifies, nevertheless, that member states, in the exercise of their sovereignty, may request that the Organization of American States provide advisory services or assistance for strengthening and developing their electoral institutions and processes, including sending preliminary missions for that purpose.

B. *The International Missions of Electoral Observations*

The electoral observation missions, pursuant to Article 24 of the Charter, shall be carried out at the request of the member state concerned. To that end, the government of that state and the Secretary General shall enter into an agreement establishing the scope and coverage of the electoral observation mission in question. The member state shall guarantee conditions of security, free access to information, and full cooperation with the electoral observation mission.

Electoral observation missions shall be carried out in accordance with the principles and norms of the OAS. The Organization shall ensure that these missions are effective and independent and shall provide them with the necessary resources for that purpose. They shall be conducted in an objective, impartial, and transparent manner and with the appropriate technical expertise.

Electoral observation missions shall present a report on their activities in a timely manner to the Permanent Council, through the General Secretariat.

C. *The Information on the Conditions for Carrying out Free and Fair Elections*

The electoral observation missions, as per Article 25 of the Charter, shall advise the Permanent Council, through the General Secretariat, if the necessary conditions for free and fair elections do not exist. In such a case, the OAS may, with the consent of the state concerned, send special missions with a view to creating or improving said conditions.

6. *Promotion of a Democratic Culture*

A. *OAS Obligations*

As per Article 26 of the Charter, The OAS will continue to carry out programs and activities designed to promote democratic principles and practices and strengthen a democratic culture in the Hemisphere, bearing in mind that democracy is a way of life based on liberty and enhancement of economic, social, and cultural conditions for the peoples of the Americas. The OAS will consult and cooperate on an ongoing basis with member states and take into account the contributions of civil society organizations working in those fields.

B. *Programs Content*

The programs and activities, pursuant to Article 27 of the Charter, will be to promote good governance, sound administration, democratic values, and the strengthening of political institutions and civil society organizations. Special attention shall be given to the development of programs and activities for the education of children and youth as a means of ensuring the continuance of democratic values, including liberty and social justice

C. *Women Participation*

States, as per Article 28 of the Charter, shall promote the full and equal participation of women in the political structures of their countries as a fundamental element in the promotion and exercise of a democratic culture.

Regarding the content of the Inter-American Democratic Charter, it is a document of great importance in the definition of essential values and fundamental components of democracy in Latin America, which commits all the member states of the OAS and serves for the protection of the democratic and constitutional order in the same.

III. DEMOCRATIC CULTURE IN VENEZUELA AND THE IMPORTAN-CE OF THE INTER-AMERICAN DEMOCRATIC CHARTER

The most important historical-political-cultural heritage that Venezuela had at the beginning of the 21st century, without doubt, was democracy as a political regime and as a way of living, which implies both the guarantee of public rights and freedoms as well as the supremacy of the rule of law.

The forty years of democratic rule at the end of the XX century produced all their effects particularly in a country with at the middle of that century was one of the Lain American countries with the lesser democratic tradition. In 2000, with all its defects and problems, it was still the Latin American country with the eldest and most experimented contemporary democracy, despite the efforts for destroying it made since 1999.

Venezuelans got used to democracy. That was the great heritage left by the traditional political parties that led the political life during the second half of the former century. The fact that they didn't understand at the end of the century the needs of their own democratic work, which made them collapse, does not mean that democracy hasn't taken roots in the people and in its institutions. That made Venezuelans used to living in freedom, and in this situation, the people usually does not accept nor tolerate authoritarianism, and rejects violence.

On the other hand, the crisis of the system of state of parties produced the political emptiness that featured the political system from the final years of the nineties, which originated a marked desire for and hope for political change for which the majority voted in 1998, that wasn't meant to terminate democracy and the public freedoms, but to improve democracy, to make it more representative and more participative. Because of that, the reaction wasn't against representative democracy, as many persons interpreted it, but against party autocracy and the absence of citizen participation. In 1999, even a constitution was sanctioned, which established a series of principles inspired in a marked reaction against the predominance of the political parties, which could lead to establish effectively a representative and more participative democracy. Nevertheless, in the Constitution, provisions were set forth that could affect the rule of law. Therefore, the Inter-American Commission on Human Rights, in its Preliminary Observations N° 23/02 dated 05/10/02 on the occasion of the on-site visit to Venezuela after the facts of April 2002, pointed out the following:

> 22. Notwithstanding these significant constitutional advances, the Commission notes that the Constitution also includes various parts that may hinder effective observance of the rule of law. These provisions include the requirement for a preliminary proceeding on the merits (*antejuicio de mérito*) for high-ranking officers of the Armed Forces prior to starting any investigation into a crime (Article 266(3)); the stipulation of the Office of the Comptroller General of the National Armed Forces without clarifying its relationship with the Office of the Comptroller General of the Republic (Article 291); and the participation of the National Electoral Council in trade union elections. Article 58, which stipulates the right to timely, accurate, and impartial information, has been criticized, among others by this Commission. Furthermore, Article 203 includes the concept of *leyes habilitantes*, or enabling statutes, and allows for the possibility of a delegation of legislative powers to the President of the Republic, without establishing limits on the content of this delegation. In so doing, new crimes may be established by Executive decrees -as has already happened- and not through statutes adopted by the National Assembly, in violation of the requirements of the American Convention on Human Rights. In addition, the Constitution has suppressed some constitutional provisions that are important for the rule of law, such as legislative review of military promotions, the provision that established the non-involvement of the Armed Forces in political decision-making, and the prohibition on the military authority and the civilian authority being exercised simultaneously.

> In any case, sometimes it seems not to be understood that what the people wanted was, precisely, more representation, not only by the parties, and more political participation and presence of the civil society made up by organizations contrary to the state. For that it was essential the effective territorial decentralization of the Public Power. It hasn't been understood that, definitively, in a people with a deep democratic culture, the change wanted was aimed at improving democracy, not destroying it; one of its essential components is the power control, and, therefore, the rejection of its concentrate and authoritarian exercise.

The Inter-American Democratic Charter analyzed hereinbefore summarizes the principles of democracy as a political regime, to which the Venezuelan people has right to and also all the American peoples and whose promotion and defense is an obligation of the governments (Art. 1). It must be remembered, in any case, that even though the Charter was approved in the General Assembly of OAS held in Lima, Peru, on 09-11-01 with the affirmative vote of Venezuela, before that, a draft was discussed in the General Assembly meeting of the OAS held in June 2001 in San Jose, Costa Rica, where the Venezuelan government expressed certain opposition.

In any case, it is true that in Venezuela there is a government elected by the people and that a Constitution and laws sanctioned by the State organs are in force. Because of that, an interruption of the constitutional order that lead to the overthrow of the government shall not be admitted, on principle. That would be contrary to the Inter-American Instruments and Declarations and could lead to the exclusion of Venezuela from the Inter-American System. Therefore, even before the facts of Caracas in April 2002 the Secretary General of the Organization of American States, Cesar Gaviria, before the public and individual manifestation of an officer of the Venezuelan Air Force on 02-07-02, in a press release dated 02-08-02 pointed out the commitment of the OAS with democracy and the rejection of "any attempt to altering the constitutional order," and expressed that "democracies built with great efforts in the Continent have mechanisms wherefore persons defend their rights, check up on the government and the state, situation familiar to Venezuelan democracy" and that "if something goes wrong, the solution ought to be found in the Constitution and Laws."

With greater reason, facing the interruption of the constitutional order produced in April 2002, the Inter-American Commission on Human Rights, in its Preliminary Observations dared 05-10-02 stated the following:

> 10. As regards the events of April, the Commission expressed its repudiation of the coup d'Etat in due course. The breakdown of the constitutional order constituted a violation of basic principles of international law in force in the Americas, reflected mainly in the Inter-American Democratic Charter, and of rights enshrined in the American Convention. Nothing justifies a break with the constitutional order or an effort to impede the operation of key institutions such as the various branches of government. The Commission recalls that in the investigation, determination of responsibilities, and punishment of the persons responsible for this attack on the democratic institutional framework, the Venezuelan State is called upon to set an example of impartiality and respect for human rights, which implies, among other things, full respect for judicial guarantees and all other rights and guarantees for persons investigated for these acts. The IACHR will closely monitor the development of these processes and its compliance with the provisions of the American Convention on Human Rights that enshrine judicial guarantees.

Nevertheless, the importance of the Inter-American Charter is that its noncompliance can be produced by a government of a member state that even though its origin is formally a popular election, serious alterations of the democratic and constitutional order, in which case it could also lead to the isolation of the state from the Inter-American system.

Such as expressed by the Inter-American Commission on Human Rights in its Preliminary Observations dated 05-10-02,

> 62. The main source of democratic legitimacy is that granted by the popular will, expressed in free, periodic, and universal elections. Yet elections in themselves are not sufficient to ensure the full observance of democracy. As indicated in the Inter-American Democratic Charter, the essential elements of representative democracy include, among others, respect for human rights and fundamental freedoms; access to and the exercise of power subject to the rule of law; the holding of periodic, free, and fair elections, based on universal suffrage and secret balloting as an expression of the popular sovereignty; a pluralistic regime of political parties and organizations; and the separation of powers and independence of the various branches of government. In addition, the following are fundamental components of the exercise of democracy: transparency in government, openness, responsible public administration on the part of governments, respect for social rights, and respect for freedom of expression

and freedom of the press. The constitutional subordination of all the institutions of the State to the lawfully-constituted civilian authority, and respect by all entities and sectors of society for the rule of law, are also fundamental for democracy. In this context, the functioning of an independent and impartial Judiciary as a guarantor of the protection of human rights, as a vehicle for obtaining justice from the victims, and as an organ of oversight and a check on the action of the other branches of government is fundamental to the rule of law.

Therefore, being the Inter-American Democratic Charter the most up-to-date international document for preserving democracy in our countries, we will analyze hereafter the situation of Venezuelan democracy when the events of April 2002 occurred in the light of the provisions of said Charter. If the text of the Charter was confronted with the political practice of the government, it could be seen the breach that was separating us from it was opening and deepening quickly.

Because of that, the General Assembly of the OAS in its emergency meeting on the occasion of the events of April 2002 resolved:

> 4. To encourage the Venezuelan government in its express will of fully observing and applying the essential elements and components of representative democracy, as set forth by Articles 3 and 4 of the Inter-American Democratic Charter.

IV. THE SITUATION OF REPRESENTATIVE DEMOCRACY AND ITS DEFORMATIONS

According to what we have pointed out, the Democratic Charter commence by stating that the effective exercise of representative democracy is the basis for the rule of law and of the constitutional regimes (Art. 2). Said statement revalued representative democracy in Latin America, despite all the efforts and suggestions made to change de adjective "representative" identifying democracy, for "participative democracy," in the meeting of Heads of State and Government of the Americas, (Third Summit of the Americas), held in Quebec city in 2001 and in the General Assembly of the OAS, held in San Jose, Costa Rica, in 2001.

In fact, in our opinion representation is the antithesis of a regime based on supposed popularity of a media leader supported by the Armed Forces. Historically, it is about the well-known relationship leader-people-military that featured the fascist and national-socialist praxis of the first half of the former century and that in the second half of said century was used to confiscate democracy to several peoples, including some Latin American countries.

In Venezuela, democracy as basis of the rule of law and of constitutional regime, without doubt, from ages had to be improved to make it representative of the people, of its organizations, regions, communities and neighborhoods, and not only of some political parties that monopolized it. That was the great political change that Venezuelans claimed for, and because of that, from the electoral process of 1998 a great majority didn't vote, and several persons vote "against" the traditional parties.

Regarding representative democracy, it has been distorted, since it is deduced from some statements of state officers, the same seems to be understood as only "representative" of the government party and didn't admit another representation. The truth is that from a pluralist-party representation democracy, we moved to a democracy representing only one party, who has monopolized the majority of the representative bodies. In this way, in Venezuela in the former four decades we haven't seen a party autocracy as the one exercised by the government party in the last three years, which didn't admit dissidence, and didn't admit that the majority it had, for example, in the National Assembly could be democratically changed by the dissidence of former followers. In that sense, it must be remembered the formal statement of a Congressman of the government party in the National Assembly when he said, straightly, that "if on January 5, 2002 the government party loses the control on the Assembly, that would be the end of democracy as support of the political regime."

That is to say, representative democracy was conceived and accepted only when it represented exclusively the government party, but not when it represented other forces and political organizations. Therefore, representative democracy in Venezuela as basis for the rule of law and of the constitutional regime, such as announced formally, was weakened, except for the solely representation of the government party.

The claim for a change in democracy based on the reaction against the exclusive representation of traditional political parties has been discriminated in favor of the exclusive representation of a political party, the governmental one. Furthermore, some violations of constitutional provisions that ruled the parties have occurred, among them the following shall be pointed out:

First, regarding the provision establishing that that the internal elections of the authorities of the parties must be organized by the National Electoral Council (Art. 297, 6), which has been ignored since said election didn't take place as per the provision.

Second, regarding the provision guaranteeing the internal renovation of the parties, in the government party such internal renovation of its directors couldn't be made, since its President is the President of the Republic and the Board of Directors was made up of high state officers he had appointed.

Third, regarding the provision ruling the constitutional imposition to public officers to be exclusively at state service, and the prohibition to serve any political party (Art. 145), it had been forgotten, and never, as in these last years, Venezuela has had a President acting more as a chief of a political party than as Head of government and state.

Fourth, the provision ruling the prohibition of public financing to public parties (Art. 67), which due to the overlapping of the government party with the state, is not absolutely in force.

On the other hand, the constitutional provision that eliminated parliamentary blocks in the National Assembly, originated a change in the denomination for "opinion groups," but hasn't mean the end of the practice of instructing the vote to congressmen. In the case of the government party, it has a strong parliamentary block subjected to party guidelines, as never seen before.

The conscience vote of which the constitution talks regarding the congressmen (art. 201), therefore, has been turned into death letter, and the provision establishing that the congressmen are only representatives of the people and are not bounded to instructions or directions has been death letter as well.

On the other hand, it is enough to remember what happened to the congressmen of the government party that decided to think by themselves in December 2001 and January 2002 and believed that they could have their own conscience to which they cannot betray. The lesser thing they were told were traitors, being removed, as they said.

In Venezuela, consequently, representative democracy hasn't been based on pluralism, tolerance, dissidence, discussion, dialogue and consensus. What we have had is a deformation of democracy representative exclusively of political parties, which Venezuelans wanted to change in 1998, transformed in a democracy of one solely party far from the provisions of the Inter-American Democratic Charter.

V. SITUATION OF THE PARTICIPATIVE DEMOCRACY AND THE DISCRIMINATION OF THE RIGHT TO CITIZEN PARTICIPATION

The Inter-American Democratic Charter, as we have said, not only reaffirms the need of an effective exercise of representative democracy as basis for the rule of law and of the constitutional regime, but also states that such representative democracy shall be strengthened and deepened by permanent, ethical and responsible participation of the citizenry within a legal framework, conforming to the respective constitutional order (Art. 2). Furthermore, the Charter adds that the participation of the citizenry in decisions relating to their own development is a right and a responsibility and a necessary condition for the full and effective exercise of democracy. Therefore, it affirms that promoting and fostering diverse forms of participation strengthens democracy (Art. 6).

The improvement of democracy of which the Venezuelan people has claimed for consists, therefore, in making it truly participative, wherefore citizenry, based on the right to political participation, could participate in the management of public matters in a permanent basis and not exclusively through political parties, as it has occurred in the last decades.

1. *Political Participation in the Constitution of 1999*

The Constitution of 1999 is totally marked by the concept of participation, wherefore it not only declares the government of the Republic and of all the political entities as participative (Art. 6), but formally establishes the right to political participation (Art. 62) and even lists the diverse ways of participating in political matters, beyond the election of public positions: through the referendum, popular consultation, revocation of the power, legislative, constitutional and constituent initiatives, the open council meeting and the citizen assembly whose decisions, the Constitution states, have biding character (Art. 70).

Not only there finishes the constitutional consolidation of political participation, but in the direct ruling of specific ways of participation in public management:

First, in the exercise of the legislative function by imposing the National Assembly the obligation of consulting the state organs, the citizens and the organized society to listen their opinions on the draft laws (Art. 211); and by the obligation of consulting the states, through their legislative councils when ruling matters regarding them (Art. 206); obligation that without doubt is translated to the President of the

Republic when a legislative delegation is produced through *leyes habilitantes* (enabling statutes) to issue executive statutes with law force (Art. 203), since on the contrary, it would be a fraud of the Constitution.

Second, in the process of choosing by the National Assembly the heads of the organs of the Citizen Power (Attorney General of the Republic, Comptroller General, and the Human Rights Ombudsman), of the Electoral Power (National Electoral Council) and the Judicial Power (magistrates of the Supreme Court of Justice). In all these cases, the Constitution -an exceptional case in contemporary constitutionalism- sets forth expressly that postulations before the National Assembly of the candidates for those positions corresponds solely to two nominations committees made up for "representatives of the diverse sectors of the society" (Arts.270, 279, 295) and not in any other way.

That participative feature of the democratic regime in Venezuela derived from those precise and categorical constitutional provisions, nevertheless, has been discriminated in the last few years.

2.   *The Mockery to the Right to Participate in the Process of Making Laws*

The most recent violation to a constitutional provision took place in 2001 on the occasion of the execution of the Enabling Statute of November 2000: The President of the Republic in Cabinet issued 48 Decrees-Laws on bestowed matters of primary importance in the country, without submitting the drafts to public consultation as required by the Constitution and as specified by the Organic Law of Public Administration of October 2001, which punishes with absolute nullity (Art. 137) legal and ruling texts issued by the National Executive without following the procedure of public consultation set forth.

The wide use of the practice of legislative bestowal threatens the participation of popular representation in sanctioning the laws. Because of that, the Secretary General of the OAS, Cesar Gaviria in his Report to the General Assembly dated 04-18-02 on the occasion of his visit to Venezuela after the events of April, 2002, stated:

> They called attention to the use of mechanisms of the enabling law. This is an old provision in Venezuelan constitutions that bestows on the Executive extensive legislative powers. The government of President Chavez made wide use of these powers, and illustrated the great resistance generated by the approval of norms without parliamentary debate and without public discussion in the Assembly.

3.   *The Violation of the Right to Citizen's Participation in the Appointment of the Organs of the National Public Powers*

The right to political participation of the society through its representatives had been violated, precisely in the process of appointment by the National Assembly of the heads of the organs of Citizen, Electoral and Judicial Powers, expressly ruled in the Constitution, whose text was ignored by the National Assembly itself when issuing the Special Law for the Ratification or Designation of Officers of the Citizen Power and Justices of the Supreme Court of Justice for the first constitutional period of November 2000.

Through this law a parliamentary commission was created made up of a majority of congressmen to choose said officers, substituting the nominations committees ruled in the Constitution that should be made up of "representatives from different sectors of society." Civil society was in this way discriminated, and the heads of the organs of the Citizen and Judicial Powers were appointed with discretionary elements (Attorney General, Human Rights Ombudsman, and Comptroller General of the Republic), and the Justices of the Supreme Court were appointed without complying with some of the objective requisites the Constitution establishes as condition to taking those offices. Through that law, the political control of the Executive branch consolidated through the dominance of the National Assembly regarding all the Public Powers.

This constitutional problem was pointed out by the Secretary General of the OAS in his *Report* to the General Assembly dated 04-18-02, by stating:

> Opposition groups and other leaders of society distance themselves from constitutional standards in different ways. In particular, they express concern about the separation and independence of the branches of government and the lack of checks and balances in the specific case of Venezuela, since they believe that the leading figures were chosen by political majorities within the Assembly. The opposition representatives in the Assembly have called attention to a recent ruling by the Supreme Court of Justice which concludes that the presidential term begins in January, 2002.

The Secretary General added in his *Report* that:

> The government and opposition should do everything within their reach to guarantee the separation of powers and effective checks and balances. Beyond the importance of establishing the supremacy of the Constitution, it is essential to re-establish complete confidence in the rule of law and ensure that all the pillars of society are to heed it. That is spelled out in Article 4 of the Inter-American Democratic Charter.

However, the problem was pointed out in a stronger way by the Inter-American Commission on Human Rights in the Press Release N° 23/02 issued on 05-10-02, in which it declared:

> 7. Regarding the Judicial Power, the Commission heard questions rose about the legitimacy of the process used to choose the highest-ranking members of the Judiciary, the Office of the Human Rights Ombudsman, the Public Ministry, and the Office of the Comptroller General of the Republic. Such procedures are not provided for in the Venezuelan Constitution. The information received indicates that those authorities were not nominated by the committees established for that purpose by the Constitution, but on the basis of a law that was passed by the National Assembly after the Constitution was approved, called the "Special Law for the Ratification or Designation of the Officers of the Citizen Power (*Poder Ciudadano*) and Members of the Supreme Court of Justice."

This matter was deeply developed by the Inter-American Commission in the Preliminary Observation dated 05-10-02:

> 25. The Commission received comments questioning the legitimacy of the election of the current members of the Supreme Court of Justice, the Office of the Human Rights Ombudsman, the Public Ministry, and the Office of the Comptroller General. As a result of the failure to follow the constitutional procedures for choosing those officials, the persons appointed to fill those positions do not have the requisite independence.

26. In this respect, the Commission was informed that the Constitution of the Bolivarian Republic adopted in 1999 provided for a "Judicial Nominations Committee" made up of different sectors of society. The current members of the Supreme Court of Justice, as well as the Human Rights Ombudsman, the Attorney General, and the Comptroller General were not nominated by such committees as required by the Constitution, but rather pursuant to a law issued by the National Assembly after the adoption of the Constitution called the "Special Law for the Ratification or Designation of Officers of the Citizen Power and Justices of the Supreme Court of Justice" for the first constitutional period. The constitutional reforms made to the way these authorities are chosen were not used in this case. Those provisions were aimed precisely at limiting undue interference, ensuring greater independence and impartiality, and allowing various voices of society to be heard in the selection of such high-level authorities.

27. The Commission also noted that questions have been raised regarding the exercise of the powers of the judicial branch without the proper independence and impartiality. On several occasions, the Supreme Court of Justice is said to have made only decisions favoring the interests of the Executive branch. Decisions were mentioned, among others, in response to questions raised about the Special Law for the Ratification or Designation of the Officers of the Citizen Power and Judges of the Supreme Court of Justice, and the decision as to the duration of the presidential term.

28. The Commission is concerned about the possible lack of independence and autonomy of the other branches of government, vis-à-vis the Executive, as they would indicate that the balance of power and the possibility of keeping a check on the abuses of power that should be characteristic of the rule of law might be seriously weakened. In this respect, the IACHR must note that the separation of powers and independence of the branches of government is an essential element of democracy, according to Article 3 of the Inter-American Democratic Charter.

29. The Commission considers it urgent to adopt the organic laws so as to establish the mechanisms provided for in the Constitution of the Bolivarian Republic of Venezuela for the selection of the members of the Supreme Court of Justice, as well as the Human Rights Ombudsman, the Attorney General, and the Comptroller General.

4. *The Support of the Supreme Court of Justice in the Process of Power Concentration*

It must be pointed out that the Human Rights Ombudsman challenged the foregoing Special Law for the Ratification or Designation of Officers of the Citizen and Judicial Powers due to its unconstitutionality; but despite that, the Supreme Court never pronounced on the claim and even decided in a sentence dated 12-12-00 that the Constitution doesn't apply regarding the requisites to be magistrates, to the magistrates who wanted to be "ratified," who were the same who were deciding. The most elemental principle in the history of law, according to which no one shall be judge and a party in the same procedure, that is to say, no one shall decide his own procedure, can be considered violated by the judicial organ in charge of looking after the integrity of the Constitution (Art. 335).

Nevertheless, the Court decided on the grounds of a constitutional transitory regime supported by the Supreme Court itself, justifying rules apart from the Constitutional text.

Precisely, regarding the constitutional "transitory regime" it must be pointed out a statement of the Inter-American Commission on Human Rights in the Preliminary Observations of 05-10-02:

> One important issue, from the constitutional standpoint, is what has been called the "transitory regime"; it is of concern to the Commission insofar as it limits the full implementation of the Constitution. The Transition Regime of the Public Power was approved by the National Constituent Assembly on December 22, 1999, before the entry into force of the new Constitution, mainly to ensure the survival of provisions tacitly derogated by the approved constitutional text, until the new statutes required are enacted. While such transition regimes are common when new constitutions are adopted, in Venezuela, this regime has endured beyond the normal time frame, and has included guidelines for executive enactment of legislative provisions beyond what is normally within the scope of a transitory regime. The information received by the Commission indicates that the transitory regime led, for example, to the failure to set in motion the mechanisms provided for in the Constitution for the designation of the magistrates of the Supreme Court of Justice, the Human Rights Ombudsman, the Attorney General, and the Comptroller General. This is all because the Supreme Court of Justice has held that for the Constitution to come fully into force, several specific statutes needs to be adopted, which has yet to happen. The failure of the Constitution to come fully into force, together with the variety of official constitutional texts, creates a situation of juridical insecurity making it difficult to fully consolidate the rule of law. The Commission hopes that the transitory regime is concluded as soon as possible, to which end it is essential that the legislative branch adopt the legislation necessary to develop the constitutional provisions.

In any case, participative democracy, in its direct constitutional provisions had been discriminated by the state organs, which, on the contrary, were in charge of assuring them effective exercise.

VI. SITUATION OF THE HUMAN RIGHTS AND THE EFFECTS OF THEIR DISRESPECT

The Inter-American Charter, in addition to establishing the right to democracy and the obligation of the governments of protecting it and defending it, and defining democracy through its representative and participative contents, in order to raise no doubts, lists the essential elements of representative democracy (Art. 3), indicating, among others, the following five:

In the *first place*, we have to mention respect for the human rights and fundamental freedoms. The relation between democracy and constitutional rights is so important that the Democratic Charter specifies that the former is indispensable for the effective exercise of the fundamental freedoms and the human rights, in their universality, indivisibility and interdependence embodied in the Constitution and in inter-American and international human rights instruments.

However, in the last three years, in Venezuela, due to the concentration of power produced and the absence of effective controls of power and political counterbalances, the human rights have suffered in their exercise and protection with an accumulation never seen before.

The Inter-American Commission on Human Rights never before has received so many denounces of violations of human rights as now, from 2000 and 2001 and the first months of 2002 regarding terrorist acts derived from kidnapping linked to Colombian guerrilla; disrespect for the freedom to form and join unions, attacks to the freedom of association, violations to the guarantee of due process, interference of the Executive branch in the other state Powers, subjection of the Judicial branch, disrespect for the right to life and to personal security because of extrajudicial executions and creation of "death squads," attacks to the freedom of expression and violations of the right to privacy of communications.

In particular, "*grupos de exterminio*" (death squads) within regional police forces has acted during months provoking the military intervention of state police forces and the action of the Attorney General of the Republic.

On this matter, the Inter-American Commission on Human Rights made a specific analysis. In the Press Release dated 05-10-02, it pointed out the following:

14. According to information received by the IACHR, and particularly based on what has been pointed out by the Human Rights Ombudsman, there are death squads ("*grupos de exterminio*") made up of State security officers operating in the states of Portuguesa, Yaracuy, Anzoátegui, Bolívar, Miranda, and Aragua. In its visit to the state of Portuguesa, the Commission observed with serious concern that the death squads are not only an illegal means of social control, but that, in the particular case of Portuguesa, they are part of a criminal organization that operates for monetary gain within the state police force, and that continues operating and threatening the family members of victims and witnesses, who are absolutely defenseless.

15. Given the gravity of the situation, the Commission demands a serious and complete investigation into these death squads, the prosecution and punishment of the persons responsible without delay, and reparations for the harm caused. In addition, it requests that the Venezuelan State grant effective measures of protection to the witnesses and the victims' next-of-kin. The Commission considers it crucial to increase the human, technical, and logistical resources earmarked for investigating these death squads, and to remove the members of the security forces involved immediately.

Furthermore, in the Preliminary Observation it made in the Press Release N° 23/02 on 05-10-02 it insisted in a marked way on the subject of the "death squads," by pointing out the following:

59. According to information received by the IACHR, and particularly what has been pointed out by the Human Rights Ombudsman, there are "death squads" (*grupos de exterminio*) made up of state security officers operating in the states of Portuguesa, Yaracuy, Anzoátegui, Bolívar, Miranda, and Aragua. According to official figures in the state of Portuguesa, which the IACHR visited, there have been 131 extrajudicial executions perpetrated by those groups since the beginning of 2001. The Commission observed with serious concern that the *grupos de exterminio* are not only an unlawful mechanism of social control, but also, in the case of Portuguesa, part of a for-profit criminal organization operating within the state police force. These organizations continue operating and threatening the relatives of victims and witnesses, who are absolutely defenseless.

60. The persecution and extermination of individuals who belong to specific groups, such as alleged criminals, is a particularly reproachable violation of the right to life and of the right to humane treatment, which has repeatedly been condemned by this Commission. The fact that security officers belong to such groups also represents a radical departure from due process and the rule of law. As an extreme crime-fighting practice, it can only result in greater citizen insecurity. The lack of due diligence in

terms of investigating, prosecuting, and punishing the members of the so-called *grupos de exterminio* is fundamental in allowing them to operate.

61. Given the gravity of the situation, the Commission demands a serious and thorough investigation of the *grupos de exterminio*, the prosecution and punishment of those responsible without delay, as well as reparation for the harm caused. In addition, the Venezuelan State asks that effective measures of protection be granted to protect witnesses and the victims' next-of-kin. The Commission considers crucial that human, technical, and logistical resources be specially earmarked to investigate these "*grupos de exterminio*" and that the members of the security forces involved be dismissed immediately.

On the other hand, the harassment exercised by groups that say they act on behalf of the government party against demonstrators, against media and against the free action of congressmen to the National Assembly and Legislative Councils recall us the fascist practices of harassment, threaten an destruction not only against constitutional rights, but against opposition groups and against democracy itself.

The forgoing outlook surely led the Secretary General of the OAS to state in his Report to the General Assembly on 04-18-02 that:

Since the events mentioned earlier, there have been increased reports of human rights violations, acts of intimidation, and significant acts of vandalism and looting, and increasing numbers of persons dead or injured. This happened before, during and after the recent crisis. We referred these cases to the IACHR and, in some cases, to the Commission's Rapporteur for Freedom of Expression as well.

VII. SITUATION OF THE RULE OF LAW AND THE ACCESS TO POWER

The *second essential element* of democracy according to the Inter-American Democratic Charter is the access to and the exercise of power, in accordance with the rule of law. This imply that for the existence of democracy the access to power ought to be based on the constitutional methods, and furthermore, the power has to be exercised in accordance with the rule of law, that is to say, once again, by respecting the Constitution and the legal order. There is no democracy where there is no respect for the Constitution.

It is clear that regarding the election of representative positions, this principle has been respected in Venezuela and in that sense, in the last years; several elections have been carried out. However, it was openly violated, as we mentioned before, regarding the access to the organs of Public Powers whose heads are not elected popularly, as the organs of the Citizen Power, Electoral Power and Judicial Power.

The Inter-American Commission on Human Rights pointed out the necessity of strengthening the rule of law, by pointing out in the Press Release of 05-10-02 and in its Preliminary Observations of the same date, the following:

17. The IACHR considers that the lack of independence of the Judiciary, the limitations on freedom of expression, the proclivity of the Armed Forces to engage in politics, the extreme polarization of society, the action of the death squads, the scant credibility of the oversight institutions due to the uncertainty surrounding the constitutionality of their designation and the partiality of their actions, and the lack of coordination among the security forces, represent a clear weakness of the basic elements of

the rule of law in a democracy, in the terms of the American Convention and the Inter-American Democratic Charter. Accordingly, the Commission calls for the rule of law to be strengthened in Venezuela as soon as possible.

VIII. SITUATION OF DEMOCRACY BROKEN FOR THE DEPENDENCE OF THE ELECTORAL POWER

In *third place,* another essential element of democracy according to the Inter-American Democratic Charter is the holding of periodic, free and fair elections based on secret balloting and universal suffrage as an expression of the sovereignty of the people. Therefore, the elective regime is essential in representative democracy wherefore the organ of electoral control is also essential to assure its effectiveness and the fair character of the elections.

The Constitution of 1999 makes the Electoral Power a component of the Public branches with organic independence, functional and budget autonomy, participation of no party in the electoral organism, impartiality and citizen participation; decentralization of the electoral administration, transparency and speed of the balloting act and scrutiny (Art. 294). However, all these principles with which free and fair election can be assured wait for the law developing them and updating them to make them reality.

In the meantime, the members of the National Electoral Council in charge of implementing representative democracy were "transitorily" appointed by a transitory legislative organ called National Legislative Commission, without the constitution of the Electoral Nomination Commission "made up of representatives from the different sectors of society" provided for in article 295 of the Constitution. Constitutional transitory regime created by the National Constituent Assembly on December 22, 1999, violating the Constitution itself popularly approved a week before (12-15-99) harmed the autonomy of the Electoral branch.

All the foregoing has served to weaken progressively representative democracy in Venezuela, since the elections have been directed by an organ in which civil society and the majority of the political parties haven't confidence in. Transitory regime regarding the conformation of the Electoral Branch according to the Constitution, in any case, has been extended *sine die* because of the decision of the parliamentary majority of discussing no law that shall rule the Electoral Nomination Committee provided for in the Constitution.

The Inter-American Commission on Human Rights, in its Preliminary Observations of 05-10-02, devoted the following considerations to the problem of the composition of the National Electoral Council:

50. During its on-site visit, the Commission received numerous observations regarding the composition of the National Electoral Council, in which the electoral power is vested according to the terms of the Constitution. Its members have yet to be selected in keeping with the procedure regulated by the Constitution. This would suggest that in practice, the Council is kept from making decisions in all matters that are important for all types of elections under its jurisdiction.

51. The organs of public power with jurisdiction to settle claims regarding the transparency and legality of elections should be endowed with the utmost impartiality, and should resolve such matters fairly and promptly, as the best way to ensure the effec-

tive exercise of the right to elect and be elected established in Article 23 of the American Convention. Accordingly, the Commission recommends that the full and definitive composition of the National Electoral Council proceed as regulated in the Constitution.

IX. SITUATION OF DEMOCRACY AND LIMITATIONS TO PLURALISM

1. *Political Pluralism and its Implications*

The *fourth* essential element of representative democracy is the pluralistic system of political parties and organizations, to which the Democratic Charter devoted another rule providing that the strengthening of the parties and other political organizations is a priority for democracy (Art. 5).

Definitively, it is about the principle of political pluralism, which is opposed to all idea of power concentration and of political organization of the society promoted by the state or from the state.

Plural democratic regime, in this way, is always opposed to state super power, trying that the parties and political organizations be always outside the sphere of the state and its influence, so as individuals and social groups freely develop their personality. Pluralism, furthermore, ought to assure free elections, governmental alternativeness and political participation and, through the latter, power decentralization. Plural regime of parties and political organizations, in short, is the antidote to totalitarianism featured by the existence of a sole source of authority that even pretend to appropriate sovereignty.

Political pluralism, therefore, implies the democratic existence of a multiplicity of political groups, parties and organizations that articulate society, outside the reach of the state. Because of that, the Constitution in several provisions refers to associations or organizations with political purposes (Art. 67), to organizations of the civil society (Art. 293, 6; 296) and to organized society (Art. 211). In contrast, the Constitution grants the Electoral Power, which is a state organ, an inadmissible interference in the organizations of the civil society, by granting it the power of organizing the elections of unions, professional groups and organizations with political purposes (Art. 293, 6). This, in itself, is an attack to political pluralism and an inconvenient transformation of the social organization into a part of the state.

That is more serious if the Electoral Power does not have effective independence regarding the Executive branch, as happened with the National Electoral Council.

In any case, society groups outside the ambit of the state power and its scope are the ones that guarantee the political pluralism as essential element for democracy. Because of that, the Constitution, as is has been said, bestows the public officers the obligation of being "at the service of the state and not at the service of any party" (Art. 145) to separate clearly the political organization of the society (the state) from the organized groups of the society (parties and organizations of the civil society), preventing even in the Constitution, even though inconveniently and contrary to the provisions of the Democratic Charter (Art. 5) the financing of the associations with political purposes with funds from the state (Art. 67).

2.   *The Inconvenient Integration of the Government Party to the State*

In Venezuela, in any case, political pluralism has been harmed, on the one hand, when the government party integrated the state in a way never known before in the Venezuelan political history. As it was said, the President of the Republic has been the President of the government party and his more close ministers have been the directors of the same. The state in several aspects, therefore, seems to be at the service of the government party and the latter to the service of the state. Other political organizations and parties different from the governmental one have been discriminated from power.

In this sense, the Secretary General of the OAS, in his Report to the General Assembly of 04-18-02 highlighted that not only "representatives of the opposition parties in the National Assembly consider their minority rights to have been violated," but that:

> The international community should provide support to Venezuela to ensure that political parties and other political groups or movements once again become the principle actors in Venezuelan politics. The current vacuum, which other social sectors have sought to fill, has clearly demonstrated its limitations. Here we could look to actions under Article 5 of the Democratic Charter.

On the other hand, the integration of the government party to the state makes us remember the application of the old technique of the "boot" regarding Public Administration trying to provoke the supposed conformation of a "new" public function made up almost exclusively by members of the government party.

In *second place,* with the concentration of power in the Executive branch, whose head has been president of the government party that has controlled all power instances, and through these ones, has tried to control the organizations of the civil society as the unions and professional groups whose elections are controlled by a state organ politically subjected, as the Electoral power.

3.   *The Inconvenient Interference of the Power in the Organization of the Society and the Regimentation of Civil Society*

On the other hand, the state, from the Executive branch tried to organize politically the society and the governors and mayor members of the government party tried to do so as well, through the so called "Bolivarian Circles," groups that are the antithesis of pluralism because of their full dependence of the organs of power.

It must be pointed out the importance that the Secretary General of the OAS gave in his Report to the General Assembly of 04-18-02 to the subject of the Bolivarian circles, by expressing the following:

> This Mission has received numerous complaints alleging that the Bolivarian Circles are responsible for these actions. The Bolivarian Circles are groups of citizens or grassroots organizations who support the President's political platform. Many sectors consider them responsible for the human rights violations, acts of intimidation, and looting.

Furthermore, the Secretary General stated the following:

> It is an absolute necessity to resort only to peaceful measures. The state, and let there be no doubt about this, must retain a monopoly on the legitimate use of force. The accusations

that certain sectors are jeopardizing the legitimate use of force must be investigated. In all cases, any use of force must occur under authorization and within the normative framework to which the military adheres.

The Inter-American Commission on Human Rights, in the Press Release of 05-10-02 gave importance to the subject of the civil society and the Bolivarian circles, by expressing the following:

13. The IACHR noted that political participation, the right of association, and freedom of expression are all rights guaranteed in the American Convention, and in this regard, the "Bolivarian Circles," as free groups of citizens or grass-roots organizations that support the President's political project, may, under certain conditions, be a suitable channel for the exercise of these rights. Nonetheless, the IACHR understands that the expression of certain partisan political ideas cannot be accorded privilege to the detriment of others, nor can there be any justification for acts of violence or restrictions on the rights of third persons with different political outlooks or given professional roles, especially if they receive public financing. The Commission reminds the Government that it is a responsibility of the State to ensure the effective exercise of the rights of all inhabitants of Venezuela. The international responsibility of the State is triggered if groups of civilians are freely violating rights, with the support or acquiescence of the Government. Therefore, the Commission calls on the Government to seriously investigate the acts of violence attributed to some Bolivarian Circles, and to adopt, with the utmost urgency, all actions necessary for preventing the recurrence of such acts. In particular, it is essential that the monopoly over the use of force be vested exclusively in the public security forces; the complete disarming of any group of civilians should take place immediately.

In its Preliminary Observation of the same date, the Inter-American Commission on Human Rights developed even more the subject in this way:

56. During its on-site visit, and even before it, the IACHR received several statements of concern over the creation, training, organization, and financing with funds from the public treasury of the so-called "Bolivarian Circles," whose main purpose is said to be to give political support to the regime of President Chávez. Some of the members of those circles have been accused of acting as shock troops to verbally and physically assault those who they identify as enemies of the political process, in particular leaders of the political opposition, including members of the National Assembly and municipal authorities, journalists and social communicators, and social leaders, especially in the trade union and university movements. It is also said that some of these circles are armed. The Government rejects these charges and asserts that the "Bolivarian Circles" are mere instruments of social action and social solidarity.

57. Political participation, the right to association, and the right to freedom of expression are rights guaranteed by the American Convention. In this regard, the "Bolivarian Circles" as free groups of citizens or grass-roots organizations that support the political project of the President, may under certain conditions be a suitable channel for the exercise of those rights. Even so, the Commission understands that the expression of certain politically partisan ideas cannot be privileged to the detriment of others, nor can it be a justification for acts of violence or restrictions on the rights of third persons with different political views or certain professional roles, especially if it is supported by public financing. The Commission reminds the Government that it is the responsibility of the State to ensure the effective exercise of the rights of all inhabitants of Venezuela. The international responsibility of the State is triggered if

groups of civilians act freely violating rights, with the support or acquiescence of the Government. Accordingly, the Commission called on the Government to investigate seriously the acts of violence attributed to some "Bolivarian Circles," and to take, as urgently as possible, all measures necessary to prevent these acts from recurring. In particular, it is essential that the monopoly of force be maintained exclusively by the public security forces; complete disarmament of any group of civilians should immediately be guaranteed.

58. According to the information collected by the IACHR, one cannot dismiss the possibility of other armed groups existing, whether Government partisans or opposition groups. It is essential to investigate the existence of such groups, and to disarm them completely, as quickly as possible.

On the other hand, regarding the right to form and join unions, it should be highlighted the interference of the state in the unions and even of the President of the Republic in the unions elections, promoting a candidate of the government to the Venezuelan Confederation of Workers.

The Secretary General of the OAS, in his Report to the General Assembly of 04-18-02 emphasized the subject of the problems of the union freedom, pointing out that:

The Venezuelan Confederation of Workers (CTV) (*Central de Trabajadores de Venezuela*) demanded that the Executive accept the CTV leaders chosen in the election called at the initiative of the national government itself. This confederation and its leaders are recognized by the International Labor Organization (ILO) and this demand can also be viewed in light of Article 10 of the Democratic Charter. The CTV leaders also call for the convocation of tripartite dialogue.

The Inter-American Commission on Human Rights gave a particular treatment to the subject of the right to form and join trade unions in the country as well. In the Press Release of 05-10-02 it stated the following:

Furthermore, the IACHR learned of a clear conflict regarding the right to form and join trade unions. The IACHR was informed that once the elections were held, in keeping with the rules of the National Electoral Council, the elected directors of the CTV union federation were not recognized by the national authorities. The American Convention protects the right to elect and to be elected, and to form and join trade unions. Accordingly, the IACHR urged the Venezuelan State to resolve as soon as possible, and in keeping with Venezuela's international obligations, the conflict that came about due to the failure of the authorities to recognize the freely elected authorities of the CTV.

Moreover, in the Preliminary Observations of 05-10-02, the Inter-American Commission on Human Rights made the following considerations:

45. On December 3, 2000, a referendum was held by the Government, through a legislative measure, in which the voters were asked whether they agreed with reforming the trade union leadership through elections to be held within six months. During that period, the directors of Venezuela's trade union federations (*centrales, federaciones*, and *confederaciones*) were suspended.

46. The referendum resulted in a significant victory of the position in favor of reforming union leadership, accompanied by widespread abstentions. In accordance with the prevailing vote in favor of the reforms, the above-mentioned directors were effectively suspended from their trade union functions, and new elections were held, in

keeping with the Elections Statute issued by the National Electoral Council (CNE) to regulate new elections for union leaders.

47.	The IACHR is of the view that having allowed the population at large to participate in that referendum, i.e., including persons other than union members, entailed a violation of the right to form and join trade unions, and the right of workers to elect their leaders. The above-mentioned actions were severely criticized by the Committee on Freedom of Association of the International Labor Organization (ILO).

48.	Once the elections were held, in keeping with the provisions laid down by the National Electoral Council, the authorities of the individual trade unions and the union federations were elected. The Commission has received information indicating that the *Confederación de Trabajadores de Venezuela* (CTV) represents the largest number of trade unions. Nonetheless, due to different interpretations of what has happened, the officers of the CTV elected in the election called by the national government have yet to be recognized by the national authorities.

49.	The Commission notes that the right to elect and to be elected and to organize in trade unions are rights recognized in the American Convention, and in the Inter-American Democratic Charter. The right to form and join trade unions, without undue interference from the state, is, in the view of the IACHR, an important element in any democracy. It requires that the conflict that has arisen due to the failure to recognize the authorities of the CTV be resolved as soon as possible, and in keeping with Venezuela's international obligations.

The Supreme Court of Justice, sadly, had been in charge of regimenting and distorting the organizations of civil society, excluding from this concept, for example, the ones of the Church; requesting them to be "representatives" of the society, when it is about instrument of participation; excluding from the concept of civil society the associations, groups and institutions receiving external subsidy (coming from international solidarity, for example), to which the character of Venezuelan has been removed; stating that they shall be regimented by the state, which is contrary to its essential free and outside-the-state character (Decision of 06-30-00 and 08-23-00), and pretending that whoever acted on behalf of the social organization shall do so "elected by someone to fulfill such representation."

On this criterion, the Inter-American Commission on Human Rights, in its Preliminary Observations of 05-10-02, called the attention of the following:

53.	The Commission wishes to call attention to the importance of the concept of civil society being understood in democratic terms, without unreasonable exclusion or unacceptable discrimination. In this regard, the IACHR has had the opportunity to learn of several decisions of the Supreme Court of Justice that have laid down a doctrine according to which non-governmental organizations that receive grants from abroad or whose boards of directors include foreigners or religious men or women, are not part of civil society, and therefore would be excluded from the right to participate in the Nominations Committees provided for in the Constitution for selecting the persons for the organs of the Citizen Power, the Electoral Power, and the Supreme Court of Justice. Acknowledging the power of the State to issue reasonable regulations of the right to association in the context of a democratic society, the Commission calls attention to this jurisprudential thesis, which, applied in discriminatory terms against independent organizations, has an exclusionary effect that is unacceptable for the open participation of civil society in Venezuela.

Political pluralism, essential element of democracy, had been seriously threatened from the state power.

4.   *The attacks against the Catholic Church*

The ecclesiastic patronage regime established in Venezuela from the 19th century, provided for in the Constitution of 1961 as a right of the state (Art. 130) was eliminated in the Constitution of 1999, which establishes the guarantee of "independence and autonomy of the churches and religious confessions with no further limitations than the ones derived from this Constitution and the law (Art. 59), consequently, all subjection of patronage of the Catholic Church was eliminated from the Constitution, and its autonomy and independence was guaranteed.

In particular, the role of the Catholic Church in Venezuela has been outstanding, giving opinions and encouraging actions regarding governmental policies.

Nonetheless, in the last years from the power of the State a harassment policy and an interference of the state in the matters of the church have been developed, accompanied by personal attacks to its leaders. There have been also attempts of dividing of the Church itself, to try to weaken its spiritual leadership.

X.   SITUATION OF DEMOCRACY FOR THE ABSENCE OF EFFECTIVE SEPARATION AND CONTROL OF POWER AND ITS DISTORTION

The *fifth* essential element of representative democracy according to the Inter-American Democratic Charter is the separation and independence of public branches. It is about the instruments of controlling and limiting the power through its distribution and separation, to serve as check and balance.

With no institutional control of power, democracy couldn't exist, since definitively all the essential elements of the same formerly analyzed depend upon the latter: only by controlling the power the respect for human rights and fundamentals freedoms exists; only by controlling the power the subjection to the rule of law can be reached; only by controlling the power, periodic, free and fair elections can be held, based on universal suffrage and secret balloting as an expression of the sovereignty of the people; and only by controlling the power a plural regime of parties and political organization could exist.

Therefore, without separation and independence of public branches both vertically and horizontal, there is no democracy.

The Constitution of 1999 provides a double distribution (separation and independence) of public branches: in the first place, *the vertical distribution*, by establishing that the Public Power is distributed among Municipal Power, State Power and National Power, each one with political autonomy; and in the second place, *the horizontal distribution* regarding the National Power, by establishing its division into five branches: Legislative, Executive, Judicial, Citizen and Electoral, each one with independence and autonomy (Art. 136).

1. *The Contradiction between the "Decentralized Federal State" and the Centralist Policy and Practice*

The vertical distribution of power is a consequence of the form of decentralized state (Art. 4) provided for in the Constitution, whose text rises decentralization as a national policy for, precisely, deepen democracy, making the power closer to population and creating the better conditions both for the exercise of democracy and for rendering effectively states purposes (Art. 158). As it has been said before, political decentralization is essential for participative democracy, since citizen participation in the management of public affairs is only possible by approaching the power to the citizen and, consequently, multiplying the primary political organization, which is the municipality.

Unfortunately, after 10 years of decentralizing policy, with lows and highs and backsets, from 1998 the country has been suffering a progressive process of centralization and concentration of resources and public competencies in the National Power, to the detriment of the autonomy of the municipalities and the states. The Constitution of 1999, in this regard, is contradictory, since parallel to the exaltation of decentralization, it reduced the autonomy of the states and municipalities and even nationalized the organization of the state legislative organ (Legislative councils), which passed from been ruled in the Constitutions of the states to a national law enacted in 2001. The centralism process, moreover, financially sank the states and, consequently, the municipalities, nationalizing in a definitive way the management of the financing funds related to AVT (FIDES) and hydrocarbons (Special allocations) which are now controlled and distributed by national organs. Democracy, therefore, as political regime, has move backward due to the attacks of centralism.

2. *The Principle of Separation of Powers and its Contrast with Concentrating Policy and Practice of the Executive Branch*

The main and essential element of democracy is the principle of separation of powers, where State powers controls over the others within a system of checks and balances as an antidote to concentration of power and authoritarianism. Democracy does not exist, when the exercise of the Public Power is concentrated in just a pair of hands.

In this regard, democracy in Venezuela suffered from a disastrous concentration of the Public Power in the sole hands of the Executive branch.

As it has been said, the National Assembly has been dominated and totally controlled by the government party, acting the President of the Republic as the President of such party. In the last years, The National Assembly in Venezuela, acted according to Presidential instructions and those partisan congressmen who thought they could consider themselves as "representatives of the people" and not of the government and that they should vote according to their conscience, with no subjection to mandates or instructions as provided for in the Constitution (Art. 201), were treated as traitors and submitted to public contempt. On the other hand, the National Assembly ruled what the President of the Republic proposed to them, as it happened with the Enabling Statute of 11-13-00, with no debate.

If the Executive branch has controlled the Legislative Power to its will, through this control it has also controlled the other branches of Government, whose heads have been appointed irregularly by a submitted National Assembly. The consequence has been that the other branches of Government have not been able to show signs of autonomy and independence.

3. *The Problems of the Judicial Branch*

The intervention of the Judicial branch decreed by the National Constituent Assembly continued even on the Supreme Court sideline and with its support, so the constitutional provision that establish a disciplinary jurisdiction (Art. 267) were not in force yet. The provisional status of judges was a common thing and with that, unfortunately, the break of their autonomy and independence for their dependence with respect to the power.

On the problem of justice administration in Venezuela, the Inter- American Commission on Human Rights in the Press Release of 05-10-02, pointed out the following:

> Another aspect related to the autonomy and independence of the Judiciary has to do with the provisional status of judges. The IACHR is aware that the problem of provisional judges in Venezuela is long-standing. According to the information provided to the IACHR during the visit, at present, 60% to 90% of the judges are provisional, which, in the Commission's view, has a negative impact on the stability, independence, and autonomy that should govern the Judiciary. The Commission expresses the importance of a process beginning immediately in Venezuela, in keeping with its domestic law and international obligations under the American Convention, to reverse the situation whereby most of the judges are provisional.

In the text of the Preliminary Observation of 05-10-02 the Inter-American Commission on Human Rights was even clearer on the subject of judges' provisional status, by stating:

> Another issue having to do with the autonomy and independence of the judicial branch is the provisional status of judges. After almost three years of re-organization of the judicial branch, a significant number of the judges -from 60% to 90%, depending on the source- are provisional. This affects the stability, independence, and autonomy that should prevail in the Judiciary.
>
> 31.   The Commission is aware that the problem of provisional judges pre-dates the present administration by several years. Nonetheless, the Commission has been informed that the problem of provisional judges has become more severe and more widespread since the current administration began the process of restructuring the Judiciary. The President of the Supreme Court of Justice informed the IACHR of progress made in correcting that situation.
>
> The Judicial branch has been established to ensure compliance with the laws, and is undoubtedly the fundamental organ for protecting human rights. In the inter-American human rights system, the adequate functioning of the Judiciary is an essential element for preventing the abuse of power by State organs, and, accordingly, for protecting human rights. In order for the judicial branch to be able to perform effectively its role in overseeing, ensuring, and protecting human rights, it is not sufficient that it exist formally; it must also be independent and impartial.
>
> The Commission expresses the importance of speeding up the process aimed at reversing the situation in which a significant number of Venezuelan judges are provisional, immediately

and in keeping with its domestic laws and its international obligations under the American Convention. The need for judges to be designated with full guarantees cannot justify the persistence of their provisional status for a lengthy period.

4.   *Subjection of the Citizen Branch*

In the Citizen Branch, the situation was not less dramatic. The Comptroller General of the Republic hasn't act as comptroller organ and, even the Comptroller General seemed to become sort of a judge, alleging that he hasn't decided anything in the well known cases of public corruption due to the absence of proofs presented to him, when in reality he rules an organ of fiscal control, which is an investigative administrative organ.

Regarding the Human Rights Ombudsman, the worst cases of constitutional rights violations, have had very little attention, as the one refereed to the police death squads, the violation of the right to political participation on the occasion of the enactment of decrees-laws bestowed in 2001, or in the attacks against the freedom of expression that have provoked the adoption of precautionary measures by the Inter-American Commission on Human Rights. Unfortunately, the international control organs needed to act because of the absence of action of the Human Right Ombudsman, despite the wide range of faculties it has in the Constitution (Art. 281).

In any case, the subjection of the organs of the Public Power to the Executive branch through the National Assembly who appointed them in an exclusionist way and following the Executive branch instructions provoked a power concentration in Venezuela that harmed the essential element of democracy, the separation and independence of the Public Powers.

XI. SITUATION OF DEMOCRACY AND THE PROBLEMS OF GO-VERNMENTAL TRANSPARENCY

The Inter-American Democratic Charter establishes as fundamental component of democracy the transparency in government activities, probity, responsible public administration on the part of governments, respect for social rights, and freedom of expression and of the press (Art. 4).

Unfortunately, these components also show a negative balance in Venezuela.

Among the fundamental components of the exercise of democracy, indeed, there is the transparency in government activities, which means that the same shall be carried out in an open, frank and confident way, submitted to citizen's scrutiny. Hidden government activities, carried out at citizenry back, distrusting the same and denying participation are contrary to the request of transparency.

In that sense, the government hasn't been transparent. On the contrary, the latter has been substituted by the secret, hidden work, as it happened with the elaboration of the decrees laws bestowed in 2001, whose text was only known by the public organs in charge of their execution after their publication in Official Gazette. The political and civil society organizations were greatly discriminated in this process, in which the constitutional request of public consultation wasn't respected.

Additionally, severe signs of corruption appeared within the public administration, putting the country in the last two years among the worst comparative levels in the world of countries with great corruption. That have been evident from the denounces made through media of actions of administrative corruption in different levels of execution of governmental programs, which weren't sanctioned in particular, due to irregularities of the Sole Social Fund, and in the management of the "Plan Bolivar 2000" that implied the management of great budget resources by the regiments of the Armed Forces in all the country, with minimum control.

The National Assembly, as the organ responsible for political control over the public administration should guarantee the accountability of public officers, instead has debated shortly on the subject.

XII. SITUATION OF DEMOCRACY AND THE LIMITATIONS TO THE FREEDOM OF EXPRESSION AND PRESS

The freedom of expression and of press has suffered severe attacks from the President of the Republic or under his incitation; and even the Supreme Court with the decision N° 1013 dated 06-12-01 has limited said freedom, contrary to the Constitution.

Said attacks have been also made through the governmental threaten and harassment to the media and their directors.

The attacks affected journalists and reporters, and the situation reached the extreme of laying siege to the paper *El Nacional*, on 01-07-02 and attacking with explosives the news paper *Así es la Noticia,* on 01-31-02.

On the freedom of expression, the Secretary General of the OAS, in his report to the General Assembly on 04-18-02, expressed that:

> Representatives of television network owners and a group of journalists believe that the Bolivarian Circles represent the greatest threat to freedom of the press and of expression. Several of these cases have already been submitted to the Inter-American Commission on Human Rights and to the Rapporteur for Freedom of Expression. It would be advisable for the government to work on these issues and to dispel many of the serious doubts that have arisen.

> Television network representatives complain of the abrupt interruption of their private television channel signals, which they consider a violation of the Organic Telecommunications Act. This produced a systematic interruption of programming, with long statements by the President and other executive officials in the days leading up to April 11. They also demand that, in keeping with the IACHR recommendation, the Government issued "a categorical denunciation of the acts of aggression to which media personnel have been subjected."

Later, he added:

> Whatever agreement is reached among the different sectors of Venezuelan society should, as the Democratic Charter indicates, fully respect freedom of expression and therefore of the press. It should be clear that any complaint or deficiency on this should be resolved in accordance with the Declaration of Chapultepec. This Secretariat publicly expressed its confidence that the government of President Chávez would resolve in a satisfactory manner concerns about security and intimidation alleged by representatives of the media.

> On the issue of television, it is important to come to an agreement on a code of conduct which, beyond the issue of laws, ensures compatibility between public interest television transmissions and the media's normal programming.

On its side, the Inter-American Commission on Human Rights, in the Press Release of 05-10-02 expressed on the freedom of expression the following:

> 9. As regards freedom of expression, the Commission, through its Rapporteur for Freedom of Expression, has been closely monitoring the protection of this right in Venezuela through its annual reports and the report provided to the IACHR on the visit by the Executive Secretary, Santiago A. Canton, in February 2002. The IACHR has found that while it is possible to direct criticisms at the authorities, they result in acts of intimidation that limit the possibility of free expression. The IACHR finds that in Venezuela newspapers have not been shut down, nor have journalists been detained. Nonetheless, free expression cannot be limited to the absence of censorship, shutdowns of newspapers, or arbitrary detentions of those who speak freely. In the particular case of journalists, the IACHR received information describing verbal and physical assaults in recent months, and recalled that it is a responsibility of the state to provide protection to citizens, including social communicators, through strong measures aimed at disarming sectors of the civilian population who operate outside the law and who have been involved in such incidents.

In the Preliminary Observations dated 05-10-02, the Inter-American Commission on Human Rights highlighted the following:

> 37. Information has been received on other ways in which the full exercise of the freedom of expression has been hindered. These include the laws that criminalize offensive speech aimed at public officials, known as contempt laws (*leyes de vilipendio* or *leyes de* desacato). The IACHR has already held that such laws are incompatible with Article 13 of the Convention.

Progressively, an open violation to the citizen right to information begins to consolidate due to the uncontrolled abuse of the so called presidential "chains," with which the Secretary of the Presidency of the Republic obliged all media to broadcast political messages of the President of the Republic as party chief and not as a state or government chief, impeding the citizenry to be informed on other events it has the right to know.

The Inter-American Commission on Human Rights, in the Press Release of 05-10-02 stated on this problem the following:

> 10. In addition, the IACHR has observed with concern the scant information or, on occasion, total lack of information, available to Venezuelan society during the institutional crisis of last April. The IACHR noted that "although there may be many justifications to explain this lack of information, to the extent that the suppression of information has resulted from editorial decisions motivated by political considerations, it should be subject to a necessary process of analysis by the Venezuelan media as to their role at that time."

In the Preliminary Observations of 05-10-02, the Inter-American Commission on Human Rights was even more explicit, indicating the following:

> 37. Another example is the abusive use of emergency broadcast systems. The IACHR issued a press release, in a timely fashion, condemning the abusive and unnecessary use of this mechanism, which, used in a highly discretionary manner, and for purposes alien to the public interest, may constitute a form of censorship. The IACHR has been pleased to receive the information provided during this visit that indicates that to date there has been a considerable decline in the use of this mechanism. Nonetheless, the IACHR expects that in the future, clear criteria will be considered for the use of such emergency broadcast systems that take account of the public interest and real emergencies or truly compelling national needs. The various

kinds of pressure brought to bear on the broadcast media by initiating administrative proceedings which, if abusive, also constitute an indirect restriction on the freedom of expression, are a third example.

38. The difficulty of public access to information continues to go unanswered; accordingly, any initiative by the government to facilitate free access to information will contribute to ensuring that the citizenry is better informed.

39. The IACHR has been concerned by the scant information, or at times total lack of information, available to Venezuelan society during the days of the institutional crisis of April. Although there may be any number of justifications to explain this lack of information, to the extent that the suppression of information resulted from politically-motive editorial decisions, this should be the subject of an essential process of reflection by the Venezuelan media about their role at that moment.

Another limitation to the citizen right to information was the governmental prohibition to journalist and reporters of flying over the city of Caracas on the occasion of the march called by the opposition on March 1st 2002. Police intelligence officers were the only ones who flew over in helicopter.

The precarious situation of the freedom of expression in Venezuela, in any case, was witnessed by the Rapporteur for the Freedom of Expression and Secretary Executive of the Inter-American Commission on Human Rights, Santiago Canton, on the occasion of his visit to Caracas in February 2002. In this occasion he pointed out that:

Anyone who read Venezuelan papers could verify that, indeed, there exists a free debate of ideas. Nevertheless, from its viewpoint, freedom of expression is truly effective when that free debate of ideas does not generate negative consequences, and added that during his visit to Venezuela, he could verify the attacks against journalists and the attempts of harassment.

XIII. SITUATION OF DEMOCRACY AND THE PROBLEM OF SUBJECTION OF THE MILITARY TO CIVIL POWER

The Inter-American Democratic Charter states, furthermore, that the constitutional subordination of all the state institutions to the civil authority legally constituted is fundamental for democracy (Art. 4). That statement points to the subordination of the military to the civilian authority. However, in contrast, in Venezuela the progressive militarization of the state, as governmental policy has broken that subordination, and the danger of a military party at the service of the President of the Republic has arisen.

It is enough to remember how through the "Plan Bolivar 2000" public resources that should be managed for activities of social character by the state Governors, came to be managed by Commanders of Garrison, with the catastrophic administrative result denounced at all levels with serious prejudice of the military institution itself. The militarization of the government, on the other hand, is shown in the illegitimate extension of the scope of military justice to judge civil crimes.

It was also shown in the appointment he had made for almost all the high positions of the Public Administration of ex military officers of his personal circle, or active military officers.

Militarization, in any case, started to show negative effects within the Armed Forces, who's active Generals started to be concerned for the politics within the Armed Forces.

It must be pointed out, finally, that politics within the Armed Forces have been encouraged from the beginning by the President of the Republic himself, when justifying the elimination from the Constitution of the prohibition they have of being "deliberative." That contributed to justify the manifestations of Generals in public acts supporting the President of the Republic as party chief and not as Commander in chief of the Armed Forces, and of his political project. That also caused public manifestations of officers of the Armed Forces rejecting the President of the Republic and his policies.

Now, on this subject of military deliberation, the Secretary General of the OAS, in his Report to the General Assembly of 04-18-02, pointed out the following:

> I also want to note the development of a dangerous practice of debate within the armed forces. Many leaders of public affairs constantly listen for what the various armed forces have to say about political developments, and even about the orders of the Commander in Chief, Constitutional President of the Republic. Some cite an article of the Constitution as grounds for such debate.

Later, he added in the same Report:

> It is essential that the government, opposition, social actors, human rights organizations and the media commit to rejecting any participation in political debate on the part of the military, and to supporting military regulations which penalize this behavior. It is also essential that we abandon the interpretation held by some that that article of the constitution can serve as the basis for actions of any officials of the armed forces. I would like to reiterate that if we do not move in this direction, we could see new acts of insubordination against the civilian authorities. This General Assembly should be categorical in pointing out the obligation of constitutional subordination of all state institutions to the legally constituted civilian authority, as enshrined in Article 4 of the Democratic Charter.

In the Press Release of 05-10-02, the Inter-American Commission on Human Rights expressed the following on the subject of the "Armed Forces and Security Forces":

> 11. As for the armed forces and the security forces, during the visit the IACHR received expressions of concern over the undue influence of the armed forces in the country's political life, as well as excessive engagement by the armed forces in political decision-making. The IACHR takes this opportunity to recall that, in keeping with Article 4 of the Inter-American Democratic Charter, the constitutional subordination of all state institutions to civil authority is fundamental.

In the Preliminary Observation of 05-10-02, the Inter-American Commission on Human Rights widely developed its considerations on the subject of the Armed Forces and security bodies, in this way:

> During its on-site visit, the IACHR was concerned to hear several accounts of the undue influence of the Armed Forces in the political life of the country, and the existence of excessive involvement by the Armed Forces in political decisions. That concern can be traced back to the fact that the 1999 Venezuelan Constitution removed a rule traditionally included in the constitutions that preceded it, according to which the Armed Forces are an "*apolitical and*

non-deliberating" body. Also of special concern to the Commission is that the government and the social sectors have incited the Armed Forces or groups of officers to support them, and even to alter the constitutional order. The IACHR recalls that, under Article 4 of the Inter-American Democratic Charter, the constitutional subordination of all state institutions to the civilian authority is fundamental.

The Armed Forces cannot be involved in political decision-making. It is essential that there be a clear step forward in applying the military and criminal codes that punish such conduct, to avoid new acts of insubordination on the part of sectors of the Armed Forces against the democratically-elected civilian authority. The reality in the region shows that the involvement of the armed forces in politics generally precedes departures from the constitution, which in almost all cases leads to serious human rights violations. It is a responsibility of all sectors, but especially the Executive, to ensure that the Armed Forces play exclusively the roles of defending the national sovereignty for which they have been established and trained.

Finally, in the Final Comments of said Preliminary Observations, the Commission highlighted:

> Priority should be accorded to rejecting any means of involvement by the Armed Forces or National Police in political decision-making and to applying the military and criminal codes that punish such conduct. A decisive step forward in this direction is essential to avoid new acts of insubordination by sectors of the Armed Forces against the democratically-elected civilian authority. The reality in the region shows that the involvement of the Armed Forces in political decision-making is generally the prelude to a breakdown in the constitutional order, which in every case leads to grave violations of human rights. It is the responsibility of all sectors, especially the Government, to ensure that the Armed Forces perform exclusively their role of defending national sovereignty, for which they have been established and trained.

XIV. SITUATION OF DEMOCRACY AND THE PRECARIOUS FUNC-TIONING OF THE RULE OF LAW

Finally, the Inter-American Democratic Charter specifies also that the respect for the rule of law by all institutions and sectors of the society is equally essential to democracy. The latter can only exist in the rule of law. However, when public institutions and the control over them do not work due to the concentration of power in a few hands it is difficult to find the rule of law. Moreover that such situation provoked the institutionalization of violence.

An example of the malfunction of checks and balances among the state power was the issue in 2001, by the President in execution of an Enabling Statute, of 48 laws of primary importance for the country, through decrees-laws in open violation of the Constitution.

Indeed, the President of the Republic when issuing the set of decrees-laws bestowed, first violated the constitutional right to citizen participation set forth in articles 62, 70, 206 and 211 of the Constitution, by submitting no legislative draft to public consultation as provided for in those provisions and, furthermore, the recently issued Organic Law on Public Administration additionally penalizes with absolute nullity legislative texts issued by the President of the Republic without public consultation. Second, a good part of said decrees-laws violated the constitutional guarantee of legal reserve set forth in the Constitution and the American Convention on Human Rights, which reserve to the legislative organ made up by congressmen or representatives elected, the ruling and limitation of human rights, such as the right to property or economic freedom, whose regime cannot be delegated. Third, several decrees-laws are distorted of functions usurpation and are constitutionally null (Art. 138), for being issued by the President of the Republic with no bestowal or with no legislative delegation, violating, furthermore, article 203 of the Constitution that requires that decrees-laws bestowed shall be subjected to directions, purposes and frame of the subject established in the Enabling Statute, and violating also article 218, which only permits that laws be derogated by other laws and never by decrees without habilitation. Additionally, several decrees-laws have intrinsic and singular vices of unconstitutionality, for example, for being confiscatory of county and state public properties and in addition, private ones, as in the Law of Coastal Zones; or the attribute of rural property, as the use, pleasure and enjoyment that the Constitution guarantees and that have been violated by the Law on Lands and Rural Development.

In a democracy ruled by the rule of law, the possibility of controlling the constitutionality of these acts of legal rank, if the institutions worked, would be guaranteed by: first, the Human Right Ombudsman, acting in defense of the violated constitutional rights; second, the Supreme Court, diligently deciding the actions of unconstitutionality; third, the Attorney General of the Republic, rising claims to determine the responsibilities of the officers who could issue or execute acts in violation of human rights, and fourth, the National Assembly initiating an open discussion to review the laws.

On the other hand, we witness how in the National Assembly, in December 2001, congressmen who dare to create a Special Commission for studying and reviewing the decrees-laws bestowed were expulsed from the government party, considering that the National Assembly never ought to review the decrees-laws and that the Commission, for the only thing it could serve for was to justify them. The reaction of the public opinion, in any case, provoked that the National Executive reformed some of the laws issued through decrees-laws, but through the irregular way of reprinting them in Official Gazette "due to material error."

From the aforementioned, in Venezuela, at the light of the Inter-American Charter, democracy was in danger, or at least, in a precarious state, which jeopardize the public freedoms and justified the close attention and the solidarity of the international community, specially within the Inter-American system, to prevent a break of the democratic commitment of the American nations and of the democratic vocation of the Venezuelan people.

The Inter-American Commission on Human Rights, on the subject, in its Press Release of 05-10-02 specified that:

> The Constitution includes various elements that may hinder the effective observance of the rule of law. The constitutional machinery does not provide, in important situations, for checks and balances as a means of controlling the exercise of public authority and of guaranteeing the observance of human rights. The main legislative powers were derived under a regime authorizing the Executive branch to exercise them, with no defined limits. Also troubling for the Commission is the so-called "transitory regime." The IACHR considers that in the case of Venezuela, the transitional provisions have lasted beyond the normal and proper time frame, and have included directives with legislative content that go beyond the nature of a transitory regime.

Finally, it must be highlighted that the same Inter-American Commission on Human Rights, in the Preliminary Observations of 05-10-02 pointed out:

> 23. Both the constitutional gains and the backsliding in the new Constitution are reflected in the day-to-day situation in Venezuela. For important situations, the constitutional machinery does not provide for checks and balances as a means of controlling the exercise of public power and to ensure the observance of human rights. Thus, for example, the main legislative powers were derived under an enabling regime granted to the Executive branch that does not establish clear limits on the nature of the matters that can be the subject of such legislative powers.

The same Inter-American Commission on Human Rights, in the Preliminary Observations of 05-10-02 also expressed the following, when urging the strengthening of the rule of law in Venezuela as soon as possible:

> 66. The IACHR considers that the lack of independence of the Judiciary, the limitations on the freedom of expression, the active role of the Armed Forces in political decision-making, the extreme degree of polarization of society, the actions of the death squads, the scant credibility of the oversight institutions due to the uncertainty surrounding the constitutionality of their designation and the partiality of their actions, the lack of coordination among the security forces, all represent a clear weakness of the fundamental pillars of the rule of law in a democracy, in the terms of the American Convention and the Inter-American Democratic Charter. Accordingly, the Commission calls for the immediate strengthening of the rule of law in Venezuela.

XV. EXTREME POLARIZATION AND SOME BASIS IN 2002 FOR AN AGREEMENT NEGOTIATED TO RESTORE DEMOCRACY

1. *The Problem of Intolerance derived from the Extreme Polarization*

The situation of democracy in Venezuela on the occasion of the political practice developed by the government, with all the distortions of democracy analyzed before, has led to an extreme political polarization in the Venezuelan society that has caused intolerance between the government and the opposition, which seriously threaten the democratic governability. This situation existed prior to the events of April 2002 and has worsened subsequently.

The situation was pointed out by the Secretary General of the OAS, Cesar Gaviria, in his Report to the General Assembly of 04-18-02 on the occasion of the in-site visit to Venezuela, expressing:

> Although a good number of representatives of organizations outside the government have accepted the call of the President for dialogue, even after the fateful events of April 11 and 12, there is excessive polarization, not only among the natural political actors, such as the government, the political parties, and opposition groups, but among almost all labor, business, and civil society groups, representatives of some other branches of government, and the media. This excessive polarization has shades of intolerance that stand in the way of democratic dialogue and the quest for agreements that would provide a degree of understanding so as to maintain social harmony. There seems to be a widespread conviction that renewed confrontation between friends and opponents of the government is inevitable and could lead to increased social protest.

Equally, the Inter-American Commission on Human Rights, in the Preliminary Observations dated 05-10-02, after the *in-loco* visit to the country, pointed out this problem in the following way:

> 14. It should be underscored that prior to the events of April, the IACHR was profoundly concerned to learn of the existence of an extreme polarization of Venezuelan society, which had its most tragic and grave expression in the events of April 10, 11, 12, 13, and 14. In the report of the Office of the Special Rapporteur for Freedom of Expression for the year 2000, the IACHR stated that during that year, President Hugo Chávez made certain statements that could be considered as intended to intimidate the press and journalists. His attitude may have contributed to creating an environment of intimidation of the press that does not foster public debate and the exchange of opinions and ideas, which are necessary for coexistence in democracy. In addition, during the visit by the Executive Secretary in February 2002, an atmosphere of intolerance and political polarization was found which, if maintained, could have threatened the full and responsible exercise of freedom of expression and the rule of law, which is aimed at safeguarding democratic institutions.

Therefore, it is evident that after the events of April 2002, one of the more concerning political problems of the current Venezuela is the excessive polarization of the society and of the governmental and opposition positions, which even more leads to be irreconcilable. Much hate has been sowed in the President's constant speech and all the Venezuelans are suffering now the fruits of the same. Hate leads to the consolidation of extremes in irreconcilable situation, and from hate to violence there is only a pace. We shall avoid that the country breaks in two halves definitively, since no one will be the winner. We all will lose and even more in the situation of economic worsening and poverty in which we are now.

What we Venezuelans should think immediately, more than identifying those guilty of the bad things happening to the country is how we shall prevent a definitive confrontation. Any help that we receive is useful, so we should start by identifying the two parties in conflict, in order to solve it.

On the one hand, there is the government, and on the other hand, there are the opposition political parties and the different groups of civil society that, fortunately in June 2002 created a Democratic Coordination of the Venezuelan Society, which even adopted a Democratic Reconstruction Agreement. Those should be the parties that have to prevent the confrontation and negotiate the reconstruction of democracy.

For that, the first thing to look for is a dialogue between parties. The Secretary General of the OAS, Cesar Gaviria, in this way, in his Report to the General Assembly of 04-18.02 expressed:

> Given the very difficult situation experienced by democratic institutions in Venezuela, I also thought it advisable to look at aspects of the country's institutional order in relation to the Democratic Charter.

Adding furthermore that:

> I would like to highlight, as well, some measures that must be taken to diffuse some of the more serious conflicts, to regain governability, to achieve political stability, and to foster economic recovery.

It is fundamental that all sectors of society, at least all those I have referred to; seek mechanisms or agreements which ensure that respect for the Constitution is the foundation and framework of action for everyone in Venezuelan public life.

Because of that, the General Assembly, on the occasion of the Report of the Secretary General, Cesar Gaviria, of 04-18-02, resolved:

3. To support the initiative of the Venezuelan Government to convoke immediately a national, all-inclusive dialogue, and to urge all sectors of Venezuelan society to participate and devote their best and most determined efforts to bring about the full exercise of democracy in Venezuela, fully abiding by the Constitution and taking into account the essential elements of representative democracy set forth in Articles 3 and 4 of the Inter-American Democratic Charter.

Time has passed with no effective dialogue, and perhaps we are now in the situation that the phase for dialogue alone as an instrument to conciliate positions passed and is over. Currently, dialogue, resolves nothing, since it is a deaf exercise in which each party talks without listening to the other. Instead of conciliating, it has produced more frustration, disappointment and polarization.

We think that Venezuelans shall undertake the phase of negotiation between the parties. As recently said father Jose Virtuoso in his speech on July 05:

The peace we are looking for in Venezuela, through dialogue and conciliation cannot be other than a consensual agreement product of a true negotiation between the parties involved.

Even though Virtuoso referred to the negotiation for the social matters, so the "Republic commits to satisfying its debts with the majorities of poor people of the country," the principle is applied to all the matters affecting the country, and particularly, to the economy and politics. For that, we proposed in July 2002 the following points for an agenda of negotiation from a political viewpoint.

2.   Negotiation to Preserve Democracy

To prevent war and further confrontation, to reaffirm and reconstruct democracy in the country, it is essential for the opposition and the government to negotiate. In my opinion, that is the major political challenge that Venezuelans face in their future.

Venezuela did not vote in 1998 and 1999 to terminate democracy. The collective manifestation of will of political change that brought Hugo Chavez to power had as a purpose and objective to improve democracy. The latter, on the one hand, had lost it representative essence, since the political parties have monopolized the representation; and on the other hand, it didn't allow space for political participation due to the state and partisan centralism.

That form of exercising democracy, which functioned badly, was the one that needed to be changed to make it more representative and more participative; that is to say, to improve it, not to terminate it.

However, the political practice of the last three years, particularly the one carried out from the government and from different centers of the public power has harmed the basis of democracy, whose legitimacy seems to remain just in the popular election as origin of the rulers. However, in the contemporary world, democracy is not limited to sole representation through suffrage. As pointed out by the Inter-American Commission on Human Rights in the Press Release of 05-10-02 on the occasion of its on-site visit to Venezuela, when making its Final Comments:

> The main source of democratic legitimacy is that granted by the popular will, expressed in free, periodic, and universal elections. Yet elections in themselves are not sufficient to ensure the full observance of democracy. As indicated in the Inter-American Democratic Charter, the essential elements of representative democracy include, among others, respect for human rights and fundamental freedoms; access to and the exercise of power subject to the rule of law; the holding of periodic, free, and fair elections, based on universal suffrage and secret balloting as an expression of the popular sovereignty; a pluralistic regime of political parties and organizations; and the separation of powers and independence of the various branches of government. In addition, the following are fundamental components of the exercise of democracy: transparency in government, openness, responsible public administration on the part of governments, respect for social rights, and respect for freedom of expression and freedom of the press. The constitutional subordination of all the institutions of the State to the lawfully-constituted civilian authority, and respect by all entities and sectors of society for the rule of law, are also fundamental for democracy. In this context, the functioning of an independent and impartial Judiciary as a guarantor of the protection of human rights, as a vehicle for obtaining justice from the victims, and as an organ of oversight and a check on the action of the other branches of government is fundamental to the rule of law.

Consequently, democracy is much more than electing rulers, since those even with an electoral origin in many cases have turned into tyrants who have terminated historical democracies. History has taught us that leaders that had popular support and reached power through votes several times originated majorities that later were despotic.

The essential condition for a negotiation between the government and the opposition in Venezuela, therefore, is the acknowledge of democracy as the only political regime Venezuelans want, which, as affirmed and developed in the Inter-American Charter is not reduced to the sole election of the rulers. That negotiation has to be aimed at satisfying a series of essential conditions of democracy that currently are omitted.

That is why the General Assembly, on the occasion of the Report of the Secretary General of 04-18-02, after his visit to Venezuela resolved:

> 5. To encourage the Government and all social sectors and institutions in Venezuela to pursue their activities in accordance with the rule of law, and to seek national reconciliation.

> 7. To provide the support and help of the OAS as required by the Government of Venezuela for the consolidation of the democratic process.

3. *Agreement to Assure the Effectiveness of Participative Democracy*

Before all and beyond the official speeches there is the need to negotiate the effectiveness of participative democracy. Political participation beyond votes in elections or referenda implies the right of citizens and organized groups of society to be consulted on the text of draft laws and by-laws. Congress and the Executive have the constitutional and legal obligation (Arts. 206 and 211) and (Organic Law on Public Administration) of consulting. *This obligatory popular consultation of draft laws before their sanctioning or approval* is the *first point of negotiation* to reach an agreement between the involved parties and to prevent confrontation and assure peace.

Moreover, according to the Constitution, political participation requires the institution of the Nominating Committees for appointing the heads of the judicial branch and the Citizen and Electoral branches. Said Nominations Committees shall be made up exclusively for representatives of the diverse sectors of society as provided for in the Constitution (Arts. 270, 279 and 295). *The government shall comply with and execute the Constitution and assure that those Committees be effective instruments of political participation. This is the second point of negotiation* for an agreement between the involved parties, in reconstructing democracy.

In addition, the State and all its components have to assume the policy of decentralization of power as the only effective way to assure the possibility of citizenry participation in the management of public affairs. The execution of article 158 of the Constitution is unavoidable and *an agreement in that sense shall be negotiated, to approach the power to the citizen and its communities, which constitutes the only way to participate in the public management. This is the third point of negotiation of the involved parties* to assure the effective democratization of all the national territory and of all the inhabited centers that made it up.

4.   Agreement to Assure the Effectiveness of the Human Rights

The exercise and guarantee of Human Rights shall be the result of an agreement between the involved parties. These ones and particularly the government shall assure that the constitutional rights are in force, in particular, the right to life, the right to freely associate and the right to property. *The fourth point of negotiation to reach a democratic agreement between the involved parties, therefore, shall consist in the effective elimination of the death squads and of all groups pretending to exercise force outside the state scope, assuring the Armed Forces the monopoly of the weapons.*

In addition, *a fifth point of negotiation implies reaching an agreement that effectively assures the property rights, through a systematic and generalized public action that prevents the occupation of lands and properties and that in the event of producing invasions, the lands be effectively restored to their legitimate owners.*

5.   Agreements to Assure the Effective Functioning of Public Powers

The access to power and its exercise shall assure that it be made according to the rule of law. The Constitution sets forth two ways to access power: in the first place, through popular election of representatives to conform the Legislative Power and the head of the Executive Power; and in the second place through the appointment of the heads of the Citizen Power (Attorney General, Comptroller General and Human Right Ombudsman), Electoral Power (National Electoral Council) and the magistrates of the Supreme Court by the National Assembly previous nomination by two Nominations Committees made up exclusively by representatives of different sectors of society. *A sixth point of negotiation between the involved parties must lead to an agreement for the immediate sanction of laws ruling the Nominations Committees for the appointment of said high officers.*

There shall also be assured the exercise of the power subjected to the rule of law, that is to say, as set forth in the Constitution. *A seventh point of negotiation shall be an agreement to assure that the congressmen to the National Assembly, effectively, be representatives of the people and the states, not subjected to mandates and instructions, but to their conscience as provided for in the Constitution.* (Art. 201), eliminating the strong control of the parliamentary blocks or opinion blocks which are contrary to the Constitution.

It must be an object of negotiation, moreover, effectively holding periodic, free, fair elections based on universal suffrage and secret balloting as expression of the popular sovereignty. *An eighth point of negotiation shall consist in reaching an agreement to assure the effective independence and autonomy of the Electoral Power, through the sanction of the Organic Law of Suffrage according to the constitutional principles.*

6.   Agreements to Effectively Assure Democratic Political Pluralism

Government and opposition shall negotiate the assurance of the effective existence of a plural regime of parties and political organizations. Political pluralism is the democratic guarantee for all political organizations to participate in the political arena and gain access to power. Therefore, *a ninth point of negotiation is reaching an agreement to make pluralism effective, assuring that officers be only and effectively at the state service and not at the service of any party (Art. 145).*

The President of the Republic, consequently, cannot continue being the president of a political party and his ministers cannot continue being members of the board of directors of the government party.

On the other hand, in order to assure political pluralism, public administration shall be at the service of all citizens (Art. 141) and not at the service of a particular group. *The tenth point of negotiation to reach an agreement between the involved parties is for the State to stop interfering in the organization of the civil society, in particular, stopping the organization of Bolivarian Circles from the public organs, such as the Presidency of the Republic or the Counties.*

The Constitution sets forth that the political parties shall elect their authorities in internal elections with the participation of their members (Art. 67). *An eleventh point of negotiation between the parties is reaching an agreement between all the political parties of submitting to the process of internal renovation of their authorities in elections in which all their members participate.*

7.   Agreements to Assure Public Branches Independence

Effectively assuring the separation and independence of public branches shall be submitted to negotiation between the government and the opposition.

In consequence, *a twelfth point of negotiation between the involved parties is reaching an agreement in which the Executive Branch relinquishes concentration of power and extreme centralization.* For that, the parties shall reach an agreement that assures the appointment of the magistrates of the Supreme Court, members of the National Electoral Council, Attorney General, Comptroller General and the Human Right Ombudsman as provided for in the Constitution.

A *thirteenth point of negotiation between government and opposition shall lead to an agreement to put an end to the transitory constitutional regime, established from 1999 on, in violation of the Constitution.*

8.   *Agreements to Assure Public Management Transparency and Responsibi-lity*

In order to assure the exercise of democracy, the transparency of governmental activities shall be negotiated. For that, *a fourteenth point of negotiation has to lead to an agreement between the involved parties that assures the Public Administration is at the service of all citizens, and not at the service of only part of them, and, in addition, that it is managed and led by public officers appointed in open competition, as provided for in the Constitution.* This agreement shall imply the exclusion from the public function of the "governmental boot" and assuring the existence of a permanent civil service that operates irrespective of the government.

On the other hand, in order to assure the probity and responsibility of the government in the public management, we shall negotiate. For that, *a fifteenth point of negotiation between the government and the opposition shall be reaching an agreement to assure effectively the control mechanism of the public management, in particular, the parliamentary control of Public Administration and the fiscal control of the public management, with an autonomous and independent General Comptroller- ship, and an efficient national system of tax control.*

9.   *Agreements to Assure the Freedom to Form and Join Unions*

It shall be object of negotiation between the involved parties the effective respect of labor rights, in particular, the right to form and join unions. For that, *a sixteenth point of negotiation between the government and the opposition is an agreement that puts an end to the state interference in the trade unions and in the state organization of the election of professional groups, which shall be outside state control.*

Additionally, it is unavoidable a negotiation between government and the opposition to effectively assure the freedom of expression and press. In a democratic society the media is an effective means of controlling the exercise of power, therefore, a *seventeenth point of negotiation between the involved parties shall assure the effective exercise of freedom of expression and the right to information, with no private or official distortions.*

10.   *Agreements to Assure the Subjection of the Armed Forces to the Civilian Authority*

It is unavoidable in a democratic society to reach an effective constitutional subjection of all state institutions to the civilian authority legally constituted, in particular, the subjection of the military authority to the civilian authority. Therefore, *an eighteenth point of negotiation is to reach an agreement to eliminate the military deliverance and accomplishing the re conduction of the activity of the National Armed Force to its constitutional functions.*

That implies a *nineteenth point of negotiation between the parties that lead to reassuming by the Armed Forces the monopoly it constitutionally has of the weapons, and disarming the civilian groups that have appeared in the last years, particularly the Bolivarian Circles.*

11. *Agreements to Assure the Effectiveness of the Constitution*

Finally, all the involved parties shall reach an agreement to respect the rule of law, which involves all the entities and sectors of the society. That leads to a *twentieth point of negotiation between the government and the opposition so an unbreakable commitment exists of assuring the respect of the Constitution and laws, eliminating all marks of transitory constitutional regime and preventing all action of civilian disobedience.*

The Secretary General of the OAS, in his Report to the General Assembly of 04-18-02 expressed as a point of agreement the following:

> It is imperative that an agreement be reached so that Article 350 of the Constitution is not interpreted as everyone's right to rebellion. Such an interpretation might well lead to worse violence than that which has already occurred. Everyone must do their part to reach that understanding.

In any case, the forgoing leads to *a twenty-one point of negotiation to reach an agreement that allows assuring the institution of a judicial branch effectively independent, with a set of magistrates separated from politics, which implies eliminating the syndrome of provisional regimes that currently exists in the Judicial branch, which conspires against its autonomy and independence.*

In this context, immediately and in particular the involved parties shall create mechanisms to clarify the true of the events of April 11 and establish the responsibilities for the deaths that occurred during a pacific walk. Before the lack of a reliable Judicial branch *a twentieth second point of negotiation shall be reaching an agreement for creating a Commission of the Truth that has credibility for that mission.*

*

None of the aforementioned agreements that could have served for the restoration of democracy were reached. The Government continued to polarize the country and during the years that have passed since 2002, the described situation of democracy worsened.

As aforementioned, the *essential elements of the representative democracy* mentioned in its article 3 of the **Inter American Democratic Charter**, that should be the corner stone of the organization and functioning of the States, includes the respect for human rights and fundamental liberties; the access to power and its exercise with subjection to the Rule of law; the celebration of periodical elections, free, fair and based on the universal and secret vote, as expression of the ruling of the people; plural regime of the political parties and organizations; and the separation and independence of public powers.

During the past years since 2002, these essential elements of democracy have continued to be ignored or fractured, specifically in the name of a supposed participative democracy and of a supposed Popular Power where the people also supposedly participate directly.

The fact is that during these last years, regarding the essential elements of democracy, it can be said that never before, there had been more violation of human rights. To realize this situation, it is enough to record the number of accusations made against the Venezuelan state before the Inter-American Commission on Human Rights. This has always been a good thermometer to determine the degree of violations of human rights by a State.

Also, the access to power has been achieved contrary to the Rule of law, by violating the separation and independence of the judicial, citizen and electoral branches of government. They are all controlled by the union established between the national Executive and the national Assembly, which is why it is not possible to control the access to power according to what is stated in the Rule of Law[42].

Particularly, the Electoral Power, was kidnapped since 2003, with the complicity of the Constitutional Chamber of the Supreme Court, reason why the elections that have taken place, have lacked of justice, and the last political reforms executed and proposed, simply aim to the substitution of the electoral representation by supposed citizen groups in the communities and communal councils whose members are not elected, but consigned from the summit of the Popular Power controlled by the President of the Republic.

The plural regime of parties has been destroyed and the Single socialist Party, imbricate in the apparatus of the State and also controlled by the President of the Republic, will takeover, not only the supposed Popular Power, but all the political and social life of the country, given the capitalism of State that has been intensified as consequence of the rich petroleum State. Because everything depends on the State, only those who are part of the Single Party could have a political, administrative, economical and social life. And this entire institutional distortion, without the existence of separation or independence between the branches of government, not

---

42   See Allan R. Brewer-Carías, *La Sala Constitucional versus el Estado democrático de derecho. El secuestro del poder electoral y de la Sala Electoral del Tribunal Supremo y la confiscación del derecho a la participación política*, Los Libros de *El Nacional*, Colección Ares, Caracas 2004; "El secuestro del Poder Electoral y la confiscación del derecho a la participación política mediante el referendo revocatorio presidencial: Venezuela 2000-2004," in *Revista Jurídica del Perú*, Año LIV N° 55, Lima, March-April 2004, pp. 353-396; "El secuestro del Poder Electoral y de la Sala Electoral del Tribunal Supremo y la confiscación del derecho a la participación política mediante el referendo revocatorio presidencial: Venezuela: 2000-2004," in *Revista Costarricense de Derecho Constitucional*, Volume V, Instituto Costarricense de Derecho Constitucional, Editorial Investigaciones Jurídicas S.A., San José 2004, pp. 167-312; "El secuestro de la Sala Electoral por la Sala Constitucional del Tribunal Supremo de Justicia, in *La Guerra de las Salas del TSJ frente al Referendum Revocatorio*," Editorial Aequitas, Caracas 2004, C.A., pp. 13-58"; "El secuestro del poder electoral y la confiscación del derecho a la participación política mediante el referendo revocatorio presidencial: Venezuela 2000-2004," Stvdi Vrbinati, *Rivista Trimestrale di Scienze Giuridiche, Politiche ed Economiche*, Year LXXI – 2003/04 Nuova Serie A – N. 55,3, Università degli studi di Urbino, Urbino, 2004, pp. 379-436; "«El secuestro del Poder Electoral y la confiscación del derecho a la participación política mediante el referendo revocatorio presidencial: Venezuela 2000-2004." in *Boletín Mexicano de Derecho Comparado*, Instituto de Investigaciones Jurídicas, Universidad Nacional Autónoma de México, N° 112. México, January-April 2005 pp. 11-73.

only in their horizontal division (Legislative, Executive, Judicial, People and Electoral) due to the control that the Executive Power has over them; but in their vertical distribution, where the proposals in circulation aim for the elimination of the federation, the substitution of the federated States by alleged "federal cities," and the elimination of municipalism and its replacement by communal councils and people assemblies. All of these in order to eliminate every trace of political decentralization, that is, of autonomous entities in the territory, which prevents every possibility for democratic participation.

But besides the essential elements of democracy mentioned above, the *Inter-American Charter*, in its article 4, also defined the following *fundamental components of the democratic exercise*: the transparency of governmental activities, integrity, responsibility of governments in the public management, and the respect of social rights and freedom of speech and press. Also, the constitutional subordination of all institutions of the State to the legally constituted civil authority, and the respect to the Rule of law of all the entities and sectors of society, were declared equally fundamental for democracy. Thus, democracy is much more than just elections and voting.

Unfortunately, all these essential elements have also been ignored or fractured in Venezuela, also in the name of a supposed Popular Power: the governmental activity deployed by the rich, and during the last years suddenly wealthy, State managed uncontrollably in a poor country, stopped being transparent due to the specific absence of fiscal control, given the submission of the Citizens Power (General Comptroller, Attorney General and the Peoples' Defendant) to the Executive power; this situation has made the true concept of integrity disappear, because it is not possible to demand any kind of responsibility to the government for the public management, among other aspects due to the submission of the judicial power; all of this, campaigning corruption in a way never seen before. On the other hand, the careful management of social rights -which has been the main governmental slogan, particularly towards the international community- has been staged in a policy of uncontrolled distribution of petroleum wealth, like it is never going to diminish, nationalizing everything in the country, dismantling the productive apparatus and without generating investments; and all these without having poverty or unemployment levels decrease.

Finally, the freedom of speech and press, since the direct censorships of the last military dictatorship of the fifties, has never been so threatened, imposing self-censorship over the persecution base to reporters and dissident media, like it has repetitively been confirmed by the Rapporteur on Freedom of Expression of the Inter-American Commission on Human Rights, and it derives from the multiple accusations made before the Commission and the recommendations and precautionary measures adopted by it.

Conversely, the militarism that has taken over the State, in a way that even though the authoritarian regime had been the result of a military *coup d'Etat*, then, another fundamental value for democracy is the constitutional subordination of all the institutions of the State to the legally constituted civil authority, by the military empowering of the State and its imbrication's with the Single Party, has been fractured, leaving the respect to the Rule of law as another value postponed by all entities and sectors of society. All of this has created a military plan which is a constitutional novelty, and has been taking the nation to a situation in which the Armed Forces, with the support of the Head of State, has taken over the civil Administration of the State, as it has been occurring during the last few years. All of these dispositions show a militarism constitutional frame truly unique in the political and constitutional history of Latin-America, not even found in the Constitutions of prior military regimes.

During the last years then, only one of the elements of democracy has been used in Venezuela, to have elections, in order to destroy all other values and essential components of democracy; thus, the democracy fraud that has taken place.

CHAPTER VIII

THE CENTRALIZATION OF POWER IN A
"CENTRALIZED FEDERATION"
(2004)

This essay is devoted to study the situation of the Federation in Venezuela, as a highly "Centralized Federation," and is based on a paper titled "Centralized Federation in Venezuela" written for the Seminar on *Federalism in the Americas and Beyond*, organized by Professor Robert Barker, Duquesne University, *Duquesne School of Law*, Pittsburgh, on November 13, 2004. Some of the reflections contained in this essay were initially written in the Presentation on *The Centralized Federation in Venezuela and Sub National Constitutions*, for the Conference on *Federalism and Sub-National Constitutions, Design and Reform*, organized by the *Center for State Constitutional Studies, Rutgers University*, New Jersey, held at the Rockefeller Foundation Study and Conference Center, in Bellagio, Italy, May 23-26, 2004. The text of this essay with the title: "Centralized Federalism in Venezuela," was published in *Duquesne Law Review*, Volume 43, Number 4, summer 2005, Duquesne University, Pittsburgh, Pennsylvania, 2005, pp. 629-643.

Federalism in Venezuela reveals a very contradictory form of government.[43] Typically, a Federation is a politically decentralized State organization based on the

---

43   See in general: Allan R. Brewer Carías, *Federalismo y Municipalismo en la Constitución de 1999 (Una reforma Insuficiente y regresiva)*, Editorial Jurídica Venezolana, Caracas, 2001; "El proceso de descentralización política en América Latina" (pp. 109-146) and "La descentralización de la Federación Venezolana (pp. 181-202), in Allan R. Brewer-Carías, *Reflexiones sobre la organización territorial del Estado en Venezuela y en la América Colonial*, Editorial Jurídica Venezolana, Caracas 1997; "La opción entre democracia y autoritarismo (pp. 41-60), "Democratización, descentralización política y reforma del Estado (pp. 105-126);"El Municipio, la descentralización política y la democracia" (pp. 127-142), in Allan R. Brewer-Carías, *Reflexiones sobre el constitucionalismo en América*, Editorial Jurídica Venezolana, Caracas, 2001; "El 'Estado federal descentralizado' y la centralización de la Federación en Venezuela. Situación y perspectiva de una contradicción constitucional" (pp. 135-138); "Algunos problemas de las Constituciones estadales (Constituciones subnacionales) en la Fede-

existence and functioning of autonomous States. The power of that decentralized state organization is distributed among the national State (the Union or the federation) and the member States. In contrast, the Federation in Venezuela is a Centralized Federation, which of course, is a contradiction in itself.

That is why, unfortunately, my Country is not a good example for explaining "Federalism in the Americas," being as it is a Federation based in a very centralized national government, with 23 formal autonomous states. Each of these 23 formal autonomous states is without their own effective public policies and without their own substantive sub-national constitutions.

But our Federation has not always been like it is now. The process of centralization of the Federation progressively occurred during the 20th Century, and has been particularly accentuated during the past five years.

The centralization process began with the installment of the authoritarian government of Juan Vicente Gómez, who ruled throughout a dictatorship that lasted approximately three decades, spanning the first half of the 20th Century. During these years no democratic institutions were developed.

The transition from autocracy to democracy began in Venezuela between 1945 and 1958, when a democratic regime, in accordance with the democratic Constitution of 1961, came into power. This democratic Constitution was the longest Constitution in force in all Venezuelan history. This Constitution, as it was of a product of a political pact signed by all democratic forces (*Pacto de Punto Fijo*, 1958), assured the dominance of a very centralized political party system. During the last 40 years of democratic development, this centralized political party system in fact impedes the reinforcement of federal institutions.

Nonetheless, important efforts were made during the Nineties in order to politically decentralize the federation. I have had the privilege of being an actor in that process by serving as the Minister of State for Decentralization (1993-1994). My efforts, however, were later abandoned, mainly due to the crisis of the centralized party system, and to the consequential political void it produced in the Country.

It was the generalized political crisis of our Democratic Party system that ultimately provoked the covenant of a National Constituent Assembly not regulated in the 1961 Constitution, resulting in the sanctioning of a new Constitution. The 1999 Constitution of the "Bolivarian Republic of Venezuela," as it is now called, was approved by referendum (Dec. 15, 1999).

This Constitution, which in fact covers with a democratic veil an authoritarian regime, regulates a very centralized system of government, where all powers of the State can be concentrated, as they now are. The Constitution has excellent declarations, including the "Decentralized Federal State," the enumeration of human rights, and the "penta separation" of State branches of government. However, each of these

---

ración" (pp. 139-149), in Allan R. Brewer-Carías, *Constitución, democracia y control del Poder,* Universidad de Los Andes, Mérida 2004.

declarations is contradicted by other regulations in the same Constitution, which allow conduct to the contrary.

I have also had the privilege of being elected as an independent candidate to the National Constituent Assembly of 1999. Thus I personally know of its achievements from within, and that is why, in relation to its real centralistic and authoritarian framework, I extended dissenting votes, all of which were duly published along with my constituents' proposals.

Our Federation has not always been a Centralized Federation. During the 19th Century, notwithstanding the political turmoil derived from the building process of the National State facing the regional *Caudillo* powers, a federal system of government was established. We also had, as in many Federations, the development of the centrifugal and centripetal political forces, which provoked the classical political pendulum movement between centralization and decentralization experienced by many Federations. In general terms, it can be said that Federalism prevails, and it prevails particularly because it's historical roots.

I. SOME ASPECTS OF THE HISTORY AND DEVELOPMENT OF THE VENEZUELAN FEDERATION

We have to bear in mind, when studying Federalism in Venezuela, that the first Constitution of an independent Latin American State was the *Federal Constitution for the States of Venezuela*, sanctioned by an elected General Congress, on December, 21 1811, at the beginning of the Independence Wars. The Constitution declared the states or provinces as sovereign states, all of which in 1810-1811 had declared independence from Spain and adopted their own provincial constitutions or form of government.

By means of this 1811 Constitution, the country adopted a federal form of government, following the influence of the United States Constitution. At that time, we must remember, a Federation was the only new constitutional instrument different to the centralized monarchical states, which was recently invented in this country. That invention was followed by the Venezuelan framers of the new state in order to unite the seven former Spanish Colonial Provinces that formed the Venezuelan State, which had never been previously united. In our territory, we did not have Viceroyalties or *Audiencias* (until 1786), and a General Captaincy for military purposes integrating the Provinces was only established in 1777. Thus, it can be said that Venezuela was the second country in constitutional history to adopt federalism, which is an important aspect of our constitutional history[44].

It was after the endless civil conflict that marked the history of Venezuela during the 19th Century that the federal form of government began to be limited. The conflict stemmed from the permanent struggles between the regional *Caudillos* and the weak central power that was been formed. This was the consequence of the central-

---

44   After the North American independence (1776) and federation (1777), the first Latin American Country to declare independence and adopt a Constitution was Venezuela in 1811, adopting the federal form of State.

izing tendencies which were derived from the consolidation of the National State, a process that was particularly reinforced during the first half of the 20th century.

During those decades, the autocratic regimes of the Country, aided by the income derived from the new exploitation of oil by the National State (oil and the subsoil always has been the public property of the State) contributed to the consolidation of the national State in all aspects. Contributions included the creation of a national army, a public administration, taxation, and legislation. These centralizing tendencies almost provoked the disappearance of the Federation, the territorial distribution of power, and the effective autonomy of the 23 States and of the Federal District, which compose the federal formal organization of the State.

The democratization process of the country really began in the second half of 20th Century, and particularly after the adoption of the 1961 Constitution, in which the Federal form of the State was kept, but with a highly centralized national organization. Due to the democratization process of the country and according to express constitutional provisions, a political decentralization process was forced to be applied, beginning in 1989, when the party system crisis exploded, with the transfer of powers and services from the national level of government to the States level. The process was forced by the democratic pressure exercised against the political parties, all of which were in the middle of a severe leadership crisis.

One of the most important reforms then adopted, was the provision of the direct election of the States Governors which until that year were just public officials appointed by the President of the Republic. In December 1989, for the first time since the 19th Century, States Governors were elected by universal, direct and secret suffrage, and regional political life began to play an important role in the country, initializing the increasing appearance of regional and local political leaders, many of whom were from outside the traditional political parties.

Ultimately, this crisis in the centralized party system, gave rise to the 1999 Constitution; which if it is true that provoked a radical change in the political players nationwide, also started the reversal of the decentralizing political efforts that were being made.

For the sanctioning of the new Constitution, a National Constituent Assembly was then elected in 1999, exclusively promoted by an anti-party new leader that appeared in the middle of the political vacuum, the President of the Republic Hugo Chávez Frías, a former Lieutenant-Colonel who led an attempted *coup d'Etat* in 1992, and who had been elected the previous year, in 1998. The National Constituent Assembly then became, the main institutional tool used by the newly elected President to conduct the take-over of all the branches of government of the State, and to reinforce the centralization of the Federation. This Constituent Assembly was elected in July 1999, and was made up of 131 members. 125 of those members were blind supporters of the President and only four dissident voices, including my own, were heard during the six months the Constituent Assembly functioned. The four dissidents were indeed, a very precarious "opposition" to the President.

Unfortunately, the 1999 constitution-making process was not conceived as an instrument of conciliation aimed at reconstructing the democratic system and assuring its effective governance. That would have required the political commitment of all the components of society and the participation of all political parties and sectors of society in order to design a new functioning democracy. Unfortunately, this did not occur. The constitutional process of 1999, in fact, served to facilitate the total takeover of all the branches of government by a new political group that crushed not only all the others, but also the autonomy of the States of the Federation.

As a result, almost all of the opportunities for inclusion and public participation vanished, and the 1999 constitution-making-process became an endless *coup d'Etat*, performed by the National Constituent Assembly. The Assembly began its activities by violating the existing 1961 Constitution by intervening and assuming all branches of government, over which it had no power, according to the referendum mandate that created the Assembly. The Constituent Assembly also decided to limit the powers of the federated States without any legitimate authority, by eliminating the State's Legislative Assemblies.

These violations of the 1961 Constitution, still in force at the time, were subsequently followed by the violation of the new 1999 Constitution voted on by the same Constituent Assembly. This took place after its popular approval by referendum held on the December 15th 1999. The violation began a week later, when the Constituent Assembly enacted a "Transitional Constitutional Regime" decree, which was not authorized in the new Constitution, and which was not submitted to, nor approved by, popular vote. It was that extra constitutional regime which allowed the Constituent Assembly to continue the endless *coup d'Etat* initiated a few month earlier, affecting the separations of powers, and allowing the new National Assembly elected in 2000 to legislate outside the constitutional framework

The final result of that process is that the new Constitution of 1999 did not have the necessary provisions to undertake the democratic changes that were most needed in Venezuela, namely, the effective separation of powers, the political decentralization of the Federation and the reinforcement of States and municipal political powers. The Constitution of 1999, in fact, continued with the same centralizing foundation embodied in the previous Constitution and, in some cases, centralizing even more aspects. For instance, if it is true that it defined the decentralization process as a "national policy devoted to strengthened democracy" (Article 158), in contrast the national public policy executed during the last five years can be characterized as a progressive centralization of government, without any real development of local and regional authorities. Consequently, in Venezuela, federalism has been postponed and democracy has been progressively weakened.

II. CONSTITUTIONAL PROVISIONS RELATING TO FEDERALISM IN THE 1999 CONSTITUTION

A Federation, above all, is a form of government in which public power is territorially distributed among various levels of government with autonomous political institutions. That is why federalism and political decentralization are intimately related concepts. Specifically, decentralization is the most effective instrument not only to guarantee civil and social rights, but to allow effective participation by citizens in the political process. In this context, the relation between local government and the population is essential. That is why all consolidated democracies in the world today are embodied in clearly decentralized forms of governments, such as

Federations, or like the new Regional States, as is the case of countries like Spain, Italy and France. That is why it can be said that the strong centralizing tendencies developing in Venezuela in recent years are contrary to democratic governance and political participation.

According to Article 4 of the 1999 Constitution, the Republic of Venezuela is formally defined "as a decentralized Federal State under the terms set out in the Constitution" governed by the principles of "territorial integrity, solidarity, concurrence and co-responsibility." Nonetheless, "the terms set out in the Constitution," are without a doubt centralizing, and Venezuela continues to be a contradictory "Centralized Federation."

Article 136 of the 1999 Constitution states that "public power is distributed among the municipal, state and national entities," establishing a Federation with three levels of political governments and autonomy (similar to Brazilian Federation): *a national level* exercised by the Republic (federal level); the *States level*, exercised by the 23 States and a Capital District; and the *municipal level,* exercised by the 338 existing Municipalities. On each of these three levels of government, the Constitution provides that it must always be "democratic, participatory, elected, decentralized, alternative, responsible, plural and with revocable mandates" (Article 6). Regarding the Capital District, it has substituted the former Federal District which was established in 1863, with the elimination of traditional federal interventions that existed regarding the authorities of the former Federal District.

The organization of the political institutions on each territorial level is formally guided by the principle of the organic separation of powers, but with a different scope. On the *national level*, with a presidential system of government, the national public power is separated among five branches of government, including: the "Legislative, Executive, Judicial, Citizen and Electoral" (Article 136). Thus, our 1999 Constitution has surpassed the classic tripartite division of power by adding to the traditional Legislative, Executive and Judicial branches, the Citizens branch, which includes the Public Prosecutor Office, the General Comptrollership Office, and the People's Rights Defendant Office, as well as an Electoral branch of government controlled by the National Electoral Council.

The new Citizens and Electoral branches, as well as the Judiciary, are reserved only to the national or federal level of government. Therefore, Venezuela does not have a Judiciary at the State level. In fact, since 1945, the Judicial branch is reserved to the national level of government, basically due to the national character of all major legislation and Codes (Civil, Commercial, Criminal, Labor and Procedural Codes). Consequently, being that all the Courts are national or federal, there is no room for State Constitution regulations on these matters.

Regarding judicial review, the Constitutional Chamber of the Supreme Tribunal of Justice is the constitutional organ with power to review and annul with *erga omnes* effect (Art. 336) all laws (national, state and municipal) including state constitutions, when contrary to the national Constitution. This concentrated method of judicial review has been exercised since 1858 through popular actions, and is also combined with the diffuse method of judicial review, similar to the United States model, which allows all courts to declare the unconstitutionality of statutes In these cases, an extraordinary recourse for revision can be brought before the Constitutional Chamber, which can make "imperative and obligatory interpretations" of the Constitution (*stare decisis* principle). In practice, these powers have even allowed the Constitutional Chamber to review decisions of the other Supreme Tribunal Chambers, like the Cassation Chambers and the Electoral Chamber, with very grave political consequences[45].

Pertaining to the Legislative branch, it must be noted that the Constitution of 1999, established a one-chamber National Assembly, thus ending the country's federalist tradition of bicameralism by, eliminating the Senate. As a result, Venezuela has also become a rare federal state without a federal chamber or Senate, where the States, through its representatives, can be equal in the sense of equal vote. In the National Assembly there are no representatives of the States, and its members are global representatives of the citizens and of all the States collectively. Theoretically, these global representatives are not subject to mandates, or instructions, but only subject to the "dictates of their conscience" (Article 201). This has effectively eliminated all vestiges of territorial representation.

Regarding the States branch of government, the 1999 Constitution established that each State has a Governor who must be elected by a universal, direct and secret vote (Article 160). Each State must also have a Legislative Council, comprised of representatives elected according to the principle of proportional representation (Article 162). According to the Constitution, it is the responsibility of each states' Legislative Council to enact its own Constitution in order "to organize their branches of government" along the guidelines of the national Constitution, which in principle guarantees the autonomy of the States (Article 159).

III. LIMITS TO THE CONTENTS OF THE SUB-NATIONAL CONSTITUTIONS

Consequently, each State has constitutional power to enact its own sub-national constitution, in order to organize the state Legislative and Executive public branches of government, and to regulate the states' own organ for audit control. In spite of these regulations on the organization and functioning of the State branches of government, the scope of States powers has also been seriously limited by the 1999 Constitution. Specifically, for the first time in federal history, the 1999 Constitution refers to a national legislation for the establishment of the general regulation on this matter.

In effect, and in relation to the States Legislative branch of government, the 1999 Constitution states that the organization and functioning of the States' Legislative Councils must be regulated by a *national statute* (Article 162), which was a manifestation of centralism never before envisioned. Just imagine, what it could mean for Federalism in the United States and in other Federations, if the Congress would have

---

45   The Supreme Tribunal of Justice is composed by six Chambers: Constitutional Chamber, Civil Cassation Chamber, Criminal Cassation Chamber, Social Chamber, Politico-Administrative Chamber and Electoral Chamber.

the power to enact legislation in order to determine the organization and functioning of all of the State legislatures.

In contrast, in Venezuela, according to the Constitution, the National Assembly has sanctioned an *Organic Law for the State Legislative Councils* (2001) in which detailed regulations were established. These regulations were related not only to the organization and functioning of the State's Legislative Councils (as the national Constitution only allowed), but also to the Council members status and attributes, as well as to the general rules for the exercise of the legislative functions, or the law enacting procedure itself. With this national regulation, the effective contents of the State Constitutions regarding their Legislative branch have been voided, and are limited to repeat what is established in the said national organic law or statute.

Additionally, the possibility of organizing the Executive branch of each state's government is also being limited by the 1999 Constitution, which has established the basic rules concerning the Governors as head of the executive branch. The Constitution has additional regulations referring to the public administration (national, states and municipal), public employees (civil service), and the administrative procedures and public contracts in all of the three levels of government. All of these rules have also been developed in two 2001 national *Organic Laws on Public Administration and on Civil Service*. Therefore, state constitutions have also been voided of real content, and their norms tending also to repeat what has been established in the national organic laws or statutes.

Finally, regarding other states organizations, in 2001, the National Assembly also sanctioned a *Law on the appointment of the States' Controller*, which limits, the powers of the State Legislative Councils without constitutional authorization. I must also point out that the national intervention regarding the various state Constitutions and their respective regulations in relation to their own state organizations, has been completed by the Constitutional Chamber of the Supreme Tribunal of Justice. Specifically, the Constitutional Chamber of the Supreme Tribunal of Justice's rulings during the past years (2001-2002), included the annulment of the articles of three state constitutions creating an Office of the State Citizens Rights' Defendant, on the grounds that citizens rights is a matter reserved to the national (federal) level of government.

As mentioned, the National Constitution establishes three levels of territorial autonomy and regulates the distribution of state powers, directly regulating the local or municipal government in an extensive manner. Therefore, the states constitutions and legislations can regulate municipal or local government only according to what is established in the national Constitution, and the *National Organic Law on Municipal Government,* which leaves very little room for the state regulation.

Thus, without any possibility for the state legislatures to regulate anything related to civil, economic, social, cultural, environmental or political rights; and with the limited powers to regulate their own branches of government, as well as other state organizations including the General Comptroller and Citizens Defenders, very little scope has been left for the contents of sub-national constitutions.

IV. THE CONSTITUTIONAL SYSTEM OF DISTRIBUTION OF POWERS WITHIN THE NATIONAL, STATE AND MUNICIPAL LEVELS OF GOVERNMENT

Federalism is based on an effective distribution of powers within the various levels of government; in Venezuela's case, between the national, state and municipal levels. Accordingly, the National Constitution enumerates the competencies attributed in an exclusive way to the national (Article 156), state (Article 154), and municipal (Article 178) levels of government. Under these regulations, however, these exclusive matters[46] are almost all reserved to the national level of government, and an important portion of the exclusive matters are attributed to the municipalities. In contrast, very few of the exclusive matters are attributed to the States.

According to Article 156, the National Power has exclusive competencies, in the following matters: 1) international relations, 2) security and defense, nationality and alien status, 3) national police, 4) economic regulations, 5) mining and oil industries, 6) national policies and regulations on education, health, the environment, land use, transportation, industrial and 7) agricultural production, 8) post, and 9) telecommunications. The administration of justice, as mentioned, also falls within the exclusive jurisdiction of the national government (Article 156.31).

Regarding local governments, Article 178 assigned the municipalities competencies, including, urban land use, housing, urban roads and transport, advertising regulations, urban environment, urban utilities, electricity, water supply, garbage collection and disposal, basic health and education services, and municipal police. Some of the powers regarding these matters are of an exclusive nature, but most of them are concurrent with the national government. The autonomy of municipalities is set forth in the constitution, but without any constitutional guarantees because municipal autonomy can be limited by national statute (Article 168).

Regarding state competencies, the National Constitution fails to enumerate substantive matters within exclusive state jurisdiction, and rather concentrates on formal and procedural ones. Furthermore, the competencies related to a limited number of matters are established in a concurrent way common to all levels of government, being in fact "exclusive" only some aspects of the competencies. This applies to municipal organizations, non-metallic mineral exploitation, police, and state's roads, administration of national roads, and commercial airports and ports (Article 164). Nonetheless, the possibility for the state legislature to regulate its own local government is also very limited, being subjected to what is established in the national *Organic Municipal Law* or statute.

According to the Constitution, State Legislative Councils can enact legislation on matters that are in the States' scope of powers (Article 162). However, these powers are referred to concurrent matters, and according to the National Constitution their exercise depends on the previous enactment of national statutes and regulations. As a result, the legislative powers of the States are also very limited.

---

46   Exclusive matters: Matters only attributed to only one of the state level.

These concurrent matters formerly provided a broad scope for possible action by state bodies. However, now subjecting their exercise to what the National Assembly must previously establish by means of national "general statutes," the possibility for states to regulate is very small. The National Constitution also states that this legislation that refers to concurrent competencies must always adhere to the principles of "interdependence, coordination, cooperation, co-responsibility and subsidiary," which theoretically allows for a wide possibility for judicial review (Article 165).

On the other hand, in terms of residual competencies, the principle of favoring the states as in all federations also has been a constitutional tradition in Venezuela. Nonetheless, in the 1999 Constitution this residual power of the states has also been limited by expressly assigning the national level of government a parallel and prevalent residual taxation power in matters not expressly attributed to the states or municipalities (Article 156.12).

Another aspect that must be mentioned is that the 1999 Constitution, following the provisions of the 1961 Constitution, has also established the possibility of decentralizing competencies via their transfer from the national level to the states. This process was regulated in the 1989 *Law on Decentralization and Transfer of Competencies*. Even though important efforts for decentralization were made between 1990 and 1994 in order to revert the centralizing tendencies, unfortunately, the process, was later abandoned. Since 2003, the transfers of competencies that were made, including health services, started the reversion process.

V. THE FINANCING RULES OF THE FEDERATION

The constitutional rules regarding the financing of the federation should also be mentioned. Virtually everything in the 1999 Constitution concerning the taxation system is more centralized than in the previous 1961 Constitution and the powers of the states in tax matters has essentially been eliminated.

The National Constitution lists the national government competencies with respect to basic taxes, including, income tax, inheritance and donation taxes, taxes on capital, production, value added, taxes on hydrocarbon resources and mines, taxes on the import and export of goods and services, taxes on the consumption of liquor, alcohol, cigarettes and tobacco (Article 156.12). The National Constitution also expressly allocates local taxation powers to the municipalities including property, commercial, and industrial activities taxes (Article 179). The National Constitution gives the national government residual competencies in tax matters (Article 156.12).

In contrast, the Constitution does not grant the states competencies in matters of taxation, except with respect to official stationery and revenue stamps (Article 164.7). Thus, the states can only collect taxes when the National Assembly expressly transfers the power to them, by a statute, which contains specific taxation powers (Article 167.5). No such statute has yet been approved and likely none will be approved in the near future.

Lacking their own resources from taxation, state financing is accomplished by the transfer of national financial resources through three different channels, which are all politically controlled by the national government. The first channel is by means of the "Constitutional Contribution," via the national level of government, which is an annual amount established in the National Budget Law equivalent to a minimum of 15% and a maximum of 20% of total ordinary national income. This percentage regarding the total ordinary national income estimated annually (Article 167.4), must be distributed among the states, according to their population. The second channel is through a nationally established system of special economic allotments for the benefit of those States in the territories of which mining and hydrocarbon projects are being developed. The benefits that accompany this statute have also been extended to include other non-mining states (Article 156.16). The third channel of financing for states and municipalities also comes from national funds, such as the *Intergovernmental Fund for Decentralization*, created in 1993 as a consequence of the national regulation of VAT, or the Interstate Compensation Fund, which is foreseen in the National Constitution (Article 167.6).

On the other hand, following a long tradition, the states and municipalities cannot borrow nor have public debt; due to the requirement of a special national statute to approve state borrowing.

VI. THE RECENTRALIZATION OF THE FEDERATION

As aforementioned, the 1999 Constitution, in a very contradictory way, although continuing with the federal form of the government, introduced elements in order to centralize power in detriment of the States of the Federation. All these centralizing elements have been used during the past decade, producing a very centralized government that has suffocated the regional and local autonomy of States and Municipalities.

This process has been completed since 2008, during which the Government has reverted the decentralization efforts of the past, and has recentralized competencies that were previously transferred, in matters like health and education.

Also in 2008, the Constitutional Chamber of the Supreme Tribunal interpreted the Constitution at the request of the Attorney General, concluding in a decision N° 565 of April 15, 2008[47], contrary to the provisions of the Constitution, that a very important "exclusive" attribution of the States to administer national highways, ports and airports was not such "exclusive" attribution, but "only" concurrent one, subjected to control of the national level of government, authorizing the central government to interfere in their exercise and even to reassume them.

Based on this decision that in an illegitimate way mutate the Constitution, after opposition candidates won in the regional elections held on December 2008, very important positions of governorship and mayors in important States and cities (Mar-

---

47 Decision of the Constitutional Chamber N° 565, April 15, 2008, Case: Procuradora General de la República, Recourse of interpretation of article 164 of the Constitution, in http://www.tsj.gov.ve/decisiones/scon/Abril/565-150408-07-1108.htm. See the comments in Allan R. Brewer-Carías, "La Sala Constitucional como poder constituyente: la modificación de la forma federal del estado y del sistema constitucional de división territorial del poder público, in *Revista de Derecho Público*, N° 114, (abril-junio 2008), Editorial Jurídica Venezolana, Caracas 2008, pp. 247-262

acaibo, Caracas), in a very quick way the National Assembly reformed the 1989 Decentralization Law[48] allowing the process of centralization that has occurred during the past weeks, reverting the decentralization process.[49]

Even the local government in Caracas has been almost extinguished by the unconstitutional recreation of a 19th century shaped "Federal District," under the name of "Capital District" governed by an executive authority appointed by the President and with the national Assembly as its legislative authority.[50]

*

As it can be deduced from what I have said, the declaration of Article 4 of the 1999 Constitution regarding the "Federal Decentralized" form of the Venezuelan government is not mere wording. It is a formula that is contradicted by all the other regulations regarding the federalism contained in the Constitution, which, on the contrary, shows that the, Federation in Venezuela is a very centralized Federation. This situation, of course, affects our democratic regime and governance deeply.

Decentralization is the most effective instrument not only to guarantee civil and social rights, but to allow effective participation of the citizens in the political process and to consolidate democracies. That is why decentralization in the contemporary world is a matter of democracies. There are no decentralized autocracies, and there have never been decentralized authoritarian governments, only democracies can be decentralized. And that is why, precisely, the authoritarian government we have in Venezuela has centralized all power at the national level of government, suffocating states and local governments.

The reality of the political situation in Venezuela is that democracy is very weak. Although democracy is based on elections, it cannot be consolidated without a real separation of powers, and without the real possibility of political participation due to the lack of decentralization. Because of an existing controlled judiciary, and a judicial review organization also controlled by the Executive, instead of enforcing the democratic constitutional principles embodied in the National Constitution, they have acted, including the Supreme Tribunal of Justice, as the main instrument of authoritarian government.

Over the past years, the most important democratic element which has existed in the Venezuelan political process has been our weak Federalist system, which nonetheless, in the recent past, has allowed more than half of the municipal Majors and one third of the elected states' governors to be opposition leaders, assuring some kind of political pluralism. Unfortunately, all of this has been recently erased in the regional elections held on October 31 2004, in which, with an abstention of more

---

48   *Gaceta Oficial*, N° 39 140, March 17, 2009

49   General Port Law, *Gaceta Oficial* N° 39.140, March 17, 2009; Civil Aviation Law, *Gaceta Oficial*, N° 39.140, March, 2009.

50   Special La won the Organization and Regime of the Capital District, *Gaceta Oficial*, N° 39.156 of April 13, 2009.

than the 75% of the electorate, the candidates for Governors supported by the President of the Republic were elected in all but two states.

Ultimately, this has resulted in a concentration of powers which is almost complete. In addition to the horizontal concentration of powers caused by the predominance of the national Executive over the Legislative, Judicial, Citizens and Electoral branches, the Venezuelan Government has also developed a vertical concentration of powers, conducted by the same national Executive, due to the centralized form of government.

Within this framework, it is very difficult to talk about Federalism in Venezuela, as well as of democracy in Venezuela. This difficulty explains the title of my paper referring to the "Centralized Federalism in Venezuela," rather than "Federalism in Venezuela."

CHAPTER IX

VENEZUELA: THE END OF FEDERALISM?
(2012)

This paper, written with the collaboration of *Jan Kleinheisterkamp*, * was the Venezuelan National Report on the Subject of "Unification of Laws in Federal Systems," for the Congress of the International Academy of Comparative Law, held in México in 2008. The text was initially published as "Unification of Laws in Federal Systems. National Report on Venezuela," in Daniel Halberstam, Mathias Reimann and Jorge A. Sánchez Cordero (Editors), *Federalism and Legal Unification: A Comparative Empirical Investigation of Twenty Systems*, International Academy of Comparative law, Instituto de Investigaciones Jurídicas, Universidad Nacional Autónoma de México, México 2012, pp. 378-391; and a revised version was published as "Chapter 20. Venezuela: The End of Federalism?" in Daniel Halberstam and Mathias Reimann (Editors), *Federalism and Legal Unification: A Comparative Empirical Investigation of Twenty Systems*, Springer, London 2014, pp. 523-543

Venezuela was the first Latin American country to gain independence from the Spanish Crown in 1810. A general congress of representatives of the former colonial provinces of the *Capitania General de Venezuela* enacted on 21 December 1811 the Federal Constitution for the States of Venezuela, the first constitution on the South American continent. This Constitution followed the general principles of modern constitutionalism derived from the North American and French Revolutions, such as the republican system; supremacy of the constitution paired with constitutional judicial control; organic separation of powers; territorial distribution of power; and declaration of fundamental rights. The 1811 Constitution established a federal form of government. Venezuela was thus the second country after the United States of America to adopt a federal system, which enabled the construction of an independent state that united the former colonial provinces. Today, the territory of the repub-

---

*   Jan KLEINHEISTERKAMP, Senior Lecturer, Department of Law, London School of Economics, Houghton Street, WC2A 2AE London, UK; Visiting Professor at the University Panthéon-Assas - Paris II, e-mail: j.kleinheisterkamp @ lse.ac. uk.

lic is divided into 23 states, a Capital District (that covers parts of the city of Caracas), and federal dependencies that comprise the islands located in the Caribbean Sea. The municipalities with jurisdiction in Caracas are organized in a Metropolitan District (*Distrito Metropolitano*), with a two tier municipal government.

Following a period of dissolution in Simon Bolivar's *Gran Colombia* as of 1821, the "State of Venezuela" re-emerged as a separate country in 1830 with a rather mixed (centralized-provincial) form of government, but lived intense struggles between the central region and provincial forces. This period ended three decades later with a 5-year "Federal War" (1858-1863), from which the Federation re-emerged with the establishment of the United States of Venezuela (1864). From that moment on, the form of government in Venezuela has always been federal, at least on paper. During the second half of the nineteenth century, successive civil wars led to various constitutional reforms in which the federal system of government was kept, yet with a progressive tendency of centralization regarding numerous elements that historically had characterized the federal system. For instance, regarding unification of laws, the states accepted in the 1864 Constitution, as part on the "Basis of the Union", "to have for all of them one same substantive legislation on criminal and civil matters".[51] In 1881, the words "the same laws on civil and criminal procedure" were added.[52] Accordingly, the Civil, Criminal, and Commercial Codes, but also the Codes of Civil and Criminal Procedure have always been federal laws.

During the first half of the twentieth century, dominated by autocratic regimes, Venezuela saw a continued process of centralization in the fields of the military, administration, taxation and legislation. The territorial distribution of power and territorial autonomy of the component states had almost disappeared, in spite of the Constitutions' continuing formal proclamations of federalism.[53] The second half of the twentieth century was characterized by democratization,[54] especially under the constitution of 1961, which upheld the federal form of government, albeit with highly centralized powers at the national level. A political decentralization process sparked by the democratic practice began in 1989 with the transfer of powers from the central government to the federal states.[55] For the first time since the nineteenth

---

51   Article 13 n° 22 *Constitución de los Estados Unidos de Venezuela* of 22 April 1864. The texts of all the Venezuelan Constitutions are published in A.R. Brewer-Carías, 1-2 *Las Constituciones de Venezuela* (Caracas 2008).

52   *Article 13* n° 19 Constitución de los Estados Unidos de Venezuela *of 27 April 1881.*

53   *See also* J. de Galíndez, "Venezuela: New Constitution", *American Journal of Comparative Law* 3: 81-82 (1954): "Only in theory does Venezuela continue to be a federal republic".

54   See M. Kornblith, "Constitutions and Democracy in Venezuela", *Journal of Latin American Studies* 23: 61, 63 (1991).

55   For the political background of this decentralization reform and its impact on the political scene in Venezuela, see M. Penfold-Becerra, "Federalism and Institutional Change in Venezuela", in: E.L. Gibson (ed.), *Federalism and Democracy in Latin America* 197-225 (Baltimore 2004). See also Point 20.2.2.1, below.

century, the governors of the federal states were elected directly,[56] and regional political life began to play an important role in the country.

Hugo Chavez, a former military officer whose *coup d'etat* had failed in 1992 and who was elected as the President of the Republic in 1998, convened a National Constituent Assembly that sanctioned today's Constitution, which was submitted to a referendum in 1999.[57] This 26th Constitution of Venezuela has caused the pendulum to swing back. Instead of undertaking the changes needed for reinforcing democracy, namely the effective political decentralization of the federation and the reinforcement of state and municipal political power, it re-launched the centralization process under an authoritarian government.[58]

I. FEDERAL DISTRIBUTION AND EXERCISE OF LAWMAKING POWERS

1. *Areas of Law Subject to (Legislative) Jurisdiction of the Central Authority*

A. *Matters Attributed to the Central Government*

Article 156 of the Constitution of 1999 enumerates all the areas of jurisdiction of the *Poder Público Nacional,* i.e., the central public power in Venezuela. As regards the legislative jurisdiction, Article 165 n° 32 explicitly provides that the central authority (National Assembly) has jurisdiction for the legislation in the areas of:

- Constitutional rights, obligations and guarantees;*
- Civil law, commercial law, criminal law, the penal system, procedural law and private international law;*
- Electoral law;*
- Expropriations for the sake of public or social interests;*
- Public credit;*
- Intellectual, artistic, and industrial property;*
- Cultural and archeological treasures;*
- Agriculture;*
- Immigration and colonization[59];*
- Indigenous people and the territories occupied by them;*
- Labor and social security and welfare[60];*

---

56 See *infra* note 30.

57 See on the 1999 constitution-making process: A.R. Brewer-Carías, "The 1999 Venezuelan Constitution-Making Process as an Instrument for Framing the development of an Authoritarian Political Regime," in: L.E. Miller (ed.), *Framing the Stale in Times of Transition. Case Studies in Constitution Making,* 505-531 (Washington 2010).

58 See A.R. Brewer-Carías, *Dismantling Democracy. The Chávez Authoritarian Experiment* (Cambridge 2010).

59 See also Article 156 n° 4: "the naturalization and the admission, extradition and expulsion of foreigners"; Article 38.

- Veterinary and phytosanitary hygiene[61];*
- Notaries and public registers;*
- Banks and insurances;*
- Lotteries, horseracing, and bets in general;*
- The organization and functioning of the organs of the central authority and the other organs and institutions of the state.[62]*

Article 156 n° 32 also specifies that the central authority also has legislative jurisdiction for all matters of "national competence", i.e., for the implementation of all other matters enumerated in Article 156 n[os] 1-31. In this list, the power to legislate is explicitly attributed to the central authority (National Assembly) for the following matters[63];

- Those related to the armed forces (n° 8)* and civil protection (n° 9)[64];
- Monetary policies (n° 11);*
- The coordination and harmonization of the different taxation authorities; the definition of principles, parameters, and restrictions, and in particular the types of tributes or rates of the taxes of the states and municipalities; as well as the creation of special funds that assure the inter-territorial solidarity (n° 13);
- Foreign commerce and customs (n° 15);*
- Mining and natural energy resources (hydrocarbon)[65];* fallow and waste land; and the conservation, development and exploitation of the woods, grounds, waters,[66] and other natural resources of the country (n° 16)[67];
- Standards of measurement and quality control (n° 17);*

---

60   See also Article 156 n° 22: "the regime and organization of the social security system".

61   "See also Article 156 n° 23: "the legislation in matters of ... public health [and] food safety..."

62   *See also* Article 156 n° 31: "the national organization and administration of justice, the Ministerio Público *and the* Defensoría del Pueblo".

63   See TSJ Sala Constitucional, decision n° 565 of 15 April 2008, file n° 07-1108, where the Supreme Tribunal interpreted the word "regimen" found in some of the provisions in Article 156 as indicating the power to legislate. See in 114 *Revista de Derecho Público,* 154-170 (2008).

64   *See also* Articles 328-332.

     "For the exclusive nature of the central authority's legislative power over the natural energy resources see in more detail the text accompanying note 37, below.

66   See also Article 304, which provides that all waters are property of the Republic and that the law establishes the necessary provisions in order to guarantee their protection, exploitation, and recovery.

67   Contrast with n° 23 (environment and water in the context of public health, housing and food safety).

- The establishment, coordination, and unification of technical norms and procedures for construction, architecture, and urbanism, as well as the legislation on urbanism (n° 19);*

- Public health, housing, food safety, environment,[68] water, tourism,[69] and the territorial organization (n° 23);

- Navigation and air transport, ground transport, maritime and inland waterway transport (n° 26)[70];

- Post and telecommunication services and radio frequencies (n° 28);*

- Public utilities such as especially electricity, potable water, and gas (n° 29).[71]

- Furthermore, the Constitution attributes to the central authority the powers to:

- Conclude, approve, and ratify international treaties (Article 154);*

- Legislate on antitrust and the abuse of market power (Articles 113 and 114).*

B.   *Nature of the Jurisdiction Attributed to the Central Government*

The Constitution does not expressly specify whether the central authority (National Assembly) has exclusive powers in these areas or whether the legislative powers are shared with the component states and the municipalities. The exclusive character of legislative powers has to be determined by interpretation for each of them separately. All of the areas of "general legislation" enumerated in Article 156 n° 32 can be considered to be of the exclusive power of the central authority, together with those other areas mentioned above that are marked with an asterisk (*), or those others where the central authority has already legislated.[72] Neither the component states nor the municipalities may legislate in these areas.[73] In all other areas that belong to the concurrent powers shared between the central government and the component states and the municipalities, the National Assembly always retains the power to enact "basic laws" (*"leyes de base"),* which establish the framework that

---

68   See also the concurrent power in this area of the municipalities, Article 178 n° 4.

69   For the concurrent nature of this power, see TSJ Sala Constitucional decision n° 826 of 16 May 2008, file n° 08-0479.

70   See also Article 156 n° 23: "the national policies and the legislation in matters of navigation".

71   See Article 164 n° 8, which attributes "exclusive" power to the states for "the creation, regulation, and organization of public utilities of the states".

72   Cf. A.R. Brewer-Carías, "La descentralización política en la Constitución de 1999: federalismo y municipalismo (una reforma insuficiente y regresiva)", 7 *Provincia* 7, 29-31 (2001).

73   See, e.g., for the exclusivity of the federal jurisdiction for matters related to retirement and pensions on the basis of Article 156 n° 32, TSJ Sala Constitucional, decision n° 518 of 1 June 2000, file n° 00-0841; decision n° 1452 of 3 August 2004, file n° 02-2585.

must be respected by the component states when enacting local "laws of development" *("leyes de desarrollo")*, Article 165 (1).[74]

Article 156 can be considered the most important source specified in the Constitution that authorizes central government regulation. On its basis, practically all
important areas of government are covered by central legislation. In summary, it
seems fair to say that the central authority (National Assembly) has legislative jurisdictions in all areas of law, either for enacting central legislation or for enacting
framework laws.

C.   *Areas of Law Remaining to the (Legislative) Jurisdiction of the Component
     States*

a.   *Overview*

Article 164 enumerates a list of matters that are formally designated to be of the
"exclusive jurisdiction" of the component states. This designation, however, is misleading since none of these matters can be regarded as truly exclusive,[75] especially
not as concerns the legislative powers.

Article 164 partially integrates the provisions of the "Decentralization Law" of
1989,[76] which already provided for the transfer of powers to the states. But different
from Article 164 of the 1999 Constitution, Article 11 of the Law of 1989 had provided explicitly that the states would have the power to legislate on these matters.[77]
With the entry into force of the 1999 Constitution, the states' pretensions to legislate
in their areas of exclusive powers have been rejected and subordinated to national
legislation.[78] The constitutional provision in Article 158, which establishes that de-

---

74   See also Exposición de Motivos de la Constitución *(the official justification of the 1999*
     Constitution): "As regards to the concurrent powers, the Constitution adopts the experience
     of comparative law on decentralization and it provides that national laws have the nature of
     basic laws, in which general, basic, and guiding concepts are laid down; and that state laws
     are laws developing these basic principles, which allows for better conditions for the delimi-
     tation of competences"; G.O. n° 5908 Extra of 19 February 2009.

75   Cf. Brewer-Carías, *supra* note 22 at 29.

76   *Ley Orgánica para la Descentralización, Delimitación y Transferencia de Competencias del
     Poder Público,* G.O. n° 4153 of 28 December 1989. See on this law see A.R. Brewer-Carias,
     "Bases legislativas para la descentralización política de la federación centralizada (1990: El
     inicio de una reforma)", in *idem* (coord.) et al., *Leyes para la Descentralización Política de
     la Federación* 7-53 (Caracas 1990).

77   Article 11, sole paragraph, of the Law of 1989 reads: "Until the states assume these powers
     through specific legislation, enacted by the respective legislative assemblies, the presently
     existing legislation continues in force".

78   See, e.g., *Dictamen de la Procuraduría de la República,* Oficio N° D.A.G.E. 000019 of 20
     October 2000, available at http://www.pgr.gob.ve/PDF/Dictamenes/CONSTITUCIO-
     NAL1.pdf, which rejects the possibility that the states can establish the legislative basis for
     the conservation, administration and exploitation of the national highways on the basis of
     Article 164 n° 10, and suggesting that, until a national law is enacted, the states and the
     federal government should conclude cooperation agreements. On these matters, the TSJ, Sala
     Constitucional Decision n° 565 of 15 April 2008, has eliminated the "exclusive" character of

centralization is a national policy, has been ignored by the central government and the "Decentralization Law" despite having been reenacted with virtually no changes in 2003 and again in 2009,[79] and can be considered dead letter.[80]

b.   *Nature of the Jurisdiction Attributed to the Component States*

The only true legislative power of the component states is to organize their own constitutional structure by adopting their own constitutions (Article 164 n° 1) "in accordance with this [federal] Constitution". This provision limits this power of self-organization, since the federal constitution imposes a general organizational structure on the component states and establishes uniform rules for the state governors (Articles 159-163, and 166).[81] Moreover, the 1999 Constitution deprives the component states of establishing in their respective state constitutions the rules of organization and functioning of their legislative assemblies, which are instead governed by a federal law of the central authority (Article 162 *in fine*)[82] as well as the basic legislation on public Administration and public servants, which has also been enacted by the central authority.[83] The only exclusive legislative powers remaining with the component states thus concern the specific legislation on the details of the organization and functioning of the governors' office and states' administrative organization.[84]

---

the states' jurisdiction, transforming it into a "concurrent" jurisdiction, available at http://www.tsj.gov.ve/decisiones/scon/Abril/565- 150408-07-1108.htm

79   G.O. n° 37753 of 14 August 2003; G.O. n° 39140 of 17 March 2009.

80   J. Sánchez Meléan, "Pasado, presente y futuro de la descentralización en Venezuela", 9 *Provincia* 20, 26 (2002); A.R. Brewer-Carías, "La descentralización política. Un modelo de Estado," in: F. Otamendi Osorio, T. Straka, & Grupo Jirahara (eds.), *Venezuela: República democrática* (Barquisimeto 2011), 645-673.

81   Cf. TSJ Sala Constitucional, decision 1182 of 11 October 2000, file n° 00-1410: "It is therefore clear that the states are constitutionally privileged by the principle of autonomy for the organization of their public power; however, it has to be understood that this autonomy is relative and therefore subject to numerous restrictions established by the Constitution and the Law". See also note 23 above. For the central regulation of the state governors see also Articles 22-32 of the "Decentralization Law" of 1989 and 2003, according to which, *inter alia,* state governors can be removed for "repeated disobedience of orders or decisions by the President of the Republic" (Article 31); for harsh criticism see A. Hernández Becerra, "Nivel territorial intermedio en Colombia y Venezuela", 15 *Provincia* 95, 105 (2006), but it has to be noted that prior to 1989, state governors were directly appointed by the President.

82   *Ley Orgánica de los Consejos Legislativos de los Estados*, G.O. N° 37282 of 13 September 2001.

83   Ley Orgánica de la Administración Pública, *G.O. N° 5890 Extra of 31 July 2008;* Ley del Estatuto de la Función Pública, *G.O. N° 37522 of 6 September 2002.*

84   Cf. Brewer-Carías, *supra* note 22 at 27.

The two other items of Article 164 which make reference to legislative powers by referring to the component states' right to enact a *"regimen"*, which could be understood as conferring legislative powers,[85] are:

- The exploitation of non-metallic minerals that are not reserved to the central authority, salt mines and oyster beds (n° 5);
- The public utilities of the component states (n° 8).

The first of these two areas is -despite being labeled as an "exclusive power" of the component states by Article 164- by and large only a concurrent power, since the central authority retains the power over "the mines and natural energy resources (hydrocarbon) ... and the conservation, development and exploitation of the ... grounds ... and the other natural treasures" according to Article 156 n° 16.[86] It follows from this provision, read in conjunction with Article 164 n° 5, that especially the exploitation of natural energy resources (hydrocarbon) - i.e. gas and petrol, the dominant source of income of Venezuela - are of exclusive jurisdiction of the central authority and subjected to the legislation enacted by the National Assembly.[87] Only the administrative procedures for the exploitation of non-precious stone, salt mines and oyster beds thus seem to fall under a genuine exclusive legislative jurisdiction of the states.[88] Furthermore, the second of the areas enumerated above (public utilities) is also merely a shared competence, since Article 156 n° 29 provides that the "general legislation" on the public utilities (at least those offered to the citizens at home) falls within the power of the central authority.

---

85 For the meaning of *"régimen"* in the constitutional catalogues of jurisdictions see note 13 above.

86 This constitutional provision thus undermines Article 11 n° 2 of the 1989 Decentralization Law (note 26 above), which provided that "in order to promote the administrative decentralization and according to the provision of Article 137 of the Constitution [of 1961] the following matters are transferred to the exclusive jurisdiction of the States:... the legislation, administration and exploitation of stones for construction and decoration or of any type other than precious ... of the earthy substances, the salt-mines and the pearl producing oyster banks".

87 The total control of the central authority over gas and petrol resources is complemented by Article 156 n° 16(3), which provides that a federal law will establish a system of special economic attributions to the states in whose territory the exploited resources are found, yet without prejudice to the possibility to also establish special attributions in favor of other states, which means that the central authority has broad discretion in its decisions regarding at least gas and petrol.

88 For the exclusivity of the jurisdiction over salt mines, albeit only in a conflict between a state and a municipality see TSJ Sala Constitucional, decision n° 78 of 30 January 2001, file n° 00-1556 ("una competencia originaria de los [Estados] ... una competencia natural y exclusive"). For such a state law see *Ley de Régimen, Administración y Aprovechamiento de Salinas y sus Productos del Estado Sucre, Gaceta Oficial Extraordinaria del Estado Sucre* n° 10 of 29 November 1993.

In summary, there are no relevant areas of law making that are reserved to the states.[89] If at all, they only have exclusive administrative powers in some areas. The states possess merely concurrent powers for some few areas in which they may enact legislation (see those items not marked with an asterisk (*) above Sect. 20.2.1).[90] In any event, all state legislation in matters of concurrent powers, which takes the form of "development laws" (leyes de desarrollo), is contingent upon the prior enactment of federal "basic laws" (leyes de base) (Article 165(1)). The latter set a binding framework for the former.[91] Article 165(1) commands that such federal "basic" framework laws have to respect the principles of interdependency, coordination, cooperation, shared responsibility and subsidiarity.[92] Yet this will not prevent the federal authority from also regulating specific details, at least as long as such detailed federal regulation can be justified under the principle of subsidiarity, i.e., if a need for centralized and thus uniform legislation can be shown. Articles 164 and 165(1) therefore only guarantee a kind of minimum core of legislative power of the states in the areas of shared competences.[93] This minimum core is rather restricted in

---

89   Brewer-Carías, *supra* note 22 at 29; K.S. Rosenn, "Federalism in the Americas in a Comparative Perspective", *University of Miami Inter-American Law Review* 26: 1,16 (1994).

90   See also Article 15 of the *Ley Orgánica de los Consejos Legislativos de los Estados*, G.O. 37282 of 13 September 2001, whose enumeration of the powers of the state parliaments, other than the power to enact and amend a state constitution and (restricted) budgetary laws, essentially mentions only the legislative power to enact "development laws" within the framework of federal "basic laws".

91   For a case in which a state claimed to be unable to legislate on matters of concurrent powers because the National Assembly had not yet enacted the necessary federal laws see TSJ Sala Constitucional, decision n° 3203 of 25 October 2005, file n° 02-2984. See also A.R. Brewer-Carias, "Centralized Federalism in Venezuela", 43 *Duquesne Law Review* 629, 639 (2005).

92   Cf. TSJ Sala Constitucional, decision 843 of 11 May 2004, file n° 03-1236, where the Supreme Tribunal affirms *obiter* that "the concurrent powers ... have to be previously delimitated by a basic national law; ... only the national legislator has the power for enacting basic regulatory laws (according to the principles of interdependency, coordination, shared responsibility and subsidiarity) in the areas of concurrent powers"; this is reaffirmed in TSJ of 15 April 2008, *supra* note 13, on the relation between Articles 156 n° 26 and 164 n° 10 regarding highways.

93   See, e.g., TSJ Sala Constitucional, decision n° 2495 of 19 December 2006, file n° 02-0265, where the State of Carabobo claimed that Article 42 of the *Ley General de Puertos* (G.O. n° 73589 of 11 December 2002) violated its powers resulting from Article 164 n° 10 of the Constitution (which grants states the "exclusive" powers for the conservation, administration, and exploitation of commercial ports "in coordination with the national government") because the federal law obliges the States either to establish an autonomous entity for the administration of each port or to grant concession to private entities for that task. The Supreme Tribunal rejected this argument, and interpreted Article 164 n° 10 as conferring merely concurrent powers, with the reasoning that such obligation is "justified" (it follows from the preceding discussion of federalism in general that this justification is made with regards to the principle of subsidiarity, although it is not specifically invoked) "by the general interest, which the Republic has to protect, in the effective and also efficient administration of decentralized public services... The reservation of the administration to a

the light of the constitutional case law which tends to interpret the powers of the central authority broadly.[94]

c. *Allocation of Residual Powers*

In line with the previous constitutions, the 1999 Constitution generally allocates residual powers with the states. Article 164 n° 11 provides that the states have "exclusive" powers "for everything that, according to this Constitution, is not allocated to the national or municipal power". This general residual power is, however, undermined by two inverse attributions of residual power to the central authority. Article 156 n° 12 grants the central authority full control over all "other taxes, excises, and revenues not attributed to the states or the municipalities by this Constitution or the law". Furthermore, Article 156 n° 33 provides for the jurisdiction of the central authority "in all other matters that correspond to it [the federal government] due to their nature or kind". This provision has been copied from the 1961 Constitution, which was intended as an implicit powers clause in favor of the federal government.[95] The federal government's power is further strengthened by the Supreme Tribunal's willingness to accept inherent powers in favor of the national level.[96] In summary, the general residual power allocated to the states is a rather theoretical one.[97] In practice, it seems that - in case of doubt - the presumption in favor of federal powers will virtually always prevail.

d. *Conflicts between Central and Component State Law*

As mentioned above, the component states do not have any exclusive legislative powers. Any legislative activity by the states can thus only take place within the

---

specialized entity safeguards that services are rendered optimally and it is in this line of reasoning that said provision is justified".

94   See note 46 below and note 28 above, and also Point 20.4.1.1, below.

95   Cf. C. Ayala Corao, "Naturaleza y Alcance de la Descentralización Estadal", in: A.R. Brewer- Carías et al. (eds.), *Leyes para la Descentralización Política de la Federación* 94 (Caracas 1990), referring to the *Exposición de Motivos* of the 1961 Constitution.

96   Cf. TSJ Sala Constitucional 15 April 2008 (note 13 above), affirming, with reference to Constitutional provisions on some public services of national interest, "that the central government [the "Administration"] has an implicit general power or general clause of public order to condition, limit, or interfere with the rights or liberties on the basis of the doctrine of inherent or implicit rights ... that allows [the interpreter]... to review the spirit of the provision attributing powers in such manner as to accept the existence of a power when this is the logical consequence of the legal provision and of the nature of the main activity exercised by the organ or entity".

97   A.R. Brewer-Carias, *La Constitución y sus Enmiendas* 28 (Caracas 1991); *idem*, "El Sistema Constitucional Venezolano", in D. García Belaunde et al. (eds.), *Los Sistemas Constitucionales Iberoamericanos* 771, 778 (Madrid 1992); Rosenn, *supra* note 39 at 16; *see also* J.M. Serna de la Garza, "Constitutional Federalism in Latin America", *California Western International Law Journal* 30: 277, 286 (2000): "the peculiar manner in which implicit powers have been understood, has created an additional instrument that can be used by the federal government to expand its powers".

framework established by the "basic laws" (Article 165) that must have been enacted by the central government prior to the state's legislation [98] By definition, these central "basic laws" must be superior to the state laws, since the latter have to remain within the framework of the former. Accordingly, in case of conflict between federal law and state law, the former will prevail.[99] The only -rather theoretical- hypothesis in which a state law could prevail over a federal law is when it can be shown that the central government did not respect the constitutional limits to its legislative powers, such as in particular the principle of subsidiarity of Article 165(1).[100]

e.   *Law-Making Powers of Municipalities*

According to Article 178 "[t]he powers of the Municipality are the governance and the administration of its interests and the management of the matters attributed to it by this Constitution and the national laws with respect to local life". For such purpose, Article 174 provides that the government and administration of the municipalities is attributed to the mayors; and Article 175 assigns the legislative function to the *Consejos Municipales* (municipal councils), which they exercise through "municipal laws" in the form of *ordenanzas* in the matters attributed to them in Article 178.[101] These "own" areas of the municipalities are, according to Article 178, matters related to zoning, historic monuments, social housing, local tourism, public space for recreation, construction, local transport, public entertainment, local environmental protection and hygiene, local public utilities, funerals, child care and other community matters. Only the matters related to local public events (n° 3) and funerals (n° 6) can be regarded as exclusive powers of the municipalities, while the other areas are concurrent and thus limited to the framework of federal and state laws.[102] According to the Law on Municipalities of 2010, the lack of federal legislation (and by logical extension also of state legislation) is supposedly no obstacle to the legislative activity of the municipalities in concurrent matters.[103]

Nonetheless, it has to be pointed out that the Municipality as the "primary political unit of the national organization" (Article 168) has been virtually rendered moot

---

98   See text accompanying note 41 above.

99   *See, e.g.,* TSF Sala Constitucional, decision n° 1495 of 1 August 2006, file n° 05-2448 in which the Supreme Tribunal, upon request by the national *Defensorio del Pueblo* (Ombudsman) suspended temporarily the *Ley de Defensa y Seguridad Ciudadana* of the State of Zulia, G.O. of the State of Zulia n° 659 Extra of 24 May 2004, due to the potential incompatibility with the *Código Orgánico de Procedimiento Penal* and the constitutional guarantees of freedom by allowing police forces to arrest suspect persons for 48 h; a final decision is not yet published. For the legal analysis of constitutionality by the *Defensoría del Pueblo* see http://www.defensoria.gob.ve/detalle.asp? sec=160104&id=110&plantilla=1

100   See text accompanying notes 42-44.

101   *For the definition of* Ordenanzas *see Article 54 n° 1 of the* Ley Orgánica del Poder Público Municipal, *G.O. n° 6015 Extra of 18 December 2010.*

102   See, e.g., *for tourism TSJ Sala Constitucional, decision n° 826 of 16 May 2008, file n° 08-0479.*

103   *Article 57 in fine of the* Ley Orgánica del Poder Público Municipal *(note 51 above).*

since 2006 by the creation of a parallel structure of *Consejos Comunales* ("communal" councils), which are elected by local "assemblies of the citizens", *Asamblea de Ciudadanos*,[104] which can be formed by interested citizens. These *Asambleas de Ciudadanos* have been attributed jurisdiction to "approve the rules of the communal living of the community",[105] the scope of which is not further defined.[106] Although these structures that have been extensively regulated in 2010,[107] and are supposed to allow "self-governance" of local communities and are therefore a potential source of diversity,[108] their members are not elected by popular, direct and secret suffrage, thus violating the constitutional principle of representative democracy. Also, it can be doubted that they will balance the high degree of centralization of the country. These community structures, understood as vehicles for the advancement of socialism, are directly coordinated, supervised, and financed by the *Ministry for the Popular Power for the Communes and Social Protection* of the National Executive. Their leaders are appointed directly by the President[109] without the participation of the states or the municipalities.[110]

---

104 The possibility to create such *Asamblea de Ciudadanos y Ciudadanas* is mentioned in Article 70 of the Constitution as one of the "means of participation and protagonism of the people in the exercise of its sovereignty", "whose decisions have binding character". The proposed reform of the Constitution, rejected in the Referendum of 2 December 2008, would have added "as long as they do not contradict the Constitution and the laws", which is probably the interpretation that has to be given to the present Article 70 anyway.

105 Article 6 n° 1 of the *Ley Orgánica de los Consejos Comunales,* G.O. n° 39335 of 10 April 2009. "Community" is defined in Article 4 n° 1 as "the social conglomerate of families and citizens which live in a specific geographic area, which share a common history and interests, know each other and have relations with each other, use the same public utilities and share similar economic, social, urbanistic, and other necessities and potentials".

106 It is worth noting that Article 6 n° 5 of the same law provide that Assembly of Citizens "exercises the social control". See in this regard the *Ley Orgánica de Contraloría Social,* G.O. n° 6011 Extra of 21 December 2010. Articles 9 and 16 of the *Decreto con Rango, Valor y Fuerza de Ley Orgánica del Servicio de Policía y del Cuerpo de Policía Nacional,* G.O. n° 5880 Extra del 9 April 2008 require the police only to inform and to consult the "communities", the *Consejos Comunales,* or the other "communitarian" organs, without mentioning the municipalities. Furthermore, Articles 47-48 provides "communities" with the possibility to create their own police force "committed to the respect of values, identity and the own culture of each community", with "the task to guarantee and ensure social peace, cohabitation, the exercise of rights and the fulfillment of the law". The National Police Law has been declared constitutional by TSJ Sala Constitucional, decision n° 385 of 15 March 2008, file n° 08-0233.

107 See in particular, *Ley Orgánica del Poder Popular,* G.O. n° 6011 Extra of 21 December 2010; *Ley Orgánica de las Comunas,* G.O. n° 6011 Extra of 21 December 2010.

108 But see *note 54 above* in fine.

109 Articles 28 to 32 of the *Ley de los Consejos Comunales* (note 55 above).

110 On this reform in general see A.R. Brewer-Carias, "El inicio de la desmunicipalización en Venezuela: La organización del Poder Popular para eliminar la descentralización, la democracia representativa y la participación a nivel local", *Revista de la Asociación Internacional de Derecho Administrativo* 49-67 (Mexico 2007); A.R. Brewer-Carias, "Introducción Gene-

II. THE MEANS AND METHODS OF LEGAL UNIFICATION

In view of the above sketched centralization of virtually all relevant law-making activity as well as the weakness of federalism in the country's history, legal unification is not an issue in Venezuela. The legal unification has been achieved exclusively through the central power of the federal government (top down). Attempts to decentralize the powers by transferring powers to the component states and municipalities have failed so far and have practically become obsolete. Voluntary coordination among component states or an impact of non-state actors on legal unification do not seem to have played a role and are rather unlikely to play one in the future in view of the tendencies to reduce federalism further more.

The curricula of the Venezuelan faculties of law, half of which are located in Caracas, are focused exclusively on federal law and are rather similar irrespective of their location.[111] In the absence of legislative diversity in Venezuela, legal education and training can be considered a factor that supports the centralization of the making and application of the law. The absence of legislative diversity also suggests that external factors are irrelevant for maintaining the high degree of centralization.

III. INSTITUTIONAL AND SOCIAL BACKGROUND

1. *The Role of the Judicial Branch*

A. *The Role of the Supreme Tribunal*

The Constitutional Chamber of the Supreme Tribunal of Justice (*Sala Constitucional del Tribunal Supremo de Justicia*) is the court with jurisdiction over all disputes over the constitutionality of statutes and acts resulting from the direct application of the Constitution and over all disputes between the central government, the states and the municipalities ("*acción de resolución de conflictos entre órganos del Poder Público*") (Articles 266.4 and 336.9). Yet, the jurisdiction of this court has to be put into a larger political context created by the 1999 Constitution and subsequent laws that have put into question the impartiality of the court, which since 1999 has been dominated by the followers of the President.[112] It is therefore

---

ral al Régimen del Poder Popular y del Estado Comunal (O de cómo en el siglo XXI, en Venezuela se decreta, al margen de la Constitución, un Estado de Comunas y de Consejos Comunales, y se establece una sociedad socialista y un sistema económico comunista, por los cuales nadie ha votado)," in: ídem (coord.) et al. (eds.), *Leyes Orgánicas sobre el Poder Popular y el Estado Comunal (Los consejos comunales, las comunas, la sociedad socialista y el sistema económico comunal)* 9-182 (Caracas 2011).

111 Fur a list of, and internet links to, most of the law faculties in Venezuela see *http://venezuela. justia.com/recursos/universidades/*

112 See, e.g., *Decreto de la Asamblea Nacional Constituyente sobre la Reorganización del Poder Judicial y el Sistema Penitenciario*, G.O. n° 36805 of 11 October 1999 (intervening in the Supreme Tribunal and allowing the removal of justices by a Special Commission created by the Constituent Assembly); Human Rights Watch, "Rigging the Rule of Law: Judicial Independence Under Siege in Venezuela", 16/3b *HRW Reports* 17-20 (2004), available at

little surprise that conflicts over powers between the central government and the states are systematically decided to the detriment of the latter.[113]

The only known recent case in which the Supreme Tribunal effectively declared that a federal law violated the legislative powers of a state under the new constitution concerns a case in which no federal interests were at stake. The presidential *Decreto con fuerza de Ley General de Puertos* of 2002[114] provided, among other things, that the entities created by the states for the administration of commercial ports are obliged to transfer 12.5 % of their gross income to the municipality in which the port is located. The Supreme Tribunal declared this provision unconstitutional, *inter alia,* because it would violate the states' exclusive right to dispose of the "exploitation" of the ports according to Article 164 n° 10, and thus of the revenues obtained thereof.[115]Examples for the Tribunal's bias in favor of the central government may be found in its refusal to hear cases in which the Central Government in 2003, after significant tensions between the President and states governed by the opposition had cut off payment of the constitutionally guaranteed share of the *Situado Constitucional,* the federal financial transfer to the states (Article 167 n° 4).[116] The Tribunal justified its refusal by stating that the alleged lack of payment is merely a question of the application of ordinary law and therefore not of constitutional nature, thus forcing the states to restart their claims before the Administrative Chamber.[117]

Another illustration is a case concerning the disarmament of the state police by the national armed forces after violent clashes between followers of the President and state police force.[118] *Inter alia*, the National Armed Forces, which are under the control of the President (Article 156 n° 8, 236 n° 5), confiscated in 2003 the assault rifles of the state police of Zulia, who had bought them in 2001 with the authorization of the federal Minister of the Interior and with federal funds for decentralization.[119] The State of Zulia requested the Supreme Tribunal to declare that the action

---

http://www.hrw.org/reports/2004/ venezuela0604/venezuela0604.pdf. *See also* A.R. Brewer-Carias, *supra* note 8 at 226-244.

113 Other than the following examples, for the bias of the Supreme Tribunal in favor of the federal government see also A.R. Brewer-Carías, "El juez constitucional vs. la supremacía constitucional", *mimeo,* available at http://www.allanbrewercarias.com, on the systematic rejection of all constitutional actions against the reform of the Constitution, which was eventually rejected in the referendum of 2 December 2007.

114 *G.O.* n° 73589 of 11 December 2002.

115 TSJ Sala Constitucional, decision n° 2495 of 19 December 2006, file n° 02-0265, *see also* note 43 above.

116 See below Point 20.4.2.2.

117 TSJ Sala Constitucional, decision n° 1682 of 18 September 2003, file n° 03-0207 (State of Monagas); and decision n° 1109 of 8 June 2004, file n° 03-0725 (State of Apure).

118 See TSJ Sala Constitucional, decision n° 1140 of 9 June 2005, file n° 03-0969.

119 For the parallel case of the destitution of the head of the metropolitan police of Caracas by the Armed Forces see TSJ Sala Constitucional, decision n° 3343 of 19 December 2002, file n° 02- 2939.

violated the State's powers to organize the state police and to guarantee the protection of public order (Articles 164 n° 6 and 332(3)), justifying the need for armory with the fact that the central government had not yet established the national police as required by the 1999 Constitution.[120] The Supreme Tribunal simply rejected the request with the argument that there was no conflict of power because the Armed Force has the powers to regulate the possession of "war weapons", which a law of 1939 defines as "all those which are used or could be used by the Army, the National Guards and the other security agencies for the defense of the Nation and the protection of public order",[121] which effectively covers all type of weapons.

B. *Component States' Law Applied by Courts*

Since 1945 Venezuela has had no state courts, since the judicial system falls within the exclusive jurisdiction of the central government (Article 156 n° 31). The only exception is the *justicia de paz*, a local system of judges for the conciliatory proceedings in neighborhoods that falls under the jurisdiction of the municipalities (Articles 178 n° 8 and 285).

All courts have jurisdiction to interpret state laws just as any another law and the recourse of cassation against their decisions eventually leads to the Supreme Tribunal's *Sala de Casación* (Article 266 n° 8). The different chambers of the Supreme Tribunal can also decide on requests for the interpretation of laws (Article 266 n° 6). These interpretations are, in principle, not actually binding. Formally, only the interpretations of constitutional provisions made by the Constitutional Chamber (*Sala Constitucional*) of the Supreme Tribunal, which is the ultimate guarantor for the uniform interpretation and application of the constitution, are "binding on the other Chambers and the other courts of the Republic" (Article 335).[122] In practice, however, the interpretations of national, state and municipal laws made by the other chambers of the Supreme Tribunal are *de facto* highly persuasive for the lower instances due to the Tribunal's authority and the system of recourses.

The Constitutional Chamber, when deciding actions on unconstitutionality regarding (national, state, and municipal) laws and regulations, has the exclusive power to review and to annul any kind of legislation - including state law and municipal

---

120 Transitional Provision 4 n° 9 of the Constitution, according to which this law should have been enacted within 1 year after the entry into force of the new Constitution. The *Ley Orgánica del Servicio de Policía y del Cuerpo de Policía Nacional* was only enacted in 2008 through a presidential decree, G.O. 5880 Extra of 9 April 2008.

121 Article 3 of the *Ley de Armas y Explosivos*, G.O. 19900 of 12 June 1939.

122 On this point see also A.R. Brewer-Carías, "Instrumentos de justicia constitucional en Venezuela (acción de inconstitucionalidad, controversia constitucional, protección constitucional frente a particulares)", in: J. Vega Gómez & E. Corzo Sosa (eds.), *Instrumentos de Tutela y Justicia Con- stitucional* 75-99 (Mexico City 2002); and A.R. Brewer-Carías, "Judicial Review in Venezuela", *Duquesne Law Review* 45: 439-465 (2007).

statutes (Article 336 n° 2)[123] - with *erga omnes* effect (Article 334(3)). Lower courts may declare the unconstitutionality of national, state and municipal statutes and regulations in particular cases and controversies; but this will only have effect *inter partes* (Article 334(2)). In these latter cases, an extraordinary recourse for revision can be brought before the Constitutional Chamber of the Supreme Tribunal so as to obtain a binding interpretation of the Constitution on the question of constitutionality of the challenged legal provision *(stare decisis* principle) (Article 334(4)).[124]

2.   Relations between the Central Government and Component States

A.   The Component States and Federal Law

Although deprived of most exclusive legislative powers, the states are nevertheless declared to be politically "autonomous" (Article 159). Accordingly, the central government cannot force the states to legislate, such as to enact "development laws" within the framework of central "basic laws" in matters of concurrent powers. So long as the states have not assumed their responsibility to legislate, the existing legislation will continue to apply,[125] and, in case of lacunae, courts will apply federal law by way of analogy.

Central government law is applied not only by the central government through specific federal agencies located and functioning in any part of the country, but also by the states and the municipalities when deciding on matters therein regulated.

Prior to 1999, Venezuela always had a bicameral Congress. In the Senate, the federal chamber of Congress, each state and the Federal District were represented by two directly elected senators, and additional senators represented minorities.[126] The 1999 Constitution eliminated the Senate and, in consequence, component states and municipalities are no longer represented in law-making at the central level. The component states' influence on the central legislative process is retained, according to the Constitution, by the National Assembly's obligation to consult the States' Legislative Council before passing laws on matters which could be of interest to the states (Article 206). Unfortunately, this provision has been systematically ignored in practice.[127]

---

123   See, e.g., TSJ Sala Constitucional, decision n° 843 of 11 May 2004, file n° 03-1236, whereby a law by which the State of Guárico intended to decentralize to the municipalities more areas than provided for in Article 165(2) was annulled.

124   See Brewer-Carias, *supra* note 72 at 84: "Accordingly, any interpretation by the Constitutional Chamber of any law or any other legal provision of the rank of a law or regulation does not have binding effect".

125   Article 11, *Parágrafo Unico,* of the 1989 and 2003 Decentralization Law (see notes 26 and 29 above).

126   Article 148 of the 1961 Constitution.

127   The 2003 law on the reform of the 1989 Decentralization Law was allegedly never submitted to the States' Legislative Council, see TSJ Sala Constitucional, decision n° 1801 of 24 August 2004, file n° 04-0331; and decision n° 966 of 9 May 2006, file n° 04-0331 (recourse of nullity eventually rejected due to inactivity of the claimants for more than 1 year). See

Furthermore, the 1999 Constitution required the creation of an intergovernmental entity called the Federal Council of Government for the purpose of planning and coordinating the policies and actions for the development of the decentralization process and transfer of powers from the central government to the components states and municipalities. The Federal Council of Government was to be headed by the Vice President of the Republic and integrated by Ministers, governors of the component states and one mayor from each component state, as well as of representatives of the civil society (Article 185). Such entity was finally created in 2010, but rather as an instrument designed to reinforce the centralization process through a central planning system.[128]

B.   *Public Finances*

Virtually everything concerning the taxation system has been centralized even more in the 1999 Constitution, so that the powers of the component states in tax matters have been basically eliminated. The Constitution lists in detail all the central government powers with respect to basic taxes (income tax, inheritance and donation taxes, taxes on capital, production, value added, taxes on hydrocarbon resources and mines, taxes on the import and export of goods and services, and taxes on the consumption of liquor, alcohol, cigarettes and tobacco) (Article 156 n° 12), and also expressly attributes to the municipalities some taxation powers with respect to local taxes (Article 179). In addition, as mentioned above, the Constitution gives to the national government (not to the states) residual competencies in tax matters (Article 156 n° 12). The Constitution does not grant the component states any power on matters of taxation, except with respect to official stationery and revenue stamps (Article 164 n° 7). Thus, the component states can only collect taxes when the National Assembly expressly transfers to them, by statute, specific taxation powers (Article 167 n° 5), which has never happened so far.

Therefore, due to the state's lack of resources from taxation, their financing is basically provided by the transfer of national financial resources through three different channels. First, it is done by means of the so-called *Situado Constitucional,* (Constitutional Contribution by the Federal Government) provided in the national Constitution, which is an annual amount within the National Budget Law equivalent to a minimum of 15 % and a maximum of 20 % of total ordinary national income, estimated annually (Article 167 n° 4). Second, a national law has established a sys-

---

also the allegations made by the State of Carabobo in its action against the *Decreto con Fuerza de Ley General de Puertos* (G.O. 37589 of 11 December 2002), which were rejected by the Supreme Tribunal with the argument that, in the meantime, the Decree had been substituted by a law for which the states allegedly have been consulted; TSJ Sala Constitucional, decision n° 2495 of 19 December 2006, file n° 02-0265.

128   See *Ley Orgánica del Consejo Federal de Gobierno,* G.O. n° 5963 *Extra of 22 February 2010.* See the comments of Penfold-Becerra, *supra* note 5 at 220: "If this Federal Council is not properly regulated by the law, it could be used by the central government as a means to divide the governors through the political use of resources accumulated in [the Intergovernmental Fund for Decentralization]". *See also* Sanchez Meléan, *supra* note 30 at 26.

tem of special economic allocations for the benefit of those component states where mining and hydrocarbon projects are being developed. According to this statute, these benefits have also been extended to include other component states (Article 156 n° 16).[129] And third, financing for states and municipalities also comes from national funds such as the Inter-Territorial Compensation Fund, which was created by the Federal Council of Government Law of 2010 and substitutes the former Intergovernmental Fund for Decentralization (FIDES), created in the Decentralization Law of 1993 (Article 167 n° 6). According to the Constitution, this Fund is administered by the Federal Council of Government (Article 185(2) *in fine)* and wholly controlled by the central authorities.[130] In fact, the central government has repeatedly and over some period of time retarded the transfer payments, thus causing serious financial problems to some states.[131]

C. *Other Institutions for Resolving Intergovernmental Conflicts*

Except the Constitutional Chamber of the Supreme Tribunal of Justice, which has jurisdiction to resolve constitutional and administrative conflicts between the central government and the component states and the municipalities, and the Federal Council of Government, which is called to plan and coordinate policies and actions for the process of decentralization and transfer of competencies, there are no other institutions (political, administrative, judicial) to help resolve conflicts between component states or between the central government and component states.

D. *The Role of Bureaucracy*

Even though national legislation on public servants was enacted in 2002,[132] which is applicable to all levels of civil servants, each level of government has its own civil service system. Thus, the civil service of the central government is separate from the civil services of the component states and of the municipalities. Being separate civil service systems, there is no formal lateral mobility (or career advancement) between them. Yet for retirement purposes (pensions), a matter falling under exclusive federal jurisdiction,[133] the length of time worked in any of the three levels of government counts for the purpose of retirement.

---

129 Ley de Asignaciones Económicas Especiales para los Estados y el Distrito Metropolitano de Caracas Derivadas de Minas y Hidrocarburos, *G.O. 37086 of 27 November 2000; substituted by* Ley de Asignaciones Económicas Especiales Derivadas de Minas y Hidrocarburos, *G.O. 5991 Extra of 29 July 2010. See A. Vigilanza García,* La Federación descentralizada. Mitos y realidades en el reparto de tributos y otros ingresos entre los entes políticos territoriales de Venezuela *(Caracas 2010).*

130 *See note 78 above.*

131 Sánchez Meléan, *supra* note 30 at 28-2; see also text accompanying note 67 above.

132 Ley del Estatuto de la Función Pública, supra *note 33.*

133 Ley del Estatuto Sobre el Régimen de Emolumentos, Pensiones y Jubilaciones de los Altos Funcionarios y Altas Funcionarías del Poder Público, *G.O. N° 39592 of 12 January 2011;* see also *note 23 above.*

E. *Social Factors*

Venezuela is a multicultural and mixed *(mestizo)* country where no important racial, ethnic, religious, linguistic or other social cleavages in the federation exist. There is a very small population of indigenous peoples (approximately 1 %), whose rights have been expressly recognized in the Constitution (Articles 119-126). The most important indigenous peoples group is located in the southern State of Amazonas, and its members have actively participated in the political process of the state and its municipalities. The Constitution also guarantees that in addition to the members of the National Assembly elected in each state, three separate members must be elected by the indigenous peoples (Article 186).[134]

There are very significant asymmetries in natural resources, development, wealth and education between the component states. The main oil exploitation (the main source of income of Venezuela) is located in the States of Zulia and Anzoátegui, and the main mining exploitations in the State of Bolívar. Since the component states are dependent on national financial allocations, one of the factors established in the Constitution for the distribution of the resources from the *Situado Constitucional* is related to the population of each state. Yet, the Constitution allows the assignation of special economic advantages to the states in whose territory the natural resources are located (Article 156 n° 16).[135]

IV. CONCLUDING REMARKS

Federalism has always been a most sensitive and controversial topic in Venezuela and accordingly has developed in a rather particular way, often described as "centralized federalism".[136] Already the *Exposición de Motivos* of the 1961 Constitution reflected the peculiarity of the Venezuelan conception of federalism:

> "'Federation' in Venezuela, properly speaking, represents a peculiar form of life, a bundle of values and feelings that the Constituency is obliged to respect to the degree that the interests of the people allow. Therefore, the following definition has been adopted: 'The Republic of Venezuela is a federal state in the terms established by this Constitution'... In other words, it is a federation to the degree and with the particular form in which this idea has been lived by the Venezuelan society".[137]

The decentralization process initiated in 1989 had brought about - probably for the first time - some new dynamism into the political landscape of Venezuela by granting new opportunities at state level to counterbalance the power of the central

---

134 See also note 76 above.

135 Ley de Asignaciones Económicas Especiales Derivadas de Minas y Hidrocarburo *(note 79 above).*

136 See Brewer-Carías, *supra* note 41.

137 *Exposición de Motivos de la Constitución de la República de Venezuela* (1961), cited by M. Arcaya, *Constitución de la República de Venezuela* 35-36 (Caracas 1971). This passage is partially also cited by M. Kornblith, "The Politics of Constitution-Making: Constitutions and Democracy in Venezuela", *Journal of Latin American Studies* 23: 61, 86 (1991).

government. Yet the 1999 Constitution and especially the political evolution since 2002 have more or less dried out the buds of living federalism created by the 1989 decentralization process.[138] Some go as far as affirming that, *de facto*, Venezuela is no longer a federation.[139]

As concerns the legislative powers, the finding that the component states of Venezuela do not have any significant legislative powers outside the restricted framework of federal laws also has to be put into the broader picture of legislative activity in Venezuela in general. In 2007, the National Assembly enacted a total of 19 laws, not including 62 approvals of treaties concluded by Venezuela with foreign countries.[140] The first of these laws was enacted by unanimous vote; it empowered the President in Article 203(4) to regulate a significant number of matters by way of "decree with force of law" for periods of 18 months.[141] The same occurred in 2010 with the approval of another enabling law authorizing the President for 18 months to regulate another significant number of matters by way of the same "decree with force of law".[142] Taken together with the broad legislative powers attributed to the central government, this means that the country is primarily governed directly by the President through decree. All in all, the discussion about federalism in Venezuela is by now virtually meaningless.

---

138 Sánchez Meléan, *supra* note 30 at 27 (citing the President himself as having declared in his weekly television show "Aló Presidente" that Venezuela is a "unitary republic"); J. Biardeau R., "El proyecto de reforma y la destrucción del Estado Federal Descentralizado", *mimeo* (20 October 2007), available at http://www.aporrea.org/ideologia/a42897.html (criticizing the planned reform of the Constitution [failed due to the negative referendum on 2 December 2007] as "not containing any elaboration of the principles of the decentralized federal State in the new geometry of power. Much is being said about popular power *[poder popular]*, but the cruel reality is that it is born as an appendix of the national executive power and without any autonomy". More optimistic in 2002 was Penfold-Becerra, *supra* note 5 at 221: "Venezuela's federal system might help counterbalance presidential power, continue to modify legislators' behavior, and even undermine the coalition that keeps Chávez in power. It is still too early to tell the impact of federalism on the eventual shape of Venezuelan democracy, but evidence indicates that federalism remains a critical source of political change in the country".

139 Serna de la Garza, *supra* note 47 at 283.

140 Asamblea Nacional, *Informe de Gestión 2007 - Balance Legislativo* (18 December 2007), available   at   http://www.asambleanacional.gov.ve/uploads/biblio/Balance_Legislativo%202007%20.pdf

141 *Ley que Autoriza al Presidente de la República para Dictar Decretos con Rango, Valor y Fuerza de Ley en las Materias que se Delegan, G.O. n° 38617 of 1 February 2007.* See on the Decree Laws enacted according to this 2008 enabling law, 1 15 *Revista de Derecho Público* (2008). Previously, the President had been given fast track powers for one year by the *Ley Habilitante* of 2000, G.O. n° 37077 of 14 November 2000; on this law see A.R. Brewer-Carias, "Apreciación general sobre los vicios de inconstitucionalidad que afectan los Decretos Leyes Habilitados" in: Academia de Ciencias Políticas y Sociales (ed.), *Ley Habilitante del 13-11-2000 y sus Decretos Leyes* 63-103 (Caracas 2002).

142 Ley que Autoriza al Presidente de la República para Dictar Decretos con Rango, Valor y Fuerza de Ley en las Materias que se Delegan, *G.O. n° 6009 Extra of 17 December 2010.*.

CHAPTER X

THE CONCENTRATION OF POWERS AND
AUTHORITARIAN GOVERNMENT

(2008-2009)

This essay with the title "The principle of separation of powers and Authoritarian Government in Venezuela," was written for the Seminar on *Separation of Powers in the Americas... and Beyond*, organized by Professor Robert Barker, *Duquesne University, School of Law*, Pittsburgh, November 7 and 8, 2008. A first version of these reflections were initially written as "Separation of Powers and Authoritarianism in Venezuela," for the lecture given in the *Constitutional Comparative Law Course* of Prof. Ruti G. Teitel, *Fordham Law School*, New York City, on February 11, 2008. A further development of this essay was written for the lecture on "Venezuela under Chávez: Blurring between Democracy and Dictatorship?, which I gave at the *University of Pennsylvania Law School*, Philadelphia, April 16, 2009. The text was published as "The Principle of Separation of Powers and Authoritarian Government in Venezuela," in *Duquesne Law Review*, Vol. 47, Number 4, Pittsburgh, Fall 2009, pp. 813-838.

I. THE PRINCIPLE OF SEPARATION OF POWERS IN MODERN CONSTITUTIONALISMO AND IN THE VENEZUELAN CONSTITUTIONAL TRADITION

The principle of separation of powers in modern constitutionalism has its origin in the Constitutions of the former Colonies of North America where, for instance, in the Constitution of Virginia of June 29, 1776, it was set forth that:

> "SEC. 3. The legislative, executive, and judiciary department shall be separate and distinct, so that neither exercises the powers properly belonging to the other: nor shall any person exercise the powers of more than one of them, at the same time..."[143]

---

143 "The Constitution or Form of Government agreed to and resolved upon by the Delegates and Representatives of the Several Counties and Corporations of Virginia" of June 29, 1776. This

This provision and the similar ones that were incorporated after 1776 in the other Constitutions of the former Colonies of North America,[144] have their theoretical backgrounds in the writings of John Locke,[145] Montesquieu[146] and J. J. Rousseau[147] which were the most important weapons used during the XVIII Century American and French Revolutions in the battle against the Absolute State: in North America to fight against the Sovereignty of the British Parliament, and in France to fight against the Sovereignty of the Monarch. The consequence of both Revolutions was the replacement of the Absolute State by a Constitutional State, submitted to the rule of law, based precisely on the principle of the separation of powers as a guarantee of liberty, even though with different trends of government: the Presidential system of government in the U.S resulting from the North American Revolution, and decades after the French revolution, the consolidation of the Parliamentary system of government in Europe.

---

article has been considered as "The most precise statement of the doctrine which had at that time appeared." M.J.C. VILE, *Constitutionalism and the Separation of Powers*, Oxford 1967, p. 118.

144 The Constitution of Massachusetts (1780) also contained the following categorical expression: "Article XXX: In the government of this Commonwealth, the legislative department shall not exercise the executive and judicial powers, or either one of them: The executive shall never exercise the legislative and judicial powers, or either one of them: The judicial shall never exercise the legislative and executive powers, or either one of them: to the end it may be a government of laws not of men."

145 See J. Locke, *Two Treatises of Government* (ed. Peter Laslett), Cambridge 1967, p. 371, 383-385, 350

146 It is always adequate to remember the famous proposition of Montesquieu, that "it is an eternal experience that any man who is given power tends to abuse it; he does so until he encounters limits... In order to avoid the abuse of power, steps must be taken for power to limit power." That is why, in the well-known Chapter VI of Volume XI of his *De l'Ésprit of laws* he formulated his theory of the division of power into three categories: "Legislative power, power to execute things which depend on international law, and power to execute things which depend on civil lawn the first case, the prince or magistrat makes laws for a period of time or for ever. In the second case, he makes peace or war, sends or receives ambassadors, establishes security, takes measures against invasion. In the third case, he punishes crimes, or settles disputes between individuals. The latter we shall call the power to judge, and the other simply the executive power of the state." He added: "When legislative power and executive power are in the hands of the same person or the same magistrate's body, there is no freedom. Neither is there any liberty if the power to judge is not separate from the legislative and executive powers... All would be lost if the same man, or the same body of princes, or noblemen or people exercised these three powers: that of making the laws, that of executing public resolutions and that of judging the wishes or disputes of individuals." Montesquieu, *De l'Esprit des Lois* (ed. G. Truc), Paris 1949, Vol. I, Book XI, Chap. IV, p. 162-164.

147 J. J. Rousseau, *Du Contrat Social* (ed. Ronald Grimsley), Oxford 1972, Book I, Chap. IV, p. 153.

The principle of separation of powers, thus, became the most important and distinguishes principle of modern constitutionalism,[148] in the sense that on the contrary, according to Madison:

"The accumulation of all powers, legislative, executive, and judiciary in the same hands, whether of one, a few, or many, and whether hereditary, self-appointed or elective, may justly be pronounced the very definition of Tyranny."[149]

That explains the provision of article 16 of the French Declaration of Rights of Man and Citizen (1789), according to which:

"Every society in which the guarantee of rights is not assured or the separation of powers not determined has no Constitution."

All these principles inspired the first modern Constitution adopted in all Latin America, the "Federal Constitution of the States of Venezuela," sanctioned on December 21, 1811 by an elected general Congress, even before the Constitution of the Spanish Monarchy of Cádiz of 1812 was sanctioned.[150] In this Constitution, the principle of separation of powers was adopted, setting forth in the Preamble that:

"The exercise of authority conferred upon the Confederation never could be reunited in its respective functions. The Supreme Power must be divided in the Legislative, the Executive and the Judicial, and conferred to different bodies independent between them and regarding its respective powers."

To this proposition, article 189 of the Constitution added that:

"The three essential Departments of government, that is, the Legislative, the Executive and the Judicial, must be always kept separated and independent one from the other according the nature of a free government, which is convenient in the connection chain that unite all the fabric of the Constitution in an indissoluble way of Friendship and Union."[151]

Consequently, since the beginning of modern constitutionalism, the principle of separation of constitutional power also was adopted in Venezuela, in particular, according to the trends of the presidential system of government within a check and balance conception, granting the Judiciary specific powers of judicial review. The later, according to the objective guaranty of the Constitution established in article

---

148 See Allan R. Brewer-Carías, *Reflexiones sobre la Revolución norteamericana (1776), la Revolución francesa (1789) y la Revolución hispanoamericana (1810-1830) y sus aportes al constitucionalismo moderno,* 2ª Edición Ampliada, Serie Derecho Administrativo N° 2, Universidad Externado de Colombia, Editorial Jurídica Venezolana, Bogotá 2008,

149 J. Madison, *The Federalist* (ed. B.F. Wright), Cambridge, Mass 1961, N°47, p. 336.

150 See Allan R. Brewer-Carías, "El paralelismo entre el constitucionalismo venezolano y el constitucionalismo de Cádiz (o de cómo el de Cádiz no influyó en el venezolano)" en *Libro Homenaje a Tomás Polanco Alcántara*, Estudios de Derecho Público, Universidad Central de Venezuela, Caracas 2005, pp. 101-189

151 See the text of the 1811 Constitution and all of the other Venezuelan Constitutions in Allan R. Brewer-Carías, *Las Constituciones de Venezuela*, Academia de Ciencias Políticas y Sociales, Caracas, Biblioteca de la Academia de Ciencias Políticas y Sociales, 2 Vols., Caracas 2008.

227, of the same 1811 Constitution, in the sense that "The laws sanctioned against the Constitution will have no value except when fulfilling the conditions for a just and legitimate revision and sanction [of the Constitution];" and in article 199, in the sense that any law sanctioned by the federal legislature or by the provinces contrary to the fundamental rights enumerated in the Constitution "will be absolutely null and void."

Since 1811, all the Constitutions in Venezuelan history have established and guarantied the principle of separation of powers, particularly between the three classical Legislative, Executive and Judicial branches of government (powers), in a system of check and balance, and always giving the Judiciary the judicial review power. For such purpose, the independence and autonomy of the branches of government have been the most important aspects regulated in the Constitutions, particularly during the democratic regimes, due to the fact that the principle of separation of powers in contemporary constitutionalism has become one of the basic conditions for democracy to exist, and for the possibility of guarantying the enjoyment and protection fundamental rights. On the contrary, without separation of powers, and without autonomy and independence between the branches of government, no democratic regime is possible to be developed and no guaranty of fundamental rights is can exist.

II. SEPARATION OF POWERS AND DEMOCRACY

In effect, the essential components of democracy are much more than the sole popular or circumstantial election of government officials, as was formally recognized in the Inter American Democratic Charter *(Carta Democrática Interamericana)* adopted by the Organization of American States in 2001,[152] in which the principle of separation and independence of powers, that is, the possibility to control the different branches of government, is enumerated as one of the *essential elements of the representative democracy,"* (article 3). The principle of separation and independence of the branches of government is conceived in a so important way, that is the one that can allow all the other "fundamental components of democracy" to be a politically possible. To be precise, democracy, as a political regime, can only function in a constitutional Rule of law system where the control of power exists; that is, check and balance based on the separation of powers with their independence and autonomy guaranteed, so that power can be stopped by power itself.

Consequently, without separation of powers and the possibility of control of power, any of the other essential factors of democracy cannot be guaranty, because only by controlling Power free and fair elections and political pluralism can exist; only by controlling Power effective democratic participation con be possible, and effective transparency in the exercise of government can be assured; only by controlling Power there can be a government submitted to the Constitution and the laws, that is, the Rule of law; only by controlling Power there can be an effective access to

---

152 See the comments on the Inter-American Democratic Charter, in Allan R. Brewer-Carías, *La crisis de la democracia venezolana. La Carta Democrática Interamericana y los sucesos de abril de 2002*, Ediciones El Nacional, Caracas 2002. pp. 137 ff.

justice functioning with autonomy and independence; and only by controlling Power there can be a true and effective guaranty for the respect of human rights.[153]

The constitutional situation in Venezuela since the Constituent making process that took place in 1999, which resulted in the complete takeover of all powers of the State and the sanctioning of the current 1999 Constitution, unfortunately has been of a very week democracy, precisely because the progressive demolishing of the principle of separation of powers. In it, a process of concentration of powers has taken place, first with the 1999 Constituent making process itself, which intervene all branches of government before sanctioning the new Constitution; and after, due to the provisions of the 1999 Constitution, which do not guaranty the effective independence and autonomy of the branches of government.

III. CONCENTRATION OF POWERS AND AUTHORITARIANISM IN DEFRAUDATION OF THE CONSTITUTION

The result has been that currently, Venezuela has an authoritarian government although not being the result of a classical Latin American military *coup d'Etat*, but of a systematic process of destruction of all the basic principles of democracy and of the Constitution. This process began with the 1998 election of Hugo Chávez Frías as President of the Republic, a position that ten years later he still hold, being in 2009 the President with the longest continued tenure in all the Venezuelan constitutional history.

Without doubts, in 1998, Chávez was elected in a free democratic election process, as an anti-party candidate, precisely during the most severe political crisis the country has had during the democratic period of the country that began in 1945. This crisis was the result of the collapse of the political parties that have controlled the political life of the country for more than 40 years;[154] being Chávez the one that filled the vacuum left by those parties and their leadership. During the electoral campaign, he blandished as his main political proposal, the obvious need for a change the country had, that he promised to achieve by convening a National Constituent Assembly in order to change the Constitution.[155]

This constitutional making procedure was not established in the 1961 Constitution then in force, so to elect such Assembly in 1999 a previous constitutional re-

---

153 See Allan R. Brewer-Carías, "Democracia: sus elementos y componentes esenciales y el control del poder," in Nuria González Martín, (Compiladora), *Grandes temas para un observatorio electoral ciudadano, Tomo I, Democracia: retos y fundamentos,* Instituto Electoral del Distrito Federal, México 2007, pp. 171-220

154 See Allan R. Brewer-Carías, *Problemas del Estado de los Partidos*, Editorial Jurídica Venezolana, Caracas 1998; "La crisis de las instituciones: responsables y salidas," in *Revista del Centro de Estudios Superiores de las Fuerzas Armadas de Cooperación,* N° 11, Caracas 1985, pp. 57-83; and in *Revista de la Facultad de Ciencias Jurídicas y Políticas,* N° 64, Universidad Central de Venezuela, Caracas 1985,pp. 129-155.

155 See on the 1998 proposals, Allan R. Brewer-Carías, *Asamblea Constituyente y Ordenamiento Constitucional,* Serie Estudios N° 53, Biblioteca de la Academia de Ciencias Políticas y Sociales, Caracas 1999.

form was needed, unless a constitutional judicial interpretation of the 1961 Constitution allows the election. The latter was what precisely the Supreme Court of Justice did in a very diligent way in January 1999, although in a very ambiguous way,[156] trying to resolve the at the moment existing dilemma between popular sovereignty willing to be expressed and constitutional supremacy[157], eventually deciding in favor of the former.

The Constituent Assembly was then elected in July 1999 after a consultative referendum that took place in April 1999, being completely controlled by Chávez supporters with more than 95% of its seats.

This Assembly, far from dedicating itself to write off the new Constitution, was the main tool the newly elected President had, in order to assault and control all the branches of government, violating the same 1961 Constitution whose interpretation helped to created it[158]. Consequently, the elected Constituent Assembly technically gave a *coup d'Etat*[159], unfortunately with the consent and complicity of the former Supreme Court of Justice, which as it always happens in these illegitimate institutional complicity cases; it was inexorably the first victim of the authoritarian government, which it helped to grab power. Just a few months later, that Supreme Court was erased from the institutional scene[160].

The 1999 Constituent Assembly was then, the instrument used by the President to dissolve and intervene all branches of government (particularly the Judiciary) and to dismiss all the public officials that have been elected just a few months before (1998), namely the representatives to the National Congress, the State's Legislative Assemblies and the Municipal Councils as well as the State Governors and munici-

---

156 See the comments to the judicial decisions in Allan R. Brewer-Carías, "La configuración judicial del proceso constituyente en Venezuela de 1999 o de cómo el guardián de la Constitución abrió el camino para su violación y para su propia extinción," in *Revista de Derecho Público*, N° 77-80, Editorial Jurídica Venezolana, Caracas 1999, pp. 453-514; and in Allan R. Brewer-Carías, *Poder constituyente originario y Asamblea Nacional Constituyente (Comentarios sobre la interpretación jurisprudencial relativa a la naturaleza, la misión y los límites de la Asamblea Nacional Constituyente)*, Colección Estudios Jurídicos N° 72, Editorial Jurídica Venezolana, Caracas 1999

157 See Allan R. Brewer-Carías, "El desequilibrio entre soberanía popular y supremacía constitucional y la salida constituyente en Venezuela en 1999," en la *Revista Anuario Iberoamericano de Justicia Constitucional*, N° 3, 1999, Centro de Estudios Políticos y Constitucionales, Madrid 2000, pp. 31-56

158 See Allan R. Brewer-Carías, *Debate constituyente (Aportes a la Asamblea Nacional Constituyente)*, Volume I (August 8-September 8, 1999), Fundación de Derecho Público-Editorial Jurídica Venezolana, Caracas 1999.

159 See Allan R. Brewer-Carías, *Golpe de Estado y proceso constituyente en Venezuela*, Universidad Nacional Autónoma de México, México 2002.

160 See the study about the effects of the December 1999 Transitory Regime established by the Constituent Assembly after the approval, by popular referendum, of the Constitution of 1999, in Allan R. Brewer-Carías, *La Constitución de 1999*. Editorial Arte, Caracas 2000; and *La Constitución de 1999. Derecho constitucional venezolano*, Volume II, Editorial Jurídica Venezolana, Caracas 2004, pp. 1150 ff.

pal Mayors. The sole exception of this intervention was the President of the Republic itself, precisely the author of the constitutional fraud. In addition, the Constitutional Assembly intervene all the other branches of government, among them, and above all, the Judiciary, whose autonomy and independence was progressive and systematically demolished[161]. The result has been the tight Executive control over the Judiciary, particularly regarding the new appointed Supreme Tribunal of Justice, being its Constitutional Chamber the most ominous instrument for the consolidation of authoritarianism in the country[162].

Through the defraudation of the Constitution in order to reach power, once all the State branches of government were controlled, the Government began another defraudation process, this time of democracy, using representative democracy for the purpose of eliminating it progressively, and supposedly substituting it by a "participative democracy" based on the establishment of popular councils of a new Popular Power controlled from the Head of the State.

This centralizing and concentrating framework of the State was the one that was pretended to be constitutionalized in the constitutional reform proposal that fortunately was rejected in the last December 2007 referendum.[163] The intention, as was announced by the then Vice President of the Republic in January 2007, was to install "the dictatorship of democracy"[164]; of course a contradiction in itself because in democracy no dictatorship is acceptable, whether of democracy or "of the proletariat" as was proposed ninety years ago (1918) in the old Soviet Union through the same sort of "councils" then called "soviets" of soldiers, workers and countrymen.

But even without succeeding in the proposed constitutional reform, the fact is that in defraudation of democracy, a new model of authoritarian State of a supposed Popular Power has taken shape in Venezuela, having its immediate origin in popular elections, providing the regime with a camouflage suit with "constitutional" and

---

161 See Allan R. Brewer-Carías, "La progresiva y sistemática demolición de la autonomía e independencia del Poder Judicial en Venezuela (1999-2004)," in *XXX Jornadas J.M Dominguez Escovar, Estado de derecho, Administración de justicia y derechos humanos*, Instituto de Estudios Jurídicos del Estado Lara, Barquisimeto 2005, pp 33-174.

162 See Allan R. Brewer-Carías, "Quis Custodiet ipsos Custodes: De la interpretación constitucional a la inconstitucionalidad de la interpretación," in *VIII Congreso Nacional de derecho Constitucional*, Peru, Fondo Editorial 2005, Colegio de Abogados de Arequipa, Arequipa, September 2005, pp. 463-489; and in Allan R. Brewer-Carías, *Crónica de la "In" Justicia Constitucional. La Sala Constitucional y el autoritarismo en Venezuela*, Caracas 2007.

163 See Allan R. Brewer-Carías, *Hacia la consolidación de un Estado Socialista, Centralizado y Militarista. Comentarios sobre el alcance y sentido de las propuestas de reforma Constitucional 2007*, Editorial Jurídica Venezolana, Caracas, 2007; and *La reforma constitucional de 2007 (Comentarios al proyecto inconstitucionalmente sancionado por la Asamblea Nacional el 2 de noviembre de 2007)*, Editorial Jurídica Venezolana, Caracas 2007.

164 Jorge Rodríguez, Vice-President of the Republic, in January 2007, expressed: "Of course we want to install a dictatorship, the dictatorship of the true democracy and the democracy is the dictatorship of everyone, you and us together, building a different country. Of course we want this dictatorship of democracy to be installed forever," in *El Nacional*, Caracas 02-01-2007, p. A-2.

"elective" shapes, designed for the destruction of the representative democracy itself.[165]

For such purpose, all the aforementioned essential elements of democracy are precisely the ones that, during the past few years have unfortunately been ignored or fractured in Venezuela, in the name of a supposed participative democracy. Never before, there had been more violation of human rights as can be deducted from the numerous petitions filed before the Inter-American Commission on Human Rights. The access to power has been achieved contrary to the Rule of law, by violating the separation and independence of the Judicial, Citizens and Electoral powers,[166] and the last political reforms creating the Communal Councils, tend to substitute electoral representation by supposed citizen assemblies and councils whose members are not elected, but appointed from the summit of the Popular Power controlled by the President of the Republic.[167] The plural regime of parties has been destroyed and an

---

165 See Allan R. Brewer-Carías, "Constitution Making in Defraudation of the Constitution and Authoritarian Government in Defraudation of Democracy. The Recent Venezuelan Experience," en *Lateinamerika Analysen*, 19, 1/2008, GIGA, Germa Institute of Global and Area Studies, Institute of latin American Studies, Hamburg 2008, pp. 119-142 and "El autoritarismo establecido en fraude a la Constitución y a la democracia y su formalización en "Venezuela mediante la reforma constitucional. (De cómo en un país democrático se ha utilizado el sistema eleccionario para minar la democracia y establecer un régimen autoritario de supuesta "dictadura de la democracia" que se pretende regularizar mediante la reforma constitucional)" in *Temas constitucionales. Planteamientos ante una Reforma,* Fundación de Estudios de Derecho Administrativo, FUNEDA, Caracas 2007, pp. 13-74

166 See Allan R. Brewer-Carías, "El secuestro del Poder Electoral y la confiscación del derecho a la participación política mediante el referendo revocatorio presidencial: Venezuela 2000-2004," in *Revista Jurídica del Perú*, Año LIV N° 55, Lima, March-April 2004, pp. 353-396; "El secuestro del Poder Electoral y de la Sala Electoral del Tribunal Supremo y la confiscación del derecho a la participación política mediante el referendo revocatorio presidencial: Venezuela: 2000-2004," in *Revista Costarricense de Derecho Constitucional*, Vol., V, Instituto Costarricense de Derecho Constitucional, Editorial Investigaciones Jurídicas S.A., San José 2004, pp. 167-312; "El secuestro de la Sala Electoral por la Sala Constitucional del Tribunal Supremo de Justicia, in *La Guerra de las Salas del TSJ frente al Referendum Revocatorio*," Editorial Aequitas, Caracas 2004, C.A., pp. 13-58; "El secuestro del poder electoral y la confiscación del derecho a la participación política mediante el referendo revocatorio presidencial: Venezuela 2000-2004," *Stvdi Vrbinati, Rivista Trimestrale di Scienze Giuridiche, Politiche ed Economiche*, Year LXXI – 2003/04 Nuova Serie A – N. 55,3, Università degli studi di Urbino, Urbino, 2004, pp.379-436; "El secuestro del Poder Electoral y la confiscación del derecho a la participación política mediante el referendo revocatorio presidencial: Venezuela 2000-2004," in *Boletín Mexicano de Derecho Comparado*, Instituto de Investigaciones Jurídicas, Universidad Nacional Autónoma de México, N° 112. México, January-April 2005 pp. 11-73.

167 See Allan R. Brewer-Carías "El inicio de la desmunicipalización en Venezuela: La organización del Poder Popular para eliminar la descentralización, la democracia representativa y la participación a nivel local," en *AIDA, Opera Prima de Derecho Administrativo. Revista de la Asociación Internacional de Derecho Administrativo*, Universidad Nacional Autónoma de México, Facultad de Estudios Superiores de Acatlán, Coordinación de Postgrado, Instituto Internacional de Derecho Administrativo "Agustín Gordillo," Asociación Internacional de Derecho Administrativo, México, 2007, pp. 49 a 67.

official single Socialist Party has been created by the State itself, completely imbricate in its apparatus and controlled by the President of the Republic. Because everything depends on the Oil rich State, only those who are part of the Single Party can be able to have a political, administrative, economic and social life.

And all this entire institutional distortion has been established without the existence of separation or independence between the public powers, not only in their horizontal division due to the control that the Executive Power has over them; but in their vertical distribution, where the Federation has been progressively dismantled. Consequently, the federated States and the municipalities have been minimized, by means of eliminating every trace of political decentralization, that is, of autonomous entities in the territory, preventing any real possibility for democratic participation.

On the other hand, all the fundamental components of democracy have also been ignored or fractured: the governmental activity deployed by the rich and suddenly wealthy State has ceased to be transparent due to the lack of any sort of control and check and balance, not being possible to demand any kind of accountability or responsibility from the government for the public interests management, so a rampant corruption has developed in a way never seen before. In addition, the freedom of speech and press has been systematically threatened, imposing in many cases self-censorship, being the reporters and dissidents persecuted.[168]

The consequence has been that all the essential elements and fundamental components of democracy, have been progressively dismantled during the past years in Venezuela, particularly the separation of powers. And on the contrary, what the country is facing is an excess of concentration and centralization of power, as it occurs in any authoritarian government, despite the electoral origin they can have. In such cases, as history has shown, an inevitable tendency toward tyranny develops particularly when there are no efficient controls over those who govern, and even worst, if they have or believe to have popular support. In the case of Venezuela, the authoritarian government that has taken roots during the last decade against the principle of separation of powers, has led to the concentration of all powers in the hands of the Executive Power which at his turn controls the National Assembly, and consequently all the other branches of government.

IV. THE CONSTITUTIONAL PROVISIONS ON SEPARATION OF PO-WERS AND THE ORIGIN OF THE DEPENDENCY OF THE BRANCHES OF GOVERNMENT

The 1999 Constitution, if it is read in a vacuum, ignoring the political reality of the country, can mislead any lector. It is the only Constitution in contemporary world that has established, not only a tripartite separation of powers between the traditional Legislative (*Asamblea Nacional*), Executive (President of the Republic, Executive offices) and Judicial (Supreme Tribunal of Justice, courts) branches of

---

168　See as an example, the case of the shot down of *Radio Caracas Televisión*, in Allan R. Brewer-Carías, "El juez constitucional en Venezuela como instrumento para aniquilar la libertad de expresión y para confiscar la propiedad privada: el *caso RCTV*" (I de III), in *Gaceta Judicial*, Santo Domingo, República Dominicana, mayo 2007, pp. 24-27.

government, but a *penta* separation of powers, adding to the latter, two more branches of government: the Electoral Power, attributed to the National Electoral Council, in charge of the organization and conduction of the elections; and the Citizens Power, attributed to three different State entities: the General Prosecutor Office (Public Ministry) (*Fiscalía General de la República*), the General Comptroller Office (*Contraloría General de la República*), and the Peoples' Defendant (*Defensor del Pueblo*) (article 136). This *penta* separation of powers in any case, was the culmination of a previous constitutional process and tendency initiated in 1961 with the consolidation in the Constitution of State organs with constitutional rank not dependents from the classical powers, as was for instance, the Public Prosecutor, the Council of the Judiciary, the Comptroller General.[169]

But as mentioned, in spite of this *penta* division of powers, the fact is that the autonomy and independence of the branches of government is not completely and consistently assured in the Constitution, its application leading, on the contrary, to a concentration of State powers in the National Assembly, and through it, in the Executive power.

In effect, in any system of separation of powers, even with five separate branches of government (Legislative, Executive, Judicial, Citizen and Electoral), in order for such separation to become effective, the independence and autonomy among them has to be assured in order to allow check and balance, that is, the limitation and control of power by power itself. This was the aspect that was not designed as such in the 1999 Constitution, and notwithstanding the aforementioned penta separation of powers, an absurd distortion of the principle was introduced by giving the National Assembly the authority not only to appoint, but to dismiss the Judges of the Supreme Tribunal of Justice, the Prosecutor General, the General Comptroller, the People's Defendant and the Members of the National Electoral Council (Articles 265, 279 and 296); and in some cases, even by simple majority of votes. This latter solution was even proposed to be formally introduced in the rejected 2007 Constitutional reform proposals, seeking to eliminate the guarantee of the qualified majority of the members of the National Assembly for such dismissals.[170]

It is simply impossible to understand how the autonomy and independence of separate powers can function and how can they exercise mutual control, when the tenure of the Head officials of the branches of government (except the President of the Republic) depend on the political will of one of the branches of government, that is, the National Assembly. The sole fact of the possibility for the National Assembly to dismiss the head of the other branches, makes futile the formal consecration of the

---

169 See the comments in Allan R. Brewer-Carías, *La Constritutión de 1999*, Caracas 2000, pp. 106 ff.

170 See Allan R. Brewer-Carías, *Hacia la consolidación de un Estado Socialista, Centralizado y Militarista. Comentarios sobre el alcance y sentido de las propuestas de reforma Constitucional 2007*, Editorial Jurídica Venezolana, Caracas, 2007; and *La reforma constitucional de 2007 (Comentarios al proyecto inconstitucionalmente sancionado por la Asamblea Nacional el 2 de noviembre de 2007)*, Colección Textos Legislativos, N° 43, Editorial Jurídica Venezolana, Caracas 2007.

autonomy and independence of powers, being the High officials of the State aware that they can be removed from office at any time, precisely if they effectively act with independence[171].

And unfortunately, this has happened in Venezuela during the past decade, so when there have been minimal signs of autonomy from some holders of State institutions, who have dared to adopt their own decisions distancing themselves from the Executive will, they have been dismiss. This occurred, for instance, in 2001 with the People's Defendant and with the Prosecutor General of the Republic, originally appointed in 1999 by the Constituent National Assembly, who were separated from their positions[172] for failing to follow the dictates of the Executive power; and this also happened with some Judges of the Supreme Tribunal who dared to vote decisions that could question the Executive action, who were immediately subjected to investigation and some of them were removed or duly "retired" from their positions[173].

The consequence resulting from this factual "dependency" of the State organs regarding the National Assembly, has been the total absence of fiscal or audit control regarding all the State entities. The General Comptroller Office has ignored the results of the huge and undisciplined disposal of the oil wealth that has occurred in Venezuela, not always in accordance with Budget discipline rules, which has provoked the classification of Venezuela in one of the lowest ranks on Government transparency in the world.[174] Nonetheless, the most important decisions taken by the Comptroller General have been those directed to disqualify many opposition candidates from the November 2008 regional and municipal elections, based on "administrative irregularities," although the Constitution establishes (that the constitutional right to run for office can only be suspended when a judicial criminal decision is

---

171 See "Democracia y control del poder," in Allan R. Brewer-Carías, *Constitución, democracia y control de poder*, Centro Iberoamericano de Estudios Provinciales y Locales. Universidad de Los Andes, Mérida 2004.

172 It the case of the General Prosecutor of the Republic, appointed in December of 1999, he thought he could initiate a criminal impeachment proceedings against the then Minister of the Interior; and the People's Defendant, also thought that she could challenge the Special Law of the 2001 National Assembly on appointment of Judges of the Supreme Tribunal without complying with the constitutional requirements. They were both duly dismissed in 2001.

173 It was the case of Franklin Arrieche, Vice-President of the Supreme Tribunal of Justice, who delivered the decision of the Supreme Tribunal of 08-14-2002 regarding the criminal process against the generals who acted on April 12, 2002, declaring that there were no grounds to judge them due to the fact that in said occasion no military coup took place; and that of Alberto Martini Urdaneta, President of the Electoral Court, and Rafael Hernandez and Orlando Gravina, Judges of the same Court who undersigned decision N° 24 of 03-15-2004 (Case: *Julio Borges, Cesar Perez Vivas, Henry Ramos Allup, Jorge Sucre Castillo, Ramón Jose Medina and Gerardo Blyde vs. the National Electoral Council*), that suspended the effects of Resolution N° 040302-131, dated 03-02-2004 of the National Electoral Council which, in that moment, stopped the realization of the presidential recall referendum.

174 See http://www.transparencia.org.ve

adopted articles 39 and 42);[175] but which the Constitutional Chamber of the Supreme Tribunal has uphold in defraudation of the Constitution.[176]

Regarding the People's Defendant, it has been perceived more as a defendant of State powers than of the peoples' rights, even if the Venezuelan State never before has been denounced so many times as has happened during the past years before the Inter American Commission on Human Rights. And finally, the Public Prosecutor has been characterized by using its powers to prosecute using in an indiscriminate way the controlled Judiciary as a tool to persecute any political dissidence.

V. THE DEFRAUDATION OF POLITICAL PARTICIPATION IN THE APPOINTMENT OF HIGH GOVERNAMENTAL OFFICERS

But the process of concentration of powers that Venezuela has experienced during the past decade has also being the result of a process of defraudation of the Constitution, particularly ignoring the limits the Constitution has established to reduce the discretional power of the National Assembly in the process of appointing the Heads of the different branches of government.

In effect, independently of the constitutional provisions regarding the possible dismissal by the National Assembly of the Heads of the non-elected branches of government, and its distortions, one of the mechanism established in order to assure their independence, was the provision in the Constitution of a system to assure that their appointment by the National Assembly was to be limited by the necessary participation of special collective bodies called Nominating Committees that must be integrated with representatives of the different sectors of society (arts. 264, 279, 295). Those Nominating Committees are in charge of selecting and nominating the candidates, guaranteeing the political participation of the citizens in the process.

Consequently, the appointment of the Justices of the Supreme Tribunal, of the Members of the National Electoral Council, of the Prosecutor General of the Republic, of the People's Defendant and of the Comptroller General of the Republic, can only be made among the candidates proposed by the corresponding "Nominating

---

175 In October 2008, the European Parliament approved a Resolution asking the Venezuelan government to end with these practices (political incapacitation in order to difficult the presence of opposition leaders in the regional and local elections) and to promote a more global democracy with complete respect of the principles established in the 1999 Constitution. See http://venezuelanoticia.com/archives/8298

176 Teodoro Petkoff has pointed out that with this decision "the authoritarian and autocratic government of Hugo Chávez has clearly shown its true colors in this episode," explaining that "The political rights to run for office is only lost when a candidate has receive a judicial sentence that has been upheld in a higher court. The recent sentence by the Venezuelan Supreme Court, upholding the disqualifications, as well as the constitutionality of article 105 [of the Organic Law of the Comptroller General Office], constitute a defraudation of the Constitution and the way in which the decision was handed down was an obvious accommodation to the president's desire to eliminate four significant opposition candidates from the electoral field." See Teodoro Petkoff, "Election and Political Power. Challenges for the Opposition," in ReVista. Harvard Review of Latin America, David Rockefeller Center for Latin American Studies, Harvard University, Fall 2008, pp. 11.

Committees," which are the ones in charge of selecting and nominating the candidates before the Assembly. These constitutional previsions seek to limit the discretional power the political legislative organ traditionally had to appoint those high officials through political party agreements, by assuring political citizenship participation.[177]

Unfortunately, these exceptional constitutional provisions have not been applied, due to the fact that the National Assembly during the past years, also defrauding the Constitution, has deliberately "transformed" the said Committees into simple "parliamentary Commissions" reducing the civil society's right to political participation. The Assembly in all the statutes sanctioned regarding such Committees and the appointment process, has established the composition of all the Nominating Committees with a majority of parliamentary representatives (whom by definition cannot be representatives of the "civil society"), although providing, in addition, for the incorporation of some other members chosen by the National Assembly itself from strategically selected "non-governmental Organizations."

The result has been the complete control of the Nominating Committees, and the persistence of the discretional political and partisan way of appointing the officials head of the non-elected branches of government, which the provisions of the 1999 Constitution intended to limit, by a National Assembly that since 2000 has been complete controlled by the Executive.

This practice even pretended to be constitutionalized through the rejected Constitutional Reform of 2007, with the proposal to formally establish exclusively parliamentary Nomination Committees, instead of being composed of representatives of the various sectors of civil society.[178]

VI. THE CATASTROPHIC DEPENDENCE AND SUBJECTION OF THE JUDICIARY

The effects of the dependency of the branches of government subjected to the Legislative Power and through it to the Executive, have been particularly catastrophic regarding the Judiciary, which after been initially intervened by the Constituent National Assembly in 1999[179], continued to be intervened with the unfortunate consent and complicity of the Supreme Tribunal of Justice itself. In this matter,

---

177 See Allan R. Brewer-Carías, "La participación ciudadana en la designación de los titulares de los órganos no electos de los Poderes Públicos en Venezuela y sus vicisitudes políticas," in *Revista Iberoamericana de Derecho Público y Administrativo*. Year 5. N° 5-2005. San José, Costa Rica 2005. pp. 76-95.

178 See Allan R. Brewer-Carías, *Hacia la consolidación de un Estado Socialista, Centralizado y Militarista. Comentarios sobre el alcance y sentido de las propuestas de reforma Constitucional 2007*, Editorial Jurídica Venezolana, Caracas, 2007; and *La reforma constitucional de 2007 (Comentarios al proyecto inconstitucionalmente sancionado por la Asamblea Nacional el 2 de noviembre de 2007)*, Colección Textos Legislativos, N° 43, Editorial Jurídica Venezolana, Caracas 2007.

179 See Allan R. Brewer-Carías, *Debate Constituyente, (Aportes a la Asamblea Nacional Constituyente)*, Volume I, (August 8-Spetember -), Caracas 1999.

in the past decade, the country has witnessed a permanent and systematic demolition process of the autonomy and independence of the judicial power, aggravated by the fact that according to the 1999 Constitution, the Supreme Tribunal which is completely controlled by the Executive, is in charge of administering all the Venezuelan judicial system, particularly, by appointing and dismissing judges.[180]

The process began with the appointment, in 1999, of new Magistrates of the Supreme Tribunal of Justice without complying with the constitutional conditions, made by the National Constituent Assembly itself, by means of a Constitutional Transitory regime sanctioned after the Constitution was approved by referendum.[181] From there on, the intervention process of the Judiciary continued up to the point that the President of the Republic has politically controlled the Supreme Tribunal of Justice and, through it, the complete Venezuelan judicial system.

For that purpose, the constitutional conditions needed to be elected Magistrate of the Supreme Tribunal and the procedures for their nomination with the participation of representatives of the different sectors of civil society, were violated since the beginning. First, as aforementioned, in 1999 by the same National Constituent Assembly once it dismissed the previous Justices, appointing new ones without receiving any nominations from any Nominating Committee, and many of them without compliance with the conditions set forth in the Constitution to be Magistrate. Second, in 2000, by the new elected National Assembly by sanctioning a Special Law in order to appoint the Magistrates, in a transitory way, without compliant with those constitutional conditions.[182] And third, in 2004, again by the National Assembly by sanctioning the Organic Law of the Supreme Tribunal of Justice, increasing the number of Justices from 20 to 32, and distorting the constitutional conditions for their appointment and dismissal, allowing the government to assume an absolute control of the Supreme Tribunal, and in particular, of its Constitutional Chamber.[183]

---

180 See Allan R. Brewer-Carías, "La progresiva y sistemática demolición de la autonomía e independencia del Poder Judicial en Venezuela (1999-2004)," in *XXX Jornadas J.M. Dominguez Escovar, Estado de derecho, Administración de justicia y derechos humanos*, Instituto de Estudios Jurídicos del Estado Lara, Barquisimeto, 2005. pp. 33-174; and "La justicia sometida al poder (La ausencia de independencia y autonomía de los jueces en Venezuela por la interminable emergencia del Poder Judicial (1999-2006)" in *Cuestiones Internacionales. Anuario Jurídico Villanueva 2007*, Centro Universitario Villanueva, Marcial Pons, Madrid 2007, pp. 25-57.

181 See the comments regarding this Transition Regime in Allan R. Brewer-Carías, *Golpe de Estado y proceso constituyente en Venezuela*, Universidad Nacional Autónoma de México, México 2002, pp. 345 ff.

182 For this reason, in its 2003 *Report on Venezuela*, the Inter-American Commission on Human Rights, observed that the appointment of Judges of the Supreme Court of Justice did not apply to the Constitution, so that "the constitutional reforms introduced in the form of the election of these authorities established as guaranties of independence and impartiality were not used in this case. See Inter-American Commission of Human Rights, 2003 *Report on Venezuela*; paragraph 186.

183 See the comments to this statute in Allan R. Brewer-Carías, *Ley del Tribunal Supremo de Justicia*, Editorial Jurídica Venezolana, Caracas 2004.

After this 2004 reform, the final process of selection of new Justices was sub-jected to the President of the Republic will, as was publicly admitted by the Presi-dent of the parliamentary Commission in charge of selecting the candidates for Mag-istrates of the Supreme Tribunal Court of Justice, who later was appointed Ministry of the Interior and Justice. On December 2004, he said the following:

> "Although we, the representatives, have the authority for this selection, the President of the Republic was consulted and his opinion was very much taken into consideration." He added: "Let's be clear, we are not going to score auto-goals. In the list, there were people from the opposition who comply with all the requirements. The opposition could have used them in order to reach an agreement during the last sessions, be they did not want to. We are not going to do it for them. There is now one in the group of postulates that could act against us..."[184]

This configuration of the Supreme Tribunal, as highly politicized and subjected to the will of the President of the Republic has eliminated all autonomy of the Judi-cial Power and even the basic principle of the separation of powers, as the corner stone of the Rule of Law and the basic of all democratic institutions.

On the other hand, as aforementioned, according to article 265 of the 1999 Con-stitution, the Magistrates can be dismissed by the vote of a qualified majority of the National Assembly, when grave faults are committed, following a prior qualification by the Citizens Power. This qualified two-thirds majority was established to avoid leaving the existence of the heads of the judiciary in the hands of a simple majority of legislators. Unfortunately, this provision was also distorted by the 2004 Organic Law of the Supreme Tribunal of Justice, in which it was established in an unconsti-tutional way that the Magistrates could be dismissed by simple majority when the "administrative act of their appointment" is revoked (article 23, 4). This distortion, contrary to the independence of the Judiciary, also pretended to be constitutionalized with the rejected 2007 Constitutional reform, which proposed to establish that the Magistrates of the Supreme Tribunal could be dismissed in case of graves faults, but just by the vote of the majority of the members of the National Assembly."[185]

The consequence of this political subjection is that all the principles tending to assure the independence of judges at any level of the Judiciary have been postponed. In particular, the Constitution establishes that all judges must be selected by public

---

184 See in *El Nacional*, Caracas 12-13-2004. That is why the Inter-American Commission on Human Rights suggested in its Report to the General Assembly of the OAS corresponding to 2004 that "these regulations of the Organic Law of the Supreme Court of Justice would have made possible the manipulation, by the Executive Power, of the election process of judges that took place during 2004." See Inter-American Commission on Human Rights, 2004 *Report on Venezuela*; paragraph 180.

185 See Allan R. Brewer-Carías, *Hacia la consolidación de un Estado Socialista, Centralizado y Militarista. Comentarios sobre el alcance y sentido de las propuestas de reforma Constitu-cional 2007*, Editorial Jurídica Venezolana, Caracas, 2007; and *La reforma constitucional de 2007 (Comentarios al proyecto inconstitucionalmente sancionado por la Asamblea Nacional el 2 de noviembre de 2007)*, Colección Textos Legislativos, N° 43, Editorial Jurídica Venezo-lana, Caracas 2007.

competition for the tenure; and that the dismissal of judges can only be made through disciplinary trials carried out by disciplinary judges (articles 254 and 267). Unfortunately, none of these provisions have been implemented, and on the contrary, since 1999, the Venezuelan Judiciary has been composed by temporal and provisional judges,[186] lacking stability and being subjected to the political manipulation, altering the people's right to an adequate administration of justice. And regarding the disciplinary jurisdiction of the judges, it has not yet been established, and with the authorization of the Supreme Tribunal, a "transitory" Reorganization Commission of the Judicial Power created since 1999, has continued to function, removing judges without due process.[187]

The worst of this irregular situation is that in 2006, there were attempts to solve the problem of the provisional status of judges by means of a "Special Program for the Regularization of Tenures," addressed to accidental, temporary or provisional judges, by-passing the entrance system constitutionally established by means of public competitive exams (article 255), by consolidating the effects of the provisional appointments and their consequent power dependency.

VII. THE SUPREMACY OF THE EXECUTIVE AND THE ABSENCE OF CHECK AND BALANCE

But if the supremacy of the National Assembly over the Judicial, Citizen and Electoral Powers is the most characteristic sign of the implementation of the Constitution of 1999 during the last decade, the distortion of the separation of powers principle transformed into a power concentration system, also derives from the supremacy that, from a political-party's point of view, the Executive Power has over the National Assembly.

In the Constitution of 1999, the presidential system has been reinforced, amongst other factors, because of the extension to six years of the presidential term; the authorization of the immediate reelection for an immediate period of the President of the Republic (article 203), and the maintaining of it election by simple majority (article 228). In the rejected Constitutional Reform of 2007, the term of the President

---

186 The Inter-American Commission on Human Rights said: "The Commission has been informed that only 250 judges have been appointed by opposition concurrence according to the constitutional text. From a total of 1772 positions of judges in Venezuela, the Supreme Court of Justice reports that only 183 are holders, 1331 are provisional and 258 are temporary," *Informe sobre la Situación de los Derechos Humanos en Venezuela*; OAS/Ser.L/V/ II.118. d.C. 4rev. 2; December 29, 2003; paragraph 11. The same Commission also said that "an aspect linked to the autonomy and independence of the Judicial Power is that of the provisional character of the judges in the judicial system of Venezuela. Today, the information provided by the different sources indicates that more than 80% of Venezuelan judges are "provisional." *Idem*, Paragraph 161.

187 See Allan R. Brewer-Carías, "La justicia sometida al poder y la interminable emergencia del poder judicial (1999-2006)," en *Derecho y democracia. Cuadernos Universitarios*, Órgano de Divulgación Académica, Vicerrectorado Académico, Universidad Metropolitana, Año II, N° 11, Caracas, septiembre 2007, pp. 122-138

was even proposed to be extended up to seven years, and the indefinite reelection of the President of the Republic was one of the main proposals contained in it.[188]

With this presidential model, to which the possibility of the dissolution of the National Assembly by the President of the Republic is added even though in exceptional cases (Articles 236,22 and 240), the presidential system has been reinforced not even finding any check and balance, for instance in the Senate, which in 1999 was eliminated.

Also, the presidential system has been reinforced with other reforms, like the provision for legislative delegation to authorize the President of the Republic by means of "delegating statutes" (enabling laws), to issue decree-laws and not only in economic and financial matters (article 203). According to this provision, the fact is that the fundamental legislation of the country sanctioned during the past decade has been contained in these decree-laws, which have been approved without assuring the mandatory constitutional provision for public hearings, established to take place before the sanctioning of all statutes.

In order to enforce this constitutional right of the citizens to participation, the Constitution specifically set forth that the National Assembly is compelled to submit draft legislation to public consultation, asking the opinion of citizens and the organized society (article 211). This is the concrete way by which the Constitution tends to assure the exercise of the political participation right in the process of drafting legislation. This constitutional obligation, of course, must also be comply by the President of the Republic when a legislative delegation takes place. But nonetheless, in 2007 and in 2008, the President of the Republic, following the same steps he took in 2001, has extensively legislated without any public hearing or consultation. In this way, in defraudation of the Constitution, by means of legislative delegation, the President has enacted decree-laws without complying with the obligatory public hearings, violating the citizens' right to political participation.[189]

VIII. THE RUPTURE OF THE RULE OF LAW AND THE REJECTED 2007 CONSTITUTIONAL REFORM

As it can be deducted from the aforementioned, in order for a democratic rule of law State to exist, the declarations contained in constitutional texts on separation of power are not enough, being indispensable the effective check and balance between

---

188   See Allan R. Brewer-Carías, *Hacia la consolidación de un Estado Socialista, Centralizado y Militarista. Comentarios sobre el alcance y sentido de las propuestas de reforma Constitucional 2007*, Editorial Jurídica Venezolana, Caracas, 2007; and *La reforma constitucional de 2007 (Comentarios al proyecto inconstitucionalmente sancionado por la Asamblea Nacional el 2 de noviembre de 2007)*, Colección Textos Legislativos, N° 43, Editorial Jurídica Venezolana, Caracas 2007.

189   See the comments in Allan R. Brewer-Carías, "Apreciación general sobre los vicios de inconstitucionalidad que afectan los Decretos Leyes Habilitados" en *Ley Habilitante del 13-11-2000 y sus Decretos Leyes*, Academia de Ciencias Políticas y Sociales, Serie Eventos N° 17, Caracas 2002, pp. 63-103.

the State powers. This is the only way to assure the enforcement of the rule of law, the democracy and the effective enjoyment of human rights.

And check and balance and control of State Powers in a democratic rule of law State can only be achieved by dividing, separating and distributing Public Power, either horizontally by means of the guarantee of the autonomy and independence of the different branches of government, to avoid the concentration of power; or vertically, by means of its distribution or spreading in the territory, creating autonomous political entities with representatives elected by votes, to avoid its centralization. The concentrations of power, as well as its centralization, then, are essentially anti-democratic state structures.

It is precisely there where the problems of the formally declared rule of law and of democracy in Venezuela -whose deformation lays in the same constitutional text of 1999-, rest; due to the fact that unfortunately, the institutional framework established in the Constitution encourages authoritarianism affecting the possibility of controlling power. This has permitted the centralization of power, provoking the dismantling process of federalism and municipalism, and twisting the possibility of the effective political participation in spite of the direct democracy mechanisms established.

This process of centralization of powers was proposed to be constitucionalized in 2007 by means of the rejected constitutional reform proposed by President Hugo Chávez, and sanctioned by the National Assembly, in which the intention was to transform the Democratic Rule of Law and Decentralized Social State established in the 1999 Constitution, into a Socialist, Centralized, Repressive and Militaristic State, grounded in a so called "Bolivarian doctrine," which was identified with "XXI Century Socialism" , and an economic system of State capitalism. [190]

In spite of its refusal by he people through referendum, one important aspect to be stressed regarding this constitutional reform proposal is that it was submitted by the President of the Republic and sanctioned by the National Assembly, evading the procedure established in the 1999 Constitution for such fundamental changes. That is, it was a reform also proposed in defraudation of the Constitution, being sanctioned through a procedure established for other purposes, in order to deceive the people. [191]

A change of the nature of the one that was proposed, according to article 347 of the 1999 Constitution, required the convening and election of a National Constituent Assembly, and could not be undertaken by means of a mere "constitutional reform"

---

190   See Allan R. Brewer-Carías, *Hacia la consolidación de un Estado Socialista, Centralizado y Militarista. Comentarios sobre el alcance y sentido de las propuestas de reforma Constitucional 2007*, Editorial Jurídica Venezolana, Caracas, 2007; and *La reforma constitucional de 2007 (Comentarios al proyecto inconstitucionalmente sancionado por la Asamblea Nacional el 2 de noviembre de 2007)*, Editorial Jurídica Venezolana, Caracas 2007.

191   See Allan R. Brewer-Carías, "Estudio sobre la propuesta de Reforma Constitucional para establecer un Estado Socialista, Centralizado y Militarista (Análisis del Anteproyecto Presidencial, Agosto de 2007)," *Cadernos da Escola de Direito e Relações Internacionais da UniBrasil*, N° 07, Curitiba, 2007, pp.

procedure, which is exclusively reserved for "a partial revision of the Constitution and a substitution of one or several of its norms without modifying the structure and fundamental principles of the Constitutional text." Consequently, following this procedure in order to achieve substantial constitutional changes, the President of the Republic and the National Assembly in 2007 tried to repeat the political tactic that has been a common denominator in the actions of the authoritarian regimen installed since 1999, of acting fraudulently with respect to the Constitution.

As was ruled in other matter by the Constitutional Chamber of the Supreme Tribunal of Justice in a decision N° 74 of 25 January, 2006, a defraudation of the Constitution (*fraude a la Constitución*) occurs when democratic principles are destroyed "through the process of making changes within existing institutions while appearing to respect constitutional procedures and forms." The Chamber also ruled that a "falsification of the Constitution" (*falseamiento de la Constitución*) occurs when "constitutional norms are given an interpretation and a sense different from those that they really possess: this is in reality an informal modification of the Constitution itself." The Chamber concluded by affirming that "A Constitutional reform not subject to any type of limitations would constitute a defraudation of the constitution."[192] This is to say, a defraudation of the Constitution occur when the existing institutions are used in a manner that appears to adhere to constitutional forms and procedures in order to proceed, as the Supreme Tribunal warned, "towards the creation of a new political regimen, a new constitutional order, without altering the established legal system"[193]

As aforementioned, this was precisely what occurred in February of 1999, in the convening of a consultative referendum on whether to convene a Constituent Assembly when that institution was not prefigured in the then existing Constitution of 1961; it occurred with the December 1999 "Decree on the Transitory Regimen of the Public Powers" with respect to the Constitution of 1999, issued by the then Constituent Assembly which was never the subject of an approbatory referendum; and it continued to occur in the subsequent years with the progressive destruction of democracy through the exercise of power and the sequestering of successive constitutional rights and liberties, all supposedly done on the basis of legal and constitutional provisions[194].

---

192 See in *Revista de Derecho Público,* Editorial Jurídica Venezolana, N° 105, Caracas 2006, pp. 76 ff.).

193 *Idem*

194 See Allan R. Brewer-Carías, "Constitution Making in Defraudation of the Constitution and Authoritarian Government in Defraudation of Democracy. The Recent Venezuelan Experience," en *Lateinamerika Analysen,* 19, 1/2008, GIGA, Germa Institute of Global and Area Studies, Institute of latin American Studies, Hamburg 2008, pp. 119-142 and "El autoritarismo establecido en fraude a la Constitución y a la democracia y su formalización en Venezuela mediante la reforma constitucional. (De cómo en un país democrático se ha utilizado el sistema eleccionario para minar la democracia y establecer un régimen autoritario de supuesta "dictadura de la democracia" que se pretende regularizar mediante la reforma constitucional)," in *Temas constitucionales. Planteamientos ante una Reforma,* Fundación de Estudios de Derecho Administrativo, FUNEDA, Caracas 2007, pp. 13-74

In the case of the 2007 Constitutional Reform attempt once again, constitutional provisions were fraudulently used for ends other than those for which they were established, that is, to try to introduce a radical transformation of the State, disrupting the civil order of the Social Democratic State under the Rule of Law and Justice through the procedure for "constitutional reform," to convert it into a Socialist, Centralized, Repressive and Militarist State in which representative democracy, republican alternation in office, and the concept of decentralized power was to disappear, and in which all power were to be concentrated in the decisions of the Chief of State[195].

This was constitutionally proscribed, and as the Constitutional Chamber of the Supreme Tribunal of Justice summarized it, in its aforementioned decision N° 74 of 25 January, 2006, referring to a symbolic case, it occurred "with the fraudulent use of powers conferred by martial law in Germany under the *Weimar* Constitution, forcing the Parliament to concede to the fascist leaders, on the basis of terms of doubtful legitimacy, plenary constituent powers by conferring an unlimited legislative power"[196]. Nonetheless, in the case of the constitutional reform of 2007, the Supreme Tribunal deliberately refused to take any decision on judicial review regarding the unconstitutional procedure that was followed by the President of the Republic, the National Assembly and the National Electoral Council.[197]

In any case, although the popular rejection of the 2007 constitutional reform has been a very important step back to the authoritarian government of President Chávez, and although according to the Constitution itself, the proposed reform cannot be formulated again in the current constitutional term of government, the President of the Republic has announced his intention to seek for the imposition of the rejected constitutional reform, again, in defraudation of the Constitution. In particular, for instance, he has suggested that in order to assure the possibility for his indefinite reelection, he will propose himself, a recall referendum of himself, seeking to convert the eventual rejection of such referendum into a plebiscite for his reelection.[198]

In any case, during July and August 2007, the President of the Republic, according to the powers to legislate by decree that were delegated upon him by his completely controlled National Assembly on January 2007, has sanctioned 26 very im-

---

195 See Allan R. Brewer-Carías, *Hacia la consolidación de un Estado Socialista, Centralizado y Militarista. Comentarios sobre el alcance y sentido de las propuestas de reforma Constitucional 2007*, Editorial Jurídica Venezolana, Caracas, 2007; and *La reforma constitucional de 2007 (Comentarios al proyecto inconstitucionalmente sancionado por la Asamblea Nacional el 2 de noviembre de 2007)*, Editorial Jurídica Venezolana, Caracas 2007.

196 See in *Revista de Derecho Público*, Editorial Jurídica Venezolana, N° 105, Caracas 2006, pp. 76 ff.

197 See Allan R. Brewer-Carías, "El juez constitucional vs. la supremacía constitucional. O de cómo la Jurisdicción Constitucional en Venezuela renunció a controlar la constitucionalidad del procedimiento seguido para la "reforma constitucional" sancionada por la Asamblea Nacional el 2 de noviembre de 2007, antes de que fuera rechazada por el pueblo en el referendo del 2 de diciembre de 2007," in *Revista de Derecho Público*, N° 112, Editorial Jurídica Venezolana, Caracas 2007, pp. 661 ff.

198 See *El Universal*, Caracas January 27, 2008.

portant new Statutes with the intention of implementing, of course in a fraudulent way, all the constitutional reform proposals that were rejected by the people in the 2007 December referendum.[199]

Unfortunately, even being all unconstitutional, those Decree Laws have been enacted and will be applied without any possibility of control or judicial review. The President is sure that no Constitutional Chamber judicial review decision will be issued, being such Chamber a wholly controlled entity that has proved to be his most effective tool for the consolidation of his authoritarian government.

This entire situation is the only explanation we can fin to understand why a Head of State of our times, as is the case of President Chávez in Venezuela, can say challenging his opponents in a political rally held two months ago, on August 28, 2008, the following:

> "I warn you, group of Stateless, putrid opposition.
>
> Whatever you do, the 26 Laws will go ahead! And the other 16 Laws... also. And if you go out in the streets, like on April 11 (2002)... we will sweep you in the streets, in the barracks, in the universities. I will close the golpista media. I will have no compassion whatsoever ... This Revolution came to stay, forever!
>
> You can continue talking stupid thinks ... I am going to intervene all communications and I will close all the enterprises I consider that are of public usefulness or of social interest! Out [of the country] Contractors and Forth Republic corrupt people!
>
> **I am the Law ... I am the State!!**"[200]

Nonetheless, this was not the first time that the President of the Republic has used this expression. In 2001, when he approved more than 48 Decree laws, also via

---

199 Regarding these 2008 Decree Laws, Teodoro Petkoff has pointed out that: "In absolute contradiction to the results of the December 2, 2007 referendum in which voters rejected constitutional reforms, in several of the laws promulgated the president presents several of the aspects of the rejected reforms almost in the same terms. The proposition of changing the name of the Venezuelan Armed Forces to create the Bolivarian National Militia was contained in the proposed reforms; the power given to the President to appoint national government officials over the governors and mayors to, obviously, weaken those offices and to eliminate the last vestiges of counterweight to the executive in general and the presidency in particular, was also contained in the reforms; the recentralization of the national executive branch of powers that today belong to the states and decentralized autonomous institutes was also part of the reforms: the enlargement of government powers to intervene in economic affairs was also contained in the reform. To ignore the popular decision about the 2007 proposal to reform the constitution in conformity with the will and designs of an autocrat, without heed to legal or constitutional norms, is, *stricto sensu*, a tyrannic act." See Teodoro Petkoff, "Election and Political Power. Challenges for the Opposition," in *ReVista. Harvard Review of Latin America*, David Rockefeller Center for Latin American Studies, Harvard University, Fall 2008, pp. 12.

200 "*Yo soy la Ley..., Yo soy el Estado!!*" See the referente in the Blog of Gustavo Coronel, *Las Armas de Coronel*, 15 de octubre de 2008: http://las armasdecoronel.blogspot.com/2008/10/yo-soy-la-leyyo-soy-el-estado.html

delegate legislation, he also said, although in a different way: **"The law is me. The State is me."**[201]

This phrase, which although attributed to Luis XIV he never delivered,[202] expressed now by a Head of State of our times, is enough to realize and understand the tragic institutional situation Venezuela is currently facing, precisely characterized by a complete absence of separation of powers and consequently, of a democratic government.[203].

---

201 *"La ley soy yo. El Estado soy yo."* See in *El Universal,* Caracas 4–12–01, pp. 1.1 and 2,1.

202 This famous phrase was attributed to Louis XIV, when in 1661 he decided to govern alone after the death of Cardinal Mazarin, but was never pronounced by him. See Yves Giuchet, *Histoire Constitutionnelle Française (1789–1958)*, Ed. Erasme, Paris 1990, p. 8.

203 This situation has been recently summarized by Teodoro Petkoff, editor and founder of *Tal Cual*, one of the important newspapers in Caracas, as follows: "Chavez controls all the political powers. More that 90% of the Parliament obey his commands; the Venezuelan Supreme Court, whose number were raised from 20 to 32 by the parliament to ensure an overwhelming official's majority, has become an extension of the legal office of the Presidency... The Prosecutor General's Office, the Comptroller's Office and the Public Defender are all offices held by "yes persons," absolutely obedient to the orders of the autocrat. In the National Electoral Council, four of five members are identified with the government. The Venezuelan Armed Forces are tightly controlled by Chávez. Therefore, form a conceptual point of view, the Venezuelan political system is autocratic. All political power is concentrated in the hands of the President. There is no real separation of Powers." See Teodoro Petkoff, "Election and Political Power. Challenges for the Opposition," in *Revista. Harvard Review of Latin America*, David Rockefeller Center for Latin American Studies, Harvard University, Fall 2008, pp. 12.

CHAPTER XI

THE CONSOLIDATION OF AUTHORITARIANISM IN
DEFRAUDATION OF DEMOCRACY

(2007)

This essay on "The Consolidation of Authoritarianism in Defraudation of Democracy, is the text of an essay (Authoritarism in Venezuela built in defraudation of the "Constitution") initially written for the *IX Congresso Ibero-Americano de Direito Constitucional e VII Simposio Nacional de Direito Constitucional,* organized by the Associação Brasileira dos Constitucionalistas Demócratas, Seção Brasileira do Instituto Ibero-Americano de Direito Constitucional, Academia Brasileira de Direito Constitucional, held on November 11-15, 2006, in Curitiba, Parana, Brasil. It was rewritten in 2007 and published in Spanish in *Temas constitucionales. Planteamientos ante una Reforma,* Fundación de Estudios de Derecho Administrativo, Caracas 2007, pp. 13-74.

I. CONSTITUTIONAL FRAUD AND THE DEFRAUDATION OF DEMOCRACY

Similar to what happened during the 1999 constitution making process, in which the judicial interpretation of the Constitution was used in order to justify the violation of the Constitution (Constitutional fraud); in the same manner, the political regime that began with said fraud in 1999, during the past years has used representative democracy in order to progressively eliminate it, and supposedly to substitute it for a "participative democracy" of the Popular Power; which is participative and democratic only by name (democracy fraud).

The democratic rule of law, due to this fraud committed against the popular will by means of the use of electoral mechanisms, has been and is being progressively substituted by a State of the Popular Power, where all the power is concentrated in the Head of State, and thus, is neither democratic, nor it is representative or participative, and on the contrary, it is severely controlled and directed from the inside, and the summit of the political power that the President of the Republic exercises (as Head of the Executive and of the governing party that will be Only one), whom without a doubt, will self proclaim as "President of the Popular Power"; to this matter, progressively, there could be no dissidence of any kind because it is criminal-ized.

It is then, as was announced by the Vice President of the Republic in January 2007, during the sanction act of the legislative delegation Law (Enabling Act) in favor of the President of the Republic, which contains an authorization even to dic-tate laws in the margin of the Constitution, which has planned, no more, no less, is the installment of "the dictatorship of democracy"[204].

In democracy, no dictatorship is acceptable, not even an alleged "dictatorship of democracy," as it has never been tolerable the supposed and failed "dictatorship of the proletariat" in the old Soviet Union installed since 1918, established around "so-viet soldiers, workers and country men." Somewhat similar to what is happening in Venezuela, ninety years later, with the creation of communal councils dependant of the President of the Republic in order to channel the Popular Power to, with the sup-posed participation of the organized people, install the "dictatorship of democracy."

Since the beginning, these supposed popular dictatorships have been and are the fraudulent instrument of the summit that controls power to, in the name of the popu-lar power, end with every trace of democracy, and impose, by force, a socialist re-gime to a country, without voting for it.

II. POPULAR AUTHORITARISM AND CONCENTRATION OF STATE POWERS

The truth is that, at the beginning of the 21st Century, regarding the Venezuelan case, Latin-America witnesses the apparition of a new model of authoritarian State supposedly of the Popular Power, that does not have its immediate origin in a mili-tary *coup d'Etat,* like in many other occasions during the decades of the last century, but in popular elections, which has provided it with a suit or style which is also mili-tarist, but this time, it is camouflaged with "constitutional" and "elective" marks, designed for the destruction of the representative democracy itself.

We are talking about a militarist authoritarism with an alleged popular support, like all fascist and communist authoritarism regimes of the last century, in many cases with some electoral origin. Neither authoritarian model, no mater how consti-tutionally and electively disguised may be or may have been, is democratic, nor can be considered to form a constitutional rule of law, because they lack the essential components of democracy, which are much more than the sole popular or circum-stantial election of government.

In particular, among all the essential elements and components of democracy, the one regarding the separation and independence of Public Powers is maybe the more fundamental pillar of the Rule of law, because it is the one that can even allow other

---

204 Jorge Rodríguez, Vice-President of the Republic, in January 2007, expressed: "Of course we want to install a dictatorship, the **dictatorship of the true democracy** and the democracy is the dictatorship of everyone, you and us together, building a different country. Of course we want this **dictatorship of democracy** to be installed forever," in *El Nacional*, Caracas 02-01-2007, p. A-2.

factors of democracy to be a political reality[205]. To be precise, democracy, as a political regime, can only function in a constitutional Rule of law system where the control of power exists; that is, one in which the classic and clear advice left as a legacy to the world by Charles Louis de Secondat, Baron of Montesquieu, decades before the French Revolution, is seriously taken to consideration with all its political consequences:

> "It is an eternal experience -he said- that every man with power tends to abuse it; and he does it until he finds limits... To avoid the abuse of power, it is necessary that, due to the disposition of things, power limits power"[206].

Decades later, as legacy from the North-American and the French Revolutions[207], this important political postulate about the division of the public power, began to be the inevitable premise of democracy as a political regime, in a way that it can not exist without said division, so that power finds limits and it can be stopped by power itself.

In consequence, for democracy as a political system to ensure the government of the people, legitimate holder of sovereignty, indirectly by means of the representatives or instruments for its direct exercise; it has to be forged over a constitutionally political system which in any case, and above all, impedes the abuse of those who have the power of the state, which is of the essence of the Rule of law. That is to say, in order for it to effectively exist and function, democracy requires the existence of a constitutional frame that establishes and allows the control of power –its essential boundary- and where power, by means of its horizontal division and its vertical or territorial distribution, can stop power, in a way that the diverse powers of the State limit each other. All of these, as an essential guaranty of all the values of democracy itself which, along with the respect to the popular will, is the force of human rights, political pluralism, republican variability and the submission of the Rule of law.

In Latin-America, in one way or another, with all the ups and downs of its efficiency, during the democratic periods that our countries have gone thru, there have always been institutions searching to assure the respect of human rights, the subjection of power to the law, elections almost regular and free, and a plural regime of parties. But if, in many cases, our democracies have not settled completely, and the Rule of Law has not absolutely taken over our political institutions, it is because in many cases we have failed to effectively establish the last of the elements mentioned about democracy and the most classical of all, referring precisely to the effective

---

205 See about the Inter-American Democratic Charter and the crisis of Venezuelan democracy, Allan R. Brewer-Carías, *La crisis de la democracia venezolana. La Carta Democrática Interamericana y los sucesos de abril de 2002*, Ediciones *El Nacional*, Caracas 2002.pp. 137 ff.

206 *De l'Espirit des Lois* (ed. G. Tunc), Paris 1949, Vol. I, Book XI, Chapter. IV, pp. 162-163.

207 See Allan R. Brewer-Carías, *Reflexiones sobre la Revolución Americana (1776) y la Revolución Francesa (1789) y sus aportes al constitucionalismo moderno*, Editorial Jurídica Venezolana, Caracas 1992.

"separation and independence of powers." That is to say, to the constitutional order that must exist in every democracy, which gives sense to the Rule of law, to control and limit power, and that particularly, can allow an effective political representation; the true possibility for citizen's political participation, a transparent and responsible government and the effective force of the empire of the law.

On the other hand, without the control of power, not only there is no and there can not be a true democracy, nor an effective Rule of law, but the efficient force of all essential factors of democracy mentioned before can not be achieved, because only by controlling Power is that there can be absolutely free and fair elections, that is, there can be efficient representativity; only controlling power is that political pluralism can exist; only controlling Power is that there can exist an effective democratic participation; by controlling Power the effective transparency in the exercise of government can be assured, with the existence of the rendering of accounts by all those in government; by controlling Power there can be a government submitted to the Constitution and the laws, that is, the Rule of law; only controlling Power there can be an effective access to justice, and it can function with valuable autonomy and independence; and only by controlling Power there can be a true and effective guaranty for the respect of human rights.

On the contrary, the excessive concentration and centralization of power, as it occurs in any authoritarian government, despite its electoral origins, can lead inevitable to a tyranny if there are no efficient controls over the governing parties, and even worst, if these have or believe to have the popular support. That was the story of humankind during the first half of the 20th Century, which showed us, precisely, those tyrants who used the vote of the majority to rise to power and apply, from there, Authoritarianism to eliminate democracy and all its elements, beginning with the respect of human rights.

Also, since the beginnings of modern constitutionalism, the principle of the separation of powers was stated in the French Declaration of the Rights of Man and of the Citizen (1789), when it proclaimed that "any society in which the guaranty of rights is not assured, nor the separation of powers is determined, has no Constitution" (article XVI). However, regardless of the two centuries that have passed, and particularly during the last five decades because of the progress in democracy, both the principle of division or organic separation of powers as manifestation of the horizontal distribution of Power, like the principle of the territorial or vertical distribution of power as a sign of the political decentralization, have been and continue to be the strongest signs, and not necessarily the most developed in the practice, of contemporary constitutionalism to assure freedom, the democratic government and Rule of law. And they are, exactly, the ones being progressive and systematically demolished in Venezuela.

That is, if in the Venezuela of today -during the first years of the 21st Century the authoritarian government has taken roots- this has its origin exactly in the way the principle of separation of powers stated in the Constitution of 1999 has deformed itself, in a way that, regarding the organic separation of powers, has allowed the concentration of powers in the hands of the Executive Power in relation to the National Assembly, and in it, regarding all other Public Powers. That is to say, the

Constitution of 1999 planted the germ of the concentration of power, and thus it was considered an authoritarian Constitution, a fact that no one took seriously.

Regarding the federal system of territorial distribution of Power regulated as well by the Constitution, contrary to the proclaimed "Federal decentralized State" (article 4, Constitution), what the constitutional text emphasized was the existing "centralized federation," worsened by the elimination of the old Senate, which existed since 1811 as an instrument to assure equal participation of the States in the preparation and control of national policies. Since 2000 then, Venezuela became a rare example of a federation without a federal Chamber, as it occurs in the few existing federations in States with very small territories. The Constitution of 1999 was an authoritarian constitution, not only for the germ of the concentration of power contained in it, but for the distinctly centralized schema also contained in it, to which no one paid any attention either.

In the Venezuelan Constitution of 1999, in fact, if we take its words textually, supposedly a democratic government system "participative and protagonist" would have been regulated, built on the principles of the organic separation of powers and the territorial distribution of the Public Power by means of a decentralized Federation. However, in reality and contrary, what was designed, by using empty misleading words, was a government system structured on the basis of the concentration of the public power and the political centralization of the State that has affected other essential elements of democracy, leading to the exact denial of the Rule of law.

What has resulted from this is the organization of a new constitutional authoritarianism in Latin-America that differs from what a democratic Rule of law should be, and built over the separation of powers and the political decentralization. In the case of Venezuela, what has developed during the last years, is a State marked, on the contrary, in part by the principle of concentration of power and constitutional authoritarism; and on the other hand, by the political centralization and effective absence of democratic participation.

III. THE PROCESS OF CONCENTRATION OF POWER SINCE 1999

The problem of the concentration of power and of authoritarism in Venezuela derives from the same text of the 1999 Constitution. That is why, when it was approved in the referendum held on December 15, 1999; I warned -in a document prepared to explain and justify the reasons for which I advocated for the "vote No" in said referendum- that in Venezuela, the following would be established, if the Constitution was to be approved:

> An institutional scheme conceived for the authoritarism derived from the combination of centralism of State, aggravated presidential system, democracy of political parties, militarism and concentration of power in the Assembly that constitutes the central element intended for the organization of the power of State. In my -added- opinion, this is not what was required in order to perfect democracy; which, on the contrary, should be based on the decentralization of

power, in a controlled and moderated presidential system, the political participation to balance the power of the State and in the subjection of the military authority to the civil authority[208].

Unfortunately, our warning has become a reality, and based on the Constitution, since 1999 an alleged "participative and protagonic" democratic system has been orchestrated, but based in the concentration and centralization of power, which is a contradiction with demolishing consequences for democracy itself and the Rule of law.

1.   *The assault to power and its initial concentration*

This process began, otherwise, with the aforementioned *coup d'Etat* committed by the 1999 Constituent National Assembly itself, which, without any authority whatsoever, assaulted and concentrated all the power of the State violating the still ruling Constitution of 1961.

This produced, not only devastating results that many, inside and outside the country, did not want to see or understand, but unusual institutional sequels like the unfinished and incomplete "constitutional trasitoriness" to which the country[209] was and in many aspects still is submitted to, as it occurs for instance in the judicial matter; and what is worst, this happened with the consent of the Constitutional Chamber of the Supreme Court of Justice, that was the most questioned product of that Assembly; with this, the fundamental principles of the democratic control of power, democracy and Rule of law[210] have been undermined.

It can be said then, that the Constitution that authorized the 1999 Constituent National Assembly, formed an *authoritarian institutional frame* that impedes the development of democracy itself and the consolidation of the Rule of law. Contrary to this institutional frame and of the constitutional practice that have implemented it during the last few years, the Constitution that Venezuela needed for this beginnings of the 21st Century, had to be one that assured the improvement of democracy by means of the design and effective implementation of the principle of the organic separation of powers, as an effective antidote to Authoritarism; and this, also, consolidating the separation of powers beyond the three classical Powers of the State (Legislative, Executive and Judicial), making, the classical control institutions that have always existed in our Latin-American countries, effective participants of the

---

208 Document dated November 30, 1999. See Allan R. Brewer-Carías, *Debate Constituyente (Aportes a la Asamblea Nacional Constituyente),* Volume III, Fundación de Derecho Público, Editorial Jurídica Venezolana, Caracas 1999, p. 339.

209 See Allan R. Brewer-Carías, *Golpe de Estado y proceso constituyente en Venezuela,* Universidad Nacional Autónoma de Mexico, Mexico, 2003. pp. 179 ff.

210 See for example, Allan R. Brewer-Carías, *La Sala Constitucional versus el Estado democrático de derecho. El secuestro del poder electoral y de la Sala Electoral del Tribunal Supremo y la confiscación del derecho a la participación política.* Los Libros de El Nacional. Colección Ares. Caracas 2004; "La progresiva y sistemática demolición institucional de la autonomía e independencia del Poder Judicial en Venezuela 1999-2004," in *XXX Jornadas J.M. Dominguez Escovar, Estado de derecho, Administración de justicia y derechos humanos.* Instituto de Estudios Jurídicos del Estado Lara. Barquisimeto, 2005. pp. 33-174.

exercise of the Public Power with constitutional rank; like the General Comptroller-ships, Public Ministry, People's or Human Rights Defendants, and electoral institutions.

2. The germ of power concentration. The Assembly's authority to remove public powers holders

Regarding the ornate verbalism in the consecration of the organic separation of powers, even with five State powers (article 136: Legislative, Executive, Judicial, Citizen and Electoral), in order for said separation could become effective, the independence and autonomy among them had to be consolidated to assure the limitation and control of power by power itself. This, however, was not designed, and notwithstanding the aforementioned separation of State institutions in five groups, there is an absurd distortion of said separation in the Venezuelan Constitution, when the National Assembly is given, as a political organ that exercises the Legislative Power and the control, not only the authority to assign, but to **remove** Judges of the Supreme Court of Justice, the Attorney General, the General Comptroller of the Republic, the People's Defendant and the Members of the National Electoral Council from their positions (Articles 265, 279 and 296); and in some cases, even by simple majority of votes.

One cannot talk about independence of powers, over which separation and the possibility of mutual control rests, when the proper existence of the holders (not elected democratically) of the institutions that exercise State powers depends on one of them, which is essentially of political character. Thus, the sole fact of the prevision in the constitutional text of such removal power in the hands of the National Assembly makes futile the formal consecration of the independence of powers, when the holders are aware that they can be removed when they act effectively with independence[211].

Unfortunately this has been stated in Venezuela, in a way that when there have been minimal signs of autonomy from some holders of State institutions, who have dared to express their opinions, they have been removed. This occurred, for instance, with the People's Defendant and the Attorney General of the Republic, originally assigned in 1999 by the Constituent National Assembly, who were separated from their positions[212] in 2000 for failing to uphold to the dictates of power; and also, with some Judges of the Supreme Court who dared to vote decisions that could question power, which resulted in their immediate investigation and some of them

---

211 See "Democracia y control del poder," in Allan R. Brewer-Carías, *Constitución, democracia y control de poder*. Centro Iberoamericano de Estudios Provinciales y Locales. Universidad de Los Andes, Mérida 2004.

212 It was the case of the General Prosecutor of the Republic, assigned in December of 1999, who thought that he could initiate the (penal) impeachment proceedings against the by then Minister of the Interior, and the People's Defendant, who also thought that she could impugn the Special Law of the 2001 National Assembly on appointment of Judges of the Supreme Court without complying with the constitutional requirements. They were both duly substituted in 2001.

were even removed from their positions, as it was the case of the First Vice-President of the Supreme Court in June of 2004; many others were duly "retired" or removed[213].

3.   The abstention of control because of the risk of removal

In other cases, the consequence resulting from this factual "dependency" of the control organs before the National Assembly, has been the total abstention in which these have incurred to exercise the control that the Constitution grants them, as it has happened with the General Comptroller of the Republic, whose existence has been motive for conjecture; and of the satisfactions of the People's Defendant with power, which has provoked his perception to be not as the defendant of the people before power, but as the defendant of power before the people.

The effects of this dependency have been catastrophic regarding the Judicial Power -to which we will refer to further on- which was intervened by the Constituent National Assembly in 1999, and continues to be intervened with the unfortunate consent and complicity of the Supreme Court of Justice itself, allowing a Judicial Power Reorganization Commission -which has been legitimated- to cohabit with it, with disciplinary powers contrary to those ordered by the Constitution. In addition to this, the political control that the National Assembly has taken over the Judges of the Supreme Court, with the always "convenient" warning of their possible investigation and removal, even by absolute majority of votes, as it was unconstitutionally established in the Organic Law of the Supreme Court of Justice of 2004.

4.   The supremacy of the Executive and the absence of check and   balance

But if the supremacy of the National Assembly over the Judicial, Citizen and Electoral Powers is the most characteristic sign of the implementation of the Constitution of 1999 during the last few years, the distortion of the separation of powers turning it into a power concentration system, also derives from the supremacy that, from a political-party's point of view, the Executive Power has over the National Assembly.

In the Constitution of 1999, the presidential system has been aggravated, amongst other factors, because of the extension, to six years, of the presidential term; the authorization of the immediate reelection of the President of the Republic

---

213 It was the case of Judge Franklin Arrieche, Vice-President of the Supreme Court of Justice, who was Speaker of the decision of the Supreme Court of Justice of 08-14-2002 (which decided that the impeachment against the generals who acted on April 12, 2002), declaring that there were no grounds to judge them due to the fact that in said occasion no military coup had taken place, but that there had been a power vacuum; and that Judges Alberto Martini Urdaneta, President of the Electoral Court, and Rafael Hernandez and Orlando Gravina, Judges of the same Court who undersigned decision N° 24 of 03-15-2004 (Case: *Julio Borges, Cesar Perez Vivas, Henry Ramos Allup, Jorge Sucre Castillo, Ramón Jose Medina and Gerardo Blyde vs. the National Electoral Council*), that suspended the effects of Resolution N° 040302-131, dated 03-02-2004 of the National Electoral Council which, in that moment, stopped the realization of the presidential recall referendum.

(article 203), which attempts against the principle of republican alternance by allowing a possible long administration term of up to 12 years; due to the complexity of the government recall referendum (article 72), which makes it practically inapplicable; and for the no adoption of the principle of the Presidential election by absolute majority and two-round system (runoff voting), maintaining the election by proportional majority (article 228), creating the possibility of governments elected with a minority of votes, which can make the system ungovernable.

With this presidential model, to which the possibility of the dissolution of the National Assembly by the President of the Republic is added (article 236, 22), even though in exceptional cases when three parliamentary censorship votes are approved against the Executive Vice-President (article 240), the presidential system is aggravated not even finding counterpoise in the eliminated old bicameralism.

5. The legislative power delegated in the Executive and the fraud to participation

Also, the presidential system has been reinforced with other reforms, like the prevision of the legislative delegation to authorize the President of the Republic by means of "enabling acts," to issue decree-laws not only in economic an financial matters (article 203), which constitutes an assault to the constitutional guaranty of the legal reserve, particularly regarding the regulation of constitutional rights. The truth is that the fundamental legislation that has taken place during the last few years (2002-2007) is contained in these decree-laws pronounced, even, without respecting the constitutional demand for the mandatory public consult required, in the Constitution, for draft laws.

In fact, the legislative power that can be delegated to the President of the Republic has, among other limits imposed in the Constitution, to assure the political participation, which is not only one of the fundamental values of the constitutional text, but one of the most relevant constitutional rights foreseen in it. The Constitution consecrates the right "of the people to participate in the formation, execution and control of the public service" having, as one of the obligations of the State to "enable the generation of the most favorable conditions for its practice" (article 62). Also, the Constitution assures the right to participate in political matters, among other means, thru "popular consult" (article 70).

Precisely, in order to define this constitutional right, the Constitution itself specifically states previsions where the National Assembly is imposed the obligation of public consult in the law creation process: *First*, with a general character, article 211 demands that the National Assembly and the Permanent Commissions must consult ("will consult"), during the proceedings and approval of draft laws, the organs of the State, citizens and the organized society to listen to their opinion on said matters; and second, article 206 demands that the National Assembly, which must consult the States ("will be consulted") by means of the Legislative Councils, when legislating in matters related to them. This is the concrete way by which the Constitution assures the exercise of the political participation right in the management of public matters in the process of formation of laws, by establishing the obligation imposed to the National Assembly for the public consult on draft laws.

This constitutional obligation of the public consult regarding the Draft laws, of course, will have to be transferred to the President of the Republic when the legislative delegation takes place. This, like every delegation, no only must transfer powers, but also duties, and among them, the constitutional obligation of the public consult of the draft law-decrees dictated in execution of the enabling law. That is, independently of the organ dictating the draft law (National Assembly or President of the Republic in virtue of the legislative authorization), the obligation of public consult is inevitable because it is an integrating part of the constitutional procedure for the creation of laws.

In 2007, the President of the Republic, following the same steps he took in 2001, but before an Assembly in which he has no opposition what so ever, requested and obtained the sanction of an Enabling Law that allows him, for a period of eighteen (18) months, to legislate in all imaginable matters. With this, again, the President of the Republic will legislate without any transparency, without the knowledge of the draft laws, without debating them, and without the realization of the public consult that the Constitution demands him to make before the National Assembly regarding new draft laws (articles 206 and 211).

In this way, in an evident Constitutional fraud, it is intended to transfer the state authority to legislate on matters of national competency from the organ exercised by the Legislative Power (National Assembly) to the Executive Power, notwithstanding that this absolutely controls the first, where it can not find opposition of any kind; legislation that, even, refers to matters affecting other powers of the State, particularly, in its horizontal division (Legislative, Executive, Judicial, People's and Electoral), and in its territorial distribution (States and Municipalities).

With these attempts to the principle of separation of powers, Venezuela, with its new Constitution filled of constitutional contradictions (a centralized Federation and without a Senate; a Legislative Power and an unlimited legislative delegation; and a penta-division of Power with an unusual concentration of power in the representative political organ), has constitutionalized the road towards Authoritarism. Thus democracy or even less the Rule of Law, can hardly be effective with this constitutional plan.

IV. THE UNENDING INTERVENTION AND SUBMISSION OF THE JUDICIAL POWER TO THE AUTHORITARIAN REGIME

1. *The continuous intervention of the judicial branch*

In Venezuela, after the unconstitutional intervention of the Judicial Power resolved by the Constituent National Assembly of 1999[214], since the sanction of the Constitution of 1999, there has been occurring a permanent and systematic demoli-

---

214 See our reserved vote to the intervention of the Judicial Power by the Constituent Nacional Assembly in Allan R. Brewer-Carías, *Debate Constituyente, (Aportes a la Asamblea Nacional Constituyente)*, Volume I, *(August 8-Spetember)*, Caracas 1999; and the critiques made to this process in Allan R. Brewer-Carías, *Golpe de Estado y proceso constituyente en Venezuela*, Universidad Nacional Autónoma de México. Mexico 2002.

tion process of the autonomy of the judicial power, submitting it to the control of the President of the Republic.[215]

Everything began with the appointment of new Judges of the Supreme Court of Justice without complying with the constitutional requirements by means of the constitutional transitory regime, dictated by the Constituent Assembly on the margin of the Constitution in December 1999; and from there, the intervention process continued commanded by the President of the Republic, who has been politically controlling the Supreme Court of Justice and, thru it, the complete Venezuelan judicial system. For this, the constitutional previsions about the conditions required to become a judge and the procedures for the appointments with the participation of sectors of society, were broken since the beginning: first, as it has been said, by the National Constituent Assembly itself when removed old Judges, by means of a transitory regime on the margin of the Constitution that approved them; and then, by the recently elected National Assembly when performing the first appointments in 2000, according to a special Law sanctioned to perform them transitorily, with context completely on the margin of the constitutional demands.

For this reason, in its 2003 *Report on Venezuela,* the Inter-American Commission on Human Rights, observed that the appointment of Judges of the Supreme Court of Justice did not apply to the Constitution, so that "the constitutional reforms introduced in the form of the election of these authorities established as guaranties of independence and impartiality were not used in this case"[216].

Then, the reform made to the 2004 Organic Law of the Supreme Court of Justice took place, approved in the middle of an ample discussion and questioning regarding the qualified majority referred to by the Constitution, for dealing with an organic law. The reform, which increased the number of Judges from 20 to 32 -the new ones elected by simple majority by the National Assembly- as was emphasized by the Inter-American Commission itself, "does not take into consideration the concerns expressed by the IACHR in its report regarding the possible threats to the independence of the Judicial Power"[217].

To the latter, the destitution or "retirement" of Judges who dared not follow the governmental line[218] must be added; all of this, has allowed the government to as-

215 See Allan R. Brewer-Carías, "La progresiva y sistemática demolición de la autonomía e independencia del Poder Judicial en Venezuela (1999-2004)," in *XXX Jornadas J.M. Domínguez Escovar, Estado de derecho, Administración de justicia y derechos humanos*; Instituto de Estudios Jurídicos del Estado Lara, Barquisimeto, 2005.pp. 33-174.

216 Inter-American Commission of Human Rights, 2003 *Report on Venezuela*; paragraph 186.

217 Inter-American Commission on Human Rights, 2004 *Report on Venezuela;* paragraph 174.

218 It was the case of Judge Franklin Arrieche, Vice-President of the Supreme Court of Justice, who was Speaker of the decision of the Supreme Court of Justice of 08-14-2002 which decided that the impeachment against the generals who acted on April 12, 2002, declaring that there were no grounds to judge them due to the fact that in said occasion no military coup had taken place, but that there had been a power vacuum; and of Judges Alberto Martini Urdaneta, President of the Electoral Court, and Rafael Hernandez and Orlando Gravina, Judges of the same Court who undersigned decision N° 24 of 03-15-2004 (Case: *Julio Bor-*

sume an absolute control of the Supreme Court of Justice in general, and of every one of its Chambers, especially the Constitutional Chamber.

In any case, after the reform of 2004, the final process of selection of the new Judges was ruled by the submission to the President of the Republic, to the point that on the eve of the appointment, Mr. Pedro Carreño, at the time President of the parliamentary Commission in charge of selecting the candidates for Judges of the Supreme Court of Justice -appointed Ministry of the Interior and Justice in January 2007- declared to the press that:

> "Although we, the representatives, have the authority for this selection, the President of the Republic was consulted and **his opinion was very much taken into consideration**" (Highlighting added). He added: "**Let's be clear, we are not going to score auto-goals**. In the list, there were people from the opposition who comply with all the requirements. The opposition could have used them to reach an agreement during the last sessions, be they did not want to. We are not going to do it for them. **There is now one in the group of postulates who is going to act for us** and we are going to take advantage of that, even in a 10 hour session"[219].

With good reason, the Inter-American Commission on Human Rights suggested in its Report to the General Assembly of the OAS corresponding to 2004 that "these regulations of the Organic Law of the Supreme Court of Justice would have made possible the manipulation, by the Executive Power, of the election process of judges that took place during 2004."[220]

It has been configured then, a Supreme Court of Justice highly politicized and subjected to the will of the President of the Republic, that has eliminated, in the practice, all the autonomy of the Judicial Power and even the basic principle of the separation of powers, as the corner stone of the Rule of Law and the force of all democratic institutions.

The President's influence on the Supreme Tribunal was admitted by himself, when he publicly complained that the Supreme Tribunal had issued an important ruling in which it "modified" the Income Tax Law, without previously consulting the "leader of the Revolution," and warning courts against decisions that would be "treason to the People" and "the Revolution." That was a very controversial case, decided by the Constitutional Chamber of the Supreme Tribunal in Decision N° 301 of February 27, 2007.[221] The President of the Republic said:

---

ges, Cesar Perez Vivas, Henry Ramos Allup, Jorge Sucre Castillo, Ramón Jose Medina and Gerardo Blyde vs. the National Electoral Council), that suspended the effects of Resolution N° 040302-131, dated 03-02-2004 of the National Electoral Council which, in that moment, stopped the realization of the presidential recall referendum.

219 See in *El Nacional*, Caracas 12-13-2004.

220 Inter-American Commission on Human Rights, 2004 *Report on Venezuela*; paragraph 180.

221 Supreme Tribunal of Justice, Constitutional Chamber, Decision N° 301 of February 27, 2007 (*Case: Adriana Vigilanza y Carlos A. Vecchio*) (Exp. N° 01-2862) in *Gaceta Oficial* N° 38.635 of March 1, 2007. See comments in Allan R. Brewer-Carías, "El juez constitucional en Venezuela como legislador positivo de oficio en materia tributaria" in *Revista de Derecho*

"Many times they come, the National Revolutionary Government comes and wants to make a decision against something that, for instance, deals with or has to pass through judicial decisions, and then they begin to move against it in the shadows, and many times they succeed in neutralizing decisions of the Revolution through a judge, or a court, and even through the very same Supreme Tribunal of Justice, behind the **backs of the Leader of the Revolution**, acting from within against the Revolution. This is, I insist, **treason to the people, treason to the Revolution.**"[222]

In order to assure the control of the Supreme Tribunal, another important provision of the new Organic Law of the Supreme Tribunal of Justice concerned dismissal of its Magistrates. According to Article 265 of the 1999 Constitution, a Magistrate can be dismissed only by the vote of a qualified majority of two-thirds of the National Assembly, following a hearing, in cases of "grave faults" (*faltas graves*) committed by the accused, following a prior qualification by the Citizens Power. The Organic Law of the Supreme Tribunal of Justice defines "grave faults" very broadly, leaving open the possibility of dismissal based exclusively on political motives.[223] Furthermore, the qualified two-thirds majority was required by the Constitution in order to avoid leaving the tenure of the Magistrates in the hands of a simple majority of Legislators. The Organic Law of the Supreme Tribunal of Justice circumvented this requirement by authorizing the dismissal of Magistrates by a simple majority vote that revokes the "administrative act of their appointment" (Article 23.4).[224] The National Assembly has already used its power to dismiss Magistrates who have ruled on sensitive issues against the Government's wishes.[225]

Público N° *109*, Editorial Jurídica Venezolana, Caracas 2007, pp. 193-212, *available at* www.allanbrewercarias.com, (Biblioteca Virtual, II.4. Artículos y Estudios N° 508, 2007) pp. 1-36; and Allan R. Brewer-Carías, "De cómo la Jurisdicción constitucional en Venezuela, no sólo legisla de oficio, sino subrepticiamente modifica las reformas legales que "sanciona," a espaldas de las partes en el proceso: el caso de la aclaratoria de la sentencia de Reforma de la Ley de Impuesto sobre la Renta de 2007" in *Revista de Derecho Público* N° 114, Editorial Jurídica Venezolana, Caracas 2008, pp. 267-276, avilable at www.allanbrewercarias.com, Section II, 4 (ArtiCles), 575 (2008).

222 *Discurso en el Primer Encuentro con Propulsores del Partido Socialista Unido de Venezuela desde el teatro Teresa Carreño* (Speech in the First Event with Supporters of the Venezuela United Socialist Party at the Teresa Carreno Theatre), March 24, 2007, available at http://www.minci.gob.ve/alocu-ciones/4/13788/primerencuentrocon.html, p. 45.

223 See Allan R. Brewer-Carías, *Ley Orgánica del Tribunal Supremo de Justicia*, Editorial Jurídica Venezolana, Caracas 2004, p. 41.

224 *Id.,* pp. 39-41.

225 That was the fate of Franklin Arrieche, Vice-President of the Supreme Tribunal of Justice, who delivered a decision dated August 14, 2002 regarding the criminal proceedings against the military generals who acted on April 12, 2002. The decision ruled that there were no grounds to prosecute the generals because no military coup had taken place. This was also the fate of Alberto Martini Urdaneta, President of the Electoral Court, and Rafael Hernandez and Orlando Gravina, Judges of the same court who signed Decision N° 24 of March 15, 2004 (Case: *Julio Borges, Cesar Perez Vivas, Henry Ramos Allup, Jorge Sucre Castillo, Ramón Jose Medina and Gerardo Blyde vs. the National Electoral Council*), a ruling that

2. *The government of the Judiciary in the hands of a controlled Supreme Tribunal*

According to the Constitution of 1999 which eliminated the old Judicature Council, organ in charge of the administration of the Judicial Power since 1961, the Supreme Court of Justice is the institution that constitutionally domains, absolutely, the Venezuelan judicial system, particularly in regards to the appointment and removal of judges, whose instability, authorized and promoted by the Supreme Court itself, and the appointment of judges without the public concurrence stipulated in the Constitution, is another component of the political subjection of the Venezuelan courts.

Regarding the independence of the Court, according to the *Basic Principles concerning the independence of the judicature*, approved by the General Assembly of the OAS[226], the principle of job security of the judges is essential and, as it has been said by the Inter-American Court on Human Rights, congruent with "the special nature of the function of the courts, because it guaranties the independence of the judges before all other branches of government and before the political-electoral changes"[227].

And said job security is assured in the Constitution of 1999, first, by the demand that the judges must be selected by public concurrence; and second, that their removal can only occur by means of disciplinary trials carried out by disciplinary judges. Unfortunately, none of these has occurred in Venezuela where, due to a strange discontinuance constructed with the complicity of the Supreme Court itself, those constitutional previsions are dead letter.

Since 1999, the Venezuelan Judicial Power has been plagued by provisional judges, situation on which, by 2003, the Inter-American Commission on Human Rights had pronounced itself[228] in its 2003 Special Report on Venezuela, considering as said provisional judges those who lack the stability in the position, and for that reason, are susceptible to the political manipulation[229], in the sense that they "do not have the stability assurance in the position and can be removed or suspended freely, which could suppose an analysis of the performance of these judges, in the

---

suspended the effects of Resolution N° 040302-131 of the National Electoral Council dated March 2, 2004, which stopped the recall of the presidential referendum at that time.

226   *Basic Principles concerning the independence of the judicature* adopted by the Séptimo Congreso de las Naciones Unidas in Milan, August 26-September 6, 1985 and confirmed by the General Assembly in its resolutions 40/32 of November, 1985 and 40/146 of December, 1985.

227   Inter-American Court on Human Rights, *Carranza vs. Argentina*; Case 10.087. Report N° 30/97, December 30, 1997; paragraph 41.

228   *Informe sobre la Situación de los Derechos Humanos en Venezuela*; OAS/Ser.L/V/II.118. d.C. 4rev. 2; December 29, 2003; paragraph 11; p. 3. It reads: "The Commission has been informed that only 250 judges have been appointed by opposition concurrence according to the constitutional text. From a total of 1772 positions of judges in Venezuela, the Supreme Court of Justice reports that only 183 are holders, 1331 are provisional and 258 are temporary."

229   *Idem*; paragraphs 11 and 12.

sense that they can not feel safe before the inadequate interferences or precisions coming from inside or outside the judicial system"[230], concluding that the high percentage of these judges alters the people's right to an adequate administration of justice.[231]

The tragic situation of the provisional status of the judges, in addition to the noticeable lack of independence affecting the judicial system in Venezuela, was also warned in 2002 by the Inter-American Commission itself in the *Preliminary Observations* expressed on May 10, 2002[232], in occasion of its visit to Venezuela, stating that: "after almost three years of reorganizing the Judicial Power, a significant number of judges have a provisional character, fluctuating from 60 to 90% according to different sources. This affects the stability, independence and autonomy that must rule the judicature[233]; adding that it had been: "informed that the problem of the provisional status of the judges had deepened and increased since the current Government began a judicial re-organization process.[234]

In the aforementioned 2003 *Special Report* on Venezuela, this same Commission also stated that "an aspect linked to the autonomy and independence of the Judicial Power is that of the provisional character of the judges in the judicial system of Venezuela. Today, the information provided by the different sources indicates that more than 80% of Venezuelan judges are "provisional."[235]

In any case, after a decade after the enactment of the Constitution, the disciplinary jurisdiction of the judges is still to be established as demanded by the Constitution (articles 254 and 267) with the tendency to assure their sole removal by means of disciplinary trials, by disciplinary judges, reason for which, with the authorization of the Supreme Court, a "transitory" Reorganization Commission of the Judicial Power (created in 1999) has continued to function, removing judges without due process, and has caused the establishment of said provisional judges.

The result has been, as mentioned by the Inter-American Commission on Human Rights in its report on the situation of human rights in Venezuela, contained in Chapter IV of the *Report* presented before the General Assembly of the OAS in 2006, that the "destitution, and substitution cases, and other kinds of measures that, because of the provisional status and reform processes, have generated difficulties for the absolute vogue of the judicial independence in Venezuela"[236]; emphasizing those "destitutions and substitutions stated as retaliations for decisions contrary to

---

230 *Idem*; paragraph 159.

231 *Idem*.

232 See "Comunicado de Prensa" dated 05-10-2000, in *El Universal*, Caracas 05-11-2002.

233 *Idem*; paragraph 30

234 *Idem*; paragraph 31

235 *Informe sobre la Situación de los Derechos Humanos en Venezuela 2003, cit.*, paragraph 161.

236 *Idem*; paragraph 291

those of the Government"[237]; concluding that for 2005, according to official numbers, "18.30% of judges are holders and 81.70% are in provisional conditions"[238].

The worst of this irregular situation is that in 2006, there have been attempts to solve the problem of this provisional status by means of a "Special Program for the Regularization of Holding," addressed to accidental, temporary or provisional judges, with a term longer than three months in the exercise of the judicial function. Such program mocks the entrance system into the judicial function which constitutionally can only occur by means of public competitive exams (article 255), because it is then limited to an evaluation of the provisional judges, some without tender or concurrence, so that more than "regularize" what it does is consolidate the effects of the provisional appointments "arbitrarily," and their consequent power dependency.

3.   *The subjection of the Venezuelan Judiciary to political*

As described above, the constitutional principles tending to assure the autonomy and independence of judges at all levels of the Judiciary are yet to be applied, particularly regarding the admission of candidates to the judicial career through "public competition" processes, with citizen participation in the procedure of selection and appointment, and regarding the prohibition of removal or suspension of judges except through disciplinary trials before a disciplinary courts and judges (Articles 254 and 267). In reality, since 1999 the Venezuelan Judiciary has been composed primarily of temporary and provisional judges, without career or stability, appointed without the public competition process of selection established in the Constitution, and dismissed without due process of law, for political reasons.[239]

This reality amounts to political control of the Judiciary, as demonstrated by the dismissal of judges who have adopted decisions contrary to the policies of the governing political authorities. Another example will serve to illustrate this point. In summary, when a contentious-administrative court ruled against the government in a politically charged case, the government responded by intervening (taking over) the court and dismissing its judges and, after the Inter-American Court of Human Rights ruled that the dismissal had violated the American Convention of Human Rights and Venezuela's international obligations, the Constitutional Chamber upheld the government's argument that the decision of the Inter-American Court cannot be enforced in Venezuela.

On July 17, 2003, the Venezuelan National Federation of Doctors brought an *amparo* action in the First Court on Contentious Administrative Matters in Caracas,[240] against the Mayor of Caracas, the Ministry of Health and the Caracas Metropolitan Board of Doctors (*Colegio de Médicos*). The petitioners asked for a declara-

---

237 *Idem*; paragraphs 295 ff.

238 *Idem*; paragraph 292

239 See Inter-American Commission on Human Rights, *Report on the Situation of Human Rights in Venezuela*, OEA/Ser.L/V/II.118, doc. 4 rev. 2, December 29, 2003, par. 174. See in http://www.cidh.oas.org/country-rep/Venezuela2003eng/toc.htm.

240 Contentious-administrative courts have competence to review administrative decisions.

tion of the nullity of certain measures of the defendant Officials through which Cuban doctors were hired for a much publicized governmental health program in the Caracas slums, without complying with the legal requirements for foreign doctors to practice the medical profession in Venezuela. The National Federation of Doctors argued that, by allowing foreign doctors to exercise the medical profession without complying with applicable regulations, the program was discriminatory and violated the constitutional rights of Venezuelan doctors.[241] One month later, in August 21, 2003, the First Court issued a preliminary protective *amparo* measure, on the ground that there were sufficient elements to consider that the constitutional guaranty of equality before the law was being violated in the case. The Court ordered, in a preliminary way, the suspension of the Cuban doctors' hiring program and ordered the Metropolitan Board of Doctors to replace the Cuban doctors already hired with Venezuelan ones or foreign doctors who had fulfilled the legal requirements to exercise the medical profession in the country.[242]

In response to that preliminary judicial *amparo* decision, the Minister of Health, the Mayor of Caracas, and even the President of the Republic made public statements to the effect that the decision was not going to be respected or enforced.[243] Following these statements, the government-controlled Constitutional Chamber of the Supreme Tribunal of Justice adopted a decision, without any appeal being filed, assuming jurisdiction over the case and annulling the preliminary *amparo* ordered by the First Court; a group of Secret Service police officials seized the First Court's premises; and the President of the Republic, among other expressions he used, publicly called the President of the First Court a "bandit."[244] A few weeks later, in response to the First Court's decision in an unrelated case challenging a local registrar's refusal to record a land sale, a Special Commission for the Intervention of the Judiciary, which in spite of being unconstitutional continued to exist, dismissed all five judges of the First Court.[245] In spite of the protests of all the Bar Associations of

---

241 See Claudia Nikken, "El caso "Barrio Adentro: La Corte Primera de lo Contencioso Administrativo ante la Sala Constitucional del Tribunal Supremo de Justicia o el avocamiento como medio de amparo de derechos e intereses colectivos y difusos" in *Revista de Derecho Público* N° 93-96, Editorial Jurídica Venezolana, Caracas, 2003, pp. 5 ff.

242 See Decision of August, 21 2003, in *id.*, pp. 445 ff.

243 The President of the Republic said: "*Váyanse con su decisión no sé para donde, la cumplirán ustedes en su casa si quieren* [...]" (You can go with your decision, I don't know where; you will enforce it in your house if you want [...]). See *El Universal*, Caracas, August 25, 2003 and *El Universal*, Caracas, August 28, 2003.

244 See Inter-American Court of Human Rights, *Apitz Barbera et al. (Corte Primera de lo Contencioso Administrativo) v. Venezuela* (Judgment of August 5, 2008), *available at* www.corteidh.or.cr, par. 239. See also, *El Universal*, Caracas, October 16, 2003; and *El Universal*, Caracas, September 22, 2003.

245 See *El Nacional*, Caracas, November 5, 2003, p. A2. The dismissed President of the First Court said: "*La justicia venezolana vive un momento tenebroso, pues el tribunal que constituye un último resquicio de esperanza ha sido clausurado.*" (The Venezuelan judiciary lives a dark moment, because the court that was a last glimmer of hope has been shut down.") *Id.* The Commission for the Intervention of the Judiciary had also massively dismissed almost

the country and also of the International Commission of Jurists;[246] the First Court remained suspended without judges, and its premises remained closed for about nine months,[247] period during which simply no judicial review of administrative action could be sought in the country.[248]

The dismissed judges of the First Court brought a complaint to the Inter-American Commission of Human Rights for the government's unlawful removal of them and for violation of their constitutional rights. The Commission in turn brought the case, captioned *Apitz Barbera et al. (Corte Primera de lo Contencioso Administrativo vs. Venezuela)* before the Inter-American Court of Human Rights. On August 5, 2008, the Inter-American Court ruled that the Republic of Venezuela had violated the rights of the dismissed judges established in the American Convention of Human Rights, and ordered the State to pay them due compensation, to reinstate them to a similar position in the Judiciary, and to publish part of the decision in Venezuelan newspapers.[249] Nonetheless, on December 12, 2008, the Constitutional Chamber of the Supreme Tribunal issued Decision N° 1.939, declaring that the August 5, 2008 decision of the Inter-American Court of Human Rights was non-enforceable (*inejecutable*) in Venezuela. The Constitutional Chamber also accused the Inter-American Court of having usurped powers of the Supreme Tribunal of Justice, and asked the Executive Branch to denounce the American Convention of Human Rights.[250]

The case just discussed, including in particular the *ad hoc* response of the Constitutional Chamber to the decision of the Inter-American Court of Human Rights, shows clearly the present subordination of the Venezuelan Judiciary to the policies,

---

all judges of the country without due disciplinary process, and had replaced them with provisionally appointed judges beholden to the ruling power.

246 See in *El Nacional*, Caracas, October 10, 2003, p. A-6; *El Nacional*, Caracas, October 15, 2003, p. A-2; *El Nacional*, Caracas, September 24, 2003, p. A-4; *and El Nacional*, Caracas, February 14, 2004, p. A-7.

247 See *El Nacional*, Caracas, October 24, 2003, p. A-2; and *El Nacional*, Caracas, July 16, 2004, p. A-6.

248 See *generally* Allan R. Brewer-Carías, "La progresiva y sistemática demolición institucional de la autonomía e independencia del Poder Judicial en Venezuela 1999–2004" in *XXX Jornadas J.M Domínguez Escovar, Estado de derecho, Administración de justicia y derechos humanos,* Instituto de Estudios Jurídicos del Estado Lara, Barquisimeto, 2005, pp. 33–174; Allan R. Brewer-Carías, "La justicia sometida al poder (La ausencia de independencia y autonomía de los jueces en Venezuela por la interminable emergencia del Poder Judicial (1999-2006))" in *Cuestiones Internacionales. Anuario Jurídico Villanueva 2007,* Centro Universitario Villanueva, Marcial Pons, Madrid, 2007, pp. 25-57, *available at* www.allanbrewercarias.com, Section, II.4 (Artículos y Estudios) N° 550 (2007).

249 Inter-American Court of Human Rights, *Apitz Barbera et al. (Corte Primera de lo Contencioso Administrativo) v. Venezuela* (Judgment of August 5, 2008), *available at* www.corteidh.or.cr.

250 Supreme Tribunal of Justice, Constitutional Chamber, Decision N° 1.939 of December 18, 2008 (Case: *Abogados Gustavo Álvarez Arias et al.*) (Exp. N° 08-1572).

wishes and dictates of the President of the Republic.[251] The Constitutional Chamber has in fact become a most effective tool for the existing consolidation of power in the person of President Chávez.[252]

It is within the aforementioned context of subjection of the Judiciary to political control that, at the Government's request, the Constitutional Chamber purported to interpret Article 258 of the Constitution, which needed no interpretation, and went further, acting beyond the scope of its competence and contradicting its own prior decisions, and "interpreted" Article 22 of the 1999 Investment Law according to the Government's position, with an eye to the various international arbitration cases pending against the State at the time of the request.

V. THE PROCESS OF CENTRALIZATION OF POWER AND THE ABSENCE OF EFFECTIVE POLITICAL PARTICIPATION

But the new plan of authoritarian government that has set roots in Venezuela for the last few years, in the midst of an electoral origin, has not only been possible thanks to the constitutionalization of a concentration plan of the Power of the State, with the consequent submission of the Judicial Power to the Executive Power, contrary to democracy and the Rule of law; but also, for the distortion of the exercise of democracy and popular participation, covered by a false populist speech that pretends to replace the representative democracy for a "participative democracy" as it was, additionally, regarding dichotomist concepts, provoking actually the absolute destruction of democracy.

---

251 This situation has been recently summarized by Teodoro Petkoff, editor and founder of *Tal Cual*, one of the important newspapers in Caracas, as follows: "Chavez controls all the political powers. More that 90% of the Parliament obey his commands; the Venezuelan Supreme Court, whose number were raised from 20 to 32 by the parliament to ensure an overwhelming officialist majority, has become an extension of the legal office of the Presidency... The Attorney General's Office, the Comptroller's Office and the Public Defender are all offices held by 'yes persons' absolutely obedient to the orders of the autocrat. In the National Electoral Council, four of five members are identified with the government. The Venezuelan Armed Forces are tightly controlled by Chávez. Therefore, form a conceptual point of view, the Venezuelan political system is autocratic. All political power is concentrated in the hands of the President. There is no real separation of Powers." See Teodoro Petkoff, "Election and Political Power. Challenges for the Opposition" in *Harvard Review of Latin America*, David Rockefeller Center for Latin American Studies, Harvard University, Fall 2008, pp. 12, *available at* http://www.drclas.harvard.edu/re-vista/articles/view/1125. See Allan R. BrewerCarías, "Los problemas de la gobernabilidad democrática en Venezuela: el autoritarismo consttucional y la concentración y centralización del poder" in Diego Valadés (Coord.), *Gobernabilidad y Constitucionalismo en América Latina*, Universidad Nacional Autónoma de México, México 2005, pp. 73-96.

252 In 2001, when approving more than 48 decree laws issued via delegate legislation, President Chávez stated: *"La ley soy yo. El Estado soy yo."* ("The law is me. The State is me.") See *El Universal,* Caracas December 4, 2001, pp. 1,1 and 2,1.

1. *The centralized Federation and the illusion of participation*

Political participation, that is, the possibility for citizens to participate in the decision making process of political matters, is only possible when power is available to the people in a state decentralization system of power based in the multiplication of local authorities with political autonomy[253]. On the contrary, in a scheme of centralized Federation like the one authorized by the Venezuelan Constitution of 1999, not only the political participation turns into a rhetoric illusion, but the system becomes an easy instrument of authoritarism[254].

For this reason, also in occasion of the approving referendum of the Constitution of 1999, in the same explanatory document of the reasons for which, at its time, we defended the "No vote" in said referendum, we warned that:

> "The great reform of the political system, necessary and essential to perfect democracy, was to dismantle the centralism of State and distribute the Public Power in the territory; the only way to make the political participation a reality. The Constituent Assembly -we added-, in order to overcome the political crisis, had to design the transformation of the State, decentralizing power and setting the basis to make it more available to people. By not doing it, **it neither transformed the State nor did it dispose of the necessary to make participation more effective**"[255].

However, despite the centralized scheme of power clearly expressed in the Constitution, this uses, in multiple occasions, the word participation and moreover, it proclaims the so called "participative democracy" as a global value, but without allowing the effective political participation of the people in the conduction of public affairs in autonomous and decentralized political entities. Thus participation is more than the exercise of the right to vote and of the implementation of several mechanisms of direct democracy like referenda, citizen's assemblies and the recently created communal councils, which are not configured as requests of the State power nor have political autonomy, but as instruments parallel to their organization, of the exclusive use and conduction of the Head of State for the centralization of power.

---

253 See our proposals for the reinforcement of the decentralization of the federation and the dismantling of its centralization in Allan R. Brewer-Carías, *Debate Constituyente (Aportes a la Asamblea Nacional Constituyente);* Volume I; Fundación de Derecho Público. Editorial Jurídica Venezolana, Caracas 1999; pp. 155 ff.

254 See the studies "La opción entre democracia y autoritarismo (Julio 2001)";pp. 41-59; "Democracia, descentralización política y reforma del Estado (Julio-Octubre 2001);pp. 105-125; and "El Municipio, la descentralización política y la democracia (Octubre 2001); pp. 127-141, in Allan R. Brewer-Carías, *Reflexiones sobre el constitucionalismo en América*; Editorial Jurídica Venezolana, Caracas 2001.

255 Document dated November 30, 1999. See Allan R. Brewer-Carías, *Debate Constituyente (Aporte a la Asamblea Nacional Constituyente),* Vol. III, Fundación de Derecho Público. Editorial Jurídica Venezolana, Caracas 1999, p. 323.

2.   *The sense of democracy and the illusion of participative democracy*

In fact, in the authoritarian speech of the "participative democracy," the later only shares the name democracy, being expertly used before the political failures faced by many of our aging democracies merely representatives and of political parties. Often, the expression is used without knowing exactly what it is about, and in general inappropriately confusing participative democracy with elements of direct democracy. But in the majority of the cases it is used as a misleading and clear strategy to end with the representative democracy itself as a political regime, aggravating the distrust in political parties and State institutions with structures and institutions far too distant from the citizen.

The confusion produced by the clamor of participation, often felt in many of our Latin American countries, which is also, by essence contrary to authoritarism, forces to reconsider true democracy in order to situate the concept of political participation where it belongs, which is precisely in the local ambit of political decentralization.

Without a doubt, the two fundamental principles of democracy in the contemporary world continue to be representation and participation. The first principle, representation, can compare to direct democracy, thus the dichotomy existing in this case is between "representative democracy" or indirect, and "direct democracy."

The second principle, participation can not, also, be compared to representation, but to political "exclusion," so the dichotomy arising from this plane is between "participative democracy" or of inclusion, and "democracy of exclusion" or exclusionist; and this is precisely what is not clear yet when talking about participative democracy, in certain cases, trying to refer to the mechanisms of direct democracy; and in others, deliberately confusing the concepts, in order to search for the elimination or minimization of representativity, and establish an alleged direct relation between a Messianic leader and the people, by means of institutional mechanisms even similar to the elected bodies of State, disposed to make the people believe that they are participating, when in fact they are being submitted to the control of the central power.

Regarding the representative democracy or indirect democracy, this is, and will continue to be of the essence of democracy[256]. Its substitution is essentially impossible in the case of democracy, without detriment that it could fortunately have been prospering during the last decades, precisely with the introduction of mechanisms of direct democracy in our political systems that complement it, but that will never replace it.

There can never be, in the contemporary world, a democracy that is only countersigned, pertaining to the plebiscite or of permanent open municipal councils; despite the fact that almost all contemporary constitutional systems have incorporated popular consult mechanisms and of citizen's assemblies in order to complement

---

256 See our proposal on the regulation of the participative and representative democratic principle in the Constitution of 1999 in Allan R. Brewer-Carías. *Debate Constituyente (Aportes a la Asamblea Nacional Constituyente),* Vol. I, *cit.;* pp 183 ff.

representativity. Also, as it is the case of the Constitution of Venezuela, all imaginable types of referenda have been regulated: consulting, approving, decisive, abrogating, and authorizing and recall; as well as the popular initiatives. Without a doubt, this has contributed to the popular mobilization and the relative direct manifestation of the will of the people; but it is clear that those mechanisms can not replace democracy driven by elected representatives. The challenge in this topic, in order to contribute to the consolidation of the democratic Rule of law, is to assure that said representatives are truly representatives of societies and their communities, and that they are elected by direct, universal and secret ballot systems, where political pluralism prevails, and by means of transparent electoral processes that assure the access to power with submission to the Rule of law.

But without a doubt, the second basic principle of democracy has more contemporary interest, which is that of political participation which, as it has been said, is not more than a democratic regime of political inclusion, where the citizen is part of its politically autonomous organized community, and contributes to the concerning decision making process. To participate means to be included, for this reason the dichotomy in the case of political participation is the political exclusion, which also leads to that of social and economic order.

Unfortunately, however, as we have mentioned, in the democratic political doctrine, too often have the concepts been confused, and when we talk of participative democracy, it is often confused and reduced to the mechanisms of direct democracy, when the participative democracy is much more than that.

To participate, in fact, in the common language, is to be part of..., is to belong, incorporate, contribute, be associated or committed to...; is to have a role, be an active part, be involved in or to lend a hand...; it is then, to relate, share or to have something to do with... The participation, then, in the political language is none other than to be part of a political community which in essence must benefit from political autonomy, in which the individual has a specific role of active character according to which it contributes in the decision making process, and can not be consumed completely, for instance, in the sole exercise of the right to vote (which is undoubtedly a minimal form of participation); or in being a member of intermediate societies, even those of political character as are the political parties; or voting in referenda (which is another minimal form of participation) particularly in citizen's assemblies controlled by the central power[257].

Democratic political participation is, truly, to be included in the political process and be an active part of it, without interventions; it is then, to be able to have access to the decision making process in public matters. And that has not been accomplished permanently in any democratic society, solely with the ballots in referenda

---

257 See Allan R. Brewer-Carías, "Democracia Municipal, Descentralización y Desarrollo Local" (Conferencia Inaugural del XXVI Congreso Iberoamericano de Municipios, Organización Iberoamericana de Cooperación Intermunicipal, Ayuntamiento de Valladolid; Valladolid, October 13-15, 2004); in *Revista Iberoamericana de Administración Pública*. N° 11. July-December 2003; INAP. Madrid 2003; pp. 11-34.

or popular consults. It is not accomplished either with manifestations, even though they are multitudinous, and even less, those that are obedient and submissive to a leader. This, which is not more than political manifestation, history has taken care of teaching it to us in all its aspects, including those proper of fascist authoritarianisms of last Century, and which can not be confused with political participation.

In order for democracy to be inclusive or of inclusion, it has to allow the citizen to be an effective part of his political community which, above all, has to be autonomous; it has to allow him to develop even a conscience of his effective pertinence, that is, to belong in the political and social order, for instance, to a community, a place, a land, a field, a district, a town, a region, a city, in short, to a State, and to be elected for that, as a representative of it.

For that, the participative democracy is not something new in the political history; it has always been there, even since the days of the Revolutions of the 19th Century in the democratic political theories and practices. Even in all the countries with consolidated democracies, it is imperceptibly established in the lowest level of the territories of the States, in the autonomous political entities, like Municipalities or Communes; that is, in the base of the territorial distribution of power.

The great issue of the political participation, in democracies with a lack of participation, is to determine where and how one can really participate, and the answer points to the entities that are the result of the political decentralization of power, and which are, above all, provided with autonomy. So that, separating and without replacing the vote and instruments of direct democracy, the political participation as democracy of inclusion, in which the citizen can personally be part in a decisive process, participating in state activities and in function of the general interest, can only exist in the most politically reduced, decentralized and autonomous territorial estates, in the local, communal or municipal level. That is to say, only in the lower autonomous territorial levels of the State organization, is that a participative organization can be structured, and that allows the incorporation of the individual citizen, groups or communities, in the public life, and particularly, in the general public decision making process or those of administrative order.

From this, results the central issue that has to be solved when talking properly about participative democracy, it is that of the determination of the territorial level required for participation as a democratic routine, and the most classical option is between the municipality, as an autonomous political entity scattered in all the remote places of a State, in every village, town and hamlet, located very close to the citizen; or the great urban or rural municipality; located far away from the citizen, and that is definitely useless.

Finally, the truth is that in most of the so called democratically developed countries prevails the existence of many municipalities, and among them, of small municipalities[258]. In contrast, in Latin-America, the municipality is extremely distant

---

258   In Germany, for instance, of its 16,098 municipalities, 76% has less than 5,000 habitants; and in Spain, about 86% of its more than 8,056 municipalities, has less than 5,000 habitants, resulting only in 16% of the population, and 61% of them has less than 1,000 habitants.. It

from the citizen[259]. In both Continents, Municipalities were tributaries of the same central postulates derived from the French Revolution, but the great difference between them was that, since the beginning of 19th Century, in Europe the Municipality was located in every hamlet, town, village and city there was, very close to the citizen; and on the other hand, in Latin-America, the colonial Municipality that exceeded the battles of the Independence, continued to be as it was created, located in the territorial level of the colonial Provinces, in the Metropolitan town councils, distant from the citizen.

In the first, the political participation is such an every day matter regarding the small issues that is imperceptible; in the second case, simply there is no participation of any kind. They have a territorial ambit so high and distant from the citizen, that makes them useless, because they are of no use to properly manage local interests or to serve instances for the political participation of the people in the decision or management of their own communal affairs.

Therefore, the participative democracy is real and indissolubly linked, not to direct democracy, but to the political decentralization, and within the later, to the municipalization; and this can not materialize solely with incorporation proposals to

must also be emphasized that, since we are in Valladolid, as an example of what means to a country to territorially have many small municipalities, being precisely the case of this Community of Castilla and Leon, that shelters little more than a quarter of the total of the Municipalities in Spain, with 2,248 municipalities (2,484,603 habitants), of which 68.5%, that is, 1,540 municipalities, have less than 500 habitants. See in *Informe sobre el Gobierno Local, Ministerio para las Administraciones Públicas.* Fundación Carles Pi i Sunyer d'Etudis Autonòmics y Locals. Madrid 1992; p. 27.

259 In Argentina, for 37 million habitants, there are 1,617 municipalities, with a population average of 22,882 habitants; in Bolivia, for 8 million habitants, there are 312 municipalities, with a population average of 25,642 habitants; in Brazil, for 168 million habitants, there are 5,581 municipalities with a population average of 30,102 habitants; in Chile, for 15 million habitants, there are 340 municipalities with a population average of 44,117 habitants; in Colombia, for 42 million habitants, there are 1,068 municipalities with a population average of 39,326 habitants; in Cuba, for 11 million habitants, there are 169 municipalities with a population average of 65,389 habitants; in Ecuador, for 12 million habitants, there are 1,079 municipalities with a population average of 11,121 habitant; in El Salvador, for 6 million habitants, there are 262 municipalities with a population average of de 22,900 habitants; in Guatemala, for 11 million habitants, there are 324 municipalities with a population average of 33,950 habitants; in Honduras, for 6 million habitants, there are 293 municipalities with a population average of 20,478 habitants; in México, for 97 million habitants, there are 2,418 municipalities with a population average of 40,116 habitants; in Nicaragua, for 5 million habitants, there are 143 municipalities with a population average of 34,965 habitants; in Paraguay, for 5 million habitants, there are 212 municipalities with a population average of 23,585 habitants; en Peru, for 25 million habitants, there are 1,808 municipalities with a population average of 13,827 habitants; in Dominican Republic, for 8 million habitants, there are 90 municipalities with a population average of 88,889 habitants; in Uruguay, for 3 million habitants, there are 19 municipalities with a population average of 157,894 habitants; and in Venezuela, for 24 million habitants, there are 338 municipalities with a population average of 71,006 habitants. See the referentes in Allan R. Brewer-Carías, Reflexiones sobre el constitucionalismo en América, Editorial Jurídica Venezolana, Caracas 2001, pp. 139 ff.

the democratic regime of instruments like referenda, consults or popular initiatives and citizen's assemblies. The participative democracy is not consumed completely nor can it be mistaken with the direct democracy, as it often occurs in many studies, about democracy, advocating its perfection[260].

The political participation, as a democratic routine or as part of democracy as a way of life, can only occur in a local level. Thus, political participation or participative democracy is intimately related to localism and political decentralization, which are the ones that can efficiently limit power, which is consubstantial to democracy. For that reason, there can not be and have never been decentralized authoritarianisms which had been able to effectively allow the political participation; on the contrary, the political centralization of power is the essence of authoritarianisms and opposing to democracy.

That is to say, political centralization impedes participation, reason for which the later can only be possible in government systems where power is politically decentralized and close to the citizen; and there is no other instance in the States for the citizen to participate, that is not the local government; the rest is falsehood and deceit, or direct democracy mechanisms which, we insist, are something else. This is why the political decentralization issue, precisely, is not as noticeable in European countries with developed and consolidated democracies, where participation is a daily thing, in the little aspects that can be dealt with in those small urban and rural municipalities.

So that, without fear of being wrong, we can affirm that not only without political or territorial decentralization, that is, without the existence of a multiplicity of local and regional local powers, politically autonomous there can not be political participation but, definitely, there can not be a participative democracy. Political decentralization is, then, the basis for participative democracy and at the same time, the force of the control of power. Centralism, on the other hand, is the basis of political exclusion by concentrating power on those few elected and, at the same time, the motive for discrediting the representative democracy regarding how many direct or countersigning democracy additives are implanted to it[261].

---

260 See for instance, in Venezuela, the set of studies published in *Participación Ciudadana y Democracia,* Comisión Presidencial para la Reforma del Estado, Caracas 1998.

261 For this reason, during a conference we gave at the XXV Congreso de la Organización iberoamericana de Municipios, in Guadalajara, Jalisco, Mexico in 2001, we said that: "the contemporary debate in our countries, regarding democracy, has to be focused in the rescue of the political decentralization process. To perfect democracy demands making it more participative and more representative; for this, the only possible way is by bringing Power closer to the citizen, and that can only be achieved by territorially decentralizing the Power of State and to take it even to the smallest of communities; that is to say, distributing Power along the national territory." I also added that, "whichever is the political decentralization way taken; it is about projects and proposals radically compared to the centralism of State and the concentration of Power, which are essentially antidemocratic." Finally, the political proposal that we presented then, and that now we insist on emphasizing, "seeks the design in our countries, of a new political system demanded by democracy, and that can only have the objective of

This is why only authoritarianisms fear and reject both the political decentralization and the democratic participation, and that is what has been taking place in Venezuela with the scam of the "participative democracy."

3. *The reaction against the Federation as a form of decentralized State*

The idea of the "participative and protagonic democracy" that has been sold by the Venezuelan authoritarian government, before being an instrument for the political decentralization, has served to dismantle what little was left of it, and finally, to finish with the still deficient representative democracy that we have left, disabling, at the same time, the actual political participation.

In Venezuela, the great political transformation that should have taken place during the constituent process of 1999, to perfect democracy[262], which must have been its key motivation, should consist of the effective substitution of the state form of the Centralized Federation, developed during the last Century, for an effectively decentralized Federation in two territorial levels, that of States and multiple autonomous Municipalities.

However, in spite of the efforts made, the reform did not go beyond nominalism, the words and declarations. That way, the Preamble as well as article 4 of the Constitution, declare the untrue, that "The Bolivarian republic of Venezuela is a decentralized federal State," but adding the normative, of course, that the later is true only "in the terms consecrated by this Constitution"; formula more or less similar to that of article 2 of the Constitution of 1961 which, however, modestly limited itself to declare that "The Republic of Venezuela is a federal State," which was also not true in political terms of vertical distribution of power[263]. To the Constitution of 1999, it has now been added that the Federation is supposedly "decentralized" which is,

---

making it more participative, with the great presence of the civil society, and more representative of the communities. This means to spread power along the territory, to the last community, so the citizen and its intermediate societies can really participate." See the conference on "El Municipio, la descentralización política y la democracia" in *XXV Congreso Iberoamericano de Municipios, Guadalajara, Jalisco, Mexico, October 23-26, 2001*, Fundación Española de Municipios y Provincias. Madrid 2003; p. 453 ff.

262   See our proposal during the discussion of the Proyecto de Constitución in Allan R. Brewer-Carías, "Propuesta sobre la forma federal del Estado en la nueva Constitución: Nuevo Federalismo y Nuevo Municipalismo" in *Debate Constituyente, (Aportes a la Asamblea Nacional Constituyente)*, Volume I, (August 8-September 8); Caracas 1999; pp. 150 to 170; and "El reforzamiento de la forma federal del Estado Venezolano en la Nueva Constitución: Nuevo Federalismo y Nuevo Municipalismo"; Report presented at The International Conference on Federalism in an Era of Globalization, Québec, Canada, October 1999, available in www.allanbrewercarias.com, Section I, 1 (Conferencias), No, 734t (1999).

263   See Allan R. Brewer-Carías, "Los problemas de la federación centralizada en Venezuela" in Revista *Ius et Praxis*, Facultad de Derecho y Ciencias Políticas, Universidad de Lima, N° 12, Peru, December 1988; pp. 49-96; and "Problemas de la Federación centralizada (A propósito de la elección directa de Gobernadores)," in *IV Congreso Iberoamericano de Derecho Constitucional*, Universidad Nacional Autónoma de México; Mexico 1992; pp. 85-131.

however, opposed by the actual text of the Constitution in which articles the power of the State is even more centralized[264].

In any case, "the terms consecrated by the Constitution" are the key to effectively determine the degree of political decentralization of the State and therefore, of the Federation; and the comparison between each of the "terms" reveals a greater centralism in the text of 1999.

Except for the nominalism, in the Constitution of 1999, in fact and as it has been said before, there was no much progress regarding what was contained in the text of 1961, in spite of the partial contitutionalization of aspects already established in the legislative reforms of 1989 (Organic Law of Decentralization, Delimitation and Transfer of Competencies of the Public Power). But there were not the progress and transformations needed to make the decentralization of the Federation a reality. Rather there was an institutional retrocession in the matter, when the Senate was eliminated, and with that, the beginning of the institutional equality of the States, establishing, for the first time in the constitutional history of Venezuela, a unicameral National Assembly (Article 186). Also, it was allowed the possibility to establish limitations to the autonomy of the States (Article 162) and even of the Municipalities (Article 168) by means of national law, which is configured as a negation, at first, of the idea itself of political decentralization, which on the other hand has to be based in the concept of the territorial autonomy assured by the Constitution. It was also established, a precarious ambit of the state competencies whose exercise, additionally, was subjected to what was regulated in the national legislation; and a tributary centralization that places the States in a more accentuated financial dependency.

The declaration about "decentralized federal State" incorporated in the Constitution of 1999 to identify the form if the State, thus, did not mean an actual improvement, it was a retrocession instead, due to the aggravation of the principles of the Centralized Federation consolidated during the 19th Century.

But even all of that has been directly threatened to disappear, in honor of the organization of the Popular Power that, apparently instead of the States of the federation, will create regions and a system of "federal cities," governed by bodies integrated by apparent representatives of the communal councils, not elected by means of the universal, direct and secret vote, but appointed arbitrarily by dint of "participation." That way, Governors and representatives members of state Legislative Councils, elected until now, by means of the universal, direct and secret vote as well, are meant to disappear, drowned also by the centralizing scheme of the Communal councils of the Popular Power.

---

264 See Allan R. Brewer-Carías, *Federalismo y Municipalismo en la Constitución de 1999 (Alcance de una reforma insuficiente y regresiva)*, Cuadernos de la Cátedra Allan R. Brewer-Carías de Derecho Público, N° 7, Universidad Católica del Táchira, Editorial Jurídica Venezolana, Caracas-San Cristóbal 2001, p. 187. See also, Allan R. Brewer-Carías, "El 'Estado Federal descentralizado' y la centralización de la Federación en Venezuela. Situación y Perspectiva de una contradicción constitucional," in *Revista de Estudios de la Administración Local (REAL)*, 292-293, May-December 2003, Madrid 2003, pp. 11-43.

4.   The reaction against Municipalism and its substitution for a centralized Popular or Communal Power

Regarding the municipal power, the great democratic reform required in the country was, essentially, to bring the autonomous local institutions closer to the citizen, municipalizing the territory; it was necessary to multiply the Municipalities instead of reducing them. None of this was done, and instead, in part, the Organic Law for the Municipal Public Power of 2005[265] prevented it, by establishing major limitations for the creation of autonomous local political entities; and on the other hand, instead of multiplying the Municipalities, what has been created are the communal councils to eliminate them (Law of Communal councils), when what should have happened was the reform of the Organic law in order to establish municipal entities as autonomous political units close to the communities and to establish the possibility of the participation in said (decentralized) autonomous political entities.

But as it has been said, the latter did not occurred like that, and on the contrary, based on elements of the direct democracy established in the Constitution, like "citizen's assemblies whose decisions are of binding character" (article 70), in its place, in 2006 the Law on Communal councils[266] was dictated, establishing a *centralized* institutional system, parallel to the municipal regime, in order to replace it, and for the hypothetical popular participation, identified "of the Popular Power," ignoring the proper existence of the municipal regime; and formally initiating the elimination process of the municipality as an instance of participative democracy. The later was announced by the President of the Republic in January of 2007, when the Ministers of his new cabinet of Ministries of the Popular Power were being sworn in, announcing "the revolutionary explosion of the communal power, the communal councils" stating that:

> "Now we must extend the local matters, and must begin to create by law, in the first place, some sort of **regional, local and national Confederation of Communal Councils.** We have to march **towards the conformation of a communal state** and the old middle-class state that still lives, that is alive and kicking, we have to continue **to dismantle it progressively while we raise the communal state, the socialist state, the Bolivarian state.**"[267]

Two days later, he added during his swearing in act for the new constitutional term, that the objective was "to transit towards the road of a communal city, where no mayor's office or municipal boards are needed, only the communal power."[268]

---

265 See *Gaceta Oficial* N° 38.204, dated June 8, 2005. the Organic Law was subject of a reform in November, 2005; *Gaceta Oficial* N° 38.327, dated December 2, 2005; and then in April, 2006, *Gaceta Oficial* N° 5,806 Extra, dated April 10, 2006, reprinted by material error in *Gaceta Oficial* N° 38.421; dated April 21, 2006. See Allan R. Brewer-Carías et al, *Ley Orgánica del Poder Público Municipal,*, Editorial Jurídica Venezolana, Caracas 2005.

266 See in Extraordinary *Oficial Gazette* N° 5.806; dated April 10, 2006.

267 Speech of Hugo Chavez, 01-08-2007.

268 Speech of Hugo Chavez, *El Nacional* 01-11-2007;p. A2

However, the great difference is that in democracy, mayors and communal councils are elected by popular vote, and instead, in the scheme of the communal power, the members of the communal councils are appointed directly by the President of the Republic or by agents of the Single Party, by means of duly controlled citizen's assemblies.

In this centralized system, Communal Councils do not have and will not have any political autonomy, because its members are not elected, as representatives of the people, by the universal, direct and secret vote; the "community" is conceived outside the municipality when, according to the Constitution, it should be the primary political unit in the national organization; and in the apparent "constitutional frame of the participative and protagonic democracy," there has also been the intention to regulate the Communal Councils as "instances for participation, articulation and integration between the different community organizations, social groups and the people," but without any autonomy or political decentralization at all. That is, as mentioned, with this non autonomous parallel structure, what has been initiated is the dismantling of representative democracy in the country.

The 2006 Law of Communal Councils, as it has been said, has established said entities without any type of relation to the Municipalities nor, then, with the democratic representation, establishing a pyramidal organization of regional and national Presidential Commissions directly governed by the President of the Republic, who controls the designation of funds. And all of that, organized in a centralized way to allegedly allow "the organized people to directly exercise the management of public politics and projects addressed to respond to the needs and aspirations of the communities in the construction of a society of equality and social justice" (article 2.) But this, as mentioned, concerns an organization conceived under a centralized hierarchic schema (without any political autonomy), completely dependent of a "Presidential Commission for the Popular Power," presided and run by the President of the Republic, with financial resources surpassing those corresponding to the Municipal Power, and that function in parallel and separated from autonomous Municipalities and their elected authorities. The Citizen's Assemblies were located in said Communal Councils as the primary instance for the exercise of power, participation and popular protagonism, whose decisions are of binding character for the respective communal council (article 4.5).

In reality, with this Law of Communal Councils, what was also initiated was the unconstitutional demunicipalization of the people's participation, replacing the Municipality, as a primary and autonomous political unit in the national organization established by the Constitution and that must be included in a political decentralization system of power (vertical distribution); by a system of entities without any political autonomy, denominated Popular Power (Communal Councils), directly linked and dependent, of a centralized schema of power, of the highest level of the National Executive Power, the President of the Republic thru a Presidential Commission of the Popular Power. Thus, Mayors and councilmen members of the Municipal Councils, elected -until now- by means of the universal, direct and secret vote, are called to disappear drowned by the centralizing schema of the Communal Councils of the Popular Power.

And within this centralist schema of the organization of the exercise of the central power, the communicating vessel that will supposedly assure participation, seems to be not other than the also announced Single Party that the Head of State would preside himself, imbricate in the state bureaucracy as it has never been seen in Venezuela, and that as a government political system has been demolished in the world with the fall of the Berlin Wall.

VI. THE FORESEEABLE END OF THE AUTHORITARIAN PROCESS: THE "DICTATORSHIP OF DEMOCRACY" FOR THE DISMANTLING OF THE REPRESENTATIVE DEMOCRACY

In order for a democratic Rule of law to exist, the declarations contained in constitutional texts that speak of "participative and protagonic democracy" or of the decentralization of the State, are not enough; neither is enough to establish an elective system that allows the election of popular representatives, by means of the vote. Besides, of course, this system has to effectively assure representation, political pluralism and power access according to the postulates of the Rule of law.

But also, in order for a true democratic Rule of law to exist, its is necessary and indispensable that the constitutional frame in which it is intended to function, effectively permits the proper control of power by power itself, even by the supreme power of the people. This is the only way to assure the force of the Rule of law, the democracy and the true exercise of human rights.

And the control of the State Power in a democratic Rule of law can only be achieved by dividing, separating and distributing Public Power, either horizontally by means of the guarantee of the autonomy and independence of the different powers of the State, to avoid the concentration of power; vertically, by means of its distribution or spreading in the State's territory, creating autonomous political entities with representatives elected by votes, to avoid its centralization. The concentrations of power, as well as its centralization, then, are essentially antidemocratic state structures.

It is precisely there where the problems of the declared Rule of Law and the alleged democracy in Venezuela -whose deformation lays in the proper constitutional text of 1999-, rest; in which, unfortunately, was established the institutional schema, encouraging authoritarianism and eliminating every form of power control; and which has also permitted the centralization of power, initiating the dismantling process of federalism and municipalism, reinforcing authoritarianism itself twisting the possibility of the effective political participation in spite of the direct democracy mechanisms recollected. It is a constitutional example of the constitutional authoritarianism with electoral origin, which, however, constitutes the negation of what a democratic Rule of law must be.

As it has been said, based over this constitutional authoritarianism, in January 2007, and in occasion of the beginning of his second constitutional term, the President of the Republic has began to expose the steps needed for the definite dismantling of democracy in Venezuela, by means of the organization system of a Single Power, denominated Popular Power or Communal Power (communal state or socialist state), totally concentrated and centralized, and politically conducted by a Single Party. And both, the Popular Power and the Single Party, in order to instate "the dictatorship of democracy," lead by a single person, who will be the President of the Popular Power and the Single Party.

For this, of course, a general reform of the Constitution will be previously needed, which was also announced in January, 2007. however, previously, in fraud o the Constitution itself, during the same month of January 2007, an Enabling Law was dictated, authorizing the President to, precisely, dictate laws contrary to the Constitution "to update and **transform the legal system that regulates State institutions**" and to establish "the **mechanisms of popular participation**, by means of the social control, the social technical inspection and the practice of the voluntary enlistment of the organized community in the application of the judicial system and the economical scope of the State; also, to **adapt the organization structure of the State institutions, to permit the direct exercise of the popular supremacy**." However, these "constitutional" laws, as it has been said, would be issued after the reform of the Constitution.[269] That is to say, during another depurated constitutional fraud, according to a Constitution that does not authorize the legislative delegation to reform the Constitution, an enabling Law is dictated with said authorization used only if during the period of force of said Law the Constitution is previously reformed.

The general lines of those reforms for the organization of the Popular Power supposedly built over the direct exercise of the supremacy by the people, are based in the elimination of democracy as a plural and representative political regime, that can allow the election by means of the universal, direct and secret ballot, of the holders of the public powers distributed in the territory (Mayors and councilmen in the Municipalities, Governors and Legislators in the States, representatives to the National Assembly and the President of the Republic).

The schema, just as it has been announce, would aim for the substitution of the direct representative democracy for an alleged indirect participative democracy, in which there would be no popular election of any kind. Its function would be based in the "neighbor assemblies" and the "communal councils" whose members would not be elected by means of the universal, direct and secret ballot, but chosen in the community, of course, with the ideological conduction of the Single Party, which would be the only one with access to the State power organizations in all their levels.

---

269 As it was written on the newspaper on January 31, 2007-02-04: "The 18 month length period of force of he enabling Law, has the object of allowing Hugo Chavez, President of the Republic, to wait for the reform of the Constitution to be approved in order to write the norms that will base the socialist model of State he wants to instate." According to the opinions of members of parliament, during the first months the law decrees written by the Executive will be adapted to the 1999 Magna Charta, and in some of them, the omissions of the Legislative Power will be filled... After the popular consult for the approval of the reforms of the Constitution, several representatives have expressed that it could happen in September, the president would have time enough to adapt the legislation to the political model he proposes. Thus, representatives assume that every legal instrument related to the State system will be announced by the end of 2007 or the beginning of 2008." *El Nacional*, Caracas 01-31-2007; p. A2.

The communal councils would appoint their representatives in the regional communal councils or those of the federal cities ("regional and local confederation of communal councils"); and the later, would be who appoint their representatives in the National Assembly for the Popular Power ("national confederation of communal councils"), which will eventually replace the current National Assembly. This way, every trace of direct, universal and secret election of representatives to state and national legislative organs, as well as governors, would disappear. And finally, the National Assembly for the Popular Power, formed as such, would then appoint a national Council (of government) for the Popular Power which, of course, would unavoidable be presided by the same person who would also be the President of the Single Party.

All of these reforms that implicate the elimination of the representative democracy in the country, have began to be implemented during 2006, with the sanction of the Law of Communal Councils (Popular Power), as parallel structure established regarding the municipal organization, in an evident fraud to the Constitution, in order to definitely replace Municipalities as primary units. The difference with these is precisely, that in them, Mayors and municipal Councilmen are elected, and the Municipalities are politically autonomous; and in stead, the members of the Communal Councils are not elected, but appointed arbitrarily by alleged "citizen assemblies" controlled from the pinnacle of the Executive Power, from which they depend, and have no political autonomy.

Once the base structure of the Popular Power was built (announced in the Law of Communal Councils), and provided of enormous resources that are not given to Municipalities, managed by a Presidential Commission, the following step would be the elimination of Municipalities, as it has been announced as well, and, simultaneously, the elimination of the States and every trace of direct election and political decentralization, and therefore the possibility of political participation. As said, what has been announced is definitely the elimination of all, municipal and regional, representative and elected bodies.[270] On a state level, due to the announcement, what would exist are certain "federal cities" or regional confederations of communal councils, whose leaders, again, would be people appointed also arbitrarily by the Communal Councils controlled by the Presidential Commission of the Popular Power.

And at any moment, as said before, there could be a proposal to eliminate even the National Assembly as national representative organ, and to establish a National Assembly of the Popular Power (national confederation of communal councils) in its place, which would be the summit of the Popular Power, formed by representatives appointed by the federal cities and Communal Council groups; all of these, of course, duly controlled, from the summit, by the mechanism of the Single Party. Everything is announced.

---

270 See the article on the declarations of the President of the Republic: "Chavez: Let's begin to eliminate mayors and governors." *El Nacional*, 01-29-2007; p. A2.

Lastly, it must be mentioned, that the President of the Republic, in the constitutional reforms he has announced and promised since 2006, there is the incorporation of the possibility of the indefinite presidential reelection in the Constitution. That reelection, of course, would not be built over a direct, universal and secret election system, but that it would be about an appointment made by the national confederation of the Popular Power which would be the National Assembly of the Popular Power. That is, in the summit of the Popular Power the same person who controls it would act as the President of the Popular Power, but not because he was elected repeated and unlimitedly in a direct way by the people by means of universal, direct and secret ballot, but because he would always be appointed as such by the Popular Power structures whose will finally converge in the national Assembly of the Popular Power to preside both, the government Council of the Popular Power and the Single Party.

In order to initiate the formation of this state organization schema, in January 2007, the President of the Republic has began to change the name and sense of the organization structure of the Public Administration, renaming all the Ministries and Ministers of the national Executive as "of the Popular Power" (e.g.: Ministry of Foreign Affairs of the Popular Power, Ministry of Infrastructure of the Popular Power, etc.).

The truth is that in general, this was the system established to assure the dictatorship of the proletariat by the Soviets in the Soviet Union since 1918, and the schema of the popular power established in Cuba, where the Popular Assembly is who appoints a State or government Council, which at the same time, always elects the same person to preside it.

In conclusion, it is about a State and Power organization schema that implies the complete elimination of the representative democracy, and its replacement by an alleged direct democracy; that is to say, the direct exercise of supremacy by the people, and the indirect election of representatives including the leadership of the State.

CHAPTER XII

THE RESTRICTIONS IMPOSED ON FREEDOM OF
EXPRESSION BY MEANS OF THE JUDICIAL CONFISCATION OF
PRIVATE ASSETS: THE RCTV CASE

(2007)

This Paper was written as a Presentation the Case of the confiscation of Radio Caracas Televisión RCTV in 2010, in which restrictions were imposed on freedom of expression by means of the judicial confiscation of private assets, and that was submitted to the *Notre Dane Law Review Symposium on Freedom of Expression in Latin America*, held in the Centre for Civil and Human Rights, University of Notre Dame, The Law, School, held on March 29, 2010.

The 2007 Venezuelan *RCTV Case* is perhaps one of the more vivid examples of the illegitimate confabulation between a subjected Judiciary and an authoritarian government, in order to reduce freedom of expression and to confiscate private property. For such purpose, the Constitutional Chamber of the Supreme Tribunal of Justice and the Political Administrative Chamber of the same Tribunal, in May 2007, instead of protecting citizens' constitutional rights, have conspired as docile instruments controlled by the Executive, in order to kidnap and violate them. In this way, the highest level of the Judiciary involved on matters of judicial review, has laundered and vouched for the governmental arbitrariness covering with a judicial veil, the closedown of *Radio Caracas Televisión* (RCTV) the most important television stations of the country, and critical of the administration of President H. Chavez

In said case, the judicial conspiracy had the purpose of reducing the freedom of expression in the country and to materialize, with impunity, the confiscation of private property assets of the TV Station which, in a way neither the Executive nor the Legislator, could have done for being forbidden in the Constitution (art. 115). The Supreme Tribunal, in the decision of both Chambers, violated express provisions of the Constitution, with the aggravating circumstance that the conspirators of this case have acted with impunity, just because they are aware that their actions cannot be controlled.

In fact, in several judicial decisions issued in May 2007, instead of controlling all the successive arbitrary and unconstitutional threats and decisions adopted by the government according to its intention to refuse the petition for the renewal or extension of the concession to use the radio electric signal in possession of RCTV for more than half a century; not only the Supreme Tribunal systematically refused to exercise any kind of control over the actions of the Executive but, acting as an obedient instrument of the government, it validated the closedown of the television station, covering up the aggression it meant for the freedom of expression and also, since the State entity (*Fundación TEVES*) created by the government to substitute RCTV was not ready to effectively transmit television signals with national coverage, it decided, ex officio acting as an arbitrary governmental agency, to confiscate the assets of RCTV which was ceasing its activities; assigning them "for temporary use", but in fact in an indefinite way and free of charge, to the State entity that began transmitting the signal in the same radio electric space.

In order to comprehend such infringement to the Constitution, and to RCTV's constitutional rights, committed by the judicial courts in charge of ensuring the supremacy of the Constitution and the legality regarding administrative actions; I will first refer to the background of the case, an then to all the judicial actions unfruitful filed searching for a response from the Judiciary Power in protection of legitimate constitutional rights which had been violated in this case.[271]

I. ON THE TELECOMMUNICATIONS REGIME

Private activities in matters of telecommunications, especially TV activities, are to be performed in Venezuela according to a legal regime that regulates both the telecommunication activities, in themselves, and the use of public domain assets, when the latter is needed for their execution. In both cases, the transformations of the contemporary world on the matter brought on an evolution on said telecommunications legal regime characterized by the following trends:

As for the regulation of all telecommunication activities as such, during the last decades, their legal regime has shown an evolution as for the State's intervention degree, which has gone from constituting an activity that, until the last third of the XX century had always, and generally, been considered as an activity reserved for the State, in most cases, categorized of public service, and which, in certain cases, excluded any private activity in them; to the current situation of an activity of general interest, in which individuals have the right to execute the activities, even thought they are subjected to certain control of the State by means of which they are authorized or enabled to execute them.

As for the regulation of the use the public domain for telecommunication activities, the evolution of the regime regarding its regulation has gone from being one

---

271 See on this Case, Allan R. Brewer-Carías, "El Juez Constitucional en Venezuela como instrumento para aniquilar la libertad de expresión plural y para confiscar la propiedad privada: El Caso RCTV", in *Revista de Derecho Público*, N°110, Editorial Jurídica Venezolana, Caracas 2007, pp. 7 ff.

which, for instance, only referred to the use of the terrestrial, aerial and maritime public domain for the rendering of telecommunication services by means of the installation of cables (subterranean, aerial and maritime); to the additional contemporary regulation of the use of the public domain asset referred to as radio electric spectrum to transmit them through waves.

The change made in Venezuela regarding the regime of all telecommunication activities took place in with the sanctioning of the 2000 Telecommunication Organic Law, which established the principle of economic freedom of telecommunications, eliminating the reserve the State had over them, and also eliminating the characterization of telecommunications services as "public service" as it was established in the old Telecommunication Law of 1941.

According to the new law, activities related to telecommunications went then, from being public activities reserved to the State (public services), to be private activities performed by individuals exercising their right to economic freedom (art. 112 of the Constitution), also performed by the State. In other words, even if some of those telecommunication activities could be considered as public services, the important aspect of the change was that these are not services reserve to the State so therefore, they can be freely developed by individuals, subjected only to administrative authorizations or permits. Actually, the Organic Law only established a reserve to the State that has been reduced to "telecommunication services for the security and defense of the nation" (Art. 8).

Being then the object of the Organic Law, to regulate activities that are not reserved to the State, its article 1° establishes that it has been sanctioned in order "to guarantee the people's right to communications and for such purpose to develop telecommunication economic activities without limitations other than those derived from the Constitution and the laws.

The consequence of this liberation of the telecommunication regime, was the establishment of the need for individuals to exercise private activities in the sector, to previously obtain the corresponding administrative permit and the concession of use and exploitation of the radio electric spectrum, if needed, that are to be given by the Administration in the cases and conditions established by the law, the regulations and the General Conditions established by the National Telecommunications Commission CONATEL (Art. 5). This regime signified the on matters of telecommunication activities, the elimination of the State's reserve and the general regime of concessions that only persists regarding the use of the public domain of the radio electric spectrum, substituting it for a regime of economic freedom limited only by the nature of the activities, which being of general interest, imposed the need to obtain some sort of administrative authorization to execute them.

Given the radical change of the telecommunication regime which went from the State's reserve, the qualification of these as public services and their exercise by means of administrative concession, to a concurrence regime in which individuals have the economic freedom; the qualification of the activities as of general interest and their exercise by means of administrative permits or authorizations; the Organic Law established, in its "transitory provisions," a regime aimed to transform the old concessions and permits granted according to the prior legislation, into the new regime of administrative permits, authorizations, concessions or just obligations to notification or the need to register, established in the new Organic Law (Art. 210). The new regime, in any case, departed from the principle of the respect for acquired rights, regulating the adaptation of the old concessions into administrative permits and concessions.

Nonetheless, the said transformation was established in the Organic Law, as obligatory, guarantying a specific administrative procedure in which the interested parties had the right to participate, in order to achieve the transformation of their legal titles within the terms to be established by CONATEL (Art. 210.7). Said procedure, which had to be ruled by the principles of transparency, good faith, equality and celerity (art. 210.1), had, necessarily, to conclude in the two-year time period following the publication of the Law, by means of a transformation administrative act issued by CONATEL, in which the concession or initial permit had to be substituted by an administrative permit and concession as provided in the new Law. The transformation could not imply granting more faculties to the operators that those they had at the time, according to their respective legal titles (Art. 210.3). The Law expressly provided, as well, that "while the adaptation takes place, all the rights and obligations acquired under prior legislation, will remain in force, in the same terms and conditions established in the respective concessions and permits" (Art. 210).

According to this prevision, RCTV opportunely requested the transformation of its titles, which were never decided by the Administration; with what the station continued to operate in agreement with its old concession, which had a duration of twenty (20) years, according to what was directly established in Decree N° 1.577 of 05-27-1987 (articles 4 and 1°), concluding on 05-27-2007. In virtue of the omission of the Administration to transform the concession, RCTV had the preferential right, according to Decree 1.577, to the extension of its concession for another twenty-year (20) term (Art. 2).

Beginning late 2006, however, the Venezuelan government, by means of direct expressions from the President of the Republic, the Minister of Communication and Information, the Minster of Telecommunications and Information Technology, and the National Communications Commission, blazed abroad that RCTV would cease to transmit its television signal on May 27, 2007; once the old, but at the time current concession it possessed expired. At first, the reason of the announced measure was mere and exclusively political, which was contrary to the Law; and at the end, the threats became specific administrative acts according to which the decision was made to not extend the concession of the TV station, because the government had decided to use the radio electric space assigned to RCTV, for five (5) decades, in order to establish a state public TV service. RCTV had the right to the extension, since according to the liberalization regime of telecommunications disposed in the 2000 Organic Law, the extension or renewal of the authorization acts is not the result of a discretional administrative decision but a decision submitted to the law, to which the holders of said concessions have the right to if all assumptions are verified in order to proceed.

The government actions originated the filing of several judicial recourses before the Political Administrative and Constitutional Chambers of the Supreme Tribunal of Justice, seeking constitutional protection (amparo) of constitutional rights, and judicial review of administrative actions including the request of precautionary preventive measures. The unfortunate result was the systematic refusal of the constitutional judge to protect the constitutional rights of the petitioners and, contrarily, to see how the Political Administrative Chamber and the Constitutional Chamber conspired to violate the constitutional rights to the freedom of the plural expression of thought, the due process, the right to the defense and the right to private property.

II. ON HOW THE CONSTITUTIONAL JUDGE DELIBERATELY REFUSED TO PROTECT THE FREEDOM OF EXPRESION AND OTHER CONSTITUTIONAL RIGHTS OPENLY THREATENED OF BEING VIOLATED BY THE HEAD OF STATE AND HIS SUBORDINATES

As a matter of fact, in view of the abuse of authority that was been announced, on February 9, 2007, RCTV, its directives, its reporters and workers brought before the Constitutional Chamber of the Supreme Tribunal of Justice (as competent court on matters of amparo actions filed against high officers of the State) an amparo action against the violation threat of its constitutional rights by the President of the Republic and the Minister for Telecommunications and Information Technology, by publically and repeatedly declaring the will of the Government, basing his words on political motives (which was even compiled and published in a *White Book*, edited in March 2007 by same the Ministry of Telecommunications), stating that from May 28, 2007; RCTV would cease operations as a opened television station in VHF. This threat was considered imminent, possible and immediate, and through which the Head of Stated and his subordinates violated:

> "(i) the freedom of thought and expression guaranteed by article 57 of the Constitution of the Bolivarian Republic of Venezuela (...) and article 13 of the American Convention on Human Rights (...) (ii) the right to due process, expressed in the right to the presumption of innocence, the right to the defense and the right to be heard by an impartial authority, guaranteed by article 49 of the Constitution and article 8(2) of the American Convention, and (iii) the right to equality and to non-discrimination, guaranteed by article 21 of the Constitution and articles 1, 2 and 5 of the Organic Law of Amparo on Rights and Constitutional Guaranties" (...)".

The Constitutional Chamber, through decision N° 920 (File: 07-0197) of 05-17-2007, declared the action inadmissible, refusing to consider the case, arguing that in matters of telecommunications, the National Telecommunications Commission (CONATEL) was the only competent entity to decide regarding the possible legal situation of the concession of RCTV, as for the use and exploitation of a public domain asset like the radio electric spectrum. Based on this the Chamber considered that the amparo action resulted "inadmissible, inasmuch that the damage is not immediate, possible and feasible by the President of the Bolivarian Republic of Venezuela, Hugo Rafael Chávez Frías, regarding the pretention addressed against his persona as supposed offender". Here, the Chamber incurred in its first error of crass ignorance about the dispositions of the Organic Law of Telecommunications, according to which, in matters of permits and television concessions, the competency corresponds expressly to the Minister of Telecommunications.

Once reduced the action of amparo, by decision of the Chamber, only against the Minister and President of CONATEL, it referred to two administrative acts issued

by the Minister on March 28, 2007 after the amparo action was filed (Resolution N°
002 and Official Letter N° 424), through which the petition filed by *Radio Caracas
Televisión RCTV, C. A.*, on January 24, 2007, had been answered, as for the transformation and renovation of the concession. In the last of said administrative acts,
the Minister decided ("*resolvió*") that:

> "the following communication is merely declarative, that is to say, it does not create,
> modifies or extinguish the legal situation regarding the concession of RCTV which expires on
> May 27, 2007; at 12 pm., legal time of Venezuela; for the length of time established in article
> 1 of the Decree N° 1.577 containing the Regulations about Concessions for Television and
> Radio Stations, which includes the accessory frequencies granted nationally for the exploita-
> tion of the concession that is about to expire".

For the Constitutional Chamber, this administrative act mean that "the circumstance originating the alleged constitutional infraction in this case had ceased", since
according to article 6.1 of the Organic Law of Amparo, "for an amparo action to
admissible, it is necessary for the reported damage to be sctual, that is to say, current", concluding then that since:

> "the fact reported as detrimental is constituted by a presumed omission assigned to the
> Minister of the Popular Power for the Telecommunications and Information Technology,
> however, during the procedure of the amparo process, the alleged offender produced the omit-
> ted response, which was why, from the moment in which the administrative act had been is-
> sued solving the request, the damage reported by the complainants ceased."

Consequently, the Chamber resolved, in this case, that the inadmissibility cause
foreseen in article 6.1 of the Organic Law of Amparo had occurred "for having
ceased the alleged constitutional infraction that had been reported". That way, the
Chamber was deliberately refusing to protect the constitutional rights that had been
violated.

However, the trial did not conclude there as was the procedural logic, implying
the archive of the files. On the contrary, after declaring the action inadmissible, the
Constitutional Chamber proceeded to formulate considerations that no party had
requested, stating that in the Resolution N° 002 of the Minister of Popular Power for
Telecommunications and Information Technology on March 28, 2007; it was decided to:

> "Declare terminated the administrative proceeding initiated according to the request made
> by Radio Caracas Televisión, on May 6, 2002; regarding the transformation of its concession,
> due to the absence of the object of said request. Consequently, said concession will remain in
> force until its expiration on May 27, 2007; in application of what is stated in article 1 of the
> Decree N° 1.577 containing the Regulations about Concessions for Television and Radio Sta-
> tions".

For that reason, on its own initiative, the Constitutional Chamber decided to inform the claimants that the adequate way to request for the protection for their constitutional rights against administrative acts, was through the contentious administrative (judicial review) actions, which in this case of RCTV, as imagined, they already
had filed before the Politico Administrative Chamber of the Supreme Tribunal on
April 17, 2007, together with an amparo petition, requesting it to declare the nullity
of the administrative acts contained in the Official Letter N° 424 and in the Resolu-

tion Nº 002 of the Minister of Popular Power for Telecommunications and Information Technology on March 28, 2007. For such reason, the Constitutional Chamber concluded that the inadmissibility clause foreseen in article 6.5 of the Organic Law of Amparo was also applicable in the case against RCTV. Regarding all other plaintiffs they were informed that they could "participate in said judicial review trial in order to protect their rights and interests".

This way, in an amparo proceeding filed on February 9, 2007, the Constitutional Chamber only came to the decision over its admissibility on May 17, 2007; that is to say, three months later, being its deliberated inaction what would provoke the inadmissibility clause of the amparo action to take place. If it had been decided in time, as it was imposed by the Constitution and the claimed rights, there would not been grounds to declare it inadmissible.

In any case, by declaring inadmissible the action filed against the violation threat to the freedom of expression, and the effective damage to the right to due process and the defense; because it had been already decided not to renew the concession, without any previous procedure; the constitutional judge, after illegitimately conspire in order to provoke the appearance of an inadmissibility clause, refused to protect the freedom of plural expression in Venezuela.

III. ON HOW THE POLITICO ADMINISTRATIVE CHAMBER OF THE SUPREME TRIBUNAL ALSO DELIBERATELY REFUSED TO PROTECT IN A PRECAUTIONARY WAY THE FREEDOM OF EXPRESSION AND OTHER CONSTITUTIONAL RIGHTS OPENLY VIOLATED BY CONATEL

On April 17, 2007, as mentioned in the Constitutional Chamber decision, RCTV, its directives, reporters and workers, had indeed filed a nullity action together with an amparo petition (precautionary) against the aforementioned administrative acts contained in Resolution Nº 002 and Official Letter Nº 0424, both dated 03/28/07 of the Ministry of Popular Power for Telecommunications and Information Technology, through which it had been decided to declare the absence of object in the request made by RCTV in the year 2002, for the transformation of it concession title granted to according to the prior legislation, in the authorization and concession according to article 210 of the new Organic Law, as well as the absence of object of the requests filed by RCTV on January 24, 2007, for the extension of the concession to render the service of open signal television until the year 2027.

Through decision Nº 00763 (File: 2007-0411) dated 05-23-2007 the Politico Administrative Chamber "in a provisional way" admitted the nullity action in order to decide on the precautionary amparo also requested, which was denied. In this way the Political Administrative Chamber also refused, deliberately, to protect the constitutional rights that had been reported as violated, which were the freedom of thought and expression, established in article 57 of the Constitution and in article 13 of the American Convention on Human Rights; due to the fact that with the challenged decisions, the petitioners were not able to freely broadcast ideas, opinions, information, entertaining content, publicity and propaganda through the frequencies assigned to RCTV throughout the country. They also had alleged the violation of Declaration of Principles about Freedom of Expression adopted by the Inter-American

Commission on Human Rights; and also, of the due process rights, as well as private property rights and economic freedom.

This amparo protection request had the purpose for the Political Administrative Chamber to order the Minister to abstain "from taking any kind of measure that would impede RCTV from operating as an open signal television station (VHF) in the frequencies in which it had been operating throughout the country" pending the adoption of the final judicial decision, and to take "all the necessary measures for RCTV to continue operating as an open signal television station (VHF) in the frequencies in which it had been operating throughout the country while the definite judicial decision was issued regarding this nullifying action."

Regarding these requests, the Political Administrative Chamber simply decided as follows:

On the matter of the alleged violation of the right to free expression of thought, the Chamber concluded that it is only "while the concession lasts" that:

> "the petitioners would be able to exercise the right to the freedom of thought and expression using the radio electric frequency assigned to RCTV, C. A. under the legal title derived from the concession; which in no way implies an alleged violation to said right, due to the fact that the claimants would be able to express their ideas, opinions and information within the diversity of the media."

The Chamber also added, with all simplicity and in a way hard to believe, that RCTV "has, as all other content generators, the freedom to continue to exercise said right through many other forms of broadcasting, like the operators of subscription television services (cable)."

And, regarding the violation of this right in its social scope, that is, the right of all society members to receive ideas, information and opinions, the Chamber rejected ir, by saying that:

> "by means of the challenged administrative acts nothing prevented, in any way, for the Venezuelan society to receive ideas, opinions, information, entertainment content, publicity and propaganda, taking into account the existence of many other privately owned television channels and media – which represent the majority of the ones existing in the country – through which such contents are transmitted, within the context of a democratic and social Rule of Law and of justice. Because such reason the alleged violation on this matter must be rejected. So is declared."

As for the violation of due process rights, regarding the argument that by issuing the challenged acts, "both the Minister as well as other high-ranking officials of the National Executive, had publicly announced, prior to that issuing, the rejection of the requested "extension and renewal" of the concession of RCTV"; the Chamber limited it self, in a simplistic way, to consider that in order to:

> "evidence the alleged violation to being heard by an impartial authority, it would be necessary to perform a detailed study of the challenged administrative acts, as well as of the actions of the aforementioned authorities, and to compare them with the arguments expressed by the plaintiffs and the provisions they refer to; which could only be done in the opportunity of the definite decision on the case, since it is prohibited for the amparo precautionary Judge to decide on matters of legality."

As for the violation of the right to the defense, by the refusal of the Minister for Telecommunications and Information Technology produce the report requested by RCTV, and to allow it access to the administrative files as requested on January 24, 2007; the Chamber simply limited it self to consider that:

> "A decision regarding the alleged violation of the right to the defense in this case would implicate the examination of the Notification N° 0424 in light of the arguments expressed by the plaintiff and the applicable legal provisions, which would be verified in the occasion of the definite decision; thus, the claim is ruled out."

And regarding the mentioned request made by RCTV on January 24, 2007; in which it had asked the Minister to complete the transformation process and to issue the new titles of the TV station, that is to say, the concession for the use and exploitation of the radio electric spectrum and the corresponding administrative permit; and the recognition of its acquired right to the extension of the titles of RCTV for an additional period of twenty (20) years; the Chamber simply limited it self to decide that what RCTV intended:

> "would involve the realization of a study of the legal regulation applicable to the case, referred by the company in its request, in order to determine if, in fact, it was necessary to initiate an administrative procedure to handle the request issued on January 24, 2007; which would be decided in the opportunity of the definite decision, reason for which the alleged violation of the right to the defense must be rejected."

As for the complaint of violation of the right to the presumption of innocence, because what was expressed in the declarations made by Executive authorities, as well as in the challenged administrative acts, constituted a sanction for the supposed infringement to the Penal Code, the Organic Law of Telecommunications, the Law of Social Responsibility in Radio and Television and other legal dispositions, without the facts being demonstrated in any way; the Chamber limited itself, in a simplistic way, to state that it was unable to find, in the challenged acts, "any kind of statement given by the Administration, in which it was evident that the content of the referred acts involved a sanction to the petitioning company for non compliance to legal provisions", declaring that "the alleged violation of the presumption of innocence of the plaintiff has not been demonstrated."

Regarding the violation of the right to equality and non-discrimination, because according to petitioners, RCTV had been treated "unequally in comparison to other operators in identical situations and which have been given a different and more beneficial treatment"; the Chamber limited itself, simply, to state that from the proofs filed in the record, such affirmation could not be appreciated, and that the petitioners had not demonstrated "the condition of equality of circumstances and of discrimination it says to have regarding the rest of the operators; for that reason, the plead regarding the alleged violation of the right to equality and non-discrimination is rejected."

Regarding the alleged violation to the guaranty of the non-retroactive of the law, by ignoring the preferential right of RCTV for the twenty year extension of its open-signal television concession in VHF, given that the Law had to be applied respecting and recognizing the rights acquired by the operators under the prior regime; the Chamber limited itself also, simply, to state that in order to determine said violation of the principle of non-retroactive, it was necessary to examine the content of the Decree N° 1.577 in light of the current Organic Law of Telecommunications, and other dispositions of inferior rank than the legal text", which "does not correspond to be examined in this stage of the process."

As for the alleged violation of the right to property and non-confiscation, by virtue of the fact that with the refusal to transform the titles granted according to the legislation prior to the Organic Law of Telecommunications, as well as the refusal to extend or renew the concession under the argument that the State was going to reserve to itself the exploitation and use of the frequency used by RCTV; the rights of RCTV to continue operating in said frequency were ignored, as well as the economical benefits said activity resulted in; the Chamber limit itself, also in a simplistic way, to advise that the radio electric spectrum is a limited telecommunications resource, and an asset of public domain inalienable and imprescriptible, held by the Republic:

> "which enforces over said asset the characteristic attributes of said ownership; that is to say, its use, enjoyment and administration according to the Law; reason for which this Chamber considers the violation claim of the right to property to be groundless."

And regarding the infringement of property rights over other goods used for the exploitation of the concession, different from the radio electric spectrum, the Chamber also in an unusually simplistic way, limited itself to comment:

> "that the expiration of the concession as a mechanism of natural extinction of itself, with a duration period know by the concessionaire beforehand, cannot be understood has a supposed damage to the right to property over said goods; for this reason, said argument is rejected."

On the other hand, the Chamber observed that in this case "even though the matter was the possible expiration of a concession, the usual figure of the reversion of the assets affected to the concession in benefit of the grantor had not been evoked to date." That is to say, the Chamber used a judicial decision in order to send a "message" to the Executive regarding something that, until that moment, "had not been evoked", particularly since it did not proceeded.

As for the allegation of the plaintiff that the loss of certain economic benefits (claim for damages for loss of profit and the recuperation of the investment) that would affect it if the disputed acts were executed, the Chamber simply limited itself to state that:

> "The determination of said loss necessarily involves the analysis of the existence or not of a preferential right in favor of the plaintiff company to obtain the extension or renewal of the concession from May 28, 2007 on, after the concession granted expires. For that reason the Chamber cannot, during this precautionary stage, issue any type of decision based on a pretended right that constitutes part of what must be resolved in the definite decision; being the allegation on this matter rejected."

Regarding the alleged violation of the right to economic freedom, because the execution of the challenged administrative decisions would prevent RCTV to exercise the activity it had been developing, without the existence of any non compliance of legal obligations and without any legal provision that could justify said decisions; the Chamber, after analyzing the public domain character of the radio electric spectrum, limited itself, also in an unusually simplistic way, to state that the arguments regarding the availability of the frequency used by the company:

> "are subjected to the proofs to be filed during the nullity process, for that reason its allegation cannot be considered during this stage of the process in order to evidence the supposed violation of the right to economic freedom. So is declared."

On the allegation of the fact that the administrative authority had the obligation to respect the object, coverage and duration period of the concession granted under the legal regulation prior to the Organic Law of Telecommunications, and therefore to transform the titles of RCTV; the Chamber, also with astonishing simplicity, limited itself to say:

> "From the proofs filed before the court one cannot deduce that the circumstance of the non-transformation of the aforementioned titles had prevented the plaintiff to continue to operate the radio electric frequency until the date of the expiration of the concession, which was expressly recognized by the challenged Resolution N° 002. So is declared."

And as for the claim made regarding that the Administration had to respect RCTV's right to the twenty (20) year extension of the concession, based on article 3 of the Decree N° 1.577, the Chamber, simply, limited itself to say that:

> "Such argument necessarily requires a decision on the legal provisions applicable to the case, which – as it had been mentioned – is prohibited to the judge of the cause during this precautionary stage, which is limited to the protection of the constitutional rights."

As consequence of all the aforementioned, the Political Administrative Chamber concluded that in the case subjected to its decision, the presumption of proper right needed in order to grant the precautionary protection was not verified. Consequently, without verifying the fulfillment of neither the *periculum in mora* nor the *fumus boni iuris*, the Chamber, simply rejected the amparo action filed together with the nullity contentious administrative recourse against the challenged administrative acts.

In any case, it is clear that an Executive order in this Case had already been given, which can be confirmed by the simplicity of the arguments used in the Chamber's decision, in fact confirming its submission to the Executive willing.

IV. ON HOW THE JUDICIAL REVIEW OF ADMINISTRATIVE ACTION JURISDICTION (CONTENTIOUS ADMINISTRATIVE), INSTEAD OF PROTECTING THE PEOPLES' RIGHTS, PRETENDED TO SUBSTITUTE THE ADMINISTRATION AND PRETENDED EX-OFFICIO TO COVER ITS ARGUMENTATIVE DEFICIENCIES.

After rejecting in the Case to grant any precautionary amparo protection regarding constitutional rights as requested conjunctly with the nullity action against the challenged administrative acts of CONATEL, the Politico Administrative Chamber of the Supreme Tribunal, in the same decision of rejection N° 00763 of May 23, 2007, continued to formulate, ex-officio, theoretical considerations about the concessions regime in matters of telecommunications, pretending thus to substitute what it probably perceived as argumentative deficiencies of the administrative authorities.

This way, the contentious administrative judge pretended to turn itself into the Administration, incurring in a judicial illegitimacy.

In fact, on the aforementioned decision, the Political Administrative Chamber issued an *"orbiter dictum"* ("something said by the way"), in which the Chamber stated that "the *concession* is a contractual form used by the Administration for the management of the *public services*, which involves a delegation made by the State to another person at its own risk for the operation of said services for a previously established period of time"; regarding which "certain elements stand out, like those of temporality, exact delimitation and economic benefits for the concessionaire for the use and exploitation of the public asset granted to the individual through the concession", adding that "once the life of the concession expires, the extinction of the relation is produced *ipso jure* and, usually, the reversion of assets affected to the concession".

The Chamber concluded stating that:

> "The limit of the right to freedom of thought and expression of RCTV, C. A. by means of the use of the radio electric frequency assigned to it, has at its limits, the duration of the concession; for which in no way there has been a violation of the referred constitutional right. RCTV, C. A. can continue to express its ideas, opinions or information and other contents by means of many other means of communication available to individuals according to the Venezuelan legal order."

With this said "by the way," the Supreme Tribunal adopted two ex-officio initiatives about issues that had not been nor was the object of judicial debate, providing beforehand its opinion regarding the substance of the trial. Once again, the contentious administrative judge pretended to lead the Administration and supply it, its deficiencies.

1.   *The issue of the public service and the telecommunications*

In fact, first, the Chamber in its *obiter dictum*, qualified the concession of use of the radio electric space for the transmission of television as a "concession of public service", which is legally incorrect. It is true that historically, telecommunication activities had been considered in many countries, and in different times, as public service activities; which, during many decades, were even regulated as activities reserved to the State, and that, in many cases, individuals could render by means of the public service concession regime granted by the State.

All of this, however, changed in the contemporary world, in which today prevails the criteria that an even when an activity is declared as public service, not always implies a reserve of said activity in favor of the State; thus existing, on the one hand, public services reserved to the State, and public services not reserved to it; with the opportunity for individuals to render the first type, by means of concession regime, and the second type to be rendered in a concurrence regime and regarding which individuals have the right and the economic freedom to perform them.

On the other hand, the reserve to the State of the telecommunication activities, because their complexity and increasing development, was eliminated as well, and these are now considered activities, regarding which, individuals have the right and economic freedom to perform; subjected to restrictions and limitations characteristic of their consideration as activities of general interest. This is the regime precisely established in the Organic Law of Telecommunications, in accordance with which telecommunication activities are not activities reserved to the State; for this reason, even if they could be qualified as "public services", they would be concurrent public services relating to which individuals have the right and economic freedom to perform, subjected to the limitations and restrictions established in the Organic Law, particularly as for the obtainment of an authorization or permits from the State through CONATEL.

Regarding these activities, therefore "a concession of public service" does not exist, since these are not reserved to the State, and are rendered by means of authorization or permits; and only in the cases in which it is necessary to use public domain assets (like the radio electric spectrum) in order to perform them, what is needed is a "concession for the use of the radio electric spectrum", that is to say, a concession regarding an *asset* of public domain, just as it is regulated in the Organic Law of Telecommunications. Therefore, it is a legal mistake of the Politico Administrative Chamber of the Supreme Tribunal to consider the concession held by RCTV as a "concession of public service". The contentious administrative judge illegitimately pretended to substitute the Administration, and was legally mistaken.

2.   *The issue of the reversion in concessions*

But the legal mistake made by the contentious administrative judge in its ex-officio decision, did not only end in the erroneous qualification of the concession for television transmissions, as a "concession of public services", contrary to the liberal regime of the 2000 Organic Law of Telecommunication, but also in referring regarding this case, illegitimately and erroneously way to the institution of the reversion in the concessions.

In fact, in its *obiter dictum* the Political Administrative Chamber, ex-officio and without any judicial debate, referred to the fact that once the term of the concession of public service has expired "the extinction of the relation is produced ipso jure", adding that "usually, the reversion of the assets affected to the concession" was produced as well.

With this, the contentious administrative judge pretended also to substitute the Administration, supplying arguments that supposedly considered that the Administration had not wielded during the case in the administrative procedure; with which incurred in a new illegitimacy, and in another legal error, since contrarily to what it indicates, once the telecommunication concessions, or of any other activity, are extinguished, the reversion does not "usually" operates, but only when it is expressly established in a statute or in the text of the concession.

It is true that one of the more classical principles of administrative law regarding concessions for public services, construction of public works and use of public works, even considered as public domain, had always been that of the necessary reversion of the service or of the constructed work to the Administration once the concession had extinguished. It was about a principle seeking to ensure continuity in the rendering of the public service or the use of a public work, once the concession was extinguished, independently of the concessionaire's participation.

However, for being a way for the extinction of the concessionaire's private property over the assets affected to service or of the constructed works, the constitutional guaranty of the property and of the need of a statute to restrict it, progressively imposed the principle stating that the reversion had to be established expressly in a legal text. Even, in that sense, was that the 1961 Constitution established the principle of the reversion in matters of concession for hydrocarbons, relating to the lands (real state) affected to them.

Thus, in the absence of an expressed legal text, the reversion could only proceed if it is regulated and disposed in the concession contract. The reversion, in fact, lost its old character of "essential element" of every concession and became an element of the relation that only operates in case of expressed pact.

This is, otherwise, the orientation followed in the Organic Law about the Promotion of the Private Investment under the Concession's regime (*Official Gazette* N° 5394 Extra. dated 10-25-1999), by providing in article 48 relating to the "reversion of works and services," that is the respective contract which must establish, among other elements, "the assets that, for being affected to the work or the service in question, will revert to the granting entity, unless these could not be completely redeemed during the mentioned period of time". To that effect, the provision also states that during a prudential period of time, prior to the termination of the contract, the granting entity must adopt the means leading to verify the delivery of the reverted assets in the *conditions agreed on* in the contract. The same provision establishes that the contract must express "the works, facilities or assets that the concessionaire must develop *not subjected* to reversion, which, if considered to be of use or public interest, could be subjected to reversion after the payment of their price to the concessionaire."

Consequently, if there is no legal provision establishing the reversion of the assets in concessions of public services, public works or of the use of the public domain, or if said reversion is not foreseen in the concession contract; once the concession is terminated, the concessionaire is not obliged to revert to the Administration, any asset that had been constructed or that had been affected to the concession, nor the Administration can pretend to appropriate or take possession of these. It can only do it by means of the expropriation, according to the Constitution and the Law. Otherwise, it would mean a confiscation, prohibited in the Constitution.

In the case of RCTV's concession for the use of the radio electric public domain, nothing had been provided; so, suggesting, as it was done by the contentious administrative judge, that the reversion "usually" took place in concession, when deciding the particular Case of the concession held by RCTV; constituted in an incitement to the confiscation of assets, that the Administration did not even mention, but would be later executed by the Constitutional Chamber of the Supreme Tribunal, precisely because no one can control its decisions.

3.   *On how the contentious administrative judge, with impunity, resolved the substance of the Case by declaring inadmissible a precautionary measure*

Lastly, the Political Administrative Chamber of the Supreme Tribunal, in its "obiter dictum" openly and with impunity provided opinion about the substance of the matter regarding the alleged nullity for the violation of the right to freedom of thought and expression of RCTV; by indicating regarding RCTV that "in no way exists in its case the violation of the aforementioned constitutional right".

In fact, in it's "be the way" saying, **ex-officio**, the Supreme Tribunal added the following:

> "The Chamber highlights that the right to freedom of thought and expression of RCTV, C. A. by means of the use of the radio electric frequency assigned to it, has as its limits the duration of the concession, for which in no way, in its case exists the violation of the referred constitutional right. RCTV, C. A. can continue to express its ideas, opinions or information and other contents by means of many other communication media available to individuals, in agreement with the Venezuelan judicial ordinance."

The trial held before the Political Administrative Chamber, where the decision refusing the requested precautionary measure was adopted, precisely has the purpose of determining the right RCTV had to continue operating the television channel and to establish its right to the freedom of expression of thought, for which were challenged the administrative acts in which was decided, first, not to continue with the transformation process of the concession of RCTV to continue to operate, and second, not to renew the right of RCTV to continue operating after May 28, 2007, by means of its adaptation and/or renewal..

On this matter, the contentious administrative judge, in its decision, ex-officio and without judicial debate, incidentally, simply stated that the concession of RCTV expired at the termination of the concession; that is to say, it had "the duration of the concession, as limit" which was until May 27, 2007; and decided once and for all, that "in no way, exists in its case the violation of the referred constitutional right; and that RCTV" supposedly, without concession, could "continue to express its ideas, opinions or information and other contents by means of many other communication media available to individuals, in agreement with the Venezuelan judicial ordinance".

With this decision adopted "by the way" and ex-officio, the Political Administrative Chamber in an unusual way and against all principles of due process, end the trial, without definitely deciding it.

On the other hand, with this judicial decision, the contentious administrative judge converted in a de fact *amicus curiae* of the Administration, cleared the path required by the Executive to not to renew the concession to which RCTV had the right to, and set the criteria, which until that moment had not been raised, like those relating to the reversion of assets in this type of concessions.

V. ON HOW THE CONSTITUTIONAL JUDGE, IN ITS SUPPOSED PROTECTION OF DIFFUSED INTERESTS IN CONFLICT, RESOLVED ALSO EX-OFFICIO, TO CONFISCATE THE ASSETS OF RCTV AND TO ASSIGN THEM IN FREE USE, *SINE DIE*, TO A STATE OWN ENTITY

Aside from the actions exercised by RCTV, its directives, reporters and workers, in May of 2007 a series of other actions were also exercised by groups of telecommunication users against the President of the Republic and of the Minister of Telecommunications. One of these actions, seek to assure the continuity of the signal transmissions in the channel assigned to RCTV, and that this company be the one to continue with the transmission of the signal. The other action, seek to assure that the new state entity to be created to substitute RCTV, Fundación TEVES, needed to assure the transmision of the new signal, with national coverage.

1. *The action attempted to assure that the new state entity could begin to transmit the signal of Channel 2, with national coverage, after May 27, 2007*

On May 22, 2007, in fact, several telecommunication User's Committees acting on behalf of their collective interests and of the rights and diffused interests of the Venezuelan people, filed before the Constitutional Chamber of the Supreme Tribunal a constitutional amparo action "for the protection of the fundamental right to legitimate expectation, of the fundamental right to the non-discrimination, and of the fundamental right to obtain a public service television of quality," adding petitions for precautionary measures, against the Ministry of Popular Power for Telecommunications and Information Technology, the Ministry of Popular Power for the Communication and the Information, and the *Fundación Televisora Venezolana Social* (TEVES).

The basic argument of the plaintiffs in this amparo action was that according to the announcements of the Minister of Telecommunications, the new television station substituting RCTV, at the beginning of its operations, was only going to be seen in the central-western region of the country, which was considered to be "express proof that the National Executive has not taken all the necessary measures... to ensure all citizens the enjoyment, nationally, of the transmissions of the new public service television station, from May 28, 2007." The petitioners considered that this was a violation of the constitutional rights to the legitimate expectation, to the non-discrimination and to obtaining a public service television of quality, supposedly guaranteed by articles 22, 19, 108 and 117 of the Constitution, stating that "Our expectative is (...) to enjoy, we insist for being a right, of a service of public service television (sic) of quality, as in fact it was offered to the Venezuelan people by the National Executive (...)". They alleged, also, that the announcement of the fact that the national transmission of the signal of the new channel, would be done through a cable television system, implied a *"clear discrimination facing the universal access to said service"*.

In their protection claim, the petitioners requested, as unnamed precautionary measures, to allow:

> "temporary access, to the Fundación Televisora Venezolana Social (TEVES), for the use and operation of the platform, formed by transmitters, antennas and repeater towers located in different places throughout the country, which have been used by the company Radio Caracas Televisión RCTV, C. A.; for the use and exploitation of the portion of the radio electric spectrum under the concession expiring next May 27, 2007; independently from its owners or possessors" and that "(...) RCTV (...) is ordered to allow the Fundación Televisora Venezolana Social (TEVES) access, use ad operation of the transmission and repetition platform to facilitate (...), that the transmissions of the new (...) television, cover the entire country, in virtue of the fact that said equipment and infrastructure, both legal and technologically, can only be used under the frequency of the channel 2 (...)".

However, it was evident that in order to assure the continuance of the transmission of the television signal in this case, it was not necessary to assign the use of the assets that belonged to RCTV to a State owned entity; on the contrary, as it was pointed out by Judge Pedro Rafael Rondón Haaz in his dissenting vote to the decision N° 956 (File: 07-0720) of May 27, 2007 of the Constitutional Chamber, to assure that with the continuity of the transmissions:

> "it would have been much more efficient if, as precautionary measure, the current operator of the radio electric spectrum had been allowed to the provisional continuance of its activities until the final decision for this process – or for any others in which such measure had been expressly requested – because it is evident that it would be much easier if RCTV simply continued in the execution of its usual activities, than the occupation of its property by a third party who has to start from scratch. That way, if the diffused right, whose protection is intended, is that of the enjoyment of the open signal currently transmitted by RCTV "throughout the country, under quality conditions, in the same terms [in] which it had been rendered", the congruent measure –which would have satisfied the immanent instrumental character to every precautionary measure- would have been the one explained supra and not the one decided."

As mentioned, the Constitutional Chamber, by means of decision N° 956 of May 27, 2007; by declaring inadmissible the amparo action filed against the Ministry of Popular Power for the Telecommunications and Information Technology, and the Fundación Televisora Venezolana Social (TEVES), resolved the requested precautionary measure by deciding, neither more nor less, on the confiscation of the private property of RCTV, company which was not a party to the process, and to which, in violation of its rights to due process and defense, no only was not summoned, nor heard, but it was not even allowed to become party to the trial by itself.

The constitutional judge was extremely careful in establish the rules of procedure to be follow, giving the plaintiffs five (5) working days to produce proofs (article 862 Civil Procedure Code), ordering the notification of the Director of CONATEL and the President of the Institute for the Defense and Protection of the Consumer and the User (INDECU), due to the fact that "in this case, there is a group of defending parties, and given the *erga omnes* effects that the decision could have if it was declared applicable". The Chamber ordered, as well, the publication of "a public notice in one of the major newspapers of national circulation, summoning all interested parties who wanted to help or oppose the claims, or in defense of their own rights or interests", but with the expressed warning that "everyone participating could only, in equal terms, allege reasons that *support the positions of those* being helped"; and that "the adjuvant with the parties, being an action of diffused interests, could only promote proofs relating to the allegations of the parties being helped." That is to say, before deciding to strip RCTV from its assets, the Chamber had resolved that said company could not allege or proof or defend itself, but could only support the positions of the plaintiffs or of the defendants.

Judge Pedro Rafael Rondón Haaz expressed his opinion in his dissenting vote, warning that the decision said nothing:

> "About the absence of RCTV, within the defendants; being the one that it intended to be order to allow TEVES the use of its equipment and facilities, without being even brought to trial for the legitimate defense of its rights, evidently, to property among others. Thus, the

company must have been summoned to trial as defendant, because a determined conduct is expected from it, or that it be condemned in the decision."

Concluding its dissenting vote by stating that:

"Consequently, the requested precautionary measure had to be denied by the Chamber because it was not the proper measure to assure its purpose, and because it implied the take over of all the assets of a third party indispensible for the execution of its own economic activities, who has been absent from the litigation, without limits, without procedure and without any kind of compensation and without even being summoned to trial."

2. The confiscation of the assets of RCTV due to the conceptual confusion of the constitutional judge about what a "universal telecommunications service is"

But after establishing the procedural terms described, the Constitutional Chamber moved on to decide the precautionary measure, arguing that article 27 of the Constitution "grants the constitutional judge the authority to immediately reestablish the infringed juridical situation or the situation that most resembles it"; observing, also, that in certain occasions, the object of the constitutional protection requires of expedite protection, for which the precautionary measures are precisely set up within judicial procedures.

The Chamber also expressed, that the constitutional judge has ample inquisitive powers in order to maintain constitutional public order; powers that "are not limited to the qualification of a determined pretention, but to the possibility of issuing measures, even ex-officio, in order to assure the constitutional rights, violated or threaten of violation ...", and not only "founded on the law, considering what was alleged and proved in the court, but also in criteria of justice and reason that would assure the effective custody of whom had demonstrated its legitimate pretention in the matter to be solved".

The Chamber went on to balance the interests involved necessary to justify a precautionary measure, in particular, "the general interests involved in the specific situation regarding the individual interests, in order to avoid affecting the totality of the supreme public interests under custody". This lead the Chamber, in this case, to make said consideration of interests according to the particular characteristics of an activity like the telecommunications, "subjected to a public law statutory regime – Organic Law of Telecommunications -, ruled by the constitutional principles established in articles 108 and 117 of the Constitution'.

Now then, the first of said articles establishes the obligation of the State to assure "public services of radio, television and library and information technology networks, in order to allow the universal access to information". According to the Chamber, the development of the aforementioned constitutional principles by the Organic Law of Telecommunications, precisely has "the objective to establish the legal framework of the general regulation of the telecommunications in order to assure the human right of the people to communication and the the development of economic activities of telecommunications necessary to achieve it, without any other limitations than those derived from the Constitution and the laws" (art. 1), emphasizing among the objectives of the Organic Law to "make possible the effective, efficient and peaceful use of the limited resources of telecommunications, like the numeration and the radio electric spectrum, as well as the proper protection of the latter" (art. 2.7); and to "incorporate and assure the fulfillment of the obligations of Universal Service, quality and goals of uniform minimal coverage, and those obligations relating to safety and defense in matters of telecommunications" (art. 2.8).

From these provisions, the Chamber deduced that the State is supposedly obligated to "seek for the effective satisfaction of the universal service of telecommunications and to assure a service of quality, to the users and consumers, in ideal conditions and of respect for the constitutional rights of all the parties involved, since communication media are a medium of reach and influence in different aspects of society, and can affect both its quality of life as well as in particular rights"; adding that said obligation does not result only in "the simple ability to grant a concession for the use of the radio electric space", but "in assuring, in situations of need, a determined communication media or to several media, legal or factual mechanisms of structural facilitation that would allow its operation in an efficient and proper manner for the rendering of the public service"; considering that "the State" can " in virtue of it, make use of those mechanisms established in the legal order to maintain, in any given time, the operational activity of such service".

Then, the Chamber went on to consider what was disposed in article 49 of the Organic Law of Telecommunications, which establishes a State obligation to assure the effective protection of the *universal service of the telecommunications*, in the following terms:

"The States assures the rendering of the Universal Service of the Telecommunications. The Universal Service of the Telecommunications is the defined group of telecommunication services that operators are obliged to render to the users in order to offer minimal standards of penetration, access, quality and economic accessibility independently from the geographic location.

The objective of the Universal Service is the satisfaction of purpose of national integration, maximization of access to the information, educational development and of health service and reduction of the access disparities of the people to the services of telecommunications".

From this norm, which without a doubt, refers to the telephony, the Chamber deduced a "duty of the State to assure the universal service of telecommunications –vgr. open signal transmissions in VHF frequency–" which in this case, the Chamber thought it implied "the maintenance of an operational structure sufficient and appropriate that would allow an efficient 'penetration, access and accessibility', in the development of the activity."

It is necessary to pause here for an instant: the Constitutional Chamber, incomprehensibly, or deliberately, confused everything in matters of telecommunications, and from a provision that is directed to assure the universal telephony service, it deduced a supposed "universal television service". The provision mentioned by the Chamber, that is to say, article 49 of the Organic Law, is copy of article 37.1 of the Spanish General Law of Telecommunications, which is, at the same time, copy of the European Union Guidelines in the matter, and only refers to telephony services. The purpose of the provision is to always assure the basic telephone service (universal) in the permits for telephony services, that is to say, the transmission of voice, fax and low speed data with voice quality; which is the one that must be accessible to all, independently to its place of residence and purchasing power, and which has to contain prefixed facilities and quality.

By applying a provision that regulates telephony services to television (remember that even in Spain, television is not regulated in the General Law), the Constitutional Chamber came to a distorted and altered conclusions, among which there is the fact that "the current reach and quality of the signal maintained by the operator of said service in exercise of the functions and duties of a television operator, according to the respective concession" had to be assured to the new operator of the television channel possessed by RCTV.

From there, the Chamber arbitrarily deduced that it could happen that:

> "the Administration can temporarily use the assets affected to the rendering of the afore-mentioned service, in behalf of maintaining the safekeeping of the rights of all the users to the rendering of a public service in quality conditions, since, due to the mandatory character in the rendering of said service, the State cannot allow the ceasing of operations in the rendering of the service (vgr. Health, water and electricity services)."

Then, the Chamber concluded in the terms of the plaintiffs, quoting declarations given by executive authorities, in the sense that:

> "the possible transmission that the Fundación Televisora Venezolana Social (TEVES) will execute, as consequence of the permit issued by CONATEL, for sonic broadcasting and open signal television, with attributes of open signal television in VHF –, due to the knowledge this Chamber has because being public, notorious and "communicational" hacts, will not have the necessary infrastructure for the transmission throughout the country (national), under conditions of quality, in the same terms in which it had been rendered."

Based then on these premises, given that in this case the reversion was not possible, and the Executive has not decided on such matter, in order to assure the purpose set by the constitutional judge, and since there was no way to take over the assets of RCTV, the Chamber proceeded to confiscate them, assigning their use, *sine die*, and free of charge to CONATEL, for which the Chamber decided:

> "temporarily and in order to guard the continuity in the rendering of a universal public service, the use of the frequency that had been assigned for open signal television in the transportation and television broadcasting network that includes, among others, microwaves, teleports, transmitters, television ancillary equipments, power and weather ancillary equipment, towers, antennas, transmission booths, plant booths, perimeter fence and service wires; without it implying to affect property rights that could correspond to Radio Caracas Televisión, C. A., over said infrastructure or equipment, except for those which are legally or conventionally property of the Republic..."

As it was said, this precautionary measure constitutes a confiscation of the assets of RCTV, because it strips said company, without any judgment regarding its property rights, and without time limit. As it was well said by Judge Pedro Rafael Rondón Haaz, in his dissenting vote to the decision, with the precautionary measure, the Chamber:

"Assigned" to CONATEL "the right to use" the equipment property of RCTV – sort of expropriation or, at least, of previous occupation with absolute lack of the applicable procedure – in order to assign its use "to the operator disposed to such effect".

According to the dissenting Judge, this

"Implies the subtraction of an attribute of the right to property (the use) of Radio Caracas Televisión RCTV C. A. regarding the assets that were affected, without any legal foundation whatsoever, which is the only source of resttriction to the private property, always with the foundations provided by the National Constitution."

To that effect, the constitutional judge, substituted the Administration, went on to list all the places of the national territory where the equipment was located, appreciating in substitution of the Legislator, that "the right to use" of the equipment unofficially assigned to CONATEL as regulating entity of the telecommunications service and without the existence of any law regulating this figure, supposedly authorized said Commission to "grant its use, temporarily, to the operator disposed for said effect, according to what is established in the Organic Law of Telecommunications".

Finally, the Chamber, substituted once more the Executive authorities, ordering the Ministry of the Defense to "guard, control and constantly watch the use of facilities and equipment such as microwaves, teleports, transmitters, television ancillary equipment, power and weather ancillary equipment, towers, antennas, transmission booths, plant booths, perimeter fences and service wires; located throughout the country and necessary for the use of the frequency that has been assigned for the open signal television in the transportation and television broadcasting network."

3. *The new confiscation of the property of RCTV by the constitutional judge, but ex-officio this time, and due to the same conceptual confusion of the constitutional judge, of what is the "universal service of telecommunications", contrary to what the petitioners had requested*

In addition to the amparo action and process aforementioned, as has been said, a series of other actions were filed by other subjects and User Committees before the Constitutional Chamber in defense of their collective rights and of the diffused interests of the Venezuelan people.

One of said actions was filed on May 24, 2007; by a group of citizens, acting "on their own behalf and of the Venezuelan society", as well as by the main spokesperson of a user's committee (OIR). It was an amparo action regarding diffused and collective interests which was exercised jointly a petition for precautionary measures, this time against the President of the Republic and the Minister of Popular Power for the Telecommunications and Information Technology, alleging the violation of the constitutional rights to freedom of expression and information, established in articles 57 and 58 of the Constitution of the Bolivarian Republic of Venezuela.

In this case, the plaintiffs formulated their claim against the constant threats for the closedown of channel 2, RCTV, repeatedly issued by the defendant officials since December, 2006; "closedown that, without a doubt, would restrict the constitutional rights to the freedom of expression and information of the Venezuelan people" seeing themselves "deprived of the possibility to enjoy of a television channel, which had been enjoyed, uninterruptedly, by all the people for 53 years, and that included the most varied programming inclined to satisfy the demands of the Venezuelan people"; considering also, that the announced closedown "has its cause, not in the alleged failure to comply with the norms of telecommunications which would make impossible the renewal of the concession, but in the fact that it seeks the punishment to said television station for including, within the messages it transmits, messages that the government considers to be adverse"; which converted the allegation in " a clear case of the violation of the freedom of expression", especially of the plaintiffs and the Venezuelan collective. Given the imminence of the violation threat of the constitutional rights claimed because of the constant and repeated threats of the closedown of RCTV, which would materialize on May 27, 2007; the plaintiffs requested:

> "The issuing of a precautionary measure in favor of the Venezuelan people, seeking to allow said channel to continue in the transmission of its programming while this procedure is being handled".

In this case, thus, the amparo action in representation of diffused interests was filed with the precautionary petition for the Constitutional Chamber to allow RCTV to continue with the transmission of its programming while the trial lasted.

In decision N° 957 (file: 07-0731) of May 25, 2007, the Constitutional Chamber admitted the proposed action only regarding the Minister of Popular Power for the Telecommunications and Information Technology, because, as for the President of the Republic, the Chamber ruled it inadmissible "because not having legal jurisdiction in this matter." In this case, the Chamber, once more, mistakenly considered that all the attributions regarding the granting, use, revocation and other relations produced between the State and the concessionaire executing the corresponding concession contract, as well as any form of extinction of it, was only of the concern of CONATEL.

By admitting the action, and before pronouncing ex-officio about the confiscation of the assets of RCTV, the Chamber also, deliberately, set the descriptive rules of the procedure to be followed, in order to mutilate RCTV's right to due process and to the defense.

Thereby, it decided that the plaintiffs were granted five (5) working days to produce the proofs, with the burden of their preclusion, for failure to introduce them within the referred time period; and that there was a group of defendants in the case, and given the *erga omnes* effects that the decision could produce if declared admitted; both the Director of CONATEL and the President of the Institute for the Defense and Protection of the Consumer and the User (INDECU) had to be summoned; and that a public notice had to be published in the newspaper calling "all interested parties who wanted to be aid or oppose the parties, or to participate in defense of their own rights or interests", but with the expressed warning that "everyone participating could only, in equal terms, allege reasons that support the positions of those being helped"; and that "the adjuvant with the parts, being an action of diffused interests, could only promote proofs relating to the allegations of the parties to be helped."

This way, it was illegitimately assured that RCTV could not appear in court by itself, and to allege and demonstrate with independence from the plaintiffs, since the precautionary measure that was requested would fall over its assets, by confiscating them, for which its right to the defense had not been assured.

In fact, the unusual of this sentence, is that the precautionary measure that the plaintiffs had requested consisted in that:

> "In view of the imminence of the violation of the constitutional rights claimed for the constant and repeated threats closedown against Radio Caracas, which would materialize on May 27, 2007; we request that the precautionary measure be declared in favor of the Venezuelan people, allowing said channel to continue transmitting its programming while the processing of this procedure lasts…"

However, the Chamber decided that petition in the opposite to what had been requested, and acting ex-officio, copied, exactly, the same motivations it used to decide on the precautionary measure of confiscation of the assets of RCTV, and to the assignment of their use, *sine die*, and free of charge to CONATEL in decision N° 956 of the same date, May 25, 2007. In that sense, the Chamber incurred in the same inexcusable mistakes of applying to television, the provisions about the "universal service of telecommunications" relating to telephony, I have mentioned before.

Also, in view of the fact that what the precautionary measure requested was to assure that RCTV was allowed to continue with the transmission of its programming while the trial lasted; the Chamber, determined in this case, that

> "all the users have the right to access and enjoy of the rendering of a telecommunications universal public service; the content of said right according to articles 108 and 117 of the Constitution, involves at first, not the continuance of a determined operator of sonic broadcasting and open signal television in VHF, but the possibility that the above-mentioned users can effectively access in conditions of equality and with the maintenance of a minimal quality standard to the corresponding service, outside the force or not of the permit or concession granted to a specific private operator."

This way, the Chamber ignored the particular and specific request to decide on a precautionary measure that would assure RCTV to be allowed to continue with the transmission of its programming while the trial lasted, regarding which it did not make any type of pronouncement, and went on to decide ex-officio, due to the fact that the Minister of Telecommunications and Information Technology and the Director of CONATEL, could not guarantee that the possible transmission that the *Fundación* TEVES could execute, as consequence of the habilitation issued for sonic broadcasting and open signal television, with attribute of open signal television in VHF, in the same terms that had been rendered by RCTV, which in this case, had not been said nor had been alleged; decided:

> "temporarily, and in order to guard the continuity in the rendering of a universal public service, the use of the frequency that has been assigned for open signal television in the transportation and television broadcasting network, which includes, among others, microwaves, teleports, transmitters, television ancillary equipment, power and weather ancillary equipment, towers, antennas, transmission booths, plant booths, perimeter fence and service wires, without it implying to affect property rights that could correspond to Radio Caracas

Televisión, C. A., over said infrastructure or equipment, except for those which are legally or conventionally property of the Republic..."

Judge Pedro Rafael Rondón Haaz also formulated a dissident vote in this case, expressing that:

"It implies the subtraction of an attribute of the right to property (the use) of Radio Caracas Televisión RCTV C. A. over the assets that were affected, without expressing any grounds of legal nature, which is the only source of limitation to private property, always with the foundations provided by the National Constitution".

Said Judge went on, then, to consider that the Chamber, contradictorily, had adopted the requested precautionary measure, but, in an illogical way, "decided a completely different one, opposite to the interests of the plaintiffs"; adding with reason, that "it is of the essence of the precautionary measures, of all of them, nominated or not, to be congruent with the petition and, thus, with the eventual decision on the merits, since its justification and purpose is to assure the eventual efficacy of said decisive act".

Then the Judge mentioned in his dissident vote to the decision of the Chamber, that:

"From this unavoidable point of view, it was legally impossible, because of the instrumentality character of any precautionary measure regarding the decision on the merits, that at the same time, the "appropriateness" of the measure requested with the claim be accepted, and the resulting decision was not only strange but contrary to the principal claim claim, reason for which the precautionary measure that was pronounced should not have been adopted".

In any case, by means of the decision, the constitutional judge, substituting the Administration, as in the aforementioned case, continued with the enumeration of the sites and places where those facilities were located; and also, substituting the Legislator, established that "the right to use" the necessary equipment for the aforementioned operations, assigned ex-officio to CONATEL as the regulating entity of the telecommunications service and without the existence of any law regulating that figure; supposedly authorized said Commission to "temporarily grant it use to the operator assigned to said effect, according to what is established in the Organic Law of Telecommunications".

Finally the Chamber, also substituting the executive authorities, ordered the Ministry of Defense "to guard, control and constantly watch the use of facilities and equipment like microwaves, teleports, transmitters, television ancillary equipment, power and weather ancillary equipment, towers, antennas, transmission booths, plant booths, perimeter fence and service wires, located throughout the country and necessary for the use of the frequency assigned for open signal television in the transportation and television broadcasting network."

That is to say, in this case, the plaintiffs went before the constitutional judge seeking the protection of their rights and the rights of the Venezuelan people, which they considered to be temporarily assured by having allowed RCTV to continue with the transmission of its programming while the trial lasted, and they found themselves with the fact that the constitutional judge, without considering in any way their petitory, ex-officio, decided on a precautionary measure that assured completely the opposite, that is to say, the ceasing of the transmissions of RCTV, the confiscation of its assets, the assignment of its use to CONATEL, so the Commission would allow their use by the new State entity TEVES so it could cover the whole country with its programming.

FINAL CONSIDERATION

Without a doubt, the case of RCTV, as it results from the analysis previously made regarding the judicial decisions adopted by the Chambers of the Supreme Tribunal of Justice, demonstrates a serious fracture of the Rule of Law in Venezuela, as well as the unfortunate loss of the fundamental role of the Judiciary as its guarantor. The decisions of the Supreme Tribunal and particularly, those of its Constitutional Chamber, show how instead of protecting the constitutional rights of the freedom of the plural expression of thought, due process and private property, the Chambers of the Tribunal have conspired, as instruments controlled by the Executive, to annihilate, kidnap and violate them, covering all the governmental arbitrariness with a purely sewn judicial veil.

The worst of the performance, in any case, is that the abuse to the Constitution, and among other violations, the confiscation of the private property, which is prohibited by the Constitution, has been committed by the Judicial Power; which results on the violations remaining formally unpunished, because, in Venezuela, the constitutional judge does not have anyone to control him. These violations to the Rule of Law have been so serious that, with just a few days of difference, the most important legal institutions in the country publicly made announcements, protesting for the demolition of the Rule of Law.

In fact, the day before the publication of the Constitutional Chamber decision, dated May 24, 2007; the Academy of Political and Social Sciences issued a "Statement about the presumed extinction of the concession of television station RCTV", in which, among other aspects of importance, acknowledged the following:

> - That the impartiality principle sustaining the Public Administration has been disrespected (article 12 of the Organic Law of the Public Administration and 30 of the Organic Law of Administrative Procedures), because a decision was issued, prior to its proper opportunity (which would be the moment to impartially evaluate the request for the renovation of the concession, if that were the case);

> - That the due process of law has been disrespected (article 49 of the Constitution), because it is evident that a decision was been adopted in advance imposing a sanction (to exclude the company from access to the concession), without opening the due procedure for said purpose, with which the principle of equality is also violated (since in case it concurred to an eventual procedure of assignment of the concession, the company knows it has been excluded beforehand), and the vice of the deviation of power is evidenced in the decision, since the power to grant the concession is used, not for the purpose intended by the norm (administration of the radio electric spectrum), but to punish (without procedure and without been qualified for it);

> - That article 19 of the Universal Declaration of the Human Rights, and article 13 of the American Convention on Human Rights, in which development the "Declaration of Principles about the Freedom of Expression" was approved by the aforementioned Commission, has also been disrespect. This Declaration, in its Principle 13, proclaims: "… the granting of radio and

television frequencies, among others, in order to press and punish or reward or privilege social communicators and communication media according to their informative policies, attempts against the freedom of expression and must be definitely prohibited by the law…"

- That the formal procedure for the transformation of the titles granted to RCTV, before the new Organic Law of Telecommunications became in effect (published in Official Gazette N° 36.970. Caracas June 12, 2000) had been un-fulfilled; and consequently, the obligation to grant RCTV the concession and administrative permit according to the said Law, has also been un-fulfilled.

On the other hand, in Communiqué directed "To the National Public Opinion. Before the absolute breaking of the Rule of Law" dated May 30, 2007; the Faculty of Judicial and Political Sciences of the Universidad Central de Venezuela, expressed among other important aspects, that:

> We watch astonished that by means of a precautionary measure property rights of an individual not been party in the judicial process are harmed, and their assets are judicially ripped in order to be assigned to be used by an new entity created by a public entity…

> According to the principles of the Democratic and Social Rule of Law State of Justice, no entity of the Judicial Power can affect, as it has been done, the right to property, since the temporary occupation and the previous occupation, can only take place in an expropriation process…

> The mistake that the decision shows is clearly evidenced just with the reading of article 588 of the Code of Civil Procedure. For that reason, the precautionary measure adopted constitutes an inexcusable mistake, and in the framework of the principle of responsibility, characteristic of the exercise of the public function, including the judicial, it constitutes a clear demonstration of abuse of power by the Constitutional Chamber…

> That no criteria of "justice and reasonability" can justify the "temporary confiscation", without limit of time, of assets property of persons that have not been a party in a process, and one does not have to be well prepared to understand that the judges signing the decision were neither just nor reasonable".

The Bar Association of Caracas, also made public a "Communiqué to the Public Opinion" dated June 1, 2007; in which it expressed the following:

> The Board of Directors of the Bar Association of Caracas, in view of the clamor of the immense majority of our members for the systematic violation of the constitutional and legal provisions, concreted in the massive violation of the Human Rights, either by action or omission of the entities of the Public Power, which submitted to the Executive Power, apply the Constitution and the Laws of the Republic with discrimination, making the Rule of Law inexistent, with which have left citizens in complete abandonment, victim of the arbitrariness executed by the Executive Power, which now intends to impose a communicational hegemony, a single thought, a single opinion and a single informative voice in its favor; by means of the distorted application of the Law, the promulgation of repressive laws and the Criminalization of the Dissidence, in a clear attempt against the Freedom of Expression, evidenced, clearly, through the CLOSEDOWN of the television channel RCTV, under pretenses of legal rank, motivated by political elements, infringing this way the right all citizens of the Country have to choose freely the television media, under the premise of the information plurality that must reign in every Democracy; justifying this arbitrariness with the unusual decisions of the Constitutional and Political Administrative Chambers of the Supreme Tribunal of Justice, where the serious action of Confiscating the Radio Electric Spectrum of the citizens and the Assets of R.C.T.V. took place; by means of a Judicial and Constitutional fraud, on behalf of the Na-

tional Executive, turning the Laws and the Judicial Power in the executing arm of the political repressions, that are decided in the High Circles of the Executive Power, all of which is characteristic of a TOTALITARIAN REGIME, that violates the Human Dignity, essential condition of any Civilized Society.

Later on, the Bar Associations of Venezuela, represented by their Chairs, gave a "Joint Statement" on June 8, 2007; in which they expressed the following:

We categorically reject the official pressure executed over the Judicial Power, produced by an unusually serious fact that materialized in a public speech given by the President of the Republic on March 24, 2007; at the *Teatro Teresa Carreño*, when he stated without roundabout means nor moderation that **to adjudicate judicial decisions that neutralize Government actions, if these decisions are taken behind the back of the leader of the "revolution", constitutes a treason to the people, treason to the revolution,** which evidences, once more, the inherence of the President in matters that are of exclusive competency of the Judicial Power.

We categorically repudiate the content of decisions N° 956 and 957 that came out of the Constitutional Chamber on May 25, 2007; according to which, by means of twisted judicial interpretations, adopt precautionary measure consisting in the **indefinite confiscation of the assets of a corporate person not a party in the process, action that constitutes, without a doubt, the abuse of power from the Constitutional Chamber,** besides of being an **un excusable mistake of law** of the Judges of the high Chamber when they obviated the legal requirements demanded by the Law in order to make precautionary measures appropriate, consequently incurring in personal liability according to articles 255 in fine and 49.8 of the Constitution, for the clear **violation of articles 49,1, and 257 of the Constitution by infringing the rights to defense and due process** to the company owning the television station.

We regret that with these judicial decision, the country has been left without a Constitutional Chamber capable of imposing, independently, the interpretation of the Constitution and its effectiveness, which implies that the Fundamental Text is seriously wounded, because decisions like these, tie the luck of the fundamental Norm to the sole will of the President of the Republic, since the interpretation that has been convenient in each case has been imposed, being converted the Constitution in a politically instrument of the official sector, transforming the constitutional conflicts in unstoppable fractures of the basic consensus that the Constitution was made to assure.

As resulting from the decisions issued by the Supreme Tribunal of Justice, where the Constitutional Chamber conspires with the National Executive in order to damage a third party, setting up with this, a constitutional fraud, that contains un excusable mistakes by gross legal ignorance and incurring in the confiscation of assets and abuse of power; the Bar Associations of Venezuela, will file before the Republican Moral Council, a request to open a repealing procedure against the Judges of the Constitutional Chamber that have signed the decisions, and will request it be given the same diligent treatment given to the procedure related to prior repeal of Judges. We claim that in our Nation the Separation of Powers does not exist, that there is no Rule of Law, nor Justice, freedom, nor equality, and consequently the great conclusion is that in Venezuela THERE IS NO DEMOCRACY.

Facing these expressions made by the most important institutions of the legal or juridical community in the country, is difficult to add something else in these final reflections regarding these abusive acts, except to refer to what was also publicly expressed by the University Council of the Universidad Central de Venezuela, in Communiqué dated May 30, 2007; which is forward by the phrase of Simon Bolivar saying that: "Justice is the queen of all republican virtues and with it equality and liberty are sustained", in which, among other concepts, the Council mentioned "the decision of the National Executive to interrupt the concession of *Radio Caracas Televisión* (RCTV) from May 28 of the current year", and expressed that:

> "Institutions cannot be sanctioned due to the real or supposed participation of any of their members in punishable events. Sanctions are applied to subjects and not over the institutions. The political argumentation, as justification for the suspension of the concession, contradicts what is established in article 19 of the Universal Declaration of the Human Rights about freedom of expression, and particularly, in the Declaration of Principles about the Freedom of Expression of the Inter-American Commission on Human Rights of the Organization of American States which expressly states: "... the granting of radio and television frequencies, among others, to pressure and punish or reward and privilege social communicators and mass media in function of their informative policies, attempts against the freedom of expression and must be definitely prohibited by the law."

CHAPTER XIII

THE INTERNATIONAL POLITICAL PERSECUTION OF DISSIDENTS BY THE AUTHORITARIAN GOVERNMENT, AND ITS STOPPAGE THROUGH GLOBAL ADMINISTRATIVE LAW PROCEDURE PROVISIONS

(2010)

This essay on "Global Administrative Law on International Police Cooperation: A Case of Global Administrative Law Procedure," was written between 2007 and 2009, in order to study how to stop the international political persecution attempst made by the authoritarian government of Venezuela against dissidents, improperly using the channels of Interpol. The ideas expressed in this article were first discussed in my Presentation before the *Seminar on Global Security Challenges. Anticipating Answers before New Threats*, organized by the *Universidad Internacional Menéndez Pelayo*, and sponsored by *Fundación Alfonso Martín Escudero*, held in La Línea de la Concepción, Campo de Gibraltar, Cádiz (Spain), on October 20, 2008. The essay was published as: "Global Administrative Law on International Police Cooperation: A Case of Global Administrative Law Procedure," in Javier Robalino-Orellana and Jaime Rodríguez-Arana Muñoz (Editors), *Global Administrative Law Towards a* Lex Administrativa, Cameron May International Law & Policy, London 2010, pp. 343-395. It was dedicated to my friends and colleagues, Professors León Henrique Cottin, Rafael Odremán, Pedro Nikken, Olivo Rodríguez, José Antonio Muci Borjas, José Eugenio Soriano, Manuel Ballbé and José Ramón Parada Vásquez, all of whom, in one way or another, insisted me to write this essay on Global Administrative Procedure on International Police Cooperation.

I. ADMINISTRATIVE LAW AND THE IMPACT OF GLOBALIZATION

Administrative law, as constitutional law, has always been, and is, above all, a law concerning the State, and public institutions with public and collective interest.[272] It is a branch of law concerning an essential component of the State, its Public Administration, its organization and functioning, as well as the legal relationship established between public entities and the citizens or individuals.[273] In addition, Administrative Law is the regulatory instrument established in democratic societies in order to guarantee the equilibrium that must always exist between the powers and prerogatives of Public Administration and the rights of individuals in order to assure the subjection of the State to the rule of law. That is why without rule of law, there would be no Administrative Law.

This has been the traditional perception of Administrative Law, which due to the process of globalization has started to change to a point in which it has ceased to be a law exclusively referred to the State or to National States and their Public Administrations, to become a law that also regulates global administrations that are no longer essentially part of a National State.

The impact of globalization has been so important in this field that nowadays, beside the traditional Public Administrations of the States, it is possible to find Public Administrations without States, that is, some sort of "Stateless Administrations"[274] or "administrative transnational entities"[275] that have assumed many regulatory functions initially corresponding to National Public Administrations; functions which have in turn acquired a global level.

Consequently, a global administrative law has begun to emerge in a manner different to the traditional "international administrative law" that developed since the beginning of last century within "international organizations" referred, first, to their internal regime (for instance, internal labor relations between them and its employees); and second, to the activities developed by those related to regulatory activities that were initially configured as "Unions." It was the case, for instance, of the Universal Postal Union established in order to channel international cooperation between National Public Administrations in the rendering of a public service like the postal one, but also in other cases like for instance related to telecommunications and international navigation. National Public Administrations continued to have the central role in those matters and International Unions had limited regulatory and decision making powers. Nonetheless, important aspects of international administrative law developed in their organization and functioning, like the previously men-

---

272 André Demichel, *Le Droit Administratif. Essai de réflexion théorique*, Paris, 1978, p.14

273 See Allan R. Brewer-Carias "El concepto del derecho administrativo en Venezuela," in *Revista de Administración Pública*, N° 100-102, Vol. 1, Madrid, 1983, p. 688. Also published in Allan R. Brewer-Carias, *Estudios de Derecho Administrativo,* Bogotá, 1986, pp. 7-24

274 See Stefano Barin, *Amministrazioni senza Stato. Profili di Diritto Amministrativo Internazionale*, Giuffré Milan, 2003.

275 See Benedict Kingsbury, Nico Krisch and Richard B. Stewart, "The Emergence of Global Administrative Law," in *Law and Contemporary Problems (The Emergence of Global Administrative Law)*, Vol 68, Summer/Autum 2005, Numbers 3 & 4, Duke University School of Law, Durham, pp. 15 ff; also published as "El surgimiento del Derecho Administrativo Global," in *Res Publica Argentina*, N° 2007-3, Buenos Aires 2007, pp. 27 ff

tioned matters related to international civil service and to the establishment of administrative courts for the resolution of disputes regarding those matters.[276]

In a different way, contemporary global administrations, with their own regulatory and decision making powers exercised within the framework of an international treaty, are subjected to a new global administrative law system that contains regulations on the administration of wide sectors of the economic and social life.[277] They were initially established in areas related to economic matters to the point that, for instance, the word "globalization" (*globalización*) mean in Spanish, as defined by the *Diccionario de la Real Academia de la Lengua* (Dictionary of the Royal Academy of Spanish Language), those "markets that transcend or exceed State boundaries, and companies that extend their activities beyond States to reach a global dimension." This was the initial area for the development of global administrations, referred to international economic organizations like, for instance, the World Trade Organization.

More recently, the scope of global administrations has progressively shifted toward other fields of action, related to other substantive aspects of administrative law. An example in the environmental protection arena is the establishment of the Compliance Committee under the Kyoto Protocol of the United Nations Framework Convention on Climate Change. In international security matters an example is the Security Council of United Nations. In the field of Nuclear Energy and Chemical Arms Control, other example is the establishment of the International Atomic Energy Agency. On matters of Industrial Property, an example is the World Intellectual Property Organization. In the field of control of banks and financial institutions' activities, the Basel Committee on Banking Supervision is another example. Concerning Peoples' status, like the one referred to refugees, an example is the High Commissioner of the United Nations on Refugees; and regarding international cooperation on police matters, which is an essential part of a classical content of administrative law, an example is the International Criminal Police Organization (INTERPOL).

It is worth noting that these global administrations, although not subjected to any national administrative law regime of a particular State, have their own global administrative law,[278] that is, their own body of international provisions regulating their organization, their functions and their activities, as well as the relationships that are established between them and other subjects of global administrative law, which are not only the different National States and their Public Administrations, but also the individuals and the citizens of such States. These global administrations pursuant

---

276 *Idem*, pp. 30-31

277 *Idem*, p. 29.

278 See. Juan Cruz Alli Aranguren, *Derecho Adminstrativo y Globalization,* Civitas, Madrid, 2004; Sabino Cassesse, *La Globalziación Jurídico*, Instituto de Administración Pública, Madrid 2006; Benedict Kingsbury, Nico Krisch and Richard B. Stewart, "The Emergence of Global Administrative Law" in *Law and Contemporary Problems (The Emergence of Global Administrative Law),* School of Law, Duke University, Vol. 68 N° 3 and 4 Summer/Autumm 2005, pp. 15 ss.

to the powers attributed to them by the international regulatory framework that governs their activities and which are, in turn, the source of global administrative law, can adopt decisions having direct effects regarding the National States and their citizens, some times even without intervention of their respective National Public Administrations, and some times even against them, configuring themselves as global administrations.

That is why José A. Muci Borjas has explained that global administrative law is compose of international or supranational provisions that have no national origin, and are not dependent on the traditional idea of sovereignty, conceived without having consideration of boundaries, and with effects surpassing the boundaries of the States.[279] This global administrative law regulates global administrations that do not belong to any national State, having been established in parallel to the Administration of National States, exercising an authority that is recognized by the national States, which traditionally only belonged to them. The result is that these global administrations are governed by a set of rules not arising from any State, having powers to limit and establish conditions upon the Pubic Administration of the States. The rules of this global administrative law also regulate, in some way, the relationships arising between the Public Administrations of the States and its citizens, thus recognizing the individuals of any National State in their capacity as subjects at an international level, with the capacity to establish direct legal relationships with the global administrations, independently from the National States' Public Administrations.[280]

In these cases, global administrations perform their activities under global administrative law procedures that allow National Public Administrations and also individuals or citizens of any State, to directly petition before global administrations, the latter for the protection of their individual rights. This could even lead to a procedure for the review of the activities of global administrations and global institutions. Consequently, in many cases, the relationship between the global administrations and the citizen of any Member State is established as a consequence of the exercise of a right to petition that is frequently set forth in global administrative law regimes, through an administrative procedure originating global administrative procedures.

Additionally, this new global administrative law has the purpose of assuring the equilibrium that in these cases is also necessary to be established, between thepowers and prerogatives of the global administrations, and the rights of the passive subjects of global administrative law, namely, the National States and the individuals or citizens of such States. In addition, global administrative law based on non-state laws, in many cases conditioned the traditional powers of the national States and their Public Administrations, which have seen, in some cases, the scope

---

279 See José Antonio Muci Borjas, *El derecho Administrativo Global y los Tratados Bilaterales de Inversión (BIT´s,)* Editorial Jurídica Venezolana, Caracas, 2007.

280 *Idem.*

of their activities to be reduced, leading also to a reduction in the scope of State administrative law.

II. THE INTERNATIONAL CRIMINAL POLICE ORGANIZATION (INTERPOL) AS A GLOBAL PUBLIC ADMINISTRATION

1. *INTERPOL as a Global Administration*

A. *International cooperation in ordinary-law crime matters*

One of these global administrations of increasing importance in contemporary world, resulting from international cooperation among National States and their Public Administrations in police matters, is the International Criminal Police Organization, INTERPOL, which was created in Vienna in 1923, having its origin in the First International Congress of Criminal Police which took place in Monaco, in 1914.

This global administration was created in order to facilitate international cooperation in police matters across borders, and to support and assist all organizations, authorities and services in charge of preventing or fighting ordinary-law crimes; a mission that the Organization fulfill even when there are no diplomatic relations between countries, and that always must to accomplished "within the limits of the existing laws in the different countries" and "within the spirit of the Universal Declaration of Human Rights," being the latter of particular importance considering that police activities essentially produce a restriction of or a limitation on individual's rights.

INTERPOL is the largest international police organization, with 188 Member countries, governed, as is any other international organization by its Constitution, adopted in 1956 by all the Member States; and by the *Regulations* adopted by the General Assembly of the Organization, and among them, the *Rules on the Processing of Information for the Purposes of International Police Cooperation* (*RPI Rules*), approved by the General Assembly on its 72nd meeting held in Benidorm (Spain) in 2003, through Resolution AG-2003-RES-04, in force since January 1, 2004 (these Rules and Regulations were modified by the General Assembly on the 74th meeting held in Berlin (Germany) in 2005, through Resolution AG-2005-RES-15, in force since January 1, 2006; the *Rules on the Control of Information and Access to INTERPOL's Files* (*RCI Rules*), approved through Resolution AG-2004-RES-08 on the 73rd meeting of the General Assembly of the Organization held in Cancún (Mexico) in 2004; and the provisions derived from the *Headquarter Exchange of Letters* between the Republic of France and INTERPOL, in force since 1984, through which was created the system of control of the Files of INTERPOL and the Commission for the Control of INTERPOL 's Files.

According to these normative instruments, that can be consulted at http://www.interpol.int/, the activities of the Organization are essentially restricted to international cooperation with regard exclusively to ordinary-law crime matters. Consequently, no intervention of INTERPOL or international cooperation can be expected on matters related to political, military, religious or racial crimes, and no request for international arrest warrants against citizens for crimes not considered to be ordinary-law crimes, can be send to the Organization.

Indeed, according to Article 2 of the Constitution of INTERPOL, its aims are:

a) to ensure and promote the widest possible mutual assistance between all criminal police authorities within the limits of the laws existing in the different countries and in the spirit of the "Universal Declaration of Human Rights"; and

b) To establish and develop all institutions likely to contribute effectively to the prevention and suppression of ordinary-law crimes.

Based on these aims, Article 3 of the Constitution set forth that: "It is strictly forbidden for the Organization to undertake any intervention or activities of political, military, religious or racial character".

It is within this competence framework and with this fundamental prohibition that INTERPOL was conceived as an international organization exclusively to assist and cooperate with criminal police organizations of Member countries and other organizations only in relation to ordinary-law crimes (*infracciones de derecho común, infractions de droit commun*) and, consequently, with the prohibition of intervening in any way in crimes having a political, military, religious or racial character.

B.   *International Organizational Regime of INTERPOL*

INTERPOL has been legally established as an international organization, as a global administration, the acts of which abide by its own Constitution and by the regulations issued by its General Assembly, without considering any frontiers. These norms have no national origin nor do they respond to the traditional idea of sovereignty.

Being an international organization and global administration, INTERPOL does not belong to, nor receive instructions from any State. In accordance with its Constitution, it has its own organization composed of the following organs: the General Assembly, the Executive Committee, the General Secretariat, the National Central Bureaus, the Advisers and the Commission for the Control of the Files (Article 5); the latter conceived as a deconcentrated administration, having additional autonomy within the global administration itself (Article 36).

Among these organs, those exercising functions as global administrations in the development of the Organization's activities, and control and vigilance on matters of ordinary-law crimes (excluding political, military, religious or racial crimes) are the General Secretariat and its various services which constitute the permanent services of same (Article 25, Constitution); and the Commission for the Control of Files which, in particular, watches over the treatment of information in order to assure its use according to the Constitution and Rules of the Organization, and to protect the fundamental rights of nationals of the member countries as to the use of this information.

The General Secretariat, beside to apply the decisions of the General Assembly and of the Executive Committee, has the following functions:

(i)   To serve as an international center for the fight against ordinary-law crime;

(ii)   To serve as a technical and information center;

(iii)   To ensure the efficient administration of the Organization; and

(iv)   To maintain contacts with national and international authorities, processing questions relative to the search for criminals through the National Central Bureaus (Article 26, Constitution).

As mentioned, in addition to the General Secretariat, the other important entity for global administrative law within the organization of INTERPOL is the Commission for the Control of Files, in charge of protecting the files of the Organization, controlling its use and assuring its adjustment to the limits regarding Police Information, particularly ensuring its confinement to the field of ordinary-law crimes.

C.   *Independence of INTERPOL as a Global Administration and the protection of international police files*

The authority conferred upon INTERPOL on matters of international police cooperation, which is recognized by the Member States and their Public Administrations, without a doubt, limits or conditions the activities of the National Police Administrations of the States, in particular when referred to relations established between said Police Administrations of the States, the Organization and the citizens of the States themselves. Consequently, the General Secretariat of INTERPOL, as a global administration in international police cooperation, has been established in parallel to National Police Administrations of the Member States, in order to exercise its own authority in matters recognized by the said Member States, which are obligated to respect such exercise of authority, formerly controlled only at a national level.

In order to ensure its character as global administration, Article 30 of the Constitution is emphatic in establishing that in the exercise of their duties, the Secretary General and the staff of INTERPOL "shall neither solicit nor accept instructions from any government or authority outside the Organization. They shall abstain from any action which might be prejudicial to their international task."

On the other hand, each of the Member States of the Organization, in accordance with its Constitution, "shall undertake to respect the exclusively international character of the duties of the Secretary General and the staff, and abstain from influencing them in the discharge of their duties" (Article 30). To that effect, each Member State of the Organization shall do their best to assist the Secretary General and the staff in the discharge of their functions (Article 30).

Within INTERPOL's organization, one of the most important entities is the Commission for the Control of Files, which as aforementioned, is an independent body in charge of protecting the files of the Organization, and controlling that its use be restricted to the field of ordinary-law crimes. This Commission was not established in the original organization of INTERPOL and has only been incorporated in the Constitution of the Organization in the reform adopted in the 77th Sessions of the Organization held in St. Petersburg in 2008. It was originally created in 1984 on the occasion of the international regularization process for the establishment of the INTERPOL's Headquarter in France, due to the need to assure within the global administrative law applied to the Organization, the existence of mechanisms devoted to protect the rights of the citizens of member countries that could be affected, for instance, by the requirements made by a National Offices or by information contained in the INTERPOL's files, which could be internationally diffused.

For such purpose, as a result of the exchange of Official Letters between INTERPOL and the Government of the Republic of France, the creation of the Commission for the Control of Files was provided for, putting an end to the discussion relating to the control of files and maintenance in the global administration organization, and outside of the reach of Member States, including the Country siege of the Headquarters.

In fact, the French administration, upon deciding the matter of the INTERPOL Headquarters, maintained that the French National Law of January 6, 1978 on Data Processing and Liberties was applicable to the personal data accumulated in the INTERPOL installations, located in Saint Cloud (France), purporting to have the right of access to said data that it wanted to exercise through the *Commission Nationale de l'informatique et des libertés* created by virtue of the said law. That is, the French National Public Administration, according to its own national administrative law provisions that were applied to the French Official Archives, pretended to have control upon INTERPOL's files and to have access to them.

In view of this, INTERPOL sustained that such national law was not applicable to police information dealt with by its General Secretariat as it was a global administration and that (a) because the said information was not the property of INTERPOL as it came from the Member States, the Organization being no more than a depositary of this information; and (b) because the application of the French Law of 1978 to the INTERPOL files could affect international police cooperation as some countries could prefer to abstain from communicating police information to INTERPOL which could be divulged to French organizations. In fact, it was a matter of setting apart the global administration that was submitted to its own global administrative law from the French National Public Administration, subject to national administrative law and establishing that the global administration could not be subject to the administrative law of any of the Member States of the Organization.

This conflict was solved by the acceptance by both parties of the principle of data protection in order to protect the activities of the international police cooperation, as well as to protect the individual rights of persons guaranteed by Article 2 of the Constitution of INTERPOL, according to which its actions must be accomplished within the framework of the Universal Declaration of Human Rights.

The solution materialized with the signature on November 3, 1982, of a new Headquarters Agreement between the French Republic and INTERPOL, which came into effect on February 14, 1984. The annex to this agreement contains the Exchange of the Official Letters, the texts of which created an internal system of control over the INTERPOL files. This event motivated France to waive the application of the 1978 National Law of Protection of Information to the Files of the Organization (Articles 7 and 9 of the Headquarter Agreement). The control of INTERPOL's Files was instead attributed to the Commission for Control of Files as part of the global administration, conceived as a professional and independent entity (article 8 of said Agreement).

The legal regime of the Commission and the system for the control of the Files of INTERPOL was later regulated in the Rules on International Police Cooperation and the Control of the Files of INTERPOL of 1982, having as its principal purpose "to protect against any abuse the police information considered and communicated within the police cooperation system established by INTERPOL, mainly in order to prevent any harm to persons' human rights" (Article 1.2). Said Cooperation Regulation was sustituted as of 2005 by the *Rules on the Processing of Information for the purpose of International Police Cooperation (RPI Rules)* and by the *Rules on the Control of Information and access to INTERPOL Files (RCI Rules)*.

D.   *Functions and independence of the Commission for the Conrol of Files*

According to article 36 of the Constitution of INTERPOL, "the Commission for the Control of Files is an independent body which shall ensure that the processing of personal information by the Organization is in compliance with the regulations the Organization establishes in this matter."This Commission shall provide the Organization with advice about any project, operation, set of rules or other matter involving the processing of personal information; and shall process requests concerning the information contained in the Organization's files.

The Commission, in accordance with Article1.a) of the *RCI Rules*, has the following substantial role:

> "To ensure that the rules and operations relating to the processing of personal information by the Organization, and particularly its projects to create new files or new methods of circulating personal information, conform to all the relevant rules adopted by the Organization, and that they do not infringe the basic rights of the people concerned, as referred to in Article 2 of the Organization's Constitution, which refers in turn to the Universal Declaration of Human Rights, or the general principles of data protection."

To that effect, the Commission must provide the Organization with advice about any project, operation, set of rules or other matter involving the processing of personal information; and shall process requests for access to INTERPOL's files and shall reply to requesting parties. Upon request, the Commission shall make the list of INTERPOL's files available to any national or permanent resident of a Member State of the Organization (Article 1.b.c).

In order to assure compliance with these functions, Article 2 of the *RCI Rules* provides that the composition of the Commission for Control of Files, will be integrated by five (5) members, appointed for a period of 3 years (Article 3) based on their expertise and in such a way as to allow the Commission "to carry out its mission completely independently" (Article 3).281 To that effect, the members of the Commission are appointed as follows: The data protection expert and the electronic data processing experts shall be appointed by the General Assembly from a list of candidates put forward by Member States and selected by the Executive Committee; the member of the Organization's Executive Committee shall be appointed by the Executive Committee; and the Chairperson shall be appointed by the other four

---

281   Said members are: a Chairperson, appointed because he holds or has held senior judicial or data protection posts; two data protection experts, who hold or have held senior positions in this field; an electronic data processing expert, who holds or has held a senior position in this field; and a member of the Organization's Executive Committee.

members (Article 2). As far as possible, the member of the Committee shall have different nationalities and shall represent at least two different regions.

Article 5.a) of the *RCI Rules* reiterates that the Commission "shall be completely independent in the exercise of its duties;" and its meetings shall be held in camera (Article 5.c). Only members of the Commission and of the Commission's Secretariat shall be considered as permanent participants in those meetings. However, "any other person whose presence the Commission considers necessary for discussion of an item on the agenda for the session, may also take part in the meetings" (Article 5.c)

In accordance with the Article 5.e of the *RCI Rules*, the Commission shall take all appropriate steps "to exercise its duties and ensure its independence," to which it is agreed that "in the exercise of their duties, the members of the Commission shall neither solicit nor accept instructions from any persons or bodies, and shall be bound by professional secrecy."

For such purpose, the *RCI Rules* guarantee the Commission to "have free and un-limited access to all personal information processed by Interpol, and to any system for processing such information, irrespective of the place, form or medium in-volved" (Article 5,e,2). In any case, the Commission shall as far as possible exercise this right without unnecessarily interfering with the daily work of the General Secretariat.

2. *Interpol and its relations with the Citizens of Member States*

Administrative Law not only establishes the legal regime of Public Administration, it also provides the legal regime to be applied to individuals in their relations with the Public Administration, seeking to establish the indispensable equilibrium between, on the one hand, the public powers and prerogatives of Public entities, and on the other hand, the private rights of the individuals. In the case of Interpol, as a global administration, the same principles apply not only because its activities are related to international police cooperation that could directly affect the individuals, citizens of all the Member State, but also because the scope of the activities of the Organization is expressly and exclusively related to ordinary-law crimes matters, which implies the obligation of the Organization to develop its global administrative activity within the spirit of the Human Rights Universal Declaration.

Consequently, the Constitution and the Rules of the Organization recognize the right of individuals, citizens of any State, to establish a direct legal relationship on an international level with Interpol's General Secretariat and its Commission for the Control of Files, as global administrations. This relationship would have to be inde-pendent from the possible relations with the national Public Administrations or the National Central Bureaus or Bureaus, and in some cases, even confronting them.

Furthermore, these direct relationships between the citizens of member countries and the Organization are expressly regulated in the internal ordinance of INTERPOL itself, guaranteeing as a global administrative right of the citizens of any member country, the right of any individual to petition before the global admin-istration, directly and without the intervention of the national Public Administrations, when affected in his rights as a consequence of the processing of international police cooperation information handled by Interpol's Services.

To that effect, in the Rules of the Organization, a global administrative procedure has been established in order to secure the protection of the citizens of any State by the global administration – for example, in opposing the intentions of the national police administrations of Members States to use INTERPOL for the persecution of political, military, religious or racial crimes, that is, crimes that do not have the character of ordinary-law crimes.

In effect, as aforementioned, according to article 2 of Interpol's Constitution, the aims of the Organization "to ensure and promote the widest possible mutual assistance between all criminal police authorities", must necessarily be achieved within the rules that govern the Organization, and within "the limits of the laws existing in the different countries and in the spirit of the Universal Declaration of Human Rights". For such purposes, the Organization has also established rules in order to protect the rights of individuals during the processing of information referred to them.

In this regard, the supervisory role of the Commission for the Control of Files was outlined in Article 5 of the Headquarter Exchange of Letters, and again in Article 22 of the Rules on International Police Cooperation, which stated that it should verify that personal information contained in the archives was to be "obtained and processed in accordance with the provisions of the Organization's Constitution and the interpretation thereof given by the appropriate organs of the Organization." These provisions have been substituted by Article 1 of the *RCI Rules* establishing that *"the Commission shall ensure that the rules and operations relating to the processing of personal information by the Organization. ... conform to all the relevant rules adopted by the Organization, and that they do not infringe the basic rights of the people concerned, as referred to in Article 2 of the Organization's Constitution, which refers in turn to the Universal Declaration of Human Rights, or the general principles of data protection."*

With regard to the processing of police information, the Commission must verify that said processing is carried out in conformity with the *RPI Rules*, and the *RCI Rules*.

It has been precisely for the purpose of assuring this protection, that article 9 (a) of the same *RCI Rules* guarantees any interested person the "right of access to personal information concerning him." In this regard, according to what is established in article 4 (a) of the same *RCI Rules*, the Commission for the Control of Interpol's Files "may receive requests from any person wishing to access personal information concerning him or the person he represents, as long as the requests meet the conditions on admissibility laid down by the Commission."

In this essay I wish to refer particularly to the global administrative procedures established in the global administrative law for the processing of international police information and cooperation that shape the regime of Interpol as a global administration. Nonetheless, first I will refer to the doctrine developed by this global administration in order to determine what must be considered a matter of "ordinary-law crime," and consequently, I will analyze the content and sense of the prohibition established in Article 3 of the Constitution of Interpol to intervene in matters concerning to political, military, religious or racial crimes.[282]

III. THE FUNDAMENTAL PROHIBITION IN INTERPOL ACTIVITY OF INTERVENING IN MATTERS RELATED TO POLITICAL, MILITARY, RELIGIOUS AND RACIAL CRIMES

In accordance with the Constitution of INTERPOL, since its creation, its acts have been restricted to international cooperation in matters of ordinary-law crimes, which implies a rigorous prohibition for INTERPOL to intervene in crimes which are not of that nature and especially in political, military, religious or racial crimes (Article 3).

This scope of the regime for the treatment and protection of police cooperation information – and especially with regard to the files of the Organization – was defined in 1946, by circumscribing the activities of INTERPOL, in accordance with Article 2(b) of its Constitution, to the prevention and repression of "ordinary-law crimes." A normative framework was thus configured at the start, in a compulsory way not only for the Organization but also for the member countries, for the purpose of guaranteeing neutrality, while still respecting the sovereignty of the States.

In any event, such an important limitation that constitutes the essence of INTERPOL action, limiting its activities to ordinary-law crimes, has imposed upon it – particularly in opposing attempts by Member States to act contrary to the prohibition – the need to interpret Article 3 of the Constitution in order to avoid becoming involved in political, religious, military or racial persecutions.

1. *Article 3 of the Constitution and Interpol neutrality: background.*

Since its creation in 1923, the activities of INTERPOL have been restricted to international cooperation in matters of ordinary-law crimes which, in spite of the absence of express statutory provision, basically excluded political crimes. This marks the neutral standing of the Organization, particularly between the two World Wars when it systematically refused to intervene in such matters, following the general tendency developed in the 19th century in matters of extradition, which was excluded for crimes of political character. In any event, this contributed to the Organization progressively gaining influence in matters of international cooperation, as well as the consideration of the administrative and judicial authorities of its Member countries.

This statutory gap, however, was covered in 1948 when an addition was made at the end of the first paragraph of Article 1 of the Constitution of the Organization by

---

282 To that effect, Interpol's General Assembly has adopted a series of interpretative resolutions which have been accompanied by several documents coming from the same organization with the titles "*Historia del artículo 3*" (GT-ART 3-2004-07; "*Marco de Interpretación del Artículo 3*" (GT-ART 3-2004.10); and "*Procedimientos dispuestos por la organización para vigilar la aplicación del artículo 3*" (GT-ART 3-2004.11), that manifest the special importance that the International Police Organization confers to this aspect. See in http://www.interpol.int/

a sentence referring to the rigorous exclusion of all matters having a political, religious or racial character. In 1948, this paragraph of Article 1 read as follows:

> "The purpose of the CIPC is to guarantee and favor the most ample reciprocal official support among all the criminal police authorities within the existing legal framework in each one of the countries, as well as create and develop all institutions able to effectively contribute to the prevention and to the repression of ordinary-law infractions, excluding rigorously any matter having a political, religious or racial character."

This rule was amended in 1956 when the INTERPOL Constitution were written and crimes having a "military" character were added to the list, thus overcoming any possible doubts there may have been as a result of the way in which the Constitution was initially drafted – that is, whether the prohibition was meant to prohibit the activity of the Organization within itself or, as in effect it did, prevent the Organization from intervening in matters having any political, military, religious or racial character, in the sense of expressly preventing Member countries from purporting to use the Organization to carry out prohibited cases.

Nevertheless, the limitation imposed upon Interpol to intervene only in cases of ordinary-law crimes, implied the exclusion of its intervention, not only in the cases of war criminals but, particularly between 1946 and 1959, also regarding cases of terrorist actions. This originated conflicts because the abstention was considered contrary to the principles of international law that had been outlined at the United Nations, to which Interpol, as an intergovernmental organization, did however not consider itself subject.

A number of controversies arose in the early 1950s, particularly with regard to the criminal practice of hijacking and taking hostages, leading the Organization to adopt an interpretation of Article 1 of its Constitution so as to enable it to establish in each case, whether or not it was an ordinary-law infraction, notwithstanding that a political or religious motivation could be claimed, and thus permitting the intervention by the Organization.

This led to the adoption by the 1951 General Assembly of the Organization of Resolution AGN/20/RES/11, in which the concept of the "*principle of predominance*"[11] was introduced in order to determine the possibility for Interpol's intervention, allowing such intervention if the crime was a preponderantly ordinary-law crime, even if committed together with other political, racial, military or religious crimes. This implied that what was forbidden were requests for information, as well as provisional arrest warrants, with regard to infractions having a *predominantly*, political, racial or religious character, even if said infractions were considered to be ordinary-law crimes in the country which formulated the request. This implied the need for the Organization to start to examine each request on a case by case basis.

However, the adoption of the theory of predominance in the interpretation of the prohibition contained in Article 3 did not initially lead to modifying the Organization's criteria for not intervening in the cases of persons accused of war crimes or crimes against humanity; this approach, however, was abandoned in 1994 by means of a resolution of the General Assembly (AGN/63/RES/9) when cooperation with the criminal court was proposed in the case of the former Yugoslavia.

The principle of predominance, on the other hand, also led to restricting the prohibition in Article 3, in connection with the possibility of the Organization intervening in cases of terrorism against the International Civil Aviation Organization (ICAO) (1970–1973 Resolutions. In the mid-1970s, this position was amplified to cover other terrorist activities beyond the field of civil aviation – such as homicide, corporal injuries, kidnapping, taking hostages, voluntary fires or attempts with explosives – but trying, at the same time, to differentiate terrorist acts from those connected with fights for national liberation in which the Organization did not intervene.

In 1979, at the 48th General Assembly, the Organization passed in Nairobi a resolution bearing the title "Acts of violence committed by organized groups", which "without forgetting" Article 3 of the Constitution, stipulated that the General Assembly condemned acts of violence committed by organized groups "alleging in some cases ideological motives."

On the other hand, after the recognition of the Organization by the United Nations in December 1982, as an intergovernmental organization, which was reaffirmed in 1983 by France when signing the Headquarters Agreement of the Organization in that country; and the recognition of the Organization as being subject to international law, it was obliged to approximate its practices to those established in the numerous international agreements regarding terrorism which then already existed.

Later, in 1984, by means of Resolutions AGN/53/RES/6 and AGN/53/RES/7, adopted at the meeting of its General Assembly in Luxemburg, the old practice of avoiding any implication in matters which could have a political character, as to terrorist acts, was abandoned and, on the contrary, the principle that National Criminal Offices as well as the General Secretariat could freely cooperate in the fight against terrorism without this resulting in violating Article 3 of the Constitution of the Organization, was accepted, abandoning the need for the examination of each case to highlighted "the ordinary-law predominance of the infraction" was abandoned.

2   Criteria established in 1984 on the Application of Article 3 of Interpol's Constitution

A.   Application of the "principle of predominance"

In any event, in the 1984 resolutions interpreting Article 3, the autonomy of Interpol as global administration was reaffirmed in a framework of respect for the sovereignty of States. That is, even though Member States, in the conformity with their sovereign powers define the political character of the infractions within their respective legislation, this may not prevent the Organization to care for the respect of its own Constitution and Rules. However, on the other hand, the right of the Organization to interpret its own legal regime may not restrict the possibility of the Member States adopting a decision different from that of the Organization in matters of political infraction.

In practice, this principle has different repercussions according to whether the Member State sends a request to the Organization, or whether it receives such a request.

In the first case, if it is a case where the country issues information or request, the denial of the Organization to deal with it on the basis of Article 3 may in no way mean that the Organization is competent to decide, instead of the State, if this infraction has or has not a political character. What the Organization does is respond to its own logic, which consists of guaranteeing respect for its Constitution and its Rules – that is, to observe the strictest neutrality. Therefore, the Member States have defined through the General Assembly the analytical framework that the General Secretariat has to follow in order to guarantee that Article 3 is respected where a political reason exists.

However, for crimes considered to be "political" – for example, to belong to a dissolved movement, opinion crimes, press crimes, insults to exercising authorities, crimes against domestic or foreign security of the state, betrayal, espionage – the prohibition provided in Article 3 is considered to operate automatically, so when the General Secretariat rejects the requests of Member States in these cases, its decision it based on its own regulations.

On the other hand, when it is considered necessary to apply the principle of preponderance according to Resolution AGN/53/RES/7, in cases in which the political, religious, military or racial infractions *predominate over the ordinary-law crime element,* then a previous examination is needed to be done, case by case, in order to determine the said predominance (AGN/53/RES/7 1.2 and 3). This must be done according to the following three principles:–

> Principle N° 1: The prohibition mentioned in Article 3 applies to infractions which shows a predominantly political, military, religious or racial character, even though in the requiring country such acts have been typified as ordinary-law infractions (AGN/20/RES/ and AGN/53/RES/7 point 1.2).
>
> Principle N° 2: The existence of the political, military, religious or racial motivation does not imply solely the application of Article 3; and the existence of an ordinary-law element is not enough to exclude the application of Article 3 (AGN//RAP/13 point 4.1).
>
> Principle N° 3: It corresponds to the States, in the exercise of their sovereignty, to determine the political, military, religious or racial character of an infraction (AGN/53/RES/6).

In any case, according to this analytical framework, even though the determination of the political character of the infraction is within the competence of the States, it is up to the Organization to appreciate the predominance of the ordinary-law crime elements based exclusively on the basis of the opinions outlined in the AGN/53/RES/7 Resolution.

In the second case, if a country receives a request for cooperation from INTERPOL, it can determine its stance and adopt the necessary measures in accordance with its own opinions from the political as well as from the legal point of view. Consequently, it is considered that it is not linked because of the decision of the General Secretariat to transmit information in which ordinary-law crime is predominant.

B. *The principle of predominance according to the Repressive or the Preventive matter regarding acts of terrorism.*

The second principle that was developed, based on Resolution AGN/53/RES/6 point II.6 of INTERPOL with regard to requests by Member States to the Organization, is that the theory of predominance is applied according to the type of cooperation act required in the sense that, if it is a matter of *prevention,* the Organization generally proceeds to the diffusion of technical information, including cases involving matters that are politically motivated. On the other hand, if it is a matter of repression with a political motive, its treatment responds to specific evaluation norms, established in the Organization. This distinction had its origin in the international community position condemning terrorist acts and fighting against terrorism (AGN/53/RES/7) and brought INTERPOL to distinguish the requests sent by Member States when they are made before the facts of terrorism (preventive) are verified with the information which was to serve to prevent the said acts (AGN/53/RES/7), or after the (repressive) terrorist act has been perpetrated.

By virtue of the above, messages alerting the preparation of terrorist acts, such as those in airports, have been intensified, and if the messages concern infractions provided in international agreements related to terrorist acts (for example, against civil aviation, the taking of hostages or against persons having international protection), INTERPOL in practice does not take into account the possible political affiliations of the potential perpetrators that have been denounced and has thus opened the doors to cooperation in these fields. The only condition established by the Organization is that the communication of information of this kind by States "is not exclusively based on the interested parties pertaining to a political movement" (AGN/53/RES/7 point II.6), but that it is also based on other data indicating the possibility that the person has participated in the preparation of an act for taking hostages or of an act against civil aviation.

Another principle derived from the Luxemburg Resolutions with regard to the predominance of ordinary-law crime in any matter puts forward the need to take into account the existence or non-existence of links between the objectives of the perpetrators and the victims, for which purpose the Organization has to examine the place where the act has been perpetrated, the nature of the victims and the magnitude of the infraction. The analysis of the place where a terrorist act has occurred is a determinant one, being the perpetration of terrorist acts outside the so called "zone of conflict" of particular interest.[12]

C. *Criteria established in matters of cooperation with international criminal courts.*

The principles for the application of Article 3 of the Constitution of INTERPOL were once again modified by Resolution AGN/63/RES/9, adopted at a meeting of the General Assembly in Rome in 1994 upon the creation (by means of Resolution 827 of May 25, 1993 of the Security Council of the United Nations) of the International Court for the judgment of persons suspected of serious violations of international humanitarian rights carried out as of 1991 in the territory of the former Yugoslavia. This resolved the matter of the relations between the Court and INTERPOL as well as its intervention in the treatment of criminal matters examined by the Court.[13]

The Organization considered it necessary to "define its posture related to the co-operation with the Court as well as related to the application of Article 3 of INTERPOL Constitution in the matters examined by the Court" (Resolution AGN/63/RAP/13), modifying the strict position previously maintained, accepting the general tendency towards a "progressive restriction in the application of exceptional provisions that provide a more favorable treatment for the authors of this type of infraction due to the political context of the act" (AGN/63/RAP/13/page 5).

By virtue of Resolution AGN/63/RES/9, the AGN/63/RAP/13 report was ratified regarding infractions sanctioned by the International Penal Court, which in addition complemented the modalities of the general interpretation of Article 3 of the AGN/53/RES/7 Resolution as follows:

(a) First, it provided that the Organization was authorized to deal with all matters examined by the Court (serious infractions of the 1949 Geneva Agreement, violation of the laws and customs of war, genocide, crimes against humanity) provided that the individual examination of the matter set out the predominance of ordinary-law crime elements. This was the first time that the Organization approached matters of this type, which, since 1946, were automatically disregarded. Additionally, in relation to violations of international humanitarian law or human rights, the Organization has systematically (since 1994) recognized the predominance of ordinary-law crime when examining matters individually.

(b) Secondly, the value of the geographic criteria was determined – that is, the place where the act was committed with regard to the zone of conflict, this being set on the same level as the opinion of the nature of the victims and the seriousness of the act. It was considered that the geographic situation did not constitute the sole criterion of appreciation as in these cases other facts are at stake, the relevance of which may be decisive when determining the predominant element – such as an examination of the existing relationship between the victims of the infractions and the possible political reason, and the seriousness of the incriminated act as, in general, the victims of these infractions are persons who do not participate or who no longer participate in the conflict AGN/63/RAP/13/p. 8).

(c) Thirdly, it is established that infractions committed by political leaders must be analyzed from the angle of the predominance of the political or ordinary-law crime element, as well as infractions committed by other persons. It was considered that, although political power must be exercised within the limits established by the law, including those of the international legislation, it must be admitted that there are numerous fields in which the exercise of a political power cannot be based on legal forms. However, the criteria concerning the seriousness of the infraction, nature of the victims and the area of the conflict served to determine the predominance of ordinary-law or political crime in each case.

(d) Fourthly, specifically, the resolution brought about various precisions on the notion of "military" infraction , establishing that "the fact that the author is a military does not mean that the act has a military character"; that "forced recruitments of prisoners or civilians in enemy armed forces (Article 2(e) of the Rules of the International Court) is related to the constitution of armed forces and that, consequently, cannot disassociate itself from military matters, may be considered as a military infraction by nature and would then authorize the application of Article 3 of the Constitution"; that "acts that are composed of elements of an infraction pertaining to ordinary-law crime and of an element constituted by the uselessness of the act from a military point of view, are not military infractions" and that "all other infractions must be examined in order to establish if ordinary-law or a military crime element prevails".

As of 1996, based on these principles of interpretation, the General Secretariat has offered its cooperation to the Court for Rwanda after the approval granted at the 63rd meeting of the General Assembly (AGN/63/PV/5).

3. General criteria for prohibiting Interpol Intervention in political, military, religious or racial crime matters.

The interpretation of Article 3 of the Constitution of INTERPOL (as can be appreciated from the evolution analyzed earlier) constitutes the core of its action and, in this regard, the General Secretariat, in addition to punctually declaring and putting into writing subject files to divulge its official position on the interpretative resolutions issued in 1951, 1984 and 1994 (GTART3/2004.10) has established the following interpretative criteria with regard to what is to be understood by crimes of political, military, religious or racial character, a matter in which the principle of predominance of the ordinary-law crime element is always examined.

Nonetheless, some acts are considered essentially as having a political, military, religious or racial character, like those pertaining to a dissolved movement; opinion crimes, press crimes, insults against authorities; crimes against domestic and foreign security of the States; desertion, treason, espionage, inquiries; infractions derived from the practice of a religion; proselytism or propaganda for a religion; and pertaining to a racial group. These types of acts are in the field of application of Article 3 of Interpol's Constitution.

A. Infractions having political character

As to infractions which, because of their very essence, have a political character, the following are the examples mentioned in the 1984 AGN/63/RAP/13 Resolution: belonging to a dissolved movement; opinion crimes; press crimes; insulting acting authorities; crimes against domestic or foreign security of the state; treason and espionage. It is an open list that makes it possible for the Organization to identify other political crimes according to its own considerations.

In the text of the report Resolution AGN/63/RAP/13 itself, the following criteria were also textually indicated with regard to particular cases.

1. Article 3 also applies to acts that may have been committed by political personalities in exercise of political power, even though these persons may be subjected to a suit after having lost their power and eventually escaping abroad. It is also important to point this out in the case of ordinary-law crimes, committed on personal capacity.

2. When politically motivated people commit crimes having no relationship to the political life of the country, of the individual or with the cause they fight, it may be considered that the facts are not covered by the immunity established in Article 3. This turns out to be true, particularly when actions are committed in other countries outside of the "conflict zone" and when it is a matter of serious actions attempting against liberty or the life of people or against property. For instance, when in order to obtain the liberty of an accomplice, police are killed or hostages are taken outside the conflict zone; and when attempts are committed against civilian – bombs in a bank, grenades in a café, etc. - outside the zone of the conflict.

3. Also, Article 3 does not apply regarding actions committed by individuals, outside of the conflict zone in order to call attention in a cause: hijacking a plane, taking hostages, kidnapping people.

4. A general evaluation criterion consist in the victims not having immediate or mediate links with the purposes pursued by the authors neither with the countries of the conflict zone or the political situation referred to.

5. The appreciation of the situation with regard to Article 3 of the Constitution must also take into account the type of cooperation act requested by the requesting National Central Bureau. If it is a matter of prevention, nothing opposes the transmission of technical information, even though linked to matters having a political motivation. Likewise, it must be possible to exchange information on potential authors of illicit acts against the civil aviation or the taking of hostages provided said information is not solely based on the interested parties belonging to a certain political movement.

In addition, requests related to serious violations of human rights committed by politicians do not enter the field of application of the prohibition provided in Article 3, as it is considered that such acts are committed at the margin of the normal exercise of political power (AGN/63/RAP/13).

In order to determine predominance it is necessary to examine if there exists or not a direct relationship between the acts perpetrated in the political reality of the country of the interested party, and the cause it combats, or the victims it creates. This can be determined by means of three benchmarks: (i) by the geographical distance from the place where the acts are committed with regard to the conflict zone;[14] (ii) as a result of the magnitude of the infraction (serious attempts against the life and liberty of persons, and against properties);[15] and (iii) because of the absence of links between the victim and the objectives pursued by the authors of the infraction, the country of the area in conflict and the political situation.[16]

B.   *Infraction having a military character*

With regard to infractions that are essentially military in character, the following have been identified: (i) desertion (Resolution AGN/53/RES/7); and (ii) the forced enrolment of war prisoners or of civilians in enemy armed forces or the constitution of armed forces (Report AGN/63/RAP/13 point 5.2.2).

As to the examination of the predominance of the ordinary-law crime element in an infraction having a military character, according to AGN/63/RAP/13, point 5.2.2, the situation is summarized as follows:

> (a) The fact that the perpetrator of an infraction is military in character does not automatically confer upon the infraction a military character. On the other hand, the unnecessary character of military actions, when said acts include elements pertaining to an ordinary-law infraction (absence of need or benefit from a military point of view), leads to the non application of Article 3.

> (b) There are elements that help to determine predominance: (i) the absence of a link between the victim and the purposes pursued by the perpetrators of the infraction, the country of the conflict zone and the political situation; and (ii) the seriousness of the acts and of the damage caused.

C. *Infraction having a religious or racial character*

With regard to infractions with a religious or racial character, the INTERPOL doctrine contained in resolution AGN/53/RES/7 has identified as such, because of their essence, to pertain to a movement that is dissolved or to practice a religion.

However, the resolutions do not contain examples of infractions that, in essence, have a racial character. In the report AGN/63/RAP/13 only one distinction between ethnicity and race is established, albeit without indicating the implications of such a distinction.

IV. THE INTERNATIONAL POLICE COOPERATION TREATMENT OF INFORMATION REGIME AND ITS INSTITUTIONAL GUARANTEE

1. *Police information cooperation and ordinary-law crimes*

The relationships established between INTERPOL, on the one hand, as global administration and the Member States, their police organizations and citizens, on the other, are basically related to Interpol's processing of information for purposes of international cooperation.

In this context, "information" is understood in the *RPI Rules* (Article 1.a) as "the item of information or set of items of information (personal or otherwise, and irrespective of the sources) pertaining to constituent elements of *ordinary-law crimes*, the investigation and prevention of such crimes, the prosecution and punishment of offences, and any information pertaining to missing persons and unidentified dead bodies" (Article 1.a). As to the term "Processing of information" it includes "any operation or set of operations (automated or manual) applied to information in any form or on any medium, from the moment it is accessed to the moment it is destroyed, and any exchange in between."

The processing of this information accumulated and filed by INTERPOL, which is to be limited to ordinary-law types of crime, may not affect the freedom of persons, especially if it exceeds the scope established by ordinary-law crimes and refers to that of political, military, religious or racial crimes.

In fact, as has already been mentioned, the fundamental objective of INTERPOL is the international police cooperation in the prevention, repression and sentencing of ordinary-law criminal infractions, refered to in Article 2 of its Constitution, without exceeding the limits of Article 3. To this end, an important accumulation, exchange and diffusion of police information is generated for the purpose of facilitating investigations related to such crimes (Article 3.1.a, *RPI Rules*), that are directly referred to persons, which can be affected in their rights. That is why, the *Rules on the Processing of Information for the purposes of International Police Cooperation (RPI Rules)* were adopted in order to set out the conditions and basic procedures according to which information is processed by the Organization, or through its channels, for the purposes of international police cooperation, or for any other legitimate purpose, "with due respect for the basic rights of individuals in conformity with Article 2 of the Organization's Constitution and the Universal Declaration of Human Rights to which the said Article refers." (Article 2.a, *RPI Rules*).

2. *Limits and Conditions for Processing of Information*

According to article 4.1 *RPI Rules*, being the General Secretariat the international centre in the fight against international ordinary-law crimes (article 26.b, Constitution), it is responsible for: processing information it receives or collects, in accordance with the rules the Organization has adopted on such matters; ensuring that the provisions of the *RPI Rules* and the texts to which they refer are observed during any operation to process information through the Organization's channels; deciding on the type and structure of the Organization's telecommunications network(s) and databases; developing and maintaining those telecommunications network(s) and databases, as well as the means necessary for National Central Bureaus, authorized national institutions and authorized international entities to have access to them; developing and verifying the security of those telecommunications network(s) and databases; and housing the Organization's databases on its premises.

The General Secretariat is also empowered to take any appropriate steps which may contribute effectively to combating international ordinary-law crime, within the limits of the tasks set for it and the provisions of the *RPI Rules*. For that purpose, it may request information (Article 4.2 *RPI Rules*) or conclude cooperation agreements involving the exchange of information (Article 4.3 *RPI Rules*).

Concerning the processing of information handled by Interpol, the Regulation defines the following terms which are those generally used: "Personal information" means any information relating to an identified or identifiable natural person; "Identifiable natural person" is one who can be identified, directly or indirectly, in particular by reference to an identification number or to one or more factors specific to his identity, or to his physiological, psychic, economic, or social characteristics (article 1.c *RPI Rules*); "Source of the information" means the entity providing the information through the Organization's channels (article 1.h *RPI Rules*); "Police information system" means all the Organization's databases and networks which can be used for processing information, through its channels, for the purposes of international police cooperation (article 1,i *RPI Rules*); and "Notices" mean international Interpol notifications containing sets of information recorded in the police information system and circulated by the General Secretariat (article 1.l *RPI Rules*).

3. *Purposes of Processing of Police Information and International Notices*

The purposes of processing information for **international police cooperation by** Interpol according to article 3,1 of the *RPI Rules*, are to prevent, investigate and prosecute ordinary-law crimes, and to assist with such investigations for the following reasons: a search for a person with a view to his arrest; to obtain information about a person who has committed or is likely to commit, or has participated or is likely to have participated (directly or indirectly) in an ordinary-law crime; to warn police authorities about a person's criminal activities; to locate a missing person; to locate a witness or victim; to identify a person or a dead body; to locate or identify objects; to describe or identify **modus operandi**, offences committed by unidentified persons, the characteristics of counterfeits or forgeries, and seizures of items connected with trafficking operations. This information may also be processed by Interpol for the purpose of identifying threats and criminal networks; and in all cases the purpose for which information is processed must be stated explicitly for each database.

In order to attain any of the aforementioned purposes of processing of information mentioned in article 3.1 of the *RPI Rules*, and to supply to the police services of Member States through their National Central Bureaus, certain information about persons or objects, Interpol can publish bulletins called "International Notices," which are considered as the main instruments of international police cooperation. These Notices are usually published by the General Secretariat in Interpol's four official languages (English, French, Spanish and Arabic), at the request of a National Central Bureau, although the General Secretariat may, however, publish blue or green notices on its own initiative. After publication these notices are circulated to the National Central Bureaus network. These Notices are used to locate, trace and arrest international fugitives; search for a missing person or, identify a person or an unidentified body.

There are nine types of notices:[283]

1. **Red notices**: Are published in order to seek the location and arrest of a person with a view to his/her extradition. Before a National Central Bureau or an authorized international entity requests publication and circulation of a red notice, it shall ensure that: the person sought is the subject of criminal proceedings or has been convicted of a crime, and references to an enforceable arrest warrant, court decision or other judicial documents are provided; assurances have been given that extradition will be sought upon arrest of the person, in conformity with national laws and/or the applicable bilateral and multilateral treaties; and sufficient information is provided to allow for the cooperation requested to be effective.

2. **Blue notices**: Are published in order to obtain information on a person of interest in a criminal investigation; and/or locate a person of interest in a criminal investigation; and/or identify a person of interest in a criminal investigation. Before a National Central Bureau, a national authorized institution or an authorized international entity requests publication and circulation of a blue notice, it shall ensure that the person is someone of interest in a criminal investigation, such as a criminal, a suspect, an accomplice, an associate or a witness; additional information on the possible criminal history, status, location or identity of the person or any other information relevant to the criminal investigation is sought; and sufficient information is provided to allow for the cooperation requested to be effective.

3. **Green notices**: Are published to warn about a person's criminal activities. Before a National Central Bureau, a national authorized institution or an authorized international entity requests publication and circulation of a green notice, it shall ensure that: the person is considered to be a possible threat to public safety and/or someone likely to commit a criminal offence; that conclusion is based on an assessment by a national law enforcement authority or an authorized international entity; -

---

283 See INTERPOL, "Implementing Rules for the Rules on the Processing of Information for the Purposes of International Police Co-Operation", VADE MECUM, 2009-01-01, Chap. 19, art 37, pp. 21-25. See in http://www.interpol.int/

the assessment is based on the person's previous criminal conviction(s) and/or other reasonable grounds; and sufficient information is provided to allow for the warning to be relevant.

4. **Yellow notices**: Are published to locate a missing person or to identify a person unable to identify himself/herself. Before a National Central Bureau, a national authorized institution or an authorized international entity requests publication and circulation of a yellow notice, it shall ensure that: if the notice is published to locate a missing person, the person has been reported missing to police, his/her whereabouts are unknown and the person's anonymity or privacy is not protected by the applicable national laws. If the notice is published to identify a person unable to identify himself/herself, the request is being made because a person has been found and he/she is unable to identify himself/herself. In any case, sufficient information is provided to allow for identification.

5. **Black notices**: Are published to identify dead bodies. Before a National Central Bureau, a national authorized institution or an authorized international entity requests publication and circulation of a black notice, it shall ensure that: the request is being made because a dead body has been found and it has not been identified; and sufficient information is provided to allow for identification

6. **Stolen Works of Art Notices**: Are published to locate works of art or items of cultural value that have been stolen, or to identify such objects discovered in suspicious circumstances. Before a National Central Bureau, a national authorized institution or an authorized international entity requests publication and circulation of a stolen work of art notice, it shall ensure that: the work of art or item of cultural value is of interest in a criminal investigation; it has some unique characteristic and/or is of considerable value; and sufficient information is provided to allow identification.

7. **Purple notices**: Are published to provide information on *modi operandi*, procedures, objects, devices and hiding places used by criminals. Before a National Central Bureau, a national authorized institution or an authorized international entity requests publication and circulation of a purple notice, it shall ensure that the circulation of the information in the form of a notice is of specific international interest to the police and is in the interests of public safety.

8. **Special notices**: Are published on the basis of an agreement with another international organization concluded pursuant to Article 41 of the Constitution. Before an international authorized entity requests publication and circulation of a special notice, it shall ensure that: the information satisfies the conditions for publishing such notices, as defined in the said agreement; and sufficient information is provided to allow for the cooperation requested to be effective. Among these Special Notices, the **Interpol -Un Security Council Special Notice** must be mentioned, issued for groups and individuals associated with Al-Qaeda and the Taliban and subject to sanctions through the freezing of assets, travel bans and arms embargoes.

9. **Orange notices**: Are published to warn about a person, an object, an event or a modus operandi representing an imminent threat to public safety and likely to cause serious damage to property and/or injury to persons. Before a National Central Bureau, a national authorized institution or an authorized international entity requests publication and circulation of a orange notice, it shall ensure that: in the case

of a person, he or she is considered to be an imminent threat to public safety and/or someone likely to commit a criminal offence; this conclusion is based on an assessment by a national law enforcement authority; this assessment is based on the person's previous criminal conviction(s) and/or other reasonable grounds; In the case of an object, modus operandi or event, it is considered an imminent threat to public safety; this conclusion is based on an assessment by a national law enforcement authority; sufficient information is provided to allow for the warning to be relevant. These Orange notices constitute alerts and it is up to each country to take appropriate measures, in conformity with its national laws.

Regarding the **Red Notices,** that is the one that can affect most the freedom and rights of persons, it is important to highlight, as it is informed in Interpol's web site, that "it is not an international arrest warrant." In these cases of Red Notices, the persons concerned are wanted by national jurisdictions (or the International Criminal Tribunals, where appropriate) and Interpol's role is "to assist the national police forces in identifying or locating those persons with a view to their arrest and extradition." These red notices allow the warrant to be circulated worldwide with the request that the wanted person be arrested with a view to extradition. In this matter of red Notice, a distinction must be drawn between two types of Red Notice: the first type is based on an arrest warrant and is issued for a person wanted for prosecution; the second type is based on a court decision for a person wanted to serve a sentence.

4.   *Some principles for the Processing of Information*

According to Article 10.1a of the *RPI Rules,* the use of information through INTERPOL can only be made when it is accumulatively "in accordance with the Constitution and the rules of the Organization applicable to the case"; when it responds to one of the purposes provided in Article 3 of this regulation and of the provisions of its Article 2"; "when it is pertinent and refers to a matter presenting a concrete interest for the police on an international level"; "when it does not affect the purposes of the Organization, its image or its interest nor its confidentiality (Article 8, *RPI Rules*) or the security of the information, that is, the integrity and the confidentiality of the information provided and dealt with through the police information system (Article 9, *RPI Rules*); and be carried out by the source which has generated it "based on the legislation in force in its country, in accordance with the international agreements subscribed and with the Constitution" of the Organization.

In order to assure the correct application of Articles 2 and 3 of Interpol's Constitution regarding the processing of information only referred to ordinary-law crimes and not to political, military, racial or religious crimes, a series of principles to determine the legality of the intervention of INTERPOL in matters of international search have been established in different Resolutions of the Organization.

For instance, in Resolution AGN/20/RES/11 (1951) concerning "request for international search," adopted in the 20th Meeting of the General Assembly celebrated in Lisbon in June 1951, was recommended to the Members States and to the heads of their National Central Bureau:

"that they see to that requests for information or search, mainly of preventive arrests having as objective infractions of a political, racial or religious character, not be transmitted at ay time to the International Office or to other National Central Bureaus even though in the requesting country, the facts would be part of an ordinary-law infraction."

In view of this, the General Assembly decided, "in order to comply as far as possible with the provisions of Article 1 of the Constitution, that should there be any doubt as to the political, racial or religious character of a request, the Head of the International Office in joint agreement with the Secretary of the CIPC" be authorized:

> "To suspend the diffusion of any request for information or search coming from a National Central Bureau or from another requesting police entity in order to be able to request all the necessary information to appreciate precise nature of the facts and the true situation of the criminals".

The General Assembly furthermore decided:

> "that the Police entity who sends a request for information or for a search to the Head of the International Office for its diffusion to the National Central Bureaus or to any other foreign National Office" shall be totally responsible as to the consequences which may derive from the political, racial or religious character of said request".

Finally, the General Assembly recommended that the Member States and the Heads of the National Central Bureaus":

> "also, as far as possible, see to that the request they receive from the foreign police authorities not seem to violate the principles enounced in paragraph 1 and 2 of this Resolution and that, if necessary, they immediately ask the International Office located in Paris to advise the General Manager"[284].

On the other hand, Resolution AGN/53/RES/7 (1984) on "the application of Article 3 of the Constitution" was adopted by the General Assembly at its 53rd Meeting celebrated in Luxemburg in September 1984, by means of which for the purpose of facilitating the interpretation of said Article recommended that the following principles be diffused to all the services in charge of prevention and repression of delinquency, that the General Secretariat as well as the National Central Bureaus must apply:

Regarding Procedures and Rules, the following procedures are set forth:

1. In accordance with Article 3 of the Constitution, "the Organization is rigorously prohibited from participating in any activity or intervention in matters having a political, military, religious or racial character.

2. A Resolution approved by the General Assembly in 1951 makes it clear that the prohibition also covers crimes having "a predominantly political, religious or racial character though in the requiring country, a qualification of ordinary-law has been assigned to these acts."

---

284 AGN/20/RAP/14

3. It is impossible to establish a more precise definition or what is called a matter having a political military, religious or racial character. Each case must be studied separately in accordance with its context.

4. As to the Secretary General having knowledge of a fact which may correspond to the application of Article 3, he shall initiate an exchange of opinions with the requesting National Central Bureau for the purpose of determining if application of Article 3 corresponds to the fact.

5. Should the intervention request be maintained, the entire responsibility derived from the character assigned to the matters has to be dealt by the OCN. Upon the diffusion, the Office of the Secretary shall include ample information.

6. In the case of a complete disagreement between the Secretary General and the National Central Bureau as to the interpretation that certain matters are worthy of with regard to Article 3, the Office of the Secretary may reject to cooperate.

7. When a National Central Bureau acting on its own account has notoriously infringed provisions of Article 3, the General Secretary reserves himself the right to transmit his own posture to the other National Central Bureaus.

8. If upon a bilateral exchange between National Central Bureaus, should the points of view related to the application of Article 3 defer, the General Secretariat will be imperatively advised.

9. The rejecting by one or of several countries to carry out the petitions coming from a National Central Bureau or from the General Secretariat (for example: a request for extradition), does not mean that the petition does not proceed neither that it must be automatically applied to Article 3 of the Constitution. However, the rejection of extraditions shall be communicated to the other National Central Bureaus by means of an Addendum to the diffusion as an indication of release (freedom). When a person is arrested for the purpose of extradition, the request for the search continues being valid, except if a communication to the contrary is received from the requesting country and up to the moment when the extradition is carried out.

These procedures and rules confirm Interpol's character as a global administration (intergovernmental organization) not subjected to the will of its Member States when applying its own Constitution and Rules, and specially that of Article 3, which rigorously prohibits the Organization from any activity or intervention in political, military, religious or racial matters. It is also particularly established that the prohibition also extends to crimes having predominantly political, religious or racial aspects, "even though the requiring country may have assigned these facts an ordinary-law crime qualification," and the Organization shall study "each case" separately in accordance with its context".

5. *Mutability of the processed information: Modification, Blocking or Destruction of Information.*

The use of information obtained through international police cooperation that is incorporated in the INTERPOL files, as established by its Constitution, must be carried out in accordance with the Universal Declaration of Human Rights and according to the prohibition contained in Article 3 of the Constitution. The consequence of this provision is that in case of its violations, the information may and must be modified, blocked or destroyed by the Organization.

To that effect, Article 15 of the *RPI Rules* provides that the modification, blocking or destruction of the information may be initiated by the source of the information or on the initiative of an entity different from the source of the information that can be an individual or citizen of a member country, but always within the limits established in the Regulations. In all these cases, the General Secretariat must prove that the information meets the conditions for its use; it must consult the source of the information and the National Central Bureaus that can be affected by the operation and it must take appropriate measures to determine the possibility and the need to carry out the requested operation.

After consultation with the source of the information or the interested National Central Bureau (Articles 10.1(c) and 12(a), *RPI Rules*), the General Secretariat must modify, block or destroy the information on its own initiative if it has pertinent and particular data making it possible to consider that "some of the criteria of the treatment of the information" provided by the *RPI Rules* or in the texts to which it refers would not be respected or the information would redound in affecting the international police cooperation, the Organization, its personnel or the fundamental rights of the person to whom the said information refers, as per Article 2 of the Constitution.

On the other hand, according to the same provision of Article 15 of the *RPI Rules*, the General Secretariat must destroy the information in whatever way possible: (a) once the purpose for which the information was obtained has been fulfilled, since there is no provision of the Regulations which allows information to be retained; (b) when the term for evaluation of the need to preserve the information has been reached, its source has not declared any need to keep it and no provision of the regulations permits that it be kept; (c) when the General Secretariat has concrete data which makes it possible to consider that the person being searched or the object of a request for information on an international level is no longer a suspect with regard to the facts that justified the filing of information concerning that person.

In the case of *international diffusions*, when the information is modified the General Secretariat must evaluate the need to keep it and, if needed, to modify it. When it is destroyed, the General Secretariat must also destroy the said international diffusion. In these cases, however, the General Secretariat may keep the information that gave rise to the international diffusion or to the request for information, during a period of five years (Article 14(c) 3, *RPI Rules*).

6.   The Data Base protection regime and Interpol's files

International police information processed by INTERPOL to comply with its cooperation activities is accumulated in the archives of the Organization and internationally divulged. These files contain information on persons that may affect their rights – for instance, as to personal liberty or privacy – making it necessary for global administrative law to regulate and protect the information, and also to make it possible to correct the information.

To that effect, as we have pointed out, Article 15 of the *RPI Rules* establishes the possibility for the General Secretariat to modify, block or destroy information contained in the files, if the source of the information so requires (e.g. a National Criminal Bureau), or upon the initiative of "an entity other than the source of the information", which may be the person interested or affected by it. In this case, the General Secretariat, after having proved that the information meets the conditions required for its use, must proceed to consult the source of the information – that is, the National Central Bureau which could be affected by the operation – and must therefore take all appropriate measures to determine the possibility and the need to proceed to the requested operation.

Consequently, it is the General Secretariat, as an organ of a global administration, the competent body to modify, block, and destroy information, even by its own initiative, and also to decide that a particular data should be preserved and maintained for purposes of police cooperation.

V. GLOBAL ADMINISTRATIVE LAW PROCEDURES DEVELOPED BEFORE INTERPOL

As a global administration, for the purpose of complying with the provisions of the global administrative law that is applied to INTERPOL, and in particular, in order to protect the rights of the citizens of member countries, the Regulations governing INTERPOL's activities have set forth two main rules of global administrative procedure: *first,* the administrative procedure established for the processing and registry of information for police cooperation, in order to assure, as previously explained, that the processing of information be made according to all the conditions established; and *second*, the administrative procedure established for the purpose of revision or review of the INTERPOL files regarding information already processed, in order to modify or eliminate the corresponding files.

In these administrative procedures, the Rules of Interpol recognize enough standing to the citizens of member countries, as subjects of global administrative law in the international level, with the possibility of entering into a direct legal relationship with the General Secretariat and the Commission for the Control of Files, as global administration, that has been configured with independence regarding the National Public Administration or the National Central Bureaus, and in some cases, confronting them.

These two sorts of global administrative procedures have been referred to in Resolution GT-ART3-2004.1, distinguishing:

In the first place, the global administrative procedure developed before the General Secretariat for the processing and recording of information related to persons in matters of ordinary-law crimes initiated at the initiative of the General Secretariat, when it receives messages or information from National Central Bureaus which are subject to investigations. The general purpose of this procedure, called *"ordinary vigilance,"* is to regulate the relationship between said Bureaus or Offices, and the Organization.

In the second place, the global administrative procedure that is also developed before the General Secretariat for the purpose of preventing the processing of information or modifying the registered information related to persons, for instance, for not referring to ordinary-law crimes, which can be initiated based on the petition of a National Central Bureau, a national individual of a country that is member country, or the Commission of Control of the Files, called *"exceptional vigilance"*.

In both cases, the procedures are global administrative procedures established in order to assure that the pertinent information regarding any individual registered in INTERPOL refers only to cases of ordinary-law crimes, and to guarantee, in accordance with Article 3 of the Constitution of the Organization, the effectiveness of INTERPOL's prohibition to act in matters of political, military, religious or racial crimes.

1. Global Administrative Procedure referred to requests for processing of information

A. General conditions of the requests

According to article 10.1.a of the *RPI Rules*, as aforementioned, the request for processing of information through Interpol's channels, including the publishing of International Notices, may only be carried out *if all* of the following conditions are met, that is, cumulatively:

1. It complies with the Constitution and relevant provisions in the Organization's Rules;

2. It is in accordance with one of the aforementioned purposes referred to in Article 3 of the *RPI Rules*, and the requirements of Article 2 of those *RPI Rules*;

3. It is relevant and connected with cases of specific international interest to the police;

4. It is not such that it might prejudice the Organization's aims, image or interests, or the confidentiality (Article 8 *RPI Rules*) or security of the information (Artile 9 *RPI Rules*);

5. It is carried out by its source "in the context of the laws existing in its country, in conformity with the international conventions to which it is a party, and with the Organization's Constitution."

The information provided to INTERPOL by a National Central Bureau, an authorized national institution, or authorized international entity is considered, **a priori**, to be accurate and relevant. However, in conformity with Articles 10.b and 12.a of the *RPI Rules*, if there is any doubt about whether the criteria for processing an item of information are being met, the General Secretariat shall consult the source of that information, or the National Central Bureau concerned, and in any case, it shall take all other appropriate steps to ensure that the criteria have indeed been met. The information may then be recorded with a view to obtaining supplementary information to allow its withholding in the police information system.

Also, in any case, and according to the same article 10 of the *RPI Rules*, the General Secretariat shall take all appropriate steps to prevent any direct or indirect prejudice the information may cause to the Member States, the Organization or its staff, and with due respect for the basic rights of individuals the information concerns, in conformity with Article 2 of the Organization's Constitution and the Universal Declaration of Human Rights.

Regarding the request for International Notices, the information provided to INTERPOL must meet the basic conditions regarding Identification and Judicial Data set forth in its *Rules* regarding the information that the Organization can obtain, process and store. In particular, for instance, regarding *Personal Information*, the request must contain the name and addresses of the affected person, as well as his nationality or Identification Document, or any other important relevant data of identification, for instance, for the purpose of extradition. Regarding the *Judicial Data*, the request formulated by the National Central Bureaus must inform about the ordinary-law crime committed; the precise date of the supposed criminal facts attributed to the interested person; the qualification of the supposed criminal offence; the precise articles of the national criminal legislation describing the offence; the maximum applicable punishment and the date of prescription of the offences; and the detail regarding the countries in which the Member State will seek for "extradition" of the affected person.

B. *Initiative in the Procedure*

The ordinary vigilance procedures as has been said are officially initiated by the General Secretariat when it receives messages or information requiring its processing for international cooperation in police matters related to ordinary-law crimes.

These messages or information may reach the General Secretariat in two ways: *first*, when the General Secretariat is the sole addressee of a message containing a request for publication of an International Notice, or when the General Secretariat is one of the several addressees or receivers of a copy of the diffused message; and second, when the General Secretariat is informed by a National Central Bureau about a copy of a message that the General Secretariat has not received, and considers that it may infringe Article 3 of the Constitution.

C. *Intervention in the procedure of the interested person*

Regarding requests for processing information filed for instance by National Central Bureaus, nothing in INTERPOL's Constitution or Regulations prevent the citizens of member countries that could be affected with the specific request in his personal rights and guaranties, to participate.

As explained previously, according to article 15 of the *RPI Rules*, the information stored in INTERPOL's files can be modified, blocked and destroyed at the initiative of the source of the information, or at the initiative of an entity different to the source of information that can be precisely the person to which the information is related. In this case, the affected person can formulate a direct petition before the Organization. For such purpose, article 4.a of the *RPI Rules*, when referring to the filing of cases before the Commission for the Control of Files, establishes an individual right to petition that the citizens of member countries can exercise in order to ask the Organization to adjust its decisions to its Constitution and Regulations.

These petitions can be filed to demand the Organization to ensure that the requests for processing information filed by National Central Bureaus comply with all the conditions established in the Rules, and in particular, with all the conditions that cumulatively must be fulfilled, which are: to be made according to the Constitution and relevant provisions in the Organization's Regulations (*Rules*), for the purposes therein established, referred to cases relevant and connected with specific police international interests; that the request be formulated in the context of the laws existing in the requesting Member State; and in addition, that the request for processing information for police cooperation must only refer to ordinary-law crimes and not to political, military, racial of religious crimes.

In all these cases of individual's initiatives, the General Secretariat must submit the matter to the Commission for the Control of Files established for the purpose of protecting the information against any abuse and of preventing any harm that can be caused to any persons' rights (article 2, 2 *RCI Rules*)

D.   *The need to consult the source of the information*

In all cases in which any doubt could exist as to the processing of the information, and in particular, about the ordinary-law crime nature of the facts, or about the matters forbidden in accordance with Article 3 of the Constitution, Article 10.1 of the *RPI Rules* establishes that the General Secretariat must always consult the source of the information or the National Central Bureau interested in knowing if the source of the information is an authorized national service.

In these cases, when the General Secretary has knowledge of a fact, in order to process the information, it is obligated to initiate a procedure for the purpose of exchanging opinions with the National Central Bureau that filed the request regarding the applicability of Article 3 of the Constitution. Said procedure must be initiated, independently from the contents of the request. Nonetheless, the procedure must not be initiated in cases dealing with crimes having a political, military, religious or racial character when they clearly qualify within the scope of the prohibitions of Article 3 of the Constitution.

On the other hand, in cases where doubts as to the application of Article 3 are raised, that is, doubts about the ordinary-law character of the crime, or about the crime having a political, military, religious or racial character; in order to respect the sovereignty of the States, the Organization must communicate to the interested National Central Bureau that it estimates that the request it made may entail the application of Article 3. In such cases, the General Secretariat, on the one hand, must require that the National Central Bureau indicate if it maintains the formulated request, and in spite of the doubts, if it confirms that the crime is an ordinary-law crime, explaining why; and on the other hand, it must request supplementary data from the National Central Bureau that may clarify the existing doubts as to whether the crime is or is not a crime pertaining to ordinary-law.

E.   *Initial registration and protective measures*

When consulting the respective National Central Bureau, the General Secretariat must take the needed and opportune measure to assure compliance with the criteria guiding its activities; and even in cases in which it considers that the request of information does not adjust to the Constitution of INTERPOL, when requesting additional data and information, it can decide to keep the information in the Police Information System.

Nonetheless, in these cases, the General Secretariat must take the appropriate measures of protection to avoid any direct or indirect damage that the information may cause to Member States, to the Organization or to its staff, and assure the due respect of the fundamental rights of those persons referred to by the said information, in accordance with what is provided for in Article 2 of the Constitution of the Organization, and in the Universal Declaration of Human Rights.

What is clear is that if the information clearly fits in the prohibition regarding crimes having a political, military, religious or racial character, the processing of the information must be denied by the General Secretariat. But also in these cases of rejected files, they must be physically kept (paper), and must be introduced into an administrative data base indicating the name of the person, the requesting National Central Bureau, and the reason and the date of the denial. If a country sends new information related to that person, an alert must be activated.

In the case of matters qualifying as ordinary-law crimes and independently from the service in charge of their examination, until the end of the exchange of opinions and a final decision is adopted, the information must be registered in the INTERPOL database, but with an *apostille* indicating that said information is being examined under the content of Article 3.

F.   *Intervention of the various Services of the General Secretariat, especially the Legal Counsel Office*

In all cases of ordinary vigilance procedures referring to the processing of information and the requests for the International Notices to be issued by INTERPOL, the General Secretariat is obliged to prove that, in all these cases, all the conditions for their registration have been complied with and, among these provisions, that Article 3 of the Constitution has been respected – that is, that the information is dealing with ordinary-law crimes and not with matters related to political, military, racial or religious crimes.

To that effect, before processing the information, all the messages, messages of diffusion and requests for publication of international diffusion sent to INTERPOL must be sent to the Operational Police Support Board and must be treated by the Center of Command and Coordination or by the Office of the Assistant Director related to the treatment of Police Data, or even including the Diffusion Services. In all these cases, the different bodies must verify the matter as being of ordinary-law crime, regarding which the vigilance in respect to Article 3 is exercised.

In cases in which it may be any doubt regarding the matter as related to political, military, religious or racial crimes, as well as requests having special political repercussion, in novel cases that could require a particular follow-up of Judicial Matters or in cases referring or pertaining to a terrorist organization not based on ordinary-law crimes, the study of the case must be assigned to the Judicial Counsel Office of the General Secretariat.

This Judicial Counsel Office is also competent to decide as to request an arbitration procedure before by the General Secretariat, for example, when in order to solve a situation, it cannot follow any of the Interpretative Resolutions or a precedent, or when the situation implies that there is a significant political risk for the Organization

G. Possible outcome of the procedure

Depending on the answer received by the General Secretariat from the respective National Central Bureau, the said office must terminate the procedure by adopting any of the following three solutions:

(a) As established in Article 10.5 of the *RPI Rules*, the General Secretariat may register the request for processing of information, and for instance, publish the corresponding International Notice once it has been proven that it is manifestly valid, that is, that it refers to a matter related to ordinary-law crimes, and that the conditions established in the Organization's Constitution and Regulations have been complied.

(b) If there is any doubt as to the character of the ordinary-law crime of the fact that has been reported, or if it deals with matters having a political, military, religious or racial character, the General Secretariat may proceed to register the request and publish the International Notice, reminding the requesting National Central Bureau that it corresponds to it to guarantee that the crime is effectively a ordinary-law crime, and provide the other Member States with the maximum information about the case in order for them to decide if they are to act fully aware of the case, indicating the position adopted by the General Secretariat.

(c) The Secretariat may refuse registration in cases of non compliance with the conditions set forth in the *RPI Rules* or in article 3 of the Constitution, indicating that the analysis made is contrary to the statements made by the requesting National Central Bureau. To that effect, it is necessary for the Secretary General to be in complete disagreement with the National Central Bureau making a request as to the interpretation to be given to certain facts regarding the prohibitions established in Article 3 of the Constitution.

In the case of information sent from a National Central Bureau directly to other National Central Bureau, received by the General Secretariat as a simple notification, the General Secretariat has the authority to exercise an *a posteriori* vigilance review for the adjustment of said messages to the prohibitions established in Article 3, in order to decide their inclusion in INTERPOL's data base. Should it decide not to enter the information in the data base, the General Secretariat must inform the other National Central Bureaus, addressees of the information, the position of the Organization, inviting them to act with maximum prudence regarding said information, in accordance with the recommendations of the Commission for Control of Files.

2. Global Administrative Procedure referred to Review, at Official Initiative, of Information already processed

Global administrative procedures concerning the so-called exceptional vigilance are those developed before the General Secretariat, in principle, once the information for police international cooperation has been processed and, consequently, consists of an opposition to the registration in order to obtain its modification, blockage or destruction.

These procedures can be initiated by a petition formulated by a National Central Bureau or by an official verification carried out by the Commission for the Control of Files, and generally, they have their origin in some error that could have been committed by the General Secretariat, or on the existence of a new element not known to the Secretariat before the registration of the information (Resolution AGN/53/RES/7).

A. *Applicable Procedure in litigations between two National Central Bureaus*

When a National Central Bureau officially opposes itself to registration by the General Secretariat of information proceeding from another National Central Bureau requesting the verification or suppression of said information, the basic procedure established, is related to the exchange of opinions between the above-mentioned National Bureaus.-,For such purpose, the General Secretariat must take into account the precedents based on pragmatic and political considerations, all in accordance with the normative texts applicable, especially, those concerning the prohibitions of Article 3 of the Constitution.

However it must be pointed out in these exceptional possible cases of global administrative procedure, can be initiated by an opposition formulated by a National Central Bureau when INTERPOL receives a request for International Notice from another National Bureau, even before it has been possible to enter said message in the database or even before the processing of the information has begun at the General Secretariat.

In these cases, when the opposition adopts the form of an express request directed to the General Secretariat, and it is based on the prohibitions contained in Article 3 of the Constitution for the purpose of not having the said message or diffusion message entered in the INTERPOL database, the procedure regulated in Article 23 of the *RPI Rules* is applied; this demanding that, in principle, the dispute be resolved by mutual consent. Should this not be reached, the Executive Committee of the Organization must be resorted to and, if necessary, the General Assembly itself in accordance with a procedure established for that purpose.

From this disposition, two supplementary procedures can be developed in the search for a political solution. With regard to the dispute between two National Offices: on the one hand, if the Secretary General considers, based on the data lying on the file, that he cannot make a decision by mutual consent with the President, he may appeal to the Executive Committee. If, on the contrary, the Secretary General makes a decision following an exchange of opinion, the National Central Bureaus may, for their part, come back to the Executive Committee and, if necessary, to the General Assembly.

On the other hand, when litigation has not been directly proposed by a Member State, the Secretary General has an ample margin available as to how to act with regard to how to direct the litigation, which can confront the General Secretariat with one or several National Bureaus. In these cases, the Secretary General may request that the matter be included in the agenda of a meeting of the Executive Committee or of the General Assembly, but he may also, at any time, request the legal opinion of the File Commission for the Control of Files on the effect of Article 2.4 of the Agreement between the Commission and the General Secretariat, which specifies that "the Commission obligates itself to verify any file regarding which the Secretary General wishes to take knowledge of his opinion even if these files have not been the object of a verification request in the case of nominal files".

Finally, when a confrontation occurs between two National Bureaus, the Secretary General may decide that the matter be resolved before recurring to the Executive Committee and to the General Assembly, and propose that the parties submit to arbitration.

As to the procedure to be followed inside the General Secretariat in cases when the political or diplomatic aspect is important, the Secretary General himself carries out an essential function because he is the one who has to receive all the analysis or acting proposals in order to adopt a decision. It is also the Secretary General who has to sign the letters and pamphlets sent to the National Bureaus.

B. *Procedure applicable to Official Verifications carried out by the Commission for Control of Files*

In accordance with Article 4 of the *RCI Rules*, another Administrative Procedure can be identified in cases of exceptional vigilance tending to check the processing and registration of an information, which is also originated at official initiative, but in this case, *ex officio* by the Commission for Control of Files when carrying out control of the files within the framework of official verifications. These are made for the purpose of verifying that the processing of information has been carried out in accordance with the provisions of the Constitution of the Organization, and in accordance with the interpretation thereof, made by the competent entities of the Organization; that the information has been registered for a precise purpose, and may not be used in a way not compatible with said purpose of the Organization; and that the registrations are exact and that they are to be kept only for a limited period of time under the conditions established by the Organization.

3. Global Administrative Procedures referred to review of information already processed initiated by individual initiative

Global administrative procedures concerning the so called exceptional vigilance can also be initiated before the General Secretariat, once the information for police international cooperation has been already processed, through petitions formulated by individuals, citizens of the member countries, in order to obtain the modification, blockage or destruction of police information registered in INTERPOL's Files. These procedures could also be initiated by individual initiative before the Commission for the Control of Files, before a request for processing an information is filed by a National Central Bureau, or once the request is filed before INTERPOL, in order to alert in advance the Secretariat General and the Commission for the Control of Files, of possible violations of the Constitution and the Regulations of the Organization, and to formulate an opposition to the possible request that a Member State can file for the processing of the information.

These global administrative procedures are of particular interest in relation to the global administrative law subject-matter because they are established to guarantee individual rights before an International Organization or a global administration, allowing citizens of any member countries to enter in direct relationship whit it.

In effect, these global administrative procedures, also called of exceptional vigilance, are initiated upon the petition of national individuals or citizens of a member country of the Organization, through a petition filed before the Commission for Control of Files, which is the key entity established within INTERPOL's organization for the control of files, and their purpose is to assure that the processing of information by the Organization does not affect the rights of individuals.

This global administrative procedure, that places the citizen of any of the 188 Member States of the Organization in the possibility of establishing a direct legal relation with the global administration, has been established for the purpose of guaranteeing those citizens their right to personal liberty and freedom, and to not to be internationally molested or persecuted by Member States through INTERPOL channels or using INTERPOL means of international cooperation, for instance, in cases of crimes related to political, military, religious or racial matters.

A. *The right to access to information handled by INTERPOL and the right to petition before the Global Administration*

Article 4(a) of the *RCI Rules* regulates the presentation of cases before the Commission for Control of Files, and establishes what could be qualified as a individual right to petition that any citizens of any member countries have in order to formulate requirements before the General Secretariat and the Commission for the Control of Files, to have access to information that is handled by INTERPOL, and to seek for the protection of their rights in cases in which Member States seek to use INTERPOL's channels of police cooperation in a way contrary to its Constitutions and Regulations, and particularly, for purposes of initiating international persecutions against individuals motivated by facts or situations having a political, military, religious or racial character.

This right of petition by individuals before INTERPOL is regulated by Article 4 of the *RCI Rules*, when providing that any person who wishes to have access to information about itself or regarding the person it represents may address the Commission for Control of Files a request related to said information.

This is ratified in Article 8 of the *RCI Rules* when establishing the "conditions and modalities of access" to the files, providing that any person who wishes to have access to his existing personal data contained in the INTERPOL files, may do so freely and at no cost.

In order to be admitted (admissibility conditions), petitions or requests for access to personal information must be made by persons who could be the object of said information, or by their duly constituted representatives or by their legal representatives. In particular, according to article 10 of the "Operating Rules of the Commission for the Control of INTERPOL's Files" dated 2008 all petitions or requests shall be considered admissible if the following conditions are met:

"(a) The request includes an original letter, signed by the requesting party and explaining the purpose of the request;

(b) It is written in one of the Organization's official languages;

(c) The request comes from the person whom it concerns, or from that person's duly authorized representative or his/her legal representative;

(d) If the request comes from the duly authorized representative of the person who is the subject of the request, the request shall be accompanied by an original power of attorney signed by the said person authorizing his/her representative to access any information about that person recorded in INTERPOL 's files;

(e) If the request comes from the legal representative of the person who is the subject of the request, it shall be accompanied by a corresponding written declaration;

(f) The request shall be accompanied by a copy of an identity document belonging to the person who is the subject of the request, in order to prove his/her identity;

(g) If the request calls into question the processing of information in INTERPOL's files, it shall set out the reasons, that is to say be accompanied by a summary of the arguments in support of the request, making specific reference to any relevant document attached. The Commission shall only be obliged to take into consideration those documents attached which have been translated into one of INTERPOL's official languages and certified if necessary."

If it is true that these petitions are regulated as a consequence of the right to have access to information already processed and registered before INTERPOL, nothing in the Regulations prevent the possibility for petitions to be filed by individuals seeking to prevent the said registration take place, avoiding the violation of their rights. That is, petitions or requests directed to INTERPOL may also be made in order to require in advance that the Organization abstains from processing requests that Member States may formulate against individuals, in violation of the provisions of the Constitution and the Regulations (*Rules*) of the Organization, and in particular, against the prohibition contained in Article 3 of the Constitution.

As to the express reference contained in Article 2 of the Constitution of INTERPOL, regarding the need for the Organization to adjust its activity to the principles contained in the Universal Declaration of Human Rights, and considering the express prohibition contained in its Article 3 that prevents INTERPOL from intervening in matters other than those related to ordinary-law crimes and, in particular, in matters related to political, military, religious or racial crimes, there is no impediment to exercising the right to petition or to access information before the Organization by a citizen or an individual, even before a National Bureau establishes a requirement for the registration and diffusion of information against the provisions of the Constitution. It is therefore not necessary for human rights violations to occur in order for them to be protected; the right to protection may also be calimed regarding threats of a violation.

Consequently, in order to internationally confront the intention that any Member State may have to use INTERPOL to pursue political persecution, a rule has been established to regulate the right of individuals to petition, permitting them to initiate an global administrative procedure and be in a position to oppose the intentions of the Member State by means of a formal request directed to the General Secretariat for INTERPOL to abstain from cooperating with any requirement of the said State with regard to political crimes.

B. *Powers of the Commission for Control of Files*

The competent organ to examine all the requests presented by a citizen of a member country, and related to the violation of Article 3 of the Constitution or of other provisions of the Regulations of the Organization. To that effect Article 10 of the *RCI Rules* provides the following as to the control exercised by the Commission:

> "a. When the Commission receives a request, it shall check that any personal information about a requesting party, or about the person he represents, that may be stored by the Organization complies with the information processing conditions which must be respected by the Organization.
>
> b. In accordance with the provisions of Article 6 of the *RCI Rules*, the Commission shall also send any recommendations it may have to the General Secretariat if it feels that action is required of the General Secretariat."

These competences of the Commission as previously said where initially established in Article 5a Exchange of Official Notes between the Organization and the French Government.[19]

The recourse, petition or individual request of the interested party filed before the Commission is consequently, automatic and once it has been presented, the Commission must then verify if the personal data that could cause effect on petitioner, and that is under the control of the Organization comply with the conditions listed in the Constitution of INTERPOL (articles 1 and 3) and the other regulations.

Petitions may also be brought directly before the General Secretariat, in which case it has the obligation to transmit them to the Commission. To that effect, Article 3.1 of the Agreement between the Commission and the General Secretariat provides that "The Secretary General must communicate to the Commission any verification requests regarding the files received in the General Secretariat together with the corresponding files (should they exist), including if said request is addressed to the Commission".

In the exercise of its attributions, the General Secretariat may take any measures it may consider necessary for the treatment of a file presented to the Commission, even prior to it having set forth a recommendation (Article 11.3 *RCI Rules*).

C. *Receipt of Requests and the right to a timely answer*

The Commission, in accordance with Article 9.b of the *RCI Rules* shall acknowledge receipt of any request, and must process the requests "at the earliest opportunity." It is thus established in INTERPOL Rules, not only the individual right to petition of the citizens for the protection of their rights, but the individual right to obtain a timely answer or response from the Organization.

Only when the Commission considers that the requests submitted to it "are clearly unreasonable," for instance because of their number or because of their repetitive or systematic nature, the Commission may refrain from carrying out the verifications and shall not be obliged to reply to the person requesting them (article 9.d *RCI Rules*).

D. *Subjection of the matter to legal study in cases of doubts*

In cases of doubt, and this doubt occurs when a petition is filed by an individual arguing that the request for processing information made by a National Central Bureau does not respect the conditions that such requests must comply according to the Constitution and Regulations of the Organization, the General Secretariat must submit the matter to a legal examination and consult the source of information. The same applies when the individual petition is filed against the requirement of a Member State to use INTERPOL's channels for international police cooperation to persecute citizens, and they file petitions before the Organization claiming that the conditions set forth in Article 3 of the Constitution would be violated.

The global administrative procedure is supervised by the Commission for the Control of Files, which as has been said, is an entity integrated by independent specialists appointed by the General Assembly. Consequently, the Commission is the entity that receives petitions, that examines the means adopted by the Secretary General, extracting its own conclusions and formulating recommendations to the General Secretariat. These recommendations formulated by the Commission to the General Secretariat, must be examined by it and decide if it must abide by them.

As has been said, INTERPOL may only process information if it is in accordance with its Constitution. This implies that upon receiving a request form a Member State or an individual petition formulated by a citizen of a member country, the first step the General Secretariat must take is analyze the application of Article 3 of the Constitution that provides the prohibition to intervene in matters having a political, military, religious or racial character. That is why, in accordance with Article 15.2.a of the *RPI Rules*, when a request to modify, block or destroy an item of information is made by an entity other than the source of the information, for instance, an individual through a particular petition, the General Secretariat shall first determine whether the conditions for processing the said information have been met, and then consult the source, or any National Central Bureau concerned, and take any other appropriate steps to determine whether it is possible and necessary to carry out the requested action.

In cases where the crime transcribed in the request for processing information formulated by a National Central Bureau is, for example, a crime having a political nature, the only way to deal with it is when the national authorities proves that the political crime is accompanied by a ordinary-law crime, or is carried out using violence or infringing damages to persons or properties. In these cases, the political crime is no longer considered "pure" and the General Secretariat must apply the "doctrine of predominance" and take into account all the pertinent facts that have no political motivation, which can incline the scale in favor of the predominance of the elements of an ordinary-law crime. However, should additional information not have been provided, indicating, for example that the crime is accompanied by acts of violence or that it has brought damage upon persons or property to the effects of evaluating the preponderance of the ordinary-law crime character; and furthermore, a petition will have been filed opposing the requirement set forth by the National Central Bureau of a Member States, in case of such doubt, the General Secretariat has the obligation to formally initiate the legal examination of the case.

During the time that can elapse until the General Secretariat receives the required additional information, it shall, in accordance with Article 10.1.c, of the *RPI Rules*, consult the source of that information or the National Central Bureau concerned, if the source of the information is an authorized national institution. It shall take all other appropriate steps to ensure that the criteria have indeed been met. The information in a precautionary way may then be recorded with a view to obtaining supplementary information to permit its retention in the police information system. In this case, the processing of certain information elements and their registration in the data base has only the purpose of introducing a warning in the information related to the person, visible to all the members consulting it, solely indicating that the information has been submitted to legal examination. In these cases, the information posted is simply no more than information, and does not imply any decision of the Organization that could affect the rights of the petitioning party. To that effect, Article 10.1.d of the *RPI Rules* provides that the General Secretariat shall also take all appropriate steps to prevent any direct or indirect prejudice the information may cause to the Member States, the Organization or its staff, and with due respect for the basic rights of individuals the information concerns, in conformity with Article 2 of the Organization's Constitution and the Universal Declaration of Human Rights.

The General Secretariat shall however, in order to not affect the rights of the Member State, give its authorities a deadline for them to provide the required additional information showing that, for instance, the case is an ordinary-law crime case in the sense that said concept is established in INTERPOL's Constitution and Rules, in order to be able to inform the Commission for the Control of Files. Said period established by the General Secretariat, is set expressly indicating that the Secretariat must, within the term, conclude the examination of the case so that if it does not receive the requested information before its expiration, by virtue of Article 15.2.b of the *RPI Rules*, it must destroy any information related to the petitioner which could be registered in their data base.

E.   *Recommendations of the Commission: the destruction of the information and the obligation of the General Secretariat to modify the information*

When the Commission finds that the initial request for processing of information filed by a National Central Bureau and related to the individual petitioner does not comply with the provisions of the Constitution and Rules of Interpol, for instance, if it refers to political, military, religious or racial crimes, and also when there has been no response by the requiring Member State providing additional information requested, the Commission must recommend that the information be eliminated from the Interpol data base and communicate this circumstance to the Member State.

In this sense, article 15,2,b of the *RPI Rules* establishes that after consulting the source of the information, or the National Central Bureau concerned (Articles 10,1 and 12,a *RPI Rules*), the General Secretariat shall modify, block or destroy an item of information on its own initiative if it has specific and relevant reasons for considering that retaining it, or allowing rights of access to it in its current state, would risk violating one of the criteria for processing information referred to in the *RPI Rules* and the texts to which they refer, or would prejudice international police cooperation, the Organization, its staff or the basic rights of the person concerned by the information, in conformity with Article 2 of the Organization's Constitution.

In addition, article 15.2.c of *RPI Rules* provides that the General Secretariat shall destroy items of information, in all their forms, not only when the purpose for which the information was processed has been achieved, or when the deadline for examining the need to retain the information has expired and the source of the information has not given an opinion on the need to retain it; but also when the General Secretariat has specific reasons for considering that the person who is wanted or is the subject of an international request for information, has been cleared of the offences which led to the information concerning him being recorded.

In any case, when the information on which a notice is based is modified, the General Secretariat must examine the need to retain the notice, and when necessary, it shall modify the notice; also when the information on which a notice was based is destroyed, the General Secretariat must also destroy the notice (Article 15.3 *RPI Rules*).

In all cases when the General Secretariat modifies, blocks access to, or destroys an item of information that has been provided by a National Central Bureau, an authorized national institution or an authorized international entity, and concerns a wanted person or a person who is the subject of a request for information, according to article 16.1 of the same *RPI Rules*, it shall inform the source of the information, and shall explain the reasons for its action. That is, it shall indicate the reasons why it was modified, blocked access to, or destroyed; it shall modify, block access to or destroy in the same way all copies of the information in any other database in the Organization's police information system; and it shall assess the consequences of that action on all operations relating to the processing of the information concerned and any related information. If necessary, it shall take any steps considered to be essential.

If the General Secretariat does not adopt the recommendations formulated by the Commission for certain information of the data base to be modified, the Commission, according to Article 11 of its *Internal Regulation*, may submit the matter of disagreement before the Executive Committee, and request that it proceed to said modification. In this respect, Article 11.4 of the said *Internal Regulation* stipulates that the Commission may only use this recourse after having heard the Secretary General or his representative, and having consulted the National Central Bureaus that could be affected.

FINAL COMMENTS

To verify the existence of a global administrative procedures established in the Rules of an Organization like INTERPOL, established as a global administration for international cooperation on police matters, is quite satisfactory, particularly if they are established for the purpose of protecting individuals, citizens of the Member States, without the intervention of the latter, and perhaps, in many cases, even confronting their intention to use the channels for police cooperation for purposes other than those established in the Constitution and Rules of the Organization.

Confronted with the general rules applicable to administrative procedures in comparative administrative law,285 these global administrative procedures follow

---

285 See for instance, Allan R. Brewer-Carías, *Principios del Procedimiento Administrativo*, Editorial Civitas, Madrid 1990; *Les principes de la procédure administrative non contentieuse. Etudes de Droit Comparé (France, Espagne, Amérique Latine)*, Economica, París

the general principles on the matter in the sense that they are designed, not only to guarantee the effectiveness of the actions of the Administration, but also to guarantee the rights of the individuals, in this case, the citizens of the Member States of the Organization.

Regarding the parties in the procedures, that is, the subjects of the global administrative law that is applicable to INTERPOL, they are not only the Member States and their Public Administrations (including the National Central Bureaus), but also all the individuals, citizens of the said Member States, which have enough standing to initiate the corresponding global administrative procedures. They have the right to file petitions directly before the Organization in order to request their fundamental rights to be guaranteed and protected, particularly their right to personal freedom when they are persecuted by Member States pretending to use the channels for international police cooperation in an incorrect way, for instance, when they are persecuted because of political, military, religious, or racial crimes, and Member States pretend to use INTERPOL to materialize said persecution.

One of the most important aspects of some of these global administrative procedures is that they are being developed upon the request of interested parties, and within them, individuals, citizens of the member countries, acting before a global administration like INTERPOL, applying a global administrative law principles derived from its Constitution and Rules, and from the Universal Declaration of Human Rights. Furthermore, within the Organization, an independent organization has been configured in order to control the processing of information, and to check for its adjustment to the Rules of the Organization, which is the Commission for the Control of Files, in charge of protecting the fundamental rights of citizens.

All this, no doubt, signifies an important advance in the rule of law principle at international and national levels, but also in the development of a global administrative law.

1992; *Principios del procedimiento administrativo en América Latina,* Universidad del Rosario, Colegio Mayor de Nuestra Señora del Rosario, Editorial Legis, Bogotá 2003.

PART THREE

THE LACK OF INDEPENDENCE OF THE JUDICIARY AND JUDICIAL REVIEW

CHAPTER XIV
DISMANTLING THE RULE OF LAW: THE POLITICAL CONTROL OF THE JUDICIARY
(2010)

This essay on "The Dismantling the Rule of Law in Venezuela, and the situation of the Judicial Power," was written for the Presentation I made on "Rule of Law and Human Rights in Venezuela," **before the** *New York City Bar Committee on Inter-American Law*, *New York City Bar*, **New York, October 5th, 2010.**

Venezuela lacks of a system of Rule of Law. The country is subjected to an authoritarian government, which is the opposite of the Rule of Law, because no effective guaranty of human rights is possible. Consequently, instead of referring to the "Rule of law and Human Rights in Venezuela," what I am going to analyze tonight is the "Process of Dismantling the Rule of Law" that the country has suffered during the past decade.

Since 1999, in effect, a tragic setback has occurred in Venezuela regarding democratic standards and the rule of law, a country that just a few decades ago was envied for its institution building and democratic accomplishments. The past decade, on the contrary, has shown a continuous, persistent, and deliberate process of demolishing the rule of law institutions[1] and of destroying democracy in a way never before experienced in all the constitutional history of the country.[2]

---

1   See in *general*, Allan R. Brewer-Carías, "La progresiva y sistemática demolición de la autonomía e independencia del Poder Judicial en Venezuela (1999-2004)," in *XXX Jornadas J.M Dominguez Escovar, Estado de Derecho, Administración de Justicia y Derechos Humanos*, Instituto de Estudios Jurídicos del Estado Lara, Barquisimeto 2005, pp. 33-174; Allan R. Brewer-Carías, "El constitucionalismo y la emergencia en Venezuela: entre la emergencia

In December of 1999, the people of Venezuela approved a new Constitution con-sidered by many as one of the best Constitutions in contemporary Latin America; an assertion with which I have never agreed, except regarding its provisions precisely referred to human rights and to the system of judicial review that unfortunately are dead words. As Member of the 1999 Constituent Assembly I participated in the drafting of the Constitution, but I was also one of the few members of the Assembly that campaigned for the rejection of the Constitution in the referendum of December 1999.

Nonetheless the most chocking fact regarding this celebrated Constitution is that it has been constantly violated by all branches of government, and more seriously, by the Supreme Tribunal of Justice and its Constitutional Chamber, which was theo-retically designed to be the guarantor par excellence of the Constitution. Contrary to that role, in Venezuela, the Constitutional Chamber, as Constitutional Jurisdiction, equivalent to a Constitutional Court, has been completely controlled by the Execu-tive, and as such, has been the main tool used to erode the rule of law and, to sustain authoritarianism, legitimizing all the constitutional violations that have occurred.

The result of this process has been the complete lack of all essential elements that a rule of law and a democratic state request, which according to the 2001 Inter-American Democratic Charter, are much more than voting in elections and referen-da.

This process of dismantling the rule of law in Venezuela began in the same year 1999, when the then newly elected President of the Republic, Hugo Chávez on the same day of his first Inauguration, convened a non-plural Constituent Assembly (February 2, 1999);[3] a decision adopted only two weeks after a very pressed and

---

formal y la emergencia anormal del Poder Judicial," in Allan R. Brewer-Carías, *Estudios So-bre el Estado Constitucional (2005-2006)*, Editorial Jurídica Venezolana, Caracas 2007, pp. 245-269; and Allan R. Brewer-Carías "La justicia sometida al poder. La ausencia de inde-pendencia y autonomía de los jueces en Venezuela por la interminable emergencia del Poder Judicial (1999-2006)," in *Cuestiones Internacionales. Anuario Jurídico Villanueva 2007*, Centro Universitario Villanueva, Marcial Pons, Madrid 2007, pp. 25-57, available at www.allanbrewercarias.com, (Biblioteca Virtual, II.4. Artículos y Estudios Nº 550, 2007) pp. 1-37. See also Allan R. Brewer-Carías, *Historia Constitucional de Venezuela*, Editorial Alfa, Tomo II, Caracas 2008, pp. 402-454.

2   See, in general, Allan R. Brewer-Carías, "El autoritarismo establecido en fraude a la Consti-tución y a la democracia y su formalización en "Venezuela mediante la reforma constitucio-nal. (De cómo en un país democrático se ha utilizado el sistema eleccionario para minar la democracia y establecer un régimen autoritario de supuesta "dictadura de la democracia" que se pretende regularizar mediante la reforma constitucional)" in the book *Temas constitucio-nales. Planteamientos ante una Reforma*, Fundación de Estudios de Derecho Administrativo, FUNEDA, Caracas 2007, pp. 13-74; and "La demolición del Estado de Derecho en Venezue-la Reforma Constitucional y fraude a la Constitución (1999-2009)," in *El Cronista del Esta-do Social y Democrático de Derecho*, Nº 6, Editorial Iustel, Madrid 2009, pp. 52-61.

3   See Decree Nº 3 of February 2, 1999, in *Gaceta Oficial* Nº 36.634 of February 2, 1999.

weak Supreme Court of Justice issued a very ambiguous ruling (January 19, 1999)[4] in which, without deciding on the merits of what was requested, cleared the way for the President to convene a referendum on the matter of the constituent assembly, violating the then in force 1961 Constitution. [5]

The result of this initial and unconstitutional decision adopted by President Chávez[6] was the election, on July 1999, of a costume-made Constituent Assembly, completely controlled by the President's followers, being used as the main tool for the political assault on all branches of government, ignoring the provisions of the then in force Constitution. This elected Constituent Assembly, technically was the result of a coup d'état given against the Constitution,[7] and in addition, it was itself the instrument used to give another coup d'état against the existing constituted pow-

---

4   See the text of the decisions in Allan R. Brewer–Carías, *Poder Constituyente Originario y Asamblea Nacional Constituyente,* Editorial Jurídica Venezolana, Caracas 1998, pp. 25 a 53; and the comment regarding its content, in pp. 55 a 114. See also in Allan R. Brewer–Carías, *Asamblea Constituyente y Ordenamiento Constitucional, Academia de Ciencias Políticas y Sociales, Caracas 1998,* pp. 153 a 228; and in *Revista de Derecho Público,* N° 77–80, Editorial Jurídica Venezolana, Caracas 1999, pp. 56 ff. and 68 ff. Regarding these decisions, Lolymar Hernández Camargo has expressed that "far from giving answer to the important question raised to the Court, opened the possibility for a consultative referendum, but without establishing the mechanism that can allow its convening, leaving that task entirely to the 'competent organs,'" in *La Teoría del Poder Constituyente. Un caso de estudio: el proceso constituyente venezolano de 1999,* UCAT, San Cristóbal 2000, pp. 54-63

5   See Allan R. Brewer–Carías, "La configuración judicial del proceso constituyente o de cómo el guardián de la Constitución abrió el camino para su violación y para su propia extinción," in *Revista de Derecho Público,* N° 77–80, Editorial Jurídica Venezolana, Caracas 1999, pp. 453 y ss.; y *Golpe de Estado y proceso constituyente en Venezuela,* UNAM, México, 2001, pp. 60 ff.

6   See the text of the popular action filed seeeking to annul on grounds of its unconstitutionality the presidencial Decree, in Allan R. Brewer–Carías, *Asamblea Constituyente y Ordenamiento Constitucional,* Academia de Ciencias Políticas y Sociales, Caracas 1999, pp. 255 a 321. See also Carlos M. Escarrá Malavé, *Proceso Político y Constituyente,* Caracas 1999, anexo 4

7   The Assembly assumed in its By-Laws, an "original constituent power." See in *Gaceta Constituyente (Diario de Debates), Agosto–Septiembre 1999,* Session, August 7, 1999, N° 4, p. 144. In the inauguration act of the Assembly, its President said "the National Constituent Assembly is original and sovereign," in *Gaceta Constituyente (Diario de Debates), Agosto–Septiembre 1999,* Sesión de 03–08–99, N° 1, p. 4. See the text also in *Gaceta Oficial* N° 36.786 of September 14, 1999. As pointed out by Lolymar Hernández Camargo, with this By-Laws, "the inobservance of the popular will that had imponed limits to the National Constituent Assembly was materialized, … The Assembly proclaimed itself as original, absolute constituent power, without limits, having the State lost its raison d'être, because if the popular will and its normative expression (the Constitution) was violated, it is not possible to qualify the State as a rule of law and much less as democratic," in *La Teoría del Poder Constituyente,* UCAT, San Cristóbal 2000, p. 73. See my dissident votes regarding the approval of the By-Laws of the Assembly in Allan R. Brewer–Carías, *Debate Constituyente, (Aportes a la Asamblea Nacional Constituyente)* tomo I, *(8 agosto–8 septiembre 1999),* Caracas 1999, pp. 15-39. See also en *Gaceta Constituyente (Diario de Debates), Agosto–Septiembre 1999,* Session of August 7, 1999, N° 4, pp. 6-13

ers.[8] The Constituent Assembly, in effect, interfered all the then elected, and non-elected branches of government, particularly the Judicial Power, whose autonomy and independence began to be progressively and systematically demolished.[9] All this happened, unfortunately, with the consent and complicity of the former Supreme Court of Justice, which endorsed the creation of a Commission of Judicial Emergency[10] that after eleven years continues to function although with another name, in violation of the new Constitution.[11]

All these acts of the Constituent Assembly were challenged before the then already bend Supreme Court, which in another much criticized decision of October 14, 1999, upheld their constitutionality, recognizing the Constituent Assembly supposed supra-constitutional power. This was the only way to justify the unconstitutional intervention of all the existing branches of governments, for which the Court paid a very high price, which was its own existence. With such decision, the Court pronounced its own death sentence, disappearing two months later as the first victim of the authoritarian government, which it helped to grab power.

This happened in December 22 of the same year 1999, in a decision adopted by the Constituent Assembly after the new Constitution was popularly approved (December 15, 1999), when the Assembly, violating both, the old (still in force) 1961 Constitution, and the new (approved but still not published) 1999 Constitution,[12] eliminated the Supreme Court itself, and dismissed its Magistrates and all the other public officials elected only a few months earlier. This was achieved through the enactment of a Transitory Constitutional Regime[13] which was not submitted to popular approval. In particular, regarding the Judiciary, the result of such Regime was

---

8   See Allan R. Brewer-Carías, "Constitution Making in Defraudation of the Constitution and Authoritarian Government in Defraudation of Democracy. The Recent Venezuelan Experience", en *Lateinamerika Analysen*, 19, 1/2008, GIGA, German Institute of Global and Area Studies, Institute of Latin American Studies, Hamburg 2008, pp. 119-142

9   On Auguts 19, 1999, the National Constituent Assembly decided to declare "the Judicial Power in emergency." *Gaceta Oficial* N° 36.772 of August 25, 1999 reprinted in *Gaceta Oficial* N° 36.782 of September 8, 1999. See in Allan R. Brewer–Carías, *Debate Constituyente*, tomo I, Fundación de Derecho Público, Editoriual Jurídica Venezolana, Caracas 1999, p. 57-73; and in *Gaceta Constituyente (Diario de Debates), Agosto–Septiembre de 1999,*, Session of August 18, 1999, N° 10, pp. 17-22. See the text of the decree in *Gaceta Oficial* N° 36.782 of September 08, 1999.

10   "Resolution" of the Supreme Court of Justice of August 23, 1999. See the comments regarding this Resolution in en Allan R. Brewer–Carías, *Debate Constituyente*, tomo I, Fundación de Derecho Público, Editoriual Jurídica Venezolana, Caracas 1999, pp. 141 ff. See also the comments of Lolymar Hernández Camargo, *La Teoría del Poder Constituyente*, UCAT, San Cristóbal 2000, pp. 75 ff..

11   See Allan R. Brewer–Carías, *Golpe de Estado y proceso constituyente en Venezuela*, Universidad Nacional Autónoma de México, México 2002, p. 160.

12   See in *Gaceta Constituyente (Diario de Debates), Noviembre 1999–Enero 2000*, Session of December 22, 1999, N° 51, pp. 2 ff. See *Gaceta Oficial* N° 36.859 of December 29, 1999; and *Gaceta Oficial* N° 36.860 of December 30, 1999.

13   See in *Gaceta Oficial* N° 36.859 of December 29, 1999.

the appointment of new Magistrates of the new Supreme Tribunal of Justice, without fulfilling the conditions established in the to-be new Constitution, completely packed with Chávez' supporters. That Supreme Tribunal has precisely been the one that during the past decade has been the most ominous instrument for consolidating authoritarianism in the country.

Today, eleven years after the 1999 constitution making-process, a centralized, militaristic, and concentrated authoritarian regime has been imposed to the Venezuelans, following a socialist model of society for which nobody has voted, that is based in a supposed "participatory democracy" which is directly controlled by the central government. Within such system, despite the political rhetoric, exuberant spending and waste of an immense public income, of a rich state in a poor country, no effective social and economic reforms or improvements have been achieved, except the building of an enormous bureaucratic State that has appropriated or confiscated all main private enterprises in the country, consolidating a corrupt and inefficient system of capitalism of State.

In this process, again, the Supreme Tribunal and particularly its Constitutional Chamber, has been the main tool in order to legitimate the violations of the Constitution.

In any case, in addition to the take-over of all the constituted powers and to the interference of all branches of government, the result of the 1999 constitution–making process was the approval of a new Constitution, which despite its advanced civil and political rights regulations, contains some provisions that have been used by the government in order to strengthen the concentration of power, the state centralization, the extreme presidentialism, the extensive state participation in the economy, and the general marginalization of civil society in public activities.

All these institutional deformations lead the President of the Republic to propose in 2007, a Constitutional Reform aimed to consolidate the authoritarian regime in the Constitution itself, formally regulating a socialist, centralized, military and police state.[14] The National Assembly sanctioned those reforms proposals in November 2, 2007, violating the Constitution because no substantive reforms of such kind are allowed to be made through the constitutional review procedure, but only by means of the convening of a Constituent Assembly. Of course, the Supreme Tribunal, very diligently, refused to decide all the multiple judicial review challenges filed against the proposal of the unconstitutional Constitutional Reform.[15] Fortunately, the

---

14   See Allan R. Brewer-Carías, *Hacia la consolidación de un Estado Socialista, Centralizado, Policial Y Militarista. Comentarios sobre el sentido y alcance de las propuestas de reforma constitucional 2007,* Colección Textos Legislativos, N° 42, Editorial Jurídica Venezolana, Caracas 2007.

15   See the comments on the various decisions in Allan R. Brewer-Carías, "El juez constitucional vs. la supremacía constitucional. O de cómo la Jurisdicción Constitucional en Venezuela renunció a controlar la constitucionalidad del procedimiento seguido para la "reforma constitucional" sancionada por la Asamblea Nacional el 2 de noviembre de 2007, antes de que fuera rechazada por el pueblo en el referendo del 2 de diciembre de 2007," in *Revista de Derecho Público,* núm. 112, Caracas, Editorial Jurídica Venezolana, 2007, pp. 661-6944

408 ALLAN R. BREWER-CARÍAS

people rejected the reforms proposal in the referendum held on December 2, 2007, but unfortunately, the rejection has been mocked by Government, which during the past three years, defrauding the Constitution, has been implementing the rejected reforms by means of ordinary legislation or through decree-laws unconstitutionally enacted.[16] The President of the Republic has been completely sure that the submissive Constitutional Chamber he has controlled would never exercise any sort of judicial review control over such unconstitutional acts.

That is why, that in this context, it is hardly surprising to hear President Chávez, when referring to the delegate legislation enacted by him, to say in August 2008, simply: "*I am the Law.... I am the State* !!;[17] repeating the same phrases he used in 2001, also referring to other series of decree-laws he enacted at that time as delegate legislation.[18] Such phrases, as we all know, were attributed in the seventeen century to Louis XIV, in France, as a sign of the meaning of an Absolute Monarchy – although in fact he never expressed them–;[19] but to hear in our times a Head of State saying them, is enough to understand the tragic institutional situation that Venezuela is currently facing, characterized by a complete absence of separation of powers and, consequently, of a democratic and rule of law government. [20]

---

16   See Lolymar Hernández Camargo, "Límites del poder ejecutivo en el ejercicio de la habilitación legislativa: Imposibilidad de establecer el contenido de la reforma constitucional rechazada vía habilitación legislativa," in *Revista de Derecho Público*, N° 115 *(Estudios sobre los Decretos Leyes),* Editorial Jurídica venezolana, Caracas 2008, pp. 51 ff.; Jorge Kiriakidis, "Breves reflexiones en torno a los 26 Decretos-Ley de Julio-Agosto de 2008, y la consulta popular refrendaría de diciembre de 2007", *Idem,* pp. 57 ff.; and José Vicente Haro García, Los recientes intentos de reforma constitucional o de cómo se está tratando de establecer una dictadura socialista con apariencia de legalidad (A propósito del proyecto de reforma constitucional de 2007 y los 26 decretos leyes del 31 de julio de 2008 que tratan de imponerla)", *Idem,* pp. 63 ff.

17   Hugo Chávezs Frís, August 28, 2008. See in Gustavo Coronel, *Las Armas de Coronel*, October 15, 2008, available at http://lasarmasdecoronel.blogspot.com/2008/10/yo-soy-la-leyyo-soy-el-estado.html

18   See in *El Universal,* Caracas, December 4, 2001, pp. 1,1 and 2,1. This is the only thing that can explain that a Head of State in 2009 could qualify "representative democracy, separation of Powers and alternate government" as doctrines that "poisons the masses mind." See "Hugo Chávez seeks to catch them young," in *The Economist*, August 22-28, 2009, p. 33.

19   See Yves Guchet, *Histoire Constitutionnelle Française (1789–1958)*, Ed. Erasme, Paris 1990, p.8.

20   See the summary of this situation in Teodoro Petkoff, "Election and Political Power. Challenges for the Opposition", en *ReVista. Harvard Review of Latin America*, David Rockefeller Center for Latin American Studies, Harvard University, Fall 2008, pp. 12. See also Allan R. Brewer-Carías, "Los problemas de la gobernabilidad democrática en Venezuela: el autoritarismo constitucional y la concentración y centralización del poder," in Diego Valadés (Coord.), *Gobernabilidad y constitucionalismo en América Latina*, Universidad Nacional Autónoma de México, México 2005, pp. 73-96.

This has lead to successive illegitimate mutations of the Constitution or constitutional distortions that have been made defrauding the Constitution itself, [21] being the first one, the decision issued by the Constitutional Chamber of the Supreme Tribunal of Justice a few weeks after approval of the 1999 Constitution, accepting the existence of not one, but of two constitutional transitory regimes: one which was approved by popular vote, and embodied in the text of the Constitution; and another not approved by the people, and adopted one week after the Constitution was popularly approved by the same Constituent Assembly. This latter Decree on the Regime of Transition of the Public Power, enacted by the Assembly without any constitutional support, eliminated the prior Congress along with its senators and representatives; assigned the legislative power to a National Legislative Commission not established in the Constitution; dissolved the states' legislative assemblies; controlled the mayor's offices and municipal councils; and, as mentioned, eliminated the former Supreme Court of Justice, appointing the magistrates of the new Supreme Tribunal but without complying with the conditions established in the Constitution. It also transformed the former Judicial Emergency Commission into a Commission for the Reorganization and Functioning of the Judiciary in order to continue with the removal of judges from office without due process, which still today continues to work.

Of course, this unconstitutional Decree was challenged before the new Constitutional Chamber which was appointed in it, being the result that the Constitutional Chamber, deciding in its own cause violating one of the most basic principles of law, argued that the Constituent Assembly had supra-constitutional power to create constitutional provisions without popular approval.[22] The consequence has been the existence in the country of two transitional constitutional regimes: one approved by the people, and the other illegitimately imposed to the people, leading to a long and endless period of constitutional instability that, eleven years later, has eroded institutional confidence and legal security.[23]

One of the unconstitutional results of the transitory constitutional regime adopted by the Constituent Assembly, as I mentioned, was the appointment of the Magistrates of the new Supreme Tribunal without fulfilling the conditions for those appointments and without guarantying the citizens' participation in the process. In this particular aspect, in effect, the 1999 Constitution provides for a direct mean of citizen participation in the nominating process of High non elected Officials, preventing the National Assembly to appoint them without being previously proposed by nominating committees; committees that were to be integrated in an exclusive way by

21 See Allan R. Brewer-Carías, "El juez constitucional al servicio del autoritarismo y la ilegítima mutación de la Constitución: el caso de la Sala Constitucional del Tribunal Supremo de Justicia de Venezuela (1999-2009)", in *IUSTEL, Revista General de Derecho Administrativo*, N° 21, junio 2009, Madrid, ISSN-1696-9650

22 See decision N° 4 of January 26, 2000, case: *Eduardo García*, in *Revista de Derecho Público*, N° 81, Editorial Jurídica Venezolana, Caracas 2000, pp. 93 ff.

23 See decision of March 28, 2000, *case: Allan R. Brewer-Carías y otros,* in *Revista de Derecho Público*, N° 81, (enero-marzo), Editorial Jurídica Venezolana, Caracas, 2000, p. 86.

representatives of "different sectors of civil society." Nonetheless, these committees have never been established in the country in the way provided in the Constitution, and have been supplanted by ordinary parliamentary commissions, extending in an illegitimate way, through legislation, the initial transitory regime. [24]

In 2000, for instance, a Special Law for the Ratification or Appointment of High Officials and Magistrates to the Supreme Tribunal of Justice[25] was enacted by the then newly elected National Assembly, but without organizing the aforementioned nominating committees, thereby confiscating the citizens' right to political participation. Such Special Law, of course, was challenged before the Constitutional Chamber (this time by the Peoples' Defendant),[26] which has never decided the merits of the case. Instead, the Chamber, in a preliminary ruling (December 2000), decided again in its own cause, establishing that the Constitution was not applicable to the Magistrates that were signing the decision, because they were not going to be "appointed" but to be "ratified;"[27] a decision that was a grotesque mockery regarding the Constitution.

This irregular situation continued in 2004, when the National Assembly eventually sanctioned the Organic Law of the Supreme Tribunal of Justice, increasing the number of magistrates from twenty to thirty-two, distorting the constitutional conditions for their appointment and dismissal, and consolidating the judicial nominating committee as a dependent parliamentary commission. This reform, as the Inter-American Commission on Human Rights emphasized in its *2004 Annual Report*, "lack the safeguards necessary to prevent other branches of government from undermining the Supreme Tribunal's independence and to keep narrow or temporary majorities from determining its composition." [28]

---

24 See Allan R. Brewer-Carías, "La participación ciudadana en la designación de los titulares de los órganos no electos de los Poderes Públicos en Venezuela y sus vicisitudes políticas", in *Revista Iberoamericana de Derecho Público y Administrativo*, Año 5, N° 5-2005, San José, Costa Rica 2005, pp. 76-95.

25 See *Gaceta Oficial* N° 37.077 of November 14, 2000.

26 See *El Universal,* Caracas, December 14, 2000, pp. 1-2.

27 The Constitutional Chamber accepted the point of view that the Magistrates could be "ratified" according to the Special Law without complying with the Constitution, because the latter only established their nomination but said noting about the "ratification" of those in office, signing the decision. See Decision of December 12, 2000 in *Revista de Derecho Público N° 84*, Editorial Jurídica Venezolana, Caracas, 2000, p. 109. See the comments in Allan R. Brewer-Carías, "La participación ciudadana en la designación de los titulares de los órganos no electos de los Poderes Públicos en Venezuela y sus vicisitudes políticas," in *Revista Iberoamericana de Derecho Público y Administrativo*, Año 5, N° 5-2005, San José, Costa Rica 2005, pp. 76-95, available at www.allanbrewercarias.com (Biblioteca Virtual, II.4. Artículos y Estudios N° 469, 2005) pp. 1-48.

28 See IACHR, *2004 Annual Report* (Follow-Up Report on Compliance by the State of Venezuela with the Recommendations made by the IACHR in its Report on the Situation of Human Rights in Venezuela [2003]), para. 174. Available at http://www.cidh.oas.org/annualrep/2004eng/chap.5b.htm

After this 2004 legal reform, the process for selecting new Magistrates, although being an exclusive competency of the National Assembly, in fact was controlled by the President of the Republic, as was publicly recognized by the representative head of the parliamentary nominating committee, when he publicly announced that fact and, in addition, said that "There is now one in the group of nominees that could act against us."[29] This configuration of the Supreme Tribunal, as highly politicized and subjected to the will of the president, has completely eliminated the autonomy of the Judiciary, and even the basic principle of separation of powers; allowing the government the absolute control of the Supreme Tribunal of Justice, and particularly, of its Constitutional Chamber.

Through the Supreme Tribunal, which is in charge of governing and administering the Judiciary, the political control over all judges has been also assured, reinforced by means of the survival of the 1999 "provisional" Commission on the Functioning and Restructuring of the Judicial System, which has been legimimazed by the same Tribunal, making completely inapplicable the 1999 constitutional provisions seeking to guarantee the independence and autonomy of judges. [30]

According to the text of the 1999 Constitution, judges can only enter the judicial career by means of public competition that must be organized with citizens' participation. Nonetheless, this provision has not yet been implemented, being the judiciary almost exclusively made up of temporary and provisional judges, without any stability. Regarding this situation, for instance, since 2003 the Inter-American Commission on Human Rights has repeatedly express concern about the fact that provisional judges are susceptible to political manipulation, which alters the people's right to access to justice, reporting cases of dismissals and substitutions of

---

29   He expressed to the press: "If it is true that the representatives have the power to choose, the opinión of the President of the Republic has been ask, and has been very much taken into account." See *El Nacional*, Caracas, December 13, 2004. The Inter-American Commission of Human Rights suggested in its *2004 Report on Venezuela* that "those provisions of the Organic Law of the Supreme Tribunal of Justice had facilitated the Executive Power to manipulate the 2004 process of election of the magistrates," paragraph párrafo 180.

30   See in general, Allan R. Brewer-Carías, "La progresiva y sistemática demolición de la autonomía e independencia del Poder Judicial en Venezuela (1999-2004)," in *XXX Jornadas J.M Dominguez Escovar, Estado de Derecho, Administración de Justicia y Derechos Humanos*, Instituto de Estudios Jurídicos del Estado Lara, Barquisimeto 2005, pp. 33-174; Allan R. Brewer-Carías, "El constitucionalismo y la emergencia en Venezuela: entre la emergencia formal y la emergencia anormal del Poder Judicial," in Allan R. Brewer-Carías, *Estudios Sobre el Estado Constitucional (2005-2006)*, Editorial Jurídica Venezolana, Caracas 2007, pp. 245-269; and Allan R. Brewer-Carías "La justicia sometida al poder. La ausencia de independencia y autonomía de los jueces en Venezuela por la interminable emergencia del Poder Judicial (1999-2006)," in *Cuestiones Internacionales. Anuario Jurídico Villanueva 2007*, Centro Universitario Villanueva, Marcial Pons, Madrid 2007, pp. 25-57, available at www.allanbrewercarias.com, (Biblioteca Virtual, II.4. Artículos y Estudios N° 550, 2007) pp. 1-37. See also Allan R. Brewer-Carías, *Historia Constitucional de Venezuela*, Editorial Alfa, Tomo II, Caracas 2008, pp. 402-454.

judges in retaliation for decisions contrary to the government's position.[31] In its *2008 Annual Report*, the Commission again verified the provisional character of the judiciary as an "endemic problem" because the appointment of judges was made without applying constitutional provisions on the matter –thus exposing judges to discretionary dismissal– which highlights the "permanent state of urgency" in which those appointments have been made.[32]

Contrary to these facts, according to the words of the Constitution in order to guarantee the independence of the Judiciary, judges can be dismissed from their tenure only through disciplinary processes, conducted by disciplinary courts and judges of a Disciplinary Judicial Jurisdiction. Nonetheless, that jurisdiction has never been created, corresponding the disciplinary judicial functions to the already mentioned transitory Commission,[33] which, as reported by the same Inter-American Commission in its *2009 Annual Report*, "in addition to being a special, temporary entity, does not afford due guarantees for ensuring the independence of its decisions,[34] since its members may also be appointed or removed at the sole discretion of the Constitutional Chamber of the Supreme Tribunal of Justice, without previously establishing either the grounds or the procedure for such formalities."[35]

The Commission has then "cleansed" the Judiciary of judges not in line with the authoritarian regime, removing judges in a discretionary way when they have issued decisions not within the complacency of the government.[36] This lead the Inter-American Commission on Human Rights, to observe in its *2009 Annual Report,* that "in Venezuela, judges and prosecutors do not enjoy the guaranteed tenure necessary to ensure their independence."[37]

---

31   See *Reporte sobre la Situación de Derechos Humanos en Venezuela*; OAS/Ser.L/V/II.118. doc.4rev.2; December 29, 2003, Paragraphs 161, 174, available at http://www.cidh.oas.org/countryrep/Venezuela2003eng/toc.htm.

32   See *Annual Report 2008* (OEA/Ser.L/V/II.134. Doc. 5 rev. 1. 25 febrero 2009), paragraph 39.

33   The Politico Administrative Chamber of the Supreme Tribunal has decided that the dismiss of temporal judges is a discretionary power of the Comission on the Functioning and Reorganization of the Judiciary, which adopts its decision without following any administrative procedure rules or due process rules. See Decision N° 00463-2007 of March 20, 2007; Decision N° 00673-2008 of April 24, 2008 (cited in Decision N° 1.939 of December 18, 2008, p. 42). The Chamber has adopted the same position in Decision N° 2414 of December 20, 2007 and Decision N° 280 of February 23, 2007.

34   See Decisión N° 1.939 of December 18, 2008 (Caso: *Gustavo Álvarez Arias et al.*)

35   Véase *Annual Report 2009*, Par. 481, en http://www.cidh.org/annualrep/2009eng/Chap. IV.f.eng.htm.

36   Decision N° 1.939 (Dec. 18, 2008) (Case: *Abogados Gustavo Álvarez Arias y otros*), in which the Constitutonal Chamber declared the non-enforceability of the decision of the Inter American Court of Human Rights of August 5, 2008, Case: *Apitz Barbera y otros ("Corte Primera de lo Contencioso Administrativo") vs. Venezuela* Serie C, N° 182.

37   See *Informe Anual de 2009*, paragraph 480, available at http://www.cidh.oas.org/annualrep/2009eng/Chap.IV.f.eng.htm

One of the leading cases showing this situation took place in 2003, when a High Contentious Administrative Court ruled against the government in a politically charged case regarding the hiring of Cuban physicians for medical social programs. In response to a provisional judicial measure suspending the hiring procedures, due to discrimination allegations made by the Council of Physicians of Caracas, [38] the government after declaring that the decision was not going to be accepted [39] seized the Court using secret police officers, and dismissed its judges after being offended by the President of the Republic.[40] The case was brought before the Inter-American Court of Human Rights and after it ruled in 2008 that the dismissal effectively violated the American Convention on Human Rights,[41] the Constitutional Chamber of the Supreme Tribunal response to the Inter-American Court ruling, at the request of the government, was that the decision of the Inter-American Court could not be enforced in Venezuela.[42] As simple as that, showing the subordination of the Venezuelan judiciary to the policies, wishes, and dictates of the President.

In December 2009, another astonishing case was the detention of a criminal judge (María Lourdes Afiuni Mora) for having ordered, based on a previous recommendation of the UN Working Group on Arbitrary Detention, the release of an individual in order for him to face criminal trial while in freedom, as guaranteed in the Constitution. The same day of the decision, the president publicly asked for the judge to be incarcerated asking to apply her a 30–year prison term, which is the maximum punishment in Venezuelan law for horrendous or grave crimes. The fact is that judge has remained to this day in detention without trial. The UN Working Group described these facts as "a blow by President Hugo Chávez to the independence of judges and lawyers in the country," demanding "the immediate release of the judge," concluding that "reprisals for exercising their constitutionally guaranteed

---

38   See Decision of August, 21 2003, in *Revista de Derecho Público*, n° 93-96, Editorial Jurídica Venezolana, Caracas, 2003, pp. 445 ff. See the comments in Claudia Nikken, "El caso "Barrio Adentro": La Corte Primera de lo Contencioso Administrativo ante la Sala Constitucional del Tribunal Supremo de Justicia o el avocamiento como medio de amparo de derechos e intereses colectivos y difusos," in *Idem*, pp. 5 ff.

39   The President of the Republic said: "*Váyanse con su decisión no sé para donde, la cumplirán ustedes en su casa si quieren ...*" (You can go with your decision, I don't know where; you will enforce it in your house if you want ..."). See *El Universal*, Caracas, August 25, 2003 and *El Universal*, Caracas, August 28, 2003.

40   See in *El Nacional*, Caracas November 5, 2004, p. A2.

41   *See* Inter-American Court of Human Rights, case: *Apitz Barbera et al. (Corte Primera de lo Contencioso Administrativo) v. Venezuela*, Decision of August 5, 2008, available at www.corteidh.or.cr. *See also*, *El Universal*, Caracas, October 16, 2003; and *El Universal*, Caracas, September 22, 2003.

42   Supreme Tribunal of Justice, Constitutional Chamber, Decision N° 1.939 of December 18, 2008 (Case: *Abogados Gustavo Álvarez Arias et al.*) (Exp. N° 08-1572), available at http://www.tsj.gov.ve/decisiones/scon/Diciembre/1939-181208-2008-08-1572.html

ALLAN R. BREWER-CARÍAS

functions and creating a climate of fear among the judiciary and lawyers' profession, serve no purpose except to undermine the rule of law and obstruct justice."[43]

The fact is that in Venezuela, no judge can adopt any decision that could affect the government policies, or the President's wishes, the state's interest, or public servants' will, without previous authorization from the same government. [44] That is why the Inter-American Commission on Human Rights, after describing in its *2009 Annual Report* "how large numbers of judges have been removed, or their appointments voided, without the applicable administrative proceedings," noted "with concern that in some cases, judges were removed almost immediately after adopting judicial decisions in cases with a major political impact," concluding that "The lack of judicial independence and autonomy vis-à-vis political power is, in the Commission's opinion, one of the weakest points in Venezuelan democracy." [45]

In this context of political subjection, the Constitutional Chamber, since 2000, far from acting as the guardian of the Constitution, has been the main tool of the authoritarian government for the illegitimate mutation of the Constitution, by means of unconstitutional constitutional interpretations, [46] not only regarding its own powers of judicial review, which have been enlarged, but also regarding substantive matters. The Supreme Tribunal has distorted the Constitution through illegitimate and fraudulent "constitutional mutations" in the sense of changing the meaning of its provisions without changing its wording. And all this, of course, without any possibility of being controlled, [47] so the eternal question arising from the uncontrolled power, – *Quis custodiet ipsos custodes* –, in Venezuela also remains unanswered.

In this regard, one of the most lethal instruments for distorting the Constitution that has been used in Venezuela has been the filing of direct actions or recourses for the abstract interpretation of the Constitution, a judicial mean that has been created

---

43 See the text of the UN Working Group in http://www.unog.ch/unog/website/news_media.nsf/%28httpNewsByYear_en%29/93687E8429BD53A1C125768E00529DB6?OpenDocument&cntxt=B35C3&cookielang=fr . In October 14, 2010, the same Working Group asked the venezuelan Gobernment to subject the Judge to a trail ruled by the due process guaranties and in freedom." See *in El Universal*, October 14, 2010, available at http://www.eluniversal.com/2010/10/14/pol_ava_instancia-de-la-onu_14A4608051.shtml

44 See Antonio Canova González, *La realidad del contencioso administrativo venezolano (Un llamado de atención frente a las desoladoras estadísticas de la Sala Político Administrativa en 2007 y primer semestre de 2008)*, Funeda, Caracas 2008, p. 14.

45 See in ICHR, *Annual Report 2009*, paragraph 483, available at http://www.cidh.oas.org/annualrep/2009eng/Chap.IV.f.eng.htm .

46 See Allan R. Brewer-Carías, *"Crónica sobre la "In" Justicia Constitucional. La Sala Constitucional y el autoritarismo en Venezuela*, Editorial Jurídica Venezolana, Caracas 2007.

47 See Allan R. Brewer-Carías, *"Quis Custodiet ipsos Custodes*: De la interpretación constitucional a la inconstitucionalidad de la interpretación," in *VIII Congreso Nacional de Derecho Constitucional*, Fondo Editorial and Colegio de Abogados de Arequipa, Arequipa, Peru, 2005, 463-89; and *Crónica de la "In"Justicia constitucional: La Sala constitucional y el autoritarismo en Venezuela*, Editorial Jurídica Venezolana, Caracas 2007, pp. 11-44 and 47-79.

by the Constitutional Chamber itself without any constitutional support.[48] These recourses can be filed by any person or very convenient, by the Attorney General; so it has been through these actions that the Constitutional Chamber eventually has "reformed" the Constitution, and has even implemented in a very illegitimate way the constitutional reforms that were rejected by the people in the referendum of 2007.

Many cases can illustrate this unconstitutional process. For instance, Article 72 of the Constitution establishes the principle of the revocation of mandates of all popularly elected offices through recall referendums, establishing that when "a number of electors equal or higher than those who elected the official, vote in favor of the revocation,"[49] the official's mandate is considered revoked. Nevertheless, clearly in an unconstitutional way, in 2003, when a recall referendum was first called by popular initiative to revoke the President's mandate, the National Electoral Council issued a regulation on the matter, adding to the constitutional provision that the number of votes to repeal, in no case could be "lower than the number of electors that voted against the revocation," changing the sense of the constitutional provisions on the matter. With that addition – established in a regulation – the right for the revocation of mandates was restricted, disrupting the nature of the recall referendum by transforming it into a "ratifying" referendum of mandates of popular election not provided in the Constitution. This constitutional fraud was endorsed by the Constitutional Chamber of the Supreme Court when it decided a recourse on the abstract interpretation of article 72 of the Constitution stating that "*if the option of the permanence [of the official] obtains more votes in the referendum, [the officer] should remain in office*, even if a sufficient number of people vote against him to revoke his mandate,"[50] and consequently, turning the "vote against the revocation" into a "vote to ratify" the official. This illegitimate distortion of the Constitution, nonetheless, in 2004 had a precise purpose, just to avoid the revocation of President Hugo Chávez's mandate. He was elected in August 2000 with 3,757,744 votes, and the number of votes casted to revoke his mandate was 3,989,008, surpassing that former number. But instead of announcing the revocation of the mandate according to the Constitution, the National Electoral Council, applying a custom-made doc-

---

48   See Decision N° 1077 of the Constitutional Chamber of September 22, 2000, case: *Servio Tulio León Briceño*. See in *Revista de Derecho Público, N° 83*, Caracas, 2000, pp. 247 ff. This ruling was later ratified in decisions of November 9, 2000 (N° 1347), November 21, 2000 (N° 1387), and April 5, 2001 (N° 457). See Allan R. Brewer-Carías, "Le recours d'interprétation abstrait de la Constitution au Vénézuéla," en

49   Decision N° 2750 of October 21, 2003, Case: *Carlos Enrique Herrera Mendoza, (Interpretación del artículo 72 de la Constitución (Exp. 03-1989);* Decision N° 1139 of June 5, 2002, Case: *Sergio Omar Calderón Duque y William Dávila Barrios,* in *Revista de Derecho Público, N° 89-92,* Editorial Jurídica Venezolana, Caracas 2002, p. 171. The same ruling was followed in Decision N° 137 of February 13, 2003, Case: *Freddy Lepage Scribani y otros* (Exp. 03-0287)..

50   See Decision N° 2750 of October 21, 2003, Case: *Carlos E. Herrera Mendoza, Interpretación del artículo 72 de la Constitución*), in Véase *El Nacional,* Caracas, August 28, 2004, pp. A-1 y A-2

trine established by the Constitutional Chamber, decided to ratify the President in its mandate due to the fact that at that moment more people (5,800,629) had voted not to revoke his mandate.[51] The recall referendum was thus illegitimately transformed into a non existing plebiscite to ratify the President.[52]

Also on electoral maters, for instance, the Constitutional Chamber distorted the mixed electoral system established in the Constitution that combines personalized and proportional representation ballots. This system requires a complex mathematical application in order to function regarding the election of representatives combining majority and list ballots. The Constitutional Chamber of the Supreme Tribunal of Justice, in 2005, before the election of the members of the National Assembly took place, legitimized a defrauding method applied by the parties supporting the government that distorted the principle of proportional representation, transforming the system into a majority one. This, among other factors, led to the opposition parties decision in 2005 to not to participate in such election, unfortunately allowing the complete control of the Assembly by the government. In 2009, the new Organic Law on Electoral Processes was sanctioned legalizing this distorted electoral method, which was applied in the last week legislative election (September 2010), but introducing another distorted element in order to neutralize even more the proportional representation method, through the configuration of the constituencies. The result of the election, as has been announced a few days ago, has been that the opposition, although obtaining more votes than the official party (52% v. 48%), has succeeded to elect only one third of the representatives in the Assembly.

The role of the Constitutional Chamber mutating the Constitution has also affected the general regime on human rights. According to the Constitution, human rights' treaties, pacts and conventions have constitutional rank and prevail in the internal order as long as they contain more favorable provisions regarding their enjoyment and exercise. However, the Constitutional Chamber in 2008, after declaring unenforceable in the country a decision of the Inter-American Court of Human Rights, resolved that Article 23 of the Constitution "does not grant supra-constitutional rank to international treaties on human rights," the Chamber also decided that in case of contradiction between a disposition of the Constitution and a provision of an international treaty, it correspond only to it to determine which one would be applicable,[53] but emphasizing that "the political project of the Constitution" could never be affected, particularly – I quote – "with ideological interpretative elements that could privilege in a decisive way, individual rights, or that welcome the supremacy of the

---

51   See in *El Nacional*, Caracas, August 28, 2004, pp. A-1 y A-2

52   See Allan R. Brewer-Carías, "La Sala Constitucional vs. el derecho ciudadano a la revocatoria de mandatos populares: de cómo un referendo revocatorio fue inconstitucionalmente convertido en un "referendo ratificatorio," in *Crónica sobre la "In" Justicia Constitucional. La Sala Constitucional y el autoritarismo en Venezuela*, Editorial Jurídica Venezolana, Caracas 2007, pp. 349-378.

53   See Decision N° 1492 of June 15, 2003, Case: *Impugnación de diversos artículos del Código Penal*, in *Revista de Derecho Público*, N° 93-96, Editorial Jurídica Venezolana, Caracas 2003, pp. 135 ff.

international judicial order over national law at the sacrifice of the sovereignty of the State." The Chamber also said that "a system of principles, supposedly absolute and supra-historic, cannot be above the Constitution" and that the theories that pretend to limit "under the pretext of universal legalities, the sovereignty and the national auto-determination" "are unacceptable."

With this decision, once again, the Constitutional Chamber illegitimately distorted the Constitution, reforming Article 23 of the Constitution by eliminating the supra-constitutional rank of the American Convention on Human Rights in cases in which it contains more favorable provisions for the benefit and exercise of human rights than the Constitution.

In addition, the Chamber also distorted another provision of the Constitution that grants power to all courts to directly apply human rights provisions of international treaties, reserving such power to the Constitutional Chamber itself.

On the other hand, regarding some fundamental rights essentials for a democracy to function, like the freedom of expression, contrary to the principle of progressiveness established in the Constitution, it has been the Supreme Tribunal of Justice the State organ in charge of limiting its scope. First, in 2000, it was the Political-Administrative Chamber of the Supreme Tribunal that ordered the media not to transmit certain information, eventually admitting limits to be imposed to the media, regardless of the general prohibition of censorship established in the Constitution.

The following year, in 2001, it was the Constitutional Chamber of the Supreme Tribunal, the one that distorted the Constitution when dismissing an *amparo* action filed against the President of the Republic by a citizen and a nongovernmental organization asking for the exercise of their right to response against the attacks made by the President in his weekly TV program. The Constitutional Chamber reduced the scope of freedom of information, eliminating the right to response and rectification regarding opinions in the media when they are expressed by the president in a regular televised program. In addition, the tribunal excluded journalists and all those persons that have a regular program in the radio or a newspaper column, from the right to rectification and response. [54]

In addition, in 2003, the Constitutional Chamber dismissed an action of unconstitutionality filed against a few articles of the Criminal Code that limit the right to formulate criticism against public officials, considering that such provisions could not be deemed as limiting the freedom of expression, contradicting a well estab-

---

54   See Allan R. Brewer-Carías, "La libertad de expresión del pensamiento y el derecho a la información y su violación por la Sala Constitucional del Tribunal Supremo de Justicia", en Allan R. Brewer-Carías (Coordinador y editor), Héctor Faúndez Ledesma, Pedro Nikken, Carlos M. Ayala Corao, Rafael Chavero Gazdik, Gustavo Linares Benzo and Jorge Olavarria, *La libertad de expresión amenazada (Sentencia 1013),* Edición Conjunta Instituto Interamericano de Derechos Humanos y Editorial Jurídica Venezolana, Caracas-San José 2001, pp. 17-57; and Jesús A. Davila Ortega, "El derecho de la información y la libertad de expresión en Venezuela (Un estudio de la sentencia 1.013/2001 de la Sala Constitucional del Tribunal Supremo de Justicia)," *Revista de Derecho Constitucional* 5, Editorial Sherwood, Caracas 2002, 305-25.

lished doctrine in the contrary ruled by the Inter-American Courts on Human Rights. The Constitutional Chamber also decided in contradiction with the constitutional prohibition of censorship, that through a statute it was possible to prevent the diffusion of information when it could be considered contrary to other provisions of the Constitution. [55]

Finally, it has been the Supreme Tribunal in 2007, the State organ that materialized the State intervention in order to terminate authorizations and licenses of radio and television enterprises to use frequencies, particularly those owned by persons considered in opposition to the government. It was the case of the arbitrarily closing of *Radio Caracas Televisión*, the oldest private TV in the country, whose assets were confiscated and its equipment assigned to a state-owned enterprise through an illegitimate Supreme Tribunal decision. [56]

On different matters, regarding the organization of the State, the same illegitimate constitutional mutation has occurred regarding the federal system of distribution of competencies among territorial entities of the State, which in Venezuela is constitutionally organized as a "decentralized federal State;" a distribution that cannot be changed except by means of a constitutional reform. Specifically, for instance, the Constitution provides that the conservation, administration, and use of roads and national highways, as well as of national ports and airports of commercial use, are of the exclusive powers of the states, which they must exercise in "coordination" with the Federal government.

One of the purposes of the rejected 2007 constitutional reform was precisely to change this competency of the States. But in spite of the popular rejection of the reform, nonetheless, it was the Constitutional Chamber, through a decision adopted four month after the referendum (April 15, 2008), the State organ in charge of implementing the reform. The Chamber, in effect, when deciding an autonomous recourse for the abstract interpretation of the Constitution filed by the Attorney General, modified the content of that constitutional provision, considering that the exclusive attribution it contained, was not "exclusive," but a "concurrent" one, to be exercised together with the federal government, which even could reassume the attribution or decree its intervention.. [57]

---

55   See *Revista de Derecho Público* 93–94, Editorial Jurídica Venezolana, Caracas 2003, 136ff. and 164ff. See comments in Alberto Arteaga Sánchez et al., *Sentencia 1942 vs. Libertad de expresión*, Caracas 2004.

56   See the Constitutional Chamber Decision N° 957 (May 25, 2007), in *Revista de Derecho Público* 110, Editorial Jurídica Venezolana, Caracas 2007, 117ff. See the comments in Allan R. Brewer-Carías, "El juez constitucional en Venezuela como instrumento para aniquilar la libertad de expresión plural y para confiscar la propiedad privada: El caso RCTV", in *Revista de Derecho Público*", N° 110, (abril-junio 2007), Editorial Jurídica Venezolana, Caracas 2007, pp. 7-32.

57   See Allan R. Brewer-Carías, "La Sala Constitucional como poder constituyente: la modificación de la forma federal del estado y del sistema constitucional de división territorial del poder público, in *Revista de Derecho Público*, N° 114, (abril-junio 2008), Editorial Jurídica Venezolana, Caracas 2008, pp. 247-262; and "La ilegitima mutación de la Constitución y la

With this interpretation, again, the Chamber illegitimately modified the Constitution usurping popular sovereignty, compelling the National Assembly to enact legislation contrary to the Constitution, which it did in March 2009, by reforming of the Organic Law for Decentralization. [58]

In other cases, the Constitutional Chamber has been the instrument of the government in order to assume direct control of other branches of government, as happened in 2002 with the take-over of the Electoral Power, which since then has been completely controlled by the Executive. This began in 2002 after the Organic Law of the Electoral Power[59] was sanctioned and the National Assembly was due to appoint the new members of the National Electoral Council. Because the representatives supporting the government did not have the qualified majority to approve such appointments by themselves, and did not reached agreements on the matter with the opposition, when the National Assembly failed to appoint the members of the National Electoral Council, that task was assumed, without any constitutional power, by the Constitutional Chamber itself. Deciding an action that was filed against the unconstitutional legislative omission, the Chamber instead of urging the Assembly to comply with its constitutional duty, directly appointed the members of the Electoral Council, usurping the Legislator's functions, but without complying with the conditions established in the Constitution for such appointments. [60] With this decision, the Chamber assured the government's complete control of the Council, kidnapping the citizen's rights to political participation, and allowing the official governmental party to manipulate the electoral results.

Consequently, the elections held in Venezuela during the past decade have been organized by a politically dependent branch of government, without any guarantee of independence or impartiality. This is the only explanation, for instance, of the complete lack of official information on the final voting results of the December 2007 referendum rejecting the constitutional reform drafted and proposed by the President. The country, nowadays, still ignored the majority number of votes that effectively rejected the constitutional reform draft tending to consolidate in the Constitution the basis for a socialist, centralized, militaristic, and police state, as proposed by President Chávez.

---

legitimidad de la jurisdicción constitucional: la "reforma" de la forma federal del Estado en Venezuela mediante interpretación constitucional," en *Memoria del X Congreso Iberoamericano de Derecho Constitucional,* Instituto Iberoamericano de Derecho Constitucional, Asociación Peruana de Derecho Constitucional, Instituto de Investigaciones Jurídicas-UNAM y Maestría en Derecho Constitucional-PUCP, IDEMSA, Lima 2009, tomo 1, pp. 29-51.

58   See *Gaceta Oficial* N° 39 140 of March 17, 2009.

59   See *Gaceta Oficial* N° 37.573 of November 19, 2002.

60   See Decision N° 2073 of August 4, 2003, Case: *Hermánn Escarrá Malaver y oros*), and Decision N° 2341 of August 25, 2003, Case: *Hemann Escarrá y otros*. See in Allan R. Brewer-Carías, "El secuestro del poder electoral y la confiación del derecho a la participación política mediante el referendo revocatorio presidencial: Venezuela 2000-2004", in *Stvdi Vrbinati, Rivista tgrimestrale di Scienze Giuridiche, Politiche ed Economiche,* Año LXXI – 2003/04 Nuova Serie A – N. 55,3, Università degli Studi di Urbino, pp.379-436.

The result of all these facts is that at the beginning of the twenty-first century, Latin America has witnessed in Venezuela the birth of a new model of authoritarian government that did not immediately originate itself in a military coup, as happened in many other occasions during the long decades of last century, but in an constituent coup d'état and in popular elections, which despite its final goal of destroying the rule of law and democracy, have provided it the convenient camouflage of "constitutional" and "elective" marks, although of course, lacking the essential components of democracy, which are much more than the sole popular or circumstantial election of governments.

In particular, among all the essential elements and components of democracy, the one regarding the separation and independence of public powers is maybe the most fundamental pillar of the rule of law, because it is the only one that can allow the other factors of democracy to become political reality. To be precise, democracy, as a rule of law political regime, can function only in a constitutional system where control of power exists, so without effective check and balance, no free and fair elections can take place; no plural political system can be developed; no effective democratic participation can be ensured; no effective transparency in the exercise of government can be assured; no real government accountability can be secure; and no effective access to justice can be guaranteed in order to protect human rights.

All these factors are lacking at the present time in Venezuela, where a new form of constitutional authoritarianism has been developed, based on the concentration and centralization of state powers, which prevent any possibility of effective democratic participation, and any possible check and balance between the branches of government. Today, all the State organs are subjected to the National Assembly, and through it, to the President. That is why the legislative elections of last week were so important, particularly bearing in mind that according to the Constitution, the presidential system of government was conceived to function only if the government has complete control over the Assembly. A government that does not have such control will find difficult to govern, and that is why the President of the Republic, just before the election, repeatedly affirmed that if the opposition was to win the control of the Assembly, that would signify war.

In any case, the fact is that the President, his official party and the National Assembly tried to configure the last week legislative elections as a plebiscite regarding the President and his socialist model and policies. And the result has been that effectively, the President lost his plebiscite, in spite of all the efforts made by the National Electoral Council to make-up the final results, presenting numbers showing a supposed tight election, trying to minimizing the importance of the fact that the opposition won the popular vote.

After a decade of demolishing the rule of law and the democratic institutions, by controlling, at the government will, all the branches of government, it will be very difficult for the government and its official party to admit the democratic need they have to share power in the Assembly. They are not used to democracy, that is to say, they are not used to any sort of compromise and consensus, but only to impose their decisions; and that is why they have already announced that they are not going to participate in any sort of dialogue. It is then possible, that in the near future, we could witness, even before the new elected representative take their sits in the Assembly in January 2011, the approval by the old Assembly of new legislation seeking to consolidate what the people has rejected, the so called "Socialism of the XXI Century" which is based on the centralized framework of the so-called "Popular Power" to be exercised by "Communes" and by the government controlled "Communal Councils," minimizing the future role of the National Assembly and of its representativeness.

One further example of the perversion of the Constitution and of the will of the people expressed in the September 2010 Legislative election, and it is very sad to pointed out, is currently in course of being materialized regarding the appointment of the new Magistrates of the Supreme Tribunal. What just a weeks ago was only a treat of the government, once lost the popular vote, for the current National Assembly – completely dominated by the official party - to immediately proceed to appoint the new magistrates of the Supreme before the inauguration of the new elected members of the National Assembly in January 2011, in order to avoid the participation in the nominating process of the opposition members of the Assembly; is now a real fact. Nonetheless, for such appointments to be done between September and December 2010, a modification of the Organic Law of the Supreme Tribunal was necessary, which has been done, not through the ordinary procedure to reform statutes, but through a completely irregular mechanism of "reprinting" the text of the statute in the *Official Gazette* based in a supposed "material error" in the copying of the text of the statute; reprinting made precisely a few days after the Government lost the majority in the National Assembly..[61]

Article 70 of the Organic Law of the Supreme Tribunal, in effect, established that the term in order to propose candidates to be nominated Magistrate of the Supreme Tribunal before the Nominating Judicial Committee "must not be *less* that thirty continuous days;" wording that has been change through a "notice" published by the Secretary of the Assembly in the Official Gazette stating that establishing that instead of the word "*less*" the correct word to be used in the antonym word "*more*" in the sense of the term "must not be more that thirty continuous days." That means that the "reform" of the statute by changing a word (less to more), transformed a minimum term was transformed into a maximum term in order to reduce the term to nominate candidates and allow the current national Assembly to proceed to make the election before the new National Assembly initiates its activities in January 2010.[62] This is the "procedure" currently used in order to reform statutes, by means of the reprinting of the text in the *Official Gazette*, without any possible judicial review

In any case, if the threats that have been repeatedly announced by government's representatives in the sense that the current National Assembly will enact such legis-

---

61   See *Gaceta Oficial* N° 39.522 of October 1, 2010.

62   See the comments in Víctor Hernández Mendible, "Sobre la nueva reimpresión por "supuestos errores" materiales de la LOTSJ en la *Gaceta Oficial* N° 39.522, de 1 de octubre de 2010," and Antonio Silva Aranguren, "Tras el rastro del engaño, en la web de la Asamblea Nacional," published as an *Addendum* to the book of Allan R. Brewer-Carías and Víctor Hernández Mendible, *Ley Orgánica del Tribunal Supremo de Justicia de 2010*, Editorial Jurídica Venezolana, Caracas 2010.

lation before January 2011, we will then be able to characterize the government, not only by its constant actions adopted defrauding the Constitution, but now, also, by defrauding the popular will as it was expressed in the last legislative election. In such case, the illegitimacy of the government will be total, and the right of the people to resist such government would become clearer.

CHAPTER XV

OVERVIEW ON THE LACK OF AUTONOMY AND INDEPENDENCE OF THE JUDICIARY (2011)

This essay was written in 2010 and 2012, in order to prepare different Legal Opinions given on the matter of the situation of the Lack of Autonomy and Independence of the Judiciary in Venezuela under the Authoritarian Government.

The Judicial Branch in Venezuela and in particular, the Supreme Tribunal of Justice that is in charge of governing and administering the whole Judiciary, currently are subject to political interference, particularly in politically sensitive cases. This political interference of the Judiciary began in 1999, when the Constituent Assembly elected in July that year, dissolved and seized control (*intervino*) of all branches of the national and state governments, and dismissed all the public officials elected just a few months before (1998), namely the members of the former Supreme Court of Justice[63] as well as all representatives to the former National Congress, the Legislative Assemblies of the States and the Municipal Councils as well as the State Governors and Municipal Mayors.[64]

In particular, the Constituent Assembly expressly declared the Judicial Branch to be "in emergency," and interfered with its autonomy. Since then, the independence

---

63   The Supreme Court of Justice was abolished by the December 22, 1999 transitory regime established by the Constituent Assembly after the approval of the 1999 Constitution by popular referendum. On the transitory regime, see generally Allan R. Brewer-Carias, *La Constitución de 1999. Derecho Constitucional Venezolano*, Vol. II, Editorial Jurídica Venezolana, Caracas 2004, pp. 1150 ff.

64   See the decrees of intervention of the branches of Government, in Allan R. Brewer-Carías, *Debate Constituyente (Aportes a la Asamblea nacional Constituyente)*, Vol. I (August-September 1999), Fundación de Derecho Publico-Editorial Jurídica Venezolana, Caracas 1999. This amounted to a *coup d'Etat. See generally* Allan R. Brewer-Carias, *Golpe de Estado y Proceso Constituyente en Venezuela*, Universidad Nacional Autónoma de México, Mexico 2002; Guayaquil, 2006.

of the Venezuelan Judiciary has been progressively and systematically dismantled,[65] being the result of this process, the tight Executive control over the Judiciary, especially the Constitutional Chamber of the newly created Supreme Tribunal of Justice.[66]

The National Constituent Assembly drafted the new Constitution that was approved in a popular referendum held on December 15, 1999, being published on December 30, 1999.[67] The Constitution provides for means designed to protect its own supremacy, being the most important of these safeguards the one related to the Judiciary and to the judicial system. In this regard, Article 253 of the Constitution proclaims that the power to render justice emanates from the citizenry and is exercised in the name of the Republic and by the authority of the law. For such purposes,

---

65   See generally Allan R. Brewer-Carías, *La progresiva y sistemática demolición de la autonomía e independencia del Poder Judicial en Venezuela (1999-2004)* in *XXX Jornadas J.M. Domínguez Escobar, Estado de derecho, administración de justicia y derechos humanos*, Instituto de Estudios Jurídicos del Estado Lara, Barquisimeto 2005, pp. 33-174; Allan R. Brewer-Carías, *El constitucionalismo y la emergencia en Venezuela: entre la emergencia formal y la emergencia anormal del Poder Judicial* in Allan R. Brewer-Carías, *Estudios sobre el Estado Constiucional (2005-2006)*, Editorial Jurídica Venezolana, Caracas 2007, pp. 245-269; and Allan R. Brewer-Carías, "La justicia sometida al poder. La ausencia de independencia y autonomía de los jueces en Venezuela por la interminable emergencia del Poder Judicial (1999-2006), in *Cuestiones Internacionales. Anuario Jurídico Villanueva 2007*, Centro Universitario Villanueva, Marcial Pons, Madrid 2007, pp. 25-57, *available at* www.allanbrewercarias.com, (Biblioteca Virtual, II.4. Artículos y Estudios N° 550, 2007) pp. 1-37. *See also* Allan R. Brewer-Carías, *Historia Constitucional de Venezuela*, Editorial Alfa, Tomo II, Caracas 2008, pp. 402-454.

66   *See* Allan R. Brewer-Carias, *"Quis Custodiet ipsos Custodes:* De la interpretación constitucional a la inconstitucionalidad de la interpretación,*"* in *VII Congreso Nacional de Derecho Constitucional*, Peru, Fondo Editorial 2005, Colegio de Abogados de Arequipa, Arequipa, September 2005, pp. 463-489, also *available at* www.allanbrewercarias.com, (Biblioteca Virtual, II.4. Artículos y Estudios N° 475, 2005) pp. 1-33; and in Allan R. Brewer-Carías, *Crónica sobre la "In" Justicia Constitucionbal. La Sala Constitucional y el autroritarismoi en Venezuela*, Editorial Jurídica Venezolana, Caracas 2007.

67   *Official Gazette* N° 36.860 of December 30, 1999. In 2007, President Chávez proposed a constitutional reform that was sanctioned by the National Assembly but rejected by the people through referendum held in December 2007. Through this failed reform, President Chávez intended to reinforce the system of centralization and concentration of power that he had managed to develop. See generally Manuel Rachadell, *Socialismo del Siglo XXI. Análisis de la reforma Constitucional propuesta por el Presidente Chávez en agosto de 2007*, FUNEDA, Editorial Jurídica Venezolana, Caracas 2008; Héctor Turuhpial Carriello, *El texto oculto de la reforma*, FUNEDA, Caracas 2008; Allan R. Brewer-Carías, *Hacia la consolidación de un Estado Socialista, Centralizado, Policial y Militarista. Comentarios sobre el sentido y alcance de las propuestas de reforma constitucional 2007*, Editorial Jurídica Venezolana, Caracas 2007. In February 2009, at the request of President Chávez, the National Assembly took the initiative of a new Constitutional Reform which purpose was to eliminate the constitutional limits that the 1999 Constitution established for the reelection of elected officials. The reform was approved by referendum held on February 14, 2009, and allows the President of the Republic of Venezuela to be elected in a continual and indefinite way.

Article 26 of the Constitution provides that the State must guarantee a "cost-free, accessible, impartial, adequate, transparent, autonomous, independent, responsible, equitable, and expeditious [system of] justice." Article 254 of the Constitution declares the principle of the independence of the Judicial Branch and establishes that the Supreme Tribunal of Justice shall have "functional, financial, and administrative autonomy."

In order to guarantee the independence and autonomy of courts and judges, Article 255 provides for a specific mechanism to ensure the independent appointment of judges, and to guaranty their stability. In this regard, the judicial office is considered as a career, in which the admission, as well as the promotion of judges within it, must be the result of a public competition or examinations to ensure that the candidates are adequately qualified. The candidates are to be chosen by panels from the judicial circuits, and the judges are to be designated by the Supreme Tribunal of Justice. The Constitution also creates a Judicial Nominations Committee (Article 270) to assist the Judicial Branch in selecting the Magistrates for the Supreme Tribunal of Justice (Article 264), and to assist judicial colleges in selecting of judges for the lower courts. This Judicial Nominations Committee is to be composed of representatives from different sectors of society, as determined by law. The Constitution also guarantees the stability of all judges, prescribing that they can only be removed or suspended from office through the disciplinary procedures developed before a specific Judicial Disciplinary Jurisdiction or Courts (Article 255). As THIS DATE (Nove 2011), none of the constitutional provisions regarding the independence of the Supreme Tribunal or and of the Judiciary based on the principles of appointment and stability of judges, has been implemented.

In particular, one of the unconstitutional results of the transitory constitutional regime adopted by the Constituent Assembly in 1999 was the appointment of the Magistrates of the new Supreme Tribunal without fulfilling the conditions for those appointments and without guarantying the citizens' participation in the process. In this particular regarding the appointment of the Supreme Tribunal Magistrates, the Constitution assigns to the National Assembly the power to elect them for a single term of 12 years (Article 264), from within the nominees proposed by a "Judicial Nominations Committee" that in theory was to be integrated only by "representatives of the different sectors of society" (Article 270). The main purpose of this constitutional procedure was to limit the discretionary power that the former Congress had in appointing Magistrates to the Supreme Court of Justice, which was often exercised on the basis of political agreements and without any sort of citizen or society control.

Unfortunately, by-passing and ignoring these constitutional provisions since 2000 the appointment of Magistrates has been made without the constitution of such Nominating Committee[68] or with a "Committee" that was provisionally organized in

---

68   *Official Gazette* N° 36.859 of December 29, 1999. On the transitory regime, see *in general*, Allan R. Brewer-Carias, *La Constitucion de 1999. Derecho Constitucional Venezolano*, Vol. II, Editorial Jurídica Venezolana, Caracas 2004, pp. 1013-1025.

2000[69] and later in the Organic Law of the Supreme Tribunal of Justice of 2004 and ir reform of 2010, as a simple parliamentary commissions controlled by and subjected to the political will of the parliamentarian majority, violating the citizens right to political participation.[70]

In this regard, in effect, in 2000 a "Special Law for the Ratification or Appointment of High Officials and Magistrates to the Supreme Tribunal of Justice"[71] was enacted by the then newly elected National Assembly, but without organizing the aforementioned nominating committees, thereby confiscating the citizens' right to political participation. Such Special Law, of course, was challenged before the Constitutional Chamber (in that occasion by the Peoples' Defendant),[72] which never decided the merits of the case. Instead, the Chamber close the case alleging lack of interest by the claimant (Peoples' defendant), after issuing a preliminary ruling (December 2000), deciding in its own cause, establishing that the Constitution was not applicable to the Magistrates that were signing the decision, because they were not going to be "appointed" but to be "ratified;"[73] a decision that was a grotesque mockery regarding the Constitution.

This irregular situation continued in 2004, when the National Assembly eventually sanctioned the Organic Law of the Supreme Tribunal of Justice, increasing the number of magistrates from twenty to thirty-two, distorting the constitutional conditions for their appointment and dismissal, and consolidating the judicial nominating committee as a dependent parliamentary commission. This reform, as the Inter-American Commission on Human Rights emphasized in its *2004 Annual Report*, "lack the safeguards necessary to prevent other branches of government from undermining the Supreme Tribunal's independence and to keep narrow or temporary majorities from determining its composition."[74]

---

69   See Special Law for the Ratification or Election of the High Officials of the Citizens Power and of the Magistrates of the Supreme Tribunal of Justice for the First Constitutional Term. *Official Gazette* N° 37.077 of November 14, 2000

70   See Allan R. Brewer-Carías, "La participación ciudadana en la designación de los titulares de los órganos no electos de los Poderes Públicos en Venezuela y sus vicisitudes políticas" in *Revista Iberoamericana de Derecho Publico y Administrativo*, Year 5, N° 5-2005, San Jose, Costa Rica 2005, pp. 76-95), *available at* www.allanbrewercarias.com, (Biblioteca Virtual, II.4. Artículos y Estudios N° 469, 2005) pp. 1-48.

71   *Gaceta Oficial* N° 37.077 del 14 de noviembre de 2000.

72   See *El Universal,* 14 de diciembre de 2000, pp. 1-2.

73   See decision of the Constitutional Chamber of November 12, 2000, in *Revista de Derecho Público N° 84*, Editorial Jurídica Venezolana, Caracas, 2000, p. 109. Se the comments in Allan R. Brewer-Carías, "La participación ciudadana en la designación de los titulares de los órganos no electos de los Poderes Públicos en Venezuela y sus vicisitudes políticas," in *Revista Iberoamericana de Derecho Público y Administrativo*, Año 5, N° 5-2005, San José, Costa Rica 2005, pp. 76-95, *disponible en* www.allanbrewercarias.com, (Biblioteca Virtual, II.4. Artículos y Estudios N° 469, 2005) pp. 1-48.

74   See IACHR, *2004 Annual Report* (Follow-Up Report on Compliance by the State of Venezuela with the Recommendations made by the IACHR in its Report on the Situation of Hu-

After this 2004 legal reform, the process for selecting new Magistrates, although being an exclusive competency of the National Assembly, in fact has been controlled by the President of the Republic, as was publicly recognized by the representative head of the parliamentary nominating committee, when he publicly announced the nominations. In 2004, in effect, according to the new Organic Law of the Supreme Tribunal,[75] the nomination and appointment by means of the new "Nominating Committee" was completely controlled by the political organs of the Government. As the President of the Parliamentary Nominating Commission in charge of selecting the candidates for Magistrates of the Supreme Tribunal (who a few months later was appointed Ministry of the Interior and Justice), stated in December 2004 to the press:

> "Although we, the representatives, have the authority for this selection, the President of the Republic was consulted and his opinion was very much taken into consideration." He added: "Let's be clear, we are not going to score own-goals. On the list, there were people from the opposition who comply with all the requirements. The opposition could have used them in order to reach an agreement during the last sessions, but they did not want to. We are not going to do it for them. There is no one in the group of candidates that could act against us [...]."[76]

On the other hand, the President's influence on the Supreme Tribunal was admitted by himself, for example, when he publicly complained that the Supreme Tribunal had issued an important ruling in which it "modified" the Income Tax Law, without previously consulting the "leader of the Revolution," and warning courts to adopt decisions that would be against the interests of the Government, considering it as a sign of "treason to the People" and "the Revolution." That was a very controversial case, decided by the Constitutional Chamber of the Supreme Tribunal in Decision Nº 301 of February 27, 2007.[77] The President of the Republic said:

man Rights in Venezuela [2003]), para. 174. Available at http://www.cidh.oas.org/annual-rep/2004eng/chap.5b.htm

75   *Official Gazette* Nº 37.942 of May 20, 2004. For comments on this law, see *generally* Allan R. Brewer-Carías, *Ley Orgánica del Tribunal Supremo de Justicia. Procesos y Procedimientos Constitucionales y Contencioso-Administrativos*, Caracas, 2004.

76   See *El Nacional*, Caracas December 13, 2004. The Inter-American Commission on Human Rights suggested in its Report to the General Assembly of the OAS for 2004 that "These provisions of the Organic Law of the Supreme Court of Justice also appear to have helped the executive manipulate the election of judges during 2004." See Inter-American Commission on Human Rights, *2004 Report on Venezuela*, par. 180. Available at http://www.cidh.oas.org/annualrep/2004sp/cap.5d.htm.

77   Supreme Tribunal of Justice, Constitutional Chamber, Decision Nº 301 of February 27, 2007 (Case: *Adriana Vigilanza y Carlos A. Vecchio*) (Exp. Nº 01-2862) (*Official Gazette* Nº 38.635 of March 1, 2007) in *Revista de Derecho Público,* Nº 101, Editorial Jurídica Venezolana, Caracas 2007, pp. 170-177. See *in general* comments in Allan R. Brewer-Carías, "El juez constitucional en Venezuela como legislador positivo de oficio en materia tributaria" in *Revista de Derecho Público Nº 109*, Editorial Jurídica Venezolana, Caracas 2007, pp. 193-212, *available at* www.allanbrewercarias.com, (Biblioteca Virtual, II.4. Artículos y Estudios Nº 508, 2007) pp. 1-36; and Allan R. Brewer-Carías, "De cómo la Jurisdicción constitucional

"Many times they come, the National Revolutionary Government comes and wants to make a decision against something that, for instance, deals with or has to pass through judicial decisions, and then they begin to move against it in the shadows, and many times they succeed in neutralizing decisions of the Revolution through a judge, or a court, and even through the very same Supreme Tribunal of Justice, behind the backs of the Leader of the Revolution, acting from within against the Revolution. This is, I insist, treason to the people, treason to the Revolution."[78]

In another occasion, the President of the Republic publicly threatened the Magistrates of the Supreme Tribunal and the Head of the Pubic Prosecutor Office to act according to his whished against a TV Channel (Globovisión), saying, on May 28, 2009:

"Mrs. Prosecutor, I am publicly summoning you in order for you, with your prosecutors, to fulfill with your obligation before the people, because it is for that that you are there. Mrs. President of the Supreme Tribunal of Justice, with all the Magistrates and courts, fulfill your obligation, it is for that that you are there and, if not, resign, so persons with courage [could] assume... He also warned that he will wait for "what must be performed be performed, and if what must occur does not occur in the corresponding levels [of government]" he himself would act against the Television Station. "I will have to act myself as I have done in other occasions facing the deficiencies and voids that we still have in some levels of the State."[79]

---

en Venezuela, no sólo legisla de oficio, sino subrepticiamente modifica las reformas legales que "sanciona", a espaldas de las partes en el proceso: el caso de la aclaratoria de la sentencia de Reforma de la Ley de Impuesto sobre la Renta de 2007" in *Revista de Derecho Público* N° 114, Editorial Jurídica Venezolana, Caracas 2008, pp. 267-276, *available at* http://www.brewercarias.com/Content/449725d9-f1cb-474b-8ab2-41efb849fea8/Content/II.4.575.pdf.

78 (Emphasis added.) (*"Muchas veces llegan, viene el Gobierno Nacional Revolucionario y quiere tomar una decisión contra algo por ejemplo que tiene que ver o que tiene que pasar por decisiones judiciales y ellos empiezan a moverse en contrario a la sombra, y muchas veces logran neutralizar decisiones de la Revolución a través de un juez, o de un tribunal, o hasta en el mismísimo Tribunal Supremo de Justicia, **a espaldas del líder de la Revolución**, actuando por dentro contra la Revolución. Eso es, repito, traición al pueblo, traición a la Revolución."* (Emphasis added.)) *Discurso en el Primer Encuentro con Propulsores del Partido Socialista Unido de Venezuela desde el teatro Teresa Carreño* (Speech in the First Event with Supporters of the Venezuela United Socialist Party at the Teresa Carreno Theatre), March 24, 2007, *available at* http://www.minci.gob.ve/alocuciones/4/13788/primer_encuentro_con.html, p. 45.

79 *"Señora Fiscal, le hago un emplazamiento público para que usted, con sus fiscales, cumpla con su obligación ante el pueblo que para eso están allí. Señora presidenta del TSJ (Luisa Estella Morales), con todos los magistrados y tribunales, cumplan con su obligación que para eso están allí y, si no, renuncien y que gente con coraje asuma..."* Seguidamente advirtió que esperará "que se cumpla lo que tiene que cumplirse y si no ocurriera lo que tiene que ocurrir en las instancias correspondientes" él mismo actuaría contra la televisora. "Voy tener que actuar yo mismo (&) como he tenido que hacerlo en algunas ocasiones ante las deficiencias y los vacíos que todavía tenemos en algunas instancias del Estado." See in *El Universal*, Caracas, June 29, 2009.. See in http://www.eluniversal.com/2009/05/29/pol_art_chavez-exige-renunci_1409179.shtml

The last expression of this executive control on the Supreme Tribunal of Justice occurred in 2010, after an illegitimate "reform" of Organic Law of the Supreme Tribunal of Justice by means of its "reprinting" due to a supposed printing (material) error,[80] allowing the appointment of new Magistrates of the Tribunal without the configuration of the Nominating Committee established in the Constitution, before the new elected members of the National Assembly in the September 2010 legislative elections start their tenure in January 2011.[81] With this legal "reform," the National Assembly, composed by representatives that by December 2010, after the Legislative elections, can be said that they did not represented the majority of the people, proceeded to fill the Supreme Tribunal of Magistrates members of the Official political party, and even with members of the same Assembly that were finishing their tenure and that did not comply with the constitutional conditions to be Magistrate. As the former magistrate of the Supreme Court of Justice, Hildegard Rondón de Sansó, wrote:

> "The biggest risk for the State of the improper actions of the Nation al Assembly in the recent nomination of the magistrates of the Supreme Tribunal of Justice, lies not only in the lacking, in the majority of the appointed of the constitutional conditions, but having taken into the apex of the Judicial Power the decisive influence of one sector of the legislative Power, due to the fact that for different Chambers, five legislators were elected."[82]

The same former Magistrate Sansó affirmed that "a whole fundamental sector of the power of the State is going to be in the hands of a small group of persons that are not jurist, but politician by profession, to whom will correspond, among other functions, the control of normative acts," adding that "the most grave I that those ap pointing, even for a single moment realized that they were designating the highest judges of the Venezuelan legal system that, as such, had to be the most competent, and of recognized prestige as the Constitution imposes."[83] She concluded, as afore-

---

80   See the comments of Víctor Hernández Mendible, "Sobre la nueva reimpresión por "supuestos errores" materiales de la Ley Orgánica del Tribunal Supremo, octubre de 2010," y Antonio Silva Aranguren, "Tras el rastro del engaño, en la web de la Asamblea Nacional," in *Revista de Derecho Público*, N° 124, Editorial Jurídica Venezolana, Caracas 2010, pp. 110-113.

81   Hildegard Rondón de Sansó, who was Magistrate of the former Supreme Court of Justice, regarding such reform, has said that "the Nomination Judicial Committee was unconstitutionally converted into an appendix of the Legislative Power." See Hildegard Rondón de Sansó, *"Obiter Dicta. En torno a una elección,"* in *La Voce d'Italia*, Caracas, December 14, 2010.

82   *"El mayor de los riesgos que plantea para el Estado la desacertada actuación de la Asamblea Nacional en la reciente designación de los Magistrados del Tribunal Supremo de Justicia, no está solo en la carencia, en la mayoría de los designados de los requisitos constitucionales, sino el haber llevado a la cúspide del Poder Judicial la decisiva influencia de un sector del Poder Legislativo, ya que para diferentes Salas, fueron elegidos cinco parlamentarios."* See Hildegard Rondón de Sansó, *"Obiter Dicta. En torno a una elección,"* in *La Voce d'Italia*, 14-12-2010.

83   *"Todo un sector fundamental del poder del Estado, va a estar en manos de un pequeño grupo de sujetos que no son juristas, sino políticos de profesión, y a quienes corresponderá, entre otras funciones el control de los actos normativos;"* agregando que *"Lo más grave es*

mentioned, recognizing within the "grave errors" accompanying the nomination, the fact of:

> "The configuration of the Nominating Judicial Committee, that the Constitution created as a neutral organ, representing the 'different sectors of society' (Article 271), but the Organic Law of the Supreme Tribunal converted it in an unconstitutional way, into an appendix of the Legislative Power. The consequence of this grave error was unavoidable: those electing elected their own colleagues, considering that acting in such a way was the most natural thing in this world, and, as example of that, were the shameful applauses with which each appointment was greeted." [84]

Unfortunately, the political control over the Supreme Tribunal of Justice has permeated to all the judiciary, due mainly to the fact that in Venezuela, it is the Supreme Tribunal the one in charge of the government and administration of the Judiciary. This has affected gravely the autonomy and independence of judges at all levels of the Judiciary, which has been aggravated by the fact that during the past decade the Venezuelan Judiciary has been composed primarily of temporary and provisional judges, without career or stability, appointed without the public competition process of selection established in the Constitution, and dismissed without due process of law, for political reasons.[85] This reality amounts to political control of the Judiciary, as demonstrated by the dismissal of judges who have adopted decisions contrary to the policies of the governing political authorities.

This political control over all judges has been assured through the Supreme Tribunal, which is in charge of governing and administering the Judiciary, reinforced by means of the survival up to 2010 of the 1999 "provisional" Commission on the Functioning and Restructuring of the Judicial System, which in addition has been legimimazed by the same Tribunal, making completely inapplicable the 1999 constitutional provisions seeking to guarantee the independence and autonomy of judges.[86]

---

que los designantes, ni un solo momento se percataron de que estaban nombrando a los jueces máximos del sistema jurídico venezolano que, como tales, tenían que ser los más aptos, y de reconocido prestigio como lo exige la Constitución." Id.

84   "la configuración del Comité de Postulaciones Judiciales, al cual la Constitución creó como un organismo neutro, representante de los "diferentes sectores de la sociedad" (Art. 271), pero la Ley Orgánica del Tribunal Supremo de Justicia, lo convirtió en forma inconstitucional, en un apéndice del Poder Legislativo. La consecuencia de este grave error era inevitable: los electores eligieron a sus propios colegas, considerando que hacerlo era lo más natural de este mundo y, ejemplo de ello fueron los bochornosos aplausos con que se festejara cada nombramiento." Id.

85   See Inter-American Commission on Human Rights, Report on the Situation of Human Rights in Venezuela, OEA/Ser.L/V/II.118, doc. 4 rev. 2, December 29, 2003, par. 174, available at http://www.cidh.oas.org/countryrep/Venezuela2003eng/toc.htm.

86   See in general Allan R. Brewer-Carías, "La progresiva y sistemática demolición de la autonomía e independencia del Poder Judicial en Venezuela (1999-2004)," in XXX Jornadas J.M Dominguez Escovar, Estado de Derecho, Administración de Justicia y Derechos Humanos, Instituto de Estudios Jurídicos del Estado Lara, Barquisimeto 2005, pp. 33-174; Allan R. Brewer-Carías, "El constitucionalismo y la emergencia en Venezuela: entre la emergencia formal y la emergencia anormal del Poder Judicial," in Allan R. Brewer-Carías, Estudios So-

The fact has been that during the past decade the Judiciary has been in a permanent situation of reorganization,[87] to the point that in March 2009, the Supreme Tribunal of Justice again declared the Judiciary in situation of "integral reorganization."[88]

The result of this permanent situation of emergency is that since 1999, the Venezuelan Judiciary has been almost exclusively made up of temporary and provisional judges,[89] and the public competition processes for the appointment of judges with citizen participation has not been implemented.

On the other hand, in general, judges lack stability, and since the constitutional provisions creating the Judicial Disciplinary Jurisdiction have not been effectively implemented by legislation, the matters of judicial discipline up to 2010 were in the hands of the "Commission of the Functioning and Restructuring of the Judiciary,"[90]

---

bre el Estado Constitucional (2005-2006), Editorial Jurídica Venezolana, Caracas 2007, pp. 245-269; and Allan R. Brewer-Carías "La justicia sometida al poder. La ausencia de independencia y autonomía de los jueces en Venezuela por la interminable emergencia del Poder Judicial (1999-2006), in Cuestiones Internacionales. Anuario Jurídico Villanueva 2007, Centro Universitario Villanueva, Marcial Pons, Madrid 2007, pp. 25-57, available at www.allanbrewercarias.com, (Biblioteca Virtual, II.4. Artículos y Estudios N° 550, 2007) pp. 1-37. See also Allan R. Brewer-Carías, Historia Constitucional de Venezuela, Editorial Alfa, Tomo II, Caracas 2008, pp. 402-454.

87   The Inter-American Court on Human Rights in its recent decision of June 30, 2009 (Case Reverón Trujillo vs. Venezuela) has concluded that "the reorganization of the Judicial Power in Venezuela, which can be considered that began with the approval of the convening of the Constituent Assembly on April 1999, has endured for more that 10 years," Paragraph 99, available at http://www.corteidh.or.cr/docs/casos/articulos/seriec_197_esp.pdf.

88   Supreme Tribunal of Justice, Resolution N° 2009-0008 of March 18, 2009, Official Gazette N° 5.915 Extra. of April 2, 2009

89   A provisional judge is one appointed pending a public competition. A temporal judge is one appointed to perform a specific task or for a specific period of time. In 2003, the Inter-American Commission on Human Rights explained that: "The Commission has been informed that only 250 judges have been appointed through competitive professional examinations as provided for in the Constitution. Of a total of 1772 judges in Venezuela, the Supreme Court of Justice reports that only 183 are tenured, 1331 are provisional, and 258 are temporary." Report on the Situation of Human Rights in Venezuela; OAS/Ser.L/V/II.118. doc.4rev.2; December 29, 2003, ¶174, available at http://www.cidh.oas.org/countryrep/Venezuela2003eng/toc.htm. The Commission also added that "one issue with an impact on the autonomy and independence of the judiciary is the provisional nature of judges within the Venezuelan legal system. Information from different sources indicates that at present, more than 80% of Venezuela's judges are 'provisional.'" Id., ¶161. The Inter-American Court on Human Rights in the decision issued on June 30, 2009 (Case Reverón Trujillo vs. Venezuela) has ruled that "in Venezuela, since August 1999 up to now, provisional judges have no stability in their tenure, are discretionally appointed and can be dismissed without any pre-established procedure. Also, when the facts of the case took place, the percentage of provisional judges in the country approximately was up to 80%."Paragraph 106, available at http://www.corteidh.or.cr/docs/casos/articulos/se-riec_197_esp.pdf

90   The Politico-Administrative Chamber of the Supreme Tribunal of Justice has ruled that the dismissal of temporary judges is a discretional power of the Functioning and Restructuring

which was not established in the Constitution, having power to remove temporary judges without due process guarantees.[91] In addition, the Judicial Commission of the Supreme Tribunal of Justice had also discretionary powers to remove all temporary judges.[92] In 2010, as explained below, the Venezuelan Judge Ethical Code Law[93] eliminated the Commission on the Functioning of the Judiciary creating instead the Disciplinary Jurisdiction, but with judges appointed by the national Assembly and even by the Supreme Tribunal, establishing a more strict political control of it.

As described above, the constitutional principles tending to assure the autonomy and independence of judges at all levels of the Judiciary are yet to be applied, particularly regarding the admission of candidates to the judicial career through "public competition" processes, with citizen participation in the procedure of selection and appointment. This provision, as aforementioned, has not yet been implemented, being the judiciary almost exclusively made up of temporary and provisional judges, without any stability. Regarding this situation, for instance, since 2003 the Inter-American Commission on Human Rights has repeatedly express concern about the fact that provisional judges are susceptible to political manipulation, which alters the people's right to access to justice, reporting cases of dismissals and substitutions of judges in retaliation for decisions contrary to the government's position. In its *2008 Annual Report*, the Commission again verified the provisional character of the judiciary as an "endemic problem" because the appointment of judges was made without applying constitutional provisions on the matter – thus exposing judges to discretionary dismissal – which highlights the "permanent state of urgency" in which those appointments have been made.[94]

Contrary to these facts, as aforementioned and according to the words of the Constitution in order to guarantee the independence of the Judiciary, judges can be dismissed from their tenure only through disciplinary processes, conducted by disci-

---

Commission of the Judiciary. This Commission was created after 1999 and adopts its decisions without following any administrative procedure. *See* Decision N° 00463-2007 of March 20, 2007; Decision N° 00673-2008 of April 24, 2008 (quoted in Decision N° 1.939 of December 18, 2008, p. 42). The same position has been established by the Constitutional Chamber in Decisions N° 2414 of December 20, 2007; and Decision N° 280 of February 23, 2007.

91   See Allan R. Brewer-Carías, "La justicia sometida al poder y la interminable emergencia del poder judicial (1999-2006)," in *Derecho y Democracia. Cuadernos Universitarios*, Órgano de Divulgación Académica, Vicerrectorado Académico, Universidad Metropolitana, Año II, N° 11, Caracas, September 2007, pp. 122-138, also published as Allan R. Brewer-Carías, "La justicia sometida al poder (La ausencia de independencia y autonomía de los jueces en Venezuela por la interminable emergencia del Poder Judicial (1999-2006))," in Cuestiones internacionales. Anuario Jurídico Villanueva, Centro Universitario Villanueva, Marcial Pons, Madrid, 2007, pp. 25–57, *available at* www.allanbrewercarias.com, (Biblioteca Virtual, II.4. Artículos y Estudios N° 550, 2007) pp. 1-37.

92   See Supreme Tribunal of Justice, Constitutional Chamber, Decision N° 1.939 of December 18, 2008 (Case: *Gustavo Álvarez Arias et al.*)

93   See *Gaceta Oficial* N° 39.493 of August 23, 2010

94   See *Annual Report 2008* (OEA/Ser.L/V/II.134. Doc. 5 rev. 1. 25 febrero 2009), para. 39

plinary courts and judges, conforming a Disciplinary Judicial Jurisdiction. Nonetheless, as mentioned that Jurisdiction was only created in 2010, corresponding to that date the disciplinary judicial functions to the already mentioned transitory Commission on the reorganization of the Judiciary,[95] which, as reported by the same Inter-American Commission in its *2009 Annual Report*, "in addition to being a special, temporary entity, does not afford due guarantees for ensuring the independence of its decisions,[96] since its members may also be appointed or removed at the sole discretion of the Constitutional Chamber of the Supreme Tribunal of Justice, without previously establishing either the grounds or the procedure for such formalities."[97]

That Commission then "cleansed" the Judiciary of judges not in line with the authoritarian regime, removing judges in a discretionary way when they issued decisions not within the complacency of the government.[98] This lead the Inter-American Commission on Human Rights, to observe in its *2009 Annual Report,* that "in Venezuela, judges and prosecutors do not enjoy the guaranteed tenure, necessary to ensure their independence."[99] The reality, as aforementioned, is that since 1999 the Venezuelan Judiciary has been mainly composed by judges without career or stability, appointed without the public competition process of selection established in the Constitution, and dismissed without due process of law, for political reasons.[100] This

---

95 The Politico Administrative Chamber of the Supreme Tribunal of Justice has considered that the dismissal of temporal judges is a discretionary power of the Commission on the Functioning and Reorganization of the Judicial System, which adopts its decisions without following any administrative procedure. See Decision N° 00463-2007 of March 20, 2007; Decision N° 00673-2008 of April 24, 2008 (cited in Decisión N° 1.939 of December 18, 2008, p. 42). The Constitutional Chamber has express the same opinion, in Decisión N° 2414 of December 20, 2007 and Decisión N° 280 of February 23, 2007.

96 See Supreme Tribunal of Justice, Decision N° 1.939 of December 18, 2008 (Case: *Gustavo Álvarez Arias et al.*)

97 See *Annual Report 2009*, Par. 481, en http://www.cidh.org/annualrep/2009eng/Chap.IV. f.eng.htm.

98 See Decision N° 1.939 (Dec. 18, 2008) (Case: *Abogados Gustavo Álvarez Arias y otros*), in which the Constitutonal Chamber decided the nonenforceability of the decision of the Inter American Court of Human Rights of Aug. 5, 2008 (Case: *Apitz Barbera y otros ["Corte Primera de lo Contencioso Administrativo"] vs. Venezuela [Corte IDH]*, Case: *Apitz Barbera y otros ["Corte Primera de lo Contencioso Administrativo"] vs. Venezuela*, Sentencia de 5 de agosto de 2008, Serie C, N° 182.

99 See *Informe Anual de 2009*, paragraph 480, in http://www.cidh.oas.org/annualrep/2009-eng/Chap.IV.f.eng.htm

100 See Inter-American Commission on Human Rights, *Report on the Situation of Human Rights in Venezuela*, OEA/Ser.L/V/II.118, doc. 4 rev. 2, December 29, 2003, ¶174, *available at* http://www.cidh.oas.org/countryrep/Venezuela2003eng/toc.htm. The Inter-American Court on Human Rights, decision of June 30, 2009 (Case Reverón Trujillo vs. Venezuela), has also concluded that "Venezuela does not offer to said [provisional] judges the inamobility guaranty (supra par. 101, 102, aand 113). As was established, the inamobility is one of the basic guaranties of judicial independence that the State is obligated to give both to the titular and provisional judges in equal form." Paragraph 121, available at http://www.corteidh.or.cr/-docs/casos/articulos/seriec_197_esp.pdf

reality amounts to political control of the Judiciary, as demonstrated by the dismissal of judges who have adopted decisions contrary to the policies of the governing political authorities.

As aforementioned, in 2010 with the sanctioning by the National Assembly of the Venezuelan Judges Ethical Code Law,[101] a Disciplinary Jurisdiction was finally created substituting the "transitional" Commission of the Functioning and Reorganization of the Judiciary, assigning the disciplinary functions to two judicial bodies: the Disciplinary Court and the Disciplinary Commission, which were created in 2011. But instead of assigning to the Supreme Tribunal the appointment of the members of such two disciplinary jurisdictional bodies, being the Supreme Tribunal the only State body with competence to do so in the Constitution, the Law attributed such appointments in a "provisional" way to the same National Assembly without complying with the conditions to appoint judges established in the Constitution, and without citizens participation, and without any intervention of any Nominating Committee.[102] In this way the matter of judicial disciplinary jurisdiction moved from a politically controlled Commission of the Functioning of the Judiciary, although in an indirect way because it was acting in the sphere of the Supreme Tribunal, to a Disciplinary Court and Tribunal directly dependent of the most political of all bodies of the State, which is the national Assembly.

In any case, and historically, one of the leading cases showing the political control exercised upon the Judiciary, and in particular, on matters of dismissing judges, took place in 2003, when a contentious-administrative court ruled against the government in a politically charged case, the government responded by intervening (taking over) the court and dismissing its judges and. After the Inter-American Court of Human Rights ruled that the dismissal had violated the American Convention of Human Rights and Venezuela's international obligations, the Constitutional Chamber upheld the government's argument that the decision of the Inter-American Court cannot be enforced in Venezuela.

In effect, on July 17, 2003, the Venezuelan National Federation of Doctors brought an *amparo* action in the First Court on Contentious-Administrative Matters in Caracas,[103] against the Mayor of Caracas, the Ministry of Health and the Caracas Metropolitan Board of Doctors (*Colegio de Médicos*). The petitioners asked for a declaration of the nullity of certain measures of the defendant Officials through which Cuban doctors were hired for a much publicized governmental health program in the Caracas slums, without complying with the legal requirements for foreign doctors to practice the medical profession in Venezuela. The National Federation of Doctors argued that, by allowing foreign doctors to exercise the medical profession without complying with applicable regulations, the program was discrimina-

---

101 See in *Gaceta Oficial* N° 39.493 of August 23, 2010

102 See the text of the legislative act of appointment of the "judges" in *Gaceta Oficial* N° 39.693 of June 10, 2011

103 Contentious-administrative courts have jurisdiction to review administrative decisions.

tory and violated the constitutional rights of Venezuelan doctors.[104] One month later, in August 21, 2003, the First Court issued a preliminary protective *amparo* measure, on the ground that there were sufficient elements to consider that the constitutional guaranty of equality before the law was being violated in the case. The Court ordered, in a preliminary way, the suspension of the Cuban doctors' hiring program, and ordered the Metropolitan Board of Doctors to replace the Cuban doctors already hired with doctors (Venezuelan or foreign) who had fulfilled the legal requirements to exercise the medical profession in the country.[105]

In response to that preliminary judicial *amparo* decision, the Minister of Health, the Mayor of Caracas, and even the President of the Republic made public statements to the effect that the decision was not going to be respected or enforced.[106] Following these statements, the government-controlled Constitutional Chamber of the Supreme Tribunal of Justice adopted a decision, without any appeal being filed, assuming jurisdiction over the case and annulling the preliminary *amparo* ordered by the First Court; a group of Secret Service police officials seized the First Court's premises; and the President of the Republic, among other expressions he used, publicly called the President of the First Court a "bandit."[107] A few weeks later, in response to the First Court's decision in an unrelated case challenging a local registrar's refusal to record a land sale, the Commission for the Functioning of the Judiciary, which in spite of being unconstitutional continued to exist, dismissed all five judges of the First Court.[108] In spite of the protests of all the Bar Associations of the country and also of the International Commission of Jurists;[109] the First Court re-

---

104 See Claudia Nikken, "El caso Barrio Adentro: La Corte Primera de lo Contencioso Administrativo ante la Sala Constitucional del Tribunal Supremo de Justicia o el avocamiento como medio de amparo de derechos e intereses colectivos y difusos," in *Revista de Derecho Público*, Nº 93-96, Editorial Jurídica Venezolana, Caracas, 2003, pp. 5 ff.

105 *See* Decision of August, 21 2003, in *id.,* pp. 445 ff.

106 The President of the Republic said: "*Váyanse con su decisión no sé para donde, la cumplirán ustedes en su casa si quieren* [...]" (You can go with your decision, I don't know where; you will enforce it in your house if you want [...]). *See El Universal,* Caracas, August 25, 2003 and *El Universal,* Caracas, August 28, 2003.

107 *See* Inter-American Court of Human Rights, *Apitz Barbera et al. (Corte Primera de lo Contencioso Administrativo) v. Venezuela* (Judgment of August 5, 2008), *available at* www.corteidh.or.cr, ¶239. *See also, El Universal,* Caracas, October 16, 2003; and *El Universal,* Caracas, September 22, 2003.

108 See *El Nacional,* Caracas, November 5, 2003, p. A2. The dismissed President of the First Court said: "*La justicia venezolana vive un momento tenebroso, pues el tribunal que constituye un último resquicio de esperanza ha sido clausurado.*" ("The Venezuelan judiciary lives a dark moment, because the court that was a last glimmer of hope has been shut down.") *Id.* The Commission for the Intervention of the Judiciary had also massively dismissed almost all judges of the country without due disciplinary process, and had replaced them with provisionally appointed judges beholden to the ruling power.

109 See in *El Nacional,* Caracas, October 10, 2003, p. A-6; *El Nacional* ONAL, Caracas, October 15, 2003, p. A-2; *El Nacional,* Caracas, September 24, 2003, p. A-4; and *El Nacional,* Caracas, February 14, 2004, p. A-7.

mained suspended without judges, and its premises remained closed for about nine months,[110] period during which simply no judicial review of administrative action could be sought in the country.[111]

The dismissed judges of the First Court brought a complaint before the Inter-American Commission of Human Rights for the government's unlawful removal of them, and for violation of their constitutional rights. The Commission in turn brought the case, captioned *Apitz Barbera et al. (Corte Primera de lo Contencioso Administrativo vs. Venezuela)*, before the Inter-American Court of Human Rights. On August 5, 2008, the Inter-American Court ruled that the Republic of Venezuela had violated the rights of the dismissed judges established in the American Convention of Human Rights, and ordered the State to pay them due compensation, to reinstate them to a similar position in the Judiciary, and to publish part of the decision in Venezuelan newspapers.[112] Nonetheless, on December 12, 2008, the Constitutional Chamber of the Supreme Tribunal issued Decision N° 1.939, declaring that the August 5, 2008 decision of the Inter-American Court of Human Rights was non-enforceable (*inejecutable*) in Venezuela. The Constitutional Chamber also accused the Inter-American Court of having usurped powers of the Supreme Tribunal of Justice, and asked the Executive Branch to denounce the American Convention of Human Rights.[113]

The case just discussed, including in particular the *ad hoc* response of the Constitutional Chamber to the decision of the Inter-American Court of Human Rights, shows clearly the present subordination of the Venezuelan Judiciary to the policies, wishes and dictates of the government.[114] The Constitutional Chamber has in fact

---

110 See *El Nacional*, Caracas, October 24, 2003, p. A-2; and *El Naciona*, Caracas, July 16, 2004, p. A-6.

111 See *generally* Allan R. Brewer-Carías, "La progresiva y sistemática demolición institucional de la autonomía e independencia del Poder Judicial en Venezuela 1999–2004," in *XXX Jornadas J.M Domínguez Escovar. Estado de derecho, Administración de Justicia y Derechos Humanos,* Instituto de Estudios Jurídicos del Estado Lara, Barquisimeto, 2005, pp. 33–174.

112 Inter-American Court of Human Rights, *Apitz Barbera et al. (Corte Primera de lo Contencioso Administrativo) v. Venezuela* (Judgment of August 5, 2008), *available at* www.corteidh.or.cr.

113 Supreme Tribunal of Justice, Constitutional Chamber, Decision N° 1.939 of December 18, 2008 (Case: *Abogados Gustavo Álvarez Arias et al.*) (Exp. N° 08-1572).

114 This situation has been recently summarized by Teodoro Petkoff, editor and founder of TAL CUAL, one of the important newspapers in Caracas, as follows: "Chavez controls all the political powers. More that 90% of the Parliament obey his commands; the Venezuelan Supreme Court, whose number were raised from 20 to 32 by the parliament to ensure an overwhelming officialist majority, has become an extension of the legal office of the Presidency... The Attorney General's Office, the Comptroller's Office and the Public Defender are all offices held by 'yes persons' absolutely obedient to the orders of the autocrat. In the National Electoral Council, four of five members are identified with the government. The Venezuelan Armed Forces are tightly controlled by Chávez. Therefore, form a conceptual point of view, the Venezuelan political system is autocratic. All political power is concentrated in the hands of the President. There is no real separation of Powers." *See* Teodoro Petkoff, *Election and*

become a most effective tool for the existing consolidation of power in the person of President Chávez.

In December 2009, another astonishing case was the detention of a criminal judge (María Lourdes Afiuni Mora) for having ordered, based on a previous recommendation of the United Nations Working Group on Arbitrary Detention, the release of an individual in order for him to face criminal trial while in freedom, as guaranteed in the Constitution. The same day of the decision, the President of the Republic publicly asked for the judge to be incarcerated asking to apply her a 30–year prison term, which is the maximum punishment in Venezuelan law for horrendous or grave crimes. The fact is that the judge has remained to this day in detention without trial. The UN Working Group described these facts as "a blow by President Hugo Chávez to the independence of judges and lawyers in the country," demanding "the immediate release of the judge," concluding that "reprisals for exercising their constitutionally guaranteed functions and creating a climate of fear among the judiciary and lawyers' profession, serve no purpose except to undermine the rule of law and obstruct justice."[115]

The fact is that in Venezuela, no judge can adopt any decision that could affect the government policies, or the President's wishes, the state's interest, or public servants' will, without previous authorization from the same government. [116] That is why the Inter-American Commission on Human Rights, after describing in its *2009 Annual Report* "how large numbers of judges have been removed, or their appointments voided, without the applicable administrative proceedings," noted "with concern that in some cases, judges were removed almost immediately after adopting judicial decisions in cases with a major political impact," concluding that "The lack of judicial independence and autonomy vis-à-vis political power is, in the Commission's opinion, one of the weakest points in Venezuelan democracy." [117]

Political Power. Challenges for the Opposition in *ReVista Harvard Review of Latin America*, David Rockefeller Center for Latin American Studies, Harvard University, Fall 2008, pp. 12, *available at* http://www.drclas.harvard.edu/revista/articles/view/1125. *See* Allan R. Brewer-Carías, "Los problemas de la gobernabilidad democrática en Venezuela: el autoritarismo constitucional y la concentración y centralización del poder," in Diego Valadés (Coord.), *Gobernabilidad y Constitucionalismo en América Latina*, Universidad Nacional Autónoma de México, México 2005, pp. 73-96.

115 Available at http://www.unog.ch/unog/website/ news_media.nsf/%28httpNewsByYear_en%29/93687E8429BD53A1C125768E00529DB6?OpenDocument&cntxt=B35C3&cookiel ang=fr. En Octubre 14, 2010, el mismo Grupo de Trabajo de la ONU solicitó formalmente al Gobierno venezolano que la Juez fuse "sometida a un juicio apegado al debido proceso y bajo el derecho de la libertad provisional". Véase en El Universa, 14 de Octiubre de 2010, en http://www.eluniversal.com/2010/10/14/pol_ava _instancia-de-la-onu_14A4608051.shtml

116 See Antonio Canova González, *La realidad del contencioso administrativo venezolano (Un llamado de atención frente a las desoladoras estadísticas de la Sala Político Administrativa en 2007 y primer semestre de 2008)*, *cit.*, p. 14.

117 See in ICHR, *Annual Report 2009*, para. 483. Available at http://www.cidh.oas.org/annual-rep/2009eng/Chap.IV.f.eng.htm.

That is why that in this context, it is hardly surprising to hear President Chávez, when referring to the delegate legislation enacted by himself, to say in August 2008, simply: *"I am the Law.... I am the State* !!;[118] repeating the same phrases he used in 2001, also referring to other series of decree-laws he enacted at that time as delegate legislation.[119] Such phrases, as we all know, were attributed in the seventeen century to Louis XIV, in France, as a sign of the meaning of an Absolute Monarchy – although in fact he never expressed them–;[120] but to hear in our times a Head of State saying them, is enough to understand the tragic institutional situation that Venezuela is currently facing, characterized by a complete absence of separation of powers and, consequently, of a democratic and rule of law government.

---

118 Hugo Chávezs Frías, on August 28, 2008. See in Gustavo Coronel, *Las Armas de Coronel*, 15 de octubre de 2008: http://lasarmasdecoronel.blogspot.com/2008/10/yo-soy-la-leyyo-soy-el-estado.html

119 See in *El Universal,* Caracas 4–12–01, pp. 1,1 and 2,1. Es también lo único que puede explicar, que un Jefe de Estado en 2009 pueda calificar a "la democracia representativa, la división de poderes y el gobierno alternativo" como doctrinas que "envenenan la mente de las masas." See "Hugo Chávez seeks to cach them young," *The Economist*, 22-28 Agosto 2009, p. 33.

120 See Yves Guchet, *Histoire Constitutionnelle Française (1789–1958)*, Ed. Erasme, Paris 1990, p.8.

CHAPTER XVI

THE CITIZEN'S ACCESS TO CONSTITUTIONAL JURISDICTION: SPECIAL REFERENCE TO THE VENEZUELAN SYSTEM OF JUDICIAL REVIEW

(2009-2010)

Paper originally written for my Presentation at the *Round-Table Conference of the International Association of Constitutional Law, International Association of Constitutional Law*, on *"Challenges to the consolidation of the Rule of Law and of Democracy in Latin America – compared experiences"*, held Porto de Galinhas, state of Pernambuco, Brazil, August 23-25, 2009. The essay was published in *Cuadernos de Soluções Constitucionais*, Nº 4, Associação Brasileira de Constitutionalistas Democratas, ABCD, Malheiros Editores, São Paulo 2012, pp. 13-29.

I.   INTRODUCTION

The Citizen's access to Constitutional Jurisdiction, or the possibility for the Citizens to litigate constitutional issues in judicial proceedings, depends on the particular system of judicial review of constitutionality that exists in each country, and on the various judicial means established for such purposes.

Venezuela, as is the case of many Latin American countries, since the nineteenth century has developed a mixed or comprehensive system of judicial review, where the two classical methods of judicial review have been combined: the so called diffuse and concentrated ones. The first, also called decentralized, allows all judges to decide not to apply a statute when it is considered to be against the Constitution, giving prevalence to the latter; and the concentrated one, in which the power to control the constitutionality of legislation is given to one single judicial organ of the State, whether it's Supreme Court or a special Constitutional Court created for such particular purpose. In the Venezuelan case, the Constitutional Chamber of the Supreme Tribunal of Justice.

Nonetheless, judicial review cannot be reduced to these two clasical methods, and other judicial means to guaranty the citizen's access to Constitutional Jurisdiction have been developed. Within them, in Latin America it must be first mentioned the specific judicial actions for the protection of human rights and constitutional guaranties that also since the XIX century have been adopted, called action for *amparo, tutela or protección, mandado de securanca,* and also the action for *habeas corpus,* and for *habeas data.*

In addition, another specific mean for judicial review, also with Latin American important developments, is the control of the unconstitutionality of Legislative omissions. And in Venezuela, finally, another mean for judicial review is the recourse for the abstract interpretation of the Constitution which also has opened the access of citizens to the Constitutional Jurisdiction.

Consequently, I will try to summarize the Venezuelan system of access of citizens to Constitutional Jurisdiction by referring to these five judicial means in a separate way: the diffuse method, the amparo proceeding, the concentrated method, the control of parliamentary omissions and the recourse for the abstract interpretation of the Constitution.

First, the question of Standing regarding in the diffuse method of judicial review of statutes, which was first established in Venezuela in the 1897 in the Civil Procedure Code, and is now expressly incorporated in the 1999 Constitution, establishing in article 334, that:

In case of incompatibility between this Constitution and a statute or other legal provision, when deciding a case, the courts, even at their own initiative, must give prevalence to the constitutional provisions.

Being am incidental mean for judicial review, in principle, only the parties to a proceeding can raise the constitutional question based on the concrete interest they hold in the trial; and that is why the decision of the judge has only *inter partes* effects in the specific case; that is, only has declarative effects.

This means that only citizens with procedural interest as set forth in the Civil Procedure Code have access to constitutional justice in these cases, that is, they have to be or a plaintiff pleading his own existing personal right or interest against a defendant, or conversely, a defending regarding the plaintiff, (art. 340 CPC). Therefore the plaintiff and the defendant are the parties entitled to raise constitutional issues in the proceeding. Third-parties are entitled to raise these issues as well, as long as they have an actual interest in supporting the reasons of one party, or, in other cases, are authorized by the Civil Procedure Code (art. 370).

Nonetheless, this principle has been modify in the Constitution of 1999 establishing the citizens' right to access to justice not only in order to enforce specific personal rights and interests, but also claiming the enforcement of "collective or diffuse interests" (art. 26), seeking the protection for instance of a number of individuals representing the entire or an important part of a society, like to protect the public welfare against attacks on the quality of life, the environment or to consumers. The same applies to the protection of *collective* interests, referred to a determined and identified sector of the population (even though not quantified), like professional groups, neighbors associations, to labor unions, to the inhabitants of a determined area.

In all these cases of petitions to decide matters of judicial review in a specific case, one of the parties can allege the protection of collective or diffuse interests, based on a common or collective right or interest, like the general damage to the quality of life of all the inhabitants of the country or parts of it.

On the other hand, representing the citizens, the Public Prosecutor, when authorized to intervene, in both civil (art.129 and ff. CCP) and criminal (art. 285, art. 105 Penal Procedural Organic Code) procedures, is entitled as well to raise constitutional issues to the ordinary judge so it will be decided in the specific case.

Additionally, the Defender of the People's Defender has wide capacity to enforce respect for and the guarantee of human rights and to protect the legitimate, collective, and diffuse rights and interests of persons against illegal actions, power deviations, and mistakes made in the managing of public services. It is entitled to sue and file for remedies. In those procedures, of course, the Defender of the People and the other parties are entitled to raise constitutional issues on behalf of citizens.

II. STANDING IN THE AMPARO PROCEEDING AND THE PROTECTION OF DIFFUSE AND COLLECTIVE RIGHTS: THE INJURED PERSON

As with the previous Constitution of 1961, the Constitution of 1999 sets forth the action for *amparo* (protection) as a *constitutional right*,[121] being the courts obliged to protect, within the scope of their jurisdictions, citizens in the exercise of their constitutional rights and guarantees (art. 27). By means of this action, the amparo proceeding initiated before the first instance courts a procedure that must be oral, public, brief, and free and without any formality. The judge is entitled to immediately restore the former legal situation or a similar situation.[122]

This action can only be filed by the citizen affected in his constitutional rights, claiming immediate legal protection; that is, the standing to raise the action of *amparo* belongs to every individual or citizen whose constitutional rights and guarantees are affected.[123] Such rights include even those not expressly listed in the Constitution or in international treaties on human rights ratified by the Republic but considered to be inherent in human beings.

Court decisions have been constant in granting the action of *amparo* a personal character. Therefore, standing belongs firstly to the citizen or "the individual direct-

121. See Allan R. Brewer-Carías, *El Derecho y la Acción de Amparo*, Vol.V of Instituciones Políticas y Constitucionales, Editorial Jurídica Venezolana, Caracas-San Cristóbal, 1998, pp. 19 ff.

122 See *Gaceta Oficial* Nº33.891 dated 01-22-88. See in general Allan R. Brewer-Carías and Carlos M. Ayala Corao, *La Ley Orgánica de Amparo sobre Derechos y Garantías Constitucionales*, Caracas 1988.

123. Individual, political, social, cultural, educative, economic, Indian and environmental rights and their guarantees are listed in arts. 19-129, Constitution. In Venezuela, there exists no limitation established in other countries (e.g. Germany, and Spain, which reduces the action of amparo to protect just "fundamental rights"). See Allan R. Brewer-Carías, *El Amparo a los derechos y garantías constitucionales (una aproximación comparativa)*, Editorial Jurídica Venezolana, Caracas 1993; and *Judicial Protection of Human Rights in Latin America*, Cambridge University Press, New Yoir, 2009.

ly affected by the infringement of constitutional rights and guarantees,"[124] not only by state organs, but also by corporations, and even by other individuals.

On mater of amparo, is also possible to file in order to claim for the protection of diffuse or collective interests, which includes, for instance, voters' political rights.[125] In these cases, the Constitutional Chamber has decided that any citizen or "individual is entitled to bring suit based on diffuse or collective interests" and has extended "standing to companies, corporations, foundations, chambers, unions and other collective entities, whose object is the defense of society, as long as they act within the boundaries of their corporate objects, aimed at protecting the interests of their members regarding those objects." [126]

In addition, the Defender of the People has the authority to promote, defend, and guard constitutional rights and guarantees "as well as the legitimate, collective or diffuse interests of the citizens" (art. 280 and 281,2C). The Constitutional Chamber has admitted the standing of the Defender of the People to bring to suit in an action of *amparo* on behalf of the citizens as a whole. In one case the Defender of the People acted against a threat by the National Legislative Commission to appoint Electoral National Council members without fulfilling constitutional requirements.

In that case, the Constitutional Chamber, decided that "the Defender has standing to bring actions aimed at enforcing diffuse and collective rights or interests" without requiring the acquiescence of the society on whose behalf he acts, but this provision does not exclude or prevent citizens' access to the judicial system in defense of diffuse and collective rights and interests, since article 26 of the Constitution in force provides access to the judicial system to every person, whereby individuals are entitled to bring suit as well, unless a law denies them that action.[127]

Finally, it must be mentioned that the Constitution of 1999, expressly incorporated the action of *habeas data*, which was originated in Brazil and followed by Peru, Colombia and many other Latin American countries. It is set forth in article 28, as follows:

Every person has the right of access to information and data about himself or his goods filed in official or private records, with exceptions established by law, as well as to know the use of them and their purpose, and to request a competent court to make them up-to-date, to rectify them or destroy them, if they were erroneous or

---

124. See for example, decision of the Constitutional Chamber dated 03-15-2000, in *Revista de Derecho Público*, Editorial Jurídica Venezolana, N° 81, 2000, pp. 322-323.

125. Decision of the Constitutional Chamber N° 483 of 05-29-2000 (Case: "Queremos Elegir" y otros), *Revista de Derecho Público*, Editorial Jurídica Venezolana, N° 82, 2000, EJV, pp 489-491. In the same sense, decision of the same Chamber N° 714 of 13-07-2000 (Case: APRUM), in *Revista de Derecho Público*, N° 83, Editorial Jurídica Venezolana, Caracas 2000, pp. 319 ff.

126. See decision of the Constitutional Chamber N° 656 of 06-05-2001 (Case: Defensor del Pueblo vs. Comisión Legislativa Nacional), in *Revista de Derecho Público*, N° 85-88, Editorial Jurídica Venezolana, Caracas 2001, pp. 453 ff.

127. *Idem.*

they affect in an illegitimate way his rights. In the same way, he may have access to documents of any kind containing information whose knowledge is interesting to communities or groups of individuals. The secrets of journalistic sources of information and other professions are excepted as determined by law.

In these cases, it is the citizen or "individual, personally or in his goods, involved" the one entitled to bring the action.[128]

III. THE GENERAL CITIZEN'S ACCESS TO CONSTITUTIONAL JURISDICTION BY MEANS OF THE *ACTIO POPULARIS* FILED AGAINST STATUTES AND ITS RESTRICTIONS

According to the European model of the concentrated method of judicial review, the citizens do not have access to Constitutional Jurisdiction in order to challenge statutes before the competent Constitutional Court or Tribunal, asking for their annulment based on constitutional questions. In the European countries where the concentrated method of judicial review is applied, in general, only a limited list of public officials has the necessary standing to file constitutional complaints before the Constitutional Jurisdiction. The citizens are excluded from such Jurisdiction.

This is also the general situation in Latin America in the countries where the concentrated method of judicial review is applied, and where in general, also only a limited number of public officials have the necessary standing to challenge the constitutionality of statutes.

Nonetheless, there are a few countries where the situation is completely the contrary, guarantying the effective and broad Citizen's access to Constitutional Jurisdiction, by means of the filing of a popular action against any statute. It is the case of Colombia, El Salvador, Nicaragua, Panama and Venezuela where the right to have access to Constitutional Jurisdiction has been guarantied to any citizen, without any special standing conditions.

In Venezuela, in this regard, the Constitutional Chamber of the Supreme Tribunal, being the "Constitutional Jurisdiction" of the country, has the power to control the constitutionality of statutes and other acts of organs exercising public power issued in direct and immediate execution of the Constitution or being ranked equal to a law; and to annul them on the grounds of unconstitutionality[129] (articles 266.1, 334, 336 of the Constitution). For such purpose, the Law has guarantied the citizen's access to judicial review by means of *popular action*[130] that can be file by anyone without any specific standing requirements. It is one of the means established in order to guarantee citizen's participation on matters of judicial review of legislation and regulations.

---

128. Decision N° 332 of the Constitutional Chamber dated 03-14-2001 (Case: Insaca vs. Director de Drogas y Cosméticos del Ministerio de Sanidad y Asistencia Social), in *Revista de Derecho Público*, N° 85-88, Editorial Jurídica Venezolana, Caracas 2001, pp. 483 ff.

129. Arts. 266,1 ; 334 and 336 of the Constitution.

130. *Idem*, pp.137 ff.

Regarding such popular action that has existed in the country since 1858, the Constitutional Chamber of the Supreme Tribunal in decision N° 1077 of August 22, 2001, stated that::

> ... In our legal order, the popular action of unconstitutionality exists when any individual having capacity to sue, has a procedural and legal interest to raise it, without the requiring the existence of any particular fact harming the plaintiff's private legal sphere. The claimant is a guardian of constitutionality and that guardianship entitles him to act, whether or not he has suffered a harm coming from the unconstitutionality of a law. [131]

The Supreme Tribunal has also considered that giving any citizen access to the Constitutional Jurisdiction seeking review of legislation, transforms him in "a guardian of constitutionality, having as such interest in filing the action, whether having or not suffered specific damages from the unconstitutional statute" [132] In another decision No. 37 of January 24, 2004, the same Constitutional Chamber considered the popular action as an "exceptional judicial mean in comparative law" due to the extremely broad standing that grants to anybody to challenge any normative State act, including statutes and regulations; being only considered inadmissible when the plaintiff has not the minimal interest whatsoever in the case. [133]

This has been the traditional criteria adopted by the Supreme Tribunal, confirmed in decision No. 796 of July 22, 2010 (Case: *Asociación civil Súmate, Francisco Javier Suárez y otros*), in which the Constitutional Chamber ratified that the popular action can be filed by any citizen, that is, any person has in principle the procedural standing and interest to challenge status and regulations" seeking judicial review on grounds of their unconstitutionality. [134]

Nonetheless, the Constitutional Chamber, in the same decision No. 796 of July 22, 2010, without any party request, in order to serve the interests of the government and disqualify those opposing it, denied in an arbitrary way the standing of the *Asociación Civil Súmate*, a very important and well known ONG on matters of electoral transparency and control, to participate on matters of constitutional control of statutes, arguing that such civil society organization at some time of its existence, *in illo tempore*, had received "financing from foreign nations in order to accomplish public activities," which the Chamber considered implied that it lacked "the standing to act in defense of foreign interests on matters of internal policy," notwithstanding that the by-laws of the Association defines its purpose an objective as to "promote democracy as a social system of living together within a framework of freedom and human rights respect."

---

131. Decision N° 1077 dated 09-22-01, Constitutional Chamber (Case: Servio Tulio León Briceño), in *Revista de Derecho Público*, Editorial Jurídica Venezolana, N° 83, Caracas 2000, pp. 247 ff.

132. *Idem*, pp.247 y ss.

133. See Caseo *Asociación Civil Mixta La Salvación SRL*, in *Revista de Derecho Público*, No. 97-98, Editorial Jurídica Venezolana, Caracas 2004, pp. 402-403.

134. Available at: http://www.tsj.gov.ve/decisiones/scon/Julio/796-22710-2010-09-0555.html .

With this arbitrary decision of the Constitutional Chamber, eventually, the popular action ceased to by "popular" in the sense that not any person has the standing to file the action, not having such standing, for instance, those "persons" leading sector considered to be opposing the "legitimate and democratic government." [135]

IV. THE CITIZEN'S INITIATIVE IN ORDER TO CONTROL THE CONSTITUTIONALITY OF PARLIAMENT'S OMISSIONS

The so-called judicial review of legislative omissions is another new institution of judicial review that following the trend initiated in Portugal,[136] has been established in many Latin American countries, like Brazil and Venezuela. In the latter country, article 336 of the 1999 Constitution grants the Constitutional Chamber the power to:

> "Declare the unconstitutionality of the omission of the municipal, state, or national legislative power in failing to issue indispensable rules or measures to guarantee the enforcement of the Constitution, or issuing them in an incomplete way; establishing the terms, and if necessary, the guidelines for their correction.

According to this provision no specific requirement of standing has been established, being possible for any citizen to claim before the Constitutional Jurisdiction against legislative omissions,[137] in a way similar to *a popular action.*

This general Citizen's access to Constitutional Jurisdiction on matters of legislative omissions, contrasts with the initial Portuguese antecedent, where for instance, the standing to sue was reduced to the President of the Republic, the Ombudsman, or the Presidents of the Autonomous Regions.[138]

V. THE CITIZENS INICIATIVE IN ORDER TO OBTAIN AN ABSTRACT INTERPRETATION OF THE CONSTITUTION BY THE CONSTITUTIONAL JURISDICTION

Finally, among the competencies of the Constitutional Chamber of the Supreme Tribunal of Justice in Venezuela, acting as "Constitutional Jurisdiction," mention must be made of the power it has to decide requests for abstract interpretation of the Constitution, without being the request related to any constitutional proceeding. The

---

135. On this decision see the comments in Allan R. Brewer-Carías, "El Juez Constitucional vs. El derecho a la participación mediante el ejercicio de la acción popular de inconstitucionalidad," ien *Revista de Derecho Público,* No. 123, (julio-septiembre 2010), Editorial Jurídica Venezolana, Caracas 2010, pp. 207-214.

136. See Allan R. Brewer-Carías, *Judicial Review in Comparative Law, op .cit.,* p. 269.

137. The Constitutional Chamber has called it "legislative silence and functioning." Decision N° 1819 of 08-08-2000 of the Political-Administrative Chamber (Case: Rene Molina vs. Comisión Legislativa Nacional), in *Revista de Derecho Público,* N° 83, Editorial Jurídica Venezolana, Caracas 2000, pp. 264 ff.

138. See Allan R. Brewer-Carías, Judicial Review in Comparative Law, *op. cit.,* p. 269.

Constitutional Chamber itself has created this judicial mean that do not exist in any other country, from its interpretation of article 335 of the Constitution.[139]

The purpose of such action of constitutional interpretation that any citizen can file providing having a personal interest on the matter has the purpose of securing a declaration by the Constitutional Chamber on the scope and content of a constitutional provision. It has been regarded as a form of citizen participation in order to clarify the doubts and ambiguities that can exist in some constitutional provisions.[140] The Constitutional Chamber, in creating the action, in decision N° 1077 dated 09-22-2000, relied on article 26 of the Constitution, which establishes the citizen's right of access to justice. From this the Chamber deduced that although this action was not set forth in the legal order, it was not forbidden either and, therefore, any citizen having a legal interest may raise before the Constitutional Jurisdiction the interpretation of a provision of the Constitution, in order to obtain a judicial decision of plain certainty on the scope and content of the specific provision.[141]

Regarding the standing to bring this action for constitutional interpretation before the Supreme Tribunal, the Constitutional Chamber gave it to any citizens providing that a particular interest must exist. In this sense, the Chamber has ruled that:

A public or private person shall have a current, legitimate legal interest, grounded in his own concrete and specific legal situation, which necessarily requires the interpretation of constitutional rules applicable to the situation, in order to end the uncertainty impeding the development and effects of said legal situation.[142]

For the action for interpretation to be allowed, the petition must specify the nature of the obscurity, ambiguity, or contradiction of the provisions of the constitutional text, or within one of them in particular, or with respect to the nature and scope of applicable principles. The decision issued by the Constitutional Chamber in these cases, have general and binding effects.[143]

---

139. See Allan R. Brewer-Carías, "Le recours d'interprétation abstrait de la Constitution au Vénézuéla", en *Le renouveau du droit constitutionnel, Mélanges en l'honneur de Louis Favoreu*, Dalloz, Paris, 2007, pp. 61-70.

140. Decision N° 1077 dated 09-22-01, Constitutional Chamber (Case: Servio Tulio León Briceño), in *Revista de Derecho Público*, N° 83, Editorial Jurídica Venezolana, Caracas 2000, pp. 247 ff.

141. *Idem.*

142. *Idem*

143. The Constitutional Chamber in decision N° 1347 dated 11-09-2000, outlined the binding character of its interpretations, by pointing out that "The interpretations of this Constitutional Chamber, in general, or those issued in proceedings of interpretative remedy, shall be understood as binding regarding the core of the studied case", in *Revista de Derecho Público*, N° 84, Editorial Jurídica Venezolana, Caracas 2000, pp. 264 ff.

CONCLUSION

From the above overview of the system of judicial review in Venezuela, the general conclusion that can be formulated is that, in general, the citizen's right to have access to Constitutional Jurisdiction has been guaranteed in a very extended way; a situation that contrast with the general trend in many countries to exclude the citizens access to the Constitutional Jurisdiction, limiting such access only to certain public officials.

Nonetheless, this broad citizen's access to judicial review does not guaranty that the Constitutional Jurisdiction will effectively enforce the Constitution. As we all know, judicial review of constitutionality[144] as the power assigned to the courts to decide upon the constitutionality of statutes and other governmental acts; can only exist in legal systems where the State, and its government and Parliament, are subjected to limits, according to the principles of the rule of law (*Estado de derecho*), and functions according to the principles of representative democracy.

That is why, judicial review is above all, an institutional tool essentially linked to democracy, understood as a political system not just reduced to the fact of having elected governments, but where separation and control of power and the respect and enforcement of human rights is possible through an independent and autonomous judiciary. And precisely, it has been because of this process of reinforcement of democracy in Latin American countries that judicial review of the constitutionality of legislation and other governmental actions has become an important tool in order to guarantee the supremacy of the Constitution, the rule of law, and the respect of human rights. It is in this sense that judicial review of the constitutionality of state acts has been considered as the ultimate result of the consolidation of the *rule of law*, when precisely in a democratic system the courts can serve as the ultimate guarantor of the Constitution, effectively controlling the exercise of power by the organs of the state.[145]

On the contrary, as happens in all authoritarian regimes even having elected governments, if such control is not possible, the same power of judicial review vested, for instance, upon a politically controlled Supreme Court or Constitutional Court, in spite of the provision guarantying the citizen's right to Constitutional Jurisdiction, it can constitute the most powerful and diabolical instrument for the consolidation of authoritarianism, the destruction of democracy, and the violation of human rights.[146]

---

144. See Allan R. Brewer-Carías, *Judicial Review in Comparative Law*, Cambridge University Press, Cambridge 1989, p. 215.

145. See Hans Kelsen, "La garantie juridictionnelle de la Constitution (La Justice constitutionnelle)," in *Revue du droit public et de la science politique en France et à l'étranger*, T. XLV, 1928, pp.197-257

146. See Allan R. Brewer-Carías, «Quis Custodiet ipsos Custodes: De la interpretación constitucional a la inconstitucionalidad de la interpretación», in *VIII Congreso Nacional de derecho Constitucional, Perú*, Fondo Editorial 2005, Colegio de Abogados de Arequipa, Arequipa, Sept. 2005, pp. 463-489.

Unfortunately this is what has been happening in my country, Venezuela, where after decades of democratic ruling through which we constructed one of the most formally complete systems of judicial review in South America, with perhaps the most broad provisions guarantying the citizen's right to Constitutional Jurisdiction, that system has been the instrument through which the politically controlled judiciary, and particularly the subjected Constitutional Chamber of the Supreme Tribunal, have been consolidating the authoritarian regime we now have; not being possible to exercise any control over the Constitutional Jurisdiction. I such a system, the citizens petitions before the Constitutional Jurisdiction in order for the Constitutional Chamber to annul statutes that have violated the Constitution have been systematically dismissed; the powers given to the Constitutional Chamber to control the legislative omissions have been used in order to provide the government with political control of other branches of government, as has happened with the Electoral Power;[147] and the self made recourse of constitutional interpretation has been used by citizens affected to the government of by representatives of the government to obtain from the Constitutional Chamber interpretations of the Constitution, that in fact have modified or mutate the Constitution in the sense seek by the government, avoiding the procedure for constitutional revisions that always need popular approval.

In a system of judicial review with various means devoted to assure the control of unconstitutional statutes and other State acts, even with the provisions in order to guaranty in a broad way citizen's access to Constitutional Jurisdiction, if the rule of law does not exists, and democracy is not effective, what outcome is that the judicial review system results in being the most perverse tool for defrauding the Constitution and the democratic system, as it has unfortunately happened in Venezuela under the authoritarian government we have had during the past decade (1999-2009), crushing any real possibility of judicial review.

---

147. See Allan R. Brewer-Carías, *Crónica sobre la "In" Justicia Constitucional. La Sala Constitucional y el autoritarismo en Venezuela*, Colección Instituto de Derecho Público, Universidad Central de Venezuela, Nº 2, Caracas 2007; "Judicial Review in Venezuela", en *Duquesne Law Review*, Volume 45, Number 3, Spring 2007, pp. 439-465.

CHAPTER XVII

THE ILLEGITIMATE JUDICIAL MUTATION OF THE CONSTITUTION

(2009)

This essay was written for the lecture I gave on "The Constitutional Judge and the Destruction of the Rule of Law", at the *Administrative Law Seminar of Professor Eduardo García de Enterría*, in the *Complutense University of Madrid*, on April 1st, 2009. The text was devoted to specifically analyze the deviations of judicial review when the Constitutional Court is controlled by the Government, as happens in Venezuela. The text was published as "El juez constitucional al servicio del autoritarismo y la ilegítima mutación de la Constitución: el caso de la Sala Constitucional del Tribunal Supremo de Justicia de Venezuela (1999-2009)," in *Revista General de Derecho Administrativo*, Nº 21, Ed. Iustel, Madrid 2009, ISSN-1696-9650; and in *Revista de Administración Pública*, Nº 180, Madrid 2009, pp. 383-418; and with the title: "La ilegítima mutación de la Constitución por el juez constitucional y la demolición del Estado de derecho en Venezuela," in *Revista de Derecho Político*, Nº 75-76, Homenaje a Manuel García Pelayo, Universidad Nacional de Educación a Distancia, Madrid, 2009, pp. 291-325.

If Constitutions are superior laws that support the validity of all the legal order, the institutional solution in order to assure its enforcement is the existence of a Supreme Court that could act as guardian of the Constitution, with powers to annul unconstitutional State acts or to declare their unconstitutionality. In democracies, these Courts have always been the main institutional guaranty of freedom and the rule of law. Nonetheless, the same Courts in authoritarian governments, far from ensuring the Rule of Law, have been the instruments used in order to demolish its foundations. Unfortunately, the latter has been the case in Venezuela during the past decade (1999-2009), notwithstanding the formal provisions contained in the Constitution on judicial review.

The 1999 Venezuelan Constitution in effect, in an express way establishes the principle of constitutional supremacy (article 7), according to which it must prevail above the will of all the constituted bodies of the State, including of course the Supreme Tribunal of Justice itself. This supremacy is ensured by means of two set of previsions: on the one hand, those regarding the absolute rigid character of the Constitution when disposing the necessary and indispensable popular intervention in order to carry out any modification or reform to its text; and on the other hand, those provisions concerning the constitutional judicial review system in order to guarantee said supremacy.

As for the institutional system for Constitutional reform, three different procedures have been established in the text: Constitutional Reform, Constitutional Amendment and Constituent National Assembly; the last needed in cases of transformation of the State, to establish a new legal order and to fully reform the Constitution (Article 347). In the other two cases the constitutional review procedures are design to introduce reforms without changing or modifying the structure and fundamental principles of the Constitution (Articles 340 and 342). The common trend in all cases is the intervention of the people through referendum by convening the Constituent Assembly or in order to approve the Constitutional reforms or the Constitutional Amendments Any modification of the Constitution carried out in a way different from these three procedures, is considered unconstitutional and illegitimate.

Regarding the constitutional justice system, as result of the principles of constitutional supremacy and rigidity, it has been established with a mixed or integral character, combining the diffused and concentrated methods of judicial review. That is, the guaranty for constitutional supremacy is assured, first, by assigning all judges of the Republic the obligation to "guaranty the integrity of the Constitution" (Article 334); and second, also, by assigning the Supreme Court of Justice as "the higher and last interpreter of the Constitution," the task of ensuring "the supremacy and effectiveness of constitutional provisions and principles", and "its uniform interpretation and application" (article 335). The Constitution also assigns to the Constitutional Chamber of the Supreme Tribunal, Constitutional Jurisdiction (Articles 266,1 and 336) through which it executes the concentrated method of judicial review of statutes and other state acts of statutory character.

In accordance to these previsions, the Venezuelan Constitutional Chamber of the Supreme Tribunal of Justice is, without a doubt, the most powerful instrument designed to ensure the supremacy of the Constitution and the Rule of Law, which, of course, as guardian of the Constitution, is submitted, as well, to the Constitution. As such guardian, and as it occurs in any Rule of Law system, the submission of the Constitutional Court to the Constitution is an absolutely understood preposition and is not subjected to discussion, since it would be inconceivable that the constitutional judge can violate the Constitution he is called to apply and warrant. As a matter of principle, it could be violated by other bodies of the State, but not by the guardian of the Constitution. For such purpose and in order to ensure that this does not occur, the Constitutional Court must of course have absolute independence and autonomy, because on the contrary, a Constitutional Court submitted to the will of the political power, instead of being the guardian of the Constitution becomes the most atrocious instrument of authoritarianism. Thus, the best constitutional justice system, in the hands of a judge submitted to political power, is a dead letter for individuals and is an instrument for defrauding the Constitution.

Unfortunately, the latter is what has been occurring in Venezuela during the last few years since 2000, where the Constitutional Chamber of the Supreme Tribunal, as Constitutional Judge, far from acting within the expressed constitutional attributions, has been adopting decisions in some cases containing unconstitutional constitutional interpretation,[148] not only about its own powers of judicial review, but regarding substantive matters, changing or modifying constitutional provisions, in may cases in order to legitimize and support the progressive building of the authoritarian State. That is to say, it has distorted the content of the Constitution, through illegitimate and fraudulent "mutation."[149] These illegitimate modifications to the Constitution, of course, have been made by its maximum guardian, who has no one to guard him, assuming a derived constituent power that does not belong to it, and is not regulated in the constitutional text. The eternal question arising from the uncontrolled power, *Quis custodiet ipsos custodes* has also acquired in this case all its meaning.

I. THE ACCEPTANCE OF A TRANSITORY CONSTITUTIONAL REGIME NOT APPROVED BY THE PEOPLE

The first constitutional mutation regarding the 1999 Constitution was decided by the Constitutional Chamber of the Supreme Tribunal of Justice, a few weeks after the approval of the Constitution, by admitting the existence of "Constitutional Transitory" provisions different to those approve by popular vote and embodied in the text of the Constitution. The 1999 Constitution was approved by referendum held on December 15, 1999, with a text that included transitory provisions. With the popular the approval of the Constitution in principle concluded the mission of the Constituent National Assembly.

However, one week after the approval of the Constitution, on December 22, 1999, the Constituent National Assembly sanctioned a Decree of the "Regime of Transition of the Public Power,"[150] in order "to give effect to the transition process towards the regime established in the Constitution of 1999", in which it decided

---

148 See Allan R. Brewer-Carías, "*Quis Custodiet Ipsos Custodes*: De la interpretación constitucional a la inconstitucionalidad de la interpretación," in *VIII Congreso Nacional de derecho Constitucional, Perú*, Fondo Editorial 2005, Colegio de Abogados de Arequipa, Arequipa, September 2005, pp 463-489; and in *Revista de Derecho Público*, N° 105, Editorial Jurídica Venezolana, Caracas 2006, pp 7-27. See also, Allan R. Brewer-Carías, *Crónica sobre la "In" Justicia Constitucional. La Sala Constitucional y el autoritarismo en Venezuela*, Caracas 2007.

149 A constitutional mutation occurs when the content of a constitutional standard is modified in such a way that, even when said standard maintains its content, it receives a different significance. See Néstor Pedro Sagües, *La interpretación judicial de la Constitución*, Buenos Aires 2006, pp 56-59, 80-81, 165 ff.; Salvador O. Nava Gomar, "Interpretación, mutación y reforma de la Constitución. Tres extractos" in Eduardo Ferrer Mac-Gregor (Coordinator), *Interpretación Constitucional*, Vol. II, Ed. Porrúa, Universidad Nacional Autónoma de México, Mexico 2005, pp. 804 ff.; and Konrad Hesse, "Límites a la mutación constitucional", in *Escritos de derecho constitucional*, Centro de Estudios Constitucionales, Madrid 1992.

150 *Gaceta Oficial* N°. 36.859 dated 12-29-1999

without any attribution foreseen in the new Constitution, to eliminate the prior Congress along with its Senators and Deputies, and instead, to assign Legislative power to a National Legislative Commission not established in the Constitution; to dissolve the Legislative Assemblies of the States, and to assign legal attributions in their place, to State Legislative Commissions which were not provided either in the Constitution; to take control of the Mayor's Offices and Municipal Councils; to eliminate the former Supreme Court of Justice, create new Chambers of the new Supreme Tribunal and to assign them a fixed number of judges -not established in the Constitution- and to appoint them without complying with what the Constitution demanded; to create a Commission for the Reorganization and Functioning of the Judiciary in order to take it over, removing judges from office without due process which, even in 2009, still coexists with the Supreme Tribunal, with its complicity; to appoint the high officials of the different Branches of government; and to dictate an Electoral Statute without any constitutional provision supporting it.

None of these reforms were constitutional because they were not approved by the people. Consequently the Transition Regime Decree was challenged before the Constitutional Chamber created in it, based in the violation of the Constitution recently approved by the people. The result was that the same Constitutional Chamber decided in its own cause, considering that the National Constituent Assembly supposedly had supra-constitutional power to create "constitutional provisions" without the popular approval, and that in consequence, in Venezuela there were two transitional constitutional regimes: the one contained in the Transitory Provisions approved by the people when they approved the Constitution via referendum; and those approved by the National Constituent Assembly without said popular appro-val.

In decision N° 6, of January 27, 2000, the Constitutional Chamber decided that, since the Transition Regime of December 22, 1999 was adopted by the Constituent Assembly prior to the publication of the Constitution on December 31, 1999 it was not subjected to this, or to the previous Constitution of 1961 still in force.[151] Later, in decision of No 186 of March 28, 2000 (case: *Allan R. Brewer-Carías* and others), when deciding the challenging of the Electoral Statute of the Public Power also adopted by the Constituent Assembly on January 30, 2000,[152] the Constitutional Chamber ratified his criteria that in order to create a new legal order and adopt a new Constitution, the Constituent Assembly supposedly had several alternatives to regulate the transitory constitutional regime: *One*, to incorporate Transitory Dispositions that would be part of the Constitution to be approved by the people via referendum; and *the other*, to dictate separate constituent acts, of constitutional scope and value, that would originate a parallel constitutional transitory regime, not approved by the people.

With these decisions, it was the Constitutional Judge the one that proceeded to illegitimately mutate the Constitution, violating popular sovereignty, by admitting

151 See in *Revista de Derecho Público*, N° 81, Editorial Jurídica Venezolana, Caracas, 2000, pp. 81 ff.
152 See in *Gaceta Oficial* N° 36,884 of February 3, 2000.

that supposedly, the National Constituent Assembly could dictate constitutional provisions not approved by the people through referendum, in this way beginning a long period of constitutional instability that, ten years later, has not ended; as it can be evidenced, for instance, with the survival of Judiciary interference Commission, exercising disciplinary functions over the judges, which the Constitution expressly demands to be exclusively done by "disciplinary judges" members of a "disciplinary jurisdiction" and through a "disciplinary procedure" (article 267). Thus, Venezuela has been under a constitutional transitory regime not approved by the people, by the grace of the Constitutional Judge who legitimized the usurpation of the popular will.

II. THE TRANSFORMATION OF THE REVOCATION REFERENDA OF ELECTIVE OFFICES INTO A "RATIFYING" REFERENDA

In Venezuela, article 72 of the Constitution established, as a political right of the people, the revocation of mandates of all popular election offices, when the repeal is required after half of the term for which the official was elected, by popular initiative of a number no lesser than 20% of the electors registered in the corresponding constituency. The Constitution determined that when a number of electors, equal or higher than 25% of the registered electors have attend to the referendum and "*a number of electors equal or higher* than that of those who elected the official, vote in favour of the revocation," its mandate is considered as revoked and the absolute void must be covered immediately through by a new election.

That is to say, the necessary votes to proceed with the revocation of a mandate must be of a number *equal or higher than the votes of the electors who elected the officer,* independently from the number of votes cast against the revocation; as it was even ratified by the Constitutional Chamber in several decisions.[153] The matter provided in the Constitution is about a "revocation" referendum of popular election mandates and not of a "ratifying" referendum (plebiscites) of said mandates, which does not exist in the constitutional text. Precisely for this reason, there is nothing in the Constitution regarding the case where a number of electors, higher than the number of votes obtained by the official at the time of his election, could vote against the revocation, that is, for the "no revocation." This could occur, but according to the Constitutional text, it would have no effect at all, because what the constitutional regulation establishes is revocation referendum: it is enough for the votes for the revocation to be equal, or greater, than those obtained by the official at the time of his election in order to be revoked.

Nevertheless, clearly in an unconstitutional way, in 2003 when a repeal referendum was first call by popular initiative for the revocation of the President mandate,

---

153 See decision N° 2750 of October 21, 2003, Case: *Carlos Enrique Herrera Mendoza, (Interpretación del artículo 72 de la Constitución (*Exp. 03-1989; and decision N° 1139 of June 5, 2002, Case: *Sergio Omar Calderón Duque and William Dávila Barrios.* See in *Revista de Derecho Público,* N° 89-92, Editorial Jurídica Venezolana, Caracas 2002, p 171. The same criterium was followed in decision N° 137 of February 13, 2003, Case: *Freddy Lepage Scribani et al.* (Exp. 03-0287).

the National Electoral Council issued a Regulation on the matter[154], in which even though it was established that a mandate is considered to be revoked "if the number of votes in favour of the revocation is equal or higher to the number of the electors that vote for the officer", the phrase: "*and does not result to be lower than the number of electors that voted against the revocation*" was added (article 60), changing the constitutional provisions on the matter. With this addition –in a Regulation of sub-legal scope– the right of the people to politically participate through the revocation of popular mandates was restricted, when establishing a condition not included in the Constitution regarding the vote for the "no revocation", disrupting the "revocation" nature of the referendum regulated by article 72 of the Constitution, and in an evident fraud to the Constitution, turning it into a "ratifying" referendum of mandates of popular election.

What was without precedent in this constitutional fraud, was that said illegitimate constitutional "reform" was endorsed by the Constitutional Chamber of the Supreme Court when it decided on an abstract interpretation recourse of the Constitution in decision N° 2750 of October 21, 2003 (Case: *Carlos E. Herrera Mendoza, Interpretación del artículo 72 de la Constitución*) stating that:

> It has to do with some kind of re-legitimating the officer and, even, in this democratic process of majorities, **if the option of his permanence obtains more votes in the referendum, he should remain in office**, even if a sufficient number of people vote against him to revoke his mandate.[155]

In this way, an illegitimate "mutation" of the Constitution was adopted by the Constitutional Judge. Actually, in a "revocation" referendum there can not be votes "in favour" of "the permanence" of the officer; what can exist are votes in favour of the "revocation" of the mandate and votes for the "no revocation". The vote "in favour" of the "no revocation" of the mandate is a negative vote (No); and a negative vote can not be turned into a positive one (Yes) for the permanence of the officer. With this mutation of the Constitution, the Constitutional Chamber changed the nature of the revocation referendum, ratifying the disruption of the nature of the revocation of mandate, turning it into a vote to "re-legitimate" or to "ratify" mandates of popular election, when this was not the intention of the Constituent. The only issue regulated in article 72 of the Constitution is the "revocation" of mandates, and for that, the only thing it demands in regards to the voting process is that "*a number of electors equal or higher* than that of those who elected the official, vote in favour of the revocation."

This illegitimate mutation of the Constitution, nonetheless, had a precise objective: to avoid the revocation of the mandate of the President of the Republic, Hugo Chavez, in 2004. He was elected in August 2000 with 3,757,744 votes; being enough for the vote in favour of the revocation to surpass this number in order to revoke his mandate. As announced by the National Electoral Council in August 27,

---

154 See *Normas para regular los procesos de Referendos Revocatorios de mandatos de Elección Popular,* of September 25, 2003. Resolution N° 030925-465 of September 25, 2003.

155 Exp. 03-1989.

2004, the number of votes in favour of the revocation of the mandate of the President of the Republic, obtained in the referendum that took place on August 15, 2004, was of 3,989,008; reason for which his mandate had been constitutionally revoked.

However, the Constitution had already been illegitimately mutated, and regardless of the fraud accusations formulated, the National Electoral Council (on August 27, 2004), because the option for vote "No" obtained more votes (5.800.629) it decided to "ratify" the President of the Republic in his position until the culmination of the constitutional term in January 2007.[156]

III. THE ELIMINATION OF THE CONSTITUTIONAL PRINCIPLE OF ALTERNATE GOVERNMENT AND THE LIMITS TO THE CONTINUOUS RE-ELECTION

Article 6 of the Constitution establishes the fundamental principles of republican government, in a clause pertaining to those denominated "rocklike", that states

> Article 6. "The government of the Bolivarian Republic of Venezuela and its political entities **is and will always be** democratic, participative, elective, decentralized, alternate, responsible, pluralist and of revocable mandates"

Consequently, among the fundamental principles of the constitutional system that can not be modified neither by means of constitutional reform or amendment are these principles of government, and within them, the principle that the government must not only "democratic" but "elective" and also "alternate."

This latter principle was incorporated for the first time in Venezuela constitutional history as a reaction to communism in power and, among other aspects, based on the very "doctrine of Simon Bolivar", in which the Republic is based according to article 1 of the Constitution, when expressing, in one of its statements, that:

---

156 In fact, on the web page of the National Electoral Council of August 27, 2004, the following note appeared: "Francisco Carrasquero Lopez, President of the National Electoral Council, addressed the country in national broadcast, to announce the definite and official results of the electoral act that took place on August 15th, *which ratified* Hugo Rafael Chavez Frias, *as President of the Republic* with a total of 5 million 800 thousand 629 votes in favour of the option "NO". 9 million 815 thousand 631 electors participated in the election, of which **3,989,008 voted in favour of the option "YES" to revoke the mandate of President Chavez**. The total showed that the option "NO" represented 59.25% of the ballot, while the option "YES" achieved 40.74% of the grand total, with a 30.02% of non-participation. It must be said that for these elections, the Electoral Registry increased significantly, reaching a universe of 14,027,607 electors with the right to vote in the Revocation Referendum. On this Friday, August 27, based on the expression of the popular will, the National Electoral Council *will ratify* Hugo Chavez Frias *in the Presidency of the Bolivarian Republic* of Venezuela, whose constitutional term will culminate in the year 2006." And in fact, during a solemn act that took place on the same day, the National Electoral Council agreed to "ratify" the President of the Republic in his position, despite the fact that a number of electors, greater than those who elected him had voted in favour of the revocation of his mandate. See *El Nacional*, Caracas, 08-28-2004, pp A-1 and A-2.

"... There is nothing as dangerous as to allow the long term permanence in office of a single citizen. The people gets used to obeying him and he gets used to rule over them... our citizens must fear, with abundant justice, that the same Magistrate who has ruled them for a long time, rules them forever".[157]

According to this doctrine, which as a "Bolivarian" one must be considered part of the values of the constitution itself (article 1), in the Venezuelan constitutionalism the word used of "alternate" government referring to "alternation" in power regarding the public positions, has always had the meaning of the people having to **take successive turns** in said positions or that the positions had to be carried out **in turns** (Spanish Royal Academy Dictionary). As stated by the Electoral Chamber of the Supreme Tribunal of Justice in decision N° 51 of March 18, 2002, the alternate principle means **"the successive exercise of a position by different persons, belonging or not to the same party."**

This principle of alternate government was historically conceived to face the perpetuation desires to remain in power, that is to say, "continuism;" and to avoid the advantages in the electoral processes of those occupying positions when being candidates to occupy the same positions. The principle of "alternate government", thus, is not equivalent that of "elective government". Election is one thing, but the need for people to take turns in office is another, and thus the principle has always been reflected in the establishment of limits to the re-election of elected officials, which is proper of the presidential government systems. This is what happened in the Constitutions of 1830, 1858, 1864, 1874, 1881, 1891, 1893, 1901, 1904, 1909, 1936, 1845 and 1947 in which it was established the prohibition of the re-election of the President of Republic for the immediate constitutional term.[158]

This prohibition, on the contrary, regarding the President of the Republic, during the democratic period that began in 1958 was extended in the Constitution of 1961 for the two following terms (10 years). The softening of the principle occurred in the 1999 Constitution, in which the possibility of the immediate presidential re-election was allowed, only once, for a new term. That is why President Chávez, after being "ratified" in 2004, was re-elected in 2006.

The alternation of government, thus, is a principle of constitutionalism that contests continuism or the permanence in power by the same person; for this reason, any provision that would allow this from happening, would be contrary to it. Thus the principle can not be confused with the "elective" principle of government or with the most general "democratic" principle established by article 6 of the Constitution. One thing is to be able to elect government officials, and another is the princi-

---

157 See Simon Bolivar, "Discurso de Angostura" (1819), in *Escritos Fundamentales*, Caracas, 1982.

158 Actually, in the constitutional history of the country, the prohibition of the immediate presidential re-election only stopped being established in the Constitutions of the authoritarian governments, that is, the Constitution of 1857; Constitutions of Juan Vicente Gomez of 1914, 1922, 1925, 1928, 1929, and 1931; and the Constitution of Marcos Perez Jimenez of 1953.

ple of alternation that impedes the succesive election of the same government official.

Thus, it is contrary to the Constitution to interpret, as it was done by the Constitutional Chamber in its decision N° 53 of February 3rd, 2009; that the principle of alternation "demands that the people, as the holder of sovereignty, has the periodical possibility to choose its government officials or representatives", confusing "alternate government" with "elective government". For this, what the Constitutional Chamber stated was wrong when deciding that the principle "would only be violated" if the possibility of election is impede. With its decision, what the Constitutional Chamber has done, once more, is to illegitimately mutate the text of the Constitution, and contrary to what has been said, the elimination of the ineligibility cause for the exercise of public positions derived from its previous exercise by any citizen, does misrepresent the alternation principle in the exercise of power.

Thus, contrary to what was decided by the Constitutional Chamber, the possibility of the continuous re-election does alter the fundamental principle of the "alternate" government, which is one of the democratic values that inform our juridical order. Said principle, would be altered if the possibility of the continuous re-election of elective positions was to be established, and which is different from the principle of the "elective" government. Because having a "rocklike" formulation in article 6 of the Constitution ("is and always will be") it can not be the object of any constitutional reform, and in the event that it could be modified, that could not be carried out neither by the proceedings of Constitutional Amendment nor Reform, but only by means of the invitation of a Constituent National Assembly.

The Constitutional Chamber, in its decision N° 53 of February 2009, actually mutated the Constitution by means of an interpretation, illegitimately modifying the sense of the principle of the "alternate" government that the Venezuelans decided must always rule their governments. In any case, with this decision, what the Constitutional Chamber did was to smooth out the road so the Referendum held a few days later on February 15, 2009 could take place in order for the people to vote for the approval or the rejection of a "Constitutional Amendment" project proposed by the National Assembly regarding articles 160, 162, 174, 192 and 230 of the Constitution to establish, in Venezuela, the principle for the possibility of continuous re-election of elective positions, antagonizing the constitutional principle of the republican alternation (article 6). The 2009 Amendment was approved in the said Referendum, and after the illegitimate "mutation" introduced by the Constitutional Chamber, the Constitution was then formally changed eliminating the effects of the principle of "alternate" government that has just remained void and ineffective in article 6 of the Constitution.

IV. THE MODIFICATION OF THE PROHIBITION TO REPEAT REFERENDA ON CONSTITUTIONAL REFORMS ON THE SAME MATTER DURING THE SAME CONSTITUTIONAL TERM

In the aforementioned decision of the Constitutional Chamber, N° 53 of February 2009 regarding the illegitimate change of the principle of alternate government, another illegitimate mutation to the Constitution was adopted, loosing the prohibition set forth in the Constitution to call for a popular referendum regarding reforms to the

Constitution already rejected by the people during the same constitutional term (article 345).

Article 345 of the Constitution, in effect, regarding "constitutional reform" procedures, establishes an express prohibition to submit to the National Assembly during the same constitutional term an initiative for constitutional reform when its matter has already been rejected by referendum. Notwithstanding, the Constitution nothing establishes regarding the effects of the rejection of a "Constitutional Amendment", or if it is possible in case a rejected "constitutional reform" to submit the matter again to referendum but through the "constitutional amendment" procedure.

In December 2007, a Constitutional Reform proposal sanctioned by the National Assembly was rejected by popular vote, in which one of the aspects that was proposed was the elimination of the prohibition established in the Constitution for the possible continuous re election of the President of the Republic. Being the expressed popular will the rejection of the proposal for a constitutional modification, according to article 345 of the Constitution it was not possible to submit during the same constitutional term, once more, the same reform to popular vote. Nonetheless, and notwithstanding this popular rejection, the same National Assembly on January 2009, took the initiative and approved this time "Constitutional Amendment" with the same specific purpose of modifying article 230 of the Constitution regarding the limits to presidential re-election, and also of modifying articles 160, 162, 174, and 192 of the Constitution regarding the re-election of the other elective officials, also eliminating the limits established.

This constitutional conflict was another of the topics interpreted by the Constitutional Chamber in its aforementioned decision N° 53 of February 2009, and instead of looking for the intention of the Constituent when establishing the rules for the non repetition of multiple referendum on the same constitutional issues (article 345), the Constitutional Chamber, confusing the sense of the prohibition, sustained that the provision established was not directed to fix limits to successive popular votes on the same matter, but only to provide limits regarding the National Assembly in the sense that it could not be asked to discuss twice in the same constitutional term modifications already rejected. The Constitutional Chamber forgot the fact that the constitutional restrictive principle was addressed to regulate popular expression of will in matters modification of the Constitution and their effects, and not regarding debates within the National Assembly.

In fact, the purpose of the constitutional prohibition to re-submit a rejected constitutional reform to multiple referendums is related to the effects of the expression of the will of the people in the sense that it cannot be asked, again and again in the same constitutional term about the same constitutional modification once it has already being rejected. Consequently, the importance of the prohibition established in a Title of the Constitution devoted to "Constitutional Reform" which, in Venezuela, can only refer to the effects of the peoples' expression as original constituent power, and not to the effects of the debate that could have taken place in the National Assembly on the matter, a body that is not a constituent power, not even derived, since it can not approve by itself any constitutional modification.

In this case, the decision N° 53 of February 2009 of the Constitutional Chamber can be considered as another one defrauding the Constitution, because the fact was that in 2007 a constitutional reform was sanctioned by the National Assembly trough the "constitutional reform" procedure in order to establish the continuous and indefinite re-election of the President of the Republic, which was rejected by the people; and that in the same constitutional term, in 2009, the same National Assembly also sanctioned a constitutional reform for the same purpose, this time trough the "constitutional amendment" procedure, only adding to the original proposal, perhaps in order to try to differentiate both proposals, all the other elected representatives.

The result was then that although the people rejected in 2007 the proposal for the continuous and indefinite re-election of the President, this modification same rejected modification of the Constitution was submitted again to referendum in 2009, and was approved. For such purpose the Constitutional Chamber issued a constitutional interpretation of article 345 of the Constitution ignoring that it has the purpose that once the people has expressed their choice, rejecting a modification to the constitutional text, citizens cannot be summoned during the same constitutional term, consecutively and without limits, to express its will on the same matter.

V. ILLEGITIMATE TRANSFORMATION FEDERAL SYSTEM, CHANGING "EXCLUSIVE" ATTRIBUTIONS INTO "CONCURRENT" ONES

Article 4 of the Constitution of 1999 establishes that the Republic "is a decentralized federal State in the terms expressed in this Constitution", a wording that contradicts the real sense of the constitutional provisions that allow the qualification of the State as that of a "Centralized federation."[159] But in spite of this limits, and notwithstanding the contradiction, the Constitution has expressly distributed some State powers between the various public and different territorial levels of government, that is to say, the Municipalities, the States and the National government, which can not be changed but by means of a constitutional reform (articles 136, 156, 164, 178 and 179).[160]

Specifically, regarding the infrastructure for circulation and transport, the Constitution provides that the conservation, administration and use of roads and national

---

159 See Allan R. Brewer-Carías, *Federalismo y Municipalismo en la Constitución de 1999 (Alcance de una reforma insuficiente y regresiva),* Editorial Jurídica Venezolana, Caracas-San Cristóbal 2001; "El Estado federal descentralizado y la centralización de la federación en Venezuela. Situación y perspectiva de una contradicción constitucional," in Diego Valadés and José María Serna de la Garza (Coordinators), *Federalismo y regionalismo,* Universidad Nacional Autónoma de México, Supreme Court of Justice of the State of Puebla, Instituto de Investigaciones Jurídicas, Mexico 2005, pp. 717-750.

160 See Allan R. Brewer-Carías, "Consideraciones sobre el régimen de distribución de competencias del Poder Público en la Constitución de 1999" in Fernando Parra Aranguren and Armando Rodríguez García (Editors), *Estudios de Derecho Administrativo. Libro Homenaje a la Universidad Central de Venezuela, Facultad de Ciencias Jurídicas y Políticas, con ocasión del Vigésimo Aniversario del Curso de Especialización en Derecho Administrativo,* Vol. I, Supreme Tribunal of Justice, Caracas 2001, pp. 107-136.

highways, as well as of national ports and airports of commercial use, exclusively correspond to the States; competency that they must exercise in "coordination with the National Power."

In the rejected Constitutional Reform proposed in 2007, one of its general purposes was to change the federal form of the State and of the territorial distribution of the competencies established in articles 156 and 164 of the Constitution, centralizing the State even more by concentrating almost all the competencies of the Public Power on the national level. Particularly, one of the purposes of the reform was to "nationalize" the referred attribution set forth in article 164.10 of the Constitution attributing the States the matters of the conservation, administration and use of national highways, roads ports and airports.[161] As it has been said, the 2007 Constitutional Reform was rejected by the people in the referendum of December 2nd, 2007, for which the attribution of the States established is the aforementioned article 164.10 of the Constitution, remained without modification. However, the Constitutional Chamber ogf the Supreme Tribunal, in decision N° 565 of April 15, 2008[162] deciding an autonomous recourse for constitutional interpretation filed by the Attorney General of the Republic ruled modifying the content of the aforementioned constitutional provision disposing that the "exclusive attribution" established in it *is not such exclusive attribution*, but a concurrent one that even the National Government can revert it in its favour, eliminating it from the States level. The Attorney General of the Republic considered that the provision "was not clear enough to establish, in an efficient and precise way, the scope and performance of the National Executive, regarding the coordination with the States about the administration, conservation and use of national roads and highways, as well as ports and airports of commercial use." The Constitutional Chamber decided, acordingly, that the National Public Administration "in exercise of its coordination authority can directly assume the conservation, administration and use of the national roads and highways, as well as all ports and airports of commercial use," and that it corresponds to the National Executive (the President of the Republic in Ministers Cabinet), to decree its intervention and assume the rendering of services and assets when considering deficient or inexistent.

With this interpretation, what the Constitutional Judge did was to illegitimately mutate the Constitutional in the sense proposed in the 2007 rejected Constitutional Reform, usurping popular sovereignty, changing the federal form of the State by misrepresenting the territorial distribution system of powers between the National

---

161 See Allan R. Brewer-Carías, *Hacia la Consolidación de un Estado Socialista, Centralizado, Policial y Militarista. Comentarios sobre el sentido y alcance de las propuestas de reforma constitucional 2007,* Editorial Jurídica Venezolana, Caracas 2007, pp. 41 ff.; and *La Reforma Constitucional de 2007 (Comentarios al Proyecto Inconstitucionalmente sancionado por la Asamblea Nacional el 2 de Noviembre de 2007),* Editorial Jurídica Venezolana, Caracas 2007, pp. 72 ff.

162 See decision of the Constitutional Chamber, N° 565 of April 15, 2008, Case: Attorney *General of the Republic, interpretation recourse of article 164,10 of the 1999 Constitution of 1999,* in http://www.tsj.gov.ve/decisio-nes/scon/Abril/565-150408-07-1108.htm

Power and the States, and particularly "nationalizing" against what expressly establishes the Constitution, attributions that are exclusively assigned to the States. The result of the interpretation requested has been that the Constitutional Chamber, has "reformed" the Constitution and has eliminated the exclusive competency of the States in the matter, turning it into a concurrent one, subjecting it to be possibly "decentralized," and in such cases with the possibility to be reverted and reassumed by the National Government. The Chamber, in order to decide, has forgotten that if it is true that the specific attribution of the States according to the Organic Law for Decentralization, Delimitation and Competency Transfer of the Public Power, was decentralized in 1989, such attribution was transformed into an "exclusive" one in the 1999 Constitution," which constitutionalized what the said Organic Law established in 1989. Nonetheless, the Constitutional Chamber without any constitutional or legal basis, disposed that "it corresponds to the National Executive, to decree the intervention in order to assume the rendering of services and assets of national roads and highways, as well as ports and airports of commercial use, in those cases where, even though said competencies had been transferred, the rendering of the service, either by the States, is deficient or inexistent."

After an illegitimate "constitutional modification" of this nature carried out through a judicial interpretation, as the very Constitutional Chamber said in its decision, it "generated a necessary revision and modification of great scope and magnitude of the current legal system," warning the National Assembly to "proceed to the revision and corresponding modification of the legal provisions related to the obligatory interpretation established in this decision, and sanctioned statutes congruent with the constitutional principles derived from the interpretation established by this Chamber in exercise of its competencies." That is to say, the Chamber forced the legislator to issue legislation against the provisions of the 1999 Constitution, and according to the illegitimate constitutional modification imposed. This provoked that, after the electoral triumph of opposition Governors and Mayors in key States and Municipalities in the elections of December 2008, substituting pro Government ones, the National Assembly in March 2009, diligently reformed, among other, the said Organic Law for Decentralization,[163] in order to eliminate the exclusive attribution of the States established in article 11, 3 and 5 of said Law; adding two new provisions allowing the National Executive to "revert, for strategic reasons, of merit, opportunity or convenience, the transfer of attributions to the States, for the conservation, administration and use of assets and services considered to be of general public interest" (article 8); and that the National Executive, could decree the intervention of the said assets and rendering of public services transferred in order to ensure users and consumers a quality service (article 9). With this, the defraudation of the Constitution made by the Constitutional Chamber was completed by the national Assembly, resulting that a constitutional assigned "exclusive" attribution was changed into a concurrent one.

---

163   *Gaceta Oficial* N° 39 140 of March 17, 2009.

VI. THE ILLEGITIMATE REFORM OF THE CONSTITUTIONAL PRO-HIBITION TO FINANCE ELECTORAL ACTIVITIES OF POLITICAL PARTIES WITH GOVERNMENT FUNDS

Article 67 of the Constitution of 1999 expressly establishes that the "the financing of political associations with Government funds will not be allowed," a provision that emphatically changed in a radical way the previous regime of public financing to the political parties, established in article 230 of the Organic Law of Suffrage and Political Participation of 1998. This Law sought to establish a greater balance and impartiality for the participation of the parties in democratic life and, especially, in electoral campaigns trying to mitigate the unbalances and perversions that could arise just with the private financing of the parties, with the risk, for instance, of the presence of "drug-financing", and the eventual indirect, irregular and corrupt public financing, just intended for government parties,[164] which can magnify in a system where there is no fiscal nor parliamentary effective control of the exercise of power. The constitutional prohibition, by derogating such article of the Organic Law, eliminated any the public funding of political parties, abandoning the inverse technique that predominates in the comparative law.[165]

This express constitutional prohibition regarding the public financing of political parties, was also one of the matters referred to in the 2007 rejected Constitutional Reform[166], in which it was proposed to modify article 67, providing the opposite, that "the State will be able to finance electoral activities." As already mentioned, the aforementioned 2007 Constitutional Reform proposal was rejected by popular vote in the referendum of December 2, 2007;[167] with which the governmental financing of political parties regarding their electoral activities continued to be prohibited in the Constitution.

However, in spite of said constitutional prohibition and of the popular rejection of its modification, the Constitutional Chamber of the Supreme Court of Justice, in decision N° 780 of May 8, 2008 (File N° 06-0785), by means of an obligatory constitutional interpretation, has illegitimately mutated the Constitution; substituting

---

164 See Allan R. Brewer-Carías, "Consideraciones sobre el financiamiento de los partidos políticos en Venezuela" in *Financiamiento y democratización interna de partidos políticos. Memoria del IV Curso Anual Interamericano de Elecciones,* San José, Costa Rica, 1991, pp. 121 to 139.

165 See in Allan R. Brewer-Carías, "Regulación jurídica de los partidos políticos en Venezuela" in *Estudios sobre el Estado Constitucional (2005-2006)*, Cuadernos de la Cátedra Fundacional Allan R. Brewer Carías de Derecho Público, Universidad Católica del Táchira, N° 9, Editorial Jurídica Venezolana. Caracas, 2007, pp. 655-686

166 See *Proyecto de Exposición de Motivos para la Reforma Constitucional, Presidencia de la República, Proyecto Reforma Constitucional. Propuesta del presidente Hugo Chávez Agosto 2007;: Proyecto de Reforma Constitucional. Prepared by the President of the Bolivarian Republic of Venezuela, Hugo Chávez Frías,* Editorial Atenea, Caracas August 2007, p. 19.

167 See Allan R. Brewer-Carías, "La proyectada reforma constitucional de 2007, rechazada por el poder constituyente originario," in *Anuario de Derecho Público 2007,* Universidad Monteavila, Caracas 2008.

itself to the popular will and of the original constituent power, disposing that "regarding the scope of the prohibition of public financing of political associations" contained in said norm, it only "limits the possibility to provide resources for the internal expenses of the different forms of political associations, but... said limitation, is not extensive to the electoral campaign, as a fundamental stage of the electoral process".

That is, the Constitutional Chamber, even facing a clear although censurable constitutional provision as the one contained in article 67 of the Constitution, whose reform was attempted without success in 2007, in this precise decision has usurped the constituent power, substituting the people, and has ruled reforming the provision by means of its interpretation, in the same sense that it was intended in the rejected Constitutional Reform, expressly allowing the governmental financing of the electoral activities of the political parties and associations, that is, in the opposite of what is provided in the Constitution.

Therefore, the Constitutional Judge simply decided that the Constitution does not say what it says, but says completely the opposite; that when it says that "the financing of political associations with Government funds will not be allowed," it is not what the Constitution establishes, but what it prohibits is solely "the financing of current and internal expenses of the political associations with resources coming from the State"; and, on the contrary, that the expenses of the electoral campaigns of said political associations, can be financed with funds coming form the State. In order to arrive to this conclusion, in a decision unnecessarily packed with author quoting about interpretation techniques, the notion of democracy, and the advantages of the public financing of the electoral campaigns of political parties, concluded in the aforementioned distinction, that one things is that the State finances "current and internal expenses" of political parties, and another is that it finances "their electoral campaigns," deducing, without any foundation, that what the Constitution prohibits is the first and not the latter.

It is an absurd conclusion, which against any democratic logic, derives from a false premise, in which, supposedly, in democratic systems it could happen that the State could finance the current and internal expenses of the parties. The latter is not conceived in democracies, reason for which it does not require of any prohibition. In democracies, what is financed is the operation of the parties, but always, with a view to the electoral campaigns, to the point of cancelling the financing if the parties do not obtain a certain percentage of votes in the elections.

The decision of the Constitutional Judge can be very commendable, allowing the financing of the electoral campaigns of the political parties with funds belonging to the State, but since it was expressly prohibited by the Constitution, just by reforming it is that the opposite could be achieved. And, in that case, that was what the Constitutional Judge did in Venezuela, that is, to reform the Constitution, usurping the original constituent power which corresponds to the people and, even against its own will expressed five months earlier by rejecting, precisely, said constitutional reform, establishing now the possibility to finance with public funds the electoral campaigns of the political parties.

VII. THE ILLEGITIMATE ELIMINATION OF THE SUPRA-CONSTITUTIONAL RANK OF INTERNATIONAL TREATIES IN MATTERS HUMAN RIGHTS

Following a contemporary universal trend, which has allowed constitutional courts the direct application of international treaties in matters of human rights for their protection, progressively widening their cast, in the text of contemporary Constitutions, the normative scope of said treaties has been progressively recognized, being possible to distinguish four different ranks recognized in the internal law: supra-constitutional, constitutional, supra-legal or legal rank.[168]

In the case of the Venezuelan Constitution of 1999, article 23 expressly disposes the following:

> Article 23. Treaties, pacts and conventions regarding to human rights, subscribed and ratified by Venezuela, have constitutional rank and prevail in the internal order, as long as they contain norms about their enjoyment and exercise, more favourable than those established in this Constitution and in the laws of the Republic, and are to be direct and immediate applicable, by the courts and other bodies of the State.

Without a doubt, this norm is one of the most important ones in matters of human rights in the country, unique in its conception in Latin-America, because first it grants international treaties in matters of human rights, not only constitutional rank, but *supra-constitutional* rank; that is, a superior rank regarding the Constitution itself, which must prevail over it in cases they contain more favourable regulations for their exercise. The article also establishes the principle of the direct and immediate application of said treaties by the courts and other authorities of the country. This provision of the Constitution was, without a doubt, a significant advance in the construction of the human rights protection framework, which has been applied by the courts for instance declaring the prevalence of the norms of the American Convention of Human Rights regarding legal and constitutional provisions. It was the case, for instance, of the right to appeal before a second judicial instance invoked before the contentious administrative jurisdiction in which in some cases (autonomous institutions or independent Administrations acts) it was excluded in the former Organic Law of the Supreme Court of Justice of 1976.

The Constitution of 1999 only establishes as a constitutional right, the right to appeal in matters of criminal procedures in favour of the person declared as guilty

---

168 Regarding this general classification, see Rodolfo E. Piza R., *Derecho internacional de los derechos humanos: La Convención Americana*, San José 1989; and Carlos Ayala Corao, "La jerarquía de los instrumentos internacionales sobre derechos humanos", in *El nuevo derecho constitucional latinoamericano*, IV Congreso Venezolano de Derecho constitucional, Vol. II, Caracas 1996 and *La jerarquía constitucional de los tratados sobre derechos humanos y sus consecuencias*, México, 2003; Humberto Henderson, "Los tratados internacionales de derechos humanos en el orden interno: la importancia del principio pro homine", in *Revista IIDH*, Instituto Interamericano de Derechos Humanos, N° 39, San José 2004, pp. 71 and ss. See also, Allan R. Brewer-Carías, *Mecanismos nacionales de protección de los derechos humanos*, Instituto Internacional de Derechos Humanos, San José, 2004, pp. 62 ff.

(article 40.1); so regarding the aforementioned contentious administrative suit, there was no express constitutional guaranty for the appeal, having been always the appeal of the First Court of Contentious Administrative decisions as inadmissible. Nonetheless, the application of article 23 of the Constitution in these cases finally leads the Constitutional Chamber of the Supreme Court to rule in 2000, on the prevailing application of the Inter-American Convention on Human Rights, considering:

> "that article 8.1 and 8. 2, h of the American Convention on Human Rights, are part of the Venezuelan constitutional order; that its dispositions, containing the right to appeal judicial decision are more favourable, concerning the benefit and exercise of said right, than that foreseen in article 49.1 of said Constitution; and that are of immediate and direct application by the courts and other State bodies."[169]

However, in decision N° 1.939 of December 18th 2008 (Case: Gustavo Alvarez Arias and others), by declaring in executable a decision of the Inter-American Court on Human Rights of August 5th 2008 referred to the case of the former judges of the First Court on the Contentious Administrative matters *(Apitz Barbera and others ("First Court on the Contentious Administrative matters") vs. Venezuela)*, the Constitutional Chamber has definitely resolved that:

> "the aforementioned article 23 of the Constitution **does not** grant "supra-constitutional rank to international treaties on human rights, thus, in case of antinomy or contradiction between one disposition of the Constitution and a provision of an international pact, it would correspond to the Judicial Power to determine which would be applicable, considering both what is established in the referred provision, and in the jurisprudence of this Constitutional Chamber of the Supreme Court of Justice, paying attention to the content of articles 7, 266.6, 334, 335, 336.11 *ejusdem* and to decision N°1.077/2000 of this Chamber."

In order to base its decision, and reject the existence of superior values not modifiable by the authoritarian political project, the Chamber clarified the following concepts:

> "On this subject, the decision N° 1309/2001 of this Chamber, among others, clarifies that law is a normative theory at the service of politics that underlines behind the axiological project of the Constitution, and that the interpretation must be engaged, if we want to maintain the supremacy of the Constitution when exercising the constitutional jurisdiction assigned to the judges, with the best political theory that underlines behind the system interpreted or integrated and with the institutional morality that serves as its axiological base (*interpretatio favor Constitutione*). The decision adds: "in this order of ideas, the standards to resolve the conflict between the principles and the provisions have to be compatible with the political project of the Constitution (Democratic and Social State of Law and Justice) and can not affect the force of said project with ideological interpretative elections that privilege individual rights decisively, or that welcome the supremacy of the international judicial order over national law at the sacrifice of the sovereignty of the State".

---

169 Decision N° 87 of March 13th, 2000. Case: *C.A. Electricidad del Centro (Elecentro) y otra vs. Superintendencia para la Promoción y Protección de la Libre Competencia. (Procompetencia)*, in *Revista de Derecho Público*, N° 81, Editorial Jurídica Venezolana, Caracas 2000, pp. 157 ff.

The decision concludes that: "a system of principles, supposedly absolute and supra-historic, can not be above the Constitution" and that the theories that pretend to limit "under the pretext of universal legalities, the sovereignty and the national auto-determination" are unacceptable.

In the same sense, the decision of this Chamber (N° 1265/2008) established that when a contradiction is evidenced between the Constitution and an international convention or treaty, "the constitutional provision that privilege the general interest and the common wellbeing must prevail, applying the dispositions that privilege the collective interests... (...) over particular interests..."[170]

With this decision, the Constitutional Chamber accomplished an illegitimate constitutional mutation, reforming article 23 of the Constitution when eliminating the supra-national rank of the American Convention on Human Rights, in the cases containing more favourable previsions for the benefit and exercise of human rights regarding those foreseen in the very Constitution.

The matter has been so about an illegitimate constitutional reform, that it was one of the express reform proposals made in 2007 by the "Presidential Council for the Constitutional Reform,"[171] in which, regarding article 23 of the Constitution, the intention was to completely eliminate the constitutional hierarchy of the previsions of the international treaties on human rights, and their prevalence over the internal order, proposing the reformulation of the provision just in the sense that: "treaties, pacts and conventions related to human rights, subscribed and ratified by Venezuela, as long as they remain current, are part of the internal order, and are of immediate and direct application by the bodies of the Public Power".

This proposal for constitutional reform, which luckily was filled before the national Assembly by the President of the Republic, was a hard blow to the principle of progressivity in the protection of the rights established in article 19 of the Constitution, which does not allow regressions in their protection.[172] However, what the authoritarian regime was not able to accomplish through a constitutional reform process, which at the end was in 2007 rejected by the people, was carried out by the Constitutional Chamber of the Supreme Court throughout its long carrier at the service of authoritarianism.[173]

---

170 See in http://www.tsj.gov.ve/decisiones/scon/Diciembre/1939-181208-2008-08-1572.html

171 See Consejo Presidencial para la Reforma de la Constitución de la República Bolivariana de Venezuela, "Modificaciones propuestas". The compelte text was Published as Proyecto de Reforma Constitucional. Versión atribuida al Consejo Presidencial para la reforma de la Constitución de la república Bolivariana de Venezuela, Editorial Atenea, Caracas July 01-2007, 146 pp.

172 See in Allan R. Brewer-Carías, Hacia la consolidación de un Estado Socialista, Centralizado, Policial y Militarista. Comentarios sobre el sentido y alcance de las propuestas de reforma constitucional 2007, Editorial Jurídica Venezolana, Caracas 2007, pp. 122 ss.

173 See Allan R. Brewer-Carías, Crónica sobre la "In" Justicia Constitucional. La Sala Constitucional y el autoritarismo en Venezuela, Colección Instituto de Derecho Público, Universidad Central de Venezuela, N° 2, Caracas 2007.

VIII. THE ELIMINATION OF JUDGES' POWER TO IMMEDIATELY AND DIRECTLY APPLY INTERNATIONAL TREATIES ON HUMAN RIGHTS

In matters of human rights, article 23 of the Constitution not only grants supra-constitutional rank to the provisions of the international treaties, pacts and conventions regarding human rights, "as long as they contain provisions more favourable to their enjoyment and exercise as those established in this Constitution and in the laws of the Republic", which, as it has been seen, it had been illegitimately mutated; but it also expressly declare that they are "of direct and immediate application by the courts and other bodies of the State" (article 23).

Regarding this provision, the Constitutional Chamber of the Supreme Court, by reaffirming its role of maximum and ultimate interpreter of the Constitution and the treaties on human rights, has established in decision N° 1492 of July 15, 2003 (Case: *Impugnación de diversos artículos del Código Penal*), that because those treatises having constitutional rank, the only one capable of their interpretation, of determine which one of their provisions prevail in the internal legal order; and of deciding which human rights, not contemplated in said international instruments, have force in Venezuela, is the Constitutional Chamber of the Supreme Tribunal.[174] With this unconstitutional decision, the Constitutional Chamber has also illegitimately mutated the Constitution, because according to its article 23, the authority to do so n not only corresponds to the Constitutional Chamber, but to all the courts of the Republic when acting as constitutional judges, for instance, when exercising the diffused control of the constitutionality of statutes or when deciding cases of amparo. The intention of the Constitutional Chamber to concentrate all constitutional justice procedures is not in accordance to the Constitution and to the judicial review system it establishes.

IX. THE DENIAL OF THE PEOPLES' RIGHT FOR THE INTERNATIONAL PROTECTION OF THE HUMAN RIGHTS AND THE NON ENFORCEABILITY OF THE DECISIONS OF THE INTER-AMERICAN COURT ON HUMAN RIGHTS

But besides the unawareness regarding the supra-constitutional scope of the American Convention on Human Rights, the Constitutional Chamber, in decision N° 1.939 of December 18, 2008 (Case: *Gustavo Álvarez Arias and others*, or more accurate, *Case: Venezuelan Government vs. Inter-American Court on Human Rights*), has ignored the effects of the decisions of the Inter-American Court on Human Rights, declaring them as un enforceable in Venezuela, contradicting the international regime of the treaties.

With said decision, issued in a proceedings initiated by the Attorney General of the Republic as a dependant organ of the National Executive, the Constitutional Chamber declared that the decision of the Inter American Court on Human Rights

---

174 See *Revista de Derecho Público*, N° 93-96, Editorial Jurídica Venezolana, Caracas 2003, pp. 135 ff.

issued on August 5, 2008 in the case of the former judges of the First Court on Contentious Administrative that were illegitimately dismissed without any sort of judicial guaranties (Case *Apitz Barbera and others ("First Court on Contentious Administrative matters) vs. Venezuela),* was non enforceable in Venezuela. In that decision, the Inter American Court decided that the Venezuelan State had violated the judicial guarantees of the said judges established in the American Convention, by removing them form their offices without due process, and condemned the State to pay for compensations, to reinstate the judges to their former positions or to some similar, and to publish the verdict in Venezuelan newspapers.[175]

Of course, in the case of the American Convention of Human Rights, once a Member State recognized the jurisdiction from the Inter American Court on Human Rights, according to article 68.1 of the Convention, they must "commit themselves to comply with the decisions of the Court in every case in which they are a part of."[176] In addition, the Venezuelan Constitution expressly contains the right to have access to the international protection in matters of human rights, with the obligation for the State to carry out the decisions of the international bodies. To that effect, article 31 of the Constitution establishes:

> Article 31. Every person has the right, within the terms established by the treaties, pacts and conventions on human rights ratified by the Republic, to file petitions or complaints before the international bodies established for such purposes, in order to ask for the protection of their human rights.
>
> The State shall adopt, in accordance with the proceedings established in this Constitution and statutes, the necessary measures for the enforcement of the decisions issued by the international bodies indicated in this article.

There have been States, however, who have resisted against the decisions of the Inter-American Court, and have intended to avoid their responsibility in their enforcement. The decision of the Inter American Court on the *Case: Castillo Petruzzi,* of May 30, 1999 (Series C, number 52), is proof of that, since after declaring that the Peruvian State had violated during a proceeding, articles 20; 7.5; 9; 8.1; 8.2.b,c,d

---

175 See www.corteidh.or.cr . Excepción Preliminar, Fondo, Reparaciones y Costas, Serie C N° 182.

176 As stated by the Inter-American Court on Human Rights in the decision of *Case Castillo Petruzzi,* on "Enforcement decision" of November 17, 1999 (Series C, number 59), "the conventional obligations of the State party entail all the powers and bodies of the State;" (paragraph 3) adding "That this obligation corresponds to a basic principle of international responsibility right of the State, endorsed by the international jurisprudence, according to which the States must comply with their conventional duties in good faith (*pacta sunt servanda*) and, as it has been mentioned by this Court, can not, due to reasons of internal order, stop complying with the established international responsibility" (paragraph 4). See in Sergio García Ramírez (Coord.), *La Jurisprudencia de la Corte Interamericana de Derechos Humanos,* Universidad Nacional Autónoma de México, Corte Interamericana de Derechos Humanos, México, 2001, pp. 628-629.

and f; 8.2.h; 8.5; 25; 7.6; 5; 1.1 and 2,[177] the Plenary Chamber of the Supreme Council of Military Justice of Peru refused to enforce the verdict, considering that it had ignored the Political Constitution of Peru, subjecting it to "the American Convention on Human Rights in the interpretation that the judges of said Court can carry out *ad-libitum.*"[178]

In 1999 Venezuela has followed the same steps of the authoritarian regime of President Fujimori in Peru, and the Constitutional Chamber of the Supreme Court in the aforementioned decision N° 1.939 of December 18, 2008 (*Case: Attorneys Gustavo Álvarez Arias and others*), has also declared the Inter American Court on Human Rights of August 5, 2008 issued in the case *Apitz Barbera and others (First Court on Contentious Administrative matters) vs. Venezuela*, as "un enforceable" in Venezuela, accusing the Inter American Court of usurping the power of the Supreme Court.[179]

---

177 Consequently, in the decision, the Inter-American Court declared "the nullity, of the process against Mr. Jaime Francisco Sebastián Castillo Petruzzi and others, for been incompatible with the Convention" ordering "the guaranty of a new trial with the complete observance of the legal due process," and also, "the State to adopt the necessary measures in order to reform the provisions that had been declared to be against the American Convention of Human Rights in the present decision, and to ensure the benefit of the rights established in the American Convention on Human Rights to all the people under its jurisdiction, without any exception". See in http://www.tsj.gov.ve/ decisiones/scon/Diciembre/1939-181208-2008-08-1572.html

178 It is precisely, because of this decision of the Plenary Chamber of the Supreme Council of Military Justice of Peru regarding the non enforceability of the decision of the Inter-American Court on Human Rights in Peru, issued on May 30, 1999, that the same Inter-American Court ruled its subsequent decision of November 7, 1999, declaring that "the State has the duty to promptly fulfil the decision of May 30, 1999 ruled by the Inter-American Court in the case Castillo Petruzzi and others." See, in Sergio García Ramírez (Coord.), *La Jurisprudencia de la Corte Interamericana de Derechos Humanos*, Universidad Nacional Autónoma de México, Corte Interamericana de Derechos Humanos, México, 2001, p. 629. This occurred during the authoritarian regime in Peru, during the mandate of President Fujimori, and which, two months after the decision of the Inter American Court of May 30, 1999, drove the Congress of Peru to approve the withdraw the recognition of the contentious competency of the Court; which was submitted the following day before the General Secretariat of the OAS. This withdrawal was declared inadmissible by the Inter American Court, in ts decision in the case *Ivcher Bronstein* of September 24, 1999, considering that "a State party can only remove itself to the competency of the Court through the formal complaint of the complete treaty." *Idem*, pp. 769-771. In any case, Peru, later in 2001, derogated the Resolution of July 1999, completely re-establishing for the State the competency of the Inter American Court.

179 The issue had been affirmed by the Constitutional Chamber in its known decision N° 1.942 of July 15, 2003 in which, when referring to the International Courts, began stating that in Venezuela, "above the Supreme Court of Justice and according to article 7 of the Constitution, there is no jurisdictional body, unless stated otherwise by the Constitution or the law, and even in this last possible case, any decision contradicting the Venezuelan constitutional order, lacks of application in the country." See Case: *Impugnación de artículos del Código*

The Constitutional Chamber in its decision, quoting a previous decision N° 1.942 of July 15, 2003, and considering that it was about an interpretation request formulated by the Republic, ruled that the Inter American Court on Human Rights could not "intend to exclude or ignore the internal constitutional order," and that it had ruled "guidelines on the government and administration of the Judiciary w matter that is of exclusive and excluding attributions of the Supreme Tribunal of Justice, and has established "rules for the Legislature in matters of judicial responsibility of the judges, transgressing the sovereignty of the Venezuelan State in its organization and in the selection of its officials; which it considered as inadmissible. The Constitutional Chamber even accused the Inter American Court of having used its decision "to intervene, unacceptably, in the judicial government and administration, which exclusively corresponds to the Supreme Tribunal," arguing that with the questioned decision, the Inter-American Court intended to "ignore the strength and force of judicial and administrative decisions that have acquired the *res judicata*, by demanding the reincorporation of the judges that have been removed from office." In order to make these affirmations, the Constitutional Chamber turned, precisely, to the aforementioned decision of 1999 of the Plenary Chamber of the Supreme Council of Military Justice of Peru, which considered un enforceable in Peru the decisions of the Inter-American Court of May 30, 1999 (Case: *Castillo Petruzzi and other*).

But the Constitutional Chamber did not stop there, but in an evident usurpation of powers -since the international relations are a matter of exclusive attribution of the Executive- requested "the National Executive to proceed to denounce the Convention, in view of the evident usurpation of functions in which the Inter American Court on Human Rights has incurred into with the ruling object of this decision." With this, the Venezuelan State concluded its process of separation from the American Convention on Human Rights, and of the jurisdiction of the Inter-American Court on Human Rights, using it very own Supreme Court of Justice for this purpose.

We must recall in fact that, in this same matter, the Constitutional Chamber has also decided adopt another illegitimate constitutional mutation, by reforming article 23 of the Constitution in the way intended in 2007 proposal for Constitutional reform formulated by the "Presidential Council for the Reform of the Constitution," by suggesting to add to article 23 of the Constitution, also in a regressive manner, that it "corresponds to the courts of the Republic to be decide upon the violations on matters established in said treaties", proposing the establishment a constitutional prohibition impeding the Inter American Court on Human Rights to decide on the violations of the American Convention on Human Rights. That is, with a provision of that kind, Venezuela would have been constitutionally excluded from the jurisdic-

---

Penal, *Leyes de desacato*, in *Revista de Derecho Público*, N° 93-96, Editorial Jurídica Venezolana, Caracas 2003, pp. 136 ff.

tion of said International Court, and of the Inter American protection human rights system.[180]

On this matter, also, what the authoritarian regime could not do by means of a constitutional reform process like the one initiated in 2007, which at the end was rejected by the people, was done by the Constitutional Chamber of the Supreme Court throughout its long carrier at the service of authoritarianism.

X. THE ILEGITIMATE CREATION OF AN AUTONOMOUS RECOURSE FOR THE ABSTRACT INTERPRETATION OF THE CONSTITUTION

Almost all of the aforementioned illegitimate mutations of the Constitutions, that have been adopted by the Constitutional Chamber of the Supreme Tribunal, have been made when deciding autonomous recourses for the abstract interpretation of the Constitution, which at its turn have their origin, also, in an illegitimate mutations to the Constitution made by the same Constitutional Chamber. In other words, it has been this autonomous recourse for the abstract interpretation of the Constitution, which is not established either in the Constitution or in any statute, the one that has served as the main tool for the adoption of some of the most distinguishable and illegitimate mutations to the Constitution, which have not their origin in constitutional interpretations made by the Constitutional Judge when deciding a particular case or action of unconstitutionality or another mean to of judicial review. Instead, they have its origin in the decision on autonomous requests for the abstract interpretation of the Constitution, in many cases filed by the National Executive through the Attorney General of the Republic.

In this regard, notwithstanding that a recourse or action for the interpretation of statutes is the only established in the Constitution, the Constitutional Chamber of the Supreme Tribunal in decision N° 1.077 of September 22, 2001, formally created its own power in order to decide "autonomous recourses for the abstract interpretation in the Constitution," establishing an unconstitutional interpretation of article 335 of the Constitution, which assigns the Supreme Tribunal and not solely to the Constitutional Chamber, its character of being the "maximum and last interpreter of the Constitution."[181] This recourse, according to the criteria followed by the Constitutional Chamber, has similarities in nature to the one expressly established for interpretation of statutes, but in these cases in order to obtain a mere declarative decision about the scope and content of a constitutional provision. The Chamber recognized standing to file this recourse to anybody when alleging an actual, personal and legitimate interest, derived from a particular and specific legal situation which necessarily requires the interpretation of a Constitution provision applicable to it, in order to put an end

---

180   See Allan R. Brewer-Carías, *Hacia la consolidación de un Estado Socialista, Centralizado, Policial y Militarista. Comentarios sobre el sentido y alcance de las propuestas de reforma constitucional 2007*, Editorial Jurídica Venezolana, Caracas 2007, p. 122.

181   See decision N° 1077 of the Constitutional Chamber dated September 22, 2000, Case: *Servio Tulio León Briceño*. See in *Revista de Derecho Público*, N° 83, Caracas, 2000, pp 247 ff. This criteria was then confirmed in decisions of November 9, 2000 (N° 1347), November 21, 2000 (N° 1387), and April 5, 2001 (N° 457), among others.

to the uncertainty that impedes the development and effects of said legal situation. The main condition for the admissibility of such recourse is the obscurity or ambiguity of the particular constitutional provision that must apply to the legal situation, or the contradiction that could exist between constitutional provisions and principles including those contained in the transition constitutional provisions adopted by the National Constituent Assembly in 1999

As was decided by the Constitutional Chamber, notwithstanding the constitutional process that in originated when a recourse for constitutional interpretation in filed, there is not need to open a contradictory hearing in order to allow the participation in the debate of people with judicial interest in a particular interpretation of the Constitution, and in decision N° 2651 of October 2, 2003 it denied the character of constitutional process to the procedure stating that in these cases "there is no *litis*, confrontation between parts, regarding which their defence has to be secured."[182] In any case, the result of the procedure is the binding character of the decision adopted by the Constitutional Chamber, particularly regarding the nucleus of the case in study.[183]

The creation by the Constitutional Chamber of this instrument for the abstract interpretation of the Constitution, without doubts, has produced a constitutional mutation, amplifying the constitutional powers of the Constitutional Chamber, by attributing to itself the power to decide a recourse that is not established in the Constitution. On the other hand, this autonomous recourse for the abstract interpretation of the Constitution has no precedent in comparative law.[184]

As we have mentioned, an autonomous recourse for the abstract interpretation of the Constitution, in the hands of an autonomous and independent Constitutional Judge, can be, without a doubt, an efficient instrument to adapt the norms of the Constitution to the changes operated in the constitutional order of a country at a point in time. However, a recourse of that nature in the hands of a Constitutional Judge absolutely dependant of the Executive Power, in an authoritarian regime like the one structured in Venezuela during the last 10 years; deciding, particularly, the interested requests filed by the Executive through the Attorney General of the Republic, is an instrument for illegitimate mutation of the Constitution, used to modify it and adapt at will, in order to strengthen authoritarianism. That is what has happened in Venezuela.

---

182 See Case: *Ricardo Delgado. Interpretation of article 174 of the Constitution.*

183 See decision N° 1347, of November 9, 2000

184 See Allan R. Brewer-Carías, "Le recours d'interprétation abstrait de la Constitution au Vénézuéla", in *Le renouveau du droit constitutionnel, Mélanges en l'honneur de Louis Favoreu*, Dalloz, Paris, 2007, pp 61-70.

CHAPTER XVIII

CONSTITUTIONAL LITIGATION IN VENEZUELA:
GENERAL TRENDS OF THE AMPARO PROCEEDING AND THE
EFFECTS OF THE LACK OF JUDICIAL INDEPENDENCE

(2010)

**Paper written for the Presentation on "Constitutional Litigation in Vene-
zuela: General Trends of the Amparo Proceeding and the effects of the lack of
Judicial Independence," delivered at the Seminar on *Constitutional Litigation:
Procedural Protections of Constitutional Guarantees in the Americas ... and Beyond*, organized by Professor Robert S. Baker, Duquesne University School of
Law, Pittsburgh, November 5, 2010. The whole text of the essay written for the
Seminar was published as "The Amparo Proceeding in Venezuela: Constitutional Litigation and Procedural Protection of Constitutional Rights and Guarantees," *Duquesne Law Review*, Volume 49, Number 2, Pittsburgh Spring 2011,
pp. 161-241.**

INTRODUCTION

The title of the 2010 International Seminar on *Constitutional Litigation and Procedural Protections of Constitutionalism in the Americas... and Beyond* organized
by Professor Robert S. Barker in the Duquesne Law School, from a Latin American
perspective, suggest the study of the amparo proceeding, which is an extraordinary
judicial remedy specifically conceived for the protection of constitutional rights
against harms or threats inflicted by authorities or by individuals. This is an institution that has been developed in Latin America, as a judicial mean for constitutional
litigation that normally concludes with a judicial order or writ of protection, indistinctly called as action, recourse or suit of *amparo, protección* or *tutela*.[185]

---

185 See Héctor Fix-Zamudio and Eduardo Ferrer Mac-Gregor (Coord.), *El derecho de amparo en
     el mundo*, Edit. Porrúa, México, 2006; Allan R. Brewer-Carías, *El amparo a los derechos y
     libertades constitucionales. Una aproximación comparativa*, Universidad Católica del Táchi-
     ra, San Cristóbal, 1993, also published in *La protección jurídica del ciudadaNº Estudios en*

This constitutional litigation mean was introduced in the American Continent during the nineteenth century, and although similar remedies were established in the twentieth century in some European countries, like Austria, Germany, Spain and Switzerland, and also in Canada, it has been adopted by all Latin American countries, except in Cuba, being considered as one of the most distinguishable features of Latin American constitutional law.[186] As such, it has influenced the introduction of a similar remedy in other countries, like The Philippines, where the writ of amparo has been created by the Supreme Court in 2007.[187]

This specific remedy provided for the protection of fundamental rights contrasts with the constitutional system of the United States, where the protection of human rights is effectively assured, following the British procedural law tradition, through the general judicial actions and equitable remedies, particularly the injunctions, which are also used to protect any other kind of personal or property rights or interests.

The amparo proceeding was first introduced in Mexico in 1857 as the *juicio de amparo*, evolving in that country into a unique and very complex institution exclusively found in Mexico, not only designed to guaranty judicial protection of constitutional guarantees against the State acts or actions, but to perform multipurpose judicial roles, including actions and procedures that in all other countries are separated processes, like judicial review, cassation review and judicial review of administrative actions.

In the rest of Latin America the amparo gave rise to a very different specific judicial remedy established with the *exclusive* purpose of protecting human rights and freedoms, becoming in many cases more protective than the original Mexican institution; being named in various ways, always meaning the same, as follows: *Amparo* (Guatemala); *Acción de amparo* (Argentina, Ecuador, Honduras, Paraguay, Uruguay, Dominican Republic, Venezuela); *Acción de tutela* (Colombia); *Proceso de amparo* (El Salvador, Peru); *Recurso de amparo* (Bolivia, Costa Rica, Nicaragua, Panama); *Recurso de protección* (Chile) or *Mandado de segurança* and *mandado de injunçao* (Brazil).[188] In all of the Latin American countries, the provisions for the

---

Homenaje al Profesor Jesús González Pérez, Tomo 3, Editorial Civitas, Madrid, 1993, pp. 2.695–2.740. See also Allan R. Brewer-Carías, *Mecanismos nacionales de protección de los derechos humanos (Garantías judiciales de los derechos humanos en el derecho constitucional comparado latinoamericano)*, Instituto Interamericano de Derechos Humanos, San José, 2005.

186 See, in general, Allan R. Brewer-Carías, *Constitutional Protection of Human Rights in Latin America. A Comparative Study of the Amparo Proceedings*, Cambridge University Press, New York 2009.

187 See, in general, Allan R. Brewer-Carías, "The Latin American Amparo Proceeding and the Writ of Amparo in The Philippines," en *City University of Hong Kong Law Review,* Volume 1:1 October 2009, pp 73–90.

188 See, in general, Allan R. Brewer-Carías, *El amparo a los derechos y garantías constitucionales (una aproximación comparativa)*, Caracas, 1993; Eduardo Ferrer Mac-Gregor, "Breves notas sobre el amparo latinoamericano (desde el derecho procesal constitucional compara-

action are embodied in the constitutions; and in all of them, except Chile, the actions of amparo have been expressly regulated by statutes; particularly in special statutes related to constitutional litigations, with the exception of Panama and Paraguay where the amparo action is regulated in the general procedural codes (*Código Judicial, Código Procesal Civil)*).

Of course, for this specific protective judicial mean to be an effective tool for constitutional litigation, as I expressed in a recent book,

> "The most elemental institutional condition needed in any country, is the existence of a really autonomous and independent Judiciary, out of the reach and control from the other branches of government, empowered to interpret and apply the law in an impartial way and protect citizens, particularly when referring to the enforcement of rights against the State. Such Judiciary has to be built upon the principle of separation of powers. If this principle is not implemented and the Government controls the courts and judges, no effective guaranty can exist regarding constitutional rights, particularly when the offending party is a governmental agency. In this case, and in spite of all constitutional declarations, it is impossible to speak of rule of law, as happens in many Latin American countries."[189]

Unfortunately, this is the current situation in Venezuela, with a Judiciary completely subjected to the Executive Power. That is why, in addition to the analysis of the current regime of the amparo proceeding in the Constitution and in the Amparo Law, I will refer to the tragic situation affecting the Judiciary as a whole, whose independence and autonomy has been progressively dismantled, turning completely ineffective the amparo proceeding.

I.   GENERAL TRENDS OF THE VENEZUELAN AMPARO PROCEEDING

In the case of Venezuela, since 1961, the Constitution establishes a "constitutional right for amparo" or to be protected by the courts,[190] that everybody have for the protection of all the rights, freedoms and guarantees declared in the constitution and in international treaties, or which, even if not listed in the text, are inherent to

---

do)," in Héctor Fix-Zamudio and Eduardo Ferrer Mac-Gregor, *El derecho de amparo en el mundo*, Edit. Porrúa, México, 2006, pp. 3–39.

189   See Allan R. Brewer-Carías, *Constitutional Protection of Human Rights in Latin America. A Comparative Study on the Amparo Proceedings*, Cambridge University Press, New York 2009, p. 418.The

190   Article 49 of the 1961 Constitution, and Article 27 of the 1999 Constitution. See on the action of amparo in Venezuela, in general, see Gustavo Briceño V., *Comentarios a la Ley de Amparo*, Editorial Kinesis, Caracas, 1991; Rafael J. Chavero Gazdik, *El nuevo régimen del amparo constitucional en Venezuela*, Editorial Sherwood, Caracas, 2001; Gustavo José Linares Benzo, *El Proceso de Amparo*, Universidad Central de Venezuela, Facultad de Ciencias Jurídicas y Políticas, Caracas, 1999; Hildegard Rondón De Sansó, *Amparo Constitucional*, Caracas, 1988; Hildegard Rondón De Sansó, *La acción de amparo contra los poderes públicos*, Editorial Arte, Caracas, 1994; Carlos M. Ayala Corao and Rafael J. Chavero Gazdik, "El amparo constitucional en Venezuela," in Héctor Fix-Zamudio and Eduardo Ferrer Mac-Gregor (Coord.), *El derecho de amparo en el mundo*, Universidad Nacional Autónoma de México, Editorial Porrúa, México, 2006, pp. 649–692.

the human person. The constitution does not set forth a separate action of habeas corpus for the protection of personal freedom and liberty (habeas corpus), which is included within the scope of the action for amparo.

Additionally, the Venezuelan Constitution has also set forth the habeas data recourse in order to guarantee the right to have access to the information and data concerning the claimant contained in official or private registries, as well as to know about the use that has been made of such information and about its purpose, and to petition the competent court for the updating, rectification or destruction of erroneous records and those that unlawfully affect the petitioner's rights (Article 28).

The amparo proceeding, has been regulated in the 1988 Organic Law on Amparo for the protection of constitutional rights and guaranties (*Ley Orgánica de Amparo sobre derechos y garantías constitucionales*),[191] in which it has been set forth that the right to amparo that can be exercised through two different judicial means: first, an "autonomous action for amparo"[192] that in general is filed before the first instance courts[193] (Article 7 Amparo Law), with a re-establishing nature, in general regarding flagrant, vulgar, direct and immediate constitutional harm upon the plaintiff's rights; and second, by means of other preexisting ordinary or extraordinary legal actions or recourses already established in the legal system to which an amparo petition is joined. That is, the amparo petition can be joined to the popular action of unconstitutionality of statutes; the judicial review of administrative actions' recourses; and to other "ordinary judicial procedures" or "preexisting judicial means," through which

---

191 See *Gaceta Oficial* n° 33.891 of January 22, 1988. See Allan R. Brewer-Carías, Carlos M. Ayala Corao and Rafael Chavero G., *Ley Orgánica de Amparo sobre Derechos y Garantías Constitucionales*, Caracas, 2007. See also Allan R. Brewer-Carías, *Instituciones Políticas y Constitucionales, Tomo V, El derecho y la acción de amparo*, Editorial Jurídica Venezolana, Caracas, 1998, pp. 163 ff.; Hildegard Rondón de Sansó, *Amparo constitucional*, Caracas, 1988; Gustavo J. Linares Benzo, *El proceso de amparo*, Universidad Central de Venezuela, Caracas, 1999; Rafael J. Chavero Gazdik, *El Nuevo regimen del amparo constitucional en Venezuela*, Editorial Sherwood, Caracas, 2001; Carlos Ayala Corao and Rafael Chavero G., "El amparo constitucional en Venezuela," in Héctor Fix-Zamudio and Eduardo Ferrer Mac-Gregor, *Idem*, Edit. Porrúa, México, 2006, pp. 649–692.

192 See Allan R. Brewer-Carías, "El derecho de amparo y la acción de amparo," in *Revista de Derecho Público*, n° 22, Editorial Jurídica Venezolana, Caracas, 1985, pp. 51 ff.

193 According to Article 7 of the Organic Law on Amparo, the competent courts to decide amparo actions are the courts of First Instance with competent on matters related to the constitutional rights or guaranties violated, in the place where the facts, acts or omission have occurred. Regarding amparo of personal freedom and security, the competent courts should be the criminal first instance courts (Article 40). Nonetheless, when the facts, acts or omissions harming or threatening to harm the constitutional right or guaranty occurs in a place where no First Instance court exists, the amparo action may be brought before and any judge of the site, which must decide according to the law, and in a twenty-four hour delay it must send the files for consultation to the competent First Instance court (Article 9). Only in cases in which facts, acts or omissions of the President of the Republic, his Cabinet members, the National Electoral Council, the Prosecutor General, the Attorney General and the General Comptroller of the Republic are involved does the power to decide the amparo actions correspond to the Constitutional Chamber of the Supreme Tribunal of Justice (Article 8).

the "violation or threat of violation of a constitutional right or guaranty may be alleged."[194]

From these regulations it results that the Venezuelan right for amparo, has certain peculiarities that distinguish it from the other similar institutions for the protection of the constitutional rights and guaranties established in Latin America,[195] being characterized by the following general trends:

First, it can be exercised for the protection of all constitutional rights, not only of civil individual rights. Consequently, the social, economic, cultural, environmental and political rights declared in the constitution and in international treaties are also protected by means of amparo. As aforementioned, the habeas corpus is an aspect of the right to constitutional protection, or one of the expressions of the amparo. Conversely, the habeas data action is conceived as a separate action.

Second, the right to amparo seeks to assure the protection of constitutional rights and guaranties against any disturbance in their enjoyment and exercise that can be originated not only in public authority's actions or omissions but also in private individuals ones. In addition, in the case of disturbance by public authorities, the amparo is admissible against statutes; against legislative, administrative and judicial acts; and against material or factual courses of action of Public Administration or public officials.

Third, the decision of the judge, as a consequence of the exercise of this right to amparo, is not limited to be of a precautionary or preliminary nature, but to reestablish the infringed legal situation by deciding on the merits, that is, the constitutionality of the alleged disturbance of the constitutional right.

Fourth, the competent courts on matters of amparo are all the first instance courts, and if no such court exists in the place of the events, any court is competent to receive the petition.

Fifth, because the Venezuelan system of judicial review is a mixed one, judicial review of legislation can also be exercised by the courts when deciding action for amparo when, for instance, the alleged violation of the right is based on a statute deemed unconstitutional. In such cases, if the protection requested is granted by the courts, it must previously declare the statute inapplicable on the grounds of it being unconstitutional. Therefore, in such cases, judicial review of the constitutionality of legislation can also be exercised when an action for amparo of fundamental rights is filed.

Finally, an extraordinary review recourse, with some similarities to the writ for certiorari has been established, granting the Constitutional Chamber of the Supreme Court the power to review final decisions issued in amparo proceedings, and also by

---

194 Allan R. Brewer-Carías, "La reciente evolución jurisprudencial en relación a la admisibilidad del recurso de amparo," in *Revista de derecho público*, n° 19, Caracas, 1984, pp. 207–218.

195 See, in general, H. Fix-Zamudio, *La protección procesal de los derechos humanos ante las jurisdicciones nacionales,* Madrid, 1982, p. 366.

any court when applying the diffuse method of judicial review resolving the inapplicability of statutes because they are considered unconstitutional (Article 336,10).

Very briefly, the following are the main aspects to be highlighted regarding the
legal provisions governing this proceeding:

Regarding the *injured party*, one of the most distinguishable principles pf the
amparo proceeding as an extraordinary judicial mean for the protection of constitutional rights is the principle of bilateralism, which implies the need for the existence
of a controversy between two or more parties. The main consequence of this principle is that the amparo proceeding can only be initiated at a party's request, which
excludes any case of *ex officio* amparo proceeding.

Consequently, in order to initiate this proceeding, an action must be brought before a court by a plaintiff as the injured party, against the injurer party or parties,
who as defendants, must be called to the procedure as having caused the harm or the
violation to the constitutional rights of the former.

The injured party, in principle is the person having the constitutional right that
has been violated; a situation that gives him a particular interest in bringing the case
before a court. That is why the amparo action has been considered as an action *in
personam* (*personalísima*) through which, seeking for the protection of constitutional rights, the plaintiff must be precisely the injured or aggrieved person.

Regarding the *justiciable constitutional rights and guarantees*[196] as a matter of
principle, in Venezuela, are protected through the amparo proceeding: first, the
rights expressly declared in the constitution; second, those rights that even not enumerated in the constitution are inherent to human beings; and third, those rights
enumerated in the international instruments on human rights ratified by the State,
that in Venezuela have constitutional rank being applied with preference in all cases
in which they provide more favorable conditions for the enjoyment of the right (article 23, Constitution). Consequently, all the rights listed in the constitution are protected though the amparo action; being those rights, the citizenship rights, the civil
rights, the political rights, the social and family rights, the cultural and educational
rights, the economic rights, the environmental rights and the indigenous people's
rights enumerated in Articles 19 to 129. Additionally, all other constitutional rights
and guaranties derived from other constitutional provisions can also be protected
even if not included in Title III, like for instance, the constitutional guaranty of the
independence of the Judiciary, or the constitutional guaranty of the legality of taxation (that taxes can only by set forth by statute).[197] Also, regarding the protected
rights, through the open clause of constitutional rights, the constitution admits the
amparo action for the protection of those other constitutional rights and guaranties

---

196 "Their quality of being suitable to be protected by courts." See Brian A. Garner (Editor in
    Chief), *Black's Law Dictionary*, West Group, St. Paul, Minn. 2001, p. 391.

197 See Allan R. Brewer-Carías, *Instituciones Políticas y Constitucionales*, Vol V, *Derecho y
    Acción de Amparo,* Caracas, 1998, pp. 209 ff. See decision of the First Court on Judicial Re-
    view of Administrative Action, *Fecadove* case, in Rafael Chavero G., *El nuevo régimen del
    amparo constitucional en Venezuela*, Ed. Sherwood, Caracas, 2001, p. 157.

not expressly listed in the constitution, but that can be considered inherent to human beings (article 22, Constitution).

Regarding the *injuries* violating constitutional rights, against which the amparo action is established, they can consist of harms or threats affecting those rights. These injuries –harms or threats– caused to constitutional rights, in order to be protected by means of the amparo proceeding, must be evident, actual and real, that is, they must affect personally and directly the rights of the plaintiff, in a manifestly arbitrary, illegal and illegitimate way, which the plaintiff must not have consented.

In addition, regarding harms, they must have a reparable character; and regarding threats, they must affect the rights in an imminent way. That is why, the type of injuries inflicted on constitutional rights, conditions the purpose of the amparo proceeding: if harms, being reparable, the amparo has a restorative effect; and if threats, being imminent, the amparo has a preventive effect.

That is, in case of harms, the amparo proceeding seeks to restore the enjoyment of the plaintiff's injured right, reestablishing the situation existing when the right was harmed, by eliminating or suspending, if necessary, the detrimental act or fact. In this regard, the amparo action has some similarities with the reparative injunctions in the United States, which seeks to eliminate the effects of a past wrong or to compel the defendant to engage in a course of action that seeks to correct those effects.[198]

However, in some cases, due to the factual nature of the harm that has been inflicted, these restorative effects cannot be obtained, in which cases the amparo decision must tend to place the plaintiff right "in the situation closest or more similar to the one that existed before the injury was caused."[199]

---

198   As has been explained by Owen M. Fiss: "To see how it works, let us assume that a wrong has occurred (such as an act of discrimination). Then the missions of an injunction – classically conceived as a preventive instrument– would be to prevent the recurrence of the wrongful conduct in the future (stop discriminating and do not discriminate again). But in *United States v. Louisiana* (380 U.S. 145, (1965)), a voting discrimination case, Justice Black identified still another mission for the injunction: the elimination of the effects of the past wrong (the past discrimination). The reparative injunction –long thought by the nineteenth-century textbook writers, such as High (A *Treatise on the Law of Injunction* 3, 1873) to be an analytical impossibility– was thereby legitimated. And in the same vein, election officials have been ordered not only to stop discriminating in the future elections, but also to set aside a past election and to run a new election as a means of removing the taint of discrimination that infected the first one (*Bell v. Southwell*, 376 F.2de 659 (5TH Cir. 1976)). Similarly, public housing officials have been ordered to both cease discriminating on the basis of race in their future choices of sites and to build units in the white areas as a means of eliminating the effects of the past segregative policy (placing public housing projects only in the black areas of the city) (*Hills v. Gautreaux*, 425 U.S. 284 (1976)). Seen Owen M. Fiss, *The Civil Rights Injunction*, Indiana University Press, 1978, pp.7–10.

199   In this sense, it has been decided by the former Venezuelan Supremo Court of Justice ruling that "one of the principal characteristics of the amparo action is to be a restorative (*restablecedor*) judicial means, the mission of which is to restore the infringed situation or, what is the same, to put the claimant again in the enjoyment of his infringed constitutional

However, as mentioned, the amparo proceeding is not only a judicial mean seeking to restore harmed constitutional rights, it is also a judicial mean established for the protection of such rights against illegitimate threats that violate those rights. It is in these cases that the amparo proceeding has a preventive character in the sense of avoiding harm, similar to the United States preventive civil rights injunctions seeking "to prohibit some act or series of acts from occurring in the future,"[200] and designed "to avoid future harm to a party by prohibiting or mandating certain behavior by another party."[201]

The main condition for the filing of an amparo actions against threats (*amenaza*) to constitutional rights, is that they must be real, certain, immediate, imminent, possible and realizable. And this is important because there are some constitutional rights that essentially and precisely need to be protected against threats, like the right to life in cases of imminent death threats, because on the contrary, they could lose all sense. In this case, the only way to guaranty the right to life is to avoid the threats to be materialized, for instance, by providing the person with effective police protection.

Regarding the *injuring party*, because as mentioned, the amparo procedure is governed by the principle of bilateralism, the party that initiates it must always file the action against an injuring party, whose actions or omissions are those that have caused the harm or threats. This means that the action must always be filed against a person or a public entity that must also be individuated as defendant.[202] That is why in the amparo proceeding, as well as the injunctions in the United States, the final result has to be a judicial order "addressed to some clearly identified individual, not just the general citizenry."[203]

It is true that the amparo proceeding was originally created to protect individuals against the State; and that is why some countries like Mexico remain with that tradi-

---

rights." See Decision of February 6, 1996, *Asamblea legislativa del Estado Bolívar* case. See in Rafael Chavero, *El nuevo régimen del amparo constitucional en Venezuela*, Ed. Sherwood, Caracas, 2001, pp. 185, 242–243.

200 See Owen M. Fiss, *The Civil Rights Injunction*, Indiana University Press, 1978, p. 7.

201 See William M. Tabb and Elaine W. Shoben, *Remedies*, Thompson West, 2005, p. 22. In Spanish the word "preventive" is used in procedural law (medidas preventivas o cautelares) to refer to the "temporary" or "preliminary" orders or restraints that in the United States the judge can issue during the proceeding. So the preventive character of the amparo and of the injunctions cannot be confused with the "medidas preventivas" or temporary or preliminary measures that the courts can issue during the trial for the immediate protection of rights, facing the prospect of an irremediable harm that can be caused.

202 The only exception to the principle of bilateralism is the case of Chile, where the offender is not considered a defendant party but only a person whose activity is limited to inform the court and give it the documents it has. That is why in the Regulation set forth by the Supreme Court (*Auto Acordado*) it is said that the affected state organ, person or public officer "can" just appear as party in the process (4). See Juan Manuel Errazuriz G. and Jorge Miguel Otero A., *Aspectos procesales del recurso de protección*, Editorial Jurídica de Chile 1989, p. 27.

203 See Owen M. Fiss, *The Civil Rights Injunction*, Indiana University Press, 1978, p. 12.

tional trend; but that initial trend has not prevented the possibility for the admission of the amparo proceeding for the protection of constitutional rights against other individual's actions. The current situation is that in the majority of Latin American countries the admission of the amparo action against individuals is accepted, as is the case in Argentina, Bolivia, Chile, the Dominican Republic, Paraguay, Peru, Venezuela and Uruguay, as well as, although in a more restrictive way, in Colombia, Costa Rica, Ecuador, Guatemala and Honduras. Only a minority of Latin American countries the amparo action remains exclusively as a protective mean against authorities, as is the case in Brazil, El Salvador, Panama, Mexico and Nicaragua. This is also the case in the United States where the civil rights injunctions, in matters of constitutional or civil rights or guaranties,[204] can only be admitted against public entities.[205]

But of course, being the amparo action originally established to defend constitutional rights against the State and authorities violations, the most common and important injuring parties in the amparo proceeding are the public authorities or public officials.

The general principle in this matter in Venezuela, with some exceptions, is that any authority can be questioned through amparo actions, and that any act, fact or omission of any public authority or entity or public officials causing an injury to constitutional rights can be challenged by means of such actions. That is also why the courts in Venezuela have decided that "there is no State act that can be excluded from revision by means of amparo.[206]

---

204   In other matters the injunctions can be filed against any person as "higher public officials or private persons." See M. Glenn Abernathy and Barbara A. Perry, *Civil Liberties under the Constitution*, Sixth Edition, University of South Carolina Press, 1993, p. 8.

205   As explained by M. Glenn Abernathy and Barbara A. Perry: "Limited remedies for private interference with free choice. Another problem in the citizen's search for freedom from restriction lies in that many types of interference stemming from private persons do not constitute actionable wrongs under the law. Private prejudice and private discrimination do not, in the absence of specific statutory provisions, offer grounds for judicial intervention on behalf of the sufferer. If one is denied admission to membership in a social club, for example, solely on the basis of his race or religion or political affiliation, he may understandably smart under the rejection, but the courts cannot help him (again assuming no statutory provision barring such distinctions). There are, then, many types of restraints on individual freedom of choice which are beyond the authority of courts to remove or ameliorate. It should be noted that the guaranties of rights in the U.S. Constitution only protect against governmental action and do not apply to purely private encroachments, except for the Thirteenth Amendment's prohibition of slavery. Remedies for private invasion must be found in statutes, the common law, or administrative agency regulations and adjudications." *Idem*, p. 6.

206   See the former Supreme Court of Justice decision dated January 31, 1991, *Anselmo Natale* case, in *Revista de Derecho Público*, n° 45, Editorial Jurídica Venezolana, Caracas, 1991, p. 118. See also the decision of the First Court on Judicial Review of Administrative Action of June 18, 1992, in *Revista de Derecho Público*, n° 46, Editorial Jurídica Venezolana, Caracas, 1991, p. 125. This universality character of the amparo regarding public authorities acts or omissions, according to the Venezuelan courts, implies that: "From what Article 2 of the Amparo law sets forth, it results that no type of conduct, regardless of its nature or character

In this regard, amparo actions can be filed against *legislative actions* or omissions, when they cause harms on constitutional rights of individuals, for instance, acts adopted by parliamentary commissions, and also *statutes*. It is true that that this has been rejected in the majority of Latin American countries, being in some countries accepted like in Venezuela regarding self-executing statutes that can harm the constitutional rights without the need for any other State act executing or applying them, or only regarding the acts applying the particular statute.

Regarding *executive authorities*, the general principle is that the action is admitted against acts, facts or omissions from public entities or bodies conforming to the Public Administration at all its levels (national, state, municipal), including decentralized, autonomous, independent bodies and including acts issued by the Head of the Executive, that is, the President of the Republic.

---

or their authors, can per se be excluded from the amparo judge revision in order to determine if it harms or doesn't harm constitutional rights or guaranties." See decision of the First Court on Judicial Review of Administrative Action of November 11, 1993, *Aura Loreto Rangel* case, in *Revista de Derecho Público*, n° 55–56, Editorial Jurídica Venezolana, Caracas, 1993, p. 284. The same criterion was adopted by the Political Administrative Chamber of the former Supreme Court of Justice in a decision of May 24, 1993, as follows: "The terms on which the amparo action is regulated in Article 49 of the Constitution (now Article 27) are very extensive. If the extended scope of the rights and guaranties that can be protected and restored through this judicial mean is undoubted; the harm cannot be limited to those produced only by some acts. So, in equal terms it must be permitted that any harming act – whether an act, a fact or an omission– with respect to any constitutional right and guaranty, can be challenged by means of this action, due to the fact that the amparo action is the protection of any norm regulating the so-called subjective rights of constitutional rank, it cannot be sustained that such protection is only available in cases in which the injuring act has some precise characteristics, whether from a material or organic point of view. The jurisprudencia of this Court has been constant regarding both principles. In a decision n° 22, dated January 31, 1991, *Anselmo Natale* case, it was decided that 'there is no State act that could not be reviewed by amparo, the latter understood not as a mean for judicial review of constitutionality of State acts in order to annul them, but as a protective remedy regarding public freedoms whose purpose is to reestablish its enjoyment and exercise, when a natural or artificial person, or group or private organization, threatens to harm them or effectively harm them. See, regarding the extended scope of the protected rights, decision of December 4, 1990, *Mariela Morales de Jimenez* case, n° 661, in *Revista de Derecho Público*, n° 55-56, Editorial Jurídica Venezolana, Caracas, 1993, pp. 284–285. In another decision dated February 13, 1992, the First Court ruled: "This Court observes that the essential characteristic of the amparo regime, in its constitutional regulation as well as in its statutory development, is its universality.., so the protection it assures is extended to all subjects (physical or artificial persons), as well as regarding all constitutionally guaranteed rights, including those that without being expressly regulated in the Constitution are inherent to human beings. This is the departing point in order to understand the scope of the constitutional amparo. Regarding Public Administration, the amparo against it is so extended that it can be filed against all acts, omissions and factual actions, without any kind of exclusion regarding some matters that are always related to the public order and social interest." See in *Revista de Derecho Público*, n° 49, Editorial Jurídica Venezolana, Caracas, 1992, pp. 120–121.

Regarding *administrative acts*, as mentioned, the Law admits the filing of amparo actions against them, providing for possibility of exercising the amparo action in two ways: in an autonomous way or conjunctly with nullity recourse for judicial review of the administrative act (Article 5).[207]

Regarding *judicial acts*, contrary to what happens in the majority of Latin American countries, in Venezuela, the amparo action is admitted against them when the corresponding court acts outside its specific competence, issuing arbitrary resolution, decision, or orders that impairs a constitutional right."

On the other hand, being a judicial means specifically established for the protection of constitutional rights, the amparo action is conceived in Venezuela as an *extraordinary judicial instrument* that, consequently, does not substitute for all the other ordinary judicial remedies established for the protection of personal rights and interest. This implies that the amparo action, as a matter of principle, only can be filed when no other adequate judicial mean exists and is available in order to obtain the immediate protection of the violated constitutional rights. This has implied the provisions of rules referred to the admissibility of the action, established in order to determine the existence or inexistence of other adequate judicial mean for the immediate protection of the rights, which justifies or not the use of the extraordinary action.

This rule of admissibility of the amparo action is similar to the general rule existing in the United States regarding the injunctions and all other equitable remedies, like the mandamus and prohibitions, all reserved for extraordinary cases,[208] in the

---

207 Regarding the latter, the former Supreme Court of Justice in the decision of July 10, 1991 (*Tarjetas Banvenez* case), clarified that in such case, the action is not a principal one, but subordinated and ancillary regarding the principal recourse to which it has been attached, and subjected to the final nullifying decision that has to be issued in it. See the text in *Revista de Derecho Público*, n° 47, Editorial Jurídica Venezolana, Caracas, 1991, pp. 169–174, and comments in *Revista de Derecho Público*, n° 50, Editorial Jurídica Venezolana, Caracas, 1992, pp. 183–184. That is why, in such cases, the amparo pretension that must be founded in a grave presumption of the violation of the constitutional right, has a preventive and temporal character, pending the final decision of the nullity suit, consisting in the suspension of the effects of the challenged administrative act. This provisional character of the amparo protection pending the suit is thus subjected to the final decision to be issued in the nullity judicial review procedure against the challenged administrative act. See in *Revista de Derecho Público*, n° 47, Editorial Jurídica Venezolana, Caracas, 1991, pp. 170–171.

208 *Ex-parte Collet*, 337 U.S. 55, 69 S. Ct 944, 93 L. Ed. 1207, 10 A.L.R. 2D 921 (1949). See in John Bourdeau *et al.*, "Injunctions," in Kevin Schroder, John Glenn and Maureen Placilla, *Corpus Juris Secundum*, Volume 43A, Thomson West, 2004, p. 20. This main characteristic of the injunction as an extraordinary remedy has been established since the nineteenth century in *In re Debs* 158 U.S. 564, 15 S.Ct 900, 39 L. Ed. 1092 (1895), in which case, in the words of Justice Brewer, who delivered the opinion of the court, it was decided that: "As a rule, injunctions are denied to those who have adequate remedy at law. Where the choice is between the ordinary and the extraordinary processes of law, and the former are sufficient, the rule will not permit the use of the latter." See in Owen M. Fiss and Doug Rendleman, *Injunctions*, The Foundation Press, Mineola, 1984, p. 8.

sense that they are available only "after the applicant shows that the legal remedies are inadequate."[209]

This extraordinary character of the amparo proceeding also conditions the general rules governing the procedure, which in general terms are related to its bilateral character; to the brief and preferred character of the procedure, and to the role of the courts directing the procedure.

In this regard, one of the most important phases in the procedure is the hearing that the court must convene, also in a very prompt period of time, with the participation of the parties before adopting its decision on the case (Article 26). This hearing which must be oral, public and contradictory, in principle must always take place and must not be suspended.

Two general sorts of *judicial adjudications* can be issued by the courts for the protection of constitutional rights: preliminary measures that can be ordered from the beginning of the procedure, with effects subject to the final court ruling; and the definitive decisions preventing the violation or restoring the enjoyment of the threatened or harmed rights.

The *preliminary measures* are conceived in order to preserve the status quo, avoiding harms or restoring the plaintiff's situation to the original one it had before the harm was inflicted. These preliminary measures, regulated in Amparo Law and the Civil Procedure Code, in order to be adopted, a few conditions must be met. The courts must consider, first, "the appearance of the existence of a good right" (*fumus boni juris*), that is, the need for the petitioner to prove the existence of his constitutional right or guaranty as being violated or threatened; second, the "danger because of the delay" (*periculum in mora*), that is, the need to prove that the delay in granting the preliminary protection will make the harm irreparable; third, the "danger of the harm" (*periculum in dammi*"), that is the need to prove the imminence of the harm that can be caused; and fourth, the balance between the collective and particular interest involved in the case.[210]

These preliminary protective measures can be decided and issued by the court in an immediate way, even without a previous hearing of the potential defendants, that is, *inadi alteram parte* or *inaudita pars*. In a similar sense, as in the United States, in cases of great urgency and when an immediate threat of irreparable injury exists, preliminary injunctions or restraining orders can be issued without giving reasonable notice to the plaintiff, but always balancing the harm sought to be preserved with the rights of notice and hearing.[211]

---

209 *Idem*, p. 59.

210 As for instance has been decided by the Venezuelan First Court on Administrative Jurisdiction, *Video & Juegos Costa Verde, C.A. vs. Prefecto del Municipio Maracaibo del Estado Zulia* case, in *Revista de Derecho Público*, n° 85-98, Editorial Jurídica Venezolana, Caracas, 2001, p. 291.

211 See for instance *Carroll v. President and Com'rs of Princess Anne*, 393 U.S. 175, 89 S. Ct. 347, 21 L. Ed.2d 325, 1968; *Board of Ed. of Community Unit School Dist. N° 101 v. Parlor*, 85 Ill. 2d 397, 54 Ill. Dec 249, 424 N.E 2d 1152, 1981; in John Bourdeau *et al.*, "Injunc-

Regarding the *definitive judicial decisions* in the amparo proceedings, their purpose for the injured party is to obtain the requested judicial protection (*amparo*) of his constitutional rights when illegitimately harmed or threatened by an injuring party.

Consequently, the final result of the process is a formal judicial decision or order issued by the court for the protection of the threatened rights or to restore the enjoyment of the harmed one, which can consist, for instance, in a decision commanding or preventing an action, or commanding someone to do, not to do, or to undo some action.[212] This is to say, the amparo, as the injunction,[213] is a writ framed according to the circumstances of the case commanding an act that the court regards as essential in justice, or restraining an act that it deems contrary to equity and good conscience.

That is why the amparo judicial order in Venezuela is very similar in its purposes and effects not only to the United States' injunction, but also to the other equitable and non-equitable extraordinary remedies, like the mandamus, prohibition and declaratory legal remedies. Accordingly, for instance, the amparo order can be first, of a prohibitory character, similar to the prohibitory injunctions, issued to restrain an action, to forbid certain acts or to command a person to refrain from doing specific acts. Second, it can also be of a mandatory character, that is, like the mandatory injunction requiring the undoing of an act, or the restoring of the status quo; and like the writ of mandamus, issued to compel an action or the execution of some act, or to command a person to do a specific act. Third, the amparo order can also be similar to the writ of prohibition or to the writ of error when the order is directed to a court,[214] which normally happens in the cases of amparo actions filed against judicial decisions. And fourth, it can also be similar to the declaratory legal remedy through which courts are called to declare the constitutional right of the plaintiff regarding the other parties.

Consequently, in the amparo proceeding, the courts have very extensive powers to provide for remedies in order to effectively protect constitutional rights, issuing

---

tions," in Kevin Schroder, John Glenn and Maureen Placilla, *Corpus Juris Secundum*, Volume 43A, Thomson West, 2004, pp. 339 ff.

212   In the United States' injunction, the order can be commanding or preventing virtually any type of action (*Dawkins v. Walker*, 794 So. 2d 333, Ala. 2001; *Levin v. Barish*, 505 Pa. 514, 481 A.2d 1183, 1984), or commanding someone to undo some wrong or injury (*State Game and Fish Com'n v. Sledge*, 344 Ark. 505, 42 S.W.3d 427, 2001). It is a judicial order requiring a person to do or refrain from doing certain acts (*Skolnick v. Altheimer & Gray*, 191 Ill 2d 214, 246 Ill. Dec. 324, 730 N.E.2d 4, 2000), for any period of time, no matter its purpose (*Sheridan County Elec. Co-op v. Ferguson*, 124 Mont. 543, 227 P.2d 597, 1951). *Idem*, p. 19.

213   See *Nussbaum v. Hetzer*, 1, N.J. 171, 62 A. 2d 399 (1948). *Idem*, p. 19.

214   See William M. Tabb and Elaine W. Shoben, *Remedies*, Thomson West, 2005, pp. 86 ff. 246 ff.; and in John Bourdeau *et al.*, "Injunctions," in Kevin Schroder, John Glenn and Maureen Placilla, *Corpus Juris Secundum*, Volume 43A, Thompson West, 2004, pp. 21 ff.; 28 ff.

final adjudication, orders to do, to refrain from doing, to undo or to prohibit,[215] or as the Amparo Law establishes in Article 32.b the decision must "determine the conduct to be accomplished."[216]

Another specific aspect that must be mentioned regarding amparo decisions in Venezuela is that it has no compensatory character[217] being in this case the function of the courts only to protect the plaintiff's rights and not to condemn the defendant to pay the plaintiff any sort of compensation for damages caused by the injury.[218] The judicial actions tending to seek for compensation from the defendant, because of its liability as a consequence of the injury inflicted to the constitutional right of the plaintiff, must be filed by means of a separate ordinary judicial remedy established for such purpose before the civil or administrative judicial jurisdiction.[219]

One last aspect that must be highlighted regarding the effects of the amparo decision refers to its obligatory character. As all judicial decisions, the amparo ruling is obligatory not only for the parties to the process but regarding all other persons or public officers that must apply them.

In order to execute the decision, the courts, *ex officio* or at the party's request, can adopt all the measures directed to its accomplishment. Yet the amparo judges in Venezuela do not have direct power to punish by imposing criminal sanctions for disobedience of their rulings. In other words, they do not have criminal contempt power, which in contrast is one of the most important features of the injunctive relief system in the United States.[220] These contempt powers are precisely what gave the

---

215 See Allan R. Brewer-Carías, *Instituciones Políticas y Constitucionales,* Vol. V, *Derecho y Acción de Amparo,* Editorial Jurídica Venezolana, Caracas, 1998, pp. 143 ff.

216 Rafael Chavero G. *El nuevo amparo constitucional en Venezuela,* Ed. Sherwood, Caracas, 2001, p. 185 ff., 327 ff.; Allan R. Brewer-Carías, *Instituciones Políticas y Constitucionales,* Vol. V, *Derecho y Acción de Amparo,* Editorial Jurídica Venezolana, Caracas, 1998, pp. 399 ff.

217 In a similar way to the United States injunctions. See *Simenstad v. Hagen,* 22 Wis. 2d 653, 126 N.W.2d 529, 1964, in John Bourdeau et al., "Injunctions," in Kevin Schroder, John Glenn and Maureen Placilla, *Corpus Juris Secundum,* Volume 43A, Thomson West, 2004, p. 20.

218 For instance in the case of an illegitimate administrative order issued by a municipal authority demolishing a building, if executed, even if it violates the constitutional right to property, the amparo action has not the purpose to compensate, being in this case inadmissible, particularly due to the irreparable character of the harm.

219 Article 27 of the Venezuelan Amparo Law also expressly provides that in cases of granting an amparo, the court must send copy of the decision to the competent authority where the public officer causing the harm works, in order to impose the corresponding disciplinary measures.

220 This is particularly important regarding criminal contempt, which was established since the *In Re Debs* case (158 U.S. 564, 15 S.Ct. 900, 39 L.Ed. 1092 (1895)), where according to Justice Brewer who delivered the court's opinion, it was ruled: "But the power of a court to make an order carries with it the equal power to punish for a disobedience of that order, and the inquiry as to the question of disobedience has been, from time immemorial, the special function of the court. And this is no technical rule. In order that a court may compel obedi-

injunction in the United States its effectiveness regarding any disobedience, being the same court empowered to vindicate its own power by imposing criminal or economic sanctions by means of imprisonment and fines. In Venezuela, in contrast, the amparo courts do not have such powers, and regarding the application of criminal sanctions to the disobedient party, the amparo courts or the interested party must seek for the initiation of a judicial criminal procedure against the disobedient to be brought before the competent criminal courts (Article 31

Finally, it must be noted that due to the general by-instance procedural principle, the amparo decisions can be appealed before the superior courts according to the general rules established in the procedural codes. In addition, as aforementioned, the Constitutional Chamber of the Supreme Court as Constitutional Jurisdiction has the power to review lower courts' decisions on constitutional matters, including amparo decisions, in a discretionary basis,[221] by means of *an extraordinary recourse for review* (Article 336.10).

II. THE FRUSTRATION ON MATTERS OF AMPARO DUE TO THE LACK OF AUTONOMY AND INDEPENDENCE OF THE COURTS

From what has been said, undoubtedly, and in theory, Venezuela has established one of the most complete and comprehensive regulations regarding the amparo proceeding.

But as afore mentioned, the country lacks the basic condition for any amparo proceeding to be effective, that is, the existence of a really autonomous and independent Judiciary, out of the reach and control from the other branches of government, that could allow the courts to interpret and apply the law in an impartial way, and to protect citizens, particularly when referring to the enforcement of rights against authorities. On the contrary, in Venezuela, the Government controls the courts and judges, being completely impossible to enforce and defend rights particularly when the offending party is a governmental agency. That is, that if it is true that in the past the amparo proceeding worked as a very important tool, widely used for the protection of constitutional rights, particularly against public authorities, nowadays, however, this is a matter of the past; it is history.

---

ence to its order it must have the right to inquire whether there has been any disobedience thereof. To submit the question of disobedience to another tribunal, be it a jury or another court, would operate to deprive the proceedings of half its efficiency." In *Watson v. Williams*, 36 Miss. 331, 341, it was said: "The power to fine and imprison for contempt, from the earliest history of jurisprudence, has been regarded as the necessary incident and attribute of a court, without which it could no more exist than without a judge. It is a power inherent in all courts of record, and coexisting with them by the wise provisions of the common law. A court without the power effectually to protect itself against the assaults of the lawless, or to enforce its orders, judgments, or decrees against the recusant parties before it, would be a disgrace to the legislation, and a stigma upon the age which invented it." See Owen M. Fiss and Doug Rendleman, *Injunctions*, The Foundation Press, 1984, p. 13. See also William M. Tabb and Elaine W. Shoben, *Remedies*, Thomson West, 2005, pp. 72 ff.

221 In a similar way to the writ of certiorari in the United States. See Jesús María Casal, *Constitución y Justicia Constitucional*, Caracas, 2002, p. 92.

That is why, instead of describing in more detail an institution like the amparo proceeding that in practice is completely ineffective when used against the State, I think it is important to analyze the situation of the Judiciary in Venezuela, in the process the country has suffered of dismantling the rule of law and the democratic regime, using constitutional provisions and even democratic tools;[222] a process in which, in a contradictory way, the Supreme Tribunal has been one of the main tools used by the authoritarian government for such purposes.

The fact is that since 1999, a tragic setback has occurred in Venezuela regarding democratic standards and the rule of law, a country that just a few decades ago was envied for its institution building and democratic accomplishments. The past decade, on the contrary, has shown a continuous, persistent, and deliberate process of demolishing the rule of law institutions[223] and of destroying democracy in a way never before experienced in all the constitutional history of the country.[224]

In December of 1999, the people of Venezuela approved a new Constitution considered by many as one of the best Constitutions in contemporary Latin America; an assertion with which I have never agreed, except regarding its provisions precisely referred to human rights and to the system of judicial review that unfortunately are dead words. As Member of the 1999 Constituent Assembly I participated in the drafting of the Constitution, but I was also one of the few members of the Assembly that campaigned for the rejection of the Constitution in the referendum of December 1999.

---

222 See Allan R. Brewer-Carías, *Dismantling Democracy. The Chávez Authoritarian Experiment*, Cambridge University Press, New York, 2010.

223 See in *general*, Allan R. Brewer-Carías, "La progresiva y sistemática demolición de la autonomía e independencia del Poder Judicial en Venezuela (1999-2004)," in *XXX Jornadas J.M Dominguez Escovar, Estado de Derecho, Administración de Justicia y Derechos Humanos*, Instituto de Estudios Jurídicos del Estado Lara, Barquisimeto 2005, pp. 33-174; Allan R. Brewer-Carías, "El constitucionalismo y la emergencia en Venezuela: entre la emergencia formal y la emergencia anormal del Poder Judicial," in Allan R. Brewer-Carías, *Estudios Sobre el Estado Constitucional (2005-2006)*, Editorial Jurídica Venezolana, Caracas 2007, pp. 245-269; and Allan R. Brewer-Carías "La justicia sometida al poder. La ausencia de independencia y autonomía de los jueces en Venezuela por la interminable emergencia del Poder Judicial (1999-2006)," in *Cuestiones Internacionales. Anuario Jurídico Villanueva 2007*, Centro Universitario Villanueva, Marcial Pons, Madrid 2007, pp. 25-57, available at www.allanbrewercarias.com, (Biblioteca Virtual, II.4. Artículos y Estudios N° 550, 2007) pp. 1-37. See also Allan R. Brewer-Carías, *Historia Constitucional de Venezuela*, Editorial Alfa, Tomo II, Caracas 2008, pp. 402-454.

224 See, in general, Allan R. Brewer-Carías, "El autoritarismo establecido en fraude a la Constitución y a la democracia y su formalización en "Venezuela mediante la reforma constitucional. (De cómo en un país democrático se ha utilizado el sistema eleccionario para minar la democracia y establecer un régimen autoritario de supuesta "dictadura de la democracia" que se pretende regularizar mediante la reforma constitucional)" in the book *Temas constitucionales. Planteamientos ante una Reforma*, Fundación de Estudios de Derecho Administrativo, FUNEDA, Caracas 2007, pp. 13-74; and "La demolición del Estado de Derecho en Venezuela Reforma Constitucional y fraude a la Constitución (1999-2009)," in *El Cronista del Estado Social y Democrático de Derecho*, N° 6, Editorial Iustel, Madrid 2009, pp. 52-61.

Nonetheless the most chocking fact regarding this celebrated Constitution is that it has been constantly violated by all branches of government, and more seriously, by the Supreme Tribunal of Justice and its Constitutional Chamber, theoretically designed to be the guarantor par excellence of the Constitution. Contrary to that role, in Venezuela, the Constitutional Chamber, as Constitutional Jurisdiction, equivalent to a Constitutional Court, has been completely controlled by the Executive, and as such, as I mentioned, has been the main tool used to erode the rule of law and, to sustain authoritarianism, legitimizing all the constitutional violations that have occurred.

The result of this process has been the complete lack of all essential elements that a rule of law and a democratic state request, which are much more than voting in elections and referenda.

This process of dismantling the rule of law in Venezuela began in the same year 1999, when the then newly elected President of the Republic, Hugo Chávez on the same day of his first Inauguration, convened a non-plural Constituent Assembly (February 2, 1999)[225] which was not established in the Constitution as a mean for constitutional review, based on a very ambiguous ruling issued by the Supreme Court of Justice (January 19, 1999),[226] without deciding the merits of what had been requested.[227] The result of this initial and unconstitutional decision adopted by President Chávez[228] was the election, on July 1999, of a costume-made Constituent Assembly, completely controlled by the President's followers, being used as the main tool for the political assault on all branches of government, ignoring the provisions of the then in force Constitution. This elected Constituent Assembly, technically was

---

225 See Decree N° 3 of February 2, 1999, in *Gaceta Oficial* N° 36.634 of February 2, 1999.

226 See the text of the decisions in Allan R. Brewer–Carías, *Poder Constituyente Originario y Asamblea Nacional Constituyente,* Editorial Jurídica Venezolana, Caracas 1998, pp. 25 a 53; and the comment regarding its content, in pp. 55 a 114. See also in Allan R. Brewer–Carías, *Asamblea Constituyente y Ordenamiento Constitucional,* Academia de Ciencias Políticas y Sociales, Caracas 1998, pp. 153 a 228; and in *Revista de Derecho Público,* N° 77–80, Editorial Jurídica Venezolana, Caracas 1999, pp. 56 ff. and 68 ff. Regarding these decisions, Lolymar Hernández Camargo has expressed that "far from giving answer to the important question raised to the Court, opened the possibility for a consultative referendum, but without establishing the mechanism that can allow its convening, leaving that task entirely to the 'competent organs,'" in *La Teoría del Poder Constituyente. Un caso de estudio: el proceso constituyente venezolano de 1999,* UCAT, San Cristóbal 2000, pp. 54-63

227 See Allan R. Brewer–Carías, "La configuración judicial del proceso constituyente o de cómo el guardián de la Constitución abrió el camino para su violación y para su propia extinción," in *Revista de Derecho Público,* N° 77–80, Editorial Jurídica Venezolana, Caracas 1999, pp. 453 y ss.; y *Golpe de Estado y proceso constituyente en Venezuela,* UNAM, México, 2001, pp. 60 ff.

228 See the text of the popular action filed seeeking to annul on grounds of its unconstitutionality the presidencial Decree, in Allan R. Brewer–Carías, *Asamblea Constituyente y Ordenamiento Constitucional,* Academia de Ciencias Políticas y Sociales, Caracas 1999, pp. 255 a 321. See also Carlos M. Escarrá Malavé, *Proceso Político y Constituyente,* Caracas 1999, anexo 4.

the result of a coup d'état given against the Constitution,[229] and in addition, it was itself the instrument used to give another coup d'état against the existing constituted powers,[230] interfering upon all the then elected, and non-elected branches of government, particularly the Judicial Power, whose autonomy and independence began to be progressively and systematically demolished.[231] All this happened, unfortunately, with the consent and complicity of the former Supreme Court of Justice that endorsed the creation of a Commission of Judicial Emergency,[232] which after eleven years continues to function although with another name, in violation of the new Constitution.[233]

All these acts of the Constituent Assembly were challenged before the then already bend Supreme Court, which in another much criticized decision of October 14, 1999, upheld their constitutionality, recognizing the Constituent Assembly supposed supra-constitutional power. This was the only way to justify the unconstitu-

---

229 The Assembly assumed in its By-Laws, an "original constituent power." See in *Gaceta Constituyente (Diario de Debates), Agosto–Septiembre 1999*, Session, August 7, 1999, Nº 4, p. 144. In the inauguration act of the Assembly, its President said "the National Constituent Assembly is original and sovereign," in *Gaceta Constituyente (Diario de Debates), Agosto–Septiembre 1999*, Sesión de 03–08–99, Nº 1, p. 4. See the text also in *Gaceta Oficial* Nº 36.786 of September 14, 1999. As pointed out by Lolymar Hernández Camargo, with this By-Laws, "the inobservance of the popular will that had imponed limits to the National Constituent Assembly was materialized, … The Assembly proclaimed itself as original, absolute constituent power, without limits, having the State lost its raison d'être, because if the popular will and its normative expression (the Constitution) was violated, it is not possible to qualify the State as a rule of law and much less as democratic," in *La Teoría del Poder Constituyente*, UCAT, San Cristóbal 2000, p. 73. See my dissident votes regarding the approval of the By-Laws of the Assembly in Allan R. Brewer–Carías, *Debate Constituyente, (Aportes a la Asamblea Nacional Constituyente)* tomo I, *(8 agosto–8 septiembre 1999)*, Caracas 1999, pp. 15-39. See also en *Gaceta Constituyente (Diario de Debates), Agosto–Septiembre 1999*, Session of August 7, 1999, Nº 4, pp. 6-13

230 See Allan R. Brewer-Carías, "Constitution Making in Defraudation of the Constitution and Authoritarian Government in Defraudation of Democracy. The Recent Venezuelan Experience", en *Lateinamerika Analysen*, 19, 1/2008, GIGA, German Institute of Global and Area Studies, Institute of Latin American Studies, Hamburg 2008, pp. 119-142

231 On Auguts 19, 1999, the National Constituent Assembly decided to declare "the Judicial Power in emergency." *Gaceta Oficial* Nº 36.772 of August 25, 1999 reprinted in *Gaceta Oficial* Nº 36.782 of September 8, 1999. See in Allan R. Brewer–Carías, *Debate Constituyente*, tomo I, Fundación de Derecho Público, Editoriual Jurídica Venezolana, Caracas 1999, p. 57-73; and in *Gaceta Constituyente (Diario de Debates), Agosto–Septiembre de 1999,,* Session of August 18, 1999, Nº 10, pp. 17-22. See the text of the decree in *Gaceta Oficial* Nº 36.782 of September 08, 1999.

232 "Resolution" of the Supreme Court of Justice of August 23, 1999. See the comments regarding this Resolution in en Allan R. Brewer–Carías, *Debate Constituyente*, tomo I, Fundación de Derecho Público, Editoriual Jurídica Venezolana, Caracas 1999, pp. 141 ff. See also the comments of Lolymar Hernández Camargo, *La Teoría del Poder Constituyente*, UCAT, San Cristóbal 2000, pp. 75 ff.

233 See Allan R. Brewer–Carías, *Golpe de Estado y proceso constituyente en Venezuela*, Universidad Nacional Autónoma de México, México 2002, p. 160.

tional intervention of all the existing branches of governments, including the Judiciary, for which the Court paid a very high price, which was its own existence. With such decision, the Court pronounced its own death sentence, disappearing two months later as the first victim of the authoritarian government, which it helped to grab power.

This happened in December 22 of the same year 1999, in a decision adopted by the Constituent Assembly after the new Constitution was popularly approved (December 15, 1999), when the Assembly, violating both, the old (still in force) 1961 Constitution, and the new (approved but still not published) 1999 Constitution,[234] eliminated the Supreme Court itself, and dismissed its Magistrates and all the other public officials elected only a few months earlier. This was achieved through the enactment of a Transitory Constitutional Regime[235] which was not submitted to popular approval. In particular, regarding the Judiciary, the result of such Regime was the appointment of new Magistrates of the new Supreme Tribunal of Justice, without fulfilling the conditions established in the to-be new Constitution, completely packed with Chávez' supporters. That Supreme Tribunal has precisely been the one that during the past decade has been the most ominous instrument for consolidating authoritarianism in the country.

Today, eleven years after the 1999 constitution making-process, a centralized, militaristic, and concentrated authoritarian regime has been imposed to the Venezuelans, following a socialist model of society for which nobody has voted, that is based in a supposed "participatory democracy" which is directly controlled by the central government. Within such system, despite the political rhetoric, exuberant spending and waste of an immense public income, of a rich state in a poor country, no effective social and economic reforms or improvements have been achieved, except the building of an enormous bureaucratic State that has appropriated or confiscated all main private enterprises in the country, consolidating a corrupt and inefficient system of capitalism of State.

In this process, again, the Supreme Tribunal and particularly its Constitutional Chamber, has been the main tool in order to legitimate the violations of the Constitution; and particularly the perversion of many of its institutions and provisions that have been used by the government in order to strengthen the concentration of power, the state centralization, the extreme presidentialism, the extensive state participation in the economy, and the general marginalization of civil society in public activities.

All these institutional deformations lead the President of the Republic to propose in 2007, a Constitutional Reform aimed to consolidate the authoritarian regime in the Constitution itself, formally regulating a socialist, centralized, military and po-

---

234 See in *Gaceta Constituyente (Diario de Debates), Noviembre 1999–Enero 2000,* Session of December 22, 1999, N° 51, pp. 2 ff. See *Gaceta Oficial* N° 36.859 of December 29, 1999; and *Gaceta Oficial* N° 36.860 of December 30, 1999.

235 See in *Gaceta Oficial* N° 36.859 of December 29, 1999.

lice state.[236] The National Assembly sanctioned those reforms proposals in November 2, 2007, violating the Constitution because no substantive reforms of such kind are allowed to be made through the constitutional review procedure, but only by means of the convening of a new Constituent Assembly. Of course, the Supreme Tribunal, very diligently, refused to decide all the multiple judicial review challenges filed against the proposal of the unconstitutional Constitutional Reform.[237] Nonetheless, fortunately, the people rejected the reforms proposal in the referendum held on December 2, 2007, but unfortunately, the rejection has been mocked by Government, which during the past three years, defrauding the Constitution, has been implementing the rejected reforms by means of ordinary legislation or through decree-laws unconstitutionally enacted.[238] The President of the Republic was completely sure that the submissive Constitutional Chamber he had controlled would never exercise any sort of judicial review control over such unconstitutional acts; which showed the complete absence of separation of powers and, consequently, of a democratic and rule of law government. [239]

This has lead to successive illegitimate mutations of the Constitution or constitutional distortions that have been made defrauding the Constitution itself, [240] being

236   See Allan R. Brewer-Carías, *Hacia la consolidación de un Estado Socialista, Centralizado, Policial Y Militarista. Comentarios sobre el sentido y alcance de las propuestas de reforma constitucional 2007,* Colección Textos Legislativos, N° 42, Editorial Jurídica Venezolana, Caracas 2007.

237   See the comments on the various decisions in Allan R. Brewer-Carías, "El juez constitucional vs. la supremacía constitucional. O de cómo la Jurisdicción Constitucional en Venezuela renunció a controlar la constitucionalidad del procedimiento seguido para la "reforma constitucional" sancionada por la Asamblea Nacional el 2 de noviembre de 2007, antes de que fuera rechazada por el pueblo en el referendo del 2 de diciembre de 2007," in *Revista de Derecho Público,* núm. 112, Caracas, Editorial Jurídica Venezolana, 2007, pp. 661-694

238   See Lolymar Hernández Camargo, "Límites del poder ejecutivo en el ejercicio de la habilitación legislativa: Imposibilidad de establecer el contenido de la reforma constitucional rechazada vía habilitación legislativa," in *Revista de Derecho Público,* N° 115 *(Estudios sobre los Decretos Leyes),* Editorial Jurídica venezolana, Caracas 2008, pp. 51 ff.; Jorge Kiriakidis, "Breves reflexiones en torno a los 26 Decretos-Ley de Julio-Agosto de 2008, y la consulta popular refrendaría de diciembre de 2007", *Idem,* pp. 57 ff.; and José Vicente Haro García, Los recientes intentos de reforma constitucional o de cómo se está tratando de establecer una dictadura socialista con apariencia de legalidad (A propósito del proyecto de reforma constitucional de 2007 y los 26 decretos leyes del 31 de julio de 2008 que tratan de imponerla)", *Idem,* pp. 63 ff.

239   See the summary of this situation in Teodoro Petkoff, "Election and Political Power. Challenges for the Opposition", en *ReVista. Harvard Review of Latin America,* David Rockefeller Center for Latin American Studies, Harvard University, Fall 2008, pp. 12. See also Allan R. Brewer-Carías, "Los problemas de la gobernabilidad democrática en Venezuela: el autoritarismo constitucional y la concentración y centralización del poder," in Diego Valadés (Coord.), *Gobernabilidad y constitucionalismo en América Latina,* Universidad Nacional Autónoma de México, México 2005, pp. 73-96.

240   See Allan R. Brewer-Carías, "El juez constitucional al servicio del autoritarismo y la ilegítima mutación de la Constitución: el caso de la Sala Constitucional del Tribunal Supremo de

the first one, the decision issued by the Constitutional Chamber of the Supreme Tribunal of Justice a few weeks after approval of the 1999 Constitution, accepting the existence of not one, but of two constitutional transitory regimes: one which was approved by popular vote, and embodied in the text of the Constitution; and another not approved by the people, and adopted one week after the Constitution was popularly approved by the same Constituent Assembly. This latter Decree on the Regime of Transition of the Public Power, enacted by the Assembly without any constitutional support, eliminated the prior Congress along with its senators and representatives; assigned the legislative power to a National Legislative Commission not established in the Constitution; dissolved the states' legislative assemblies; controlled the mayor's offices and municipal councils; and, as mentioned, eliminated the former Supreme Court of Justice, appointing the magistrates of the new Supreme Tribunal but without complying with the conditions established in the Constitution. It also transformed the former Judicial Emergency Commission into a Commission for the Reorganization and Functioning of the Judiciary in order to continue with the removal of judges from office without due process, which still today continues to work.

Of course, this unconstitutional Decree was challenged before the new Constitutional Chamber which was appointed in it, being the result that the Constitutional Chamber, deciding in its own cause violating one of the most basic principles of law, argued that the Constituent Assembly had supra-constitutional power to create constitutional provisions without popular approval.[241] The consequence has been the existence in the country of two transitional constitutional regimes: one approved by the people, and the other illegitimately imposed to the people, leading to a long and endless period of constitutional instability that, eleven years later, has eroded institutional confidence and legal security.[242]

One of the unconstitutional results of the transitory constitutional regime adopted by the Constituent Assembly, as I mentioned, was the appointment of the Magistrates of the new Supreme Tribunal without fulfilling the conditions for those appointments and without guarantying the citizens' participation in the process. In this particular aspect, the 1999 Constitution provides for a direct mean of citizen participation in the nominating process of High non elected Officials, preventing the National Assembly to appoint them without being previously proposed by nominating committees; committees that were to be integrated in an exclusive way by representatives of "different sectors of civil society." Nonetheless, these committees have never been established in the country in the way provided in the Constitution, and

Justicia de Venezuela (1999-2009)", in *IUSTEL, Revista General de Derecho Administrativo*, N° 21, junio 2009, Madrid, ISSN-1696-9650

241 See decision N° 4 of January 26, 2000, case: *Eduardo García*, in *Revista de Derecho Público*, N° 81, Editorial Jurídica Venezolana, Caracas 2000, pp. 93 ff.

242 See decision of March 28, 2000, *case: Allan R. Brewer-Carías y otros*, in *Revista de Derecho Público*, N° 81, (enero-marzo), Editorial Jurídica Venezolana, Caracas, 2000, p. 86.

have been supplanted by ordinary parliamentary commissions, extending in an illegitimate way, through legislation, the initial transitory regime. [243]

In 2000, for instance, a Special Law for the Ratification or Appointment of High Officials and Magistrates to the Supreme Tribunal of Justice[244] was enacted by the then newly elected National Assembly, but without organizing the aforementioned nominating committees, thereby confiscating the citizens' right to political participation. Such Special Law, of course, was challenged before the Constitutional Chamber (this time by the Peoples' Defendant),[245] which has never decided the merits of the case. Instead, the Chamber, in a preliminary ruling (December 2000), decided again in its own cause, establishing that the Constitution was not applicable to the Magistrates that were signing the decision, because they were not going to be "appointed" but to be "ratified;"[246] a decision that was a grotesque mockery regarding the Constitution.

This irregular situation continued in 2004, when the National Assembly eventually sanctioned the Organic Law of the Supreme Tribunal of Justice, increasing the number of magistrates from twenty to thirty-two, distorting the constitutional conditions for their appointment and dismissal, and consolidating the judicial nominating committee as a dependent parliamentary commission. This reform, as the Inter-American Commission on Human Rights emphasized in its *2004 Annual Report*, "lack the safeguards necessary to prevent other branches of government from undermining the Supreme Tribunal's independence and to keep narrow or temporary majorities from determining its composition." [247]

After this 2004 legal reform, the process for selecting new Magistrates, although being an exclusive competency of the National Assembly, in fact was controlled by the President of the Republic, as was publicly recognized by the representative head

---

243 See Allan R. Brewer-Carías, "La participación ciudadana en la designación de los titulares de los órganos no electos de los Poderes Públicos en Venezuela y sus vicisitudes políticas", in *Revista Iberoamericana de Derecho Público y Administrativo*, Año 5, N° 5-2005, San José, Costa Rica 2005, pp. 76-95.

244 See *Gaceta Oficial* N° 37.077 of November 14, 2000.

245 See *El Universal,* Caracas, December 14, 2000, pp. 1-2.

246 The Constitutional Chamber accepted the point of view that the Magistrates could be "ratified" according to the Special Law without complying with the Constitution, because the latter only established their nomination but said noting about the "ratification" of those in office, signing the decision. See Decision of December 12, 2000 in *Revista de Derecho Público N° 84*, Editorial Jurídica Venezolana, Caracas, 2000, p. 109. See the comments in Allan R. Brewer-Carías, "La participación ciudadana en la designación de los titulares de los órganos no electos de los Poderes Públicos en Venezuela y sus vicisitudes políticas," in *Revista Iberoamericana de Derecho Público y Administrativo*, Año 5, N° 5-2005, San José, Costa Rica 2005, pp. 76-95, available at www.allanbrewercarias.com (Biblioteca Virtual, II.4. Artículos y Estudios N° 469, 2005) pp. 1-48.

247 See IACHR, *2004 Annual Report* (Follow-Up Report on Compliance by the State of Venezuela with the Recommendations made by the IACHR in its Report on the Situation of Human Rights in Venezuela [2003]), para. 174. Available at http://www.cidh.oas.org/annual-rep/2004eng/chap.5b.htm

of the parliamentary nominating committee, when he publicly announced that fact and, in addition, said that "There is now one in the group of nominees that could act against us."[248] This configuration of the Supreme Tribunal, as highly politicized and subjected to the will of the president, has completely eliminated the autonomy of the Judiciary, and even the basic principle of separation of powers; allowing the government the absolute control of the Supreme Tribunal of Justice, and particularly, of its Constitutional Chamber.

Through the Supreme Tribunal, which is in charge of governing and administering the Judiciary, the political control over all judges has been also assured, reinforced by means of the survival of the 1999 "provisional" Commission on the Functioning and Restructuring of the Judicial System, which has been legimimazed by the same Tribunal, making completely inapplicable the 1999 constitutional provisions seeking to guarantee the independence and autonomy of judges. [249]

According to the text of the 1999 Constitution, judges can only enter the judicial career by means of public competition that must be organized with citizens' participation. Nonetheless, this provision has not yet been implemented, being the judiciary almost exclusively made up of temporary and provisional judges, without any stability. Regarding this situation, for instance, since 2003 the Inter-American Commission on Human Rights has repeatedly express concern about the fact that provisional judges are susceptible to political manipulation, which alters the people's right to access to justice, reporting cases of dismissals and substitutions of judges in retaliation for decisions contrary to the government's position.[250] In its *2008 Annual Report*, the Commission again verified the provisional character of the

---

248 He expressed to the press: "If it is true that the representatives have the power to choose, the opinión of the President of the Republic has been ask, and has been very much taken into account." See *El Nacional*, Caracas, December 13, 2004. The Inter-American Commission of Human Rights suggested in its *2004 Report on Venezuela* that "those provisions of the Organic Law of the Supreme Tribunal of Justice had facilitated the Executive Power to manipulate the 2004 process of election of the magistrates," paragraph párrafo 180.

249 See in general, Allan R. Brewer-Carías, "La progresiva y sistemática demolición de la autonomía e independencia del Poder Judicial en Venezuela (1999-2004)," in *XXX Jornadas J.M Dominguez Escovar, Estado de Derecho, Administración de Justicia y Derechos Humanos*, Instituto de Estudios Jurídicos del Estado Lara, Barquisimeto 2005, pp. 33-174; Allan R. Brewer-Carías, "El constitucionalismo y la emergencia en Venezuela: entre la emergencia formal y la emergencia anormal del Poder Judicial," in Allan R. Brewer-Carías, *Estudios Sobre el Estado Constitucional (2005-2006)*, Editorial Jurídica Venezolana, Caracas 2007, pp. 245-269; and Allan R. Brewer-Carías "La justicia sometida al poder. La ausencia de independencia y autonomía de los jueces en Venezuela por la interminable emergencia del Poder Judicial (1999-2006)," in *Cuestiones Internacionales. Anuario Jurídico Villanueva 2007*, Centro Universitario Villanueva, Marcial Pons, Madrid 2007, pp. 25-57, available at www.allanbrewercarias.com, (Biblioteca Virtual, II.4. Artículos y Estudios N° 550, 2007) pp. 1-37. See also Allan R. Brewer-Carías, *Historia Constitucional de Venezuela*, Editorial Alfa, Tomo II, Caracas 2008, pp. 402-454.

250 See *Reporte sobre la Situación de Derechos Humanos en Venezuela*; OAS/Ser.L/V/II.118. doc.4rev.2; December 29, 2003, Paragraphs 161, 174, available at http://www.cidh.oas.org/countryrep/Venezuela2003eng/toc.htm .

judiciary as an "endemic problem" because the appointment of judges was made without applying constitutional provisions on the matter – thus exposing judges to discretionary dismissal – which highlights the "permanent state of urgency" in which those appointments have been made. [251]

Contrary to these facts, according to the words of the Constitution in order to guarantee the independence of the Judiciary, judges can be dismissed from their tenure only through disciplinary processes, conducted by disciplinary courts and judges of a Disciplinary Judicial Jurisdiction. Nonetheless, that jurisdiction has never been created, corresponding the disciplinary judicial functions to the already mentioned transitory Commission, [252] which, as reported by the same Inter-American Commission in its *2009 Annual Report*, "in addition to being a special, temporary entity, does not afford due guarantees for ensuring the independence of its decisions, [253] since its members may also be appointed or removed at the sole discretion of the Constitutional Chamber of the Supreme Tribunal of Justice, without previously establishing either the grounds or the procedure for such formalities." [254]

The Commission has then "cleansed" the Judiciary of judges not in line with the authoritarian regime, removing judges in a discretionary way when they have issued decisions not within the complacency of the government. [255] This lead the Inter-American Commission on Human Rights, to observe in its *2009 Annual Report,* that "in Venezuela, judges and prosecutors do not enjoy the guaranteed tenure, necessary to ensure their independence," [256] being subjected to the changes in government

One of the leading cases showing this situation took place in 2003, after the First Court of the Contentious Administrative Jurisdiction issued a preliminary amparo measure suspending administrative actions, pending the trial, because presumptively being discriminatory. In effect, based on the previous democratic tradition of the country in matters of control and review of Public Administration actions, on July 17, 2003, the Venezuelan National Federation of Doctors brought before the afore-

---

251 See *Annual Report 2008* (OEA/Ser.L/V/II.134. Doc. 5 rev. 1. 25 febrero 2009), paragraph 39

252 The Politico Administrative Chamber of the Supreme Tribunal has decided that the dismiss of temporal judges is a discretionary power of the Comission on the Functioning and Reorganization of the Judiciary, which adopts its decision without following any administrative procedure rules or due process rules. See Decision N° 00463-2007 of March 20, 2007; Decision N° 00673-2008 of April 24, 2008 (cited in Decision N° 1.939 of December 18, 2008, p. 42). The Chamber has adopted the same position in Decision N° 2414 of December 20, 2007 and Decision N° 280 of February 23, 2007.

253 See Decisión N° 1.939 of December 18, 2008 (Caso: *Gustavo Álvarez Arias et al.*)

254 See *Annual Report 2009*, Paragraph 481, available at http://www.cidh.org/annualrep/2009eng/Chap.IV.f.eng.htm.

255 Decision N° 1.939 (Dec. 18, 2008) (Case: *Abogados Gustavo Álvarez Arias y otros*), in which the Constitutonal Chamber declared the non-enforceability of the decision of the Inter American Court of Human Rights of August 5, 2008, Case: *Apitz Barbera y otros ("Corte Primera de lo Contencioso Administrativo") vs. Venezuela* Serie C, N° 182.

256 See *Informe Anual de 2009*, paragraph 480, available at http://www.cidh.oas.org/annualrep/2009eng/Chap.IV.f.eng.htm

mentioned Judicial Review of Administrative Actions highest Court in Caracas (First Court), a nullity claim against the Mayor of Caracas and the Ministry of Health and the Caracas Metropolitan Board of Doctors (*Colegio de Médicos*) actions hiring Cuban doctors for an important popular governmental health program in the Caracas slums, but without complying with the legal conditions established for doctors to practice the medical profession in the country. The National Federation of Doctors considered that the program was discriminatory and against the rights of licensed doctors to exercise their medical profession, allowing doctors to exercise it without complying with the Medical Profession Statute regulations. The consequence was the filing an amparo petition against both public authorities, seeking the collective protection of the Venezuelan doctors' constitutional rights.[257]

One month later, in August 21, 2003, the First Court issued a preliminary protective amparo measure, considering that there were sufficient elements to deem that the equality before the law constitutional guaranty was violated in the case. The Court ordered in a preliminary way the suspension of the Cuban doctors' hiring program and ordered the Metropolitan Board of doctors to substitute the Cuban doctors already hired, by Venezuelan ones or foreign Doctors who had fulfilled the legal regulations in order to exercise the medical profession in the country.[258]

Nonetheless, in response to that preliminary judicial amparo decision, instead of enforcing it, the Minister of Health, the Mayor of Caracas, and even the President of the Republic made public statements to the effect that the decision was not going to be respected or enforced.[259] Following these statements, the government-controlled Constitutional Chamber of the Supreme Tribunal of Justice adopted a decision, without any appeal being filed, assuming jurisdiction over the case and annulling the preliminary amparo ordered by the First Court; a group of Secret Service police officials seized the First Court's premises; and the President of the Republic, among other expressions he used, publicly called the President of the First Court a "bandit."[260] A few weeks later, in response to the First Court's decision in an unrelated case challenging a local registrar's refusal to record a land sale, a Special Commission for the Intervention of the Judiciary, which in spite of being unconstitutional

---

257 See Claudia Nikken, "El caso "Barrio Adentro": La Corte Primera de lo Contencioso Administrativo ante la Sala Constitucional del Tribunal Supremo de Justicia o el avocamiento como medio de amparo de derechos e intereses colectivos y difusos," in *Revista de Derecho Público*, nº 93-96, Editorial Jurídica Venezolana, Caracas, 2003, pp. 5 ff.

258 See Decision of August, 21 2003, in *Idem*, pp. 445 ff.

259 The President of the Republic said: "*Váyanse con su decisión no sé para donde, la cumplirán ustedes en su casa si quieren ...*" (You can go with your decision, I don't know where; you will enforce it in your house if you want ..."). See *El Universal*, Caracas, August 25, 2003 and *El Universal*, Caracas, August 28, 2003.

260 *See* Inter-American Court of Human Rights, case: *Apitz Barbera et al. (Corte Primera de lo Contencioso Administrativo) v. Venezuela*, Decision of August 5, 2008, available at www.corteidh.or.cr. *See also*, *El Universal*, Caracas, October 16, 2003; and *El Universal*, Caracas, September 22, 2003.

continued to exist, dismissed all five judges of the First Court.[261] In spite of the protests of all the Bar Associations of the country and also of the International Commission of Jurists;[262] the First Court remained suspended without judges, and its premises remained closed for about nine months,[263] period during which simply no judicial review of administrative action could be sought in the country.[264]

The dismissed judges of the First Court brought a complaint to the Inter-American Commission of Human Rights for the government's unlawful removal of them and for violation of their constitutional rights. The Commission in turn brought the case, captioned *Apitz Barbera et al. (Corte Primera de lo Contencioso Administrativo vs. Venezuela)* before the Inter-American Court of Human Rights. On August 5, 2008, the Inter-American Court ruled that the Republic of Venezuela had violated the rights of the dismissed judges established in the American Convention of Human Rights, and ordered the State to pay them due compensation, to reinstate them to a similar position in the Judiciary, and to publish part of the decision in Venezuelan newspapers.[265] Nonetheless, on December 12, 2008, the Constitutional Chamber of the Supreme Tribunal issued Decision N° 1.939, declaring that the August 5, 2008 decision of the Inter-American Court of Human Rights was non-enforceable (*inejecutable*) in Venezuela. As simple as that, showing the subordination of the Venezuelan judiciary to the policies, wishes, and dictates of the President. The Constitutional Chamber also accused the Inter-American Court of having usurped powers of the Supreme Tribunal of Justice, and asked the Executive Branch to denounce the American Convention of Human Rights.[266]

---

261 *See El Nacional*, Caracas, November 5, 2003, p. A2. The dismissed President of the First Court said: "*La justicia venezolana vive un momento tenebroso, pues el tribunal que constituye un último resquicio de esperanza ha sido clausurado.*" ("The Venezuelan judiciary lives a dark moment, because the court that was a last glimmer of hope has been shut down.") *Id.* The Commission for the Intervention of the Judiciary had also massively dismissed almost all judges of the country without due disciplinary process, and had replaced them with provisionally appointed judges beholden to the ruling power.

262 *See* in *El Nacional*, Caracas, October 10, 2003, p. A-6; *El Nacional*, Caracas, October 15, 2003, p. A-2; *El Nacional*, Caracas, September 24, 2003, p. A-4; and *El Nacional*, Caracas, February 14, 2004, p. A-7.

263 *See El Nacional*, Caracas, October 24, 2003, p. A-2; and *El Nacional*, Caracas, July 16, 2004, p. A-6.

264 See, in general, Allan R. Brewer-Carías, "La justicia sometida al poder (La ausencia de independencia y autonomía de los jueces en Venezuela por la interminable emergencia del Poder Judicial (1999-2006))," in *Cuestiones Internacionales. Anuario Jurídico Villanueva 2007*, Centro Universitario Villanueva, Marcial Pons, Madrid 2007, pp. 25–57, available at www.allanbrewercarias.com, (Biblioteca Virtual, II.4. Artículos y Estudios N° 550, 2007).

265 Inter-American Court of Human Rights, case *Apitz Barbera et al. (Corte Primera de lo Contencioso Administrativo) v. Venezuela*, Decision of August 5, 2008, *available at* www.corteidh.or.cr.

266 Supreme Tribunal of Justice, Constitutional Chamber, Decision N° 1.939 of December 18, 2008 (Case: *Abogados Gustavo Álvarez Arias et al.*) (Exp. N° 08-1572).

In general terms, this was the global governmental response to an amparo judicial preliminary decision that affected a very sensitive governmental social program; a response that was expressed and executed through the government-controlled judiciary.[267] The result was that the subsequent newly appointed judges replacing those dismissed, began to "understand" how they needed to behave in the future.

This emblematic case, contrast with the very progressive text of the constitution in force in Venezuela (1999), and shows that with a Judiciary controlled by the Executive, the declaration of constitutional rights is a death letter, and the provision of the action for amparo is no more that an illusion. As mentioned, this has been the tragic institutional result of the deliberated process of dismantling democracy to which Venezuela has been subjected during the past decade, through the imposition of an authoritarian government, defrauding the constitution and democracy itself.[268]

Last year, in December 2009, another astonishing case was the detention of a criminal judge (María Lourdes Afiuni Mora) for having ordered, based on a previous recommendation of the UN Working Group on Arbitrary Detention, the release of an individual in order for him to face criminal trial while in freedom, as guaranteed in the Constitution. The same day of the decision, the president publicly asked for the judge to be incarcerated asking to apply her a 30–year prison term, which is the maximum punishment in Venezuelan law for horrendous or grave crimes. The fact is that judge has remained to this day in detention without trial. The UN Working Group described these facts as "a blow by President Hugo Chávez to the independence of judges and lawyers in the country," demanding "the immediate release of the judge," concluding that "reprisals for exercising their constitutionally guaranteed functions and creating a climate of fear among the judiciary and lawyers' profession, serve no purpose except to undermine the rule of law and obstruct justice."[269]

The fact is that in Venezuela, no judge can adopt any decision, particularly amparo decision against public authorities, that could affect the government policies, or the President's wishes, the state's interest, or public servants' will, without previ-

---

267 See Allan R. Brewer-Carías, "La progresiva y sistemática demolición institucional de la autonomía e independencia del Poder Judicial en Venezuela 1999–2004," in *XXX Jornadas J.M Domínguez Escovar, Estado de derecho, Administración de justicia y derechos humanos,* Instituto de Estudios Jurídicos del Estado Lara, Barquisimeto, 2005, pp. 33–174.

268 See generally Allan R. Brewer-Carías, *Dismantling Democracy. The Chávez Authoritarian Experiment,* Cambridge University Press, New York 2010.

269 See the text of the UN Working Group in http://www.unog.ch/unog/website/news_media.nsf/%28httpNewsByYear_en%29/93687E8429BD53A1C125768E00529DB6?OpenDocument&cntxt=B35C3&cookielang=fr. In October 14, 2010, the same Working Group asked the venezuelan Gobernment to subject the Judge to a trail ruled by the due process guaranties and in freedom." See in *El Universal,* October 14, 2010, available at http://www.eluniversal.com/2010/10/14/pol_ava_instancia-de-la-onu_14A4608051.shtml

ous authorization from the same government. [270] That is why the Inter-American Commission on Human Rights, after describing in its *2009 Annual Report* "how large numbers of judges have been removed, or their appointments voided, without the applicable administrative proceedings," noted "with concern that in some cases, judges were removed almost immediately after adopting judicial decisions in cases with a major political impact," concluding that "The lack of judicial independence and autonomy vis-à-vis political power is, in the Commission's opinion, one of the weakest points in Venezuelan democracy." [271]

In this context of political subjection, the Constitutional Chamber, since 2000, far from acting as the guardian of the Constitution, has been the main tool of the authoritarian government for the illegitimate mutation of the Constitution, by means of unconstitutional constitutional interpretations, [272] not only regarding its own powers of judicial review, which have been enlarged, but also regarding substantive matters. The Supreme Tribunal has distorted the Constitution through illegitimate and fraudulent "constitutional mutations" in the sense of changing the meaning of its provisions without changing its wording. And all this, of course, without any possibility of being controlled, [273] so the eternal question arising from the uncontrolled power, – *Quis custodiet ipsos custodes* –, in Venezuela also remains unanswered.

In this regard, one of the most lethal instruments for distorting the Constitution that has been used in Venezuela has been the filing of direct actions or recourses for the abstract interpretation of the Constitution, a judicial mean that has been created by the Constitutional Chamber itself without any constitutional support. [274] These recourses can be filed by any person or very convenient, by the Attorney General; so it has been through these actions that the Constitutional Chamber eventually has "reformed" the Constitution, and has even implemented in a very illegitimate way the constitutional reforms that were rejected by the people in the referendum of 2007.

---

270 See Antonio Canova González, *La realidad del contencioso administrativo venezolano (Un llamado de atención frente a las desoladoras estadísticas de la Sala Político Administrativa en 2007 y primer semestre de 2008)*, Funeda, Caracas 2008, p. 14.

271 See in ICHR, *Annual Report 2009*, paragraph 483, available at http://www.cidh.oas.org/-annualrep/2009eng/Chap.IV.f.eng.htm .

272 See Allan R. Brewer-Carías, *"Crónica sobre la "In" Justicia Constitucional. La Sala Constitucional y el autoritarismo en Venezuela*, Editorial Jurídica Venezolana, Caracas 2007.

273 See Allan R. Brewer-Carías, *"Quis Custodiet ipsos Custodes*: De la interpretación constitucional a la inconstitucionalidad de la interpretación," in *VIII Congreso Nacional de Derecho Constitucional*, Fondo Editorial and Colegio de Abogados de Arequipa, Arequipa, Peru, 2005, 463-89; and *Crónica de la "In"Justicia constitucional: La Sala constitucional y el autoritarismo en Venezuela*, Editorial Jurídica Venezolana, Caracas 2007, pp. 11-44 and 47-79.

274 See Decision N° 1077 of the Constitutional Chamber of September 22, 2000, case: *Servio Tulio León Briceño*. See in *Revista de Derecho Público*, N° 83, Caracas, 2000, pp. 247 ff. This ruling was later ratified in decisions of November 9, 2000 (N° 1347), November 21, 2000 (N° 1387), and April 5, 2001 (N° 457). See Allan R. Brewer-Carías, "Le recours d'interprétation abstrait de la Constitution au Vénézuéla," en *Le renouveau du droit constitutionnel, Mélanges en l'honneur de Louis Favoreu*, Dalloz, Paris, 2007, pp. 61-70

Many cases can illustrate this unconstitutional process. For instance, Article 72 of the Constitution establishes the principle of the revocation of mandates of all popularly elected offices through recall referendums, establishing that when "a number of electors equal or higher than those who elected the official, vote in favor of the revocation,"[275] the official's mandate is considered revoked. Nevertheless, clearly in an unconstitutional way, in 2003, when a recall referendum was first called by popular initiative to revoke the President's mandate, the National Electoral Council issued a regulation on the matter, adding to the constitutional provision that the number of votes to repeal, in no case could be "lower than the number of electors that voted against the revocation," changing the sense of the constitutional provisions on the matter. With that addition – established in a regulation – the right for the revocation of mandates was restricted, disrupting the nature of the recall referendum by transforming it into a "ratifying" referendum of mandates of popular election not provided in the Constitution. This constitutional fraud was endorsed by the Constitutional Chamber of the Supreme Court when it decided a recourse on the abstract interpretation of article 72 of the Constitution stating that "*if the option of the permanence [of the official] obtains more votes in the referendum, [the officer] should remain in office*, even if a sufficient number of people vote against him to revoke his mandate,"[276] and consequently, turning the "vote against the revocation" into a "vote to ratify" the official. This illegitimate distortion of the Constitution, nonetheless, in 2004 had a precise purpose, just to avoid the revocation of President Hugo Chávez's mandate. He was elected in August 2000 with 3,757,744 votes, and the number of votes casted to revoke his mandate was 3,989,008, surpassing that former number. But instead of announcing the revocation of the mandate according to the Constitution, the National Electoral Council, applying a custom-made doctrine established by the Constitutional Chamber, decided to ratify the President in its mandate due to the fact that at that moment more people (5,800,629) had voted not to revoke his mandate. [277] The recall referendum was thus illegitimately transformed into a non existing plebiscite to ratify the President.[278]

---

275 Decision N° 2750 of October 21, 2003, Case: *Carlos Enrique Herrera Mendoza, (Interpretación del artículo 72 de la Constitución (Exp. 03-1989);* Decision N° 1139 of June 5, 2002, Case: *Sergio Omar Calderón Duque y William Dávila Barrios,* in *Revista de Derecho Público,* N° 89-92, Editorial Jurídica Venezolana, Caracas 2002, p. 171. The same ruling was followed in Decision N° 137 of February 13, 2003, Case: *Freddy Lepage Scribani y otros* (Exp. 03-0287).

276 See Decision N° 2750 of October 21, 2003, Case: *Carlos E. Herrera Mendoza, Interpretación del artículo 72 de la Constitución),* in Véase *El Nacional,* Caracas, August 28, 2004, pp. A-1 y A-2

277 See in *El Nacional,* Caracas, August 28, 2004, pp. A-1 y A-2

278 See Allan R. Brewer-Carías, "La Sala Constitucional vs. el derecho ciudadano a la revocatoria de mandatos populares: de cómo un referendo revocatorio fue inconstitucionalmente convertido en un "referendo ratificatorio," in *Crónica sobre la "In" Justicia Constitucional. La Sala Constitucional y el autoritarismo en Venezuela,* Editorial Jurídica Venezolana, Caracas 2007, 349-378.

Also on electoral maters, for instance, the Constitutional Chamber distorted the mixed electoral system established in the Constitution that combines personalized and proportional representation ballots. This system requires a complex mathematical application in order to function regarding the election of representatives combining majority and list ballots. The Constitutional Chamber of the Supreme Tribunal of Justice in 2005, before the election of the members of the National Assembly took place, legitimized a defrauding method applied by the parties supporting the government that distorted the principle of proportional representation, transforming the system into a majority one. This, among other factors, led to the opposition parties decision in 2005 to not to participate in such election, unfortunately allowing the complete control of the Assembly by the government. In 2009, the new Organic Law on Electoral Processes was sanctioned legalizing this distorted electoral method, which was applied in the last week legislative election (September 2010), but introducing another distorted element in order to neutralize even more the proportional representation method, through the configuration of the constituencies. The result of the election, as has been announced a few days ago, has been that the opposition, although obtaining more votes than the official party (52% v. 48%), has succeeded to elect only one third of the representatives in the Assembly.

The role of the Constitutional Chamber mutating the Constitution has also affected the general regime on human rights. According to the Constitution, human rights' treaties, pacts and conventions have constitutional rank and prevail in the internal order as long as they contain more favorable provisions regarding their enjoyment and exercise. However, the Constitutional Chamber in 2008, after declaring unenforceable in the country a decision of the Inter-American Court of Human Rights, resolved that Article 23 of the Constitution "does not grant supra-constitutional rank to international treaties on human rights," the Chamber also decided that in case of contradiction between a disposition of the Constitution and a provision of an international treaty, it correspond only to it to determine which one would be applicable, [279] but emphasizing that "the political project of the Constitution" could never be affected, particularly – I quote – "with ideological interpretative elements that could privilege in a decisive way, individual rights, or that welcome the supremacy of the international judicial order over national law at the sacrifice of the sovereignty of the State." The Chamber also said that "a system of principles, supposedly absolute and supra-historic, cannot be above the Constitution" and that the theories that pretend to limit "under the pretext of universal legalities, the sovereignty and the national auto-determination" "are unacceptable."

With this decision, once again, the Constitutional Chamber illegitimately distorted the Constitution, reforming Article 23 of the Constitution by eliminating the supra-constitutional rank of the American Convention on Human Rights in cases in which it contains more favorable provisions for the benefit and exercise of human rights than the Constitution.

---

279 See Decision N° 1492 of June 15, 2003, Case: *Impugnación de diversos artículos del Código Penal*, in *Revista de Derecho Público*, N° 93-96, Editorial Jurídica Venezolana, Caracas 2003, pp. 135 ff.

In addition, the Chamber also distorted another provision of the Constitution that grants power to all courts to directly apply human rights provisions of international treaties, reserving such power to the Constitutional Chamber itself.

On the other hand, regarding some fundamental rights essentials for a democracy to function, like the freedom of expression, contrary to the principle of progressiveness established in the Constitution, it has been the Supreme Tribunal of Justice the State organ in charge of limiting its scope. First, in 2000, it was the Political-Administrative Chamber of the Supreme Tribunal that ordered the media not to transmit certain information, eventually admitting limits to be imposed to the media, regardless of the general prohibition of censorship established in the Constitution.

The following year, in 2001, it was the Constitutional Chamber of the Supreme Tribunal, the one that distorted the Constitution when dismissing an *amparo* action filed against the President of the Republic by a citizen and a nongovernmental organization asking for the exercise of their right to response against the attacks made by the President in his weekly TV program. The Constitutional Chamber reduced the scope of freedom of information, eliminating the right to response and rectification regarding opinions in the media when they are expressed by the president in a regular televised program. In addition, the tribunal excluded journalists and all those persons that have a regular program in the radio or a newspaper column, from the right to rectification and response.[280]

In addition, in 2003, the Constitutional Chamber dismissed an action of unconstitutionality filed against a few articles of the Criminal Code that limit the right to formulate criticism against public officials, considering that such provisions could not be deemed as limiting the freedom of expression, contradicting a well established doctrine in the contrary ruled by the Inter-American Courts on Human Rights.[281] The Constitutional Chamber also decided in contradiction with the constitutional prohibition of censorship, that through a statute it was possible to prevent

---

280 See Allan R. Brewer-Carías, "La libertad de expresión del pensamiento y el derecho a la información y su violación por la Sala Constitucional del Tribunal Supremo de Justicia", en Allan R. Brewer-Carías (Coordinador y editor), Héctor Faúndez Ledesma, Pedro Nikken, Carlos M. Ayala Corao, Rafael Chavero Gazdik, Gustavo Linares Benzo and Jorge Olavarria, *La libertad de expresión amenazada (Sentencia 1013),* Edición Conjunta Instituto Interamericano de Derechos Humanos y Editorial Jurídica Venezolana, Caracas-San José 2001, pp. 17-57; and Jesús A. Davila Ortega, "El derecho de la información y la libertad de expresión en Venezuela (Un estudio de la sentencia 1.013/2001 de la Sala Constitucional del Tribunal Supremo de Justicia)," *Revista de Derecho Constitucional* 5, Editorial Sherwood, Caracas 2002, 305-25.

281 See Decision N° 1492 of June 15, 2003, Case: *Impugnación de diversos artículos del Código Penal,* in *Revista de Derecho Público,* N° 93-96, Editorial Jurídica Venezolana, Caracas 2003, pp. 135 ff.

the diffusion of information when it could be considered contrary to other provisions of the Constitution. [282]

Finally, it has been the Supreme Tribunal in 2007, the State organ that materialized the State intervention in order to terminate authorizations and licenses of radio and television enterprises to use frequencies, particularly those owned by persons considered in opposition to the government. It was the case of the arbitrarily closing of *Radio Caracas Televisión*, the oldest private TV in the country, whose assets were confiscated and its equipment assigned to a state-owned enterprise through an illegitimate Supreme Tribunal decision.[283]

On different matters, regarding the organization of the State, the same illegitimate constitutional mutation has occurred regarding the federal system of distribution of competencies among territorial entities of the State, which in Venezuela is constitutionally organized as a "decentralized federal State;" a distribution that cannot be changed except by means of a constitutional reform. Specifically, for instance, the Constitution provides that the conservation, administration, and use of roads and national highways, as well as of national ports and airports of commercial use, are of the exclusive powers of the states, which they must exercise in "coordination" with the Federal government.

One of the purposes of the rejected 2007 constitutional reform was precisely to change this competency of the States. But in spite of the popular rejection of the reform, nonetheless, it was the Constitutional Chamber, through a decision adopted four month after the referendum (April 15, 2008), the State organ in charge of implementing the reform. The Chamber, in effect, when deciding an autonomous recourse for the abstract interpretation of the Constitution filed by the Attorney General, modified the content of that constitutional provision, considering that the exclusive attribution it contained, was not "exclusive," but a "concurrent" one, to be exercised together with the federal government, which even could reassume the attribution or decree its intervention. [284]

---

282   See *Revista de Derecho Público* 93–94, Editorial Jurídica Venezolana, Caracas 2003, 136ff. and 164ff. See comments in Alberto Arteaga Sánchez et al., *Sentencia 1942 vs. Libertad de expresión*, Caracas 2004.

283   See the Constitutional Chamber Decision N° 957 (May 25, 2007), in *Revista de Derecho Público* 110, Editorial Jurídica Venezolana, Caracas 2007, 117ff. See the comments in Allan R. Brewer-Carías, "El juez constitucional en Venezuela como instrumento para aniquilar la libertad de expresión plural y para confiscar la propiedad privada: El caso RCTV", in *Revista de Derecho Público*", N° 110, (abril-junio 2007), Editorial Jurídica Venezolana, Caracas 2007, pp. 7-32.

284   See Allan R. Brewer-Carías, "La Sala Constitucional como poder constituyente: la modificación de la forma federal del estado y del sistema constitucional de división territorial del poder público, in *Revista de Derecho Público*, N° 114, (abril-junio 2008), Editorial Jurídica Venezolana, Caracas 2008, pp. 247-262; and "La ilegitima mutación de la Constitución y la legitimidad de la jurisdicción constitucional: la "reforma" de la forma federal del Estado en Venezuela mediante interpretación constitucional," en *Memoria del X Congreso Iberoamericano de Derecho Constitucional,* Instituto Iberoamericano de Derecho Constitucional, Aso-

With this interpretation, again, the Chamber illegitimately modified the Constitution usurping popular sovereignty, compelling the National Assembly to enact legislation contrary to the Constitution, which it did in March 2009, by reforming of the Organic Law for Decentralization. [285]

In other cases, the Constitutional Chamber has been the instrument of the government in order to assume direct control of other branches of government, as happened in 2002 with the take-over of the Electoral Power, which since then has been completely controlled by the Executive. This began in 2002 after the Organic Law of the Electoral Power[286] was sanctioned and the National Assembly was due to appoint the new members of the National Electoral Council. Because the representatives supporting the government did not have the qualified majority to approve such appointments by themselves, and did not reached agreements on the matter with the opposition, when the National Assembly failed to appoint the members of the National Electoral Council, that task was assumed, without any constitutional power, by the Constitutional Chamber itself. Deciding an action that was filed against the unconstitutional legislative omission, the Chamber instead of urging the Assembly to comply with its constitutional duty, directly appointed the members of the Electoral Council, usurping the Legislator's functions, but without complying with the conditions established in the Constitution for such appointments. [287] With this decision, the Chamber assured the government's complete control of the Council, kidnapping the citizen's rights to political participation, and allowing the official governmental party to manipulate the electoral results.

Consequently, the elections held in Venezuela during the past decade have been organized by a politically dependent branch of government, without any guarantee of independence or impartiality. This is the only explanation, for instance, of the complete lack of official information on the final voting results of the December 2007 referendum rejecting the constitutional reform drafted and proposed by the President. The country, nowadays, still ignored the majority number of votes that effectively rejected the constitutional reform draft tending to consolidate in the Constitution the basis for a socialist, centralized, militaristic, and police state, as proposed by President Chávez.

ciación Peruana de Derecho Constitucional, Instituto de Investigaciones Jurídicas-UNAM y Maestría en Derecho Constitucional-PUCP, IDEMSA, Lima 2009, tomo 1, pp. 29-51

285 See *Gaceta Oficial* N° 39 140 of March 17, 2009
286 See *Gaceta Oficial* N° 37.573 of November 19, 2002
287 See Decision N° 2073 of August 4, 2003, Case: *Hermánn Escarrá Malaver y oros*), and Decision N° 2341 of August 25, 2003, Case: *Hemann Escarrá y otros*. See in Allan R. Brewer-Carías, "El secuestro del poder electoral y la conficación del derecho a la participación política mediante el referendo revocatorio presidencial: Venezuela 2000-2004", in *Stvdi Vrbinati, Rivista tgrimestrale di Scienze Giuridiche, Politiche ed Economiche*, Año LXXI – 2003/04 Nuova Serie A – N. 55,3, Università degli Studi di Urbino, pp.379-436

FINAL REMARKS

The result of all these facts is that at the beginning of the twenty-first century, Latin America has witnessed in Venezuela the birth of a new model of authoritarian government that did not immediately originate itself in a military coup, as happened in many other occasions during the long decades of last century, but in an constituent coup d'état and in popular elections, which despite its final goal of destroying the rule of law and democracy, have provided it the convenient camouflage of "constitutional" and "elective" marks, although of course, lacking the essential components of democracy, which are much more than the sole popular or circumstantial election of governments.

In particular, among all the essential elements and components of democracy, the one regarding the separation and independence of public powers is maybe the most fundamental pillar of the rule of law, because it is the only one that can allow the other factors of democracy to become political reality. To be precise, democracy, as a rule of law political regime, can function only in a constitutional system where control of power exists, so without effective check and balance, no free and fair elections can take place; no plural political system can be developed; no effective democratic participation can be ensured; no effective transparency in the exercise of government can be assured; no real government accountability can be secure; and no effective access to justice can be guaranteed in order to protect human rights.

All these factors are lacking at the present time in Venezuela, where a new form of constitutional authoritarianism has been developed, based on the concentration and centralization of state powers, which prevent any possibility of effective democratic participation, and any possible check and balance between the branches of government. Today, all the State organs are subjected to the National Assembly, and through it, to the President. That is why the legislative elections of last September 2010 were so important, particularly bearing in mind that according to the Constitution, the presidential system of government was conceived to function only if the government has complete control over the Assembly. A government that does not have such control will find difficult to govern, and that is why the President of the Republic, just before the election, repeatedly affirmed that if the opposition was to win the control of the Assembly, that would signify war.

In any case, the fact is that the President, his official party and the National Assembly tried to configure the last September 2010 legislative elections as a plebiscite regarding the President and his socialist model and policies. And the result has been that effectively, the President lost his plebiscite, in which the Venezuelan people sent a clear message of rejection.

After a decade of demolishing the rule of law and the democratic institutions, by controlling, at the government will, all the branches of government, particularly the Judiciary, it will be very difficult for the government and its official party to admit the democratic need they have to share power in the Assembly. They are not used to democracy, that is to say, they are not used to any sort of compromise and consensus, but only to impose their decisions; and that is why they have already announced that they are not going to participate in any sort of dialogue. It is then possible, that in the near future, we could witness, even before the new elected representative take their sits in the Assembly in January 2011, the approval by the old Assembly of new legislation seeking to consolidate what the people has rejected, the so called "Socialism of the XXI Century" which is based on the centralized framework of the so-called "Popular Power" to be exercised by "Communes" and by the government controlled "Communal Councils," minimizing the future role of the National Assembly and of its representativeness.

One further example of the perversion of the Constitution and of the will of the people expressed in the September 2010 Legislative election, and it is very sad to pointed out, is currently in course of being materialized regarding the appointment of the new Magistrates of the Supreme Tribunal. What just a weeks ago was only a treat of the government, once lost the popular vote, for the current National Assembly – completely dominated by the official party - to immediately proceed to appoint the new magistrates of the Supreme before the inauguration of the new elected members of the National Assembly in January 2011, in order to avoid the participation in the nominating process of the opposition members of the Assembly; is now a real fact. Nonetheless, for such appointments to be done between September and December 2010, a modification of the Organic Law of the Supreme Tribunal was necessary, which has been done, not through the ordinary procedure to reform statutes, but through a completely irregular mechanism of "reprinting" the text of the statute in the *Official Gazette* based in a supposed "material error" in the copying of the text of the statute; reprinting made precisely a few days after the Government lost the majority in the National Assembly.[288]

Article 70 of the Organic Law of the Supreme Tribunal, in effect, established that the term in order to propose candidates to be nominated Magistrate of the Supreme Tribunal before the Nominating Judicial Committee "must not be *less* that thirty continuous days;" wording that has been change through a "notice" published by the Secretary of the Assembly in the Official Gazette stating that establishing that instead of the word "*less*" the correct word to be used in the antonym word "*more*" in the sense of the term "must not be more that thirty continuous days." That means that the "reform" of the statute by changing a word (less to more), transformed a minimum term was transformed into a maximum term in order to reduce the term to nominate candidates and allow the current national Assembly to proceed to make the election before the new National Assembly initiates its activities in January 2010.[289] This is the "procedure" currently used in order to reform statutes, by means of the reprinting of the text in the *Official Gazette*, without any possible judicial review.

In any case, this is currently happening, so with this sort of actions, we will then be able to characterize the government, not only by its constant actions adopted per-

---

288   See *Gaceta Oficial* N° 39.522 of October 1, 2010

289   See the comments in Víctor Hernández Mendible, "Sobre la nueva reimpresión por "supuestos errores" materiales de la LOTSJ en la *Gaceta Oficial* N° 39.522, de 1 de octubre de 2010," and Antonio Silva Aranguren, "Tras el rastro del engaño, en la web de la Asamblea Nacional," published as an *Addendum* to the book of Allan R. Brewer-Carías and Víctor Hernández Mendible, *Ley Orgánica del Tribunal Supremo de Justicia de 2010*, Editorial Jurídica Venezolana, Caracas 2010.

verting or defrauding the Constitution, but now, also, defrauding the popular will as it was expressed in the last legislative election. This is the tragic institutional situation we are currently experiencing in Venezuela, where of course, no amparo proceedings can be effectively filed in order to face the arbitrary actions of the government.

Pittsburgh, November 5, 2010

CHAPTER XIX

ON THE SITUATION OF THE JUDICIARY IN VENEZUELA
AS AN INSTRUMENT FOR POLITICAL PERSECUTION

(2013)

This essay was written for my Presentation at the Forum on *Political Use of the Judicial System, The State of Justice in Latin America*, organized by the American Forum for Freedom and Prosperity and the Inter American Institute for Democracy, at the United States Capitol, Rayburn House Office Building, Washington, October 8th, 2013.

The most important institutional legacy left by Hugo Chávez Frías in Venezuela, after fourteen years of authoritarian government has been the complete control his government managed to establish upon the Judicial branch of Government, erasing from the political landscape of the country the very notion of separation of powers. The "State of Justice," which is an expression used in the text of the Constitution is essentially nonexistent, and the "Political Use of the Judicial System," which is the title of this Forum, is the most common trend of the Judiciary in the country.

The submission of the Judicial System to the government began in 1999, after the unconstitutional convening of a costume-made Constituent Assembly, completely controlled by the followers of Hugo Chávez, then the newly elected President of the Republic. That Constituent Assembly was used as his main tool for materializing a Coup d'Etat, in order to assure the political assault on all branches of government, of course depict the opposition of the very few independent members that were elected; only four of 131. I was one of those four members, challenging since then, the unconstitutional assault of power.

One of the first decisions adopted by the Constituent Assembly was the political intervention of the Judiciary, by appointing a so called "Commission of Judicial Emergency," which although with other name continued to function in an endless transitional way until 2011, in charge of dismissing and appointing judges in a discretionary way, that is, in charge of preventing the enforcement of the constitutional provisions of the new 1999 Constitution on matters of independence, autonomy and impartiality of judges.

The same Constituent Assembly, in December 1999, in contempt of the Constitution, that is, violating both, the old (still in force) 1961 Constitution, and the new (approved but still not published) 1999 Constitution, eliminated the former Supreme Court, dismissed all its Justices, and proceeded to appoint new Justices of the new Supreme Tribunal of Justice, but without fulfilling the conditions established in the to-be new Constitution, beginning the Supreme Tribunal to be completely packed with the President's supporters.

It has been precisely that Supreme Tribunal, which in Venezuela, according to the Constitution is the body in charge of governing and managing the Judiciary, the one that during the past fourteen years has been the most ominous instrument for consolidating authoritarianism in the country, as well as the main tool in order to legitimate the violations of the Constitution, being the government sure that that controlled Tribunal will never exercise any sort of judicial review over the unconstitutional acts of government, as in fact has been the situation during the past fourteen years.

This is the only reason that could explain why a Head of State of our times could publicly exclaim in Television "*I am the Law.... I am the State* !!; as Chavez did in 2001, and again, in 2008; and expression that is enough to understand the tragic institutional situation that Venezuela has been facing, characterized by a complete absence of separation of powers and, consequently, of a democratic and rule of law government, and of course of a State of Justice.

The consequence of the political control on the Judiciary has been the complete absence of judicial review over the government actions; a situation that was completely consolidated in 2004, when the new Organic Law of the Supreme Tribunal of Justice was sancioned increasing the number of magistrates from twenty to thirty-two, distorting again the constitutional conditions for their appointment and dismissal. The reform, as was pointed out by the Inter-American Commission on Human Rights its *2004 Annual Report*, "lack the safeguards necessary to prevent other branches of government from undermining the Supreme Tribunal's independence and to keep narrow or temporary majorities from determining its composition."

And in fact, after the reform, the process for selecting the new Magistrates, was completely controlled by the President of the Republic, as was publicly recognized by the head of the parliamentary nominating committee, when he publicly recognized and accepted the personal involvement of the President in the nominating process, announcing, regarding the selected Justices, that "There is now one in the group of nominees that could act against us." As simple as that, completely eliminating with this highly politicized Supreme Tribunal, not only the autonomy of the Judiciary, but the basic principle of separation of powers.

Through that Supreme Tribunal, which in substitution of the former National Council of the Judiciary, is in charge of governing and administering the Judiciary, the political control over all judges has been also assured and progressively reinforced, making in fact completely inapplicable the provisions of the 1999 Constitution regarding the independence and autonomy of judges, that was supposed to be guarantied by means of their selection through public competitions and their removal only by courts of a disciplinary jurisdiction. On the contrary, since 2000, no public competition has been made in order to appoint judges, being the judiciary almost exclusively made up of temporary and provisional judges that can be dismissed in a discretional way. Lacking of stability, the judges have been the object of political manipulation.

This political control exercised upon the Judiciary, is the only explanation to all the cases of political persecution against dissidents developed in the country. It has been the case of the persecution, for instance, *first,* of judges that have decided cases not satisfactory for the government or that had not please some high officials; *second*, against enterprises and their shareholders, particularly in the media world, because their opposition to the government policies; *third,* against innocent people that were blamed of crimes they did not commit, just in order to liberate the real criminals because their support to the government; and *fourth*, in order to persecute political outspoken individuals that have criticized the authoritarian government.

One of the leading cases showing the persecution against judges because daring to decide in an independent way, was the case of the members of the First Court on Judicial Review of Administrative Action, which in 2003 issued a preliminary injunction suspending in a temporary way, the decision of the government to hire Cuban doctors for medical social programs in Caracas without the required license, a policy that was challenged by the Venezuelan Federation of Doctors. The response of the government against the judicial ruling, not only was the official announcement made by the President of the Republic that the decision was not going to be enforced, but the subsequent search of the Court by the secret police, and the abruptly dismissal of all its judges, remaining the court closed for almost one year. The demonstrative effect of such actions was devastating, resulting since then in the factual inexistence of any possibility of judicial review regarding administrative actions. The case was brought before the Inter-American Court of Human Rights and after it ruled in 2008 that the dismissal of the judges had effectively violated the American Convention on Human Rights, the Supreme Tribunal response to the international ruling, at the request of the government, was that such decision was no enforceable in the country.

The other leading case regarding the judicial persecution of judges took place in December 2009, after a criminal judge (María Lourdes Afiuni Mora) adopted a decision, following a formal recommendation of the UN Working Group on Arbitrary Detention, ordering the release of an individual in order for him to face criminal trial while in freedom, as it is guaranteed in the Constitution. The decision did not personally pleased the President of the Republic, who only one hour later appeared in Television, asking for the detention of the judge, and for her condemnation to 30 year of prison, a term, reserved for horrendous crimes. The fact is that the judge, from that day, has remained in detention, without trial, although recently in house arrest. After such reaction, the same UN Working Group described these facts as "a blow by President Hugo Chávez to the independence of judges and lawyers in the country," demanding "the immediate release of the judge," concluding that "reprisals for exercising their constitutionally guaranteed functions and creating a climate of fear among the judiciary and lawyers' profession, serve no purpose except to undermine the rule of law and obstruct justice."

The fact is that in Venezuela, no judge can adopt any decision that could affect the government policies, or the President's wishes, or the will of high public servants. This explain the assertion made by the Inter-American Commission on Human Rights, in its *2009 Annual Report* , explaining "how large numbers of judges have been removed, or their appointments voided, without the applicable administrative proceedings," noting "with concern that in some cases, judges were removed almost immediately after adopting judicial decisions in cases with a major political impact," and concluding that "The lack of judicial independence and autonomy vis-à-vis political power is, in the Commission's opinion, one of the weakest points in Venezuelan democracy."

Regarding the second group of cases in which the Judiciary has been used for political persecution, they are referred to the exercise of freedom of expression, concluding in the shutdown of TV stations that had a line of political opposition regarding the government and the persecution of their main shareholders. One leading case was the *Radio Caracas Televisión* case, referred to a TV station that, in 2007, was the most important television station of the country, critical of the administration of President Hugo Chavez. The case is the most vivid example of the illegitimate collusion or confabulation between a politically controlled Judiciary and an authoritarian government in order to reduce freedom of expression, and to confiscate private property. For such purpose, it was the Constitutional Chamber of the Supreme Tribunal of Justice and the Political Administrative Chamber of the same Tribunal that in May 2007, instead of protecting the citizens' right of freedom of expression, conspired as docile instruments controlled by the Executive, in order to kidnap and violate them. In this case, it was the highest level of the Judiciary that covered the governmental arbitrariness with a judicial veil, executing the shout down of the TV Station, reducing the freedom of expression in the country, and with total impunity, proceeded to confiscate private property in a way that neither the Executive nor the Legislator, could have done, because being forbidden in the Constitution (art. 115). In the case, it was the Supreme Tribunal, which violated the Constitution, with the aggravating circumstance that the conspirators knew that their actions could not be controlled. This case has also been recently submitted before the Inter American Court of Human Rights.

Other cases of political persecution, also related to freedom of expression are the cases against Guillermo Zuloaga and Nelson Mezerhane; two very distinguish businessman that were the principal shareholders of Globovisión, the other independent TV station that after the takeover of Radio Caracas Television, remained with a critic line of opinion regarding the government. They both were harassed by the Public Prosecutor Office and by the Judiciary; accused of different common crimes that they did not commit; they were detained without any serious base, their enterprises were occupied and their property confiscated. They both had to leave the country, without any possibility of obtaining Justice. Their cases have also been submitted before the Inter American Commission of Human Rights.

The Judiciary, particularly on criminal matters, has also been used as the government instrument to pervert Justice, distorting the facts in specific cases of political interest, converting innocent people into criminals, and liberating criminals of all suspicion. It was the unfortunate case of the mass killings committed by government agents and supporters as a consequence of the enforcement of the so-called Plan Avila, a military order that encouraged the shooting of peoples participating in the biggest mass demonstration in Venezuelan history which on April 11, 2002, was asking for the resignation of President Chávez. The soothing provoked a general military disobedience by the high commanders, in a way witnessed by all the country in TV, which ended with the military removal of the President, although just for a few hours, until the same military reinstated him in office. Nonetheless, in order to change history, the shooting and mass killing were re-written, and those responsible that everybody saw in live in TV, because being government supporters were gratified as heroes, and the Police Officials trying to assure order in the demonstration, like the Officers Simonovic and Forero, were blamed of crimes that they did not commit, and condemned of murder with the highest term of 30 years of prison. The former Chief Justice of the Criminal Chamber of the Supreme Tribunal of Justice, general Eladio Aponte Aponte, confessed last year 2012 in a TV Program in Miami, when answering about if there were "political persons in prison in Venezuela, saying **"Yes, there are people regarding which there is an order not to let them free,"** referring particularly to **"the Police Officers,"** mentioning Officer Simonovic. The same former Justice, answering a question about *"Who gives the order,"* simply said: **"The order comes from the President's Office downwards,"** adding that **"we must have no doubts, in Venezuela there are no sewing point if it is not approved by the President." He finally said, answering a question if he** *"received the order not tolet free Simonovis"* he explained that: **"the position of the Criminal Chamber"** was **"To validate all that arrived already done; that is, in a few words, to accept that these gentlemen could not be freed.".**

To hear this answers given by one who until recently was the highest Justice in the Venezuelan Criminal System, produce no other than indignation, because it was him, as Chief Criminal Justice, the one in charge of manipulating justice, in the way he confessed; condemning the Police Officers to 30 years in prison, just because obeying orders from the Executive.

Many other cases can be highlighted, related to the use of the Judiciary in order to persecute civil opponents to the government. It was also the case of a former opposition presidential candidate, Manuel Rosales who in 2006, as Governor of the Zulia State, competed against President Chavez, when he was the candidate for reelection. In a TV program, he called Rosales, among other tings, as a bandit, a corrupt, a thief, and a mafia member, threatening him to put him in jail, and to erase him from the political map of Venezuela. Not long after, the Public Prosecutor office acted accordingly, filing an accusation against Rosales for corruption charges, having the corresponding obedient court issued an order of detention. He had to leave the country.

Other case of political persecution using the Judiciary regarding a prominent civil opposition individual is the case of Diego Arria Saliceti, former Governor, former Ambassador and former President of the General Assembly of the United Nations. After giving public declarations criticizing the government of Hugo Chávez, in 2010 the government proceeded to "rescue" his rural state, being Chávez himself the one that explained the procedure also in TV, saying that the idea was to take back for the revolution the land of some of those living dead of the fourth republic, threatening

Arria, when he said that he was going to fight against the confiscation, that the only way to "have back his property was to overthrow Chávez, because it was of the revolution." The fact is that the judicial claim filed in the case, has never even been admitted, and in 2012, in order to assure that it will never be admitted,, the Constitutional Chamber of the Supreme Tribunal decided to take the case, where it will remain for ever without decision.

Other case of political persecution using the Judiciary is my own case, which I mention at the express request of Guillermo Lousteau, one of the organizers of this Forum. Since 1998, I have opposed to the authoritarian project and policies of Hugo Chávez. At that time, I was the President of the National Academy of Political and Social Sciences, and Chávez was, for the first time, a presidential candidate Since then I challenged its authoritarian proposals for the unconstitutional convening of the National Constituent Assembly; I later was elected member of the Constituent Assembly challenging and opposing to all his authoritarian initiatives, and in 2001. I challenged the legislation he imposed by means of decree laws, abusing his powers of delegate legislation, which ignited the general protest against him, asking for his resignation.

And it was precisely the fact that I was formally asked, as a constitutional lawyer, to give a legal opinion related to the political crisis provoked by the military removal of President Chavez on April 12, 2002, being my legal opinion contrary to what the transitional brief government decreed, the excuse used for my persecution, accusing me without any sort of base or proof of conspiring to change violently the Constitution, with the only weapon that I have ever had, my pen and my freedom of speech.

After been accused only based on news papers cuttings with comments and gossips of journalist in 2005, a judicial process began in which all my judicial rights and guaranties, particularly, my rights to a due process, to defense, to the presumption of innocence, to judicial protection, to freedom of expression, and to the free exercise of the legal profession, were massive and systematically violated. The case was also brought before the Inter American Court of Human Rights, and last month as the victim, in the case *Allan R. Brewer-Carías vs. Venezuela,*

I had the opportunity not only of addressing for the first time in eight years before an independent court, but of hearing the witness presented by the State, which literally confessed the political persecution.

First, a former official of the Army, Coronel Bellorín, who confirmed before the Inter American Court that in 2002 he filed a report before the Public Prosecutor naming a few lawyers, one of which was myself, that were named in the news papers as having given their legal opinion against the decree of constitution of the brief government of transition of April 2002. Undoubtedly, he had the order – as all officials with the grade of Coronel needs to have for such an action - to involve civilians in an exclusive military favt; but at the same time he said that he did not want to involve anybody. In addition, he confirmed that his report before the Public Prosecutor was only based in news papers cuttings, containing just opinions and gossips of journalist.

We also hear the confession of the former General Public Prosecutor of Venezuela, Isaías Rodríguez, who said before the Inter-American Court that the 2005vindictment against the lawyers, including myself, for "conspiring to change violently the Constitution," was exclusively based on those news papers cuttings containing just gossips and comments of journalists, the contents of which he said to the Judges, were simple "tales", imagined by journalists, whom he said, not always are to be trusted. So during the past eight years, the witnesses of the State have confirmed before the Inter American Court that I have been persecuted in a political motivated judicial process, just because journalist tales or gossips.

The whole judicial process was the main instrument used by the government to get rid of a political opponent of the authoritarian government, seeking to silence me, and impeding me to return to my country.

The important aspect to be stressed, as it results from all these cases, is the fact that the political control developed over the Judiciary, and the political use of the Judicial System in Venezuela, has not been made in a clandestine way, but conducted openly, and systematically announced in order to subject the courts to the orders of the government.

This intensified after the government briefly lost the absolute control of the Supreme Tribunal in 2003, and Chávez himself, urged in a TV program to get rid of the Justices of the Supreme Tribunal that could vote based on "political positions," that is, in a way contrary to his actions. After the sanctioning of the Supreme Tribunal statute in 2004, he himself packed the Tribunal with Justices openly affiliated with the government. In this way, the political control of the Supreme Tribunal was assured, and through it, the political control of all the mainly provisional or temporal existing judges.

Since then, even the Justices of the Supreme Tribunal openly have proclaimed their submission to the Executive, and to the government policies, which has occurred, for instance, in the annual ceremonies for the opening of the Judicial Year. In 2005, for instance, Justice Oberto in his speech requested all judges not in connection with the Bolivarian Project, just to leave their posts; and in 2010, Justice Carrasquero praissed that "the constitutional rigidity and the principles of representative democracy, have served as utilitarian dogmas for the politicians in order to maintain" what he called "former constitutional law principles." It was also the case in 2011, of Justice Vegas expressing that the Supreme Tribunal and all the courts in general were to "severely apply the laws in order to sanction conducts contrary to the construction of Bolivarian socialism." And, finally, it was the case of Chief Justice Morales, when after the announcement of the illness of President Chávez, publicly referring to the powers of the head of State, expressed that the institutional conviction of the members of the Tribunal was to consider that Chávez's "Power represented all other Public Powers," adding that President's conception of the Republic was the source of inspiration of the courts' activities.

This submission was also confirmed last year (2012), by who the former Justice, President of the Criminal Chamber of the Supreme Tribunal, General Eladio Aponte Aponte, confessed in public that the autonomy of the Judiciary in Venezuela was no more than a fallacy, being the Judiciary completely controlled by the Executive, mentioning for instance, a weekly meeting held in the office of the Vice President of the Republic in order to decide what was going to be done by the Judiciary, and in which sense the orders were going to be given for judges to decide according to the political panorama.

All these facts shows the absolute lack in Venezuela of the most essential pillar of democracy, that is, the existence of a system of separation of powers, which at the same time is the most fundamental element of the rule of law, regarding which the President of the Supreme Tribunal of Justice, a few years ago, in 2010, just exclaimed in a Press Conference, that "the separation of powers weakens the State" and that such principle "has to be reformed."

Within this situation, it is not difficult to imagine what could be the real and effective possibility for any one dissenting from the government, which for any reason has become its target, to defend him self before any court in the country. And now, and for the near future, not even before the Inter American Court of Human Rights, due to the unconstitutional denunciation, laste year, of the American Convention by the Government

These are, unfortunately, some aspects of the current situation of the "State of Justice in Venezuela", where the "Political Use of the Judicial System," has been the main trend of the functioning of the Judiciary in the past decade.

PART FOUR
THE CONSTITUTIONAL ECONOMIC SYSTEM AND ITS DISTORTION UNDER THE AUTHORITARIAN GOVERNMENT

CHAPTER XX
THE DESTRUCTION OF THE ECONOMY: STATIZATION, NATIONALIZATION, EXPROPRIATION AND CONFISCATION OF PRIVATE ASSETS
(2009)

This essay on the the processes of "Statizaton," Nationalization, Expropiation and Confiscation of Private assets and Enterprises," is an essay analyzing the *Recent Compulsory Take Over Process of Private Economic Activities in Venezuela*, that follows in contemporary time the paths of the nationalization of the oil industry in 1975, but with the main difference that not always compensation have been satisfied. One initial aspect of the essay ("The 'Statization' of the Pre 2001 Primary Hydrocarbons Joint Venture Exploitations: Their Unilateral termination and the Assets' Confiscation of Some of the Former Private parties") was published in *Oil, Gas & Energy Law Intelligence*, www.gasandoil.com/ogel/ ISSN: 1875-418X, Issue Vol 6, Issue 2, (OGEL/TDM Special Issue on Venezuela: The battle of Contract Sanctity vs. Resource Sovereignty, edited By Elizabeth Eljuri), April 2008; and in Spanish in Víctor Hernández Mendible (Coordinador), *Nacionalización, Libertad de Empresa y Asociaciones Mixtas*, Editorial Jurídica Venezolana, Caracas 2008, pp. 123-188.

I.   PRINCIPLES OF THE VENEZUELAN ECONOMIC SYSTEM IN THE 1999 CONSTITUTION

The 1999 Venezuelan Constitution contains express provisions devoted to regulate the Economic Constitution[1] of the country, based on a system of mixed economy, in which private enterprise and the right of property and economic freedom are recognized, but also declaring the principles of social justice, and allowing the state to intervene in the economy, significantly in some cases.

1.   *The mixed economic system*

The system of mixed "social market economy"[2] has been developed since the beginning of the Oil production, combining economic freedom, private initiative, and a free–market economic model (as opposed to a state-directed economy) with the possibility of state intervention in the economy to uphold principles of social justice.

This has been possible particularly because of the special position of the state as owner of the subsoil and the oil industry, which has been nationalized since 1975.[3] This has made the state the most powerful economic entity in the nation, leading it to intervene in the country's economic activities in important ways.

It is precisely within this context that Article 299 of the 1999 Constitution sets forth that the social-economic regime of Venezuela shall be based on the principles of social justice, democratization, efficiency, free competition, environmental protection, productivity, and solidarity, with a view to ensuring overall human development and a dignified and useful existence for the community. Thus, Article 299 expressly establishes that the state must "jointly with private initiative" promote "the harmonious development of the national economy for the purpose of generating sources of employment, a high national level of added value, in order to elevate the standard of living of the population and strengthen the nation's economic sovereign-

1   See Allan R. Brewer-Carías, "Reflexiones sobre la Constitución Económica," in *Estudios sobre la Constitución Española. Homenaje al Profesor Eduardo García de Enterría,* Madrid 1991, 3839-53.

2   See Henrique Meier, "La Constitución económica," *Revista de Derecho Corporativo* 1, Caracas 2001, 9-74; Ana C. Núñez Machado, "Los principios económicos de la Constitución de 1999," *Revista de Derecho Constitucional* 6, Editorial Sherwood, Caracas 2002, 129-40; Claudia Briceño Aranguren and Ana C. Núñez Machado, "Aspectos económicos de la nueva Constitución," in *Comentarios a la Constitución de la República Bolivariana de Venezuela,* Vadell Hermanos Editores, Caracas 2000, 177ff.; Jesús Ollarves Irazábal, "La vigencia constitucional de los derechos económicos y sociales en Venezuela," in *Libro Homenaje a Enrique Tejera París, Temas sobre la Constitución de 1999,* Centro de Investigaciones Jurídicas (CEIN), Caracas 2001, 159-92.

3   See Organic Law That Reserves to the State the Industry and Commerce of Hydrocarbons, *Official Gazette* Extra, N° 1.769, Aug. 29, 1975. See Allan R. Brewer-Carías, "Introducción al régimen jurídico de las nacionalizaciones en Venezuela," *Archivo de Derecho Público y Ciencias de la Administración* 3, Instituto de Derecho Público, Facultad de Ciencias Jurídicas y Políticas, Universidad Central de Venezuela, Caracas 1981, 23-44.

ty, guaranteeing legal certainty, solidity, dynamism, sustainability, permanence, and economic growth with equity, in order to guarantee a just distribution of wealth by means of strategic democratic, participative and open planning."

The economic system is therefore based on economic freedom, private initiative, and free competition in combination with the state as promoter of economic development, regulator of economic activity, and planner together with civil society. As the Constitutional Chamber of the Supreme Tribunal of Justice stated in Decision N° 117 (February 6, 2001),[4] this is "a socioeconomic system that is in between a free market (in which the state acts as a simple programmer [*programador*] for an economy that is dependent upon the supply and demand of goods and services) and an interventionist economy (in which the state actively intervenes as the 'primary entrepreneur')." The Constitution promotes "joint economic activity between the state and private initiative in the pursuit of, and in order to concretely realize the supreme values consecrated in the Constitution," and to pursue "the equilibrium of all the forces of the market, and joint activity between the State and private initiative." In accord with that system, the Supreme Tribunal ruled that the Constitution "advocates a series of superior normative values with respect to the economic regime, consecrating free enterprise within the framework of a market economy and, fundamentally, within the framework of the Social State under the Rule of Law (the *Welfare State*, the State of Well-being or the Social Democratic State). This is a social State that is opposed to authoritarianism."[5] Nonetheless, in practice, particularly during the past decade (1999–2009), this framework has been changed as a result of the authoritarian government that developed, inclining the balance toward state participation in the economy through a process of progressive state appropriation ("statization") of the economy, reduction of economic freedoms, and an increase in the country's dependency on oil production.[6]

2.   *Reduced property rights and economic freedoms*

Title 3 of the 1999 Constitution also contains a declaration of economic rights (Chapter 7, Articles 112–118), including economic freedom and the right to private property.

---

4   See *Revista de Derecho Público* 85–88, Editorial Jurídica Venezolana, Caracas 2001, 212-18.

5   The values alluded to, according to the doctrine of the Constitutional Chamber, "are developed through the concept of free enterprise" (*libertad de empresa*), which encompasses both a subjective right "to dedicate oneself to the economic activity of one's choice" and a principle of economic regulation, "according to which the will of the business (*voluntad de la empresa*) to make its own decisions is manifest. The State fulfills its role of intervention in this context. Intervention can be direct (through businesses) or indirect (as an entity regulating the market)," *id.*

6   As reported by Simón Romero, "Chávez Reopens Oil Bids to West as Prices Plunge," *New York Times*, Jan. 12, 2009, 1: in 2009, Venezuela was "reliant on oil for about 93 percent of its export revenue in 2008, up from 69 percent in 1998."

Regarding economic freedom, Article 112 of the Constitution declares the right of all persons to develop the economic activity of their choice, without other limits than those established by statute for reasons of human development, security, sanitation, environmental protection, and other social interests. In any case, the state must promote private initiative, guaranteeing the creation of wealth and its just distribution, as well as the production of goods and services to satisfy the needs of the population; freedom to work; and free enterprise, commerce, and industry – without prejudice to the power of the state to promulgate measures to plan, rationalize, and regulate the economy and promote the overall development of the country.

In 2007, by means of the draft constitutional reforms (rejected by referendum held in December of that same year), the president proposed to eliminate this constitutional provision, substituting it with one defining as a matter of state policy the obligation to promote "the development of a Productive Economic Model, that is intermediate, diversified and independent . . . founded upon the humanistic values of cooperation and the preponderance of common interests over individual ones, guaranteeing the meeting of the people's social and material needs, the greatest possible political and social stability, and the greatest possible sum of happiness."

The proposal added that the state, in the same way, "shall promote and develop different forms of businesses and economic units from social property, directly or communally, as well as indirectly or through the state." According to that norm, the state was to promote "economic units of social production and/or distribution, that may be mixed properties held between the State, the private sector, and the communal power, so as to create the best conditions for the collective and cooperative construction of a Socialist Economy."[7]

Article 115 of the Constitution, although following the orientation of the previous 1961 Constitution in the sense of guaranteeing the right to property, did not establish private property as having a social function to be accomplished, as did the 1961 Constitution.[8] Nonetheless, it provides that property shall be subject to such contributions, restrictions, and obligations as may be established by law in the service of the public or general interest. However, Article 115 defines the attributes of the right to property that traditionally were enumerated only in the Civil Code (Article 545); that is, the right to use, enjoy, and dispose of property are now in the Constitution.

The 2007 constitutional reforms proposed radical changes to this constitutional regime regarding property rights. The president sought to eliminate private property as a constitutionally protected right and to substitute recognition of private property as "assets for use and consumption or as means of production," together with other

7   See Allan R. Brewer-Carías, *La Reforma Constitucional de 2007 (Sancionada inconstitucionalmente por la Asamblea Nacional el 2 de Noviembre de 2007)*, Editorial Jurídica Venezolana, Caracas 2007,127ff.

8   See Allan R. Brewer-Carías "El derecho de propiedad y libertad económica. Evolución y situación actual en Venezuela," in *Estudios sobre la Constitución. Libro Homenaje a Rafael Caldera,* Caracas 1979, 2:1139-246.

forms of properties and, in particular, public property. The proposed reform regarding Article 115 of the Constitution recognized and guaranteed "different forms of property" instead of guaranteeing the right to private property, enumerating them as follows: public property, which belongs to state entities; social property, which belongs to the people jointly and to future generations; collective property, which pertains to social groups or persons and is exploited for their common benefit, use, or enjoyment, and may be of social or private origin; mixed property, ownership of which is by the public, social, collective, and private sectors in different combinations, for the exploitation of resources or the execution of activities, subject always to the absolute economic and social sovereignty of the nation; and private property, which is owned by "natural or legal persons, only regarding assets for use or consumption, or as means of production legitimately acquired."[9]

With respect to expropriation, Article 115 of the Constitution establishes that expropriation can be decreed for any kind of property only for reasons of public benefit or social interest, and then by means of a judicial process and payment of just compensation.[10] Consequently, the Constitution prohibits confiscation (expropriation without compensation), except in cases permitted by the Constitution itself, regarding property of persons responsible for crimes committed against public property or who have illicitly enriched themselves in exercising public office. Confiscations may also take place regarding property deriving from business, financial, or any other activities connected with illicit trafficking of psychotropic or narcotic substances (Articles 116 and 271).

Article 307 of the Constitution declares the regime of large private real estate holdings (*latifundio*) to be contrary to social interests, charging the legislator with taxing idle lands and establishing necessary measures to transform them into productive economic units, as well as to recover arable land. The same constitutional provision entitles peasants to own land, thus constitutionalizing the obligation of the state to protect and promote associative and private forms of property to guarantee agricultural production and to oversee sustainable arrangements on arable lands to guarantee their food-producing potential. In exceptional cases, the same article requires that the legislature use federal tax revenue to fund financing, research, technical assistance, transfer of technology, and other activities aimed to raise productivity and competitiveness of the agricultural sector.

3   The almost-unlimited possibility of state intervention in the economy

In the economic arena, the Constitution is marked by statism, as it attributes to the state the fundamental responsibility in the arrangement and provision of basic public services in health, education, and social security areas and those pertaining to

---

9   See Allan R. Brewer-Carías, *La Reforma Constitucional de 2007 (Sancionada inconstitucionalmente por la Asamblea Nacional el 2 de Noviembre de 2007)*, Editorial Jurídica Venezolana, Caracas 2007, 122ff.

10   See José L. Villegas Moreno, "El derecho de propiedad en la Constitución de 1999," in *Estudios de derecho administrativo: Libro homenaje a la Universidad Central de Venezuela*, Imprenta Nacional, Caracas 2001, 2:565-82.

homes: distribution of water, gas, and electricity. It is also derived from the regulation of state power to control and plan economic activities.

Consequently, the articles of the Constitution regarding the economy are those destined for state intervention. Only succinct rules are devoted to regulating economic freedom (Article 112) and private property (Article 115); the necessary balance between public and private sectors is absent. In the latter, only activities not fundamental to generating wealth and employment are privileged, such as agricultural (Article 305), crafts (Article 309), small and medium enterprises (Article 308), and tourism (Article 310).

In effect, the Constitution also regulates various forms of state economic intervention that have developed in Venezuela in the past decades. The Constitution regulates the state as a promoter – that is, without substituting private initiatives – to foster and order the economy to ensure the development of private initiative. Article 112 sets forth that in any case, the state must promote private initiative, guaranteeing the creation of wealth and its just distribution, as well as the production of goods and services to satisfy needs of the population; freedom to work; and free enterprise, commerce, and industry – without prejudice to the power of the state to promulgate measures to plan, rationalize, and regulate the economy and promote the overall development of the country.

In this same regard, Article 299 sets forth that the state, jointly with private initiative, shall promote the harmonious development of the national economy to the end of generating sources of employment, a high rate of domestic added value, an increased standard of living for the population, and strengthened economic sovereignty of the country. It also guarantees the reliability of the law, as well as the solid, dynamic, sustainable, continuing, and equitable growth of the economy, to ensure just distribution of wealth through participatory democratic strategic planning with open consultation.

Specifically regarding agricultural activities, Article 305 of the Constitution establishes that the state shall promote sustainable agriculture as the strategic basis for overall rural development and, consequently, shall guarantee the population a secure food supply, defined as the sufficient and stable availability of food within the national sphere and timely and uninterrupted access to the same for consumers. A secure food supply must be achieved by developing and prioritizing internal agricultural and livestock production, understood as production deriving from the activities of agriculture, livestock, fishing, and aquaculture. Food production is in the national interest and is fundamental to the economic and social development of the nation. To that end, the state shall promulgate such financial, commercial, and technological transfer; land tenancy; infrastructure; training; and other measures as may be necessary to achieve strategic levels of self-sufficiency. In addition, it shall promote actions in the national and international economic context to compensate for the disadvantages inherent to agricultural activity. The state shall protect the settlement and communities of nonindustrialized fishermen, as well as their fishing banks in continental waters and those close to the coastline, as defined by law.

Regarding rural development, Article 306 imposes on the state the duty to promote conditions for overall rural development, for the purpose of generating employment and ensuring the rural population an adequate level of well-being, as well as their inclusion in national development. It shall likewise promote agricultural activity and optimum land use by providing infrastructure projects, supplies, loans, training services, and technical assistance.

Regarding industrial activities, Article 308 obligates the state to protect and promote small– and medium–sized manufacturers, cooperatives, savings funds, family-owned businesses, small businesses, and any other form of community association for purposes of work, savings, and consumption, under an arrangement of collective ownership, to strength the country's economic development based on the initiative of the people. Training, technical assistance, and appropriate financing are guaranteed. However, Article 309 provides that typical Venezuelan crafts and folk industries enjoy special protection of the state, to preserve their authenticity, and receive credit facilities to promote production and marketing.

On commercial matters, Article 301 reserves to the state the use of trade policy to protect the economic activities of public and private Venezuelan enterprises. In this regard, more advantageous status than that established for Venezuelan nationals will not be granted to foreign persons, enterprises, or entities. Foreign investment is subject to the same conditions as domestic investment.

Finally, Article 310 of the Constitution declares tourism an economic activity of national interest and of high priority in the country's strategy of diversification and sustainable development. As part of the foundation of the socioeconomic regime the Constitution contemplates, the state will promulgate measures to guarantee the development of tourism and will create and strengthen a national tourist industry.

Regarding economic planning, Article 112 empowers the state to promulgate measures to plan, rationalize, and regulate the economy and promote the overall development of the country. The president must formulate the National Plan of Development and, once approved by the National Assembly, direct its execution (Articles 187.8 and 236.18).

The Constitution establishes no provisions for the state to promote highly qualified or heavy industries, though it does establish that the state can reserve for its own exploitation, through an organic law and by reasons of national convenience, the petroleum industry (already nationalized since 1975) and other industries, operations, and goods and services that are in the public interest and of a strategic nature. The state shall promote the domestic manufacture of raw materials deriving from the exploitation of nonrenewable natural resources, with a view to assimilating, creating, and inventing technologies; generating employment and economic growth; and creating wealth and well-being for the people (Article 302).

As aforementioned, on the basis of a similar constitutional provision establishing the power of the state to reserve for its own exploitation services or resources (Article 97 of the 1961 Constitution), the oil industry was nationalized in 1975 and is managed by the state-owned enterprise Petróleos de Venezuela S.A. Article 303 of the 1999 Constitution set forth that for reasons of economic and political sovereignty and national strategy, the state shall retain all shares of that public enterprise, with the exception of its subsidiaries, strategic joint ventures, enterprises, and any other venture established or to be established as a consequence of carrying on the business of Petróleos de Venezuela. This last possibility has been considered a loosening of the strict nationalization process carried out through the 1975 organic law that reserves to the state the industry and commercialization of hydrocarbons.[11] The 2000 Organic Law on Hydrocarbons allowed for the establishment of mixed companies for the exploitation of primary hydrocarbons activities, although with the state as majority shareholder[12] – that law was implemented in 2006–7.[13]

With respect to public enterprises in general, Article 300 of the Constitution refers to the statutes to determine the conditions for the creation of functionally decentralized entities to carry out social or entrepreneurial activities, with a view to ensuring the reasonable economic and social productivity of the public resources invested in such activities.

All the aforementioned provisions regarding the participation of the state in the economy were proposed to be radically changed in the 2007 draft constitutional reforms, which attempted to reduce the whole economic role of the state to promote and develop economic and social activities "under the principles of the socialist economy" (Article 300).

Thus, under the Constitution, the state is responsible for almost everything and is able to regulate everything. Private enterprise appears to be shunned. The 1999 Constitution did not assimilate the previous decades' experience of regulating, controlling, and planning an entrepreneurial state. The necessity of granting privileges to private enterprises and stimulating the generation of wealth and employment to society was not understood.

Globally, the result of the constitutional text regarding the economy is a Constitution created for state intervention in the economy, not for the development of the economy by private sectors under the principle of subsidiary state intervention.

Nonetheless, the government in 1999, while the Constitution was been drafted, sanctioned a statute in order to encourage investments in the country, particularly foreign investments.

---

11   See Allan R. Brewer-Carías, "El régimen de participación del capital privado en las industrias petrolera y minera: Desnacionalización y regulación a partir de la Constitución de 1999," in *VII Jornadas Internacionales de Derecho Administrativo Allan R. Brewer-Carías, El Principio de Legalidad y el Ordenamiento Jurídico-Administrativo de la Libertad Económica,* Fundación de Estudios de Derecho Administrativo FUNEDA, Caracas 2004, 15-58.

12   Ley Orgánica de Hidrocarburos, *Official Gazette* N° 38.493, Aug. 4, 2006.

13   See Allan R. Brewer-Carías, "The 'Statization' of the Pre-2001 Primary Hydrocarbons Joint Venture Exploitations: Their Unilateral Termination and the Assets Confiscation of Some of the Former Private Parties," in *Oil, Gas & Energy Law Intelligence* 6. Available at http://www.gasandoil.com/ogel/; and "La estatización de los convenios de asociación que permitían la participación del capital privado en las actividades primarias de hidrocarburos sucritos antes de 2002, mediante su terminación anticipada y unilateral y la confiscación de los bienes afectos a los mismos," in *Nacionalización, libertad de empresa y asociaciones mixtas,* coord. Víctor Hernández Mendible, Editorial Jurídica Venezolana, Caracas 2008, 123-88.

II THE COMPULSORY MEANS FOR THE ACQUISITION OF PRIVATE ASSETS IN VENEZUELA

One of the general trend of the economic policy of the authoritarian government that has taken shape in Venezuela, following the framework established in the 1999 Constitution, has been the progressive "statization" of the economy, that is, the appropriation by the State of private industries and services. This process has been fueled during the past decade, in addition of been an express public policy, because the possibility for the State to dispose without control, the outstanding fiscal revenues that have derived from the increase of the oil price, in an Oil Producer country like Venezuela, where the Oil Industry was already nationalized since 1975.

This process of "statization" has been made through the acquisition of industries and services by means of private law procedures, as it happened with the electricity and telephone companies; and also, through the use of the public law instruments allowed in the Constitution like the nationalization of economic sectors, which always imply the expropriation of the private assets of the reserved economic sector. But in many cases, the process of forced appropriation of private assets has occurred as a result of confiscations that nonetheless are forbidden in the Constitution.

In the Venezuelan legal system, the term "nationalization" refers to the institution of public law that combines the reserve of an economic activity to the State with the acquisition, normally through expropriation, of private assets used in such activities. I first explained this institution in 1974, when I wrote that "an authentic nationalization of an economic sector results when the measure of reservation and the expropriation technique are adopted in conjunction. The latter [expropriation] is the mechanism to make the reservation effective."[14]

The possibility for the State, through an organic law and because motives of national convenience or interest, to reserve for itself some industries and services was established in article 97 (equivalent to Article 302 of the 1999 Constitution) of the 1961 Constitution, which was initially used for the nationalization of the industry of natural gas that was reserved to the State in 1971;[15] and of the iron mineral exploitation industry also reserved for the State in 1974.[16]

The oil industry and commerce were nationalized in 1975 by means of the 1975 Organic Law Reserving to the State the Industry and Commerce of Hydrocarbons,[17]

---

14 See Allan R. Brewer-Carías, "Comentarios en torno a la nacionalización petrolera" in *Revista Resumen,* N° 55, Vol. V, Caracas, 1974. p. 22. (English translation). See also, Román J. Duque Corredor, *El Derecho de la Nacionalización Petrolera*, Colección Monografías Jurídicas N° 10, Editorial Jurídica Venezolana, p. 22.

15 *Ley que Reserva al Estado la Industria del Gas Natural),* in *Gaceta Oficial* N° 29.594 of August 26, 1971

16 Decree-Law N° 580 of November 26, 1974 (*Decreto Ley que Reserva al Estado la Industria de la Explotación del Mineral de Hierro),* in *Gaceta Oficial* N° 30.577 of December 16, 1974

17 *Gaceta Oficial (Extraordinary)* N° 1.769 of August 29, 1975. The 1975 Organic Nationalization Law reserved to the State all matters "related to the exploration of the national territory in search for petroleum, asphalt and any other hydrocarbons; to the exploitation of reservoirs

which reserved the activity to the State, disposed the termination of the then existing concessions for the exploration and exploitation of oil in the country that were assigned to foreign enterprises, and provided a procedure for the expropriation of private assets engaged in the activity, including the payment of compensation to the private participants in the industry. That reservation was maintained in article 302 of the 1999 Constitution, in which is established that "The State reserves for itself, by means of the corresponding organic law and for reasons of national convenience, the oil activity and other industries, exploitations, services and assets of public interest and strategic character..." The Oil Industry reservation to the State was also kept in the 2001 Organic Hydrocarbons Law, whose article 9 establishes that "The activities relating to the exploration in search of hydrocarbon reservoirs encompassed in this Decree-Law, to their extraction in natural state, to their initial production, transport and storage, are denominated as primary activities for purposes of this Decree-Law. In accordance with what is provided in article 302 of the Constitution of the Bolivarian Republic of Venezuela, the primary activities indicated, as well as those relating to works required by their management, remain reserved to the State in the terms established in this Decree-Law."[18]

On the other hand, as provided in Article 115 of the Constitution, expropriation is the compulsory acquisition of any privately owned assets, rights, or property by the State, through a specific procedure and with the payment of just compensation, regardless of whether the economic sector has been reserved to the State, or the interests in question are taken individually or as part of a more broadly applicable measure. The 2002 Expropriation Law[19] defines expropriation in its article 2, as "an institution of Public Law, by which the State acts for the benefit of a cause of public utility or social interest, with the purpose of obtaining the compulsory transfer of the right to property or any other right of private individuals [*particulares*] to its [the State's] patrimony, through a final judicial decision and timely payment of just compensation."[20]

An expropriation can be effected through an act of general effects like a special statute, as was the case, for instance, with the expropriations decided in the 1970s in connection with the reservation to the State of the iron industry and of the oil industry. In those cases, the statutes implementing the nationalization declared the reser-

---

thereof, the manufacturing or upgrading, transportation by special means and storage; internal and external trade of the exploited and upgraded substances, and the works required for their handling [...]" (Article 1). Article 5 ordered that these activities be exercised directly by the National Executive or entities owned by it, and authorized private participation through operating agreements or association agreements in certain circumstances.

18   2001 Organic Law of Hydrocarbons in *Gaceta Oficial* N° 37.323 of November 13, 2001

19   *Gaceta Oficial* N° 37.475 of July 1, 2002

20   (English translation (emphasis added).) ["[...] *una institución de Derecho Público, mediante la cual el Estado actúa en beneficio de una causa de utilidad pública o de interés social, con la finalidad de obtener la transferencia forzosa del derecho de propiedad o algún otro derecho de los particulares, a su patrimonio, mediante sentencia firme y pago oportuno de justa indemnización.*"]

vation and also ordered the expropriation of the interests of the former concessionaries providing for specific rules of procedure.

The 2002 Expropriation Law[21] establishes the general procedure for expropriation and contemplates the possibility of an expropriation decree applying to more than one asset of more than one individual or entity (articles 5 and 6). While this law regulates a procedure for expropriation, Article 4 contemplates that other procedures may be provided by special laws. This possibility includes special laws that expropriate multiple assets of multiple subjects.

Moreover, the Supreme Court of Justice has held that "the institution of expropriation applies not only when the State resorts to it, through the organisms authorized to do so, in compliance with the Law that governs it, but also within its conceptual amplitude, its principles are applied by extension to all the cases of deprivation of private property, or of patrimonial diminution, for reasons of public utility or public interest."[22]

In Venezuela, all property, rights, and assets may be subject to lawful expropriation and are protected from unlawful expropriation This follows from Article 115 of the Constitution, which provides the constitutional guaranty of the right to property, and refers to the conditions for the expropriation of "any type of assets," and is also reflected in Article 2 of the 2002 Expropriation Law which refers to the compulsory transfer of the "right to property or any other right of private parties." One of the important changes introduced in the 1999 Constitution and in the 2002 Expropriation Law was precisely to clarify that expropriation, as a compulsory means for the State to acquire assets, can refer not only to "the right to property" (*derecho de*

---

21 *Gaceta Oficial* N° 37.475 of July 1, 2002. See text and comments on this law in Allan R. Brewer-Carías, "Introducción General al Régimen de la Expropiación" in Allan R. Brewer-Carías, Gustavo Linares Benzo, Dolores Aguerrevere Valero y Caterina Balasso Tejera, *Ley De Expropiación por Causa de Utilidad Pública o Interés Social*, Colección Textos Legislativos N° 26, 1ª Ed., EJV, Caracas 2002, pp. 7-100. The 2002 Expropriation law replaced the 1947 Law on Expropriation without altering its fundamental rules. *Gaceta Oficial* N° 22.458 of November 6, 1947. For general comments on this law, see *generally* Allan R. Brewer-Carías, Enrique Pérez Olivares, Tomás Polanco e Hildegard Rondón de Sansó, "Expropriation in Venezuela" in A. Lowenfeld (ed.), *Expropriation in the America A. Comparative Legal Study*, New York, 1971, pp. 199-240. For the text of the 1947 law and administrative doctrine and judicial case law regarding expropriation, up to 1965 *see generally* Allan R. Brewer-Carías, *La Expropiación por Causa de Utilidad Pública o Interés Social (Jurisprudencia, Doctrina, Administrativa, Legislación)*, Colección de Publicaciones del Instituto de Derecho Público, Vol. 2, Facultad de Derecho, Universidad Central de Venezuela, Caracas, 1966, pp. 416 ff. For case law on the subject up to 1975, see *generally* Allan R. Brewer-Carías, *Jurisprudencia de la Corte Suprema 1930-1974 y Estudios de Derecho Administrativo, Tomo VI: La Propiedad y la Expropiación por Causa de Utilidad Pública e Interés Social*, Ediciones del Instituto de Derecho Público, Facultad de Derecho, Universidad Central de Venezuela, Caracas 1979, pp. 690 ff.

22 See Supreme Court of Justice, Politico-Administrative Chamber, Decision of October 3, 1990 (*Case: Inmobiliaria Cumboto, C.A.*) in *Jurisprudencia Ramírez & Garay*, CXIV, Caracas 1990, pp. 551-552.

propiedad) but also to "any other right" of private parties (*algún otro derecho de los particulares*) (Article 2), or to "assets of any nature" (*bienes de cualquier naturaleza*) (Article 7). Accordingly, expropriation is related to the constitutional guaranty of the right to property, any other rights or assets of any nature, which cannot be compulsorily taken by the State except through a judicial procedure (juridical guaranty) and by means of just compensation (patrimonial or economic guaranty). Expropriation without compensation is a "confiscation" and is unconstitutional except in limited circumstances. That is, any taking of private property, rights or assets by the State, or any extinction of private individual rights by the State without following the expropriation procedures and requirements or the other means that the State has to acquire property (requisition, seizure, reversion, authorized confiscation) is considered a "confiscation" in the Venezuelan system, which is prohibited in the Constitution. Confiscation has been traditionally prohibited in Venezuela, and it is only allowed as a sanction as a consequence of a criminal conviction (Article 116).

Any "limitations," "contributions, restrictions and obligations" on property, rights, or assets become an expropriation of such interests when they deprive the owner of the essence of his asset or where such regulations annihilate the property, right, or asset in question. For example, based on Articles 115 and 116 of the Constitution, the Constitutional Chamber of the Supreme Tribunal has stated that "such limits must be established on the basis of a legal text, as long as said restrictions do not constitute an absolute or irrational impairment of such property right. That is, impeding the patrimonial capacity of the individuals in such way that it eventually extinguishes it."[23] Moreover, the Supreme Court has explained that:

> "Article 99 of the Constitution establishes the guaranty of the right to property. [...] the limitation imposed on that right cannot represent an impairment that implies absorption of its attributions to the extent that it eliminates it. [...] This is, the right to property may be limited, restricted with respect to most of its content, attributions and scope, but this cannot exceed the limit -it is emphasized- by virtue of which such right is left completely empty, there is a central core of that right that is not susceptible of being impaired by the legislator, since if this were so, we would find ourselves before another legal institution (for example expropriation)."[24]

And with regards to the prohibition of confiscation, the Court has explained that:

> "the prohibition of confiscation is related to the principle of reasonability that must guide the adjustment between the actions of the State and the impact on the legal sphere of those subject to the law, for which care must be taken that the activity does not formally or substan-

---

23   Supreme Tribunal of Justice, Constitutional Chamber, Decision N° 3003 of October 14, 2005 (Exp. 04-2538)

24   See Supreme Court of Justice, Decision of April 29, 1997 in *Revista de Derecho Público*, N° 69-70, Editorial Jurídica Venezolana, Caracas 1997, pp. 391-392.

tially reach the confiscation of the assets of the person, which occurs with the total dispossession of the assets or their equivalent."[25]

III THE 2006-2007 "STATIZATION" PROCESS OF THE PRIVATE ENTERPRISES PARTICIPATING IN THE NATIONALIZED OIL INDUSTRY ACCORDING TO THE 1975 NATIONALIZATION ORGANIC LAW

The 1975 Nationalization Organic Law, although it reserved to the State the Oil Industry, established the possibility for private enterprises to participate in the primary hydrocarbons activities in two ways: Operating Agreements and Exploration at Risk and Profit Sharing Agreements which where subscribed with State-owned oil companies in the nineties. Although the 2001 Organic Hydrocarbons Law changed the legal framework for the participation of private enterprises in the oil industry reducing it to mixed companies, repealing the 1975 Nationalization Organic Law, in light of the general principle regarding the non-retroactive nature of laws (Article 24 of the 1999 Constitution), their norms remained in force regarding such Agreements as validly executed by the State.

Starting in 2006, the Venezuelan State initiated an oil "statization" process through the gradual elimination or reduction, by law, of private capital participation in the oil industry activities as it was conceived before the 2001 Organic Hydrocarbons Law was enacted. I use the word "statization" (*estatización*) in order to distinguish this process from the "nationalization" one, which in the Venezuelan constitutional system combines the decision to reserve to the State certain activities followed by the expropriation (by means of compensation) of the assets affected to the corresponding the activities. In the process developed in 2006-2007, the reserve to the State was already established in the 2001 Hydrocarbon Law, and the termination of the Agreements was made without compensation.[26]

This process of eliminating or sharply reducing private capital's participation in the industry, in effect, was achieved through three legislative instruments:

Firstly, by the *Law Regulating Private Participation in Primary Activities,* of April 2006, that declared the extinction or rather the early and unilateral termination of the existing Operating Agreements.

Secondly, by the *Decree-Law N° 5200 Concerning the Migration of the Association Agreements of the Orinoco Belt and of the Exploration at Risk and Profit Sharing Agreements into Mixed Companies*, of February 2007, which decided the early

---

25 Supreme Tribunal of Justice, Constitutional Chamber, Decision N° 2152 of November 14, 2007 in *Revista de Derecho Público* N° 112, Editorial Jurídica Venezolana, Caracas 2007, pp. 519 ff

26 See regarding the concept of nationalization in Venezuela, Allan R. Brewer-Carías, "Introducción al Régimen Jurídico de las Nacionalizaciones en Venezuela," in *Archivo de Derecho Público y Ciencias de la Administración*, Vol. III, 1972-1979, Tomo I, Instituto de Derecho Público, Facultad de Ciencias Jurídicas y Políticas, Universidad Central de Venezuela, Caracas 1981, pp. 23-44

and unilateral termination of the existing Association and Exploration at Risk and Profit Sharing Agreements entered into between 1993 and 2001, although providing, however, in the latter case, the possibility for such association agreements to migrate to or transform themselves into new mixed companies with minimum 50% State equity participation according to the 2001 Organic Hydrocarbon Law, Articles 22 and 27 to 32); and

Thirdly, by the *Law on the Effects of the Migration Process to Mixed Companies of the Orinoco Belt Association Agreements and the Exploration at Risk and Profit-Sharing Exploration Agreements*, of October 2007, that "confiscated" the interests, shares, participation and rights of the companies which had participated in such Agreements and Associations, but had not reached the imposed agreements for their migration to mixed companies

Pursuant to the first two laws, by extinguishing the existing public contracts, it could be said that according to the Constitution, an expropriation process was to be initiated concerning the contractual rights corresponding to the private contracting companies, although carried out directly by a statute, without following the general procedure set forth in the Expropriations Law by reason of public and social utility (2001). This two Laws, however, pursuant to Article 115 of the Constitution, generated inalienable rights for the contracting companies to be fairly compensated for the damages (expropriation of contractual rights) arising from such early and unilateral termination of the public contracts validly entered into by the State.

Nevertheless, according to the last of the above-mentioned laws, what could have initially been seen as the beginning of an expropriation process, by unilateral and early termination of the contracts, became a "confiscation" of rights in the case of the companies that did not reach an agreement with the State to continue operating under the new imposed formula of mixed companies.

1. The Extinction of the Operating Agreements

In fact, regarding the Operating Agreements executed pursuant to the former legislation between Petróleos de Venezuela S.A. (PDVSA) affiliates and private companies for the exploitation of primary hydrocarbons, the *Law Regulating Private Participation in Primary Activities*[27] passed on April 18, 2006 has as its specific purpose, to declare by Law their extinction, because their exercise as provided in article 1, had:

> "[...] been denaturalized by the Operating Agreements that arose as a result of the so-called Oil Opening, to a point where it violated the higher interests of the State and the basic elements of sovereignty."

Hence, Article 2 of the Law declared that the content of the above-mentioned Operating Agreements that arose as a result of the Oil Opening process was "incompatible with the rules set forth in the oil nationalization regime," providing moreover

---

27   *Gaceta Oficial* N° 38.419 of April 18, 2006.

"that they will be extinguished and the execution of their precepts will no longer be possible as of the publication of this Law in the *Official Gazette*" (Art. 2).

This means that on its April 18, 2006 publication date, a National Assembly statute terminated and extinguished all existing Operating Agreements, thus prematurely and unilaterally terminating validly executed public contracts. This was not the unilateral administrative rescission of a public contract by the contracting Administration, in this case PDVSA affiliates, but an early and unilateral termination of such contracts by a decision of a State legislative body, through a new Law. In such cases, the State's liability for the damages caused by the unilateral and premature termination of the contracts and the co-contractors' right to compensation are unquestionable under the public contracts ("administrative contracts") régime, since the termination constitutes an expropriation of rights, even if the decision had been taken by means of a legislative act[28].

Moreover, the Law in question provided, in advance, that:

"[...] no future contract shall authorize any private, natural or legal person to participate in activities of exploration, production, storage or initial transportation of liquid hydrocarbons, or in the benefits derived from the production of such hydrocarbons, unless such person is a minority shareholder of a mixed company, incorporated pursuant the Organic Hydrocarbons Law where the State is assured shareholding and operational control of the company" (Art. 3).

By this provision, the new statute legislatively ratified the principle set forth in the 2001 Hydrocarbons Organic Law, whereby private capital could only participate in primary activities by incorporating into mixed companies with the State regulated by the Law, which was exactly what was proposed in the Constitutional Reform Draft that was rejected by referendum in 2007[29].

The consequence of declaring the extinction of the existing Operating Agreements, apart from the State's obligation to indemnify the former contractors for the damages caused by the early and unilateral termination of the Agreements and the expropriation of their contractual rights, over which, however, the Law provided nothing in its text, was that, pursuant to Article 4 of the Law:

"[...] the Republic, either directly or through its wholly-owned companies, will reassume the exercise of the oil activities performed by private parties, in order to guarantee the continuity of such activities and by reason of their public utility and social interest, without prejudice to the incorporation of mixed companies to such end, subject to approval by the National

---

28   See Allan R. Brewer-Carías, "Algunas reflexiones sobre el equilibrio financiero en los contratos administrativos y la aplicabilidad en Venezuela de la concepción amplia de la Teoría del Hecho del Príncipe," in *Revista Control Fiscal y Tecnificación Administrativa*, Año XIII, N° 65, Contraloría General de la República, Caracas 1972, pp. 86-93.

29   See the comments in Allan R. Brewer-Carías, *La Reforma Constitucional de 2007 (Comentarios al Proyecto inconstitucionalmente sancionado por la Asamblea Nacional el 2 de Noviembre de 2007)*, Colección Textos Legislativos, N° 43, Editorial Jurídica Venezolana, Caracas 2007, pp. 129 ff.

Assembly and prior favorable report by the National Executive through the Ministry of Energy and Petroleum and by the National Assembly's Permanent Energy and Mines."

To such end the National Assembly had already adopted in March 2006 the "Accord approving the Terms and Conditions for the creation and operation of Mixed Companies"[30].

2. The beginning of the process for the early and unilateral termination of the association agreements and their transformation into mixed companies

The "Enabling" Law (Legislative Delegation Law) of February 1, 2007[31] authorized the President of the Republic to dictate legislation that would allow the State to:

> "[...] either directly or through wholly-owned companies, assume control of the activities performed by the associations operating in the Orinoco Belt, including upgrades and exploration at-risk and profit-sharing assignments, to regulate and adjust their activities within the legal framework governing the national oil industry, through mixed companies or wholly-owned State enterprises."

This legislative delegation sought, firstly, the State's assuming "control of the activities performed by the associations operating in the Orinoco Belt, including upgrades and at-risk and profit-sharing exploration assignments;" a provision that was in fact unnecessary, since that control already existed through the decision-making methodology regulated by the Association Agreements, even when the State only had a minority participating interest in them. But apart from that, secondly, what was sought by the legislative delegation was what the Legislator failed to do with the 2001 Organic Hydrocarbons Law, and which could not be done, because it could not endow it with retroactive effect by applying the 2001 Organic Law to the previous Association Contracts that had been validly executed in accordance with the previous legislation. Therefore the authorization sought to "regulate and adjust their activities within the legal framework governing the national oil industry, through mixed companies or wholly-owned State enterprises."

Upon executing such legislative delegation on February 26, 2007, the National Executive passed the *Decree-Law N° 5200 Concerning the Migration of the Association Agreements of the Orinoco Belt and of the Exploration at Risk and Profit Sharing Agreements into Mixed Companies*, thereby ordering the unilateral and early termination of the association agreements executed between 1993 and 2001, which, for the contractors that did not agree to the terms unilaterally fixed by the State, implied the expropriation of their contractual rights and the consequent right to be fairly compensated for the damages caused by the execution of such Law.

---

30   *Gaceta Oficial*, N° 38.410 of March, 31, 2006
31   *Gaceta Oficial* N° 38.617 of February 1, 2007

A. *Early termination of the Association Agreements and the attempt to have them migrate to mixed companies*

In fact, the Law in question provided that:

"[…] the associations between Petróleos de Venezuela S. A. affiliates and the private sector operating in the Orinoco Belt, and in the so-called Exploration at Risk and Profit Sharing Agreements shall be adjusted to the legal framework governing the national oil industry by becoming mixed companies pursuant to the provisions set forth in the Organic Hydrocarbons Law." (Art. 1).

This meant, purely and simply, to assign retroactive effects to the 2001 Organic Hydrocarbons Law, since it unilaterally imposed the obligation on the Association Agreements incorporated in accordance with the prior legislation to obligatory adapt to the new Law, and to its terms.

To such end, this Law, once again, provided the early and unilateral termination of public contracts that had been validly executed as Association Agreements between 1993 and 2001, between PDVSA affiliates and different private companies for the performance of primary activities; providing, moreover, not only that they were to adjust to the new legal framework of the 2001 Organic Law, to which *ex post facto* it gave retroactive effects, but it also provided that:

"[…] all activities performed by strategic associations in the Orinoco Belt, involving the companies Petrozuata, S.A., Sincrudos de Oriente, S.A., Sincor, S.A., Petrolera Cerro Negro S.A. and Petrolera Hamaca, C.A; the Exploration at Risk and Profit Sharing Agreements of Golfo de Paria Oeste, Golfo de Paria Este and la Ceiba, as well as the companies or consortia incorporated in their execution; Orifuels Sinovensa, S.A., as also the affiliates of such companies that conduct business activities in the Orinoco Belt, and throughout the production chain, **will be transferred** to the new mixed companies."

So, not only was it unilaterally decided to prematurely terminate the contracts, but it was required that if the private investor partners in the Associations that were being extinguished agreed to their transfer to new mixed companies, they could only opt to be shareholders of the mixed companies with up to a maximum participation of 40% in their equity, and having as State shareholder the *Corporación Venezolana de Petróleo, S.A.* or another affiliate of Petróleos de Venezuela, S.A. (PDVSA), with a minimum 60% share of the equity (Art. 2).

If the investing partner of an Association Agreement agreed to become a minority shareholder of the new mixed company, Article 6 of the Law provided that:

"[…] since this is a particular circumstance of public interest, and pursuant to the sole paragraph of Article 37 of the Organic Hydrocarbons Law, the choice of the minority partners in the migration process of the associations will be made directly."

The application of this exception to the general principle of selection by means of competitive bidding as required by the 2001 Organic Law could only happen, of course, if the private company that was part or partner of the Association Agreement decided to continue in the operation by forming part, as a minority shareholder, of the new mixed company. Otherwise, according to the Organic Hydrocarbons Law, if the company was not a party to one of the former Association Agreements, but rather a new private shareholder of the new mixed company that was to take on the operations of a former Association Agreement, it would have to have been selected by means of competitive procedures (Art. 37).

If the shareholding companies of the Association Agreements that were unilaterally and prematurely terminated by this Migration Law did not reach an agreement with the National Executive to form part, as shareholders, of the new mixed companies, the effect of the Law was to expropriate their contractual rights, whereupon they were entitled, pursuant to Article 115 of the Constitution, to be fairly compensated for the damages caused by the unilateral and early termination of the public contracts.

B. *The State's immediate taking over of the operations*

The legislative decision to unilaterally and prematurely put an end to the association contracts implied the need to ensure the State's immediate assumption of the actual industrial operation of each association Agreement.

To such end, the Law provided that the State shareholding company of the potential mixed companies was to be *Corporación Venezolana del Petróleo, S.A.* or the Petróleos de Venezuela, S.A. affiliate designated to such effect, had to form within 7 days following the publication of the Decree-Law, that is by March 5, 2007, "a Transition Commission for each association," also providing that such Commission had to include "the current board of directors of the respective association, in order to guarantee *the transfer to the state company* of control over all the activities performed by the associations," in a process that ended of April 30, 2007 (Art. 3).

To such end, the Law provided that the private sector companies that had formed part of the association agreements were to cooperate with *Corporación Venezolana de Petróleo, S.A.* in ensuring a safe and smooth changeover of the operator (Art. 3).

In regard to the situation of the workers on the contractor payroll of the associations to be transformed, the Law provided that as of its entry into force they were to enjoy job stability and would be covered by the Oil Industry Collective Bargaining Agreement in force for the workers of Petróleos de Venezuela, S.A. (Art. 10)

Article 2 of the Law, attributed to the Ministry of People's Power for Energy and Petroleum the power, in each case, to unilaterally determine:

> "[...] the appraisal of the Mixed Company, the shareholding participation of the Petróleos de Venezuela, S.A. affiliated designated to such effect, and the appropriate economic and financial adjustments" (Art. 2).

So it was for the State to unilaterally determine, through the respective Ministry, the value of the new mixed company to be set up to substitute each Association Agreement; the shareholding participation percentage corresponding to the PDVSA affiliate to be shareholder in each mixed company substituting each Agreement, which shareholding could in no case be less than 60% of total equity; and "the appropriate economic and financial adjustments."

Moreover, Article 7 of the Law expressly provided that the infrastructure, transportation services and improvements of the Orinoco Belt associations and of the so-called Exploration at Risk and Profit-Sharing Agreements, were to be "freely used according to the guidelines which, by means of a Resolution, are issued by the Ministry of People's Power for Energy and Petroleum," for which purpose, "the costs derived from the use of such services, will be determined by common agreement between the parties, failing which, the Ministry of People's Power for Energy and Petroleum will set the conditions for their rendering."

C. *The deadline for private companies to decide on their incorporation into the mixed companies*

Although the Law provided that the transfer of the Association Agreements to the State be immediate, as well as the consequent assumption of the operation of the Agreements by the corresponding state company, Article 4 of the Law gave the private sector companies that had been part of the extinguished Orinoco Belt Association Agreements and the so-called Exploration at Risk and Profit Sharing Agreements, a four (4) month term starting on the date the Law was published (February 26, 2007), that is, until June 26, 2007, to "agree on the terms and conditions of their *possible participation* in the new Mixed Companies," understood to be with the respective Ministry, also providing that in such case they would be conceded "two (2) extra months to submit the aforementioned terms and conditions to the National Assembly for the corresponding authorization, pursuant to the Organic Hydrocarbons Law."

Now, once the four-month term had elapsed, on June 26, 2007 "without having reached an agreement on the incorporation and operation of the Mixed Companies," then the Republic, through Petróleos de Venezuela, S.A. or any of its affiliates, was to *directly take over the activities* exercised by the associations to ensure their continuity, by reason of their character of public use and social interest (Art. 5).

The Law also provided that the acts, business and agreements conducted or executed to incorporate the Mixed Companies provided in the Law, as well as the assignment or transfer of assets and any other operations that generated enrichment or supposed the transfer, transmission or sale of assets destined to form part of the patrimony of such companies, would be exempt from the payment of taxes, rates, special contributions or any other tax liability created by the Authorities.

Nothing was mentioned in the *Migration Law* about the rights to be indemnified to the private companies that did not reach the agreement to continue as partners of the new mixed companies. However, as mentioned above, the result of the retroactive application of the 2001 Law on Association Agreements, validly executed before such Law's coming into force, was an early and unilateral termination of the Association Agreements, and an expropriation initiated by Law of the contractual rights of the contractors under such Agreements, the aforesaid pursuant to Article 115 of the Constitution, and gave rise to the right to be fairly compensated for the damages caused.

D. *Rights of the new mixed companies*

Article 8 of the Law provided that the National Executive had, by Decree, to transfer to the Mixed Companies resulting from the migration process "the right to conduct their primary activities, and to also adjudicate to them the ownership or other rights over movable or immovable property belonging privately to the Republic, that may be required for the efficient exercise of such activities." Such rights, however, can be revoked "if the operators fail to comply with their obligations, in such a way as to achieve the purpose for which such rights were transferred" (Art 8).

Similarly, by Resolution, the Ministry of People's Power for Energy and Petroleum had to designate "the areas in which the Mixed Companies were to conduct their primary activities, which were to be divided into lots with a maximum area of one hundred square kilometers (100 km^2)" (Art. 9).

E. *Applicable law and jurisdiction*

Finally, Article 13 of the Migration Law provided that

> "All facts and activities associated with this Decree-Law shall be governed by National Law, and the disputes deriving there from shall be submitted to Venezuelan jurisdiction, as provided in the Constitution of the Bolivarian Republic of Venezuela."

In regard to this provision, it should first be remembered that all the effects produced by any law passed in Venezuela, by virtue of the principle of territoriality are in principle governed by national legislation; thus if nothing is expressly provided otherwise in the text of the law, all juridical situations deriving from any law are governed by "National Law."

Apart from this, the Law set forth, with faulty drafting, that disputes arising from its provisions are to be submitted to Venezuelan jurisdiction and, once again, such disputes could not be resolved in any other way, unless the legislator expressly renounced Venezuelan jurisdiction. Therefore, disputes arising in regard to the migration of the former Associations to the new mixed companies, or from the agreements reached by the former partners of Association Agreements upon incorporating their companies as minority partners of the new mixed companies, can only be resolved by national jurisdiction.

Moreover, for example, disputes arising from decisions in the Decree-Law and their application are, without doubt, in principle also subject to Venezuelan jurisdiction, for example, in regard to the possibility of challenging the regulations of the Migration Law before the Constitutional Jurisdiction, by reason of their unconstitutionality, or challenging before the Contentious-Administrative Jurisdiction the administrative actions dictated by the National Executive pursuant to the Migration Law.

But this provision of article 13 of the Law, in no way implies the annulment of the existing clauses of the Association Agreements whose early and unilateral termination was resolved by Law, providing the submission of controversies deriving from the execution, performance and breach of the Association Agreements, to arbitral jurisdiction, even in Venezuela, as authorized by Article 151 of the Constitution. In other words, according to such constitutional provision, the contractors are entitled to have the disputes deriving from the execution, performance, breach and early and unilateral termination of those Association Contracts, which are in fact public contracts ("administrative contracts"), in the event that they contain arbitration clauses or clauses concerning the application of a foreign legislation or jurisdiction, aired in the manner provided therein. The contrary would mean giving retroactive effect to the Migration Law, which is prohibited by Article 24 of the Constitution which disallows the attribution of retroactive effects to legislative provisions.

Therefore, Article 13 of the 2007 Law cannot be interpreted as a regulation that could signify the "annulment" of the previous contractual clauses themselves relative to the solution of disputes that were provided in the Association Agreements that are deemed terminated, derived precisely, for example, from the State's breach of the Agreements, such as would arise from its premature termination.

3. The "confiscation" of interests, shares, participations and rigнTs of companies that did not reach an agreement with the state to migrate to mixed companies

A. *The definitive extinction of the former Agreements and Associations*

According to the aforesaid, pursuant to the *Law Concerning the Migration of the Association Agreements of the Orinoco Belt and of the Exploration at Risk and Profit Sharing Agreements into Mixed Companies* (Decree Law N° 5200) of February 2000, the activities exercised by the former strategic associations of the Orinoco Belt, comprising the companies Petrozuata, S.A., Sincrudos de Oriente, S.A., Sincor, S.A., Petrolera Cerro Negro S.A and Petrolera Hamaca, C.A.; the Exploration at Risk and Profit Sharing Agreements of Golfo de Paria Oeste, Golfo de Paria Este and la Ceiba, as well as the companies or consortia incorporated in their execution; Orifuels Sinovensa, S.A., as also the affiliates of such companies that conducted business activities in the Orinoco Belt, and throughout the production chain, were ordered to be transferred to the new mixed companies; and from such order, it resulted that some of them were incorporated into mixed companies in which private capital participated.

In such cases, according to the *Law on the Effects of the Migration Process to Mixed Companies of the Orinoco Belt Association Agreements and the Exploration at Risk and Profit Sharing Agreements* of October 5, 2007[32], the agreements that had given rise to the associations referred to in the *Law of the Migration of the Orinoco Belt Association Agreements and Exploration at Risk and Profit Sharing Agreements to Mixed Companies* "were extinguished" as of the publication date of the "decree that ordered the transfer of the right to exercise primary activities to the mixed companies incorporated pursuant to such Law" in the Official Gazette of the Republic (Art. 1).

Insofar as the agreements in which, according to the same *Law Concerning the Migration of the Association Agreements of the Orinoco Belt and of the Exploration at Risk and Profit Sharing Agreements into Mixed Companies* (Decree Law N° 5200) of February 2007, none of the private companies that were formerly part of the corresponding associations, had reached an agreement to migrate to mixed companies within the term established in Article 4 of such Law, pursuant to the Law on the Effects of the Migration Process to Mixed Companies of the Orinoco Belt Association Agreements and the Exploration at Risk and Profit Sharing Agreements of October 5, 2007, such agreements were to be extinguished "as of the publication date" of such Law in the Official Gazette of the Republic (Art. 1)

---

32   *Gaceta Oficial* N° 38.785 of October 8, 2007

As was said, the *Migration Law* (Decree Law N° 5.200) had made no mention of the rights to indemnity and compensation of the private companies that had not reached an agreement to continue as partners of the new mixed companies, by virtue of the early and unilateral termination of the Agreements and Associations, which they had according to the provisions of Article 115 of the Constitution. However, this was an expropriation initiated by a special law, by passing the provisions of the general Law of Expropriations, which implied, in accordance with the Constitution, the companies' right to be indemnified.

However, instead of proceeding to do this, the State chose to definitively "confiscate" such rights by purely and simply declaring the agreements extinguished as of the publication date of the *Law on the Effects of the Migration Process to Mixed Companies of the Orinoco Belt Association Agreements and the Exploration at Risk and Profit Sharing Agreements* of October 5, 2007.

B. *Confiscation of the rights of the private companies that participated in the Agreements and Associations by appealing to the principle of "reversion"*

For purposes of executing such confiscation, Article 2 of the *Law on the Effects of the Migration Process* expressly provided that "the interests, shares and participations" in the associations referred to in Article 1 of the Migration Law in the companies incorporated to develop the corresponding projects, and in "the assets used to conduct the activities of such associations, including property rights, contractual and other rights," which, until June 26, 2007 (pursuant to the term established in Article 4 of the aforementioned Law), "belonged to the private sector companies with whom agreement was not reached for migrating to a mixed company, **are hereby transferred, based on the principle of reversion**, without the need for any additional action or instrument, to the new mixed companies incorporated as a result of the migration of the respective associations, except for the provisions of Article 2 herein." This provision, according to the Venezuelan constitutional régime constitutes a confiscation of such assets, which is prohibited in the Constitution (Art. 116).

In other words, the State, by Law, ordered the forced transfer of privately-owned assets to the newly incorporated mixed companies without compensation or process, in all the cases where *some* of the other private companies of the respective agreement or association will have agreed to form part of the mixed companies. Article 4 of the Law clarified that in such cases "the transfers of interests, shares, participations and rights" provided in the Law "shall not generate tax liabilities in the Bolivarian Republic of Venezuela for any person or entity."

But in the cases where "*none* of the companies making up the private part of the association agreements reached an agreement to migrate to a mixed company within the established term," pursuant to Article 3 of the *Law on the Effects of the Migration Process* "the interests, shares, participations and rights" of the same were ordered kept "as property of the affiliate of Petróleos de Venezuela, S.A. that took over the activities of the association in question, until the National Executive determines the affiliate that will definitively perform such activities."

This is, anyway, as was said, a forced transfer of privately-owned assets to the State, declared by the Legislator, without any compensation or process whatsoever, which constitutes a **confiscation** prohibited under Article 116 of the Constitution.

On the other hand, in these cases, in no way the take over can be justified by recurring to the "principle of reversion," a figure that is essentially associated with the figure of administrative "concessions" which do not exist in hydrocarbons matters, and that is applicable only when the corresponding contract arrives to its term, once the assets being duly amortized.

In fact, one of the classic principles of administrative law in relation to the concession of public services, to the construction and use of public works and the exploitation of public domain assets, has been the necessary reversion of the service or of the works constructed to the conceding Administration once such concession is extinguished according to the term of the contract. This was a principle that sought to ensure the continuation of the rendering of the service, of the use of a public work or of an exploitation of public assets, independently of the concessionary's participation, once the concession was extinguished at its term.

However, when it is a means of extinction of the private property of the concessionary over the assets used for the service or of the works constructed, property guarantees and legal reserves impose the need for the principle of reversion being set forth in the express legal text[33]. In matters of hydrocarbons concessions, for example, the principle was established in the 1961 Constitution itself (Art. 103) and the old Hydrocarbons Law (Art. 80), pursuant to which the 1971 "Law on assets subject to reversion in the hydrocarbons concessions"[34]. In absence of an express legal text, therefore, the reversion can only proceed if it has been expressly regulated in the concession contract[35].

This was, moreover, the orientation followed by the Organic Law for the Promotion of Private Investment under the Concessions régime[36], when providing in Article 48 relative to the "reversion of works and services" which is the respective *contract* that must establish, among other elements, "the assets which, since they are associated with the work or the service in question, *will revert to the conceding entity, unless it had not been possible to amortize them during the aforementioned term*." To such end the regulation also provides that during a prudent period prior to the termination of the contract, the conceding entity shall adopt provisions such that upon delivery of the assets to be reverted, the *conditions accorded* in the contract are verified. The regulation also provides that the contract express "the works, facilities or assets *not subject* to reversion to be executed by the concessionary, which, if

---

33   Moreover, in this sense, it was the 1961 Constitution (Article 103) that established the principle of the concession in hydrocarbons matters, in regard to the land (immovable property) affected by such concessions.

34   See *Gaceta Oficial* N° 29577 of 06-08-1971

35   As has been said by Eduardo García de Enterría and Tomás R. Fernández, under this perspective, the reversion "loses its old character of being an essential element of every concession and comes to be regarded as an accidental element of the business, that is, it is admissible only in the case of an express accord, like one more piece, when conceived in this way, of the economic formula that all concessions consist in," in their *Curso de Derecho Administrativo*. I. Thirteenth Edition, Thomson-Civitas, Madrid 2006, p. 763

36   *Gaceta Oficial* N° 5394 Extra. of 25-10-1999

deemed to be of public usefulness or interest, may be subject to reversion after due payment of their price to the concessionary."

Therefore, if there is no legal provision that establishes the reversion of assets in concessions of public services, public works or the use or exploitation of assets of the public domain, or if such reversion is not provided in the concession contract, then upon termination of the concession, the concessionary is not obliged to revert any asset to the Administration that has been acquired or constructed or that has been associated with the concession, nor may the Administration pretend to appropriate or take possession of them. It would only be able to do so through expropriation, according to the Constitution and the Law.

In general terms, it must be said that the Orinoco Belt Association Agreements and Exploration at Risk and Profit Sharing Agreements to Mixed Companies, after establishing a term of 35 years for their termination, expressly provided that at the Date of Termination, the foreign partners were to transfer to the State Own partner company, without compensation, their part on the Join Venture, including the interest in any entity or association and the rights and interest in all the assets and contracts of common property of the Parties regarding the projects. This provision can be consider similar to the reversion institution of concessions, but in this cases, the obligatory transfer of assets is only applicable when the Agreements arrives to their precise Date of Termination, that is, after the fixed 35 years of Duration have been elapsed, which means that it is not applicable in any other case of anticipated termination of the contracts not provided in the contracts. Otherwise, it would be a confiscation forbidden by the Constitution, such as has been decreed in the *Law on the Effects of the Migration Process*[37].

C. *Applicable legal regime and jurisdiction*

Just as provided in the *Migration Law* (Art. 13), Article 5 of the *Law on the Effects of the Migration Process* also provided that "all the facts and activities subject to its provisions, shall be governed by the laws of the Bolivarian Republic of Venezuela, and the controversies derived there from shall be submitted to its jurisdiction, as provided in the Constitution of the Bolivarian Republic of Venezuela."

---

37   This Law, moreover, does not refer to "hydrocarbons concessions," which disappeared from the legal order decades ago. In a December 3, 1974 decision of the former Supreme Court of Justice (Case: *Challenge to the Law of assets affected by reversion in the oil concessions*), when referring to the reversion established in Articles 103 of the 1961 Constitution and 80 of the old Hydrocarbons Law, the Court said that "both laws contemplate the transfer of assets to the State without compensation upon extinction of the concession, and it is evident also that both the confiscation by means of which determined assets are seized from a person without any indemnity whatsoever, and the expropriation, which supposes a special compensation procedure, are figures different to reversion, by virtue of which the assets belonging to the grantor, as well as those of the concessionary, that are for the concession, return to the hands of the grantor when for any reason the concession reaches its end." See *Gaceta Oficial* N° 1718 Extra. of January 20, 1975, pp. 22-23.

In regard to this provision, it must also be remembered that any effect produced by any law passed in Venezuela, by virtue of the principle of territoriality, is in principle governed by the national legislation; therefore if nothing to the contrary is provided in the text of the law, all the legal situations deriving from any law are governed by the "National Law."

What is more, this Law also provides, with poor drafting, that the controversies deriving from its provisions will be submitted to Venezuelan jurisdiction and, again, this could not be any other way, unless the legislator were to expressly renounce Venezuelan jurisdiction. Therefore, the disputes arising on occasion of the migration of the former Associations to the new mixed companies, or the agreements that may have been reached by the former partners of the Association Agreements upon incorporation, pursuant to the Law's provisions, as minority partners, can only be resolved by national jurisdiction.

Moreover, for example, the controversies deriving from the decisions contained in the Law and its application are doubtless in principle subject to Venezuelan jurisdiction, for example, insofar as the possibility of challenging, by reason of unconstitutionality, the provisions of the Law on the Effects of the Migration Process before the Constitutional Jurisdiction, or of challenging the administrative acts which, pursuant to such Law, may be dictated by the National Executive, before the Contentious Administrative Jurisdiction.

But this by no means implies the annulment of the clauses that may be contained in the Association Agreements whose early and unilateral termination led to ordering the forced transfer of privately-owned property to the State, for example, relative to the submission of disputes deriving from the execution, performance and breach of the Association Agreements, to arbitral jurisdiction, even outside Venezuela, as authorized by Article 151 of the Constitution. So the contractors, in such cases, are entitled to seek the resolution of disputes deriving from the execution, performance and breach of such Association Agreements, being public contracts, in the event that they contain arbitration clauses either by application of the legislation or by a foreign jurisdiction, in the manner provided in them. If it were not so, it would mean giving retroactive effect to the *Law on the Effects of the Migration Process*, which is prohibited by Article 24 of the Constitution which prohibits giving retroactive effect to legislative provisions.

Therefore, Article 5 of the *Law on the Effects of the Migration Process* cannot signify the "annulment" of prior contractual dispute-resolution clauses set forth in the Association Agreements, whose private rights are being confiscated, deriving precisely, for example, from the State's breach of the Agreements, which is what is occurring with this confiscation.

IV. THE 2008-2009 NATIONALIZATIONS AND "STATIZATIONS"

1. *The Nationalization of the Iron and Steel Industry*

On April 30, 2008, through Law-Decree N° 6.058[38] issued by the National Executive according to the legislative delegation contained in the 2007 Enabling Law,[39] the iron and steel exploitation and transformation industry located in the Guayana region was nationalized. The motives for the nationalization decision was the link of the industry with strategic activities of the Nation, having Guayana the highest iron mineral reserves of the country, that since 1975 were nationalized (art. 1). As a direct consequence of the reservation to the State of this is exploitation and transformation industry, and in order to complete the nationalization process by means of expropriation, all business activities of the company SIDOR C.A. as well as any of its subsidiaries and affiliates were declared as of "public utility and social interest" (article 3).

Therefore the reservation to the State for the purpose of nationalizing the iron and steel industry, produced as a consequence the order to transform the company SIDOR C.A., its subsidiaries and affiliates according to article 100 of the Organic Law of Public Administration, into a State owned companies, with a State's shareholder participation of at least 60% (art. 3).

With regards of the managerial transformation, article 4 of the Decree Law establishes that the Republic, through the Popular Power Ministry for Basic and Mining Industries or any of its decentralized organizations, would be the legal stockowner of the percentage belonging to the public sector in the newly created State owned companies. To ensure the proper transfer of all activities resulting from this "transformation" and in accordance with article 5 of the Law, the Popular Power Ministry for Basic and Mining Industries or any of its decentralized organizations, within seven days of publication of the Law was to establish a "Transitional Commission" for each company, to be incorporated in SIDOR's Executive Board. From the nationalized Private Companies' point of view, Article 5 of the Law mandated the obligation to fully cooperate with the nationalization process in order to guarantee a successful and safe transition, which ended on June 30, 2008. Article 10, of the law exempted from any direct or indirect tax contribution, all business agreements, title transfers, and negotiations, needed to conclude the transformation process of the private companies into state owned companies and, or any operation that could result in economic gains.

Since the process was a nationalization one, in order to ensure the compelling transfer of property, as well as the compensation payment due to the shareholder private companies being nationalized, article 6 of the Law, gave them sixty (60) continuous days, beginning on the publication date of the organic Decree Law, that is, until August 12, 2008, to agree on the terms and conditions of the possible ownership participation on the "new" state owned companies. A Technical Committee

---

38   *Gaceta Oficial* N° 38.928 of May 12, 2008
39   *Gaceta Oficial* N° 38.617 of Febrary 1, 2007

with the participation of state and private representation was formed, to set, in sixty (60) continuous days, which could be extended by mutual consent, a fair value to base the appropriate compensation owned to the nationalized companies (Art. 7). On March 25, 2009, it was announced that the State and the Argentinean enterprise (Techint) that had the majority ownership of the shares of SIDOR C.A., reached an agreement in order to fix the compensation and establish a schedule for its payment.

In any case, the Decree Law established that if no agreement for the "transformation" of the private companies into state owned companies, was reached by August 12, 2008, as in fact occurred, then the Republic, through the Popular Power Ministry for Basic and Mining Industries or any of its decentralized organizations, was to assume total control and management of the private companies in order to ensure the continuous operation of the nationalized industry; which effectively occurred. Articles 9 and 11 provided that all lay offs was to be frozen from the publication of the organic law and until the "transformation" process was over, all employees of the iron and steel industry would be covered under their respective collective contracts.

Additionally, in case no agreement whatsoever was reached for the "transformation" into stated owned companies, article 8 provided an expropriation clause for the shares of such companies, based on the Expropriation Law for Public and Social Use. Nonetheless, that same article 8 provided that in order to estimate the "compensation or fair value" of the assets being expropriated, no lost profit or indirect damages would be taken into account.

Finally, article 12 of the Organic Law provides that all facts and activities related to the Organic Law-Decree, would be subjected to national legislation, and that any controversy pertaining to the same would be submitted to Venezuelan jurisdiction, according to the provisions set forth in the Constitution. This provisions only prevented the private companies that were nationalized, to seek for arbitration proceeding with regards to property transfer, compensation or payments plans agreed or State imposed to the nationalized companies according to the new Decree Law; but of course could not prevent the possibility for the private parties to submit to arbitration controversies derived from the nationalization of their investment in Venezuela according to the promotion and protection of investments legislation existing before the decree law, or to contracts entered into before the nationalization process, providing for such arbitration.

2. The Nationalization of the Cement Industry

Following the same trend used to nationalize the iron and steel industry, on May 27, 2008 through Law-Decree N° 6.091 as part of the delegate legislation authorized in the 2007 Enabling Law, the cement industry was also nationalized. The motive for the nationalization decision was the relation of the industry with strategic activities for the development of the Nation (art. 1). As a direct consequence of the reservation to the State of this industry, and in order to complete the nationalization process by means of expropriation, the activities developed by *Cemex Venezuela, S.A.C.A., Holcim Venezuela C.A.* and *C.A. Fabrica Nacional de Cementos, S.A.C.A.* (*Grupo Lafarge de Venezuela*), as well as any of its subsidiaries and affiliates, were declare as of public utility and social interest (Article 3).

Therefore the reservation to the State for the purpose of nationalizing the cement industry, produced as a consequence the order to transform the said thee companies (*Cemex, Holcim, Lafarge*), its subsidiaries and affiliates, in accordance with article 100 of the Organic Law of Public Administration, into a State owned companies, with a State's shareholder participation of at least 60% (Article 3).

With regards of the managerial transformation, article 4 of the Decree Law establishes that the Republic, through the Popular Power Ministry for Basic and Mining Industries or any of its decentralized organizations, would be the legal stockowner of the percentage belonging to the public sector in the newly created State owned companies. To ensure the proper transfer of all activities resulting from this "transformation" and in accordance with article 5 of the Law, the Popular Power Ministry for Basic and Mining Industries or any of its decentralized organizations, within seven days of publication of the Law was to establish a "Transitional Commission" for each company, to be incorporated in the Executive Board of the nationalized companies. In fact no such Committee was established and the enterprises were occupied by public officials. In any case, Article 5 of the Law mandated the private shareholders to fully cooperate with the nationalization process in order to guarantee a successful and safe transition, which must be ended on December 31, 2008 (article 6). Article 10, of the law exempted from any direct or indirect tax contribution, all business agreements, title transfers, and negotiations, needed to conclude the transformation process of the private companies into state owned companies and, or any operation that could result in economic gains.

Since the take over process of the cement industry was formally a nationalization one, in order to ensure the compelling transfer of property, as well as the compensation payment due to the shareholder private companies being nationalized, article 6 of the Decree Law, gave them sixty (60) continuous days, beginning on the publication date of the organic Decree Law, that is, until September 18th, 2008 to agree on the terms and conditions of the possible ownership participation on the "new" state owned companies. A Technical Committee with the participation of state and private representation was formed, to set, in sixty (60) continuous days, which could be extended by mutual consent, a fair value to base the appropriate compensation owned to the nationalized companies (Art. 7).

The government signed Memorandum of Understanding with two of the shareholders of the nationalized enterprises (Holcim and Lafarge), in which the compensation price was agreed, as wall as the payment conditions. These agreements were not effective, and al least one of these enterprises initiated an international arbitration procedure. The third enterprise (Cemex) did not reach any agreement with the State, and submitted the differences to international arbitration. In this latter case, however, the State signed an Agreement for technical assistance with the company, with limited duration, that allowed the nationalized industry to continue its operation but using the systems of the private company.

The Decree Law also established that if no agreement for the "transformation" of the private companies into state owned companies, was reached by December 31, 2008, as in fact occurred, then the Republic, through the Popular Power Ministry for Basic and Mining Industries or any of its decentralized organizations, was to assume total control and management of the private companies in order to ensure the continuous operation of the nationalized industry; which effectively occurred well before that date. Articles 9 and 11 also provided that all lay offs was to be frozen from the publication of the organic law and until the "transformation" process was over, all employees of the iron and steel industry would be covered under their respective collective contracts.

Additionally, in case no agreement whatsoever was reached for the "transformation" into stated owned companies, article 8 provided an expropriation clause for the shares of such companies, based on the Expropriation Law for Public and Social Use. Nonetheless, that same article 8 provided that in order to estimate the "compensation or fair value" of the assets being expropriated, no lost profit or indirect damages would be taken into account.

Finally, article 12 of the Organic Law provides that all facts and activities related to the Organic Law-Decree, would be subjected to national legislation, and that any controversy pertaining to the same would be submitted to Venezuelan jurisdiction, according to the provisions set forth in the Constitution. This provisions only prevented the private companies that were nationalized, to seek for arbitration proceeding with regards to property transfer, compensation or payments plans agreed or State imposed to the nationalized companies according to the new Decree Law; but of course could not prevent the possibility for the private parties to submit to arbitration controversies derived from the nationalization of their investment in Venezuela according to the promotion and protection of investments legislation existing before the decree law, or to contracts entered into before the nationalization process, providing for such arbitration, as indeed occurred.

3. The "Statization" of assets and services related to the Hydrocarbon Primary Activities

In May 2009, the National Assembly, also due to its strategic character, sanctioned the Organic Law reserving for the State the assets and services related to the primary activities of the oil industry[40] established in the Hydrocarbon Law (article 1), which were formerly conducted by *Petróleos de Venezuela, S.A. (PDVSA)* and its subsidiaries, but were assumed by third parties, although being essential to the industry (article 2). Consequently, article 1 of the Law provided that said activities were to be "directly executed by the Republic, by *Petróleos de Venezuela, S.A. (PDVSA)*, or any of its designed subsidiaries, or by mixed companies under *Petróleos de Venezuela, S.A. (PDVSA)* control."

Article 7, of the Law, assigned "public order" character to its provisions by which such provisions "shall have preference over any other legal dispositions related to the matter." On the other hand, Article 5 established that all the aforementioned assets and services provided or required were to be considered as "public services and of public and social interest." Such assets and services are enumerated in article 2 of the Organic Law, as follow:

---

40   *Gaceta Oficial* N° 39.173 of May 7, 2009.

1. Water, steam or gas injections, aimed to increase the oilfield's energy and improve the recovery factor.

2. Gas compression.

3. All goods and services connected to activities in the *Lago de Maracaibo*: boats for personnel transport, divers, and maintenance; cargo ships, including diesel, industrial waters, and any other supplies, crane ships, tug boats, buoys, padding and filling cranes, pipe and wire lines, ships maintenance, workshops, docks, floating docks, and ports of any nature.

In order to materialize the statization process, article 3 of the Law, empowers the Popular Power Ministry for Energy and Oil, to determine by unilateral administrative acts (Resolutions); the assets and services comprises in the aforementioned provisions of articles 1 and 2 of the law.

In any such cases of Resolutions issued, according to article 3 of the Organic Law, all previous contracts and agreements signed between private companies with state own companies referred to the reserved activities, will be considered as *ipso jure* extinguished by virtue of the Law." For the purpose of this early termination of such contracts and agreements, the law recognized them as "administrative contracts" (Article 3).

The reservation for the State of the assets and services related to the primary hydrocarbon activities, in a different way as the previous nationalization processes, provided in this case that as of the date of the publication of the Law (May 7, 2009) "*Petróleos de Venezuela S.A., (PDVSA)* or any of its subsidiaries will take possession of any assets and control of all operations related to the reserved activities," which effectively occurred. That was, according to the Law "explanation of motives," an "expedite mechanism, according to the needs of the oil industry, allowing *Petróleos de Venezuela S.A.*, (PDVSA) or any of its subsidiaries, to take over assets and control the operations of related the reserved activities, as a previous step to complete the expropriation process."

To ha effect, the Law authorized the Popular Power Ministry for Energy and Oil to take all available measures in order to ensure the continuous operation of the reserved activities, being authorized to ask for support from any State organ or entity. In the case, it was the National Guard the one chosen to achieve this goal. Additionally all actors involved in the process were compelled by the Law to fully and peacefully collaborate in the transfer of operations, facilities, documents, and property affected by the law provisions, otherwise they could be subjected to administrative or criminal sanctions (Art. 4).

In order to ensure the transfer to the State of all assets and services, Article 8 provided that any permits, certifications, authorizations and valid registries belonging to the private operating companies, or pertaining to any of the reserved activities, would *ipso juris* be transferred to Petróleos *de Venezuela S.A. (PDVSA)* or to it designed subsidiary.

Additionally, in order to facilitate the transfer, Article 9 establishes that any act, business or agreement, related to the transfer of assets and operations enshrined under the Organic Law, would be exempt of any national taxes.

As well, the Organic Law, as part of the transfer process, on article 10, gives power to the Popular Power Ministry for Energy and Oil to make any decisions regarding the transfer of all working personnel from the "statisized" companies to *Petróleos de Venezuela, S.A., (PDVSA)* or any of its subsidiaries. All labor rights were guaranteed by the Law, which could be paid directly by *Petróleos de Venezuela, S.A., (PDVSA)* or any of its subsidiaries, but deducted from the compensation amount that could correspond to the expropriated companies. The law also guaranteed all personnel benefits, rights and agreements under the Collective Oil Convention for all transferred personnel to Pedtóleos de Venezuela S.A or its subsidiaries (article 10).

The statization and immediate take over of all goods, services and assets, implied the State's obligation to fairly compensate the shareholders of the private companies assumed by the State. But for such purpose, the Law only referred to the expropriation process as a mere possibility providing that the State could (*"podrá"*) decree total or partial expropriation of all shares and assets belonging to any company doing business or conducting any of the reserved, in accordance with the Expropriation Law for Public and Social Use. In such cases, *Petróleos de Venezuela S.A., (PDVSA)* or any of its subsidiaries would be the expropriating entity, and the competent courts to decide expropriation process will be the competent courts in these cases (Art. 6).

In this case of the statization of the assets and services related to the primary activities of the oil industry, however, the Law established a restricted criteria regarding the just and fair compensation provided for on article 115 of the Constitution, since in order to estimate the fair value of the assets being expropriated, article 6 of the Law provided that in no case lost profits or indirect damages could be taken into account, and the valuation would be based on "book value less all wages, payroll and environmental passives determined by the proper authorities." Article 6 ads that the time taken to effectively take possession would be taken into account to establish such fair value. Additionally payments could be done either with cash, bonds or obligations issued by public entities (Art. 6).

Finally, article 11 of the Organic Law provides that all facts, activities and contracts referred in the Law, and any controversy pertaining to the same would be submitted to the national law and the Venezuelan courts. This provisions only could prevent the private companies that were nationalized, to seek for arbitration proceeding with regards to property transfer, compensation or payments plans agreed or State imposed to the statized companies according to the Law; but of course could not prevent the possibility for the private parties to submit to arbitration controversies derived from the statization of their investment in Venezuela according to the promotion and protection of investments legislation existing before the Organic law was issued, or to contracts entered into before the statization process, providing for such arbitration.

In any event, the following day of the publication of the Organic Law, on May 8, 2009, the Popular Power Ministry for Energy and Oil passed Resolution N° 051[41] listing all services, sectors, goods and companies "affected by the take over measures," (article 1), instructing Petróleos de Venezuela, S.A. or any of its subsidi-

---

41   *Gaceta Oficial* N° 39.174 of May 8, 2009

aries "to take control over operations and immediate possession of the mentioned facilities, documents, capital assets and equipment" (article 2).

In order to assure this immediate take over, the Law provided that in order to register all information related to all goods, services and assets, affected, within the following 15 days an inventory must be made to be signed by *Petróleos de Venezuela, S.A.* or any of its subsidiaries and the private companies, or be made through a judicial inspection or notarized act (Article 2). On that same Resolution, the Popular Power Ministry for Energy and Oil reserves to itself the right to apply any necessary measures to guarantee the continuous operation of the affected business, as well as the right to identify other assets, services, companies, or sectors that follow under the provisions of the Organic (Article 3).

A few days later, on May 13, 2009,[42] the Popular Power Ministry for Energy and Oil passes another Resolution No 54, naming an additional list of companies conducting business, and in possession of essential capital assets (Gas compression) connected with primary hydrocarbon activities in accordance with the Hydrocarbon Organic Law, and that was believe to follow the pattern as of the reserved activities, being considered the list as a declarative not compelling one (Art.1).

In order to materialize the statization process, article 2 of the Resolution instructed *Petróleos de Venezuela, S.A.* or any of its subsidiaries "to take control over operations and immediate possession of facilities, documents, capital assets and equipment" of the enterprises. In this case it was also provided that in order to register all information related to all goods, services and assets, affected, within the following 15 days an inventory must be made to be signed by *Petróleos de Venezuela, S.A.* or any of its subsidiaries and the private companies, or be made through a judicial inspection or notarized act (Article 2). The Resolution set forth that in the event that after further evaluation no interest was shown to effectively take over the affected companies of assets, the Resolution will cease to affect those companies or assets.

On that same Resolution, the Popular Power Ministry for Energy and Oil reserves to itself the right to apply any necessary measures to guarantee the continuous operation of the affected business, as well as the right to identify other assets, services, companies, or sectors that follow under the provisions of the Organic (Article 3).

The fact with all these provisions and actions was the immediate take over of all the assets and services unilaterally enumerated by the State, without any compensation paid or any expropriation process initiated. It simply was another confiscation of private property prohibited in the Constitution.

4. *The Reservation to the State of the Petrochemical Activities*

On June 2009, the Law for the Development of the Petrochemical Activities was sanctioned,[43] reserving for the State the Basic and Intermediate Petrochemical, as

---

42   *Gaceta Oficial* N° 39.177 of May 13, 2009
43   *Official Gazette* N° 39.203 of June 18, 2009

well as the works, assets and installations required for its accomplishment (article 5). Basic Petrochemical is defined as the industrial processes related with chemist of physical transformation of the basic components of hydrocarbons implying a molecular change, understood as the products obtained from hydrocarbons that have a very defined chemical formula (article 4.2); and Intermediate Petrochemical is defined as the industrial processes related to the chemical or physical transformation obtained from the basic petrochemical (Article 4.3).

The reservation for the State of the Petrochemical activities implies that they can only be accomplished by the State, directly by the national Executive, by enterprises of its exclusive ownership, or by mixed enterprises in which the State controls its decisions having a participation on the capital of the enterprise of not less that the fifty per cent of the shares. Regarding the mixed enterprises modality, they are subject to prior authorization of the National Assembly, once informed by the Ministry of Energy and Oil about the specific circumstances and conditions in each case (Article 5).

In the same Law, it was declared that because of economic and political sovereignty and national strategy reasons, the State shall kip the ownership of all the shares of *Petroquímica de Venezuela S.A.,* or of any other entity that in its substitution could be established in order to manage the petrochemical industry (Article 6).

V. THE STATE APPROPRIATIONS OF WHAT IT HAS CONSIDERED STRATEGIC ECONOMIC ACTIVITIES

Since the enactment of the Land and Farming Law,[44] not only the possibility for the state to occupy and expropriate private land was extended, leading to the massive appropriation of private land by the state, without compensation, but also the possibility for the state to take over rural land simply ignoring its condition of private own property supported in the due registered titles, imposing in many cases to the owner, without legal support, the impossible burden to proof a property tradition for almost two hundred years.[45]

On the other hand, since 2007, a massive process of expropriation, in many cases without due compensation, and of forced occupation of assets and industries by public authorities, with the support of the national guard, have taken place, based on "strategic" or "alimentary sovereignty" motives. In the latter case, the process has been based on the provisions of the Organic Law on Farming and Alimentary Security and Sovereignty,[46] which assigns expropriation powers to the executive without

---

44 See Ley de Tierras y Desarrollo Agrario in *Official Gazette* N° 5.771 Extra. of May 18, 2005.

45 See Antonio Canova González, Luis Alfonso Herrera Orellana and "Karina Anzola Spadaro, *¿Expropiaciones o Vías de hecho? (La degradación continuada del derecho fundamental de propiedad en la Venezuala actual)*, FUNEDA, Caracas 2009, 115ff. See also Allan R. Brewer-Carías, "El régimen de las tierras baldías y la adquisición del derecho de propiedad privada sobre tierras rurales en Venezuela," in *Estudios de derecho administrativo* 2005-2007, Editorial Jurídica Venezolana, Caracas 2007, 327-74.

46 See Ley Orgánica de soberanía y seguridad alimentaria, *Official Gazette* N° 5.889, Extra., July 31, 2008. See the comments in José Ignacio Hernández G., "Planificación y soberanía

the need of a previous declaration of a specific public interest or public utility, and allowing the State to occupy private industries without compensation.[47]

Also, the Law for the defense of persons in their access to goods and services[48] has allowed indiscriminate occupations of private property and industries, in all sectors of the economy, supporting its take over by public authorities, in many cases *sine die* and without compensation.[49]

A similar pattern has been followed by the Venezuelan Government in other economic activities, but by means of using regulatory powers, as has occurred in the financial sector, or in the housing construction sector, but with the addition of using the Public Prosecutor's Office as an instrument by the Executive Power in order to harass private citizens and private entrepreneurs. The *modus operandi* of the Government, developed in particular in 2010, has become to unlawfully utilize Venezuela's criminal courts without just cause, for the issuance of preliminary judicial orders, such as orders of arrest, seizure and occupation of private assets, whose only purpose is to force Venezuelan citizens to leave the country, and facilitate the *de facto* take over of their enterprises and private property. These acts are "legitimated" by the State, -up by means of administrative procedures which have no judicial backing whatsoever.[50] Thus, the State is able to obviate the need for a judicial order and can also avoid paying the due compensation that is guaranteed in the Constitution (art. 115) in cases of expropriations.

---

alimentaria," in *Revista de Derecho Público (Estudios sobre los Decretos Leyes)* 115, Editorial Jurídica Venezolana, Caracas 2008, 389-394.

47 See Carlos García Soto, "Notas sobre la expansión del ámbito de la declaratoria de utilidad pública o interés social en la expropiación," in *Revista de Derecho Público*, N° 115 (Estudios sobre los Decretos Leyes), Editorial Jurídica Venezolana, Caracas 2008, 149-151; Antonio Canova González, Luis Alfonso Herrera Orellana and Karina Anzola Spadaro, *¿Expropiaciones o Vías de hecho? (La degradación continuada del derecho fundamental de propiedad en la Venezuala actual)*, FUNEDA, Caracas 2009, 143ff.

48 See Decreto Ley N° 6,092 para la defensa de las personas en el acceso a los bienes y servicios, *Official Gazette* N° 5.889 Extra. of July 31, 2008,

49 See Juan Domingo Alfonzo Paradisi, "Comentarios en cuanto a los procedimientos administrativos establecidos en el decreto N° 6.092 con rango valor y fuerza de Ley para la defensa de las personas en el acceso a los bienes y servicios," in *Revista de Derecho Público* 115, *(Estudios sobre los Decretos Leyes)*, Editorial Jurídica Venezolana, Caracas 2008, 246ff.; Karina Anzola Spadaro, "El carácter autónomo de las 'medidas preventivas' contempladas en el artículo 111 del Decreto Ley para la defensa de las personas en el acceso a los bienes y servicios," in *id.*, 271-79; Antonio Canova González, Luis Alfonso Herrera Orellana and Karina Anzola Spadaro, *¿Expropiaciones o Vías de hecho? (La degradación continuada del derecho fundamental de propiedad en la Venezuala actual)*, FUNEDA, Caracas 2009, 163ff.

50 See in general, Antonio Canova González, Luis Alfonso Herrera Orellana, and Karina Anzola Spadaro, *¿Expropiaciones o vías de hecho? (La degradación continuada del derecho fundamental de propiedad en la Venezuela actual,"* Funeda, Universidad Católica Andrés Bello, Caracas 2009; Allan R. Brewer-Carías, *Dismantling Democracy. The Chávez Authoritarian Experiment*, Cambridge University Press, New York, 2010, pp. 245-262.

THE PRO-ARBITRATION TREND OF THE 1999 CONSTITUTION AND THE ANTI-ARBITRATION POLICY OF THE AUTHORITARIAN GOVERNMENT: VENEZUELA BEFORE ICSID

(2013)

This Essay was written based on different Legal Opinions I gave between 2008 and 2012, as a Legal Expert, in some Arbitration Cases before various ICSID Arbitral Tribunals.

INTRODUCTION

The Venezuelan government signed the 1964 *Convention on the Settlement of Investment Disputes between States and Nationals of Other States (ICSID),*[51] on Aug 18, 1993, being approved the following year, in 1994, by Law of approval sanctioned by the Venezuelan Congress.[52] The Law of approval entered into force on June 1, 1995, after the deposit of its ratification was made on May 2, 1995.

On the various forms of written consent by ICSID Contracting States, in addition to an express provision that can be included in a public contract signed by the State (for instance a concession of public works), or in a Bilateral Treaty or Agreement for the Protection of Investments (BIT), as was stated in the *Report of the Executive Directors on the Convention on the Settlement of Investment Disputes Between States and Nationals of other States" dated March 18, 1965*, to the member governments of the World Bank for their consideration with a view to its signature and ratification, "a host state might in its *investment promotion legislation* offer to sub-

---

51 Available at http://icsid.worldbank.org/ICSID/StaticFiles/basicdoc/partA-preamble.htm

52 See the *Ley Aprobatoria del Convenio sobre Arreglo de Diferencias Relativas a Inversiones entre Estados y Nacionales de otros Estados*, in *Official Gazette* N° 4.832 Extra. of December 29, 1994.

mit disputes arising out of certain classes of investments to the jurisdiction of the Centre, and the investor might give his consent by accepting the offer in writing."

And this was precisely the case of Venezuela, when the Law on the Promotion and Protection of Investments was enacted by Decree Law N° 356 of October 13, 1999, [53] in which article 22 was included, containing a unilateral written expression of consent of the State, in the form of an open offer given to international investors to submit investment disputes to international arbitration, including ICSID arbitration. Based on that provision, during the past years many cases were filed before the ICSID Center against Venezuela, and also many of them have been decided by ICSID Tribunals. In particular, and specifically on matter of Jurisdiction of the ICSID Center based on article 22 of the 1999 Investment Law, up to June 2013, the following five decisions were issued: ICSID Case N° ARB/07/27, *Mobil Corporation, Venezuela Holdings, B.V., Mobil Cerro Negro Holding, Ltd., Mobil Venezuela de Petróleos Holdings, Inc., Mobil Cerro Negro Ltd. and Mobil Venezolana de Petróleos, Inc. v. Bolivarian Republic of Venezuela*, decision on Jurisdiction dated June 10, 2010 (***Mobile* ICSID Case**);[54] ICSID Case N° ARB/08/15, *Cemex Caracas Investments B.V. and Cemex Caracas II Investments B.V. v. Bolivarian Republic of Venezuela*, decisions on Jurisdiction dated December 30, 2010 (***Cemex* ICSID Case**);[55] ICSID Case N° Arb/08/3, *Brandes Investment Partners, LP v. The Bolivarian Republic of Venezuela,* decision dated August 2, 2011 (***Brandes* ICSID Case**);[56] ICSID Case N° ABC/10/5, *Tidewater Inc. et al.* v. *The Bolivarian Republic of Venezuela*, decision dated February 8, 2013 (***Tidewater* ICSID Case**)[57]; and ICSID Case N° ARB/10/14, *Opic Karimun Corporation v Bolivarian Republic of Venezuela*, decision dated May 23, 2013 (***Opic Karimun* ICSID Case**),[58] In all these decisions, the ICSID Tribunals concluded that although article 22 of the 1999 Investment Law in effect contain an obligation imposed upon the State to go to international arbitration, which means that in it, the State expressed its consent, being possible to grammatically interpret the condition it establish in two valid ways, the intention of the State to submit disputes to international arbitration, lacked to be sufficiently evidenced. In the end, due to lack of evidences, the ICSID Tribunal eventually declared that they had no Jurisdiction in those cases. Nonetheless, the procedural situation on the first four cases was different to the situation on the *Opic Karimun* ICSID Case,

---

53   Law on the Promotion and Protection of Investments (*Ley de promoción y Protecciuón de Inversiones*) enacted by Decree Law N° 356 of October 13, 1999, in *Official Gazette* N° 5.300 Extra. Of October 22d, 1999.

54   Available   at
     http://icsid.worldbank.org/ICSID/FrontServlet?requestType=CasesRH&actionVal=showDoc
     &docId=DC1510_En&caseId=C256

55   Available   at
     http://icsid.worldbank.org/ICSID/FrontServlet?requestType=CasesRH&actionVal=showDoc
     &docId=DC1831_En&caseId=C420

56   Available at http://italaw.com/documents/BrandesAward.PDF

57   Available at http://italaw.com/sites/default/files/case-documents/italaw1277.pdf

58   Available at http://italaw.com/sites/default/files/case-documents/italaw3013.pdf

were enough evidence proving the intention of the State to consent to ICSID Arbitration was submitted before the Tribunal, which originated an important Dissenting Vote of arbitrator Professor Guido Santiago Tawil, expressing that he was unable to join the conclusions of the majority "on the interpretation of the evidence produced in this case regarding Venezuela's consent to ICSID arbitration under Article 22 of the Investment Law." (¶ 1)[59]

After the first three aforementioned cases were decided, in January 24, 2012 the Government of Venezuela officially withdraws in an irrevocable way from the *Convention on the Settlement of Investment Disputes between States and Nationals of Other States*. After receiving the written notice of denunciation of the Convention, the World Bank as the depositary of the ICSID Convention, notified all ICSID signatory States of Venezuela's denunciation of the Convention. In accordance with Article 71 of the ICSID Convention, the denunciation took effect six months after the receipt of Venezuela's notice, that is, on July 25, 2012.

The "Official Communiqué" of the Government justifying Venezuela's withdrawing from the ICSID Convention[60] mentioned that its ratification in 1993 was a decision adopted by "a week government without popular legitimacy pressed by traditional transnational economic sectors that participated in the dismantling of the national sovereignty of Venezuela." This statement referred to the government lead by President Ramón J. Velasquez (1993-1994), in which I served as Minister for Decentralization.

Contrary to such assertion, that Government lead by a President Velasquez was a very important transitional one, configured after his appointment by Congress in June 1993, once the acting President Carlos Andrés Pérez was removed from office by decision of the same Congress, with the support of all the political parties, in order to complete the constitutional term of former President Pérez. That transitional Government had the important task of assuring the continuity of the democratic rule of the country and, in particular, the successful development of the general elections that took place on December 1993. That Government was able to continue conducting the State in the midst of a grave political and economic crisis, having for such purpose all the needed legitimacy derived from the Constitution. Important decisions were adopted in many fields,[61] and also on matters of promotion of investments. In that respect, the signing of the ICSID Convention, according to the general prevailing policy of attracting foreign investments to the country, was a very important one for such purpose.

The "Official Communiqué" of the Venezuelan Government of January 24, 2012, in order to justify the Venezuela's withdrawing from the Convention, in addi-

---

59   Available at: http://italaw.com/sites/default/files/case-documents/italaw3014.pdf

60   The text of the Official Communiqué is available at http://www.noticierodigital.com/2012/01/ramirez-ratifica-salida-de-venezuela-del-ciadi/

61   See the collective book: *Ramón J. Velásquez. Estudios sobre una trayectoria al servicio de Venezuela,* Universidad Metropolitana. Universidad de Los Andes-Táchira, Caracas 2003.

tion expressed that the text of article 151 of the 1999 Venezuelan Constitution[62] supposedly "invalidates, in its spirit and in its wording, the provisions of the ICSID Convention." This assertion only evidenced the most complete ignorance by the Government of President Hugo Chávez of the sense and meaning of such constitutional provision, in which, on the contrary, it is expressly established the principle of relative jurisdictional sovereign immunity of the State[63] following previous constitutional provisions included in the Constitution since 1947, allowing international arbitration in public contracts except when considered inappropriate according to their nature. The restriction, on the other hand, only refers to matters of arbitration related to public contracts, and in principle is not directed to regulate arbitration resulting from the consent of the State express in a statute.

In effect, Article 151 of the 1999 Constitution establishes that

> "Article 151: In contracts of public interest, unless inappropriate according with their nature, a clause shall be deemed included even if not been expressed, according to which the doubts and controversies that may arise on such contracts and that could not be resolved amicably by the contracting parties, shall be decided by the competent courts of the Republic, in accordance with its laws and could not give rise by any motive or cause to foreign claims."

This provision is basically a reproduction of the content of article 127 of the 1961 Constitution, which was kept in the new 1999 Constitution due to my personal proposal made before the National Constituent Assembly,[64] in particular, in order to contradict the "bizarre" and "inappropriate" proposal contained in a document submitted by President of the Republic, Hugo Chávez before the Assembly[65], proposing some constitutional changes. Among those, Chávez first proposed to completely eliminate from the Constitution the "Calvo Clause,"[66] and second, he proposed to

---

62 See the text of the Constitution in *Official Gazette* N° 5.908 Extra. Of February 2, 2009. See the general comments in Allan R. Brewer-Carías, *La Constitución de 1999 y la Enmienda Constiucional N° 1 de 2009*, Editorial Jurídica Venezolana, Caracas 2011; and in *Constitucional Law. Venezuela*, Supplement 97, International Encyclopaedia of Laws, Kluwer, Belguium 2012.

63 See in general, Tatiana B. de Maekelt, "Inmunidad de Jurisdicción de los Estados," in *Libro Homenaje a José Melich Orsini*, Vol. 1, Universidad Central de Venezuela, Caracas 1982, pp. 213 ff.

64 I was Elected Member of the 1999 Constituent Assembly. See my proposal regarding article 151 in Allan R. Brewer-Carías, "Propuesta sobre la cláusula de inmunidad relativa de jurisdicción y sobre la cláusula Calvo en los contratos de interés público," in *Debate Constituyente (Aportes a la Asamblea Nacional Constituyente)*, Vol. I (8-Agosto-8 Septiembre 1999), Fundación de Derecho Público/Editorial Jurídica Venezolana, Caracas 1999, pp. 209-233.

65 See Hugo Chávez Frías, *Ideas Fundamentales para la Constitución Bolivariana de la V República*, Caracas agosto 1999.

66 The *Calvo* Clause had its origin in the work of Carlos Calvo, who formulated the doctrine in his book *Tratado de Derecho Internacional*, initially published in 1868, after studying the Franco-British intervention in Rio de la Plata and the French intervention in Mexico. The *Calvo* Clause was first adopted in Venezuela in the 1893 Constitution as a response to diplomatic claims brought by European countries against Venezuela as a consequence of con-

return to the principle of absolute jurisdictional sovereign immunity but exclusively regarding public contracts entered by the "Republic," eliminating all jurisdictional restriction regarding other public interest contracts signed by other public entities, that by the way, are the most common and important public contracts in the country, like for instance those signed in the oil and mining industry. That presidential proposal was without doubts, excessive permissive towards international arbitration on matters of pubic law.

The two clauses contained in the text of article 151 of the Constitution have been in the text of all Venezuelan Constitutions since 1893[67] . The first clause is the one referred to the principle of jurisdictional sovereign immunity of the State regarding public contracts. Initially it was referred to public contracts entered by the Republic and the States (Venezuela has the federal form of Government), and was conceived as an "absolute" jurisdictional immunity clause. It was first changed in 1901, expanding its initial scope in order to include, not only the "national" and "states" public interest contracts, but also the "municipal" contracts and any other public contract entered by other organs ("public powers") of the State. And later, in 1947 it was also changed regarding the scope of the immunity, transforming it into a "relative" jurisdictional sovereign immunity clause, following the general trend prevailing in comparative constitutional law.[68]

The proposal of Mr. Chávez in 1999 regarding this constitutional clause was to reestablish the absolute sovereign jurisdictional immunity principle abandoned in 1947, but in a limited way only regarding some "national" public interest contracts, that is, only those entered by the Republic, eliminating any kind of restriction on jurisdictional matters regarding public interest contracts entered by the states, the municipalities and other public entities. This presidential proposal, as I argued, was excessive and inconveniently permissive, particularly due to the fact that commonly, the public interest contracts are entered precisely by other entities different to the Republic, and particularly by public corporations and public enterprises.[69]

In any case, leaving aside that failed proposal made by the President of the Republic in 1999, the way the clause has been in the Constitution since 1947, that is, following the "relative" jurisdictional sovereign immunity, cannot be considered as something extraordinary or unusual, particularly because it follow the general prin-

---

tracts signed by the State and foreign citizens. See Allan R. Brewer-Carías, *Historia Constitucional de Venezuela*, Vol I, Editorial Alfa, Caracas 2008, pp. 411.

67   See the text of the 1893 Constitution as well as all the other Constitution in the history of the country in Allan R. Brewer-Carías, *Las Constituciones de Venezuela*, Academia de Ciencias Políticas y Sociales, Caracas 2008, 2 vols.

68   See in general the classical book of Ian Sinclair, *The Law of Sovereign Immunity. Recent Developments*, Académie International de Droit International, Recueil des Cours 1980, The Hague 1981.

69   See in Allan R. Brewer-Carías, "Propuesta sobre la cláusula de inmunidad relativa de jurisdicción y sobre la cláusula Calvo en los contratos de interés público," in *Debate Constituyente (Aportes a la Asamblea Nacional Constituyente)*, Vol. I (8-Agosto-8 Septiembre 1999), Fundación de Derecho Público/Editorial Jurídica Venezolana, Caracas 1999, pp. 209-233.

ciple of relative immunity in contemporary world. According to this Clause, the State is authorized in the Constitution to submit to international arbitration matters of public interest contracts except if the "nature" of their object prevents it, which is referred to the matters generally known as of *ius imperii*. That is why the argument of the Government for withdrawing from ICSID Convention, as well as the suggestion given the by ICSID tribunals in the *Mobil* and *Cemex* casees, arguing that "Venezuela remained reluctant *vis-à-vis* contractual arbitration in the public sphere, as demonstrated by [...] Article 151 of the 1999 Constitution" (*Mobil* ICSID case, ¶¶ 131; 127, 128; *Cemex* ICSID case, ¶ 125), simply did not really understood the content of the provision of said article 151, from which no "reluctant" attitude towards arbitration can be deducted. On the contrary, the constitutional provision of article 151 is, precisely, the one that allows international arbitration involving the Venezuelan State according to the principle of relative sovereign jurisdictional immunity that is the one generally accepted in contemporary world. Consequently, nothing in the Venezuela legal and constitutional order authorizes the Government to say that article 151 of the 1999 Venezuelan Constitution supposedly "invalidates, in its spirit and in its wording, the provisions of the ICSID Convention," which means to consider that an expression of consent for international arbitration as the one contained in article 22 of the Investment Law would be inconceivable in light of article 151 of the Constitution. On the contrary, it is the trend set forth in such article the one that authorizes for the State to go to international arbitration.

The second clause contained in article 151 of the Constitution, inserted in the constitutional text also in 1893, and that has remained without change, is the already mentioned "Calvo Clause", according to which in Venezuela is excluded and is inadmissible any diplomatic claims regarding public interest contracts signed between the different organs of the State and foreign entities or persons. The President of the Republic in his "bizarre" 1999 proposal before the Constituent Assembly, pretended to completely eliminated from the Constitution this centenary "clause," and consequently to allow the possibility that in public interest contracts, their execution could gave rise to foreign diplomatic claims against the Republic.[70] From that proposal, it is impossible to deduct any restrictive approach of the President toward arbitration matters. On the contrary, his proposals were inadmissible, being contrary to the interest of the State.

Finally, it must be mentioned, that article 151 of the Constitution establishing the relative sovereign jurisdictional sovereign immunity clause and the *Calvo* Clause, is a provision referred to "public interest contracts," that is, basically, those entered by the three territorial divisions of the State (Republic, States, Municipalities). The clause allows the possibility for the State to give its consent to submit to international arbitration, for instance, disputes related to commercial matters derived from such public interest contracts.

In ICSID arbitration cases, based on jurisdiction through a State's consent given by a statute, as is the case of article 22 of the Investment Law, the ICSID Tribunals

---

70   *Idem.*

are not to deal with public interest contracts regulated in article 151 of the Constitution. The Tribunals in such cases only deal with the consent given by the Venezuelan State in a statute (Article 22 of the 1999 Investment Law) to submit matters related to investment, generally of industrial, commercial or finance nature, to international arbitration.

In any case the decision of the government to "escape from ICSID,"[71] of course ignored the importance of the ICSID Convention for the purpose of attracting investment, which resulted evidenced by the fact that between 1993 and 1998, many bilateral treaties on investments (BITs) were signed, specifically providing for international arbitration, and in particular, for ICSID International Arbitration.[72] Its importance also results from the fact that it was the same Government that in 2012 rejected international arbitration, the one that in 1999 sanctioned by means of a Decree Law N° 356 of October 3, the 1999 Investment Law containing express recognition of ICSIS international arbitration. In it, the current Government went farther an expressed, in Article 22 of the Law, the express written consent of the Republic of Venezuela to submit investments disputes to the ICSID arbitration Center, under Article 25.1 of the ICSID Convention. This is a historical fact that in spite of the decision to "escape from ICSID," cannot be denied.

Article 22 of the 1999 Investment Law was not a provision that was officially adopted by the Government without knowing its significance, or that "under the influence of globalization currents was filtered within the Venezuelan regime" as it has been affirmed without foundations.[73] On the contrary, it was a conscious decision adopted by a Government that at the time was seeking to promote and encourage international investments in the country, giving investors legal security assurances, like for the disputes to be decided by arbitral tribunals.

For such purpose, in article 22 of the 1999 Investment Law, the State gave its consent to submit investments disputes to ICSID arbitration, expressed in the form of an open offer of arbitration (*oferta abierta de arbitraje*) subject to acceptance by the investor-claimant to a relevant dispute, to go to international arbitration, or, at

---

71   See James Otis Rodner, "Huyendo del CIADI,", in *El Universal*, Caracas February 7, 2012, available at http://www.eluniversal.com:80/opinion/120207/huyendo-del-ciadi

72   See lists of all those treaties at Venezuelan Ministry of for Foreign Relations at http://www.mre.gov.ve/metadot/index.pl?id=4617;isa=Category;op=show; ICSID Database of Bilateral Investment Treaties at http://icsid.worldbank.org/ICSID/FrontServlet; UNCTAD, Investment Instruments On-line Database, Venezuela Country-List of BITs as of June 2008 at http://www.unctad.org/Templates/Page.asp?intItemID=2344&lang=1. See also, in José Antonio Muci Borjas, *El derecho administrativo global y los tratados bilaterales de inversión (BITs),* Caracas 2007; Tatiana B. de Maekel, "Arbitraje Comercial Internacional en el sistema venezolano," in Allan R. Brewer-Carías (Editor), *Seminario sobre la Ley de Arbitraje Comercial*, Academia de Ciencias Políticas y Sociales, Caracas 1999, pp. 282-283; Francisco Hung Vaillant, *Reflexiones sobre el arbitraje en el sistema venezolano*, Caracas 2001, pp. 104-105.

73   See Hildegard Rondón de Sansó, *Aspectos jurídicos fundamentales del arbitraje internacional de inversión*, Ed. Exlibris, Caracas 2010, p. 132.

his will, to resort to national courts. Not only the signing of the ICSID Convention in 1993, but the text of Article 22 of the 1999 Investment Law, reflected the pro-arbitration trend existing in Venezuela at the time, developed over the past few decades, which crystallized not only in Article 258 of the 1999 Constitution, sanctioned in parallel to the 1999 Investment Law, compelling the State to promote arbitration. This same trend was reflected in an important number of other statutes sanctioned during the same year 1999.

In the ICSID *Mobil* and *Cemex* cases, the tribunals decided that in those particular cases, article 22 of the Investment Law did not provide a basis for their jurisdiction. In the ICSID *Brandes* case, the tribunal without any motivation also ruled that article 22 of the Investment Law did not provide basis for jurisdiction at all. Nonetheless, and contrary to those assertions, since 2005 I have been of another opinion, considering that article 22 of the 1999 Investment Law contains the consent of the Venezuela State, as an open offer, to go to international arbitration. My intention in this essay is to reaffirm my conviction, stressing the erroneous motivation of the aforementioned three ICSID tribunals rulings, as well as of the erroneous content of Supreme Tribunal Decision N° 1.541 of 2008 issued by the Constitutional Chamber, at the request of the Government, interpreting Article 22 of the Investment Law in the sense asked by the Government.

I.   THE VENEZUELAN STATE'S EXPRESSION OF CONSENT TO ICSID ARBITRATION JURISDICTION IN ARTICLE 22 OF THE 1999 IN-VESTMENT LAW

As already mentioned, since 2005 it has been my opinion that Article 22 of the 1999 Investment Law contains a unilateral written expression of consent, in the form of an open offer by the Republic of Venezuela, for international investors to submit investment disputes to international arbitration, including ICSID arbitration. I first expressed that opinion when analyzing in general terms the 1999 Investment Law in a *Seminar* held in Caracas, organized by the *Academy of Political and Social Sciences* that was sponsored by the *Venezuelan Arbitration Committee*. That can be considered the first general academic approach made regarding the 1999 Investment Law made in Venezuela, in order to study its provisions, convening a numerous group of Scholars in order to study the different aspects of the Law, from the point of view of the different branches of law. Previous to such occasion, nonetheless, it must be mentioned that perhaps the first specific analysis of the Venezuelan Law, particularly of its article 22, was made in 2000, immediately after its enactment, by two well known Venezuelan lawyers, Fermín Toro Jiménez and Luis Brito García, when they filed a popular action challenging the constitutionality of article 22 of the Law before the Supreme Tribunal of Justice. They based their argument in the fact that such provision authorized investors to live aside the national courts and resort to international arbitration, which could only occur if the State in the same provision had already expressed its consent to arbitrate before international arbitration forum. The claimants argued that by leaving the decision to submit the disputes on investments with the State to international arbitration, on the exclusive hands of the international investors, it violated the Constitution. The Constitutional Chamber of the

Supreme Tribunal dismissed the case hupholding the constitutionality of article 22 in decision N° 186 of February 14, 2001.[74]

The 2005 Seminar on "*Arbitraje comercial interno e internacional. Reflexiones teóricas y experiencias prácticas*" was inaugurated by the then President of the Academy Professor Alfredo Morles Hernández, who gave a general overview (*Presentación*) on arbitration. That Presentation altogether with all the papers submitted to the Seminar was all published in a book by the Academy.[75] That academic event followed a previous one, also organized by the Academy in 1998, on the "*Ley de Arbitraje Comercial,*" in which it was my duty to make the "Presentation," as I was at that time the President of the Academy. All the papers submitted to that Seminar, were also published in the book.[76] In both Seminars, all the Papers submitted were academic papers given by Law Professors, with only academic purposes.

It was in the context of the 2005 Seminar on arbitration organized by the Academy in 2005, that I was asked by the Coordinator of the Seminar to submit comments on the 1999 Investment Law, from the exclusive point of view of public internal law, which I did, writing the aforementioned paper on "*Algunos comentarios a la ley de promoción y protección de Inversiones: Contratos Públicos y Jurisdicción*" ("Some Comments on the Law of promotion and Protection of Investments: Public Contracts and Jurisdiction").[77]

As the title of the paper announced, what I wrote, in fact, were "Some Comments" on the Law, making specific emphasis on the legal stabilization intention of the Law; the general legal guaranties given for the protection of investments); the figure of the public contracts for legal stabilization for investments; and the provisions established in the Law for the solution of disputes or controversies on matters of investments. All such comments were expressed in a brief paper written without footnotes, and only based in the analysis of text of the Law. The purpose was merely to divulgate comments on the institutions provided in the Law, which up to that moment, was one statute that have had very little attention in the legal academic

---

74   See the decision N° 186 of the Constitutional Chamber of the Supreme Tribunal of Justice of February 14, 2001, available at http://www.tsj.gov.ve/decisiones/scon/Febrero/186-140201-00-1438%20.htm.

75   See Irene Valera (Coord.), *Arbitraje comercial interno e internacional. Reflexiones teóricas y experiencias prácticas,* Academia de Ciencias Políticas y Sociales, Caracas 2005.

76   See Allan R. Brewer-Carías (Coord.), *Seminario sobre la Ley de Arbitraje Comercial*, Academia de Ciencias Políticas y Sociales, Caracas 1999.

77   See Allan R. Brewer-Carías, "Algunos comentarios a la Ley de promoción y protección de Inversiones: contratos públicos y jurisdicción", in Irene Valera (Coordinadora), *Arbitraje Comercial Interno e Internacional. Reflexiones teóricas y experiencias prácticas*, Academia de Ciencias Políticas y Sociales, Comité Venezolano de Arbitraje, Caracas 2005, pp. 279-288. This Paper was later included in my book *Estudios de Derecho Adminbistrativo 2005-2007*, Editorial Jurídica Venezolana, Caracas 2007, pp. 453-462, and is also available at http://allanbrewercarias.com/Content/449725d9-f1cb-474b-8ab2-41efb849fea8/Content/II,%204,%20473.%20Protección%20de%20Inversiones.%20Contratos%20públicos%20y%20jurisdicción%20bis%2010-05.pdf, pp. 7-9.

world. Those "Some Comments," consequently, were just general comments made regarding the text of the Law from the internal public law point of view, without even quoting for such purpose any decisions of national courts on the matter. That is why no mention was made, for instance, to the Decision N° 186 of the Supreme Tribunal of February 14, 2001 dismissing a popular action of unconstitutionality and upholding the constitutionality of article 22 of the Investment Law,[78] particularly because the discussion about the incorporation of arbitration in the 1999 Constitution as part of the judicial system was a matter I considered already without discussion.

Instead, in that occasion in 2005, in the Seminar organized by the Academy, when studying in particular article 22 of the Law and realizing that it contained a general expression of consent given by the Venezuelan State for international arbitration, researching for antecedents of such State's consent to arbitration given through a national statute, I only referred to an ICSID tribunal decision that was drown to my attention, issue in the case *Southern Pacific Properties (Middle East) Ltd. v. Arab Republic of Egypt* (ICSID Case N° ARB/84/3, Decision on Jurisdiction of April 14, 1988) (*SPP case*).[79]

The matter of the State's consent included in Article 22 of the Venezuelan Law and the solution given in the aforementioned *ICSID SPP* case decision, at that time was for me, from the internal public law point of view, one of the most interesting aspects of the Law, being in fact a novelty in Venezuelan law. It was the first time that I found in the text of a statute in Venezuela, that the State was unilaterally giving its consent for jurisdiction on matters of international arbitration. Never before I knew about any other Law in which the State assumed in a unilaterally way an obligation to submit controversies to international arbitration, that is, with international effects. This was the aspect that at that time called my attention, and doing some research for antecedents of such unilateral expressions of consent, I found the *ICSID SPP* case, which I mentioned in my "Some Comments."

In effect, in the Paper I wrote for the Seminar of the Venezuelan Academy in 2005, I expressed the following regarding the interpretation of the 1999 Investment Law confronted with article 25,1 of the ICSID Convention:

> "The main subject for discussion in this case, is to determine in which form the "written consent" can be given. In the *Case: Southern Pacific Properties (Middle East) v. Arab Republic of Egypt,* the Centre, in its Decision on Jurisdiction dated April 14 1988, as a source of the consent imposed by article 25,1 of the Convention, interpreted the value that internal law provisions have, when recognizing the jurisdiction of the Centre for the settling of disputes concerning foreign investments. The Center, in that case, interpreted as follows: "The Convention does not prescribe any particular form of the consent, not does require that consent be given on a case-by-case basis. To the contrary, the drafters of the Convention intended that consent

78 Available at http://www.tsj.gov.ve/decisiones/scon/Febrero/186-140201-00-1438%20.htm
79 See *Southern Pacific Properties (Middle East) Ltd. v. Arab Republic of Egypt,* Case ARB/84/3, May 20, 1992. Decision Award on the Merits, in which mention is made to all the previous decisions on Jurisdiction, available at http://icsid.worldbank.org/ICSID/FrontServlet?requestType=CasesRH&actionVal=showDoc&docId=DC671_En&caseId=C135

could be given in advance through investment legislation. Accordingly, the Tribunal cannot accept the contention that the phrase "where it applies" in Article 8 of Law N° 43 requires a further or *ad hoc* manifestation of consent of the Centre's jurisdiction (Paragraph 101, 3 *ICSID Reports*, at 155-56).

Article 8 of the Egyptian N° 43 Law, established the following:

"Investment Disputes in respect of the implementation of the provisions of this Law shall be settled in a manner to be agreed upon with the investor, or within the framework of the agreements in force between the Arab Republic of Egypt and the investor's home country, or within the framework of the Convention for the Settlement of Investment Disputes between the State and the nationals of other countries to which Egypt has adhered by virtue of Law 90 of 1971, where such Convention applies".

In my opinion, this last expression of the Egyptian law is identical in its sense to the provision of article of the Venezuelan Law: "disputes to which the provision [of the ICSID Convention] are *applicable*".

This mean that according to the jurisprudence of the Center, when an internal law has a provision which refers to the Center jurisdiction the settling of disputes related to investments, the condition of article 25,1 of the ICSID Convention is fulfilled by that sole circumstance, and that for article 25,1 be applicable, it is only required that the dispute arose directly from an investment between Contracting State and a national of other Contracting State in the Convention, not being necessary *"a further or ad hoc manifestation of consent of the Center's jurisdiction."*[80]

As I mentioned, from the internal constitutional and administrative law point of view, the matter of the State expression of consent to ICSID arbitration through a *national statute* was, without doubts, a novelty matter in Venezuela. It was one of the instruments for the State to give consent to arbitration according to the ICSID Convention that authorized the States to give direct consent for international arbitration in an unilateral way through statutes, having as precedent, the case ***ICSID SPP***, decided by an ICSID Tribunal by decision of April 14, 1988, precisely regarding

---

80   In the article, I quoted the 1985 ICSID Centre decision on Jurisdiction issued in the case *Southern Pacific Properties (Middle East) v. Arab Republic of Egypt,* referred to Article 8 of the Egyptian Law N° 43, considering as "an express 'consent in writing' to the Centre's jurisdiction within the meaning of Article 25.1 of the Washington Convention in those cases where there is no other agreed-upon method of dispute settlement and no applicable bilateral treaty." *Decision on Jurisdiction, 27 November 1985,* ¶ 98, *3 ICSID Reports,* Cambridge University Press, 1995. ¶ 116. At that time, I read the relevant parts of the decision in Doak Bishop, James Crawford and W. Michael Reisman, *Foreign Investment Disputes. Cases, Materials and Commentary,* Kluwer Law International, The Hague 2005, p. 384. In its subsequent Decision on Jurisdiction of 14 April 1988, the Tribunal held the following: "The ordinary grammatical meaning of the words in Article 8, taken together with other Laws and Decrees enacted in Egypt, showed that Article 8 *mandated the submission* of disputes to the various methods described therein, in hierarchical order, where such methods were applicable" and concluded that "Article 8 was legally sufficient manifestation of written consent to the jurisdiction of the Centre, and that no separate ad hoc written consent was required." Also at that time, I read the relevant parts of the decision in E. Lauterpacht and E. Rayfusse (Ed.), *ICSID Reports, Vol 3. Cambridge University Press,* 1995, p. 106.

matters of Jurisdiction. In it the Tribunal, determined that the aforementioned Article 8 of the Egyptian Law N° 43 constituted "an express 'consent in writing' to the Centre's jurisdiction within the meaning of Article 25.1 of the Washington Convention even in those cases where there is no other agreed-upon method of dispute settlement and no applicable bilateral treaty."[81]

I considered that Article 22 of the Investment Law had similarities to that provision of the Egyptian law, and that the *ICSID SPP* case provided support for the idea that consent may be given through a statute as opposed to a BIT.[82] Article 22 of the 1999 Investment Law, in effect, states:

> "Article 22. Controversies that may arise between an international investor, whose country of origin has in effect with Venezuela a treaty or agreement on the promotion and protection of investments, or **controversies in respect of which the provisions of** the Convention Establishing the Multilateral Investment Guarantee Agency (MIGA) or **the Convention on the Settlement of Investment Disputes Between States and Nationals of Other States (ICSID)** *are applicable, shall be submitted to international arbitration according to the terms of the respective treaty or agreement*, if it so establishes, *without prejudice to the possibility of using, as appropriate, the contentious means contemplated by the Venezuelan legislation in effect.*"[83]

Both Articles in the Egyptian (E) and Venezuelan (V) Laws establish the same expression of consent of the State to submit disputes on investments to international arbitration, by using the same wording, particularly in the following three expressions: **"Shall be settled"** (E) or **"shall be submitted"** (V) [by/to ICSID Center] **"within the framework of the Convention"**(E) or **"under the terms provided for**

---

81   *Southern Pacific Properties (Middle East) Ltd. v. Arab Republic of Egypt,* ICSID Case N° ARB/84/3, Decision on Jurisdiction of April 14, 1988, ¶ 116.

82   In its Decision on Jurisdiction of 14 April 1988, the Tribunal held that "[t]he ordinary grammatical meaning of the words in Article 8, taken together with other Laws and Decrees enacted in Egypt, showed that Article 8 *mandated the submission* of disputes to the various methods described therein, in hierarchical order, where such methods were applicable" and concluded that "Article 8 was legally sufficient manifestation of written consent to the jurisdiction of the Centre, and that no separate *ad hoc* written consent was required." *Southern Pacific Properties (Middle East) Ltd. v. Arab Republic of Egypt,* ICSID Case N° ARB/84/3, Summary of Decision on Jurisdiction of April 14, 1988, 3 ICSID Reports, p. 106. See also in E. Lauterpacht and E. Rayfusse (Ed.), *ICSID Reports, Vol 3. Cambridge University Press,* 1995, p. 106

83   Spanish Text: *Artículo 22. Las controversias que surjan entre un inversionista internacional, cuyo país de origen tenga vigente con Venezuela un tratado o acuerdo sobre promoción y protección de inversiones, o las controversias respecto de las cuales sean aplicables las disposiciones del Convenio Constitutivo del Organismo Multilateral de Garantía de Inversiones (OMGI – MIGA) o del Convenio sobre Arreglo de Diferencias Relativas a Inversiones entre Estados y Nacionales de Otros Estados (CIADI), serán sometidas al arbitraje internacional en los términos del respectivo tratado o acuerdo, si así éste lo establece, sin perjuicio de la posibilidad de hacer uso, cuando proceda, de las vías contenciosas contempladas en la legislación venezolana vigente."* The term *"controversias"* has also been translated as "disputes" (instead of "controversies") and the expression *"si así éste lo establece"* has also been translated as "if it so provides" or "should it so provide" (instead of "if it so establishes").

in the respective treaty or agreement"(V); "where such Convention applies"(E) or were such treaties or Convention "are applicable" (V).

In my opinion, the content and structure of both Articles were very similar, and the last expression of the Egyptian law "where such Convention applies," is identical in its meaning to the provision Article 22 of the Venezuelan Law concerning "disputes to which the provisions [of the ICSID Convention] are applicable." This means that, according to the jurisprudence of ICSID, when an internal law containing an expression of consent to submit disputes to international arbitration has a provision which refers to ICSID jurisdiction, the condition of Article 25.1 of the ICSID Convention is fulfilled. For such Article 25.1 to be applicable, it is only required that the dispute arose directly from an investment between the Contracting State and a national of another Contracting State in the Convention, so due to the mandatory provision to submit to arbitration, no "further or *ad hoc* manifestation of consent of the Center's jurisdiction" is necessary.[84]

While, in general, consent of the States to ICSID arbitration is less commonly given through statutes than through BITs, the *SPP* case provides an example of a statute providing such consent.[85] Based on such similarities, in 2005, I considered that Article 22 of the Venezuelan Investment Law was no different; conclusion that is shared by other commentators;[86] although others have a different point of view.[87]

---

84   Allan R. Brewer-Carías, "Algunos comentarios a la Ley de promoción y protección de Inversiones: contratos públicos y jurisdicción," *loc. cit.*, pp. 286-287.

85   It is therefore not surprising that similar legislations passed in other States have "received less attention from practitioners, academics and international organizations responsible for legal and policy issues related to foreign investments." See Ignacio Suarez Ansorena, "Consent to Arbitration in Foreign Investment Laws," in I. Laird and T. Weiler (Eds.), *Investment Treaty Arbitration and International Law*, Vol 2, JurisNet LLC 2009, pp. 63, 79.. It is important to note that the constitutionality of the law was upheld in 2001 by the Constitutional Chamber of the Supreme Tribunal of Justice.

86   See, e.g., Andrés A. Mezgravis, "Las inversiones petroleras en Venezuela y el arbitraje ante el CIADI," in Irene Valera (Coordinadora), *Arbitraje Comercial Interno e Internacional. Reflexiones teóricas y experiencias prácticas*, Academia de Ciencias Políticas y Sociales, Comité Venezolano de Arbitraje, Caracas 2005, p. 392. Other commentators also have reached the same conclusion about the similarity between Article 8 of the Egyptian N° 43 Law and Article 22 of the 1999 Venezuelan Investment Law. *See, e.g.*, Victorino Tejera Pérez, "Do Municipal Investment Laws Always Constitute a Unilateral Offer to Arbitrate? The Venezuelan Investment Law: A Case Study," in Ian A. Laird and Todd J. Weiler (Ed.), *Investment Treaty Arbitration and International Law*, Vol 2, JurisNet LLC 2009, pp. 104-105; Victorino Tejera Pérez, *Arbitraje de Inversiones*, Magister Thesis, Universidad Central de Venezuela, Caracas 2010, p. 175. See also: See for instante Gabriela Álvarez Ávila, "Las características del arbitraje del CIADI", en *Anuario Mexicano de Derecho Internacional*, Vol II 2002, Instituto de Investigaciones Jurídicas, Universidad Nacional Autónoma de México, UNAM, México 2002 (ISSN 1870-4654). http://juridicas.unam.mx/publica/rev/de-rint/cont/2/cm/; Guillaume Lemenez de Kerdelleau, "State Consent to ICSID Arbitration: Article 22 of the Venezuelan Investment Law" in *TDM*, Vol. 4, Issue 3, June 2007; M.D. Nolan and F.G. Sourgens, "The Interplay Between State Consent to ICSID Arbitration and denunciation of

On the other hand, the interpretation of article 22 of the Investment Law as an open offer of consent of the Venezuelan State for international arbitration was consistent with the policy defined by Congress and the National Executive of Venezuela in 1999 in order to promote and protect international investments. For such purpose, Article 22 of the Investment Law expressed the consent of the Venezuelan State to submit to international arbitration controversies regarding international investment.

Being a provision of a national law, the text of article 22 had to be interpreted according to the principles of interpretation established in Venezuelan law, particularly in article 4 of the Civil Code. Nonetheless, being a national law that gives consent to international arbitration it also has to be interpreted following principles on international law. That is why the three ICSID Arbitral Tribunal decisions on Article 22 of the Venezuelan Investment already mentioned have considered relevant to give consideration of international law along with national law (See *Mobil* ICSID case, ¶¶ 85, 95) *Cemex* ICSID case, ¶¶ 79, 88), and *Brandes* ICSID case, ¶ 36). Consequently, it ss possible to sustain that both Venezuelan law and international law are relevant in interpreting the Investment Law, bearing in mind that as such Tribunals concluded in the three cases, on matter of interpretation, Venezuelan law does not conflict with international law. That implied, among other principles, that the Tribunals, applying general principles of interpretation in a very similar way, considered that the text of the Article must be analyzed totality and not only in its separate parts.

Consistent with the conclusion that the wording of the law and the connection of the words used is central, and considering the general pro-arbitration content of the Venezuelan legislation issued at the same time by the Government, in my opinion, the only reasonable conclusion is that Article 22 is an expression of a general offer of consent given by the Venezuelan State to submit investment disputes to international arbitration when accepted by international investors; giving the international investor, at his will, the option to go to arbitration or to resort before the national courts.

In effect, the necessity of analyze the wording of article 22 in its context, is a principle of Venezuelan law established in Article 4 of the Civil Code,[88] resulting from it that the expression of consent to international arbitration contained in Article

---

the ICSID Convention: The (Possible) Venezuela Case Study" in *TDM*, Provisional Issue, September 2007.

87   See for instance, Omar E. García-Bolívar, "El arbitraje en el marco de la ley de promoción y Protección de Inversiones: las posibles interpretaciones", in *Revista de Derecho*, Tribunal Supremo de Justicia, N° 26, Caracas 2008, pp. 313 ff; and more recently, Hildegard Rondón de Sansó, *Aspectos jurídicos fundamentales del arbitraje internacional de inversión*, Ed. Exlibris, Caracas 2010, pp. 123 ff. Sansó, in particular, criticizes my opinion, pp. 146-148.

88   Spanish text: Civil Code, "Artículo 4: *A la Ley debe atribuírsele el sentido que aparece evidente del significado propio de las palabras, según la conexión de ellas entre sí y la intención del legislador. Cuando no hubiere disposición precisa de la Ley, se tendrán en consideración las disposiciones que regulan casos semejantes o materias análogas; y, si hubiere todavía dudas, se aplicarán los principios generales del derecho.*"

22 of the Investment Law derives from the meaning of the words used in the provision, considered within the pro-arbitration policy of the Government at the time and within the general context of the whole text, and not from only one part of it. Notably, the language "**shall be submitted to international arbitration**" ("*serán sometidas al arbitraje internacional*") used in the provision, is an expression of command that conveys the mandatory nature of Article 22. The phrase "**if it so establishes**" ("*si así éste lo establece*") means that such command of Article 22 is subjected to a condition in the sense that it applies if the respective treaty or agreement (Article 22 refers to other treaties alongside the ICSID Convention) contains provisions establishing a framework for international arbitration, that is, "establishes arbitration."[89]

This condition is satisfied by the ICSID Convention, being the open offer of consent expressed in Article 22 confirmed in its last phrase which is a disclaimer: "without prejudice to the possibility of using, as appropriate, the contentious means contemplated by the Venezuelan legislation in effect" ("*sin perjuicio de la posibilidad de hacer uso, cuando proceda, de las vías contenciosas contempladas en la legislación venezolana vigente*"). All of these factors in combination give the international investor the possibility to unilaterally decide, at his will, to submit the particular dispute to international arbitration or to submit the dispute before the national courts. Given the command included in the first part of the Article, the option that the investor has can only exist and make sense if the State has already given its consent to international arbitration by virtue of the State's ratification of the ICSID Convention.

Article 22 of the Investment Law's expression of a unilateral consent by the State to submit disputes with international investors to the jurisdiction of ICSID arbitration on the other hand, was intentionally included by the Government (National Executive), acting as a Legislator, when it enacted the Decree Law N° 356 of October 3, 1999 sanctioning such Law. This intention of the National Executive was also consistent with the general policy defined by the Government at the time of its enactment for the purpose of attracting and promoting international investments in the country, which also lead, at the same time, to the drafting of the constitutional mandate of Article 258 of the 1999 Constitution. This Article 258 imposed on all organs of the State (not only the legislative organs but also the Judiciary)[90] the task to promote arbitration. Other pieces of legislation, from which the pro-arbitration principle is derived, also were issued at the time.[91]

---

89   See Victorino Tejera Pérez, "Do Municipal Investment Laws Always Constitute a Unilateral Offer to Arbitrate? The Venezuelan Investment Law: A Case Study," loc cit. pp. 95; Victorino Tejera Pérez, *Arbitraje de Inversiones*, Magister Thesis, Caracas 2010, cit..

90   See Eugenio Hernández Bretón, "Arbitraje y Constitución. El arbitraje como derecho fundamental," in Irene Valera (Coordinadora), *Arbitraje Comercial Interno e Internacional. Reflexiones teóricas y experiencias prácticas*, Academia de Ciencias Políticas y Sociales, Comité Venezolano de Arbitraje, Caracas 2005, p. 27.

91   *Idem*, p. 31. See also Francisco Hung Vaillant, *Reflexiones sobre el arbitraje en el derecho venezolano*, Editorial Jurídica Venezolana, Caracas 2001, pp. 66-67.

What is absolutely clear from the aforementioned, regarding the content of Article 22 of the Investment Law, is that the reference it contains regarding ICSID international arbitration is not a mere declaration of principles, or a "mere reference in a national law to ICSID" as was suggested by the Supreme Tribunal of Justice in Decision N° 1541 of October 17, 2008, issued at the request of the Attorney general seeking an "official" interpretation of article 22 of the Investment Law.[92] Nor was Article 22 of the Investment Law intended to simply acknowledge the possibility of dispute resolution in ICSID Center. On the contrary, Article 22 of the Investment Law amounts to the binding consent given by the Venezuelan State to arbitral jurisdiction.

II. THE PRO-ARBITRATION TREND IN THE EVOLUTION OF THE VENEZUELAN LEGAL REGIME IN THE YEARS PREVIOUS TO THE ENACTMENT OF THE 1999 INVESTMENT LAW

At the moment at which the Investment Law was enacted, it can be said that the hostility or unfavorable attitude toward arbitration that existed in Venezuela since the last decade of the 19th century was already completely overcome. The 1999 Investment Law was therefore a piece of legislation completely reconcilable with its historical background, including the State's ratification between 1993 and 1998 of numerous treaties for the protection and promotion of investments (that also provided for international arbitration), as well as the other legal provisions regarding arbitration adopted at the time. Therefore, in 1999, and from a **systematic** and **historical** perspective, article 22 of the Investment Law by which the State offered unilateral consent to arbitration in order to promote investment, can be said that was an essential part of the *raison d'être* of the 1999 Investment Law, in complete accord with the political official trend in favor of international arbitration. Furthermore, using the **teleological** and **sociological** element of statutory interpretation, the economic and social situation prevailing at the time the 1999 Investment Law was enacted, explains that the former Congress and the National Executive, acting as legislators, intended to promote investments. Offering consent to international arbitration was a means to do so.

That economic policy and the whole legal order existing in 1999, in effect, tended to promote foreign investment and international arbitration,[93] being such policy

---

92 See Decision N° 1.541 of October 17, 2008 of the Constitutional Chamber of the Supreme Tribunal of Justice, available at http://www.tsj.gov.ve/decisiones/scon/Octubre/1541-171008-08-0763.htm, pp. 10-14. It was also published in *Official Gazette* N° 39.055 of November 10, 2008. In this paper, when referring to the Decision N°1541 of 2008, I will quote the pages of the version published in the web site of the Tribunal. See the critical comment on this decision in Eugenio Hernández Bretón, "El arbitraje internacional con entes del Estado venezolano," in *Boletín de la Academia de Ciencias Políticas y Sociales*, N° 147, Caracas 2009, p. 156.

93 See Victorino Tejera Pérez, "Do Municipal Investment Laws Always Constitute a Unilateral Offer to Arbitrate? The Venezuelan Investment Law: A Case Study," *loc. cit.,* p. 113; Victorino Tejera Pérez, *Arbitraje de Inversiones*, Magister Thesis, Universidad Central de Venezuela, Caracas 2010, p. 154.

clearly reflected in the 1999 Investment Law as a whole, primarily devoted to promoting and protecting foreign investment by regulating limiting) the actions of the State in the treatment of such investment. Submission of disputes to international arbitration is precisely one of the principal means of protecting foreign investors and investments. Even the 2008 Decision N° 1.541 of the Supreme Tribunal, recognized that one of the ways States have in order to attract foreign investment is to make a unilateral promise to submit disputes to arbitration The Tribunal said: "It is not possible to ignore that States seeking to attract investments must in their sovereignty decide to grant certain guarantees to investors, in order for such relationship to take place. Within the variables used to achieve said investments, it is common to include an arbitration agreement, which in the investors' judgment provides them with security in relation to the —already mentioned— fear of a possible partiality of State tribunals in favor of [the tribunals'] own nationals" (p. 29).

1. *The historical background of the matter of arbitration: from hostility towards acceptance*

The historical background of the Investment Law were summarized in 2005 by the President of the Academy of Social and Political Sciences, professor Alfredo Morles Hernández, in the already mentioned *Seminar* organized in 2005[94] in order to analyze and study the 1999 Investment Law. In his opening statement (*Presentación*), what Alfredo Morles said confirms that by 1999, the prevailing attitude towards arbitration in the Government was a favorable one, despite the voices that still existed that opposed to State arbitration as a principle. The statements of Professor Morles also confirm his own favorable attitude towards arbitration. In the last part of the statement of Morles he said:

> "Now, all this hostile culture towards arbitration in general, and all the suspicious and prejudicial attitude of the legal community regarding the its use, **has been giving way to a new situation, favored in the international field by the equalitarian treatment between Nations and because the action of international organizations like UNCITRAL, in which a wide participation of the Nations of all Regions exists** [...]." (Emphasis added).[95]

After reviewing all the elements of that "new trend" favoring international arbitration, particularly the ratification during the past decades of all the most important international conventions on the matter, making particular emphasis on the ICSID Convention which Professor Morles considered as being "the object of a practically universal acceptance," he clarifies that if it is true that "during a length of time the Latin American counties showed reticence in adhering" "this tendency from some time on has reverted."[96]

---

94   See Alfredo Morles Herández, "Presentación," in Irene Valera (Coord.), *Arbitraje comercial interno e internacional. Reflexiones teóricas y experiencias prácticas*, Academia de Ciencias Políticas y Sociales, Caracas 2005, pp. 7-14.

95   *Idem*, p. 12

96   *Idem*, pp. 12-13

Professor Morles ended his statement by pointing out that "lawyers and judges have to abandon, that is, forget the reticence towards arbitration; and learn the convenience of its use, for the simple reason that as well as the majority of citizens lack the resources to pay for expensive justice, they also don't have the patience to tolerate justice that is even more slow and suspicious."[97]

From what Professor Morles said in his Presentation, when read in totality, what is clear is that its "central theme" was not to consider the matter of traditional hostility towards arbitration, but on the contrary, to stress the "new situation" in favor of international arbitration that substituted the former "hostile culture," and to express the need for the legal community to overcome, that is to "abandon" and "forget," all "reticence towards arbitration" which he considers as an "ideal, rapid and transparent system of conflict resolution."[98]

Professor Morles' position related to the possibility of the renunciation of jurisdictional immunity in public contracts entered by the Republic referring to external public debt (emprésito público) was very different. [99] Since 1970, Professor Morles has criticized the legal opinion of the General Attorney's Office (expressed in 1977) that it was permissible to incorporate in external public debt contracts clauses renouncing the State's jurisdictional immunity which at the time was extensively incorporated in public contracts.[100]

Therefore, it is an historical fact that, particularly after the sanctioning of the 1961 Constitution and well before 1999, the Republic had accepted in a very extensive way, specifically with respect to public contracts, its ability to renounce its jurisdictional immunity.

2. The constitutional evolution on jurisdictional immunity of the State and the healing of old diplomatic wounds

In any case, it is useful to recall the evolution of the constitutional provisions in Venezuela on matters of international arbitration and jurisdictional immunity. During the 19th century and the first two decades of the 20th century, international arbitration was the general rule that the Constitutions imposed to be established in a clause that had to be incorporated in all international treaties for the solution of all differences between the Contracting parties.[101] The clause was reestablished in 1947,

---

97   *Idem*, pp. 13-14

98   *Idem*, p. 14

99   *Idem*, pp. 13-14

100 See Alfredo Morles Hernández, "La inmunidad de jurisdicción y las operaciones de crédito público," in *Estudios sobre la Constitución, Libro Homenaje a Rafael Caldera*, Universidad Central de Venezuela, Caracas 1979, Vol. III, p. 1717.

101 In the 1864 (Article 112), 1874 (Article 112), 1881 (Article 109), 1891 (Article 109), 1893 (Article 141), 1901 (Article 133), 1904 (Article 120), 1909 (Article 138), 1914 (Article 120), and 1922 (Article 120) Constitutions, an Article was included establishing that in international treaties a clause was to be incorporated with the following text: "All the differences between the contracting parties must be decided, without recurring to war, by arbitration of friendly State or States." See in Allan R. Brewer-Carías, *Las Constituciones de Venezuela*,

although with a wider scope, referring to all international compromises (and not only treaties) and to the solution of controversies by pacific means (and not only arbitration) recognized in international law.

The Constitution has included, since 1893, an important Article with three specific clauses: first, the prohibition for public interest contracts (public interest contracts) to be transferred to foreign States; second, the absolute immunity for jurisdiction clause establishing the obligation of its incorporation in all public contracts; and third, the so called "*Calvo* clause" excluding any diplomatic claims regarding such public contracts. Following this provision, it was precisely, at the turn of the 20th Century, that arbitration was rejected in Venezuela on matters of public law by application of the "*Calvo* Clause," and as a result of events of 1902 that gave rise in Venezuela to the "*Drago* Doctrine."[102] In effect, ten years after the 1893 constitutional reform, a hostile action took place in 1902, with the military blockade of the Venezuelan ports by forces of Germany, Great Britain and Italy made seeking for the compulsory collection of public debts giving rise to the application in Venezuela of the "*Drago* Doctrine."[103] In any case, all such clauses have remained up to date in the Constitution, although the second one was transformed in 1947 and since 1961, from an absolute jurisdictional sovereign immunity into a relative sovereign immunity for jurisdiction clause.

After all the experiences occurred at the turn of the 20th century, since 1961 and due to the reestablishment in the Constitution (Article 127) of the principle of relative sovereign immunity of jurisdiction, based on a similar provision contained in Article 108 of the 1947 Constitution, the insertion of binding arbitration clauses in public contracts became a generally accepted practice, recognized as valid.[104]

Academia de Ciencias Políticas y Sociales, Caracas 2008. See J. Eloy Anzola, "El fatigoso camino que transita el arbitraje," in Irene Valera (Coordinadora), *Arbitraje Comercial Interno e Internacional. Reflexiones teóricas y experiencias prácticas*, Academia de Ciencias Políticas y Sociales, Comité Venezolano de Arbitraje, Caracas 2005, p. 410.

102 The *Drago* Doctrine was conceived in 1902 by the then Argentinean Minister of Foreign Relations, Luis María Drago, who –in response to threats of military force made by Germany, Great Britain and Italy against Venezuela– formulated his thesis condemning the compulsory collection of public debts by the States. See generally Victorino Jiménez y Núñez, *La Doctrina Drago y la Política Internacional*, Madrid 1927.

103 See Allan R. Brewer-Carías, *Historia Constitucional de Venezuela*, Vol I, Editorial Alfa, Caracas 2008, pp. 411.

104 See Allan R. Brewer-Carías, *Contratos Administrativos*, Colección Estudios Jurídicos N° 44, Editorial Jurídica Venezolana, Caracas 1992, pp. 262-265. The possibility for arbitration clauses to be incorporated in public contracts was first examined in Venezuela in 1960 even before the 1961 Constitution was enacted. See Antonio Moles Caubet, "El arbitraje en la contratación administrativa," in *Revista de la Facultad de Derecho*, N° 20, Universidad central de Venezuela, Caracas 1960, p. 22. See also Alberto Baumeister Toledo, "Algunas consideraciones sobre el procedimiento aplicable en los casos de arbitrajes regidos por la ley de Arbitraje Comercial," in Allan R. Brewer-Carías (Ed.), *Seminario sobre la Ley de Arbitraje Comercial*, Academia de Ciencias Políticas y Sociales, Caracas 1999, pp. 95-98; Allan R. Brewer-Carías, "El arbitraje y los contratos de interés públicos," in Allan R. Brewer-Carías

3. The general acceptance of arbitration on matters of private law

On the other hand, on matters of private law, after arbitration was initially established as a constitutional right in the 1830 Constitution (Art. 140),[105] and was authorized as binding in the 19th Century in the civil procedure regulations as a means of alternative dispute resolution, at the beginning of the 20th century, in the 1916 Civil Procedure Code, arbitration was established only as a non-binding method of dispute resolution, that is, without making the arbitration agreement mandatory (Articles 502-522). It was in 1986, with the amendments of the Civil Procedure Code, that the parties were allowed to make a binding agreement to submit controversies to arbitral tribunals, and to exclude the jurisdiction of ordinary courts (Articles 608-629).[106] In addition, special statutes allowed for arbitration in areas related to copyright, insurance, consumer protection, labor, and agrarian reform.[107]

In addition, Venezuela ratified the 1979 Inter-American Convention on Extraterritorial Validity of Foreign Judgments and Arbitral Awards,[108] the 1975 Inter-American Convention on International Commercial Arbitration,[109] and the 1958 United Nations Convention on the Recognition and Enforcement of Foreign Arbitral Awards (New York Convention).[110] This was followed in 1995, by the ratification

---

(Coord.), *Seminario sobre la Ley de Arbitraje Comercial*, Academia de Ciencias Políticas y Sociales, Caracas 1999, pp 167-186; Francisco Hung Vaillant, *Reflexiones Sobre el Arbitraje en el Sistema Venezolano*, Editorial Jurídica Venezolana, Caracas 2001, pp. 125-130.

105 See J. Eloy Anzola. "Luces desde Venezuela: La administración de justicia no es monopolio exclusivo del Estado," in *Spanish Arbitration Review, Revista del Club Español de Arbitraje*, N° 4, 2009, p. 62.

106 On the importance and impact of the 1986 Civil Procedure Code reform on matters of arbitration, see Víctor Hugo Guerra Hernández. "Evolución del arbitraje commercial interno e internacional," in Irene Valera (Coordinadora), *Arbitraje Comercial Interno e Internacional. Reflexiones teóricas y experiencias prácticas*, Academia de Ciencias Políticas y Sociales, Comité Venezolano de Arbitraje, Caracas 2005, pp. 42-44; Arístides Rengel Romberg, "El arbitraje comercial en el Código de Procedimiento Civil y en la nueva Ley de Arbitraje Comercial (1998)," in Allan R. Brewer-Carías (Ed.), *Seminario sobre la Ley de Arbitraje Comercial*, Academia de Ciencias Políticas y Sociales, Caracas 1999; J. Eloy Anzola, "El fatigoso camino que transita el arbitraje," in Irene Valera (Coordinadora), *Arbitraje Comercial Interno e Internacional. Reflexiones teóricas y experiencias prácticas*, Academia de Ciencias Políticas y Sociales, Comité Venezolano de Arbitraje, Caracas 2005, p.408.

107 See the laws listed, including the Copyright Law (1993), Insurance Companies Law (1994), Consumer Protection Law (1995), Organic Labor Law (1990), in Francisco Hung Vaillant, *Reflexiones Sobre el Arbitraje en el Sistema Venezolano*, *op. cit.*, pp. 90-101; Paolo Longo F., *Arbitraje y Sistema Constitucional de Justicia*, Editorial Frónesis S.A., Caracas, 2004, pp. 52-77; Víctor Hugo Guerra Hernández. "Evolución del arbitraje commercial interno e internacional," *loc. cit.*, pp. 44-46); and in 2008 Decision N° 1.541, pp. 12-13.

108 *Official Gazette* N° 33.144 of January 15, 1985.

109 *Official Gazette* N° 33.170 of February 22, 1985.

110 *Official Gazette* N° 4832 Extra of December 29, 1994. For an account of international instruments relevant to Venezuela's recognition of international arbitration, see Decision N° 1541 of 2008, pp. 13-14.

of the ICSID Convention,[111] as well as by the signing of all the Bilateral Treaties on promotion and protection of investments (BITs) that were signed during the 90's providing for international arbitration. Finally, in 1998, Venezuela adopted the Commercial Arbitration Law,[112] which is based on the Model Law on International Commercial Arbitration of UNCITRAL.[113]

On the other hand, and specifically on maters of foreign investments, and according to the regime existing at the time, the Executive Decree 2.095 of February 13, 1992 containing the Regulation on the "Common Regime on the Treatment of Foreign Capitals and on Trademarks, patents, Licenses and Royalties, approved in Decisions Nos. 291 and 292 of the Commission of the Cartagena Agreement," established in a general way that "the solution of controversies or conflicts derived from direct foreign investments or sub-regional investors or from the transfer of foreign technology, the jurisdictional or conciliation and arbitration mechanisms established in the law can be used."[114] Consequently, it was a generalized practice to provide for arbitration for the possible solution of investments disputes.

4.   The general acceptance of arbitration on matters of public contracts and the sense of the provisions of Article 4 of the Commercial Arbitration Law and of Article 151 of the Constitution

Specifically regarding the extensive use of the mechanisms of arbitration according to the relative jurisdictional immunity clause in public contracts, due to the constitutional provision in the 1961 Constitution that was highlighted by Professor Morles,[115] as pointed out by the ICSID tribunals in the *Mobil* and *Cemex* case, shows that in 1993 "the environment in Venezuela had become more favorable to international arbitration" (ICSID *Mobil* case, ¶ 130; ICSID *Cemex* case, ¶ 125) in the sense that "the traditional hostility towards international arbitration had receded in the 1990s in favor of a more positive attitude" (ICSID *Mobil* case, ¶ 131). Nonetheless, the ICSID Tribunal in the *Mobil* case added, in an incomprehensible way, that: "However, Venezuela remained reluctant *vis-à-vis* contractual arbitration in the public sphere, as demonstrated by [Article 4 of] the 1998 Arbitration Law and Article 151 of the 1999 Constitution" (Emphasis added) (ICSID *Mobil* case, ¶¶ 131; 127, 128). The same was asserted in the *Cemex* case (ICSID *Cemex* case, ¶ 125). These Tribunals have not really understood the content of both provisions from which no "reluctant" attitude towards arbitration can be drawn.

---

111 *Official Gazette* N° 35.685 of April 3, 1995.

112 *Official Gazette* N° 36.430 of April 7, 1998.

113 See *generally* Arístides Rengel Romberg, "El arbitraje comercial en el Código de Procedimiento Civil y en la nueva Ley de Arbitraje Comercial (1998)," *loc. cit.*, pp. 47 ff.

114 *Official Gazette* N° 34.930 of March 25, 1992

115 See Alfredo Morles Hernández, "La inmunidad de jurisdicción y las operaciones de crédito público," *loc. cit.*, p. 1717.

Article 4 of the Commercial Arbitration Law[116] is an elemental administrative procedural provision, providing the following:

> "Article 4. When in an arbitral agreement one of the parties is a company in which the republic, the States, the Municipalities or the Public Corporations have a participation equal of higher that the 50% of the capital, or a company in which the legal persons aforementioned have a participation equal or higher that the 50 % of the capital, for the validity of the contract the approval of the members of the Board of Directors of the company and the authorization of the Minister of control will be required. The arbitration agreement must specify the sort of arbitration and the number of arbiters, which in no case can be less than three".[117]

The provision imposes only that arbitration agreement can be entered into by decentralized entities in the public sector, according to their by-laws, and that for their validity the approval of the Board of Directors of the contracting entity must be given, as well as the authorization by the Ministry in charge of controlling the specific decentralized entity (*Ministro de tutela*).[118] This provision therefore only establishes administrative procedural requirements.[119] It is therefore incomprehensible to find from such provisions a "reluctant attitude" of Venezuela towards arbitration or that such provision establishes that the country "remained reluctant" towards contractual arbitration (ICSID *Mobil* case, ¶¶ 129, 131; ICSID *Cemex* case, ¶ 125).

More incomprehensible is the reference in the ICSID Mobil decision (ICSID *Mobil* case, ¶¶ 131; 127, 128) to Article 151 of the Constitution in order to prove the "reluctance" of Venezuela towards contractual arbitration. Such provision establish-

---

116 Se in *Official Gazette* N° 36.430 of April 7, 1998.

117 Spanish version: *Artículo 4. Cuando en un acuerdo de arbitraje al menos una de las partes sea una sociedad en la cual la República, los Estados, los Municipios y los Institutos Autónomos tengan participación igual o superior al cincuenta por ciento (50%) del capital social, o una sociedad en la cual las personas anteriormente citadas tengan participación igual o superior al cincuenta por ciento (50%) del capital social, se requerirá para su validez de la aprobación de todos los miembros de la Junta Directiva de dicha empresa y la autorización por escrito del ministro de tutela. El acuerdo de arbitraje especificará el tipo de arbitraje y el número de árbitros, el cual en ningún caso será menor de tres (3).*

118 The "*Ministerio de tutela*" expression used in article 4 of the Commercial Arbitration Law cannot be translated, as made by the ICSID Tribunal in the decision in the *Mobil* case, as "Ministry of Legal Protection (ICSID *Mobil* case, ¶ 128). In that Article of the Commercial Arbitration Law, the expression *Ministerio de tutela*, following the well established sense of the administrative law French expression "*contrôle de tutelle*" in order to differentiate it from the "hierarchical control," refers to the Ministry of the National Executive to which a decentralized entity is assigned or attached. In Venezuela, all public enterprises or public corporations must be assigned or attached to a Ministry, which is called *Ministerio de tutela* or *Ministerio de adscripción*. See for instance the expression as has been used in the Organic Law of Public Administration, Articles 78, 97.5, and 120-122. Decree Law N° 6217 of July 15, 2008, in *Official Gazette* N° 5890 Extra. of July 31, 2008. See the comments in Allan R. Brewer-Carías *et al.*, *Ley Orgánica de la Administración Pública*, Editorial Jurídica venezolana, Caracas 2008, pp. 77-79.

119 See on this Article, the comments in Allan R. Brewer-Carías, "El arbitraje y los contratos de interés nacional," *loc. cit.*, pp. 169-204.

es, as it is generally admitted in international law, on the one hand, the principle of relative immunity for jurisdiction on matters of public contracts; and on the other hand, the principle that foreign States cannot initiate diplomatic claims against the Venezuelan State as a consequence of public contracts entered with foreign corporations ("*Calvo* clause").[120] Therefore, there is nothing extraordinary or unusual.

On the other hand, and as aforementioned explained, those two provisions (article 4, Commercial Arbitration Law; Article 151, Constitution) are precisely among those that are an essential and important manifestations of the pro-arbitration trend of the Venezuelan legal system. Consequently, and contrary to the erroneous comment contained in the ICSID Tribunal decisions in the *Mobile* and *Cemex* cases, from the general evolution in favor of arbitration, it is perfectly possible - using the same words of the decisions – (*Mobile ICSID* case, ¶ 138; *Cemex ICSID* case, ¶ 126) to draw "the conclusion that Venezuela, in adopting Article 22, intended to give in advance its consent to ICSID arbitration" particularly if the disclaimer included in the last part of the article giving the investor the right to unilateral chose to go to arbitration or to resort before the national courts, is not ignored. The inclusion of this last phrase of article 22 ("without prejudice to the possibility of using, as appropriate, the contentious means contemplated by the Venezuelan legislation in effect"), which the ISCID tribunals in the *Mobile* and *Cemex* cases did not consider at all, is the one that precisely confirm the intention of Venezuela to give its advance consent to ICSID arbitration in general. That was the way chosen by the drafters of the 1999 Investment Law enacted by the National Executive to confirm that the first part of the article was an expression of consent as an open offer, by giving the investor the option to go to arbitration or to resort to the national courts.

The fact is that the inclusion of the disclaimer in the provision, only meant to ratify that the State's consent for international arbitration given in the first part of the Article, was given without excluding the possibility for the investor to resort to national courts, when not accepting the open offer made by the State. In other words, this disclaimer contained in the last part of the provision means that despite the consent given by the Republic, as an open offer for international arbitration, the investor has the option to unilaterally accept the offer to submit the dispute to international arbitration, or to use, as appropriate, the contentious means contemplated by the Venezuelan legislation. This option established in the last part of the article can only have sense and meaning if the first part of the article is interpreted as a unilateral expression of consent that acts as an open offer given by the State. This means that the open offer of consent, is given by the State "*sin perjuicio de la posibilidad de hacer uso*" (without prejudice to the possibility of using), as appropriate,[121] the con-

---

120 See on this Article, our proposal before the National Constituent Assembly, in Allan R. Brewer-Carías, "Propuesta sobre la cláusula de inmunidad relativa de jurisdicción y sobre la cláusula Calvo en los contratos de interés público," in *Debate Constituyente (Aportes a la Asamblea Nacional Constituyente)*, Vol. I (8-Agosto-8 Septiembre 1999), Fundación de Derecho Público/Editorial Jurídica Venezolana, Caracas 1999, pp. 209-233.

121 The expression "as appropriate" is referred to the matters that in Venezuela cannot be submitted to arbitration, like the use of the power of taxation or the power of expropriation. See

tentious means contemplated by the Venezuelan legislation in effect," leaving to the investor, as a right, the election to submit disputes arising under the Investment Law to international arbitration or to Venezuelan courts.

The sense of the disclaimer of last part of article 22, is the direct consequence of the language used, in the sense that it disclaim, explain or clarify that the investor has always the possibility to resort to national courts, meaning that after the State has expressed its consent to international arbitration, the investor has the option of accepting the offer given by the State or to submit the dispute to national courts. Otherwise, if one considers that no consent for arbitration was given by the State in the first part of the article, then the disclaimer would have no sense, because according to the Venezuelan Constitution the possibility to resort to national courts is always possible.

This provision of the disclaimer based on the expression "without prejudice," of course cannot be interpreted as having no meaning or purpose, for instance considering that it only applies when the investor has already proceeded to arbitration, or when international arbitration has already commenced. If it were for such purpose, the disclaimer of article 22 would have been superfluous, without any need to be expressed. On the contrary, the final part of article 22 has sense, only when considered as a provision giving the investor the right, as an absolute option, to unilaterally resort (or not) at his will, to international arbitration, once the State gave its consent in the first part of the article. That is, the right provided in the disclaimer could only possibly be granted, if the first part of the Article is a unilateral expression of consent that acts as an open offer, given by the State.

It is well known that the expression *"sin perjuicio de"* knowm in the Spanish Grammar is known as a *"locución adverbial"* (adverbial expression or diction), mainly used in legal texts, equivalent to the expressions *"dejando a salvo," "sin detrimento de"* or *"sin menoscabo de"* and used to specify that when a particular conduct is ordered in the specific legal provision, it does not mean that it excluded or affects other possible conduct. That is, that the inclusion of a conduct in the norm, does not affect other possible conducts allowed in the legal order, expressed in the provision. In order to have sense and meaning, therefore, a conduct must be regulated expressly in the provision in order to clarify that it does not affect other conducts that can be also accomplished. This is the sense of a norm providing for a particular conduct "without prejudice to" the possibility of doing other thing, or not affecting the possibility of doing other thing.

It is precisely the sense of Article 22 of the Investment Law when providing for the State consent for international arbitration which is given without excluding the possibility for the investor to resort to national courts by not accepting the open offer made by the State. The adverbial expression allowing the investor to go to na-

---

for instance, Allan R. Brewer-Carías, *Contratos Administraivos*, Caracas 1997, p. 265. These are the same State powers that cannot be subjected to transactions. See Allan R. Brewer-Carías, "Las transacciones fiscales y la indisponibilidad de la potestad y competencia tributarias," en *Revista de Derecho Tributario*, N° 18, Caracas, mayo-junio 1967, pp. 1-36.

tional courts has sense only if it has the choice to opt to go to international arbitration accepting the open offer expressed by the State in the provision, or to resort to national courts for the resolution of international investments disputes. In the case of article 22 of the Investment Law, if no open offer for arbitration is contained in the first parte of the article, the disclaimer of the second part would have no sense, because national courts are always available for the resolution of disputes according to the Constitution, and there is no need to expressed it in the provision, except in order to emphasize that the consent given by the State for international arbitration do not prevent for the investor to opt to resort to national courts, at his will.

In any case, when interpreting a provision of a statute, the interpreter, including international arbitration tribunals, is obliged to analyze its whole text and its actual wording, and not only a part of the article; not being allowed to ignore another part of the article, and much less to arrive to an interpretative conclusion only based on the speculative point of view of the interpreter, including tribunals, on how it would have written the article if it would have been in the position of its drafter. And that exercise could not be admitted because it would be an invalid speculation due to the fact that in a "legal clinic or laboratory," in a *ex post facto* way, it would be impossible to reconstruct the political environment surrounding the drafting of a Law, and much less, the one existing in a new government seeking for international investments as was the case in 1999 regarding the Investment Law. The judges' arguments and speculations on how would have been the better way to write or not to write an articles of a law, is not the correct way to resolve a disputes regarding the interpretation of a statute. That is why, it is completely unacceptable for a tribunal to base its ruling by stating in an hypothetical way, as was the case of the ISCID tribunals in the *Mobile* and *Cemex* cases, on how "would have been easy for the drafters of Article 22 to express that intention clearly by using any of those well known formula" (*Mobile ICSID* case, ¶ 139; *Cemex ICSID* case, ¶ 137). National courts and Arbitral tribunal decisions are not conceived as a means to give writing rules to the drafters of statutes on how to write or not to write them, but to interpret their provisions following the rules of interpretation, even if they are not written in the way the tribunal would have written them.

In any case, apart the writing lessons, the conclusions of the ICSID tribunals in the *Mobile* and *Cemex* cases, eventually were to say that from the wording of article 22 the intention of the Government to express the State consent to submit investments disputes to international arbitration only subjected to the condition that a treaty or an agreement provide a framework or mechanisms for arbitration, "is not established" (*Mobile ICSID* case, ¶ 140; *Cemex ICSID* case, ¶ 138), and that they could not conclude specifically and only in such cases, "that Venezuela, in adopting the 1999 Investment Law, consented in advance [or "unilaterally"] to ICSID arbitration for all disputes covered by ICSID Convention" ruling therefore, that such article "does not provide basis for jurisdiction of the Tribunal in **the present case**" (*Mobile ICSID* case, ¶ 140; *Cemex ICSID* case, ¶ 138). Nonetheless, as mentioned above, the ICSID Tribunal decision in the *Brandes* case, without any reasoning, arguments or motivation, proclaimed in a general and universal way, and not only for the "present case," that "it is obvious that Article 22 of the Law on Promotion and protection of Investments does not contain the consent of the Bolivarian Republic of Venezuela to

ICSID jurisdiction" (*Brandes ICSID* case, ¶ 118). The difference between this decision in the *Brandes* if compared with the decisions in the *Mobile* and *Cemex* cases, at least from the point of view of the general standard rules governing judicial decisions, as aforementioned, completely lacks of the reasons or motives on which it is based.

5. The legal doctrine of the Attorney General's Office on acceptance of arbitration on matters of public contracts

Since the 1970s, it has been a generally accepted practice to include in public contracts the relative immunity clause, as was pointed out by Professor Morles.[122] Almost two decades later, the Office of the Attorney General of the Republic, as the constitutionally-appointed entity responsible for advising the National Executive on legal matters, intended to review the issue of jurisdictional sovereign immunity included in public external debt contracts (*contratos de emprestitos públicos*) entered into by the Republic.[123] In such regard, a formal Legal Opinion was given by the Attorney General's Office that same year, through Letter N° 4211 of December 19, 1996, directed to the Minister of Finance[124] reviewing the previous legal criteria expressed by the same Office in the 1970's regarding the "commercial" nature of the external public debt contracts, proposing that the Republic cease renouncing its entitlement to jurisdictional immunity in such contracts. This Opinion was unsuccessful in changing the legal principles that have been well-established since 1970's, and was, in any event, abandoned four months later, in April 1997. But again, however, the subject matter of the Opinion was jurisdictional immunity in public debt contracts and not the availability or constitutionality of international arbitration.[125] .

In effect, on April 21, 1997,[126] the Attorney General recognized the relevance of the relative jurisdictional sovereign immunity clause contained in Article 127 of the

---

122 See Alfredo Morles Hernández, "La inmunidad de jurisdicción y las operaciones de crédito público," *loc. cit.*, p. 1717.

123 In that regard, Jesús Petit Da Costa, the Attorney General of the Republic at the time, published in September 1996 an Op-Ed in a mayor News paper of Caracas, containing its "personal opinion" regarding the possibility of subjecting the Republic, not to the jurisdiction of arbitral tribunals generally, but only to the jurisdiction of "foreign tribunals." In any case, theThe Article titled "*Blindar con la Constitución*" (*El Universal*, Caracas, September 14, 1996), had nothing to do with arbitration, and does not refer to international arbitration at all ("arbitration" is a word that is not even used in the Article), and only refers to "foreign tribunals" (*tribunal extranjero*) meaning courts of other foreign States.

124 Letter N° 4211 of December 19, 1996 directed to Luis Raúl Matos Azocar, Ministry of Finance.

125 In addition, in the Opinion, the Attorney General, only ratified his personal assertion made in the Article published three months before, expressing the same concerns

126 See excerpt of the Opinion in Margot Y. Huen Rivas, "El arbitraje internacional en los contratos administrativos," in *VIII Jornadas Internacionales de Derecho Administrativo "Allan Randolph Brewer-Carías," Los contratos administrativos. Contratos del Estado*, Fundación de Estudios de Derecho Administrativo, FUNEDA, Vol. I, Caracas 2005, pp. 434-435; and Juan Carlos Balzán, "El arbitraje en los contratos de interés a la luz de la cláusula de inmuni-

1961 Constitution (equivalent to article 151 of the 1999 Constitution regarding to public contracts, and provided that the security of the Republic or its internal sovereignty is not compromised, admitting that 'the submission to a foreign jurisdiction cannot signify a violation of Article 127 of the Constitution."[127]

6. The inclusion of arbitration clauses in public contracts since the 1990's with the knowledge and consent of the Attorney General's Office

According to this legal doctrine, and even before the quickly defunct Opinion of 1996, the Attorney General's Office consistently gave its acceptance for the inclusion of arbitration clauses in many State acts. First, in 1994, in the Decree Law N° 138 of April 20, 1994, which was another important statute on promotion of investments sanctioned by the Government, containing the Organic Law on Concessions of Public Works and National Public utilities,[128] issued by the President of the Republic with the legal consent of the General Attorney Office. This law includes an Article expressly establishing that "the National Executive and the concessionaire could agree that the doubts and controversies that may arise resulting from the interpretation and execution of the concession contract would be decided by an arbitral tribunal whose composition, competency, procedure and applicable law shall be determined by the parties" (Article 10).[129]

Second, in 1995, the Attorney General's Office also accepted an international arbitration clause that was included in the Congressional Resolution (*Acuerdo*) establishing the Framework of Conditions for the "Association Agreements for the Exploration at Risk of New Areas and the Production of Hydrocarbons under the Shared-Profit Scheme" ("*Convenios de Asociación Para la Exploración a Riesgo de Nuevas Areas y la Producción de Hidrocarburos Bajo el Esquema de Ganancias Compartidas*"), dated July 4, 1995.[130] This provision was challenged on the grounds of its supposed unconstitutionality before the Supreme Courts of Justice through a popular action brought, among others, by Ali Rodríguez Araque then member of Congress, and appointed 1999 as Minister of Energy and Mines. Rodríguez Araque opposed, together with the other co-claimants, the inclusion of the arbitration clause

---

dad de jurisdicción prevista en el artículo 151 de la Constitución," in *VIII Jornadas Internacionales de Derecho Administrativo "Allan Randolph Brewer-Carías," Los contratos administrativos. Contratos del Estado*, Fundación de Estudios de Derecho Administrativo, FUNEDA, Vol. II, Caracas 2006, pp. 345.

127 *Id*. This was later included even more expressly in the 2005 Law on the Financial Administration of the Public Sector, Article 104. *See Offical Gazette* N° 37.978 of July 13, 2004.

128 See *Official Gazette* N° 4719 Extra. of April 26, 1994.

129 See in Luis Fraga Pittaluga, "El arbitraje y la transacción como métodos alternativos de Resolución de conflictos administrativos," in *IV Jornadas Internacionales de Derecho Administrativo Allan Randolph Brewer Carías, La relación jurídico-administrativa y el procedimiento administrativo*, Fundación de Estudios de Derecho Administrativo, FUNEDA, Caracas 1998, p. 178. This means that Fraga considered in 1998 that "the admission of arbitration in administrative field is an irreversibly tendency," *Id*. p. 177.

130 *Official Gazette* N° 35.754 of July 17, 1995.

in the Congressional Resolution and in the Association Agreements. Based on these antecedents, and knowing Mr. Rodríguez personally, I assume that in 1999, acting as the Minister of Energy and Mines, he must have opposed to the inclusion of Article 22 of the Investment Law because providing it provided the State's consent to arbitration.

In August 1999, the Supreme Court of Justice dismissed the action filed by Rodríguez Araque and others, upholding the constitutionality of the Congressional Resolution authorizing the Framework of Conditions for the "Association Agreements for the Exploration at Risk of New Areas and the Production of Hydrocarbons under the Shared-Profit Scheme," holding that such authorization and, in particular, the inclusion of arbitration clauses in public law contracts, were valid under Article 127 of the 1961 Constitution in force at the time (equivalent to Article 151 of the 1999 Constitution).[131] This decision of the Supreme Court of Justice, since then, has been considered as the leading judicial precedent on the matter of arbitration in public contracts and on the sense of the relative sovereign immunity of jurisdiction clause in the country.[132]

During the same time period, Article 4 was included in the Commercial Arbitration Law of 1998). As previously mentioned Article 4 expressly admits the inclusion of arbitral clauses in public contracts, upon approval by the competent organ according to the by-laws of the entity and written authorization by the Ministry in charge of controlling the activities of the specific decentralized entity. The provision is no more that the express ratification and express acceptance by Congress of the possi-

---

131   See decision in Allan R. Brewer-Carías (Compilator), *Documentos del Juicio de la Apertura Petrolera (1996-1999)*, Caracas, 2004 *available at* http://allanbrewercarias.com/Content/449725d9-f1cb-474b-8ab2-41efb849fea3/Content/I,%202,%2022.%20%20APERTURA%20PETROLERA.%20DOCU MENTOS%20DEL%20JUICIO.pdf,_pp. 280-328. I acted as counsel to PDVSA in that judicial proceeding, defending the constitutionality of that *Acuerdo*, and in particular, the constitutionality of the arbitration clause included in the Association Agreements. The Constitutional Chamber of the Supreme Tribunal of Justice has confirmed the ruling made under the 1961 Constitution, holding that Article 151 of the 1999 Constitution allows the incorporation of arbitration provisions in contracts of public interest. See 2008 Decision N° 1.541, pp. 23-24) and Decision N° 97 of February 11, 2009 (*Interpretation of Articles 1 and 151 of the Constitution. Fermín Toro Jiménez, Luis Brito García et al.*). See the comments on the August 1999 upholding the Congress Resolution approving the Framework of the Association Agreement I made when rejecting the constitucional proposal of President Chávez regarding Article 151 of the Constitution, in Allan R. Brewer-Carías, "Propuesta sobre la cláusula de inmunidad relativa de jurisdicción y sobre la cláusula Calvo en los contratos de interés público," in *Debate Constituyente (Aportes a la Asamblea Nacional Constituyente)*, Vol. I (8-Agosto-8 Septiembre 1999), Fundación de Derecho Público/Editorial Jurídica Venezolana, Caracas 1999, pp. 220-229.

132   See Juan Carlos Balzán, "El arbitraje en los contratos de interés a la luz de la cláusula de inmunidad de jurisdicción prevista en el artículo 151 de la Constitución," *loc. cit.*, pp. 349-357; Margot Y. Huen Rivas, "El arbitraje internacional en los contratos administrativos," *loc. cit.*, pp. 438-39.

bility to include arbitration clauses in public contracts.[133] It does not deal with the competence of public entities to include arbitration clauses in public contracts, which is accepted, being only an administrative procedural provision establishing one of the most elemental rules of management in Public Administration, which is control.

On the other hand, the availability of arbitration as a remedy has been recognized in a number of subsequent judicial decisions, a number of which were issued before the Investment Law was enacted in 1999.[134] For example, in January 15, of the same year 1998, the Supreme Court of Justice in Politico Administrative Chamber issued another decision (*Industrias Metalúrgicas Van Dam, C.A. vs. República de Venezuela. Ministerio de la Defensa* case), in which an arbitration clause were recognized in public contracts, although because the military object of the contract in the specific case, in a restrictive way regarding the "technical aspects" of the contract excluding matters of matters of national security and defense.[135]

In any case, what is important to highlight is that the general situation during the decades (and not only years) prior to 1999, shows a clear tendency of surpassing the historic "reticence" that could have existed regarding arbitration clauses and State jurisdictional immunity in public law contracts before the 1961 Constitution was enacted and before the Civil Procedure Code was reformed in 1986. This reticence was supplanted by a general acceptance of the possibility for public entities to include in public contracts arbitral clauses, as was expressly ratified in the 1998 Commercial Arbitration Law. At that time, the official doctrine of the Attorney General's Office, the general constitutional, administrative and international law legal doctrine, and the jurisprudence of the Supreme Court of Justice were clearly in favor of these principles.

---

133 See Allan R. Brewer-Carías, "El arbitraje y los contratos de interés nacional," in *Seminario sobre la Ley de Arbitraje Comercial*, Biblioteca de la Academia de Ciencias Políticas y Sociales, Caracas 1999, pp. 169-204

134 See the cases quoted in Juan Carlos Balzán, "El arbitraje en los contratos de interés a la luz de la cláusula de inmunidad de jurisdicción prevista en el artículo 151 de la Constitución," pp. 333-335, 349 and in José G. Villafranca, "Precisión jurisprudencial en torno a la inmunidad de jurisdicción en demandas por responsabilidad patrimonial (Comentario a la sentencia de la CSJ-SPA de fecha 30-07-1998)," in *Revista de Derecho Administrativo*, N° 4, Editorial Sherwood, Caracas 1998, p. 347-360.

135 See excerpt quoted in Juan Carlos Balzán, "El arbitraje en los contratos de interés a la luz de la cláusula de inmunidad de jurisdicción prevista en el artículo 151 de la Constitución," *loc. cit.*, pp. 349-350.

III. PRINCIPLES OF INTERPRETATION OF ARTICLE 22 OF THE INVESTRMENT LAW AS A STATE'S UNILATERAL OPEN OFFER OF CONSENT FOR INTERNATIONAL ARBITRATION

1.   *The inclusion of international and national arbitration provisions in the 1999 Investment law*

As aforementioned, regarding the content of Article 22 of the 1999 Investment Law, the reference it contains regarding ICSID international arbitration is not a mere declaration of principles, or a mere reference in a national law to ICSID international arbitration Center as suggested by some commentators[136] and by the Supreme Tribunal of Justice Decision N° 1541 of 2008.[137] Nor was Article 22 of the Investment Law intended just to acknowledge the possibility of dispute resolution by means of arbitration. On the contrary, Article 22 of the Investment Law amounts to the binding consent of Venezuela to arbitral jurisdiction. On the other hand, arbitration as a means for dispute resolution was included in many other statutes adopted by the Government at the same time, and there are other references to the availability of arbitration in the same 1999 Investment law.

In effect, beside Article 22, arbitration is also provided in Article 18.4 of the Law regarding the contracts for legal stabilization. Following the 1998 Commercial Arbitration Law regulations, the State and an international investor could establish arbitration, in a bilateral act – the contract for legal stabilization – as the means to resolve contractual controversies.[138]

Arbitration is also provided for in Article 21 of the Investment Law regarding the solution of controversies relating to the Investment Law that may arise between the Venezuelan State and the country of origin of the international investor.[139] In these cases, when the diplomatic means fail, the Law imposes the obligation on the State to seek for the submission of the dispute to an Arbitral Tribunal whose composition,

---

136 See Hildegard Rondón de Sansó, *Aspectos jurídicos fundamentales del arbitraje internacional de inversión*, Ed. Exlibris, Caracas 2010, pp. 129, 139

137 Other commentators have expressed the same criticism of this decision. See, e.g., Eugenio Hernández Bretón, "El arbitraje internacional con entes del Estado venezolano," in *Boletín de la Academia de Ciencias Políticas y Sociales*, N° 147, Caracas 2009, p. 156.

138 Article 18.4 of the 1999 Investment Law provides that: "Any disputes that arise between the companies of investors which signed the legal stabilization contract and the Venezuelan State, concerning the interpretation and application of the respective contract may be submitted to institutional arbitration pursuant to the Law on Commercial Arbitration."

139 Article 21 of the 1999 Investment Law states that: "Any dispute that arises between the Venezuelan State and the country of origin of the International investor with which no treaty or agreement on investments is in effect, concerning the interpretation and application of the provisions of this Decree Law shall be resolved through diplomatic channels. In no agreement is reached within twelve months following the date on which the dispute began, the Venezuelan State shall recommend that the dispute be placed before an Arbitral Tribunal, whose composition, mechanism for the appointment thereof, procedure and expense regime shall be agreed upon with the other State. The decisions of this Arbitral Tribunal shall be final and binding."

mechanism of designation, procedure and cost regime has to be negotiated in a bilateral act with the other State. In these two first cases (Articles 18.4 and 21), in order to proceed to arbitration, the Law is clear in providing for the need of a separate bilateral act to be negotiated between the parties.

On the contrary, in other two provisions of the same 1999 Investment Law which provide for arbitration, Articles 22 and 23, the State has given **in advance** its consent for arbitration, as an open offer in the same way as it is provided in almost all BITs, using similar wording that the dispute "shall be submitted" to international arbitration. Both the Investment Law and BITs provide that investors, at their will, may unilaterally choose to go to arbitration or to resort to the national courts.[140] In the case of Article 22, as aforementioned, the State expressed in advance, as an open offer, its consent to go to international arbitration subject to the only condition that the treaties or agreements provide mechanisms or a framework for international arbitration.

This interpretation of Article 22 of the Investment Law as containing a unilateral written expression of consent of the Republic of Venezuela to submit disputes with international investors to the jurisdiction of ICSID arbitration is shared by the majority of the Venezuelan legal commentators[141] as well as many foreign authors.[142] For example, one commentator stated in 2007 that the Investment Law leaves "no doubt at all on the viability of arbitration to resolve controversies between States and foreign investors .... [because it] establishes in a very clear way that the investor, in case of controversy, has the possibility to opt between resort to the ordinary judicial mean or to ICSID, provided that (i) Venezuela and the country from which the in-

---

140   See in this regard, Tatiana B. de Maekelt, "Tratados Bilaterales de Protección de Inversiones. Análisis de las cláusulas arbitrales y su aplicación," in Irene Valera (Coord.), *Arbitraje Comercial Interno e Internacional. Reflexiones teóricas y experiencias prácticas*, Academia de Ciencias Políticas y Sociales, Comité Venezolano de Arbitraje, Caracas 2005, pp. 340-341.

141   See for instance Andrés A. Mezgravis, "Las inversiones petroleras en Venezuela y el arbitraje ante el CIADI", in Irene Valera (Coordinadora), *Arbitraje Comercial Interno e Internacional. Reflexiones teóricas y experiencias prácticas*, Academia de Ciencias Políticas y Sociales, Comité Venezolano de Arbitraje, Caracas 2005, p. 388; Eugenio Hernández Bretón, "Protección de inversiones en Venezuela" in *Revista DeCITA, Derecho del Comercio Internacional, Temas de Actualidad, (Inversiones Extranjeras)*, N°3, Zavalía, 2005, pp. 283-284; José Antonio Muci Borjas, *El Derecho Administrativo Global y los Tratados Bilaterales de Inversión (BITs)*, Caracas 2007, pp. 214-215; José Gregorio Torrealba R, *Promoción y Protección de las Inversiones Extranjeras en Venezuela*, Funeda, Caracas 2008. pp. 56-58, 125-127; Victorino Tejera Pérez, "Do Municipal Investment Laws Always Constitute a Unilateral Offer to Arbitrate? The Venezuelan Investment Law: A Case Study," pp. 90, 101, 109; Victorino Tejera Pérez, *Arbitraje de Inversiones*, Magister Thesis, Caracas 2010, *cit.*, pp. 162, 171, 173, 177, 193.

142   See for instance Gabriela Álvarez Ávila, "Las características del arbitraje del CIADI", en *Anuario Mexicano de Derecho Internacional*, Vol. II 2002, Instituto de Investigaciones Jurídicas, Universidad Nacional Autónoma de México, UNAM, México 2002; Guillaume Lemenez de Kerdelleau, "State Consent to ICSID Arbitration: Article 22 of the Venezuelan Investment Law" in *TDM*, Vol. 4, Issue 3, June 2007.

vestors is a national have signed a treaty on promotion and protection of investments, or (ii) the provisions of the Constitutive Convention of MIGA or of ICSID Convention are applicable, in which case – in our opinion – the country of nationality of the investor must also have signed and ratified at least one of such Conventions."[143]

The contrary opinion in the sense that Article 22 of the Investment Law does not constitute a standing, general consent of the Republic to arbitrate all investments disputes before ICSID" is shared only by a few authors,[144] which consider in general, that since the ICSID Convention supposedly does not provide for a consent to ICSID arbitration, a separate instrument of consent is required as a condition in Article 22. This is of course a misrepresentation of the wording of Article 22, because the condition established in it only refers to the need for mechanisms of arbitration to be provided in the treaties or agreements, not for a separate consent as it is required for instance in Article 21 of the same 1999 Investment Law. To adopt this interpretation would amount to accepting, in an inadmissible tautological way, that the right given to the investor to opt between going to arbitration or before the national court, does not actually allow the investor to choose between those options, which would make the disclaimer of the last phrase of Article 22 completely meaningless.[145]

These opinions fail to analyze the content of Article 22 as a whole, in the general context of the Law, particularly the last part of the provision, which as aforementioned has been generally ignored, and not even mentioned or analyzed in the referred ICSID *Mobil, Cemex* and *Brandes* cases. They fail to acknowledge that the provision gives the investor the right, as an absolute option, to unilaterally resort (or not) at his will, to international arbitration. This is a right that could only possibly be granted if the first part of the Article is a unilateral expression of consent that acts as an open offer, given by the State. This means that when the words of Article 22 (including those used in the last phrase of Article 22: "without prejudice to the possibility of using, as appropriate, the contentious means contemplated by the Venezuelan legislation in effect") are contrasted with those of Article 23 of the same Law,[146]

---

143 See Juan C. Bracho Ghersi, "Algunos Aspectos fundamentales del Arbitraje Internacional," in *Cuestiones actuales del Derecho de la empresa en Venezuela,* Grau, García, Hernández, Mónaco, Caracas 2007, pp. 18..

144 See for instance, Omar E. García-Bolívar, El arbitraje en el marco de la ley de promoción y Protección de Inversiones: las posibles interpretaciones," in *Revista de Derecho*, Tribunal Supremo de Justicia, N° 26, Caracas 2008, pp. 313 ff. Moer recently, see Hildegard Rondón de Sansó, *Aspectos jurídicos fundamentales del arbitraje internacional de inversión*, Ed. Exlibris, Caracas 2010, pp. 123 ff.

145 See Victorino Tejera Pérez, *Arbitraje de Inversiones*, Magister Thesis, Caracas 2010, *cit.*, p. 190; Victorino Tejera Pérez, "Do Municipal Investment Laws Always Constitute a Unilateral Offer to Arbitrate? The Venezuelan Investment Law: A Case Study," *loc. cit.*, pp. 107. See also Eugenio Hernández Bretón, "El arbitraje internacional con entes del Estado venezolano," *loc. cit.*, pp. 141-168..

146 Article 23 of the Investment Law states: "Any dispute arising in connection with the application of this decree Law, once the administrative remedies have been exhausted, may be sub-

the wording of Article 22 is stronger than Article 23, which contains a unilateral consent to arbitration on the part of the Republic. Article 22 and also Article 23, both give investors the option to submit disputes arising under the Investment Law to arbitration: In the case of Article 22, to international arbitration courts or to Venezuelan courts; and in the case of Article 23, to Venezuelan courts or Venezuelan arbitral tribunals. In both cases, the decision is made **at the election of the investors**.

That is, Article 23 contains an arbitration clause or an unilateral consent to arbitration on the part of the Republic by giving investors the option to submit disputes under the investment Law to Venezuelan courts or Venezuelan arbitral tribunals; and also Article 22 provides the same option, but between international arbitration and national courts, not being correct to ignore the choice offered in that provision. In a similar way, regarding clauses for arbitration in BIT's executed by Venezuela, which define the scope of the dispute to be resolved, giving the foreign investor the option to initiate arbitration before ICSID or in another forum, and leaves no doubt that Venezuela is consenting to arbitration of that dispute before ICSID, also Article 22 of the Investment Law is an express consent to arbitration given by the State, leaving also to the international investor the option to initiate arbitration before ICSID or in Venezuelan courts, leaving no doubt that Venezuela is consenting to arbitration of that dispute before ICSID.

This is what has precisely been decided in the *Mobil* and *Cemex* cases, in which the Tribunals determined without doubt, that Article 22 contains a unilateral declaration of the State establishing an obligation to go to arbitration, although subjected to a condition. Consequently, Article 22 of the Investment Law has been considered in both ICSID tribunals' decisions as a unilateral expression of consent given by the Venezuelan State to submit disputes to international arbitration, although subjected to a condition. This also is true of the *Brandes* decision. The reason why these Tribunals nevertheless determined that this did not provide consent for the international investor to resort to ICSID arbitration will be discussed below was only based in the lack of evidence regarding the intent of the State when enacting the Law and assuming the obligation, but not in the fact that the obligation to go to arbitration (although conditional) was not established in article 22.

The sanctioning of the Investment Law by the Government in 1999 had the clear intention to serve as an instrument for the development and promotion of private (foreign and domestic) investment in Venezuela, in accordance with the mandate included in parallel in article 258 of the 1999 Constitution to promote alternative mechanisms for dispute resolution. For such purpose, Article 22 of the Investment Law offered assurance that the resolution of investment disputes by arbitration was a means for their promotion, leaving the option for the investor to go to international arbitration or to resort to the national courts. That is why the National Council for the Promotion of Investment (CONAPRI), a mixed public-private association for the

---

mitted by the investor to the National Courts or Arbitral Tribunals of Venezuela, at the election of the investor."

promotion of private investment in the country, incorporated by the Attorney General of the Republic in 1990[147] in its March 2000 *Report* on the "Legal Regime of the Foreign Investments in Venezuela" devoted an entire Chapter to examine the various types of arbitration established in the legal system, that were offered to investors for the resolution of investment disputes, repeating the same terms and words used in the Law.[148]

In this context, the *Mobil* and *Cemex* ICSID Tribunals, after accepting that article 22 of the Investment Law contained a conditional obligation for the State to go to arbitration, ruled on whether the article provided consent *in particular regarding those cases*, based on matters of evidence regarding the intention of the State when issuing the statute, but not as a universal ruling applicable to all circumstances. That is, it is not accurate to say that the ICSID Tribunal decisions in the cases *Mobil* and *Cemex* supposedly had found, in general, that Article 22 of the Investment Law does **not** provide a basis for ICSID jurisdiction. This is simply not true because the conclusion of the Tribunals was that Article 22 "*does not provide basis for jurisdiction of the Tribunal in the present case*". That is, in these two ICSID Tribunals decisions did not found, in general, that Article 22 does **not** provide a basis for ICSID jurisdiction; being the last conclusion of the Tribunal that Article 22 "does not provide basis for jurisdiction of the Tribunal in the present case." Nonetheless, as mentioned, the ICSID tribunal decision in the *Brandes* case, without any reasoning, arguments or motivation, and without explaining any "findings in the paragraphs" of its decision, it not only copied and ratified the aforementioned conclusion of the ICSID tribunals in the *Mobil* and *Cemex* cases, but went further, proclaiming in a general and universal way, and not only for the "present case," that "it is obvious that Article 22 of the Law on Promotion and Protection of Investments does not contain the consent of the Bolivarian Republic of Venezuela to ICSID jurisdiction" (ICSID *Brandes* case, ¶ 118).

In summary, after having studied the matter in detail and from the stand point of Venezuelan public law, and after having read the ICSID tribunals' decisions interpreting Article 22 of the Investment Law (*i.e.,* the *Mobil, Cemex, Brandes* cases) as a provision establishing an obligation for the State (although conditional) to go to arbitration, I remain convinced and ratify my prior opinion that from the stand point of national Venezuelan law, Article 22 of the Investment Law contains **an expression of consent of the State given as an open offer to submit investment disputes to international arbitration, and in particular to ICSID arbitration, leaving in the hands of the international investor the right to unilaterally decide to go to arbitration or to resort to the national courts.**

---

147 Decree N° 1102 published in *Official Gazette* N° 34.549 of 1990.

148 See Consejo Nacional de Promoción de Inversiones (CONAPRI), *Régimen Legal para la Inversión Extranjera en Venezuela,* Caracas marzo 2000, pp. 29-36.

2. *Article 22 of the Investment Law is a Unilateral Declaration of the State according to the Principles of Statutory Interpretation in Venezuelan Law*

In effect, Article 22 of the Investment Law, as is evident from its wording, and as admitted by the ICSID tribunal in the *Mobil* case (ICSID *Mobil* case, ¶ 103), is a "compound" provision that contains a number of parts: the first one, concerning bilateral or multilateral treaties or agreements on the promotion and protection of investments; the second one, dealing with the MIGA Convention; and the third one, dealing with the ICSID Convention.[149] Because Article 22 addresses three different sets of treaties or agreements, providing for all of them at the same time, it needs to be interpreted in the same way as other legal provisions.

It is hardly surprising, however, that it does not follow any particular model or pattern of other national legislations that address only consent to ICSID jurisdiction. On the other hand, iIt makes no sense to draw inferences from a comparison between Article 22 and expressions of consent to arbitration in bilateral investment treaties executed by Venezuela or even in contracts. Article 22 of the 1999 Investment Law is not a bilateral treaty nor was it the product of a negotiation with another State. Bilateral contracts, constructed by two parties, are the product of an interchange of proposals that are negotiated between them. No doubt we have to suppose that the public officials of the Republic knew how to draft an obligatory consent to international arbitration when that was their intention, but there is also no doubt that for such purpose they chose to use the language contained in the Investment Law different to any model. That choice does not mean there is no consent. Article 22 of the Investment Law is a piece of national legislation, unique because it was the first time in Venezuelan recent legislative history that the State, in an internal law, discussed unilateral consent to international arbitration. Definitively, in that perspective, the Republic had no previous experience in drafting this type of statute.

That is why Article 22 of the Investment Law cannot, as a principle, be interpreted by just comparing its content with any sort of bilateral established and negotiated clauses for arbitration included in BITs or in "model clauses" that are to be negotiated by two Contracting States as "consent clauses." Article 22 must be interpreted not by reference to any pattern or model, but in accordance with its own structure and terms, taking into account its compound nature. Nonetheless, because the aims expressed in Article 1 of the Investment Law as affirmed in the *ICSID Mobile* and *Cemex* cases "are in general comparable to those of the treaties on promotion and reciprocal protection of investments and are reflected in the text of the law itself" which contains provisions "which are comparable to those incorporated in BITs" (as expressed in the ICSID *Mobil* case, ¶¶ 121, 122; and in the ICSID *Cemex* case, ¶ 119), the unilateral open offer of consent by the State to arbitration contained in both BITs and the Investment Law are of paramount importance. Although the *Mobil*

---

149 See on the various alternatives of application of Article 22 of the Investment Law, Victorino Tejera Pérez, "Do Municipal Investment Laws Always Constitute a Unilateral Offer to Arbitrate? The Venezuelan Investment Law: A Case Study," pp. 92-94; Victorino Tejera Pérez, *Arbitraje de Inversiones*, Magister Thesis, Caracas 2010, *cit.*, pp. 166-170.

case failed to mention this feature of the Investment Law, Article 22 unquestionably represents such an expression which leaves to the international investors the option to accept or reject the State's offer.[150]

3. The rules of interpretation of statutes under Venezuelan Law

The interpretation of Article 22 of the 1999 Investment Law as an instrument of national law that purports to express consent to international arbitration by reference to international treaties and agreements, including ICSID Convention, do to its international effects can be considered as properly governed by principles of international law, although the provision can also be interpreted from the standpoint of Venezuelan Law, which is also relevant due to the fact that it is a national statute. In this regard, the Tribunal in the *ICSID Mobil* case interpreted Article 22 on the basis of the "rules of international law governing the interpretation of unilateral acts formulated within the framework and on the basis of a treaty" (ICSID *Mobil* case, ¶ 95), although considering that the national law should not "be completely ignored" being called to "play a useful role" regarding "the intention of the State having formulated such acts" (ICSID *Mobil* case, ¶ 96).[151]

In Venezuela, the main rules on statutory interpretation are set forth in Article 4 of the Civil Code. This article, as aforementioned provides that the interpreter must attribute to the law "the sense that appears evident from the *proper meaning of the words*, according to *their connection* among themselves and the *intention of the Legislator*." The article goes on to state that, "when there is no precise provision of the Law, the provisions regulating similar cases or analogous matters shall be taken into account; and should doubts persist, general principles of law shall be applied."

In Decision N° 895 of July 30, 2008, the Politico-Administrative Chamber of the Supreme Tribunal of Justice referred to four relevant elements to be taken into account in the interpretation of legal provisions.[152] The first element is the **literal, grammatical or philological** one, which must always be the starting point of any interpretation. The second element of interpretation is the **logical, rational or reasonable** one, which aims at determining the *raison d'être* of the provision within the legal order. The third element is the **historical** one, through which a legal provision is to be analyzed in the context of the factual and legal situation at the time it was adopted or amended and in light of its historical evolution. The fourth element is the **systematic** one, which requires the interpreter to analyze the provision as an integral part of the relevant system.

---

150 As it is pointed out by Tatiana B. de Maekelt, "Tratados Bilaterales de Protección de Inversiones. Análisis de las cláusulas arbitrales y su aplicación," pp. 340-344; Andrés A. Mezgravis, "Las inversiones petroleras en Venezuela y el arbitraje ante el CIADI", *loc. cit.*, p. 357; José Gregorio Torrealba, *Promoción y protección de las inversiones extranjeras en Venezuela, op. cit.*, pp. 128-129.

151 See also ICSID *Cemex* case (ICSID Mobil case, ¶¶ 88, 89) and ICSID *Brandes* case (ICSID, *Brandes* case, ¶ 36.

152 See in *Revista de Derecho Público*, N°115, Editorial Jurídica Venezolana, Caracas 2008, pp. 468 ff.

The Politico-Administrative Chamber noted that interpretation of statutes is not a matter of choosing among the four elements, but of applying them together, even if not all of the elements are of equal importance. Nonetheless although the ICSID tribunal in the *Brandes* case said to having interpreted Article 22 of the Investment Law "according to the parameters set by the Republic's legal system" (ICSID *Brandes* case, ¶ 36), in fact followed a different approach, applying what it referred to as an "initial analysis" of the elements mentioned in Article 4 of the Civil Code: first the "purely grammatical analysis" and "if this initial analysis fails to define clearly the meaning of the provision, it then becomes necessary to examine the contents..." (ICSID *Brandes* case, ¶ 35). This approach is not in accordance with the principles of statutory interpretation that must be always applied together. In this sense, the Constitutional Chamber of the Supreme Tribunal in a recent decision N° 1067 of November 3, 2010 (Case *Astivenca Astilleros de Venezuela C.A,*), has ruled regarding the elements for interpretation derived from Article 4 of the Civil Code, that "the normative elements must be harmonized as a whole, in the sense that it one must not ignore the other, but all must be kept in mind in order to make a correct valuation of the content of the legal text.[153]"

In addition, it must be mentioned that the Supreme Tribunal of Justicein Decision N° 895 of 2008, has identified two other elements of interpretation: the **teleological** one – that is, the need to identify and understand the social goals or aims that led to the law being adopted – and the **sociological** one, which helps to understand the provision within the context of the social, economical, political and cultural reality where the text is going to be applied.[154]

From the standpoint of Venezuelan law, only the principles that govern the *interpretation of statutes* may have some bearing on the interpretation of Article 22, not being proper to interpret the provision following the rules established for contractual clauses (*cláusula compromisoria*) providing arbitration but seeking to exclude in an absolute way the possibility to resort to national courts.[155] There is a basic conceptual distinction between Venezuelan principles of statutory interpretation and alleged

---

153 See in http://www.tsj.gov.ve/decisiones/scon/Noviembre/1067-31110-2010-09-0573.html, pp. 39 of 60.

154 See in *Revista de Derecho Público*, N°115, Editorial Jurídica Venezolana, Caracas 2008, pp. 468 ff.

155 This refers, specifically, to the Politico- Administrative Chamber of the Supreme Tribunal of Justice, decisions imposing the need for arbitral clauses that pretend to exclude completely the possible resort to national courts, to be clear and unequivocal. See Decision N° 1209 of June 20, 2001 (Case: *Hoteles Doral C.A. v. Corporación L. Hoteles C.A*) at http://www.tsj.gov.ve/decisiones/spa/Junio/01209-200601-0775.htm; Decision N° 00098 of January 29, 2002 (Case: *Banco Venezolano de Credito, S.A.C.A. v. Venezolana de Relojeria, S.A. (Venrelosa) y Henrique Pfeffer C.A*) at http://www.tsj.gov.ve/decisiones/spa/Enero/00098-290102-1255.htm; Decision N° 00476 of March 25, 2003 (Case: *Consorcio Barr, S.A v. Four Seasons Caracas, C.A.*) at http://www.tsj.gov.ve/decisiones/spa/Marzo/00476-250303-2003-0044.htm; Decision N° 00038 of January 28, 2004 (Case: *Banco Venezolano de Crédito, S.A. Banco Universal*) at http://www.tsj.gov.ve/decisiones/spa/Enero/00038-280103-2003-1296.htm.

specific requirements for the efficacy of a contractual agreement to arbitrate under the domestic legal order. The latter have no application in a case of article 22 of the Investment Law, where the matter at stake is whether the State's expression of consent embodied in a statute meets the requirements of an international treaty (the ICSID Convention) to set in motion the jurisdiction of international tribunals operating under that treaty.[156]

In the *Cemex* case, the ICSID Tribunal noted that in all of the BITs concluded by Venezuela before 1999, a "compulsory arbitration clause" was always incorporated (ICSID *Cemex* case, ¶ 120), but failed to compare such solution with the one included in Article 22 of the Investment Law. More importantly, both the Investment Law and BITs also provide for the right of the international investor to unilaterally accept the arbitration offer or to resort to the national courts in order to resolve investments disputes. This is valid in the terms of Article 4 of the Civil Code. Even if you do not apply the analogy between BITs and the Investment Law, contrary to was asserted in the *Mobil* and *Cemex* ICSID case, it is perfectly possible – using the same words of such decisions (ICSID *Mobil* case, ¶ 123; ICSID *Cemex* case, ¶ 120) – to draw from the law as a whole the conclusion that Article 22 must be interpreted as establishing consent by Venezuela to submit ICSID disputes to arbitration particularly if the disclaimer of the last part of Article 22 ("without prejudice to the possibility of using, as appropriate, the contentious means contemplated by the Venezuelan legislation in effect") is not ignored. Both decisions of the ICSID Tribunals, in an incomprehensible way ignore it, and therefore consider the disclaimer as meaningless. The fact that the *Mobil* and *Cemex* decisions did not consider this when interpreting Article 22 or give the last part of the provision a meaningful interpretation, renders its text "meaningless," which cannot be accepted under Venezuelan law.

On the other hand, the fact that another State or States in the world have written national laws containing the expression of consent in a way that is different to the way chosen by Venezuela, cannot demonstrate that the State in article 22 did not

---

156 As Professor Hung Vaillant states that, according to the pro-arbitration principle in Article 258 of the Constitution, "[...] *se debe tratar de sostener la validez en to- dos aquellos casos de duda, siempre que tal admission no conduzca a una violación de normas de orden público ni atente contra las buenas costumbres. En resumen, en caso de duda, se deberá pronunciar a favor de la existencia del Arbitraje.* [...]" ("[...] one should try to sustain its validity [of Arbitration] in all those cases of doubt, as long as such admission does not lead to a violation of norms of public order or impairs good customs. In sum, in case of doubt, one should pronounce in favor of the existence of Arbitration. [...]"). Francisco Hung Vaillant, *Reflexiones sobre el Arbitraje en el Sistema Venezolano*, Caracas 2001, p. 66. Professor Vaillant makes this statement in the context of discussing the general principles that govern arbitration under Venezuelan Law., pp. 63-69. In that section, Professor Vaillant addresses those principles that should serve to *"establecer la solución adecuada cada vez que existe una antinomia o una laguna legal; así como también en aquellos casos en los cuales es necesario interpretar un texto oscuro de una cláusula o de un pacto arbitral."* ("to provide for an adequate solution each time that there is an antinomy or a legal gap; as well as in those cases in which it is necessary to interpret an obscure text of an arbitration clause or of an arbitration agreement"). *Idem*, p. 63.

manifest its clear and unequivocal consent to arbitrate in the provision. The wording used in the Law in 1999 is in its text, and this cannot be replaced; so there is no need to compare the way the State enacts its laws with the way used for instance in Albania, in the Central African Republic or in Côte d'Ivoire.. The way legislation is made in other States cannot demonstrate anything regarding Venezuela's drafting of its own statutes. Nonetheless, in order to interpret correctly a compound provision such as Article 22 of the Investment Law, one must use the rules and tools established in the legal order of the relevant State – here, Venezuela. And even if you do compare the Investment Law to laws of other States, however, it would be useful to do this with one law that actually is similar to the Investment Law, that is the Egyptian law, which was the object of an ICSID decision that found this Egyptian law as a national law in which consent to international arbitration exist.

Consequently, according to Venezuelan law, Article 22 must be interpreted not by reference to any international pattern or model, but in accordance with its own structure and terms, taking into account its compound nature, and the purpose for its enactment. It is also, as all statutes, to be interpreted in harmony or in conformity with the Constitution[157] and with the pro-arbitration trend existing in Venezuela in 1999, when it was enacted, which had been extensively developed and promoted by the then new Government. Nonetheless, being an instrument of national law that expresses consent of the State to international arbitration, as mentioned, it may also be interpreted according to the applicable international conventions and to the rules of international law governing unilateral declarations of the State.

Consequently, if it is from the stand point of being a national law Article 22 of the Investment Law must be interpreted following the rules of statutory interpretation and construction in Venezuelan Law, that is, according to Article 4 of the Civil Code, it must be read in all its content, taking into account its context, purpose and intent.[158]

It was in that sense that it can be said that when interpreting article 22 of the Investment Law, the ICSID Tribunals in the *Mobil* and *Cemex* cases, concluded that such provision established or contained an obligation for the State to go to arbitration (although subjected to a condition), or in their own words, a "conditional obligation to go to arbitration" (ICSID *Mobil* case, ¶ 102),[159] which is equivalent to say

---

157 This is a general principle accepted in Venezuelan judicial review system. See José Peña Solís, "La interpretación conforme a la Constitución," *Libro Homenaje a fernando Parra Aranguren*, Tomo II, Universidad Central de Venezuela, Caracas 2001. On the application of this principle regarding arbitration matters, see Eugenio Hernández Bretón, "Arbitraje y Constitución. El arbitraje como derecho fundamental," *loc. cit.*, pp. 31; Andrés A. Mezgravis, "Las inversiones petroleras en Venezuela y el arbitraje ante el CIADI," *loc. cit.*, p. 390.

158 The Tribunal in the *ICSID Mobil* considered that the interpretation of Article 22 according to the national statutory rules of interpretation "play a useful role" regarding "the intention of the State having formulated such acts" (ICSID *Mobil* case, ¶ 96).

159 What is clear from the aforementioned is that the provision related to ICSID arbitration in Article 22, is not at all a mere reference in a law to ICSID, nor a part of a list of options without any effect.

that the provision is an expression of consent given by the State subjected to a condition. This obligation or consent was established in an unequivocal way in the sense that the provision clearly contained such obligation or consent. The ICSID tribunals, nonetheless, considered that it was the condition established in the article, the one that was equivocal because supposedly allowed for two possible grammatical interpretations (ICSID *Mobil* case, ¶¶ 109, 111). Those were that the condition could be for the State to go to international arbitration if the treaties or agreements "provide for international arbitration" or that such treaties or agreements were to "provide for the submission to international arbitration." This assertion, in any case, was a wrong grammatical proposition because the second interpretation would result in a tautology, equivalent to say that "I will go to international arbitration if the treaty obliged me to go to arbitration." This option would render the provision meaningless. The correct and only valid interpretation of the condition, in my opinion, is the first option, equivalent to say "I will go to arbitration if the treaty provides a framework for international arbitration." In any case, the consequence of the assertion made by the ICSID tribunals considering that the condition set forth in Article 22 allowed for two possible interpretations, lead the tribunals to try to established the intent of the State when adopting the Law, concluding in those cases, and only in them, that because of lack of evidence it could not be deducted from article 22 the expression of consent to go to ICSID international arbitration.

4.   The Principle that Consent for Arbitration has to be expressed in Writing

Another matter that must be clarified regarding consent for arbitration in Venezuelan law is the matter of the "form" or condition that is required in order for the Republic to express consent for arbitration. In Venezuela, in this matter, the only applicable "dogma," as explained by the Supreme Tribunal of Justice in its decision N° 1541 of 2008 is that the expression of consent must be in writing (pp. 31-34). No provision in any law requires that the writing consent must also be "clear," "express" or "unequivocal" as suggested in other parts of the same decision (pp. 31-48).

In this sense, Venezuelan law is perfectly consistent with international principles, in the sense that an expression of consent for arbitration needs only to be expressed in writing in order to comply with the Commercial Arbitration Law. This is what has been definitively decided by the Constitutional Chamber of the Supreme Tribunal in a decision issued on November 3, 2010 (Case *Astivenca Astilleros de Venezuela C.A,*), affirming that in any judicial decision regarding the verification of "the validity, efficacy and applicability of the arbitral clause it must be limited to verify the written character of the arbitration agreement."[160]

---

160   The Constitutional Chamber has established an obligatory interpretation in the sense of ruling that the judicial "verification of arbitral clauses must be limited to verify the written character of the arbitration agreement, excluding any analysis related to the consent devices that could derived from the written clause." See decision N° 1067 of November 3, 2010 (Case *Astivenca Astilleros de Venezuela C.A,*), at http://www.tsj.gov.ve/decisiones/scon/Noviembre/1067-31110-2010-09-0573.html, pp. 35 of 60 and 38 of 60.

On the other hand, as aforementioned, Article 4 of the Civil Code, which establishes the rules for the interpretation of statutes, provides that in the absence of a precise provision of the Law, the provisions regulating similar cases or analogous matters shall be taken into account. Consequently, regarding the way consent for arbitration must be given, in the absence of a general and precise provision, the Venezuelan 1998 Commercial Arbitration Law, which is inspired by the UNCITRAL Model Law, must be applied. Like the ICSID Convention, that Law requires only that the consent or agreement to arbitration be evidenced "in writing."[161]

As mentioned, in Venezuelan law there no legal principle is established in the sense that in addition to being in writing, consent for arbitration must be clear and unequivocal. That is, there is no legal provision in Venezuelan law requiring the consent for arbitration to be clear and unequivocal. Even in cases of commercial arbitration establishing arbitration clauses, following the pro-arbitration trend of the Venezuelan legal system, in case of doubt, one must find in favor of arbitration.[162] For example, as Francisco Hung, has argued that "in all those cases in which doubts can rise regarding the interpretation of the will to submit to arbitration in an arbitral clauses or agreements, those called to decide must prefer the application of the '*favor arbitri*' principle, and declare the arbitral [tribunal] competent," that is "in cases

---

161 Article 6 of the Commercial Arbitration Law: "The arbitration agreement must be evidenced **in writing** in any document or group of documents placing on record the will of the parties to submit themselves to arbitration. A reference in a contract to a document containing an arbitration clause shall constitute an arbitration agreement, provided that said contract is evidenced in writing and the reference implies that said clause is a part of the contract. In adhesion contracts and standard-form contracts, the manifestation of the will to submit the contract to arbitration must be made in an express and independent manner." In this regard, and according to this Law, as Alberto Baumeister has pointed out when analyzing the "form of the arbitral clause" that it is only required to be in writing in the contract or in any document assuring that the parties have agreed to submit disputes to arbitration. See Alberto Baumeister, "Algunos tópicos sobre el procedimiento en la Ley de Arbitraje Comercial,", in Irene Valera (Coord), *Arbitraje comercial interno e internacional. Reflexiones teóricas y experiencias prácticas*, Academia de Ciencias Políticas y Sociales, Caracas 2005, pp. 140-141. For additional support for the contention that the arbitration clause need only be in writing, see Francisco Hung Vaillant, *Reflexiones Sobre el Arbitraje en el Sistema Venezolano*, *op. cit.*, pp. 203-204; Alfredo De Jesús O., "Validez y eficacia del acuerdo de arbitraje en el derecho venezolano," in Irene Valera (Coordinadora), *Arbitraje Comercial Interno e Internacional. Reflexiones teóricas y experiencias prácticas*, Academia de Ciencias Políticas y Sociales, Comité Venezolano de Arbitraje, Caracas 2005, pp. 73, 94-97, 130; Andrés A. Mezgravis, "La promoción del arbitraje: un deber constitucional reconocido y vulnerado por la jurisprudencia," in *Revista de Derecho Constitucional*, Nº 5, Editorial Sherwood, Caracas 2001, p. 133.

162 The "pro-arbitration" principle of interpretation regarding arbitration in the Venezuelan legal system has been established as an obligatory doctrine of interpretation by the Constitutional Chamber of the Supreme Tribunal in decision in decision Nº1067 of November 3, 2010 (Case *Astivenca Astilleros de Venezuela C.A,) cit.*, pp. 34 of 60 and 40 of 60.

of doubt, the decision must be in favor of arbitration."[163] This is based on the **intention** of the parties, taking into account the **good faith** intention.[164]

It must be mentioned, that the matter of consent for arbitration was considered in a few decisions of the Politico Administrative Chamber of the Supreme Tribunal, not regarding the merits on the "conditions" of consent for arbitration, but only the way in which it is expressed in order to decide conflicts of jurisdiction between national courts and arbitral tribunals. In particular, those decisions are: Decision N° 1.209 of June 20, 2001 (Case: *Hoteles Doral C.A. v. Corporación L. Hoteles C.A.*) (Exp. N° 2000-0775); Decision N° 00098 of January 29, 2002 (Case: *Banco Venezolano de Crédito, S.A.C.A. v. Venezolana de Relojería, S.A. (Venrelosa) y Henrique Pfeffer C.A., Abraham Ricardo Pfeffer Almeida, Marianela de la Coromoto Núñez de Pfeffer et al.g*) (Exp. N° 2000-1255); Decision N° 00476 of March 25, 2003 (Case: *Consorcio Barr, S.A. v. Four Seasons Caracas, C.A.*) (Exp. N° 2003-0044); and Decision N° 00038 of January 28, 2004 (Case: *Banco Venezolano de Crédito, S.A. Banco Universa v. Armando Días Guía y Marisela Riera de Guía*) (Exp. N° 2003-1296). From these decisions issued in resolving conflicts of jurisdiction and not resolving the merits of matter of arbitration, deductions have been made in the sense that in the country exits a requirement that **consent for arbitration** has to be "clear and unequivocal,"[165] which is incorrect.

---

163 See Francisco Hung Vaillant, "Apostillas a cinco sentencias en materia arbitra dictadas por el Tribunal Supremo de Justicia," in *Derecho privado y procesal en Venezuela. Homenaje a Gustavo Planchart Manrique*, Tomo II, UCAB, Escritorio Tinoco, Caracas 2003, pp. 654. See the comments on the pro-arbitration trend of the Venezuelan legal system in Andrés A. Mezgravis, "La promoción del arbitraje: un deber constitucional reconocido y vulnerado por la jurisprudencia," in *Revista de Derecho Constitucional*, N° 5, Editorial Sherwood, Caracas 2001, p. 133; Andrés Mezgravis, "El principio pro arbitraje en el ordenamiento jurídico venezolano", in *Ámbito Jurídico* Año IV, N°55, abril 2002; Carlos Alberto Urdaneta Sandoval, "Aspectos del arbitraje en la contratación administrativa," in *VIII Jornadas Internacionales de Derecho Administrativo "Allan Randolph Brewer-Carías," Los contratos administrativos. Contratos del Estado*, Fundación de Estudios de Derecho Administrativo, FUNEDA, Vol. I, Caracas 2005, p. 359; Eugenio Hernández Bretón, "Arbitraje y Constitución. El arbitraje como derecho fundamental," *loc. cit.*, p. 30. As mentioned this has been the obligatory principle established by the Constitutional Chamber of the Supreme Tribunal in decision N°1067 of November 3, 2010 (Case *Astivenca Astilleros de Venezuela C.A,*), *cit.* pp. 34 of 60 and 40 of 60.

164 See Andrés A. Mezgravis, "La promoción del arbitraje: un deber constitucional reconocido y vulnerado por la jurisprudencia," *loc. cit.*, p. 133; Francisco Hung Vaillant, *Reflexiones Sobre el Arbitraje en el Sistema Venezolano*, Editorial Jurídica Venezolana, Caracas 2001, pp. 63-69, 341.

165 See the critical comments on these decisions, in Alfredo de Jesús O., "Validez y eficacia del acuerdo de arbitraje en el derecho venezolano," *loc. cit.*, pp. 73-75, 78; Andrés Mezgravis, "El principio pro arbitraje en el ordenamiento jurídico venezolano", in *Ámbito Jurídico* Año IV, N°55, abril 2002, p. 16; Andrés A. Mezgravis, "La promoción del arbitraje: un deber constitucional reconocido y vulnerado por la jurisprudencia," *loc. cit.*, pp. 133-134; Francisco Hung Vaillant, "Apostillas a cinco sentencias en materia arbitra dictadas por el Tribunal Supremo de Justicia," in *Derecho privado y procesal en Venezuela. Homenaje a Gustavo*

In fact, this assertion has no basis. First, in Venezuela, the decisions of the Supreme Tribunal of Justice in Politico Administrative Chamber in these matters of arbitration do not refer to the substance of arbitration or to the consent for arbitration, being the Chamber only called upon to decide conflict of jurisdiction between courts or between arbitral tribunals and the courts. Second, in Venezuela the decisions of the Politico Administrative Chamber of the Supreme Tribunal, notwithstanding their importance, cannot be qualified as "precedents" because they do not have an obligatory character. Only the Constitutional Chamber of the Supreme Tribunal, acting as Constitutional Court when exercising its competencies on judicial review, can issue obligatory decisions on constitutional matters (*decisions vinculantes*) when is interpreting the Constitution (Article 335 of the Constitution).[166] Third, the decisions of the Politico Administrative Chamber are issued for the purpose of granting jurisdiction or to national courts or to arbitration courts, based on the interpretation of the valid consent clauses for arbitration in the sense of determining if they exclude or not in an absolute, clear and unequivocal way the possibility to resort to national courts. Fourth, in a Constitution like the Venezuelan one that establishes arbitration as integral part of the judicial system (Article 253) and that imposes an obligation on the State to promote arbitration (Article 258), arbitration cannot be considered as an exception to a supposed constitutional mandate of jurisdiction in national courts.[167] And fifth, there are not Venezuelan judicial "precedents" that have developed on matters of commercial arbitration that the consent for arbitration must be "clear, express and unequivocal."

In effect, in the 2001 *Hoteles Doral C.A. v. Corporación de L'Hoteles C.A* case,[168] the Supreme Tribunal does not explained that, as arbitration supposedly constitutes an exception to the constitutional jurisdiction of national courts, it is required that there be 'manifest, express and indisputable' consent to arbitration." In such case, as can be read in the full Spanish text of the decision (not in the cuttings

---

Planchart Manrique, Tomo II, UCAB, Escritorio Tinoco, Caracas 2003, pp. 654 ff; J. Eloy Anzola, "El fatigoso camino que transita el arbitraje," in Irene Valera (Coordinadora), *Arbitraje Comercial Interno e Internacional. Reflexiones teóricas y experiencias prácticas*, Academia de Ciencias Políticas y Sociales, Comité Venezolano de Arbitraje, Caracas 2005, pp.425-426.

166 See on this obligatory decisions (*decisiones vinculantes*) Allan R. Brewer-Carías, "La potestad de la Jurisdicción Constitucional de interpretar la Constitución con efectos vinculantes," in Jhonny Tupayachi Sotomayor, (Coord.), *El precedente constitucional vinculante en el Perú (Análisis, comentarios y doctrina comparada)*, Editorial Adrus, Arequipa 2009, pp. 791-817.

167 On the contrary, in Venezuela arbitration is considered an integral part of the "system of justice" (Article 253). The Constitutional Chamber of the Supreme Tribunal, in its decision N° 1067 of November 3, 2010 (Case *Astivenca Astilleros de Venezuela C.A,*) has ruled establishing an obligatory doctrine excluding the consideration of arbitration as an exception regarding ordinary jurisdiction, considering that arbitration is an integral part of the judicial system (pp. 19 of 60 to 26 of 60; 29 of 60),

168 See Decision N° 1209 of June 20, 2001, Case: *Hoteles Doral C.A. v. Corporación L. Hoteles C.A,* at http://www.tsj.gov.ve/decisiones/spa/Junio/01209-200601-0775.htm.

made for translation), the lower court "declared its lack of jurisdiction to decide the case, by considering the existence of an arbitral clause (*cláusula compromisoria de arbitraje*) capable of subtracting the decision of the dispute of the ordinary jurisdiction" (pp. 3-4). The Politico Administrative Chamber in order to determine the competent jurisdiction, proceeded to determine the "validity of the arbitral clause" just in order to determine "the efficacy or not of the arbitral clause in the sense that it could exclude or not the Judicial Power from its constitutional rank competence to decide cases (p. 4), and to determine "from the contractual clauses if it exist or not, a manifest, express and unquestionable will to exclude any judicial decision on the disputes" and instead to submitted to arbitration (p. 5). That is, the Supreme Tribunal only elaborated on the unequivocal and express manifestation of will of the parties to completely exclude the competence of the courts (not on the consent for arbitration), concluding, in the case, that it did not "exist a manifest and unequivocal will to submit to the jurisdiction of private arbiters, that is, it does not exist an undoubted disposition to renounce to the free access to the judicial organs of the ordinary jurisdiction" (p. 5); and then interpreting that because in the specific arbitral clause in the case, "the possibility to resort to the judicial means remained opened" in the sense that in such clause "the submission to arbitration was an option for the parties" (p. 19), concluded that in the case "there was no pact renouncing in an absolute way to the possibility or alternate option to access to the ordinary organs of the Judiciary, which does not exclude their competence to decide on the *litis*" (pp. 19-20). Consequently the decision adopted by the Supreme Tribunal in the *Hoteles Doral C.A. v. Corporación de L'Hoteles C.A* case, was a completely different matter and of course in it, the Tribunal did not required the consent to arbitration to be 'manifest, express and indisputable.'".

In 2002 *Banco Venezolano de Credito, S.A.C.A. v. Venezolana de Relojeria, S.A. (Venrelosa) y Henrique Pfeffer C.A, Abraham Ricardo Pfeffer Almeida, Marianela de la Coromoto Núñez de Pfiffer et al.,*[169] the Supreme Tribunal did not upheld the principle of "consent to arbitration" be "manifest, express and indisputable" and did not stated that arbitration 'requires the compliance and verification of the manifestation of an unequivocal and express will of the parties involved." In such case, as can also be read in the full Spanish text of the decision (not in the cuttings made for translation), what the Supreme Tribunal quoting what the Tribunal had decided in the already mentioned *Hoteles Doral C.A. v. Corporación de L'Hoteles C.A* case (pp. 8-9), was that in the specific commercial contract, the arbitral clause leaved opened the option for one of the parties to resort to the courts, arguing that it such clause "it doesn't exists a manifest and unequivocal will to submit to the jurisdiction of private arbiters, that is, it does not exist an undoubted disposition to renounce to the free access to the judicial organs of the ordinary jurisdiction" (p. 16). The Supreme Tribunal determined that the specific arbitral clause in the case was conceived as an "optional arbitration" in the sense of "submission to arbitration in a optional

---

169 See Decision N° 00098 of January 29, 2002, Case: *Banco Venezolano de Credito, S.A.C.A. v. Venezolana de Relojeria, S.A. (Venrelosa) y Henrique Pfeffer C.A.,* at http://www.tsj.gov.ve/decisiones/spa/Enero/00098-290102-1255.htm

and partial way, that is, always leaving open the possibility that either parties could opt to resort to the judicial mean" (p. 16), interpreting that because in the specific arbitral clause in the case, "the submission to arbitration – contained in it - is an option in order for the parties to select it as an alternate mechanism for controversies solutions (p. 17), concluded that in the case "there was no pact renouncing in an absolute way to the possibility or alternate option to access to the ordinary organs of the Judiciary, which does not exclude their competence to decide on the *litis*." (pp. 17). Consequently the decision adopted by the Supreme Tribunal in the *Banco Venezolano de Credito, S.A.C.A. v. Venezolana de Relojeria, S.A. (Venrelosa) y Henrique Pfeffer C.A, Abraham Ricardo Pfeffer Almeida, Marianela de la Coromoto Núñez de Pfiffer et al.,* case, was also a completely different matter and of course, in it, the Tribunal did not required the compliance and verification of the manifestation of an unequivocal and express will of the parties involved. .

In 2003, in the *Consorcio Barr S.A v. Four Seasons Caracas, C.A.* case[170] the Tribunal did not held that in order to find a valid arbitration agreement, an unequiv-ocal and express consent must exist. In such case, as can also be read in the full Spanish text of the decision (not in the cuttings made for translation), the lower court declared its jurisdiction to decide the case, by considering "that the arbitral clause (*Cláusula compromisoria*) in the case, was not in accordance with article 5 of the Commercial Arbitration Law, because its wording does not express the exclud-ing and undoubted character of the election of manifestation of will to subtract the solution of controversies or disputes originated in relation to the contract from the judicial jurisdiction, due to the fact that in the same contract, in the jurisdictional clause, the parties declared to be subjected to the nonexclusive jurisdiction of the courts of the Bolivarian Republic of Venezuela" (p.12). What the Supreme Tribunal considered that needed to be determined in this case was if the arbitral clause had "the derogatory force regarding the Venezuelan jurisdiction" (p. 16), concluding that from its wording "the exclusion of the ordinary jurisdiction is not demonstrated be-cause it result confusing that in it the same it is agreed to resort to the judicial mean" (p. 18), being in such content and for the exclusive purpose of "derogating the juris-diction that correspond to the Venezuelan courts to decide the case [that] the lacks of the legal efficacy needed for such purposes. So is declared" (p. 18). And it was for such purpose of determining if in the case it existed an absolute exclusion of the jurisdiction of the Venezuelan courts that the Supreme Tribunal considered that for such purpose, for "the validity of the arbitral clause in must exist a unequivocal and express manifestation of will of the involved parties to subtract the decision of the case from the ordinary courts" (p. 18). Consequently, the decision adopted by the Supreme Tribunal in the *Consorcio Barr, S.A v. Four Seasons Caracas, C.A.* case was also a completely different matter, and of course, in it, the Tribunal did not hold that in order to find a valid arbitration agreement, an unequivocal and express con-sent must exist.

---

170 See Decision N° 00476 of March 25, 2003, Case: *Consorcio Barr, S.A v. Four Seasons Caracas, C.A.*, at http://www.tsj.gov.ve/decisiones/spa/Marzo/00476-250303-2003-0044.htm;

In 2004 *Banco Venezolano de Crédito, S.A. Banco Universal v. Armando Díaz Egu y Marisela Riera de Díaz* case[171] the Supreme Tribunal did not held that arbitration was not mandatory because there was no manifest and unequivocal' submission to arbitration In this case, the decision of the Supreme Tribunal originated because a lower court decided in the case to declare its jurisdiction to decide the case, because observing that in the existing arbitral clause the parties did not "expressly renounced to the ordinary jurisdiction in order to resolve the conflicts" observing that the arbitral clause was only to be applied only when in enforcement actions (*ejecución de garantías*) and only where there is "opposition from the defendants" (p. 3). In the case, the Supreme Tribunal, quoting again what it had decided in the already mentioned *Hoteles Doral C.A. v. Corporación de L'Hoteles C.A* case (pp. 3-4), refused to remove the case to arbitration because in such "cases of enforcements actions established in the contract, it doesn't exists a manifest and unequivocal attitude of a submission to arbiters, due to the fact that it is only to be applied in case of opposition by the defendants," (pp. 5), confirming the lower court decision. Consequently the decision adopted by the Supreme Tribunal en the *Banco Venezolano de Crédito, S.A. Banco Universal v. Armando Díaz Egu y Marisela Riera de Díaz* case was also a completely different matter, and of course, in it, the Tribunal did not held that arbitration was not mandatory because there was no 'manifest and unequivocal' submission to arbitration.

On the other hand, the so-called fundamental requirement of 'clear, express and unequivocal' consent to arbitrate is not a general opinion in the legal Venezuelan doctrine. Precisely, Professor Francisco Hung Vaillant has stated that, according to the pro-arbitration principle in Article 258 of the Constitution, "one should try to sustain its validity [of Arbitration] in all those cases of doubt, as long as such admission does not lead to a violation of norms of public order or impairs good customs. In sum, in case of doubt, one should pronounce in favor of the existence of Arbitration;[172] addressing those principles that should serve "to provide for an adequate solution each time that there is an antinomy or a legal gap; as well as in those cases in which it is necessary to interpret an obscure text of an arbitration clause or of an arbitration agreement."[173]

In conclusion, none of the aforementioned four decisions of the Politico-Administrative Chamber of the Supreme Tribunal of Justice sustain such assertions; and nothing can be deduct from them by picking isolated phrases out of context. All

---

171   See Decision N° 00038 of January 28, 2004, Case: *Banco Venezolano de Crédito, S.A. Banco Universal,* at http://www.tsj.gov.ve/decisiones/spa/Enero/00038-280103-2003-1296.htm

172   See Francisco Hung Vaillant, *Reflexiones sobre el Arbitraje en el Sistema Venezolano,* Caracas 2001, p. 66.

173   *Idem.* p. 63. Professor Ivor D Mogollón-Rojas, assertion based on the need for a "written" and "documented" agreements to arbitrate than must be included in contracts as a proof "express and unequivocal consent to submit to arbitration," is made only and basically in order to stress the core of his statement which is that no "tacit acceptance for arbitration" is acceptable. See Ivor D. Mogollón, *El arbitraje comercial venezolano,* Vadell Hermanos Editores, Caracas 2004, pp. 61-62.

these decisions, as mentioned, do not deal in the internal legal order with the substantive requirements for the validity of arbitration, for consent to arbitration, or for the validity of bilateral expressions of consent to arbitration (*cláusula compromisoria*). The decisions deal, only and exclusively with the issue of the parties' ability to exclude **in a total an absolute way** the possibility for one of the parties to resort to national courts, The fact that the Politico Administrative Chamber of the Supreme Tribunal when deciding jurisdictional conflicts, used to impose a rule that there must be "clear, express and unequivocal" expression in excluding the availability of an option is a completely different matter than an expression that provides **for** the consent to arbitration.

But in any case, regarding such "doctrine" and in the context that the Politico Administrative Chamber of the Supreme Tribunal used to apply it, the Constitucional Chamber of the Supreme Tribunal in its decision N° 1067 of November 3, 2010 (Case *Astivenca Astilleros de Venezuela C.A,*) has formally decided, in an obligatory way for all courts that from the moment of the publication of the decision, that is November 3, 2010,

> "the jurisprudence criteria sustained on these matters by the Politico Administrative Chamber of the Supreme Tribunal up to this date, are not applicable" (Vid. Among others, the decisions Numbers 1209 and 832, of June 20, 2001 and June 12, 2002, Cases: "*Hoteles Doral, C.A*" and "*Inversiones San Ciprian, C.A.*")" (pp. 43 of 60).[174]

From what has been previously said, and as a conclusion, is possible to affirm that in Venezuela there is not at a requirement for the consent for arbitration to be "clear and unequivocal," and the only thing that has happened is that a confusion has been generated on the matter based on the aforementioned jurisprudence of the Politico Administrative Chamber of the Supreme Tribunal of Justice, ruling exclusively acting in the resolution of conflict of jurisdiction between national courts and national arbitral tribunals, giving always jurisdiction to the national courts when the clause providing for arbitration was not clear and unequivocal, excluding any sort of jurisdiction of national courts. That is, when the arbitral clause in a contract (without any consideration regarding its validity or the efficacy of the expression of consent) excluding the jurisdiction of national courts was considered not to be clear or unequivocal, then in cases of conflict of jurisdiction, the Chamber used to gave always jurisdiction to the national courts. Also, when the arbitral clause provided the possibility for the parties to resort to the national courts, not having a clear and unequivocal expression of absolute rejection of the jurisdiction of national courts, the Supreme Tribunal used to give always jurisdiction to the national courts.

This was the jurisprudence of the Politico Administrative Chamber of the Supreme Court, which does not refer at all, to the requirements for the validity of consent of arbitration clauses, which was changed by means of the aforementioned decision decision adopted by the Constitutional Chamber of the Supreme Tribunal Decision N° 1067 of the November 3, 2010 (Case: *Astivenca Astilleros de Venezuela*

---

174   See at http://www.tsj.gov.ve/decisiones/scon/Noviembre/1067-31110-2010-09-0573.html, pp. 43 of 60

C.A)[175]. It is enough to read completely the text of such decision in order to understand the sense of the obligatory interpretation (*interpetación vinculante*) it contains
for all courts established according to article 335 of the Constitution, expressed by
the Chamber, in which it has established the rule that the judicial "verification of
arbitral clauses must be limited to verify the written character of the arbitration
agreement, excluding any analysis related to the consent devices that could derived
from the written clause;" adding, regarding the already mentioned "doctrine" applied by the Politico Administrative Chamber of the Supreme Tribunal in order to
resolve conflicts of jurisdiction, that "the jurisprudence criteria sustained on these
matters by the Politico Administrative Chamber of the Supreme Tribunal up to this
date, are not applicable" (Vid. Among others, the decisions Numbers 1209 and 832,
of June 20, 2001 and June 12, 2002, Cases: "*Hoteles Doral, C.A*". and "*Inversiones
San Ciprian, C.A.*")," reaffirming that in any judicial decision regarding the verification of "the validity, efficacy and applicability of the arbitral clause it must be limited to verify the written character of the arbitration agreement." The *Hoteles Doral
C.A.* case was precisely the leading case of the "doctrine" overruled by the Constitutional Chamber, in which is based the supposed "doctrine" of "clear and unequivocal" consent, which resulted from a completely different concept of arbitration that
the Chamber overruled.

As it has been argued, and is useful to remember, the Political Administrative
Chamber in order to establish the aforementioned "doctrine," considered arbitration
as an "exception" regarding the constitutional attributions of ordinary courts in order
to resolve controversies submitted by citizens to their decision (the Constitutional
Camber made reference among others to the decision No 1.209/01 of the Politico
Administrative Chamber). On the contrary, in the decision of the Constitutional
Chamber adopted in the 2010 *Astivenca* Case, issued in a procedure for constitutional revision of a decision of the Politico Administrative Chamber of the Supreme
Tribunal (N° 687 of May 21, 2009) precisely deciding on a conflict of jurisdiction, it
argued that arbitration was a "fundamental right," considered as an entirely "part of
the judicial system" and of "jurisdiction," and as an effective mean for obtaining
justice (*tutela judicial efectiva*). Consequently, the Constitutional Chamber considered arbitration as an effective institution for jurisdictional protection that cannot be
considered as an "exceptional" institution regarding the jurisdiction exercised by the
Judicial Power. The Chamber ruled, based on the considerations it made "on the
principle competence-competence and in the coordination and subsidiary relations
of the Judicial Power organs regarding the arbitral system," that "the organs of the
Judicial Power can only make a formal, preliminary or summary 'prima facie' exam
or verification of the conditions of validity, efficacy and applicability of the arbitral
clause, which must be limited to verify the written character of the arbitral agreement, and exclude any other analysis related to the vices of consent that derives
from the written clause." In other words, the Chamber ruled that due to the fact that
article 258 of the Constitution imposes the promotion of arbitration (as decided by
the same Chamber quoting decision N° 1.541/08), "any legal provision or judicial

---

175   See at http://www.tsj.gov.ve/decisiones/scon/Noviembre/1067-31110-2010-09-0573.html

interpretation that could contradict it, must be considered contrary to the fundamental text, and thus, unconstitutional;" and consequently, "the organs of the Judicial Power when they have not noticed a manifest nullity, inefficacy or inapplicability, must sent the disputes submitted to their consideration to arbitration."

The result of this new doctrine is that the courts must rule in principle in favor of arbitration, considered part of the judicial system and of jurisdiction, from which result that arbitration cannot be considered any more by the courts as an exemption to jurisdiction. That is why, the rule imposed by the Constitutional Chamber to the courts when analyzing prima facie arbitral clauses, is to verify just the written character of the arbitral clause without any other consideration regarding the validity or efficacy in order to reject arbitration. The result of this new doctrine has been the pro arbitration trend adopted even by the Politico Administrative Chamber, which precisely can be appreciate in many of the decisions it has adopted after the *Astivenca* Case ruling, in which, in many cases, the Chamber ruled to maintain the cases in the arbitral jurisdiction. In those cases, the argument of the Politico Administrative Chamber was not that in order to submit disputes resolution to arbitral tribunals, the consent for arbitration was supposedly to be "clear and unequivocal." On the contrary, in many of the cases, the decision of the Chamber was only to consider that there were not enough "inaccurate or incomplete" statements or "unambiguous" intent to remove the decisions from the arbitral tribunals, leaving the matter for their decision.

In addition, the procedural settings of international arbitration cases are entirely different. In such cases, the parties are not in a Venezuelan court debating whether a national court must be deprived of jurisdiction by a contractual arbitration clause. On the contrary, Article 22 does not have the effect of preventing investors from resorting to litigation remedies that may be available under Venezuelan law. Article 22 expressly permits recourse to local courts as an option for the investors when expressing in its last phrase: "[...] without prejudice to the possibility of using, whenever it should be appropriate, the contentious means contemplated by the Venezuelan legislation in effect." As the language of Article 22 contains no option for the Republic of Venezuela to resort to the national court, the premise of those decisions – that no longer can be applied by the courts – is not present in international arbitration proceeding. Article 22 does not preclude resort to "the contentious means contemplated by the Venezuelan legislation in effect," being that, on the contrary, an option only for the international investor, because the Republic of Venezuela has already expressed its unilateral consent to arbitration. The very purpose of arbitration provisions is to give the investor the option to resort to arbitration instead of being required to litigate the dispute in the courts of the host-State. In fact, one might argue that if the Republic wanted for there to be the option for an international investor to have recourse **only** to national courts (if there was no applicable treaty) it would need to be expressed in a "clear, express and unequivocal" way. As explained above, this has since been overruled. What is clear, express and unequivocal is that in Article 22 of the Investment Law, it is expressly, unequivocally and clearly provided that, because it contains the consent of the State for international arbitration, it is possible for the international investor to opt between going to international arbitration of to resort to national courts.

In addition, and despite its inapplicability since November 3, 2010, the cases decided by the Politico Administrative Chamber of the Supreme Tribunal, were not and are not binding. The other Venezuelan judges could and may depart from such decisions. According to Article 321 of the Code of Civil Procedure, Judges shall try to follow the "**cassation** doctrine established in analogous cases, in order to defend the integrity of the legislation and the uniformity of the jurisprudence," but even in this case, it is not established as a mandate. Therefore, such judicial decisions could not and can not be considered to have established a general rule of the Venezuelan Law on matters of resolving conflicts of jurisdiction, and much less on matters of consent for arbitration which was not their purpose.[176] In any case, as already mentioned, the Constitutional Chamber of the Supreme Tribunal has ruled in an obligatory way that such doctrine could no longer be applied by the courts, establishing on the contrary that the only condition of validity of arbitral clauses is to be in writing.

But in any case, a reading of the full text of these four cases reveals that all that they decided was that in the specific commercial contracts on which the cases were based, the arbitral clauses included an option for one of the parties to resort to the courts. The court concluded that such a clause "doesn't present a manifest and unequivocal will to submit to the jurisdiction of private arbiters, that is, it does not exists an **undoubted disposition to renounce to the free access to the judicial** organs of the ordinary jurisdiction" (See, e.g., p. 16). The Politico Administrative Chamber of the Supreme Tribunal determined that the specific arbitral clause in the cases was conceived as an "optional arbitration" in the sense of "submission to arbitration in an optional and partial way that is, always leaving open the possibility that either parties could opt to resort to the judicial mean" (p. 16). But the fact was that on the contrary, the validity of the consent for arbitration was not in question in those cases; what was in question was that the consent for arbitration did not completely and absolutely exclude the option to resort to the national courts.

Contrary to the so-called and no longer applicable requirement of "clear, express and unequivocal" consent to arbitrate" that has been deducted from those decisions, the general opinion in Venezuelan legal doctrine is to the contrary, as has been definitively established by the Constitutional Chamber of the Supreme Tribunal of Justice in its decision N° 1067 of November 3, 2010 (Case *Astivenca Astilleros de Venezuela C.A,*). For example, in this regard Professor Francisco Hung Vaillant, has stated that, according to the pro-arbitration principle in Article 258 of the Constitution, now adopted in an obligatory way by the Constitutional Chamber, "one should try to sustain [the] validity [of arbitration clauses] in all those cases of doubt, as long as such admission does not lead to a violation of norms of public order or impairs

---

176 The decisions have also been criticized because the Commercial Arbitration Law (Article 6) only requires that the consent be in writing. See Andres Mezgravis "La Promoción del Arbitraje: un deber constitucional reconocido y vulnerado por la jurisprudencia", in *Revista de Derecho Constitucional* N° 5, Diciembre 2001, Editorial Sherwood, Caracas 2001, pp. 133-135; Francisco Hung Vaillant, "Apostillas a cinco sentencias en materia arbitra dictadas por el Tribunal Supremo de Justicia," in *Derecho privado y procesal en Venezuela. Homenaje a Gustavo Planchart Manrique*, Tomo II, UCAB, Escritorio Tinoco, Caracas 2003, pp. 654.

good customs. In sum, in case of doubt, one should pronounce in favor of the existence of arbitration. ... [which should] provide for an adequate solution each time that there is an antinomy or a legal gap; as well as in those cases in which it is necessary to interpret an obscure text of an arbitration clause or of an arbitration agreement."[177]

IV. THE PRO-ARBITRATION PUBLIC POLICY DEFINED BY THE GOVERNMENT IN 1999, REFLECTED IN THE 1999 CONSTITUTION

1.   *The pro-arbitration trend of all the legislation enacted in 1999*

The enactment of the 1999 Investment Law was the result of a defined economic policy of the new government that began in February that year. It was intended to attract investments, and particularly, foreign investments. In effect, President Hugo Chávez, who was first elected in December 1998 and took office on February 2, 1999, requested the Congress to sanction an Organic Law enabling him (the President of the Republic) to enact a group of statutes on matters related to Public Administration, Finance, Taxation and the Economy. The last of which mainly was devoted to promote, protect and encourage investment in the country.

Consequently, following the draft submitted by same National Executive, a few weeks later, on April 1999, the Congress sanctioned the enabling Organic Law of April of that year 1999.[178] This law authorized the President of the Republic not only to "enact provisions in order to promote the protection and promotion of national and foreign investments with the purpose of establishing a legal framework for investments and to give them greater legal security" (Article 1.4.f); but also to "reform the decree-Law on Public Works and National Public Utilities Concessions to stimulate private investments" for both existing and prospective projects (Art. 1.4.h) and to issue the necessary measures for the exploitation of gas, modernizing the legislation on the matter (Art. 1.4.i).

---

177 See Francisco Hung Vaillant, *Reflexiones sobre el Arbitraje en el Sistema Venezolano*, Caracas 2001, p. 63, 66. Other autjors refered to the matter: José Luis Bonnemaison only copied one of the decisions of the Politico Administrative Chamber of the Supreme Tribunal, but does not give his personal opinion. See José Luis Bonnemaison, *Aspectos fundamentals del arbitraje commercial, Tribunal Supremo de Justicia*, Caracas 2006, **p. 24.** Ivor D Mogollón-Rojas, bases his assertion on the need for a "written" and "documented" agreements to arbitrate that must be included in contracts as a proof that an "express and unequivocal consent to submit to arbitration" has been made, basically in order to stress the core of his statement which is that no "tacit [or implicit] acceptance for arbitration" is acceptable. See Ivor D. Mogollón, *El arbitraje comercial venezolano*, Vadell Hermanos Editores, Caracas 2004, pp. 61-62. Carlos J. Sarmiento Sosa, also refers to the written consent for arbitration only to stress that there cannot be a "presumed or implicit arbitral agreement." Carlos J. Sarmiento Sosa, *Ley de arbitraje comercial*, Livrosca, Caracas 1999, p. 12.

178 See *Ley Orgánica que Autoriza al Presidente de la República Para Dictar Medidas Extraordinarias en Materia Económica y Financiera Requeridas por el Interés Público* (Organic Law Authorizing the President of the Republic to Issue Extraordinary Measures in Economic and Financial Matters Required by the Public Interest), in *Official Gazette* N° 36.687 of April 26, 1999.

It was the National Executive that defined the economic policy of the country focused on the promotion and protection of investments in general, and on matters of public works and public utilities, hydrocarbons, gas and mines, for which purpose it received a very wide and comprehensive legal authorization to enact statutes by means of delegate legislation. It was precisely within this legislative authorization that the Executive Power issued the Decree Law containing the 1999 Investment Law, as well as many other Decree Laws all of which were not issued by the President of the Republic "exercising the power vested in him by the new Political Constitution", as erroneously asserted in the *Brandes* case decision (ICSID *Brandes* case, ¶ 25). The "new" Constitution was sanctioned after the April 1999 Enabling Law and after the Investment Law was approved.

A month after the August 1999 Supreme Court of Justice decision rejecting the challenge to the Hydrocarbons Association Agreements was published, the President of the Republic proceeded to enact four important Decree Laws executing the provisions of the Enabling Law already mentioned, containing statutes on matters of investments (Articles 1.4.f,; 1.4.h; 1.4.i; and 1.4.j), and in all of them, providing for arbitration as a means for the solution of disputes between the State and private persons.[179] Of these four authorizations, three Decree Laws – those regarding Gassed Hydrocarbons, Promotion and Protection of Investments through Concessions and the Investment Law – are of particular importance.

In the Law on Gassed Hydrocarbons,[180] Article 127 of the 1961 Constitution that provides that in all the licenses given to private persons in order to execute activities of exploration and exploitation of gassed hydrocarbons, a clause shall be deemed to be included (even if not expressed in writing), establishing that "the doubts and controversies of any kind that may arise resulting from the license, and that could not be resolved amicably by the parties, *including by arbitration*, shall be decided by the competent courts of the Republic, in accordance with its laws, not being able to give rise by any motive or cause to foreign claims" (Article 25.6.b). This Law expressly recognizes the possibility to submit to arbitration disputes on matters relating to licenses given by the State for the exploration or exploitation of non-gas hydrocarbons.[181]

---

179 See *Official Gazette* N° 5.382 Extra of September 28, 1999 (controversies concerning mining titles may be arbitrated). The other three laws are the laws concerning Gassed Hydrocarbons, the Promotion and Protection of Investments through Concessions and the Investment Law.

180 Decree Law N° 310 of September 12, 1999, *Official Gazette* N° 36.793 of September 23, 1999.

181 Other commentators have agreed with this interpretation of the Law. *See, e.g.*, J. Eloy Anzola, "El fatigoso camino que transita el arbitraje," in Irene Valera (Coordinadora), *Arbitraje Comercial Interno e Internacional. Reflexiones teóricas y experiencias prácticas*, Academia de Ciencias Políticas y Sociales, Comité Venezolano de Arbitraje, Caracas 2005, p.419) ("We must presume that it was made with the clear intention of admitting arbitration as a mean of solution of conflicts in the exploration and exploitation contracts according to the constitutional text ....in order to incentivize private participation that without doubt will be

In the Law on the Promotion of Private Investments through the Regime of Concessions, [182] it was provided that the parties, in public concessions contracts:

> "Can agree in the respective contract to submit their differences to the decision of an Arbitral Tribunal, whose composition, competence, procedure and applicable law shall be determined by mutual agreement, in conformity with the provisions applicable on the matter."

This pro-arbitration disposition of the government in the sensitive area of public contracts of concessions for public works and public utilities has been subsequently re-affirmed by a number of Venezuelan court decisions.[183]

The third statute establishing arbitration enacted by the President of the Republic using the delegated legislation powers was precisely the Decree-Law Nº 356 of October 13, 1999 on the Law on the Promotion and Protection of Investments. This law contains consent to arbitration in a number of places in the text: first, Article 21 (state-to-state arbitration); second, in Article 22 (international arbitration or national litigation with an international investor); and third, Article 23 (national litigation or arbitration with a national or international investor). In these last two cases, the consent of the State to submit disputes to arbitration is expressed in the Law, and it is for the investor – as its right – to decide to go to arbitration or to the national courts.

The prevailing attitude of the Government in 1999 regarding the solution of disputes on matter of investments was, without doubt, a pro-arbitration one, as demonstrated in the aforementioned legislation. This pro-arbitration attitude was confirmed not only by the parallel discussion on the matter of the State's obligation to promote arbitration contained in the new Constitution in August-November 1999, but also by the text submitted by the President of the Republic himself to be included in the new Constitution. [184]

---

more comfortable seeking justice before an arbitral tribunal without the need to resort to local tribunals.")

182 Ley Orgánica sobre promoción de la inversión privada bajo el régimen de concesiones, *Official Gazette* Nº 5.394 Extra. of October 25, 1999. See Diego Moya-Ocampos Pancera and Maria del Sol Moya-Ocampos Pancera, "Comentarios relativos a la procedencia de las cláusulas arbitrales en los contratos de interés público nacional, en particular: especial las concesiones mineras," en *Revista de Derecho Administrativo*, Nº 19, Editorial Sherwood, Caracas 2006, p. 174. See *in general* on this Law, Alfredo Romero Mendoza "Concesiones y otros mecanismos no tradicionales para el financiamiento de obras públicas", in Alfredo Romero Mendoza (Coord.), *Régimen Legal de las Concesiones Públicas. Aspectos Jurídicos, Financieros y Técnicos*, Editorial Jurídica Venezolana, Caracas 2000, pp. 28-29.

183 See for example the summary in Alfredo Romero Mendoza (Coord.), *Régimen Legal de las Concesiones Públicas. Aspectos Jurídicos, Financieros y Técnicos*, pp. 12, 28, 29, 155.

184 I was a Member of the National Constituent Assembly that was responsible for drafting many aspects of the new Constitution in 1999. In that capacity, I contributed to the drafting of the 1999 Constitution, and in particular, the drafting of Article 151 which establishes the possibility for arbitration in public contracts, rejecting the project proposed by the President of the Republic. See on the discussion of my contributions to the National Constituent Assembly's drafting of the 1999 Constitution in Allan R. Brewer-Carías, *Debate Constituyente (Aportes a la Asamblea Nacional Constituyente)*, 3 Vols., Fundación de Derecho

2.   *The pro-arbitration trend of the 1999 Constitution and the bizarre proposal submitted to the Constituent Assembly by President Chávez in 1999*

The 1999 Constitution incorporates arbitration as an alternative means of adjudication and as a component of the judicial system (Article 253), requiring the State in article 258 to promote it, in particular through legislation ("The law shall promote arbitration, conciliation, mediation and any other alternative means of dispute resolution");[185] and guarantying arbitration as a fundamental right.[186] The text of the Constitution itself imposes upon all the organs of the State the duty to promote arbitration, establishing as a constitutional (fundamental) right of the citizens the ability to submit disputes to arbitration. All of this confirms that, at the time, there was no prevailing "culture of hostility" to arbitration. On the contrary, the 1999 Constitution, the laws sanctioned by the new Government in 1999, the legal system as a whole, and the international instruments to which Venezuela was a party, embraced and promoted arbitration.[187]

The proposal submitted by President Chávez to the National Constituent Assembly in August 1999 proposing the text of an Article to replace Article 127 (current Article 151 of the 1999 Constitution), contrary to any assumed "restrictive" character regarding arbitration, was excessively permissive towards international arbitration.[188] That was precisely the reason for this author, as member of the national Constituent Assembly, to oppose firmly such proposal, and instead to propose to include in the new Constitution the same text of Article 127 of the 1961 Constitu-

---

Público/Editorial   Jurídica   Venezolana,   Caracas   1999.   Available   at http://allanbrewercarias.com/

185 On the recognition of arbitration as an alternative means of adjudication in the 1999 Constitution, and the promotion of arbitration as a constitutional obligation of all organs of the State, see Eugenio Hernández Bretón, "Arbitraje y Constitución. El arbitraje como derecho fundamental," *loc cit.*, p. 27; 2008 N°1.541 Decision, (p. 11); Supreme Tribunal of Justice, Constitutional Chamber, Decision N° 186 of February 14, 2001 (Case: Constitutional Challenge of Articles 17, 22 and 23 of the 1999 Investment Law, Fermín Toro Jiménez and Luis Brito García).

186 On arbitration as a fundamental right, see Eugenio Herández Bretón, "Arbitraje y Constitución. El arbitraje como derecho fundamental," *loc. cit.,* pp. 25, 27-28 (noting the 1830 Constitution provides that arbitration is a citizens' fundamental right). In the same sense, J. Eloy Anzola, "El fatigoso camino que transita el arbitraje," in Irene Valera (Coord.), *Arbitraje Comercial Interno e Internacional. Reflexiones teóricas y experiencias prácticas*, Academia de Ciencias Políticas y Sociales, Comité Venezolano de Arbitraje, Caracas 2005, p.409-410.

187 ICSID arbitration continued to be incorporated in the bilateral treaties for promotion and protection of investments signed and ratified after 1999. See for instance Venezuela-France Bilateral Investment Treaty in *Official Gazette* N° 37.896 of March 11, 2004.

188 See Hugo Chávez Frías, *Ideas Fundamentales para la Constitución Bolivariana de la V República,* Caracas agosto 1999. See also the quotations of the proposal of President Chávez in Hildegard Rondón de Sansó, *Aspectos jurídicos fundamentales del arbitraje internacional de inversión*, Ed. Exlibris, Caracas 2010, pp. 150. Sansó finds that from such proposal is not possible to deduct that the intention was to open the doors to international arbitration, p. 151.

tion.[189] Fortunately my proposal prevailed in the current Article 151 of the 1999 Constitution, which in any case was not really debated.

Because it was coherent with the pro-arbitration trend of the various Decree Laws issued by President Chávez in September 1999, including the Investment Law provisions of Articles 21, 22 and 23, President Chávez was at the same time proposing to reduce the jurisdictional immunity principle only to be applied in contracts entered by the "Republic" (and not by the States, Municipalities and decentralized public entities). Such contracts are almost inexistent (almost all public contracts are entered by decentralized public entities), except on matters of public external debt. It was only regarding those contracts that the Republic, and only the Republic (not the states, the municipalities, the public corporations or the public enterprises), as proposed by Chávez, would never agree to submit to foreign jurisdictions in a contract of public interest. Nonetheless, regarding public contracts entered by other entities of the State (that are the overwhelming majority of public contracts) and regarding international treaties or agreements and national laws providing for international arbitration, the President significantly proposed to eliminate all limits to arbitration, allowing arbitration without even the consideration of the "nature" of the contract or the matter involved. From this, the proposal of President Chávez makes clear that Venezuela had all the intention to make an open and unlimited offer to arbitrate disputes in an international forum; that is, the Government at the time effectively intended to provide a general, open-ended consent to submit to arbitration in all investments disputes.

In order to realize these assertions it is important to really understand the consequences that President Chávez's proposal would have had, by comparing the text of Article 127 of the 1961 Constitution (maintained as Article 151 of the 1999 Constitution), with the proposal of Chávez:

> **Article 127. 1961 Constitution**: "In contracts of public interest, unless inappropriate according with their nature, a clause shall be deemed included even if not been expressed, according to which the doubts and controversies that may arise on such contracts and that could not be resolved amicably by the contracting parties, shall be decided by the competent courts of the Republic, in accordance with its laws and could not give rise by any motive or cause to foreign claims."

> **Article proposed by President Chávez**: "In contracts entered into by the Republic that are of public interest, a clause shall be deemed included even if not expressed, according to which the doubts and controversies that may arise on such contracts, shall be decided by the competent courts of the Republic in accordance with the laws."[190]

---

189 The notion of "contracts of public interest" was fixed in the same Constitution (Article 126) as comprising "contracts of national, states and municipal public interest." That is, contracts of public interest not only entered by the Republic, but also by the States and by the Municipalities, as well as by public national, states and municipal entities (public corporations and public enterprises). See Allan R. Brewer-Carías, *Contratos Administrativos*, Editorial Jurídica Venezolana, Caracas 1997, pp. 28 ff.

190 See Hugo Chávez Frías, *Ideas Fundamentales para la Constitución Bolivariana de Venezuela*, August 5, 1999.

The proposal submitted by President Chávez was extremely bizarre and inappropriate regarding the principle of immunity jurisdiction of the State. The proposal meant that in contracts entered by all other public entities or juridical persons (as distinct from the Republic), such as the states, the municipalities, the autonomous institutions and other juridical persons of public law as well as by any public enterprises, no limit would exist regarding any matter related to the principle of immunity jurisdiction. President Chávez proposed provision was more liberal than the provision in the 1961 Constitution, only including those contracts entered by the "Republic" itself, and not by decentralized public entities.

Second, the proposal of President Chávez implied the complete elimination from the Constitution of the more than a century old "Calvo clause," admitting the possibility that public interest contracts could gave rise to foreign diplomatic claims against the Republic. From his proposals one cannot conclude that President Chávez was "opposed" to international arbitration. On the contrary, with such proposal, as I argued in the debate in the National Constituent Assembly in September 1999,[191] he attempted to eliminate from the Constitution the restrictions on the matters of relative jurisdictional immunity.

Far from being inconceivable, the constitutional proposal of President Chávez was completely coherent with the intention to provide a general, open-ended consent to submit to arbitration in all investments disputes. By making his constitutional proposal at the same time that he enacted the Investment Law, President Chávez without doubt had the intention to make an open and unlimited offer to arbitrate disputes in an international forum.

3. *The ratification of the pro-arbitration trend in the legislation enacted by President Chávez in 1999*

The extremely favorable trend regarding arbitration resulting from all the aforementioned Decree Laws issued by President Chávez in 1999 on matters of investments, in general, and in particular, regarding investments in administrative concessions and licenses for public works and public utilities, and in the field of gassed hydrocarbons and mines, was ratified two years later, in 2001, in a new set of Legislation that included the general admission of arbitration as a means for the solution of disputes. For example, the Organic Taxation Code of October 2001 included a general admission of arbitration as a means for the solution of disputes between taxpayers and the State.[192]

Subsequently, also in 2001, arbitration was generally admitted by establishing it as a means for the solution of disputes between the State and private parties in the

---

191 See Allan R. Brewer-Carías, "Propuesta sobre la cláusula de inmunidad relativa de jurisdicción y sobre la cláusula Calvo en los contratos de interés público," in *Debate Constituyente (Aportes a la Asamblea Nacional Constituyente)*, Vol. I (8-Agosto-8 Septiembre 1999), Fundación de Derecho Público/Editorial Jurídica Venezolana, Caracas 1999, pp. 209 233.

192 Articles 312-326. Organic Code on Taxation, *Official Gazette* N° 37.305 of October 17, 2001.

very important nationalized oil public sector, in cases related to the constitution of mixed companies for the exploitation of primary hydrocarbons activities. President Chávez, through the Decree Law N° 1.510 of November 2, 2001, issued the Organic Hydrocarbons Law[193] in execution of a new Organic Enabling Law approved by the newly elected National Assembly in November 2000,[194] in which the provision of Article 151 of the 1999 Constitution was ratified. This Law provided that contracts establishing mixed companies for the exploitation of hydrocarbons, "shall be deemed [to] include even if not … expressed," a clause establishing that "the doubts and controversies of any kind that may arise resulting from the execution of activities and that could not be resolved amicably by the parties, *including arbitration* …." will be resolved by the courts (Article 34.3.b). This provision expressly recognized in the Law the possibility to submit to arbitration the solution of disputes resulting from activities in the hydrocarbon sector when mixed companies are constituted with private investors.[195]

All of these Decree Laws and acts of the National Assembly between 1999 and up to 2001 confirm that in Venezuela, "without doubt, a clear legislative tendency existed in order to admit arbitration in contract related to the commercial activity of Public Administration."[196]

4.   *The elemental procedural administrative provisions assuring the correct legal opinion to be issued on matters of arbitral clauses in public contracts*

It was within this pro-arbitration trend of the Government on maters of investments, that President Chavez approved through Decree Laws an Instruction No 4 in March 12, 2001 establishing elemental rules for the "internal review" of drafts of public contracts containing arbitration clauses.[197] Far from being any sign of the intention of the government against arbitration clauses for the State,[198] this Presidential instruction was no more that the correct administrative response to the extension of arbitration clauses included in public contracts entered into only by the "Republic" encouraged as a general policy of the same Government. On the other hand, further Articles enacted by the President regarding rules of management in public

---

193   *Ley Orgánica de Hidrocarburos, Official Gazette* N° 37.323 of November 13, 2001

194   *Ley Orgánica Habilitante* of November 2000, *Official Gazette* N° 37.076 of November 13, 2000.

195   The same occurred with the reform of the Organic Statute of the Development of Guayana, also sanctioned by means of Decree Law N° 1531 of November 7, 2001, *Official Gazette* N° 5561 Extra. of November 28, 2001 and the Organic Law on Drinking Water Services and Sanitation enacted by the National Assembly in December 2001. See *Ley Orgánica para le prestación de los servicios de agua potable y de saneamiento, Official Gazette,* N° 5.568 Extra. of December 31, 2001.

196   See Juan Carlos Balzán, "El arbitraje en los contratos de interés a la luz de la cláusula de inmunidad de jurisdicción prevista en el artículo 151 de la Constitución," *loc. cit.,* p. 299.

197   *Official Gazette* N° 37.158 of March 14, 2001.

198   As pointed out by Hildegard Rondón de Sansó, *Aspectos jurídicos fundamentales del arbitraje internacional de inversión,* Ed. Exlibris, Caracas 2010, pp. 151-152..

administration, assigning to the Attorney General's office the function of reviewing any contracts containing submission to arbitration on public interests, were perfectly and completely reconcilable with the attitude reflected in laws, decrees and statements made both before and after the Investment Law with the notion that Article 22 of the Investment Law intended to constitute a standing, general consent of the Republic to arbitrate all investments disputes before ICSID.

Regarding public debt contracts which were a matter of discussion in the previous years, in an Opinion given on March 14, 2003, the same Attorney General's Office reiterated the opinion of the relative character of the clause of jurisdictional immunity in lending agreements, and suggested that

> "in future contracts in which the Republic is a party, in lieu of the ordinary jurisdictional means, arbitral clauses should be incorporated, due to the fact that currently the arbitral means constitute an expedited, efficient and economic form for the resolution of conflicts that could arise from contractual relationships."[199]

This attitude and opinion of the Attorney General's Office was far from "reticent" regarding arbitration in public contracts, and was completely coherent with the general pro-arbitration policy of the Government, particularly since 1999, when the Investment Law was enacted.

V. THE CORRECT INTERPRETATION OF ARTICLE 22 OF THE 1999 INVESTMENT LAW

As discussed below, when the text of Article 22 is interpreted according to the rules of interpretation set forth in Article 4 of the Civil Code, the sense that evidently appears from the proper meaning of the words used, in accordance with their connection and with the **intention of the legislator**, the conclusion is that it **states the unilateral consent of the Republic of Venezuela to the submission of disputes to ICSID arbitration**, leaving to qualified investors the right to decide whether to give their own consent or to resort to the Venezuelan courts.

In the Spanish phrase "*serán sometidas a arbitraje internacional*" (shall be submitted to international arbitration), the tense of the verb indicates that it is an expression of command. The phrase conveys the fact that international arbitration of disputes is a mandatory system, in the sense that, once properly invoked by the other party to a dispute, the Republic of Venezuela has **a duty** or **obligation to comply** with the applicable procedural rules and **to abide** by the decision of the arbitral tribunal. In this regard, the English translation "shall be submitted" for "*serán sometidas*," which is common ground between the parties, shows that the translators correctly understood the Spanish original as conveying this mandatory obligation.[200]

---

199 Quoted in Margot Y. Huen Rivas, "El arbitraje internacional en los contratos administrativos," *loc. cit.,* pp. 435-436; and in Juan Carlos Balzán, "El arbitraje en los contratos de interés a la luz de la cláusula de inmunidad de jurisdicción prevista en el artículo 151 de la Constitución," *loc. cit.,* p. 346-347.

200 "Shall can express (A) the subject's *intention to perform a certain action* or cause it to be performed, and (B) *a command.*" The use of shall to express *a command* "is chiefly used in

Consequently, the text of this provision (*"shall be submitted to international arbitration"*) is a **unilateral express statement of consent to ICSID arbitration freely given in advance by the Republic of Venezuela;**[201] or in the words of the ICSID Tribunal in the *Mobil* case, Article 22 "creates a conditional obligation" to go to arbitration (ICSID Mobil case, ¶ 102). None of the other aspects of the text or the other elements of interpretation led to a different conclusion.

The mandate to submit disputes to ICSID arbitration refers to "disputes to which apply the provisions of the [ICSID Convention]." As an initial observation, the term "disputes" appears for a second time in Article 22, in parallel to the first reference to "disputes" between an international investor whose country of origin has in effect a treaty or agreement for the promotion and protection of investments and the Republic of Venezuela. Grammatically, this duplicate and parallel reference indicates that the second category of "disputes" related to the ICSID Convention is not necessarily subsumed within the first category of "disputes" related to investment treaties or agreements. Therefore, when Article 22 refers to the "disputes" related to the ICSID Convention no reference is made to "international investor," as this term is defined in the Investment Law.

The second category of "disputes" comprises those in respect of which the provisions of the ICSID Convention are applicable. According to Article 25.1 of the ICSID Convention, ICSID jurisdiction "shall extend to any legal dispute arising directly out of an investment, between a Contracting State [...] and a national of another Contracting State, which the parties to the dispute consent in writing to submit to the Centre." As the ICSID Convention does not itself supply consent, it is unreasonable to interpret Article 22, which expressly provides that disputes shall be submitted to arbitration, as looking to the ICSID Convention to supply the consent that Article 22 itself purports to supply. Consequently, the only way to give effect to the mandate in Article 22 that disputes "shall be submitted" to ICSID arbitration is to interpret the phrase "disputes to which apply the provisions of the [ICSID Convention]" as referring to any disputes that meet all the requirements for ICSID jurisdiction **other than consent**, which is supplied by Article 22 itself. Any other interpretation would render this portion of Article 22 circular and would deprive it of any effect, in violation of the principle of effective interpretation or *effect utile*.

---

regulations or legal documents. In less formal English must or are to would be used instead of shall in the above sentences." See A. J. Thomson and A. V. Martinet, *A Practical English Grammar*, Fourth Edition, Oxford University Press 2001, pp. 208, 246..

201 In the same sense, see e.g., Gabriela Álvarez Ávila, "Las características del arbitraje del CIADI," in *Anuario Mexicano de Derecho Internacional*, Vol. II, Instituto de Investigaciones Jurídicas, Universidad Nacional Autónoma de México, UNAM, México 2002, pp. 4-5, 17 footnote 23, available at http://juridicas.unam.mx/publica/rev/derint/cont/2/cm/; Eugenio Hernández Bretón, "Protección de inversiones en Venezuela," in *Revista DeCITA, Derecho del Comercio Internacional, Temas de Actualidad, (Inversiones Extranj eras)*, N°3, Zavalía, 2005, pp. 283-284; José Antonio Muci Borjas, *El Derecho Administrativo Global y los Tratados Bilaterales de Inversión (BITs)*, Caracas 2007, pp. 214-215; José Gregorio Torrealba R, *Promoción y Protección de las Inversiones Extranjeras en Venezuela*, Funeda, Caracas 2008. pp. 56-58, 125-127.

The portion of Article 22 referring to the ICSID Convention ends with the phrase "if it so establishes" ("*si así éste lo establece*") also translated as "if it so provides". This phrase, interpreted according to the the the sense that **evidently appears from the proper meaning of the words** used, in accordance with **their connection** with the entirety of that section and consistent with the **intention of the Legislator**, refers to the need for the "respective treaty or agreement" **to contain provisions establishing international arbitration**[202] in order for the preceding express command (shall be submitted) to be capable of being executed; and for the last part of the Article that leaves the option to the international investor to decide whether or not to resort to international arbitration, to be effective. As the ICSID Convention paradigmatically establishes a framework or system of international arbitration for the settlement of investment disputes, the condition "if it so establishes" is clearly satisfied in the case of the portion of Article 22 that refers to the ICSID Convention. On the other hand, the phrase "should it so provide" refers primarily to the possibility that treaties or agreements for the promotion and protection of investments might not provide for international arbitration of disputes to which they apply.

As already mentioned, Article 22 is a compound provision that combines three rules concerning three different kinds of international instruments: first, treaties or agreements on the promotion and protection of investments; second, the MIGA Convention; and third, the ICSID Convention. Although the phrase "should it so provide" applies to each of the three rules, the condition that it embodies (that the treaty or agreement establish international arbitration) is satisfied in the case of the ICSID and MIGA Conventions,[203] which clearly provide for arbitration, and is also satisfied in the case of those treaties or agreements for the promotion and protection

---

202 In this sense, Victorino Tejera Pérez considers that the expression "if it so establishes" means "if it [respective treaty or agreement] establishes arbitration." See Victorino Tejera Pérez, "Do Municipal Investment Laws Always Constitute a Unilateral Offer to Arbitrate? The Venezuelan Investment Law: A Case Study," *loc. cit.*, p. 95; Victorino Tejera Pérez, *Arbitraje de Inversiones*, Magister Thesis, Caracas 2010, *cit.*, p. 170.

203 The MIGA Convention contemplates two kinds of disputes: (a) disputes between the Agency and a Member country (Article 57), which shall be settled in accordance with the procedures set out in Annex II to the Convention and (b) disputes involving MIGA and a holder of a guarantee or reinsurance (Article 58), which shall be submitted to arbitration in accordance with such rules as shall be provided for or referred to in the contract of guarantee or reinsurance. Article 22 of the Investment Law can refer only to disputes of the first kind (those that could arise between MIGA and a Member State), because disputes of the second type do not involve the Venezuelan State or any other Venezuelan instrumentality. In the case of disputes that could arise between MIGA and a Member State, Annex II of the Convention provides a procedure for settlement that calls for negotiation followed by arbitration, with conciliation as a permissible alternative. According to Article 57(b)(ii) of the MIGA Convention, this procedure may be superseded by an agreement between the State and MIGA concerning an alternative method for the settlement of such disputes, but such an agreement must be based on Annex II, which means that it must also contain resort to arbitration. As the MIGA Convention provides for international arbitration in either situation, the condition "should it so provides" is satisfied and Article 22 requires submission of such disputes to international arbitration according to the terms of the MIGA Convention.

of investments that do provide for international arbitration.[204] On the contrary, the condition is not satisfied in the case of treaties or agreements for the promotion and protection of investments that do not provide for international arbitration of disputes between the host State and foreign investors. Accordingly, "should it so provide" (if it so establishes) reflects a contingency only in the case of treaties or agreements for the promotion and protection of investments, which may or may not provide for international arbitration of such disputes.

Consequently, it is an error to suppose that the phrase "should it so provide" refers to the State's **consent** to arbitration. First, there is nothing in the text of Article 22 suggesting or supporting such an interpretation. The antecedent sentence ("shall be submitted to international arbitration under the terms of the respective treaty or agreement") makes no reference to consent; it refers to international arbitration. The "so" in "should it so provide" refers to "international arbitration" and cannot refer to a concept ("consent") that is not included in the antecedent sentence. Thus, the interpretation that the "so" refers to the act of consent, is unfounded. Second, it should be remembered that the "it" in "should it so provide" refers, in the context we are addressing in this case, to the ICSID Convention. Therefore, interpreting "should it so provide" as though it meant "should the ICSID Convention provide consent to arbitration" would turn this phrase into an impossible condition (one that cannot be fulfilled), because the ICSID Convention does not itself provide for a Contracting State's consent to ICSID arbitration. It is precisely because the ICSID Convention requires consent by a separate written instrument, such as a piece of national legislation like Article 22,[205] that it cannot be presumed that the drafters of Article 22 intended the absurdity of subjecting the mandate relating to ICSID arbitration to a condition that was not and could not be fulfilled. Under Venezuelan law, any interpretation of a statute that leads to absurdity or that would deprive a statutory provision of any effect must be rejected.[206] The principle of effective interpretation (*effet utile*) has been recognized to be a critical canon for the interpretation of statutes. For example, the Civil Cassation Chamber of the Supreme Tribunal of Justice has declared that "it would be absurd to suppose that the Legislator does not try to use the

---

204 The Spanish text, which uses the subjunctive mood, makes clear that it refers not only to treaties or agreements of this kind to which the Republic of Venezuela was a party at the time the Investment Law was adopted, but also treaties or agreements to which it may become a party at any time in the future. Historically, while most agreements of this kind concluded by States around the world provide for international arbitration of investor-State disputes, some agreements do not. The Republic of Venezuela may become a party to treaties or agreements of this kind that do not provide for the resolution of controversies through arbitration.

205 It is settled that under Article 25.1 of the ICSID Convention an ICSID Contracting State may express its written consent to submit to the jurisdiction of the Centre by way of the Contracting State's legislation for the promotion of investments.

206 See Supreme Tribunal of Justice, Constitutional Chamber, Decision N° 1.173 of June 15, 2004 (Case: Interpretación del Artículo 72 de la Constitución de la República Bolivariana de Venezuela) (Exp. 02- 3.215), in *Revista de Derecho Público* N° 97-98, Editorial Jurídica Venezolana, Caracas 2004, pp. 429 ff.

most precise and adequate terms in order to express the purpose and scope of its provisions, or deliberately omits elements that are essential for their complete understanding."[207]

On the other hand, the final part of Article 22 ("without prejudice to the possibility of using, when applicable the systems of litigation provided for in the Venezuelan laws in force") further confirms that Article 22 is an expression of consent to arbitration. That statement indicates that Article 22 does not have the effect of preventing the investor from using domestic litigation remedies. If Article 22 were a mere declaration of the State's willingness to agree to arbitration in a separate document as opposed to a firm expression of consent to arbitration by the State, there would have been no need to disclaim that Article 22 did not prevent the investor from resorting to domestic remedies.

The interpretation of Article 22 as containing an open offer by the State to submit investment disputes to ICSID arbitration not only results from the **literal or grammatical** element of statutory interpretation, but also from applying the **logical, rational or reasonable** element of interpretation derived from the fact that the State's offering of unilateral consent to arbitration in order to promote investment was part of the *raison d'être* of the Investment Law.

The Constitutional Chamber of the Supreme Tribunal of Justice in Decision N° 1.173 of June 15, 2004 has held that the determination of the intention of the Legislator must "start from the will of the creator of the provision, as it results from the debates prior to its promulgation."[208] Being the Investment Law enacted through a Decree Law and not as the result of a parliamentary debate, the "creator" of such Law was not the National Assembly, but the President acting in Council of Ministers, that is, with all the Cabinet (Article 236.8 of the Constitution). Such intention, therefore, resulted from the debates prior to the promulgation of the Law that were sustained in the Council of Ministers itself, in the Economic Cabinet, and from the proposals made by the drafter of the Law, who in this case, was Ambassador Werner Corrales-Leal. At that time Corrales was Head of the Permanent Representation of Venezuela before the WTO and the UN Offices headquartered in Geneva and was charged by the Government to prepare a draft of the Investment Law.[209] This is par-

---

207   See Supreme Tribunal of Justice, Civil Cassation Chamber, Decision N° 4 of November 15, 2001 (Case: *Carmen Cecilia López Lugo v. Miguel Angel Capriles Ayala et al.*), ar http://www.tsj.gov.ve/decisiones/scc/Noviembre/RECL-0004-151101-99003-99360.htm, p. 7.

208   See Supreme Tribunal of Justice, Constitutional Chamber, Decision N° 1.173 of June 15, 2004 (Case: Interpretación del Artículo 72 de la Constitución de la República Bolivariana de Venezuela) (Exp. 02-3.215), in *Revista de Derecho Público*, N° 97-98, Editorial Jurídica Venezolana, Caracas 2004, pp. 429 ff.

209   See in Eduardo Camel A., "Ley de promoción de Inversiones viola acuerdos suscritos por Venezuela", *El Nacional*, Caracas September 15, 1999. The character of Corrales as drafter was officially recognized, for instance, in a press released of the Ministry of Foreign Affairs, *Oficina de Comunicaciones y Relaciones Institucionales*, "Resúmen de Medios nacionales e

ticularly important, in the absence of an *Exposición de Motivos* of the Law formally explaining its motives and content. All those elements contribute to establish the intention of the National Executive as the "creator" of the Law.

That is why, in the ***Opic Korimun* ICSID Case**, arbitrator professor Guido Santiago Tawil, in his Dissenting Vote to such decision, concluded as follows:

> "12. Absent in the case of the Investment Law (enacted by Presidential decree) a formal Congressional debate, "direct evidence" of the intention of the legislator would have normally appeared in the form of documents existing in the official administrative files, the minutes of the Economic Cabinet or the minutes of the Council of Ministers. Such evidence could have only been produced by Respondent, who did not disclose them, notwithstanding the multiple requests made to this respect.

> 13. Having the Tribunal come to the conclusion that Messrs. Corrales and Capriles contributed to the drafting of the Investment Law, and that their intention was that Article 22 of the Investment Law would constitute consent of Venezuela to ICSID jurisdiction in respect of disputes brought by investors against the Respondent under the Investment Law -which is consistent with the documentary evidence available in the record-, denial of jurisdiction for lack of consent based in the absence of "direct evidence" that could only take the form of documents in possession, custody or control of the Respondent, duly requested and not produced, appears in my view as a threshold too high for the Claimant to comply with and with which I am, respectfully, unable to agree."[210]

In effect, the intention of the National Executive when enacting the Investment Law, in a consistent way with the general policy defined by the Government at the time of its enactment for the purpose of attracting and promoting international investments in the country, was the same reflected in all the other pieces of legislation enacted by the Executive at the same time, all according to the pro-arbitration principle that prevail en 1999. If according to Article 4 of the Civil Code, the interpretation of a statute results from "the sense that appears evident from the proper meaning of the words, according to their connection among themselves and the **intention of the Legislator;**" the latter is one of the key elements in the interpretation to be taken into consideration.

Being the Investment Law the product of a bureaucratic drafting process and not of a parliamentary process with recorded debates in a legislative body, the intention of the drafters are a valid source to determine the intention of the "legislator," or of the "creator" of the statute. In this case of the Investment Law it was not the product of a diffuse "creator" (Parliament, Congress, Legislative Assembly) composed by representatives, parliamentary commissions, legislative assistance, interacting in close or open debates that are normally involve in the sanctioning of a statute; but was the product of an executive bureaucratic process, that in that case allows to identify a "drafter" of the law. Consequently in that sense it is possible to understand

---

Internacionales", April 29, 2009, p. 23. See also, in Alberto Cova, "Venezuela incumple Ley de Promoción de Inversiones,' in *El Nacional*, April 24, 2009.

210 Available at: http://italaw.com/sites/default/files/case-documents/italaw3014.pdf

that **"the will of the creator of the provision"** eventually is **the will of the drafter of the provision.**

That is to say, whenever a statute, even when approved by a Congress, can be identify with its drafter (and that is why so many statutes and laws have or takes the name of its drafters), it is compulsory for the interpreter to seek for the intention of the "drafter" in order to establish the intention of the legislator. In such cases, there is no other "creator" of the Law different to its drafter. And this is the case, in general, regarding decree laws or executive regulations, which normally are approved without a "debate" like the parliamentary ones. Commonly, it is the respective Minister of the Executive in charge of drafting and proposing of the text, the one that can eventually express the will or the intention of the body approving the text. But it can also be a public official, specialized in the subject or matter of the text, by assignment or delegation by the President, the one in charge of drafting a proposal of a statute or regulation. It was the case of the 1999 Investment Law, in which the Ambassador before the specialized United Nations Agencies on Commerce in Geneva, Mr. Corrales was charged by the Executive of drafting the Law. In these cases, the opinion or the intention of the drafter is essential to identify the intention of the legislator. Consequently, the intention of the drafter is absolutely relevant to determine the intention of the legislator, not being at all inappropriate to look to the intention of the drafter.

In each case, and according to each circumstance, in order to determine the intention of the legislator, the interpreter has the obligation to precise and identity the some times diffuse "creator" of the text. And that is what must be done in a case like the one of the 1999 Decree Law on the Investment Law, in the absence of any "Statements of Purposes" or other official document explaining the motives of the statute as for instance the Minute (*Acta*) of the Council of Minister (different to the deliberations, which are the only reserved part of its actions). According to the public information available, being Mr. Corrales and Mr. Capriles the drafters of the Law, acting by delegation of the President of the Republic, the only way to determine the will of the legislator or of the Council of Ministers as "creator" of the law, is to determine the intention the drafters. Consequently, in the case of the 1999 Investment Law, this intention of the legislator, being the National Executive who enacted the Law, is not other that the intention expressed by the drafters of such law; and in particular regarding its Article 22, the expressed intention is to express a unilateral consent by the State to submit disputes with international investors to the jurisdiction of ICSID arbitration, as a main tool in order to attract and promote international investments in the country.

This intention, on the other hand and as aforementioned, was completely consistent with the pro arbitration trend that characterized all the legislation enacted by the Congress and the Executive at the same time of the Investment law, particularly by means of decree laws, in execution of the Enabling Organic Law of April of 1999 authorizing the President of the Republic to "enact provisions in order to promote the protection and promotion of national and foreign investments with the purpose of establishing a legal framework for investments and to give them greater legal security," as well as in the 2000 Enabling Law with similar purposes. It was the case of the *1999 Law on Gassed Hydrocarbons*, recognizing the possibility to submit to arbitration disputes on matters relating to licenses given by the State for the exploration or exploitation of non-gas hydrocarbons;[211] of the *1999 Law on the Promotion of Private Investments through the Regime of Concessions*, in which it was provided that the parties, in public concessions contracts, could agree to submit their differences to the decision of an Arbitral Tribunal;[212] of the *2001 Organic Taxation Code* that included a general admission of arbitration as a means for the solution of disputes between taxpayers and the State; the *2001 Organic Hydrocarbons Law* in which the possibility to submit to arbitration the solution of disputes resulting from activities in the hydrocarbon sector when mixed companies are constituted with private investors is expressly recognized.[213] In all these laws, referred all of them to key sectors of the economy, there is a clear legislative tendency admitting arbitration. The pro arbitration trend that characterized the legislation enacted between 1999 and 2001, derived not from its provision as compulsory (this was only the case of Article 22 of the 1999 Investment Law), but of its consistent regulation in all those laws as a means for conflict resolution

Consequently, considering Article 22 **systematically** and in a **historical** perspective, expressing consent to international arbitration was in accord with the trend in favor of international arbitration described above, including the State's ratification between 1993 and 1998 of treaties for the protection and promotion of investments that accepted international arbitration, as well as the other legal provisions regarding arbitration adopted at the time.

Furthermore, using the **teleological** and **sociological** element of statutory interpretation, the economic and social situation prevailing at the time the Investment Law was enacted explains the legislator's intent to promote investments and the offering of consent to international arbitration as a means to do so. The economic policy and the whole legal order existing in 1999 tended to promote foreign investment and international arbitration. This general intent is clearly reflected in the Investment Law as a whole, which is primarily devoted to promoting and protecting foreign investment by regulating the actions of the State in the treatment of such

---

211 Decree Law N° 310 of September 12, 1999, *Official Gazette* N° 36.793 of September 23, 1999.

212 Ley Orgánica sobre promoción de la inversión privada bajo el régimen de concesiones, *Official Gazette* N° 5.394 Extra. of October 25, 1999. See *in general* on this Law, Alfredo Romero Mendoza "Concesiones y otros mecanismos no tradicionales para el financiamiento de obras públicas", in Alfredo Romero Mendoza (Coord.), *Régimen Legal de las Concesiones Públicas. Aspectos Jurídicos, Financieros y Técnicos*, Editorial Jurídica Venezolana, Caracas 2000, pp. 28-29.

213 *Ley Orgánica de Hidrocarburos, Official Gazette* N° 37.323 of November 13, 2001. See Diego Moya-Ocampos Pancera and Maria del Sol Moya-Ocampos Pancera, "Comentarios relativos a la procedencia de las cláusulas arbitrales en los contratos de interés público nacional, en particular: especial las concesiones mineras," en *Revista de Derecho Administrativo*, N° 19, Editorial Sherwood, Caracas 2006, p. 174.

investment. Submission of disputes to international arbitration is precisely one of the principal means of protecting foreign investors and investments.[214]

VI. THE INTENTION OF THE GOVERNMENT IN 1999 TO EXPRESS THE STATE CONSENT FOR INTERNATIONAL ARBITRATION IN ARTICLE 22 OF THE INVESTMENT LAW

And that was precisely the intention of the drafters of the Investment law and of the National Executive when considering it and approving it in September 1999: to express in Article 22 the consent of the Republic to submit disputes to international arbitration, particularly before the ICSID. This offer was an open offer, subject only to the condition that the respective treaties or agreements, like the ICSID Convention, establish a framework or mechanism for international arbitration. It created a right for the investors to go at their will to international arbitration or to resort to the national courts.

1. The absence of a formal "Statement of Purposes" and the motives of the Investment Law as exposed by its drafters

Contrary to the practice observed in almost all other Decree Laws issued by the President of the Republic at the time, the Decree Law on the Investment Law does not have a "Statement of Purposes" (*Exposición de Motivos*). This does not mean that the Law itself had no "motives" or purposes, or that the National Executive had no specific intention by issuing the Decree law. The Investment Law had precise motives, not only to promote and protect investments but to promote arbitration, to guarantee arbitral resolution of disputes, thus, limiting the scope of the national courts on the matter. The intention of the Investment Law is in this sense expressed in its first Article, in which is clear that its provisions are "directed to regulate the action of the State regarding investments and investors, whether nationals or foreign," that is, the Law:

> "comes to fix the extension of the competencies of the State in a way such as to assure such investments and investors the stable legal cadre that guarantees the enough security, devoted to achieve the harmonic increase, the diversification and complementation of investments in favor of the objectives of national development"(Article 1).[215]

And this is what the Law precisely works out in Article 22: to limit – not to exclude – the jurisdiction of the national courts on matters of investments by providing

---

214 Even the Decision N° 1541 of 2008 p. 28 recognizes that one of the ways States attract foreign investment is to make a unilateral promise to submit disputes to arbitration ("It is impossible to be unaware that States which attempt to attract investment must, on a national sovereignty level, decide to grant certain guarantees to investors, in order to ensure that the relationship materializes and, within the variables used to encourage these investments, it is common to include an arbitration agreement which, in the opinion of the investors, provides them with security to mitigate the fear of possible partiality by State courts in favor of nationals of their own country...").

215 See Eugenio Hernández Bretón, "Protección de Inversiones en Venezuela," in *Boletín de la Academia de Ciencias Políticas y Sociales*, N° 142, Caracas 2004 pp. 221-222.

for international arbitration; but always leaving in the hands of the investors the choice of venue.

In this regard, in the absence of a published "Statement of Purposes" for the De-cree Law on the Investment Law, and being the product of a bureaucratic drafting process and not of a parliamentary process with recorded debates in a legislative body, the intention of the drafters are a valid source to determine the intention of the "legislator." [216] This is particularly so of the "preparatory work" of the text of the Decree.[217] In this sense, it is a matter of public knowledge that the 1999 Investment Law was drafted under the direction of the then Ambassador Werner Corrales-Leal, Head of the Permanent Representation of Venezuela before the WTO and the UN entities headquartered in Geneva.[218] Ambassador Corrales, who since 1998 had an important role in the formulation of Venezuelan policy toward investments, includ-ing the negotiations of a failed bilateral investment treaty with the U.S.[219] was en-trusted with the task of drafting the Investment law[220] being ratified in such task by

---

216 The Constitutional Chamber of the Supreme Tribunal of Justice has held that the determina-tion of the intention of the Legislator must **start from the will of the creator of the provi-sion**, as it results from the debates prior to its promulgation." See Supreme Tribunal of Justi-ce, Constitutional Chamber, Decision N° 1.173 of June 15, 2004 (Case: *Interpretación del Artículo 72 de la Constitución de la República Bolivariana de Venezuela*) (Exp. 02-3.215), in *Revista de Derecho Público N° 97-98*, Editorial Jurídica Venezolana, Caracas 2004, pp. 429 ff.

217 It is what in the Vienna Convention on the law of treaties of 1969 is called as "supplemen-tary means of interpretation" which includes referring to treaties, its "preparatory work" and the "circumstances of its conclusion" (Article 32).

218 See in Eduardo Camel A., "Ley de promoción de Inversiones viola acuerdos suscritos por Venezuela", *El Nacional*, Caracas September 15, 1999. The character of Corrales as drafter was officially recognized, for instance, in a press released of the Ministry of Foreign Affairs, *Oficina de Comunicaciones y Relaciones Institucionales*, "Resúmen de Medios nacionales e Internacionales", April 29, 2009, p. 23. See also, in Alberto Cova, "Venezuela incumple Ley de Promoción de Inversiones,' in *El Nacional*, April 24, 2009.

219 For instance see Gioconda Soto, "Cancillería llama a consultas a Corrales y Echeverría,"in *El Nacional*, June 10, 1998; Fabiola Zerpa, "Venezuela rechaza presiones para firmar Acuerdo con EEUU," *El Nacional*, Caracas June 12, 1998; Alfredo Carquez Saavedra, "Tratado de inversiones con EE.UU. divide a negociadores venezolanos," in *El Nacional*, Caracas June 16, 1998.

220 In January 1999 Ambassador Corrales as head of the Permanent Representation of Venezuela before the WTO and the UN entities headquartered in Geneva, filed before the Government a document titled *"Formulación de un Anteproyecto de ley de promoción y Protección de In-versiones (Términos de referencia), enero 1999."* This document is cited in Werner Corrales Leal and Marta Rivera Colomina, "Algunas ideas sobre el Nuevo régimen de promoción y protección de inversiones en Venezuela," in Luis Tineo and Julia Barragán (Comp.), *La OMC como espacio normativo. Un reto para Venezuela*, Asociación Venezolana de Derecho y Economía, Caracas, p. 195; also in Victorino Tejera Pérez, "Do Municipal Investment Laws Always Constitute a Unilateral Offer to Arbitrate? The Venezuelan Investment Law: A Case Study," *loc. cit.*, p. 116; Victorino Tejera Pérez, *Arbitraje de Inversiones*, pp. 155-156.

the then new Chávez administration.[221] As Head of that Permanent Representation, Ambassador Corrales prepared reports and opinions for the Government.

One of those reports, dated April 1999 and written by Ambassador Corrales with Marta Rivera Colomina, an official at the Permanent Representation, contains ideas for the design of the legal regime of promotion and protection of investments in Venezuela.[222] The document explains that "a regime applicable to foreign investments, must leave open the possibility to resort to international arbitration, which today is accepted almost everywhere in the world, either by means of the mechanism provided for in the Convention on the Settlement of Investment Disputes between States and Nationals of Other States (ICSID) or by means of the submission of the dispute to an international arbitrator or an *ad hoc* arbitral tribunal like the one proposed by UNCITRAL."[223]

This view was made even more explicit in an essay written by the same authors explaining "Some ideas on the new regime on the promotion and protection of Investments in Venezuela" (*"Algunas ideas sobre el Nuevo régimen de promoción y protección de inversiones en Venezuela"*) published shortly after the 1999 Investment Law came into effect. The authors and co-drafters of the Investment Law in that essay, stated that "a regime applicable to foreign investments, must leave open the possibility to **unilaterally** resort to international arbitration, which today is accepted almost everywhere in the world, either by means of the mechanism provided for in the Convention on the Settlement of Investment Disputes between States and Nationals of Other States (ICSID) or by means of the submission of the dispute to an international arbitrator or an *ad hoc* arbitral tribunal like the one proposed by UNCITRAL."[224] The reference to **unilateral** resort to international arbitration makes it clear, without doubt, that the persons entrusted with drafting the 1999 Investment Law intended Article 22 to express the State's consent to ICSID arbitration, which is the only way for the investor to have the option to unilaterally resort to such international arbitration, or to decide to go before the national courts. Given that the State through the Government (the Executive) was the one giving the instructions to the drafters and also was involved (through the Executive Cabinet) in

---

221 As mentioned in the ICSID *Mobil* case, the Republic has "doubt[ed]" the character of Corrales as the drafter of the Law (ICSID *Mobil* case, ¶ 133).

222 See Werner Corrales-Leal and Martha Rivera Colomina, "Algunas ideas relativas al diseño de un régimen legal de promoción y protección de inversiones en Venezuela," April 30, 1999. Document prepared at the request of the Minister of CORDIPLAN.

223 *Id.*, pp. 10-11.

224 See Werner Corrales-Leal and Marta Rivera Colomina, "Algunas ideas sobre el nuevo régimen de promoción y protección de inversiones en Venezuela" p. 185. In the absence of "legislative history" of the decree Law, Victorino Tejera Pérez considers that this article of Corrales and Rivera "could even be assimilated to a supplementary means of interpretation, as established in Article 32 of the Vienna Convention on Treaty Law." See Victorino Tejera Pérez, *Arbitraje de Inversiones*, p. 187; Victorino Tejera Pérez, "Do Municipal Investment Laws Always Constitute a Unilateral Offer to Arbitrate? The Venezuelan Investment Law: A Case Study," p. 115.

approving the Investment Law once it was drafted, this was therefore an expression of intent on behalf of the State. Put differently, providing for unilateral resort to arbitration in connection with the 1999 Investment Law presupposes that said law provides the State's consent that is necessary for the investor to have the right to unilaterally resort to international arbitration.

As was pointed out by Professor Guido Santiago Tawil in his Dissenting Vote as arbitrator in the *Opic Korimun* **ICSID Case,** referring to the aforementioned essays written by Mr. Corales), considered that they were "consistent with the testimony provided by Mr. Corrales regarding the intention to provide consent to arbitration through Article 22 of the Investment Law." Mr. Tawil considered that the first of those articles "appeared months before the enactment of the Investment Law" and the other "was published immediately after such enactment took place and many years before any dispute on the matter arose, which evidences "the context and purpose" of Article 22. On the contrary, Venezuela failed to submit any contemporary documentary or witness evidence to the contrary, even when requested to do so." [225]

On the contrary, the ICSID tribunals in its Decisions in the *Mobil* and *Cemex* cases, referring to these contemporaneous works of Corrales when the Law was being drafted, said that Corrales "did not say that the drafters or Article 22 intended to provide for consent in ICSID arbitration in the absence of any BITs" (ICSID *Mobil* case, ¶ 136; ICSID *Cemex* case, ¶ 132), which is an erroneous way to read those essays. Corrales and his colleague wrote in their own words, and with the authorization of the Republic for them to conceive of an Investment Law, that they considered necessary, in the benefit of the investors, to "leave open the possibility to unilaterally resort to international arbitration," this being possible only if the State has provided in the same text of Article 22 of the Investment Law for consent to ICSID arbitration in the absence of any BITs.

As was correctly noted by the ICSID tribunal in the *Cemex* case the "the word 'unilaterally' did not appear in the first article of 30 April, 1999. It was added to the second article in 2000 (ICSID *Cemex* case, ¶ 131, Footnote 118), precisely because the second article was published **after** the Investment Law was approved and published (while the first article was published **before** the Investment Law was approved by the Republic). With the adding of that word, the authors and co-drafters of the Law, emphasized the inclusion of this word, in order to stress that the only way for the investor to have that possibility to "unilaterally resort to arbitration," is if he has the right, as an option, to go to arbitration or to resort to national courts. This, in its turn, can only occur when the State has expressed its consent to go to arbitration, also unilaterally, and as an open offer in the same text of Article 22. Consequently, the only way to understand the reason for the erroneous assertion of the ICSID tribunals in the *Mobil* and *Cemex* cases, is to realize that when reading Article 22, the tribunals simply ignored the disclaimer included in the last phrase of the provision, which is not even considered in the whole text of the decisions, as discussed in detail above.

---

225 Available at: http://italaw.com/sites/default/files/case-documents/italaw3014.pdf

2. The discussion of the Draft of the Investment Law in the Council of Ministers in 1999

The Draft of the 1999 Investment Law was coordinated in Venezuela by the Central Office of Coordination and Planning, and not by a particular Ministry. It was considered in meetings of the Economic Cabinet of the Council of Ministers, particularly in the meeting held on August 24, 1999 with the assistance of Ambassador Werner Corrales presenting the text.[226] The specific matter of Article 22 as expression of the State consent for arbitration was discussed. Specifically, in that meeting, as was reported to the press by the General Director of Central Office of Coordination and Planning (Cordiplán) that "the possibility for arbitration is maintained."[227]

In the press it was reported that:

> "The Director General of Cordiplán Fernando Hernández, as the spokesman of the economic group of President Chávez, assured that this legal draft 'will offer national and foreign investors legal and fiscal security, in order to create confidence.' One of the aspects regarding this law regarding which Hernández was asked is the one related to the resolution of controversies. Specifically, he was asked about the judicial body before which investors entering into contracts with the Republic would have to go. 'International arbitration is maintained,' Hernández said without giving details."[228]

The Ministry of Production and Commerce replaced the previous Ministry of Industry and Commerce in August 1999. Juan de Jesús Montilla, who was appointed as Minister [229] in substitution of the former Minister of Industry and Commerce (Gustavo Márquez), commented a few months later in mid 2000 on the provisions of the 1999 Law Investment Law without mentioning the unilateral offer expressed by the Republic for arbitration. No conclusion can be legitimately drawn from the Minister's silence, particularly since the drafters of the Law have expressed the contrary. Nonetheless, as mentioned, Minister Montilla was not a member of the National Executive or Council of Ministers during the months in 1999 when the Law was drafted (before September 1999). Therefore, although he signed the Decree Law on October 3, 1999, as the new Minister of Production and Commerce, he did not participate in the conception of the Investment Law and was not involved in its Drafting, and not even his Office was involved (given it succeeded the previous Ministry of Industry and Commerce).[230] Consequently, the fact that this Minister Montilla

---

226 In the press it was reported as a consequence of this Meeting and in relation to the discussions of the Draft, that "In the Draft, international arbitration is provided as an option for the resolution of conflicts." See "El proyecto prevé el arbitraje internacional como opción para resolver conflictos. Evalúan Ley de Inversiones," in *El Universal*, August 25, 1999.

227 See Andrés Rojas Ramírez, "Decreto para la protección de Inversions contradice Constitución de Chávez", *El Nacional*, Caracas August 25, 1999.

228 *Id.*

229 See Decree N° 288 published in *Gaceta Oficial* N° 36.779 of September 3, 1999

230 See in Victorino Tejera Pérez, *Arbitraje de Inversiones*, Magister Thesis, Caracas 2010, *cit.*, p. 158. As is mentioned by Tejera Pérez, even the predecessor of Montilla, the Minister of Industry and Commerce, Gustavo Marquez, who attended the meetings where the Decree

over six months after the approval of the Investment Law did not mention that the Investment Law included unilateral offer by the Republic permitting foreign investors to resort to arbitration cannot lead to the conclusion that it does not contain consent to arbitration.[231] Nonetheless, in an incomprehensibly way, the ICSID Tribunal in the *Cemex* case, considered that when the Minister said what he said (that "the solution in the case of controversies or disputes where it is set forth that these shall be resolved in national courts or within a framework of acknowledgment of the commitments that have been undertaken in international agreements"), this supposedly is a statement that is "contrary" to say that "Article 22 intended to provide for consent to ICSID arbitration in the absence of any BIT" (*ICSID Cemex* ¶¶ 132, 133). This conclusion had no basis at all.

In the meetings of the Economic Cabinet of the Council of Ministers in which the draft of the Investment Law were considered, one of the High Officials who attended was Alvaro Silva Calderón, then Vice Minister of Energy and Mines.[232] In that meeting, I understand that Vice Minister Calderón opposed the inclusion in Article 22 of the open offer of expression of consent by the State to go to international arbitration. This was a position that was coherent with his well known personal opinion opposing the idea of the State subjection to international investment arbitration.[233] Nonetheless, and despite his opposition, in the meeting, Vice Minister Calderón's personal opinion and opposition did not prevail, and instead, the proposal made by Werner Corrales and his legal adviser Gonzalo Capriles in favor of the State expressing consent in Article 22 for international arbitration, was the one accepted by the Cabinet[234] According to the Organic Law on Central Administration of 1995,[235] in force when the Investment Law was being discussed in the Economic Cabinet, the documents considered and the opinions expressed in the meetings of the Economic Cabinet (acting as a Sector Cabinet with respect to the Investment Law)

Law was considered, declined to comment on the drafting of the Law, explaining that his Ministry was not involved in the drafting of it. *Id.*, p. 158 Footnote 557.

231　On this particular point, the *Cemex* tribunal is simply incorrect.

232　As it is referred to in Victorino Tejera Pérez, *Arbitraje de Inversiones*, Magister Thesis, Caracas 2010, *cit.*, p. 158.

233　See for instance, Alvaro Silva Calderón, "Apreciaciones sobre el arbitraje jurídico en Venezuela," available at http://www.pdvsa.com/interface.sp/database/fichero/free/5000/639.PDF, pp. 14-16. Alvaro Silva Calderón was one of the representatives of the Republic in the recourse of interpretation on Article 22 of the 1999 Investment Law ending with the Supreme Tribunal 2008 Decision N°1.541. He also participated in 1995 challenge of the constitutionality of the arbitration clause of the Association Agreements of the *Apertura petrolera*. See in Allan R. Brewer-Carías (Compiler), *Documentos del Juicio de la Apertura Petrolera (1996-1999)*, Caracas, 2004, p. 125.

234　See the information in Victorino Tejera Pérez, *Arbitraje de Inversiones*, Magister Thesis, Caracas 2010, *cit.*, pp. 155-158, who personally interviewed Corrales and Capriles (Footnote 558.

235　See *Official Gazette* N° 5.025 Extra of December 20, 1995.

were not secret. Only "the deliberations of the Council of Ministers" themselves were secret.[236]

Ambassador Corrales was also publicly reported to have been the one who made the presentation of the Draft of the Investment Law in another meeting of the Economic Cabinet of the Government, held on September 14, 1999.[237] The Law eventually was approved by President Chavez in the Council of Ministers session held on October 3, 1999,[238] with the assistance of the acting Minister of Energy and Mines, Alí Rodríguez. Based on Minister Rodríguez's prior strong and public objections to international investment arbitration, I assume that he issued a dissenting vote and opposition to the inclusion in Article 22 of the express consent of the State of an open offer to investors to go to international arbitration. His personal and political opinion opposing the idea of the *Apertura Petrolera* in general, and in particular of the State subjection to international investment arbitration, was well known and expressed in 1996 when he was a Member of the Congress[239] and opposed the inclusion of arbitration clauses in the Congress resolution on the General Conditions regarding the Association Agreements of the *Apertura Petrolera*.[240] At the same time, he also was the leading person who filed the popular action brought before the Supreme Court challenging the constitutionality of the arbitration clause authorized by the former Congress to be included in such Association Agreements for oil exploitation.

In effect, in that popular action, Alí Rodriguez and other co-claimants requested the Supreme Court to declare

> "the nullity of Clause Seventeen of Article 2 of the Congress Resolution (Acuerdo) because it provides ... 'The way to resolve controversies on matters others that those attributed to the Control Committee and that could not be resolved by the parties' agreement, shall be arbitration, which will be achieved according to the procedural rules of the International Chamber of Commerce, in force at the moment of the signing of the Agreement.' Such provi-

---

236 The 1999 Organic Law of Central Administration established the same principles regarding the Sector Cabinets, as bodies different from the Council of Ministers. In the 2008 Organic Law on Public Administration, the Sector Cabinets were transformed into Sector Boards with the same functions, but with power of only advisory bodies for the study of matters to be consider in the Council of Ministers (Articles 67, 68).

237 See Eduardo Camel Anderson, "Ley de promoción de inversiones viola acuerdos suscritos por Venezuela," in *El Nacional*, Caracas September 15, 1999.

238 This is the date of the decree Law. Nonetheless, on September 29, 1999, the Vice Minister of Production and Commerce, Eduardo Ortíz Bucarán, informed the press that the Law had been approved in Council of Ministers ten days earlier. See in Maribel Osorio, "Ley de Inversiones otorga al Presidente facultad para otorgar incentivos," in *El Nacional*, September 29, 1999.

239 See the Dissenting Vote in the Congress approval of the Conditions for Association Agreements of the *Apertura Petrolera*, in the Bi-cameral Report of the Energy and Mines Commissions (Senate and Chamber of Representatives) of June 19, 1996, in http://www.minci.gob.ve/doc/convasociacion19061996.pdf

240 See in *Official Gazette* N° 35.754 of July 17, 1995.

sion is a flagrant contravention to article 127 of the Constitution [equivalent to article 151 of the 1999 Constitution] that does not authorize the submission to legal provisions other than the Venezuelan; so we respectfully ask."[241]

In the Final Arguments expressed in the process before the Supreme Court in such case, which took place on January 22, 1998, Alí Rodriguez himself submitted a written argument in which he insisted in asking for the annulment of the Clause, in which, he denounced, that by providing "that always, the doubts and controversies shall be submitted to arbitration according to the rules of the International Chamber of Commerce of Paris," it has allowed that "some Association Agreements have established [for the State] the unconditional renunciation to allege the jurisdictional immunity, arbitrarily declaring that such contractual forms are of mere contractual nature establishing that always such arbitration will take place abroad." He added that "article 127 of the Constitution does not leave the farthest doubt by establishing in a niter way that, in public interest contracts, the doubts and controversies shall be decided by the competent tribunals of the republic, in conformity with the laws." With the challenged clause, Alí Rodríguez argued that "the sovereign abdicate its condition as such, and leaves in the private hands the solution of the doubts and controversies on matters of contracts that are indissolubly *public*, as it were a simple lawsuit between private parties a purely commercial matters."[242]

In that regard, if Rodríguez opposed the Investment Law (as I assume he must have given his position on international arbitration), President Chavez overruled any such opposition and signed into law the Investment Law containing consent to international arbitration. It is perhaps due to potential disagreements in the Council of Ministers, presumably manifested by Alí Rodríguez as Acting Minister of Energy and Mines, that the Decree Law No 356 of October 3, 1999 was only published twenty days later in the *Official Gazette* of October 22, 1999[243] without its corresponding "*Exposición de Motivos*" (Statement of Purposes), although a Draft of such Statement of Purpose was reportedly written.[244] Finally, it must be mentioned that Ambassador Corrales continued his official activities related to the promotion of investments from his position in Geneva until 2002.[245]

---

241   See in Allan R. Brewer-Carías (Compilator), *Documentos del Juicio de la Apertura Petrolera (1996-1999)*, Caracas, 2004 *available at* http://allanbrewercarias.com/Content/449725d9-f1cb-474b-8ab2-efb849fea3/Content/I,%202,%2022.%20%20APERTURA%20PETRO-LERA.%20DOCUMENTOS%20DEL%20JUICIO.pdf, p. 25 .

242   *Id.* pp. 104-105

243   *Official Gazette* N° 5.390 Extra. of October 22, 1999.

244   A Draft of the "Statement of Purpose" of the Investment Law was prepared by Gonzalo Capriles, Legal Expert hired by Cordiplán to work with Ambassador Corrales, with the title: "*Borrador de Exposición de Motivos de la Ley de promoción y protección de Inversiones,*" 1999. See the reference in Victorino Tejera Pérez, *Arbitraje de Inversiones en Venezuela*, Master Thesis, cit. Caracas 2010, p. 154, Footnote 154.

245   See for instance Adriana Cortes, "Venezuela oficializó restricciones a la importación de productos agrícolas," in *El Nacional*, Caracas March 13, 2000.

From all the elements aforementioned, it can be said, contrary to what was concluded in the ICSID tribunals in the *Mobil* and *Cemex* cases, that "the legislative history of Article 22 in this respect" effectively provides very important "information on the intention of the drafters in the Investment Law," and that, in those cases, as in this case, the Tribunal had, indeed, "direct information" on the preparation of the Law as it was discussed in the Executive Council of Ministers. The intention of Ambassador Corrales, who was operating at the specific instance and direction of the Republic as a co-drafter of the Investment Law regarding the unilateral expression of consent for Arbitration given by the Venezuelan State contained in Article 22 of the Law, was clarified in a speech he gave on March 28, 2009 at a Conference organized in Caracas by the *Centro Empresarial de Conciliación y Arbitraje (CEDCA)* on "Investment Arbitration in Comparative Law." At that conference, he explained the following:

> "Today this forum is discussing whether Article 22 of the official version of the Investments law really includes a **unilateral or open offer of arbitration**. ….
>
> In my scope of competence at least, I can state the **intention of offering the possibility of open unilateral arbitration and this can be verified** in several articles on the matter which we published in international journals and which we also took to international congresses. ….Referring to the protection of investors, after dealing with contributions to development, in the first article of 1998, it states more or less something like "the possibility to arbitration must be opened", and in the second article it states "the unilateral possibility of arbitration must be opened to foreign investors".
>
> With this, I hope to leave sufficiently clear that my purpose as co-drafter was to offer in the broadest and most transparent manner the possibility of the investors resorting to international arbitration as a unilateral offer made by the Venezuelan state. And I add that whoever participates in public policies -including those who participate in the drafting or administration of a law or any legal policy instrument- must act with very clear objectives and be always respectful of the principles therein created. At that time we thought –as I continue to believe- that it was absolutely necessary for a public policy closely linked to promoting development such as the case of an investment policy, must aid in the investments acting in pro of development and we thought – as I think today that it is absolutely indispensable for legal instruments to protect the investments from the possibility that the justice system of the country receiving the investment not be independent, as is unfortunately the case we are seeing in Venezuela today."[246]

This statement of Corrales, contrary to what the ICSID tribunals said in the *Mobil* and *Cemex* cases, is fully supported "by the contemporaneous written documents" already discussed, as well as by the "contemporaneous" references published in the press regarding the discussions of the draft in the Council of Ministers. As revealed in these documents, Corrales and Capriles, acting with the express permission of the Republic, intended to include an open, unilateral offer to arbitration in the Investment Law. That is why, there is no other way than to express astonishment, to read what the ICSID Tribunal decided in the *Brandes* case, without any sort

---

246 See in CEDCA, BUSINESS MAGAZINE (June 2009), *Legal Report*, Caracas 2009, pp. 77-82.

of reasoning or motivation, to consider "to be unnecessary, for the purpose of re-solving this dispute, to establish the actual role played by Mr. Corrales in the draft-ing of the LPPI, his knowledge of the issue under discussion and the relevance of his publications about this issue" (¶ 103), affirming that "What is apparent to the Tribu-nal is that Mr. Corrales' opinion cannot provide the basis for finding that Article 22 of the LPPI contains the consent of the Bolivarian Republic of Venezuela to submit to ICSID arbitration (¶ 103).

On this regard, in any case, the Republic failed to present before the Tribunals any evidence that the drafters of the Law had not the intention of providing the State's consent for ICSID Arbitration. As was also pointed out by professor Guido Santiago Tawil in his Dissenting Vote as arbitrator in the *Opic Korimun* **ICSID Case:**

> "9. The Tribunal has explained in paragraphs 109-124 of the Award the relevance of Mr. Corrales testimony and how the Respondent decided not to present evidence contradicting such testimony regarding its intention with respect to Article 22. It has also explained in para-graphs 134-145 of the Award how, differing from *Conoco* or *Mobil,* specific document requests were made by Claimant in this case, how the Tribunal directed Respondent to pro-duce those documents in its possession, custody or control, that although such documents must have existed they were not produced a,nd how the Tribunal considered itself entitled to infer that contemporaneous documents of the Respondents relating to the preparation of the Investment Law would not assist the Respondent to support its contention in this matter.
>
> 10. Notwithstanding so, my fellow arbitrators have concluded that, absent direct evidence of Respondent's intention to consent to ICSID jurisdiction, such negative inference is not enough to determine on its own that Article 22 was intended by Venezuela to be the consent to jurisdiction required by Article 25 of the ICSID Convention.[paras. 125 and 146].
>
> 11. I am unable to agree with such conclusion. The record evidences that while the Claimant has made substantial efforts to prove that Article 22 of the Investment Law provides consent to arbitrate, the Respondent provided no assistance in determining the purpose and in-tention of such provision, notwithstanding its duty to "cooperate with the Tribunal in the pro-duction of the evidence" under Rule 34(3) of the Arbitration Rules."[247]

In my opinion, without doubt, article 22 of the Investment Law was drafted with the purpose of expressing the consent of the State to ICSID international arbitrarion, being such assertion the only logic and rational explanation of the effcorts directly and indifrectly made by the State to change the meaning of article 22 of the Investment Law, without reforming the statute, by means of seeking for a judicial interpretation in contrary sense.

---

247 Available at: http://italaw.com/sites/default/files/case-documents/italaw3014.pdf

VII. THE EFFORTS MADE SINCE 2000 IN ORDER TO CHANGE THE MEANING OF ARTICLE 22 OF THE INVESTMENT LAW BY MEANS OF JUDICIAL INTERPRETATION WITHOUT REFORMING THE STATUTE

Since the 1999 Investment Law was adopted, and particularly after it began to be effective once claims were brought before the ICSID Center, some commentators have thought that article 1999 needed to be revised, in order to "get rid of all the problems it shall create."[248] The fact was that the government never reviewed the Law. Conversely, various attempts were made by individual opponents of the pro-arbitration policy of the Government and to the principle of relative jurisdictional immunity, to obtain a different interpretation from the Venezuelan courts.[249] Eventually, after various failed efforts, the Venezuelan Government itself filed before the Constitutional Chamber of the Supreme Tribunal of Justice a petition for the interpretation of the provision, and obtained, in record time, the Decision N° 1.541 of October 17, 2008 on the supposed interpretation of Article 258 of the Constitution and effectively on the interpretation of Article 22.

Nonetheless, prior to that decision, the same Supreme Tribunal issued other previous decisions concerning Article 22 of the 1999 Investment Law that must be also analyzed in order to understand how the interested legal community reacted to the content of Article 22 of the Investment Law. Only a few months after the approval of the Law, a few judicial review actions began to be filed before the Supreme Tribunal, seeking the annulment of the provision or for a new interpretation. For such purpose, and following a long tradition, the Venezuelan mixed system of judicial review contained all the necessary judicial tools, combining the classical diffuse method of judicial review (American model) established in Article 334 of the Constitution,[250] with the concentrated method of control of constitutionality of statutes (European model), established in Articles 335 and 336 of the Constitution . According to those constitutional Articles, the Supreme Tribunal is the "highest and final interpreter" of the Constitution, having within its role to assure its "uniform interpretation and application" and to guarantee the "supremacy and effectiveness of constitutional norms and principles." For such purpose, the Constitution created the Constitutional Chamber within the Supreme Tribunal, whose role is to exercise "Constitutional Jurisdiction." (Articles 266,1 and 262), having the exclusive power to de-

---

248 See for instante Hildegard Rondón de Sansó, "La muerte definitiva del 22," *Quinto Día*, August 26, 2012, p. 13.

249 See on these decisions Hildegard Rondón de Sansó, *Aspectos jurídicos fundamentales del arbitraje internacional de inversión*, Ed. Exlibris, Caracas 2010, pp. 152 ff..

250 1999 Constitution, Article 334 [...] In the event of an incompatibility between this Constitution and a law or any other legal norm, the Constitutional provisions shall be applied, corresponding to the courts in any case, even *ex officio* (*sua sponte*), to decide what is needed.

clare the nullity of statutes and other State acts issued in direct and immediate execution of the Constitution, or having the force of law (statute) (Article 334).[251]

In effect, following a long tradition,[252] the Venezuelan system of judicial review is a mixed system,[253] which combines the classical diffuse method of judicial review (American model) established in Article 334 of the Constitution,[254] with the concentrated method of control of constitutionality of statutes (European model), established in Articles 335 and 336 of the Constitution. According to Articles 335 and 336, in the Venezuelan legal order, the Supreme Tribunal is the "highest and final interpreter" of the Constitution. Its role is to assure a "uniform interpretation and application" of the Constitution and "the supremacy and effectiveness of constitutional norms and principles." For such purpose, the Constitution created a Constitutional Chamber within the Supreme Tribunal, whose role is to exercise "constitutional jurisdiction" (Articles 266.1 and 262). That Chamber has the exclusive power to declare the nullity of statutes and other State acts issued in direct and immediate execution of the Constitution, or having the force of law (statute) (Article 334).[255]

To implement the concentrated method of judicial review, the Constitution provides for different means of recourse to the courts, including the action for unconstitutionality of statutes (*acción de inconstitucionalidad*), which any citizen can file directly before the Constitutional Chamber.

In addition to the means of judicial review established in the Constitution, the Constitutional Chamber of the Supreme Tribunal of Justice has created a petition (*recurso*) for abstract interpretation of the Constitution (petition for **constitutional interpretation**), which has been extensively used.[256] The petition for **constitutional**

---

251 These include "acts of government," internal acts of the National Assembly, and executive decrees having the rank of statutes.

252 *See* generally Allan R. Brewer-Carías, *Instituciones Políticas y Constitucionales*, Vol. VI, La Justicia Constitucional, Universidad Católica del Táchira, Editorial Jurídica Venezolana, San Cristóbal-Caracas, 1998; Allan R. Brewer-Carías, *Estado de Derecho y Control Judicial*, Instituto de Administración Pública, Madrid 1985; Allan R. Brewer-Carías, *Justicia Constitucional. Procesos y Procedimienos Constitucionales*, Ed. Porrúa, México 2006..

253 *See* Allan R. Brewer-Carías, *Judicial Review in Comparative Law,* Cambridge University Press, Cambridge 1989, pp. 275-277; Allan R. Brewer-Carías, *El Sistema Mixto o Integral de Control de Constitucionalidad en Colombia y Venezuela,* Bogotá 1995..

254 1999 Constitution, Article 334. "[...] In the event of an incompatibility between this Constitution and a law or any other legal norm, the Constitutional provisions shall be applied, corresponding to the courts in any case, even *sua sponte*, to decide what is needed. [...]").

255 These include "acts of government," internal acts of the National Assembly, and executive decrees having the rank of statutes.

256 *See* Supreme Tribunal of Justice, Constitutional Chamber, Decision N° 1077 of September 22, 2000 (Case: *Servio Tulio León Briceño*) in *Revista de Derecho Público* N° 83, Caracas, 2000, pp. 247 ff. *See* Allan R. Brewer-Carías, "Quis Custodiet Ipsos Custodes: De la interpretación constitucional a la inconstitucionalidad de la interpretación," in *VIII Congreso Nacional de Derecho Constitucional, Peru,* Fondo Editorial 2005, Colegio de Abogados de Arequipa. Arequipa, September 2005, pp. 463-489; Allan R. Brewer-Carías, "Le recours

interpretation was created by the Constitutional Chamber without any constitutional or legal support. The Constitutional Chamber attributed to itself the sole power to decide it.[257]

In cases dealing with interpretations **of the Constitution**, the Constitutional Chamber is empowered to give binding effect to its decisions (Article 335). According to Decision N° 1.309 of June 19, 2001 (Case: *Hermann Escarrá*),[258] the decisions of the Constitutional Chamber on petitions of abstract interpretation of the Constitution have effects *erga omnes*, that is to say, they are binding on all courts of the Republic of Venezuela, but they apply only prospectively (*pro futuro, ex nunc*), that is, they do not have retroactive effects.

There is a second type of petition of interpretation in Venezuela: the petition (*recurso*) of **interpretation of statutes**. Unlike the prior one, this type of petition is provided for in the Constitution (Article 266.6) and in the 2004 Organic Law of the Supreme Tribunal of Justice (Article 5, paragraph 1.52). The competence to decide these petitions corresponds to the Chamber of the Supreme Tribunal (Politico-Administrative, Civil, Criminal, Social or Electoral Chamber) that has competence over the subject-matter of the statute.[259] When a petition for interpretation results in the interpretation of a statute, such interpretation applies only prospectively.

A petition (*recurso*) of interpretation has the purpose of obtaining from the Supreme Tribunal a declarative ruling to clarify the content of legal or constitutional provisions. To have standing to file a petition of interpretation, a petitioner must invoke an actual, legitimate and juridical interest in the interpretation based on a particular and specific situation in which he stands, which requires interpretation of the legal or constitutional provision in question. The Constitutional Chamber has held that in a petition for constitutional interpretation, the petitioner must always point to "the obscurity, the ambiguity or contradiction between constitutional provisions."[260] In Decision N° 2.651 of October 2, 2003, the Constitutional Chamber

---

d'interprétation abstrait de la Constitution au Vénézuéla," in *Renouveau du droit constitutionnel, Mélanges en L'honneur de Louis Favoreu*, Dalloz, Paris, 2007, pp. 61-70.

257 No provision of the 2004 Organic Law of the Supreme Tribunal of Justice attributes this power to the Constitutional Chamber of the Supreme Tribunal of Justice. *See* Allan R. Brewer-Carías, *Ley Orgánica del Tribunal Supremo de Justicia. Procesos y Procedimientos Constitucionales y Contencioso-Administrativos*, Editorial Jurídica Venezolana, Caracas 2004, pp. 103-109.

258 Ratified in Supreme Tribunal of Justice, Constitutional Chamber, Decision N° 1.684 of November 4, 2008 (Case: *Carlos Eduardo Giménez Colmenárez*) (Exp. N° 08-1016), available at http://www.tsj.gov.ve/decisiones/scon/Noviembre/1684-41108-2008-08-1016.html, pp. 9-10.

259 Before 2000, the only petition (*recurso*) of interpretation existing in the Venezuelan legal order was the petition of interpretation of statutes in cases expressly provided by them. It was established in Article 42,24 of the 1976 Organic Law of the Supreme Court of Justice, and exclusively attributed to the Politico-Administrative Chamber of that court. This changed in the 1999 Constitution.

260 Allan R. Brewer-Carías, *"Quis Custodiet Ipsos Custodes*: De la interpretación constitucional a la inconstitucionalidad de la interpretación," in *VIII Congreso Nacional de Derecho Cons-*

ruled that the proceeding did not have an adversarial nature, and left it to the court's discretion whether to call to the proceeding those that could have something to say on the matter.[261]

As a matter of principle, when deciding a petition of statutory interpretation, the Chambers of the Supreme Tribunal (other than the Constitutional Chamber) are not empowered to establish a binding interpretation of constitutional provisions. Conversely, when the Constitutional Chamber decides a petition of interpretation of the Constitution, it is not empowered to establish binding interpretations of statutory provisions except when it is as a consequence of the interpretation of the Constitution. Accordingly, a petition of statutory interpretation, for instance, of an Article of the 1999 Investment Law, could only be filed before the Politico-Administrative Chamber of the Supreme Tribunal. Consistent with this, the Constitutional Chamber declined to assume jurisdiction to resolve a petition of interpretation of Article 22 of the 1999 Investment Law filed by three Venezuelan lawyers in 2007.[262] It was within this judicial review system that various attempts were made in order to obtain a judicial interpretation of Article 22 of the Investment Law different to the one expressed in that Article and to the sense of what was intended by be expressed by the Government when the Law was sanctioned. These intents were the following:

1.   *The first attempt, in 2000, to change the meaning of Article 22 of the 1999 Investment Law through a popular action challenging its constitutionality and seeking its annulment*

The first case filed before the Supreme Tribunal in connection with Article 22 of the 1999 Investment Law was an action of unconstitutionality brought before the Constitutional Chamber by two very well known lawyers, Fermín Toro Jiménez and Luis Brito García. This action challenged Articles 17, 22 and 23 of the 1999 Investment Law. The Constitutional Chamber eventually upheld the constitutionality of the challenged provisions in Decision N° 186 of February 14, 2001,[263] allowing me

---

titucional, Peru, Fondo Editorial 2005, Colegio de Abogados de Arequipa. Arequipa, September 2005. pp. 463-489,

261   Supreme Tribunal of Justice, Constitutional Chamber, Decision N° 2.651 of October 2, 2003 (Case: *Ricardo Delgado,* Interpretation of Article 174 of the Constitution), available at http://www.tsj.gov.ve/decisiones/scon/Octubre/2651-021003-01-0241.htm, pp. 30-32.

262   Supreme Tribunal of Justice, Constitutional Chamber, Decision N° 609 of April 9, 2007 (Case: *Interpretation of Article 22 of the 1999 Investment Law*), available at http://www.tsj.gov.ve/decisiones/scon/Abril/609-090407-07-0187.htm.

263   See Supreme Tribunal of Justice, Constitutional Chamber, Decision N° 186 of February 14, 2001 (Case: Challenging the constitutionality Articles 17, 22 and 23 of the 1999 Investment Law, Fermín Toro Jiménez, Luis Brito García), available at http://www.tsj.gov.ve/decisiones/scon/Febrero/186-140201-00-1438%20.htm. Also in *Revista de Derecho Público*, N° 85-88, Editorial Jurídica Venezolana, Caracas 2001, pp. 166-169. See the comments on this decision in José Gregorio Torrealba, *Promoción y protección de las inversions extranjeras en Venezuela, op. cit.,* pp. 123-124; in Eloy Anzola, "El fatigoso camino que transita el arbitraje," in Irene Valera (Coordinadora), *Arbitraje Comercial Interno e Internacional. Reflexiones teóricas y experiencias prácticas*, Academia de Ciencias Políticas y Sociales, Comité Vene-

630 ALLAN R. BREWER-CARÍAS

to conclude that in doing so, the Tribunal eventually accepted the constitutionality of the open offer of consent that the State gave in Article 22 for international arbitration. In effect, when the Constitutional Chamber rejected the allegations of Fermin Toro and Luis Brito considering unconstitutional the provision of article 22 of the Investment Law, because the norm gave the investors the right to reject submitting the disputes to national courts (leaving aside national courts) resorting to arbitration, implying that the provision contained an order or command compelling the State to be submitted to international arbitration at the will of the investors. That meant, in my opinion, the acceptance by the Supreme Tribunal of the text of the Article 22 as it was written with all its consequences, that is, the open offer given by the State for international arbitration, and the disclaimer contained in its last part, giving the investor the option to accept or not offer the open offer, and to resort at its will to national courts.

The claimants in the popular action, acting by them selves were Fernín Toro Jiménez and Luis Brito García. The former had been a Professor of International Law for many years, having had very close tides with the new Government of President Chavez. At the time of the drafting of the Investment Law he was Head of the Diplomatic Academy of the Ministry of Foreign Affairs, and years after he was the Venezuelan Ambassador before the United Nations in New York. He has had a very well known opinion regarding the interpretation of article 127 of the Constitution of 1961 (equivalent to article 151 of the 1999 Constitution) in the sense of considering that in it, "public interest contracts" are equivalent to "international treaties"[264] He also considers that in Venezuela, even with the text of such constitutional article establishing the principle of relative jurisdictional immunity of the State (depending of the nature of the contract), on the contrary and according with the tradition initiated in 1893, the State has "absolute jurisdictional immunity regarding public interest contracts entered with natural or juridical persons of foreign nationality" independently of the "nature" of the contract.[265] Toro Jiménez has said that the opinion of Luis Brito García appears to coincide with his, although expressed with "vacillations."[266]

Nonetheless, the opinion of Luis Brito Grcía, also a well known lawyer and writer in Venezuela, expressed since 1968 has been in the same direction. He has expressed his concerns about the subjection of disputes arising from public interest contracts to foreign courts and to be decided according to laws different to the Ven-

---

zolano de Arbitraje, Caracas 2005, p. 413.; Diego Moya-Ocampos Pancera and Maria del Sol Moya-Ocampos Pancera, "Comentarios relativos a la procedencia de las cláusulas arbitrales en los contratos de interés público nacional, en particular: especial las concesiones mineras," en *Revista de Derecho Administrativo*, N° 19, Editorial Sherwood, Caracas 2006, p. 173.

264 See Fermín Toro Jiménez, *Manual de Derecho Internacional Público*, Vol 1, Universidad Central de Venezuela, Caracas 1982, pp. 324, 437, 438, 441, 443, 444.

265 *Id.* pp. 444, 446, 451, 500, 501.

266 *Id.* pp. 441, 445.

ezuelan law, a situation that he considered as "unacceptable,"[267] arguing in addition that the exception established in article 127 of the Constitution (equivalent to article 151 of the 1999 Constitution) could only be applicable if one considers that contracts of public interest are equivalent to international treaties.[268] Brito finishes his argument, in particular regarding arbitration clauses in public interest contract expressing his criterion that "it is not possible to include in contracts of public interest clauses in which is established that the controversies arising from such contracts would be submitted to arbitration."[269]

Based in these opinions that although expressed many years ago, have been since then constantly in the thought and writings of Toro Jiménez and Brito García, then is possible to understand why they personally filed an action of unconstitutionality against provisions of a statute such as articles 22 and 23 of the Investment Law, that contrary to their thoughts and believes, not only established arbitration as a mean to resolve controversies on investments between the State and a private investor, but in both cases contains the consent given in advance by the State, as an open offer, to submit disputes to arbitration leaving in the hands of the investors to decide to go to arbitration and not to resort to the national courts, allowing them to decide unilaterally to withdraw the case from the possible jurisdiction of national courts. They did not file an action against the possibility in itself of the State being subject to arbitration, as it is also provided in other articles of the Law (articles 18.4 and 21), but only regarding the provisions expressing the consent of the State to go to arbitration.

Because they have for a longtime opposed in their wittings to the State subjected to international or national arbitration, therefore, these two Venezuelan authors and lawyers were the first to formally argue acknowledging the existence in the challenged articles in the Investment Law of the unilateral consent given by the State to go to ICSID arbitration, by giving international investors, and exclusively to them, the right to opt in an unilateral way, in cases of investments disputes, between resorting to arbitration or before the national court; reacting in writing against that decision adopted by the Government when enacting such Law. That is why these two authors and lawyers, in their personal character, as citizens, on April 27, 2000, just five months after the Law was published, filed a popular action challenging the constitutionality of articles 22 and 23 of the Decree Law, as a mean to seek for their annulment by the Supreme Tribunal of Justice, and consequently, to change of the law without needing for it to be formally reformed.

Based on the summary and quotations of the text of the popular action included in the Decision of the Supreme Tribunal N° 186 of February 14, 2001 rejecting the petitioners request, the petitioners based their request on the argument that Article 22 being a provision of "obligatory application" was contrary to Articles 157 and

---

267 Luis Brito García, "Régimen constitucional de los contratos de interés público," in *Revista de Control Fiscal y Tecnificación Administrativa*, N° 50, Contraloría General de la República, Caracas 1968, pp. 124.

268 *Id.* p, 124

269 *Id.* pp. 125-126.

253 of the Constitution, because it "attempts to authorize private parties [*los particulares*] to put aside the application of Venezuelan public law provisions, in favor of arbitral organs, which as it is known, freely apply equity criteria without necessarily following positive law provisions" (pp. 3, 4, 5, 21). The petition also was based on the fact that Article 23 of the Investment Law also was an "obligatory application," which "also is unconstitutional because it attempts to authorize to put aside the administration of justice, which is obligated to the precise application of public order provisions, in favor of resort to 'Arbitral Tribunals,' which in its condition as arbitrators would put aside non-negotiable and sovereign order public provisions [...]" (pp. 3, 4, 5, 21).

From these statements, it is evident that the petitioners understood both, Article 22 and Article 23 of the Law, as open offers of consent made unilaterally by the State to submit controversies on investments to arbitration (international arbitration in the case of Article 22, and national arbitration in the case of Article 23), giving the investors the right - in the words of the petitioners - "to put aside the application of Venezuelan public law provisions in favor of arbitral organs" or "Arbitral Tribunals." The only way to understand the petitioners complain of the unconstitutionality of Articles 22 and 23 is based on the fact that they made possible for "private parties" to decide by themselves to leave aside the application of Venezuelan public law provisions in favor of arbitral organs. This is only possible if the State in such provisions gave already its consent to submit disputes to arbitration. On the contrary, if the State would not have expressed its consent to go for arbitration in such provisions of "obligatory application" - as qualified by the petitioners -, if would have been impossible to say that the provisions (unilaterally) authorizes private parties to go to arbitration, that is "to put aside the application of Venezuelan public law provisions in favor of arbitral organs" or "Arbitral Tribunals."

The Constitutional Chamber, of course, denied the petition, finding that these provisions were consistent with the Constitutional right to arbitration as an "alternative means of justice." (p. 22-23).

In rejecting the petition of annulment as it concerned Article 22, the Constitutional Chamber reasoned that:

> "the plaintiffs incur in the mistake of considering that by virtue of the challenged provisions previously quoted [Articles 22 and 23 of the 1999 Investment Law], there is an attempt to give an authorization to leave aside public law provisions in favor of arbitral organs, taking away from national courts their power to decide the potential disputes that may arise in connection with the application of the Decree Law on the Promotion and Protection of Investments. In fact, this Chamber considers that the prior statement **is an error because it is the Constitution itself which incorporates within the system of justice the alternative means of justice, among which, the arbitration is obviously placed.**" (p. 22).

That is, the Constitutional Chamber accepts that it is the Constitution, that in article 253 incorporates the alternative means of justice, among which, arbitration, so the authorization given in the Law "to leave aside public law provisions in favor of arbitral organs, taking away from national courts their power to decide the potential disputes that may arise in connection with the application" of the Investment Law, as happened in the challenged provisions, was in conformity to the Constitution, warning the petitioners that "from the constitutional provision they claim as violated [article 253], the alternative means of justice are also part of the Venezuelan system of justice" (p. 23). The Constitutional Chamber decision, in addition, referred to article 151 of the Constitution as the founding provision for admitting the possibility for the State to be subjected to arbitration (p. 25)

The Constitutional Chamber noted that the Constitution incorporates alternative means of adjudication, including arbitration, within the Venezuelan system of justice. It highlighted that arbitration –national and international– has a constitutional basis in Article 258 of the 1999 Constitution, and specifically concluded that "**the arbitral settlement of disputes, provided for in** the impugned articles 22 and 23, does not conflict in any manner with the Fundamental Text." (p. 25).

The Constitutional Chamber it its decision referred to the mandate to promote arbitration in Article 258 of the Constitution ("The law shall promote arbitration, conciliation, mediation and any other alternative means of dispute resolution") and explained that:

> "[...] the law, in this case an act with rank and force of such, promoted and developed the referred constitutional mandate, **by establishing arbitration as an integral part of the mechanisms for settlement of controversies** that arises between an international investor, whose country of origin has in effect with Venezuela a treaty or agreement on the promotion and protection of investments, or **controversies with respect to which the provisions of** the Convention Establishing the Multilateral Investment Guarantee Agency (OMGI-MIGA) or **the Convention on the Settlement of Investment Disputes between States and Nationals of Other States (ICSID) are applicable**" (p. 24).

It must be noticed that the Constitutional Chamber, when referring to article 22 of the Investment Law and confirming that arbitration was "an integral part of the mechanisms" for settlement of investments disputes, it refers simply to "controversies with respect to which the provisions of the ICSID Convention "**are applicable**" (p. 24), without copying, using or referring to any other phrases of the article, assuming, with that assertion, that the ICISD Convention applies by virtue of the same provision and because of the consent the State gave in it, which is the justification to the clarification immediately made, in the sense that being a provision that gave the State consent for arbitration, this did not prevent the investor to resort to the national courts, by saying:

> "It must be made clear that in accordance with the challenged norm itself, the possibility of using the contentious means established under the Venezuelan legislation in effect remains **open**, when the potential dispute arises and these avenues are appropriate" (p. 24).[270]

The only meaning of this clarification is to consider that it was made by the Constitutional Chamber because in the decision it was accepted that the State had given its general consent for arbitration, as an open offer, which did not prevent for the

---

270 See the comments in this same sense in Victorino Tejera Pérez, "Do Municipal Investment Laws Always Constitute a Unilateral Offer to Arbitrate? The Venezuelan Investment Law: A Case Study," *loc. cit.*, p. 94; Victorino Tejera Pérez, *Arbitraje de Inversiones*, Magister Thesis, Caracas 2010, *cit.*, p. 168-169.

investor at his will to decide to use the contentious means established in the legislation, allowing then the Chamber to conclude in its decision "that the provision for arbitration under the terms developed in the challenged norm, as it is affirmed by the claimants, does not violate the sovereign power of national courts to administer justice, but in fact – it is reiterated - the programmatic provisions outlined above contained in the Constitution of the Bolivarian Republic of Venezuela, are effectively implemented" (p. 24). In this context, the Constitutional Chamber by upholding the constitutionality of Article 22 in effect did address the "meaning and scope of the provision" in the sense of accepting the consent expressed in it by the Republic, leaving in the hands of the investors to decide to go to international arbitration or to resort to the national courts.

Consequently, in this first attempt to change the meaning of articles 22 and 23 of the Investment Law containing open offers of the State' consent to go to arbitration for the resolution of investments disputes, the Constitutional Chamber rejected the popular action of unconstitutionality filed by Toro Jiménez and Brito García, accepting in particular that Article 22 contains the express consent of the State to submit to international arbitration controversies regarding investment. The quoted reasoning of the Supreme Tribunal would make no sense unless the Constitutional Chamber understood Article 22 as expressing the State's consent to international arbitration, in the same sense that article 23 does it.

In this context, consequently, the Constitutional Chamber by upholding the constitutionality of Article 22 did address the "meaning and scope of the provision." In any case, the opinion on the meaning of article 22 given by the claimants in the popular action Fermín Toro and Luis Brito, remained in the files of the Supreme Tribunal after such upholding the constitutionality of the challenged provisions of the Law. Professors Toro and Brito did not publish in a separate way their comments on the Law after challenging it, and their written arguments were not commonly known.

Nonetheless, in the Venezuelan Public Law Journal (*Revista de Derecho Público*) that same year 2001, after analyzing the Constitutional Chamber Decision N° 186 (not the arguments filed by Toro and Brito), when reporting on the decision, the most important and interesting parts of it, from the stand point of internal public law, references were made, on the one hand, to the challenging of the provision establishing "public contacts for legal stabilization" (art. 17); and on the other hand, to the provision referred to the "admission of international arbitration" (art. 22). The corresponding excerpt of the Decision were published after my review and under my personal direction in the Section of *Jurisprudencia Administrativa y Constitutional* (Constitutional and Administrative Jurisprudence),[271] highlighting the pertinent excerpt considered important in the matter after the sanctioning of the 1999 Constitution. That is why the excerpt regarding the part of the decision dealing with Article

---

271 Section prepared by Secretary General of the *Journal*, Ms. Maria Ramos Fernández, published in the *Revista de Derecho Público*, N° 85-86/87-88, Caracas 2001, pp. 220-225 and pp. 166-169.

was preceded by the phrase: "International Arbitration is admitted in the Constitution as parte of the system of justice, and thus, the solution of controversies established in articles 22 and 23 of the Decree law of Promotion and Protection of Investments is not contrary in any way to the Fundamental Text."[272]

2. The second attempt, in 2007, to obtain a different interpretation of Article 22 of the Investment Law

On February 6, 2007, a group of lawyers (Omar Enrique Valentier, Omar Enrique García and Emilio Enrique García Bolívar) filed a petition or recourse for statutory interpretation of Article 22 of the 1999 Investment Law before the Constitutional Chamber of the Supreme Tribunal, which was rejected by Decision N° 609 of April 9, 2007 because the Chamber lacked competence to decide on the matter.[273] The stated purpose of the petition was to obtain an interpretation of Article 22 "to determine whether [Article 22] established or not the consent necessary to allow foreign investors to initiate international arbitrations against the Venezuelan State" (p. 2).

The petitioners expressed that they were not asking for the Constitutional Chamber to declare Article 22 unconstitutional, a matter that they said, had been resolved in Decision N° 186 of February 14, 2001. Instead they argued that "one thing is that the Article at issue is constitutional and another very different is that such Article establish a general and universal consent to allow any foreign investor to request that its disputes with the Venezuelan State be resolved by means of international arbitration, a matter with respect to which the wording of the Article is not clear" (p. 2). The petitioners formulated before the Court the following specific questions:

> "Does Article 22 of the Law on the Promotion and Protection of Investments contain the arbitral consent by the Venezuelan State in order for all the disputes that may arise with foreign investors to be submitted to arbitration before ICSID?
>
> In case of a negative [answer] (sic), what is the purpose and use of Article 22 of the Law on the Promotion and Protection of Investments?" (p. 2).

In Decision N° 609 of April 9, 2007, the Constitutional Chamber ruled that it had *no* competence to decide on the interpretation of Article 22 of the Investment Law, which corresponded to the attributions of the Politico Administrative Chamber of the Tribunal (p. 12-13). This was a ratification of the Constitutional Chamber's position that it had no competence to decide petitions of interpretation of statutes in an isolated way; its competence being limited to petitions of interpretation of the Constitution and of instruments within the "block of constitutionality, "and of statutes but as a consequence of interpreting constitutional provisions. The Constitutional Chamber concluded that the matter referred to in the Investment Law was "a matter of public law, on the relations (in this case, the solution of controversies) derived from foreign investments in the Venezuelan State, which means that competence,

---

272 See in *Revista de Derecho Público*, N° 85-88, Caracas 2001, p. 166..

273 Available at available at http://www.tsj.gov.ve/decisiones/scon/Abril/609-090407-07-0187.htm.

according to the subject-matter, corresponds to the Politico-Administrative Chamber of this Supreme Tribunal, on the basis of number 6 of article 266 of the Constitution and number 52 of article 5 of the Organic Law of the Supreme Tribunal of Justice." Accordingly, the Constitutional Chamber ordered that the file be transferred to the Politico-Administrative Chamber of the same Supreme Tribunal of Justice.

3.   The third attempt, in 2007, to obtain a different interpretation of Article 22 of the Investment Law

The case on the interpretation of Article 22 of the 1999 Investment Law, rejected by the Constitutional Chamber of the Supreme Tribunal of Justice, once sent to the Politico Administrative Chamber of such Tribunal was decided through Decision N° 927 of June 5, 2007,[274] declaring the request inadmissible because the petitioners lacked standing.

The Politico-Administrative Chamber reasoned that the petitioners had failed to demonstrate the existence of a particular juridical situation affecting them in a personal and direct way that could justify a judicial decision on the scope and application of Article 22 (p. 14). The Politico-Administrative Chamber noted that the petitioners had based their interest only on their activities as lawyers, and had not referred expressly to any personal and direct interest in the requested interpretation. The Chamber also emphasized that a petition of interpretation must not be used for mere academic purposes (p. 15).

4.   The fourth and final attempt, in 2008, to obtain a different interpretation of Article 22 of the Investment Law

After the aforementioned failed attempts by various individuals to obtain judicial decisions interpreting Article 22 of the 1999 Investment Law, the Republic itself, succeeded in obtaining a "custom made" judicial decision issued by the Constitutional Chamber of the Supreme Tribunal of Justice. This was Decision N° 1.541 of October 17, 2008, issued in response to a petition of interpretation of Article 258 of the Constitution filed on June 12, 2008 by representatives of the Attorney General of the Republic (Hildegard Rondón de Sansó, Alvaro Silva Calderón, Beatrice Sansó de Ramírez et al).[275] As mentioned in the petition, this request was prompted by the ICSID cases against the Republic of Venezuela pending at the time the petition was filed (p. 10). Although labeled as a request for constitutional interpretation of Article 258 of the Constitution, the Constitutional Chamber, contradicted its previous ruling, and went on to issue a statutory interpretation of Article 22 of the 1999 Investment Law. As already discussed, this was a matter that the Constitutional Chamber itself had acknowledged to be within the exclusive competence of the Politico-Administrative Chamber.

---

274   Available at http://www.tsj.gov.ve/decisiones/spa/Junio/00927-6607-2007-2007-0446.html.

275   Available at http://www.tsj.gov.ve/decisiones/scon/Octubre/1541-171008-08-0763.htm. It was also published in *Official Gazette* N° 39.055 of November 10, 2008. In this paper, when referring to the Decision N°1541 of 2008, I will quote the pages of the version published in the web site of the Supreme Tribunal.

The Constitutional Chamber's 2008 "custom made" decision has been highly criticized.[276] It was issued as an "obligatory interpretation" (*interpretación vinculante*) of Article 258 of the Constitution, although ostensibly it was an interpretation of Article 22 of the Investment Law. The Constitutional Chamber confirmed that such Article, by itself, does not constitute a general offer to submit disputes to international arbitration before ICSID. For such purpose, in fact, it changed the sense of the provision, depriving it of its content in a certain way pretending to "revoke" the unilateral expression of consent of the State to go to international arbitration it contained, without a formal reform of the statute – which of course has no legal effect.[277] This left without meaning the last part of the provision, the one that allows the investors to opt to go to arbitration or to resort to the national courts.

In effect, in the 2008 Decision Nº 1.541[278] the Supreme Tribunal admitted that it is possible for a State to express its consent to submit the resolution of disputes to international arbitration in a statute (pp 34-38), but it adopted, in a judicial process developed without input from any parties other than the Government, the Government's opinion that Article 22 does not have that effect. The Constitutional Chamber decided the matter in a very unusual abbreviated proceeding within only 120 days (including 30 days of judicial vacation) and without any adversarial hearings. The petition was filed on June 12, 2008 and it was notified to the Constitutional Chamber on June 17, 2008. Only one month later, on July 18, 2008, the Chamber issued a decision admitting the petition, after omitting the oral hearing on the ground that it was a "merely legal" matter. The Constitutional Chamber set a maximum term of 30 days to decide the case, which would begin to count five days after a newspaper notice giving interested parties five days to file their arguments. The newspaper notice was published on July 29, 2008. On September 16, 2008, three individuals filed arguments as third parties (*escrito de coadyuvancia*), but their participation was

---

276 See for example Tatiana B. de Maekelt; Román Duque Corredor; Eugenio Hernández-Bretón, "Comentarios a la sentencia de la Sala Constitucional del Tribunal Supremo de Justicia, de fecha 17 de octubre de 2008, que fija la interpretación vinculante del único aparte del art. 258 de la Constitución de la República," in *Boletín de la Academia de Ciencias Políticas y Sociales*, Nº 147, Caracas 2009, pp. 347-368; Eugenio Herández Bretón, "El arbitraje internacional con entes del Estado venezolano," in *Boletín de la Academia de Ciencias Políticas y Sociales*, Nº 147, Caracas 2009, pp. 148-161; Victorino Tejera Pérez, "Do Municipal Investment Laws Always Constitute a Unilateral Offer to Arbitrate? The Venezuelan Investment Law: A Case Study," pp. 92-109; Victorino Tejera Pérez, *Arbitraje de Inversiones*, Magister Thesis, Caracas 2010, *cit.*, pp. 180-193.

277 See the comments on the inefficacy of such revocation without reforming the Law regarding international arbitration, in Andrés A. Mezgravis, "El estándar de interpretación aplicable al consentimiento y a su revocatoria en el arbitraje de inversiones," in Carlos Alberto Soto Coaguila (Director), *Tratado de Derecho Arbitral*, Universidad Pontificia Javeriana, Instituto peruano de Arbitraje, Bogotá 2011, Vol. II, pp. 858-859.

278 See in general, the comments on this Decision in Tatiana B. de Maekelt; Román Duque Corredor; Eugenio Hernández-Bretón, "Comentarios a la sentencia de la Sala Constitucional del Tribunal Supremo de Justicia, de fecha 17 de octubre de 2008, que fija la interpretación vinculante del único aparte del art. 258 de la Constitución de la República," pp. 347-368.

denied by the Constitutional Chamber on grounds of lack of standing (pp. 1-4). The final decision in the case was issued one month later, on October 17, 2008.

In the Venezuelan judicial review system the recourse of constitutional interpretation was established without any constitutional support by the jurisprudence of the same Constitutional Chamber for the sole purpose of interpreting obscure, ambiguous or inoperative constitutional provisions. As aforementioned, Article 258 requires no such interpretation, as it can be confirmed from its own text in which there is nothing obscure, ambiguous or inoperative. As has been pointed out by Professor J. Eloy Anzola, one of the Venezuelan leading experts on arbitration matters in his comments on the decision, it was obvious that the representatives of the Republic when filing its request for interpretation, "did not hide the real intention of the recourse" that was to obtain "the interpretation of legal norm instead of a constitutional one,"[279] in the sense "that Article 22 of the Investment Law does not contain such consent. It is there where the decision is heading." (pp. 73-74).

The Decision N° 1541 of 2008 states that it is possible for a State to express its consent to submit the resolution of disputes to international arbitration in a statute (pp. 41-44), but it accepted the Government's position that Article 22 does not have that effect.

The Constitutional Chamber decided the matter in a very unusual abbreviated proceeding within only 120 days (including 30 days of judicial vacation) and without any adversarial hearings. The petition was filed on June 12, 2008 and it was notified to the Constitutional Chamber on June 17, 2008. Only one month later, on July 18, 2008, the Chamber issued a Decision admitting the petition, after omitting the oral hearing on the ground that it was a "merely legal" matter.[280] The Constitutional Chamber set a maximum term of 30 days to decide the case, which would begin to count five days after a newspaper notice giving interested parties five days to file their arguments.[281] The newspaper notice was published on July 29, 2008. On September 16, 2008, three individuals filed arguments as third parties (*escrito de coadyuvancia*), but their participation was denied by the Constitutional Chamber on

---

279 See J. Eloy Anzola, "Luces desde Venezuela: La Administración de la Justicia no es monopolio exclusivo del Estrado,"in *Spain Arbitration Review, Revista del Club Español de Arbitraje*, N° 4, 2009, pp. 64, 64.

280 Supreme Court of Justice, Constitutional Chamber: Ruling Related to the Admissibility of the Autonomous Petition for Constitutional Interpretation of the Norm Contained in the Sole Paragraph of Article 258 of the Constitution, Expediente N° 08-0763, July 18, 2008. Magistrate Pedro Rafael Rondón dissented from the decision to admit the petition. He explained that Article 258 was not obscure, and added that the petition was being used to obtain a legal opinion from the Constitutional Chamber, contravening prior decisions of the same Chamber. Finally, he noted that the petition included a request for interpretation of a statutory provision (Article 22) which exceeded the competence of the Constitutional Chamber. Dissent, Decision of July 18, 2008.

281 *Id.*, p. 8.

grounds of lack of standing.[282] The final decision in the case was issued one month later, on October 17, 2008.

As aforementioned, the petition of constitutional interpretation was established by the jurisprudence of the Constitutional Chamber for the sole purpose of interpreting obscure, ambiguous or inoperative constitutional provisions. Article 258 requires no such interpretation. It states that:

> "The law shall promote arbitration, conciliation, mediation and any other alternative means of dispute resolution."

As there is nothing obscure, ambiguous or inoperative in this provision, it is obvious that the real purpose of the petition of constitutional interpretation filed by the representatives of the Republic of Venezuela was not to obtain a clarifying interpretation of Article 258. Instead, they used this petition as a vehicle for obtaining an interpretation of Article 22 of the Investment Law in the sense that it does not contain the State's unilateral consent to arbitration. In particular, the Republic of Venezuela requested a declaration that "article 22 of the 'Investment Law' may not be interpreted in the sense that it constitutes the consent of the State to be subjected to international arbitration" and "that Article 22 of the Investment Law does not contain a unilateral arbitration offer, in other words, it does not overrule the absence of an express declaration made in writing by the Venezuelan authorities to submit to international arbitration, nor has this declaration been made in any bilateral agreement expressly containing such a provision [...]."[283]

The Constitutional Chamber noted that the 1999 Constitution allows the Republic of Venezuela to give its unilateral consent to have disputes, particularly disputes regarding foreign investments, resolved by international arbitration.[284] However, the Constitutional Chamber then went on to interpret Article 22 of the Investment Law and concluded, as the Representatives of the Republic of Venezuela had requested, that this provision did not constitute such an expression of unilateral consent.[285]

There have been numerous critics of this decision that agree with my interpretation that it did not concern Article 258 of the Constitution but an improper request to interpret Article 22.[286]

---

282 Decision N° 1541 of 2008, pp. 5-7.

283 Decision N° 1541 of 2008, p. 9.

284 Decision N° 1541 of 2008, pp. 32, 40.

285 Decision N° 1541 of 2008, pp. 48-53. The flaws in the Constitutional Chamber's reasoning are addressed elsewhere in this Opinion.

286 See the critics mentioned in Eugenio Herández Bretón, "El arbitraje internacional con entes del Estado venezolano," in *Boletín de la Academia de Ciencias Políticas y Sociales*, N° 147, Caracas 2009, pp. 148-161; Victorino Tejera Pérez, "Do Municipal Investment Laws Always Constitute a Unilateral Offer to Arbitrate? The Venezuelan Investment Law: A Case Study," pp. 92-109; Victorino Tejera Pérez, *Arbitraje de Inversiones*, Magister Thesis, Caracas 2010, *cit.*, pp. 180-193.

In addition, Magistrate Pedro Rafael Rondón Haaz, who dissented from the Constitutional Chamber decision to admit the petition (*recurso*), also dissented from 2008 Decision N° 1.541, stressing that the Constitutional Chamber had acted *ultra-vires* when engaging in the interpretation of a statutory provision (Article 22) (pp. 56-59). He reiterated his earlier dissent and stated that:

> Article 258 does not raise any reasonable doubt. It does not require a clarifying interpretation because it only contains a request directed to the Legislator in order to promote arbitration.

> The petition of interpretation at issue had the purpose of obtaining from the Constitutional Chamber a "legal opinion" by means of an *a priori* judicial review process that does not exists in Venezuela. It sought the exercise of a legislative function by the Constitutional Chamber.

> The decision of the majority does not interpret or clarify Article 258 of the Constitution because this clear provision does not give rise to any doubts.

> The Constitutional Chamber exceeded its competence when it engaged in the interpretation of Article 22 of the 1999 Investment Law. The interpretation of statutory provisions is of the exclusive competence of the Politico-Administrative Chamber of the Supreme Tribunal of Justice.

> The Constitutional Chamber contradicted its own jurisprudence and exceeded its powers of constitutional interpretation, as well as its powers of judicial review concerning international treaties.

The dissenting Magistrate correctly noted that the Constitutional Chamber in interpreting Article 22 exercised a "legislative function" by providing, through an *a priori* judicial review procedure, rules that the Legislature must follow in the future in order to express the State's consent to international arbitration through a statute (pp. 56-59). Of course those effects are limited to the Venezuelan courts, that is, the effects of 2008 Decision N° 1.541 under Venezuelan law **do not affect the powers of an ICSID tribunal to interpret Article 22 independently in ruling on its own jurisdiction**.

The political purpose of 2008 Decision N° 1,541, perhaps is the only factor that can explain its arbitrariness and lack of coherence and logical legal analysis. By its own admission, the Constitutional Chamber was operating on the understanding that it was bound to further the interests of the State. (p. 41) ("national sovereignty and self-determination …oblige the organs of the Government to establish the most favorable conditions for the achievement of the interests and purposes of the State"). The Court betrayed its prejudice against the impartiality of arbitral jurisdiction, noting that "settlement of disputes will be made by arbitrators who, in a considerable number of cases, are related to and **tend to favor the interests of multinational corporations, thus becoming an additional instrument of domination and control of national economies [...]**" and adding that "it is somewhat unrealistic simply to make an argument of the impartiality of arbitral justice." (p. 24) (emphasis added). Given these statements, this decision is neither objectively reasonable nor neutral nor is it in any way reliable.

The following year, the Supreme Tribunal of Justice officially "responding" to criticisms formulated by Luis Brito García[287] against the Constitutional Chamber of the Supreme Tribunal decision N° 97 of February 11, 2009 in which the Tribunal dismissed a recourse for the interpretation of Articles 1 and 151 of the Constitution filed by Fermín Toro Jiménez and the same Luis Brito García, published a "Press Communiqué (*Boletín de Prensa*) on its web site on June 15, 2009 ("*Author*: Prensa TSJ").[288] In this Press Communiqué the Supreme Tribunal decided to express some conclusions on the scope of previous decisions adopted by the Constitutional Chamber, without any sort of request made by anybody, without any constitutional process and without any parties or contradictory procedure. It was then a "decision by means of a Press Communiqué,"[289] in which the Supreme Tribunal referred, among other issues, precisely to Article 22 of the Investment Law "declaring" that:

> "The [Supreme Tribunal] decisions eliminate the risk that signified to interpret Article 22 of the Investment Law as an open offer or invitation of Venezuela to be submitted to the jurisdiction of other countries, as it has been tried to argue in the International Forum, by subjects with interests contrary to the Bolivarian Republic of Venezuela, as is the case of the big energy transnational."

This "Press Communiqué" is not a proper judicial decision and does not have force of law.[290] In addition, it confuses submission to an international tribunal with submitting a dispute to "the jurisdiction of other countries."

The "custom-made" 2008 Decision N° 1.541 can only be fully understood by taking into account that unfortunately the Judicial Branch in Venezuela and in particular, the Constitutional Chamber of the Supreme Tribunal, are subject to political interference in all politically sensitive cases. Since 1999, the independence of the Venezuelan Judiciary has been progressively and systematically dismantled, resulting from the tight Executive control over the Judiciary, and especially of the Constitutional Chamber of the Supreme Tribunal of Justice.[291] Since 2000, the appoint-

---

287 See Carlos Díaz, interview to Luis Britto García, "Perdimos el derecho a ser juzgados según nuestras leyes, nunca las juntas arbitrales foráneas han favorecido a nuestro país," *La Razón*, Caracas 14-06-2009, published on June 20, 2009 by Luis Britto García in http://luisbrittogarcia.blogspot.com/2009/06/tsj-lesiono-soberania.html

288 See in http://www.tsj.gov.ve/informacion/notasdeprensa/notasdeprensa.asp?codigo=6941.

289 See Luis Britto García, "¡Venezuela será condenada y embargada por jueces y árbitros extranjeros!," in http://www.aporrea.org/actualidad/a80479.html. Publication date: June 21, 2009.

290 See, e.g., Víctor Raúl Díaz Chirino, "El mecanismo de arbitraje en la contratación pública," in Allan R. Brewer-Carías (Coord.), *Ley de Contrataciones Públicas*, 2d. ed. Editorial Jurídica Venezolana, Caracas 2011, pp. 356-357.

291 Since 2004, and from the academic point of view, I have systematically studied this situation. See for instance, "La progresiva y sistemática demolición de la autonomía e independencia del Poder Judicial en Venezuela (1999-2004)" in *XXX Jornadas J.M Dominguez Escovar, Estado de Derecho, Administración de Justicia y Derechos Humanos*, Instituto de Estudios Jurídicos del Estado Lara, Barquisimeto 2005, pp. 33-174; "La justicia sometida al poder. La ausencia de independencia y autonomía de los jueces en Venezuela por la interminable

ment of Magistrates to the Supreme Court of Justice have been conducted in an un-constitutional manner and in a way that violates the citizens' right to political participation,[292] to a point that the President himself admitted his own influence on the Supreme Tribunal, when he publicly complained that the Supreme Tribunal had issued an important ruling in which it "modified" a Law in 2007, without previously consulting the "leader of the Revolution," and warning courts against decisions that would be "treason to the People" and "the Revolution."[293] The last expression of this executive control on the Supreme Tribunal of Justice occurred in 2010, after an illegitimate "reform" of Organic Law of the Supreme Tribunal of Justice by means of its "reprinting" due to a supposed printing error,[294] allowing the appointment of new

---

emergencia del Poder Judicial (1999-2006)" in *Cuestiones Internacionales. Anuario Jurídico Villanueva 2007,* Centro Universitario Villanueva, Marcial Pons, Madrid 2007, pp. 25-57, *available at* www.allanbrewercarias.com, (Biblioteca Virtual, II.4. Artículos y Estudios N° 550, 2007) pp. 1-37; Allan R. Brewer-Carías, *Dismantling Democracy. The Chávez Authoritarian Experiment,* Cambridge University Press, 2010, pp. 226-244; "Sobre la ausencia de independencia y autonomía judicial en Venezuela, a los doce años de vigencia de la constitución de 1999 (O sobre la interminable transitoriedad que en fraude continuado a la voluntad popular y a las normas de la Constitución, ha impedido la vigencia de la garantía de la estabilidad de los jueces y el funcionamiento efectivo de una "jurisdicción disciplinaria judicial")", in *Independencia Judicial,* Colección Estado de Derecho, Tomo I, Academia de Ciencias Políticas y Sociales, Acceso a la Justicia, Fundación de Estudios de Derecho Administrativo (Funeda), Universidad Metropolitana (Unimet), Caracas 2012.

292 See for instance, what was publicly expressed by the Representative head of the Nomination Committee of magistrates in *El Nacional,* Caracas December 13, 2004. The Inter-American Commission on Human Rights suggested in its Report to the General Assembly of the OAS for 2004 that "These provisions of the Organic Law of the Supreme Court of Justice also appear to have helped the Executive manipulate the election of judges during 2004." See Inter-American Commission on Human Rights, *2004 Report on Venezuela,* par. 180, available at http://www.cidh.oas.org/annualrep/2004sp/cap.5d.htm. See Allan R. Brewer-Carías, "La participación ciudadana en la designación de los titulares de los órganos no electos de los Poderes Públicos en Venezuela y sus vicisitudes políticas" in *Revista Iberoamericana de Derecho Publico y Administrativo,* Year 5, N° 5-2005, San Jose, Costa Rica 2005, pp. 76-95, *available at* www.allanbrewercarias.com, (Biblioteca Virtual, II.4. Artículos y Estudios N° 469, 2005) pp. 1-48

293 See the President's speech identifying the alleged "treason" of judicial decisions taken "behind the back of the Leader of the Revolution" in *Discurso en el Primer Encuentro con Propulsores del Partido Socialista Unido de Venezuela desde el teatro Teresa Carreño* (Speech in the First Event with Supporters of the Venezuela United Socialist Party at the Teresa Carreno Theatre), March 24, 2007, *available at* http://www.minci.gob.ve/alocuciones/4/13788/primer_encuentro_con.html, p. 45. The decision to which he is referring specifically is the Supreme Tribunal of Justice, Constitutional Chamber, Decision N° 301 of February 27, 2007 (Case: *Adriana Vigilanza y Carlos A. Vecchio*) (Exp. N° 01-2862) (*Official Gazette* N° 38.635 of March 1, 2007) in *Revista de Derecho Público,* N° 101, Editorial Jurídica Venezolana, Caracas 2007, pp. 170-177.

294 See the comments of Víctor Hernández Mendible, "Sobre la nueva reimpresión por "supuestos errores" materiales de la Ley Orgánica del Tribunal Supremo, octubre de 2010," y Antonio Silva Aranguren, "Tras el rastro del engaño, en la web de la Asamblea Nacional," in *Revista de Derecho Público,* N° 124, Editorial Jurídica Venezolana, Caracas 2010, pp. 110-113.

Magistrates of the Tribunal without the input of the Nominating Committee established in the Constitution, before the new National Assembly elected in September 2010 convene in January 2011.[295] With this legal "reform," the National Assembly proceeded to fill the Supreme Tribunal of Magistrates with individuals who did not comply with the constitutional conditions to be Magistrate.[296]

Unfortunately, the political control over the Supreme Tribunal of Justice has permeated to all the judiciary, due mainly to the fact that in Venezuela, it is the Supreme Tribunal that is in charge of the government and administration of the Judiciary. This has affected gravely the autonomy and independence of judges at all levels of the Judiciary, which has been aggravated by the fact that during the past decade the Venezuelan Judiciary has been composed primarily of temporary and provisional judges, without career or stability, appointed without the public competition process of selection established in the Constitution, and dismissed without due process of law, for political reasons.[297] The fact is that, in Venezuela, no judge can adopt any decision that could affect the government policies, or the President's wishes, the state's interest, or public servants' will, without previous authorization from the same government,[298] That is why the Inter-American Commission on Human Rights in its *2009 Annual Report*: "The lack of judicial independence and autonomy vis-à-vis political power is, in the Commission's opinion, one of the weakest points in Venezuelan democracy."[299] It is within the aforementioned context that the Government's 2008 request to the Constitutional Chamber of the Supreme Tribunal must be viewed.

Without doubt, the 2008 Decision N° 1.541 was the product of a politically influenced judiciary that was called upon by the Republic of Venezuela to try to bolster its position in pending ICSID cases. The Constitutional Chamber acted *ultra vires* when it undertook to interpret Article 22 of the 1999 Investment Law at the request of the Government of the Republic,[300] because the Politico-Administrative Chamber

---

295   Hildegard Rondón de Sansó, who was Magistrate of the former Supreme Court of Justice, regarding such reform, has said that "the Nomination Judicial Committee was unconstitutionally converted into an appendix of the Legislative Power." See Hildegard Rondón de Sansó, *"Obiter Dicta. En torno a una elección,"* in *La Voce d'Italia*, Caracas, December 14, 2010.

296   See Hildegard Rondón de Sansó, *"Obiter Dicta. En torno a una elección,"* in *La Voce d'Italia*, 14-12-2010.

297   See Inter-American Commission on Human Rights, *Report on the Situation of Human Rights in Venezuela*, OEA/Ser.L/V/II.118, doc. 4 rev. 2, December 29, 2003, par. 174, *available at* http://www.cidh.oas.org/countryrep/Venezuela2003eng/toc.htm.

298   See Antonio Canova González, *La realidad del contencioso administrativo venezolano (Un llamado de atención frente a las desoladoras estadísticas de la Sala Político Administrativa en 2007 y primer semestre de 2008)*, Funeda, Caracas 2008, p. 14.

299   See in ICHR, *Annual Report 2009*, paragraph 483, available at http://www.cidh.oas.org/-annualrep/2009eng/Chap.IV.f.eng.htm .

300   See Allan R. Brewer-Carías, "La Sala Constitucional vs. La competencia judicial en materia de interpretación de las leyes," in *Revista de Derecho Público*, N° 123, Editorial Jurídica Venezolana, Caracas 2010, pp. 187-196.

has exclusive competence (*competencia*) to interpret statutes by means of a recourse of interpretation of statutes; and to interpret such article with the excuse of interpreting Article 258 of the Constitution that needs no interpretation at all.

5.   *The incorrect interpretation adopted by the Supreme Tribunal of Justice in 2008 at the request of the Government*

The Supreme Tribunal of Justice through its Constitutional Chamber in Decision 1541 of October 17, 2008, ruled that Article 22 only recognizes international arbitration where the treaty or agreement itself contains an obligatory submission to arbitration arguing that while the ICSID Convention provides a mechanism for international arbitration, it does not itself provide for the arbitration of any dispute without the separate instrument of consent (pp. 45-48). This is contrary to the wording of the Article, the connection of the words used in it, considering the whole of its text, and the intention of the National Executive when enacting the Law.

In particular, to interpret the expression "if so provides" in Article 22, in the sense if the respective treaty or agreement provides according to its terms, that the dispute shall be submitted to international arbitration, would mean to ignore the final provision of the Article in which a right is given to the international investor to unilaterally opt for international arbitration of to resort before the national courts. The disclaimer of the last phrase of the Article, which the Constitutional Chamber did not even consider, would have no meaning whatsoever, if the condition set forth in the provision were to refer to the need for a consent to be necessarily established in the respective treaty or agreement. This is particularly so because interpreting "if it so establishes" as an equivalent of "if the ICSID Convention establishes consent" would turn this phrase into an impossible condition (a condition that cannot be fulfilled), depriving Article 22 of any meaningful effect. In addition, the interpretation of the condition included in Article 22 of the Investment Law proposed by the Supreme Tribunal of Justice is fundamentally flawed. It is incorrect to interpret "if it so establishes" as a requirement that the State's consent that is already given in the Law needs to be incorporated in the ICSID Convention, because "so" cannot refer to a term ("consent") that is not used in the preceding sentence containing the command ("shall be submitted to international arbitration according to the terms of the respective treaty or agreement"). It is unreasonable to interpret Article 22, as looking to the ICSID Convention to supply the consent that Article 22 itself purports to supply.

The final part of Article 22 ("without prejudice to the possibility of using, as appropriate, the contentious means contemplated by the Venezuelan legislation in effect") is a confirmation that Article 22 is an expression of consent to arbitration, in the sense that it indicates that the unilateral expression of consent of Article 22 does not have the effect of preventing the investor from using domestic litigation remedies. On the contrary, it confirms the unilateral consent given by the State as an open offer that can be accepted or not, at his will, by the investor. If Article 22 were a mere declaration of the State's **willingness** to agree to arbitration in a separate document as opposed to a firm expression of consent to arbitration by the State, there would have been no need to disclaim that Article 22 did not prevent the investor from resorting to domestic remedies.

Consequently, the Supreme Tribunal of Justice proposed reading of Article 22 is to ignore the condition included by the Legislator, and most important, the very right given to the international investor to make a choice which is a result clearly impermissible under either Venezuelan or international legal principles.

On the other hand, the Decision N° 1541 of 2008 (p. 48) attempts to show that interpreting Article 22 as expressing the State's consent to international arbitration would be "unacceptable" in any legal order. Those attempts miss the mark, and show an internal contradiction in the decision. While on the one hand the Constitutional Chamber concedes that a State can express its consent unilaterally and generically in investment legislation (p. 44) a method of consent that is clearly allowed in the ICSID Convention and is firmly established in international practice, on the other hand, the Chamber offers arguments that amount to denying that very same point. In particular, the Decision N° 1541 of 2008 argues that, if Article 22 were interpreted as a general offer of consent and that offer were accepted by an investor, a wide range of matters within the scope of the statute would automatically (*de pleno derecho*) be submitted to arbitration, without the State being able to assess the benefits or disadvantages of arbitration in each case, in violation of an alleged principle of "informed" consent (p. 41). Yet this is precisely what happens, as the intended consequence, whenever a State chooses to consent to arbitration, generically, by means of a national statute or a treaty. In the same vein, the Decision N° 1541 of 2008 argues that interpreting Article 22 as containing "[…] a general offer to submit disputes to the Convention on Settlement of Investment Disputes between States and Nationals of Other States in matters related to foreign investment would absurdly imply that the State cannot select a forum or jurisdiction which is more convenient or favorable to its interests (Forum Shopping) […]." (p. 49). This is not an absurdity at all; it is the normal effect of a generic expression of consent, which is uniformly accepted under the ICSID Convention. A State that gives generic consent to arbitration in treaties or in statutes has given up the right to assess the benefits or disadvantages of international arbitration on a case-by-case basis, in exchange for the investment promotion benefits derived from a generic offer of international arbitration to foreign investors.

The Decision N° 1541 of 2008 also argues that interpreting Article 22 as a generic offer of consent would in effect abrogate bilateral and multilateral investment treaties that provide for different dispute resolution methods, because investors protected by those treaties could invoke the most-favored-nation clause (MFN) contained in them to take advantage of ICSID arbitration, thereby avoiding the dispute resolution mechanisms provided for in the treaty (p. 49). This argument has no basis. Assuming that an investment treaty to which Venezuela is a party has an MFN clause that covers dispute settlement, and assuming that ICSID arbitration is more favorable than the dispute-settlement method contemplated in such treaty, an investor claiming under that treaty would already have the right to invoke ICSID arbitration, because the MFN clause of that treaty would incorporate by reference the dispute-settlement provisions of other investment treaties to which Venezuela is a party, which provide for ICSID arbitration. Under the logic of the Decision N° 1541 of 2008, the treaty of the example would have been "abrogated" by the other treaties, independently of how Article 22 is interpreted, a conclusion that shows that the argument proves nothing. Besides, the argument in the Decision N° 1541 of 2008 amounts to asserting that a State cannot consent to ICSID jurisdiction by statute if it has entered into investment treaties that provide for different methods of dispute resolution, a conclusion that has no basis.

Furthermore, there is no basis for the argument in the Decision N° 1541 of 2008 (pp. 51-52), that interpreting Article 22 as an open offer of consent would create an inconsistency with Articles 5, 7, 8 and 9 of the Investment Law. There is, in fact, no contradiction between the open offer of consent in Article 22 and any of those other provisions.

Article 5 guarantees that the provisions of the Investment Law shall not derogate from any higher level of protection under international treaties or agreements for the promotion and protection of investments. This means that the level of protection under the Investment Law was intended to be a floor, leaving room for higher levels of protection under treaties. Article 5 also provides that, in the absence of any such treaty or agreement, and notwithstanding the MFN clause in the Investment Law, an investor will benefit only from the protection established in that Law (the Investment Law) until such time as the investor is covered by a treaty or agreement containing an MFN clause (in which case the investor will benefit from that particular treaty and any other more favorable treatment required by other treaties, as well as from the Investment Law). Article 5 also requires the State to seek, in the negotiation of such treaties, the greatest level of protection for Venezuelan investors and to ensure that, in any case, such level of protection is not inferior to that granted to the investors of the other contracting State in Venezuela. There is nothing in these provisions that contradict giving consent to ICSID jurisdiction in Article 22.

Article 7 of the Investment Law establishes a basic principle of national treatment. International investments and investors are to have the same rights and obligations as national investments and investors, except as otherwise provided in special statutes and in the Investment Law itself. There is no contradiction between this principle and an open offer of consent to ICSID jurisdiction in Article 22 because, even though such offer necessarily benefits only foreign investors,[301] the offer of consent is an exception provided for in the Investment Law itself.

Article 8 of the Investment Law prohibits discrimination against international investors based on the country of origin of their capital, subject to exceptions for agreements on economic integration or tax matters. There is no contradiction between this provision and the open offer of consent to ICSID jurisdiction in Article 22, which applies to foreign investors in general, without regard to the origin of their capital. Any investor that is a national of a State that is or becomes a party to ICSID can accept the offer of consent. If Article 8 were inconsistent with Article 22, it

---

301 Under Article 25 of the ICSID Convention the investor must be a national of a State other than the State party to the dispute (Venezuela in the situation at issue), except when for reasons of foreign control the parties have agreed that a national of the Contracting State party to the dispute "should be treated as a national of another Contracting State for the purposes of this Convention."

would also be inconsistent with Article 5, because Article 5 presupposes the existence of different legal regimes for international investors, depending on whether
they are nationals of countries having treaties or agreements for the promotion or
protection of investments with Venezuela, or are protected only by the Investment
Law.

Article 9 of the Investment Law establishes the principle that international investments and investors will have the right to the most favorable treatment under
Articles 7 and 8 of the same Law. This means that they are entitled to the better of
national treatment under Article 7 or most-favored-nation treatment (non-
discrimination on the basis of the country of origin of their capital) under Article 8,
with the exceptions authorized by those provisions. Since, as already discussed, the
open offer of consent in Article 22 is not inconsistent with either Article 7 or 8, it
cannot be inconsistent with Article 9.

The two hypothetical examples posed by the Decision N° 1541 of 2008 (p. 52)
do not show any contradiction between the open offer of consent in Article 22 and
any of the other provisions just discussed. In the first hypothetical example, the
Constitutional Chamber argues that, if Article 22 is interpreted as containing an
open offer of consent, a State member of ICSID that does not have a treaty on investments with Venezuela (and has not consented to ICSID jurisdiction in an investment law of its own) would be in a better position *vis-à-vis* a State member of
ICSID that has such a treaty, because the first State would not be subject to ICSID
claims by Venezuelan investors, while the second State would. Once again, this
argument proves nothing. The Investment Law does not guarantee equal treatment
for States; it guarantees certain levels of treatment for investors, primarily international investors. Nor does any provision of the Investment Law require reciprocity,
that is, that Venezuelan investors must have the right to submit controversies to IC
SID against States whose nationals may benefit from the open offer of consent in
Article 22. Since consent to ICSID jurisdiction by statute is by nature a unilateral
act, to challenge such consent on grounds of lack of reciprocity amounts to denying,
contrary to uniform practice, the possibility of any consent by statute.

In the second example, the Decision N° 1541 of 2008 argues that, if Article 22 is
interpreted as an expression of consent, an investor of a country that is a party to the
ICSID Convention but does not have a treaty on investments with Venezuela would
be in a better position than an investor of a country that is not a party to the ICSID
Convention but has a treaty with Venezuela providing for non-ICSID arbitration.
The "better position" would result from ICSID arbitration being supposedly more
favorable to an investor than the non-ICSID arbitration provided in the treaty. In
fact, ICSID arbitration may or may not be more favorable to an investor than another arbitration regime that may be established in a treaty. But even assuming that, in a
particular case, ICSID arbitration is more favorable than the arbitration regime in a
treaty, the hypothesis is not inconsistent with any provision of the Investment Law,
which does contemplate the possibility of parallel regimes under treaties and under
the Investment Law. Under the same logic, the State could not become a party to a
treaty that does provide for ICSID arbitration, because investors protected by such
treaty would receive better treatment than investors protected by a treaty that provides for a different arbitration regime.

Not only is the Decision N° 1541 of 2008 legally unsound, but it is internally contradictory. The following examples serve to illustrate the point:

First, while the Decision N° 1541 of 2008 concedes and pays lip service to the proposition that international law applies to the interpretation of Article 22 (p. 38), it later advocates an interpretation entirely based on alleged principles of "national order." Later, the decision undermines the merits of its own analysis by stating that there is little value ("utility") in an analysis limited to considerations of "internal order." (p. 39)

Second, as already noted, the Decision N° 1541 of 2008 concedes that a State can express its consent to arbitration unilaterally and generically through its investment legislation (p. 44), but it then argues that Article 22 cannot be interpreted as an expression of consent on the ground that it would deprive the Republic of Venezuela from analyzing the advantages of arbitration "in each case" (p. 41) and from choosing "a forum or jurisdiction that is most convenient or advantageous to their interests" ("Forum Shopping")" (p. 49). Put differently, for the Constitutional Chamber, the problem with interpreting Article 22 as an expression of consent is that it would prevent the State from forum shopping on a case by case basis.

Finally, although the Decision N° 1541 of 2008 devotes several paragraphs to reiterating the existence of a constitutional mandate to promote arbitration (Article 258 of the Constitution) (pp. 9-11), it ultimately reaches an interpretation of Article 22 that does nothing of the kind.

The lack of a coherent and logical legal analysis contrasts with various statements in the Decision N° 1541 of 2008 that make it evident that this ruling was the product of a political agenda that the Constitutional Chamber was called upon to defend. By its own admission, the Constitutional Chamber was operating on the understanding that it was bound to further the interests of the State. Most notably, the Chamber stated:

> [A]lthough the Republic and the government, in accordance with the Constitution and current law, are limited in the scope of their authority before other international law provisions based on jurisprudential principles, such as the limitations set forth in Article 13 of the Constitution of the Bolivarian Republic of Venezuela "[...] territory may not be assigned, transferred, leased or in any way conveyed, even temporarily or partially, to foreign governments or other parties subject to international law [...]," also that **national sovereignty and self determination allow and obligate the Federal Government to establish conditions which are most favorable to the interests and purposes of the State** as set forth in the Constitution.[302]

---

302 Decision N° 1541 of 2008, 40-41 (emphasis added). The protection of national sovereignty and self- determination were a constant theme informing various statements in this decision. For example, when holding that the interpretation of all laws must be made in accordance with the Constitution, the Court went on to explain that this meant "*safeguarding the Constitution from all deviations in principles and separation from the political plan which is the will of the people incarnate*" adding that "*part of the protection and guarantee of the Constitution of the Bolivarian Republic of Venezuela therefore rests on an* in fieri, *political perspective resistant to the ideological connections with theories which could restrict it, under*

The protection of national sovereignty and self-determination were a constant theme informing various statements in the 2008 Decision N° 1.541. For example, when holding that the interpretation of all laws must be made in accordance with the Constitution, the Court went on to explain that this meant "to protect the Constitution itself from any deviation of principles and from any separation from the political project that it embodies by the will of the people" adding that "part of the protection and guarantee of the Constitution of the Bolivarian Republic of Venezuela is rooted, then, in a political perspective in fieri, **disinclined toward ideological linkages to theories that may limit, under the pretext of universal validity, the national sovereignty and self-determination**, as required by article 1° eiusdem (…)." (p. 40 (emphasis added). Earlier, 2008 Decision N° 1.541 had expressed some skepticism about a generalized perception of impartiality of arbitral jurisdiction, noting that "the displacement of the jurisdiction from State tribunals to those of arbitration frequently occurs because the settlement of disputes will be made by arbitrators who[,] in [a] considerable [number of] cases[,] are related to and **tend to favor the interests of multinational corporations, thus becoming an additional instrument of domination and control of national economies** [...]" and adding that "it is somewhat unrealistic simply to make an argument of the impartiality of arbitral justice in detriment of the justice provided by the judicial authorities of the Judiciary, to justify the applicability of the jurisdiction of contracts of general interest." (p. 24) (emphasis added).

The following year, the Supreme Tribunal of Justice officially "responding" to critics formulated by Luis Brito García[303] against the Constitutional Chamber of the Supreme Tribunal decision N° 97 of February 11, 2009 dismissing a recourse for the interpretation of articles 1 and 151 of the Constitution filed by Fermín Toro Jiménez and himself (Luis Brito García) , in an unusual way published a "Press Communiqué (*Boletín de Prensa*) in its web site on 15 de junio de 2009 ("*Author*: Prensa TSJ"), with the following title: "The inmunity of Venezuela regarding foreign courts is consolidated" (*Se consolida la inmunidad de Venezuela frente a tribunales*

---

the pretext of universal truths, sovereignty and national self determination, as required by Article 1° eiusdem (...)." Id., p. 40 (emphasis added). Earlier, the Decision N° 1541 of 2008 had expressed some skepticism about a generalized perception of impartiality of arbitral jurisdiction, noting that "moving the jurisdiction of the state courts to arbitration courts, in many situations, is due to the fact that dispute resolution is conducted by arbiters which, in a number of cases, are connected to and **tend to favor the interests of transnational corporations, and thus become an additional instrument of domination and control of national economies**" and adding that "it is not very realistic to simply use the argument of the impartiality of arbitral justice to the detriment of justice administered by the jurisdictional branches of the Judiciary to justify the admissibility of the jurisdiction of general interest contracts." *Id.*, p. 24 (emphasis added).

303 See Carlos Díaz, interview to Luis Britto García, "Perdimos el derecho a ser juzgados según nuestras leyes, nunca las juntas arbitrales foráneas han favorecido a nuestro país," *La razón*, Caracas 14-06-2009, published on June 20, 2009 by Luis Britto García in http://luisbrittogarcia.blogspot.com/2009/06/tsj-lesiono-soberania.html

extranjeros). [304] In such Press Communiqué the Supreme Tribunal decided, presumably in a meeting of all the Magistrates of it's the Chambers, to express some conclusions on the scope of previous decisions adopted by the Constitutional Chamber of the Tribunal, without any sort of request made by anybody, without any constitutional process and without any parties or contradictory procedure. It was then a "decision by means of a Press Communiqué,"[305] in which the Tribunal referred, among other issues, precisely to article 22 of the Investment Law containing the express unilateral consent of the State to submit investments disputes to international arbitration, "declaring" in a contrary sense and confusing "international arbitral tribunals" with "other countries jurisdictions," that:

> "The [Tribunal] decisions eliminate the risk that signified to interpret article 22 of the Investment Law as an open offer or invitation of Venezuela to be submitted to the jurisdiction of other countries, as it has been tried to argue in the International Forum, by subjects with interests contrary to the Bolivarian Republic of Venezuela, as is the case of the big energy transnational."[306]

The Supreme Tribunal in the same "decision by means of a Press Communiqué,"[307] reaffirmed that "any decision or arbitral ruling can be the object of judicial review if it pretend to be executed in Venezuela, as the Constitutional Chamber in decisions N° 1.939/08, in the case: *Corte Interamericana de Derechos Humanos vs. Jueces de la Corte Primera de lo Contencioso Administrativo*", and in the decision N° 1.541/08, which at its turn was ratified in the decision N° 1.942/03." [308]

6. *The insufficient interpretation of Article 22 of the 1999 Investment Law made by the ICSID Tribunals in the Mobil and Cemex Cases*

The matter of the interpretation of Article 22 has also been considered by the ICSID Tribunals in the *Mobil* and *Cemex* cases, in which the tribunals did not decide that Article 22 does not constitute a standing, general consent of the Republic to arbitrate all investments dispute before ICSID. On the contrary, in the *Mobil* case, the ICSID Tribunal decided that Article 22 effectively "creates an obligation to go to arbitration," although it refers to it as "a conditional obligation" (ICSID *Mobil* case,

---

304   See in http://www.tsj.gov.ve/informacion/notasdeprensa/notasdeprensa.asp?codigo=6941

305   See Luis Britto García, "¡Venezuela será condenada y embargada por jueces y árbitros extranjeros!," in http://www.aporrea.org/actualidad/a80479.html. Publication date: June 21, 2009.

306   See in http://www.tsj.gov.ve/informacion/notasdeprensa/notasdeprensa.asp?codigo=6941.

307   See on such sort of judicial "decision," Allan R. Brewer-Carías, "Comentarios sobre el 'Caso: Consolidación de la inmunidad de jurisdicción del Estado frente a tribunales extranjeros,' o de cómo el Tribunal Supremo adopta decisiones interpretativas de sus sentencias, de oficio, sin proceso ni partes, mediante 'Boletines de Prensa,'" in *Revista de Derecho Público*, N° 118, Editorial Jurídica Venezolana, Caracas 2009, pp. 319-330. See on what is called an "unfortunate Press Communiqué," Víctor Raúl Díaz Chirino, "El mecanismo de arbitraje en la contratación pública," in Allan R. Brewer-Carías (Coord.), *Ley de Contrataciones Públicas*, 2d. ed. Editorial Jurídica Venezolana, Caracas 2011, pp. 356-357 .

308   See in http://www.tsj.gov.ve/informacion/notasdeprensa/notasdeprensa.asp?codigo=6941.

¶ 102). This condition to which the obligation is subjected according to the decisions, results from the phrase "if it so provides" or "establishes". The ICSID Tribunals in these two cases completely ignored the existence of the disclaimer included in the last phrase of Article 22, holding that it can be interpreted in two ways, in the sense that the treaty, agreement or convention can (i) provide "for international arbitration," or (ii) "for mandatory submission of disputes to international arbitration" (ICSID *Mobil* case, ¶ 109) ("creates an obligation for the State to submit disputes to international obligation," ICSID *Cemex* case, ¶ 101).

The ICSID Tribunals then concluded, exclusively regarding the condition established in the provision, that "both interpretations are grammatically possible" (ICSID *Mobil* case, ¶ 110; ICSID *Cemex case*, ¶ 102). This assertion, as aforementioned cannot be correct because the second option is a denial in itself not only of the premise that the Article effectively contains a "conditional obligation," but of the disclaimer included in the last phrase of the provision that gives the investor the right to go to arbitration or to resort to the national courts. That is, if it is true that in the first option, the existence in Article 22 of a "conditional obligation" to go to arbitration remains subject only to the condition that the treaties or agreements provide for international arbitration, the second option denies the "conditional obligation" given its requirement of "mandatory submission". This second interpretation would result in a tautology which is grammatically incorrect.

As aforementioned, the ICSID Tribunals also fail in their grammatical analysis to consider and analyze the last part of the Article. By ignoring it, they erase the part of the Article that precisely confirms the existence in the Article of the "conditional obligation" to go to arbitration. This is improper under Venezuelan law because it leaves the last part of the provision to be interpreted as "meaningless."[309]

As it has also been decided by the Venezuelan Supreme Tribunal, "it would be absurd to assume that the legislator would not try to use the most precise and adequate terms to express the purpose and scope of its provisions, or deliberately omit elements that are essential for their complete understanding."[310] This means, from the stand point of the interpreter and according to a well established principles of interpretation of statutes, that one must assume that the legislator did not deliberately draft the provision in an ambiguous way or omit elements that are essential for the complete understanding of the provision. However, one cannot ignore the words, phrases or elements that the legislator used in the provision.

On the other hand, it also is a well established principle of statutory interpretation that the interpreter, when interpreting a statute, must reject and avoid all absurd

---

309 The same is true, of course, for the *Brandes* decision, which also did not ascribe meaning to the disclaimer.

310 Decision N° 4 of November 15, 2001 (*Carmen Cecilia López Lugo v. Miguel Ángel Carpiles Ayala et al.* case), available at http://www.tsj.gov.ve/decisiones/scc/Noviembre/RECL-0004-151101-99003-99360.htm.

interpretations.[311] As mentioned, each and every part of Article 22 has a meaning and purpose, and when interpreting it, no part can be just ignored, as occurred in the ICSID Tribunal decisions which ignore the last part of Article 22. Given the failure of the *Mobil* and *Cemex* tribunals to consider and to give any meaning to a crucial part of Article 22 that is essential for its interpretation, without interpreting the provision "in a manner compatible with the effect sought" by the State making the Law (ICSID *Mobil* case, ¶ 118), these decisions failed to properly interpret the provision in accordance with Venezuelan or international law. In the end, the tribunals' conclusions are for the purpose **of those cases** (and only those cases), and the Tribunal in this case must make an independent decision for itself.

7. The absence of interpretation of Article 22 of the 1999 Investment Law in the ICSID tribunal Brandes Case

The ICSID tribunal *Brandes* case, reached the same conclusion that the *Mobil* and *Cemex* cases, but in an astonishing way, and in contrast with those decisions, without making any effort to interpret Article 22 of the 1999 Investment Law. Instead, the ICSID tribunal limited itself only to refer to the tools and principles for interpretation of the Article, without applying them in the case. It pointed out in its decision: (i) that Article 22 was to be interpreted beginning with the principles of the Venezuelan legal system "starting with the Political Constitution" (ICSID *Brandes* case, ¶ 36, 81) but also in accordance with the principles of international law (ICSID *Brandes* case, ¶¶ 36, 81); (ii) that nonetheless, when applying the principles of Venezuelan law the elements of Article 4 of the Civil Code, were not to be applied together as imposed by the Venezuelan Article 4 of the Civil Code, but in a lineal way, beginning with the grammatical analysis (ICSID *Brandes* case, ¶ 35); (iii) that Article 22 of the Investment Law was required to be interpreted taking into account its relationship with "other legal norms of the Republic" (ICSID *Brandes* case, ¶ 30, 35, 97); and (iv) that it was essential for the Tribunal to analyze other Articles of the Investment Law constituting the immediate context for Article 22 (ICSID *Brandes* case, ¶ 88).

After announcing all these tools and principles of interpretation, but without applying any one of them to the case, the Tribunal issued its decision without analyzing the text of the Article, the words it contains, and the relationship of the words used in it to each other. The Tribunal also does not establish the relationship between the words used in the Article within the content of its entire text, including the last phrase of the disclaimer. That is, the Tribunal, without making any effort to even apply the first step announced in the decision, defined as the "purely grammatical analysis" (ICSID *Brandes* case, ¶ 35), and without any reasoning and motivation, just concludes that "the wording of Article 22 of the LPPI is confusing and imprecise, and that it is not possible to affirm, based on a grammatical interpretation,

---

311 See Supreme Tribunal of Justice, Constitutional Chamber, Decision N° 1.173 of June 15, 2004 (Case: *Interpretación del Artículo 72 de la Constitución de la República Bolivariana de Venezuela*) (Exp. 02-3.215), in *Revista de Derecho Público N° 97-98*, Editorial Jurídica Venezolana, Caracas 2004, pp. 429 ff.

whether or not it contains the consent of the Bolivarian Republic of Venezuela to ICSID jurisdiction" (ICSID *Brandes* case, ¶ 86). The astonishing aspect of this conclusion is that the same Tribunal concluded that it was "unnecessary to summarize" the "laborious and thorough efforts of the parties to scrutinize the meaning of Article 22" (ICSID *Brandes* case, ¶ 85). Within the parameters of any judicial decision in the Venezuelan legal system, this decision would be an unmotivated judicial one, susceptible to being annulled. It is not possible to reach a conclusion like the one expressed by the tribunal under Venezuelan law without explaining which part of the provision is "confusing," which other part is "imprecise," and as any tribunal of justice must do when deciding cases of justice, to make its best effort to try to explain what is imprecise in a provision, and to explain what is confusing in it. This is precisely the role that any tribunal has, not being allowed just to issue a decision without stating the reasons on which it is based.

The only minor and indirect interpretative effort the *Brandes* Tribunal makes regarding Article 22 of the Investment Law is to its "context" (ICSID *Brandes* case, ¶ 87), pointing out that the Investment Law has similarities in its structure and contents with many BITs (ICSID *Brandes* case, ¶ 89). The tribunal fails to refer to the most important similarity for the purpose of interpreting Article 22 of the Investment Law, which is the open offer as expression of consent made by the State in all BITs to date leaving in the hands of the international investor the right to go to arbitration or to resort to national courts. Instead, it asks only why the consent formula of the BITs is not used (ICSID *Brandes* case, ¶ 90).

A law containing an unilateral offer as expression of consent to go to arbitration is not a bilateral treaty on investments, and despite the similarities in the structure or content of the Law with the BITs, the Law must be examined and interpreted as a unilateral effort by a Government seeking to attract investments without negotiating anything with another State (ICSID *Brandes* case, ¶ 94). In this way it differs from BITs that are negotiated between two parties. It is this distinction that the ICSID tribunal in the *Brandes* case failed to consider. It is only because it ignored the essential part of Article 22 that gives the investor the choice to resort to arbitration or to a Venezuelan court that the ICSID tribunal in the *Brandes* case then arrived to the conclusion that "Despite the similarities between the content of the LPPI and that of a BIT, the Tribunal does not find in the Article that it has analyzed (sic) nor in any other Article of the LPPI (sic), any provision that would allow it to assert that it provides for Venezuela's consent to ICSID jurisdiction" (ICSID *Brandes* case, ¶ 92). Of course the Tribunal cannot find the consent of the State if it ignores the right given to the investor to make a choice. The only way to understand this unfounded conclusion is then to recognize that the Tribunal, in its decision, did not actually "analyze" in any way Article 22, or other relevant Articles of the Investment Law (such as Articles 21 and 23).

The *Brandes* tribunal also decides that it is "unnecessary, for the purpose of resolving this dispute, to establish the actual role played by Mr. Corrales in the drafting of the LPPI, his knowledge of the issue under discussion and the relevance of his publications about this issue" because "Mr. Corrales' opinion cannot provide the basis for finding that Article 22 of the LPPI contains the consent of the Bolivarian Republic of Venezuela to submit to ICSID arbitration" (ICSID *Brandes* case, ¶ 103).

Again, it is astonishing how the tribunal can simply and abruptly arrive at these "conclusions," without any reasoning, analysis, and worst of all, without expressing any reason to disqualify in a general and universal way one of the two key people involved in the drafting of the Investment Law, who was put in charge of that task at the request and direction of the Government.

In the end, after extensively copying and enumerating – without analyzing them– the "valid arguments" of the parties, the ICSID Tribunal in the *Brandes* case just concludes without addressing at all the "fundamental" issue, that it "has not found anything that may lead it to depart from the conclusions arrived at by those tribunals [in the *Cemex* and *Mobil* cases] with respect to the specific matter at issue here" (ICSID *Brandes* case, ¶ 114). In the following Paragraph the Tribunal copied the final ruling in those cases (ICSID *Brandes* case, ¶ 115), in which those Tribunals have concluded that Article 22 "does not provide a basis for the jurisdiction of the Tribunal in the present case" (ICSID *Mobil* case, ¶ 140; ICSID *Cemex* case, ¶ 138), without pretending to preclude or prejudice other cases. Nonetheless, the ICSID Tribunal in the *Brandes* case, without any reasoning, arguments, and without explaining any "findings in the paragraphs" of its decision, went further, proclaiming in a general and universal way, and not only for the "present case," that "it is obvious that Article 22 of the Law on Promotion and protection of Investments does not contain the consent of the Bolivarian Republic of Venezuela to ICSID jurisdiction" (ICSID *Brandes* case, ¶ 118). This decision, at least from the point of view of the general standard rules governing judicial decisions in internal law, fails to state the reason on which it is based, that is, it lacks foundation.

The ICSID tribunals in the three decisions, concluded that in cases of unilateral obligations like the one included in article 22 of the Investment Law, derived from the supposed existence of an ambiguity regarding the condition established that could have two possible grammatical interpretation, it was compulsory, after analyzing the principle of effect utile (ICSID *Mobil* case, ¶ 112 ff; ICSID *Cemex* case, ¶ 104), to seek for the "effect sought by the State" when enacting the Law "), which could only be determined establishing the "intention of the State when adopting article 22" (ICSID *Mobil* case, ¶ 118, 119; ICSID *Cemex* case, ¶ 111, 112). Examining the evidences filed in those cases regarding the intention of the State, and bearing in mind the "general evolution in favor of BITs regarding arbitration in the country, the tribunals concluded that they could not draw "the conclusion that Venezuela, in adopting Article 22, intended to give in advance its consent to ICSID arbitration in the absence of such BITs" (ICSID *Mobil* case, ¶ 131; ICSID *Cemex* case, ¶ 126); and "that the legislative history of Article 22 does not establish that, in adopting the Investment Law, Venezuela intended to consent in general and in advance to ICSID arbitration" (ICSID *Mobil* case, ¶ 138; ICSID *Cemex* case, ¶ 135). The *thema decidendum* eventually was referred to evidences in order to establish the intention.

CHAPTER XXII

THE IMPOSITION OF A SOCIALIST (COMMNIST)
ECONOMIC SYSTEM BY STATUTE, WITHOUT REFORMING
THE CONSTITUTION

(2011)

This Paper is part of the essay written for my Presentation in the Panel on "Doing Business in Hostile Environments: The case of Venezuela, Ecuador and Bolivia," in the *Columbia Latin-American Week*, organized by *Columbia International Arbitration Association (CIAA) and Columbia Latin-American Business Law Association (CLABLA)*, held at *Columbia Law School*, Jerome Greene Hall at 116th Street and Amsterdam Ave., April 11 2011.

Based on what is established in the 1999 Constitution, it is not possible to create in Venezuela, by law, political institutions of a Popular or Communal State in order to empty the powers of other organizations of the State or a socialist economic system in order to substitute the mixed economic system provided in the Constitution.

An attempt was made to change this Constitutional model of the State, through a constitutional reform sanctioned by the National Assembly in 2007, with the objective of establishing a socialist, centralized, militaristic, and police State,[312] called the

---

312 See Allan R. Brewer-Carías, *Hacia la Consolidación de un Estado Socialista, Centralizado, Policial y Militarista. Comentarios sobre el sentido y alcance de las propuestas de reforma constitucional 2007,* Colección Textos Legislativos, Nº 42, Editorial Jurídica Venezolana, Caracas 2007.

Popular Power State or Communal State,[313] which, nevertheless, once it was put to popular vote, was rejected by the people on December 7, 2007.[314]

Nevertheless, in disdain of the popular will and defrauding the Constitution, even before the aforementioned referendum was held, the National Assembly in open violation of the constitution began to dismantle the Constitutional State, to be substituted by a Socialist State, structuring in parallel a Popular Power State or Communal State, through the sanctioning of the Communal Councils Law of 2006[315], later reformed and elevated to organic law rank in 2009.[316]

Subsequently, the drive to establish a socialist State in Venezuela was rejected again in the September 26, 2010 parliamentary elections, which the President and the governmental majority of the National Assembly, with a massive campaign for their candidates, posed such elections as a "plebiscite" on the President, his performance and his socialist policies, already previously rejected by the people in 2007; "plebiscite" which the President and his party lost overwhelmingly because the majority of the country voted against them.

However, the President and his party, having lost the absolute control they had over the National Assembly in the elections, which will prevent them in the future from imposing at will the legislation they want, before the newly elected deputies to the Assembly took possession of office in January 2011, again defrauding the popular will and the Constitution, the delegitimized previous National Assembly, in December 2010, hastily proceeded to sanction a set of organic laws through which they have finished defining, outside of the Constitution, the legislative framework for a new State, parallel to the Constitutional State, which is no more than a socialist, centralized, military and police State called the "Communal State."

The organic laws that were approved in December 2010 are the laws on the Popular Power[317]; the Communes[318]; the Communal Economic System[319]; the Public

---

313 See Allan R. Brewer-Carías, *La reforma constitucional de 2007 (Comentarios al Proyecto inconstitucionalmente sancionado por la Asamblea Nacional el 2 de noviembre de 2007)*, Colección Textos Legislativos, N°43, Editorial Jurídica Venezolana, Caracas 2007.

314 See Allan R. Brewer-Carías, "La proyectada reforma constitucional de 2007, rechazada por el poder constituyente originario", in *Anuario de Derecho Público 2007*, Año 1, Instituto de Estudios de Derecho Público de la Universidad Monteávila, Caracas 2008, pp. 17-65

315 See *Official Gazette* N° 5.806 Extra. 04-10-2006

316 See *Official Gazette* N° 39.335 de 12-28-2009. See decision N° 1.676 12-03-2009 Constitutional Chamber, Supreme Tribunal of Justice about the constitutionality of the organic character of the Communal Councils Organic Law, in http://www.tsj.gov.ve/decisiones/scon/diciembre/1676-31209-2009-09-1369.html

317 See *Official Gazette* N° 6.011 Extra. 12-21-2010.The Constitutional chamber through decision N° 1329 12-16-2009 declared the constitutionality of the organic character of this Law. Nevertheless, by December 31, 2010, the decision has not yet been published in the Supreme Tribunal's webpage.

318 See *Official Gazette* N° 6.011 Extra. 12-21-2010. The Constitutional chamber through decision N° 1330 12-17-2010 declared the constitutionality of the organic character of this Law. See http://www.tsj.gov.ve/decisiones/scon/Diciembre/1330-171210-2010-10-1436.html

and Communal Planning[320]; the Social Comptrollership.[321] Furthermore, in the same framework of organizing the Communal State, based on the Popular Power, was approved the reform of the Organic Law of Municipal Public Power and the Public Policy Planning and Coordination of the State Councils.[322]

The delegitimized National Assembly also passed an enabling Law authorizing the President through delegated legislation, to enact laws on all imaginable subjects, including laws of organic nature, emptying the new National Assembly of matters on which to legislate for a period of 18 months until 2012.

However the general defining framework of the Socialist State that is being imposed on Venezuelans, and for which nobody has voted, is based on the exercise of the sovereignty of the people exclusively in a direct manner through the exercise of the Popular Power and the establishment of a Communal State as contained in the Organic Law for Popular Power (LOPP), for which these notes are intended, whose provisions, according to Article 6:

> "Are applicable to all organizations, expressions and areas of Popular Power, exercised directly or indirectly by the people, communities, and social sectors of society, in general, and to situations that affect the collective interest, accepting the principle of legality in the formation, implementation and control of public management."

That is, the provisions of this organic law are all-encompassing; apply to everyone and everything, as an essential part of the new "socialist principle of legality" in the creation, implementation and control of public management.

I.   THE COMMUNAL STATE, POPULAR POWER AND SOCIALISM

The main purpose of these laws is the organization of the "Communal State" which has the commune as its fundamental unit, unconstitutionally supplanting the municipality as the "primary political unit of the national organization" (Art. 168 of the Constitution), through whose organization Popular Power is exercised, and which is manifested in the exercise of popular sovereignty only directly by the people, not by representatives. It is therefore a political system in which representative democracy is ignored, openly violating the Constitution.

The Socialist State sought through these laws, called the Communal State, in parallel to the Constitutional State, is based on this simple scheme: as Article 5 of the Constitution provides that "Sovereignty resides untransferably in the people, who exercise it directly as provided in this Constitution and the Law, and indirectly, by suffrage, through the organs exercising Public Power", being the Constitutional

---

319 See *Official Gazette* N° 6.011 Extra. 12-21-2010. The Constitutional chamber through decision N° 13291 12-17-2010 declared the constitutionality of the organic character of this Law.

320 See *Official Gazette* N° 6.011 Extra. 12-21-2010.The Constitutional chamber through decision N° 1326 12-16-2009 declared the constitutionality of the organic character of this Law.

321 See *Official Gazette* N° 6.011 Extra. 12-21-2010.The Constitutional chamber through decision N° 1329 12-16-2009 declared the constitutionality of the organic character of this Law. See http://www.tsj.gov.ve/decisiones/scon/Diciembre/%201328-161210-2010-10-1437.html

322 See *Official Gazette* N° 6.015 Extra. 12-28-2010.

State structure based on the concept of representative democracy, that is, the exercise of sovereignty indirectly through the vote; the Communal State is now structured based on the direct exercise of sovereignty.

This has even been "legitimized" by the Supreme Tribunal Constitutional Chamber's decisions analyzing the organic character of the laws, such as the one issued in connection with the Organic Law of Municipalities, in which it stated that it had been enacted:

> "developing the constitutional principle of participative and decentralized democracy postulated in the constitutional preamble and recognized in Articles 5 and 6 of the Constitution of the Bolivarian Republic of Venezuela, from whose content the principle of sovereignty is extracted, whose holder is the people, who is also empowered to exercise it "directly" and not only "indirectly" by Public Power organizations; as well as in Article 62, which governs the right of the people to participate freely in public affairs; and especially in Article 70, which expressly recognizes self-management means as popular and active participation mechanisms in the exercise of its sovereignty."[323]

Based on these principles, Article, 8.8 of the LOPP defines the Communal State as:

> "Social and political organization based on the democratic and social State of law and justice established in the Constitution of the Republic, in which power is exercised directly by the people, with an economic model of social property and endogenous sustainable development that allows reaching the supreme social happiness of the Venezuelan people in a socialist society. The basic unit forming the Communal State is the Commune.[324]

What is being sought is to establish a Communal State alongside the Constitutional State: the first one based on the direct exercise of sovereignty by the people; and the second, based on the indirect exercise of sovereignty by the people through elected representatives by universal suffrage; in a system in which the former will gradually strangle and empty competencies from the second. All of this is unconstitutional, particularly because in the structure of the Communal State that is established, at the end, the exercise of sovereignty is indirect through "representatives" that are "elected" in Citizens' Assemblies to exercise Popular Power in the name of the people, called "spokespersons", but that are not elected by the people through universal, secret and direct suffrage.

The system that is being structured, in short, controlled by a Ministry from the National Executive Branch of Government, far from being an instrument of decen-

---

323 See sentence N°1.330, Case: Organic Character of the Law of the Communes 12/17/2010, in http://www.tsj.gov.ve/decisiones/scon/Diciembre/1330-171210-2010-10-1436.html

324 The Organic Law of Municipalities, however, defines the Communal State as follows: "Form of sociopolitical organization, based on the democratic and social state of law and justice established in the Constitution of the Republic, whose power is exercised directly by the people through communal self-governments, with an economic model of social property and endogenous and sustainable development that achieves the supreme social happiness of the Venezuelan people in a socialist society. Forming the basic unit of the Communal State is the commune" (Art.4.10).

tralization – concept that is indissolubly linked to political autonomy – is a central-ized and tightly controlled system of the communities by the central power. That is the reason that explains the aversion to suffrage. Under this framework, a true par-ticipative democracy would be one that guarantees members of the communal coun-cils, the communes and all organizations of the Popular Power to elect their repre-sentatives through universal direct and secret suffrage and not through a show of hands by assemblies controlled by the official party and the executive branch, con-trary to the decentralized Democratic and Social State of Law and Justice estab-lished in the Constitution.

It is in this context, seeking to establish in parallel to the Constitutional State in which the people exercise public power indirectly through representatives elected by direct universal and secret suffrage, that a Communal State is being imposed to the Venezuelans, in which the people allegedly would exercise Popular Power directly through spokespersons who are not elected by direct universal and secret suffrage, but in citizen's assemblies. In this regard, Article 2 of the LOPP, defines Popular Power as:

> "The full exercise of sovereignty by the people in the political, economic, social, cultural, environmental, international, and in all areas of development of society through its diverse and dissimilar organization forms that constitute the Communal State."

All of which is but a fallacy, because ultimately this "building" of the Communal State denies people the right to elect, by direct universal and secret suffrage, those who are going to "represent" them in all these areas, including internationally. It is rather a "building" of organizations to prevent people from really exercising their sovereignty and to impose on them through a tightly centralized control, policies for which they never have a chance to vote.

Moreover, under Article 4 of the LOPP, the purpose of this Popular Power that is exercised by the organs of the Communal State, is to "guarantee the life and social welfare of the people, through the creation of social and spiritual development mechanisms, ensuring equal conditions for everyone to freely develop their person-ality, direct their destiny, enjoy human rights and achieve supreme social happiness; without discrimination based on ethnicity, religion, social status, gender, sexual orientation, identity and expression of gender, language, political opinion, national origin, age, economic status, disability or any other personal, legal or social circum-stance, which has the effect of nullifying or impairing the recognition, enjoyment or exercise of human rights and constitutional guarantees." Of course all these princi-ples of equality are broken since the Communal State system, parallel to the Consti-tutional State, is structured on a unique concept which is socialism, so that anyone who is not a socialist is automatically discriminated. It is not possible, therefore, under the framework of this law to reconcile pluralism guaranteed by the Constitu-tion and the principle of non discrimination on grounds of "political opinion" re-ferred to in this article, with the remaining provisions of this Law pursuing the op-posite, that is, the establishment of a Communal State, whose bodies can only act on the basis of socialism and in which any citizen who has another opinion is excluded.

That is, through this Organic Law the defining framework of a new model of a State parallel and different from the Constitutional State, has been established, called the Communal State, based exclusively and exclusionist on Socialism as the political doctrine and practice, which is the political organization through which the exercise of Popular Power is produced which in turn is "the full exercise of sovereignty by the people."

This Popular Power is based, as declared in Article 3 of the LOOP, "in the sovereign principle of progressiveness of rights established in the Constitution, whose exercise and development is determined by the level of political and organizational consciousness of the people" (Art.3). With this statement, however, far from the universality, prevalence and progressiveness of human rights as guaranteed by the Constitution, what has been established is the total disappearance of the universal concept of human rights, the abandonment of its prevalent character and the deterioration of the principles pro homines and favor libertatis, by conditioning its existence, scope and progressiveness "by the level of political and organizational consciousness of the people", that is, by what the organizations of Popular Power which seek to "organize" the people, all subjected to Socialism, stipulate and prescribe. With it, the conception of human rights as areas that are innate to man and immune against power disappear, moving to a conception of human rights dependent on the orders of the central power, which ultimately controls the entire "building" of the Communal State or Socialist State, as a clear demonstration of totalitarianism which is at the basis of this Law.

In the same sense, Article 5 of the LOPP states that "people's organization and participation in exercising its sovereignty is based on Simon Bolivar the Liberator's doctrine, and is based on socialist principles and values",[325] thus, as has been mentioned, relates the organization of the Communal State in parallel to the Constitutional State, with the socialist political ideology, that is, with socialism, which is defined in Article 8.14 as:

> "a mode of social relations of production, centered in coexistence with solidarity and the satisfaction of material and intangible needs of all of society, which has as fundamental basis, the recuperation of the value of work as a producer of goods and services to meet human needs and achieve supreme social happiness and integral human development. This requires the development of social ownership of the basic and strategic means of production, so that all families, Venezuelan citizens, possess, use and enjoy their patrimony, individual or family property, and exercise full enjoyment of their economic, social, political and cultural rights."[326]

The first thing that must be observed in relation of this provision is the untenable claim of linking "the doctrine of Simon Bolívar" with socialist principles and values.

---

325 The same expression was utilized in the Organic Law of the Communes with respect to their constitution, shaping and functioning (art.2), in the Communal Council's Law (Art.1) and in the Organic Law of Social Comptrollership (Art. 6)

326 The same definition is found in Article 4.14 of the Organic Law of the Communes. Many are the definitions of socialism, but in all, its basic elements can be identified: (i) a system of social and economic organization, (ii) based on collective or State ownership and administration of the means of production, and (iii) State regulation of economic and social activities and distribution of goods, (iv) seeking the gradual disappearance of social classes.

In the work of Bolivar and in relation to his conception of the State nothing can be found about it,[327] it is used only as a pretext to continue to manipulate the Bolivar "cult" to justify authoritarianism, as has occurred so many times before in the history of the country.[328] On the other hand, this provision openly violates the Constitution's guarantee to the right to property (Art. 115) which does not allow for restrictions to only collective or social property, excluding private ownership of the means of production.

Article 5 of the LOPP, moreover, defines as "socialist principles and values" the following:

> "participatory and active democracy, collective interest, equity, justice, social and gender equality, complementarity, cultural diversity, human rights, shared responsibility, joint management, self-management, cooperation, solidarity, transparency, honesty, effectiveness, efficiency, effectiveness, universality, responsibility, social duty, accountability, social control, free debate of ideas, voluntariness, sustainability, environmental protection and defense, guarantee of the rights of women, children and adolescents and of any vulnerable person, geographical integrity and national sovereignty defense." (Art. 5) [329]

This catalog of "principles", of course, is not necessarily linked to socialism, nor is it an exclusively catalog of "socialist principles and values" as it aims to show, in a misappropriation made by the legislator. What the drafter of the rule did, in fact, was to copy the entire set of principles that are defined throughout the Constitution (Preamble and articles 1, 2, 3, 4, 6, 19, 20, 21, 22, 26, 84, 86, 102, 112, 137, 141, 153, 165, 257, 293, 299, 311, 316, 326, for example), which are the values of the Constitutional State. Only in some cases they have not dared to use the classic terminology such as "freedom of expression" and have wanted to replace it with "free

---

327 See Allan R. Brewer-Carías, "Ideas centrales sobre la organización el Estado en la Obra del Libertador y sus Proyecciones Contemporáneas" in *Boletín de la Academia de Ciencias Políticas y Sociales*, N° 95-96, January-June 1984, pp. 137-151.

328 It has been the case of Antonio Guzmán Blanco in the nineteenth century and Cipriano Castro, Juan Vicente Gómez, Eleazar López Contreras and Marcos Perez Jimenez in the twentieth century. John Lynch has noted that: "The traditional worship of Bolívar has been used as a convenient ideology by military dictators, culminating with the regimes of Juan Vicente Gómez and Eleazar López Contreras, who at least more or less respected the basic thoughts of the Liberator, even when they distorted their meaning." Lynch concludes by noting that in the case of Venezuela today, to proclaim the Liberator as basis for policies of the authoritarian regime is a distortion of his ideas. See John Lynch, Simón Bolívar: A Life, Yale University Press, New Haven 2007, p. 304. .See also, Germán Carrera Damas, El culto a Bolívar, esbozo para un estudio de la historia de las ideas en Venezuela, Universidad Central de Venezuela, Caracas 1969; Luis Castro Leiva, De la patria boba a la teología bolivariana, Monteávila, Caracas 1987; Elías Pino Iturrieta, El divino Bolívar. Ensayo sobre una religión republicana, Alfail, Caracas 2008; Ana Teresa Torres, La herencia de la tribu. Del mito de la independencia a la Revolución bolivariana, Editorial Alfa, Caracas 2009. About the history related to these books see Tomás Straka, La épica del desencanto, Editorial Alfa, Caracas 2009.

329 These same principles are listed in relation to the communes in Article 2 of the Organic Law of the Communes, and in relation to social comptrollership in Article 6 of the Organic Law of Social Comptrollership.

discussion of ideas", which of course is not the same, especially since that freedom is not tolerated in a socialist State which knows only a single ideology.

To develop and strengthen Popular Power, ignoring basic constitutional principles and values that all levels of government in Venezuela must have, that they be "elective, decentralized, alternative, responsible, pluralistic and of revocable mandates" as required by article 6 of the Constitution, is that the LOPP has been issued, to supposedly generate:

> "Objective conditions through various means of participation and organization established in the Constitution, in the Law and those that may arise from popular initiative so that citizens may exercise their full right to sovereignty, participatory and active democracy, and the establishment of forms of community and communal self-government for the direct exercise of power" (Art. 1)."

According to the Constitution, the "creation of new decentralized organs at the parish, community, "barrios" and neighborhood levels", is only possible with "a view to guaranteeing the principle of shared responsibility in the public administration of local and state governments, and to develop self-management and joint management processes in the administration and control of state and municipal public services." (Art. 184.6) This means that the mechanisms of participation that can be established under the Constitution are not to empty the Constitutional State structures, that is, the "local and state governments" (like the municipalities), but to strengthen them in governance. Moreover, under the Constitution, there can be no other government than elective, decentralized and pluralistic, yet in the LOPP a parallel State is defined which is the Communal State, structured on "Governments" or "self-governments" that are neither elected nor decentralized nor pluralistic.

On these, Article 14 of the LOPP merely defines "the communal self-government and aggregation systems that arise among their instances" as "a field of action of Popular Power in the development of its sovereignty, by the direct involvement of organized communities, in the formulation, implementation and control of public functions, according the law regulating the matter."

In this context, moreover, the "community" is defined in the LOPP as a "basic and indivisible spatial nucleus made up of people and families living in a specific geographical area, linked by common characteristics and interests who share a history, needs and potentialities on cultural, economic, social, geographical and other measures"(art. 8.4).[330]

II. THE IMPLANT OF A SOCIALIST (COMMUNIST) ECONOMIC SYSTEM

One of the main components of these regulations referred to the Communal State, is the implant in the country, without reforming the Constitution, of a socialist

---

[330] The same definition is repeated in the Organic Law of the Communes (Art 4.4) and in the Organic Law of the Communal Councils (Art. 4.1)

(communist) economic system, named the Communal Economic System, defined in article 18 of the Organic Law on the Popular Power, as an:

> "area of Popular Power that allows organized communities the establishment of economic and financial institutions and means of production, for the production, distribution, exchange and consumption of goods and services, as well as of knowledge and expertise developed under communal forms of social ownership, to satisfy collective needs, social reinvestment of the surplus, and contribute to the country's overall social development in a sustainable manner in accordance with the provisions of the Economic and Social Development Plan of the Nation and the law governing the matter".

This area of Public Power has been regulated by the Organic Law of the Communal Economic System,[331] which is defined in the Organic Law of the communes as a set of social relations of production, distribution, exchange and consumption of goods and services, as well as knowledge and expertise developed by the instances of Popular Power, Public Power, or by agreement between them, through socio-productive organizations under communal forms social property" (Art. 4.13). This is also the definition contained in article 2 of the Organic Law on the Communal Economic System (art. 2).

Consequently, the communal economic system is one that is exclusively developed through "socio-productive organizations" of social communal property, which according to the statute, are only public enterprises of the Communal State and of the Constitutional State, as well as productive family units and interchange (trueque) groups; in which private property is excluded regarding the production means and commercialization of goods ands services.

Consequently the socialist economic system that has been implanted in the country by statute is completely contrary to the economic system of mixed economy guaranteed in the Constitution in which on the contrary, private property and economic freedom are established as fundamental principles of the constitutional system. That is, the economic system established in the Organic Law completely changing the structure of the State could only be established through the convening of a National Constituent Assembly (not even a Constitutional Reform or Amendment), in order to transform the existing mixed economy system into a State economic system controlled by the state, mixed with provisions of primitive and local societies that in the global world of today are simply inexistent. In these provisions, the proposal is to establish misery as a way of life, in order to regulate and justify the interchange (trueque) as a system, thinking perhaps in agricultural and recollecting societies, where at the end of the day, it could be possible to imagine the interchange of a fish for a rabbit, or a professional opinion for a shirt pressing; and propose the creation of local "communal currencies" different from the bolívar that is the official currency provided for in the Constitution. These provisions reminds us the old tickets used in the Haciendas, more than a century ago, with which the rural worker could buy goods in the confined territory of the farm, as provided by the owner. This communal economic system is conceived in the law as a "fundamental tool for the

---

331 See *Official Gazette* N° 6.011 Extra. 12-21-2010.

construction of a new society," which supposedly is only ruled by "socialist princi-ples and values" which the Law, without any historical support declares that suppos-edly are inspired in the Simón Bolívar doctrine (art. 5).

The communal economic system, as established in the Law, as mentioned, is based exclusively on public property, state property (public domain) regarding the production means, so in practice, it is not a right of "society," but of the state appa-ratus, whose development is ruled by a system of centralized planning that elimi-nates any possibility of economic freedom and private initiative, converting the so-cio-productive organizations in mere appendix of the State.

In this sense, public policy planning in the terms established in the Organic Law of Public and Popular Planning,[332] is also defined in Article 17 of the Organic Law of the Public Power as "an area for action that assures, through shared government action among the public institutions and the instances of Popular Power, the imple-mentation of the strategic guidelines of the Economic and Social Development Plan of the Nation for the use of public resources and achievement, coordination and harmonization of plans, programs and projects to achieve the country's transfor-mation, balanced territorial development and fair distribution of wealth." From this provision, the distinction between constitutional State bodies that are designated as "public institutions" and Popular Power instances stand out, confirming the intent of the law to establish a parallel State, the Communal State, with the purpose of empty-ing the content and ultimately stifle the Constitutional State.

On the other hand, in connection with this planning competence, in terms of "participatory planning" the LOPP defines it as the "form of citizens' participation the design, formulation, implementation, evaluation and control of public policies" (Art. 8.11), and in terms of "participatory budget" it is defined "as the mechanism through which citizens propose, debate and decide on the formulation, implementa-tion, monitoring and evaluation of public budgets, in order to materialize the pro-jects leading to the development of communities and the general welfare" (Art. 8.12).

On the other hand, regarding the communal economic system in its socialist con-text, the "socialist model of production" is defined in the Organic Law on the Com-munal Economic System, as:

> "The model of production based on social property, oriented towards the elimination of the social division of work that appertains to the capitalist model. The socialist model of pro-duction is directed to satisfy the growing needs of the population, through new ways of gen-eration and appropriation, as well as the social re-inversion of surplus (art. 6.12) (emphasis added).

From this text, it is clear that the purpose of the Law, is to change the capitalist system and substitute it by force of a law, into a socialist system, imposing a com-munist system, for which the drafters of the Law, perhaps based themselves in some old communist Manual of unsuccessful or failed revolutions, have paraphrased in

---

332 See *Official Gazette* N° 6.011 Extra. 12- 21-2010.

the text of the Law what Carl Marx and Frederic Engels wrote one hundred sixty years ago, in 1845 and 1846 on the "communist society" in their well known book, The German Ideology. [333]

The drafters of the Organic Law on the Communal Economic System, perhaps haven't realized that contemporary societies cannot be reduced to those that used to live from hunt and fishing, or from the survival sowing and raising animals, and that in contemporary globalized societies it is impossible not to base production on the social division of work. They seem not to have realized that after so many years of stagnation and misery trying to impose a communist society, the development of a capitalist system is what has allowed China to catapult the country economically, although subjected to a State capitalist dictatorship. They also seem not to have realized that in Cuba, the communist regime itself cry out for its elimination for which in 2011 has began to throw to the streets dozen of thousands of former public employees, in order to force them to develop private initiatives based in the supposed "slavery" of social division of work and in the supposed product of "slavery" which is private property, convinced that in the current world is impossible to "eliminate the social division of work." Precisely, the contrary to what the drafters of the Venezuelan Law proposed (art. 6.12), ignoring that precisely, by means of the social division of work is that industrial production is possible, and with it, employment generation and wealth.

Instead, in order to eliminate any mean tending to generate wealth, freedom to work and employment, the Venezuelan Law declares as an essential piece of the new economic communal system, the necessary "social re-investment of surplus," as a fundamental principle to guide the socio productive organizations, defined as "the use of the surplus produced by the economic activities of the socio-productive organizations, directed to satisfy the collective needs of the community or the Commune, and to contribute to the integral social development of the country"(art. 6.19). With this principle, the drafters of the Law incorporated in its provisions, other of the pillars of the communist system, as it was conceived by Marx and Engels, as opposed to the capitalist system, as it is the "social re-investment of the surplus" resulting from the economic activity. It must be remembered that, on the contrary, industrial societies have developed from the economic point of view, thanks to the accumulation of the economic surplus created by private entrepreneurs and to its re-investment in order to generate more economic growth, which eventually gave birth to industrialization. It is a system in which if it is true that the social re-investment of part of the surplus is achieved through the tax system, it is based on the free private initiative that generate wealth, and that at the same time, is the one that can help to multiply employment and work, and in general, more economic growth.

---

333 See in Karl Marx and Frederich Engels,"The German Ideology," en *Collective Works*, Vol. 5, International Publishers, New York 1976, p. 47. Also available at: http://www.educa.madrid.org/cms_tools/files/0a24636f-764c-4e03-9c1d-6722e2ee60d7/Texto%20Marx%20y%20Engels.pdf

Based on the utopist and behind the times communist principles of "social property of production means," elimination of the social division of work," and "social re-investment of surplus," the Organic Law of the Communal Economic System has been conceived, without a doubt, in order to implant in Venezuela a communist system contrary to the capitalist system. And for such purpose, the law establishes a omni-comprehensive regulation that must be applied "to all organized communities, communal councils, communes and all the instances of Popular Power, specially to the socio-productive organizations established within the communal economic system;" as well as to "all the organs and entities of the Public Power and private sectors organizations, in their relations with the Popular Power" (art. 3). That is to say, the communist system established in the Law must be applied to all the organs, and entities of the Constitutional State and to all the institutions, enterprises and persons of the private sector; all subjected to a centralized planning system controlled by the state, in which private initiative is banished.

The Law also has established a regime for the acquisition of legal personality of the communal enterprises, parallel to the one established in the Commercial Code, by means of registration before the Ministry for the Communes (art 16). Accordingly, no publicity is regulated regarding such Registry, and no rules are established regarding the attributions of the public official in charge of the registration, except that no registry is possible "when the socio productive project have purposes different to those established in the law" (art. 18). That is, those socio productive organizations that declare themselves as not being socialist, which are not according to the socialist model of production, are not allowed to be registered.

Finally, the extended regulation of the Law regarding the "alternate and solidarity interchange system" must be highlighted, consisting of a communal swap system (art 43) between what are called "prosumidores" (producers-consumers) for the purpose of interchanging "knowledge, information, goods and services," which must be done by means of "an alternate communal currency," being all kind of financial practices prohibited, like the charge of "interest or commissions" (art. 40). In this way, according to the Law, each commune can have its own communal currency, as an "alternate instrument regarding the legal currency in the specific geographical site of the Republic" (art. 52). Of course, these provisions regarding "communal currencies," contradict the global achievements obtained more than a century ago, derived from the regulations that created central banks to whom the monopoly to create currency was given. With these provisions, it seems that the drafters of the Law not only have ignored history, but pretend to return the country we had one hundred years back, confined to the local spheres, bypassing globalization. They even don't realized what the European countries have been doing in order to maintain a supranational currency like the Euro.

PART FIFTH
THE 2007 CONSTITUTIONAL REFORM ATTEMPT AND THE 2009 CONSTITUTIONAL AMENDMENT

CHAPTER XXIII
THE 2007 FAILED ATTEMPT TO CONSOLIDATE AN AUTHORITARIAN, SOCIALIST, CENTRALIZED, REPRESSIVE AND MILITARIST STATE IN THE CONSTITUTION

(2007)

This essay written in order to analyze the *Constitutional Reform Draft* submitted by the late President Chávez to the National Assembly in 2007, which was rejected by the people in the Referendum held on December 2007, and that was designed for the consolidation of an Authoritarian, Socialist, Centralized, Repressive and Militarist State and Government. The reflections contained in this essay were incorporated in my book published in Spanish: *Hacia la consolidación de un Estado socialista, centralizado, policial y militarista. Comentarios sobre el sentido y alcance de las propuestas de reforma constitucional 2007*, Editorial Jurídica Venezolana, Caracas 2007, 157 pp. The text also oriented the text written after the popular rejection of the Reform Draft, published in my book: *La reforma constitucional de 2007 (Comentarios al proyecto inconstitucionalmente sancionado por la asamblea nacional el 2 de noviembre de 2007)*, Editorial Jurídica Venezolana, Caracas 2007, 224 pp.; and in the following articles: "La reforma constitucional en Venezuela de 2007 y su rechazo por el poder constituyente originario," in *Revista Peruana de Derecho Público*, Año 8, Nº 15, Lima, Julio-Diciembre 2007, pp. 13-53; and "La proyectada reforma constitucional de 2007, rechazada por el poder constituyente originario," in *Anuario de Derecho Público 2007*, Año 1, Instituto de Estudios de derecho Público de la Universidad Monteávila, Caracas 2008, pp. 17-65.

I.   A NEW FRAUD UPON THE CONSTITUTION AND ITS REJECTION BY POPULAR VOTE

On November 2nd 2007, the National Assembly of Venezuela, following the proposals made by the President of the "Bolivarian Republic of Venezuela" Hugo Chávez Frías, sanctioned a major constitutional reform[1] in order to transform the *Democratic Rule of Law and Decentralized Social State* established in the 1999 Constitution, into a *Socialist, Centralized, Repressive and Militaristic State*. In the referendum for the approval of the constitutional reform that took place on December 2, 2007, the people rejected the proposed reform.[2]

This rejected constitutional reform was intended to transform the most essential and fundamental aspects of the State, making it possible to consider it one of the most important reforms draft in all of Venezuelan constitutional history. With it, the Decentralized, Democratic, Pluralistic and Social State built and consolidated since the Second World War, would have been radically changed in order to create a Socialist, Centralized, Repressive and Militaristic State, grounded in a "Bolivarian doctrine," which has been identified with "XXI Century Socialism"[3] , and an economic system of State capitalism. This reform was sanctioned following the proposal of the President of the Republic, Hugo Chávez Frías, evading the procedure established in the Constitution for such fundamental change. Thus, it was a reform that defrauded the Constitution, which was sanctioned through a procedure established for other purposes, in order to deceive the people.

The most important consequence of this draft reform from the perspective of citizens was that with it, an official State ideology and doctrine was intended to be formally established in Venezuela. Its was denominated "Socialist" and supposedly "Bolivarian" ideology, which as a State doctrine (in spite of its imprecision -and thus the danger-) would have admit no dissidence. It must not be forgotten that the citizens have a constitutional duty to enforce and assure the enforcement of the Constitution (article 131), thus, if this reform had been approved, all citizens will have had the duty to actively contribute to the implementation of the State official doctrine. Because of this, even a neutral position would not have been admissible. Thus, any thought, any expression of thoughts, any action or omission that could have been considered contrary to the official socialist and "Bolivarian" doctrine, or that the authorities might have consider as not contributing to the development of Socia-

---

1   See Allan R. Brewer-Carías, *La reforma constitucional de 2007 (Comentarios al proyecto inconstitucionalmente sancionado por la Asamblea Nacional el 2 de noviembre de 2007)*, Colección Textos Legislativos, Nº 43, Editorial Jurídica Venezolana, Caracas 2007, 224 pp.

2   According to the information given by the National Electoral Council on December 2, 2007, of 16.109.664 registered electors only 9.002.439 went to vote (44.11% of abstention); and of the voting electors, 4.504.354 rejected the proposal (50.70%). This mean that only 4 379 392 votes where for the approval of the proposal (49.29%). hat mean that only 28% of the registered voters voted for the approval.

3   See *Proyecto de Exposición de Motivos para la Reforma Constitucional, Presidencia de la República, Proyecto Reforma Constitucional. Propuesta del Presidente Hugo Chávez* Agosto 2007, p. 19.

lism, could have been determined to be a violation of a constitutional duty, subject to possible criminalization, and the imposition of criminal sanctions. It was a matter of a unique and official way of thinking, which would not admit any sort of dissidence.

This rejected reform draft was the conclusion of a process that the President began in January of 2007, when he announced that he would propose a series of reforms to the Constitution of 1999[4], and designated for such purpose a Presidential Council for the Reform of the Constitution[5]. This Council was presided over by the President of the National Assembly, and composed of high officials from each of the Branches of Government, including the Second Vice President of the National Assembly and four additional Deputies, the President of the Supreme Tribunal of Justice, the People's Defender, the Minister of Labor, the Attorney General and the Prosecutor General. The Council was instructed by the President in the designating decree, to "work according to the Chief of State's guidelines in strict confidentiality" (art. 2)[6] contrary to the principles of any form of constitutional reform in a democratic country.

Guidelines for the proposed reforms emerged from various discussions and speeches of the President of the Republic. These pointed to, *on the one hand,* the formation of a State of Popular Power or of Communal Power, or, a Communal State *(Estado del Poder Popular o del Poder Communal, o Estado Comunal)* built upon the *"Consejos Comunales"* (Communal Councils) as primary political units or social organizations. These Communal Councils, whose members are not elected by means of universal direct and secret suffrage, were already created by statute in 2006[7] in parallel to the municipal entities, supposedly to channel citizen participation in public affairs. However, they operate within a system of centralized management by the cusp of the National Executive Power without any territorial autonomy[8]. On the other hand, the guidelines for reform suggested by Presidential discussions also referred to the structuring of a Socialist state and the substitution of the system of economic freedom and mixed economy that has been always in place, with a State and collectivist economic system subject to centralized planning, that

---

4   See the 1999 Constitution in *Gaceta Oficial* N° 36.860 of 30 December, 1999, republished in the *Gaceta Oficial* N° 5452 Extraordinaria de of 24 March, 2000. See also commentaries on the Constitution in Allan R. Brewer-Carías, *La Constitución de 1999. Derecho Constitucional Venezolano,* 2 volumes, Editorial Juridical Venezolano, Caracas 2004.

5   Decree N° 5138 of 17 January, 2007, in *Gaceta Oficial* N° 38.607 of 18 January, 2007 establishing the "Consejo Presidencial para la Reforma de la Constitución."

6   Id., art. 2. This was also declared publicly by the President of the National Assembly when she took her seat as part of the Council. *El Universal,* Caracas 20 February, 2007.

7   Ley de Consejos Comunales *Gaceta Oficial Extra.* N° 5.806, 10 April, 2006.

8   See Allan R. Brewer-Carías, "El inicio de la desmunicipalización en Venezuela: La organización del Poder Popular para eliminar la descentralización, la democracia representativa y la participación a nivel local," in *AIDA,Revista de la Asociación Internacional de Derecho Administrativo,* Universidad Nacional Autónoma de México, Asociación Internacional de Derecho Administrativo, México 2007, pp. 49 a 67.

minimizes the role of the individual and eliminates any vestige of economic liberty or private property as constitutional rights.

In accordance with all of these orientations, the 2007 rejected Constitutional Reform was intended to produce a radical transformation of the State creating a completely new juridical order. A change of that nature, according to article 347 of the Constitution of 1999, required the convening and election of a National Constituent Assembly, and could not be undertaken by means of a mere "constitutional reform" procedure. The procedure for "constitutional reform" is applicable only to, "a partial revision of the Constitution and a substitution of one or several of its norms without modifying the structure and fundamental principles of the Constitutional text." This limited constitutional change is obtained through its debate and sanctioning in the National Assembly followed by its approval in a popular referendum.[9].

Nonetheless, despite these constitutional provisions, with the 2007 rejected Constitutional Reform, a repetition of a political tactic that has been a common denominator in the actions of the authoritarian regimen that since 1999 has taken over all branches of government in Venezuela, took place, acting fraudulently with respect to the Constitution[10]. This is to say, to use existing institutions in a manner that appears to adhere to constitutional form and procedure in order to proceed, as the Supreme Tribunal has warned, "towards the creation of a new political regimen, a new constitutional order, without altering the established legal system"[11]. This occurred in February of 1999, in the convening of a consultative referendum on whether to convene a Constituent Assembly when that institution was not prefigured in the then existing Constitution of 1961[12]. It occurred with the December 1999 "Decree on the Transitory Regimen of the Public Powers" with respect to the Constitution of 1999, which was never the subject of an approbatory referendum[13]. It has continued to occur in subsequent years with the progressive destruction of democracy through the exercise of power and the sequestering of successive public rights and liberties, all supposedly done on the basis of legal and constitutional provisions.[14]

---

9   See Allan R. Brewer-Carías, *Hacia la consolidación de un Estado Socialista, Centralizado y Militarista. Comentarios sobre el alcance y sentido de las propuestas de reforma Constitucional 2007*, Editorial Jurídica Venezolana, Caracas, 2007.

10 See the decision of the Constitutional Chamber of the Supreme Tribunal of Justice N° 74 of 25 January, 2006, in *Revista de Derecho Público*, Editorial Jurídica Venezolana, N° 105, Caracas 2006, pp. 76, et seq.

11 See, *Id.*

12 See Allan R. Brewer-Carías, *Asamblea Constituyente y Ordenamiento Constitucional*, Academia de Ciencias Políticas y Sociales, Caracas 1999.

13 See Allan R. Brewer-Carías, *Golpe de Estado y proceso constituyente en Venezuela*, Universidad Nacional Autónoma de México, México 2002.

14 See Allan R. Brewer-Carías, "Constitution Making Process in Defraudation of the Constitution and Authoritarian Government in Defraudation of Democracy. The Recent Venezuelan Experience," Paper delivered in the First Plenary Session, of the VII International Congress of Constitutional Law, on the subject of "The Constitution between conflict and stability." Athens, June 2007. See also, Allan R. Brewer-Carías, "El autoritarismo establecido en fraude

In this instance, once again, constitutional provisions were fraudulently used for ends other than those for which they were established, that is, to pretend making a radical transformation of the State, disrupting the civil order of the Social Democratic State under the Rule of Law and Justice through the procedure for "constitutional reform," in order to convert the State into a Socialist, Centralized, Repressive and Militarist State in which representative democracy, republican alternation in office, and the concept of decentralized power would have disappeared, and in which all power was concentrated in the decisions of the Head of State. This was, and is constitutionally proscribed, and as the Constitutional Chamber of the Supreme Tribunal of Justice summarized it, in its decision N° 74 of 25 January, 2006, referring to a symbolic case, it occurred "with the fraudulent use of powers conferred by martial law in Germany under the *Weimar* Constitution, forcing the Parliament to concede to the fascist leaders, on the basis of terms of doubtful legitimacy, plenary constituent powers by conferring an unlimited legislative power."[15] In the case of the 2007 rejected Constitutional Reform process, the various acts adopted (the Presidential initiative, the sanction by the National Assembly, the convening of referendum by the National Electoral Council) were all challenged for judicial review through actions of unconstitutionality and amparo, and in all cases the Supreme Tribunal in a very diligent way declared all as non admissible.[16]

Nonetheless, the instant fraud upon the Constitution was initially evidenced in the proposals elaborated by the President's Council for Constitutional Reform which began to circulate in June of 2007 despite the "pact of confidentiality" ordered by the President [17], demonstrating the thinking and intentions of the highest government and State officials who composed the Council. Those proposals were later

---

a la Constitución y a la democracia y su formalización en Venezuela mediante la reforma constitucional. (De cómo en un país democrático se ha utilizado el sistema eleccionario para minar la democracia y establecer un régimen autoritario de supuesta "dictadura de la democracia" que se pretende regularizar mediante la reforma constitucional)," in *Temas constitucionales. Planteamientos ante una Reforma,* Fundación de Estudios de Derecho Administrativo, FUNEDA, Caracas 2007, pp. 13-74.

15 See the Constitutional Chamber of the Supreme Tribunal of Justice decision N° 74 of 25 January, 2006 in *Revista de Derecho Público* N° 105, Editorial Jurídica Venezolana, Caracas 2006, pp. 76 ff.

16 Véase el estudio de dichas sentencias en Allan R. Brewer-Carías, *El juez constitucional vs. la supremacía constitucional. O de cómo la Jurisdicción Constitucional en Venezuela renunció a controlar la constitucionalidad del procedimiento seguido para la "reforma constitucional" sancionada por la Asamblea Nacional el 2 de noviembre de 2007, antes de que fuera rechazada por el pueblo en el referendo del 2 de diciembre de 2007,* New York, 4 de diciembre de 2007, en www.allanbrewercarias.com, Parte I,2 (Documentos, 2007)

17 The document circulated in June of 2007 under the title, *Consejo Presidencial para la Reforma de la Constitución de la República Bolivariana de Venezuela, "Modificaciones propuestas."* The complete text was published under the title, *Proyecto de Reforma Constitucional. Versión atribuida al Consejo Presidencial para la reforma de la Constitución de la República Bolivariana de Venezuela,* Editorial Atenea, Caracas 1 July, 2007, 146 pp.

given concrete form in the First Draft Constitutional Reforms presented by the President of the Republic to the National Assembly on the 15th of August of 2007[18], proposing a radical transformation of the State in order to create a new juridical order[19]. Finally, the defrauding of the Constitution was consummated in November 2007, by the sanctioning of the Constitutional Reform by the National Assembly, in which:

FIRST, the State was proposed to be converted into a Centralized State of concentrated power under the illusory guise of a Popular Power, implying a definitive elimination of the federal form of the State, rendering political participation impossible, and degrading representative democracy. All of this was envisaged to be done by means of the supposed organization of the population to participate in the Councils of the Popular Power ("*Consejos del Poder Popular*") such as the Communal Councils ("*Consejos Comunales*"). These were institutions wholly lacking of autonomy, whose members are not to be elected; they were to be controlled from the head of the national government, and in their functioning they were to be managed by a single national official socialist party, which is an instrument the Government created during 2007.

SECOND, in addition, the State was proposed to be converted into a Socialist State, with a political official doctrine of socialist character, named in addition as "Bolivarian doctrine," by mean of which any thoughts different to the official one was rejected and, thus, any dissidence, due to the fact that the official political doctrine was incorporated in the Constitution itself, as a State and Society's doctrine and policy, was proscribed constituting a constitutional duty for all citizens to comply and assure its compliance. As a consequence, the basis for criminalizing all dissidence was been formally established.

THIRD, the State was proposed to be converted into a State owned, socialist and centralized economy, by means of the elimination of economic liberty and private

---

18   The full text was published as the *Proyecto de Reforma Constitucional. Elaborado por el ciudadano Presidente de la República Bolivariana de Venezuela, Hugo Chávez Frías*, Editorial Atenea, Caracas agosto 2007, 58 pp.

19   In this sense the Director of the National Electoral Council, Mr. Vicente Díaz, stated on July 16th, 2007, that "the presidential proposal to reform the constitutional text modifies fundamental provisions and for that reason it would be necessary to convene a National Assembly to approve them." This member of the electoral council was consulted on this matter on, Unión Radio, on August, 16, 2007, available at: http://www.unionradio.com.ve/Noticias/Noticia.aspx?noticiaid=212503. The initiation of the reform process in the National Assembly could have been challenged before the Constitutional Chamber of the Supreme Tribunal on the basis of its unconstitutionality. Nonetheless, the President of the Constitutional Chamber of the Supreme Tribunal of Justice -who was in addition a member of the Presidential Council for the Reform of the Constitution-, made it clear that "no legal action related to modifications of the constitutional text would be heard until such modifications had been approved by citizens in referendum.," adding that "any action must be presented after a referendum, when the constitutional reform has become a norm, since we cannot interpret an attempted norm. Once a draft reform has become a norm we can enter into interpretations of it and hear nullification actions." See report by Juan Francisco Alonso, *El Universal*, 18 August, 2007.

initiative as constitutional rights, as well as by the disappearance of the constitutional right to private property; the conferring of the means of production to the State, to be managed through a centralized planning; the configuring of the State into an institution on which all economic activity depends, and to whose bureaucracy the totality of the population is subject. All of these reforms collided with the ideas of liberty and solidarity that are proclaimed in the Constitution of 1999, and, in addition, established a State that serves as a substitute for society itself and private economic initiative, which it minimizes.

FOURTH, the State was proposed to be also converted into a Repressive (Police) State, due to the regressive character of the regulations established in the reform regarding human rights, particularly, civil rights, and the expansion of the emergency powers in the hands of the President which was authorized inclusive to indefinitely "suspend" constitutional rights.

FIFTH, finally, the State was proposed to be converted into a Militarist State, on the basis of the role that was assigned to the "Bolivarian Armed Force" (*"Fuerza Armada Bolivarian"*) which was configured to function wholly under the Chief of State, with the additional creation of a new component of the armed force, the "Bolivarian National Militia" (*"Milicia Nacional Bolivariana"*).

All these reforms implied the radical transformation of the Venezuelan political system, seeking to establish a Centralized Socialist, Repressive and Militaristic State of Popular Power, departing fundamentally from the concept of a civil Social Democratic State under the Rule of Law and Justice based upon a mixed economy that were regulated in the Constitution of 1999.

Moreover, under the sanctioned reforms, representative democracy at the local level and territorial political autonomy would have materially disappeared, being substituted by a supposed "participative and protagonist democracy" that was in fact to be controlled centrally and totally by the Chief of State, and which proscribed any form of political decentralization and territorial autonomy.

In this way, eight years after the sanctioning of the 1999 Constitution by a National Constituent Assembly totally controlled by the President of the Republic, in 2007 the Constitution was proposed to be changed again, this time through a National Assembly also wholly controlled by his followers.

Nonetheless, as aforementioned, on December 2, 2007, according to article 344 of the Constitution, the Constitutional Reform sanctioned by the National Assembly on November 2, 2007,[20] was submitted to a referendum held on December 2, 2007,

---

20   Véase sobre la propuesta de reforma constitucional de 2007: Allan R. Brewer-Carías, *Hacia la consolidación de un Estado Socialista, Centralizado, Policial y Militarista, Comentarios sobre el sentido y alcance de las propuestas de reforma constitucional 2007,* Colección Textos Legislativos, N° 42, Editorial Jurídica Venezolana, Caracas 2007, 157 pp; y *La Reforma Constitucional de 2007 (Comentarios al proyecto inconstitucionalmente sancionado por la Asamblea Nacional el 2 de noviembre de 2007),* Colección Textos Legislativos, N° 43, Editorial Jurídica Venezolana, Caracas 2007, 224 pp.

in which the popular vote expressing the will of the original constituent power rejected it.

According to the Constitution, the consequence of the will expressed by the people was that no new constitutional reforms on the same matters could be again proposed during the constitutional term (2006-2012).

Yet, even though the 2007 Constitutional Reform was rejected by the people, it is important to analyze its contents, which clearly shows the shape of the authoritarian government Venezuela has had during the past decade (1999-2009). For such purpose, I will analyze the meaning and scope of the reform, as was sanctioned by the National Assembly, comparing in each case the proposed changes with the corresponding provision of the 1999 Constitution, in the following parts: 1. *Proposed changes to the fundamental principles of the organization of the State,* that sought to transform the democratic decentralized State into the Socialist centralized State; 2. *Proposed changes to the political system* that sought to transform representative democracy by a supposed popular participation conducted by a Central Power. 3. *Proposed changes to the form of the State* that sought to definitively eliminate the vestiges of a centralized Federation through the total centralization of the State. 4. *Proposed changes to the Organization of the National Power* that sought to accentuate the presidential system. 5. *Proposed changes to the economic Constitution* that sought to transform a social State and promoter of a mixed economy, into a socialist State with a centralized confiscatory state economy. 6. *Proposed changes to the human rights regime,* with a regressive content regarding individual rights, in order to establish a Repressive State, guardian of the official, unique ideology; and 7. *Proposed changes to the regimen of the Armed Forces,* that sought to transform the State into a Militarist State.

II. PROPOSED CHANGES TO THE FUNDAMENTAL PRINCIPLES OF THE ORGANIZATION OF THE STATE: FROM THE DEMOCRATIC DECENTRALIZED STATE TO THE CENTRALIZED SOCIALIST STATE

Throughout 2007, and particularly in his Speech at the Presentation of the *Draft Constitutional Reforms* before the National Assembly[21], the President of the Republic said that the reforms' main objective was "the construction of a Bolivarian and socialist Venezuela"[22]. This is to say, as he explained, to sow "socialism in the political and economic realms"[23]. This is something that the Constitution of 1999 did not do. When the Constitution of 1999 was sanctioned, said the President, "We were not

---

21   See *Discurso de Orden pronunciado por el ciudadano Comandante Hugo Chávez Frías, Presidente Constitucional de la República Bolivariana de Venezuela en la conmemoración del Ducentécimo Segundo Aniversario del Juramento del Libertador Simón Bolívar en el Monte Sacro y el Tercer Aniversario del Referendo Aprobatorio de su mandato constitucional,* Sesión especial del día Miércoles 15 de agosto de 2007, Asamblea Nacional, División de Servicio y Atención legislativa, Sección de Edición, Caracas 2007.

22   Id., p. 4

23   Id., p. 33.

projecting the road of socialism [...] Just as candidate Hugo Chávez repeated a million times in 1998, 'Let us go to a Constituent [Assembly]', so candidate President Hugo Chávez said [in 2006]: 'Let us go to Socialism' and, thus, everyone who voted for candidate Chávez then, voted to go to socialism"[24].

Thus, the Draft Constitutional Reforms presented by the President on this basis, and sanctioned by the National Assembly on November 2nd 2007, proposed according to what the President said in his Speech: the construction of "Bolivarian Socialism, Venezuelan Socialism, our Socialism, and our socialist model."[25] It was a socialism whose "basic and indivisible nucleus" was "the community" ("*la comunidad*"), one "where common citizens shall have the power to construct their own geography and their own history."[26] This was all based on the premise that, "real democracy is only possible in socialism"[27]. However, this supposed "democracy" referred to, was one which, as the President proposed and was included in the rejected 2007 Constitutional Reform regarding article 136, was "not born of suffrage or from any election, but rather is born from the condition of organized human groups as the base of the population." Of course, this was a "democracy" that was not a democracy, as there can be no democracy without the election of representatives.

The President in his Speech summarized all his reform proposals in this manner: "on the political ground, deepen popular Bolivarian democracy; on the economic ground, create better conditions to sow and construct a socialist productive economic model, our model; the same in the political field: socialist democracy; on the economic, the productive socialist model; in the field of Public Administration: incorporate new forms in order to lighten the load, to leave behind bureaucracy, corruption, and administrative inefficiency, which are heavy burdens of the past still upon us like weights, in the political, economic and social areas."[28].

The proposals for the construction of socialism, were, moreover, linked by the President to Simón Bolivar's 1819 Draft Constitution. The President stated that Bolivar's draft was "perfectly applicable to a socialist project: one perfectly well can take the original Bolivarian ideology as a basic element of a socialist project"[29].

---

24 Id., p. 4. This is to say it is sought to impose the wishes expressed by only 46% of inscribed voters in the Electoral Register who voted to reelect the President, upon the remaining 56% of registered voters who did not vote for the presidential re-election. According to official statistics from the National Electoral Council, out of a universe of 15,784,777 registered voters, only 7,309,080 voted to re-elect the President.

25 See *Discurso de Orden pronunciado por el ciudadano Comandante Hugo Chávez Frías, cit.* p. 34

26 Id., p. 32.

27 Id., p. 35.

28 Id., p. 74

29 Id., p. 42. It should be remembered that only one month before the President's Speech on Presenting the Proposed Constitutional Reforms, the former Minister of Defense, General in chief Raúl Baduel, who was in office until July 18, 2007, stated in his speech on leaving the Ministry of Popular Power for the Defense, that the president's call to "construct Socialism

Nonetheless, all one need to do is read Bolivar's 1819 "Angostura Discourse" on presenting the draft Constitution of Angostura, to realize that nothing there expressed has to do with a "socialist project" of any kind. [30].

The rejected 2007 Constitutional Reform, without doubt, proposed to alter the basic foundations of the State. This is true particularly with respect to the proposals on: the constitutional amplification of the so-called "Bolivarian doctrine"; the substitution of the democratic, social State under the rule of law for the Socialist State; the elimination of decentralization as a policy of the State designed to develop public political participation; the dismantling of the organization of the Public Administration; and, the elimination of budgetary discipline and the unity of the treasury.

1. *Bolivarian Doctrine as a Supposed Doctrine of the Socialist State*

One of the innovations of the Constitution of 1999 was the change in the name of the "Republic of Venezuela" to the name, the "Bolivarian Republic of Venezuela" (article 1). This substituted the name the Republic has had since 1811, with the sole exception of the period between 1821 and 1830 when the denomination disappeared because Venezuela itself disappeared as an independent state and was integrated into the Republic of Colombia, precisely upon the proposal of Simón Bolívar. This latter political organization could then be considered as the "Bolivarian conception" of the State: one in which Venezuela, as such, simply ceased to exist.

That is why, the name change in 1999, in principle, had nothing to do with Simón Bolívar and his thought, nor with the construction of socialism -since just as the President stated in his August 15th, 2007 Speech, in 1999 socialism had not been proposed. The name change at that time had in reality a partisan political motivation, drawing the name from the political group established by the President of the Republic, but which could not legally use the name of the "Bolivar" as a functioning political party. In this manner, it was the "Bolivarian party" that gave the Republic its name[31] and the teaching of the *"ideario bolivariano"* (Bolivarian Thoughts) became obligatory in schools (Article 170).

But in 2007, the President of the Republic, with his proposed reforms, and the National Assembly, through its sanctioning of the 2007 Constitutional Reform, iden-

---

for the XXI Century, implied a necessary, pressing and urgent need to formalize a model of Socialism that is theoretically its own, autochthonous, in accord with our historical, social, political and cultural context." He added, "Up until this moment, this theoretical model does not exist and has not been formulated." It is hard to imagine that it could have been formulated just one month later.

30   See Simón Bolívar, *Escritos Fundamentales*, Caracas, 1982. See also, Pedro Grases (Ed), *El Libertador y la Constitución de Angostura de 1819,* Caracas, 1969; and, José Rodríguez Iturbe (ed.), *Actas del Congreso de Angostura,* Caracas, 1969.

31   According to the Ley de Partidos Politicos, *Gaceta Oficial* N° 27.725, April 30, 1965, political parties cannot use the name of the Founders of the country nor the homeland symbols. The political organization the President formed before campaigning for the 1998 presidential election was called *Bolivarian Movement 200*. That name could not be used to call the political party he founded, the Fifth Republic Movement (Movimiento V República).

tified the "Bolivarian doctrine" with the socialist political and economic model of the State, and this was identified with the Republic itself. It is in this sense, then, that the expression "*Bolivariano*" must be understood. The proposed reform to article 100 of the Constitution of 1999 declared the Bolivarian Republic as "the historical product of a confluence of various cultures." It was in the same sense of the complete identification between Socialism and "Bolivarianism" that the 2007 Constitutional Reform, identified the Armed Force as the Bolivarian Armed Forces *("Fuerza Armada Bolivariana"*) (Articles 156.8; 236.6; 328; 329); and the components of the armed forces as the Bolivarian National Army, the Bolivarian National Navy, the Bolivarian National Air Force, the Bolivarian National Guard, and the Bolivarian National Militia (article 329).

Moreover, the proposed reform to article 328 of the Constitution stated that the functioning of the Bolivarian Armed Forces was to be realized "by means of the study, planning and execution of Bolivarian military doctrine," that is to say, according to the Socialist doctrine, in order that they be enabled to guarantee the independence and sovereignty of the Nation, to preserve it from external or internal attack, and assure the integrity of the national geographic space.

In addition, the proposed reform of article 103 of the Constitution pretended to seal the relationship between Bolivarianism and Socialism, by stating that the priority investment that the State has to made in education, must to be done "according to the humanistic principles of the Bolivarian socialism."

2.   *The substitution of the Social Democratic State under the rule of law and justice ("Estado social y democrático de derecho y de justicia") for a socialist state*

Article 2 of the Constitution of 1999, following the tradition of contemporary constitutionalism, defines Venezuela as a "Social democratic state under the rule of law and justice." This is a phrase *("Estado democrático y social de derecho y de justicia"*) that was constructed precisely in order to design a non-socialist State, just as it was adopted in the post war contemporary constitutions like the Constitution of the Federal Republic of Germany of 1949 (CONST. F.R. GER., 1949, art. 20,1); in the Spanish Constitution of 1978 after the raising of democracy (CONST. SPAIN 1978, art. 1°) and in Latin America, for example, in the Constitution of Colombia of 1991 (CONST. COL. 1991, art. 1°).

This corresponds to a conception of a liberal, non-socialist State in a mixed economy, which follows the contemporary trends of the "social State," which is one with obligations to resolve problems of social justice. This leads the State to intervene in economic and social activity, as a provider of benefits, assistance and services *("Estado prestacional"*). This social character of the State derives principally from the fundamental values of equality and non-discrimination (Articles 2 and 21); and from the declaration of the principle of social justice as a foundation of the economic system (Article 299). The democratic State, is the concept through which the whole of the political organization of the Nation rests upon the principle of representative democracy, which derives from the Preamble of the Constitution of 1999 (with the term "democratic society"), and is present in its articles 2, 3, 5 and 6, which identify the fundamental value of constitutionalism as democracy that is exercised through representatives ("elective democracy"), as well as through instruments of direct democracy. The Rule of Law State ("*Estado de derecho*") is the concept of a State under the Rule of Law, or Legality, as is provided in the Preamble to the Constitution of 1999. The concept implies that all acts of the State and the Public Administration must adhere to the principle of legality (Article 141), and are subject to independent judicial control (Articles 7, 137,258, 334 and 336). The state is also defined, for this reason, as a State of Justice, in which justice, beyond the mere affording of formal procedure is guaranteed (Article 26).

Even though the 2007 Constitutional Reform makes no mention of article 2 of the Constitution of 1999, it is evident that its sense is radically altered by the creation of a Socialist State in place of the traditional Social Democratic State under the Rule of Law and Justice state. This is so because the model of a Socialist State is absolutely incompatible with that of the Social Democratic State under the Rule of Law and Justice. This confirms, again, the deception of reforming the Constitution in order to establish a Socialist state without proposing to change its article 2; justifying the claims that supposedly fundamental aspects of the State have been left untouched by the reform, and that, thus, the convening of a National Constituent Assembly is unnecessary to approve them.[32] This is to say, the 2007 Constitutional Reform was the result of one more fraud upon the Constitution.

In that Constitutional Reform, references to the Socialist State are contained in many articles, and in particular in the following: in article 16 of the Constitution where "the Communes and Communities" ("*Comunas y Comunidades*") were created as "the basic and indivisible spatial nuclei of the Venezuelan Socialist State"; in article 70, which added to the definition of the "means of political participation and protagonism of the people in the direct exercise of their sovereignty" the only objective to be directed "for the construction of socialism"; and, in the same article, where a stipulation was added to the mention of various forms of citizens' political associations, requiring that they be, "constituted to develop the values of mutual cooperation and socialist solidarity"; in article 112, where it was established that the economic model created, to achieved "the best conditions for the collective and cooperative construction of a Socialist Economy"; and, in article 113 that stated the need to constitute "mixed corporations and/or socialist units of production."

In addition in the rejected constitutional reform, in article 158 it was stated that "the State must promote people's participation as a national policy, devolving its power and creating the best conditions for the construction of a Socialist democracy"; article 168 referred to the socialist means of production; articles 184 and 300 mentioned the Socialist economy; article 299 mentioned the socialist principles which was to found the socio economic system; and articles 318 and 320 referred to the Socialist State and to the socialist development of the nation.

---

32   The President of the National Assembly stated this on August 23, 2007, upon the approval of the *Draft Constitutional Reform*, as a whole, in the first debate. See *El Universal*, Caracas, August 24, 2007.

3. *The elimination of decentralization as a state policy*

The Constitution of 1999, in its article 4, states that "The Bolivarian Republic of Venezuela is a federal decentralized State in the terms consecrated by this Constitution." The Constitution incorporated some elements of the Organic Law of Decentralization, Delimitation and Transfer of Competencies of the Public Powers of 1989 [33] which promoted the transfer of certain competencies of the National Public Power to the State Powers. As a policy of the State, decentralization was also reflected in a variety of other norms contained in the Constitution of 1999. These include, for example: article 6, that defines the government as "decentralized"; article 16, in its reference to "municipal autonomy and political administrative decentralization"; article 84 that refers to a decentralized national public health system; articles 269 and 272 on the decentralized administration of justice and the penitentiary system; article 285 on a decentralized electoral administration; and article 300 on the functional decentralization of the economic administrative organization of the State.

In addition, article 158 of the 1999 Constitution defined decentralization as a general *national policy* to be implemented to "deepen democracy, to bring power closer to the population, creating the best conditions for the exercise of democracy and for the effective and efficient meeting of state commitments" with respect to *all* public activities.

Following the political practice of recent years, the 2007 Constitutional Reform, contrary to what was is established in the 1999 Constitution, definitively and totally tended to centralize the State and eliminate any vestige of decentralization in public policy and organization in territorial autonomy and representative democracy at the local level, which is to say, in the primary political units in the land. This without any doubt changed a fundamental characteristic of the State which could not constitutionally be achieved through the procedure of "constitutional reform."

The 2007 rejected Constitutional Reform eliminated all vestiges of "political decentralization" by beginning with the fundamental principle of territorial decentralization and autonomy established in article 16 of the Constitution. Autonomy and decentralization are basic elements of participative democracy, and Article 16 of the 1999 Constitution requires the territorial political division of the Republic to guarantee "municipal autonomy and public administrative decentralization." The Reform, however, sought to create a new territorial division that guarantied only "the participation of the Popular Power," eliminating any reference to political autonomy or decentralization.

The 2007 rejected Constitutional Reform, as previously mentioned, tended to derogate and eliminate article 158 of the Constitution, which defined the national policy of decentralization to "deepen democracy"; establishing in its place, only that: "The State shall promote, as a national policy, the protagonist participation of

---

33   Ley Orgánica de Descentralización, Delimitación y Transferencia de Competencias del Poder Público de 1989, *Gaceta Oficial* N° 4.153, of December 28, 1989. This law was reformed in 2003, *Gaceta Oficial* N° 37.753 of August 14, 2003; and in 2009, *Gaceta Oficial,* N° 39 140 of March 17, 2009.

the people, transferring power to them, and creating the best conditions for the construction of a Social Democracy." This fundamental change, as the President of the Republic stated in his August 15th Speech to the National Assembly, constituted "the development of what we understand by decentralization, because the Fourth Republic concept of decentralization is very different from the concept we must work with. For this reason -the President said-, we have here stated 'the protagonist participation of the people, transferring power to them, and creating the best conditions for the construction of social democracy."[34]

In addition, the expression "decentralization" was to be eliminated with the proposed reform of articles 272 (decentralization of prisons); 295 (decentralized electoral administration) and 300 (decentralized public enterprises).

4.   *The fragmentation of the public administration of the state*

One of the most important innovations in the Constitution of 1999 is that of having incorporated a normative framework of fundamental principles specifically designed to regulate the Public Administration of the State and to rationalize it. In particular, Article 141 provided, first, that the Public Administration was to operate at the service of citizens; second, that it was to be based upon the principles of honesty, public participation, speediness, effectiveness, and efficiency, transparency, accountability, and responsibility in the exercise of public functions; and third, that it was to fully operate under the law, thus implicating the constitutional formulation of the principle of legality.

The 2007 Constitutional Reform eliminated the requirement that the public administrative apparatus, as a single universe, must exist at the service of citizens, replacing this norm with another in which is stated that the Public Administration exists solely at the service of the State, and thus terminating the right of citizens to have an Administration that operates at their service. In this sense, it was further proposed to establish in article 141 that: "The public administrations are organizational structures destined to serve as instruments of the public powers, for the exercise of their functions and for the provision of services."

The new language proposed to be adopted for article 141 would signify the fragmentation of Public Administration, and the departure from a universal regulation of one apparatus, to a regulation of various "public administrations." These, in a manner contrary to any proper legislative technique, were classified in a way that was more suited to a "course materials" than to a Constitution. In the 2007 Constitutional Reform, "public administrations" were classified into two "categories": "the bureaucratic or traditional public administrations," which were those that attend to structures established and regulated under the Constitution of 1999 and the laws, and the "Missions" ("*las Misiones*"), which were "organizations of a variety of natures, created to meet the most deeply felt and urgent needs of the population." Their provision of services, according to the norm, required the use of exceptional systems,

---

34   See *Discurso de Orden pronunciado por el ciudadano Comandante Hugo Chávez Frías, cit.* p. 50.

including experimental systems, which were to be "established by the Executive Power by means of organizational and functional regulations."

Thus 2007 Constitutional Reform, instead of seeking to correct the almost one decade old administrative disaster produced by a lack of budgetary and administrative discipline due to the creation of "funds" assigned to "missions" that existed outside of the general organization of the State, would constitutionalize the administrative disorder by characterizing the administrative structures of the State as "bureaucratic or traditional" but renouncing the path of converting precisely these institutions into the proper instruments for meeting the most deeply felt and urgent needs of the population. Moreover, all of this leaved the organization of the Public Administration to the sole volition of the President of the Republic, to be exercised by means of regulations.

5.   The abandonment of budgetary discipline and the unity of the treasury

Even though the 2007 Constitutional Reform did not contain express changes to articles 313 and 314 of the Constitution -the principal articles that establish the general principle of budgetary discipline- sought to eliminate this fundamental principle of State economic and financial administration as a consequence of changes proposed to article 321.

In effect, under articles 313 and 314, the economic and financial administration of the entire National Public Administration must be governed by a budget approved annually through legislation of the National Assembly, providing an estimate of public revenues, and the public authorized spending. Thus, article 314 declares, that "there shall be no form of spending that has not been provided for in the annual Budget law," being the only exceptions those provided by additional budget credits for unforeseen expenses and under funded items, which also require approval of the National Assembly. That system is designed to guarantee that ordinary revenues are sufficient to cover ordinary expenses and, that "the income generated from the exploitation of the wealth derived from the subsoil and minerals, in general, will tend to be used to finance real productive investments, education and health" (Article 311).

The rejected 2007 Constitutional Reform of article 321 was intended to bring the whole system of budgetary discipline into complete chaos, through constitutional provisions. In this sense, it eliminated the constitutional provision requiring the creation of "a fund for macroeconomic stabilization destined to guarantee the expenses of the State at the municipal, regional and national levels, in the event of fluctuations in ordinary revenues," and that such a funds must function under "basic principles of efficiency, equity, and non-discrimination between the public entities that bring resources to it." Instead, it established that the "At the end of each year, the Chief of State shall establish, in coordination with the Central Bank of Venezuela, the level of reserves needed for the national economy, as well as the amount of surplus reserves. The surplus reserves shall be destined to funds established by the National Executive for productive investments, development and infrastructure, financing of the Missions, and, definitively, to the integral, endogenous, humanist and socialist development of the nation." By means of the reform, the Chief of State was at the same time, the person designated to be charged with the administration of international reserves (article 318).

In this way, through the 2007 Constitutional Reform, the definitive rupture of the unity of the Treasury was to be constitutionalized, establishing a financial mechanism parallel to the budget consisting in "funds" created solely by the National Executive destined for the Missions. As has been said, these Missions are also under the charge of the National Executive, and exist as public administrative organizations parallel to the "bureaucratic and traditional Public Administration."

III. PROPOSED CHANGES IN THE POLITICAL SYSTEM: FROM REPRESENTATIVE DEMOCRACY TO A SUPPOSED "PARTICIPATORY DEMOCRACY" CONDUCTED BY THE CENTRAL POWER

1. The elimination of representative democracy at the local level and its substitution by a supposed "protagonist participation"

Article 5 of the 1999 Constitution establishes that "sovereignty resides untransferably in the people, who exercise it directly in the manner provided in this Constitution and the Law, and indirectly, by means of suffrage through the organs that exercise the Public Power." This norm followed Venezuela's republican tradition that began with the Constitution of 1811[35] by providing for the exercise of popular sovereignty through political representation (indirect democracy), adding the provision for the direct exercise of democracy as complementary component. The 1999 Constitution also establishes mechanisms for popular participation contained in article 62, which consecrates the right of all citizens to "freely participate in public affairs, directly or through their representatives," as well as through the "means of participation" set forth in article 70.

In order for democracy to exist as such, it must above all be representative, although it may additionally contain mechanisms of direct democracy. For this reason, the Constitution of 1999 requires that representative democracy always have its source in elections that must be popular, universal, direct and secret (art. 70); that such elections be directed to selecting the titular heads of almost all of the organs that exercise the Public Powers; and, of course, that these be the officials of the branches of Government established in the Constitution according to the principles of the separation and distribution of powers (art. 136).

This form of representative democracy is, of course, not contradictory to participative democracy, and both are different to the mechanisms of direct democracy: such as referenda (consultative, approbatory, abrogating, and recall (Articles 71 ff.) that serve to perfect democracy; and to the various "forms of political participation" regulated in the Constitution. The latter include popular consultations, legislative, constitutional and constituent initiatives, the *cabildos abiertos* (Open Town Hall meetings), and the citizens assemblies (Article 70).

---

35 Regarding the presence of this principle in all of Venezuela's constitutions, see Allan R. Brewer-Carías, *Las Constituciones de Venezuela,* Academia de Ciencias Políticas y Sociales, Caracas 1997.

In any case, "participative democracy" cannot substitute representative democracy: that is a falsehood, especially if "participation" is conducted from above. In order for democracy to be participative in addition to being essentially representative, it is necessary to allow the citizen to really have the possibility to participate in public affairs which is only possible when he or she has access to power. And this is possible only when power is near to the citizen, which necessarily implies the presence of a well established and well developed system of autonomous local government in every locality and urban or rural settlement. This means that political participation can only be founded upon political decentralization, through the creation of autonomous political entities that permit local self-government. In this sense, it is only possible to participate politically when, through the decentralization of government, local authorities are established by means of elections through suffrage at the smallest territorial level. As a whole, this implies the spreading of public power in the territory of the State.

This is, of course, contrary to the concentration of Power and centralism which the rejected Constitutional Reform of 2007 attempted to consolidate under cover of the themes of socialism and "protagonist participation." The reform, as stated, attempted to eliminate from the Constitution all references to political decentralization, and to definitively substitute representative democracy at the local level with a supposed "participative democracy." This would have finished off democracy itself as a political regimen, substituting it for an authoritarian one that centralizes and concentrates Power, and impedes political participation because of the non-existence of autonomous local entities.

This, as stated, was sought to be achieved through the proposals to eliminate all vestiges of local territorial autonomy and political decentralization, thereby precluding the possibility of participative democracy. As mentioned, democratic participation requires the existence of autonomous territorial political entities, so without them, what can be developed is a simple and controlled mobilization of the population by the Central Power. But popular mobilization cannot be confound with democratic participation, and mobilization of the people is precisely what occurs in the Communal Councils recently created by law[36] that were sought to be constitutionalized. The members of the Communal Councils were not elected by means of suffrage (Article 136) but instead were designated under the control of the National Executive Power itself. The proposal to reform article 16 of the Constitution sought to constitutionally consolidate this system created and controlled from above, down, through its reference to new territorial divisions that supposedly guarantee "the participation of the Popular Power."

---

36   Ley de los Consejos Comunales (2006). See Allan R. Brewer-Carías, "El inicio de la desmunicipalización en Venezuela: La organización del Poder Popular para eliminar la descentralización, la democracia representativa y la participación a nivel local," in *AIDA, Opera Prima de Derecho Administrativo. Revista de la Asociación Internacional de Derecho Administrativo*, Universidad Nacional Autónoma de México, Asociación Internacional de Derecho Administrativo, México, 2007, pp. 49 a 67.

According to the rejected 2007 Constitutional Reform of article 16 of the Constitution of 1999, a new "Popular Power" ("*Poder Popular*") -a proposed new level of State powers (in addition to the national, States and municipal levels)- was to be created supposedly from the bottom, up: beginning with the Communities ("*Comunidades*"), each of which, "shall constitute a basic and indivisible spatial nucleus of the Venezuelan Socialist State, where ordinary citizens will have the power to construct their own geography and their own history." The Communities are to be grouped into "Communes" ("*Comunas*") that were "geographic areas or extensions," and, "geo-human cells of the territory." The Communes, in turn, were to be grouped into "Cities" ("*Ciudades*"), conceived as, "the primary political unit in the organization of the national territory." The latter were to be understood as "all of the popular settlements within the Municipality (*Municipio*)."

In this manner, it was supposedly from the Community and the Commune that, "the Popular Power shall develop forms of political-territorial communal aggregation that are to be regulated by Law and shall constitute forms of Self-government and any other expression of direct democracy."

The rejected Constitutional Reform of article 136 of the Constitution was precise in its reference to the Popular Power. It provided that this power "is expressed through the constitution of communities, communes, and the self-government of the cities, by means of the communal councils, workers' councils, peasant councils, student councils, and other entities established by law." However, although "the people" ("el pueblo") were designated as the "depositary of sovereignty," to be, "exercised directly through the Popular Power," it was precisely stated, that the Popular Power "does not arise from suffrage or from any election, but arises from the condition of the organized human groups that form the base of the population."

What was sought, then, definitively, in that reform was to put an end to representative democracy at the local level, and with this, to put an end to any vestige of political territorial autonomy - the essence of decentralization-, which is necessary to allow political participation. For such purpose, the reforms were proposed under the name of a "participative democracy," intending to substitute representation with a supposed "direct democracy" of "participation" in "citizens' assemblies," "communities," "communes" and "cities" that were not autonomous political territorial entities, but were to be controlled from the Central Power.

2.   *The extension of the right to vote*

The 2007 Constitutional Reform proposed to extend the right to vote to all citizens over the age of 16 years (Article 64).

3.   *The proposed elimination of the principle of republican alternation in office by the establishing of the possibility of the indefinite re-election of the president of the republic*

According to article 4 of the Constitution of 1999, the Republic's government and all of the political entities that compose it are required to be 'democratic and alternating' ('*democrático, alternativo*'). On the basis of this principle the Constitution established term limits governing the re-election of all its officers.

With respect to the President of the Republic, article 230 of the Constitution of 1999, in a radical departure from the previous constitutional tradition forbidding immediate presidential election, allowed, although only for one time and at the end of the first term, the immediate re-election of the President. Regarding members ("*Diputados*") of the National Assembly, Article 192 provides that they may be re-elected for no more than "two consecutive terms." Article 160 provides that State Governors "may be immediately re-elected for a new term, but only once," and article 162 provides that members of the States' Legislative Councils may be re-elected for only "two consecutive terms." Finally, article 174 provides that Mayors "may be immediately re-elected for a new term, but only once."

Regarding these matters, the 2007 Constitutional Reform of article 230 of the Constitution, not only would have increase the length of the presidential term from six to seven years, but also sought in particular to establish the possibility that the President of the Republic "be re-elected." This would have signified the inclusion in the Constitution of the principle of indefinite re-election of the President, contradicting the democratic principle of alternation in office, and featuring the perpetuation in power of the President of the Republic.

Nonetheless, and in spite of the rejection of this reform, the following year, the National Assembly approved a "Constitutional Amendment" with the same purpose, and extending the reelection principle to all the elected officials that was submitted to a referendum on February 15th 2009, also in defraudation of the Constitution.

4.   *The contradictory restrictions to the citizens' right to political participation*

Regarding the principle of political participation, the 1999 Constitution directly establishes regulations assuring the participation of civil society in public affairs that now in some cases, with the rejected Constitutional Reform, and in the name of a "participatory democracy," were being eliminated or restricted.

This was the case with the mechanism created to assure civil society participation in the appointment of high non elected State officials (of the Judiciary, the Citizens Power and the Electoral Power); with political participation by means of referenda; and, with citizens political participation in matters of constitutional review.

A.   *The elimination of the constitutional cases of civil society representatives' participation in the nomination of high State officials.*

The 2007 rejected Constitutional Reform proposed the elimination of civil society representatives' direct participation in public affairs (established in the 1999 Constitution, as an institutional novelty) in the nomination of the Justice of the Supreme Tribunal, the members of the National Electoral Council, the Peoples' Defender, the Comptroller General and the Prosecutor General. The nomination is to be made before the National Assembly by various Nomination Committees that were required to be composed only of "representatives of the various sectors of society" (arts. 264, 279, 295).

These provisions of the 1999 Constitution were distorted through political praxis and subsequent legislation by the National Constituent Assembly (1999) followed by the National Assembly (2000). This transformed the Nominating Committees into mere amplified Parliamentary Commissions (2002-2004), thus limiting civil society's right to political participation.[37] This trend was intended to be constitution-alized with the rejected 2007 Constitutional Reform, which sought to establish that the Nomination Committees, instead of being composed of representatives of the various sectors of civil society, would be composed almost completely of State officials.

In this sense, regarding article 270 on the Judicial Nominating Committee, the proposed reform established a parliamentary commission that was similar to what was regulated in the 2004 Organic Law of the Supreme Tribunal of Justice[38]. The reform provided that the National Assembly would convene Judicial Nominating Committee, and that it would be "composed of members of the Assembly, representatives of the Popular Power and representatives related to juridical activities" adding that the "Popular Power Councils, social sectors and organizations related to juridical activities can nominate candidates."

Regarding the Electoral Nominating Committee for the National Electoral Council, the rejected 2007 Constitutional Reform to article 295 also established a parliamentary commission similar to what is regulated in the 2002 Organic Law of the Electoral Power. The reform provided that the National Assembly would convene the Committee and that it would be "composed of members of the Assembly, and of representatives of the Popular Power, of social organizations and of sectors." This is to say, that it would be composed basically of representatives of State organs, abandoning the principle of the exclusive participation of civil society. Regarding the nomination of candidates, the provision in the 1999 Constitution that provides that a number of them are to be proposed by the Law faculties around the country was eliminated in the reform, and instead it proposed to assign the nominations of candidates to representatives of the Popular Power and to representatives of institutions and the educational and social sectors.

Finally, regarding the Citizens Power Nominating Committee to appoint the Peoples' Defender, the Comptroller General and the Prosecutor General, the rejected 2007 Constitutional Reform to article 279 also established that the National Assembly would convene a Committee "composed of members of the Assembly, and of representatives of the different sectors of the Popular Power," and eliminated any reference to civil society.

---

37   See Allan R. Brewer-Carías, "La participación ciudadana en la designación de los titulares de los órganos no electos de los Poderes Públicos en Venezuela y sus vicisitudes políticas [Citizen participation in the appointment of high officials in un-elected offices in the Public Powers of Venezuela, and political vicisitudes]," en *Revista Iberoamericana de Derecho Público y Administrativo*, Año 5, N° 5-2005, San José, Costa Rica 2005, pp. 76-95

38   See Allan R. Brewer-Carías, *Ley Orgánica del Tribunal Supremo de Justicia [The Organic Law of the Supreme Court of Justice]*, Editorial Jurídica Venezolana, Caracas, 2006, pp. 32 et. Seq.

B.   *Limits to political participation by means of referendums and restrictions upon direct democracy*

Articles 5 and 62 of the 1999 Constitution establish that the right to political participation can be exercised indirectly by the election of representatives, and in a direct form through the means regulated in the Constitution. Political participation is exercised directly in particular, through those means provided in article 70 and by means of referendums, enumerated in articles 71 to 74 as: consultative, recall, approbatory and abrogatory referendums.

The important aspect of these provisions is the establishment of the popular initiative to convene the referendum, attributing: to 10% of registered voters the right to ask for the convening of the consultative referendums (Article 71); to 20% of registered voters the right to ask for the convening of the recall referendums (Article 72); to 15% of registered voters the right to ask for the convening of the approbatory referendums of certain international treaties (Article 73); to 10% of registered voters the right to ask for the convening of referendums for the abrogation of statutes (Article 74); and to 5% of registered voters the right to ask for the convening of the referendums for the abrogation of executive decree-laws (Article 74).

Regarding these articles, the 2007 rejected ional Reform sought to limit the political right to participate, by increasing the percentage of registered voters required to file the popular initiative to convene a referendum, making it more difficult, as follows: to 20% instead of 10% of registered voters for the consultative referendums (Article 71); to 30% instead of the 20% of registered voters for recall referendums (Article 72); to 30% instead of 25% of registered voters for approbatory referendums for laws (Article 73): to 30% instead of 15% of registered voters for the right to ask for the convening of the approbatory referendums of certain international treaties (Article 73); to 30% instead of the 10% of the registered voters for referendums for the abrogation of statutes (Article 74); and to 30% instead of the 5% of the registered voters for referendums for the abrogation of executive decree-laws (Article 74).

Regarding the recall referendum, the 2007 Constitutional Reform, regarding article 72 sought to change the system in order to make it less participatory and more difficult to initiate recall elections. The reform established: first, that instead of directly convening a recall election as a popular right exercised by not less that 20% of registered voters, a petition was to be filed before the National Electoral Council in order to activate a proceeding through which then a number not less than 30% of the registered voters could petition for a recall referendum; second, instead of fixing the electoral participation in recall votes at least 25% of the registered voters, the reform was to require the participation of 40% of the registered voters; and third, for a recall to be achieved, in addition, to requiring number of votes for the recall to be equal or higher to the number of votes through which the official in question was originally elected as is provided in the Constitution of 1999, the reforms was to add the new requirement that the final vote in favor of a recall must be higher that the total number of votes against it, even though the number of votes for the recall would be higher than the number of votes that elected the official to begin with. In this way, the recall referendum was to be distorted and converted in a "ratification" referendum, as was already in a *de facto* way transformed in 2004.[39]

C.   *Limits on the right to political participation in the constitutional review procedures*

The 1999 Constitution provides for three means or procedures for constitutional review according to the importance of the reforms to be implemented: Amendment, the Constitutional Reform and the National Constituent Assembly.

Amendment is the procedure to be applied when it is only a matter of addition or modification of one or various articles without altering the fundamental structure of the Constitution (Article 340). The initiative for the amendment process in the case of a popular initiative lies with at least the 15% of the registered voters. The rejected 2007 Constitutional Reform sought to augment the requirement to 20% of the registered voters (Article 341.1), making the process more difficult to initiate. In addition the Constitutional Reform proposed that the National Assembly, distorting the character of the popular initiative, was to approve Amendments.

Amendments must be approved by referendum in which at least 25% of the registered voters must participate. The rejected 2007 Constitutional Reform sought to raise this percentage to 30% of the registered voters.

The "Constitutional Reforms" procedure according to article 342 of the 1999 Constitution is intended to partially review the Constitution and to substitute one or various articles while not modifying the structure and fundamental principles of the constitutional text. The initiative for the constitutional reform procedure, in the case of the popular initiative, corresponds to al least the 15% of the registered voters. The rejected 2007 Constitutional Reform sought to augment the requirement to 25% of the registered voters (Article 342), making this procedure also more difficult to initiate

Finally, regarding the "National Constituent Assembly," according to article 347 of the 1999 Constitution, this is intended to "transform the State, create a new legal order and write a new Constitution." The initiative for the convening of a Constituent Assembly, in the case of a popular initiative, lies with at least 15% of the registered voters. The rejected 2007 Constitutional Reform sought to augment the requirement to 30% of the registered voters (Article 342), making it also much more difficult to initiate.

---

39   See Allan R. Brewer-Carías, "La Sala Constitucional vs. el derecho ciudadano a la revocatoria de mandatos populares: de cómo un referendo revocatorio fue inconstitucionalmente convertido en un 'referendo ratificatorio'," in the book *Crónica Sobre la "In" Justicia Constitucional. La Sala Constitucional y el autoritarismo en Venezuela*, Colección Instituto de Derecho Público, Universidad Central de Venezuela, Nº 2, Editorial Jurídica Venezolana, Caracas 2007, pp. 349-378.

5. The restriction of the right to political participation by reducing it to the implementation of the socialist ideology

Article 62 of the 1999 Constitution declares it to be a political right of citizens "to freely participate in public affairs, directly or through their elected representatives," and refers to "the people's participation in the conception, execution and control of public management," as a "necessary means to obtain protagonism in order to guarantee complete individual and collective development." For this purpose, the norm establishes the "obligation of the State and duty of Society to provide for the generation of more favorable conditions for its practice."

This norm is complemented by article 70 of the 1999 Constitution which provides for the following means for peoples participation and the exercise of popular sovereignty. In the political field, among others: the election of public officials, referenda, popular hearings, mandate recall, legislative and constitutional review initiatives, open town hall meetings, and citizens' assemblies whose decisions are of an obligatory nature; and in the social and economic field: means of citizens' attention, the self-management, the co-management; cooperatives in all their forms including those of a financial character, saving institutions, communitarian enterprises and other associative means guided by mutual cooperation and solidarity."

In the rejected 2007 Constitutional Reform, while the means of participation were proposed to be augmented in a certain fashion, the end resulting was that political participation tended to be restricted. On the one hand, the enumeration of means of participation in article 70 was enlarged to include "the Councils of Popular Power, the communal councils, the workers councils, the students councils, the peasant councils, the artisans' councils, the fisherman councils, the sportive councils, the youth councils, the senior citizens councils, the women's' councils, and the disabled peoples' councils"; but on the other hand, all of them resulted being restrictive with respect to citizens' right to freely participate in public affairs, due to the fact that the means of political participation were to have only one purpose, which is, "the construction of socialism." Consequently, those that do not wanted to construct socialism, were goring to be excluded from the right to political participation, which was only reserved to develop "socialist solidarity" and was not free, as is provided in article 62 of the Constitution.

6. The system of political parties, political association, and the issue of public financing of electoral activities

In a marked reaction against political parties, the Constitution of 1999 omitted reference to the express phrase "political parties" and instead established a set of provisions regulating "associations for political purpose," guaranteeing citizens, "the right to associate for political ends by means of democratic methods, organization, functioning and leadership" (Article 67).

One of the traditional problems associated with the political parties referred to the financing of their activities through public funds established in the Organic Law of Suffrage and Political Participation[40], which led to inequitable concentrations of such funds in hands of the official (governmental) parties. The drafters of the 1999 Constitution reacted to this problem in article 67 by simply prohibiting in an inconvenient way public financing of all "associations for political purposes." This was considered as a regression in the context of contemporary democratic trends regarding public (State) financing of political activity, because it could open the door to irregular and illegitimate public financing of political parties supporting the government.

The 2007 rejected Constitutional Reform sought to modify the prohibition of State funding of political parties, proposing to include, instead, that "the State may finance electoral activities" without indicating if it was referred to political parties in general, or also to self nominated candidates. The proposal also provided for the enactment of a law to establish "means for the financing, for the use of public space, and for access to social communications media in elections campaigns." In any event, if with the Constitutional Reform a unique official State ideology was going to be established, the financing of electoral activities other than those tending to consolidate Socialism could have been considered as contrary to the Constitution. Nonetheless, this proposed reform was also achieved thorough constitutional interpretation established by the Supreme Tribunal in 2008.[41]

One the other hand, the 2007 rejected Constitutional Reform attempted to eliminate from article 67 the general prohibition directed to "the directors of associations with political ends" to "contract with public sector entities." In a system in which the proposal was to consolidate a single official socialist party, such elimination could have developed in a total inter-weaving of the party and the State.

The Constitutional Reform proposal also established in article 67, a general prohibition against, "the financing of associations with political ends or of persons participating in electoral processes by any foreign public or private entity."

IV. PROPOSED CHANGES IN THE FORM OF THE STATE: FROM THE CENTRALIZED FEDERATION TO THE TOTALLY CENTRALIZED STATE

From the time the Republic was created in 1811, and from when it was subsequently re-constituted in 1830, the form of the Venezuelan State, in formal terms, has always been that of a Federation. This is, a State whose Public Powers are distributed between autonomous political-territorial entities on three levels: the national level (the Republic), the state level (the States), and the municipal level (the Munic-

---

40   Ley Orgánica del Sufragio y Participación Política, *Gaceta Oficial* N° 5.233 Extra, May 28, 1998.

41   See the comments in Allan R. Brewer-Carías, "El juez constitucional como constituyente: El caso del financiamiento de las campañas electorales de los partidos políticos en Venezuela," in *Revista de Derecho Público*, N° 117, Editorial Jurídica Venezolana, Caracas 2009, pp. 195 ff.

ipalities). The respective autonomies of each of these levels have been constitutionally guaranteed.

Despite all of its vicissitudes and a tendency to centralize the Federation, this has always been the form of the Venezuelan State, implying a vertical distribution of the Public Powers. While not being expressly eliminated in formal terms, the federal form of State was to materially disappear under the 2007 rejected Constitutional Reform. This was intended, again, to perpetrate a fraud upon the Constitution.

1. The destruction of the federal form of the state

A. Emptying of the Federation of territorial content

While not eliminating the federal form the State in express terms, the rejected 2007 Constitutional Reform was design to empty the content of the federation, as such, resulting in its material disappearance as the form of the State.

With respect, in particular, to the States and Municipalities established in article 16 of the Constitution of 1999, and upon which the concept of the federal system is built, the 2007 Constitutional Reform sought to eliminate the constitutional guarantee of municipal autonomy and political administrative decentralization, laying groundwork for emptying those territorial entities of meaning and of their jurisdictional competencies. The reforms also proposed to strip the Municipalities of their traditional constitutional characterization as the primary political units of the Republic (Article 168), and instead proposed that "the primary political unit of the National territory shall be the city, by which is understood all of the populated settlements within the Municipality, which are composed of geographic areas or extensions called Communes."

According to the proposed reform for article 15 of the Constitution, these Communes forming the Popular Power (as a new vertical level of government), "shall be the geo-human cells of the territory and shall be composed of Communities, each of which shall constitute an indivisible spatial nucleus of the Venezuelan Socialist State, in which the citizens shall have the power to construct their own geography and their own history." This concluded with the statement that, "from the Community and the Commune, the Popular Power shall develop forms of Political-Territorial communal aggregation that are to be regulated by Law, and which shall constitute forms of Self-government and any other expression of Direct Democracy."

The reform of article 16 added, moreover, that "the Communal City (*"Ciudad Comunal"*) shall be constituted when, within the totality of its perimeter, the organized Communities, the Communes, and communal Self-government have been established, subject to a popular referendum to be convened by the President in Council of Ministers."

Furthermore, the proposed reform to article 136, which addressed the Popular Power, sets forth that "The Popular Power is expressed through the constitution of communities, communes, and the self-government of the cities, by means of the communal councils, workers' councils, peasant councils, student councils, and other entities established by Law," expressing that, the Popular Power "does not arise from suffrage or from any election, but arises from the condition of the organized human groups that form the base of the population." This definitively involved the elimination of representative democracy and local political autonomy, that is to say the elimination of political decentralization as a condition of political participation. What was sought to be achieved here through the 2007 rejected Constitutional Reform was that at local level, the Titular Heads of the Public Powers ceased to be elected democratically, which was contrary to the constitutional principle of representative democracy.

B.   *A new territorial division of the Republic that is tied to the Central Power and is built upon unelected authorities*

The whole territorial scheme contained in the 2007 Constitutional Reform, as stated, definitively proposed the dismemberment of the federal form of the State, which has implied an organization of the territory into "political entities" that have enjoyed political territorial autonomy, and that have had governments that must be, as article 6 of the Constitution required, "elective" as well as having other constitutionally required characteristics.

Instead of the political organization of the Republic built upon a division of the national territory into States, the Capital District and Municipalities with democratic governments elected through suffrage, as laid out in the Constitution of 1999, the 2007 rejected Constitutional Reform regarding for article 16 of the Constitution provided the following: "the national territory, conforming to the political-territorial purposes, and in accord with the new geometry of power, [is constituted] by a Federal District in which the Capital of the Republic shall have its seat, by the States, by the Maritime Regions, by the Federal Territories, by the Federal Municipalities and by the Island Districts."

On the other hand, in stead of the territory to be organized in municipalities as set forth in the 1999 Constitution, in the 2007 Constitutional Reform what was stated was that "the States are organized in municipalities" (Article 16), which would have disappeared if part of their territories were to be engulfed by the previously new entities. That is why in the 2007 Constitutional Reform, the municipality as the political primary unity in national organization also were to disappear.

Leaving aside, for the moment, the reforms proposed for the local order, as already discussed -under which the Municipality would simply empty its attributes into the Communities, Communes and Cities from which it is proposed that the Popular Power be developed- the proposed reforms for article 16 sought to authorize the President of the Republic, in Council of Ministers, to "upon a previous accord approved by a simple majority of the Deputies of the National Assembly" ... "create by means of decree, Maritime Regions (*regiones marítimas*), Federal Territories (*territorios federales*), Federal Municipalities, *(municipios federales)* Insular Districts *(distritos insulares),* Federal Provinces *(provincias federales)* Federal Cities *(ciudades federales)* and Functional Districts *(distritos funcionales)*, and any other entity established by Law." Under this proposed reform, therefore, the territorial political division of the Republic would have ceased to be a subject matter of constitutional rank, contrary to what has always been, nor even be a subject matter regulated by legislation; here were going to become the subject solely of Executive regulation. It is difficult to find more power centralization than the one proposed.

All these territorial entities, according to the proposed reforms, were not conceived as political entities with any kind of autonomy. They were to be subject to the Central Power and the "National Power" was the one that was to designate "their respective authorities."

C. *The new conception of the Capital City without political autonomy or local democratic government*

One of the important reforms introduced in the 1999 Constitution was to definitively assure a regimen of decentralized and democratic local government in Caracas, the capital of federal city, Caracas. This is a regimen that guarantees municipal autonomy and the political participation of the diverse entities that compose its urban area. To this end, a two tiered metropolitan government structure was created in order to assure a general (metropolitan) government for the city, and, at the same time, assure the existence of democratic elected local governments, enjoying political autonomy. The Constitution of 1999 thus eliminated the Federal District which was a vestige of the traditional nineteenth century federation conception, in which the capital city had no self-government.

The 2007 rejected Constitutional Reform, in a regressive way sought to return to the same nineteenth century model in which local government in the capital city was absent, a model that has been overcome in all of the Federations of the world. For such purpose, the Constitutional Reform, regarding article 18 of the Constitution, proposed to eliminate the Capital District and the district's municipal organization, substituting it for a revived Federal District without any constitutional guarantee of municipal or territorial autonomy, nor any guarantee of a "democratic and participative character of government" as it is establish for the capital city by the Constitution of 1999. The intention was to pass the city into control of the National Power, just as the original Federal District was conceived in 1863, so that in the capital of the Republic which is the seat of the National Power, only the national government organs could act, and no local, democratic government with political autonomy of any kind could exists. This reform, nonetheless, was unconstitutionally made through legislation in 2009, by crating the Capital District under a framework of a 19th century Federal District. [42]

Thus, in place of article 18 of the Constitution, what was proposed in the rejected Constitutional Reform, was a norm regulating the city of Caracas as the capital of the Republic and the seat of the organs of the National Power, which as a "political territorial unit" was to be regulated by legislation an to be called, "*Cuna de Bolívar y Reina del Guaraira Repano*"[43] (Birthplace of Bolívar and the Queen of *Guaraira Repano].*" That organization, which was to be dependent upon the Central Power, was conceived as being without any local political autonomy what so ever. The pro-

---

42 See the comments in Allan R. Brewer-Carías et al, *Leyes sobre Régimen de Gobierno del Distrito Capital y del Area Metropolitana de Caracas*, Editorial Jurídica venezolana, Caracas 2009.

43 *Wuarairarepano or Guaraira Repano* is the indigenous name of the Avila Mountain

posed norm adds that, "The National Power, through the Executive Power, and with the collaboration and participation of all of the entities of the National, State and Municipal Public Powers, in addition to those of the Popular Power, its Communities, Communes, and Communal Councils and other social organizations, shall provide for all that is necessary for urban reorganization, the restructuring of roadways, environmental recuperation, optimal results in public and personal security, the comprehensive strengthening of neighborhoods, urban development, the provision of systems for health, education, sports, culture and entertainment, the total restoration of the historic city center and historical sites, the construction of a system of small and mid-sized Satellite Cities along the territorial axes, and in general the achievement of the greatest humanization possible in the *Cuna de Bolívar y Reina del Wuarairarepano.*" This is to say, what the Reform sought definitively was to nationalize and centralize the entire regimen of government in Caracas.

In addition, in the same article 18, a provision regarding the establishment of a national system of cities was included, as well as an article declaring the Right to a City *("Derecho a la Ciudad")* which was to be understood as "the equitable benefit that each of the inhabitants receives, in conformity with the strategic role that the City formulates with relative to both the urban regional context, as well to the National System of Cities."

2. The abandonment of the principle of the vertical distribution of national, state and municipal public powers, with the incorporation of the popular power

In the history of Venezuelan constitutions, the federal form of the State materialized through the vertical distribution of the Public Powers, was first expressed formally in the Constitution of 1858, by stating that "The Public Powers are divided into the National and the Municipal [Powers]" (Article 9). Subsequently, in the Constitution of 1925, the "Municipal Power" was added to this formulation. The final result was the provision of article 136 of the Constitution of 1999 stating that, "The Public Powers are distributed between the Municipal Powers, the State Powers, and the National Powers."

In the 2007 rejected Constitutional Reform, regarding article 136, a radical change to this traditional distribution of powers was proposed, by adding in addition to the municipal, state and national powers, a new territorial level, that of the Popular Power, which was to express itself through the Councils of Popular Power, that is through "the communal councils, the workers councils, the students councils, the peasant councils, the artisan councils, the fisherman councils, the sportive councils, the youth councils, the senior citizens councils, the women councils, and the disables councils, and other entities established by law." Through these councils the people as the depository of sovereignty, was to exercised it directly, but stressing that the Popular Power "does not arise from suffrage or from any election, but arises from the condition of the organized human groups that form the base of the population."

In addition, the concept of Popular Power was incorporated in the rejected Constitutional Reform regarding the composition of the Nominating Committees for the appointment of the Justices of the Supreme Tribunal, and the Heads of the Citizen

Power and the Electoral Power, in the sense that in addition to members of the National Assembly, they were to have among others, representatives of the different sectors of the Popular Power.

3. The "nationalization" of competencies attributed to the Federated States by the Constitution of 1999

Article 136 the 1999 Constitution, when organizing the "Federal" State, distributes and assigns various competencies among the three levels of government: National, State, and municipal, which are to be exercised autonomously, according with the principle of the vertical distribution of power. In this matter, nonetheless, the main tendency has been the centralization of almost all competencies within the National Power, which has left very few, assigned to the States at the intermediate level, and has left competencies relating to local life at the level of the municipalities.

The 2007 rejected Constitutional Reform, in these matters, sought to materially centralize all of the competencies of the Public Powers at the National Level, by assigning new competencies to the National Powers, centralizing the competencies held by the States under the 1999 Constitution, and by creating an obligation imposed upon States and Municipalities to transfer their competencies to the Communal Councils. The result of all these reforms would have been to leave the States as vitiated entelechies.

But among the subject matters sought to be attributed to the National Power in the rejected Constitutional Reform, implying the complete centralization of competencies in the National Power and the definitive drowning of state and municipal competencies, were those referred to in articles 156.10 and 156.11 of the Constitution. The first of these, sought to confer competency to the National Power with respect to, "the regulation and administration of the territory, and of the territorial regimen of the Federal District, of the States, of the Municipalities, of the Federal Dependencies and of other regional entities" (Article 156.10). The second sought to confer competency to the National Power with respect to, "the creation, regulation and administration of federal Provinces, federal and Communal Territories, and federal and Communal Cities" (article 156.11). Under these reforms, the States and Municipalities would have ceased being "political entities" and have become totally dependent units upon the national level, as organs without autonomy of any kind, which is to say, as peripheral administrations of the Central Power, subject to the regulation and administration of the National Power.

The proposed Constitutional Reform also proposed attributing to the National Power, competency for administrative legislation (Article 156,32), which was to imply the total centralization of all legislation governing Public Administration, whether National, State or Municipal.

On the other hand, the Constitutional Reform sought to eliminate a number of competencies that the 1999 Constitution attributes to the States and Municipalities, re-assigning them to the National Power. In particular, the changes proposed for article 156, 27, sought to "nationalize," or attribute to the National Power, the competency that article 164, 10 assigns to the States as a part of the policy to advance in the area of decentralization, for the "conservation, administration, and use of national roads and highways." The approval of this reform would have also imply a modification of sections 9 and 10 of article 164 of the Constitution, which assign the to States competency for the "conservation, administration, and use of national roads and highways, and of ports and airports of commercial use, in coordination with the National Executive" which will be eliminated. Nonetheless, these reforms, also in an illegitimate way, were accheived in 2008 through judicial interpretation made by the Supreme Tribunal of Justice. [44]

Finally, in the area of shared national and municipal competencies, article 156,14 of the Constitution of 1999 assigns to the National Power the creation and organization of land taxes on rural lands and real property transactions, while their "collection and control corresponds to the municipalities, in accord with this Constitution." The 2007 Constitutional Reform proposed here to eliminate all references to the municipal role, and simply added "collection of land taxes on rural lands" to the competencies of the National Power.

Following this centralistic orientation, the 2007 Constitutional Reform proposed to eliminate the competency of the States in the area of the regimen and exploitation of non-metallic minerals, salt deposits, and oyster beds (Article 164,5), which was to be transferred to the national level, and could only be delegate to the States (Article 157,17).

In a definitive coup *de grace* to the federal form of the State, the rejected 2007 Constitutional Reform proposed to eliminate the residual competency of the States, something that is inherent in every Federation, which is established in article 164.11 of the Constitution of 1999, regarding "all those that do not correspond to the national or municipal competency, according to this Constitution." The rejected Constitutional Reform sought to substitute this provision with one that established the rule inversely and to attribute residual competency to the National Power. This change was proposed in the reform to article 156 that states that the competency of the National Public Power embraces, "all other subject areas that this Constitution attributes to the National Power, or that by their kind or nature correspond to it, or that are not expressly attributed to state or municipal competencies."

4.   *The obligation of states and municipalities to release (decentralize) their competencies and transfer them to the organs of the popular power*

In article 184, the Constitution of 1999 establishes the principle that the law must create open and flexible mechanisms through which the States and Municipalities can decentralize, and transfer the rendering of their respective public services, to communities and organized neighborhood organizations, once they have demonstrated their capacity to provide those services. The intention of this article is, in this manner, to promote the transfer of the provision of services in the areas of health,

---

44   See the comments in Allan R. Brewer-Carías, "La Sala Constitucional como poder constituyente: la modificación de la forma federal del estado y del sistema constitucional de división territorial del poder público," en *Revista de Derecho Público*, N° 114, (abril-junio 2008), Editorial Jurídica Venezolana, Caracas 2008, pp. 247-262.

education, housing, sports, culture, social programs, the environment, the mainte-nance of industrial areas, the maintenance and conservation of urban areas, neigh-borhood prevention and protection, works in construction, and other public services. This policy intends to promote the participation of communities and citizens through neighborhood associations and non-governmental organizations, in the formulation of the investment proposals of state and municipal authorities, as well as to partici-pate in the implementation, evaluation and monitoring of public works, social pro-grams, and public services provided within their jurisdictions. In addition, the policy is also intended to promote the creation of new subjects of decentralization, at the level of the Parishes, communities, neighborhoods and localities. This needs to be done to guarantee the principle of "co-responsibility" ("*corresponsabilidad*") in public business in local and state government, and, to develop self-management and co-management in the administration and control of state and municipal services.

The rejected Constitutional Reform materially redefined the federal decentralized democratic State in this area and sought to convert it into a Communal centralized non-democratic State. The reform regarding article 184, proposed to establish that the "decentralization and transferring" required by the Constitution to be regulated by law, was to be done into "the organized Communities, the communal Councils, the Communes, and other Entities of the Popular Power." This implied "the assump-tion of the activity of municipal and/or state public enterprises by the communal organizations" (Article 184.2), and also "the transference of the administration and control of state and municipal public services to the Communal organizations, on thee basis of the principle of co-responsibility in public business" (Article 184.7).

The rejected 2007 Constitutional Reform defined the structure of "the organized Community" ("*la Comunidad organizada*"), which "shall have as its maximum au-thority the Assembly of Citizens ("*Asamblea de ciudadanos y ciudadanas*") of the Popular Power, which, in that capacity, was to designate and revoke the organs of the Communal Power (*Poder Comunal*) in the communities, Communes, and other political-territorial entities constituting the city, as the primary political unit of the territory." It was also stated that "The Communal Council constitutes the executive organ for the decisions of the citizen's assemblies, formulating and composing the diverse communal organizations and social groups," The proposed reform to article 184 continues stating, that the Communal Council "shall assume the role of the Jus-tice of the Peace and the provision of "neighborhood prevention and protection ser-vices," which have traditionally been competencies of the Municipalities. Finally, it was proposed that "a Fund for the financing of the projects of the Communal Coun-cils' shall be created through legislation."

This institutional framework must, of course, be adequately linked to what the same rejected Constitution Reform proposed with respect to article 136 of the Con-stitution, relative to the Popular Power and the elimination of any vestige of repre-sentative democracy.

5.   *The elimination of the constitutional guarantee for municipal autonomy*

Under article 168 of the 1999 Constitution, the Municipalities constitute the pri-mary political unit (*unidad política primaria*) of national organization. They have juridical personality, and enjoy autonomy. This status comprehends: the election of

their authorities, the management and administration of matters within their competencies, the creation, collection, and investment of revenues, and, the constitutional
protection that provides that Municipal acts "may not be challenged except before
the competent courts, according with the Constitution and the laws." This implies
that Municipal acts are not subject to any form of review -other than judicial- by the
organs of the National Power or of the States.

The rejected 2007 Constitutional Reform attempted to eliminate this final element of the legal and institutional autonomy of the Municipalities established in
article 168 of the Constitution of 1999. This reform would have leave opened the
possibility of establishing by law that the acts of Municipalities could be challenged
and reviewed by organs of the Executive Powers of the States or of the National
Power, and would eliminate the guarantee that Municipal acts can only be reviewed
by judicial authorities.

V. PROPOSED CHANGES IN THE ORGANIZATION OF THE NATION-AL POWER

1. *Proposed Reforms regarding the international activities of the Republic*

The 2007 rejected Constitutional Reform sought to substantially modify articles
152 and 153 of the Constitution, where the basis for the international activities of the
Republic, as well the participation of Venezuela in the economic integration process
is defined.

Regarding article 152, in the reform, the guidelines for the international activity
of the State were also defined. The article indicates that such activity were to be
based on the exercise of the sovereignty of the Venezuelan State, and was to be
ruled by the following principles: "political independence, equality among States,
free determination and non- intervention in internal affairs, the pacific solution of
international conflicts, the defense and respect for human rights and solidarity between the countries in their struggle for their emancipation and the welfare of human
kind." In addition, it was established that the Republic must develop "the most firm
and decisive defense of these principles before international organizations and institutions, seeking their permanent democratization and the construction of a just and
equilibrated order," and that the external policy must be oriented "in an active way
towards the configuration of a multi-polar world, free from the hegemony of any
center of imperial, colonial and neo-colonial power"

On the other hand, the innovative constitutional basis the 1999 Constitution established in order to allow the Republic participate in the Latin American economic
integration processes with legal support was proposed to be completely eliminated
in the 2007 rejected Constitutional Reform. Instead, what was established were few
principles of foreign affairs in holding that, "The Republic must promote the integration, the Confederation and the union of Latin America and the Caribbean in
order to configure a political, economic and social great regional block." The provision added, that "in order to attain that objective, the State will privilege the structure of new models of integration and union on our continent, allowing the creation
of geopolitical spaces, within which peoples and governments of our America could
construct a single Grand national (*Grannacional*) project, that *Simón Bolívar* called

'A Nation of Republics'." For those purposes, the reforms allowed the Republic "to subscribe to international treaties and covenants based in the most ample political, social, economic, cultural, Grand national, productive, complementarily, solidarity and just trade cooperation."

2. Proposed Reforms to the executive power and the accentuation of presidential system of government

With the 2007 rejected Constitutional Reform, the presidential system was accentuated, particularly because the extension of the President's term of office, the possibility for the indefinite re-election of the President of the Republic, the establishment of new Vice presidents and the expansion of presidential powers and attributions.

A. The extension of the President's term and the unlimited reelection

The 2007 Constitutional Reform, in addition to propose the assuring of the possibility for the indefinite re-election of the President of the Republic, sought to extend the Presidential term of office from six to seven years (Article 230). This was contrary to Venezuelan Constitutional tradition based in the "alternate" character of government, not allowing the continuous and indefinite election of the President and other elected officials. Never has there been such a lengthy presidential term in the whole of the country's constitutional history. The fact is that never in the whole of its political history has a President exercised the Executive Power continuously for as many years as the current President has governed the country: from 1999 to 2009. Nonetheless, regarding the continuous and indetifite reelection rejected proposal, it was eventually achieved through a Constitutional Amendment in 2009.[45]

B. The new executive organs: the Vice Presidents

One of the innovations of the Constitution of 1999 was the creation of the office of the "Executive Vice President" (*"Vicepresidente Ejecutivo"*), although without any parliamentarian trend, particularly because article 225 of the Constitution establishes expressly that the Vice President is freely named and removed by the President of the Republic, thus rendering him completely subject to the political will of the Chief of the National Executive and the State.

The rejected 2007 Constitutional Reform regarding article 225, sought to multiply the number of Vice-presidents by changing the title from "Executive Vice President" to "First Vice President" (*"Primer Vicepresidente"*), and by enabling the President to designate the number of Vice-presidents he "deems necessary." The new Vice Presidents would have also exercised the Executive Power, and as was publicly announced, would have been assigned to determined territories, sectors, or subject matters, and in particular, in order to conduct the "new geometry of power." Consequently, these public officials would have reinforced the direct action of the Presi-

---

45   See the comments in Allan R. Brewer-Carías, "El Juez Constitucional vs. La alternabilidad republicana," in *Revista de Derecho Público*, N° 117, Caracas 2009, pp. 205 ff.

dent in the territory or in determined subject areas, independently of the vertical distribution of the Public Powers that could exist, accentuating the centralized State controlled by the President.

C. *The extension of the powers attributed to the President of the Republic*

Article 236 of the Constitution of 1999 enumerates the competencies of the President of the Republic, which the 2007 Constitutional Reform sought to expand and amplify, as follows:

1. In addition to the power to direct the "Government," as is provided in article 236, 2, the reform sought to give him the power to direct "the State," and to coordinate relations between the other National Public Powers while acting in his capacity as Head of State. This reform sought to assign to the President the power to direct the actions of the State, which constitutionally implied that the President was to direct not only the actions of the National Executive Power, but those of all the organs of the National Power (including the other national branches of government) and all of the state and municipal Powers. This would have implied the complete centralization of the State.

2. In the same trend, a new power was proposed to be conferred to the President in article 236.3 not only in matters of territorial organization and management of land, but regarding the "regime of the Federal District, the States, the Municipalities, the federal dependencies and other regional entities." With these powers all vestiges of autonomy and territorial division would have disappeared, due to the fact that the matter not even was a power of the legislator, but exclusively of the Executive.

3. Regarding article 236.4, the reform sought to assign the President the power to create, "the Federal Provinces, Federal Territories, federal cities, functional districts, federal municipalities, maritime regions and insular districts, as provided in the Constitution, and to designate their authorities as established by law." This implied the creation of territorial entities that would have been totally dependent upon the National Executive, and would be superimposed upon those entities that form the political division of the territory.

4. Regarding article 236.19 that attribute to the President the competence to "formulate a National Plan for Development and direct its execution" subject to the approval by the National Assembly (Article 236.18), the reform sought to eliminate the requirement of the Plan's approval in the National Assembly. This change would have eliminated all participation in the planning process of the popular representation (in the National Assembly).

5. Regarding articles 236.5 and 236.6 of the Constitution, the Constitutional Reform sought to reinforce the role of the President, to "command the Bolivarian Armed Forces as Commander in Chief, exercising Supreme Hierarchical Authority in all of its Corps, Components and Units, determining its contingent," adding in article 236.7 the power to "promote officials in all [of the Armed Force's] ranks and hierarchies and designate their corresponding positions." Under these reforms, the whole of the Bolivarian Armed Forces, all of its Corps, its Components and its Units would have become directly and hierarchically subject to the will of the Head of State President, and of course, subject to his political project.

6. In the rejected Constitutional Reform, the President was empowered to "decree the suspension and restriction of constitutional guaranties" in cases of state of exception (article 236,9), in contrast to what is established in the 1999 Constitution where the President is only authorized to "restrict" the guaranties but not to "suspend" them. This attribution was also ratified in the proposed reform to article 337, which expanded the President's powers in cases of states of exception (articles 338, 339).

7. Finally, in addition to the classical attribution to the President to "administer the National Treasury," the Constitutional reform also proposed to assign the President the power to administer "the international reserves, as well as to establish and regulate the monetary policy, in coordination with the Central Bank."

On the other hand, in addition to the reforms proposed to article 236 of the Constitution, in other articles, the Constitutional reform assigned the President new and broad competencies as follows:

8. In article 11 of the Constitution, a new competency was established by the reform, for the President to create by "decree Special Military Regions in order to guarantee the sovereignty, the security and the defense in any part of the territory and geographic spaces of the Republic," as well as to create by, "decree Special Authorities in the event of contingencies, disasters, or any other requiring immediate and strategic intervention of the State."

9. In article 16, it was assigned to the President the power to create by decree, Communal Cities when in within the totality of its perimeter, organized communities, communes and communal self government were established.

10. Also in article 16, the reforms sought to confer to the President in Council of Ministers, upon the prior consent of a simple majority of the Deputies of the National Assembly, the competency to "create by decree maritime regions, federal territories, federal municipalities, insular districts, federal provinces, federal cities and functional districts, as well as any other entity established in the Constitution or in statute."

11. Also in the reforms to article 16, it was assigned to the National Government (directed by the President), the power to develop and activate a District Mission with the corresponding Functional-strategic Plan for the purpose of creating a Functional District.

12. In the same article 16 the reform assigned the "National Executive Power," whose head is the same President of the Republic, competency in order to designate and dismiss the authorities of the maritime regions, federal territories, federal district, federal municipalities, insular districts, federal provinces, federal cities and functional districts, as well as any other entity established in the Constitution or by statute.

13. In article 18, the reform sought to attribute competency to the Executive Power -with the collaboration and participation of all entities of the National, State and Municipal Public Powers, as well as of the Popular Power, its Communities, Communes, Councils, and other social organizations- to provide for all "all that is necessary for urban reorganization; the restructuring of roadways; environmental recuperation; the achievement of optimal results in public and personal security; the

comprehensive strengthening of neighborhoods; urban development; the provision of systems for health, education, sports, culture and entertainment; the total restoration of the historic city center; and, the construction of a system of small and mid-sized Satellite Cities along its territorial axes of expansion." Under these provisions, the Legislative Power would have been left materially void of competency in all of these areas, since they would be assigned to the exclusive competence of the Executive Power, for action by decree, without the need for prior formal Legislation.

14. According to the 2007 Constitutional Reform, in article 141 competencies were to be conferred to the Executive Power to establish Missions as "public administrations" by means of organizational and functional regulations. Missions were understood to be, "organizations of varied of natures, created to meet the most deeply felt and urgent needs of the population, requiring the use of exceptional systems, including experimental systems." The consequence of this reform was that all of the Public Administration and its regimen would have been of the exclusive competency of the National Executive and would lie beyond the reach of the Legislator. These rejected constitutional reforms, nonetheless, were illegitimately made through a Decree Law in 2008.[46]

15. In article 318 of the rejected Constitutional Reform, competency were to be conferred to the President of the Republic or to the Executive Power to establish "monetary policies and exercise the monetary competencies of the National Power" in coordination with the Central Bank of Venezuela. This power was conferred so that the President or the Executive Power: may jointly, with the Central Bank of Venezuela, "achieve stability in prices and preserve the internal and external value of the currency"; and may share with the Central Bank of Venezuela the functions "of participating in the formulation and execution of monetary policy, the design and execution of exchange policy, the regulation of money and credit, and the fixing of interest rates." As administrator of the National Public Treasury (*Hacienda Pública Nacional*), competency was proposed to be afforded additionally to the President to administer and direct the Republic's international reserves which are to be managed by the Central Bank of Venezuela.

16. In article 321, competency was assigned to the "Chief of State" to, within the framework of his functions in the administration of international reserves, establish, in coordination with the Central Bank of Venezuela, at the end of each year, the level of reserves necessary for the national economy, as well as the amount of surplus reserves, which were to be directed to funds "established by the National Executive for productive investments, development and infrastructure, financing of the Missions, and, definitively, to the integral, endogenous, humanist and socialist development of the nation." This is to say that under the proposed reforms, all competencies in the area of monetary and fiscal policy would have been in the hands of the Chief of the National Executive power.

---

46   See the comments in Allan R. Brewer-Carías, "El sentido de la reforma de la Ley Orgánica de la Administración Pública,," in *Revista de Derecho Público*, Nº 115, Caracas 2008, pp. 155-162.

D.   *The proposed reform of the Council of State*

One of the innovations of the 1999 Constitution was the creation of the Council of State as a superior consultative entity of the government and Public Administration of intergovernmental character, with attributions to recommend policies of national interest in all the matter submitted to it by the President of the Republic (Article 251). The Council is headed by the Executive Vice President, integrated by other national high officials and by a representative of the States governors.

With the 2007 rejected Constitutional Reform, the shape of this Council was to be changed radically, in order to convert it in a consultative entity just for the national Government, with "functional autonomy" but whose opinions were to have not obligatory character, and presided by the President of the Republic, and integrated by all the high national powers officials (Article 252).

3.   *Proposed Reforms regarding the legislative power and the political permeability between the executive and the legislator*

The 1999 Constitution, following a traditional principle derived from the separation of powers, in order to assure the separation between the Executive and the legislative powers in the presidential system of government, established that the members of the National Assembly could not be appointed to executive positions, without losing their legislative tenure (art. 191). This means that once appointed to an executive post, the ex-member of the legislative body cannot return to the Assembly.

In the rejected Constitutional Reform, this separation was been diluted. Instead of the mentioned rule, the Reform sought to establish the contrary one, that is, that members of the National Assembly could accept executive positions without losing their legislative tenure. When designated by the President of the Republic, it was proposed that they could return to the Assembly once finished with an executive appointment, in order to finish the period of the legislative tenure for which they were elected (article 191). This provision, of course, was inconceivable in presidential systems of government. It is normal in parliamentary systems where the Parliament is in charge of forming the government with its members.

4.   *Proposed reforms regarding the judicial power*

A.   *Proposed reforms regarding the appointment and dismissal of the Justices of the Supreme Tribunal of Justice*

In addition to the aforementioned reforms regarding the composition of the Nominating Committee for the appointment of the Magistrates of the Supreme Tribunal of Justice (article 264), in the rejected 2007 Constitutional reform, the regime for their dismissal was also changed.

According to article 265 of the 1999 Constitution, the Magistrates can be dismissed by the vote of a qualified majority of the National Assembly, when grave faults are committed, following a prior qualification by the Citizens Power. This qualified two-thirds majority avoids leaving the bare existence of the heads of the judiciary in the hands of a simple majority of legislators. Unfortunately, this provision was distorted by the 2004 Organic Law of the Supreme Tribunal of Justice, in which it was established in an unconstitutional way that the Magistrates could be dismissed by simple majority when the "administrative act of their appointment" is revoked.

This distortion, contrary to the independence of the Judiciary, was proposed to be constitutionalized with the rejected Constitutional Reform, by establishing that the Magistrates of the Supreme Tribunal could be dismissed in case of graves faults, upon the vote of the majority of the members of the national Assembly."

    B.   *Proposed reforms regarding the attributions of the Supreme Tribunal*

In the rejected Constitutional Reform, the competencies of the Supreme Tribunal were proposed to be modified with respect to the prejudgment of high officials of the State, and judicial review of the decrees establishing a state of exception.

In the first case, the list of High officials benefiting from the privilege of the prejudgment by the Supreme Tribunal in order to be accused and submitted to trial, was extended in particular, to high military officials in positions of Command (Article 266.2).

In the second case, the rejected Constitutional Reform sought to eliminate the attribution the 1999 Constitution assigned the Constitutional Chamber of the Supreme Tribunal to constitutionally control executive decrees establishing states of exception even on an *ex officio* basis, which is to say, on its own initiative (article 339).

5.   *Proposed Reforms regarding the citizens power*

    A.   *Proposed reforms regarding the appointment and dismissal of the Heads of the Citizen Power*

The 1999 Constitution limited the powers of the National Assembly to appoint and dismiss the Peoples' Defender, the Comptroller General and the Prosecutor General.

Regarding the appointment of these High officials, the National Assembly is obliged to appoint those nominated by a Nominating Committee of the Citizens Power. That Committee is to be composed exclusively of representatives of the various sectors of society. As mentioned before, the rejected Constitutional Reform ought to change the composition of the Committee, transforming it into a parliamentary commission composed of members of the National Assembly, some other public officials, like the representative of the Popular Power, and some representatives of social organizations (article 279).

But, in addition, regarding the appointment of the High officials, the rejected Constitutional Reform sought to eliminate the guarantee of the qualified majority of the members of the National Assembly for such appointments (Article 279), seeking to establish a simple majority for that purpose as well.

    B.   *Proposed reforms regarding the powers of the Office of the Comptroller General*

Regarding the Office of the Comptroller General of the Republic, the rejected Constitutional Reform sought to eliminate the autonomy of the Comptrollers of the States and Municipalities, subjecting them to a National System of Fiscal Control and to the powers of the Comptroller General, even regarding their appointment which was to be attributed to the latter (Articles 163, 176, and 289.1,2,6).

6. *Proposed reforms regarding the electoral power*

A. *Proposed reforms regarding the appointment and dismissal of the members of the National Electoral Council*

In the same sense as the proposed changes in the nomination before the National Assembly of the members of the National Electoral Council, the provision of the Constitution of 1999 establishing that the Electoral Nominating Committee be composed of representatives of the various sectors of society (art. 292), has also to be changed. The rejected Constitutional Reform provided that the National Assembly, in order to make the appointments must itself convene a Nominating Committee that was to be composed of members of the Assembly itself, of representatives of the Popular Power, and representatives of other social organizations (art. 295). That is to say, the Nominating Committee was to be composed of a majority of public officials. The reform also sought to eliminate the requirement that the candidates must be nominated by civil society and law Faculties of the country, and instead it is established that such nominations are to be made by the Councils of Popular Power and other educational and social sectors (Article 296). These proposed reforms follow the trend established in the 2002 Organic Law of the Electoral Power which in an unconstitutional way converted the Nominating Committee into a parliamentary Commission.

On the other hand, the provision of the 1999 Constitution imposing the need for a majority of two thirds of the members of the Assembly to appoint members of the National Electoral Council (Article 296), was also to be eliminated in the rejected Constitutional Reform, and instead established that a vote by a simple majority was sufficient (Article 295). The reform also established that a majority of votes of the members of the National Assembly was sufficient to dismiss the members of the Electoral Power (Article 296).

B. *Proposed reforms regarding the attributions of the Electoral Power*

The 1999 Constitution assigned to the Electoral Power the attribution to not only organize the general elections, but also to organize those of trade unions, professional associations and political parties (organizations with political ends), and in addition, to intervene in the elections of civil society organizations (Article 292,6). This could be considered as an unacceptable intervention of the State into the functioning of private entities.

The rejected Constitutional Reform, sought to eliminate the intervention of the Electoral Council into the elections of trade unions, establishing in this regards the possibility for the Council to cooperate and assist in such elections, when asked to by trade unions or by the Supreme Tribunal of Justice.

In addition, the rejected Constitutional Reform proposed to eliminate the obligatory character of the directives issued by the Electoral Council regarding politico-electoral financing and publicity (Article 293.3).

VI. PROPOSED CHANGES IN THE ECONOMIC CONSTITUTION: FROM A SOCIAL AND MIXED ECONOMY STATE TO A SOCIALIST STATE WITH A CENTRALZIED STATE ECONOMY

According to the trends in constitutionalism developed since the middle of the last century, the economic constitution of Venezuela has been established upon the economic model of the mixed economy, which is based upon the principle of liberty as opposed to the directed economy, in a similar way to the economic models that exist in all western nations. This economic system, then, is founded upon economic liberty, private initiative, and free competition, without excluding the participation of the State as a promoter of economic development, as a regulator of economic activity, and as a planner together with the participation of civil society.

Following this orientation, the Constitution of 1999 establishes a mixed economic system, which is to say, a social market economy. This is an economic system that is based upon economic liberty, but which is required to be developed according to principles of social justice, and therefore requires the intervention of the State. This socio-economic regimen, in accord with article 299 of the Constitution, rests on the following principles: social justice, democratization, efficiency, free competition, environmental protection, productivity and solidarity. These are directed to the ends of assuring comprehensive human development, existence with dignity, and the maximum benefit for the collectivity. For these purposes, this very article of the Constitution expressly sets forth that the State, must, "jointly with private initiative," promote "the harmonious development of the national economy for the purpose of generating sources of employment, a high national level of added value, in order to elevate the standard of living of the population and strengthen the nation's economic sovereignty, guaranteeing legal certainty, solidity, dynamism, sustainability, permanence, and economic growth with equity, in order to guarantee a just distribution of wealth by means of strategic democratic, participative and open planning."

As the Constitutional Chamber of the Supreme Tribunal of Justice stated in its decision N° 117 of 6 February 2001[47] this is "a socioeconomic system that is intermediate between a free market (in which the State acts as a simple programmer (*programador*) for an economy that is dependent upon the supply and demand of goods and services) and an interventionist economy (in which the State actively intervenes as the 'primary entrepreneur')." The Constitution promotes, "joint economic activity between the State and private initiative in the pursuit of, and in order to concretely realize the supreme values consecrated in the Constitution," and in order to pursue "the equilibrium of all the forces of the market, and, joint activity between the State and private initiative." In accord with this system, the Courts ruled, the Constitution "advocates a series of superior normative values with respect to the economic regimen, consecrating free enterprise within the framework of a market economy and, fundamentally, within the framework of the Social State under

---

47   See in *Revista de Derecho Público,* N° 85-88, Editorial Jurídica Venezolana, Caracas, 2001, pp. 212-218

the Rule of Law (the *Welfare State*, the State of Well-being or the Social Democratic State). This is a social State that is opposed to authoritarianism."[48]

The practical application of this constitutional model brought about the development of an economy that is based on economic freedom and private initiative but that is subject to important and necessary intervention by the State in order a ensure the constitutionally, required orientation of economic regime based upon principles of social justice. State intervention has grown because the State owns title, within the public domain, to the petroleum rich sub-soil, as it always has in Venezuela's legal history.

In 2007, the rejected Constitutional Reform proposed to radically alter this model, to accentuate the existing disequilibrium between the public and private sectors, and to transform the system into one of a State economy based on central planning within a socialist State and socialist economy.

1. *The elimination of economic liberty as a constitutionally protected right to the free exercise of economic activities*

As one of the fundamental principles of the constitutional system, article 112 of the Constitution of 1999 establishes the right of every person to freely dedicate to the economic activity of his choice, without limitations beyond those that are established in the Constitution and the laws on the basis of reasons related to human development, to security, to public health, to the protection of the environment, or to other social interest. Because of this, under the 1999 Constitution, the State is obligated to promote, "private initiative, in order to guarantee the creation and just distribution of wealth, the production of goods and services meeting the needs of the population, the freedom to work, free enterprise, and commercial and industrial liberty, while not diminishing [the State's] power to take measures in order to plan, rationalize, and regulate the economy to promote comprehensive development within the nation."

The rejected Constitutional Reform proposed to eliminate both the constitutional right to develop economic activities and economic freedom, by seeking to substitute the above norm with one that defines, as only as a matter of state policy, the obligation to promote, "the development of a Productive Economic Model, that is intermediate, diversified and independent," Moreover, that model was to be, "founded upon the humanistic values of cooperation and the preponderance of common interests over individual ones, guaranteeing the meeting of the people's social and material needs, the greatest possible political and social stability, and the greatest possible sum of happiness." The proposal added that the State, in the same way, "shall

---

48   The values that are alluded to, according to the doctrine of the Constitutional Chamber, "are developed through the concept of free enterprise" (*libertad de empresa*) which encompasses both the notion of a subjective right "to dedicate oneself to the economic activity of ones choice," and a principle of economic regulation according to which the will of the business (*voluntad de la empresa*) to make its own decisions is manifest. The State fulfills its role of intervention in this context. Intervention can be direct (through businesses) or indirect (as an entity regulating the market)." *Idem.*

promote and develop different forms of businesses and economic units from social property, both directly or communally, as well as indirectly or through the state," According to this norm, additionally, the state was to promote, "economic units of social production and/or distribution, that may be mixed properties held between the State, the private sector, and the communal power, so as to create the best conditions for the collective and cooperative construction of a Socialist Economy"

This is to say, regarding article 112, which is located in the constitutional Chapter on economic rights, the rejected reforms sought simply to derogate and eliminate the right to the free exercise of economic activities as a constitutional right and the economic freedom itself. This would of course have been contrary to the principle of progressivism in human and constitutional rights that is guaranteed in article 19 of the Constitution of 1999. It also would have constituted a fundamental transformation of the State that cannot be accomplished through the "constitutional reform" procedure.

On the other hand, the 1999 Constitution confers a set of attributes to the State in order for it to regulate the exercise economic rights. In particular, the Constitution provides a regimen for the prohibition of monopolies, declaring activities that tend to establish them, or that can lead to their existence, as contrary to the fundamental principles of the Constitution (Article 113). The abuse of a position of market dominance, independent of the cause of such dominance, is also declared as being contrary to the fundamental principles of the constitution. In each of these cases, the norm affords the State the power to take those measures necessary to avoid the harmful and restrictive effects of monopoly, the abuse of market dominance, and the concentration of demand, for the purpose of protecting consumers and producers, as well as to ensure the protection of effective conditions for competition in the economy.

The rejected Constitutional Reform in these matters also proposed to radically alter the regimen of economic activity. The reform for article 113 provided for a series of limitations that far exceed the restrictions on monopoly and abuse of market dominance, but rather moved to establish a privileged public or state economy and privileged socialist means of production, within a capitalism of State.

In the context of this orientation, the rejected Constitutional Reform included a norm that prohibited activities, agreements, practices, conduct, and omissions by individuals that could damage the methods and systems of social and collective production and affect social and collective property. This norm was also to prohibit acts by individuals that prevent or make difficult the just and equitable confluence of goods and services. This norm would have therefore rendered the very possibility of private economic activity, subjected to decisions within the absolute discretion of public authorities.

The rejected Constitutional Reform also added to this norm that in cases involving the exploitation of natural resources or other assets within National dominion that are of a strategic character, or, that involve the providing of essential services, the State may reserve the exploitation of resources or the providing of services to itself, either directly or through State owned corporations. This was to be made, however, "without prejudice to the establishment of corporations were to be direct social property, of mixed corporations, and / or socialist units of production that ensure social and economic sovereignty, that respect the oversight of the State, and meet their imputed social responsibilities in accordance with the terms of legislation corresponding to their respective sector of the economy."

2. The elimination of property as a constitutionally protected right

In addition to economic liberty, another fundamental pillar of the Constitution of 1999 is the constitutional guarantee of the right to private property, conceived as the right of every person "to the use, enjoyment, benefit, and disposition of his or her assets" (article 115). The right to an asset is subject to "those contributions, restrictions, and obligations established by law for the purposes of public utility or general interest," and, it is "only for the cause of public utility or social interest, and on the basis of a final judicial decision and timely payment of just indemnification," that any asset may be expropriated.

The rejected Constitutional Reform sought to alter radically the regimen of the right to private property, by eliminating private property as a constitutionally protected right, and by only "recognizing" together with many sorts of properties, "private property" ("*la propiedad privada*") and only referred to "assets for use and consumption or as means of production," resulting minimized and marginalized in comparison to the other properties recognized and in particular to public property.

With respect to article 115 of the Constitution, the rejected Constitutional Reform, in effect, recognized and guarantees "different forms of property," instead of guaranteeing the right to private property, enumerating those different forms as follows:

1. "Public property (*la propiedad pública*) is that which belongs to the entities of the State; social property *(la propiedad social)* is that which belongs to the people jointly and to future generations, and can be of two kinds: a) "Indirect social property *(propiedad social indirecta)* when exercised by the State in the name of the community," and b) "Direct social property *(propiedad social directa),* when the State assigns property, in its different forms, and within the ambit of demarcated territories, to one or several communities, or to one or several communes, so that it constitutes communal property *(propiedad comunal)*; or the property is assigned to one or several cities, so that it constitutes, "citizens property" *(propiedad ciudadana)."*

2. "Collective property *(propiedad colectiva)* is property pertaining to social groups or persons, exploited for their common benefit, use, or enjoyment, that may be of social or private origin."

3. "Mixed property *(propiedad mixta)* is property that is constituted between the public sector, the social sector, the collective sector and the private sector, in different combinations, for the exploitation of resources or the execution of activities, subject always to the absolute economic and social sovereignty of the nation."

4. "Private property *(propiedad privada)* is that which is owned by natural or legal persons, is recognized as assets for use or consumption, or as means of production legitimately acquired."

As a consequence of these rejected reforms, private property was to be reduced to assets for use or consumption, or means of production. What is to be understood by assets for consumption remained to be defined, but in common parlance, were those assets that are not used to produce others goods, that is to say, that are used to meet the specific needs of the consumer who acquires them. "Means of production" in common usage refers to a set of work objects that whose use is coordinated in the process of production and that a man uses to create material assets.

With respect the guarantee of private property to be only taken by expropriation, the rejected Constitutional Reform regarding to article 115 sought to add express "authority to organs of the State to previously occupy assets that are the object of expropriation during judicial proceedings," and thus constitutionalized a mechanism for prior occupation.

3.   The elimination of the "latifundio"

Article 307 of the Constitution of 1999 declares the *latifundio* as contrary to social interests. In common usage, *latifundio* refers to large tracts of privately owned rural land subject to agricultural exploitation on a large scale, but that make inefficient use of the available resources. In order to correct this situation, the Constitution refers to the Legislator that must pass legislation "in the area of taxation, in order to levy taxes on idle lands and to establish the measures necessary to transform these into productive economic units, and, equally, recover lands with agricultural potential."

The norm contained in article 307 also establishes property rights for rural workers ("*campesinos*") and other agricultural and livestock producers working the land, in those cases, and according to the forms established in respective legislation. However, the article places an obligation on the State to protect and promote associational and private forms of property in order to guarantee agricultural production, and to safeguard the sustainable organization of arable lands with the objective of ensuring their agricultural and alimentary potential. The same article states that the Legislator shall on an exceptional basis create non-tax based contributions for the purpose of facilitating the funding of financing, research, technical assistance, technical transfers and other activities aimed at promoting the competitiveness and productivity of the agricultural sector.

The rejected Constitutional Reforms regarding article 307 sought to eliminate any concept of the public policy of promoting the disappearance of the *latifundio* through tax measures by taxing idle lands, and as well as to eliminate the policy of transforming the *latifundios* into productive economic units, while recovering lands with agricultural potential. Instead, the rejected Constitutional Reform established that, "the Republic shall determine by Law the form in which the *latifundios* will be transferred into the property of the State, or into that of public entities or public corporations, cooperatives, communities, or social organizations that are capable of administering them and of making the lands productive." Consequently, with the reform, it was not a matter of making any privately own *latifundio* productive, but rather to transfer the property to the State.

The rejected 2007 Constitutional Reform also added to this norm that for the purposes of guaranteeing agricultural production, the State shall protect and promote social property, and legislation shall be enacted to tax productive lands that are not devoted to agriculture or livestock.

Finally, it was proposed that a clause be added stating that "farms whose owners execute irreparable actions of environmental destruction, or dedicate farms to the production of psychotropic substances or narcotics, or trade in persons, or use the farms, or permit the farms to be used as areas for the commission of crimes against the security and defense of the Nation, shall be confiscated."

4.   *The regimen governing State intervention into the economy*

One of the classical forms of active State intervention in the economy is done through the constitution of public corporations or public enterprises. Regarding the regulation of such corporations, article 300 of the Constitution of 1999 only refers to national legislation for the establishment of conditions for the creation of public corporations as "entities that are functionally decentralized." The purpose of the public enterprises, under article 300, is to realize social or entrepreneurial activities aimed at assuring the reasonable economic and social productivity of the public resources invested.

The rejected 2007 Constitutional Reform sought to alter the idea of this regulation by eliminating any reference to decentralization, and, by reducing the scope of possible purposes serving as the basis for creating public enterprises or entities to the single purpose of promoting and realizing the ends of the socialist economy. In particular, the Constitutional Reform proposed that the norm in article 300 refer only to the creation of "regional corporations or entities for the promotion and realization of economic and social activities under the principles of the socialist economy," and that these establish "mechanisms for oversight and accounting that ensure transparency in the management of the public resources invested in them, and, their reasonable economic and social productivity."

Regarding trade policy, article 301 of the 1999 Constitution requires the State to defend the economic activity of national public and private enterprises, and established that foreign investments were to be subject to the same regulatory conditions as national investments. In the rejected Constitutional Reform, however, not only was the defense of the economic activities of public and private enterprises placed within the scope of the objectives of the State's trade policy, but also were added the defense of the communal, mixed, collective and social enterprises. With the proposed reform, in addition, all reference to foreign investment was eliminated.

With respect to economic activities to be reserved to the State, article 302 of the Constitution of 1999, sets forth that, "by means of the respective organic legislation and for reasons of national interest, the State shall reserve to itself the activity in petroleum," adding that activities in other "industries, forms of exploitation, and areas of goods and services that are in the public interest and are of a strategic character" may also be reserved to the State. In this way, the reserving to the State of the petroleum industry that had already been effectuated through the Organic Law of the nationalization of petroleum in 1975, acquired constitutional rank in the text of 1999. However, the constitutional text of 1999 tied the terms of the reserve to what was established in the organic law, which could be changed legislatively, as in fact occurred in 2000. The reservation of the petroleum industry to the State was thus neither rigid, nor absolute, but was flexible, in accord with what was established in the corresponding organic law.

712 ALLAN R. BREWER-CARÍAS

The rejected Constitutional Reform sought to radically change the conception of this regulation by establishing the reserve in the Constitution itself, for reasons of national interest, with respect to "the exploitation of liquid, solid and gaseous hydrocarbons, as well as to the initial recollection, transport and manufacturing and the works required for it." In the reform, it was added to the norm that "the State shall promote national manufacture to process the raw material, assimilating, creating or innovating national technology, in particular referred to the Orinoco Oil Belt (*Faja Petrolífera del Orinoco*), gas belts in land and off shore and the petrochemical corridors, in order to develop productive forces, to impulse economic growth and achieve social justice." In addition, it is added to the norm, that "the State by means of organic legislation can reserve for itself any other activity related to hydrocarbons."

In the same article, the reforms sought to add that the activities reserved to the State were to be accomplished "directly by the national Executive, or through entities or enterprises of its exclusive property, or by means of mixed enterprises in which the State have the control and majority of shares," therefore constitutionalizing the mixed enterprises regime established in 2006 and 2007.

In addition, in the rejected Constitutional Reform, regarding article 113, it was provided that the State could also reserve for itself, directly or by means of enterprises of its property, the exploitation or execution of natural resources or any other public of the domain of the Nation (*dominio de la Nación*) considered to be by the Constitution or by the law of a strategic character, as well as the rendering of vital public services (public utilities) considered as such in the Constitution or in the law.

Finally, regarding the State reserved activities, the rejected constitutional reform regarding article 303, sought to establish the absolute prohibition to privatize any of them.

Another important innovation of the 1999 Constitution was the regulation of principles and policies in the area of sustainable agricultural production and nutritional security through 305. The rejected Constitutional Reform proposed to add to this article that "if necessary to guarantee nutritional security, the Republic may assume indispensable sectors of agricultural, livestock, fishing and aquatic production, and transfer their operation to autonomous entities, public corporations and social, cooperative, or communal organizations." Further, the proposal added that the Republic might in this context, "fully utilize its powers of expropriation, encumbrance, and occupation according to the terms established by this Constitution and the Law."

5. *The proposed changes in the State's fiscal and economic regimen*

In the area of the fiscal regimen, for the first time in Venezuelan constitutionalism, the 1999 Constitution incorporates a set of norms relating to the Central Bank of Venezuela and the macro-economic policy of the State (arts. 318 a 321). In particular the Constitution attributes the National Power's competencies relating monetary policy to the Central Bank of Venezuela requiring exercising it exclusively, and obligatorily for the fundamental objectives of achieving stability in prices and preserving the internal and external values of the currency. The Constitution guarantees the Bank's autonomy in the formulation of policies within its competency. In addition, in order that the Bank could adequately meet its objectives, the Constitution assigns to it competencies to formulate and execute monetary policy, to participate in the design and execution of exchange policy, to regulate money and credit, to set interests rates, to administer international reserves, and to assume all of those attributes established by law.

A. *The elimination of the autonomy of the Central Bank of Venezuela and the Executive's assumption of monetary policy*

Contrary to the provisions of the 1999 Constitution, the rejected Constitutional Reform totally and radically sought to change the regimen governing monetary policy and the Central Bank of Venezuela by seeking to eliminate the Bank's competencies and autonomy, and rendering the Bank totally and directly dependent upon the National Executive.

To this end, the following reforms were proposed regarding article 318 of the Constitution:

In the first place, to require that "The national monetary system be directed towards at the achievement of the essential ends of the Socialist State and the well being of the people, above any other consideration."

In the second place, those competencies to fix monetary policies of the National Power that the Constitution of 1999 "exclusively" assigns to the Central Bank would instead be attributed to the National Executive and the Central Bank "in strict and obligatory coordination."

In the third place, the autonomy of the Bank was formally eliminated through proposed language stating that the Bank "is a person in public law without autonomy in the formulation and execution of the corresponding policies." To this was added that the Bank's functions were to be subordinated to general economic policy and to the National Development Plan (-which is dictated by the Executive alone, without the intervention of the National Assembly-), in order to achieve the superior objectives of the Socialist State and the greatest possible sum of happiness for the whole of the people."

In the fourth place, in the rejected reform for article 118, it was established that the functions of the Central Bank were to be "shared with the Executive Power," and that for the adequate fulfillment of its specific objectives, the Central Bank of Venezuela "shall have, among its functions, shared with the National Executive Power," only the power to "participate in the formulation and execution of monetary policy, in the design and execution of exchange policy, in the regulation of money and credit, and the fixing of interest rates."

In the fifth place, competency to "administer international reserves" was entirely removed from the Central Bank of Venezuela," so the norm would have state instead that, "the international reserves of the Republic shall be managed by the Central Bank of Venezuela, under the administration and direction of the President of the Republic, as administrator of the National Public Treasury."

B. *Macro-economic policy at the mercy of the National Executive*

Article 320 of the Constitution of 1999 establishes detailed regulation in relation to the coordination of macro-economic policy, first relating to economic stability and second to a "Macro-economic Stabilization Fund" ("*Fondo de Estabilización Macroeconómica*"). The rejected Constitutional Reform sought radically to change both regulations.

Article 320 sets forth that "the State must promote and defend economic stability, avoid economic vulnerability and safeguard the price stability in order to assure social well being." The provision establishes the obligation "of the ministry responsible for the finances and of the Central Bank of Venezuela" to contribute "to the harmonization of fiscal policy with monetary policy, facilitating the achievement of the macro-economic objectives." The Constitution further states that "in the exercise of its functions, the Central Bank of Venezuela shall not be subordinated to the directives of the Executive Power and shall not validate or finance deficit fiscal policies."

In addition, the constitutional norm requires that the coordinated action of the Executive Power and the Central Bank of Venezuela is to be realized "through an annual policy agreement" which must include the "final growth objectives and their social repercussions, the foreign exchange balance, inflation, fiscal, exchange and monetary policy, as well as the levels of intermediate and instrumental variables necessary for the achievement of the indicated final objectives." Article 320 set forth the formal procedures required for the approval of the agreement, which included the signature of the President of the Central Bank of Venezuela, the signature of the head of the Ministry of Finances, and the presentation of the agreement to the National Assembly at the time of the Assembly's approval of the budget. The Constitution provides that the institutions signatories to the agreement are responsible to ensure that it's "policy actions are consistent with its objectives," and that it specifies, "the anticipated results, and the policies and actions directed towards reaching those results."

The rejected 2007 Constitutional Reform sought to eliminate the entire detailed regulatory framework designed to guarantee economic stability and coordination between the National Executive and the Central Bank; proposing instead that article 320 contained the following language: "the State must promote and defend economic stability, avoid economic vulnerability and safeguard the monetary and price stability, in order to assure social well being. Equally, the State shall safeguard the harmonization of fiscal and monetary policies to achieve the macro-economic objectives." These changes would have eliminated any principle of coordination between the National Executive and the Central Bank. Under these reforms, the Central Bank would have remained without autonomy as an executing arm of what is disposed by the National Executive.

With respect to the regimen governing the Fund for Macro-Economic Stabilization, article 321 of the 1999 Constitution refers to it as "destined to guarantee the expenditures of the State at the municipal, regional and national levels in the event of fluctuations in ordinary revenues." The article requires that the functioning of the fund be tied to "basic principles of efficiency, equity, and non-discrimination among the public entities that bring resources to it." The rejected Constitutional Reform, totally eliminated the Fund for Macro-economic Stabilization, and in stead, it was proposed that article 321 be re-written to attribute the function of the "administration of international reserves" "to the Head of State" and to authorize the Head of State "in coordination with the Central Bank of Venezuela, to establish the level of reserves needed for the national economy, at the end of each year, as well as the amount of surplus reserves." The express indication was added that the surplus reserves shall be destined to funds established by the National Executive for productive investments, development and infrastructure, financing of the Missions, and, definitively, to the integral, endogenous, humanist and socialist development of the nation."

VII. PROPOSED CHANGES IN MATTERS OF HUMAN RIGHTS

With respect to human rights, the 1999 Constitution introduced very important and notable reforms, sealed by the principle of progressiveness in their protection, which was expressly included in article 19.

Unfortunately, in this matter of human rights, a few important and radical changes were incorporated in the rejected 2007 Constitutional Reform, like the already referred to restrictive changes in matters of political rights and political participation, and on matters of economic freedom and property rights. In addition, in matters of emergency or states of exception, the rejected Constitutional Reform also had a notable regressive character, contrary to the principle of progressiveness, and through which the State was proposed to be configured as a repressive (Police) State. Other reforms in matters of human rights referred to the right of non-discrimination and to labor rights. Reforms in the latter category do not require a constitutional reform since they can be achieved through legislation.

1.   The extension of the principle of equality

In article 21 of the 1999 Constitution, the principle of equality and non-discrimination was extensively regulated, with a very rich content.

In the rejected 2007 Constitutional Reform, the principle was extended with respect to the enumeration of the forms of forbidden discrimination. While the 1999 Constitution referred to discriminatory motives based upon "race, sex, religion and social condition," the 2007 Constitutional reform draft proposed to add discriminatory motives based upon "ethnic, gender, age, sex, health, creed, political orientation, sexual orientation, social and religious conditions."

2.   Proposed changes in the states of exception regime and on the suspension and restriction of constitutional guaranties

Chapter II of Title VIII of the 1999 Constitution ("Protection of the Constitution"), is directed to establish the régime governing the exceptional circumstances that could originate states of exception or emergency that could gravely affect the security of the Nation, of its institutions and of persons, and impose the need to adopt exceptional measures (Article 337).

With the rejected Constitutional Reform, the protective regulations established in the 1999 Constitution regarding human rights were proposed to be radically changed, including the revocation of the Organic Law on the States of Exception of 2001 in the only derogatory Disposition of the reform.

A.   *The expansion of the cases allowing the declaration of states of exception*

According to article 338 of the 1999 Constitution, a "state of alarm" can be de-creed "when catastrophes, public calamities and other similar situations could con-stitute a serious peril for the security of the nation or its citizens."

In the rejected Constitutional Reform, the states of alarm were extended, estab-lishing two sorts: first, one that established hypothetical situations that could origi-nate the new form of a state of alarm, in cases where "a certain and imminent possi-bility exists for the occurrence of situations capable of originating catastrophes, pub-lic calamities and other similar situations, in order to adopt the necessary measures to protect the nation and its citizens"; and second, calling the previous regulated "state of alarm" a "state of emergency."

B.   *The elimination of the terms of duration of the states of emergency*

The 1999 Constitution establishes that the states of exception (alarm, emergency, or commotion) must necessarily be limited to a duration which varies from 30 to 90 days, with the possibility an extension. The rejected 2007 Constitutional Reform sought to eliminate from article 338 the terms of duration from the various states of exception (30 days for the state of alarm; 60 days for the state of economic emer-gency; and 90 days for the states of interior or exterior commotion). It proposed to convert them into situations without temporal limits, whose enforcement was subject to the sole will and discretion of the President of the Republic.

The consequence of this reform was that also, the National Assembly was to lose the power it has according to the 1999 Constitution, to approve or deny extensions of the duration of the states of emergency.

C.   *The possibility of the suspension and not only of the restriction of constitu-tional guaranties*

The 1999 Constitution expressly eliminated the possibility for the President of the Republic to "suspend" the constitutional guaranties of human rights, as had been authorized in the 1961 Constitution, and had in the past led to unacceptable institu-tional abuses[49]. In cases of states of exception, the power of the President of the Republic was then reduced to only temporarily "restrict" (art. 236.7) the constitu-tional guaranties.

With the rejected 2007 Constitutional Reform, in a specifically regressive way, the possibility for the President to suspend constitutional guarantees was proposed to be re-established, which was and is inadmissible in a democratic society.

---

49   See for example, Allan R. Brewer-Carías, "Consideración sobre la suspensión o restricción de las garantías constitucionales Considerations on the suspensión or restriction of constitu-tional guarantees," *Revista de Derecho Público*, N° 37, Editorial Jurídica Venezolana, Cara-cas, enero-marzo 1989, pp. 5-25.

D. *Changes regarding the constitutional guarantees of human rights that can be defected in situations of exception*

Within the constitutional guarantees that according to the 1999 Constitution could not be affected in cases of a declaration of states of exception, are the right to life, the prohibition against incommunicado detentions, the prohibition of torture, the right to due process of law, the right to be informed, and all the other intangible human rights." The latter term could be considered to include the guarantees that according to the International Covenant of Civil and Political Rights and to the American Convention of Human Rights could not be suspended, such as the guarantee of equality and non- discrimination, the guarantee to not to be condemned to prison on the basis of contractual obligations; the guarantee against retroactive or *ex post facto* laws the right to personality, to religious liberty, the principle of legality, the protection of the family; the rights of the child, the guarantee against being arbitrarily deprived of nationality, the exercise of the political rights, and the right to have access to public functions.

In the rejected 2007 Constitutional Reform, the prohibition against suspending or restricting due process of law rights, the right to be informed and all the other intangible human rights right were to be eliminated from article 337. Added to the reduced list of non affected rights were: the prohibition of the disappearance of persons, the right to self defense, the right to personal integrity, the right to be judged by the competent natural court, and to not be condemned to punishment in excess of 30 years.

F. *The elimination of the control mechanisms of the states of exception*

The 1999 Constitution, in the provisions regarding the states of exception, establishes three sorts of mechanism for controlling the executive powers: through the national Assembly, through the Constitutional Chamber of the Supreme Tribunal, and through international organizations. All of these mechanisms for control were proposed to be eliminated in the rejected 2007 Constitutional Reform.

First, the reform eliminated the possibility for the National Assembly to control and revoke the executive decree declaring states of exception (including the possibility to extend their term), and established only that the President of the Republic could put end to the effects of the decree "when their motivating cause ceases (Article 339). The decree declaring the state of exception was to be presented to the Assembly, but in the reform, the Assembly retained no power whatsoever to revoke it, as it is established in the 1999 Constitution.

Second, the rejected Constitutional Reform also eliminated from article 339 the obligatory constitutional control attributed to the Constitutional Chamber of the Supreme Tribunal regarding decrees of states of exception. Nonetheless, the competency of the Supreme Tribunal remained in article 336.6, which attributed the Constitutional Chamber the power to review the constitutionality of the decrees, even *ex officio*, on the basis of its own initiative,

Third, the rejected 2007 Constitutional Reform also proposed to eliminate the constitutional provision established in article 339 of the 1999 Constitution, that requires that executive decrees of states of exception comply with "the conditions, principles and guarantees established in the International Covenant on Civil and Political Rights and in the American Convention on Human Rights" (Article 339).

3.   *Proposed changes in labor rights: a useless constitutional "reform"*

The rejected Constitutional Reform also proposed changed to two articles from the chapter of the Constitution of 1999 regarding labor rights. First, article 87 referred to the regimen for social security for non-dependent workers; and second, article 90 of the Constitution concerning the maximum length of the work day. The content of the proposed reforms, however, was not a matter for constitutional review and required no constitutional modification for their implementation that could be achieved through legislation developing the norms contained in the Constitution of 1999.[50]

VIII. PROPOSED CHANGES IN THE REGIMEN OF THE ARMED FORCES: FROM A CIVILLY MANAGED STATE TO A MILITARIST STATE

Another area of innovation in the Constitution of 1999 was the regimen of the National Armed Forces, established within the regimen of security and defense. The changes in 1999 demonstrated an accentuation of militarism.

The rejected 2007 Constitutional Reform in addition to changing the name of the institution of the National Armed Forces to the Bolivarian Armed Forces (proposed reforms for articles 156,8; 236,6; 328 and 329), and changing the names of the institution's components: the Army, the Navy, the Air Force, and the National Guard, to the Bolivarian National Army, the Bolivarian National Navy, the Bolivarian National Air Force, the Bolivarian National Guard, and the Bolivarian National Militia (Article 329), proposed radical changes in the character of the military as an institution. The proposed reforms for articles 328 and 329 of the Constitution sought to transform the military from a professional, apolitical institution, that does not deliberate, and that operates at the service of the Republic, into a militia that operates at the service of the Chief of State and at the service of his or her political partiality.

Article 328 of the 1999 Constitution establishes that the National Armed Forces is "an institution that is essentially professional, without political affiliation, and organized by the State in order to guarantee the independence and sovereignty of the Nation and to assure the integrity of its geographic space." In order to achieve its purposes, the National Armed Forces must assure the military defense, the coopera-

---

50   The only reasonable explanation for the inclusion of these futile constitutional "reforms" among the 2007 proposals derives from a decision of the National Electoral Council that the national referendum to the approve the constitutional reforms will be effectuated in one single block (*en bloque*), which is to say, all the reforms are to be approved or disapproved together as a single set of provisions in the referendum, rather than having each reform voted on separately. Because of this, the labor "reforms" serve as a disincentive for the "NO" vote on all of the Constitutional reforms. A "NO" vote would mean a vote against these improvements in the labor area, even though, as stated, these changes do not in fact need to a Constitutional reform to be implemented.

tion in the maintenance of internal order, and the active participation in national development. The norm in article 328 adds that, "in the fulfillment of its function," the National Armed Forces operates "exclusively at the service of the Nation, and not at the service of any person or political partiality." The article sets forth "discipline, obedience and subordination." as fundamental pillars of the institution.

The rejected 2007 Constitutional Reform regarding article 328, sought in the first place, to eliminate the constitutional clause that states that the Armed Forces "is an institution that is essentially professional, without political affiliation." In its place, it was proposed that the Constitution stated that the Armed Forces were "a corps that is essentially patriotic, popular, and anti-imperialist." Under this reform, the military as a professional institution would have disappeared, as would the prohibition against the institution's assumption of a political partisanship. The definition of the institution as "patriotic, popular, and anti-imperialist" would have opened an avenue for the integration of the Armed Forces into the political party of its Commander in Chief who would, under the proposed reforms for article 236,6 exercised Supreme Hierarchical Authority in each of its Corps, Components and Units.

In the second place, while article 328 sets forth the objectives of the Armed Forces in the following terms: "to guarantee the independence and sovereignty of the Nation, and assure the integrity of its geographic space," the rejected reform proposed to add "to reserve [the Nation] from any internal or external attack."

In the third place, instead of stating that the objectives of the Armed Forces are to be achieved "through military defense, through cooperation in the maintenance of internal order, and through active participation in national development," the rejected reform established that the objectives must be obtained "by means of study, planning and execution of Bolivarian military doctrine, by means of the application of principles of comprehensive military defense and the popular war of resistance (*"guerra popular de resistencia"*), by means of permanent participation in the tasks of maintaining citizen security and the conservation of internal order, and in the same sense, by means of actively participating in the plans for the economic, social, scientific and technical development of the Nation." In this way, the "Bolivarian Military Doctrine" sought to be incorporated into the Constitution as an essential element of the Armed Forces, although the exact content of this term remains unknown. Guerrilla elements were proposed to be incorporated in the term "popular war of resistance and the Armed Forces was proposed to be converted into a national police organization, charged with citizen security and conservation of internal order. In addition providing that the Armed Forces are to, among its other functions, "active[ly] participate in the plans for the economic, social, scientific and technical development of the Nation" the rejected reform sought to constitutionalize the militarization of the State and the Public Administration.

In the fourth place, instead of providing, as the Constitution of 1999 does, that in fulfilling its function the Armed Forces operates "exclusively at the service of the Nation, and not of any person or political partiality," the rejected 2007 Constitutional Reform proposed that the Armed Forces "in the fulfillment of its function, shall always be at the service of the Venezuelan people in defense of their sacred interests, and in no case shall be at the service of any oligarchy or foreign imperial power." The consequence of this change would have been to eliminate the constitutional prohibition now placed upon the Armed Forces from operating in the service of any person or political preference. This proposal, again, sought to open a path to the integration of the Armed Forces into the political party of his Commander in Chief, who, under the proposed reforms for 236.6 of the Constitution, would exercise Supreme Hierarchical Authority in each of its Corps, Components and Units, and, who could then place the Armed Forces at his service or at the service of the government's party.

It should be remembered, also, that the rejected reform for article 236,7, sought to attribute to the President of the Republic, acting in his or her capacity as Commander in Chief the power to "promote officials in all [of the Armed Force's] ranks and hierarchies and to assign them to their corresponding positions." This power would have constituted an instrument for securing a political hold on such officials.

In the fifth place, where article 328's asserts that the fundamental pillars of the Armed Forces are the Constitution and the laws, discipline, obedience and subordination, the rejected Constitutional Reform proposed to add, "its historic pillars stand in the mandate of Bolívar: "Liberate the homeland, take up the sword in defense of the social guarantees and be deserving of the people's blessings."

Article 329 of the Constitution of 1999, states that "the Army, the Navy and the Air Force have, as an essential responsibility, the duty to plan, execute and oversee those military operations that are required to assure the defense of the Nation." The National Guard, under this norm, is to "cooperate in the development of those operations and shall have as a basic responsibility, the duty to carry out operations necessary for maintaining the internal order of the country." The provision adds that "the Armed Forces may exercise those administrative police and criminal investigative activities that are assigned by law."

The rejected Constitutional Reform proposed to change article 329 as follows. In the first place, it proposed to increase the number of military components of the Bolivarian Armed Forces to five, including land, air and sea corps, and to administratively organize these into the Bolivarian National Army, the Bolivarian National Navy, the Bolivarian National Air Force, the Bolivarian National Guard, and the Bolivarian National Militia.

In the second place, the reform established that the Bolivarian Armed Forces "could accomplish police activities attributed by law."

All of these reforms sought to complete a process of accentuating the political character of the Armed Forces and the militarism of the State that began in the Constitution of 1999 itself. The provision asserting the "apolitical and non-deliberating character" of the armed forces established in 132 de la Constitution de 1961 had already disappeared from the 1999 constitutional text, as had the essential obligation of the armed forces to ensure "the stability of the democratic institutions and respect of the Constitution and the laws, whose obedience is always above any other obligation" contained in the same 1961 article. The traditional prohibition against the simultaneous exercise of military and civil authority contained in article 131 of the Constitution of 1961, and the control held by the former Senate over military promotions in the upper levels under article 331 of the Constitution of 1961 had also already disappeared in the Constitution of 1999.

In any case, notwithstanding the popular rejection to all these reforms proposed in the 2007 Constitutional Reform, they were all implemented in a fraudulent and illegitimate way by means of a Decree Law enacted by the President of the Republic in 2008, reforming the Organic law of the Bolivarian Armed Forces. [51]

IX. THE IRREGULAR AND DEFRAUDING IMPLEMENTATION OF MANY OF THE REJECTED CONSTITUTIONAL REFORMS BY MEANS OF LAWS AND DECREE LAWS

Once rejected the 2007 Constitutional Reform by popular vote, the President of the Republic and the main officials of the National Assembly, publicly announced that in spite of such rejection, by means of statutes and decree laws they were going to implement them, which effectively occurred in many matters through decree laws and statutes contrary to the Constitution.

In effect, many of the rejected constitutional reforms were illegitimately and fraudulently implemented by means of decree laws issued by the President of the Republic in execution of the February 1999 Enabling Law,[52] sanctioned in parallel to the announcement by the President of the beginning of the 2007 Constitutional Reform process. After its popular rejection, the legislative delegation powers contained in the Enabling Law was then used in a fraudulent way to implement many of the rejected constitutional reforms,[53] particularly in economic and social matters in order to structure a Socialist centralized State.

This process even began before the Constitutional Reform Draft was submitted by the National Assembly, when a Decree Law N° 5841 was enacted in June 12, 2007,[54] containing the Organic Law creating the Central Planning Commission. This was the first formal State act devoted to build the Socialist State that the 2007 Constitutional Reform proposal aimed to consolidate.[55] Once this Reform was rejected

---

51   See Jesús María Alvarado Andrade, "La nueva Fuerza Armada Bolivariana (comentarios a raíz del Decreto N° 6.239, con rango, valor y fuerza de Ley Orgánica de la Fuerza Armada Nacional Bolivariana),"in *Revista de Derecho Público*, N° 115, Editorial Jurídica Venezolana, Caracas 2008, pp. 205 ff.

52   *Gaceta Oficial*, 38.617, of February 1st, 2007

53   See Lolymar Hernández Camargo, "Límites del poder ejecutivo en el ejercicio de la habilitación legislativa: Imposibilidad de establecer el contenido de la reforma constitucional rechazada vía habilitación legislativa," in *Revista de Derecho Público*, N° 115 *(Estudios sobre los Decretos Leyes)*, Editorial Jurídica venezolana, Caracas 2008, pp. 51 ff.; Jorge Kiriakidis, "Breves reflexiones en torno a los 26 Decretos-Ley de Julio-Agosto de 2008, y la consulta popular refrendaría de diciembre de 2007," *Idem*, pp. 57 ff.; and José Vicente Haro García, "Los recientes intentos de reforma constitucional o de cómo se está tratando de establecer una dictadura socialista con apariencia de legalidad (A propósito del proyecto de reforma constitucional de 2007 y los 26 decretos leyes del 31 de julio de 2008 que tratan de imponerla)," *Idem*, pp. 63 ff.

54   *Gaceta Oficial* N° 5.841 Extra. of June 22, 2007.

55   See Allan R. Brewer-Carías, "Comentarios sobre la inconstitucional creación de la Comisión Central de Planificación, centralizada y obligatoria," in *Revista de Derecho Público*, N° 110, (abril-junio 2007), Editorial Jurídica Venezolana, Caracas 2007, pp. 79-89.

by the December 2, 2007 Referendum, ten days latter, on December 13, 2007 the National Assembly approved the *2007-2013 Economic and Social Development National Plan* that was established in article 32 of the Decree Law enacting the Planning Organic Law, in which the basis of the "planning, production and distribution system oriented towards socialism," are established providing that "the relevant matter is the progressive development of social property of the production means." For such purpose, the proposals of rejected 2007 Constitutional Reform to assign the State all powers to control and assume farming, livestock, fishing and aquiculture production, and in particular, the production of food, where materialized by the Decree Law on the Organic law on Farming and Food Security and Sovereignty,"[56] in which it was assigned to the State not only to power to authorize food imports but to prioress its production and also to directly assume its distribution and commercialization.

In the same sense, through Decree Law N° 6.130 of June 3, 2008, the Popular Economy Promotion and Development Law was enacted, establishing a "socio-productive communal model," with different socio-productive organizations following the "socialist model."[57] In the same openly socialist orientation another Decree Law was issued enacting the Access to Goods and Services Persons Defense Law, which derogated the previous Consumer and Users Protection Law,[58] with the purpose of regulating all the commercialization chain and all the different economic aspects related to goods and services, extending the State powers of control to the point of establishing the possibility to confiscate goods and services.

Regarding the 2007 Constitutional reforms related to representative democracy in order to eliminate it at the local level, the same began to be implemented in 2006, before those proposals, with the sanctioning of the Communal Councils Law,[59] that created them, as social units and organizations directed by not elected officials, without any sort of territorial autonomy, supposedly devoted to canalized citizens participation, but in a centralized conducted system from the apex of the National Executive.

Regarding the elimination of the decentralizing principle that has been one of the fundamental principles of Venezuelan constitutionalism, one of the purpose of the rejected 2007 Constitutional Reform, was to complete the dismantling of the Federal form of the State through the centralization of attributions that were assigned to the States, the creation of administrative entities to be established and directed by the

---

56   *OficialGazette* N° 5.889 Extra. of July 31, 2008.

57   *OficialGazette* N° 5.890 Extra. of July 31, 2008.

58   *OficialGazette* N° 37.930 of May 4, 2004.

59   Ley de Consejos Comunales, *Oficial Gazette,* N° 5806 Extra. of April 10, 2006. See Allan R. Brewer-Carías, "El inicio de la desmunicipalización en Venezuela: La organización del Poder Popular para eliminar la descentralización, la democracia representativa y la participación a nivel local," in *AIDA, Opera Prima de Derecho Administrativo. Revista de la Asociación Internacional de Derecho Administrativo*, Universidad Nacional Autónoma de México, México, 2007, pp. 49 a 67

National Executive, the attribution of powers to the President of the Republic in order to interfere in regional and local affairs, and the voiding of State and Municipal competency by means of their compulsory transfer to the Communal Councils.

In order to implement these reforms, not only the last mentioned aspect has been achieved forcing the States and Municipalities to transfer its attributions to local institutions controlled by the Central Power (Communal Councils), but by means of Decree Law N° 6.217 of July 15, 2008 on the Organic Law of Public Administration[60] that is now directly applicable to the States' and Municipalities' Public Administrations, by means of implementing the principle of centralized planning, they have been subjected to what the National Executive may decide through the Central Planning Commission. This Organic Law also assigns to the President of the Republic, as was proposed in the rejected 2007 Constitutional Reform, the power to appoint Regional Authorities with powers to plan, execute, follow up and control land use and territorial development policies, subjecting all programs and projects to central planning approval.

Regarding the vertical distribution of State attributions between the national level and the States, the proposed 2007 Constitutional Reform, among other aspects, sought to eliminate the "exclusive" attribution assigned to the States in article 164.10 of the Constitution, to "maintain, administrate and profited use of national roads and highways, as well as ports and airports of commercial use, in coordination with the National Power." In this case, the fraudulent implementation of the rejected constitutional reform was made by the Constitutional Chamber of the Supreme Tribunal of Justice, when deciding recourse for constitutional interpretation filed by the Attorney General representing the National Executive. In decision N° 565 of April 15, 2008,[61] the Supreme Tribunal simply "modified" the content of the mentioned constitutional provision, and through an obligatory interpretation provided, mutating the Constitution, that such "exclusive" attribution was not as such, but only a "concurrent" one, that the National Power could revert, eliminating the competency of the States. The disruption of the legal order provoked by such decision forced the Constitutional Chamber to urge the National Assembly to approve legislation in accordance with the "constitutional reform" that it produced. This was effectively accomplished in May 2009. by means of the reform of the Organic Law on Decentralization, Delimitation and Transfer of Public Attributions,[62] eliminating the exclusive attributions of the States established in its article 11.3 and 11.5, and adding two new provisions authorizing the National Executive to revert the transfer of competencies already made to the States (article 8); and to decree the intervention of trans-

---

60   *G.O.* Extra N° 5.890 de 31-07-2008. Véase Allan R. Brewer-Carías, "El sentido de la reforma de la Ley Orgánica de la Administración Pública," *Revista de Derecho Público*, N° 115, EJV, Caracas 2008, pp. 155 ff.

61   *Cfr.* Sentencia de la Sala Constitucional N° 565, Caso *Procuradora General de la República*, recurso de interpretación del artículo 164.10 de la Constitución de 1999 de fecha 15 de Abril de 2008, en http://www.tsj.gov.ve/de-cisiones/scon/Abril/565-150408-07-1108.htm.

62   *Gaceta Oficial* N° 39 140 of March 17, 2009.

ferred assets and public services (article 9). With these reforms, the fraud upon the Constitution was completed, disrupting the federal regime of government.[63]

Within the same centralizing trend, the 2007 rejected Constitutional Reform sought to eliminate the Capital District, created in the federal framework of the Constitution as a political entity where Public National authorities have their siege, instead recreating the former "Federal District" as an entity without self government, completely dependent from the National level of government, and in particular, from the President of the Republic. Notwithstanding the popular rejection to the reform, on April 2009 it was implemented by the National Assembly in defraudation of the Constitution, sanctioning a Special Law on the Organization and Regime of the Capital District.[64] In it, instead of creating a democratic entity to govern the Capital District, the Law established an organization completely dependent of the National level of government in the same territorial jurisdiction that "used to be the one of the extinct Federal District" equivalent to the one of the current *Libertador* Municipality in the capital city of Caracas. According to this Law, the Capital District, now and in a contrary sense to what is provided in the Constitution, has no self elected authorities of government, and is governed by the National level of government by means of a "special regime" consisting in the exercise of the legislative function by the National Assembly itself, and a Chief of Government in charge of the executive branch (article 3) appointed by the President of the Republic. This means that through a national statute, in the same territory of the *Libertador* Municipality, a new national structure has been unconstitutionally superposed.

Another of the 2007 rejected Constitutional reforms was referred to military matters, seeking to transform the National Armed Force into a National Bolivarian Armed Force, creating beside the Army, the Navy, the Air force and the National Guard, a new fifth component, called the "National Bolivarian Militia." Although this was rejected in the December 2, 2007, the President of the Republic, by means of a Decree Law reformed the Organic Law on the Armed Force,[65] transforming the National Armed Force into a "Bolivarian National Armed Force" subjected to a "military Bolivarian Doctrine," and creating in it the "National Bolivarian Militia," all of this according to what was proposed and rejected by the people in the 2007 Constitutional Reform.

---

63   See Allan R. Brewer-Carías, "La Sala Constitucional como poder constituyente: la modifica-
      ción de la forma federal del estado y del sistema constitucional de división territorial del po-
      der público, in *Revista de Derecho Público*, N° 114, (abril-junio 2008), Editorial Jurídica
      Venezolana, Caracas 2008, pp. 247-262.

64   *Gaceta Oficial* N° 39.156 of April 13, 2009.

65   Decree Law N° 6.239, on the Organic Law of the National Bolivarian Armed Force, in *Offi-
      cial Gazette* N° 5.891 Extra. of July 31, 2008.

CHAPTER XXIV

THE ALTERNATE PRINCIPLE OF GOVERNMENT AND
THE 2009 CONSTITUTIONAL AMENDMENT ON
CONTINEOUS REELECTION

(2009)

This essay was written in 2009 dealing with the *2009 Constitutional Amendment* that was approved after the rejection of the same constitutional review proposal in 2007, by a referendum held on February 2009, through which the alternate character of government was changed, establishing in the Constitution the possibility for the continuous and indefinite reelection of the President of the Republic. It was initially written with the title "Venezuela 2009 Referendum on Continuous Reelection: Constitutional implications" for my Presentation in the *Panel Discussion on Venezuela Referendum: Public Opinion, Economic Impact And Constitutional Implications*, Moderated by Christopher Sabatini, *Americas Society/Council of the Americas*, held in New York, February 9, 2009. The text was published in Spanish as "El Juez Constitucional vs. La alternabilidad republicana (La reelección continua e indefinida)," in *Revista de Derecho Público*, N° 117, (enero-marzo 2009), Caracas 2009, pp. 205-211.

On February 15th 2009, a referendum took place in Venezuela approving Constitutional Amendment in order to change the principle of alternate democratic government, allowing the continuous and indefinite reelection of elected public official. This Constitutional Amendment was made defrauding the prohibition established in the Constitution to submit to popular vote the same constitutional reform proposal during the same constitutional term, and eliminating a non changeable constitutional principle like the alternate one.

I. THE REPUBLICAN PRINCIPLE OF ALTERNATE GOVERNMENT AND THE VENEZUELAN NON REELECTION TRADITION

In effect, since the beginning of the Republic, the general restriction for elected officials to be reelected in a continuous way has been a tradition in the Venezuelan Constitutional history, having Venezuela adopted since 1811, as occurred in all Latin America countries, the presidential system of government.[66]

The restriction to presidential reelection was first established in the 1830 Constitution, as a reaction to continuity in office (*continuísmo*), precisely in order to confront individuals' anxieties to perpetuate themselves in power, and to avoid the advantages that public officials in office could have in electoral processes.

The reaction against continuity in power was clearly expressed by Simón Bolívar in his famous Angostura Speech (1819) when he said:

> "The continuation of the authority in the same individual has frequently been the end of democratic governments. Repeated elections are essentials in popular systems, because nothing is more dangerous than to leave for a long term the same citizen in power. The people get used to obey him, and he gets used to command them; from were usurpation and tyranny is originated....Our citizens must fear with more than enough justice that the same Official, who has governed them for a long time, could perpetually command them."[67]

This principle of limiting the term of elected Officials called in Venezuelan constitutional law as the alternate principle ("*alternabilidad,)*" from the Latin word "*alternatium*," which means "interchangeably" or "by turns." In Spanish it has the same meaning and when referring to public offices or public positions means the idea that elected public offices must be occupied by turns, and not continuously by the same elected person. It is in this same sense that the Supreme Tribunal of Justice of Venezuela in a decision of 2002 issued by its Electoral Chamber, said that *alternabilidad* means "the successive exercise of public offices by different persons" (Decision N° 51 of March 18, 2002.)[68] The principle, consequently, is not the same

---

66 Restrictions to presidential reelection are traditional in the presidential system of government, and not in the parliamentary system of government mainly followed in Europe. See Allan R. Brewer-Carías, *Reflexiones sobre la Revolución Norteamericana (1776), la Revolución Francesa (1789) y la Revolución Hispanoamericana (1810-1830) y sus aportes al constitucionalismo moderno*, Universidad Externado de Colombia, Bogotá 2008, pp. 106 ff.

67 "La continuación de la autoridad en un mismo individuo frecuentemente ha sido el término de los gobiernos democráticos. Las repetidas elecciones son esenciales en los sistemas populares, porque nada es tan peligroso como dejar permanecer largo tiempo en un mismo ciudadano el poder. El pueblo se acostumbra a obedecerle y él se acostumbra a mandarlo; de donde se origina la usurpación y la tiranía. ... nuestros ciudadanos deben temer con sobrada justicia que el mismo Magistrado, que los ha mandado mucho tiempo, los mande perpetuamente." See in Simón Bolívar, *Escritos Fundamentales*, Caracas, 1982.

68 Quoted in the Dissenting Vote to the Constitutional Chamber of the Supreme Tribunal of Justice Decision N° 53, of February 2, 2009 (*Interpretation of articles 340,6 and 345 of the Constitution* Case), in http:/www.tsj.gov.ve/decisions/scon/Febrero/53-3209-2009-08-1610.html

as the "elective" principle or to be elected for public offices. To be elected is one thing, and another is to occupy public offices by turns.

The principle has always been establishing in a "rock like" or immutable constitutional clause (*Cláusula pétrea*), in the sense that it must never be changed. That is why Article 6 of the Constitution says: "The government of the Republic and of its political entities **is and will always be"** *alternativo*, in addition to "democratic, participatory, elective, decentralized, responsible, and plural and of repeal mandates,"[69] which mean that it cannot be changed.

The principle has been included in almost all the Venezuelan Constitutions since 1830 (1830, 1858, 1864, 1874, 1881, 1891, 1893, 1901, 1904, 1909, 1936, 1845 and 1947),[70] establishing a general prohibition for the immediate reelection of the President of the Republic for the next term. In the 1961 Constitution the prohibition for reelection was extended up to two terms (10 years), and it was in the current 1999 Constitution that the provision was made more flexible, by establishing for the first time in more than a century the possibility for the immediate reelection of the President, but only once, for the next term (article 230).

The fact is that in Venezuelan history, the only Constitutions not providing for the prohibition for presidential reelection was the short lived 1857 Constitution, the authoritarian Constitutions of the period of Juan Vicente Gómez (1914-1933), and the 1953 Constitution of Marcos Pérez Jiménez, who were two of the dictators we had during the last century. And now, after the Constitutional Amendment to the 1999 Constitution approved by referendum held on February 15th 2009, it was proposed by Hugo Chávez Frías.

On the other hand, another fact to bear in mind is that each time that the principle of non-reelection has been changed through disputed constitutional reforms, the outcome have been a political crisis ending in the overthrow of the government. It occurred in 1858 with the pretension of continuity of President José Tadeo Monagas, who after reforming the Constitution in 1857 was outset a few months later by the Julián Castro March Revolution. It happened in 1891 when President Raimundo Andueza Palacios also reformed the Constitution in order to allow him to be reelected, being overthrown the next year in 1892 by the Joaquin Crespo Legalist Revolution. It also occurred, although in another context, in 1945, with the constitutional reform promoted by President Isaías Medina Angarita that failed to establish the direct presidential election, allowing the continuation of the indirect presidential election of the government candidates by, Congress, a fact that contributed to the 1945 October Revolution. And, finally, it occurred in 1957 when Marcos Pérez Jiménez convened a referendum (plebiscite) to approve his own reelection, which led,

---

69   "Article 5. El gobierno de la República Bolivariana de Venezuela y de las entidades políticas que la componen es y será siempre democrático, participativo, electivo, descentralizado, alternativo, responsable, pluralista y de mandatos revocables."

70   See the text of all the Constitutions in Allan R. Brewer-Carías, *Las Constituciones de Venezuela,* 2 vols., Academia de Ciencias Políticas y Sociales, Caracas 2008.

the next year, to the Democratic Revolution of 1958.[71] This shows that nor always the countries follow the lessons of history, and frequently the result has been the unwanted repetition of similar facts.

In any case, the restriction established in the current 1999 Constitution for the reelection of the President of the Republic (article 230); and the similar provisions establishing reelection restrictions in the cases of Governors and Mayors and of representatives to the National Assembly and to the State Legislative Councils (articles 160, 162, 174, 192), are the ones that were proposed by the national Assembly to be changed through a Constitutional Amendment that the Venezuelan people approved in the referendum held on February 15, 2009.

II. THE LIMITS IMPOSED BY THE CONSTITUTION REGARDING THE CONSTITUTIONAL REVIEW MEANS

The 1999 Constitution establishes three institutional mechanisms for constitutional review, distinguishable according to the importance and magnitude of the changes proposed, which includes the "Constitutional Amendment," the "Constitutional Reform," and the National Constituent Assembly. The "Constitutional Amendment" procedure is established for the purpose of adding or of modifying one or more provisions to the Constitution without altering its fundamental structure (article 340); and the "Constitutional Reforms," is designed for partial revisions of the Constitution and for the substitution of one or several provisions but also without modifying its structure and fundamental principles (article 342). Both procedures, have in common that they need to be approved by referendum, and cannot be used to change fundamental constitutional principles or the structure of the Constitution. Only through a National Constituent Assembly the Constitution can be reviewed in order to "transform the State, to create a new legal order, and to write a new Constitution" (Articles 347).

On the other hand, the Constitution establishes the effects of the popular rejection of a "constitutional reform," in the sense that a similar proposal cannot be filed again before the National Assembly in the remainder of the constitutional term (Article 345). Nothing is established in the Constitution regarding the effects of the rejection of "constitutional amendments," and also, nothing is established regarding the possibility to file the same rejected "constitutional reform" proposal, through the procedure of a "constitutional amendment," as it is now occurring.

The case was a matter of interpretation and of determining the intention of the Constituent power, which in my opinion was to establish a limit regarding the possibility of repeatedly asking the direct expression of the will of the people by referenda. That is, once the people have express their popular will through a referendum, it is not possibly to asked the people again and again, without limits, on the same matters in the same constitutional term.

---

71 See Allan R. Brewer-Carías, *Historia Constitucional de Venezuela*, 2 vols., Editorial Alfa, Caracas 2008.

The matter of the continuous presidential reelection had been already proposed through the "constitutional reform" draft formulated by the President of the Republic in 2007 and was rejected by the people in the Referendum held on December 2007.[72] Nonetheless, at the suggestion of the same President of the Republic, one year later, the National Assembly voted on January 15[th,] 2009 a modification of the Constitution, using this time the "Constitutional Amendment" procedure, initially intended to establish the possibility for the indefinite and continuous reelection of the President of the Republic, which was later extended to all elected public offices.

III. THE BINDING CONSTITUTIONAL INTERPRETATION ISSUED BY THE SUPREME TRIBUNAL

Two questions with constitutional implication result from this new "amendment" proposal, which were the object of endless constitutional discussions and legal contention in the country:

First, the possibility to use a "constitutional amendment" procedure through which no fundamental constitutional principle can be changed, in order to alter and change the principle of *alternabilidad* of the government that is a fundamental republican principle formulated in article 6 of the Constitution; and

Second, the possibility to use the "constitutional amendment" procedure to include the continuous election of the President of the Republic, changing the limits imposed in the Constitution (reelection only once, for the next period), which was a proposal already submitted to referendum in December 2007, and rejected by the people.

It was on these matters that the Constitutional Chamber of the Supreme Tribunal of Justice issued on February 3, 2009, two decisions N° 46 and N° 53[73] in which a binding interpretation of the Constitution was established, as follows:

First, regarding the possibility of submitting to popular vote a modification of the Constitution via "constitutional amendment" on the same matter already rejected by the people in a "constitutional reform" procedure held during the same constitutional term. The Constitutional Chamber argued that the limit imposed in the Constitution was directed only to the National Assembly to discuss again a constitutional reform on the same subject once rejected by the people, without considering the

---

72   See Allan R. Brewer-Carías, *La reforma constitucional de 2007 (Comentarios al proyecto inconstitucionalmente sancionado por la Asamblea Nacional el 2 de noviembre de 2007)*, Editorial Jurídica Venezolana, Caracas 2007.

73   See the Constitutional Chamber of the Supreme Tribunal of Justice Decision N° 53, of February 3, 2009 (*Interpretation of articles 340,6 and 345 of the Constitution* Case), in http:/www.tsj.gov.ve/decisions/scon/Febrero/53-3209-2009-08-1610.html. See the comments on that decision in Allan R. Brewer-Carías, *El Juez Constitucional vs. La alternabilidad republicana. Notas sobre la sentencia de la Sala Constitucional de 03-02 2009 que declara constitucional el proceso de Enmienda Constitucional 2008-2009 que altera el principio de alternabilidad del gobierno, al establecer la reelección indefinida de cargos electivos y que se someterá a referendo el 15-02-2009*, in www.allanbrewerca-rias.com, Section I, 2 (Documents), 2009.

substantive aspect of the prohibition regarding the limits to ask again and again the people, to express in an endless way their will, through referenda.

Second, regarding the possibility of using the "constitutional amendment" procedure in order to change the fundamental principle of *alternabilidad* in government, which means that public offices must be occupied by turns, and not continuously by the same elected person, the Constitutional Chamber said that what the principle of *alternabilidad* imposes "is for the people as sovereign to have the possibility to periodically elect their representatives," confusing alternate government ("*gobierno alternativo*") with elective government ("*gobierno electivo*") that is, the principle that elected public offices must be occupied by turns, with the principle of election of representatives, considering that the principle of *alternabilidad* can only be infringed if the possibility to have elections is impeded.

With these decisions, what the Supreme Tribunal made, in addition to resolving the constitutional challenges to the February 15th referendum was, through a constitutional interpretation, to modify or mutate the text of the Constitution, changing the sense of the prohibition of subsequent calling for referendum on the same matters, and also changing the sense of a constitutional principle like the principle of *alternabilidad* in government considering it alike to the principle of elective government, ignoring the difference established in the Constitution (article 6).

IV. THE REMAINING CONSTITUTIONAL IMPLICATIONS

One constitutional implication of the February 15th 2009 Referendum remained unsolved and it was the one resulting from the question itself that was proposed to the people, which was approved, and in which it was not clear the real intention to establish the possibility of continuous reelection in public offices.

The question approved in the referendum, in fact, was the follow:

> "*Do you approve of the amendment of articles 160,162,174,192 and 230 of the Constitution of the Republic prepared by initiative of the National Assembly, which extends the political rights of the people in order to allow any citizen in exercise of a public office by popular election to become a candidate to the same office for the constitutionally established term, his or her election depending exclusively from the popular vote?*[74]

Having been the purpose of the constitutional amendment to eliminate the restriction for reelection of all elected public officials and representatives established in the five aforementioned articles of the Constitution, to allow them be reelected without limits in a continuous and indefinite way, is not clear to realized why this was not clearly stated in the question submitted to referendum, in which the words "reelection," "indefinite" or "continuous" reelection was not used.

---

74   "¿Aprueba usted la enmienda de los artículos 160, 162, 174, 192 y 230 de la Constitución de la Republica tramitada por iniciativa de la Asamblea Nacional, que amplia los derechos políticos del pueblo con el fin de permitir que cualquier ciudadano o ciudadana en ejercicio de un cargo de elección popular pueda ser sujeto de postulación como candidato o candidata para el mismo cargo por el tiempo establecido constitucionalmente, dependiendo su elección exclusivamente del voto popular?."

On the other hand, as established in the Constitution, in any case of constitutional amendments, when approved, it must be published as a continuation of the Constitution without altering the original text, although the amended articles must have a footnote referring to the number and date of their amendments. With the question as it was formulated, the result has been to eliminate the limits imposed in articles 162 and 192 of the Constitution regarding the representatives to the State Legislative Councils and to the National Assembly to be reelected only for up to two terms; and in articles, 160, 174, and 230 regarding the President of the Republic, the Governors of the States and the Municipal mayors to be reelected only once for an immediate new term.

This constitutional amendment was considered by the President of the Republic as a process "vital for the revolution,"[75] but in reality what has resulted in a constitutional modification of a vital principle for the future of democracy.

---

75   In his weekly program *Aló President*, January 11, 2009

CHAPTER XXV

THE "BOLIVARIAN REVOLUTION" AND VENEZUELAN CONSTITUTIONAL LAW

(2012)

This essay was written for my Presentation on "The "Bolivarian Revolution" and Venezuelan Constitutional Law," at the *33d. Conference of the German Society of Comparative Law, Legal limits of liberty and legal protection* **held in Trier, Germany, September 16, 2011. It was pulished in Uwe Kischel und Christian Kirchner (Coord.),** *Ideologie und Weltanschauung im Recht,* **Gesellschaft für Rechtsvergleichtung e.V., Rechtsvergleichung und Rechtsvereinheitlichung, Mohr Siebeck, Tübingen 2012, pp. 121-148**

The Venezuelan Constitution, last reformed in 1999, instituted the country as a Democratic and Social State of Law and Justice (Article 2), organized as "a decentralized federal State" (Article 4).[76]

The political framework of the organization of the State, in based, on the one hand, in the principle of separation or powers (between five and not only three powers, adding to the traditional ones, the Electoral and the Citizens powers), with their autonomy and independence; and on the other hand, based on a vertical distribution of public powers in three territorial levels of government: National level, State level and Municipal level (Art. 136). In each level, the government must always be "elective, decentralized, alternative, responsible, plural, and of revocable mandate" (Article 6).

The political system of government is based on the principles of representative democracy, political decentralizing and political pluralism, according to which, no political institution of the State can be created without ensuring its elective character through elected representatives of the people by means of universal, direct and se-

---

76 See the study of the constitution regarding the regulation of this State Constitutional Model, in Allan R. Brewer-Carías, *La Constitución de 1999. Derecho Constitucional venezolano*, 2 vols., Caracas 2004.

cret suffrage; without guaranteeing its political autonomy, which is essential to its decentralized nature; and without guaranteeing its plural character in the sense that it cannot be linked to a particular ideology.

And finally, the economic system is conceived as a mixed economic one, declaring economic liberty and free private initiative, altogether with the guaranty of private property, allowing the State participation in the economy, and in all case with the purpose of satisfying social justice.

These are the constitutional ground norms embodied in the 1999 Constitution that consequently cannot be changed by the government without changing the Constitution itself.

Nonetheless, in the name of a so-called "Bolivarian Revolution," all these basic principles have been changed without a formal constitutional reform and, on the contrary, defrauding or in degradation of the 1999 Constitution, progressively implementing a new XXI century "Communist State."

It must be noted that in 1999, the national Constituent Assembly changed the very name of the country from the "Republic of Venezuela," which had been the name of the country since 1811, into the "Bolivarian Republic of Venezuela" (Article 1); a name that has been very conveniently used to support what now is called the "Bolivarian Revolution."

It must be remembered that Venezuela has a very long constitutional tradition, being this country the first to adopt a Modern Constitution following the principles of modern constitutionalism derived from the French and the American revolutions, which were embodied in the Federal Constitution of the Venezuelan States of December 21, 1811. That Constitution and all the papers of the independence process from Spain were conceived and written without the participation of Simón Bolívar, who in fact began his influence in the country as a military, fighting and commanding the national forces against the Spanish Armed forces. This is the reason for his name being indissolubly attached to the Venezuelan Independence, as well as to the independence of other Latin American countries such as Colombia, Ecuador, Bolivia and Peru which were historically called the "Bolivarian" republics.

His name, of course has been used many times for political purpose, so this is not the first time in Venezuela's political history that rulers, mainly of military and authoritarian roots, have evoked Simón Bolívar to attract followers and to give some "doctrinal" basis to their regimes. It was the case of Antonio Guzmán Blanco in the nineteenth century and of Cipriano Castro, Juan Vicente Gómez, Eleazar López Contreras, and Marcos Pérez Jiménez in the twentieth century. Professor John Lynch, one of the great Bolivar's biographers, has pointed out that:

> "The traditional cult of Bolivar has been used as a convenient ideology by military dictators, culminating with the regimes of Juan Vicente Gómez and Eleazar López Contreras; these

had at least more or less respected the basic thought of the Liberator, even when they misrepresented its meaning."[77]

Adding that:

> "In 1999 Venezuelans were astonished to learn that their country had been renamed 'the Bolivarian Republic of Venezuela' by decree of President Hugo Chávez, who called himself a 'revolutionary Bolivarian.' Authoritarian populist, or neocaudillos, or Bolivarian militarists, whatever their designation, invoke Bolívar no less ardently than did previous rulers, though it is doubtful whether he would have responded to their calls…But the new heresy, far from maintaining continuity with the constitutional ideas of Bolívar, as was claimed, invented a new attribute, the populist Bolívar, and in the case of Cuba gave him a new identity, the socialist Bolívar. By exploiting the authoritarian tendency, which certainly existed in the thought and action of Bolívar, regimes in Cuba and Venezuela claim the Liberator as patron for their policies, distorting his ideas in the process."[78]

That is, never before had the adherence to Bolivar led to changing the republic's name and to the invention of a "Bolivarian doctrine" to justify the government's policies, as Chávez has done regarding his "XXI century Socialism" one.[79]

This "Bolivarian Revolution" led the President of the Republic himself, in 2007, to propose a constitutional reform before the National Assembly,[80] in order to express and formally incorporate in the text of the Constitution the socialist "Bolivari-

---

77   See John Lynch, *Simón Bolívar: A Life*, Yale University Press, New Haven, CT, 2007, p. 304. See also Germán Carrera Damas, *El culto a Bolívar, esbozo para un estudio de la historia de las ideas en Venezuela*, Universidad Central de Venezuela, Caracas 1969; Luis Castro Leiva, *De la patria boba a la teología bolivariana*, Monteávila, Caracas 1987; Elías Pino Iturrieta, *El divino Bolívar. Ensayo sobre una religión republicana*, Alfail, Caracas 2008; Ana Teresa Torres, *La herencia de la tribu. Del mito de la independencia a la Revolución bolivariana*, Editorial Alfa, Caracas 2009. See also the historiography study on these books in Tomás Straka, *La épica del desencanto*, Editorial Alfa, Caracas 2009.

78   See John Lynch, *Simón Bolívar: A Life*, Yale University Press, New Haven, CT, 2007, p. 304. See also A.C. Clark, *The Revolutionary Has No Clothes: Hugo Chávez's Bolivarian Farce*, Encounter Books, New York 2009, pp. 5-14.

79   The last attempt to completely appropriate Simón Bolívar for the "Bolivarian Revolution," was the televised exhumation of his remains that took place at the National Pantheon in Caracas on July 26, 2010, conducted by President Chávez himself and other high officials, including the Prosecutor General, among other things, for the purpose of determining if Bolivar died of arsenic poisoning in Santa Marta in 1830, instead of from tuberculosis. See Simon Romero, "Building a New History By Exhuming Bolívar," *The New York Times*, August 4, 2010, p. A7.

80   See on the constitutional reforms proposals, Allan R. Brewer-Carías, *Hacia la consolidación de un Estado socialista, centralizado, policial y militarista. Comentarios sobre el sentido y alcance de las propuestas de reforma constitucional 2007*, Editorial Jurídica Venezolana, Caracas 2007; *La reforma constitucional de 2007 (Comentarios al proyecto inconstitucionalmente sancionado por la Asamblea Nacional el 2 de noviembre de 2007)*, Editorial Jurídica Venezolana, Caracas 2007.

an doctrine" or "Bolivarian Socialism" [81] as the fundamental doctrine of the Socialist State he proposed to establish.

Of course, no relation can be found in any of Simón Bolívar writings with any aspect related to socialism. Just to remember, as Karl Marx was born in this city of Trier, if Bolívar would have expressed any idea related to socialism, Marx would have detected it when he wrote, ten years after publishing his book with F. Engels on *The German Ideology*[82] where the word "communism" perhaps was first used, the entry on "Simón Bolívar y Ponte" for the *New American Cyclopedia* published in New York in 1857. [83] The fact is that in such article no mention at all is made regarding socialist ideas of Bolívar, being it one of the most critical works on Bolívar ever written.

In any case, in order to begin to implement the so-called "Bolivarian Revolution" President Chávez presented to the national Assembly a complete draft of Constitutional Reforms, with the purpose of establishing a socialist, centralized, militaristic, and police State,[84] called the "Popular Power State" or "Communal State," affecting the most essential and fundamental aspects of the state,[85] as follows:

First, the democratic and decentralized State was to be converted into a centralized state of concentrated power under the illusory guise of a popular power, imply-

81   All his proposals to construct socialism were linked to the president to Simón Bolívar's 1819 Constitution of Angostura, which he considered "perfectly applicable to a socialist project" in the sense of considering that it was possible to "take the original Bolivarian ideology as a basic element of a socialist project." Of course, this assertion has no serious foundations: it is enough to read Bolívar's 1819 Angostura discourse on presenting the draft constitution to realize that it has nothing to do with a "socialist project" of any kind. See Simón Bolívar, *Escritos fundamentales*, Caracas 1982. See also Pedro Grases ed., *El Libertador y la Constitución de Angostura de 1819,* Caracas 1969; José Rodríguez Iturbe, ed., *Actas del Congreso de Angostura,* Caracas 1969.

82   See in Karl Marx and Frederick Engels, "The German Ideology," in *Collective Works*, Vol. 5, International Publishers, New York 1976, p. 47. Véanse además los textos pertinentes en http://www.educa.madrid.org/cms_tools/files/0a24636f-764c-4e03-9c1d-6722e2ee60d7/Texto%20Marx%20y%20Engels.pdf

83   See *The New American Cyclopaedia*, Vol. III, 1858, on "Bolivar y Ponte, Simón." Available at http://www.marxists.org/archive/marx/works/1858/01/bolivar.htm

84   See Allan R. Brewer-Carías, *Hacia la Consolidación de un Estado Socialista, Centralizado, Policial y Militarista. Comentarios sobre el sentido y alcance de las propuestas de reforma constitucional 2007*, Colección Textos Legislativos, N° 42, Editorial Jurídica Venezolana, Caracas 2007.

85   See Rogelio Pérez Perdomo, "La Constitución de papel y su reforma," in *Revista de Derecho Público* 112 *(Estudios sobre la reforma constitucional)*, Editorial Jurídica Venezolana, Caracas 2007, p. 14; G. Fernández, "Aspectos esenciales de la modificación constitucional propuesta por el Presidente de la República. La modificación constitucional como un fraude a la democracia," *Id*, p. 22; Alfredo Arismendi, "Utopía Constitucional," in *id.*, p. 31; Manuel Rachadell, "El personalismo político en el Siglo XXI," in *id.*, p. 66; Allan R. Brewer-Carías, "El sello socialista que se pretendía imponer al Estado," in *id.*, p. 71-75; Alfredo Morles Hernández, "El nuevo modelo económico para el Socialismo del Siglo XXI," in *id.*, p. 233-36.

ing definitive elimination of the federal form of the state,[86] rendering political partic-ipation impossible, and degrading representative democracy. For such purpose, the reform established a new "popular power" (*poder popular*) (art. 16), composed by communities (*comunidades*), each of which "shall constitute a basic and indivisible spatial nucleus of the Venezuelan Socialist State, where ordinary citizens will have the power to construct their own geography and their own history;" which were to be grouped into communes (*comunas*).[87] The main aspect of these reforms is that it was expressly stated that the popular power "does not arise from suffrage or from any election, but arises from the condition of the organized human groups that form the base of the population." Consequently, representative democracy at the local level and territorial political autonomy was to disappear, substituted with a supposed participatory and protagonist democracy that would, in fact, be controlled by the president and that proscribed any form of political decentralization and territorial autonomy.[88] Even anticipating the constitutional reform proposal, perhaps being sure of its approval, in 2006 the Law on the Councils of the Popular Power (*Consejos del Poder Popular*) was sanctioned.[89]

Second, the state was to be converted into a socialist state for the purpose of the "construction of a Socialist democracy" (art. 158); thus establishing a political offi-cial doctrine of socialist character – Bolivarian doctrine – allowing the criminaliza-tion of all dissidence was formally established.

---

86   See Manuel Rachadell, "El personalismo político en el Siglo XXI," in *Revista de Derecho Público* 112 *(Estudios sobre la reforma constitucional)*, Editorial Jurídica Venezolana, Cara-cas 2007, 67; Ana Elvira Araujo, "Proyecto de reforma constitucional (agosto a noviembre 2007). Principios fundamentales y descentralización política," in *id.*, 77-81; José Luis Ville-gas, "Impacto de la reforma constitucional sobre las entidades locales," in *id.*, 119-23.

87   The communes were created in the statute on the Federal Council of Government. See *Ley Orgánica del Consejo Federal de Gobierno, Gaceta Oficial* N° 5.963 Extra. of Feb. 22, 2010).

88   This fundamental change, as the president stated on August 15, 2007, constituted "the devel-opment of what we understand by decentralization, because the Fourth Republic concept of decentralization is very different from the concept we must work with. For this reason, we have here stated 'the protagonist participation of the people, transferring power to them, and creating the best conditions for the construction of social democracy.'" See *Discurso de or-den pronunciado por el ciudadano Comandante Hugo Chávez Frías*, *op. cit.*, 50.

89   See Giancarlo Henríquez Maionica, "Los Consejos Comunales (una breve aproximación a su realidad y a su proyección ante la propuesta presidencial de reforma constitucional)," in *Re-vista de Derecho Público* 112 *(Estudios sobre la reforma constitucional)*, Editorial Jurídica Venezolana, Caracas 2007, pp. 89-99; Allan R. Brewer-Carías, "El inicio de la desmunicipa-lización en Venezuela: La organización del poder popular para eliminar la descentralización, la democracia representativa y la participación a nivel local," in *AIDA, Opera Prima de De-recho Administrativo. Revista de la Asociación Internacional de Derecho Administrativo*, Universidad Nacional Autónoma de México, Asociación Internacional de Derecho Adminis-trativo, Mexico City 2007, pp. 49-67. The 2006 law was replaced by *Ley Orgánica de los Consejos Comunales, Gaceta Oficial* N° 39.335, Dec. 28, 2009. See the comments on this Law in Allan R. Brewer-Carías, *Ley de los Consejos Comunales*, Editorial Jurídica Venezo-lana, Caracas 2010.

Third, the mixed economic system was to be converted into a state-owned, socialist, centralized economy by means of eliminating economic liberty and private initiative as constitutional rights, as well as the constitutional right to private property; conferring the means of production to the state, to be centrally managed; and configuring the state as an institution on which all economic activity will depend.[90].

Fourth, the state was to be converted into a repressive (police) state, given the regressive character of the regulations established in the reform regarding human rights, and also into a militarist state, on the basis of the role assigned to the "Bolivarian Armed Force" (*Fuerza Armada Bolivariana*), which was configured to function wholly under the president, and the creation of the new "Bolivarian National Militia (*Milicia Nacional Bolivariana*). As the President himself explained, the motivation for the drafting of the constitutional reforms in 2007, was to construct a "Bolivarian Socialism, Venezuelan Socialism, our Socialism, and our socialist model," having "the community" (*la comunidad*), as its "basic and indivisible nucleus," and considering that "real democracy is only possible in socialism." [91]

The proposed constitutional reform, without doubt, would have altered the basic foundations of the state.[92] This is true particularly with respect to the proposals of the substitution of the democratic and social state with the socialist state; the elimination of decentralization as a policy of the state designed to develop public political participation; and the elimination of economic freedom and the right to property.[93]

All these constitutional reforms, were submitted to popular vote, and were all rejected by the people in the referendum that took place on December 2, 2007.[94]

---

90   See Gerardo Fernández, "Aspectos esenciales de la modificación constitucional propuesta por el Presidente de la República. La modificación constitucional como un fraude a la democracia," in *Revista de Derecho Público* 112 *(Estudios sobre la reforma constitucional)*, Editorial Jurídica Venezolana, Caracas 2007, p. 24; Alfredo Arismendi, "Utopía Constitucional," in *id.*, p. 31; José Antonio Muci Borjas, "La suerte de la libertad económica en el proyecto de Reforma de la Constitución de 2007," in *id.*, pp. 203-208; Tamara Adrián, "Actividad económica y sistemas alternativos de producción," in *id.*, pp. 209-14; Víctor Hernández Mendible, "Réquiem por la libertad de empresa y derecho de propiedad," in *id.*, pp. 215-18; Alfredo Morles Hernández, "El nuevo modelo económico para el Socialismo del Siglo XXI," in *id.*, pp. 233-236.

91   See *Discurso de orden pronunciado por el ciudadano Comandante Hugo Chávez Frías, op cit.*, 32, 34, 35.

92   See Eugenio Hernández Bretón, "Cuando no hay miedo (ante la Reforma Constitucional)," in *Revista de Derecho Público* 112 *(Estudios sobre la reforma constitucional)*, Editorial Jurídica Venezolana, Caracas 2007, oo. 17-20; Manuel Rachadell, "El personalismo político en el Siglo XXI," in *id.*, pp. 65-70.

93   See on these reforms, Allan R. Brewer-Carías, *Dismantling Democracy. The Chávez Authoritarian Experiment*, Cambridge University Press, 2010.

94   See Allan R. Brewer-Carías, "La proyectada reforma constitucional de 2007, rechazada por el poder constituyente originario", in *Anuario de Derecho Público 2007,* Año 1, Instituto de Estudios de Derecho Público de la Universidad Monteávila, Caracas 2008, pp. 17-65. According to information from the National Electoral Council on Dec. 2, 2007, of 16,109,664 registered voters, only 9,002,439 voted (44.11% abstention); of voters, 4,504,354 rejected the

One constitutional aspect that must be analyzed regarding the rejected constitutional reforms is that the proposals in themselves were unconstitutional because the procedure of "constitutional reform" cannot be used for so important changes. The Constitution, in effect, provides for three different methods of constitutional review: constitutional amendments, constitutional reforms, and the convening of a national Constituent Assembly, so major constitutional changes can only be approved by means of the former. In the case of the 2007 constitutional reform draft, it was sanctioned by the national Assembly evading the procedure established in the Constitution for such fundamental change, which imposes the convening of a Constituent Assembly. The reform defrauded the Constitution[95] as one more step of the "permanent coup d'état" that since 1999 has occurred in Venezuela.[96] The procedure followed was challenged on grounds of unconstitutionality before the Constitutional Chamber of the Supreme Tribunal of Justice, which refused to exercise judicial review on these matters declaring that such actions could no even be filed.[97]

In any case, the rejection of the Constitutional reform draft in the 2007 referendum, did not prevent the Government of beginning to implement them in order to establish the Socialist State, first through the progressive political process of concentrating and controlling all public powers by the National Executive, through the National Assembly, as has occurred regarding the Judiciary;[98] and second, through

---

proposal (50.70%). This means that there were only 4,379,392 votes to approve the proposal (49.29%), so only 28% of registered voters voted for the approval.

95   See Rogelio Pérez Perdomo, "La Constitución de papel y su reforma," in *Revista de Derecho Público* 112 *(Estudios sobre la reforma constitucional)*, Editorial Jurídica Venezolana, Caracas 2007, 14; Gerardo Fernández, "Aspectos esenciales de la modificación constitucional propuesta por el Presidente de la república. La modificación constitucional en fraude a la democracia," in id., 21-25; Fortunato González, "Constitución histórica y poder constituyente," in *id.*, pp. 33-36; Lolymar Heránez Camargo, "Los límites del cambio constitucional como garantía de pervivencia del Estado de derecho," in *id.*, 37-45; Claudia Nikken, "La soberanía popular y el trámite de la refroma constitucional promovida por iniciativa presidencial el 15 de agosto de 2007," in *id.*, 51-58.

96   See José Amando Mejía Betancourt, "La ruptura del hilo constitucional," in in *Revista de Derecho Público* 112 *(Estudios sobre la reforma constitucional)*, Editorial Jurídica Venezolana, Caracas 2007, p. 47. The term was first used by Francois Mitterand, *Le coup d'État permanent*, Éditions 10/18, Paris 1993.

97   See Allan R. Brewer-Carías, "El juez constitucional vs. la supremacía constitucional O de cómo la jurisdicción constitucional en Venezuela renunció a controlar la constitucionalidad del procedimiento seguido para la 'reforma constitucional' sancionada por la Asamblea Nacional el 2 de noviembre de 2007, antes de que fuera rechazada por el pueblo en el referendo del 2 de diciembre de 2007," in Eduardo Ferrer Mac Gregor y César de Jesús Molina Suárez (Coordinarores), *El juez constitucional en el Siglo XXI,* Universidad nacional Autónoma de México, Suprema Corte de Justicia de la Nación, México 2009, Tomo I, pp. 385-435.

98   See Allan R. Brewer-Carías, "La justicia sometida al poder [La ausencia de independencia y autonomía de los jueces en Venezuela por la interminable emergencia del Poder Judicial (1999-2006)]" en *Cuestiones Internacionales. Anuario Jurídico Villanueva 2007,* Centro Universitario Villanueva, Marcial Pons, Madrid 2007, pp. 25-57

the enactment of ordinary legislation by the National Assembly and decrees laws issued by the President of the Republic as delegate legislation. [99]

This process began even before the draft reforms were even submitted to the National Assembly. In June 2006 the National Assembly had passed the Law on the Communal Councils,[100] parallel to the municipal entities, supposedly to channel citizen participation in public affairs, but subjected to a system of centralized management by the national executive power and without any political or territorial autonomy.[101] The following year, in June 2007, the Central Planning Commission was created,[102] and in December 13, the National Assembly approved the 2007–13 Economic and Social Development National Plan, providing that the "planning, production and distribution system oriented towards socialism," being "the relevant matter" the progressive development of "social property of the production means." Through another Law the State assumed all powers in order to control farming, livestock,

---

99   See Lolymar Hernández Camargo, "Límites del poder ejecutivo en el ejercicio de la habilitación legislativa: Imposibilidad de establecer el contenido de la reforma constitucional rechazada vía habilitación legislativa," in *Revista de Derecho Público* 115 *(Estudios sobre los Decretos Leyes)*, Editorial Jurídica Venezolana, Caracas 2008, pp. 51ff.; Jorge Kiriakidis, "Breves reflexiones en torno a los 26 Decretos-Ley de julio-agosto de 2008, y la consulta popular refrendaría de diciembre de 2007," in *id.*, pp. 57ff.; José Vicente Haro García, "Los recientes intentos de reforma constitucional o de cómo se está tratando de establecer una dictadura socialista con apariencia de legalidad (A propósito del proyecto de reforma constitucional de 2007 y los 26 decretos leyes del 31 de julio de 2008 que tratan de imponerla)," in *id.*, pp. 63ff.; Ana Cristina Nuñez Machado, "Los 26 nuevos Decretos-Leyes y los principios que regulan la intervención del Estado en la actividad económica de los particulares," in *id.*, pp. 215-20; Aurilivi Linares Martínez, "Notas sobre el uso del poder de legislar por decreto por parte del Presidente venezolano," in *id.*, pp. 79-89; Carlos Luis Carrillo Artiles, "La paradójica situación de los Decretos Leyes Orgánicos frente a la Ingeniería Constitucional de 1999," in *id.*, pp. 93-100; Freddy J. Orlando S., "El "paquetazo," un conjunto de leyes que conculcan derechos y amparan injusticias," in *id.*, pp. 101-104

100 *Ley de Consejos Comunales, Gaceta Oficial, Extra.* 5.806, Apr. 10, 2006. This statute was replaced by Ley Orgánica de los Consejos Comunales. See *Gaceta Oficial* N° 39.335, Dec. 28, 2009.

101 See Allan R. Brewer-Carías, "El inicio de la desmunicipalización en Venezuela: La organización del poder popular para eliminar la descentralización, la democracia representativa y la participación a nivel local," in *AIDA, Revista de la Asociación Internacional de Derecho Administrativo,* Universidad Nacional Autónoma de México, Asociación Internacional de Derecho Administrativo, Mexico City 2007, 49-67.

102 Decree Law N° 5,841 was enacted on June 12, 2007, *Gaceta Oficial* N° 5.841, Extra., June 22, 2007. See Allan R. Brewer-Carías, "Comentarios sobre la inconstitucional creación de la Comisión Central de Planificación, centralizada y obligatoria," in *Revista de Derecho Público* 110, Editorial Jurídica Venezolana, Caracas 2007, pp. 79-89; Luis A. Herrera Orellana, "Los Decretos-Leyes de 30 de julio de 2008 y la Comisión Central de Planificación: Instrumentos para la progresiva abolición del sistema político y del sistema económico previstos en la Constitución de 1999," in *Revista de Derecho Público* 115, *(Estudios sobre los Decretos Leyes)*, Editorial Jurídica Venezolana, Caracas 2008, pp. 221-32

fishing, and aquaculture, and in particular the production of food,[103] allowing the State to directly assume distribution and commercialization of goods, and the occupation of industries without compensation.[104] In 2008, another Law on the Popular Economy Promotion and Development was passed, establishing a "socio-productive communal model," with different socio-productive organizations following the "socialist model;"[105] as well as the general law on matters of Consumer and Users Protection In the same openly socialist orientation.[106] These Laws extended the state powers of control to the point of establishing the possibility of confiscating goods and services by means of their takeover and occupation of private industries and services through administrative decisions.[107]

---

103 Decree Law on the Organic Law on Farming and Food Security and Sovereignty. *Gaceta Oficial* N° 5.889, Extra., July 31, 2008. See José Ignacio Hernández G., "Planificación y soberanía alimentaria," in *Revista de Derecho Público* 115, *(Estudios sobre los Decretos Leyes),* Editorial Jurídica Venezolana, Caracas 2008, pp. 389-94; Juan Domingo Alfonso Paradisi, "La constitución económica establecida en la Constitución de 1999, el sistema de economía social de mercado y el decreto 6.071 con rango, valor y fuerza de Ley Orgánica de seguridad y soberanía agroalimentaria," in *id.,* pp. 395-415; Gustavo A. Grau Fortoul, "La participación del sector privado en la producción de alimentos, como elemento esencial para poder alcanzar la seguridad alimentaria (Aproximación al tratamiento de la cuestión, tanto en la Constitución de 1999 como en la novísima Ley Orgánica de soberanía y seguridad alimentaria)," in *id.,*pp. 417-24.

104 See Carlos García Soto, "Notas sobre la expansión del ámbito de la declaratoria de utilidad pública o interés social en la expropiación," in *Revista de Derecho Público* 115, *(Estudios sobre los Decretos Leyes),* Editorial Jurídica Venezolana, Caracas 2008, pp. 149-51; Antonio Canova González, Luis Alfonso Herrera Orellana, and Karina Anzola Spadaro, *¿Expropiaciones o vías de hecho? (La degradación continuada del derecho fundamental de propiedad en la Venezuela actual,"* Funeda, Universidad Católica Andrés Bello, Caracas 2009.

105 Decree Law, N° 6,130 of June 3, 2008, *Gaceta Oficial* N° 5.890, Extra., July 31, 2008. See Jesús María Alvarado Andrade, "La desaparición del bolívar como moneda de curso legal (Notas críticas al inconstitucional Decreto N° 6.130, con rango, valor y fuerza de la ley para el fomento y desarrollo de la economía comunal, de fecha 3 de junio de 2008," in *Revista de Derecho Público* 115, *(Estudios sobre los Decretos Leyes),* Editorial Jurídica Venezolana, Caracas 2008, pp. 313-20.

106 Decree Law N° 6,092 enacting the Access to Goods and Services Persons Defense Law. *Gaceta Oficial* N° 5,889 Extra of July 31, 2008; José Gregorio Silva, "Disposiciones sobre el Decreto-Ley para la defensa de las personas en el acceso a bienes y servicios," in *id.,* pp. 277-79; Carlos Simón Bello Rengifo, "Decreto N° 6.092 con rango, valor y fuerza de la ley para la defensa de las personas en el acceso a los bienes y servicios (Referencias a problemas de imputación)," in *id.,* pp. 281-305; Alfredo Morles Hernández, "El nuevo modelo económico del socialismo del siglo XXI y su reflejo en el contrato de adhesión," in *id.,* pp. 229-32.

107 See Juan Domingo Alfonso Paradisi, "Comentarios en cuanto a los procedimientos administrativos establecidos en el Decreto N° 6.092 con rango, valor y fuerza de Ley para la defensa de las personas en el acceso a los bienes y servicios," in *Revista de Derecho Público* 115, *(Estudios sobre los Decretos Leyes)*, Editorial Jurídica Venezolana, Caracas 2008, pp. 245-60; Karina Anzola Spadaro, "El carácter autónomo de las 'medidas preventivas' contempladas en el artículo 111 del Decreto-Ley para la defensa de las personas en el acceso a los bienes y servicios," in *id.,* pp. 271-76. See, in general, Antonio Canova González, Luis Alfonso

A primary purpose of the 2007 constitutional reforms was to complete the dismantling of the federal form of the state by centralizing power attributions of the states, creating administrative entities to be established and directed by the national executive, attributing powers to the president to interfere in regional and local affairs, and voiding state and municipal competency by means of compulsory transfer of that competency to communal councils.[108] The implementation of these rejected constitutional reforms was completed with the approval in 2010 of the Law on the Federal Council of Government,[109] forcing the states and municipalities to transfer its attributions to local institutions controlled by the central power (communal councils),

The last set of unconstitutional legislation implementing the 2007 rejected reform was approved in December 21, of 2010, by formally establishing a Communal State (or Socialist or Communist state) based upon the exercise of a new Popular Power that has no constitutional basis, created in parallel to the existing Constitutional decentralized State based upon the Public Power (National, state, municipal) expressly established in the Constitution.[110] For such purpose the National Assembly passed eight important Laws referred to the Popular Power; the Communes; the Communal Economic System; the Public and Communal Planning; and the Social Comptrollership;[111] and reformed the Organic Law on Municipalities, and the Laws of the States and Local Councils on Public Policy Planning and Coordination.[112]

These laws were approved after President Chávez himself confessed in January 2010 that the supposedly "Bolivarian revolution," was no more than the resurrection of the historically failed "Marxist revolution," but in this case led by a president who -he said- has never even read Marx's writings.[113] This presidential announcement

---

Herrera Orellana, and Karina Anzola Spadaro, *¿Expropiaciones o vías de hecho? (La degradación continuada del derecho fundamental de propiedad en la Venezuela actual,"* Funeda, Universidad Católica Andrés Bello, Caracas 2009

108 See Manuel Rachadell, *"La centralización del poder en el Estado federal descentralizado,"* in Revista de Derecho Público, 115, *(Estudios sobre los Decretos Leyes)*, Editorial Jurídica Venezolana, Caracas 2008, pp. 111-131.

109 See *Ley Orgánica del Consejo Federal de Gobierno, Gaceta Oficial* N° 5.963 Extra. of Feb. 22, 2010.

110 See Gustavo Linares Benzo, "Sólo un Poder Público más. El Poder Popular en la reforma del 2007," in *Revista de Derecho Público* 112 *(Estudios sobre la reforma constitucional)*, Editorial Jurídica Venezolana, Caracas 2007, pp. 102-105; Arturo Peraza, "Reforma, Democracia participativa y Poder Popular," in *id.*, pp. 107-13.

111 See *Gaceta Oficial* N° 6.011 Extra. 12-21-2010. See on all these organic laws, Allan R. Brewer-Carías *et al.*, *Leyes Orgánicas sobre el Poder Popular y el Estado Comunal*, Editorial Jurídica Venezolana, Caracas 2011.

112 See *Gaceta Oficial* N° 6.015 Extra. 12-28-2010.

113 In his annual speech before the National Assembly on Jan. 15, 2010, in which Chávez declared to have "assumed Marxism," he also confessed that he had never read Marx's works. See María Lilibeth Da Corte, "Por primera vez asumo el marxismo," in *El Universal*, Caracas Jan. 16, 2010, http://www.eluniversal.com/2010/01/16/pol_art_por-primera-vez-asu_1726209.shtml.

provoked in April 2010, that the governmental United Socialist Party of which the President presides, in its First Extraordinary Congress then adopted its "Declaration of Principles" in which it officially declared itself as a "Marxist," "Anti-imperialist" and "Anti-capitalist" party; prescribing that its actions are to be based on "scientific socialism" and on the "inputs of Marxism as a philosophy of praxis," in order to substitute the "Capitalist Bourgeois State" with a "Socialist State" based on the Popular Power and the socialization of the means of production.[114]

With these declarations it can be said, finally, that the so called "Bolivarian Revolution" has been unveiled; a revolution for which nobody in Venezuela has voted except for its rejection, first, in the December 2, 2007 referendum, in which the President's proposals for constitutional reforms in order to establish a Socialist, Centralized, Police and Militaristic state received a negative popular response;[115] and second, in the parliamentary elections of September 26, 2010, in which the Government lost the support of the majority of the popular vote, after an electoral campaign developed as a sort of "plebiscite" on the President, his performance and his socialist policies.

In such election, although the opposition won the majority of the popular vote in the election, it did not won the majority of seats in the National Assembly, due to distorting electoral regulations. Nonetheless, it won enough parliamentary seats in the National Assembly (approximately 40%), preventing the Government on the possibility of passing laws or decisions requiring a qualified vote, like the Organic Laws.

This meant that the President and his party, having lost the absolute control they used to have since 2005 over the National Assembly, before the newly elected deputies to the Assembly could have taken possession of office in January 2011, in December 2010 they forced the National Assembly to proceed to sanction of the aforementioned set of organic laws through which they have finished defining the legislative framework for a new State. In this way, by-passing the Constitution and in parallel to the Constitutional State, the National Assembly regulated a socialist, centralized, military and police State, called the "Communal State" of the "Popular Power" already rejected by the people in 2007. The delegitimized National Assembly also passed an enabling Law authorizing the President, through delegated legislation, to enact laws on all imaginable subjects, including laws of organic nature, emptying the new National Assembly of matters on which to legislate for a period of 18 months until 2012.

---

114 See "Declaración de Principios, I Congreso Extraordinario del Partido Socialista Unido de Venezuela," Apr. 23, 2010, at http://psuv.org.ve/files/tcdocumentos/Declaracion-de-principios-PSUV.pdf

115 See on the 2007 constitutional reforms proposals, Allan R. Brewer-Carías, *Hacia la consolidación de un Estado socialista, centralizado, policial y militarista. Comentarios sobre el sentido y alcance de las propuestas de reforma constitucional 2007,* Editorial Jurídica Venezolana, Caracas 2007; *La reforma constitucional de 2007 (Comentarios al proyecto inconstitucionalmente sancionado por la Asamblea Nacional el 2 de noviembre de 2007),* Editorial Jurídica Venezolana, Caracas 2007.

The main purpose of these laws, as aforementioned, was the organization of the "Communal State" which has the commune as its fundamental unit, unconstitutionally supplanting the municipalities as the "primary political units of the national organization" (Art. 168 of the Constitution), through whose organization the Popular Power is exercised, although not through representatives. In this Communal State representative democracy is ignored, openly violating the Constitution.

One thing that has to be highlighted is that after failing to create the Communal State in substitution of the Constitutional State, the December 2010 Laws have created it in parallel or alongside the Constitutional State. The Socialist State based on the direct exercise of sovereignty by the people; and the Constitutional State, based also on the indirect exercise of sovereignty by the people through elected representatives by universal suffrage; in a system in which the former will gradually strangle and empty competencies from the second.

All of this is unconstitutional, particularly because in the structure of the Communal State that is established, in the end, the exercise of sovereignty is factually indirect, through supposed "representatives" that are not popularly elected through universal and direct suffrage, but "elected" in Citizens' Assemblies, that are subjected to the control of the Central Power, being the whole system structured, directly controlled by a Ministry from the National Executive Branch of Government. Consequently, far from being an instrument of participation and decentralization is a centralized and tightly controlled system of the communities by the central power.

On the other hand, this Communal State is established imposing a unique official socialist concept and doctrine, contrary to any sort of pluralism, so that anyone who is not a socialist is automatically discriminated and excluded.

The December 2010 Laws on the Communal State and the Popular Power also reformed the Economic Constitution, establishing in parallel to the mixed economic system regulated in the Constitution, the so-called Communal Economic System to be developed "under communal forms of social ownership, to satisfy collective needs, social reinvestment of the surplus, and contribute to the country's overall social development in a sustainable manner" (art. 18).[116] This system must be exclusively developed through "socio-productive organizations under communal social property forms" created as public enterprises, family productive units, or bartering groups, in which private initiative and private property are excluded.

The socialist productive model established in the Law (art. 3.2), is precisely defined as a "production model based on social property, oriented towards the elimination of the social division of work that appertains to the capitalist model," directed to satisfy the increasing needs of the population through new means of generation and appropriation as well as the reinvestment of social surplus" (art. 6.12). This is nothing different than to legally impose a communist system by copying isolated paragraphs perhaps of a forgotten old manual of a failed communist revolution paraphrasing what Karl Marx and Friedrich Engels wrote 150 years ago (1845-1846) on

---

116 Organic Law of the Communal Economic System .See *Gaceta Oficial* N° 6.011 Extra. (12-21-2010

the "communist society,"[117] precisely based upon those three basic concepts: the social property of production means, the elimination of social division of work, and the social reinvestment of surplus (art. 1).

This Communal or Socialist State, regulated on the fringes of the Constitution, as mentioned, has been established as a "Parallel State" to the Constitutional State, but with provisions that, if implemented, will enable the Communal State to drown the Constitutional State, for which purpose the Law has provided that all organs of the Constitutional State are subjected to the mandates of the organizations of Popular Power, establishing a new principle of government, so-called in the Law, the principle of "govern obeying," no other than obeying the wishes of the central government[118] thorough the controlled organization of the Communal State.

As the Popular Power organizations have no political autonomy, since their "spokespersons" are not democratically elected by universal, direct and secret ballot, but appointed by citizen Assemblies politically controlled and operated by the governing party and the National Executive who controls and guides all the organizational process of the Communal State in the sphere of socialist ideology, there is no way there can be a spokesperson who is not a socialist.

Consequently, this "govern obeying" principle is a limitation to the political autonomy of the elected bodies of the Constitutional State such as the National Assembly, Governors and Legislative Councils of States and Mayors and Municipal Councils, upon who ultimately is imposed an obligation to obey any provision made by the National Government and the ruling party, framed exclusively in the socialist sphere as a political doctrine.

Therefore, in the unconstitutional framework of these Popular Power Laws, the popular will expressed in the election of representatives of the Constitutional State bodies has no value whatsoever, and the people have been confiscated of their sovereignty by transferring it to assemblies who do not represent them.

The result of these Laws is that the National Assembly has imposed on the Venezuelan people, against the popular will and defrauding the Constitution, a Socialist State model, called "the Communal State," in order to supposedly exercise Popular Power directly by the people, as an alleged form of direct exercise of sovereignty.

By regulating this Communal State of the Popular Power through ordinary legislation, in addition to defrauding the Constitution, a technique that has been consistently applied by the authoritarian regime in Venezuela since 1999 to impose its de-

---

117 See in Karl Marx and Frederich Engels, "The German Ideology," in *Collective Works*, Vol. 5, International Publishers, New York 1976, p. 47. Véanse además los textos pertinentes en http://www.educa.madrid.org/cms_tools/files/0a24636f-764c-4e03-9c1d-6722e2ee60d7/Texto%20Marx%20y%20Engels.pdf

118 Article 24 of the Law establishes the following principle: "Proceedings of the bodies and entities of Public Power. All organs, entities and agencies of Public Power will govern their actions by the principle of "govern obeying", in relation to the mandates of the people and organizations of Popular Power, according to the provisions in the Constitution of the Republic and the laws."

cisions outside of the Venezuelan Constitution,[119] it now adds fraud to the popular will by imposing on Venezuelans through organic laws a State model for which nobody has voted.

What is clear about all this is that there are no masks to deceive anyone, or by reason of which someone pretends to be deceived or fooled about what essentially the "Bolivarian revolution" in Venezuela is nothing else but a communist Marxist revolution, carried out deliberately by misusing and defrauding constitutional institutions.

---

119 See Allan R. Brewer-Carías, *Reforma constitucional y fraude a la Constitución (1999-2009)*, Academia de Ciencias Políticas y Sociales, Caracas 2009; *Dismantling Democracy. The Chávez Authoritarian Experiment*, Cambridge University Press, New York 2010.

CHAPTER XXVI

THE "BOLIVARIAN REVOLUTION" AND THE PROCESS OF "DECONSTITUTIONALIZATION" OF THE VENEZUELAN CONSTITUTIONAL STATE

(2012)

This Paper on "The "Bolivarian Revolution" in Venezuela and the Regime's Contempt for Constitutional Law. The Popular Power and the Communal State, or the Creation of a XXI Century Neo-Communist State by-passing the Constitution," is based on the ideas expressed in the essay included in the previous Chapter, and that was followed in my Presentations on "The "Deconstitucionalization" of the Venezuelan State and the Creation of a Communal State By-Passing The Constittuion," delivered at the *Inter-American Bar Association*, Washington, September 21, 2012; at the *Venezuelan Democracy Caucus, Western Hemisphere Subcommittee*, Washington, DC, November 8, 2011; ant at the Seminar on *Venezuela 2012. The Next Generation Hosts a Roundtable Discussion on Challenges to and Prospects for Growth and Stability*, Liechtenstein Institute on Self-Determination at Princeton University, Princeton NJ, November 18th, 2011. The ideas expressed in such Papers were later followed in the paper written for my Presentation at the Seminar on *Current Constitutional issues in the Americas ... and Beyond, Duquesne University School of Law*, Pittsburgh, 9/10 November 2012, which was published as "The Process of "Deconstitutionalization" of the Venezuelan Constitutional State, as the Most Important Current Constitutional Issue in Venezuela," in *Duquesne Law Review*, Volume 51, Number 2, Spring 2013, Pittsburgh 2013, pp. 349-386.

The Constitutional State was conceived in the 1999 Venezuelan Constitution, which is still formally in force, as a Democratic and Social Rule of Law State of Justice (Art. 2).

As a **Democratic State**, the Constitution organized the State based upon the two most classic principles of modern constitutionalism. On the one hand, the principle of separation of powers between five autonomous branches of government (Legislative, Executive, Judicial, Electoral, Citizens); and on the other hand, as "a decentralized federal State"[120] (Art. 4), the principle of the vertical distribution of public powers in three territorial levels of government: National, State and Municipal levels (Art. 136). In each of such levels the corresponding governments must always be of an "elective, decentralized, alternative, responsible, plural, and of revocable mandate" character (Article) That is, the political organization of the Nation must be based on the democratic principles (Articles 2, 3, 5 and 6), as a "democratic society" (Preamble), of representative and participatory character.

As a *Social State*, according to the extended declaration of rights, particularly of social rights, it has social obligations established to procure social justice; an objective which can brings the State to intervene in social and economic activity as a welfare state. That is why this Social State must seek for the application of the fundamental values of equality and solidarity, the preeminence of human rights (Preamble, Article 1° and 21°) and the achievement of "social justice" as one of the basis of the economic system (Article 299).[121] That is why the economic system was conceived in the Constitution as a mixed one, declaring economic liberty and free private initiative, altogether with the guaranty of private property, allowing the State participation in the economy, and in all case with the purpose of satisfying social justice.

As a *Rule of Law State* (*Estado de derecho*), the Constitution expressly provides that all the organs of the State must always act subjected to and act according to the provisions established in the Constitution and in the statutes enacted by the National Assembly (article 141). For such purpose, the Constitution is considered to be the "supreme law" of the land, and "the ground of the entire legal order," as it is declared in its Article 7, which in addition prescribes that the provisions of the Constitution are obligatory for all branches of government as well as for individuals (articles 7, 131). In order to assure such supremacy and enforceability, the Constitution has been conceived as a very rigid one in the sense that in order for its modification or reform, being possible to modify it only through three procedure set forth in the Constitution for its revision, depending on the importance and the scope of the modification proposed and always with popular participation,[122] which are: first, the

120 See the study of the Constitution regarding the regulation of this Constitutional State Model, in Allan R. Brewer-Carías, *La Constitución de 1999. Derecho Constitucional venezolano*, 2 vols., Caracas 2004; and *La Constitución de 1999 y la Enmienda Constitucional de 2009*, Editorial Jurídica Venezolana, Caracas 2011.

121 On the social values in the Constitution see Jacqueline Lejarza A., "El carácter normativo de los principios y valores en la Constitución de 1999," in *Revista de Derecho Constitucional*, N° 1 (septiembre-diciembre), Editorial Sherwood, Caracas, 1999, pp. 195-220; Liliana Fasciani "De la Justicia a la Justicia Social," in Jesús María Casal, Alfredo Arismendi and Carlos Luis Carrillo Artiles Coords, *Tendencias Actuales del Derecho Constitucional. Homenaje a Jesús María Casal Montbrun*, Vol. I, Universidad Central de Venezuela/Universidad Católica Andrés Bello, Caracas 2008, pp. 161-196.

122 See Allan R. Brewer-Carías, "La intervención del pueblo en la revisión constitucional en América latina", in *El derecho público a los 100 números de la Revista de Derecho Público 1980-2005*, Editorial Jurídica Venezolana, Caracas 2006, pp. 41-52

convening of a national "Constituent Assembly" for the whole transformation of the State, the "Constitutional reform" procedure for major constitutional changes, and the "Constitutional Amendment" for minor constitutional changes (arts. 340 ss).[123]

Finally, as a **State of Justice**, the organs of the State are the ones called to guarantee and enforce the Constitution, and above all, the fundamental rights (political, social, educational, cultural, economic, environmental rights) it declares, in order to assure their enjoyment by all persons without any sort of discrimination (article 21).

Also, as a State of Justice, the Constitution itself in order to assure its supremacy and the functioning of the State in all its qualifications (Democratic, Rule of Law, Social and Justice State), assigns all courts and judges the duty "of guaranteeing the integrity of the Constitution" (Article 334) with the power to decide not to apply a statute that they deemed to be unconstitutional when deciding a particular case.

In addition, Article 335 of the Constitution also assigns the Supreme Tribunal of Justice the duty of guaranteeing "the supremacy and effectiveness of the constitutional rules and principles," as "the maximum and final interpreter of the Constitution," with the duty to seek for "its uniform interpretation and application." For such purposes, the Constitution has organized a very extended and comprehensive system of judicial review in order to assure the enforceability of the Constitution, which combines the diffuse method of judicial review with the concentrated method of judicial review, assigning the latter to the Constitutional Chamber of the Supreme Tribunal of Justice.[124]

Constitutionally speaking, therefore, the Venezuelan State was constitutionalized according to all the general principles of modern constitutionalism, namely, the principles of separation of powers, representative democracy, political pluralism, political decentralization and participation, controlled government, and human rights guarantees;[125] established in a rigid way in the sense that no change to those principles can be made without reforming the Constitution. That is, for instance, from the democratic perspective, the alternate form of government cannot be eliminated at any level of government without a constitutional reform, and no political institution of the State can be created without ensuring its elective character through elected representatives of the people by means of universal, direct and secret suffrage; without guaranteeing its political autonomy, which is essential to its decentralized na-

---

123 See Allan R. Brewer-Carías, "Los procedimientos de revisión constitucional en Venezuela," in Eduardo Rozo Acuña (Coord.), *I Procedimenti di revisione costituzionale nel Diritto Comparato*, Urbino, Italia, 1999, pp. 137-181; "Modelos de revisión constitucional en América Latina," in *Boletín de la Academia de Ciencias Políticas y Sociales*, enero-diciembre 2003, N° 141, Caracas 2004. pp.115-156.

124 See Allan R. Brewer-Carías, "Judicial Review in Venezuela", in *Duquesne Law Review*, Volume 45, Number 3, Spring 2007, pp. 439-465.

125 See Allan R. Brewer-Carías, *Reflexiones sobre la revolución norteamericana (1776), la revolución francesa (1789) y la revolución hispanoamericana (1810-1830) y sus aportes al constitucionalismo moderno*, 2ª Edición Ampliada, Universidad Externado de Colombia, Editorial Jurídica Venezolana, Bogotá 2008.

ture; and without guaranteeing its plural character in the sense that it cannot be linked to a particular ideology.

Nonetheless, and in sharp contrast with the constitutional framework of the Constitutional State, the most important current constitutional issue in Venezuela is not its constitutionalization in the very publicized 1999 Constitution, but the deconstitutionalization process of the Constitutional Democratic, Social and Rule of Law State of Justice resulting from the now one decade long systematic institutional demolition process, which has been carried on by the authoritarian government installed in the country since 1999, in the name of a so called "Bolivarian Revolution"[126] imposing a series of political and "constitutional" changes in contempt of the Constitution and of its supremacy.

That is, during the past decade, almost all the basic principles of the organization of the State and of the political system of the country embodied in the Constitution have been changed without following the formal constitutional review procedures set forth in the Constitution; the Constitutional Chamber of the Supreme Court of Justice has failed to enforce the Constitution regarding the functioning of the State, refusing to guaranty its rigidity, allowing "constitutional reforms" to be sanctioned by means of ordinary legislation or even introducing "constitutional mutations" to the Constitution changing its meaning through constitutional interpretations.

This Paper has the purpose of highlighting the most recent expressions of such process of deconstitutionalization of the Constitutional State in Venezuela, which is the most important current constitutional issue in the country. That process has been developed thanks to the actions and to the omissions of the Constitutional Chamber of the Supreme Tribunal of Justice, which as Constitutional Jurisdiction, has refused to consider constitutional issues as such, allowing instead, in the name of the "Bolivarian Revolution," the introduction of changes in all the basic principles embodied in the Constitution without a formal constitutional reform. The Supreme Tribunal, on the contrary, defrauding or in degradation of the 1999 Constitution, has progressively allowd the implementation of the so called new "21st century Socialism" replacing the Constitutional State by a Communal State, without formally reviewing the Constitution.

---

126 See Allan R. Brewer-Carías, *Dismantling Democracy. The Chávez Authoritarian Experiment*, Cambridge University Press, Cambridge 2012.

I.   THE GENERAL FRAMEWORK FOR THE "DECONSTITUTIO-NALIZATION" PROCESS OF THE STATE: THE "BOLIVARIAN" LA-BEL IN ORDER TO DISGUISE THE IMPLANTATION OF A SOCIAL-IST OR COMMUNIST STATE, WITHOUT REFORMING THE CONSTITUCION

One of the most distinguished and apparently formal changes to the Venezuela Constitution adopted in 1999 was the new name given to the Republic as "Bolivarian Republic of Venezuela" (article 1), in substitution of the two hundred years old name of "Republic of Venezuela."

That change of name and the parallel initiation of the political changes derived from the "Bolivarian Revolution," were made by a National Constituent Assembly that was convened and elected in the same year of 1999 without being provided in the 1961 Constitution; that is in violation of the constitutional review procedures established in it.[127] That 1999 elected Constituent Assembly was completely controlled by the followers of the then recently elected (1998) President Hugo Chávez who, after 13 years, still remains as the head of the Executive Power.

The motivation for the new name given to the country in 1999 was formally to refer to the ideas and actions of Simón Bolívar, who not only was the "Liberator" of Venezuela at the beginning of the XIX century in the wars that followed the declaration of independence form Spain, but also of other Latin American countries such as Colombia, Ecuador, Bolivia and Peru which have been historically called the "Bolivarian" republics. Among them, Venezuela is the one with the oldest constitutional tradition, beginning with the sanctioning of the Federal Constitution of the United Provinces of Venezuela of December 21, 1811.[128]

---

127 See on the 1999 constitutional making process: Allan R. Brewer-Carías, *Golpe de estado y proceso constituyente en Venezuela,* Universidad Nacional Autónoma de México, Mexico City 2002; "The 1999 Venezuelan Constitution-Making Process as an Instrument for Framing the development of an Authoritarian Political Regime," in Laura E. Miller (Editor), *Framing the State in Times of Transition. Case Studies in Constitution Making*, United States Institute of Peace Press, Washington 2010, pp. 505-531; "Constitution Making in Defraudation of the Constitution and Authoritarian Government in Defraudation of Democracy. The Recent Venezuelan Experience", in *Lateinamerika Analysen*, 19, 1/2008, GIGA, German Institute of Global and Area Studies, Institute of Latin American Studies, Hamburg 2008, pp. 119-142.

128 This 1811 Constitution was the first Modern republican and democratic Constitution of Latin America, sanctioned by an elected Congress following the principles of modern constitutionalism derived from the French and the American revolutions. That Constitution and all the papers of the independence process from Spain were conceived and written without the participation of Simón Bolívar, who in fact began his influence in the country as a military, fighting and commanding the national forces against the Spanish military invasion of the country in 1812. This is the reason for his name being indissolubly attached to the Venezuelan Independence, as well as to the independence of other Latin American countries. See Allan R. Brewer-Carías, *Los inicios del proceso constituyente hispano y americaNº Caracas 1811 – Cádiz 1812,* (Prólogo de Asdrúbal Aguiar), Editorial bid & co. Editor, Colección Historia, Caracas 2012

During and after the wars against Spain (1813-1824), Bolívar participated in the subsequent constitution-making processes of the country first, in 1819, reformulating the constitutional framework of the State proposing a new Constitution called of *Angostura*; and second, in 1821 by proposing the constitution of a new State, the Republic of Colombia which comprised the territories of what is today Venezuela, Colombia and Ecuador. These Constitutions (1819, 1821), in contrast with the 1811 Federal Constitution, organized a centralized State with militaristic roots derived from the bitter independence wars.

In any case, being the name of Bolívar so closely linked with the initial organization of the State after the Independence, it has been used for political purposes by many rulers and in many occasions in Venezuelan history, in order to attract followers or to give some "doctrinal" basis to political regimes, mainly with military and authoritarian roots. It was the case in the nineteenth century, of Antonio Guzmán Blanco, and during the twentieth century, of Cipriano Castro, Juan Vicente Gómez, Eleazar López Contreras, and Marcos Pérez Jiménez; [129] and now, at the beginning of the twenty first century, of Hugo Chávez Frías, who has unearthed the name of Bolivar not only in order to change the very name of the country, but also to serve as the support for a new, but at the same time very old political doctrine, Socialism, which was completely unknown in Bolivar's times; but in the past.

Professor John Lynch, the most important non Venezuelan biographer of Bolívar, pointed out regarding those military rulers using the name of Bolívar during the nineteenth and twentieth centuries, that they have "at least more or less respected the basic thought of the Liberator, even when they misrepresented its meaning."[130] Nonetheless, referring to the current situation of the Chávez regime, the same Professor Linch concluded his comments on the political use of the name of Bolívar that:

"In 1999 Venezuelans were astonished to learn that their country had been renamed 'the Bolivarian Republic of Venezuela' by decree of President Hugo Chávez, who called himself a 'revolutionary Bolivarian.' Authoritarian populist, or neocaudillos, or Bolivarian militarists, whatever their designation, invoke Bolívar no less ardently than did previous rulers, though it is doubtful whether he would have responded to their calls...But the new heresy, far from maintaining continuity with the constitutional ideas of Bolívar, as was claimed, invented a new attribute, the populist Bolívar, and in the case of Cuba gave him a new identity, the socialist Bolí-

---

129 See in general Allan R. Brewer-Carías, *Historia Constitucional de Venezuela*, Ed. Alfa, 2 vols., Caracas 2008.

130 See John Lynch, *Simón Bolívar: A Life*, Yale University Press, New Haven, CT, 2007, p. 304. See also Germán Carrera Damas, *El culto a Bolívar, esbozo para un estudio de la historia de las ideas en Venezuela*, Universidad Central de Venezuela, Caracas 1969; Luis Castro Leiva, *De la patria boba a la teología bolivariana*, Monteávila, Caracas 1987; Elías Pino Iturrieta, *El divino Bolívar. Ensayo sobre una religión republicana*, Alfail, Caracas 2008; Ana Teresa Torres, *La herencia de la tribu. Del mito de la independencia a la Revolución bolivariana*, Editorial Alfa, Caracas 2009. See also the historiography study on these books in Tomás Straka, *La épica del desencanto*, Editorial Alfa, Caracas 2009.

var. By exploiting the authoritarian tendency, which certainly existed in the thought and action of Bolívar, regimes in Cuba and Venezuela claim the Liberator as patron for their policies, distorting his ideas in the process."[131]

An effectively, never before the adherence to Bolivar had led to changing the republic's name, and to the invention of a new "Bolivarian doctrine" in order to justify the government's policies, as the retired Lieutenant General Chávez has done regarding what he has called the "Bolivarian Revolution" linked to his idea of a "21st Century Socialism"[132] implemented under the tutelage of the Cuban dictators. Of course, is needless to say that no relation can be found in any of Simón Bolívar writings with any aspect related to "socialism." Just to remember, if Bolívar would have expressed any idea related to socialism, Karl Marx himself would have detected it when he wrote the entry on "Simón Bolívar y Ponte" for the *New American Cyclopedia* published in New York in 1857,[133] eleven years after publishing his book with Fredrick Engels on *The German Ideology.*[134] It was in this 1847 book were they used the word "communism" perhaps for the first time;[135] and the fact is that ten years later, in the 1857 article on Bolívar, Marx made no mention at all regarding any "socialist" ideas of Bolívar, being that article, by the way, one, if not the most critical work on Bolívar ever written.

On the other hand, and beside any ideological issues, in all Venezuelan constitutional history, the only "Bolivarian Republic" that has existed, strictly speaking, has been the State that resulted from the "union of the peoples of Colombia" proposed by Simón Bolívar in 1819, and materialized in the 1821 Constitution of the Republic of Colombia (comprising the territories of today's Venezuela, Nueva Granada and Ecuador). With that constitution, the Republic of Venezuela just disappeared as an autonomous state,[136] a situation that endured up to 1830, until Bolivar's death.

---

131 See John Lynch, *Simón Bolívar: A Life*, Yale University Press, New Haven, CT, 2007, p. 304. See also A.C. Clark, *The Revolutionary Has No Clothes: Hugo Chávez's Bolivarian Farce*, Encounter Books, New York 2009, pp. 5-14.

132 The last attempt to completely appropriate Simón Bolívar for the "Bolivarian Revolution," was the televised exhumation of his remains that took place at the National Pantheon in Caracas on July 26, 2010, conducted by President Chávez himself and other high officials, including the Prosecutor General, among other things, for the purpose of determining if Bolivar died of arsenic poisoning in Santa Marta in 1830, instead of from tuberculosis. See Simon Romero, "Building a New History By Exhuming Bolívar," *The New York Times,* August 4, 2010, p. A7.

133 See *The New American Cyclopaedia*, Vol. III, 1858, on "Bolivar y Ponte, Simón." Available at http://www.marxists.org/archive/marx/works/1858/01/bolivar.htm

134 The book was written between 1845 and 1846. The Communist Manifest was published in February 1848.

135 See in Karl Marx and Frederich Engels, "The German Ideology," in *Collective Works*, Vol. 5, International Publishers, New York 1976, p. 47. See the pertinent text at http://www.educa.madrid.org/cms_tools/files/0a24636f-764c-4e03-9c1d-6722e2ee60d7/Texto%20Marx%20y%20Engels.pdf

136 See the texts of all these Laws in Allan R. Brewer-Carías, *Las Constituciones de Venezuela*, Academia de Ciencias Políticas y Sociales, Caracas 2008, Vol. 1, pp. 643-46.

Consequently, the renaming of the Republic in 1999 as "Bolivarian Republic," this time fortunately without affecting the country's sovereignty, can only be explained as an intent to give the Republic, a "definitive" national doctrine supposedly based on the thoughts of Bolívar, which has been no more that the label used by the new rulers of the country in order to impose their own socialist doctrine disguised as a "Bolivarian" one.

For such purpose, the first step adopted was to give the country the name of Bolivar, initially with an exclusive political or partisan purpose derived from the name given in 1982 to the political movement used by Chávez to gain power, which was called the "Bolivarian Revolutionary Movement 200 (MBR-200)." Because such an organization, once transformed into a formal political party was not allowed to use the name of Bolivar,[137] the decision taken was to incorporate the name of Bolívar in the Constitution of the country.[138] The party itself became the Fifth Republic Movement (Movimiento V República, MVR) that was later transformed into the United Socialist Party of Venezuela (PSUV), which declared itself as a "Marxist" party following the "Bolivarian doctrine."[139]

In 1999 I was one of the few members of the 1999 Constituent Assembly that voted against the country's renaming proposal,[140] not only because I considered it was partisan motivated, but also because I considered that a republic organized as "a federal decentralized State" was essentially anti-"Bolivarian," Bolivar being the one that in the first decades of Latin American independence promoted the idea of centralized governments – non federal – in the new republics.[141] In any case, the new name was given to the Republic, later linked with socialism as a political doctrine

The consequence of the 1999 constitutional reform, in any case, was that everything related to the new political regime was called "Bolivarian," beginning, for instance, with the creation ten years ago of the "Bolivarian Circles" that were the first social or communal organizations promoted and supported by the government in order to react against any opposition to the government and to threaten anybody

---

137 According to the Political Parties Law, *Gaceta Oficial* N° 27.725, Apr. 30, 1965, political parties cannot use the name of the founders of the country or homeland symbols. The political organization the president formed before campaigning for the 1998 election was Movimiento Bolivariano 200. That name could not be used to identify the political party he founded, which became Movimiento V República.

138 *Mutatis mutandi*, in a certain way it happened with the use of the name of Augusto C. Sandino in the name of the *Frente Sandinista de Liberación* and of the Sandinista Republic of Nicaragua.

139 See "Declaration of Principles" of the United Socialist Party of Venezuela (Apr. 23, 2010), available at http://psuv.org.ve/files/tcdocumentos/Declaracion-de-principios-PSUV.pdf.

140 See Allan R. Brewer-Carías, *Debate constituyente (Aportes a la Asamblea Nacional Constituyente)* Fundación de Derecho Público–Editorial Jurídica Venezolana, Caracas 1999, 3 (Oct. 18–Nov. 30), pp. 237; 251-52.

141 See Allan R. Brewer-Carías, "Ideas centrales sobre la organización el Estado en la Obra del Libertador y sus Proyecciones Contemporáneas," in *Boletín de la Academia de Ciencias Políticas y Sociales*, N° 95-96, January-June 1984, pp. 137-151.

with different views.[142] This lead to the bitter polarization of the country, between "Bolivarian" and those who are not, and, consequently, supposedly, between patriots and anti-patriots, good people and bad people, pure people and corrupt people, revolutionary and antirevolutionary or oligarchs; and now between socialists and non socialists; all that, by manipulating history and popular feelings regarding the image of Bolivar.

In 2007, the constant promotion of the "Bolivarian Revolution," led the President of the Republic himself, to draft and propose a constitutional reform before the National Assembly, in order to formally include in the text of the Constitution, the link between the "Bolivarian doctrine" and Socialism as the fundamental doctrine of the State, even for international relations.

This constitutional reform based on then so-called "21st century socialism," failed to be implanted, being rejected by the people through popular vote in a Referendum that took place on December 2, 2007.[143] Nonetheless, and despite its rejection by the peoples votes, in the following year (2008), the 2007 constitutional reform proposals began to be implemented by the authoritarian government in violation of the Constitution through a massive amount of decree laws issued by the President, and by means of Organic Laws sanctioned by the National Assembly, reforming in this way the Constitution but without formally reviewing it. The last set of unconstitutional legislation implementing the 2007 rejected reform was approved in December of 2010, by formally creating a Communal State (or Socialist or Communist state) based upon the exercise of a Popular Power without any constitutional basis, in parallel to the existing Constitutional decentralized State based upon the Public Power (National, state, municipal) expressly established in the Constitution.[144]

These laws related to the implantation of Socialism as the doctrine of the new Communal State, were sanctioned in 2010, after Chávez confessed himself in January 2010, that the supposedly "Bolivarian revolution," was no more than the phantasmagoric resurrection of the historically failed "Marxist revolution," but in this

---

142   The general assembly of the Organization of American States, in its Report of Apr. 18, 2002, said about the Bolivarian Circles, that they "are groups of citizens or grassroots organizations which support the President's political platform. Many sectors consider them responsible for the human rights violations, acts of intimidation, and looting." See the reference in Allan R. Brewer-Carías, *La crisis de la democracia en Venezuela*, Libros El Nacional, Caracas 2002.

143   The definitive voting figures in such referendum have never been informed to the country by the government controlled National Electoral Council. See Allan R. Brewer-Carías, "Estudio sobre la propuesta de Reforma Constitucional para establecer un estado socialista, centralizado y militarista (Análisis del anteproyecto presidencial, Agosto de 2007)," *Cadernos da Escola de Direito e Relações Internacionais da UniBrasil* 7, Curitiba 2007, pp. 265-308.

144   See Gustavo Linares Benzo, "Sólo un Poder Público más. El Poder Popular en la reforma del 2007," in *Revista de Derecho Público* 112 *(Estudios sobre la reforma constitucional)*, Editorial Jurídica Venezolana, Caracas 2007, pp. 102-105; Arturo Peraza, "Reforma, Democracia participativa y Poder Popular," in *id.*, pp. 107-13.

case led by a president said he has never even read Marx's writings.[145] This public announcement lead to the adoption in April 2010, by the governmental United Socialist Party of Venezuela (which the President presides), in its First Extraordinary Congress, of a "Declaration of Principles" in which the party was officially declared as a "Marxist," "Anti-imperialist" and "Anti-capitalist" party. According to the same document, the party's actions are based on "scientific socialism" and on the "inputs of Marxism as a philosophy of praxis," in order to substitute the "Capitalist Bourgeois State" with a "Socialist State" based on the Popular Power and the socialization of the means of production.[146] Of course, none of these ideas can be found in the works of Simón Bolivar, his name only being used as a pretext to continue to manipulate the Bolivar "cult" to justify authoritarianism, as has occurred so many times before in the history of the country.[147]

With these declarations it can be said, finally, that the so called "Bolivarian Revolution" was unveiled; a revolution for which nobody in Venezuela has voted except for its rejection in the December 2, 2007 referendum, in which the President's proposals for constitutional reforms in order to establish a Socialist, Centralized, Police and Militaristic state, received a negative popular response.[148]

II. THE INTENT TO RADICALLY TRANSFORM THE CONSTITUTIONAL STATE INTO A SOCIALIST, CENTRALIZED AND COMMUNAL STATE, IN 2007, IN VIOLATION OF THE CONSTITUTION, BY MEANS OF A "CONSTITUCIONAL REFORM" PROCEDURE THAT WAS REJECTED BY THE PEOPLE, A THAT WAS DECLARED BY THE CONSTITUTIONAL JUDGE NON JUSTICIABLE.

As aforementioned, a major step taken in order to formally consolidate in the Constitution an authoritarian government by establishing a socialist, centralized and communal state in substitution of the democratic decentralized social State, was the 2007 constitutional reform proposal in order to establish a "Popular Power State" or

---

145 In his annual speech before the National Assembly on Jan. 15, 2010, in which Chávez declared to have "assumed Marxism," he also confessed that he had never read Marx's works. See María Lilibeth Da Corte, "Por primera vez asumo el marxismo," in *El Universal*, Caracas Jan. 16, 2010, http://www.eluniversal.com/2010/01/16/pol_art_por-primera-vez-asu_1726209.shtml.

146 See "Declaración de Principios, I Congreso Extraordinario del Partido Socialista Unido de Venezuela," Apr. 23, 2010, at http://psuv.org.ve/files/tcdocumentos/Declaracion-de-principios-PSUV.pdf

147 See *supra* notes 11, 12.

148 See on the 2007 constitutional reforms proposals, Allan R. Brewer-Carías, *Hacia la consolidación de un Estado socialista, centralizado, policial y militarista. Comentarios sobre el sentido y alcance de las propuestas de reforma constitucional 2007*, Editorial Jurídica Venezolana, Caracas 2007; *La reforma constitucional de 2007 (Comentarios al proyecto inconstitucionalmente sancionado por la Asamblea Nacional el 2 de noviembre de 2007)*, Editorial Jurídica Venezolana, Caracas 2007.

"Communal State,"[149] which was submitted by the President of the Republic before the National Assembly. As mentioned, the reform was approved by the Assembly, but once submitted to popular vote, it was rejected by the people on December 2, 2007.

As mentioned, the constitutional reform was intended to radically transform the most essential and fundamental aspects of the state,[150] being one of the most important reforms proposals in all of Venezuelan constitutional history. With it, the decentralized, democratic, pluralistic, and social state built and consolidated since the Second World War, would have been radically changed to create instead a socialist, centralized, repressive, and militaristic state grounded in the so-called "Bolivarian doctrine," identified with "21st century socialism" and a socialist economic system of State Capitalism. As mentioned, this reform was sanctioned evading the procedure established in the Constitution for such fundamental change, which imposed the convening of a Constituent Assembly. In fact, the reform designed defrauding the Constitution,[151] was one additional step in the "permanent coup d'état" that since 1999 has being occurred in Venezuela.[152]

The most important consequence of the proposed reform was the adoption of an official state ideology and doctrine to be formally established in Venezuela, which was the socialist and supposedly "Bolivarian" doctrine, which could have implied if approved by the people, to impose a duty on all citizens to actively contribute to its implementation, eliminating any vestige of political pluralism, and allowing for the

---

149 See Allan R. Brewer-Carías, *Hacia la Consolidación de un Estado Socialista, Centralizado, Policial y Militarista. Comentarios sobre el sentido y alcance de las propuestas de reforma constitucional 2007,* Colección Textos Legislativos, N° 42, Editorial Jurídica Venezolana, Caracas 2007.

150 See Rogelio Pérez Perdomo, "La Constitución de papel y su reforma," in *Revista de Derecho Público* 112 *(Estudios sobre la reforma constitucional),* Editorial Jurídica Venezolana, Caracas 2007, p. 14; G. Fernández, "Aspectos esenciales de la modificación constitucional propuesta por el Presidente de la República. La modificación constitucional como un fraude a la democracia," *Id,* p. 22; Alfredo Arismendi, "Utopía Constitucional," in *id.,* p. 31; Manuel Rachadell, "El personalismo político en el Siglo XXI," in *id.,* p. 66; Allan R. Brewer-Carías, "El sello socialista que se pretendía imponer al Estado," in *id.,* p. 71-75; Alfredo Morles Hernández, "El nuevo modelo económico para el Socialismo del Siglo XXI," in *id.,* p. 233-36.

151 See Rogelio Pérez Perdomo, "La Constitución de papel y su reforma," in *Revista de Derecho Público* 112 *(Estudios sobre la reforma constitucional),* Editorial Jurídica Venezolana, Caracas 2007, 14; Gerardo Fernández, "Aspectos esenciales de la modificación constitucional propuesta por el Presidente de la república. La modificación constitucional en fraude a la democracia," in id., 21-25; Fortunato González, "Constitución histórica y poder constituyente," in *id.,* pp. 33-36; Lolymar Herández Camargo, "Los límites del cambio constitucional como garantía de pervivencia del Estado de derecho," in *id.,* 37-45; Claudia Nikken, "La soberanía popular y el trámite de la refroma constitucional promovida por iniciativa presidencial el 15 de agosto de 2007," in *id.,* 51-58.

152 See José Amando Mejía Betancourt, "La ruptura del hilo constitucional," in *id.,* 47. The term was first used by Francois Mitterand, *Le coup d'État permanent,* Éditions 10/18, Paris 1993.

ALLAN R. BREWER-CARÍAS

formal criminalization of any dissidence regarding the unique and official way of thinking.

Guidelines for the proposed reforms emerged from various discussions and speeches of the president. These pointed out, on the one hand, o the formation of a state of "popular power" or of "communal power," or a "communal state" (*Estado del poder popular o del poder communal, o Estado comunal*) built upon communal councils (*consejos comunales*) as primary political units or social organizations. The communal councils, whose members are not elected by means of universal, direct, and secret suffrage, in a way contrary to the democratic principles established in the Constitution, were created by statute since 2006,[153] with a status parallel to the municipal entities, supposedly to channel citizen participation in public affairs. However, since their creation, they have operated within a system of centralized management conducted by the national executive power and without any political or territorial autonomy.[154]

On the other hand, the guidelines for the proposed constitutional reform also referred to the structuring of a socialist state and the substitution of the existing system of economic freedom and mixed economy, by a state and collectivist socialist economic system subject to centralized planning, minimizing the role of individuals and eliminating any vestige of economic liberties or private property as constitutional rights.

These proposals had the purpose of radically transform the state by creating a completely new juridical order; a change that according to Article 347 of the 1999 Constitution, required the convening and election of a Constituent Assembly and could not be undertaken by means of mere constitutional reform procedures. This later procedure for constitutional reform can only be applied to "partial revisions of the Constitution and for substitution of one or several of its provisions without modifying the structure and fundamental principles of the Constitutional text." In such case, the limited constitutional change is achieved through debate and sanctioning in the National Assembly, followed by approval in popular referendum.

Nonetheless, ignoring these constitutional provisions, the same political tactic used since 1999, was repeated, by acting fraudulently with respect to the Constitution. That is, the use of the existing institutions with the appearance of its adherence to constitutional form and procedure, in order to proceed, as the Supreme Tribunal had warned, "towards the creation of a new political regime, a new constitutional

---

153 *Ley de Consejos Comunales, Gaceta Oficial, Extra.* 5.806, Apr. 10, 2006. This statute was replaced by Ley Orgánica de los Consejos Comunales. See *Gaceta Oficial* N° 39.335, Dec. 28, 2009.

154 See Allan R. Brewer-Carías, "El inicio de la desmunicipalización en Venezuela: La organización del poder popular para eliminar la descentralización, la democracia representativa y la participación a nivel local," in *AIDA, Revista de la Asociación Internacional de Derecho Administrativo,* Universidad Nacional Autónoma de México, Asociación Internacional de Derecho Administrativo, Mexico City 2007, 49-67.

order, without altering the established legal system."[155] This occurred in February 1999 in the convening of a consultative referendum on whether to convene a Constituent Assembly when that institution was not prefigured in the then-existing Constitution of 1961.[156] It occurred with the December 1999 Decree on the Transitory Regime of the Public Powers, with respect to the 1999 Constitution, which was never the subject of an approbatory referendum.[157] It has continued to occur in subsequent years with the progressive destruction of democracy through the factual elimination of any effective separation of powers, and the sequestering of successive public rights and liberties, all supposedly based on legal and constitutional provisions.[158]

In this instance, once again, constitutional provisions were fraudulently used for ends other than those for which they were established. The "constitutional reform" procedure was used to radically transform the state, thus disrupting the civil order of the social-democratic state to convert the state into a socialist, centralized, repressive, and militarist state in which representative democracy, republican alternation in office, and the concept of decentralized power would have disappeared, with all power instead concentrated in the decisions of the head of state.[159] That could only be achieved through the convening of a Constituent Assembly, which was avoided.

The consequence was that the various State acts adopted in the irregular constitutional review procedure (the presidential initiative, the sanction of the reform by the National Assembly, the convening of referendum by the National Electoral Council)

---

155 See the decision of the Constitutional Chamber of the Supreme Tribunal of Justice N° 74 (Jan. 25, 2006), in *Revista de Derecho Público* 105, Editorial Jurídica Venezolana, Caracas 2006, 76ff.

156 See Allan R. Brewer-Carías, *Asamblea constituyente y ordenamiento constitucional*, Academia de Ciencias Políticas y Sociales, Caracas 1999.

157 See Allan R. Brewer-Carías, *Golpe de estado y proceso constituyente en Venezuela,* Universidad Nacional Autónoma de México, Mexico City 2002.

158 See Allan R. Brewer-Carías, "Constitution-Making Process in Defraudation of the Constitution and Authoritarian Government in Defraudation of Democracy: The Recent Venezuelan Experience," paper presented at the VII International Congress of Constitutional Law, Athens, June 2007. See also Allan R. Brewer-Carías, "El autoritarismo establecido en fraude a la Constitución y a la democracia y su formalización en Venezuela mediante la reforma constitucional. (De cómo en un país democrático se ha utilizado el sistema eleccionario para minar la democracia y establecer un régimen autoritario de supuesta 'dictadura de la democracia' que se pretende regularizar mediante la reforma constitucional)," in *Temas constitucionales. Planteamientos ante una reforma,* Fundación de Estudios de Derecho Administrativo, Caracas 2007, 13-74.

159 As is constitutionally proscribed, and as the Constitutional Chamber of the Supreme Tribunal of Justice summarized in Decision N° 74 (January 25, 2006), a symbolic case, it occurred "with the fraudulent use of powers conferred by martial law in Germany under the *Weimar* Constitution, forcing the Parliament to concede to the fascist leaders, on the basis of terms of doubtful legitimacy, plenary constituent powers by conferring an unlimited legislative power." See the Constitutional Chamber of the Supreme Tribunal of Justice, Decision N° 74 (Jan. 25, 2006) in *Revista de Derecho Público* 105, Editorial Jurídica Venezolana, Caracas 2006, 76ff.

were all challenged through judicial review actions of unconstitutionality and actions of *amparo,* filed before the Constitutional Chamber of the Supreme Tribunal. The response of the Chamber regarding the actions filed, being as it is completely controlled by the Government, was to declared the issues as non justiciables, allowing the deconstitutionalizing the Constitutional State.[160]

The purposes of the approved "constitutional reform" for the radical transformation of the state and the creation a new juridical order, were evidenced, first, from the proposals elaborated by the president's Council for Constitutional Reform that began to circulate in June 2007,[161] and later, from the final draft filed by the President before the National Assembly on August 15, 2007,[162] in which it was proposed:[163]

---

160 On these decisions, see Allan R. Brewer-Carías, "El juez constitucional vs. la supremacía constitucional. O de cómo la jurisdicción constitucional en Venezuela renunció a controlar la constitucionalidad del procedimiento seguido para la 'reforma constitucional' sancionada por la Asamblea Nacional el 2 de noviembre de 2007, antes de que fuera rechazada por el pueblo en el referendo del 2 de diciembre de 2007," in *Revista de Derecho Público* 112 *(Estudios sobre la reforma constitucional)*, Editorial Jurídica Venezolana, Caracas 2007, 661-94.

161 The document circulated in June 2007 under the title *Consejo Presidencial para la Reforma de la Constitución de la República Bolivariana de Venezuela, "Modificaciones propuestas."* The complete text was published as *Proyecto de reforma constitucional. Versión atribuida al Consejo Presidencial para la reforma de la Constitución de la República Bolivariana de Venezuela*, Editorial Atenea, Caracas 2007, 146.

162 The full text was published as *Proyecto de Reforma Constitucional. Elaborado por el ciudadano Presidente de la República Bolivariana de Venezuela, Hugo Chávez Frías,* Editorial Atenea, Caracas 2007. The director of the National Electoral Council, Vicente Díaz, stated on July 16, 2007, "The presidential proposal to reform the constitutional text modifies fundamental provisions and for that reason it would be necessary to convene a National Assembly to approve them." This council member was consulted on this matter on Unión Radio, Aug. 16, 2007, at http://www.unionradio.com.ve/Noticias/No-ticia.aspx?noticiaid=212503. The initiation of the reform process in the National Assembly could have been challenged before the Constitutional Chamber of the Supreme Tribunal on the basis of unconstitutionality. Nonetheless, the president of the Constitutional Chamber – who was also a member of the Presidential Council for the Reform of the Constitution – made clear that "no legal action related to modifications of the constitutional text would be heard until such modifications had been approved by citizens in referendum," adding that "any action must be presented after a referendum, when the constitutional reform has become a norm, since we cannot interpret an attempted norm. Once a draft reform has become a norm we can enter into interpretations of it and hear nullification actions." See Juan Francisco Alonso, *El Universal*, Caracas Aug. 18, 2007

163 On the reform proposals, see Allan R. Brewer-Carías, *Hacia la consolidación de un estado socialista, centralizado, policial y militarista. Comentarios sobre el sentido y alcance de las propuestas de reforma constitucional 2007,* Colección Textos Legislativos N° 42, Editorial Jurídica Venezolana, Caracas 2007; *La reforma constitucional de 2007 (Comentarios al proyecto inconstitucionalmente sancionado por la Asamblea Nacional el 2 de noviembre de 2007)*, Colección Textos Legislativos N° 43, Editorial Jurídica Venezolana, Caracas 2007. See also all the articles published in *Revista de Derecho Público* 112 *(Estudios sobre la reforma constitucional)*, Editorial Jurídica Venezolana, Caracas 2007.

First, to convert the decentralized federal state into a centralized state of concentrated power, under the illusory guise of a popular power, which implied the definitive elimination of the federal form of the state,[164] rendering political participation impossible, and degrading representative democracy.

For such purpose, the reform established a new "popular power" (*poder popular*) (art. 16), composed by communities (*comunidades*), each of which "shall constitute a basic and indivisible spatial nucleus of the Venezuelan Socialist State, where ordinary citizens will have the power to construct their own geography and their own history;" which were to be grouped into communes (*comunas*).[165]

The main aspect of these reforms was that they provided that the popular power "is expressed through the constitution of communities, communes, and the self-government of the cities, by means of the communal councils, workers' councils, peasant councils, student councils, and other entities established by law." However, although "the people" (*el pueblo*) were designated as the "depositary of sovereignty," to be "exercised directly through the popular power," it was expressly stated that the popular power "does not arise from suffrage or from any election, but arises from the condition of the organized human groups that form the base of the population." Consequently, representative democracy at the local level and territorial political autonomy was to disappear, substituted with a supposed participatory and protagonist democracy that would, in fact, be controlled by the president and that proscribed any form of political decentralization and territorial autonomy.[166]

Even anticipating the constitutional reform proposal, perhaps being the government sure of its approval, in 2006 the Law on the Councils of the Popular Power (*Consejos del Poder Popular*) was sanctioned.[167] In the same trend of such Law, the

---

164 See Manuel Rachadell, "El personalismo político en el Siglo XXI," in *Revista de Derecho Público* 112 *(Estudios sobre la reforma constitucional)*, Editorial Jurídica Venezolana, Caracas 2007, 67; Ana Elvira Araujo, "Proyecto de reforma constitucional (agosto a noviembre 2007). Principios fundamentales y descentralización política," in *id.*, 77-81; José Luis Villegas, "Impacto de la reforma constitucional sobre las entidades locales," in *id.*, 119-23.

165 The communes were created in the statute on the Federal Council of Government. See *Ley Orgánica del Consejo Federal de Gobierno*, Gaceta Oficial N° 5.963 Extra. of Feb. 22, 2010).

166 This fundamental change, as the president stated on August 15, 2007, constituted "the development of what we understand by decentralization, because the Fourth Republic concept of decentralization is very different from the concept we must work with. For this reason, we have here stated 'the protagonist participation of the people, transferring power to them, and creating the best conditions for the construction of social democracy.'" See *Discurso de orden pronunciado por el ciudadano Comandante Hugo Chávez Frías, op. cit.,* 50.

167 See Giancarlo Henríquez Maionica, "Los Consejos Comunales (una breve aproximación a su realidad y a su proyección ante la propuesta presidencial de reforma constitucional)," in *Revista de Derecho Público* 112 *(Estudios sobre la reforma constitucional)*, Editorial Jurídica Venezolana, Caracas 2007, pp. 89-99; Allan R. Brewer-Carías, "El inicio de la desmunicipalización en Venezuela: La organización del poder popular para eliminar la descentralización, la democracia representativa y la participación a nivel local," in *AIDA, Opera Prima de Derecho Administrativo. Revista de la Asociación Internacional de Derecho Administrativo,*

reforms proposals conceived "the communes and communities" (*comunas y comunidades*) as "the basic and indivisible spatial nucleus of the Venezuelan Social-ist State" (art. 15); adding that the only objective of the constitutional provision for political participation, was "for the construction of socialism," requiring that all citizens' political associations be devoted "to develop the values of mutual coopera-tion and socialist solidarity" (art. 70).

Second, to convert the democratic and pluralist state into a socialist state, with the obligation to "promote people's participation as a national policy, devolving its power and creating the best conditions for the construction of a Socialist democra-cy" (art. 158); thus, establishing a political official doctrine of socialist character – Bolivarian doctrine –. The consequence of this would have been that any thoughts different from the official one was to be rejected, as the official political doctrine was to be incorporated into the Constitution itself, establishing a constitutional duty for all citizens to ensure its compliance, imposing the teaching in the schools of the "*ideario bolivariano*" (Bolivarian ideology), and stating that the primary investment of the state in education was to be done "according to the humanistic principles of the Bolivarian socialism." As a consequence, the basis for criminalizing all dissi-dence was formally to be established.

Third, to convert the mixed economic system into a state-owned, socialist, cen-tralized economy by means of eliminating economic liberty and private initiative as constitutional rights, as well as the constitutional right to private property; confer-ring the means of production to the state, to be centrally managed; and configuring the state as an institution on which all economic activity depended and to whose bureaucracy the totality of the population is subject. In this sense, the reform estab-lished that the socialist economic model created was to achieve "the best conditions for the collective and cooperative construction of a Socialist Economy" (art. 112), through "socialist means of production" (art. 168) by constituting "mixed corpora-tions and/or socialist units of production" (art. 113), or "economic units of social production" as to "create the best conditions for the collective and cooperative con-struction of a socialist economy," or "different forms of businesses and economic units from social property, both directly or communally, as well as indirectly or through the state" (art. 112). The reforms sought simply to derogate and eliminate the right to the free exercise of economic activities as a constitutional right and eco-nomic freedom itself.[168] The reforms then referred to the "socialist principles of the

---

Universidad Nacional Autónoma de México, Asociación Internacional de Derecho Adminis-trativo, Mexico City 2007, pp. 49-67. The 2006 law was replaced by *Ley Orgánica de los Consejos Comunales, Gaceta Oficial* N° 39.335, Dec. 28, 2009. See the comments on this Law in Allan R. Brewer-Carías, *Ley de los Consejos Comunales*, Editorial Jurídica Venezo-lana, Caracas 2010.

168 See Gerardo Fernández, "Aspectos esenciales de la modificación constitucional propuesta por el Presidente de la República. La modificación constitucional como un fraude a la demo-cracia," in *Revista de Derecho Público* 112 *(Estudios sobre la reforma constitucional)*, Edi-torial Jurídica Venezolana, Caracas 2007, p. 24; Alfredo Arismendi, "Utopía Constitucio-nal," in *id.*, p. 31; José Antonio Muci Borjas, "La suerte de la libertad económica en el pro-yecto de Reforma de la Constitución de 2007," in *id.*, pp. 203-208; Tamara Adrián, "Activi-

socioeconomic system" (art. 229) and to the "socialist state" and the "socialist development of the nation" (arts. 318, 320). All the reforms collided with the ideas of liberty and solidarity proclaimed in the 1999 Constitution and established a state that substitutes itself for society and private economic initiative.

Fourth, to convert the liberal state into a repressive (police) state, given the regressive character of the regulations established in the reform regarding human rights, particularly civil rights, and the expansion of the president's emergency powers, under which he was authorized to indefinitely suspend constitutional rights.

Fifth, and finally, to convert the civil state into a militarist state, on the basis of the role assigned to the "Bolivarian Armed Force" (*Fuerza Armada Bolivariana*), which was configured to function wholly under the president, and the creation of the new "Bolivarian National Militia (*Milicia Nacional Bolivariana*). All were to act "by means of the study, planning and execution of Bolivarian military doctrine" – that is, according to socialist doctrine.

All the reforms implied the radical transformation of the Venezuelan political system; sought to establish a centralized socialist, repressive, and militaristic state of popular power; and departed fundamentally from the concept of a civil social-democratic state under the rule of law and justice based on a mixed economy. None of those reforms could be approved thorugh a "constitutional reform" procedure.

The motives for the reforms were all very explicitly expressed by the President of the Republic in 2007, beginning with his speech of presentation of the draft reforms before the National Assembly, in which he said that the reforms' main objective was "the construction of a Bolivarian and socialist Venezuela" – that is, to sow "socialism in the political and economic realms."[169] He clearly expressed that in his presidential campaign in 1999, he did not propose such thing as "projecting the road of socialism" to be incorporated in the Constitution, but conversely, in 2006, as candidate for reelection, he said: "Let us go to Socialism," deducting from that that "everyone who voted for [reelecting] candidate Chávez then, voted to go to socialism."[170]

---

dad económica y sistemas alternativos de producción," in *id.*, pp. 209-14; Víctor Hernández Mendible, "Réquiem por la libertad de empresa y derecho de propiedad," in *id.*, pp. 215-18; Alfredo Morles Hernández, "El nuevo modelo económico para el Socialismo del Siglo XXI," in *id.*, pp. 233-236.

169 See *Discurso de orden pronunciado por el ciudadano Comandante Hugo Chávez Frías, Presidente Constitucional de la República Bolivariana de Venezuela en la conmemoración del ducentécimo segundo aniversario del juramento del Libertador Simón Bolívar en el Monte Sacro y el tercer aniversario del referendo aprobatorio de su mandato constitucional*, special session, Aug. 15, 2007, Asamblea Nacional, División de Servicio y Atención legislativa, Sección de Edición, Caracas 2007, 4, 33.

170 Id., 4. That is, it sought to impose the wishes of only 46% of registered voters who voted to reelect the president on the remaining 56% of registered voters who did not vote for presidential reelection. According to official statistics from the National Electoral Council, of 15,784,777 registered voters, only 7,309,080 voted to reelect the president.

This was then the motivation for the drafting of the constitutional reforms in 2007, aiming to construct "Bolivarian Socialism, Venezuelan Socialism, our Socialism, and our socialist model," having "the community" (*la comunidad*), a "basic and indivisible nucleus," and considering that "real democracy is only possible in socialism." However, the democracy referred to was not at all a representative democracy because it was "not born of suffrage or from any election, but rather is born from the condition of organized human groups as the base of the population." [171]

The president in that speech summarized the aims of his reform proposals explaining that on the political ground, the purpose was to "deepen popular Bolivarian democracy"; and on the economic ground, to "create better conditions to sow and construct a socialist productive economic model," which he considered "our model." That is, "in the political field: socialist democracy; on the economic, the productive socialist model; in the field of public administration, incorporate new forms in order to lighten the load, to leave behind bureaucracy, corruption, and administrative inefficiency, which are heavy burdens of the past still upon us like weights, in the political, economic and social areas." [172]

All his proposals to construct socialism were linked by the president to Simón Bolívar's 1819 Constitution of Angostura, which he considered "perfectly applicable to a socialist project" in the sense of considering that it was possible to "take the original Bolivarian ideology as a basic element of a socialist project." [173] Of course, this assertion had no serious foundations: it is enough to read Bolívar's 1819 Angostura discourse on presenting the draft constitution to realize that it has nothing to do with a "socialist project" of any kind. [174]

The rejected constitutional reform, without doubt, would have altered the basic foundations of the state. [175] This is true particularly with respect to the proposals on

---

171 See *Discurso de orden pronunciado por el ciudadano Comandante Hugo Chávez Frías, op cit.,* 32, 34, 35.

172 *Id.,* 74.

173 *Id.,* 42. Only one month before the president's speech on the proposed constitutional reforms, the former minister of defense, General in Chief Raúl Baduel, who was in office until July 18, 2007, stated on leaving the Ministry of Popular Power for the Defense that the president's call to "construct socialism for the twenty-first century, implied a necessary, pressing and urgent need to formalize a model of Socialism that is theoretically its own, autochthonous, in accord with our historical, social, political and cultural context." He added, "Until this moment, this theoretical model does not exist and has not been formulated." It is hard to imagine that it could have been formulated just one month later.

174 See Simón Bolívar, *Escritos fundamentales*, Caracas 1982. See also Pedro Grases ed., *El Libertador y la Constitución de Angostura de 1819,* Caracas 1969; José Rodríguez Iturbe, ed., *Actas del Congreso de Angostura,* Caracas 1969. The contrary at least would have been noticed by Karl Mark who, on the contrary, in 1857 wrote a very critical entry regarding Bolivar, without discovering any socialist trends in his life, for the *The New American Cyclopaedia*, Vol. III, 1858, on "Bolivar y Ponte, Simón." Available at http://www.marxists.org/archive/marx/works/1858/01/bolivar.htm

175 See Eugenio Hernández Bretón, "Cuando no hay miedo (ante la Reforma Constitucional)," in *Revista de Derecho Público* 112 *(Estudios sobre la reforma constitucional)*, Editorial Jurídi-

the constitutional amplification of the Bolivarian doctrine; the substitution of the democratic, social state with the socialist state; the elimination of decentralization as a policy of the state designed to develop public political participation; and the elimination of economic freedom and the right to property.[176] All these constitutional reforms, approved by the National Assembly defrauding the Constitution, as aforementioned, were submitted to popular vote, and were all rejected by the people in the referendum that took place on December 2, 2007.[177]

Of course, as mentioned, none of these reforms changing so radically the State could be achieved through the constitutional review procedure ("constitutional reform") used by the President and the National Assembly. Major constitutional changes as those proposed in 2007 can only be approved by means of the convening of a Constituent Assembly.

That is why, the unconstitutional procedure that was followed for the reform, as mentioned, was of course challenged on grounds of unconstitutionality before the Constitutional Chamber of the Supreme Tribunal of Justice, which because being completely controlled by the Executive, refused to exercise judicial review on these matters declaring that such actions could no even be filed (*"improponible"*).[178]

Nonetheless, as aforementioned, the constitutional reform was rejected by popular vote in the referendum that took place on December 2, 2007,[179] a fact that the

---

ca Venezolana, Caracas 2007, oo. 17-20; Manuel Rachadell, "El personalismo político en el Siglo XXI," in *id.*, pp. 65-70.

176   See on these reforms, Allan R. Brewer-Carías, *Dismantling Democracy. The Chávez Authoritarian Experiment*, Cambridge University Press, 2010.

177   See Allan R. Brewer-Carías, "La proyectada reforma constitucional de 2007, rechazada por el poder constituyente originario", in *Anuario de Derecho Público 2007,* Año 1, Instituto de Estudios de Derecho Público de la Universidad Monteávila, Caracas 2008, pp. 17-65. According to information from the National Electoral Council on Dec. 2, 2007, of 16,109,664 registered voters, only 9,002,439 voted (44.11% abstention); of voters, 4,504,354 rejected the proposal (50.70%). This means that there were only 4,379,392 votes to approve the proposal (49.29%), so only 28% of registered voters voted for the approval.

178   See Allan R. Brewer-Carías, "El juez constitucional vs. la supremacía constitucional O de cómo la jurisdicción constitucional en Venezuela renunció a controlar la constitucionalidad del procedimiento seguido para la 'reforma constitucional' sancionada por la Asamblea Nacional el 2 de noviembre de 2007, antes de que fuera rechazada por el pueblo en el referendo del 2 de diciembre de 2007," in Eduardo Ferrer Mac Gregor y César de Jesús Molina Suárez (Coordinarores), *El juez constitucional en el Siglo XXI,* Universidad nacional Autónoma de México, Suprema Corte de Justicia de la Nación, México 2009, Tomo I, pp. 385-435.

179   See Allan R. Brewer-Carías, "La proyectada reforma constitucional de 2007, rechazada por el poder constituyente originario", in *Anuario de Derecho Público 2007,* Año 1, Instituto de Estudios de Derecho Público de la Universidad Monteávila, Caracas 2008, pp. 17-65. According to information from the National Electoral Council on Dec. 2, 2007, of 16,109,664 registered voters, only 9,002,439 voted (44.11% abstention); of voters, 4,504,354 rejected the proposal (50.70%). This means that there were only 4,379,392 votes to approve the proposal (49.29%), so only 28% of registered voters voted for the approval.

766 ALLAN R. BREWER-CARÍAS

authoritarian government simply ignored, by implementing it through ordinary legislation and constitutional interpretations.

III. THE FRAUDULENT IMPLEMENTATION OF THE REJECTED 2007 CONSTITUTIONAL REFORM

In effect, the formal popular rejection of the 2007 constitutional reforms proposals through the December 2007 referendum, which in any democratic state would have lead the government to listen and follow the will of the people, on the contrary, in Venezuela did not prevent the Government of beginning to implement them, without even bothering to try again to formally change the Constitution, in order to establish the Socialist State.

On the contrary in defiance of the popular will, once the 2007 constitutional reforms proposal were rejected by popular vote, the president and other main officials of the National Assembly publicly announced that despite such rejection, they were going to implement the reforms.

This has been achieved during the past five years, *first* through the progressive political process of concentrating and controlling all public powers by the National Executive, through the National Assembly, as has occurred regarding the Judiciary;[180] *second*, through the enactment of ordinary legislation by the National Assembly, and decrees laws issued by the President of the Republic as delegate legislation,[181] which the Supreme Tribunal has refused to control; *third*, through the implementation of a nationalization, expropriation and confiscation process of private industries, private assets and private properties;[182] and *fourth*, through constitutional

180 See Allan R. Brewer-Carías, "La justicia sometida al poder [La ausencia de independencia y autonomía de los jueces en Venezuela por la interminable emergencia del Poder Judicial (1999-2006)]" en *Cuestiones Internacionales. Anuario Jurídico Villanueva 2007,* Centro Universitario Villanueva, Marcial Pons, Madrid 2007, pp. 25-57.

181 See Lolymar Hernández Camargo, "Límites del poder ejecutivo en el ejercicio de la habilitación legislativa: Imposibilidad de establecer el contenido de la reforma constitucional rechazada vía habilitación legislativa," in *Revista de Derecho Público* 115 *(Estudios sobre los Decretos Leyes),* Editorial Jurídica Venezolana, Caracas 2008, pp. 51ff.; Jorge Kiriakidis, "Breves reflexiones en torno a los 26 Decretos-Ley de julio-agosto de 2008, y la consulta popular refrendaría de diciembre de 2007," in *id.*, pp. 57ff.; José Vicente Haro García, "Los recientes intentos de reforma constitucional o de cómo se está tratando de establecer una dictadura socialista con apariencia de legalidad (A propósito del proyecto de reforma constitucional de 2007 y los 26 decretos leyes del 31 de julio de 2008 que tratan de imponerla)," in *id.*, pp. 63ff.; Ana Cristina Nuñez Machado, "Los 26 nuevos Decretos-Leyes y los principios que regulan la intervención del Estado en la actividad económica de los particulares," in *id.*, pp. 215-20; Aurilivi Linares Martínez, "Notas sobre el uso del poder de legislar por decreto por parte del Presidente venezolano," in *id.*, pp. 79-89; Carlos Luis Carrillo Artiles, "La paradójica situación de los Decretos Leyes Orgánicos frente a la Ingeniería Constitucional de 1999," in *id.*, pp. 93-100; Freddy J. Orlando S., "El "paquetazo," un conjunto de leyes que conculcan derechos y amparan injusticias," in *id.*, pp. 101-104.

182 See Antonio Canova González, Luis Alfonso Herrera Orellana, and Karina Anzola Spadaro, *¿Expropiaciones o vías de hecho? (La degradación continuada del derecho fundamental de*

"mutations," that is, changes introduced in the Constitution by means of interpretation made by the Constitutional Chamber of the Supreme Tribunal of Justice as Constitutional Jurisdiction.[183]

The result has been that absolutely all the mentioned general trends and basic purposes of the popularly rejected 2007 constitutional reform draft have been implemented in the country in contempt of the Constitution, and on the sight of the entire democratic world.

This occurred, first, by means of decree laws issued by the president in execution of the February 2007 enabling law[184] (legislative delegation) sanctioned by the National Assembly as was proposed by the president at the beginning of 2007, with the prospect of the constitutional reform process. As aforementioned, perhaps assuming that the presidential constitutional-reform proposal was going to be approved by the people, the president began to implement it through decree laws, and continue to do so after the popular rejection of the reforms.[185] This happened particularly in economic and social matters, beginning the structuring of the socialist centralized state,[186] in a process of delegate legislation developed in absolute secrecy with no

---

propiedad en la Venezuela actual," Funeda, Universidad Católica Andrés Bello, Caracas 2009.

183   See Allan R. Brewer-Carías, "El juez constitucional al servicio del autoritarismo y la ilegítima mutación de la Constitución: el caso de la Sala Constitucional del Tribunal Supremo de Justicia de Venezuela (1999-2009)", in *Revista de Administración Pública*, N° 180, Madrid 2009, pp. 383-418; "La fraudulenta mutación de la Constitución en Venezuela, o de cómo el juez constitucional usurpa el poder constituyente originario,", in *Anuario de Derecho Público*, Centro de Estudios de Derecho Público de la Universidad Monteávila, Año 2, Caracas 2009, pp. 23-65; José Vicente Haro, "La mutación de la Constitución 'Bolivariana'," in Gonzalo Pérez Salazar and Luis Petit Guerra, *Los retos del derecho procesal constitucional en Latinoamérica, I Congreso Internacional de Derecho Procesal Constitucional, 19 y 20 Octubre de 2011*, Vol I, Universidad Monteávila Funeda, Caracas 2011, pp. 93-141.

184   *Gaceta Oficial*, 38.617, Feb. 1, 2007.

185   See Lolymar Hernández Camargo, "Límites del poder ejecutivo en el ejercicio de la habilitación legislativa: Imposibilidad de establecer el contenido de la reforma constitucional rechazada vía habilitación legislativa," in *Revista de Derecho Público* 115 *(Estudios sobre los Decretos Leyes)*, Editorial Jurídica Venezolana, Caracas 2008, pp. 51ff.; Jorge Kiriakidis, "Breves reflexiones en torno a los 26 Decretos-Ley de julio-agosto de 2008, y la consulta popular refrendaría de diciembre de 2007," in *id.*, pp. 57ff.; José Vicente Haro García, "Los recientes intentos de reforma constitucional o de cómo se está tratando de establecer una dictadura socialista con apariencia de legalidad (A propósito del proyecto de reforma constitucional de 2007 y los 26 decretos leyes del 31 de julio de 2008 que tratan de imponerla)," in *id.*, pp. 63 ff.

186   See Ana Cristina Nuñez Machado, "Los 26 nuevos Decretos-Leyes y los principios que regulan la intervención del Estado en la actividad económica de los particulares," in *Revista de Derecho Público* 115 *(Estudios sobre los Decretos Leyes)*, Editorial Jurídica Venezolana, Caracas 2008, pp. 215-20.

public consultation and participation, in violation of Article 210 of the Constitution.[187]

As aforementioned, the process began even before the draft reforms were even submitted to the National Assembly, when Decree Law N° 5,841 was enacted on June 12, 2007,[188] containing the organic law creating the Central Planning Commission. This was the first formal state act devoted to build the socialist state.[189] Once the 2007 constitutional reform was rejected in referendum, a few days later, on December 13, 2007, the National Assembly approved the 2007–13 Economic and Social Development National Plan, established in Article 32 of the Decree Law enacting the Planning Organic Law,[190] in which the basis of the "planning, production and distribution system oriented towards socialism" was established, providing that "the relevant matter is the progressive development of social property of the production means."

For such purpose, the proposed 2007 rejected constitutional reforms to assign the state all powers over farming, livestock, fishing, and aquaculture, and in particular the production of food, was then materialized in the Decree Law on the Organic Law on Farming and Food Security and Sovereignty.[191] That law assigned to the state power not only to authorize food imports but also to prioritize production and directly assume distribution and commercialization. The law also expanded expropriation powers of the executive violating the constitutional guarantee of the previ-

---

187   See Aurilivi Linares Martínez, "Notas sobre el uso del poder de legislar por decreto por parte del Presidente venezolano," in *Revista de Derecho Público* 115 *(Estudios sobre los Decretos Leyes),* Editorial Jurídica Venezolana, Caracas 2008, pp. 79-89; Carlos Luis Carrillo Artiles, "La paradójica situación de los Decretos Leyes Orgánicos frente a la Ingeniería Constitucional de 1999," in *id.*, pp. 93-100; Freddy J. Orlando S., "El "paquetazo," un conjunto de leyes que conculcan derechos y amparan injusticias," in *id.*, pp. 101-104.

188   *Gaceta Oficial* N° 5.841, Extra., June 22, 2007.

189   See Allan R. Brewer-Carías, "Comentarios sobre la inconstitucional creación de la Comisión Central de Planificación, centralizada y obligatoria," in *Revista de Derecho Público* 110, Editorial Jurídica Venezolana, Caracas 2007, pp. 79-89; Luis A. Herrera Orellana, "Los Decretos-Leyes de 30 de julio de 2008 y la Comisión Central de Planificación: Instrumentos para la progresiva abolición del sistema político y del sistema económico previstos en la Constitución de 1999," in *Revista de Derecho Público* 115, *(Estudios sobre los Decretos Leyes),* Editorial Jurídica Venezolana, Caracas 2008, pp. 221-32.

190   *Gaceta Oficial* N° 5.554 of Nov. 13, 2001.

191   *Gaceta Oficial* N° 5.889, Extra., July 31, 2008. See José Ignacio Hernández G., "Planificación y soberanía alimentaria," in *Revista de Derecho Público* 115, *(Estudios sobre los Decretos Leyes),* Editorial Jurídica Venezolana, Caracas 2008, pp. 389-94; Juan Domingo Alfonso Paradisi, "La constitución económica establecida en la Constitución de 1999, el sistema de economía social de mercado y el decreto 6.071 con rango, valor y fuerza de Ley Orgánica de seguridad y soberanía agroalimentaria," in *id.*, pp. 395-415; Gustavo A. Grau Fortoul, "La participación del sector privado en la producción de alimentos, como elemento esencial para poder alcanzar la seguridad alimentaria (Aproximación al tratamiento de la cuestión, tanto en la Constitución de 1999 como en la novísima Ley Orgánica de soberanía y seguridad alimentaria)," in *id.*, pp. 417-24.

ous declaration of a specific public interest or public utility involved, and allowing the State occupation of industries without compensation,[192] what has repeatedly occurred during the past years.[193]

Another Decree Law, N° 6,130 of June 3, 2008, enacted the Popular Economy Promotion and Development Law, establishing a "socio-productive communal model," with different socio-productive organizations following the "socialist model."[194] In the same openly socialist orientation, Decree Law N° 6,092 was also issued enacting the Access to Goods and Services Persons Defense Law,[195] which derogated the previous Consumer and Users Protection Law,[196] with the purpose of regulating all commercialization and different economic aspects of goods and services, extending the state powers of control to the point of establishing the possibility of confiscating goods and services by means of their takeover and occupation of private industries and services through administrative decisions,[197] which has also repeatedly occurred during the past years.[198]

Regarding the 2007 rejected constitutional reforms related to eliminating local-level representative democracy, as aforementioned, the same began to be implemented in 2006, even before its formal proposal, with the sanctioning of the Com-

192 See Carlos García Soto, "Notas sobre la expansión del ámbito de la declaratoria de utilidad pública o interés social en la expropiación," in *id.*, pp. 149-51.

193 See, in general, Antonio Canova González, Luis Alfonso Herrera Orellana, and Karina Anzola Spadaro, *¿Expropiaciones o vías de hecho? (La degradación continuada del derecho fundamental de propiedad en la Venezuela actual,*" Funeda, Universidad Católica Andrés Bello, Caracas 2009.

194 *Gaceta Oficial* N° 5.890, Extra., July 31, 2008. See Jesús María Alvarado Andrade, "La desaparición del bolívar como moneda de curso legal (Notas críticas al inconstitucional Decreto N° 6.130, con rango, valor y fuerza de la ley para el fomento y desarrollo de la economía comunal, de fecha 3 de junio de 2008," in *Revista de Derecho Público* 115, *(Estudios sobre los Decretos Leyes),* Editorial Jurídica Venezolana, Caracas 2008, pp. 313-20.

195 *Gaceta Oficial* N° 5,889 Extra of July 31, 2008; José Gregorio Silva, "Disposiciones sobre el Decreto-Ley para la defensa de las personas en el acceso a bienes y servicios," in *id.*, pp. 277-79; Carlos Simón Bello Rengifo, "Decreto N° 6.092 con rango, valor y fuerza de la ley para la defensa de las personas en el acceso a los bienes y servicios (Referencias a problemas de imputación)," in *id.*, pp. 281-305; Alfredo Morles Hernández, "El nuevo modelo económico del socialismo del siglo XXI y su reflejo en el contrato de adhesión," in *id.*, pp. 229-32.

196 *Gaceta Oficial* N° 37.930, May 4, 2004.

197 See Juan Domingo Alfonso Paradisi, "Comentarios en cuanto a los procedimientos administrativos establecidos en el Decreto N° 6.092 con rango, valor y fuerza de Ley para la defensa de las personas en el acceso a los bienes y servicios," in *Revista de Derecho Público* 115, *(Estudios sobre los Decretos Leyes),* Editorial Jurídica Venezolana, Caracas 2008, pp. 245-60; Karina Anzola Spadaro, "El carácter autónomo de las 'medidas preventivas' contempladas en el artículo 111 del Decreto-Ley para la defensa de las personas en el acceso a los bienes y servicios," in *id.*, pp. 271-76.

198 See, in general, Antonio Canova González, Luis Alfonso Herrera Orellana, and Karina Anzola Spadaro, *¿Expropiaciones o vías de hecho? (La degradación continuada del derecho fundamental de propiedad en la Venezuela actual,*" Funeda, Universidad Católica Andrés Bello, Caracas 2009

munal Councils Law, which created them as social units and organizations not directed by popularly elected officials, without any sort of territorial autonomy, supposedly devoted to channeling citizens' participation but in a centralized conducted system from the apex of the national executive.[199] This Law was later reformed and elevated to organic law rank in 2009.[200]

A primary purpose of the 2007 constitutional reforms was to complete the dismantling of the federal form of the state by centralizing power attributions of the states, creating administrative entities to be established and directed by the national executive, attributing powers to the president to interfere in regional and local affairs, and voiding state and municipal competency by means of compulsory transfer of that competency to communal councils.[201] The implementation of the rejected constitutional reforms regarding the organization of the "Popular Power" based on the strengthening of the communes and communal councils was completed with the approval in 2010 of the Law on the Federal Council of Government.[202]

To implement these reforms, not only the last mentioned aspect was achieved, forcing the states and municipalities to transfer its attributions to local institutions controlled by the central power (communal councils), but also by means of Decree Law N° 6217 of July 15, 2008, on the Organic Law of Public Administration[203] that is now directly applicable to the States' and Municipalities' Public Administrations, the National Executive has implemented the principle of centralized planning, subjecting regional and local authorities to the Central Planning Commission. This Organic Law also assigns to the president, as proposed in the 2007 reforms, the power

---

199 Ley Orgánica de los Consejos Comunales, *Gazeta Oficial* N° 39.335, Dec. 28, 2009. See Juan M. Raffali A., "Límites constitucionales de la Contraloría Social Popular," in Revista de Derecho Público, 115, *(Estudios sobre los Decretos Leyes)*, Editorial Jurídica Venezolana, Caracas 2008, pp. 133-47.

200 See *Gaceta Oficial* N° 39.335 12-28-2009. See decision N° 1.676 12-03-2009 Constitutional Chamber, Supreme Tribunal of Justice about the constitutionality of the organic character of the Communal Councils Organic Law, in http://www.tsj.gov.ve/decisiones/scon/diciembre/1676-31209-2009-09-1369.html. See Allan R. Brewer-carías, *Ley Orgánica de los Consejos Comunales*, Editorial Jurídica Venezolana, Caracas 2010.

201 See Manuel Rachadell, "*La centralización del poder en el Estado federal descentralizado,*" in Revista de Derecho Público, 115, *(Estudios sobre los Decretos Leyes)*, Editorial Jurídica Venezolana, Caracas 2008, pp. 111-131.

202 See *Ley Orgánica del Consejo Federal de Gobierno, Gaceta Oficial* N° 5.963 Extra. of Feb. 22, 2010.

203 *Gaceta Oficial* N° 5.890, Extra., July 31, 2008. See Allan R. Brewer-Carías, "El sentido de la reforma de la Ley Orgánica de la Administración Pública," in *Revista de Derecho Público* 115, *(Estudios sobre los Decretos Leyes)*, Editorial Jurídica Venezolana, Caracas 2008, pp. 155-161; Cosimina G. Pellegrino Pacera, "La reedición de la propuesta constitucional de 2007 en el Decreto N° 6.217, con Rango, Valor y Fuerza de Ley Orgánica de la Administración Pública," in *id.*, pp. 163-68; Jesús Caballero Ortíz, "Algunos comentarios sobre la descentralización funcional en la nueva Ley Orgánica de la Administración Pública," in *id.* Pp. 169-74; Alberto Blanco-Uribe Quintero. "Afrenta a la Debida Dignidad frente a la Administración Pública. Los Decretos 6.217 y 6.265," in *id.*, pp. 175-79.

to appoint regional authorities with powers to plan, execute, follow up on, and control land use and territorial development policies, thus subjecting all programs and projects to central planning approval.

Regarding the vertical distribution of state attributions between the national level and the states, one of the general purposes of the rejected 2007 constitutional reform was to change the federal form of the state and the territorial distribution of the competencies established in Articles 156 and 164 of the Constitution, thus centralizing the state even more by concentrating almost all competencies of the public power at the national level. Particularly, "nationalizing" the competency set forth in Article 164.10 of the Constitution, which attributed to the states exclusive jurisdiction on the conservation, administration, and use of national highways, roads, ports, and airports.[204]

Despite the rejection of the constitutional reforms in the December 2007 referendum in order to change such provision, the Constitutional Chamber of the Supreme Tribunal, in Decision N° 565 (April 15, 2008),[205] issuing an abstract constitutional interpretation at the request of the attorney general of the republic, modified the content of the constitutional provision, arguing that the "exclusive" attribution "was not exclusive" but "concurrent" – meaning that the national government could also exercise that competency interfering with the states' powers. With that interpretation, the Chamber illegitimately modified the Constitution, usurping popular sovereignty, and changed the federal form of the state by misrepresenting the territorial distribution system of powers between the national power and the states.[206] The Chamber, consequently, urged the National Assembly to issue legislation against the provisions of the 1999 Constitution, which was effectively accomplished in May 2009 by reforming the Organic Law on Decentralization, Delimitation, and Transfer of Public Attributions,[207] eliminating the aforementioned exclusive attribution of the states.[208]

---

204 See Allan R. Brewer-Carías, *Hacia la consolidación de un estado socialista, centralizado, policial y militarista. Comentarios sobre el sentido y alcance de las propuestas de reforma constitucional 2007,* Editorial Jurídica Venezolana, Caracas 2007, 41ff.; and *La Reforma Constitucional de 2007 (Comentarios al proyecto inconstitucionalmente sancionado por la Asamblea Nacional el 2 de noviembre de 2007),* Editorial Jurídica Venezolana, Caracas 2007, 72 ff.

205 See Decision N° 565 of the Constitutional Chamber (Apr. 15, 2008) (Case: *Procurador General de la república, Interpretación del artículo 164.10 de la Constitución),* available at http://www.tsj.gov.ve/decisio-nes/scon/Abril/565-150408-07-1108.htm.

206 See Decision N° 565 of the Constitutional Chamber (Apr. 15, 2008) (Case: *Procurador General de la República, Interpretación del artículo 164.10 de la Constitución),* available at http://www.tsj.gov.ve/decisio-nes/scon/Abril/565-150408-07-1108.htm.

207 *Gaceta Oficial* N° 39.140, Mar. 17, 2009.

208 See Allan R. Brewer-Carías, "La Sala Constitucional como poder constituyente: La modificación de la forma federal del estado y del sistema constitucional de división territorial del poder público," in *Revista de Derecho Público* 114, Editorial Jurídica Venezolana, Caracas 2008, pp. 247-62; Manuel Rachadell, *"La centralización del poder en el Estado federal des-*

ALLAN R. BREWER-CARÍAS

The rejected 2007 constitutional reforms also sought to eliminate the Capital District that the 1999 Constitution had created as a political entity in substitution of the former Federal District, which was dependent on the National level of government. Notwithstanding popular rejection of the 2007 reform proposals, in April 2009, such reform was unconstitutionally implemented by the National Assembly, defrauding once more the Constitution by sanctioning the Special Law on the Organization and Regime of the Capital District.[209] In it, instead of organizing a democratic political entity to govern the capital district, in Caracas, the capital of the Republic, the law established an organization completely dependent on the national level of government in the same territorial jurisdiction that "used to be one of the extinct Federal District." According to this law, the capital district, contrary to what is provided for in the Constitution, has no elected authorities of government and is governed by the national level by means of a "special regime" consisting of the exercise of the legislative function by the National Assembly itself and a chief of government as the executive branch (Article 3) appointed by the president. This means that through a national statute, in the same territory of Caracas, a new national structure has been unconstitutionally imposed.

Finally, although the 2007 constitutional proposed reforms regarding the military and the Armed Force that sought to transform them into the Bolivarian Armed Force organized for the purpose of reinforcing socialism were rejected in the December 2007 referendum, the radical changes it contained have been implemented by the president, also usurping the constituent power, by means of a Decree Law reforming the Organic Law on the Armed Force,[210] creating the "Bolivarian National Armed Force" subjected to a "military Bolivarian Doctrine," and creating in it the "National Bolivarian Militia" – all of this according to what was proposed and rejected by the people in the 2007 Constitutional Reform.[211]

Almost all these laws and decree laws have been challenged on grounds of their unconstitutionality before the Constitutional Chamber of the Supreme Tribunal, which has never decided on the matter. Its omission has been, without doubt, the main source of the deconstitutionalization of the Constitutional State.

---

centralizado," in Revista de Derecho Público, N° 115 (Estudios sobre los Decretos Leyes), Editorial Jurídica Venezolana, Caracas 2008, p. 120.

209 Gaceta Oficial N° 39.156, Apr. 13, 2009. See the comments on this Law in Allan R. Brewer-Carías et al., Leyes sobre el Distrito Capital y el Área Metropolitana de Caracas, Editorial Jurídica Venezolana, Caracas 2009.

210 Decree Law N° 6.239, on the Organic Law of the National Bolivarian Armed Force, in Gaceta Oficial N° 5.933, Extra., Oct. 21, 2009.

211 See Alfredo Arismendi A., "Fuerza Armada Nacional: Antecedentes, evolución y régimen actual," in Revista de Derecho Público, N° 115 (Estudios sobre los Decretos Leyes), Editorial Jurídica Venezolana, Caracas 2008, pp. 187-206; Jesús María Alvarado Andrade, "La nueva Fuerza Armada Bolivariana (Comentarios a raíz del Decreto N° 6.239, con rango, valor y fuerza de Ley Orgánica de la Fuerza Armada Nacional Bolivariana)," in id., pp. 207-14.

IV. THE CONCLUSION OF THE DECONSTITUTIONALIZATION PROCESS OF THE CONSTITUTIONAL STATE: THE CREATION OF THE COMMUNAL STATE OF THE POPULAR POWER THROUGH ORDINARY LEGISLATION

In September 26, 2010 a parliamentary election was held in the country, the result of which was that the opposition to the government won the popular vote, although not the majority of seats in the National Assembly, due to distorting electoral regulations. This result meant, in fact, that the majority of popular vote expressed was against the proposals debated in the electoral campaign for the establishment of a socialist State in Venezuela, a matter that the President and the governmental majority of the National Assembly, with a massive campaign for their candidates, posed as a sort of "plebiscite" on the President, his performance and his socialist policies.

In disdain of the popular will expressed in the parliamentary elections ratifying the previously rejection by the people of the reforms in the 2007 referendum, the President and his party, having lost the absolute control they used to have since 2005 over the National Assembly, before the newly elected deputies to the Assembly could have taken possession of office in January 2011, in late December 2010 forced the National Assembly to proceed to sanction a set of organic laws through which they finished defining the legislative framework for a new State, different to the Constitutional State. In this way, by-passing the Constitution and in parallel to the Constitutional State, the National Assembly regulated a socialist, centralized, military and police State, called the "Communal State" or the State of "Popular Power" already rejected by the people in the referendum of December 2007.

The organic laws that were approved on December 21, 2010 are the laws on the Popular Power; the Communes; the Communal Economic System; the Public and Communal Planning; and the Social Comptrollership.[212] Furthermore, in the same framework of organizing the Communal State[213] based on the Popular Power, the Organic Laws of Municipal Public Power, of the Public Policy Planning and Coordination of the State Councils,[214] and of the Local Council Public Planning Laws, were reformed.

The delegitimized National Assembly also passed an enabling Law authorizing the President, through delegated legislation, to enact laws on all imaginable subjects, including laws of organic nature, emptying the new National Assembly of matters on which to legislate for a period of 18 months until June 2012.

---

212 See *Gaceta Oficial* N° 6.011 Extra. 12-21-2010.The Constitutional chamber through decision N° 1329 12-16-2009, among others, declared the constitutionality of the organic character of these Laws. See http://www.tsj.gov.ve/decisiones/scon/Diciembre/%201328-161210-2010-10-1437.html

213 See on all these organic laws, Allan R. Brewer-Carías *et al.*, *Leyes Orgánicas sobre el Poder Popular y el Estado Comunal*, Editorial Jurídica Venezolana, Caracas 2011, pp. 361 ff.

214 See *Gaceta Oficial* N° 6.015 Extra. 12-28-2010.

All these laws were also challenged on grounds of their unconstitutionality before the Constitutional Chamber of the Supreme Tribunal, which has never decided on the matter. As aforementioned, its omission has been, without doubt, the main source of the deconstitutionalization of the Constitutional State

The general defining framework of the Socialist State imposed on Venezuelans through such unconstitutional legislation, and for which nobody has voted, is supposedly based on the exercise of the sovereignty of the people but exclusively in a "direct" manner through the exercise of the Popular Power and the establishment of a Communal State. This is provided in the Organic Law for Popular Power, which is to be applied to everyone and everything as an essential part of the new "socialist principle of legality" in the creation, implementation and control of public management.

The main purpose of these laws is the organization of the "Communal State" which has the commune as its fundamental unit, supplanting in an unconstitutional way the municipalities as the "primary political units of the national organization" (Art. 168 of the Constitution) The exercise of Popular Power is made through the Communes, as expression of the exercise of popular sovereignty although not through representatives. It is therefore a political system in which representative democracy is ignored, openly violating the Constitution.

The Socialist State or Communal State sought to be established through these laws, in parallel to the Constitutional State, is supposedly based on Article 5 of the Constitution that provides that "Sovereignty resides untransferably in the people, who exercise it directly as provided in this Constitution and the Law, and indirectly, by suffrage, through the organs exercising Public Power," but by-passing the basic rule of the Constitutional State structure grounded on the concept of representative democracy, that is, the exercise of sovereignty indirectly through the vote.

The Communal State is now structured based only on the supposedly direct exercise of sovereignty[215] through the Communes, "with an economic model of social property and endogenous sustainable development that allows reaching the supreme social happiness of the Venezuelan people in a socialist society (art. 8.8). [216]

What is being sought is to establish a Socialist or Communal State alongside the Constitutional State: the first one supposedly based on the direct exercise of sover-

---

215 This has even been "legitimized" by the Supreme Tribunal Constitutional Chamber's decisions analyzing the organic character of the laws, such as the one issued in connection with the Organic Law of Municipalities. See decision N°1.330, Case: Organic Character of the Law of the Communes 12/17/2010, in http://www.tsj.gov.ve/decisiones/scon/Diciembre/1330-171210-2010-10-1436.html

216 The Organic Law of Municipalities, however, defines the Communal State as follows: "From of sociopolitical organization, based on the democratic and social state of law and justice established in the Constitution of the Republic, whose power is exercised directly by the people through communal self governments, with an economic model of social property and endogenous and sustainable development that achieves the supreme social happiness of the Venezuelan people in a socialist society. Forming the basic unit of the Communal State is the commune" (Art.4.10).

eignty by the people; and the second, based on the indirect exercise of sovereignty by the people through elected representatives by universal suffrage; in a system in which the former will gradually strangle and empty competencies from the latter. All of this is contrary to the Constitution, particularly because in the structure of the Communal State that is established, in the end, the exercise of sovereignty is factually indirect, through supposed "representatives" that are not popularly elected through universal and direct suffrage, but "elected" in Citizens' Assemblies. They are the ones called to exercise Popular Power in the name of the people, with the name of "spokespersons", but that as already mentioned, are not elected through universal, secret and direct suffrage.

This system that is being structured, directly controlled by a Ministry from the National Executive Branch of Government, far from being an instrument of participation and decentralization – a concept that is indissolubly linked to political autonomy – is a centralized and tightly controlled system of the communities by the central power, in which the members of the communal councils, the communes and all organizations of the Popular Power are not elected but "appointed" through a show of hands by assemblies controlled by the official party and the executive branch.

This Communal State system, parallel to the Constitutional State, is structured on a unique concept which is socialism, so that anyone who is not a socialist is automatically discriminated. It is not possible, therefore, under the framework of these laws to reconcile pluralism and the principle of non discrimination on grounds of "political opinion" guaranteed by the Constitution, with the provisions of these Law pursuing the opposite, that is, the establishment of a Communal State whose bodies can only act on the basis of socialism and in which any citizen who has another opinion is excluded. That is, through these Organic Laws, in a way evidently contrary to the Constitution, the defining framework of a new model of a State parallel and different from the Constitutional State has been established, called the Communal State, based exclusively on Socialism as the political doctrine and practice.

Regarding the Communal State, on the other hand, article 5 of the Organic Law on the Popular Power states that "people's organization and participation in exercising its sovereignty is based on Simon Bolivar the Liberator's doctrine, and is based on socialist principles and values,"[217] - a link that, as aforementioned, is untenable – matching the organization of the Communal State (established in parallel to the Constitutional State) with the socialist political ideology, for which purpose the Law defined socialism, as:

> "a mode of social relations of production, centered in coexistence with solidarity and the satisfaction of material and intangible needs of all of society, which has as fundamental basis, the recuperation of the value of work as a producer of goods and services to meet human needs and achieve supreme social happiness and integral human development. This requires the development of social ownership of the basic and strategic means of production, so that

---

217 The same expression was used in the Organic Law of the Communes with respect to their constitution, shaping and functioning (art.2), in the Communal Council's Law (Art.1) and in the Organic Law of Social Comptrollership (Art. 6)

all families, Venezuelan citizens, possess, use and enjoy their patrimony, individual or family property, and exercise full enjoyment of their economic, social, political and cultural rights (Article 8.14)."[218]

Article 7 of the same Organic Law on the Popular Power defines as a purpose of the Popular Power, to strengthen "the organization of the people in order to consolidate the revolutionary democracy and build the bases of a socialist society, democratic, of law and justice," and to "establish the bases that allow organized communities to exercise social comptrollership to ensure that the investment of public resources is efficiently performed for the collective benefit; and monitor that the activities of the private sector with social impact develop within legal rules that protect users and consumers." This, of course, is a well known procedure established in other authoritarian regimes in order to construct a general system of social espionage to be developed among peoples in order to institutionalize the denunciation and persecution of any deviation regarding the socialist framework imposed on the citizenship.[219]

According to the Law of the Communes[220] these communes are conceived as a "local entity" or "socialist space" of the Communal State, where citizens exercise the Popular Power" (art. 1). Nonetheless, according to the Constitution, this expression of "local entity" can only be applied to local political entities of the Constitutional State with autonomous and self-governments entities composed of elected representatives by universal, direct and secret ballot (art. 169). This means that there can be no "local entities" directed by persons that are not elected by the people but appointed by other bodies.

And this is precisely what happens with the so-called "governments of the communes", which under this legislation on Popular Power and its organizations, their origin is not guaranteed through democratic representative election by universal, direct and secret suffrage, thus being an unconstitutional conception.

Within the areas of communal power, the Law has specifically regulated the Communal economy that must be developed "under communal forms of social ownership, to satisfy collective needs, social reinvestment of the surplus, and contribute to the country's overall social development in a sustainable manner" (art. 18). This area of Public Power has been regulated by the Organic Law of the Communal Economic System,[221] which must be exclusively developed through "socio-productive

---

218   The same definition is found in Article 4.14 of the Organic Law of the Communes. Many are the definitions of socialism, but in all, its basic elements can be identified: (i) a system of social and economic organization, (ii) based on collective or State ownership and administration of the means of production, and (iii) State regulation of economic and social activities and distribution of goods, (iv) seeking the gradual disappearance of social classes.

219   See Luis A. Herrera Orellana, "La Ley Orgánica de Contraloría Social: Funcionalización de la participación e instauración de la desconfianza ciudadana,", in Allan R. Brewer-Carías *et al*, *Leyes Orgánicas sobre el Poder Popular y el Estado Comunal*, Editorial Jurídica Venezolana, Caracas 2011, pp. 361 ff.

220   See *Gaceta Oficial* N° 6.011 Extra. (12-21-2010).

221   See *Gaceta Oficial* N° 6.011 Extra. (12- 21-2010.

organizations under communal social property forms" created as public enterprises, family productive units, or bartering groups, in which private initiative and private property are excluded. This system radically changes the mixed economic system of the 1999 constitutional framework, substituting it with a state controlled economic system, mixed with provisions belonging to primitive societies, and even allowing the creation of local or "communal" currencies in a society that must be ruled only "by socialist principles and values" that the Law declares to be inspired, without any historical support, on the "Simón Bolívar's doctrine" (art. 5).

The socialist productive model established in the Law (art. 3.2), is precisely defined as a "production model based on *social property*, oriented towards the elimination of the social division of work that appertains to the capitalist model," directed to satisfy the increasing needs of the population through new means of generation and appropriation as well as the *reinvestment of social surplus*" (art. 6.12). This is nothing different than to legally impose a communist system by copying isolated paragraphs perhaps of a forgotten old manual of a failed communist revolution, paraphrasing what Karl Marx and Friedrich Engels wrote 170 years ago (1845-1846) on the "communist society,"[222] precisely based upon those three basic concepts: the social property of production means, the elimination of social division of work, and the social reinvestment of surplus (art. 1).

SOME CONCLUSIONS

This Communal State, regulated on the fringes of the Constitution, has been established through ordinary legislation, as a parallel State to the Constitutional State, but with provisions that, once implemented, will enable the Communal State to drown the Constitutional State, for which purpose the Law has provided that all organs of the Constitutional State that exercise Public Power are subjected to the mandates of the organizations of Popular Power, establishing a new principle of government, so-called in the Law, the principle of "govern obeying," no other than obeying the wishes of the central government.[223]

As the Popular Power organizations have no political autonomy, since their "spokespersons" are not democratically elected by universal, direct and secret ballot, but appointed by citizen Assemblies politically controlled and operated by the governing party and the National Executive who controls and guides all the organiza-

---

222 See in Karl Marx and Frederich Engels,"The German Ideology," en *Collective Works*, Vol. 5, International Publishers, New York 1976, p. 47. Véanse además los textos pertinentes en http://www.educa.madrid.org/cms_tools/files/0a24636f-764c-4e03-9c1d-6722e2ee60d7/Texto%20Marx%20y%20Engels.pdf

223 Article 24 of the Law establishes the following principle: "Proceedings of the bodies and entities of Public Power. All organs, entities and agencies of Public Power will govern their actions by the principle of "govern obeying", in relation to the mandates of the people and organizations of Popular Power, according to the provisions in the Constitution of the Republic and the laws."

tional process of the Communal State in the sphere of socialist ideology, there is no way there can be a spokesperson who is not a socialist.

Consequently, this "govern obeying" principle is a limitation to the political autonomy of the elected bodies of the Constitutional State such as the National Assembly, Governors and Legislative Councils of States and Mayors and Municipal Councils, upon who ultimately is imposed an obligation to obey any decision adopted by the National Government and the ruling party, framed exclusively in the socialist sphere as a political doctrine.

Therefore, in the unconstitutional framework of these Popular Power Laws, the popular will expressed in the election of representatives of the Constitutional State bodies has no value whatsoever, and the people have been confiscated of their sovereignty by transferring it to assemblies who do not represent them.

With these Organic Laws of Popular Power framework, there is no doubt about the political decision taken in December 21, 2010 by the completely delegitimized National Assembly that was elected in 2005, and that no longer represented the majority of the popular will as it was expressed in the September 26, 2010 legislative election, against the President of the Republic, the National Assembly itself and socialist policies they have developed. These policies are aimed to impose on Venezuelans, against popular will and defrauding the Constitution, a Socialist State model, called "the Communal State" and conceived as a Socialist State, in order to supposedly exercise Popular Power directly by the people, as an alleged form of direct exercise of sovereignty (which is not true because it is exercised through "spokespersons" who supposedly "represent" them but without being elected in universal, direct and secret suffrage.

By regulating this Communal State of the Popular Power through ordinary legislation, in addition to defrauding the Constitution, a technique that has been consistently applied by the authoritarian regime in Venezuela since 1999 to impose its decisions outside of the Venezuelan Constitution,[224] it now adds fraud to the popular will by imposing on Venezuelans through organic laws a State model for which nobody has voted.

The new State framework radically and unconstitutionally changes the text of the 1999 Constitution, which has not been reformed as the regime had wished in 2007, and in open contradiction to the popular rejection that the majority expressed in the attempt the regime developed to reform the Constitution in the referendum of December 2, 2007, even in violation of the Constitution, and the popular rejection that the majority of the people expressed regarding the socialist policies of the President to the Republic and his National Assembly on the occasion of the parliamentary elections of 26 September 2010.

---

224 See Allan R. Brewer-Carías, *Reforma constitucional y fraude a la Constitución (1999-2009)*, Academia de Ciencias Políticas y Sociales, Caracas 2009.

What is clear about all this is that there are no masks to deceive anyone, or by reason of which someone pretends to be deceived or fooled about what essentially the "Bolivarian revolution" is; nothing else but a communist Marxist revolution, carried out deliberately by misusing and defrauding constitutional institutions, which subsist due to the abstention or omission of the Constitutional Chamber of the Supreme Tribunal to exercise its power of judicial review.

Chapter XXVII

ABOUT THE "POPULAR POWER" AND THE COMMUNAL STATE
IMPOSED TO THE PEOPLE BESIDES THE CONSTITUTION AND
WITHOUT THE PEOPLE'S APPROVAL

(2010)

This essay about "The Popular Power and the Communal State in Venezuela (Or how a Socialist State is imposed on the Venezuelan people, violating the Constitution and defrauding the will of the people)," was written in December 2010. Once the Popular Power Organic Laws were sanctioned. Reflections on such legislation were published in Spanish in various articles: "La Ley Orgánica del Poder Popular y la desconstitucionalización del Estado de derecho en Venezuela," in *Revista de Derecho Público*, Nº 124, (octubre-diciembre 2010), Editorial Jurídica Venezolana, Caracas 2010, pp. 81-101; "Las leyes del Poder Popular dictadas en Venezuela en diciembre de 2010, para transformar el Estado Democrático y Social de Derecho en un Estado Comunal Socialista, sin reformar la Constitución," in *Cuadernos Manuel Giménez Abad*, Fundación Manuel Giménez Abad de Estudios Parlamentarios y del Estado Autonómico, Nº 1, Madrid, Junio 2011, pp. 127-131. An extensive analysis of the Laws was latter published as "Introducción General al Régimen del Poder Popular y del Estado Comunal (O de cómo en el siglo XXI, en Venezuela se decreta, al margen de la Constitución, un Estado de Comunas y de Consejos Comunales, y se establece una sociedad socialista y un sistema económico comunista, por los cuales nadie ha votado)," in the book: Allan R. Brewer-Carías, Claudia Nikken, Luis A. Herrera Orellana, Jesús María Alvarado Andrade, José Ignacio Hernández y Adriana Vigilanza, *Leyes Orgánicas sobre el Poder Popular y el Estado Comunal (Los consejos comunales, las comunas, la sociedad socialista y el sistema económico comunal)* Colección Textos Legislativos Nº 50, Editorial Jurídica Venezolana, Caracas 2011, pp. 9-182.

The 1999 Venezuelan Constitution, following the provisions of the previous 1961 Constitution, instituted the country as a **Democratic and Social Rule of Law and Justice State**, "which holds as higher values of its legal system and its performance, life, liberty, justice, equality, solidarity, democracy, social responsibility and, in general, the preeminence of human rights, ethics and political plurality" (Art. 2). For such purposes it organized the Republic as "a **decentralized federal State**" which "is governed by the principles of geographical integrity, cooperation, solidarity, concurrence and shared responsibility" (Art. 4).

Such is the Constitutional State in Venezuela: a decentralized **Federal Democratic and Social Rule of Law and Justice State**[225], based on a vertical distribution of public powers in three territorial levels of government: National level, State level and municipal level (Art. 136), according to which each level must always have a government of an "elective, decentralized, alternative, responsible, plural, and of revocable mandate" character, as required by Article 6 of the Constitution.

Constitutionally speaking, therefore, it is not possible to create in Venezuela, by law, political institutions in order to empty the powers of other organizations of the State (at any level: national, States, municipal and other local entities), and, even less, to establish new political organizations without ensuring the elective character of their governments and people's representatives by means of universal, direct and secret suffrage; nor without assuring their own political autonomy, which is essential to their federal and decentralized nature; and not guaranteeing its plural character in the sense that they cannot be linked to a particular ideology such as socialism.

An attempt was made to change this Constitutional model of the Federal State, through a constitutional reform draft that was sanctioned by the National Assembly in 2007, with the objective of establishing a socialist, centralized, militaristic, and police State[226], called the "Popular Power State" or "Communal State"[227], which, nevertheless, once it was put to popular vote, was rejected by the people on a referendum held on December 7, 2007.[228]

Nevertheless, in disdain of the popular will and defrauding the Constitution, even before the aforementioned referendum was held, the National Assembly in open

---

225   See the study of the constitution regarding the regulation of this constitutional federal state model, en Allan R. Brewer-Carías, *La Constitución de 1999. Derecho Constitucional venezolano*, 2 vols., Caracas 2004; and *La Constitución de 1999 y la Enmienda Constitucional de 2009*, Editorial Jurídica Venezolana, Caracas 2011.

226   See Allan R. Brewer-Carías, *Hacia la Consolidación de un Estado Socialista, Centralizado, Policial y Militarista. Comentarios sobre el sentido y alcance de las propuestas de reforma constitucional 2007*, Colección Textos Legislativos, N° 42, Editorial Jurídica Venezolana, Caracas 2007; and "Estudio sobre la propuesta de Reforma Constitucional para establecer un estado socialista, centralizado y militarista (Análisis del anteproyecto presidencial, Agosto de 2007)," in *Cuadernos da Escola de Direito e Relações Internacionais da UniBrasil* 7, Curitiba 2007, pp. 265-308.

227   See Allan R. Brewer-Carías, *Hacia la consolidación de un Estado socialista, centralizado, policial y militarista. Comentarios sobre el sentido y alcance de las propuestas de reforma constitucional 2007*, Editorial Jurídica Venezolana, Caracas 2007; *La reforma constitucional de 2007 (Comentarios al Proyecto inconstitucionalmente sancionado por la Asamblea Nacional el 2 de noviembre de 2007)*, Colección Textos Legislativos, N°43, Editorial Jurídica Venezolana, Caracas 2007.

228   See Allan R. Brewer-Carías, "La proyectada reforma constitucional de 2007, rechazada por el poder constituyente originario", in *Anuario de Derecho Público 2007*, Año 1, Instituto de Estudios de Derecho Público de la Universidad Monteávila, Caracas 2008, pp. 17-65

violation of the Constitution began to dismantle the Constitutional Federal State, seeking its substitution by a Socialist State, by structuring in *parallel* a "Popular Power State" or "Communal State," through the sanctioning of the Communal Councils Law of 2006[229], later reformed and elevated to organic law rank in 2009[230].

Nonetheless, the drive to establish a socialist State in Venezuela was rejected again as it resulted from the September 26, 2010 parliamentary elections, which the President and the governmental majority of the National Assembly, with a massive campaign for their candidates, posed such elections as a "plebiscite" on the President, his performance and his socialist policies, already previously rejected by the people in 2007; "plebiscite" which the President and his party lost overwhelmingly because the majority of the country voted against them.

As a result from such parliamentary election, the President and his party lost the absolute control they previously had over the National Assembly, preventing them in the future from imposing at will the legislation they want. Nonetheless, before the newly elected deputies to the Assembly took possession of office in January 2011, defrauding the popular will and the Constitution, the already delegitimized previous National Assembly, in December 2010, hastily proceeded to sanction a set of organic laws through which they have finished defining, outside of the Constitution, the legislative framework for a new State, parallel to the Constitutional Federal State, which is no more than a socialist, centralized, military and police State called the "Communal State."

The organic laws that were approved in December 2010 are the laws on the Popular Power; the Communes; the Communal Economic System; the Public and Communal Planning; the Social Comptrollership.[231] Furthermore, in the same framework of organizing the Communal State, based on the Popular Power, the Organic Laws of Municipal Public Power, of the Public Policy Planning and Coordination of the State Councils, and of the Local Council Public Planning Laws, were reformed.[232] Finally, in 2012 the Law on the States and Municipalities Power and

---

229 See *Official Gazette* N° 5.806 Extra. 04-10-2006. See on this Law: Allan R. Brewer-Carías, "El inicio de la desmunicipalización en Venezuela: La organización del poder popular para eliminar la descentralización, la democracia representativa y la participación a nivel local," in *AIDA, Revista de la Asociación Internacional de Derecho Administrativo*, Universidad Nacional Autónoma de México, Asociación Internacional de Derecho Administrativo, Mexico City 2007, 49-67

230 See *Official Gazette* N° 39.335, of Dec. 28, 2009. See on this Law the comments in Allan R. Brewer-Carías, *Ley Orgánica de Consejos Comunales*, Editorial Jurídica Venezolana, Caracas 2010.

231 See *Official Gazette* N° 6.011 Extra. of Dec. 21, 2010. See on these Laws the comments in Allan R. Brewer-Carías, Claudia Nikken, Luis A. Herrera Orellana, J. M. Alvarado Andrade, José Ignacio Herández, Adriana Vigilanza, *Leyes Orgánicas sobre el Poder Popular y el Estado Comunal (Los Consejos Comunales, las Comunas, la Sociedad Socialista y el Sistema Económico Comunal)*, Editorial Jurídica Venezolana, Caracas 2011.

232 See *Official Gazette* N° 6.015 Extra. of Dec. 28, 2010. Nevertheless by December 31st 2010 it had not yet been published.

Competencies Transfer System to Popular Power Organizations was also approved but through a decree Law.[233]

In 2012, the delegitimized National Assembly also passed an enabling Law authorizing the President through delegated legislation, to enact laws on all imaginable subjects, including laws of organic nature, emptying the new National Assembly of matters on which to legislate for a period of 18 months until June 2012.

The general defining framework of the Socialist State that is being imposed on Venezuelans, and for which nobody has voted, is supposedly based on the exercise of the "sovereignty of the people" exclusively in a direct manner through the implementation of the Popular Power and the establishment of a Communal State as contained in the Organic Law for Popular Power (LOPP), whose provisions, according to its Article 6 "are applicable to all organizations, expressions and areas of Popular Power, exercised directly or indirectly by the people, communities, social sectors of society in general and situations that affect the collective interest, accepting the principle of legality in the formation, implementation and control of public management."

That is, the provisions of this organic law are all-encompassing; apply to everyone and everything, as an essential part of the new "socialist principle of legality" in the creation, implementation and control of public entities, in parallel of the Federal State.

I.   THE COMMUNAL STATE, POPULAR POWER AND SOCIALISM

The main purpose of these laws is the organization of the "Communal State" which has the commune as its fundamental unit, unconstitutionally supplanting the municipality as the "primary political unit of the national organization" (Art. 168 of the Constitution). Through them, the Popular Power is exercised, manifested in the exercise of popular sovereignty only directly by the people, not by representatives. It

---

233. See *Official Gazette* Nº 39954 of June 28, 2012. See on this Decree Law the comments of José Luis Villegas Moreno, "Hacia la instauración del Estado Comunal en Venezuela: Comentario al Decreto Ley Orgánica de la Gestión Comunitaria de Competencia, Servicios y otras Atribuciones, en el contexto del Primer Plan Socialista-Proyecto Nacional Simón Bolívar 2007-2013, (pp. 1290138); Juan Cristóbal Carmona Borjas, "Decreto con rango, valor y fuerza de Ley Orgánica para la Gestión Comunitaria de Competencias, Servicios y otras Atribuciones, (pp.139-146); Celilia Sosa G,. "El carácter orgánico de un Decreto con fuerza de Ley (no habilitado) para la gestión comunitaria que arrasa lentamente con los Poderes estadales y municipales de la Constitución"(pp. 147-157), José Ignacio Hernández, "Reflexiones sobre el nuevo régimen para la Gestión Comunitaria de Competencias, Servicios y otras Atribuciones,"(pp. 157-164), Alfredo Romero Mendoza, "Comentarios sobre el Decreto con rango, valor y fuerza de Ley Orgánica para la Gestión Comunitaria de Competencias, Servicios y otras Atribuciones"(pp. 167-176), and Enrique J. Sánchez falcón, "El Decreto con Rango, Valor y Fuerza de Ley Orgánica para la Gestión Comunitaria de Competencias, Servicios y otras Atribuciones o la negación del federalismo cooperativo y descentralizado,"(pp. 177-184), in *Revista de Derecho Público*, Nº 130 (Estudios sobre los decretos leyes 2010-2011), Editorial Jurídica Venezolana, Caracas 2012.

is therefore a political system in which representative democracy is ignored, openly violating the Constitution.

The Socialist State sought through these laws, called the Communal State, in parallel to the Constitutional Federal State, is based on this simple scheme: as Article 5 of the Constitution provides that "Sovereignty resides untransferably in the people, who exercise it directly as provided in this Constitution and the Law, and indirectly, by suffrage, through the organs exercising Public Power", being the Constitutional federal State structure based on the concept of representative democracy, that is, the exercise of sovereignty indirectly through the vote; the Communal State is now structured based on the direct exercise of sovereignty, ignoring representation.

This has even been "legitimized" by the Supreme Tribunal Constitutional Chamber's decisions analyzing the organic character of the laws, such as the one issued in connection with the Organic Law of Municipalities, in which it stated that it had been enacted:

"developing the constitutional principle of participative and decentralized democracy postulated in the constitutional preamble and recognized in Articles 5 and 6 of the Constitution of the Bolivarian Republic of Venezuela, from whose content the principle of sovereignty is extracted, whose holder is the people, who is also empowered to exercise it "directly" and not only "indirectly" by Public Power organizations; as well as in Article 62, which governs the right of the people to participate freely in public affairs; and especially in Article 70, which expressly recognizes self-management means as popular and active participation mechanisms in the exercise of its sovereignty."[234]

Based on these principles, Article, 8.8 of the LOPP defines the Communal State as:

"Social and political organization based on the democratic and social State of law and justice established in the Constitution of the Republic, in which power is exercised directly by the people, with an economic model of social property and endogenous sustainable development that allows reaching the supreme social happiness of the Venezuelan people in a **socialist** society. The basic unit forming the Communal State is the Commune."[235]

What is being sought is to establish a Communal State alongside the Constitutional Federal State: the first one based on the supposedly direct exercise of sovereignty by the people; and the second, based on the indirect exercise of sovereignty

---

234 See decision N°1.330, Case: Organic Character of the Law of the Communes 12/17/2010, in http://www.tsj.gov.ve/decisiones/scon/Diciembre/1330-171210-2010-10-1436.html

235 The new Organic Law of the Municipal Power, however, defines the Communal State as follows: "Form of sociopolitical organization, based on the democratic and social state of law and justice established in the Constitution of the Republic, whose power is exercised directly by the people through communal self governments, with an economic model of social property and endogenous and sustainable development that achieves the supreme social happiness of the Venezuelan people in a socialist society. Forming the basic unit of the Communal State is the commune" (Art.4.10).

by the people through elected representatives by universal suffrage; in a system in which the former will gradually strangle and empty competencies from the second. All of this is unconstitutional, particularly because in the structure of the Communal State that is established, at the end, the exercise of sovereignty is indirect through "representatives" that are "elected" in Citizens' Assemblies to exercise Popular Power in the name of the people, called "spokespersons", but that are not elected by the people through universal, secret and direct suffrage.

The system that is being structured, in short, controlled by a Ministry from the National Executive Branch of Government, far from being an instrument of decentralization –concept that is indissolubly linked to federalism and political autonomy– is a centralized and tightly controlled system of the communities by the central power. That is the reason that explains the aversion to suffrage. Under this framework, a true participative democracy would be one that guarantees members of the communal councils, the communes and all organizations of the Popular Power to elect their representatives through universal direct and secret suffrage, and not through a show of hands by assemblies controlled by the official party and the executive branch, contrary to the decentralized Democratic and Social Rule of Law and Justice Federal State established in the Constitution.

It is in this context, seeking to establish in parallel to the Constitutional Federal State in which the people exercise public power indirectly through representatives elected by direct universal and secret suffrage, that a Communal State is being imposed to the Venezuelans, in which the people allegedly would exercise Popular Power directly through spokespersons who are not elected by direct universal and secret suffrage, but in citizen's assemblies. In this regard, Article 2 of the LOPP defines Popular Power as:

> "The full exercise of sovereignty by the people in the political, economic, social, cultural, environmental and international areas, as well as in all areas of development of society, through the diverse and dissimilar organization forms that constituted the Communal State."

All of which is but a fallacy, because ultimately this "building" of the Communal State denies people the right to elect, by direct universal and secret suffrage, those who are going to "represent" them in all these areas, including internationally. It is rather a "building" of organizations to prevent people from really exercising their sovereignty and to impose on them through a tightly centralized control, policies for which they never have a chance to vote.

Moreover, under Article 4 of the LOPP, the purpose of this Popular Power that is exercised by the organs of the Communal State, is to "guarantee the life and social welfare of the people, through the creation of social and spiritual development mechanisms, ensuring equal conditions for everyone to freely develop their personality, direct their destiny, enjoy human rights and achieve supreme social happiness; without discrimination based on ethnicity, religion, social status, gender, sexual orientation, identity and expression of gender, language, political opinion, national origin, age, economic status, disability or any other personal, legal or social circumstance, which has the effect of nullifying or impairing the recognition, enjoyment or exercise of human rights and constitutional guarantees." Of course all these principles of equality are broken since the Communal State system, parallel to the Constitutional Federal State, is structured on a unique concept which is **socialism**, so that anyone who is not a socialist is automatically discriminated. It is not possible, therefore, under the framework of this law to reconcile pluralism guaranteed by the Constitution and the principle of non discrimination on grounds of "political opinion" referred to in this article, with the remaining provisions of this Law pursuing the opposite, that is, the establishment of a Communal State, whose bodies can only act on the basis of socialism and in which any citizen who has another opinion is excluded.

The result from all these laws, after President Chávez confessed himself in January 2010 as a convinced Marxist, has been the resurrection, in the name of a supposedly "Bolivarian revolution," of the historically failed "Marxist revolution," although led by a president said he has never even read Marx's writings.[236] This public announcement, in any case, lead to the adoption in April 2010, by the governmental United Socialist Party of Venezuela (which the President presides), in its First Extraordinary Congress, of a "Declaration of Principles" in which the party was officially declared as a "Marxist," "Anti-imperialist" and "Anti-capitalist" party. According to the same document, the party's actions are based on "scientific socialism" and on the "inputs of Marxism as a philosophy of praxis," in order to substitute the "Capitalist Bourgeois State" with a "Socialist State" based on the Popular Power and the socialization of the means of production.[237]

Consequently, through the Organic Law on the Popular Power, the defining framework of a new model of a Socialist State parallel and different from the Constitutional Federal State, has been established, called the Communal State, based exclusively and exclusionist on Socialism as the political doctrine and practice, which is the political organization through which the exercise of Popular Power is produced which in turn is "the full exercise of sovereignty by the people."

This Popular Power is based, as declared in Article 3 of the LOOP, "in the sovereign principle of progressiveness of rights established in the Constitution, whose exercise and development is determined by the level of political and organizational consciousness of the people" (Art.3). With this statement, however, far from the universality, prevalence and progressiveness of human rights as guaranteed by the Constitution, what has been established is the total disappearance of the universal concept of human rights, the abandonment of its prevalent character and the deterioration of the principles *pro homines* and *favor libertatis*, by conditioning its existence, scope and progressiveness "by the level of political and organizational consciousness of the people", that is, by what the organizations of Popular Power which

---

236 In his annual speech before the National Assembly on Jan. 15, 2010, in which Chávez declared to have "assumed Marxism," he also confessed that he had never read Marx's works. See María Lilibeth Da Corte, "Por primera vez asumo el marxismo," in *El Universal*, Caracas Jan. 16, 2010, http://www.eluniversal.com/2010/01/16/pol_art_por-primera-vez-asu_1726209.shtml.

237 See "Declaración de Principios, I Congreso Extraordinario del Partido Socialista Unido de Venezuela," Apr. 23, 2010, at http://psuv.org.ve/files/tcdocumentos/Declaracion-de-principios-PSUV.pdf

seek to "organize" the people, all subjected to Socialism, stipulate and prescribe. With it, the conception of human rights as areas that are innate to man and immune against power disappear, moving to a conception of human rights dependent on the orders of the central power, which ultimately controls the entire "building" of the Communal State or Socialist State, as a clear demonstration of totalitarianism which is at the basis of this Law.

In the same sense, Article 5 of the LOPP states that "people's organization and participation in exercising its sovereignty is based on Simon Bolivar the Liberator's doctrine, and is based on socialist principles and values",[238] thus, as has been mentioned, relates the organization of the Communal State in parallel to the Constitutional State, with the socialist political ideology, that is, with **socialism**, which is defined in Article 8.14 as:

> "a mode of social relations of production, centered in coexistence with solidarity and the satisfaction of material and intangible needs of all of society, which has as fundamental basis, the recuperation of the value of work as a producer of goods and services to meet human needs and achieve supreme social happiness and integral human development. This requires the development of social ownership of the basic and strategic means of production, so that all families, Venezuelan citizens, possess, use and enjoy their patrimony, individual or family property, and exercise full enjoyment of their economic, social, political and cultural rights."[239]

The first thing that must be observed in relation of this provision is the untenable claim of linking "the doctrine of Simon Bolívar" with socialist principles and values. In the work of Bolivar and in relation to his conception of the State nothing can be found about socialism.[240] On the contrary, Karl Marx himself would have detected it when he wrote the entry on "Simón Bolívar y Ponte" for the *New American Cyclopedia* published in New York in 1857,[241] eleven years after publishing his book with Fredrick Engels on *The German Ideology*.[242] It was in this 1847 book were they

---

238 The same expression was utilized in the Organic Law of the Communes with respect to their constitution, shaping and functioning (art.2), in the Communal Council's Law (Art.1) and in the Organic Law of Social Comptrollership (Art. 6)

239 The same definition is found in Article 4.14 of the Organic Law of the Communes. Many are the definitions of socialism, but in all, its basic elements can be identified: (i) a system of social and economic organization, (ii) based on collective or State ownership and administration of the means of production, and (iii) State regulation of economic and social activities and distribution of goods, (iv) seeking the gradual disappearance of social classes.

240 See Allan R. Brewer-Carías, "Ideas centrales sobre la organización el Estado en la Obra del Libertador y sus Proyecciones Contemporáneas" in *Boletín de la Academia de Ciencias Políticas y Sociales*, N° 95-96, January-June 1984, pp. 137-151.

241 See *The New American Cyclopaedia*, Vol. III, 1858, on "Bolivar y Ponte, Simón." Available at http://www.marxists.org/archive/marx/works/1858/01/bolivar.htm

242 The book was written between 1845 and 1846. The Communist Manifest was published in February 1848.

used the word "communism" perhaps for the first time;[243] and the fact is that ten years later, in the 1857 article on Bolívar, Marx made no mention at all regarding any "socialist" ideas of Bolívar, being that article, by the way, one, if not the most critical work on Bolívar ever written.

Consequently the name of Bolívar is used only as a pretext to continue to manipulate the Bolivar "cult" to justify authoritarianism, as has occurred so many times before in the history of the country,[244] although in the past, it has been used "at least more or less respecting the basic thought of the Liberator, even when they misrepresented its meaning."[245] The fact is that never before, the adherence to Bolivar had led to changing the republic's name, and to the invention of a new "Bolivarian doctrine" in order to justify the government's policies, as it has happened with the so-called "Bolivarian Revolution" linked to the idea of a "21st Century Socialism,"[246] as well as to the creation of the Communal State.

On the other hand, the already mentioned provision of article 8.14 of the LOPP defining socialism openly violates the Constitution's guarantee to the right to property (Art. 115) which does not allow for restrictions to only collective or social property, excluding private ownership of the means of production

---

243 See in Karl Marx and Frederich Engels, "The German Ideology," in *Collective Works*, Vol. 5, International Publishers, New York 1976, p. 47. See the pertinent text at http://www.educa.madrid.org/cms_tools/files/0a24636f-764c-4e03-9c1d-6722e2ee60d7/Texto%20Marx%20y%20Engels.pdf

244 It has been the case of Antonio Guzmán Blanco in the nineteenth century and Cipriano Castro, Juan Vicente Gómez, Eleazar López Contreras and Marcos Perez Jimenez in the twentieth century. John Lynch has noted that: "The traditional worship of Bolívar has been used as a convenient ideology by military dictators, culminating with the regimes of Juan Vicente Gómez and Eleazar López Contreras, who at least more or less respected the basic thoughts of the Liberator, even when they distorted their meaning." Lynch concludes by noting that in the case of Venezuela today, to proclaim the Liberator as basis for policies of the authoritarian regime is a distortion of his ideas. See John Lynch, *Simón Bolívar: A Life*, Yale University Press, New Haven 2007, p. 304. .See also, Germán Carrera Damas, *El culto a Bolívar*, esbozo para un estudio de la historia de las ideas en Venezuela, Universidad Central de Venezuela, Caracas 1969; Luis Castro Leiva, *De la patria boba a la teología bolivariana*, Monteávila, Caracas 1987; Elías Pino Iturrieta, *El divino Bolívar. Ensayo sobre una religión republicana*, Alfail, Caracas 2008; Ana Teresa Torres, *La herencia de la tribu. Del mito de la independencia a la Revolución bolivariana*, Editorial Alfa, Caracas 2009. About the history related to these books see Tomás Straka, *La épica del desencanto*, Editorial Alfa, Caracas 2009.

245 See John Lynch, *Simón Bolívar: A Life*, Yale University Press, New Haven, CT, 2007, p. 304.

246 The last attempt to completely appropriate Simón Bolívar for the "Bolivarian Revolution," was the televised exhumation of his remains that took place at the National Pantheon in Caracas on July 26, 2010, conducted by President Chávez himself and other high officials, including the Prosecutor General, among other things, for the purpose of determining if Bolivar died of arsenic poisoning in Santa Marta in 1830, instead of from tuberculosis. See Simon Romero, "Building a New History By Exhuming Bolívar," *The New York Times*, August 4, 2010, p. A7.

Article 5 of the LOPP, moreover, defines as "socialist principles and values" the following:

> "participatory and active democracy, collective interest, equity, justice, social and gender equality, complementarity, cultural diversity, human rights, shared responsibility, joint management, self-management, cooperation, solidarity, transparency, honesty, effectiveness, efficiency, effectiveness, universality, responsibility, social duty, accountability, social control, free debate of ideas, voluntariness, sustainability, environmental protection and defense, guarantee of the rights of women, children and adolescents and of any vulnerable person, geographical integrity and national sovereignty defense." (Art. 5) [247]

This catalog of "principles", of course, is not necessarily linked to socialism, nor is it an exclusively catalog of "socialist principles and values" as it aims to show, in a misappropriation made by the legislator. What the drafter of the rule did, in fact, was to copy the entire set of principles that are defined throughout the Constitution (Preamble and articles 1, 2, 3, 4, 6, 19, 20, 21, 22, 26, 84, 86, 102, 112, 137, 141, 153, 165, 257, 293, 299, 311, 316, 326, for example), which are the values of the Constitutional Federal State. Only in some cases they have not dared to use the classic terminology such as "freedom of expression" and have wanted to replace it with "free discussion of ideas", which of course is not the same, especially since that freedom is not tolerated in a socialist State which knows only a single ideology.

For the purpose of developing and strengthening the Popular Power, ignoring the basic constitutional principles and values that all levels of government in Venezuela (for instance that they be "elective, decentralized, alternative, responsible, pluralistic and of revocable mandates" as required by article 6 of the Constitution), is that the LOPP has been issued, to supposedly generate:

> "Objective conditions through various means of participation and organization established in the Constitution, in the Law and those that may arise from popular initiative so that citizens may exercise their full right to sovereignty, participatory and active democracy, and the establishment of forms of community and communal self-government for the direct exercise of power" (Art. 1)."

According to the Constitution, the "creation of new decentralized organs at the parish, community, 'barrios' and neighborhood levels", is only possible with "a view to guaranteeing the principle of shared responsibility in the public administration of local and state governments, and to develop self-management and joint management processes in the administration and control of states and municipal public services" (Art. 184.6). This means that the mechanisms of participation that can be established under the Constitution are not to empty the Constitutional Federal State structures, that is, the "local and states governments" (like the municipalities), but to strengthen them in governance. Moreover, under the Constitution, there can be no other government than *elective, decentralized and pluralistic*, yet in the LOPP a

---

247   These same principles are listed in relation to the communes in Article 2 of the Organic Law of the Communes, and in relation to social comptrollership in Article 6 of the Organic Law of Social Comptrollership.

parallel State is defined which is the Communal State, structured on "governments" or "self-governments" that are neither elected nor decentralized nor pluralistic.

On these, Article 14 of the LOPP merely defines "the communal self-government and aggregation systems that arise among their instances" as "a field of action of Popular Power in the development of its sovereignty, by the direct involvement of organized communities, in the formulation, implementation and control of public functions, according the law regulating the matter."

In this context, moreover, the "community" is defined in the LOPP as a "basic and indivisible spatial nucleus made up of people and families living in a specific geographical area, linked by common characteristics and interests who share a history, needs and potentialities on cultural, economic, social, geographical and other measures"(art. 8.4).[248]

II. THE PURPOSE OF POPULAR POWER

Article 7 of the LOPP defines the following purpose of Popular Power, that is, supposedly "the full exercise of sovereignty by the people" through "its various and dissimilar organization forms that build the communal State." (Art. 2):

First, "promote the strengthening of the organization of the people, in order to consolidate the revolutionary democracy and build the bases of a **socialist** society, democratic, of law and justice." In relation to what the Constitution provides about the organization of the State, the addition of "socialist" imposed by this provision breaks the principle of pluralism, which is guaranteed by the Constitution, paving the way for political discrimination against any citizen who is not a socialist, who is denied, therefore, the right to political participation.

Second, "Create conditions to ensure that popular initiative, in exercising social management, assumes duties, responsibilities and competencies for administering service delivery and implementation of work, by transferring from the different political and geographical authorities to community and communal self-governments, and aggregation systems which may arise thereof." Under Article 184.1 of the Constitution, this transfer of competences can only refer to "the transfer of services in the areas of health, education, housing, sports, culture, social programs, the environment, maintenance of industrial areas, maintenance and upkeep of urban areas, neighborhood prevention and protective services, public works and provision of public services." To this end, "they shall have the power to enter into agreements, whose content shall be guided by the principles of interdependence, coordination, cooperation and shared responsibility."

Third, "Strengthen the culture of participation in public affairs to ensure the exercise of popular sovereignty."

Fourth, "Promote values and principles of socialist ethic: solidarity, common good, honesty, social duty, voluntary nature, defense and protection of the environment and human rights." Again, these, really, are not the values of any "socialist

---

248 The same definition is repeated in the Organic Law of the Communes (Art 4.4) and in the Organic Law of the Communal Councils (Art. 4.1)

ethic", but as mentioned earlier, they are values of democracy and of Western civilization and typical of the Constitutional State.

Fifth, "Contribute with State policies in all its instances, in order to work in coordination with the implementation of the Economic and Social Development Plan of the Nation and other plans established in each of the geo-political levels and in political-administrative levels established by law."

Sixth, "Establish the bases that allow organized communities exercise social comptrollership to ensure that the investment of public resources is efficiently performed for the collective benefit; and monitor that the activities of the private sector with social impact develop within legal rules that protect users and consumers." For the purposes of this provision, Article 8.6 of the LOPP, defines social comptrollership as the exercise of the prevention, surveillance, supervision, monitoring and control functions, practiced by individual or collective citizens, over the management of Public Power and of instances of Popular Power and of private activities that affect collective interests (Art. 8.6). However, nothing in the Constitution authorizes the allocation of competencies to public entities of the community dependent on the national executive, and to individuals in general to practice surveillance, supervision or social comptrollership over private activities. This is a feature that can only be exercised by political authorities of the State in a limited way. As it has been established in these laws on the Popular Power, it is no more than a general system of social espionage and surveillance to be developed among peoples in order to institutionalize the denunciation and persecution of any deviation regarding the socialist framework imposed on the citizenship.

Seventh, "Deepening shared responsibility, self-management and joint-management." For the purposes of this rule, the Law defines co-responsibility, as the "shared responsibility among citizens and State institutions in the process of formation, implementation, control and evaluation of social, community and communal management, for the welfare of organized communities" (Art. 8.7). Self-management is defined as the set of actions by which organized communities assume direct management of projects, implementing public work and services to improve the quality of life in its geographical area" (Art. 8.2). And joint management, is defined as "the process by which organized communities coordinate with public authorities at any level or instances, joint management for implementation of work and services needed to improve the quality of life in its geographical area" (Art. 8.3).

Moreover, for the purposes of these rules, "organized community" is defined in the LOPP as one "made up of popular organizational expressions, councils of workers, peasants, fishermen and any other social grassroots organization, coordinated with an instance of Popular Power[249] duly recognized by law and registered in the competent Ministry of Popular Power on matters of citizen participation" (Art. 8.5). The Constitution, however, referring to community organizations subject to decen-

---

249 The definition of "organized community" is similar in the Organic Law of the Communes: formed by "popular organizational expressions, councils of workers of, peasants, and fishermen and any other grassroots organization, linked to an instance of Popular Power" (art. 4.5)

tralization, conceived only the following as geographical entities: "parishes, communities and neighborhoods," without any subjection to the National Executive, which are those that are allowed, under Article 186.6, to assume "co-responsibility in the governance of local and state governments and develop self and joint management processes in the administration and control of state and municipal public services."

III. THE INSTANCES OF POPULAR POWER

1. The diverse instances of popular power and their legal status

The instances of Popular Power for the "full exercise of sovereignty by the people" and that make up the "diverse and dissimilar organization forms that build the communal State" (Art. 2), as specified in Article 8.9 of the LOPP, are "made up of the different aggregation and articulations of communal systems, to expand and strengthen communal action for self-government: communal councils, communes, communal cities, communal federations, communal confederations and, in accordance with the Constitution and the law and its regulation governing the matter, may arise from popular initiative[250], "being grassroots organizations of Popular Power" those "consisting of citizens in pursuit of collective welfare" (Article 8.10).

All these Popular Power instances recognized by the LOPP, as provided in Article 32, acquire legal status through their registration in the Popular Power National Executive Ministry of the Communes, taking into account the procedures that are to be established in the regulations of the Law. Consequently, the decision to register a communal council, a commune, or a communal city, hat is its existence, is ultimately in the hands of the National Executive, who, of course, strictly applying the letter of the law, that if it is dominated by "spokespersons" who are not socialist, there will be no registration, nor, therefore, its recognition as a legal entity, even if it's the result of a genuine and popular initiative.

2. The Popular Power instances' spokespersons and their non representative character

None of the persons exercising the authority over Popular Power instances, and who are called "spokespersons" are expected to be elected in elections made through direct, universal and secret ballot. They are not even expected to be elected by "indirect" suffrage, as in no case they have root in a previous and initial direct election.

In fact, the LOPP does not indicate how the spokespersons of Popular Power instances are to be designated. What is stated in the regulations of the laws enacted regarding the instances of Popular Power is a designation by bodies that do not have their origin in direct, secret and universal elections. In particular, for example, the Organic Law of Communal Councils, provides that spokespersons are "elected" by

---

250 The Organic Law of the Communes, however, defines Popular Power instances as those "constituted by an aggregation of different communal systems: communal councils, communes, communal cities, communal federations, communal confederations and others that according to the Constitution and the law may arise from the initiative."(Article 4.12)

citizen's assemblies (Articles 4.6 and 11), and not by means of a direct, universal and secret ballot as prescribed by the Constitution, but by an alleged "popular vote" which is not organized by the National Electoral Council, and is performed in open assemblies in which there is no guarantee of suffrage or secrecy. The Law, however, does indicate that all levels of Popular Power that are "elected by popular vote", are revocable from the first half of the period for which they were elected, under the conditions established by law (Art. 17).

In fact, It should be said that Citizens Assemblies are at the base of these instances of Popular Power, which, while not specifically regulated by the LOPP, nor named in any of its articles, are defined as the "highest instance of participation and decision of organized communities, established in accordance to the law regulating the form of participation for the direct exercise of Popular Power, by the integration of people with legal quality, whose decisions are of a binding nature for the community, for different forms of organization, for the communal government and for the instances of Public Power, according to what is established in the laws that develop the creation, organization and operation of community self-governments, and the aggregation systems that may arise" (Art. 8.1).

3.   Communal aggregation systems

Article 15.4 of the LOPP, defines communal aggregation systems, as those instances that may arise from popular initiative, from community councils and among Communes, on which Article 50 of the Organic Law of the Communes (LOC) specifies that "the instances of Popular Power may constitute communal aggregation systems among them with the purpose of articulating the exercise of "self-government"(although not elected), strengthening the capacity for action on geographical, political, economic, social, cultural, ecological and security and defense of national sovereignty aspects according to the Constitution and the law."

The purpose of communal aggregation systems under Article 59 of the LOC, are to:

A.   Expand and strengthen communal "self-government" action.

B.   Carry out investment plans in its geographical area, following guidelines and requirements set forth in the respective communal development plans.

C.   Assume the competencies granted to them by the transference of administration, and implementation of public works and public services.

D.   Encourage the development of the communal economic system, through the articulation of networks for production and service areas, by social organizations in the community of direct or indirect communal property.

E.   Exercise social comptrollership functions on various plans and projects implemented within its geographical area by the instances of Popular Power or Public Power.

The LOC, however, says nothing about the conditions for the creation of communal aggregation systems and their operation, which is referred to by what will be established in the Regulations of the LOC and the guidelines issued by the Popular Power Ministry of the Communes.

In any event, the LOC lists in Article 60, the various types of communal systems as follows:

A.   The Communal Council: an instance for the articulation of social movements and organizations of a community.

B.   The Commune: an instance for articulation of several communities organized in a specified geographical area.

C.   The Communal City: established by popular initiative, through the aggregation of several Communes in a specified geographical area.

D.   Communal Federation: an instance for articulation of two or more cities corresponding to an instance of a Development District.

E.   Communal Confederation: articulation instance of communal federations within the scope of a development axis within a geographical area.

F.   All others formed by popular initiative

In particular, regarding the Communal City and the Communal Federation and Confederation, the conditions for their creation must be developed in the Regulation governing each Law.

However, all these instances of Popular Power envisaged for "the exercise of self-government", Article 15 of the LOPP only refers in some detail to the Communal Councils and to the Communes, which have otherwise been regulated by the Organic Law of the Communal Councils and by the Organic Law of the Communes; and to the Communal Cities.

4.   *The Communal Councils.*

The communal councils are defined in the Law as the "instance of participation, articulation and integration among citizens, and various community organizations, social and popular movements that allow organized people exercise community government and direct management of public policy and projects aimed to meet the needs, potentials and aspirations of communities, in the construction of the new model of the socialist society of equality, equity and social justice" [251](art. 15.1)

This legal definition highlights the fact that Community Councils can only and exclusively have as an objective to contribute to "the construction of a new model of **socialist** society", in violation of the principle of pluralism established by Article 6 of the Constitution, so any citizen who does not follow or accepts the socialist doctrine has no place in this new parallel State that is sought with this Law.

This instance of Popular Power constituted by the Communal Councils is regulated by the referred Law of the Communal Councils[252], whose "spokespersons", also by reforming the Organic Law of Municipal Public Power of December 2010, have been assigned the function of appointing the members of the Parish Councils, which were therefore "degraded" by ceasing to be the "local entities" they were

---

251   The same definition is established in Article 2 of the Organic Law on Communal Councils (art. 2).

252   See *Official Gazette* N° 39.335 of Dec. 28, 2009.

when their governments were elected through universal, direct and secret suffrage; becoming now mere "advisory, evaluating and coordination bodies between the Popular Power and the Municipal entities of Public Power"(Art. 35), whose members are also appointed by the spokespersons of the community councils of the respective parish (Art. 35), and only from among those supported by the Citizens' Assembly "of the respective municipal council" (Art. 36).

For such purpose, in an evident unconstitutional manner, the Reformed Law of Municipal Power ordered the "cessation" in their roles of "members and their alternates, and secretaries of the existing parish councils, being the Mayor's Office responsible for the management and future of the staff, as well as the corresponding assets. (Second Repeal Provision)

5. *The Communes*

The Communes, on the other hand, which are conceived in the LOPP as the "basic unit" of the Communal State is defined in Article 15.2 as the "**socialist space** that as a local entity is defined by the integration of neighboring communities with a shared historical memory, cultural traits and customs that are recognized in the territory they occupy and in the productive activities that serve as their support and over which they exercise sovereignty principles and active participation as an expression of popular power, in accordance with a regime of social production and the model of endogenous and sustainable development contemplated in the Economic and Social Development Plan of the Nation".[253] This same definition of the Commune as a socialist space is in Article 5 of the Organic Law of Municipalities; notion which implies that it is forbidden for anyone who is not a socialist or who does not believe in socialism or is in communion with socialism as a political doctrine. The legal concept of the Commune, therefore, is contrary to democratic pluralism guaranteed by the Constitution, being openly discriminatory and contrary to equality as guaranteed in Article 21 of the Constitution.

On the other hand, the LOPP defines the commune as a "local entity" and the same description is in Article 1 of the Organic Law of the Communes, which defines it "as the local entity where citizens in exercising Popular Power, exercise the full rights of sovereignty and develop active participation through forms of self-government for the construction of the Communal State under the Social Democratic State of Law and Justice" (Art. 1). Also in the December 2010 reform of the Organic Law of Municipal Public Power, the communes were included in the list of "local territorial authorities", providing, that being governed by different Popular Power legislation, and having to be constituted "among various municipalities", are exempted from the provisions of the Organic Law of Municipal Public Power.

Now, as to qualify communes as "local entities", the delegitimized legislator of December 2010 forgot that under the 1999 Constitution (Articles 169, 173), this expression of "local entity" can only be applied to political entities of the Constitutional Federal State which necessarily need to have "governments" composed of

---

253   The same definition is established in Article 5 of the Organic Law of the Communes

elected representatives by universal, direct and secret ballot (Articles 63, 169) adhered to the principles laid down in Article 6 of the Constitution, that is, that "shall always be democratic, participatory, elective, decentralized, alternative, responsible and pluralist, with revocable mandates." According to the 1999 Constitution, therefore, there can be no "local entities" with governments that are not democratic in the mentioned terms, especially if "representatives" are not directly elected by the people and are appointed by other public bodies.

And this is precisely what happens with the so called "governments of the communes", which under this legislation on Popular Power and its organizations, their origin is not guaranteed through democratic election by universal, direct and secret suffrage, thus being an unconstitutional conception.

It should also be stressed that, as provided in Article 28 of the LOPP, the government of the communes can transfer its management, administration and services to organizations of Popular Power. To this end, grassroots organizations of Popular Power must make their respective formal requests, fulfilling the preconditions and requirements established in the laws governing the matter.

This instance of Popular Power made up by the communes has been regulated by the Organic Law of the Communes.[254]

6. *Communal Cities*

According to the Law, Communal cities "are those created by popular initiative, through the aggregation of several communes, in a given territory" (Art. 15.3). Being the communes, according to the Law, the "socialist space" and "basic unit" of the Communal State, Communal Cities as aggregation of several communes or several socialist spaces are also designed under the law as "**socialist**" Cities, which as such, are forbidden, in fact, to any citizen or neighbor who is not a socialist.

IV. THE ORGANIZATIONS AND ORGANIZATIONAL EXPRESSIONS OF POPULAR POWER

In addition to Popular Power instances, the law establishes some provisions tending to regulate two organizational forms which are specific to Popular Power: the organizations and organizational expressions of Popular Power

1. *Organizational Forms of Popular Power*

A. *The organizations of Popular Power*

Under Article 9 of the LOPP, Popular Power organizations "are the various forms of organizing people, constituted from the locality by popular initiative, which integrate, citizens with common goals and interests, to overcome difficulties and promote common welfare so that the people involved assume their rights and duties and develop higher levels of political awareness. Popular Power organizations will act democratically and will seek popular consensus among its members".

---

254 See *Official Gazette* N° 6.011 Extra. of Dec. 21, 2010.

These Popular Power organizations are constituted at the initiative of citizens, in accordance to their nature, common interests, needs, potentialities and any other common point of reference as set out in the law governing their area of activity (Art. 12).

These Popular Power Organizations, like Popular Power instances, under Article 32 of the LOPP, acquire their legal status by registering with the Ministry of Popular Power competent on matters of citizen participation, taking into account the procedures established in the Regulations of the law. It's in the hands of the National Government, therefore, the formal recognition of these organizations, so that all those who are not socialists because they are contrary to the purposes prescribed in the Law (Article 1) would be rejected. In those registered organizations, citizens who do not share the socialist ideology, would not be accepted.

B. *Organizational expressions of Popular Power*

With respect to the "organizational expressions of Popular Power", as provided in Article 10 of the LOPP, they are "the integration of citizens with common goals and interests, constituted from the locality, their location or social area development reference, which temporarily and based on the principles of solidarity and cooperation, seek the collective interest."

These expressions of Popular Power are constituted by popular initiative and in response to the needs and potentialities of the communities, in accordance with the Constitution and the law. (Art.13)

Under the Third final provision, the exercise of people's participation and the stimulus to the initiative and organization of Popular Power established by Law should apply in indigenous towns and communities, according to their habits, customs and traditions.

2. *The purpose of organizations and organizational expressions of Popular Power*

These organizations and organizational expressions of popular power, according to Article 11 of the LOPP, have as their purpose the following:

First, "strengthen participatory and active democracy, according to Popular Power insurgency, as a historical event for the construction of the **socialist** society, democratic, of law and justice." As noted above, the addition of "socialist" that this provision imposes on society breaks the principle of pluralism guaranteed by the Constitution, paving the way for political discrimination against any citizen who is not a socialist, to whom the political right to participate, is denied.

Second, "promote the development and consolidation of the communal economic system, by establishing socio-productive organizations for the production of goods and services to satisfy social needs, the exchange of knowledge and expertise and the social reinvestment of the surplus." The LOPP, for these purposes, defines as "communal economic system" a set of social relations of production, distribution, exchange and consumption of goods and services, as well as knowledge and expertise developed by the instances of Popular Power, Public Power, or by agreement among them, through socio-productive organizations under communal forms social property"(Art. 8.13).

Third, "promote unity, solidarity, primacy of collective interests over individual interests and consensus in their areas of influence."

Fourth, "promote research and dissemination of values, historical and cultural traditions of the communities."

And fifth, "exercise social control."

V. AREAS OF POPULAR POWER

The LOPP identifies the following "areas of Popular Power" that are defined in the Organic Law and that in the traditional terminology of public law is nothing more than competencies that are assigned to Popular Power: Public Policy Planning, Communal Economy, Social Comptrollership, Organization and Management of the Territory and Communal Justice.

1. *Public Policy Planning*

Public policy planning in the terms established in the Organic Law of Public and Popular Planning,[255] is defined in Article 17 of the LOPP as "an area for action that assures, through shared government action among the public institutions and the instances of Popular Power, the implementation of the strategic guidelines of the Economic and Social Development Plan of the Nation for the use of public resources and achievement, coordination and harmonization of plans, programs and projects to achieve the country's transformation, balanced territorial development and fair distribution of wealth."

From this provision, the distinction between constitutional State bodies that are designated as "public institutions" and Popular Power instances stand out, confirming the intent of the law to establish a parallel State, the Communal State, with the purpose of emptying the content and ultimately stifle the Constitutional Federal State.

On the other hand, in connection with this planning competence, in terms of "participatory planning" the LOPP defines it as the "form of citizens' participation the design, formulation, implementation, evaluation and control of public policies" (Art. 8.11), and in terms of "participatory budget" it is defined "as the mechanism through which citizens propose, debate and decide on the formulation, implementation, monitoring and evaluation of public budgets, in order to materialize the projects leading to the development of communities and the general welfare" (Art. 8.12).

All this public policy planning, in any case is to be developed within a centralized planning system completely controlled by the Central government. For such purpose, even before the 2007 draft constitutional reforms were submitted to the National Assembly, in June 2007, a Decree Law N° 5,841 was enacted,[256] containing

---

255 See *Official Gazette* N° 6.011 Extra. of Dec. 21, 2010.
256 *Gazette* N° 5.841, Extra., of June 22, 2007.

the Organic Law creating the Central Planning Commission. This was the first formal state act devoted to build the socialist state,[257] so once the 2007 constitutional reform was rejected in referendum, a few days later, on December 13, 2007, the National Assembly approved the 2007–13 Economic and Social Development National Plan, established in Article 32 of the Decree Law,[258] in which the basis of the "planning, production and distribution system oriented towards socialism" was established, providing that "the relevant matter is the progressive development of social property of the production means."

2. *Communal Economy*

Communal economy, as defined in Article 18 the LOPP, is an "area of Popular Power that allows organized communities the establishment of economic and financial institutions and means of production, for the production, distribution, exchange and consumption of goods and services, as well as of knowledge and expertise developed under communal forms of social ownership, to satisfy collective needs, social reinvestment of the surplus, and contribute to the country's overall social development in a sustainable manner in accordance with the provisions of the Economic and Social Development Plan of the Nation and the law governing the matter".

This area of Public Power has been regulated by the Organic Law of the Communal Economic System,[259] which is defined in the Organic Law of the communes as a set of social relations of production, distribution, exchange and consumption of goods and services, as well as knowledge and expertise developed by the instances of Popular Power, Public Power, or by agreement between them, through socio-productive organizations under communal forms social property" "(Art. 4.13). This Communal Economic System,[260] on the other hand, must be exclusively developed through "socio-productive organizations under communal social property forms" created as public enterprises, family productive units, or bartering groups, in which private initiative and private property are excluded.

---

257 See Allan R. Brewer-Carías, "Comentarios sobre la inconstitucional creación de la Comisión Central de Planificación, centralizada y obligatoria," in *Revista de Derecho Público* 110, Editorial Jurídica Venezolana, Caracas 2007, pp. 79-89; Luis A. Herrera Orellana, "Los Decretos-Leyes de 30 de julio de 2008 y la Comisión Central de Planificación: Instrumentos para la progresiva abolición del sistema político y del sistema económico previstos en la Constitución de 1999," in *Revista de Derecho Público* 115, *(Estudios sobre los Decretos Leyes)*, Editorial Jurídica Venezolana, Caracas 2008, pp. 221-32.

258 *Official Gazette* N° 5.554 of Nov. 13, 2001.

259 See *Official Gazette* N° 6.011 Extra. of Dec. 21, 2010

260 See the comments on thjs matter in Allan R. Brewer-Carías, "Sobre la Ley Orgánica del Sistema Económico Comunal o de cómo se implanta en Venezuela un sistema económico comunista sin reformar la Constitución," in *Revista de Derecho Público*, N° 124, (octubre-diciembre 2010), Editorial Jurídica Venezolana, Caracas 2010, pp. 102-109.*Official Gazette* N° 6.011 Extra. of Dec. 21, 2010

This system radically changes the mixed economic system of the 1999 constitutional framework, substituting it with a state controlled economic system, mixed with provisions belonging to primitive societies, and even allowing the creation of local or "communal" currencies in a society that must be ruled only "by socialist principles and values" that the Law declares to be inspired, without any historical support, on the "Simón Bolívar's doctrine" (art. 5).

The socialist productive model established in the Law (art. 3.2), is precisely defined as a "production model based on *social property*, oriented towards the *elimination of the social division of work* that appertains to the capitalist model," directed to satisfy the increasing needs of the population through new means of generation and appropriation as well as the *reinvestment of social surplus*" (art. 6.12). This is nothing different than to legally impose a communist system by copying isolated phrases perhaps of a forgotten old manual of a failed communist revolution, paraphrasing what Karl Marx and Friedrich Engels wrote 170 years ago (1845-1846) on the "communist society,"[261] precisely based upon those three basic concepts: the social property of production means, the elimination of social division of work, and the social reinvestment of surplus (art. 1).

3. *Social Comptrollership*

In terms of social comptrollership, Article 19 of the LOPP defines it as a "area of Popular Power designed to carry out surveillance, monitoring, supervision and control over Public Power management, Popular Power instances and activities of the private sector that affect the common good, practiced individually or collectively by citizens, in the terms established by the law governing the matter. This area of Public Power has been regulated by the Organic Law of Social *Comptrollership*,[262] where it is defined as "a function shared among instances of Public Power and citizens, and organizations of Popular Power, to guarantee that Public investment is carried out transparently and efficiently for the benefit of the interests of society, and that private sector activities do not affect social or collective interests". (Art. 2)

This Law, imposing the socialist doctrine as an official and compulsory one, by organizing this social comptrollership system, what eventually has created is an obscure general system of social espionage and surveillance, which is attributed to individuals or to communal organizations, based on the denunciation and persecution against any private person that could be considered as not acting in accordance with the socialist imposed doctrine, and that for such reason could be considered as acting against the "common good" or affecting the "social or collective interests."

---

261 See in Karl Marx and Frederich Engels, "The German Ideology," en *Collective Works*, Vol. 5, International Publishers, New York 1976, p. 47. Véanse además los textos pertinentes en http://www.educa.madrid.org/cms_tools/files/0a24636f-764c-4e03-9c1d-6722e2ee60d7/Texto%20Marx%20y%20Engels.pdf

262 See *Official Gazette* N° 6.011 Extra. of Dec. 21, 2010.

4. *Organization and Management of the Territory*

The organization and management of the territory under Article 20 of the LOPP, is an "area of Popular Power, with the participation of organized communities, through their spokesmen or spokeswomen, in the various activities of the organization and management of the territory, in the terms established by law governing the subject."

5. *Communal Justice*

With respect to Communal justice, Article 21 the LOPP defines it as an "area of Popular Power, through alternative means of justice of the peace that promote arbitration, conciliation, mediation and other forms of conflict resolution in situations resulting directly from the exercise of the right to participation and communal coexistence, in accordance to the constitutional principles of Democratic and Social State of Law and Justice, and without violating the legal competencies of the ordinary justice system.[263]

Article 22 of the LOPP, refers to a special law, the regulation of the special communal jurisdiction, which must establish the organization, operation, procedures and rules of communal justice and its special jurisdiction. The Organic law of the communes is more explicit in stating that "the pertinent law shall determine the nature, legal procedures, rules and conditions for the creation of a special communal jurisdiction, which envisages its organization and operation, as well as instances with jurisdiction to hear and decide at the communal level, where communal judges shall be elected by universal, direct and secret suffrage from communal area residents over the age of fifteen "(art. 57).

The action of this communal jurisdiction, as required by Article 22 of the LOPP, "will be framed within free, accessible, impartial, suitable, transparent, autonomous, independent, responsible, equitable and expeditious principles, without undue delay and without formalities for useless repetitions."

With these provisions Municipalities are totally emptied of their assigned constitutional competence on matters of justice of peace (Art. 178.7), idea which was attempted before in the rejected constitutional reform of 2007, seeking to control the justices of peace that according to Article 258 of the Constitution shall be elected by universal suffrage, directly and by secret ballot.[264]

VI. RELATIONS BETWEEN PUBLIC AND POPULAR POWER (OR THE *"MATAPALO"* -KILLER TREE- TECHNIQUE")

As noted, the Communal State established in the LOPP, whose bodies directed by "spokespersons" that are not "representatives" directly elected by the people exercise Popular Power, has been established as a "Parallel State" to the Constitutional

---

263 The same definition is established in Article 56 of the Organic Law of the Communes.

264 See the Organic Law of Justice of the Peace in *Official Gazette* N° 4.817 Extra. of Dec. 21, 1994.

State whose bodies on the contrary are elected through direct universal and secret popular vote and exercise Public Power. These two established Parallel States, one in the Constitution and the other in an unconstitutional Law, with provisions that, if implemented, will enable the Communal State to drown and empty the Constitutional State, behaving as does in botany the *Ficus benjamina L.* tree, native of India, Java and Bali, known as the "killer tree" that can grow as a strangler surrounding and choking the host tree, forming a hollow tree, destroying it.

To this end, in the LOPP, provisions are established to regulate relations between the State of Public Power (Constitutional State) and State of Popular Power (Communal State), which generally provides that "are governed by the principles of equality, territorial integrity, cooperation, solidarity, co-responsibility, within the decentralized federal system enshrined in the Constitution of the Republic "(art. 26). These provisions are:

First, a legal obligation established on organs, entities and agencies of Public Power to promote support and accompany people's initiatives for the creation, development and consolidation of various forms of organizations and self-government of the people (Art. 23)[265] . In particular, even the Organic Law of the Communes stipulates that "bodies of the Citizen Power branch of government will support community control councils for the purpose of contributing to the fulfillment of their duties" (Art. 48).

Second, all organs of the Constitutional State that exercise Public Power, are subjected to the mandates of the organizations of Popular Power, establishing a new principle of government, to "govern obeying". Article 24 of the LOPP, in fact states:

> *Article 24.* Proceedings of the bodies and entities of Public Power. All organs, entities and agencies of Public Power will govern their actions by the principle of "govern obeying", in relation to the mandates of the people and organizations of Popular Power, according to the provisions in the Constitution of the Republic and the laws.

As Popular Power organizations have no political autonomy, since their "spokespersons" are not democratically elected by universal, direct and secret ballot, but appointed by citizen assemblies controlled and operated by the governing party and the National Executive who controls and guides all the organizational process of the Communal State in the sphere of socialist ideology, there is no way there can be a spokesperson who is not a socialist, ultimately this "govern obeying" principle is a limitation of the political autonomy of the elected bodies of the Constitutional State such as the National Assembly, Governors and Legislative Councils of States and Mayors and Municipal Councils, upon who ultimately is imposed an obligation to obey any provision made by the National Government and the ruling party, framed exclusively in the socialist sphere as a political doctrine. Popular will, expressed in the election of representatives of the Constitutional State, therefore, has no value

---

265 A similar regulation is in article 62 of the Organic Law of the Communes, for the "establishment, development, and consolidation of the communes as a self-government form"

whatsoever, and the people have been confiscated of their sovereignty by transferring it to assemblies who do not represent them.

Thirdly, in particular, an obligation is established for the Executive Branch "in accordance with the development and consolidation initiatives originated from Popular Power," to plan, articulate and coordinate "joint actions with social organizations, organized communities, communes and the aggregation and articulation systems that may arise among them, in order to maintain consistency with the strategies and policies at the national, regional, local, municipal and community level" (art. 25).

Fourthly, an obligation is established for the agencies and entities of Public Power in their relationships with Popular Power, to give "priority to organized communities, the communes and the aggregation and articulation systems that may arise among them, in response to the requirements the they formulate to fulfill their needs and exercise their rights under the terms and periods established by law" (Art. 29). It also provides that authorities of organs, entities and agencies of Public Power in their different territorial political levels, should take "measures to ensure that socio-productive organizations of socio-communal property have priority and preference in government procurement processes for the acquisition of goods, services and execution of public works" (art. 30)[266]

Fifth, an obligation is established for the Republic, states and municipalities in accordance to the law governing the process of transference and decentralization of powers and competencies. The obligation of transferring "to organized communities, communes and aggregation systems that may arise among them: management functions, administration, service control and implementation of public works attributed to them in the Constitution of the Republic, to improve efficiency and results in benefit of the collective" (art. 27) [267] With it, legally emptying the competencies of states and municipalities, leaving empty structures with government representatives elected by the people but have with no matters on which to rule.

Sixth, the Law establishes that agencies and grassroots organizations of Popular Power covered by the LOPP, are exempt from any kind of payment of national taxes and registration fees, and for that purpose, laws and ordinances may be established in the states and municipalities, respectively, for the exemptions provided here for grassroots organizations of Popular Power (Art. 31).

---

266 In particular, article 61 of the Organic Law of the Communes, states that "all the organs and entities of the Public Power committed to financing projects for the communes and its aggregation systems, will give priority to those that aim to promote communities with less relative development, to guarantee a balanced development

267 The same rule is repeated in the Organic Law of the Communes (art. 64). By December 31, 2010, the second discussion of the draft organic law of the System of Competencies and Power Transfer from the States and Municipalities to Popular Power organizations was still pending before the National Assembly.

FINALREMARKS

With this Organic Law of Popular Power framework, there is no doubt about the political decision taken in December 2010 by the completely delegitimized National Assembly that was elected in 2005, and that no longer represented the majority of the popular will as it was expressed on the 26 September 2010 parliamentary elections against the President of the Republic, the National Assembly itself and socialist policies they have developed; to impose on Venezuelans, against popular will and defrauding the Constitution. The political decision has been to impose in Venezuela a Socialist State model, called "the Communal State," conceived as a Socialist State, in order to supposedly exercise Popular Power directly by the people, as an alleged form of direct exercise of sovereignty (which is not true because it is exercised through "spokespersons" who "represent" them and who are not elected in universal, direct and secret suffrage).

This Communal State has been established in parallel to the Constitutional Federal State (the Decentralized Federal Democratic and Social of Law and Justice provided in the Constitution of 1999) established for the exercise of Public Power by people both indirectly through elected representatives in universal, direct and secret elections, as well as directly through mechanisms authorized in the Constitution, which includes Citizens Assemblies.

This regulation, in parallel, of two States and two ways of exercising sovereignty, one, the Constitutional State governed by the Constitution and the other the Communal or Socialist State governed by unconstitutional organic laws, has been arranged in such a way that the latter will act as the "killer tree," strangling the former, surrounding it in order to destroy it. That is why, in 2012, a Decree Law has been enacted for the "Communitarian Management of Competencies, Services and other attributions"[268] in order to regulate the process of transfer of powers, competencies and resources, from the National Power and the political entities (States and Municipalities) to the organized people, which will assume such powers through Social Property Communal Enterprises. The result of the application of this Law will be the voiding of powers and competencies of the Constitutional Federal State in the benefit of the Communal State.

In this way, in addition to defrauding the Constitution, a technique that has been consistently applied by the authoritarian regime in Venezuela since 1999, to impose its decisions outside of the Venezuelan Constitution,[269] now adds fraud to the popu-

---

268 See *Official Gazette* N° 39954 of June, 28, 2012

269 See on the 1999 constitutional making process: Allan R. Brewer-Carías, *Golpe de estado y proceso constituyente en Venezuela,* Universidad Nacional Autónoma de México, Mexico City 2002; "The 1999 Venezuelan Constitution-Making Process as an Instrument for Framing the development of an Authoritarian Political Regime," in Laura E. Miller (Editor), *Framing the State in Times of Transition. Case Studies in Constitution Making,* United States Institute of Peace Press, Washington 2010, pp. 505-531; "Constitution Making in Defraudation of the Constitution and Authoritarian Government in Defraudation of Democracy. The Recent Venezuelan Experience", in *Lateinamerika Analysen,* 19, 1/2008, GIGA, German Institute of Global and Area Studies, Institute of Latin American Studies, Hamburg

lar will, by imposing on Venezuelans through organic laws, a State model for which nobody has voted and that radically and unconstitutionally changes the text of the 1999 Constitution, which has not been reformed as they had wished, and in open contradiction to the popular rejection that the majority expressed in the attempt to reform the Constitution in December 2007, even in violation of the Constitution, and the popular rejection that the majority of the people expressed regarding the policies of the President to the Republic and his National Assembly on the occasion of the parliamentary elections of 26 September 2010.

What is clear about all this is that there are no masks to deceive anyone, or by reason of which, someone pretends to be deceived or fooled.

2008, pp. 119-142; *Reforma constitucional y fraude a la Constitución (1999-2009)*, Academia de Ciencias Políticas y Sociales, Caracas 2009; and *Dismantling Democracy. The Chávez Authoritarian Experiment*, Cambridge University Press, New York 2010. See also Alessandro Pace, "Muerte de una Constitución," in *Revista Española de Derecho Constitucional*, Año 19, N° 57, Madrid 1999, pp. 271-283.

CHAPTER XXVIII

THE SITUATION OF THE VENEZUELAN STATE AFTER
THE APRIL 2013 PRESIDENTIAL ELECTIONS:
THE CHÁVEZ'S INSTITUTIONAL LEGACY

(2013)

This essay on "The Situation of the Venezuelan State after the April 2013 Presidential Elections: The Chávez's Institutional Legacy, "was written for the Presentation I gave at the Program on "Presidential election and beyond," organized by the *Venezuelan American Association of the United States,* **New York, April 9, 2013.**

As we all know, the Venezuelan Presidential Elections that were held on April 14, 2013, were due to the death of Hugo Chávez Frías, who after being President of the Republic for two terms since 1999, and after being reelected on October 2012, never managed to take his oath of office, missing the Inauguration ceremony that was scheduled for January 10th, 2013. The fact is that since December 10th, 2012, he was confined to a bed in a Hospital in Habana, Cuba where he was operated upon, not being seen alive in public any more since then.

This mean that since December 2012, it was absolutely clear that the late President was already unable to govern, a situation that nonetheless was deliberately hidden by government officials in Caracas, even by making believe that he was ruling the country from Havana, a fact that was completely false. The result is that in fact nobody really knows exactly when he died. Even the Supreme Tribunal of Justice, in his decision of March 8, 2013 through which it allowed Vice President Nicolás Maduro to continue ruling the country as acting President, in a very careful way did not affirm that the former President actually died on March 5th, 2013, as it was officially announced, it only said that was the day that the Vice President announced.[270]

The result of all the secrecy surrounding the condition of the former President and of the manipulation of the information regarding his incapacity to govern, were

---

[270] See the text of the decision N° 141 of March 5, 2013 in http://www.tsj.gov.ve.decisiones/scon/Marzo/141-9313-2013-13-0196.html

two "custom made" judicial decisions issued by the Supreme Tribunal of Justice, in January 9th, 2013[271] and in March 8th, 2013, in which, contrary to express constitutional provisions, the Tribunal ruled to ensure, first, the continuity on the tenure of Vice President Maduro who was in charge of the Executive Power, affirming that the late President was supposedly in charge of the government, which was absolutely impossible; and second, that the same Vice President Maduro, after he announced the death of the former President, was the one to assume the Presidency with the possibility of running as a candidate in the Presidential Elections that were to follow, without stepping down from such official position.

Thanks to those unconstitutional rulings, Nicolás Maduro, as acting President, illegally using all sort of public resources and funds and without any control by the National Electoral Council, runned in the presidential election as *the official candidate of the State*. Yes, I repeat, as the official candidate of the Venezuelan State, and not of a particular political party, facing the candidate of the opposition, the former Governor of the Miranda State Henrique Capriles, who confronted the most vulgar abuse of power ever seen before in an electoral campaign in the country. Even the Ministry of Defense had openly endorsed Maduro in the name of the Armed Forces.[272] Perhaps that is why Nicolás Maduro, a few days before the election, affirmed, threatening in the most typical style of the former President, that if for any "historical accident" Capriles could won the election, in no more that two months there was going to be a "popular uprise" against his policies.[273]

But in spite of the efforts to try to copy the rude style of the late President, the Apriel 2013 election was conditioned, above all, by the fact that for the first time in fourteen years of elections, the former President, having being the President with the longest tenure and political presence in all of Venezuelan political history, was not physically participating in it.[274]

In addition, as any authoritarian leader of his kind, and in his case, after having mastered the use of the media, like nobody else, the former President could not really be imitated. Nobody could really claim to be him or similar to him. No body could effectively claim to inherit his political legacy.

Nonetheless, as we all know, the candidate Maduro was openly trying to imitate him, to sell himself as his "son," and to hide himself in his shadow. One of the last

---

271 See the text of the decision N° 2 of January 9, 2013 in http://www.tsj.gov.ve/decisiones/scon/Enero/02-9113-2013-12-1358.html

272 See the expressions of Diego Molero Bellavía, Minister of Defense, in *CNN es la Noticia*, 5-3-2013, available at http://cnnespanol.cnn.com/2013/03/05/ministro-de-la-defensa-venezolano-hace-un-llamado-a-la-unidad/

273 See in "Maduro: habrá un "alzamiento popular" si triunfa Capriles," ANSA, Caracas March, 28, 2013, available at http://redigitaltv.com/?p=97014&utm_campaign=nacional-y-politica&utm_medium=twitter&utm_source=twitter

274 Chavez ruled the country more years than any of the other well known authoritarian rulers, more that Antonio Guzmán Blanco in the XIX century, and Juan Vicente Gómez in the XX century. See Allan R. Brewer-Carías, *Historia Constitucional de Venezuela*, Editorial Alfa, Caracas 2008, Vol. II.

sign of such attempt was his announcement a few days before the election that the dead President appeared before him, flying, and transfigured into a little bird, giving him his benediction for the Presidential campaign.[275] This sort of expressions made by any other than Chávez, only generaed sorrow or laugh, but for sure evidenced the dangerous risk that the outcome of this election could eventually result in a tragic comedy with a phantom directing the policies of the country.

In this context, any way, the situation of the presidential campaign in Apriel 2013 was that if it is true that who was in fact running against Henrique Capriles was not the former President, the constant use by Maduro of the Chávez's legacy, placed Capriles in the situation of really running against all the apparatus of the State, the same State that through the Supreme Tribunal and the National Electoral Council had admitted the candidacy of Maduro in violation of the Constitution, particularly because as Vice President he was forbidden to be a candidate.

Now, independently from the result of the elections, in which both candidates currently have real chances of winning, the fact is that both, Capriles and Maduro as well as all Venezuelans, in the near future, will have to face the reality of the institutional mess that we are inheriting from the former President long government. This is precisely the aspect that I want to address, related to the "beyond" the election.

We must not forget that with all of its defects, still in the 90's, Venezuela was still one of the most envied democracies in Latin America, with a steady economic growth and permanent social policies led by Social Democratic and Social Christian parties; a situation that is in sharp contrasts with the situation of the country in April 2013, that had the record of being among the countries with the highest index of violence and lack of security; of governmental inefficiency; of greater number of public employees compared to its population; of militarization of the Public Administration; of infrastructure destruction; of military expenses; of human rights violations; of impunity; of lack of economic liberty; of participation of the State in economic activities; of imports' dependency; of public internal and external debt; of lowest international reserves; of oldest currency exchange control; of inflation and currency devaluation; of dependency on oil production; of greater State control on the media and of less freedom of expression; of the biggest political polarization; of institutional destruction; of absence of separation of powers and check and balances; of absence of government accountability and fiscal control; of corruption; and of absence of transparency in government. And the gravest of all, a country were the value of work had disappeared from society as a consequence of the policies that have been applied by the government supposedly to take care of the poor, which were based on direct subsidies and distribution of money and goods that eventually had worsened the situation of the poor with the mirage of pocket money.[276]

---

275 See " Maduro dice que Chávez se apareció en forma de "pajarito chiquitico" y lo bendijo," in *Noticias 24*, April 2, 2013, available at http://www.noticias24.com/venezuela/noticia/159655/maduro-dice-chavez-se-apareció-en-forma-de-pajarito-chiquitico-y-lo-bendijo/

276 As Luis Ugalde, the former Rector of the Andrés Bello Catholic University of Caracas said regarding the Chávez's legacy: *"Con 1 billón (1 millón de millones) de dólares en las manos,*

The most recent record derived from the Chávez's legacy, has been the formal exclusion of the country from the international community having lost its voting rights in the bodies of the United Nations Organization because of lack of payment of the required contributions.[277]

So for the April 2013 Presidential election, the position of the two running candidates appeared to be clear: In the case of Maduro, having been in the government since 1999, and purporting to be the heir of Chávez, he was proposing to continue with the policies that have lead to the catastrophic situation the country had in 2013, to the point that any other different political offer he made, for instance, to improve the grave situation of lack of security and lower the extremely high rate of crime in the country, necessarily falled into a vacuum. In the case of Capriles, on the contrary, he proposed to change all those failed policies, and to reestablish the rule of law in the country.

Within that situation that all Venezuelans were going to face in the future, the one more important to highlight in April 2013, was the situation of the State that the new President will encounter, specifically from the standpoint of the Constitution, which in spite of all the propaganda, seems to have lost all its value as a fundamental law of the country.

In this regard, the first problem that the new President was going to manage, was the catastrophic consequences of the so called "Bolivarian Revolution," the result of which has been, on the one hand, what I have called the process of deconstitutionalization of the Constitutional State, and on the other hand, the result of the conduction of the Constitutional State permanently ignoring the Constitution.

The common aspect of these two situations is that all the political changes that have been introduced in the country during the tenure of the late President, have been made in contempt of the Constitution and of its supremacy. This means, first, that all the changes introduced in all the basic principles of the organization of the

---

su pésima gestión ha llevado a Venezuela a los primeros lugares de endeudamiento interno y externo, de inflación (el triple del promedio latinoamericano), corrupción, creación de multimillonarios ineptos y parásitos a la sombra del poder político, récord en las importaciones de productos agropecuarios e industriales y ruina de la productividad con atrofia de las exportaciones. Nos ha puesto en los primeros lugares del mundo en el crimen en las calles y en las cárceles y nuestra sociedad enferma prolonga la agonía gracias al suero petrolero" [...] "Con ilimitada demagogia se le inculca a la población que para salir de la pobreza no son necesarios el esfuerzo propio y la productividad; basta la ayuda de un presidente compasivo y generoso con el reparto del ingreso petrolero. Al contrario –decimos-, lo que el pobre necesita para dejar de serlo es apoyo decidido a su educación y formación productora, a su organización social y la creación de millones de puestos de trabajo con inversión y enorme creatividad empresarial exitosa de decenas de miles de emprendedores." See in Luis Ugalde, "Salud y Compasión," El Nacional, Caracas, April 4, 2013, available at http://www.el-nacional.com/luis_ugalde/Salud-compasion_0_165583664.html

277 See "Venezuela pierde temporalmente su derecho a votar en la ONU por impago de cuotas," in Globovisión, Caracas April 3, 2013, available in http://globovision.com/articulo/venezuela-pierde-temporalmente-su-derecho-a-votar-en-onu-por-impago-de-cuotas

State, and of the political system of the country set forth in the Constitution, have been made without following its formal review procedure; and second, that the functioning of the organs of State even when they were not changed, have been gravely distorted, in contempt of the Constitution.

The first of these situations, that is, the changes introduced on the State organization without formally changing the Constitution, can be considered as the basic trend of the government policies during the past decade.[278]

The 1999 Constitution defines the Venezuelan State as a Democratic and Social State of Law and Justice (Article 2), organized as "a decentralized federal State" (Article 4),[279] theoretically based, among other well known principles, on the principle of separation or powers, with five and not only three different powers, each of them with their supposed autonomy and independence.

In the Constitution, in addition, the State power is also divided in a vertical way in three territorial levels of government (National, States and the Municipal) according to the federal principle (Art. 136), each of them with a government that according to the Constitution must be of an "elective, decentralized, alternative, responsible, plural, and of revocable mandate" character (Article 6).

On the other hand, the political system of the country is arranged in the Constitution based on the principles of representative democracy, political decentralization, participation, and political pluralism, according to which no political institution of the State can be created without ensuring its representative character by means of universal, direct and secret suffrage; without guaranteeing its political autonomy, and without guaranteeing its plural character in the sense that it cannot be linked to a particular ideology.

Regarding the economic system, it is conceived in the Constitution as a mixed one, guaranteeing economic freedom and free private initiative and enterprise, altogether with private property rights, and allowing the State to participate in the economy in order to satisfy social justice.

All these principles are the ones embodied in a rigid way in the Constitution, in the sense that they cannot be changed without formally reviewing its text.

Nonetheless, and without any constitutional review procedure, the fact is that what the country has inherited from the late President, is that all those basic principles have been changed in the name of the so-called "Bolivarian Revolution," in order to progressively implement a new so-called 21st century "Communist State," without reviewing the Constitution

---

278 See Allan R. Brewer-Carías, "The process of "deconstitutionalization"of the Venezuelan Constitutional State as the Most Important Current Constitutional Issue in Venezuela," in *Duquesne Law Review*, Vol 51, N° 2, Spring 2013, Duquesne University School of Law, Pittsburgh, pp. 349-386.

279 See the study of the constitution regarding the regulation of this State Constitutional Model, in Allan R. Brewer-Carías, *La Constitución de 1999. Derecho Constitucional venezolano*, 2 vols., Editorial Jurídica Venezolana, Caracas 2004; and *La Constitución de 1999 y la Enmienda Constitucional de 2009*, Editorial Jurídica Venezolana, Caracas 2011.

That is why, this process of de-constitutionalization of the Constitutional State, is the most important current constitutional feature in the country[280] that the next President will have to face; and that has been progressively implemented using the name of Bolívar to serve as the support of a political socialist doctrine, that of course was completely unknown in Bolivar's times. [281]

We have to recognize that the initial intention of the late President was to have implemented his "Bolivarian Revolution" by formally reforming the Constitution. For such purpose, in 2007 he proposed before the National Assembly[282] a Constitutional Reform Draft in order to incorporate in the same text of the Constitution, not only the "Bolivarian socialist doctrine"[283] as the official doctrine of the country, but the framework of the new Socialist State that he intended to establish. That 2007 Constitutional Reform Draft,[284] in effect, formally sought to substitute the Constitutional State by a new "Communal State" or State of the "popular power" (*Estado del poder popular o del poder communal, o Estado comunal*) organized based on the

---

280 See Allan R. Brewer-Carías, "The process of "deconstitutionalization"of the Venezuelan Constitutional State as the Most Important Current Constitutional Issue in Venezuela," in *Duquesne Law Review*, Vol 51, N° 2, Spring 2013, Duquesne University School of Law, Pittsburgh, pp. 349-386.

281 One of the last attempt to completely appropriate Simón Bolívar for the "Bolivarian Revolution," was the televised exhumation of his remains that took place at the National Pantheon in Caracas on July 26, 2010, conducted by the late President Chávez himself and other high officials, including the Prosecutor General, among other things, for the purpose of determining if Bolivar died of arsenic poisoning in Santa Marta in 1830, instead of from tuberculosis. See Simon Romero, "Building a New History By Exhuming Bolívar," *The New York Times*, August 4, 2010, p. A7.

282 See on the constitutional reforms proposals, Allan R. Brewer-Carías, *Hacia la consolidación de un Estado socialista, centralizado, policial y militarista. Comentarios sobre el sentido y alcance de las propuestas de reforma constitucional 2007*, Editorial Jurídica Venezolana, Caracas 2007; *La reforma constitucional de 2007 (Comentarios al proyecto inconstitucionalmente sancionado por la Asamblea Nacional el 2 de noviembre de 2007)*, Editorial Jurídica Venezolana, Caracas 2007.

283 All his proposals to construct socialism were linked by Chávez to Simón Bolívar's 1819 *Discurso de Angostura*, which he considered "perfectly applicable to a socialist project" in the sense of considering that it was possible to "take the original Bolivarian ideology as a basic element of a socialist project." Of course, this assertion has no serious foundations: it is enough to read Bolívar's 1819 Angostura discourse on presenting the draft constitution to realize that it has nothing to do with a "socialist project" of any kind. See Simón Bolívar, *Escritos fundamentales*, Caracas 1982. See also Pedro Grases ed., *El Libertador y la Constitución de Angostura de 1819*, Caracas 1969; José Rodríguez Iturbe, ed., *Actas del Congreso de Angostura*, Caracas 1969.

284 The first Draft circulated in June 2007 under the title *Consejo Presidencial para la Reforma de la Constitución de la República Bolivariana de Venezuela, "Modificaciones propuestas."* The complete text was published as *Proyecto de reforma constitucional. Versión atribuida al Consejo Presidencial para la reforma de la Constitución de la República Bolivariana de Venezuela*, Editorial Atenea, Caracas 2007, 146. The presidencial proposals were published as *Proyecto de Reforma Constitucional. Elaborado por el ciudadano Presidente de la República Bolivariana de Venezuela, Hugo Chávez Frías*, Editorial Atenea, Caracas 2007

creation of communes and communal councils (*consejos comunales*) as the primary political units of social organization, trying to resuscitate the one hundred year old soviets of the Russian Revolution.

Considered globally, the proposed reform sought to establish a socialist, centralized, militaristic, and police State,[285] for which purpose all the most essential and fundamental principles and aspects of the political organization of the Democratic and Social State of rule of law and justice were proposed to be modified.[286]

That is, *First,* the reforms proposed to convert the democratic and decentralized State regulated in the Constitution into a centralized state of concentrated power that under the illusory guise of a popular power, sought to definitively replace the federal form of the state,[287] as well as any form of political decentralization; thus, rendering political participation impossible, and progressively eliminating representative democracy.[288] The main aspect of the reforms as was expressly affirmed in its text was that the popular power "does not arise from suffrage or from any election, but arises from the condition of the organized human groups that form the base of the population." That is to say that representative democracy and territorial political autonomy was to disappear, substituted with a supposed "participatory democracy" that, in fact, in a very undemocratic way, was to be controlled by the National Executive.[289]

---

285 See Allan R. Brewer-Carías, *Hacia la Consolidación de un Estado Socialista, Centralizado, Policial y Militarista. Comentarios sobre el sentido y alcance de las propuestas de reforma constitucional 2007,* Colección Textos Legislativos, N° 42, Editorial Jurídica Venezolana, Caracas 2007.

286 See Rogelio Pérez Perdomo, "La Constitución de papel y su reforma," in *Revista de Derecho Público* 112 *(Estudios sobre la reforma constitucional),* Editorial Jurídica Venezolana, Caracas 2007, p. 14; G. Fernández, "Aspectos esenciales de la modificación constitucional propuesta por el Presidente de la República. La modificación constitucional como un fraude a la democracia," *Id,* p. 22; Alfredo Arismendi, "Utopía Constitucional," in *id.,* p. 31; Manuel Rachadell, "El personalismo político en el Siglo XXI," in *id.,* p. 66; Allan R. Brewer-Carías, "El sello socialista que se pretendía imponer al Estado," in *id.,* p. 71-75; Alfredo Morles Hernández, "El nuevo modelo económico para el Socialismo del Siglo XXI," in *id.,* p. 233-36.

287 See Manuel Rachadell, "El personalismo político en el Siglo XXI," in *Revista de Derecho Público* 112 *(Estudios sobre la reforma constitucional),* Editorial Jurídica Venezolana, Caracas 2007, 67; Ana Elvira Araujo, "Proyecto de reforma constitucional (agosto a noviembre 2007). Principios fundamentales y descentralización política," in *id.,* 77-81; José Luis Villegas, "Impacto de la reforma constitucional sobre las entidades locales," in *id.,* 119-23.

288 For such purpose, the reform established a new "popular power" (*poder popular*) (art. 16), composed by communities (*comunidades*), each of which were to constitute "a basic and indivisible territorial nucleus of the Venezuelan Socialist State, where ordinary citizens will have the power to construct their own geography and their own history;" which were to be grouped into communes (*comunas*). The communes were later created in the Law on the Federal Council of Government. See *Ley Orgánica del Consejo Federal de Gobierno, Gaceta Oficial* N° 5.963 Extra. of Feb. 22, 2010).

289 This fundamental change, as the president stated on August 15, 2007, constituted "the development of what we understand by decentralization, because the Fourth Republic concept of decentralization is very different from the concept we must work with. For this reason, we

In this respect, it must be mentioned that anticipating to the expected results of the proposed constitutional reforms, perhaps being sure of its approval – which did not occur -, the previous year, in 2006, the National Assembly sanctioned the Law on the Communal Councils (*Consejos Comunales*) [290] along the same undemocratic and unconstitutional trends, seeking since then, the dismantling the traditional local governments or municipalities of the country.

The *second* global change proposed in the 2007 Constitutional Reforms Draft, was to convert the Constitutional Democratic and Social State into a Socialist State for the purpose of the "construction of a Socialist democracy" (art. 158); thus establishing a political official doctrine of socialist character –the supposed "Bolivarian doctrine"– denying pluralism and allowing the possible formal official criminalization of all dissidence, legalizing political persecution.

The *third* main change proposed in the same 2007 Constitutional Reforms Draft, along with the Socialist doctrine, tended to convert the mixed economic system of the country into a wholly state-owned, socialist and centralized economy by means of eliminating economic freedom and private initiative as constitutional rights, as well as the constitutional right to private property; conferring all the means of production to the State, to be centrally managed; and configuring the State as an institution on which all economic activity was to depend. [291]

And finally, the *fourth* constitutional reform proposal of 2007, was to convert the State into a repressive or police state, given the regressive character of the proposed

---

have here stated 'the protagonist participation of the people, transferring power to them, and creating the best conditions for the construction of social democracy.'" See *Discurso de orden pronunciado por el ciudadano Comandante Hugo Chávez Frías, op. cit.,* 50.

290 See Giancarlo enríquez Maionica, "Los Consejos Comunales (una breve aproximación a su realidad y a su proyección ante la propuesta presidencial de reforma constitucional)," in *Revista de Derecho Público* 112 *(Estudios sobre la reforma constitucional)*, Editorial Jurídica Venezolana, Caracas 2007, pp. 89-99; Allan R. Brewer-Carías, "El inicio de la desmunicipalización en Venezuela: La organización del poder popular para eliminar la descentralización, la democracia representativa y la participación a nivel local," in *AIDA, Opera Prima de Derecho Administrativo. Revista de la Asociación Internacional de Derecho Administrativo,* Universidad Nacional Autónoma de México, Asociación Internacional de Derecho Administrativo, Mexico City 2007, pp. 49-67. The 2006 law was replaced by *Ley Orgánica de los Consejos Comunales, Gaceta Oficial* N° 39.335, Dec. 28, 2009. See the comments on this Law in Allan R. Brewer-Carías, *Ley de los Consejos Comunales,* Editorial Jurídica Venezolana, Caracas 2010.

291 See Gerardo Fernández, "Aspectos esenciales de la modificación constitucional propuesta por el Presidente de la República. La modificación constitucional como un fraude a la democracia," in *Revista de Derecho Público* 112 *(Estudios sobre la reforma constitucional)*, Editorial Jurídica Venezolana, Caracas 2007, p. 24; Alfredo Arismendi, "Utopía Constitucional," in *id.*, p. 31; José Antonio Muci Borjas, "La suerte de la libertad económica en el proyecto de Reforma de la Constitución de 2007," in *id.*, pp. 203-208; Tamara Adrián, "Actividad económica y sistemas alternativos de producción," in *id.*, pp. 209-14; Víctor Hernández Mendible, "Réquiem por la libertad de empresa y derecho de propiedad," in *id.*, pp. 215-18; Alfredo Morles Hernández, "El nuevo modelo económico para el Socialismo del Siglo XXI," in *id.*, pp. 233-236.

reforms on matters of human rights, and also into a militarist state, based on the role assigned to the "Bolivarian Armed Force" (*Fuerza Armada Bolivariana*), configured to function wholly under the direct control of the President of the Republic, creating a new very dangerous and phantasmagorical "Bolivarian National Militia" (*Milicia Nacional Bolivariana*), as a political military force.

As the late President himself explained, the motivation for the drafting of the constitutional reforms in 2007, was to construct –in his own words- a "Bolivarian Socialism, Venezuelan Socialism, our Socialism, and our socialist model," having "the community" (*la comunidad*), as its "basic and indivisible nucleus," and considering that "real democracy is only possible in socialism." [292]

That is why I have said that the proposed constitutional reform tended to formally alter the basic foundations of the Democratic Constitutional State,[293] and the economic system of the country,[294] the consequence being that they needed to approve only by convening a National Constituent Assembly and not by means of a "constitutional reform procedure" which was the one chosen by the President and the National Assembly.

Notwithstanding, the authoritarian way to govern imposed the use of a wrong constitutional review procedure,[295] as one additional sign of the "permanent coup d'état" that since 1999 characterized the political situation in Venezuela.[296] The consequence was that the chosen procedure was challenged multiple times before the Supreme Tribunal on grounds of its unconstitutionality, but being the Tribunal completely controlled by the Executive, the result was also the issuing of multiple deci-

---

292   See *Discurso de orden pronunciado por el ciudadano Comandante Hugo Chávez Frías, op cit.*, 32, 34, 35.

293   See Eugenio Hernández Bretón, "Cuando no hay miedo (ante la Reforma Constitucional)," in *Revista de Derecho Público* 112 *(Estudios sobre la reforma constitucional)*, Editorial Jurídica Venezolana, Caracas 2007, pp. 17-20; Manuel Rachadell, "El personalismo político en el Siglo XXI," in *id.*, pp. 65-70.

294   See on these reforms, Allan R. Brewer-Carías, *Dismantling Democracy. The Chávez Authoritarian Experiment*, Cambridge University Press, 2010.

295   See Rogelio Pérez Perdomo, "La Constitución de papel y su reforma," in *Revista de Derecho Público* 112 *(Estudios sobre la reforma constitucional)*, Editorial Jurídica Venezolana, Caracas 2007, 14; Gerardo Fernández, "Aspectos esenciales de la modificación constitucional propuesta por el Presidente de la república. La modificación constitucional en fraude a la democracia," in id., 21-25; Fortunato González, "Constitución histórica y poder constituyente," in *id.*, pp. 33-36; Lolymar Heránndez Camargo, "Los límites del cambio constitucional como garantía de pervivencia del Estado de derecho," in *id.*, 37-45; Claudia Nikken, "La soberanía popular y el trámite de la refroma constitucional promovida por iniciativa presidencial el 15 de agosto de 2007," in *id.*, 51-58.

296   See José Amando Mejía Betancourt, "La ruptura del hilo constitucional," in in *Revista de Derecho Público* 112 *(Estudios sobre la reforma constitucional)*, Editorial Jurídica Venezolana, Caracas 2007, p. 47. The term was first used by Francois Mitterand, *Le coup d'État permanent*, Éditions 10/18, Paris 1993.

sions by the Tribunal refusing to exercise judicial review on these matters, even declaring that the requests could no even be filed ("*improponible*"). [297]

But apart from the adopted unconstitutional procedure, the most important aspect of the 2007 constitutional reforms proposals is that they were submitted to popular approval in a referendum that took place on December 2, 2007,[298] resulting in an overwhelming popular rejection of the reforms.

This was, without doubt, the most important political failure for Chávez, and of course the most important political fact - the expression of the will of the people – regarding his policies. But nonetheless, this result had no importance whatsoever for the authoritarian government that refused to listen or to follow the peoples' decision. The popular rejection of the reforms was in fact mocked by the Government, and not only did not prevent it to begin the implementation of the reforms without even bothering to try again to change the Constitution, but encouraged the Government to impose its decision over the people without any hesitation.

And this is precisely what has occurred since 2008, having the country experienced and endured the following: *First,* a progressive political process of concentrating and controlling all public powers at the National Executive, which has been assured through the politically controlled National Assembly, and the political submission of the Judiciary to the Executive, having the latter been converted into one of its appendixes.[299] *Second,* a permanent process of enactment of the basic legislation of the country by means of laws issued by Decree-Laws of the President of the Republic, as delegated legislation, by-passing the process of sanctioning ordinary legislation.[300] *Third,* an indiscriminate process of nationalization, expropriation and confis-

---

297 See Allan R. Brewer-Carías, "El juez constitucional vs. la supremacía constitucional O de cómo la jurisdicción constitucional en Venezuela renunció a controlar la constitucionalidad del procedimiento seguido para la 'reforma constitucional' sancionada por la Asamblea Nacional el 2 de noviembre de 2007, antes de que fuera rechazada por el pueblo en el referendo del 2 de diciembre de 2007," in Eduardo Ferrer Mac Gregor y César de Jesús Molina Suárez (Coordinarores), *El juez constitucional en el Siglo XXI,* Universidad nacional Autónoma de México, Suprema Corte de Justicia de la Nación, México 2009, Tomo I, pp. 385-435.

298 See Allan R. Brewer-Carías, "La proyectada reforma constitucional de 2007, rechazada por el poder constituyente originario", in *Anuario de Derecho Público 2007,* Año 1, Instituto de Estudios de Derecho Público de la Universidad Monteávila, Caracas 2008, pp. 17-65. According to information from the National Electoral Council on Dec. 2, 2007, of 16,109,664 registered voters, only 9,002,439 voted (44.11% abstention); of voters, 4,504,354 rejected the proposal (50.70%). This means that there were only 4,379,392 votes to approve the proposal (49.29%), so only 28% of registered voters voted for the approval.

299 See Allan R. Brewer-Carías, "La justicia sometida al poder [La ausencia de independencia y autonomía de los jueces en Venezuela por la interminable emergencia del Poder Judicial (1999-2006)]" en *Cuestiones Internacionales. Anuario Jurídico Villanueva 2007,* Centro Universitario Villanueva, Marcial Pons, Madrid 2007, pp. 25-57

300 See Lolymar Hernández Camargo, "Límites del poder ejecutivo en el ejercicio de la habilitación legislativa: Imposibilidad de establecer el contenido de la reforma constitucional rechazada vía habilitación legislativa," in *Revista de Derecho Público* 115 *(Estudios sobre los Decretos Leyes),* Editorial Jurídica Venezolana, Caracas 2008, pp. 51ff.; Jorge Kiriakidis, "Bre-

cation of private industries, private assets and private properties, that have been implemented without guaranteeing the right to just compensation.[301] And *fourth*, a constant process of constitutional "mutations" made through decisions issued by the Constitutional Chamber of the Supreme Tribunal of Justice, by means of constitutional interpretations, following the government's will.[302]

The result of such processes have been that absolutely all the previous mentioned general trends and basic purposes of the rejected 2007 Constitutional Reform Draft were in fact implemented in the country, in open contempt of the Constitution and of the popular will, originating the current deconstitucionalization process of the State.

That process, as already mentioned, began in 2006 with the creation of the Communal Councils,[303] and particularly since 2007, with the creation of the Central Planning Commission in violation of the economic freedom established in the Con-

---

ves reflexiones en torno a los 26 Decretos-Ley de julio-agosto de 2008, y la consulta popular refrendaría de diciembre de 2007," in *id.*, pp. 57ff.; José Vicente Haro García, "Los recientes intentos de reforma constitucional o de cómo se está tratando de establecer una dictadura socialista con apariencia de legalidad (A propósito del proyecto de reforma constitucional de 2007 y los 26 decretos leyes del 31 de julio de 2008 que tratan de imponerla)," in *id.*, pp. 63ff.; Ana Cristina Nuñez Machado, "Los 26 nuevos Decretos-Leyes y los principios que regulan la intervención del Estado en la actividad económica de los particulares," in *id.*, pp. 215-20; Aurilivi Linares Martínez, "Notas sobre el uso del poder de legislar por decreto por parte del Presidente venezolano," in *id.*, pp. 79-89; Carlos Luis Carrillo Artiles, "La paradójica situación de los Decretos Leyes Orgánicos frente a la Ingeniería Constitucional de 1999," in *id.*, pp. 93-100; Freddy J. Orlando S., "El "paquetazo," un conjunto de leyes que conculcan derechos y amparan injusticias," in *id.*, pp. 101-104

301 See Antonio Canova González, Luis Alfonso Herrera Orellana, and Karina Anzola Spadaro, *¿Expropiaciones o vías de hecho? (La degradación continuada del derecho fundamental de propiedad en la Venezuela actual*," Funeda, Universidad Católica Andrés Bello, Caracas 2009.

302 See Allan R. Brewer-Carías, "El juez constitucional al servicio del autoritarismo y la ilegítima mutación de la Constitución: el caso de la Sala Constitucional del Tribunal Supremo de Justicia de Venezuela (1999-2009)", en *Revista de Administración Pública*, N° 180, Madrid 2009, pp. 383-418; "La fraudulenta mutación de la Constitución en Venezuela, o de cómo el juez constitucional usurpa el poder constituyente originario,", en *Anuario de Derecho Público*, Centro de Estudios de Derecho Público de la Universidad Monteávila, Año 2, Caracas 2009, pp. 23-65; José Vicente haro, "La mutación de la Constitución 'Bolivariana',", in Gonzalo Pérez Salazar and Luis Petit Guerra, *Los retos del derecho procesal constitucional en Latinoamérica, I Congreso Internacional de Derecho Procesal Constitucional, 19 y 20 Octubre de 2011*, Vol I, Universidad Monteávila Funeda, Caracas 2011, pp. 93-141.

303 *Ley de Consejos Comunales, Gaceta Oficial, Extra.* 5.806, of Apr. 10, 2006. This statute was replaced by Ley Orgánica de los Consejos Comunales. See *Gaceta Oficial* N° 39.335, Dec. 28, 2009. See Allan R. Brewer-Carías, "El inicio de la desmunicipalización en Venezuela: La organización del poder popular para eliminar la descentralización, la democracia representativa y la participación a nivel local," in *AIDA, Revista de la Asociación Internacional de Derecho Administrativo*, Universidad Nacional Autónoma de México, Asociación Internacional de Derecho Administrativo, Mexico City 2007, 49-67

stitution,[304] leading to the approval of the 2007–13 Economic and Social Development National Plan, in which it is expressly provided, contrary to the pluralistic foundation of the Constitution, that the "planning, production and distribution system [must be] oriented towards socialism," being "the relevant matter" of the economic system the progressive development of "social property of the production means."

Subsequently, since 2008, by means of other Laws and Decree Laws, the State assumed all powers in order to control farming, livestock, fishing, and aquaculture, and in particular, the production of food,[305] allowing the State to directly assume the distribution and commercialization of all goods, and the occupation of private industries without compensation.[306] The same year 2008, the Law regulating the Promotion and Development of the Popular Economic System was sanctioned following the "socialist model,"[307] establishing a "socio-productive communal model," with

---

304 Decree Law N° 5,841 was enacted on June 12, 2007, *Gaceta Oficial* N° 5.841, Extra., of June 22, 2007. See Allan R. Brewer-Carías, "Comentarios sobre la inconstitucional creación de la Comisión Central de Planificación, centralizada y obligatoria," in *Revista de Derecho Público* 110, Editorial Jurídica Venezolana, Caracas 2007, pp. 79-89; Luis A. Herrera Orellana, "Los Decretos-Leyes de 30 de julio de 2008 y la Comisión Central de Planificación: Instrumentos para la progresiva abolición del sistema político y del sistema económico previstos en la Constitución de 1999," in *Revista de Derecho Público* 115, *(Estudios sobre los Decretos Leyes)*, Editorial Jurídica Venezolana, Caracas 2008, pp. 221-32

305 Decree Law on the Organic Law on Farming and Food Security and Sovereignty. *Gaceta Oficial* N° 5.889, Extra., July 31, 2008. See José Ignacio Hernández G., "Planificación y soberanía alimentaria," in *Revista de Derecho Público* 115, *(Estudios sobre los Decretos Leyes)*, Editorial Jurídica Venezolana, Caracas 2008, pp. 389-94; Juan Domingo Alfonso Paradisi, "La constitución económica establecida en la Constitución de 1999, el sistema de economía social de mercado y el decreto 6.071 con rango, valor y fuerza de Ley Orgánica de seguridad y soberanía agroalimentaria," in *id.*, pp. 395-415; Gustavo A. Grau Fortoul, "La participación del sector privado en la producción de alimentos, como elemento esencial para poder alcanzar la seguridad alimentaria (Aproximación al tratamiento de la cuestión, tanto en la Constitución de 1999 como en la novísima Ley Orgánica de soberanía y seguridad alimentaria)," in *id.*, pp. 417-24.

306 See Carlos García Soto, "Notas sobre la expansión del ámbito de la declaratoria de utilidad pública o interés social en la expropiación," in *Revista de Derecho Público* 115, *(Estudios sobre los Decretos Leyes)*, Editorial Jurídica Venezolana, Caracas 2008, pp. 149-51; Antonio Canova González, Luis Alfonso Herrera Orellana, and Karina Anzola Spadaro, *¿Expropiaciones o vías de hecho? (La degradación continuada del derecho fundamental de propiedad en la Venezuela actual,"* Funeda, Universidad Católica Andrés Bello, Caracas 2009.

307 Decree Law, N° 6,130 of June 3, 2008,. *Gaceta Oficial* N° 5.890, Extra., July 31, 2008. See Jesús María Alvarado Andrade, "La desaparición del bolívar como moneda de curso legal (Notas críticas al inconstitucional Decreto N° 6.130, con rango, valor y fuerza de la ley para el fomento y desarrollo de la economía comunal, de fecha 3 de junio de 2008," in *Revista de Derecho Público* 115, *(Estudios sobre los Decretos Leyes)*, Editorial Jurídica Venezolana, Caracas 2008, pp. 313-20.

different socio-productive organizations; and the general law on matters of Consumer and User Protection was reformed with the same openly socialist orientation.[308]

These Laws extended the state control powers to the point of establishing the possibility of confiscating private industries and services by means of their takeover and occupation only through administrative decisions,[309] also violating the Constitution that on the contrary requires for such actions judicial participation. Accordingly, since 2008, the process of State appropriation of private assets has been systematically applied in the country, with no possibility at all for any judicial surveillance.

All of these "constitutional reforms" adopted by means of ordinary legislation, have also distorted and dislocated the federal form of government by centralizing the power assigned to the states, in some cases creating national administrative entities in order to assume such attributions, and authorizing the President of the Republic to interfere in regional and local affairs; and also, by voiding the states and municipal powers forcing them to compulsory transfer their competency to the newly created communal councils as local non representative institutions controlled by the central power.[310] These reforms were complemented with the approval in 2010 of the Law on the Federal Council of Government,[311] providing the means to force the states and municipalities to such transfers of their constitutional attributions.

The last set of legislation implementing the rejected Constitutional Reform Draft of 2007, was approved two years ago, in December 2010, by formally creating the "Communal State" framework as a Socialist or Communist State, not in substitution

---

308   Decree Law N° 6,092 enacting the Access to Goods and Services Persons Defense Law. *Gaceta Oficial* N° 5,889 Extra of July 31, 2008; José Gregorio Silva, "Disposiciones sobre el Decreto-Ley para la defensa de las personas en el acceso a bienes y servicios," in *id.*, pp. 277-79; Carlos Simón Bello Rengifo, "Decreto N° 6.092 con rango, valor y fuerza de la ley para la defensa de las personas en el acceso a los bienes y servicios (Referencias a problemas de imputación)," in *id.*, pp. 281-305; Alfredo Morles Hernández, "El nuevo modelo económico del socialismo del siglo XXI y su reflejo en el contrato de adhesión," in *id.*, pp. 229-32.

309   See Juan Domingo Alfonso Paradisi, "Comentarios en cuanto a los procedimientos administrativos establecidos en el Decreto N° 6.092 con rango, valor y fuerza de Ley para la defensa de las personas en el acceso a los bienes y servicios," in *Revista de Derecho Público* 115, *(Estudios sobre los Decretos Leyes)*, Editorial Jurídica Venezolana, Caracas 2008, pp. 245-60; Karina Anzola Spadaro, "El carácter autónomo de las 'medidas preventivas' contempladas en el artículo 111 del Decreto-Ley para la defensa de las personas en el acceso a los bienes y servicios," in *id.*, pp. 271-76. See, in general, Antonio Canova González, Luis Alfonso Herrera Orellana, and Karina Anzola Spadaro, *¿Expropiaciones o vías de hecho? (La degradación continuada del derecho fundamental de propiedad en la Venezuela actual*," Funeda, Universidad Católica Andrés Bello, Caracas 2009

310   See Manuel Rachadell, *"La centralización del poder en el Estado federal descentralizado,"* in Revista de Derecho Público, 115, *(Estudios sobre los Decretos Leyes)*, Editorial Jurídica Venezolana, Caracas 2008, pp. 111-131.

311   See *Ley Orgánica del Consejo Federal de Gobierno, Gaceta Oficial* N° 5.963 Extra. of Feb. 22, 2010.

of the Constitutional Decentralized State as was intended in 2007, but parallel to it, and to its existing National, State, Municipal levels of government. [312]

For such purposes, five important and very unconstitutional Organic Laws were sanctioned, referred to "the Popular Power;" "the Communes;" "the Communal Economic System;" "the Public and Communal Planning;" and "the Social Comptrollership; [313] and three important statutes were reformed in the same framework of organizing the Communal State:[314] the Organic Law of Municipal Public Power, the Law on State Councils for Public Policy Planning and Coordination, and of the Law on Local Council Public Planning. [315]

The main purpose of these Laws on the Communal State, is to organized it, based in the "Communes" as its fundamental unit, seeking to supplant in a unconstitutional way the municipalities that are the ones conceived in the Constitution as the "primary autonomous political units of the national organization" (Art. 168). These new Communes, on the contrary, are conceived without any autonomy, being directly controlled by a Ministry of the National Executive, so instead of being instruments for participation and decentralization, its organization in a centralized system of entities tightly controlled by the National Executive, is conceived to be the instrument for the imposition of a unique official socialist doctrine of the government, contrary to any sort of pluralism, so that all those that are not socialist are automatically discriminated and excluded.

These Laws on the Communal State are particularly important regarding the economic communal system created, ignoring the mixed economic system established in the Constitution, and establishing in parallel a system based only on "socialist productive model"[316] only based as it is expressly defined in the Law (art. 3.2) - I quote - , as a "production model based on *social property*, oriented towards the *elimination of the social division of work* that appertains to the capitalist model," and based on the principle of the *reinvestment of social surplus*" (art. 6.12).

It is enough to read carefully this legal definition to understand that what has been legally imposed in Venezuela, is simply a "communist system," [317] being such legal definition nothing else than the copying of isolated phrases of a perhaps forgot-

---

312 See Gustavo Linares Benzo, "Sólo un Poder Público más. El Poder Popular en la reforma del 2007," in *Revista de Derecho Público* 112 *(Estudios sobre la reforma constitucional)*, Editorial Jurídica Venezolana, Caracas 2007, pp. 102-105; Arturo Peraza, "Reforma, Democracia participativa y Poder Popular," in *id.*, pp. 107-13.

313 See *Gaceta Oficial* N° 6.011 Extra. Dec. 21, 2010.

314 See on all these organic laws, Allan R. Brewer-Carías (Coord.) *et al.*, *Leyes Orgánicas sobre el Poder Popular y el Estado Comunal*, Editorial Jurídica Venezolana, Caracas 2011, 719 pp.

315 See *Gaceta Oficial* N° 6.015 Extra. Of Dec. 28, 2010.

316 Organic Law of the Communal Economic System .See *Gaceta Oficial* N° 6.011 Extra. Dec 21, 2010.

317 See Allan R Brewer-Carías, "Sobre la Ley Orgánica del Sistema Económico Comunal o de cómo se implanta en Venezuela un sistema económico comunista sin reformar la Constitución," in *Revista de Derecho Público*, N° 124, (octubre-diciembre 2010), Editorial Jurídica Venezolana, Caracas 2010, pp. 102-109

ten old manual of a failed communist revolution using the same words that Karl Marx and Friedrich Engels wrote 150 years ago (1845-1846) in their book on *The German Ideology.*[318] In that book they used perhaps for the first time, the word "communism," and they defined the "communist society"[319] precisely by using the three phrases copied in the aforementioned article of the Law: *social property of production means, elimination of social division of work*, and *social reinvestment of surplus*.

All these statutes were approved in just one session of the Legislative Assembly after the late President, himself, confessed a few months earlier, that his supposedly "Bolivarian revolution," in fact was not other than the historically failed "Marxist revolution," but in this case led by a president who -he said- never even read Marx's writings.[320] Three months after this presidential announcement, the governmental United Socialist Party of which the former President used to preside, adopted in its First Extraordinary Congress a "Declaration of Principles" in which it officially declared itself as a "Marxist," "Anti-imperialist" and "Anti-capitalist" party; establishing that its actions are based on "scientific socialism" and on the "inputs of Marxism as a philosophy of praxis," in order to substitute the "Capitalist Bourgeois State" with a "Socialist State" based on the Popular Power and the socialization of the means of production.[321]

This is, my friends, the government and the State that the former President Chávez left as his most valuable institutional legacy when he died, with which the President elected in April 2013 had to deal with; a State and a political system that were imposed in an authoritarian way upon the Venezuelan people without reforming their Constitution, only through ordinary legislation, defrauding the popular will expressed in the December 2, 2007 referendum,[322] and, above all, for which nobody in the country have ever voted for, nor approved.

---

318 See in Karl Marx and Frederich Engels, "The German Ideology," in *Collective Works*, Vol. 5, International Publishers, New York 1976, p. 47. Véanse además los textos pertinentes en http://www.educa.madrid.org/cms_tools/files/0a24636f-764c-4e03-9c1d-6722e2ee60d7/Texto%20Marx%20y%20Engels.pdf

319 The book was written between 1845 and 1846. The "Communist Manifest" was published in February 1848.

320 In his annual speech before the National Assembly on Jan. 15, 2010, in which Chávez declared to have "assumed Marxism," he also confessed that he had never read Marx's works. See María Lilibeth Da Corte, "Por primera vez asumo el marxismo," in *El Universal*, Caracas Jan. 16, 2010, http://www.eluniversal.com/2010/01/16/pol_art_por-primera-vez-asu_1726209.shtml.

321 See "Declaración de Principios, I Congreso Extraordinario del Partido Socialista Unido de Venezuela," Apr. 23, 2010, at http://psuv.org.ve/files/tcdocumentos/Declaracion-de-principios-PSUV.pdf

322 The definitive voting figures in such referendum have never been informed to the country by the government controlled National Electoral Council. See Allan R. Brewer-Carías, "Estudio sobre la propuesta de Reforma Constitucional para establecer un estado socialista, centralizado y militarista (Análisis del anteproyecto presidencial, Agosto de 2007)," *Cadernos da Escola de Direito e Relações Internacionais da UniBrasil* 7, Curitiba 2007, pp. 265-308. See on

This means that being the "Communal State" created and organized in parallel to the Constitutional State, we Venezuelans, including the next President to be elected, are going to deal not only with one State organization, but with two State organizations that are functioning in parallel in the same national territory: On the one hand, a Socialist State based on the supposed direct exercise of sovereignty by the people through Citizens Assemblies, Communes and non elected Communal Councils; and on the other hand, the Constitutional State, based on representative democratic principles exercised through elected representatives by universal suffrage, but with a very distorted system of separation of powers.

These parallel systems of two States were conceived, not only in a way contrary to the provisions of the Constitution, but in a way designed to allow for the Socialist or Communal State to take control and gradually strangle the Constitutional State, by progressively emptying its powers and competencies. For such purpose the Organic Law of the Popular Power simply provides that all organs of the Constitutional State are subjected to the mandates of the organizations of Communal State, establishing for such purpose a "new" principle of government, the so-called in the Law as the principle of "govern obeying" (*gobernar obedeciendo*), which is no other than obeying the wishes of the central government[323] through the controlled organization of the Communal State. This is, of course, again, an unconstitutional limitation to the political autonomy of the elected bodies of the Constitutional State such as the National Assembly itself, the States' Governors and the Legislative Councils, as well as the Mayors and the Municipal Councils, upon which ultimately is imposed an obligation to obey any provision made to enforce the socialist doctrine, through the organization of a non elected Communes and Communal Council currently controlled by the Government and the ruling party.

This is the entire framework of the "Communal State" created in parallel to the Constitutional State that the new government will face,[324] that was imposed by the government having the assurance that no judicial review would ever be exercised regarding the statutes creating it, due to the very strict and tight political control exercised by the Executive upon the Supreme Tribunal.

---

the 2007 constitutional reforms proposals, Allan R. Brewer-Carías, *Hacia la consolidación de un Estado socialista, centralizado, policial y militarista. Comentarios sobre el sentido y alcance de las propuestas de reforma constitucional 2007,* Editorial Jurídica Venezolana, Caracas 2007; *La reforma constitucional de 2007 (Comentarios al proyecto inconstitucionalmente sancionado por la Asamblea Nacional el 2 de noviembre de 2007),* Editorial Jurídica Venezolana, Caracas 2007.

323   Article 24 of the Law establishes the following principle: "Proceedings of the bodies and entities of Public Power. All organs, entities and agencies of Public Power will govern their actions by the principle of "govern obeying", in relation to the mandates of the people and organizations of Popular Power, according to the provisions in the Constitution of the Republic and the laws."

324   See Allan R. Brewer-Carías, *Reforma constitucional y fraude a la Constitución (1999-2009),* Academia de Ciencias Políticas y Sociales, Caracas 2009; *Dismantling Democracy. The Chávez Authoritarian Experiment,* Cambridge University Press, New York 2010.

And it has been, because of this absence of an autonomous and independent Supreme Tribunal that in parallel to the deconstitutionalization of the Constitutional State, during the past decade the government has openly distorted the must essential pillar of democracy and of the Constitutional State, which is the principle of separation of powers that has lost all value in Venezuela.

That means that the new President to be elected was going to face a system of government where there is was no separation of powers, having that principle been completely demolished,[325] with the result that all the powers of the State were entirely controlled by the former President, within a grid of loyalties that he personally constructed -which again, in my opinion, nobody could really inherit-, including the Legislative and the Judicial Power, as well as the Public Prosecutor Office, the General Comptrollership Office, the People's Defendant and the National Electoral Council (Citizens and Electoral Powers). This, of course, was another of the most complicated political problem and situation that all Venezuelans inherited from the late President.

The problem was highlighted by the Inter American Commission on Human Rights in its 2009 *Annual Report*, when after analyzing the situation of human rights in Venezuela and the institutional deterioration of the country, said that it "reveals the absence of due separation of and independence between the branches of government in Venezuela."[326] This situation, on the other hand, is the one that explains why the President of the Supreme Tribunal of Justice, simply exclaimed in a Press Conference, the same year, that "the separation of powers weakens the State" and that such principle "has to be reformed."[327]

Perhaps the assertion of the President of the Supreme Tribunal was made in order to support what in August 2008 the late President Chávez when he affirmed: "*I am the Law ... I am the State,*"[328] (*Yo soy la Ley... Yo soy el Estado*) when he announced that despite the general opposition against his abusive use of delegate legislation, he was going to enforce forty statutes through Decree Laws, threatening to persecute all those that could oppose him. And this was not the first time he used such expression; also in 2001, when he approved the first forty eight executive De-

---

325 See Allan R. Brewer-Carías, "The Principle of separation of Powers and the Authoritarian Government in Venezuela", en *Duquesne Law Review*, Volume 47, Spring 2009, Pittsburgh, pp. 813-838.

326 See IACHR, *2009 Annual Report*, para. 472, available at http://www.cidh.oas.org/annualrep/2009eng/Chap.IV.f.eng.htm

327 See in Juan Francisco Alonso, "La división de poderes debilita al estado. La presidenta del TSJ [Luisa Estela Morales] afirma que la Constitución hay que reformarla," *El Universal*, Caracas December 5, 2009, available at http://www.eluniversal.com/2009/12/05/pol_art_mo-ra-les:-la-divisio_1683109.shtml. The complete text is available at http://www.tsj.gov.ve/informacion/notasde prensa/notasdeprensa.asp?codigo=7342

328 "*Yo soy la Ley..., Yo soy el Estado!!*" See the quotation in the Blog of Gustavo Coronel, *Las Armas de Coronel*, October 15, 2008, available at: http://lasarmasdecoro-nel.blogspot.com/2008/10/yo-soy-la-leyyo-soy-el-estado.html

cree Laws, he affirmed, although in a different way: *"La Ley soy yo... El Estado soy yo."*[329]

I am sure that to hear these expressions that as we know were attributed to Louis XIV although he never expressed them in such a way, is enough to realize and understand the tragic institutional legacy left by the former President, which the country was facing, precisely characterized by a complete lack of separation of powers and, consequently, of a democratic regime, a situation that was achieved through a permanent and subsequent process of defrauding or perverting the Constitution, and the rule of law.

Consequently, independently of the results of the April 2013 Presidential election, the fact is that the elected President had to face such institutional situation that for sure, was to be prolonged itself well beyond the electoral exercise.

---

329 *"La ley soy yo. El Estado soy yo"*. See in *El Universal,* Caracas December 4, 2001, pp. 1,1 and 2,1.

PART SIXTH
REFLECTIONS ON THE ORIGINS OF CONSTITUTIONALISM IN VENEZUELA AT THE BEGINNING OF THE 19TH CENTURY

CHAPTER XXIX
REFLECTIONS ON THE "*INTERESTING OFFICIAL DOCUMENTS RELATING TO THE UNITED PROVINCES OF VENEZUELA,*" PUBLISHED IN LONDON IN 1812

(2012)

This Chapter has its origin in the essay I wrote for the Lecture I gave on the "The Connection Between the United States Independence and the Hispanic American Independence Movement, and the Role Played by some Key Books Published at the beginning of the Xix Century," at the Law Library of Congress, Mumford Room, Washington D.C., on November 22nd, 2011, on the occasion of the Bicentenary of the publication of the book: *Interesting Official Documents Relating to the United Provinces of Venezuela*, London 1812. The text was later rewritten and published as the "General Introduction" of the book *Constitutional Documents of the Independence*, with the facsimile edition of the book *Constitutional Documents of the Independence1811. Interesting Official Documents Relating to the United Provinces of Venezuela*, London 1812, Editorial Jurídica Venezolana, Bilingual Edition, Caracas 2012, pp. 59-299.

The most important written testimony of the first constitution-making process developed in modern times in Latin America two hundred years ago, as a consequence on the independence process of Venezuela in 1811, is a book published the following year (1812) in London titled: ***Interesting Official Documents Relating to the United Provinces of Venezuela***, containing the collection of the most important official constitutional documents and other political papers supporting the independence process and the establishment of the new State of the United Provinces of Venezuela. This is the book that for the first time is now here republished, and to which the comments of this General Introduction are directed.

It is a real masterpiece edition with many vignettes of good taste, "with a nice presentation and interesting content,"[1] reflecting the political and constitutional process that gave rise to a new modern State in Hispanic America, all produced even before the *Cortes Generales* of Spain sanctioned the modern Constitution of the Spanish Monarchy of Cádiz, of March 18, 1812.

This important book, although referred to Venezuela, nonetheless was not edited and published in Caracas where the political facts reported in had and were occurring. It was edited and published in London, but not only in English but in a unique bilingual Spanish-English edition, printed by W. Glidon, Rupert-Street, Haymarket, for various booksellers: Longman and Co. Paternoster-Row; Durlau, Soho-Square; Hartding, St. Jame's Street; and W. Mason, N° 6, Holywell Street, Strand, & c. & c.

The double text of all the documents contained in the book was set in a parallel way along its pages, having the Spanish text on even pages, and the English text on odd pages. In the upper party of its front page, a simplified title of the book was included, as: *Documentos interesantes relativos a Caracas / Interesting Documents relating to Caracas*; being included in the lower part of the page, an engraving of T. Wogeman with an allegory "of contemporary taste," which according to the description of Carlos Pi Sunyer, had "a female figure representing America, another figure that symbolizes the republic and that has a tablet on which is written the word 'Colombia' and a cherub with a roll of parchment with the title 'Constitution of Venezuela.'"[2] In fact, more that an vignette with an allegory, it really was the official "coat of arms" of the new independent and sovereign State which was formally adopted by the General Congress, and ordered to be included in the official Flag of the State.[3]

This extraordinary and very beautiful piece was intended to explain in English and Spanish in Europe, when the facts were happening, the reasons and motives of the political actions that since 1808 had taken place in Caracas or the independence of Venezuela, which eventually were the beginning of the independence of all Span-

---

1   See Carlos Pi Sunyer. *Patriotas Americanos en Londres (Miranda, Bello y otras figuras),* (Ed. y prólogo de Pedro Grases), Monteávila Editores, Caracas 1978, p. 211

2   See Carlos Pi Sunyer. *Patriotas Americanos en Londres (Miranda, Bello y otras figuras),* (Ed. y prólogo de Pedro Grases), Monteávila Editores, Caracas 1978, p. 211

3   On July 5th, 1811, the same day of the Declaration of Independence, the General Congress of Venezuela appointed a Commission composed by Francisco de Miranda, Lino de Clemente and José de Satta y Bussy, in order to design the Flag of the new sovereign and independent State. The proposal was submitted and approved on July 9th, 1811, on a Flag with three colors: yellow, bleu and red disposed in nonequal strips, wider the first, less wiuder the second and less the third. On the yellow stripe, in its upper left side, a coat of arms was included with an Indian female figure sitting on a rock handling with his left hand an flagpole with a bonnet on the top, sourraunded by a few symbols of development: commerce, sciences, arts, an aligator and vegetales; in her back an inscription: "Venezuela Libre," an on her feets, a ribbon with the word "Colombia," equivalent at that time to "America." The Flag was officially hoisted for the first time on July 14th 1811. See "Evolución histórica de la Bandera Nacional," available at: http://www.efemeridesvenezolanas.com:80/html/evolucion.htm

ish America from Spain. Those reasons were specifically summarized in the text of the "Declaration (*Manifiesto*) made to the World by the Confederation of Venezuela in South America," which is included in the book, dated July 30, 1811, explaining "reasons on which she has founded her Absolute Independence of Spain, and of every other Foreign Power whatever." In addition, in the book, in addition to the initial *Preliminary Remarks* that forwarded the documents, effectively contained the most important documents adopted and sanctioned by the General Congress of the Confederation of Venezuela, namely some texts of the Declarations of the Rights of the People of July 1st, 1811; the Declaration of Independence of July 5th, 1811, and the Federal Constitution of the United Provinces of Venezuela of December 21st, 1811. The General Congress that approved all those texts was the first Constituent Assembly convened in Hispanic America, integrated by elected deputies representing seven of the nine provinces of the General Captaincy of Venezuela. Such Congress, by declaring the independence of the Provinces from Spain, specifically denied all the Spanish authorities, not only those of the Colonies but those governing from Spain, in particular the Council of Regency of the Spanish Monarchy, and the very *Cortes Generales* of Cadiz themselves.[4] As reported by Juan Garrido Rovira, the 1811 Constituent Assembly:

> "assumed the challenge of the times and check marked the political-cultural ideals of the centuries, among others: Political independence; special consecration of the freedom of thought; separation of powers; suffrage, representation and participation of the citizens in the government; social fairness; consecration and respect of the rights and duties of the man; limitation and control of power; political and civil equality of free men; recognition and protection of the rights of the indigenous towns; prohibition of the traffic of slaves; popular, responsible and alternative government; autonomy of the judicial power on moral basis; the nation over the factions."[5]

The book refers, therefore, to the most important documents that could contribute, in 1812, to explain the situation of Venezuela in its struggle for the already declared independence from Spain. That is why in the book, particular importance have the texts of the *Declaration of Independence* of July 5th, 1811, containing "the solemn declaration that the General Congress of Venezuela made on the absolute independence of this part of Southern America;" of the *Constitution of the Confederation of States of Venezuela* of December 21st, 1811;[6] and of the already mentioned the "*Manifesto* that the Confederation of Venezuela in Southern America made to the World" dated July 30th, 1811, "made and ordered to be published by accord of the General Congress of the United Provinces of the Confederation" and signed in the "Federal Palace of Caracas" devoted to express the reasons on which

---

4   On the constitutional aspects of the process of independence of Venezuela since 1810. See Allan R. Brewer-Carías, *Historia Constitucional de Venezuela*, Tomo I, Editorial Alfa, Caracas 2008, pp. 195-278.

5   See Juan Garrido Rovira, *El Congreso Constituyente de Venezuela*, Bicentenario del 5 de julio de 1811, Universidad Monteávila, Caracas 2010, p.12.

6   See the text of these documents in Allan R. Brewer-Carías, *Las Constituciones de Venezuela*, Academia de Ciencias Políticas y Sociales, Caracas 2008, Tomo I, pp. 545-579.

"its absolute independence from Spain and any other foreign domination." All these documents -as was stated in the *Manifesto*- had the purpose of assure that "the Free Men and Fellows of our Destiny!" would give "an unbiased and disinterested glance" to what at that time was happening in Venezuela.[7]

Given the lack of literature in the English language reporting those facts of the independence process that had formally begun in Spanish America from the events occurred in Caracas, the book -as declared in the *Preliminary Remarks*- pursued to describe the situation in Venezuela, as the first Spanish province in the New World:

> "to break up the chains that bound it to the Mother Country after two years spent in vain efforts for reform and relief and after having suffered as many shames and indignities it could possibly stand, and has now at last proclaimed the sacred and incontestable right of every people to adopt the means most conducive for its national welfare and most effective to repel the attacks of the foreign enemy."

Towards that end, in the same *Preliminary Remarks* was expressed that "the emergency of the causes that compelled" the Provinces "to adopt this extreme measure appears in the *Manifesto* that was addressed to the World unbiased. It was also mentioned that "the justice of the views of its representatives, directed to the health of the constituency people, is clearly shown in the Constitution which was established for the formation and administration of the laws and shown as well in the result of its solemn declarations," stating that since the independence, "the inhabitants of Venezuela have seen, for the first time, their rights established and their liberties secured."

In short, the *Preliminary Observation* further stated that "in the documents that make up this volume, one shall find no less great principles nor less fair consequences than in the most celebrated actions of the *Cortes*, whose liberality and philanthropy is quite inferior to that of the Americans;" noting that "the example given by Venezuela to the rest of Spanish America" was "like the dawn of a clear sky." Consequently, the document expressed the wishes of the drafters that "hopefully, no sinister occurrence will delay or prevent the progress" of the Spanish American cause of independence.

Nonetheless, in this case, the political ironies of the life of nations would have it that a sinister occurrence or a unfortunate events did in fact took place, so tragically, by the time the book describing the process of independence of Venezuela to whom the *Interesting Official Documents* referred actually began to circulate in England, the government of the independent Republic was already a thing of the past. This provoked that after its edition was completed, eventually the book was completely forgotten at least for a century, when some attention was given to one of its copies "discovered" at the beginning of the twentieth century, by a member of the Academy of History of Venezuela who took it to Caracas. The fact is that, in any event,

---

7   In the citations that we make of the documents, the following abbreviations are used: **OP**: Preliminaries, **AI**: Act of Independence of July 5, 1811, **M**: *Manifesto* made to the World by the Confederation of Venezuela in South America, on July 30, 1811.

since 1812 the book edited with such care by the agents of the new Republic became an obsolete text, and was never reprinted.

This 2011 edition, consequently, is the first reprint ever made in two centuries of this book;[8] a propitious mean to celebrate not only the Bicentenary of its publication, but the Bicentenary of the facts recorded in it, that is, the Independence of Venezuela and the beginning of the Independence process of all Hispanic America.

I.   THE BACKGROUND OF THE 1811 INDEPENDENCE PROCESS OF VENEZUELA: THE POLITICAL CRISIS OF SPAIN SINCE 1808

Of all Latin American countries, as already mentioned, Venezuela was the first one to declare its independence from Spain in 1811, subsequently establishing a new State, with a federal form of government, the first of its kind after the one established three decades before in the United States of America, by uniting seven colonial Provinces that were part of the General Captaincy of Venezuela.

Within the colonial territorial organization of Spanish America, the general captaincies were territorial division commonly used for the organization of less important provinces, outside the jurisdiction of the Viceroyalties in which on the contrary were included the rich and more important provinces.[9] Consequently, the Spanish American revolution started in the new Continent, not in the opulent and illustrated capitals of the Viceroyalties, but in the poor and marginal Province of Caracas, which capital, the city of Caracas, was also the capital of the General Captaincy; at the same time that in the Spanish Peninsula various *de facto* local governments were in the process of fighting a bloody war of independence against the French that had invaded the territory; being such situation among the main reasons that caused the political uprising in the other side of the Atlantic. Those facts were known and their news reflecting "the hopeless state of Spain" circulates in the provinces at the time the French entered Andalusia; to which was added "the dread of falling into the hands of the same usurpers," all of which as pointed out in the *Preliminary Remarks* of the book,

> "were the chief causes of the Americans resolving no longer to trust to the administration of their European governors, conceiving their own affairs more secure when confided to their own assemblies or Juntas, whom they created after the manner of the Provinces of Spain."

In those years of the early nineteenth century, the Revolution had already ended in France after the Terror period, and the Republic been overshadowed and hijacked

---

8   The text of the documentos, Orly in their Spanish version were published in the book *La Constitución Federal de Venezuela de 1811 y documentos afines*, Academia Nacional de la Historia, Caracas 1959.

9   In the area of the Caribbean there were two Viceroyalties: The Viceroyalty of Nueva España – México – and the Viceroyalty of Nueva Granada – Colombia –. The Provinces of the General Captaincy of Venezuela not only were not politically subjected to any of those Viceroyalties, but lacking a uniform political and judicial government were subjected to two different *Audiencias,* which were the highest Colonial governmental bodies: the central provinces to the *Audiencia* of Santo Domingo, the oldest of all in Hispanic America; and the occidental provinces, those located in the Andes region, to the *Audiencia* of Santa Fe.

by a new authoritarian regime that made Napoleon Bonaparte in 1802 a Consul for life, proclaiming him, in 1804, Emperor for life, of course, according to the hereditary principle, suppressing in 1808 the very republic itself. All Europe was threatened and much of it was occupied or controlled by the Emperor, who was conducting a state that was at war. Spain, on the border, did not escape the grips of Napoleon and his continental diplomacy game.[10] In such context, and following the Treaty of Fontainebleau signed on October 27, 1807 by the representatives of the Spanish Crown and the Napoleonic Empire, the two countries agreed on the distribution of Portugal, whose princes had fled to Brazil. In a secret clause of the Treaty, the grant of the territory of the Algarve -under hereditary title- to Manuel Godoy, the favorite minister of Charles IV, was included, as well as the invasion of Portugal by the Napoleonic troops through Spain.

But the truth is that ten days before the signing of the Treaty, Napoleon's troops were already in Spain and had crossed the Portugal border, which meant that by March 1808, more than 100,000 men of Napoleon's armies were already in Spain. At the same time, King Charles IV had known of his son Ferdinand's plot to seize him from the throne (and snatch Godoy), for which presumably the King had forgiven him. On the other hand, since February 1808, there was already a regent in Portugal (*Junot*), who was acting on behalf of the Emperor, whereby the Treaty of Fontainebleau and the distribution of Portugal's territory, had become invalid. Napoleon initially thought that the Spanish royal family would follow the example of that of Portugal,[11] and would fly to Cadiz and thence to America, but eventually changed his mind, imposing the delivery to France of all the territory of Spain north of the Ebro, including the Pyrenees, as a condition for the distribution of the middle Portuguese Kingdom to Spain.

---

10   See Joseph Fontana, *La crisis del antiguo Régimen 1808–1833,* Barcelona 1992.

11   Before the French troops (which since November 1807 had already invaded Spain) arrived at the Portugal border, Prince John of Braganza (who was regent of the kingdom of Portugal due to the illness of his mother Queen Mary) and his Court took shelter in Brazil, settling the royal government at Rio de Janeiro on March 1808. Eight years later -in 1816- Prince John took the Crown of the United Kingdom of Portugal, Brazil and Algaves (with its capital in Rio de Janeiro) as John VI. On the peninsula, Portugal was governed by a Regency Council that was controlled by the commander of the British forces. Once Napoleon was defeated in Europe, John VI returned to Portugal leaving his son Peter as regent for Brazil. Although the Cortes reinstated the territory of Brazil to its previous status and required from the Regent Pedro to return to the Peninsula, he -like the Portuguese Cortes- also convened a Constituent Assembly in Brazil proclaiming Brazil's independence on September 1822 and where, on October 12 that year, he was proclaimed Emperor of Brazil (as Peter I of Braganza and Borbon). In 1824, the Imperial Constitution of Brazil was passed. Two years later, in 1826, the Brazilian Emperor returned to Portugal following the death of his father, John VI, to assume the Portuguese kingdom as Peter IV, although for a short time. See Felix A. Montilla Zavalía, "La experiencia monárquica americana: Brasil y México", en *Debates de Actualidad*, Asociación argentina de derecho constitucional, Año XXIII, N° 199, enero/abril 2008, pp. 52 ss.

The presence of French troops in Spain and the concentration of Spanish troops in Aranjuez led to all sorts of rumors, including the mentioned possible flight of the Monarch to Andalusia and the Americas, which the King had discarded. However, such rumors had to be clarified by the monarch who announced in a proclamation to the Spanish subjects that the concentration of troops in Aranjuez neither had to defend his person nor accompany him on a journey "that your malice has made you assume as one required." The concentration of troops in Aranjuez, however, was truly a part of an ongoing conspiracy against the government of Godoy, lead, among others, by the very Prince of Asturias –Ferdinand, future Ferdinand VII- who sought also the abdication of his father -Charles IV-, with the complicity of French agents and the help of the popular hatred that had developed against Godoy, due to the French occupation of the kingdom.

On the night of March 18, 1808 riots erupted in Aranjuez,[12] originating a popular revolt that led to the arrest of Godoy and the destruction of his properties by the mob and, finally, and to the abdication of Charles IV in his son Ferdinand as was announced on March 19, 1808 as part of his intrigues. Nonetheless, on the same night Charles IV was already telling his servants that he had not abdicated, and two days later, on March 21, 1808, he regretted his abdication stating in a proclamation that:

> "I contest and declare that everything stated on my decree of March 19 abdicating the crown on my son, was forced to prevent greater evils and bloodshed of my dear subjects and, therefore, is of no value."

He also wrote to Napoleon, clarifying the situation, saying:

> "I did not yield on my son. I did it by force of circumstances, when the thunder of guns and the cries of the revolted garrison made me recognize the need to choose life or death, since the latter would have been followed by that of the queen."

Despite these declarations, Charles IV would not only ever recover the crown, but three days later, Ferdinand VII would enter Madrid triumphantly, initiating a short-days reign in which one of his first decrees was to order the requisition of Godoy's assets, originating a popular rage against those assets that overturned throughout the Kingdom. But within hours of the arrival of the new King in Madrid, on March 23, 1808, the General Joachim Murat, Lieutenant General of the French troops in Spain also arrived in the city, ordering for Godoy to be saved from a definite lynching, ignoring the very presence of the new King in the city that was already occupied by the French. Moreover, under the command of Murat the former King Charles IV and his family were transferred, on April 9, 1808 to El Escorial, and then further to Bayonne, on April 30, 1808, where Napoleon awaited for them. At Bayonne, Ferndinand VII had already arrived on April 20, and also did the very Minister Godoy on April 26, 1808. All of them had turned to the Emperor in pursue

---

12 See an account of the March events in Madrid and Aranjuez and the entire documents concerning the abdication of Charles IV in J.F. Blanco y R. Azpúrua, *Documentos para la Historia de la Vida Pública del Libertador...*, op. cit., Tomo II, pp. 91 a 153.

of support and recognition, whereby Napoleon had become the referee of the Spanish monarchy political crisis.

While the kingdom was under his control, he decided to take it over following these subsequent path: First, on May 5, 1808, he obtained a new abdication of Charles IV, this time, on behalf of Napoleon himself; second, on the next day, May 6, 1808 he made Ferdinand VII abdicate the crown in his father Charles IV,[13] without telling him what he had done just before; and third, by the signing of the Treaties of Bayonne, a few days later, on May 10, 1808, Charles IV and Ferdinand VII solemnly transferred all their rights to the Crown of Spain and the Indies to the Emperor Napoleon[14] "as the only one that -in the present state of things as they have become- can restore order" in exchange for asylum, pensions and property in France.[15] Besides, since May 25, 1808 Napoleon had also named Joachim Murat -Grand Duke of Berg and Cleves- as Lieutenant General of the Kingdom,[16] expressing to the Spanish people:

> "Your monarchy is old: My mission is intended to renew it: your institutions shall improve; and I will have you enjoy the benefits of a reform, without experiencing failures, unrests and commotions."

He promised, moreover, "a constitution that reconciles the holy and sovereign authority of the ruler with the liberties and privileges of the People."[17]

Consequently, the Emperor's brother -Joseph Bonaparte- was installed in Madrid as the new King of Spain, keeping the political forms through the granting of a council and issuing a statute known as the Constitution of Bayonne of July 1808. Said constitution, however, did not give any institutional stability to the Kingdom since before it was granted Spain had already begun, on May of 1808, its war of independence against France, in which local *de facto* governments had the key role, assuming the people's representation at the prompting of the people's initiatives.[18]

In fact, the factual abduction of the Spanish monarchs in France provoked a popular rebellion that exploded in Madrid on May 2, 1808, which generated bloody events due to the repression unleashed by the French garrison.[19] The Emperor vowed to avenge the dead Frenchmen, and without doubt, the seizure of the kingdom of Spain was part of that revenge. But what was avenged was the Spaniards that were killed in the tragic shootings of May 3. The Spanish people spread rebellion throughout all Spain; and what worked as the common denominator for it was the reaction against the French troops. Therefore, as the uprising became widespread

---

13   *Idem,* Tomo II, p. 133.

14   *Idem,* Tomo II, p. 142.

15   *Idem,* Tomo II, pp. 142 a 148

16   *Idem,* Tomo II, p. 153.

17   *Idem,* Tomo II, p. 154.

18   See A. Sacristán y Martínez, *Municipalidades de Castilla y León,* Madrid, 1981, p. 490

19   See F. Blanco y R. Azpúrua, *Documentos para la Historia de la Vida Pública del Libertador..., op. cit.,* Tomo II, p. 153.

in the towns and cities, Armament and Defense *Juntas* began to be spontaneously established during the war in all the capitals of the provinces, assuming the *de facto* power of the people. They were formed by the leading individuals of each locality, and were charged with the supreme direction of local affairs, and with the holding and organizing the resistance against the French. From here then the War of Independence broke out.

These *Juntas*, although composed of individuals nominated by popular acclamation, had as a common agenda to defend the monarchy symbolized in the person of Ferdinand VII, for which reason these committees always acted on behalf of the King. Nevertheless, the fact was that a political revolution developed, through which the absolutist system of government was replaced by popular, democratic and fully autonomous municipal system of *Juntas*.[20] These local *Juntas*, through delegates, joined in the formation of Provincial *Juntas*, representing the municipalities grouped in a particular territory; and at their turn, these Provincial Juntas, formed a Supreme or Central *Junta* that was established in Seville. In 1810, this *Junta Central* of Government of the Kingdom was the one that was forced to settle in Cádiz, in the extreme south of Andalucía, where it appointed a Council of Regency to govern the Realm, convening, at the same time, the elections of representatives of all the Spanish provinces in order to form the *Cortes Generales* (Parliament) for the purpose of drafting a new Constitution, which is known as the 1812 Cádiz Constitution.

The news about the occupation of Spanish territory by the armies of Napoleon and the adoption of the Constitution of Bayonne on July 6, officially became known in Caracas one month later, in August 15, 1808, when such facts were formally given to the Captain-General of Venezuela by royal decrees, among which was that the Royal Decree of proclamation of Ferdinand VII of April 20, 1808,[21] which was precisely opened at the meeting of the *Ayuntamiento* of Caracas of that day (July 15, 1808),[22] four months after it had been issued.

Of course, by that time -two months earlier, in May 1808- other serious events already mentioned had also taken place in the Spanish Peninsula, such as the abdication of the Crown by Ferdinand VII in his father and the transfer of the Crown by Charles IV to Napoleon. These events made the initial news entirely useless because, besides, a week before receiving them, as noted, Joseph Napoleon had proclaimed himself "King of the Spains and the Indies," and had decreed the Constitution of Bayonne on July 6, 1808. No wonder, therefore, the devastating political effects on Venezuela of the late news about the royal political disputes among father and son; the forced abdication of the throne by the violence of Napoleon; and the occupation of Spanish territory by the Emperor's armies; all of which became worse due to the fact that the late knowledge of these news had been because they were

---

20   See O. C. Stoetzer, *Las Raíces Escolásticas de la Emancipación de la América Española*, Madrid, 1982, p. 270.

21   See J. F. Blanco y R. Azpúrua, *Documentos para la Historia de la Vida Pública del Libertador...*, *op. cit.*, Tomo II, pp. 126, 127.

22   *Idem*, Tomo II, pp. 127 y 16.

delivered by relevant French emissaries who had come to Caracas for such purpose, exacerbating thereby the uncertainties.

Upon receiving the news, the Captain-General of Venezuela Juan de Casas, who since 1807, as Deputy Lieutenant, had assumed the office upon the death of the holder (Manuel de Guevara y Vasconcelos[23]), made a solemn declaration of July 18, 1808, stating that because "no illegitimate and intruder government can destroy the legitimate and true power... in no ways is the form of government or the Reign of the Lord Master Ferdinand VII altered in this district."[24] What's more, on July 27, the City Council or *Ayuntamiento* of Caracas joined in by stating that "we do not and shall not recognize sovereignty other than his (Ferdinand VII) and of the legitimate successors to the House of Bourbon."[25]

The Captain-General Casas, on that same date, addressed the *Ayuntamiento* urging it to erect in this city "a *Junta* after the example of that of Seville."[26] For that purpose the Council acknowledged the act by which the Seville *Junta* was established,[27] and agreed to study a "proposal," the writing of which was assigned to two of the City Council members, which being approved on July 29, 1808, was submitted for approval to the "President, Governor and Captain-General."[28]

---

23   It was precisely during the administration of Guevara y Vasconcelos and when de casas was his Deputy Lieutenant, when José María España, one of the ringleaders of the so-called conspiracy of Gual y España (1797)), and the first of the victims of the republican ideas in Venezuela, had been hung with great display of terror in the main square of Caracas (1799); and also when Francisco de Miranda landed in La Vela de Coro in 1806, with his small independence expedition, staying in Coro for five days.

24   *Idem,* Tomo II, p. 169. It was precisely during the administration of Guevara y Vasconcelos and his King's Lieutenant, Casas, when, for example, José María España, one of the ringleaders of the so-called conspiracy of Gual y España (1797) and the first of the victims of the republican ideas in Venezuela, had been hung with great display of terror in the main square of Caracas (1799); and also, when Francisco de Miranda landed in La Vela de Coro in 1806 with his small independence expedition, staying in Coro for five days.

25   *Idem,* Tomo II, p. 169.

26   On June 17, 1808, for example, the Supreme Council of Seville explained to the Spanish dominions in America the "major events that have led to the creation of the Supreme Board of Seville which, on behalf of Ferdinand VII, rules the kingdoms of Seville, Cordoba, Granada, Jaén, provinces of Extremadura, Castilla la Nueva and the remaining territories to be shaking off the yoke of the Emperor of the French". See the text of the proclamation "of the main facts that have motivated the creation of the Supreme Council of Seville which, on behalf of Ferdinand VII, ruled the kingdoms of Seville, Cordoba, Granada, Jaén, provinces of Extremadura, Castilla la Nueva and the remaining territories to be shaking off the yoke of the Emperor of the French." of June 17, 1808 in J. F. Blanco y R. Azpúrua, *Documentos para la Historia de la Vida Pública del Libertador...*, *op. cit.,* Tomo II, pp. 154–157, y 170-174. See C. Pérez Parra, *Historia de la Primera República de Venezuela,* Biblioteca de la Academia Nacional de la Historia, Caracas, 1959, Tomo I. pp. 311 y ss., y 318.

27   See the City Hall minute of July 28, 1808 in J.F. Blanco y R. Azpúrua, *Documentos para la Historia de la Vida Pública del Libertador...*, *op. cit.,* Tomo II, p. 171.

28   See the text of the prospectus and approval of July 29, 1809. Ibid., pp. 172-174; and C. Pérez Parra, History of the First Republic, *Historia de la Primera República...*, *op. cit.,* p. 318.

The Captain-General, however, never came to consider the proposal not even withstanding the representation that had been sent to him on November 22, 1808 by the most notables citizens in Caracas and which was designated to deal with the Captain-General on "the formation and organization of the Supreme *Junta*." In said representation, the fact of the installation of councils under the name of Supreme *Juntas* in the provincial capitals of the peninsula was recorded. About such *Juntas* it was said:

> "The nation's noble efforts for the defense of religion, the king and the freedom and integrity of the state have rested and rests; and these very ones will sustain Thou under the authority of the Central Sovereign, which installation is claimed to have been done. The provinces of Venezuela do not have less loyalty nor less ardor, courage and perseverance than those of the European Spain."

Therefore the *Ayuntamiento* reported to the Captain-General that it believed it was:

> "Absolutely necessary to put into effect the decision of the President, Governor and Captain-General reported to the Honorable Ayuntamiento for the formation of a Supreme Junta which will be subject to the Sovereign Junta of Spain and will be able to exercise the supreme authority in this City while our beloved King Ferdinand VII returns to the throne."[29]

To this end and to "prevent all cause for concern and disorder," the *Ayuntamiento* decided to name "people's representatives" for dealing with the President, Governor and Captain-General on the project and the organization of the Supreme *Junta*."[30] The Captain-General, Juan de Casas, after having declared for the desirability of the constitution of the Caracas *Junta*, eventually not only did not agreed to the request made to him, but further saw it as an offense to public order and safety, persecuting and judging the petitioners.[31]

The result was that although the agitating creoles failed to have the *Ayuntamiento* established as a Supreme *Junta* for the Preservation of the Rights of Ferdinand VII, since August 15th, 1808 nothing could stop the progression of the revolution in the midst of the general unrest of the province, particularly due to the news that kept coming in, even though late in the following year (1809), on the general invasion of Spain by French armies. By that time, the invasion had come to encompass almost the entire peninsula, having been the operations of the provisional government of the *Junta Central of Spain* reduced to the Island of Leon, in Cádiz.

All these facts regarding the political crisis of the Spanish Crow, being one of the main reasons that caused the independence process in the provinces of Venezuela, were explained in the documents published in the London book of 1812. For exam-

---

29   See text in J.F. Blanco y R. Azpúrua, *Documentos para la Historia de la Vida Pública del Libertador...*, *op. cit.*, Tomo II, pp. 179–180; C. Parra Pérez, *Historia de la Primera República ...*, *op. cit.*, Tomo I, 133.

30   J.F. Blanco y R. Azpúrua, *Documentos para la Historia de la Vida Pública del Libertador...*, Tomo II, pp. 179–180.

31   *Idem.*, Tomo II, pp. 180–181; L. A. Sucre, *Gobernadores y Capitanes Generales de Venezuela*, Caracas, 1694, pp. 312–313.

ple, in the *Declaration of Independence* the Representatives "Provinces of Caracas, Cumana, Varinas, Margarita, Barcelona, Merida, And Truxillo" assembled in Congress, declared that the independence was the product of the "the full and absolute possession" of the rights of such "united Provinces" that were "forming the American Confederation of Venezuela, in the South Continent;" which they:

> "recovered justly and legally from the 19th of April, 1810, in consequence of the occurrences in Bayona, and the occupation of the Spanish Throne by conquest, and the succession of a new Dynasty, constituted without our consent."

And in the same *Declaration of Independence* it was stated that:

> "The Cessions and Abdications at Bayona, the Revolutions of the Escorial and Aranjuez, and the Orders of the Royal Substitute, the Duke of Berg, sent to America, suffice to give virtue to the rights, which till then the Americans had sacrificed to the unity and integrity of the Spanish Nation."

This link between the political crisis in Spain and the independence process, as one of the main causes of the latter, was also stated and argued extensively in the *Manifesto* of 1811, noting that when "Caracas learnt the scandalous scenes that passed in El Escurial and Aranjuez," it already "perceived what were her rights, and the state in which these were placed by those great occurrences," and while "every one is aware of the occurrences which happened at the Escorial, in 1807," however, "perhaps every one is not acquainted with the natural effects of these events."

Therefore, in the *Manifesto* a summary of the most important aspects of such events was given, with an appropriate clarification, however, their explanation by the Congress was not intended "to enter into the discovery of the origin of the discord that existed in the family of Charles IV," leaving to England and France to "attribute it to themselves" for which "both governments have their accusers and defenders." So the *Manifesto* expressed that it was not the intention of the Congress to refer to the "marriage agreed on between Ferdinand and the daughter-law of Buonaparte, the peace of Tilsit, the conferences at Erfuhrt, the secret treaty of St. Cloud, and the emigration of the house of Braganza to the Brazils;" considering instead that what was of the "most materially concerns" to the Venezuelans was the fact that at "El Escorial, Ferdinand VII was declared a traitor against his father, Charles IV."

On this, the Congress said in the *Manifiesto*:

> "A hundred pens, and a hundred presses published at the same time in both worlds, his perfidy, and the pardon which at his prayer, was granted to him by his father, but this pardon as an attribute of the sovereignty and of paternal authority, only absolved the son from corporal punishment; the king, his father, had no power to free him from the infamy and inability which-the constitutional laws of Spain impose on the traitor, not only to hinder him from obtaining the royal dignity, but even the lowest office or civil employment. Ferdinand, therefore, never could be king of Spain, or of the Indies."

The account of the subsequent events was made in the same *Manifiesto*, as follows:

> "To this condition the heir of the crown remained reduced, till the month of March, 1808, when, whilst the court was at Aranjuez, the project frustrated at the Escorial was converted in-

to insurrection and open mutiny, by the friends of Ferdinand. The public exasperation against the ministry of Godoy, served as a pretext to the faction of Ferdinand, and as a plea indirectly to convert into the good of the nation, what was perhaps calculated under other designs. The fact of using force against his father; his not rather recurring to supplication and convincing arguments; his having excited mutiny on the part of the people; his having assembled them in front of the palace in order to surprise it, to insult the minister, and force the king to abdicate his crown; far from giving him any title to it; only tended to increase his crime, to aggravate his treachery, and complete his inability to ascend the throne, vacated by means of violence, perfidy, and factions. Charles IV outraged, disobeyed, and threatened with force, had no other alternative left him, suitable to his decorum, and favourable to his vengeance; than to emigrate to France to implore the protection of Buonaparte, in favour of his offended royal dignity. Under the nullity of the abdications of Aranjuez, all the Bourbons assemble in Bayona, carried there against the will of the people, to whose safety they preferred their own particular resentments; the Emperor of the French, took advantage of them, and when he held under his controul, and within his influence, the whole family of Ferdinand, as well as several of the first Spanish dignitaries and substitutes for deputies in the Cortes; he caused the son to restore the crown to his father, and the latter then to make it over to him the Emperor, in order that he might afterwards confer it on his brother Joseph Napoleon."

All this - the 1811 it was affirmed in the *Manifesto* - was unknown or known only superficially in Venezuela "when the emissaries of the new king reached Caracas" arguing about "the innocence of Ferdinand, compared with the insolence and despotism of the favourite Godoy;" impelling and directing the conduct of Caracas "when the local authorities wavered on the 15th of July, 1808;" having "being left to choose between the alternative of delivering herself up to a foreign power, or of remaining faithful to a king, who appeared unfortunate and persecuted." In such situation, the General Congress said in the *Manifiesto* that:

> "the ignorance of events triumphed over the true interests of the country, and Ferdinand was acknowledged, under a belief that, by this means, the unity of the nation being maintained, she would be saved from the threatened oppression, and a king be ransomed, of whose virtues, wisdom and rights, we were falsely prepossessed."

The result, as expressed in the same *Manifiesto*, was that:

> "Ferdinand, disqualified and unable to obtain the crown; previously announced by the leaders of Spain as dispossessed of his rights to the succession; incapable of governing in America, held in bondage, and under the influence of a foreign power; from that time, became by illusion, a legitimate but unfortunate prince; it was feigned a duty to acknowledge him; as many as had the audacity to call themselves such, became his self-created heirs and representatives, and taking advantage of the innate fidelity of the Spaniards of both worlds, and forming themselves into intrusive governments, they appropriated to themselves the sovereignty of the people, in the name of a chimerical king, began to exercise new tyrannies, and even of the commercial Junta of Cadiz sought to extend her control over America."

The issue also came under consideration in the *Declaration of Independence*, which noted that:

> "All the Bourbons concurred to the invalid stipulations of Bayona, abandoning the country of Spain, against the will of the People; -they violated, disdained, and trampled on the sacred duty they had contracted with the Spaniards of both Worlds, when with their blood and treasure they had placed them on the Throne, in despite of the House of Austria. By such a

conduct, they were left disqualified and incapable of governing a Free People, whom they delivered up like a flock of Slaves,

The intrusive Governments that arrogated to them- selves the National Representation, took advantage of the dispositions which the good faith, distance, oppression, and ignorance, created in the Americans, against the new Dynasty that had entered Spain by means of force; and, contrary to their own principles, they sustained amongst us the illusion in favour of Ferdinand, in order to devour and harass us with impunity: at most, they promised to us liberty, equality, and fraternity, conveyed in pompous discourses and studied phrases, for the purpose of covering the snare laid by a cunning, useless, and degrading Representation.

As soon as they were dissolved, and had substituted and destroyed amongst themselves the various forms of the Government of Spain; and as soon as the imperious law of necessity had dictated to Venezuela the urgency of preserving itself, in order to guard and maintain the rights of her King, and to offer an asylum to her European brethren against the ills that threatened them; their former conduct was divulged: they varied their principles, and gave the appellations of insurrection, perfidy, and ingratitude, to the same acts that had served as models for the Governments of Spain; because then was closed to them the gate to the monopoly of administration, which they meant to perpetuate under the name of an imaginary King."

These ideas were also resumed in the *Preliminary Remarks* of the London book, even with another language and insisting that "reform has been the watch-word" arguing that in Europe "whole nations have been seen to struggle for redress of grievances," so that "even those who have been longest accustomed to clank the galling chains of Despotism, have pondered on their long forgotten rights, and have felt that they were yet men."

So it could not be expected that the Spanish America whose inhabitants have been:

"so long trampled upon, and enslaved, where a reform was in short the most wanting, would alone standstill, and bear with her former hardships; that she would calmly behold, whilst the governments of Spain, were busied in meliorating their own condition, that she was yet debarred from all relief, her claims unheard, and that she was even left in a more degraded state, than Under the corrupt administration of the late ministers of Charles IV."

On the contrary, in the *Preliminary Remarks* it was added that Spanish Americans had also "felt the electric shock" of the contrasts, so that being confident "of the justice of their demands," for which they have "asked redress, but it was denied;" they began to pursue them, particularly in regard to the double oppression "by the crown, and by monopolies," and to the "burdensome and unreasonable restrictions, destructive of all enterprize " with laws that had lost their useful purpose and "did not inflict punishment on the guilty, nor afford protection to the innocent." In that situation -it was argued in said *Preliminary Remarks*- what was found at every step were "arbitrary acts" which were "common;" lacking the natives a "fair participation in offices of trust and emolument;" and prevailing an ignominious system of government "disgraceful to the Statute books of Spain and the Indies, opposed to the common rights of mankind, and hostile to the dictates of truth and reason."

In short the *Preliminary Remarks* concluded, saying that the condition of the Spanish Americans "could be considered in no other state than in that of feudal vassallage to Spain." In the colonial provinces, on the other hand, there were huge gaps in all "branches of industry, occasioned by wanton ignorance" as they were subjected to a "system of monopoly, generated by a false principle of preference to few, but hostile to productive labour," denouncing in particular that in the Province of Caracas "it was not allowed to teach mathematics, to have a printing-press, a school for the tuition of navigation, or the study of *jus publicum*; and that in Merida, one of the provinces of Venezuela, an university was not tolerated." All of which could not be deny by "the most unblushing advocates for arbitrary power" "nor can they ever be palliated by the ingenious and specious pieces written in Cadiz to prove the utility and advantages of dependence and monopoly."

Hence, in the *Preliminary Remarks* it was argued that it could not be expected that only the provinces of the Americas be denied of their rights and the ability to "guard against the rapid encroachments of power, and to repair the breach;" to demand from them "that for the distribution of justice" they had "to traverse an ocean of two thousand leagues;" that in moments so critical as those in which they were, they were "to depend, as political nothings, on a nation, herself threatened with destruction from a powerful foe;" and that they remain "like a vessel deprived of her helm, left to be buffeted by the rude tempests ready to assail them, and be exposed to become the prey of the first ambitious nation that may have the strength to effect their conquest."

II. THE DEPOSITION OF THE COLONIAL AUTHORITIES, THE INDE-PENDENCE AND THE CONSTITUTION MAKING PROCESS IN 1810 AND 1811

In any case, after the events of 1808, the feeling among the people in the Caracas province that the provincial government was pro-bonapartist had begun to rise and was also attributed to the Field Marshal, Vicente Emparan and Orbe, who had been appointed by the Supreme Governing *Junta* of Spain as Governor of the Province of Venezuela, in March 1809, succeeding Governor de Casas.[32] This Kingdom's Supreme Central and Governing *Junta*, as mentioned, had been established at Aranjuez on September 25, 1808 and had been moved to Seville later on December 27, 1809, comprising representatives of the various provinces of the Kingdom, taking charge of the national interests.[33] That was why on January 12, 1809, the *Ayuntamiento* of Caracas recognized such Central *Junta* in Venezuela, as the supreme government of the empire.[34]

It was days later that the Central Supreme *Junta* by the very important but to late Royal Order of January 22, 1809, decided that:

---

32   See L. A. Sucre, *Gobernadores y Capitanes Generales...*, *op. cit.*, p. 314.

33   See text in J. F. Blanco y R. Azpúrua, *Documentos para la Historia de la Vida Pública del Libertador...*, *op. cit.*, Tomo II, pp. 174 y 179.

34   See Parra Pérez, *Historia de la Primera República ...*, *op. cit.*, Tomo II, p. 305.

"The vast and beautiful domains which Spain has in the Indies are not properly colonies or factories, like those of other nations, but an essential and integral part of the Spanish monarchy.... "[35]

As a result of this important statement it was considered that the Provinces of the Americas should have its representation and be part of the Central Supreme *Junta,* for which matter the way to elect Spanish American representatives and vocals was implemented by appointment through the American *Ayuntamientos,* but in an absolute minority in relation to the mainland representatives.[36]

In any case, in early 1809, adverse events against the Supreme Central and Governing *Junta* had already appeared in the Peninsula, being the *Junta* itself accused of usurping authority. This led, ultimately, to the convening of the General *Cortes* to give legitimacy to the national representation which the *Junta* made by decree of May 22 and June 15, 1809 fixing the meeting of the *Cortes* on March 1, 1810 at the Island of Leon.[37] In those *Cortes,* in any event, the Kingdom's Provincial *Juntas* and the representatives of the Provinces of the Indies should be represented and had to be elected in accordance with regulations issued on October 6th, 1809. As to the representatives of Spanish America and after endless discussions about their number and form of election arose, the final choice of them was actually made, being chosen as *suplentes,* among the Spanish Americans residents in Cadiz.[38]

In the mean time, in May 1809, as mentioned, the new President, Governor and Captain-General of Venezuela -Vicente Emparan and Orbe- had already arrived in Caracas. He was known in the provinces of Venezuela as he had served as Governor General of Cumana between 1792 and 1804 with so much liberal ideas that he was credited with helping Manuel Gual to board clandestinely to Trinidad, the other party responsible for the conspiracy of 1797.

Nonetheless, he was the Governor, and he received the warning given the same month of his appointment by the Supreme Governing *Junta* of Spain to all the Provinces of America on the dangers of the spreading of the Emperor's machinations to

---

35   See text in J.F. Blanco y R. Azpúrua, *Documentos para la Historia de la Vida Pública del Libertador...*, *op. cit.,* Tomo II, pp. 230–231; O. C. Stoetzer, *Las Raíces Escolásticas de la Emancipación...*, *op. cit.,* p. 271.

36   This was protested in America. See for example the "Memorial de Agrarios" de C. Torres de 20 de noviembre de 1809 en J. F. Blanco y R. Azpúrua, *Documentos para la Historia de la Vida Pública del Libertador...*, *op. cit.,* Tomo II, pp. 243–246; and O.C. Stoetzer, *Las Raíces Escolásticas de la Emancipación...*, *op. cit.,* p. 272. To that end a process of election was established and applied, e.g., in the province of Guayana. See texts in J. F. Blanco y R. Azpúrua, *Documentos para la Historia de la Vida Pública del Libertador...*, *op. cit.,* Tomo II, pp. 260–261.

37   See text in J.F. Blanco y R. Azpúrua, *Documentos para la Historia de la Vida Pública del Libertador...*, *op. cit.,* Tomo II, pp. 234–235.

38   See E. Roca Roca, *América en el Ordenamiento Jurídico...*, *op. cit.,* p. 21; J. F. Blanco y R. Azpúrua, *Documentos para la Historia de la Vida Pública del Libertador...*, *op. cit.,* Tomo II, pp. 267–268.

the Americas.[39] This was enough, as mentioned in the *Preliminary Remarks* of the London book, "to suspect the whole of the viceroys and governors," which was confirmed by the subsequent events, as these officers

> "all proclaimed the doctrine that America ought to share the same fate as the Peninsula, and that when the one was conquered, the other was to submit; in short, the commanders abroad were prepared for this alternative, they had been previously chosen by the Prince of Peace, and were ready to be moulded to the views on which he had acted."

Consequently, the fear that arose in Caracas on the full subjugation of the Peninsula, no doubt, was what prompted the beginning of the conspiracy for the independence of the Province of Venezuela; an event of which even Emparan was aware, prior to arriving in Caracas.[40] His government action, on the other hand led him to alienate himself even from the clergy and the *Ayuntamiento*, events which contributed to accelerate the reaction of the Creoles. Thus, by the end of 1809 there was put a plan in the Province to overthrow the government and in which partook the most outstanding youth of Caracas, including Simón Bolívar, the future Liberator of Venezuela, Colombia, Ecuador, Perú and Bolivia, who had returned from Spain in 1807, and were all friends of the Captain-General.[41] The Captain took several actions as he discovered the plan but the orders were weak, arousing protests from the *Ayuntamiento*.[42]

Similarly, on January 29, 1810 after the French victories in Andalusia, the Central Governing *Junta* had decided to recall the Kingdom's authority by appointing a Regency Council with the supreme power although limited by its submission to the *Cortes* which was scheduled to meet months later.[43] Thus, the decision was announced that "the *Cortes* will reduce their functions to the exercise of the legislative power, which properly belongs to them, entrusting the Regency with the exercise of the executive power."[44]

In exercise of the authority it had received, the Regency Council addressed a "speech" on February 14, 1810 to the Spanish Americans with which said Council accompanied a royal decree mandating attendance to the Extraordinary *Cortes* by the deputies of the Peninsula and simultaneously by the deputies of the Spanish dominions in America and Asia.[45]

Meanwhile, there were no news in the Provinces of America about the events occurred in Spain, which the territory was held by the French except for Cadiz and the

---

39   See text at J.F. Blanco y R. Azpúrua, *Documentos para la Historia de la Vida Pública del Libertador...*, *op. cit.*, Tomo II, pp. 250–254.

40   See G. Morón, *Historia de Venezuela*, Caracas, 1971, Tomo III, p. 205.

41   C. Parra Pérez, *Historia de la Primera República ...*, *op. cit.*, Tomo I, pp. 368–371.

42   *Idem.*, p. 371.

43   See J. F. Blanco y R. Azpúrua, *Documentos para la Historia de la Vida Pública del Libertador...*, *op. cit.*, Tomo II, pp. 265–269.

44   *Idem*, Tomo II, p. 269.

45   See text at *Idem*, Tomo II, pp. 272–275.

Island of Leon. Such news and the ones referring to the dissolution of the Central and Governing Supreme *Junta* due to the establishment of the Regency Council, as mentioned, only became known in Caracas on April 18, 1810.[46]

The thought of the disappearance of the Supreme Government in Spain and the need to seek the establishment of a government for the Province of Venezuela to secure itself against the Napoleon's schemes, no doubt, were the final trigger for the beginning of the Spanish American independence revolution.

In Caracas, what was certain is that the Governor could not stop the conspiracy, so much so that on that April 19, after rejecting the new proposal to establish a *Junta* and after terminating the session of the *Ayuntamiento*, he was forced by the mob to return to the Council as he was leaving from it to attend the services of Good Thursday in the Cathedral of Caracas, being told: "To the *Cabildo* (Town Hall), Sir, the people are calling you to the Council to express their desire."[47] The result of such civil insurrection or coup d'état against the colonial authorities,[48] deposing the Governor and General Captain, and establishing a new autonomous government,[49] was the decision adopted by the members of the *Ayuntamiento* to replace the Council itself, incorporating new members as representatives of the people into a *Junta*

---

46   See *Idem,* Tomo II, pp. 380 y 383.

47   See on these events Juan Garrido Rovira, *La Revolución de 1810*, Universidad Monteávila, Caracas 2009, pp.97 ss.

48   See the relevant documents on the facts of April 19, 1811 in *El 19 de Abril de 1810,* Instituto Panamericano de Geografía e Historia, Caracas, 1957. See also Juan Garrido Rovira, *La Revolución de 1810*, Universidad Monteávila, Caracas 2009; Enrique Viloria Vera and Allan R. Brewer-Carías, *La Revolución de Caracas de 1810*, Centro de Estudios Ibéricos y Americanos de Salamanca, Caracas 2011. Several months before the Caracas events, in August 10, 1809, an insurrection took place in Quito in which a group of natives under the command of John Pius Montúfar, Marquis of Selva Alegre, also deposed the colonial authorities and established a Supreme Council also swearing loyalty to Ferdinand VII, in what has been regarded as the first sign for independence in the Spanish American colonies. However, the movement ended up not taking shape and three months later Peru's Viceroy's troops had taken over the capital and restored the Spanish government. See the documents of Montúfar and of Rodríguez de Quiroga, Grace and Justice Minister of the Quito Supreme Council in José Luis Romero y Luis Alberto Romero (Coord.), *Pensamiento Político de la Emancipación*, Biblioteca Ayacucho, Tomo I, Caracas 1985, pp.47–50.

49   The news of the Caracas revolution only reached London on June 1810, and it was Francisco de Miranda who sent the reports to the local press (*Morning Chronicle, Courier*). See Mario Rodríguez, *"William Burke" and Francisco de Miranda. The Word and the Deed in Spanish America's Emancipation*, University Press of America, Lanham, New York, London 1994, p. 276. In the July 31, 1810 issue of *El Español*, published in London and directed by José Blanco-White, he made an important commentary on the Caracas Revolution, at the end of a comment referred to a book of Alexander Humboldt (*Ensayo politico sobre el Reino de Nueva España*, Paris 1808-1809), verifying the provisional character of the new government, recognizing the rule of Ferdinand VII, giving some advice to the Council of Regency of Spain if they wanted to prevent to "universally excite the independent spirit of the Americans." See the text in Juan Goytisolo, *Blanco White. El Español y la independencia de Hispanoamérica,* Taurus 2010, pp. 111 ss.

Suprema de Venezuela Conservadora de los Derechos de Fernando VII, kidnapped by Napoleon.[50]

Regarding this decision, the General Congress in the 1811 *Manifesto* expressed that in that day "the Colossus of despotism was cast down in Venezuela, the empire of the laws proclaimed, and the tyrants expelled, with all the felicity, moderation, and tranquillity, that they themselves have confessed; so much so, as even to have filled with admiration and friendship for us, the rest of the impartial world."

That day, as was considered by the General Congress in the *Manifiesto*, should have been "when the independence should have been declared;" a day when Venezuela with "one strong and generous hand [...] deposed the agents of her misery and her slavery," and placing:

> "the name of Ferdinand the 7th at the head of her new government, swore to maintain his rights, promised to acknowledge the unity and integrity of the Spanish nation, opened her arms to her European, brethren, offered them an asylum in their misfortunes and calamities, equally hated the enemies of the Spanish name, sought the generous alliance of England, and prepared to take part in the felicity or misfortune of the nation from whom she could, and ought to have eternally separated."

The Venezuelan people -the *Manifesto* indicated- acknowledged "the imaginary rights of the son of Maria Louisa" and respecting the "misfortunes of the nation" they gave "official notice to the same Regency we disowned," offering

> "not to separate from Spain, as long as she maintained a legal government, established by the will of the nation, and in which America had that part, given to her by justice, necessity, and the political importance of her territory."

In any case, this occurred just six months after the Instruction for the election of the constituents of the Cádiz *Cortes* had been issued in Spain (October 6, 1809) and five months before their installation on September 24, 1810. That is, by the time that general assembly of representatives began its activities, already in one of the Colonies a political rebellion was in course in which the Municipal body of Caracas had ignore the Spanish colonial authorities, and established, following the same pattern of the Spanish *Juntas* established in almost all the provinces of Spain during the war of independence, an autonomous *Junta* of government. Nonetheless, the American *Junta* had an important distinction, and was the fact that it had additional inspiration

---

50   On July 28, 1808, a previous attempt was made in the *Ayuntamiento* of Caracas to establish a Junta following the pattern of the Juntas formed in Spain, but it failed because of the opposition of the Captain General. See the text in José Félix Blanco y Ramón Azpúrua, *Documentos para la Historia de la Vida Pública del Libertador de Colombia, Perú y Bolivia. Puestos por orden cronológico y con adiciones y notas que la ilustran*, Ediciones de la Presidencia de la República, Caracas 1977, Tomo II, p. 171. Coincidentally, on July 20, 1808 (?), Francisco de Miranda in a letter sent to the Marquis del Toro, member of the *Ayuntamiento* of Caracas, proposed to the municipal council to take charge of the government of the province. See the text in Francisco de Miranda, *Textos sobre la Independencia*, Biblioteca de la Academia Nacional de la Historia, Caracas 1959, pp. 100-101. See also Giovanni Meza Dorta, *Miranda y Bolívar*, bid&co. Editor, Caracas 2007 p. 43.

in the new republican principles based on the sovereignty of the people and representation derived from the North American and French Revolutions that had occurred only two and three decades before.

In effect, as mentioned, the *Ayuntamiento* of Caracas, on its April 19, 1810 session (the day after the publication of the political situation in the Peninsula) deposed the established authority, having its minutes recorded the first constitutional act of a new government and the beginning of the legal formation of a new state,[51] assuming the "supreme command" or "supreme authority" of the Province[52] "by the approval of the very people."[53]

Thus a "new government" was thereby established and recognized in the Capital City and to it were submitted "all the employees of the military political and other branches."[54] Moreover, the *Ayuntamiento* moved to dismiss the former authorities of the country and to provide public safety and preservation of the rights of the captive monarch. This it did by "resuming the sovereign power on itself."[55]

The motivation of this revolution was discussed in the text of the Minute, in which it was considered that because of the dissolution of the Supreme Governing *Junta* of Spain -which supplied for the absence of the monarch- the people had been left in "total orphan hood", a reason for which it was found that:

> "The natural right and every other right dictate the necessity to seek means for the preservation and defense; and to erect, at the very heart of these countries, a system of government capable of mending the said faults by exercising sovereignty rights which, by the same reason, have rested in the people."

In reaching this decision, of course, the *Ayuntamiento* had to ignore the authority of the Regency Council,[56] considering that:

---

51   See generally T. Polanco, "Interpretación jurídica de la Independencia" en *El Movimiento Emancipador de Hispanoamérica, Actas y Ponencias,* Caracas, 1961, Tomo IV, pp. 323 y ss.

52   See the minute text of the Caracas City Hall of April 19, 1810 in Allan R. Brewer-Carias, *Las Constituciones de Venezuela, op. cit.,* pp. 531-533.

53   This is provided in the "Newsletter" sent by the City Hall on April 19, 1810 to the authorities and corporate entities of Venezuela. See J. F. Blanco y R. Azpúrua, *Documentos para la Historia de la Vida Pública del Libertador..., op. cit.,* Tomo II, pp. 401–402. See also in *Textos Oficiales de la Primera República de Venezuela,* Biblioteca de la Academia Nacional de la Historia, 1959, Tomo I, p. 105.

54   *Idem.*

55   As specified in the declaration of the Supreme Council to the Inspector General Fernando Toro on April 20, 1810. See J.F. Blanco y R. Azpúrua, *Documentos para la Historia de la Vida Pública del Libertador..., op. cit.,* Tomo II, p. 403 y Tomo I, p. 106, respectivamente.

56   What was asserted again, in a correspondence sent to the very Regency Board of Spain, explaining the facts, reasons and grounds for the establishment of the new government. J. F. Blanco y R. Azpúrua, *Documentos para la Historia de la Vida Pública del Libertador..., op. cit.,* Tomo II, p. 408; and *Textos oficiales..., op. cit.,* Tomo I, pp. 130 y ss. Particularly, in a letter of May 3, 1810, the Supreme Council of Caracas addressed the Supreme Council of Cadiz and the Regency, questioning the assumption by these entities "that replacing each other indefinitely, they are only similar in attributing to themselves entirely a delegation of

"It cannot exercise any control or jurisdiction over these countries because it has neither been established by the vote of these faithful people, when these people have been already declared not settlers but integral parts of the Crown of Spain and as such called to the exercise of domestic sovereignty and to the reform of the national Constitution."

In any case, the *Ayuntamiento* felt that while the latter exercises could be waived, the Regency Council was impotent and its members could not rely on themselves because of the circumstances of the war, conquest and usurpation of the peninsula by the French arms. Thence at the Extraordinary City Council Assembly, once the President, Governor and Captain-General was forced to resign, the authority rested with the *Ayuntamiento*, which was expressed also in the minutes of another meeting of it on the same day of April 19, 1810 to mark the "establishment of the new government," in which it was decided that the new employees had to give oath before the *Ayuntamiento*, thereby promising:

"To keep, fulfill and enforce and cause to have them kept, fulfilled and enforced any and all orders given by the Supreme Sovereign Authority of these Provinces in the name of our Lord and King Ferdinand VII."[57]

It was thus established, in Caracas, "a Governing *Junta* of these Provinces comprised of the *Ayuntamiento* of this Capital and the vocals appointed by the people's vote;"[58] and in a Proclamation which spoke of "the Revolution of Caracas" and referred to "the political independence of Caracas", the Governing *Junta* promised:

"To grant the new government with the appropriate interim form it should have, while a constitution adopted by legitimately established national representatives moves to sanction, consolidate and present with political dignity to the face of the universe an organized and orderly province of Venezuela in a way that makes its people happy and may provide useful and decent example to the Americas."[59]

This Caracas *Junta* was formally organized two months later, in June 1810, as mentioned, following the general pattern of similar *Juntas*, being in both cases, the initial motivation of these constituent acts basically the same, and among other factors, as mentioned, the extreme political instability that since 1808 had been affect-

---

sovereignty, which not having been made neither by the recognized monarch nor by the large community of Spaniards in both hemispheres, can not fail but to be null and void, illegal and contrary to the principles enshrined in our legislation" (*Textos oficiales...*, *op. cit.*, Tomo I, p. 130); adding that "little will be needed to show that the Central Council lacked a true national representation because its authority emanated originally from nothing but from the turbulent acclamation of some provincial capitals and because the people of the hemisphere never had in it the rightful representative part that its legitimately owed to them. In other words, we disregard the new Regency Council" (*Idem*, p. 134).

57   See text at *Idem*, J.F. Blanco y R. Azpúrua, *Documentos para la Historia de la Vida Pública del Libertador...*, *op. cit.*, Tomo I, p. 393.

58   So it is called in the *Manifesto* of May 1, 1810. See in *Textos Oficiales...*, *cit.*, Tomo I. p. 121.

59   See text in J. F. Blanco y R. Azpúrua, *Documentos para la Historia de la Vida Pública del Libertador...*, *op. cit.*, Tomo II, p. 406, y en *Textos Oficiales...*, *op. cit.*, Tomo I, p. 129.

ing the Spanish government, due to the absence of Ferdinand VII from Spain, who was held captive in France by Emperor Napoleon Bonaparte; the invasion of the Peninsula by the French Army; and the appointment of Joseph Bonaparte as King of Spain by the Emperor after enacting a new Constitution for the Realm, in Bayonne in 1808.

In any case, what apparently was the beginning of a local reaction of a municipal organization of the capital of one of the poorest Spanish provinces in America against the Napoleonic invasion in the Iberian Peninsula quickly became the first successful expression of independence from Spain. Days after the April 19th, 1811 events, on April 27, 1810 it was ordered that they be reported to all the *Ayuntamientos* in America, inviting them to participate in "the great work of the Spanish-American Confederation,"[60] promoting the revolution among the other Provinces of America. The "example given by Caracas" was immediately followed by almost all the Provinces of the General Captaincy,[61] with the exception of Coro and Maracaibo,[62] as well as in other jurisdictions, like Buenos Aires on May 25, 1810, and Bogota, Nueva Granada on July 20, 1810.[63]

Accordingly, on April 27, 1810 in Cumana, the *Ayuntamiento* assumed the representation of Ferdinand VII and "his legitimate succession". On July 5, 1810 the *Ayuntamiento* of Barinas decided to go forth and establish "a Higher Supreme *Junta* that would receive the authority of the people that composed it by being a separate province". On September 16, 1810, the *Ayuntamiento* of Merida decided "on behalf of the people" to adhere to the joint efforts done by the Supreme and Superior *Juntas* which had already been established in Santa Fe, Caracas, Barinas, Pamplona and Socorro and resolved (with a people's representation) to establish a *Junta* "that would assume the sovereign authority." The *Ayuntamiento* of Trujillo agreed to install "a Supreme *Junta* for the preservation of our Holy Religion; for the rights of our beloved, legitimate and sovereign master Ferdinand VII and his dynasty; and for the rights of the Homeland." On October 12, 1811 in the City Council of New Barcelona "the distinguished and honorable people of Barcelona" came together and decided to declare the independence of the province from Spain and to join together

---

60   See details of the events and the writings of Rafael Seijas, Aristides Rojas, L. Vallenilla Lanz, Christopher L. Mendoza and others, in *El 19 de abril de 1810, op. cit.,* pp. 63 ss.

61   See at *Las Constituciones Provinciales, op. cit.,* pp. 339 y ss.

62   See the Supreme Council correspondence in regard to the attitude of the Coro City Hall and Maracaibo's Governor at *Textos Oficiales...,* cit., Tomo I, pp. 157 a 191. See besides the texts that are published by J. F. Blanco y R. Azpúrua, *Documentos para la Historia de la Vida Pública del Libertador...,* op. cit., Tomo II, p. 248 a 442, y 474 a 483.

63   See for instance, *Actas de Independencia. Mérida, Trujillo y Táchira en 1810,* Halladas y publicadas por Tulio Febres Cordero, 450 Años de la Fundación de Mérida, 1558-2008, Mérida 2007; Ángel F. Brice (Ed.), *Las Constituciones Provinciales,* Academia Nacional de la Historia, Caracas, 1959.

with Caracas and Cumana. The next day a Provincial Junta was created to represent the rights of the people.[64]

In any case, the Venezuela's Supreme *Junta* began to assume the legislative and executive functions, on an interim basis, establishing in the Proclamation of April 25, 1810 these bodies for the Judiciary: "The Superior Court of Appeals, Petitions and Resorts for grievances will be established in the houses the *Audiencia* had before;" and the Police Tribunal, that was "in charge of the smooth application and administration of justice in all civil and criminal cases, will be headed by the magistrates."[65]

As mentioned, this revolutionary movement initiated in Caracas, on April 1810, undoubtedly followed the same pattern of the French Revolution and it was also inspired by the American Revolution,[66] so much that it may even be considered that it was a revolution of the native bourgeoisie, aristocracy or oligarchy, which like the *Trier État* in France was the only active nationwide force.[67] Initially then, the independence revolution in Venezuela was the instrument of the colonial aristocracy - that is, of the Caucasians or aristocrats - used to react against colonial authority and take over the government of the land that had been discovered, conquered, settled and cultivated by their ancestors.[68] It was not, therefore, a popular revolution at its beginnings, as the *pardos* people, despite being the majority of the population, were just beginning to be admitted to the civil and social circles as a result of the decree of "*Gracias, al Sacar*". This decree was in force since 1795 and, notwithstanding the complaints of the white people, it allowed the *pardos*, by paying a sum of money, to acquire rights previously reserved to the renowned whites.[69]

---

64   See the Independence Proceedings of the several cities of the Captaincy General of Venezuela at *Las Constituciones Provinciales,* Academia Nacional de la Historia, 1959, pp. 339 y ss.

65   *Textos oficiales ..., op. cit.,* Tomo I, pp. 115–116.

66   See José Gil Fortoul, *Historia Constitucional de Venezuela,* Tomo primero, *Obras Completas,* Vol. I, Caracas, 1953, p. 209.

67   See José Gil Fortoul, *Historia Constitucional de Venezuela, op. cit.,* Tomo primero, p. 200; Pablo Ruggeri Parra, *Historia Política y Constitucional de Venezuela,* Tomo I, Caracas, 1949, p. 31.

68   In this sense, for example, L. Vallenilla Lanz is categorical, considering that "in every procedure in support of the Revolution (of independence) nothing should be seen other than the struggle of the noblemen against the Spanish authorities, the struggle from the landowners against the monopoly of trade, the long ago by that powerful and compelling social class which no wonder believed the sole owner of these lands that had been discovered, conquered, settled and cultivated by their ancestors. In all these cases, not only the predominance and influence enjoyed by the native nobility was based, but also the legitimate right to self-government without the need to resort to exotic principles so much in conflict with their privileges and caste prejudices." See Vallenilla Laureano Lanz, *Cesarismo Democrático.* Estudio sobre las bases sociológicas de la Constitución efectiva en Venezuela, Caracas 1952, pp. 54 y 55.

69   On the "*Gracias, al Sacar*" Royal Decree of 10/02/1795 see J. F. Blanco y R. Azpúrua, *Documentos para la Historia de la Vida Pública del Libertador...,* op. cit., Tomo I, pp. 263 a 275. *Cf.* Federico Brito Figueroa, *Historia Económica y Social de Venezuela. Una estructura*

Hence, considering the pre-independence social situation, it may, no doubt, be described as "unusual" the fact that in the *Ayuntamiento* of Caracas (having become a Supreme *Junta*) there had been given representation not only to the social strata out of the *Ayuntamiento* (such as the representatives of the clergy and the so-called "representatives of the people") but also to a representative of the *pardo* people.[70] These political actions were criticized publicly in the *Official Declaration* published in Philadelphia by the former and deposed Captain-General Emparan on July 6, 1810[71] which was refuted in the "Rebuttal to the Proclamation of Former Captain-General Emparan" ordered to be published as a "reply from the Government of Venezuela." This reply was written by Ramón García de Sena,[72] the brother of Manuel García de Sena, the translator of the works of Paine, who was editor of *"El Publicista Venezolano,"* a journal of the General Congress of 1811. He would later be an outstanding officer of Venezuela's army and a Secretary of War and Navy in 1812. Ramón Garcia de Sena also appears as signing the very extensive "Constitution of the Republic of Columbian Barcelona" dated January 12, 1812.[73]

The immediate success of the spreading of the revolutionary ideas initiated in Caracas provoked the design of the second task of the new *Junta*, which was to es-

---

para su estudio, Tomo I, Caracas, 1966, p. 167; and L. Vallenilla Lanz, *Cesarismo Democrático, op. cit.,* pp. 13 y ss. In this regard, it should be noted that in the social situation existing at the pre-independence period there were indications of class struggles between whites or aristocrats (who constituted 20 % of the population and the browns and blacks who constituted 61 % of the population); these indications will later materialize in the rebellion of 1814. See F. Brito Figueroa, *op. cit.,* tomo I, pp. 160 y 173. *Cf.* Ramón Díaz Sánchez, "Evolución social de Venezuela (hasta 1960)", en M. Picón Salas y otros, *Venezuela Independiente 1810–1960,* Caracas, 1962, p. 193.

70 See Gil Fortoul, *Historia Constitucional de Venezuela, op. cit.,* Tomo primero, pp. 203, 208 y 254. It should be borne in mind, as noted by A. Grisanti, that "The council was represented by the provincial oligarchies extremely jealous of their political, administrative and social prerogatives, and who held power by the dominance of few noble or ennobled families, who monopolized the city posts ..." See Angel Grisanti, Prólogo al libro *Toma de Razón, 1810 a 1812,* Caracas, 1955. The change of attitude in the Caracas City Hall is therefore undoubtedly due to the influence of its enlightened members who received the egalitarianism from the French Revolution: *Cf.* L. Vallenilla Lanz, *Cesarismo Democrático, op. cit.,* p. 36. The author stresses in connection with this as follows: "It is in the name of the Encyclopedia, in the name of rationalist philosophy, in the name of Condorcet's and Rousseau's humanitarian optimism that the revolutionaries of 1810 and the constituents of 1811, proceeding entirely from the upper social classes, enacted civil and political equality of all free men", *op. cit.,* p. 75.

71 In the *El Mercurio Venezolano* # 1 dated January 1811 the said *Manifesto* of Emparan was commented upon and a response to it was offered at the following number of the journal. See the facsimilar edition at <http://cic1.ucab.edu.ve/hmdg/bases/hmdg/textos/Mercurio/Mer_Enero1811.pdf>.

72 See text at *El Mercurio Venezolano,* N°II, Febrero 1811, pp. 1-21, edición facsimilar publicada en <http://cic1.ucab.edu.ve/hmdg/bases/hmdg/textos/Mercurio/Mer_Febrero1811.pdf>.

73 See *Las Constituciones Provinciales* (Estudio Preliminar por Ángel Francisco Bice), Biblioteca de la Academia Nacional de la Historia, Caracas 1959, p. 249.

tablish a well constituted central power by uniting all the provinces of the General Captaincy. The fact was that the outcome of the rapid and expansive revolutionary process of the provinces of Venezuela provoked that by June 1810, the idea of a "Confederation of Venezuela"[74] had already begun to be spoken of officially, and the Caracas *Junta* (comprising representatives of Cumana, Barcelona and Margarita) had been already acting as a Supreme Junta without obviously fully exercising the government in the entire expanded territory of the General Captaincy. Hence there was the need to form a "well-established central authority", that is, a government that would unite the provinces. For that matter the Supreme Junta found that the "time to organize it had come" and summoned:

> "All kinds of free men to the first of the joys of the citizen which is to agree by its vote to delegate the personal and property rights that are originally found in the common mass of the population."

In this way, the *Junta* called to elect and convene the representatives (*diputados*) who were to form "the Representatives General *Junta* of the Provinces of Venezuela" and pursuant thereto it issued on June 11, 1810 the Election Regulations of said Congress[75] which, moreover, anticipated the abdication of the powers of the Supreme *Junta* on behalf of the General Congress. Consequently, the Supreme *Junta* of Caracas was to remain only as the Provincial *Junta* of Caracas (Chapter III, art. 4). These regulations on elections, no doubt, were the first electoral statute approved in Latin America.

In parallel to the issuing of the Supreme *Junta* Elections Regulations, the *Junta* appointed Simón Bolívar and Luis López Mendez as commissioners to represent the new government in the United Kingdom, who with Andrés Bello as Secretary, traveled to London, while such Junta continued with the foreign policy it began since its installation. The commissioners had the mission to strengthen relations with England and request immediate aid to resist the threat of France. The commissioners were basically able to obtain the aid, specifically expressed in the commitment of England to defend the government of Caracas from the "attacks or plots of the tyrant of France."[76]

---

74 See the "Refutación a los delirios políticos del Cabildo de Coro, de orden de la Junta Suprema de Caracas" ["refutation of the political delusions of the City Hall of Coro, by order of the Caracas Supreme *Junta*] dated June 1, 1810, at *Textos Oficiales...*, *op. cit.*, Tomo I, p. 180.

75 See text at *Textos Oficiales...*, *op. cit.*, Tomo II, pp. 61–84; y en Allan R. Brewer–Carías, *Las Constituciones de Venezuela, op. cit.*, Tomo I, pp. 535-543.

76 See the newsletter sent on December 7, 1810 by the Colonial Secretary of Great Britain to the heads of the British West Indies at J. F. Blanco y R. Azpúrua, *Documentos para la Historia de la Vida Pública del Libertador...*, *op. cit.* Tomo II, p. 519. Similarly, the article published in the Gazette of Caracas on Friday, October 26, 1810 on the negotiations of the commissioners. See at J. F. Blanco y R. Azpúrua, *Documentos para la Historia de la Vida Pública del Libertador...*, *op. cit.*, Tomo II, p. 514.

As recorded by Francisco de Miranda with whom they associated in London, the Venezuelan commissioners had continued what the Precursor had begun "twenty years ago [...] for our emancipation and independence."[77] In any case, Bolivar and Miranda returned to Caracas on December 1810 and Francisco de Miranda was elected representative for El Pao to form the General Congress of Venezuela which was installed on March 2, 1811.[78] As aforementioned, it would be Andrés Bello, who remained in London as Secretary of the Delegation of Venezuela, to further develop relations with the English and Spanish community that were interested in the fate of Spanish America, and to take over the final editing process and publication of the London book *Interesting Official Documents* in 1811 and 1812.

In any case, amidst the situation of total split between the provinces of Venezuela and the Metropolis, by the end of 1810, indirect elections in two levels were held, with a relative universal system of vote, in seven of the nine provinces that existed in the territory of the General Captaincy of Venezuela.[79] The result was the election of 44 representatives (*diputados*) from the provinces of Caracas (24), Barinas (9), Cumana (4), Barcelona (3), Mérida (2), Trujillo (1) and Margarita (1).[80] The elected representatives formed the "General *Junta* of Representatives for the Provinces of Venezuela"[81] that assumed the character of a National Congress of representatives. On March 2, 1811, the representatives were installed in such National Congress through the following oath:

> "You hereby swear to God under the Holy Gospels that you are about to receive and hereby promise to the Nation that you shall preserve and defend the nation's rights and those of our Lord F. VII without the slightest influence from France and regardless of any type of government existing in the peninsula of Spain and without any interest other than the representation that the General Congress of Venezuela stands for."[82]

After the installation of the General Congress the use of the expression of the "Confederation of the Provinces of Venezuela" began to spread out in all the provinces, which had kept their own political specificities having the following month -

---

77   See the Letter from Miranda to the Supreme Council of August 3, 1810 at J. F. Blanco y R. Azpúrua, *Documentos para la Historia de la Vida Pública del Libertador...*, op. cit., Tomo II, p. 580.

78   See C. Parra Pérez, *Historia de la Primera República...*, op. cit., Tomo I, Caracas 1959, pp. 15 y 18.

79   The partaking provinces were the provinces of Caracas, Barinas, Cumaná, Barcelona, Mérida, Trujillo y Margarita. See José Gil Fortoul, *Historia Constitucional de Venezuela, op. cit.,* Tomo primero, p. 223, y en J. F. Blanco y R. Azpúrua, *Documentos para la Historia de la Vida Pública del Libertador...*, op. cit., Tomo II, pp. 413 y 489.

80   See C. Parra Pérez, *Historia de la Primera República ...*, op. cit., Tomo I, p. 477.

81   See Gil Fortoul, *Historia Constitucional de Venezuela, op. cit.,* Tomo primero, p. 224.

82   *Idem,* Tomo I, p. 138; Tomo II, p. 16.

at the session of April 6, 1812 - the General Congress decided to urge the "provincial legislatures" to accelerate the formation of their relevant constitutions.[83]

In any case, the Congress replaced the Supreme *Junta* adopting the principle of separation of powers to organize the new government, designating on March 5, 1811 three citizens to exercise the State Executive Branch taking weekly turns in office and also establishing a High Court of Justice.

On March 28, 1811, Congress appointed a committee to draft the Constitution of the Province of Caracas which would serve as standard for the other Provinces of the Confederation.[84] This commission was slow to develop the project, so some provinces, as indicated below, proceeded to make their own in order to organize themselves politically. On July 1, 1811 Congress proclaimed the *Declaration of the Rights of the Peoples,*[85] a proclamation that can be taken as the third declaration of constitutional rights in modern constitutionalism.

On July 5, 1811, Congress being comprised of the representatives of the provinces of Margarita, Merida, Cumana, Barinas, Barcelona, Trujillo and Caracas, adopted the *Declaration of Independence* and renamed the new nation as the American Confederation of Venezuela,[86] provoking the initial abandonment of the compromise manifested on April 19th 18122 to seek for the conservancy of the rights of Ferdinand VII. This provoked the need for the General Congress to justify and explain the reasons for the breakdown of the oath, considering Ferdinand VI in the *Manifiesto* as a "presumptive king, unfit to reign."

Thus, in the 1811 *Manifesto*, in fact, there was said that even when all "the evils of this disorder, and the abuses of such an usurpation might be considered as not imputable to Ferdinand," who had been "already acknowledged in Venezuela, at the same time that he was unable to remedy so much insult, such excesses, and so much violence committed in his name," it was considered:

> "it necessary to remount to the origin of these same rights, that we may then descend to the nullity and invalidity of the generous oath by which we conditionally acknowledged him; notwithstanding we have, in spite of ourselves, to violate the spontaneous silence we had imposed upon us, respecting every thing that was anterior to the transactions of El Escurial and Aranjuez."

The matter was regarded as a moral and legal one, so that in the *Manifesto* it was considered necessary "that no handle should be left for the scruples of conscience,

---

83 See *Libro de Actas del Supremo Congreso de Venezuela 1811–1812,* Biblioteca de la Academia Nacional de la Historia, Caracas, 1959, Tomo II, p. 401.

84 See Allan R. Brewer-Carías, La Constitución de la Provincia de Caracas de 30 de enero de 1812, Academia de Ciencias Políticas y Sociales, Caracas 2011.

85 See Allan R. Brewer–Carías, *Las Constituciones de Venezuela, op. cit.,* pp. 549-551. See references in the work of Pedro Grases, *La conspiración de Gual y España y el ideario de la Independencia,* Caracas 1978.

86 See the text of the meetings of July 5, 1811 in *Libro de Actas... cit.,* pp. 171 a 202. See the text of the Declaration of Independence at Allan R. Brewer–Carías, *Las Constituciones de Venezuela, cit.,* pp. 545-548.

for the illusions of ignorance, and for the malice of wounded ambition," confronting the issue by explaining the reasons of Venezuela to have detached itself from the "conditional oath by which" Ferdinand VII was recognized in April 1810, and that "the representative body that now declares its independence of every other foreign power, previously acknowledged Ferdinand VIIth" in July 1811. For such purpose it was said that such "promissory oath" was "no more than an accessory bond, which always pre-supposes the validity and legitimacy of the contract ratified by the same," so, were there not been "vice which may render it null and illegitimate, [...] the obligation to comply with them, is founded on an evident maxim of the natural law."

And as for the "oath" before God it was stated that:

> "God can at no time guarantee any thing that is not binding in the natural order of things, nor can it be supposed he will accept of any contract, opposed to those very laws he himself has established, for the felicity of the human race."

In any case, it was argued that "even when the oath were to add any new obligation to that of the contract thereby confirmed, the nullity of the one, would at all times be inseparable to the nullity of the other," so that "if he who violates a sworn contract, is criminal and worthy of punishment, it is, because he has violated good faith, the only bond of society; without the perjury doing more than serving to increase the crime, and to aggravate the punishment." Additionally, it was said "that natural law which obliges us to fulfill our promises, and that divine one which forbids us to invoke the name of God in vain, do not in any manner alter the nature of the obligations contracted under the simultaneous and inseparable effects of both laws; so that the infraction of the one, supposes the infraction of the other."

Under these principles -certainly laid down by the hands of the jurists who were members of the General Congress- in the *Manifesto* was analyzed the "conditional oath by which the Congress of Venezuela has promised to preserve the rights legally held by Ferdinand VII without attributing to it any other, which, being contrary to the liberty of the people, would of consequence invalidate the contract, and annul the oath," for which purpose it begun by finding that, at last, "impelled by the conduct of the governments of Spain, the people of Venezuela became sensible of the circumstances, by which the tolerated rights of Ferdinand VII were rendered void in consequence of the transactions of El Escorial and Aranjuez; as well as those of all his house, by the cessions and abdications made at Bayonne;" concluding that:

> "from the demonstration of this truth, follows, as a corollary, the invalidity of an oath, which, besides being conditional, could not subsist beyond the contract to which it was added, as an accessory bond. To preserve the rights of Ferdinand, was all that Caracas promised on the 19th of April, at a time she was ignorant he had lost them and even if he retained them, with regard to Spain, it remains to be proved, whether, by virtue of the same, he was able to cede America to another dynasty, without her own conset."

In any case, it was "the advices, which in spite of the oppression and cunning of the intrusive governments of Spain, Venezuela was enabled to obtain of the conduct of the Bourbons, and the fatal effects the same was about to entail on America," what allowed to have formed:

"a body of irrefragable proofs, evincing, that as Ferdinand no longer retained any rights, the preservation thereof, which Venezuela promised, as well as the oath by which she confirmed this promise, consequently are, and ought to be done away (Jurabis in veritate, et in judicio, et in justitia, Jerem. Cap. 4). Of the first of the position, the nullity of the second, becomes a legitimate consequence."

But the 1811 *Manifesto* went beyond that by affirming in it that "the Escorial, Aranjuez, or Bayona, were the first theatres of the transactions, which deprived the Bourbons of their rights to America. Already in Basil (*Treaty of Basilea* of 15 of July 1795) and in the court of Spain, the fundamental laws of the Spanish dominion in these countries," having ceaded Charles IV "contrary to one of them" (*Ley 1, tít. 1 de la Recopil. de Indias*) "the island of St. Domingo to France, and disposed of Louisiana to the same foreign power."

Therefore, it was stated in the *Manifesto* that these:

"unheard of, and scandalous in fractions, authorized the Americans, against whom they were committed, as well as the whole of the Columbian people, to separate from the obedience and lay aside the oath, by which they had bound themselves to the crown of Castile, in like manner, as they were entitled to protest against the eminent danger, which threatened the integrity of the monarchy in both worlds, by the introduction of French troops into Spain previous to the transactions of Bayona; invited there, no doubt, by one of the Bourbon factions, in order to usurp the national sovereignty in favour of an intruder, a foreigner, or a traitor."

Returning to the actions in Venezuela which took place from July 15, 1808 to July 5, 1811, and upon the possible claims that the oath given for the preservation of the rights of Ferdinand VII could be raised against the Venezuelans "in order to perpetuate those evils, which the dear bought experience of three years has proved to be inseparable to so fatal and -ruinous an engagement," the General Congress stated in the *Manifiesto* that the time had come to "abandon a talisman invented by ignorance, and adopted by a misguided fidelity, for ever since it was, it has not failed to heap upon us all the evils attendant on an ambiguous state, and on suspicion and discord," considering that "Ferdinand the Seventh, is the universal watch-word for tyranny in Spain, as well as America."

The disregard for Ferdinand VII as alleged king, and therefore, for the oath that had been given in 1810 to preserve his rights, were evident in the mind of the General Congress of Venezuela in 1811, whose members in the *Manifesto*, opposed "three centuries of injuries, [...] by three years of lawful, generous and philanthropic efforts," also protested, in passing, that if "gall and poison" had been the agents of the "solemn, true and candid manifestation" of protest against the pledge to preserve the rights of Ferdinand VII, they would have:

"began by destroying the rights of Ferdinand, in consequence of the illegitimacy of his origin, declared by his mother in Bayona, and published in the French and Spanish papers; we should have proved the personal defects of Ferdinand, his ineptitude to reign, his weak and degraded conduct in the Cortes of Bayona, his inefficient and insignificant education, and the want of proofs which he never gave to found the gigantic hopes of the governments of Spain, which had no other origin than the illusion of America, nor any other support than the political interest of England, much opposed to the Bourbons"[87]

But it was proclaimed in the *Manifesto* that since "decency is the guide of our conduct "its editors were ready to sacrifice" the "best reasons," particularly considering that sufficient were the alleged ones "to prove the justice, necessity and utility of our resolution, to the support of which nothing is wanting, but the examples by which we will strive to justify our independence."

So, it was proclaimed in the *Manifesto* that

"Even when the rights of the Bourbons had been incontestible, and indelible the oath, which we have proved not to exist; the injustice, force and deceit, with which the same was snatched from us, would suffice to render it void and of no effect, as soon as it was discovered to be opposed to our liberty, grievious to our rights, prejudicial to our interests, and fatal to our tranquility."

In short, it was stated in the *Manifesto* in general that:

"Three distinct oligarchies have declared war against us, have **contemned our claims, have excited civil dissensions amongst us, have sown** the seeds of discord and mistrust in our great family, have plotted three horrible conspiracies against our liberty, have interrupted our trade, have suppressed our agriculture, have traduced our conduct, and have sought to raise against us an Europian power, by vainly imploring its aid to oppress us. The same flag; the same language, the same religion, and the same laws, have, till now, confounded the party of liberty, with that of tyranny; Ferdinand VII as liberator, has been opposed to Ferdinand VII as oppressor; and, if we had not resolved to abandon a name, at the same time synonimous with crime and virtue, America would at length be enslaved by the same force that is wielded for the independence of Spain."

The same concerns were expressed in the *Declaration of Independence*, stating that when the Venezuelans:

"faithful to our promises, were sacrificing our security and civil dignity, not to abandon the rights which we generously preserved to Ferdinand of Bourbon, we have seen that, to the relations of force which bound him to the Emperor of the French, he has added the ties of blood and friendship; in consequence of which, even the Governments of Spain have already declared their resolution only to acknowledge him conditionally."

It was then stated in the *Declaration of Independence* that "this mournful alternative" had

"remained three years, in a state of political indecision and ambiguity, so fatal and dangerous, [...] till necessity has obliged us to go beyond what we at first proposed, impelled by the hostile and unnatural conduct of the Governments of Spain, which have disburdened us of

---

87   The *Manifesto* made clear that "the public opinion in Spain and the Kingdom's revolution experience, would provide us with abounding evidence of the mother's behavior and the attributes of the child, without resort to the minister Azanza proclamation (made public after the Bayonne journey and distributed in this capital city despite the former oppression) and without resort to the secret memoirs of Maria Luisa."

our conditional oath, by which circumstance, we are called to the august representation we now exercise."

In any case, after the Declaration of Independence was issued, ant the Manifiesto was published, the General Congress sanctioned on December 21st, 1811 under the inspiration of the United States Constitution and of the French Declaration of the Rights of Man,[88] the first Federal Constitution for the States of Venezuela and all Latin American countries.[89] In it, the division of the Supreme Power in three categories was specifically provided (legislative, executive and judiciary),[90] with a presidential system of government; establishing the supremacy of the law as "the free expression of the general will,"[91] and the sovereignty - that rested in the people of the country - was exercised by the representatives.[92] Its 228 sections were intended to govern the legislature (Sections 3 to 71), the Executive (Sections 72 to 109), the

---

88 See José Gil Fortoul, *Historia Constitucional de Venezuela, op. cit.,* Tomo Primero, pp. 254 y 267.

89 See *Libro de Actas del Supremo Congreso de Venezuela 1811–1812,* (Estudio Preliminar: Ramón Díaz Sánchez), Biblioteca de la Academia Nacional de la Historia, 2 vols. Caracas 1959. See the text at Allan R. Brewer–Carías *Las Constituciones de Venezuela, op. cit.,* pp. 555-579. Also in *La Constitución Federal de Venezuela de 1811 y documentos afines,* Biblioteca de la Academia Nacional de la Historia, Caracas 1959. See also Juan Garrido Rovira, "La legitimación de Venezuela (El Congreso Constituyente de 1811)", en Elena Plaza y Ricardo Combellas (Coordinadores), *Procesos Constituyentes y Reformas Constitucionales en la Historia de Venezuela: 1811–1999,* Universidad Central de Venezuela, Caracas 2005, tomo I, pp. 13–74.

90 In the *Preliminar* of the constitution there is explicitly stated that "The exercise of this authority, entrusted to the Confederation, shall never be found at once in its various functions. The Supreme Power shall be divided into the legislative, executive and judicial branches and shall be entrusted to separate bodies free from each other and in their respective powers ... " In addition, section 189 insisted that "the three essential government departments, namely the legislative, executive and judicial, must be retained as separate and independent from each other as required by the nature of a free government which is what is convenient to the connection string that ties all the fabric of the Constitution in an indissoluble mode of Friendship and Union".

91 "The law is the free expression of the general will or the majority of the citizens, as indicated by the body of their legally constituted representatives. It is founded on justice and the common good, and must protect the public freedom and individuality against all oppression and violence". "The acts, other than the ones established by the law, perpetrated wrongfully against anyone are wicked, and if through them the constitutional authority or freedom of the people are encroached they shall be tyrannical" (Sections 149 and 150).

92 "A society of men gathered under the same laws, customs and government compose a sovereignty." "The sovereignty of a country or the supreme power to fairly regulate or administer the interests of the community resides, then, essentially and originally in the general aggregate of the people and is exercised through their agents or representatives appointed or established under the Constitution." "Neither an individual, nor a particular family, nor any village, town or partition may attribute itself with the sovereignty of society, which is irrevocable, inalienable and indivisible in its essence and origin; nor may any person exercise any public function of government if it has not achieved it under the Constitution (Sections 143, 144 and 145)."

Judiciary (Sections 110 to 118), the Provinces (Sections 119 to 134) and the Human Rights to be observed in the entire extension of the State (Sections 141 to 199). The provinces declared themselves as sovereign states, having each also adopted its own constitution or form of government (Provincial Constitutions) under the same principles of modern constitutionalism.[93]

In any case, with a constitutional text of this kind, after the political and constitutional revolutions that a few decades before had taken place in North America and in France, this was the first time that a republican constitutional process of this kind had occurred in modern history,[94] a process that occurred even before the sanctioning of the very important Constitution of the Spanish Monarchy of Cádiz, in March 1812, also following the same modern constitutional principles;[95] a process which occur, precisely when the relations between the governing authorities in Spain and the new independent authorities in Caracas were in its worst shape

By declaring the independence, as the drafters of the *Declaration of Independence* explicitly made clear, they did not want to begin by "by alleging the rights inherent in every conquered country, to recover its state of property and independence;" preferring to forget "the long series of ills, injuries, and privations, which the sad right of conquest" had "indistinctly caused, to all the descendants of the Discoverers, Conquerors, and Settlers of these Countries [...] Drawing a veil over the three hundred years of Spanish dominion in America," they proceeded to put forward the "the authentic and well-known facts, which ought to have wrested from one world, the right over the other, by the inversion, disorder, and conquest, that have already dissolved the Spanish Nation." In this, in the *Manifiesto* was also considered America, as "condemned for more than three centuries, to have no other existence than to serve to increase the political preponderance of Spain, without the least influence or participation in her greatness;"

It was then in the *Manifesto* of 1811, where the General Congress did refer liberally to the general situation of America in connection with Spain, beginning by pointing out that it was the "instinct of self-security" the one that finally ordered the

---

93   See *Las Constituciones Provinciales* (Estudio Preliminar por Ángel Francisco Bice), Biblioteca de la Academia Nacional de la Historia, Caracas 1959; Allan R. Brewer-Carías, *Historia Constitucional de Venezuela*, Tomo I, Editorial Alfa, Caracas 2008, pp. 239 ss.

94   On the constitutional aspects of the process of independence of Venezuela since 1810 see Allan R. Brewer-Carias, *Historia Constitucional de Venezuela*, Tomo I, Editorial Alfa, Caracas 2008, pp. 195-278.

95   See Allan R. Brewer-Carías, "La Constitución de Cádiz de 1812 y los principios del constitucionalismo moderno: su vigencia en Europa y en América," en *Anuario Jurídico Villanueva*, III, Año 2009, Villanueva Centro Universitario, Universidad Complutense de Madrid, Madrid 2009, pp. 107-127; "El paralelismo entre el constitucionalismo venezolano y el constitucionalismo de Cádiz (o de cómo el de Cádiz no influyó en el venezolano)," en *Libro Homenaje a Tomás Polanco Alcántara*, Estudios de Derecho Público, Universidad Central de Venezuela, Caracas 2005, pp. 101-189, y en *La Constitución de Cádiz. Hacia los orígenes del Constitucionalismo Iberoamericano y Latino,* Unión Latina-UCAB, Caracas 2004, pp. 223-331.

Americans "that the moment of acting had arrived, and that it was time to reap the fruits of three hundred years of inaction and patience." For such purpose, they took into consideration that just as the "discovery of the new world" had been "one of the most interesting occurrences to the human race," so too "the regeneration of this same world, degraded from that period by oppression and servitude" would be "no less meaningful," so that America, "raising herself from the dust, and freed of her chains" will offer a revolution to be "most useful to the human race" allowing "America, when constituted and governed by her own self," to "open her arms to receive the people of Europe [...] friends, and not as tyrants; as men in need, not as lords; not to destroy, but to build; not as tigers, but as men."

As explained on the *Manifesto*, "It was written in her ineffable designs, that one half of the human race should not groan under the tyranny of the other," finding, however, that what had happened in Europe and America during those three hundred years proved that "all, all accelerated the progress of evil in one world, and that of good in the other." The *Manifesto* noted, for example, "the unfairness" "the injustice" of "dependence and degradation" of America "when every nation has viewed as an insult to political equity, that Spain, unpeopled, corrupted, and sunk in a state of inaction and sloth by a despotic government, should have exclusively usurped from the industry and activity of the rest of the continent, the precious and incalculable resources of a world, constituted in the fief and monopoly of a small portion of the other."

America, therefore, was an option to the anarchy-ridden Spain and it was an "advantageous alternative, that enslaved America presented on the other side of the ocean, to her mistress Spain, when cast down by the weight of every evil, and undermined by every destructive principle of society, she called upon her to ease her of her chains, that she might fly to her succour."

The claims of America were, however, not heard, particularly those of Venezuela and as stated in the *Manifesto*, Venezuela was "the first to pledge to Spain, the generous aid which she considered as a necessary homage"; the first "to know the disorders that threatened the destruction of Spain;" and "the first to provide for her own safety, without breaking the bonds that held her to the mother country." Nonetheless, Venezuela was also the first to perceive the effects of Spain's "ambitious ingratitude"; and "was the first on whom war was made by her brethren." From there it was, hence, concluded in the *Manifesto* that Venezuela was therefore "the first to recover her independence and civil dignity in the new world."

It was precisely "In order to justify this measure of necessity and justice" that the *Manifesto* was drawn up "to present to the universe, the reasons" for the independence and drawing attention to the fact that "the interest of Europe cannot clash with the liberty of a quarter of the globe, that now shews itself to the felicity of the other three," and that "none but a South Peninsula can oppose the interests of its government, to those of its nation, in order to raise the old hemisphere against the new one, now that the impossibility of oppressing it any longer." The Spain's repressive demeanor against Venezuela was considered in the *Manifesto* enough to justify "not only our independents but even also the declaration of an irreconcilable enmity against those who directly, or indirectly, have contributed to fee unnatural system now adopted against us;" the drafters being aware that "we cannot extricate our-

selves from the condition of slaves, without being branded with the calumny of being ingrates, rebels, and unthankful."

In this regard, other aspects treated in the *Manifiesto* when justifying the independence of the provinces from Spain, referred to the supposed titles that Spain
might have had on the Americas as well as the assertion that the rights over those
lands were first with the Americans descendants of the Conquerors. To this end, the
constant principle "of natural, and a law of positive right" invoked was that "America does not belong to the territory of Spain;" and that while:

> "the rights which the Bourbons, justly or unjustly, had to it, notwithstanding they were
> hereditary, could not be disposed of without the consent of the people, and particularly of
> those of America, who, on the election between the French and Austrian dynasties, might
> have done in the 17th century, what they have now done in the 19th."

As for "The bull of Alexander IV and the just titles which the house of Austria
alledged in the American code," it was also reported in the *Manifesto*, that it "had no
other origin, than the right of conquest, partially ceded to the conquerors and settlers, for the aid they had rendered to the crown in order to extend its dominion in
America."

At any event, it was alleged in the *Manifiesto*, it seemed that:

> "the fury of conquest had ceased; when the thirst for gold was satisfied; when the conti-
> nental equilibrium was declared in favour of Spain, by the advantageous acquisition of Amer-
> ica; the feudal government destroyed and rooted up from the time of the reign of the Bour-
> bons in Spain, and every right extinct that did not originate in the new concessions or man-
> dates of the prince, the conquerors and settlers then became absolved of theirs."

So in strict legal sense, "as soon as the lameness and invalidity of the rights arrogated to themselves by the Bourbons, is demonstrated," then "the titles by which the
Americans, descendents of the conquerors, possessed these countries," should have:

> "revive; not in detriment to the natives and primitive proprietors, but to equalise them in
> the enjoyment of liberty, property, and independence, which they always held by a right
> stronger than that of the Bourbons, or of any others to whom they may have ceded America,
> without the consent of the Americans, its natural owners."

This was emphasized in the *Manifesto* but also noting the fact that not belonging
America "to the territory of Spain," as a "principle of natural, and a law of positive
right, [...] no title, just or unjust, which exists of her slavery, can apply to the Spaniards of Europe; and all the liberality of Alexander VI, could not do more, than declare the Austrian kings promoters of the faith, in order to find out for them a preter-
natural right, whereby to make them Lords of America," because:

> "Neither the pre-eminence of the parent state, nor the prerogative of the mother country,
> could at any time ground the origin of Lordship on the part of Spain. The first was lost, from
> the time that the monarch, acknowledged by the Americans, left the country and renounced
> his rights, and the second, always amounted to nothing more than a scandalous abuse of
> words; as was that of calling our slavery, felicity: that of saying the fiscals were the protectors
> of the Indians; and that the sons of Americans were divested of every right and civil dignity."

The *Manifesto* also noted that "By the mere act of men passing from one country to another to settle it, those who do not leave their homes, acquire no property, nor do they expose themselves to the hardships inseparable to emigration;" instead:

> "those who conquer and obtain possession of a country by means of their labour, industry, cultivation, and connection with the natives thereof, are they who have a preferable right to preserve it and transmit it to their posterity born therein; for if the country where one is born, were considered as an origin of sovereignty, or a title of acquisition; the general will of nations, and the fate of the human race, would then be riveted to the soil, in like manner as are the trees, mountains, rivers and lakes."

And somewhat ironically, to reinforce the assertion, it was stated in the *Manifesto* that "Neither could it ever be considered as a title of property to the rest of a nation, for one part thereof to have past over to another country to settle it;" because:

> "for by a right of this nature, Spain herself would belong to the Phoenicians, their descendants, or to the Carthagenians, wherever they may be found∗; even the whole of the nations of Europe, would have to change their abodes to make room and re-establish so singular a territorial right; home would then become as precarious as are the wants and caprices of men."

Consequently, in view of all of this there was - as stated in the *Declaration of Independence* – that:

> "It is contrary to order, impossible to the Government of Spain, and fatal to the welfare of America, that the latter, possessed of a range of country infinitely more extensive, and a population incomparably more numerous, should depend and be subject to a Peninsular Corner of the European Continent."

Finnaly, in view of all the "solid, public, and incontestible reasons of policy," to justify the cause of independence, the conclusion was according to the *Declaration of Independence*, that the Venezuelans "in compliance with the imprescriptible rights enjoyed by nations, to destroy every pact, agreement, or association, which does not answer the purposes for which governments were established; we believe that we cannot, nor ought not, to preserve the bonds which hitherto kept us united to the Government of Spain; and that, like all the other nations of the world, we are free, and authorised not to depend on any other authority than our own." This was precisely what led them ("We, the Representatives of the United Provinces of Venezuela"), while simultaneously meeting with the "indispensable duty" to "provide for our own preservation, security, and felicity, by essentially varying all the forms of our former constitution," to:

> "declare solemnly to the world, that its united Provinces are, and ought to be, from this day, by act and right, Free, Sovereign, and Independent States; and that they are absolved from every submission and dependence on the Throne of Spain, or on those who do, of may call themselves its Agents and Representatives; and that a free and independent State, thus constituted, has full power to take that form of Government which may be conformable to the general will of the People."

∗   In this comparison, no notice is taken of the disputes respecting primitive history.

This was, without doubt, the clearest manifestation of the right of rebellion or insurrection exercised in the *Declaration of Independence*, as an "indispensable duty to provide for our own preservation, security, and felicity, by essentially varying all the forms of our former constitution," and which was expressed in more detail in the General Congress 1811 *Manifesto*. In it, the Congress, among the reasons for the independence of Venezuela referred to the "right of insurrection of the peoples" against despotic governments. To this end, it was relied on the statement that: "never had, nor can have, any other duration than the utility and felicity of the human race, that kings are not of any priviledged nature, nor of an order superior to other men;" and "kings are not of any priviledged nature, nor of an order superior to other men; that their authority emanates from the will of the people."

So, after long and reasoned quotes on the rebellion of the people of Israel in ancient history, which would not have been "questioned by God," the conclusion in the *Manifesto* was made with the question of whether the condition of the "Christian people of Venezuela could be still in a worse plight," in the sense that "after being declared free by the government of Spain, after 300 years of captivity, exactions, hardships and injustice, shall they not be allowed to do what the God of Israel, whom they equally adore, formerly permitted to his people, without being spurned, and without vengeance being deprecated upon them?"

The response in the *Manifesto* to this question was no other than "It is his divine hand that guides our conduct, and to his eternal judgements our resolution shall be submitted," asserting that "If the independence of the Hebrew people was not a sin against the written law, that of a Christian people cannot be such against the law of grace;" and arguing that "At no time has the Apostolical see excommunicated any nation that has risen up against the tyranny of those kings or governments, which had violated the social compact," so that:

> "The Swiss, Dutch, French, and North Americans, proclaimed their independence, overturned their constitution, and varied their forms of government, without having incurred any other spiritual censures than those which the church might have fulminated for the infringements on the belief, discipline or piety, but without their being connected with political measures, or alluding to the civil transactions of the people."

In the *Preliminary Remarks* to the book the issue over the right of peoples to revolt and to its representation was reiterated again, based on the "invariable principle that "Societies ought to be self-governed." To that end, reference was made in the *Preliminary Remarks* to the work of John Locke to whom, as indicated in the book:

> "all legitimate government is derived from the consent of the people, that men are naturally equal, and that no one has a right to injure another in his life, health, liberty, or possessions, and that no man, in civil society, ought to be subject to the arbitrary will of others, but only to known and established laws, made by general consent, for the common benefit. That no taxes are to be levied on the people, without the consent of the majority, given by themselves, or by their representatives. That the ruling power ought to be govern by declared and received laws, and not by extemporary dictates, and undetermined resolutions. That kings and princes, magistrates, and rulers of every class, have no just authority but what is delegated to them by the people; and which when not employed for their benefit, the people have always a right to resume in whatever hands it may be placed."

Thereby the *Preliminary Remarks* referred precisely to "these sacred rights" which were those exercised by "the people of Venezuela" when they "resolved to administer their own concerns," and to decide "to be no longer dependent on governors who were ready to deliver them up to the French,"[96] relying confidently in that:

> "in the pages of impartial history, they will be found to have acted correctly. They have made use of that right which the most enlightened Spaniards have acknowledged to exist, and Don Gaspar Jovellanos, in the famous opinion which he laid before the Central Junta on the 7th Oct. 1808, expressly says, 'that when a people discovers the imminent danger of the society of which it is member, and knows that the administrators of the authority who ought to govern and defend it, are suborned and enslaved, it naturally enters into the necessity of defending itself,' and of consequence acquires an extraordinary and legitimate 'right of insurrection.' And can it be argued, that these are maxims only formed for the Spaniards of Europe, and that they do not extend to the Americans.?"

In the *Preliminary Remarks*, another reference was made to the criterion of John Locke,[97] referring to him as "our inimitable Locke"[98] indicating that he observed in fact "that revolutions happen not upon every little mismanagement of public affairs." On the contrary:

> "Great mistakes in the ruling part, many wrong and inconvenient laws, and all the slips of human frailty, will be borne by the people without muting or murmer. But if a long train of abuses, prevarications, and artifices, all tending the same way, make the design visible to the people, and they cannot but feel what they lie under, and see whither they are going, it is not to he wonde ed, that they should then rouze themselves, and endeavour to put the rule into such, hands which may secure to them the ends for which government was at first erected."

Finally, resort was also made to Montesquieu in the *Preliminary Remarks* to whom was credited establishing "as a maxim, if not an immutable law" that "that nations can be saved only by the recovery of their lost principles;" then concluding that:

> "the only mode left to the Americans was, to have governors of their own choice, answerable to them alone for their conduct; and under such circumstances they have always been ambitious of forming an equal and component part of the Spanish Nation. It was there- fore for their own security and in order to get out of the orphan state in which they were plunged, that the people of Venezuela, resolved to place their confidence in a body of Representatives of their own choice, and that their labours have advanced the public happiness, is evinced by the expressions of the people themselves, by the contrasted state of what the country was, and what it now is."

---

96   Reference was made to "Joseph Napoleon's orders to the various governments in America."

97   Reference was made to the *Tratado sobre el Gobierno civil* [Treaty on the Civil Government], Lib. 3 § 225.

98   Carlos Pi Sunyer said that this phrase could bolster the view that the *Preliminary Remarks* may have been written by an Englishman, which however he dismissed, attributing the use of it more to the fact that the text was addressed to the English audience. Carlos Pi Sunyer. *Patriotas Americanos en Londres...*, *op. cit.*, p. 216.

III. THE REACTION OF THE SPANISH AUTHORITIES AGAINST THE PROVINCES OF VENEZUELA: THE BLOCKADE AND THE MILITARY INVASION TO "PACIFY" THE PROVINCES

The process of independence of the Provinces of Venezuela, with all its justifications, as was pointed out in the *Manifiesto*, developed from 1808 up to 1811, after the events of the El Escorial, Aranjuez and Bayonne, inserted within the progression of three periods that were forced out from the Venezuelans, which the General Congress said had started "from the 15th July 1808," the "resolutions of the 19th April 1810" and "of the 5th July 1811;" composing three epochs that "will form the first period of the glories of regenerated Venezuela, when the impartial pen of history shall record the first lines of the political existence of South America."

This period of "three years" which elapsed "since we ought to be free and independent, till the period when we resolved to be so," and, in particular, "from the 19th of April 1810 to the 5th July 1811," was considered in the *Manifesto* as the "most interesting of the history of our revolution," although it was marked by "a bitter and painful alternative of acts of ingratitude, insults and hostilities on the part of Spain." In regard to that, the *Manifesto* began an account on how local authorities in Caracas accepted "the dispatches of the kingly substitute Murat" and "supporting" his orders they required Venezuelans "allegiance to the new king." This ignited the revolution.

Indeed, the first of the dates mentioned in the *Manifesto* as the beginning of the independence process is that of July 15, 1808, as aforementioned, was precisely when the news formally came to the *Ayuntamiento of Caracas* about the assumption to the Crown of Ferdinand VII on March 20, 1808, after the Aranjuez events; which provoked the proposal made before the *Ayuntamiento* by the Captain-General of Venezuela for the formation and organization of the Supreme *Junta*. About this project, the *Manifesto* of 1811 referred to the late reaction of the new Captain-General Vicente de Emparan before the *Audiencia*, saying "that in Caracas there was no other law nor will *but* his own," which fully manifested in several arbitrary acts and excesses." Among these, emphasis was made in the *Manifiesto* on the expelling from the Provinces of "Captain Don Francisco Rodriguez, and the assessor of the board of trade, Don Miguel Jozé Sanz, all embarked for Cadiz and Puerto Rico;" the condemnation "of a considerable multitude of good men, snatched from their homes under the pretence of vagrants [...] without either form or appearance of trial [...] to the labour of the public works;" and the Emparan's decisions "revoking and suspending the resolutions of the Audiencia, when not conformable to his caprice and absolute will." And all these actions, as reported in the *Manifiesto*, "after supporting his ignorance and pride to the utmost lengths: after many scandalous disputes between the Audiencia and the municipal body, and after all the law characters being reconciled to these despots, in order that they might be more secure and inexpugnable against us," and plotting "to organize and carry into effect, under the shadow of fallacy, the projects of espionage and ambiguity."[99]

In the 1811 *Manifesto*, therefore, specific reference was made to orders such as the one issued on April 30, 1810, so that

> "under the pretence of attending only to the war, both Spain and America might be sunk toper into a state of ignorance, it was ordained that rights and premiums should not be heard of, and that nothing was to be done, but sending to Spain, money, American men, provisions, colonial productions, submission, and obedience."

Furthermore, the *Manifesto* reported that "under the most severe threats of punishment, a political inquisition with all its horrors, was established against those who should read, possess, or receive other papers, not only foreign, but even Spanish, that were not out of the Regency's manufacture." The *Manifesto* even denounced that all correspondence had been "ordered to be opened; an excess unknown even under the despotism of Godoy, and only adopted to cause the espionage over America to be more tyrannical."

As aforementioned, in the midst of the general political crisis in the Crown and in the relation between Spain and the American provinces, after declaring that they were no more Colonies but parties of the Spanish empire, once the Cortes were convened, a decree was issued to assure the representation of the Spanish American provinces. On this "representation," nonetheless, the 1811 *Manifesto* sensitively recorded and stressed, to the contrary, about the lack of representation that was intended to give to the Spanish American provinces in the *Cortes*, to the point of stating that:

> "If the three hundred years of our former servitude, have not sufficed to authorize our emancipation, there would be sufficient cause in the conduct of the governments, which arrogated to themselves the sovereignty of a conquered nation, which never could have any property in America, declared an integral part of the same, whilst they attempted again to involve it in conquest."

Added in the *Manifesto* was that: "If the governors of Spain had been paid by her enemies, they could not have done more against the felicity of the nation, bound in its close union and good correspondence with America;" stressing out how "with the greatest contempt of our importance, and of the justice of our claims, when they could not deny us the appearance of a representation, they subjected it to the despotic influence of their agents over the municipalities to whom the election was committed."

Worse yet was it when the Americans got to compare their representation status within Spain where "at the same time [...] they allowed even for the provinces in possession of the French, as well as the Canaries and Balearic islands, a representative for each fifty thousand souls, freely elected by the people" but in America

---

99   There is an indication in the *Manifesto* that the foregoing is the result of true testimonies that rested in the files "even after the vigilance with which they were looted" by the Spanish authorities.

"scarcely a million sufficed to have the right of one representative, named by the Viceroy or Captain General, under the signature of the municipality."

In any case, the fact is that after the 19th of April 1811 Revolution of Caracas, the Supreme Junta of Venezuela addressed the Regency Council of Spain on May 3, 1810 in response to the papers that had been received from the Cadiz Supreme *Junta* and the Regency Council, and which were requiring the "recognition" of the latter as the "legitimate repository of the Spanish sovereignty." In such letter, the *Junta* reported not only about the events and decisions of the new government in Caracas, but it also purported to formally inform that the government of Venezuela "disregarded" such Regency as the government of Spain.[100] On the Regency -whose government was called in the *Manifesto* as "intrusive and illegitimate"- the address indicated that while the Regency declared the Americans free "in the theory of their plans," it "subjected them in practice to a *tiny and insignificant representation*, assuming that those to whom nothing is owed are to be content with whatever their master gives them."

The Regency expected to maintain the illusion of the Spanish Americans who already knew as was pointed out in the *Manifiesto*,

> "how little we should expect from the intruder representatives of Ferdinand: We did not ignore that if we were not to rely on the viceroys, ministers and governors, more so could we neither be subjected to a captive King with no titles or authority nor be subjected to a void and illegitimate government or to a nation unable to assert a right over another or to a mainland angle of Europe which has been almost entirely occupied by a foreign power."

The *Manifesto* in addition said, that it had been to no effect the declaration and proclamation in Spain that Spain "had received a new existence since the abandonment of her authorities, since the cessions of the Bourbons, and the introduction of the new dynasty," and that recovering "their absolute independence and liberty" they offered this example to the Americans, "that they might recover the same rights there proclaimed."[101]

It was then considered in the *Manifiesto* that the *Junta Central* -even when it "began to vary the language of liberality and sincerity [...] perfidiously adopted the talisman of Ferdinand, at first invented by good faith," suppressing, "but with cunning and sweetness, the plain and legal project of Caracas to imitate the representative conduct of the governments of Spain," referring to the "project agitated in 1803 to form a Junta, intended for the administration of governments and public safety, like those of Spain," and with "they began to set on foot a new species of despotism,

---

100 See the text drafted by José de Las LLamosas y Martín Tovar Ponte who later was deputy for San Sebastian in the General Congress at *El Mercurio Venezolano*, Nº I, Enero de 1811, pp. 7-14, edición facsimilar publicada en <http://cic1.ucab.edu.ve/hmdg/bases/hmdg/textos/Mercurio/Mer_Enero1811.pdf>.

101 In the *Manifesto* there are cited as supports "Various forms that came out with the first impulse of the revolution in Spain. The Count of Floridablanca, answering the Central Council to the Council of Castile. A *Manifesto* of the same Central Council. And the University of Seville, answering the latter's query."

under the factitious name of a king, acknowledged only from a principle of generosity, and destined to effect our ill and disaster, by those who had usurped the sovereign power."

The *Manifesto* then gave an account of how during those years "the defeats and misfortunes of the Spanish armies were concealed; pompous and imaginary triumphs over the French, in the Peninsula and on the Danube" while at the same time:

> "parties and factions were imagined, every one was calumniated who did not consent to be initiated in the mysteries of perfidy; fleets and emissaries from the French were figured, as being in our seas and amongst us; our relations with the neighbouring colonies were circumscribed and restricted; our trade was newly fettered; and the whole, to the end of keeping us in a state of continual agitation, that we might not fix our attention on our real interests."

However, despite this, according to the *Manifiesto*, the Venezuelans began "to lose confidence in the governments of Spain and their agents" and began to discover "the horrid futurity that threatened" them, noting that "the true fate of Spain, the disorders of her government, the energy of her inhabitants, the formidable power of her enemies, and the groundless hopes of her salvation."

The *Manifesto* reported that the even though Venezuelans were shut up in their "own houses, surrounded by spies, threatened by infamy and banishment, scarcely were we able to bewail our own situation, or to do more than secretly to complain against our vigilant and cunning enemies;" and that were "exhaled in the moments of bitterness and oppression [...] shut up within the walls of our own houses, and debarred from all communication with our fellow-citizens," the fact was that "scarcely was there one individual of Caracas, who did not think, that the moment of being for ever free had arrived, or else that, of irrevocably sanctioning a new and horrid slavery."

That is why, all Venezuelans, said the *Manifiesto*, started to:

> "discover the nullity of the acts of Bayonne, the invalidity of the rights of Ferdinand, and of all livered up as slaves, those, who had placed them on the throne, in opposition to the pretensions of the house of Austria; the connivance of the intrusive mandataries of Spain, to the plans of the new dynasty; the fate that these same plans prepared for America, and the necessity of taking some resolve, that might shield the new world from the calamities that were about to result from its relations with the old one."

In the *Manifesto* it was also reported, in contrast, that in Spain:

> "they beheld nothing but disorder, corruption, factions, defeats, misfortunes, treacheries, dispersed armies, whole provinces in the power of die enemy, the ready phalanxes of the latter, and at the head of all, a weak and tumultuary government, formed out of such rare elements."

Consequently, as pointed out in the *Manifesto*, such was the general and uniform noticed "on the faces of all the people of Venezuela by the agents of oppression, sent out to support, at every hazard, the infamous cause of their constituents; every word produced a proscription, every discourse cost banishment to its author, and every effort or attempt to do the same in America, as had been done in Spain, if it did not cause the blood of Americans to flow, it was at least sufficient, for the ruin, infamy, and desolation of many families."[102]

The *Manifesto* also reported that in Spain they were "wrong calculation" at the time in which "needy and desolate, her fate dependent on the generosity of America, and almost in the act of being blotted out from the list of nations;" she nonetheless began to take actions with the appearance of being "transported back to the 16th and 17th ages," beginning again "to conquer America, with arms more terrible than iron and lead." The Americans, meanwhile, captured every day new evidence of the fate that threatened them, being placed "in the sad alternative of being sold to a foreign power, or obliged for ever to groan under a fresh and irrevocable servitude" In any case, the *Manifiesto* said, the noise had resounded in the ears of Caracas of "the irruption of the French into Andalusia, the dissolution of the Central Junta," and the "abortive institution of another Protean government, under the name of Regency." The Council of Regency, as was also mentioned in the *Manifiesto*, then announced to the Americans "under ideas more liberal" some proposals or "brilliant promises, by theories barren of reform," that their "fate was no longer in the hands of viceroys, ministers, or governors;" seeking "to strengthen the illusions of the American people" with proposals that "in other occasion would have dazzled the Americans." But at the same time, the Spanish agents "received the most strict orders to watch over our conduct, over our opinions, and not to suffer these to exceed the limits, traced by the eloquence that gilded over the chains, prepared in the captious and cunning letter of emancipation."

In that contradictory situation, the *Manifesto* affirmed regarding the decisions adopted in the Provinces of Venezuela leading to their "political transformation," that:

> "every day we received fresh motives sufficiently strong, for each to have caused us to do what we have done, after three ages of misery and degradation. In every vessel that arrived from Spain, new agents, came out to strengthen with fresh instruction, those, who sustained the cause of ambition and perfidy. For the very same purpose, refusal was sent out for the officers, and other Europeans to return to Spain, not withstanding they asked it to fight against the French."

It must be remembered that during those very years 1808 to 1811, while in the former Spanish American colonies of Venezuela there was developing a process of institution building of an independent state, the institutional situation in Spain was in general terms precarious. After the widespread uprisings against the French invasion since May 1808 and the subsequent and spontaneous formation of Interim Boards in towns and cities to defend the nation, the need to form one unit of direction for the war and the politics was imperative by September 1808 and it led to the formation of a Central Junta composed of reputable people, some of which had even been part of the reign of Charles IV.

---

102 In the *Manifesto* there is quoted the "Deportation of several reputable officers and citizens of rank and honesty, enacted on March 20, 1810 by Emparan."

The choice between forming a Regency Council, or a Central *Junta* to deal with the conduct of the affairs of the kingdom in the absence of Fernando VII, resulted in the need to convoke the General Cortes, an act that was consulted to the country in 1809. Upon the advancement of the French troops, the Central Junta that operated in Seville had to retreat to the Isle of León (San Fernando), where it ended up appointing a Regency Council on January 29, 1810 while terminating its own functions and calling the nation to Parliament through the election of representatives under the Rules later issued by the Regency Council on October 6, 1810; these rules also included representatives from the Spanish American colonies' territories, which territories were sought to be unified to the Kingdom.

Before that, however, on August 1, 1810, the Regency Council had declared a strict blockade status for the Province of Caracas because its people "committed an act of defiance by declaring themselves *free* from the metropolis and by creating a governing board purported to exercise the relevant independent authority."[103] Undoubtedly, the events in Caracas had been those of a true political revolution; a coup d'état against the Spanish authorities by the Municipality which had assumed the supreme power of the Province disregarding any authority in the Peninsula, even the Regency Council.

This confronting situation between Spain and Venezuela was profusely highlighted in the *Manifiesto* of 1811 with which the General Congress of Venezuela told the world the reasons for the Independence. In it, in fact, it was reported that not only "the arrogant mandataries of our country, were not however, the only ones, authorized to support the horrid plot of their constituents" but that

> "from the sad and ominous reign of the Junta of Seville, the Central one, and the Regency; and under the system of political freemasonry, founded on the machiavelic pact, they all accorded in mutually substituting, replacing, and assisting each other, in the plans combined against the felicity and political existence of the new world."

The Peninsula leaders' demeanor over America was reported in the *Manifesto*, considering that it was "harder and more insulting [...] compared with that she appears to exercise with regard to France;" and referring to the "intrusive, illegitimate, weak and tumultuary governments" which in the Peninsula had been called "themselves the agents of the King, or representatives of the nation." Finally, it was reported that "America alone, is condemned to endure the unheard of condition, of being warred upon, destroyed, and enslaved," because "it appears that the independence of America, creates more irritation to Spain, than the foreign oppression that threatens her; for against her, are preferably employed, measures that have not even been used against the very provinces, that have proclaimed the new king."

---

103   See at J. F. Blanco y R. Azpúrua, *Documentos para la Historia de la Vida Pública del Libertador... op. cit.,* Tomo II, p. 571. The blockade was run by the Regional Commissioner Cortabarría from Puerto Rico, starting January 21, 1811. See at J. F. Blanco y R. Azpúrua, *Documentos para la Historia de la Vida Pública del Libertador..., op. cit.,* Tomo III, p. 8; C. Parra Pérez, *Historia de la Primera República..., op. cit.,* Tomo I, p. 484.

The same feelings were expressed in the *Declaration of Independence* in which it was said that despite the moderation and generosity shown by the provinces to Spain, they "were declared in a state of rebellion; we were blockaded; war was declared against us; agents were sent amongst us, to excite us one against the other, endeavouring to take away our credit with the other Nations of Europe, by imploring their assistance to oppress us." This was followed, referring to the Venezuelans that were appointed in Cádiz as representatives of the Provinces to the Cortes, by denouncing that

> "we are condemned to a mournful in-communication with our brethren; and, to add contempt to calumny, empowered agents are named for us, against our own express will, that in their Cortes they may arbitrarily dispose of our interests, under, the influence and force of our enemies."

On these matters, in addition, and regarding to the initial system of electing the representatives of the American provinces to the *Cortes* of Cádiz in 1810, which were to be appointed by the *Ayuntamientos*, the Declaration of Independence insisted that:

> "In order to crush and suppress the effects of our Representation, when they were obliged to grant it to us, we were submitted to a paltry and diminutive scale; and the form of election was subjected to the passive voice of the Municipal Bodies, degraded by the despotism of the Governors: which amounted to an insult to our plain dealing and good faith, more than a consideration of our incontestable political importance."

And in the *Declaration of Independence* it was added that the Spanish governments, always deaf to the cries for justice that were made from the Americas, only sought to "to discredit all our efforts, by declaring as criminal, and stamping with infamy, and rewarding with the scaffold and confiscation, every attempt, which at different periods some Americans have made, for the felicity of their country."

According to the *Manifesto*, the reaction of one of the Ministers of the Indies Council against Venezuela amounted to try again to "conquering Venezuela, with the same arms as those of the Alfingers and the Weslers"[104] the German factors to whom Charles V had "let out these provinces" for the purposes of continuing "the system of Spanish domination in the Americas" thereby ultimately stating that "the name of Ferdinand" had lost "every consideration amongst us, and consequently ought to be abandoned for ever."

As has been mentioned, the Spanish headquarters for the confrontation against Venezuela was established on the island of Puerto Rico by the Regency, which was, as stated in the *Manifesto*,

> "the haunt of all the agents of the Regency, the place of equipment for all the expeditions, the head quarters of all the anti-American forces, the workshop of all the impostures, calumnies, triumphs, and threats of the Regents; the refuge of all the wicked, the rendezvous port of a new set of Filibustiers, in order that there might not be wanting any of the calamities of the sixteenth century, to the new conquest of America, in the nineteenth."

---

104 The *Manifesto* made reference to the "First tyrants of Venezuela authorized by Charles V and promoters of the civil war between its original inhabitants."

In charge of the operations against the Province was the Governor of Puerto Rico, Salvador Meléndez y Bruna, named in the *Manifesto* as the "*Bajá* Meléndez" or "the tyrant of Borriquen" who was accused of declaring war on the Provinces and thereby also becoming "himself into the gratuitous jail-keeper, of the emissaries of peace and confederation," and of "in the most barefaced manner," plundering "more than one hundred thousand dollars of the public funds, belonging to Caracas, that had been embarked on board the ship Ferdinand the seventh, in order to purchase stores and military clothing in London."

In the Province, instead, it was said in the *Manifiesto*, "notwithstanding so much insult, robbery, and ingratitude," the new government business continued unchanged according to the oath for the preservation of the rights of Ferdinand VII, so that "the sublime act of her national representation was proclaimed in the name of Ferdinand VII." It was then declared that "under his fantastical authority, all the acts of our government and administration were sustained, though they required no other origin than the people who had constituted them;" and that under "the laws and regulations of Spain [...] a horrible and sanguinary conspiracy of the Europeans" was judged; laws that "were even infringed to save their lives, in order that the philanthropic memory of our revolution might not be stained with the blood." It was also stated in the *Manifiesto* that even under the name of Ferdinand "endeavors were made to inform and reduce the imperious mandataries of Coro and Maracaybo, who perfidiously kept separated from our interests," announcing that "we will reconquer Guayana, twice snatched from our confederation, as was Maracaybo, against the general wishes of its inhabitants."

From all these events, the *Manifiesto* affirmed, that it seemed "that nothing was now left to be done for the reconciliation of Spain, or for the entire and absolute separation of America," and even though "Venezuela was desirous of draining every means left within her reach, in order that justice and necessity should leave her no other safe alternative than that of independence, which ought to have been declared from the 15th of July 1808, or from the 19th of April 1810, "given the impact that the revolution principles had had in the Americas," and particularly "from the Orinoko, as far as El Magdalena; and from Cape Codera, as far as the Andes," the country had 'to endure fresh insults, before we fly to the painful extreme of breaking with our brethren for ever." Thus, the 1811 *Manifesto* expressed that:

> "Caracas, without having done more than imitate many of the provinces of Spain; and used the same rights which the Council of Regency declared in her favour, as well as that of all America; without having had in this conduct, other designs than those inspired by the supreme law of necessity not to be involved in an unknown fate, and to relieve the Regents of the trouble of attending to the government of countries, as well extensive as remote, at the same time that they protested that they would attend to nothing but the war; without having torn asunder her unity and political integrity with Spain; without having disowned, as was possible and proper, the .lame rights of Ferdinand; far from applauding for convenience, if not from sentiments of generosity, so just, necessary, and modest a resolution, and without answering even, or submitting to the judgment of the nation our complaints and claims, is declared in a state of war, her inhabitants are proclaimed rebels, and unnaturalized; every communication is cutoff with her brethren; England is deprived of her trade, the excesses of Melendez are approved, and he is authorized to commit whatever his malignity of heart may suggest to him, however opposed to reason and justice, as is proved by the order of the 4th of

Sept. 1810, unheard of for its enormity, even amongst the despots of Constantinople or Indostan; and not to deviate in the least from the plots of the conquest, a new Encomendero is sent out under the name of a pacificator, who, with more prerogatives than the conquerors and settlers themselves was to take his post in Puerto Rico, and thence to threaten, rob, pirate, deceive, excite civil disturbances, and all in the name of Ferdinand VII."

The *Manifesto*, in this paragraph, precisely referred to the Regency's decision to appoint Antonio Ignacio de Cortavarría or Cortabarría as Regional Commissioner based in Puerto Rico, in charge of the "pacification" of the provinces of Venezuela. Until then, as noted in the *Manifesto*, although orders had been given to governor Melendez of Puerto Rico "the progress of the system of subversion, anarchy, and depredation, which the Regency proposed to itself on hearing of the movements of Caracas" had been slow; but since "the principal focus of the civil war, being transferred nearer" of the Provinces, the progress became more intense as they were directed by "the chiefs hired by Cortavarria and Melendez" with the "the discord newly fanned by Miyares, rendered vain and arrogant by the imaginary and promised Captain-generalship of Venezuela."[105]

The outcome from all the actions that was deployed from Puerto Rico was not only the shedding of American blood on the coast of Coro, but "the robberies and assassinations" committed in such coast "by the pirates of the Regency," the "miserable blockade, intended to seduce and rise up our shore settlements; [...] the insults committed on the English flag; [...] the falling off of our trade; [...] the horrid perfidy in Guyana, and the insulting deportation of its leading characters to the Moorish dungeons jails in Puerto Rico;" being "the generous and impartial offices of reconciliation sincerely interposed by a representative of the British Government in the Antilles"[106] scorned by the "pseudo-pacificator."

From this all –it was denounced in the *Manifesto*- derived:

"all the evils, all the atrocities, and all the crimes, which are, and ever will be, inseparable to the names of Cortavarria and Melendez in Venezuela, which have impelled her government to go beyond what was proposed, when it took upon itself the fate of those who honoured it with their confidence."

In particular, the *Manifesto* emphatically denounced what it called "the mission of Cortavarria in the 19th Century, and th estate of Spain who decreed it, compared with America, against whom it is directed," which showed "to what an extreme the illusion of ambition blinds those, who on the depravation of the people, found all the origin of their authority." Just by the appointment of said peacemaker Cortabarría – as reported in the *Manifiesto*-, "alone sufficed to authorized our conduct," thereby unwittingly playing in the minds of the drafters of the *Manifesto* "the spirit of Charles V, the memory of Cortes and Pizarro, and the manes of Montezuma and

---

105 The document referred to Fernando Mijares appointed Captain-Generalof Venezuela to replace Emparan but who never held office in the capital.

106 The *Manifesto* referred to the Office of the Hon. Sir Admiral Cochrane, the Secretary of State.

Atahualpa [...] when we see the *Adelantados, Pesquisidores*, and *Encomenderos*" but after "300 years of submission and sacrifices."

On the mission of Contabarria the *Manifiesto* concluded by noting that:

> "The scandalous plenitude of power confided to a man, authorized by an intrusive and illegitimate government, that under the insulting name of pacificator, he might despotize, excite, rob, and (to crown the insult) that he might offer pardon to a people, noble, innocent, tranquil, generous, and masters of their own rights; could only be credited in the impotent delirium of a government that tyranises over a nation disorganized and stunned by the horrid tempest that overtakes her."

It must be remembered that the Cortes of Cadiz after being were convened in 1810, they were installed on September 24, 1810 in the Island of León, being moved five months later to Cádiz, gathering at the Chapel of San Felipe Neri. They were integrated by representative elected in the Spanish Peninsula Provinces, and also with some American "representatives" which were appointed as alternates in the very Island of León from within the Spanish Americans residing at the Peninsula.

The work of the Constituent Cortes of Cadiz concluded with the adoption of the March 18, 1812 Constitution of the Spanish Monarchy, the content of which revolutionized Spain laying the groundwork for the collapse of the Ancien Regime and the beginning of modern constitutionalism embodied in the principles of national sovereignty, separation of powers, freedom of the press and the abolition of privileges and the Inquisition. But like the 1811 Federal Constitution of Venezuela was short lived, so did the Constitution of Cadiz. In effect, after the secret Treaty signed in Valençay on December 8, 1813 between Napoleon and Ferdinand VII, the first renounced to the throne of Spain, whereby Fernando VII could go to back to his country, what he did on March 29, 1814, among other, for the purpose of swearing the new Constitution imposed on him by the Regency Council. He had spent 6 years in exile, and returned, but unfortunately, not to continue the work of the constituents of Cadiz but to end it. On May 4, 1814 he repealed the Cadiz *Cortes* and voided the 1812 Constitution, restored absolutism and persecuted all those who would defend the void Constitution. On October 1, 1814 Charles IV again abdicated his rights for the second time in his son to the throne of Spain and the Empire of the Indies.

However, the constitutional foundations of the new Constitutional Monarchy were set. It must be remembered that after the installation of the *Cortes* of 1810, the first of its decrees (Decree N° 1) was to declare "void and with no value nor effect the crown's transfer said to be made on behalf of Napoleon," acknowledging Ferdinand VII as King.[107] In addition, "being unsuitable that the Legislature, Executive and Judiciary branches remained united", the General *Cortes* reserved for them the Legislature, and the Regency Council assigned itself the exercise of the Executive power.[108] In the installation session of the *Cortes* in the Island of León, 207 deputies convened, including 62 Spanish Americans alternates, and among them presumably

---

107 See J. F. Blanco y R. Azpúrua, *Documentos para la Historia de la Vida Pública del Libertador...*, op. cit., Tomo II, pp. 657.

108 See in E. Roca Roca, *América en el Ordenamiento Jurídico ...*, op. cit., p. 193.

two for the Province of Caracas, Esteban Palacios and Fermín de Clemente, who had also been appointed as alternate members recruited in the Peninsula,[109] according to the rules set forth by the Regency Council only 15 days earlier, on September 8, 1810.

It is true that the deputy representatives who had been appointed in Cádiz for Venezuela had asked for directions to the Supreme *Junta* of Caracas, on February 1, 1811, the *Junta* replied not only considering the meeting of the *Cortes* "as illegal as the establishment of the Regency Council," but also alleging that "Mr. Palacios and Mr. Clemente had no authority to represent the provinces of Venezuela" and that "their actions as members were and would be considered void."[110] Already by January 23, 1811, the Supreme Junta had addressed the people rejecting the appointment of such alternate members, calling the *Cortes* as "the funny *Cortes* of Spain."[111]

Therefore, the constitutional breakdown resulting from the independence of Venezuela had not only operated from the part of the Supreme Junta of Caracas against the Regency but it continued against the *Cortes*, which got directly involved in the conflict, for which they were considered in Venezuela as "illegitimate and funny," denying in them any ability to represent the provinces of Venezuela.

It was then stated in the *Manifesto* that it was irritating:

> "to see so much liberality, so much civism, and so much disinterest in the Cortes, with regard to Spain, disorganized, exhausted, and nearly conquered; and at the same time, so much meanness, so much suspicion, prejudice, and pride, towards America; tranquil, faithful, generous, decided to aid her bretheren."

In addition, and comparing the treatment given by the Spanish government to the provinces in both sides of the Atlantic, in the *Manifiesto* was stated that

> "not one of the provinces surrendered, or satisfied with the dominion of the French [have] been treated like Venezuela; [...] not one of them has yet been declared traiterous, in rebellion, and unnaturalized as was Venezuela; [and for none of them has been created a public commission of diplomatic mutineers, to arm Spaniard against Spaniard, to fan the flame of civil war, and to burn and delapidate all that cannot be held in the name of Ferdinand the seventh."

---

109 See J. F. Blanco y R. Azpúrua, *Documentos para la Historia de la Vida Pública del Libertador...*, *op. cit.*, Tomo II, pp. 656. See further, Eduardo Roca Roca, *América en el Ordenamiento Jurídico ...*, *op. cit.*, pp. 22 y 136.

110 See the text in the *Gaceta de Caracas*, martes 5 de febrero de 1811, Caracas, 1959, Tomo II, p. 17. See also C. Parra Pérez, *Historia de la Primera República ...*, *op. cit.*, Tomo I, p. 484.

111 "Our ancient tyrants tend new bonds to seize us. A shameful and despicable mission tells us to ratify the appointment of alternate members they assigned to Venezuela. The funny Cortes of Spain follow the same steps than their mother the Regency: instead of assuming the position of requesting our pardon for the many offenses and insults with which they have persecuted us and reducing themselves to implore our generous protection in light of the powerless and weak situation they are in, they, on the contrary, maintain hostilities against the Americas and rush, godless and barbarously, all means to enslave us." See Official Texts ..., *op. cit.*, Volume II, p. 17.

In the open conflict between the Spanish government and the new Venezuelan State, for example, the *Cortes* themselves went so far as to "reward" the provinces of the former General Captaincy of Venezuela that had not joined the independence movement (Maracaibo, Coro, Guyana). Consequently, the *Cortes* granted the City of Guayana the adornment of their coat of arms with cannon trophies, bales, rifles, flags and other military insignia as a reward for having apprehended the New Barcelona rebels in the action of September 5, 1811 (Decree N° CXXXIII of February 6, 1812); and they awarded it with the title of the "very noble and very loyal" one in connection with the events in Venezuela that took place from the 15th to 16th of March of 1812 (Decree N° CCXII of December 8, 1812). The *Cortes* also distinguished the City of Coro with the title of the "very noble and fair," with the relevant shield, giving the members of the *Ayuntamiento* of the city the award of "The Accomplishment of the City of Coro" in connection with the city's demeanor during the commotions that had "inflicted on several provinces of Venezuela" and their defense against the insurgents in Caracas on November 28, 1812 (Decree N° CCXXXVVII of March 21, 1813). Also the city of Maracaibo, received the title of the "very noble and fair" for the same reasons than the City of Coro, granting the members of its *Ayuntamiento* "The Accomplishment of the City of Coro" (by Decree N° CCXXXVIII of March 21, 1813). As noted above, this recognition by the *Cortes* of Cádiz arose from the fact that the provinces of Maracaibo and Guayana, and the city of Coro had not joined the independence revolution nor had they been part of the General Congress which in 1811 enacted the Federal Constitution for the States of Venezuela.[112]

On the *Cortes,* the 1811 *Manifesto* said that after the "strange and short-lived governments" that had followed in Spain since the *Junta* of Seville "they recurred to a system of apparent liberality," assembling the representatives in an "accelerated and tumultuously" way; *Cortes* that were

> "so desired by the nation, yet opposed by the commercial government of Cadiz, but which were at length considered necessary, in order to restrain the torrent of liberty and justice, which in every quarter burst the mounds of oppression and iniquity in the new world."

Yet when analyzing its composition, the Venezuelan General Congress in the *Manifesto* asked itself skeptically "by what kind of deception, fatal to Spain, it is believed, that the part of the nation which passes the ocean, or is born under the tropics, acquires a constitution suitable to servitude, and incapable of ceding to the efforts of liberty," affirming, as was clearly evidenced in the newspapers of the Province of Venezuela:

> "the defects under which the Cortes laboured respecting America, and the illegal and insulting measures by them adopted, to give us therein a representation which we could not but oppose, even though we were, as the Regency had loudly boasted us to be, integral parts of the nation, and had no other complaints to allege against their government, than the scandalous usurpation of our rights, at a moment they most required our aid."

---

112 See the text of the decrees in Eduardo Roca Roca, *América en el Ordenamiento Jurídico ...*, *op. cit.,* pp. 79–80.

The General Congress noted in the *Manifesto* that it was gushing on that the *Cortes* would have received news of the reasons that the *Junta* of Caracas had given to "their perfidious envoy"[113] when "the former missions being frustrated, the great shipments of newspapers, filled with triumphs, reforms, heroic acts, and lamentations, being rendered useless, and the inefficacy of blockades, pacificators, squadrons, and expeditions, made known" in the Peninsula:

> "it was thought necessary to dazzle the self love of the Americans, by seating near the throne of the Cortes, members whom the latter had never named, nor who could be chosen by those who created them into their substitutes, as in like manner they did others for the provinces in possession of the French."

So then, the 1811 General Congress *Manifesto* reported regarding "the eloquent manifest" written by the Cortes on the 9th of January, 1811, against America,[114] that it was:

> "worded in a style worthy of a better object, but under the brilliancy of diction, the back ground of the perspective, designed to deceive us, was discovered. Fearing that we should be beforehand to protest against the whole of these nullities, they began to calculate on what was already known, not to risque what was yet hidden. The misfortunes of Ferdinand, were the pretexts that had obtained for his pseudo-representatives, the treasures, submission and slavery of America, after the events of Bayona; and Ferdinand seduced, deceived and prostituted

---

113 The General Congress was referring to the "abominable and noted behavior of Montenegro," envoy by the Spanish government.

114 Reference was made to the *Manifesto* issued by General and Special *Cortes* to the Nation dated January 9, 1811, where the reasons were given for Spain's independence from Napoleon's claims. See the text published in *El Mercurio Venezolano*, Vol I, Caracas, febrero 1811. See the newspaper's text in facsimile version in <http://cic1.ucab.edu.ve/hmdg/bases/hmdg/textos/Mercurio/Mer_Febrero1811.pdf>. It should be noted that the editor of *El Mercurio* in 1811 was precisely Francisco Isnardy, Secretary of the General Congress, who as such signed the *Manifesto* of the Congress of 1811. On the note preceding the text of the *Manifesto* of the General Cortes -undoubtedly from the pen of Isnardy- the following text was drafted mimicking what Napoleon could have said and was included in the *Manifesto* of the General Congress upon such *Manifesto* saying that "In one of our newspapers *("Mercurio Venezolano"*, February 1811), we have discovered the true spirit of the manifesto in point, which reduced to the following reasoning may be regarded as an assertive commentary to it: 'The Americas are under threat of being subjected to a foreign nation or alternatively continue to be enslaved to us; to regain their rights and not depend on anyone, they have found it necessary not to violently break the bonds which bind them to these nations; Ferdinand has been the convening signal that the New World has adopted and we have followed; he is suspected of collusion with the Emperor of the French and if we blindly let ourselves recognize him, we will give the people of the Americas -who still regard us as their representatives- an excuse to openly deny this representation; since these crafts are already beginning to be unveiled in some parts of the Americas, let us express in advance that we will not recognize Ferdinand except under certain conditions; these conditions will never happen and while Ferdinand, in fact or in law, is not our king, we shall be it for the Americas and that country so much coveted by us and so hard to keep in slavery, will not go so quickly out of our hands."

to the designs of the Emperor of the French, is now the last resourse to which they fly, to extinguish the flames of liberty, which Venezuela had kindled in the South Continent."

But despite this demonstration of the *Cortes* "destined to stir up, and excite commotions in America" the General Congress said in the *Manifesto* that it was its belief that "within the walls of the *Cortes*, justice is overlooked, our efforts are eluded, our resolutions contemned, our enemies upheld, the voices of our imaginary representatives suppressed, the inquisition is renewed against them [115] at the same time liberty of the press is proclaimed, and it is controversially discussed, whether the Regency could or not, declare us and an integral part of nation."

On the other hand, the persecution developed against the Provinces of Venezuela "from the island of Puerto Rico" did not end with the establishment of the *Cortes*, for which cause the *Manifesto* of the General Congress recorded that "Melendez, named king of Puerto Rico by the Regency," was left by a decree of the *Cortes*:

> "with the equivalent investiture of governor, synonimous names in America; because it now appeared, too monstrous to have two kings, in a small island of the Spanish Antilles. Cortavarria alone, was sufficient to elude the effects of a decree, only dictated by an involuntary sentiment of decency. Thus it happened, that when the investiture, granted by the Regency to Melendez was declared iniquitous, arbitrary, and tyrannical, and a revocation was extended to all the countries of America, then situated as was Puerto Rico, nothing was said of the plenipotentiary Cortavarria, authorized by the same Regency against Venezuela, with powers, the most uncommon and scandalous, ever remembered in the annals of organical despotism."

And just after the decree of the *Cortes*, as it was reported in the 1811 General Congress *Manifesto*, was that "the effects of that discord, promoted, sustained, and aimed from the fatal observatory of Puerto Rico, were more severely felt;" that "the fishermen and coasters were inhumanly assassinated in Ocumare, births pirates of Cortavarria;" that "Cumana and Barcelona where blockaed, threatened and summoned;" being a "a new and sanguinary conspiracy, against Venezuela," plotted and organized "by a vile emissary, who perfidiously entered the pacific bosom of his country, in order to devour it." The *Manifesto* also referred to the deceptions practiced "on the most innocent and lavorious classes of the imported colonists of Venezuela;" and that "by the suggestions of the Pacificator of the *Cortes*, and posterior to the said decree, [...] the political unity of our Constitution was interrupted in Valencia" promoting thereby disagreements among the provinces:

> "in order that on the same day, Venezuela might be deluged in blood, and sunk in affliction and desolation: be hostilely assaulted from every point within the reach of the conspirators, who were scattered amongst us by the same government, which issued the decree in favor of Puerto Rico and of all America. The name of Ferdinand VII is the pretext under which the new World is about to be laid waste, if the example of Venezuela does not henceforward cause the banners o fan unshaken and decided liberty, to be distinguished from those of a malicious and dissembled fidelity."

---

115 In the *Manifesto* it was reported that there were "positive news that Mr. Mejia, Deputy for Santa Fe, has been imprisoned by the Inquisition for his liberal ideas."

In any case, the threat of the envoy from Puerto Rico, Domingo Monteverde as head of the Spanish invader army, and the need to defend the Republic, led the General Congress, on April 4, 1812 to delegate the executive branch with all the necessary powers,[116] appointing, on April 23, 1812, Generalissimo Francisco de Miranda with dictatorial powers. In this way, the war of independence forced, quite rightly, to put aside the Constitution. As Secretary of War, José de Sata y Bussy (who had been deputy for San Fernando de Apure in the General Congress) notified in a letter addressed to Miranda that same day of April 23 1812:

> "The executive branch of the Union has just appointed you Chief-General of the arms of the entire Venezuelan Confederation with absolute authority to take all necessary actions you deem fit to save our country which has been invaded by the enemies of the Colombian freedom; and under this concept neither the law nor the regulations hitherto governing these republics shall bind you but instead you shall need to ask no more than to the Supreme Law of saving the country; and to this end the power of the Union has delegated under your responsibility its natural and extraordinary capacities given to it from the national representation by decree of the 4th of this month."[117]

At the session of April 4, 1812, it was agreed that "the measure and rule" of the powers granted to the executive branch was the health of the nation; and that that being the supreme law it "should silence every other;"[118] yet it was also agreed to notify the "Provincial Legislatures" the validity of the Federal Constitution notwithstanding the extraordinary authority bestowed on the Executive Branch.[119] The Congress, on April 4, 1812, had also asked the same "Provincial Legislatures" to force and urge the deputies of their provinces to attend, without excuse or delay, to the city of Valencia on July 5, 1812 in order to determine what would be most beneficial for the public cause.[120] Nonetheless, this meeting never took place.

In this way it is that in the Venezuelan constitutional history, the first break of the constitutional line was produced only a few months after the sanctioning of the Constitution of 1811 because of the need to save the Republic. The dictatorship, however, was short-lived as on July 25, 1812 Miranda signed a Capitulation and accepted the occupation of the province territory of Caracas by Monteverde.[121] Previously, Colonel Simón Bolívar had lost the garrison of Puerto Cabello, which he was in charge of, and since mid-July -before the capitulation- he reported the events

---

116 See *Libro de Actas del Congreso de Venezuela 1811–1812*, Biblioteca de la Academia Nacional de la Historia, tomo II, Caracas, 1959, pp. 397 a 399.

117 See *Archivo del General Miranda, op. cit*, Tomo XXIX, pp. 396 y 397.

118 See *Libro de Actas del Congreso de Venezuela..., op. cit.*, pág. 398.

119 *Idem*, p. 400.

120 *Ibidem*, pp. 398–399.

121 See the documents at *Archivo del General Miranda*, tomo XXIV, *op, cit.*, pp. 509 a 530. Also in J.F. Blanco y R. Azpúrua, *Documentos para la Historia de la Vida Pública del Libertador..., op. cit.*, pp. 679 y ss.

to Miranda.[122] Among the many causes for the fall of the First Republic, the loss of Puerto Cabello was, no doubt, one of them.

After the signing of the Capitulation, Monteverde disregarded its terms and Miranda was detained the night of July 30th, 1812, and Bolivar was able to leave La Guaira in late August to Curacao and then to Cartagena.

As for the constitution making process provoked by the Independence process, as mentioned, is most important result was the 1811 Federal Constitution that conditioned the development of the Venezuelan political and constitutional institutions still to this day, having in one way or another, influenced all the Venezuelan Constitutions up to the present in force sanctioned in 1999.[123] Nonetheless, as for its enforcement, the reality is that by when the book *Interesting Official Documents* was being edited in London, the work for the establishment of a Venezuelan independent State was left half done because as soon as the Republican government was installed in the capital city of Valencia, on March 1, 1812, the Royalist reaction conducted by Monteverde against the Republic began to be felt, which was favored by the devastating effects of the earthquake that ravaged Caracas on March 26th, 1812 and which the Friars and the Archbishop of Caracas attributed to a punishment of God for the revolution of Caracas.[124]

After the Capitulation signed on July 1812, no constitutional rule was applied in the provinces of Venezuela, not even the ones of the Cádiz 1812 Constitution that formally was swear in Caracas six months later, on December 3, 1812, in a military – not civic - ceremony. Such Constitution, in any case, had limited application even in the Peninsula because during its years of enforcement (1812-1814) the country was still largely occupied by the French, and the King remained absent; and when he did return in 1814, he disregarded the sovereignty of the *Cortes* of Cadiz, and formally annulled and repealed the Constitution.

---

122 *Idem.* pp. 415 a 430.

123 Since the 1811 Constitution, and during the last two hundred years, the Venezuelan independent state has been subjected to twenty-six Constitutions sanctioned successively in 1811, 1819, 1821, 1830, 1857, 1858, 1864, 1874, 1881, 1891, 1893, 1901, 1904, 1909, 1914, 1922, 1925, 1928, 1929, 1931, 1936, 1945, 1947, 1953, 1961 and 1999. This excessive number of "constitutions" was the product of the absence of the "amendment" constitutional revision technique, so in their great majority they were mere partial and punctual reforms generally provoked by circumstantial political factors. That is, this number of constitutions does not correspond to similar number of fundamental political pacts originating new political regimes and forms of constitutional government. See the texts of all the Venezuelan Constitutions since 1811, in Ulises Picón Rivas, *Índice Constitucional de Venezuela*, Caracas, 1944; Luis Mariñas Otero, *Las Constituciones de Venezuela*, Madrid, 1965; Allan R. Brewer–Carías, *Las Constituciones de Venezuela*, Academia de Ciencias Políticas y Sociales, 2 Vols., Caracas 2008.

124 See J.F. Blanco y R. Azpúrua, *Documentos para la Historia de la Vida Pública del Libertador...*, *op. cit.,* Tomo III, pp. 614 y ss.

IV. THE DRAFTERS OF THE *INTERESTING OFFICIAL DOCUMENTS* OF THE VENEZUELAN INDEPENDENCE, THEIR IMPRISONMENT AT THE FALL OF THE REPUBLIC, AND THE SUBSEQUENT COMPTENT OF THE CONSTITUTION

As for the constitutional documents that resulted from the Venezuelan independent process published in the London book as the *Interesting Official Documents Relating to the United Provinces of Venezuela,* in which the constitutional framework of the new State was defined, they were conceived and written by a formidable team of Venezuelan lawyers, who at that time, in addition to being fluent in English and French, and with access to all the new books that managed to get into the provinces, were the principal actors personally participating in the process of independence in a very active way since its beginnings on April 19, 1810; being all politically persecuted for such crime and particularly for of having written such "dangerous" documents.

Among them, mention must be made of Juan Germán Roscio (1763-1821), an experienced *pardo* attorney and theorist, who was one of the "representatives of the people", called to be incorporated in the Caracas *Junta* of 1810.[125] He quickly became Secretary of State (Foreign Affairs) of the new *Junta*, and editor of the *Gaceta de Caracas*, which was not only the official journal of the government, but the main journal of the country. From those positions, he maintained close relations with Andrés Bello, the first editor of the *Gaceta* and who worked with him in the Department of Foreign Affairs until he traveled to London in July 1810, as Secretary of the Commissioners sent by the *Junta* to London seeking support from the British government.[126] Bello, as we all know was a prolific writer, considered as the most prominent intellectual or the First Humanist of Spanish America,"[127] who developed his main intellectual activities in Chile where he settled some decades later. After the commissioners returned to Caracas, Bello remained in London, being as mentioned, the key instrument for the editing and publication of the book.

Roscio, who was a close friend of Bello, also supervised through him the edition of the *Interesting Official Documents* book, being himself one of the main co-drafter of the documents, as well as of other documents like the already mentioned Regulation for the Election of Representatives of the Provinces of Venezuela to the General Congress, and of course, of the very important *Manifiesto* issued by the General Congress to the World explaining reasons of the independence process.

---

125 See Luis Ugalde s.j., *El pensamiento teológico-político de Juan Germán Roscio*, Universidad Católica Andrés Bello, bid & co. Editor, Caracas 2007, p. 39.

126 Andrés Bello delivered José M. Blanco White, the editor in London of the journal named "*El Español,*" a letter of Roscio dated January 28, 1811, which was answered by the latter on July 11, 1811. Both letters were published in *El Español*. See the text in José Félix Blanco and Ramón Azpúrua, *Documentos para la Historia de la Vida Pública del Libertador...*, *op. cit.*, Tomo III, pp. 14-19.

127 See Pedro Grases, *Andrés Bello: El primer Humanista de América*, Ediciones El Tridente, Buenos Aires 1946; *Escritos Selectos*, Biblioteca Ayacucho, Caracas 1988, p. 119.

The other co-drafters of the *Interesting Official Documents* were Francisco Javier Ustáriz, Francisco Isnardy, and Miguel José Sanz, all active members of the General Congress in Caracas, and all of them together with Roscio and Miranda, considered by Monteverde after the Capitulation signed by the latter, as part of the "monsters of America" responsible for all the evils of the former colonies. They were all captured after Miranda's Capitulation in July 1812, and sent to prison. Miranda resulted to be the most prominent victim of betrayal by his own people and subordinates, particularly by Simón Bolívar, the former Commander of Puerto Cabello; Manuel María de las Casas, the military chief of the Port of La Guaira; and Miguel Peña, the civil chief of said Port.[128] After Miranda's imprisonment, Monteverde issued a passport to Bolívar, who then managed to escape from possible persecution to Cartagena in the provinces of Nueva Granada. As Monteverde himself wrote on August 26, 1812 in a letter sent to the Spanish authorities:

> "I cannot forget the interesting services of Casas, nor of Bolívar and Peña, and because of their persons have not been touched, giving only to the second his passport to foreign countries, due to that in these circumstances, his influence and connection could be dangerous."[129]

As for the "monster of America" they were the direct victims of the new "rule of conquest" imposed by the new Spanish conquerors in the provinces of Venezuela; precisely at the same time that in London the book was beginning to be available; a book that none of them ever gotten to see.

After being detained in Puerto Cabello and later, in the prison of San Felipe El Morro in Puerto Rico, Miranda died in Cádiz in 1816 without being subjected to any sort of trial.[130] Roscio, from his part, who was also imprisoned and sent to Cádiz, managed to be released the previous year, in 1815, traveling to Philadelphia where he published in 1817 another very important book with his late reflections of the independence process titled: *"El triunfo de la libertad sobre el despotismo, En la confesión de un pecador arrepentido de sus errores políticos, y dedicado a desagraviar en esta parte a la religión ofendida con el sistema de la tiranía* [The Triumph of Freedom over Despotism in the Confession of a Repentant Sinner from

---

128 See Giovanni Meza Dorta, *Miranda y Bolívar, Dos visions*, 3a ed., bid & co. Editor, Caracas 2011, pp. 143 ss., 153 ss.; Mario Rodriguez, *William Burke" and Francisco de Miranda, cit.* p. 488.

129 See the text of the letter in Giovanni Meza Dorta, *Miranda y Bolívar, Dos visions*, 3a ed., bid & co. Editor, Caracas 2011, Appendix 18, pp. 204-206.143 ss.

130 See the letters he sent fron the prisons in Puerto Cabello, Rico and Cádiz to all Spanish authorities, including the *Cortes Generales* and even King Ferdinand VII, dated March 8, 1813, June 6, 1813, June 30, 1814 and September 25, 1814 helplessly claiming for justice, in Francisco de Miranda, *América Espera, cit*, pp. 474, 480, 484, 487, 491. See specifically the first letter he sent to the Audiencia of Caracas on March 8, 1813 where he argues on the violation of the new Cádiz Constitution of 1812 and on the terms of the capitulation, in Francisco de Miranda, *Textos sobre la Independencia, cit.*, pp. 163-172.

his Political Mistakes and Dedicated to make Amends in this Part, of the Offended Religion with the System of Tyranny].[131]

This "System of Tyranny" argued by Roscio was no other than the one developed by Spain after the independence of Venezuela was declared, in order to achieve the "pacification" of the Venezuelan provinces. For such purpose, the *Junta Suprema* of Spain, and later the Council of *Regencia*, as mentioned, reacted in a very aggressive way against the independence processes, assigning to a "pacification" military task with headquarters located in Puerto Rico, the invasion of the Venezuelan provinces, from where the Spanish Commander Domingo de Monteverde sailed, arriving in the coasts of Venezuela in February of 1812.[132] One month later, on the eve of the terrible earthquake (March 26th, 1812) that devastated Caracas[133] and also with devastating effects in the institutions of the new State, on March 25th 1812 Monteverde managed to take the town of Carora.

The physical and moral destruction of the provinces originated a terrible political and social crisis that was followed by the entire institutional destruction of the Republic, being the republican order eliminated. After the Capitulation between Miranda and Monteverde was signed in July 1812, after seven months of enforcement, the Federal Constitution of 1811 was substituted by the military rule of Conquest, producing among other facts, the destruction of the historical memory of the new Republic. The Archives of the Province, in effect, were sacked, provoking the disappearance of the original manuscript of the *Interesting Official Documents* of Independence. Some copies were saved due to their publication in the *Gaceta de Caracas,* and particularly because all the copies were previously sent to London for its publication in the book, being printed at the same time that their original manuscripts were disappearing.

Having the Federal Constitution of 1811 been repealed by military force, the invading authorities should have sought the swearing in Venezuela of the Cadiz Con-

---

131   In the press of Thomas H. Palmer. The second edition of 1821 was also made in Philadelphia in the Press of M. Carey & Sons.

132   See the documents at the *Archivo del General Miranda,* La Habana, 1950, tomo XXIV, pp. 509 a 530. Also in José Félix Blanco y Ramón Azpúrua, *Documentos para la Historia de la Vida Pública del Libertador de Colombia, Perú y Bolivia. Puestos por orden cronológico y con adiciones y notas que la ilustran,* La Opinión Nacional, Vol. III, Caracas 1877, Edición facsimilar: Ediciones de la Presidencia de la República, Caracas 1977, 1983, pp. 679 y ss. Also in José de Austria, *Bosquejo de la Historia Militar de Venezuela,* Biblioteca de la Academia Nacional de la Historia, Tomo I, Caracas 1960, pp. 340 ss.

133   See on the earthquake, the description of Louis Delpech published in *Le Journal de Paris,* in May 1813. See the text in Jesús Rosas Marcano, *La independencia de Venezuela y los periódicos de Paris, 1808-1825,* Caracas 1964, pp. 135-140. See an English version of the letter in Mario Rodríguez, *"William Burke" and Francisco de Miranda. The Word and the Deed of the Spanish America's Independence,* University Press of America, 1994, pp. 451-454. See also the important Message of the Legislature of the Province of Caracas of April 9, 1812, *Idem.,* p. 436; and the comments on the events of Miguel José Sanz, "Bases para un gobierno provisional en Venezuela," in Pedro Grases (Ed.), *Pensamiento Político de la Emancipación Venezolana,* Biblioteca Ayacucho, Caracas1988, pp. 111 ss.

stitution, recently enacted (March 1812) when these events occurred. For that matter the newly appointed Governor of the former Province of Venezuela, Captain-General Fernando Mijares (position that he materially failed to effectively ever exercise), sent to Monteverde from Puerto Cabello, a few days after the signing of the capitulation, on 13 August 1812, twenty copies of the constitutional monarchic text, with the corresponding orders and provisions given by the *Cortes* for its publication and enforcement.[134] Monteverde failed to do so immediately, being only a few months later that he published the Constitution but in a "military fashion" assuming an omnipotent power contrary to the very text of the Constitution of Cadiz.[135] About it, the same Monteverde reported antagonistically to the Metropolitan Government that if he had come to publish the Constitution of Cadiz, it had been "out of respect and obedience, but not because I considered the province of Venezuela still worthy of partaking on the effects of such a benign code."[136]

Further, the following year, Simon Bolivar gave an account in Cartagena on the events regarding the non-application of the Constitution of Cadiz in Venezuela, on his "Brief Statements on the Deeds of the Spanish Commander Monteverde, during the Year of his Rule in the Provinces of Venezuela" dated September 20, 1813, in which he said:

> "But there is one fact that confirms better than any other the complicity of the Cadiz Government. The Cortes created the Constitution of the Monarchy -a work, for certain, that was the fruit of the enlightenment, knowledge and experience of those who composed the Cortes- and Monteverde kept it as something that did not matter or as opposed to his ideas and the ideas of his advisers. He finally resolves to publish it in Caracas. But what did he publish it for? Not only to make fun of it but also to insult and contradict it with deeds entirely contrary to the Constitution. He invites everyone, announces peace and tells them that the Ark of Peace has been brought, and thenceforth the innocent neighbors gather and many leaving the dens in where they were hiding. They trusted him in good faith but since the purpose was to surprise those that had escaped him, there was, on the one hand, the proclamation of the Spanish Constitution -based on the sacred rights of liberty, property and security-, while on the other hand, Spanish and Canarian units came the same day and seized the unaware who had come to witness and celebrate the publication. And they were disgracefully driven into the vaults.
>
> This is a fact so well known as are all those which have been indicated in this paper and which will be expanded in the proposed proclamation. In the province of Caracas, the Spanish Constitution is of no avail; the Spanish themselves make fun of it and call it names. After the Constitution, arrests are made absent summary information; shackles and chains are put at will by commanders and judges; life is taken away without formalities, without trial..."[137]

---

134 See José de Austria, *Bosquejo de la Historia militar...*, *op. cit.*, Tomo I, p. 364.

135 See Manuel Hernández González, "La Fiesta Patriótica. La Jura de la Constitución de Cádiz en los territorios no ocupados (Canarias y América) 1812-1814," en Alberto Ramos Santana y Alberto Romero Ferrer (eds), *1808-1812: Los emblemas de la libertad*, Universidad de Cádiz, Cádiz 2009, pp. 104 ss.

136 See José de Austria, *Bosquejo de la Historia militar...*, *op. cit.*, Tomo I, p. 370.

137 *Ibídem*, Tomo II, pp. 111 a 113.

In Venezuela, therefore, in 1812, the institutional situation was a *de facto* one since the collapse of the republican constitutional government was followed, simultaneously, by the displacement of the colonial institutions themselves. Thus, Monteverde, throughout his campaign in Venezuela between 1812 and 1813, ignored the appeal that had been made by the very *Cortes* of Cadiz since October 1810, in the sense that in the provinces where rebellions had occurred, and this in fact was only the case of Caracas, there should be "a general oblivion of all that had unduly happened" if the "recognition of the legitimate sovereign authority" established in Spain was made.[138] The terms of the Capitulation signed between Miranda allowing the military occupation of the Provinces, nonetheless, was violated by Monteverde, persecuting and imprisoning in an indiscriminate way all those who have collaborated with the independence, to the point that in report he addressed to the Council of Regency on January 17, 1813, he said that:

> "Since I entered this Capital City and became aware of the character of its inhabitants, I realized that indulgence was a crime and that tolerance and feint would turn insolent and reckless the criminal men."[139]

He added his appreciation about "the apathy I noticed the day the Constitution was proclaimed and the lack of enthusiastic attendance at public events" which allegedly had him depart from his attempts to rule "gently and kindly." He convened a meeting with the population and ordered "the arrest of those who were known as addicts to the 1810 revolution" even in contempt of the very *Audiencia* of Caracas that "had released individuals viewed as suspects by the people and that over irritated my dispositions," instructing the military commanders not to release the prisoners to justice.[140]

Therefore, on December 30, 1812, in a letter addressed to the military commander of Puerto Cabello, Monteverde, in contempt of the *Audiencia* orders and defying it, ordered:

> "Under no circumstances will you release some of the men who are imprisoned in that place for reason of disloyalty, without my prior order, even when the Royal Audience decides the release, in which case you will report to me in furtherance to the corresponding resolution."[141]

The *Audiencia* accused Monteverde of infringing the law for which reason, after accepting that "I am charged of disturbing these lands, that I bring unrest to them

---

138 See Decreto V, 15 de octubre de 1810, en Eduardo Roca Roca, *América en el Ordenamiento Jurídico de las Cortes de Cádiz,* Granada, 1986, p. 199.

139 See the text in J.F. Blanco y R. Azpúrua, *Documentos para la Historia de la Vida Pública del Libertador...,* op. cit., Tomo IV, p. 623–625.

140 *Idem*, p. 623–625.

141 See the text in José de Austria, *Bosquejo de la Historia militar...,* op. cit., Tomo I, pp. 365 y 366.

and put them in shock, in violation of the laws established for their peace;"[142] he explain himself noting that:

> "As well as Coro, Maracaibo and Guayana deserve to be under the protection of the Constitution of the Monarchy, Caracas and all others who made up the General Captaincy of Caracas, should not, by now, be part of its benefits until furnishing proof of having abhorred their evils; and under this concept they should be treated by the Rule of Conquest, that is, by the corresponding harshness and toils. Otherwise everything that has been gained shall be lost."[143]

In those years between 1812 and 1814, therefore, the situation in Venezuela was one of total war -a war to death- having neither the Federal Constitution of 1811 nor the Cadiz Constitution of 1812 any effective enforcement. Monteverde led a military dictatorship,[144] repressive and ruthless against those who had sided with the revolution of 1810. That is why the response of the patriots may be summarized in that terrible proclamation of Simon Bolivar, from Merida, on July 8, 1813:

> "The victims will be avenged: the executioners killed. Our goodness is exhausted already and as our oppressors force us to a deadly war, they shall disappear from America, and our land shall be purged off from the monsters that infest it. Our hatred is implacable, and war shall be to death."[145]

In the Provinces of Venezuela, therefore, there was no other constitution than the military commands of Royalists and Patriots. Monteverde ruled with the most brutal *rule of conquest*; and Bolivar and the patriots ruled with the dictatorial law of the "vigorous plan" or the "sovereign power" of who had been proclaimed the Liberator. Such proclamation, as Bolivar said, "So good events have it provided me with."[146]

The lawless situation even lead the Archbishop of Caracas, Narciso Coll y Prat in a Circular Edict of December 18, 1813, to recommending the observance of the "Law of Independence" adopted on July 5, 1811:

> "This law was without effect while the Spanish forces occupied these very Provinces, but as soon as the republic forces won over -and the people's acquiescence joined their victory- this law regained all its empire and it's now the one presiding the Venezuelan state."[147]

But the Cadiz *Cortes* and their envoys felt differently. They formally saluted Domingo Monteverde and the troops under his command by Decree of October 21, 1812, for "the important and distinguished services in the pacification of the Prov-

---

142 See J.F. Blanco y R. Azpúrua, *Documentos para la Historia de la Vida Pública del Libertador...*, *op. cit.*, Tomo IV, pp. 623–625.

143 *Idem.*

144 See J. Gil Fortoul, *Historia Constitucional de Venezuela*, Obras Completas, Caracas, 1953 Tomo I, p. 214.

145 *Idem*, Tomo I, p. 216.

146 See J. Gil Fortoul, *Historia Constitucional de Venezuela, op. cit.*, Tomo I, p. 221.

147 J.F. Blanco y R. Azpúrua, *Documentos para la Historia de la Vida Pública del Libertador...*, *op. cit.*, Tomo IV, p. 726.

ince of Caracas."[148] Two months later, on December 15 of that year 1812, Bolivar would give out to the people his celebrated *Manifiesto de Cartagena* or "A Memorial addressed to the citizens of New Granada by a Caracas native,"[149] in which he described the reasons for the loss of Venezuela, attributing them to the weakness of the political system adopted in the Constitution of 1811 - the text of which had been already published in London a few months earlier in that same year 1812, in the book *Interesting Official Documents Relating to the United Provinces of Venezuela.*

The wars of independence in Venezuela, in any case, were the beginning of the Latin American militarism. The military rule initiated by Monteverde, as a consequence of the wars of independence led by Bolívar, continued in the following years leading to a generalized and unfortunate disdain for the First Republic and its institution – all embodied in the *Interesting Official Documents* published in the book, which were considered weak, and were blamed as being the main cause of its fall. Such attitude even lead to their qualification as being of a *Patria Boba* (Foolish Motherland),[150] historically resulting in an unfortunate militarist cult of the same Bolivar, that has remained in many of the "Bolivarian" countries up to present times.

That is why that the name of Simón Bolívar has been evoked many times in Venezuela's political history by rulers, mainly of military and authoritarian roots, in order to attract followers and to give some "doctrinal" basis to their regimes. This was the case of Antonio Guzmán Blanco in the nineteenth century and of Cipriano Castro, Juan Vicente Gómez, Eleazar López Contreras, and Marcos Pérez Jiménez in the twentieth century. That is why Professor John Lynch, the most important European biographer of Bolívar, has pointed out that "the traditional cult of Bolivar has been used as a convenient ideology by military dictators, culminating with the regimes of Juan Vicente Gómez and Eleazar López Contreras," explaining that "these had at least more or less respected the basic thought of the Liberator, even when

---

148 See en Eduardo Roca Roca, *América en el Ordenamiento Jurídico...*, *op. cit.*, p. 81.

149 See text in Simón Bolívar, *Escritos Fundamentales*, Monte Ávila Editores, Caracas, 1982, pp. 57 y ss.; y en *Proclamas y Discursos del Libertador*, Caracas, 1939, pp.11 y ss.

150 See for instance, regarding the *Nueva Granada,* the use of the expresión in *La Patria Boba*, a book containing works of J.A. Vargas Jurado (*Tiempos Coloniales*), José María Caballero (*Días de la Independencia)*, y J.A. de Torres y Peña (Santa Fé Cautiva), Bogotá 1902. The work of Caballero was published as *Diario de la Independencia*, Biblioteca de Historia Nacional, Bogotá 1946, and *Diario de la Patria Boba,* Ediciones Incunables, Bogotá 1986. See also, José María Espinosa, *Recuerdos de un Abanderado, Memorias de la Patria Boba 1810-1819*, Bogotá 1876. See also Mario Rodríguez, *"William Burke" and Miranda, cit,* pp. 526, 529. See in Venezuela, Germán Carrera Damas, *El culto a Bolívar, esbozo para un estudio de la historia de las ideas en Venezuela*, Universidad Central de Venezuela, Caracas 1969; Luis Castro Leiva, *De la patria boba a la teología bolivariana*, Monteávila, Caracas 1987; Elías Pino Iturrieta, *El divino Bolívar. Ensayo sobre una religión republicana*, Alfail, Caracas 2008; Ana Teresa Torres, *La herencia de la tribu. Del mito de la independencia a la Revolución bolivariana*, Editorial Alfa, Caracas 2009. See also the historiography study on these books in Tomás Straka, *La épica del desencanto*, Editorial Alfa, Caracas 2009.

they misrepresented its meaning."[151] Nonetheless, referring to situation in Venezuela at the beginning of the 21st Century, the same Professor Lynch concluded his comments on the use of the name of Bolívar saying that:

> "In 1999, Venezuelans were astonished to learn that their country had been renamed 'the Bolivarian Republic of Venezuela' by decree of President Hugo Chávez, who called himself a 'revolutionary Bolivarian.' Authoritarian populist, or neocaudillos, or Bolivarian militarists, whatever their designation, invoke Bolívar no less ardently than did previous rulers, though it is doubtful whether he would have responded to their calls...But the new heresy, far from maintaining continuity with the constitutional ideas of Bolívar, as was claimed, invented a new attribute, the populist Bolívar, and in the case of Cuba gave him a new identity, the socialist Bolívar. By exploiting the authoritarian tendency, which certainly existed in the thought and action of Bolívar, regimes in Cuba and Venezuela claim the Liberator as patron for their policies, distorting his ideas in the process."[152]

In any case, with all that militaristic initial weight, the civilian construction of the first years of the Republic and the extraordinary civic effort to establish a democratic republic, all embodied in the Federal Constitution of Venezuela of December 1811, and in all the documents published in the London 1812 book, unfortunately were buried with the pejorative and absolutely unjust qualification used on those times as of the *Patria Boba*, with the only for the purpose of disqualifying democracy, selling the idea of the need in our countries for a military or authoritarian ruler.[153]

V. THE PUBLICATION OF THE BOOK *INTERESTING OFFICIAL DO-CUMENTS* IN LONDON IN 1812 AS THE WRITTEN TESTIMONY OF THE INDEPENDENCE PROCESS, AND THE ROLE PLAYED IN THE PROJECT BY FRANCISCO DE MIRANDA

But despite all those deviations, it was in the book: *Interesting Official Documents Relating to the United Provinces of Venezuela*, where for the first time ever, not only in English but also in Spanish, all the main constitutional documents of the extraordinary Venezuelan independence process of 1811 were published together, as the result of an official project that was designed by the new authorities at the beginning of 1812.

Being an official venture, the book had no authorship, its content being the collection of the documents written and democratically approved by the representative of the people to secure the constitutional foundations of the new State.

The book was preceded by an introductory *Preliminary Remarks* explaining its general purpose, also without authorship. Not being in itself one of the "official

---

151 See John Lynch, *Simón Bolívar: A Life*, Yale University Press, New Haven, CT, 2007, p. 304.

152 *Idem*. See also on the subject, A.C. Clark, *The Revolutionary Has No Clothes: Hugo Chávez's Bolivarian Farce*, Encounter Books, New York 2009, pp. 5-14.

153 See for instante, the classical book of Laureano Vallenilla Lanz, *Cesarismo Democrático. Estudio sobre las bases sociológicas de la Constitución efectiva en Venezuela*, Caracas 1952.

documents," attempts have been made to determine its author. For instance, Carlos Pi Sunyer had attributed the authorship of the *Preliminary Remarks* to Andrés Bello himself, based on a reference made by Fray Servando Maria de Mier, one of the London friends of Miranda, in the sense that the text on "the insurrection of Vene-zuela" would have been "a solid and eloquent booklet of the Secretary of the Dele-gation that remained in London after the visit of the Commissioners." As mentioned, Andrés Bello at that time was precisely the secretary of the 1810 Venezuelan Com-missioners to London.[154] Others like Caracciolo Parra-Pérez considered that Miguel José Sanz was probably the one who wrote the *Preliminary Remarks* of which he said "were undoubtedly reviewed by Bello."[155] In any case, it is enough to read the *Preliminary Remarks*, all together with all the others of the official documents con-tained in the book, to realize that it was without doubt written by many pens, partic-ularly of those who participated directly in the drafting of the *official documents* themselves. That is, considering that the book was one published under the auspices of the Government to express the Government's position regarding the independ-ence process, it is not possible to believe that the very authors of the documents would have not partaken in any way in the making of the *Preliminary Remarks* in which their very points of view were summarized.[156]

Andrés Bello, of course, being in London, and in charge of the editing process of the book, must have done important editing efforts, even adding remarks like for instance the references to the works of "our inimitable Locke," and perhaps of those of Montesquieu.

The fact is that all the documents included in the book, dated between July and December 1811, were sent to Andrés Bello in London in the first months of 1812, without doubts by Juan Germán Roscio, the secretary of State of the new govern-ment and the closest friend of Bello in Venezuela. Bello managed to edit and publish the book in a very expeditious way, that is, in a matter of a few months, including the supervision of the translation of the texts into English.

Of course, the whole task, in any event, was not an easy one. To sail between La Guaira and Southampton in England, was quite a complicated journey that generally took several weeks or months; and copies of documents were generally handwritten, as was also the case of translations. In any case, even in London at the time, printing books in general was also a major typographic enterprise. Nonetheless, despite all

---

154 This is the view of Carlos Pi Sunyer, *Patriotas Americanos en Londres...*, *op. cit.*, pp. 211-223. See the comment in Ivan Jasksic, *Andrés Bello. La pasión por el orden*, Editorial Uni-versitaria, Imagen de Chile, Santiago de Chile 2001

155 See Caracciolo Parra-Pérez, See "Estudio Preliminar" in *La Constitución Federal de Vene-zuela de 1811 y Documentos Afines,* Biblioteca de la Academia Nacional de la Historia, Ses-quicentenario de la Independencia, Caracas 1952, p. 12

156 Further, reading the *Preliminary Remarks* and the *Manifesto*, it is evident the presence of the same pen that participated in the drafting of some writings of William Burke, as for example, the considerations about the meaning of the Pledge to Fernando VII or the term *patria* (Motherland) in relation to Spain. See William Burke, *Derechos de la América del Sur y México,* Vol. 1, Academia de la Historia, Caracas 1959, pp. 239 y 243.

these factors, the truth is that publication of the book in London as planned, supported and financed by envoys of the newly independent Venezuelan government, was made in record time.

But life not always follows the path designed by man, and books do not always get out of the printing press as planned by its authors or editors. In this case, a book that was conceived to serve as an written explanation of the independence process of Venezuela, due to the political events that occurred in the new State while the book was being edited and printed in London, resulted in a tragic sort of "post mortem" official publication. It began to be available only when the newly born Republic had already crumbled and its institutions designed in the documents published in the book were disappearing as a consequence of the military invasion of the provinces made by the Spanish army from the "pacification" headquarter that the Spanish Regency had established in Puerto Rico.

One thing is clear in the publication process of the book, and it is that its edition was for sure completed after the date of the earthquake that devastated Caracas that occurred on March 26th, 1811 which is evidenced by the footnote placed at the bottom of the page of the English text to Article 67 of the Constitution of 1811,[157] and thus, after the enactment of the Constitution of Cadiz of March 18, 1812. On the other hand, it is sure that the final composition of the book also was completed before the news of the Capitulation signed on July 25, 1811 between Francisco de Miranda and the Commander of the Spanish Army, Domingo Monteverde, through which the Republic of Venezuela ended as a sovereign state,[158] made it to London. Otherwise some note would also have had been added to the text, unless it had deliberately not been made to avoid the publishing project to crumble.[159] The crumbling of the Republic and in some way of the immediately "useless" editorial project that was developed in London, of course, also produced devastating effects upon Bello, who remained in London and for a few decades without great difficulties and without much academic activities.[160]

But despite all these effects, in the long run, the book produced very important effects, particularly due to the fact that the original manuscripts of the documents it

---

157 The footnote informed that the Congress had decided to made Valencia, instead of Caracas, the Federal Capital of the Republic (February 15th, 1812) where the representatives had been assembled "at the time of the late earthquake at Caracas" (March 26th, 1812).

158 Se the text of the capitulation in Francisco de Miranda, *América Espera* (J.L Salcedo bsastardo, Ed), Biblioteca Ayacucho, Caracas 1982, pp. 465 ss.

159 In that sense, Carlos Pi Sunyer, assuming that the book had come off the press by the end of 1812, said: "It is likely that at the time to be published, Bello had already known about the events that led to the fall of the first Republic of Venezuela; because on October 12, Lopez Mendez directs a communication to Lord Castlereagh, referring to them, written in Bello's handwriting, a time when it is believed that the book had been not yet issued or that it had just been issued" See Carlos Pi Sunyer. *Patriotas Americanos en Londres...* op. cit., p. 222.

160 See Ivan Jasksic, *Andrés Bello. La pasión por el orden*, Bid & co. Edotores, Caracas 2007, pp. 88 ss.

contained, among them the texts of the Federal Constitution and of the Declaration of Independence, disappeared after the Spanish invasion in 1812.

In the particular case of the original manuscript of the *Declaration of Independence* of July 5, 1811, it remained in fact disappeared for almost one hundred years, to the point that in 1903, on the eve of the celebration of the centenary of the Independence, the Venezuelan government, in absence of the original text, officially declared that the only real and authentic copy of the Declaration of Independence was precisely the one published in the London book of 1812, hence, its historical importance.

For such purpose, after one copy of the book was acquired in Europe by a member of the Venezuelan Academy of History, and after the matter being studied by the Academy, it gave its formal opinion on the authenticity of the text included in the London book. This opinion was followed by the official decision of the Government, adopted by decree of President of the Republic Cipriano Castro,[161] in which it was stated that since the book was out of print and there was only one copy existing in Venezuela (the one acquired by the National Academy of History), the publication of the original edition comprising only the Spanish version of the documents was ordered.[162]

Nonetheless, it must be mentioned that in 1907, four years after the official decision of the government regarding the authentic copy of the Declaration of Independence, the lost original manuscript, as well as all the texts of the 1811 *Interesting Official documents* were found with the casual discovery of two big bound volumes of the Minutes of the sessions of the General Congress of 1811. They were found by chance, as almost all discoveries occur, in the city of Valencia, where the Federal Capital of the Republic began to function in March 1812. In that city, the two big volumes containing such precious documents had remained for a century in private hands, being used without noticing their content, as hard cushions placed upon a bench in order for young pupils to sit high for the purpose of playing the piaNo[163]

---

161 Published al *Official Gazette* N° 8863 of May 28, 1903

162 See *Prólogo a los Anales de Venezuela,* Academia Nacional de la Historia, Caracas, 1903. The Spanish version of the *Observaciones Preliminares* that precedes the book's various documents was published in J.F. Blanco y R. Azpúrua, *Documentos para la Historia de la Vida Pública del Libertador...,* op. cit., Tomo III, pp. 391-395. The complete text of the Spanish version of the documents were also published in 1959 in the book headed: *La Constitución Federal de Venezuela de 1811 y Documentos Afines* ("Estudio Preliminar" por Caracciolo Parra-Pérez), Biblioteca de la Academia Nacional de la Historia, Sesquicentenario de la Independencia, Caracas 1952, 238 pp. It was reprinted by Fundación Polar in Caracas, 2009.

163 The Books containing the manuscripts of the Minutes of the Congress were in possession of two families in Valencia, and the historian Francisco González Guinand participated in their rescue in 1907. See Ramón Días Sánchez, Ëstudio Preliminar" in *Libro de Actas del Supremo Congreso de Venezuela 1811-1812,* Academia Nacional de la Historia, Caracas 1959, pp. 11-13.

After those discoveries, the fact is that the 1812 bilingual edition of the book remained completely ignored, and never again was republished. Published in London, and without a Republic to which promote, the copies of the first edition almost disappeared.

In any case, the choice of London for the publishing of the book was not a casual one; it undoubtedly was a Miranda choice, being as he was, at that time, by far, not only a "Man of the World,"[164] but the most important person known in Europe related to the South American independence process. He was such an extraordinary person, that William Spencer Robertson, his most important biographer, identified as:

> "Precursor, Knight-Errant, and Promoter of Spanish-American liberty. He was the first cultured South American to make a tour of either the United States or Europe. His life has a unique interest because he was the only personage of his time to participate in the struggle for the independence of the Thirteen Colonies, the French revolution, and the war for the liberation of Spanish America."[165]

Miranda, in effect, was born in Caracas in 1750, leaving Venezuela in 1776 one year before the General Captaincy of Venezuela was created (1777). He went to Spain, rejecting the bigotry and oppression that prevailed in the province, which had affected the status of his father, who was born in the Canary Islands. Upon his arrival in Madrid, he enrolled in a military regiment of the Spanish Crown and went to Cádiz, at which time he met John Turnbull (1776) one of his main protectors and who years after would become one of his most important financial supporters, and even who prepared, with the aide of his son, his failed escape from La Carraca, the Cadiz prison in 1816, the year of his death. This close relation led Miranda to named Turnbull as his executor.[166]

His initial military actions were in Northern Africa and later, from its base in Cuba, in North America, in the taking of Pensacola and the Bahamas (1781), which gave him promotions, but also enemies. Since his first years in Spain, since 1778, he had been accused and persecuted by the Inquisition Tribunal, among other motives, because having bought "prohibited books,"[167] to which was added an accusation of supposedly smuggling goods from Jamaica to La Havana during a secret military mission assigned to him in 1781,[168] charges from which he was declared not guilty in 1799.[169]

---

164 See *Miranda: A Man of the World*, Dedicated to the Bicentennial of the U.S., Instituto de Estudios Históricos Mirandinos, 1976.

165 See William Spence Robertson, *The Life of Miranda*, The University of North Carolina Press, Chapel Hill 1929, vol. 1, p. ix.

166 See his testament of August 1 1810 in Francisco de Miranda, *América Espera* [Ed. J.L. Salcedo Bastardo], Biblioteca Ayacucho, Caracas 1892, pp. 329

167 See the references to the decisions in Tomás Polanco Alcántara, *Miranda*, Caracas 1997, pp. 22, 28 30.

168 See in Tomás Polanco Alcántara, *Miranda, cit.*, p. 27

169 *Idem*, p 160 ss

He managed to evade the order of detention that was issued against him on March 11, 1782,[170] and made the decision to travel to North America, with the agreement of the Commander of the Spanish army in the Caribbean, Juan Manuel Cajigal, to whom he explained that it was not "prudent" to remain in Cuba, being a "indispensable precaution" to avoid detention.[171] He spent one year in North America (1783-1784) where he personally met with the most important leaders of the American Revolution (Washington, Hamilton, Jefferson, among others) with whom he began to discus his liberation plans for "Colombia." Knowing about the Spanish persecution deployed against him,[172] he sailed to London (1785), where among others, he met Colonel William Steuben Smith, who was Aide de Camp to George Washington and with whom he began a military observation journey to Prussia (1785).

The publications in London about Miranda alerted again the Spanish authorities of his presence in Europe, which prevented him from returning to London, due to the danger of being detained.[173] Miranda then traveled to Saxony, Austria, Italy, Egypt, Trieste, Constantinople, the Black Sea and Crimea (1786), where, after meeting with Prince Gregory Potemkin of Russia, he traveled with him to Kiev as a guest of the Russian government. He was received by the Empress Catherine of Russia from whom he received effective support for his projects regarding Spanish America. With a Russian passport, he traveled from Petersburg to Sweden, Norway and Denmark, where, again, he heard of the Spanish government intent to detain him in Stockholm. He then proceeded to the Netherlands and Switzerland arriving in Paris via Marseille, using another name (M. de Meroff).

He managed to return to England on the eve of the French revolution, in June 1789, hoping to find support for his projects of freeing Spanish America. There he met with the Prime Minister, William Pitt (1790); but not finding the support he had expected, he traveled back to Paris, with the same ideas and with the intention of going back to Russia (1792). In Paris, the Revolution was already installed, so the invasion of Champagne by the Prussian forces compelled him to accept a military command post in the French forces under the command of General Charles Dumouriez, with the rank of field marshal (1792). For his military actions, he was appointed Commander-In-Chief of the Northern Army. Nonetheless, the Neerwinden military disaster which forced the French army to evacuate the Netherlands and which resulted in treason charges against Dumouriez for wanting to restore the Monarchy, led to a trial against him in which he intended to involve Miranda in his performance. Miranda was persecuted by Robespierre, detained and submitted to trial before the Revolutionary Tribunal of Paris, but was declared not guilty in the process that unfolded against him. In December 22, 1797 he signed, in

---

170 *Idem*, p. 31

171 See his letter to Cajigal dated April 16, 1783 in Francisco de Miranda, *América Espera, cit.* pp. 57-58

172 See Tomás Polanco Alcántara, *Miranda, cit.*, p. 62

173 *Idem*, p. 115

Paris, with other "representative of the peoples and provinces of America" (José del Pozo y Sucre, José de Salas) the "Act of Paris" proclaiming the "independence" of the American provinces,[174] returning to London, where the Prime Minister, William Pitt (1798), this time began to pay attention to his plans of Spanish American independence.[175]

During those years, Miranda was perhaps one of the most pursued and searched of all Spanish-Americans by the Spanish Crown, being in turn, one of the most important promoters and forerunners of the independence movement regarding Spanish America.

After fixing his residence in London in 1799, he stayed until 1805 when he went back to New York, in order to organize, in 1806, an important expedition with independence purposes to the coast of Venezuela, where he came twice ashore, proclaiming independence and libertarian ideas;[176] although eventually failing in his purposes.[177] He returned to London in 1808 only to reinforce his independence projects and to return to Venezuela, after three decades of absence in December 1810 once the independence revolution had started.

His seal in that process in Venezuela is of course indelible, even imprinted in the process of publication of our London book. Although Miranda was in Caracas from December 1810 until July 1812, precisely during the writing process of all the documents published in the book and during its editing process, its publication in London was only possible due to the solid and tight set of political and editorial relations and contacts that he had established during his years of residence in London, particularly from 1799 until he began his journey of return to Caracas in October 1810.

These relations involved many persons not only interested in the emancipation of South America from Spain, and deeply involved in the political process for independence, but also in the intellectual life of London. In that group, no doubt, Francisco de Miranda was the key person, whose contacts and organization made possible the publication of the book, although at the time of the editing process he was in Venezuela, as Commander in Chief or *Generalísimo* of the Republican Army defending the Republic against the invasion by the Spanish military forces.

---

174 See in Francisco de Miranda, *América Espera, cit.,* p. 195 ; Francisco de Miranda, *Textos sobre la Independencia*, Biblioteca de la Academia Nacional de la Historiaa, Caracas 1959, pp 49-57

175 See Tomás Polanco Alcántara, *Miranda, cit.*, pp. 145 ss.

176 See the Proclaims in Francisco de Miranda, *América Espera, cit.* p. 356 ss

177 See his letter to Castlereagh explaining the reasons of the failure of the expedition, in Francisco de Miranda, *América Espera, cit.* p. 366 ss

VI. THE *INTERESTING OFFICIAL DOCUMENTS* RELATED TO THE VENEZUELAN INDEPENDENCE, THEIR INSPIRATION ON THE IDEAS OF THE FRENCH AND AMERICAN REVOLUTION, AND THE ROLE PLAYED BY A CERTAIN "WILLIAM BURKE"

In any case, and thanks to the grid of relations left by Miranda in London, the documents published two hundred years ago in the very important London book were and still are not only the fundamental documents on the Venezuelan Independence but most important documents ever published in English regarding the process of the independence of Spanish America. They are the most conspicuous evidence of the effective impact that the modern principles of constitutionalism, derived from the American and French Revolutions, produced in the constitution making process of Venezuela and Hispanic America in 1811,[178] where for the first time in history those principles were conjointly applied and developed.[179]

According to those principles, the new constitutional State created in Venezuela two hundred years ago, followed the general trends of the constitutional process of the United States. In Venezuela, also a General Congress[180] integrated by elected representatives of the "United Provinces," of the former General Captaincy of Venezuela, not only declared Independence in 1811, but also sanctioned a "Federal Constitution for the United States of Venezuela;"[181] being Venezuela the first country in modern constitutional history to adopt the federal form of State after the United States of America.

---

178 See Allan R. Brewer-Carias, *Reflexiones sobre la Revolución Norteamericana (1776), la Revolución Francesa (1789) y la Revolución Hispanoamericana (1810-1830) y sus aportes al Constitucionalismo Moderno*, 2ª Edición Ampliada Universidad Externado de Colombia, Editorial Jurídica Venezolana, Bogotá 2008.

179 As Juan Garrivo Rovira has pointed out, the Venezuelan 1811 Constituent Assembly, "assumed the challenge of the times and check marked the political-cultural ideals of the centuries, among others: Political independence; special consecration of the freedom of thought; separation of powers; suffrage, representation and participation of the citizens in the government; social fairness; consecration and respect of the rights and duties of the man; limitation and control of power; political and civil equality of free men; recognition and protection of the rights of the indigenous towns; prohibition of the traffic of slaves; popular, responsible and alternative government; autonomy of the judicial power on moral basis; the nation over the factions." In *El Congreso Constituyente de Venezuela*, Bicentenario del 5 de julio de 1811, Universidad Monteávila, Caracas 2010, p.12.

180 See Ramón Díaz Sánchez (Editor), *Libro de Actas del Supremo Congreso de Venezuela 1811-1812,* Academia Nacional de la Historia, Caracas, 1959; Pedro Grases (Compilador), *El pensamiento político de la Emancipación Venezolana,* Ediciones Congreso de la República, Caracas 1988; Tulio Chiossone, *Formación Jurídica de Venezuela en la Colonia y la República,* Universidad Central de Venezuela, Caracas, 1980.

181 See Caraccciolo Parra Pérez (Editor), *La Constitución Federal de Venezuela de 1811 y Documentos afines,* Academia Nacional de la Historia,bCaracas, 1959, pp. 79 ff.; and Allan R. Brewer-Carías, *Las Constiuciones de Venezuela,* Acadeia de Ciencias Políticas y Sociales, Vol. I, Caracas 2008, pp. 553-581.

Venezuela was also, after the United States, the first country to follow all the general principles of modern constitutionalism in its Constitution, namely, the principles of constitutional supremacy, sovereignty of the people, political representation and republicanism; including a declaration of fundamental rights or bill of rights;[182] the organization of the State according to the principle of separation of power with a system of checks and balances, and the superiority of the law as expression of the general will; the establishment of a presidential system of government and elected representatives to the senate and the representatives chamber (*diputados*); the organization, within the federation, of a complete system of local governments; and the provision of a Judicial Power integrated by judges imparting justice in the name of the nation with judicial review powers.[183]

But the main question that I want now to highlight regarding this inspiration, of course, relates to the way through which all those ideas and principles managed to enter in the provinces and could pass through the strict Spanish colonial control of the Inquisition, influencing the elites of the country, and being embodied precisely in the *Interesting Official Documents* published in the London book.

The fact is that during Spanish colonial times, as it happens nowadays in all authoritarian systems of government, books, as well as pens and pencils, were and are considered dangerous weapons, and could not spread freely throughout the provinces. This was and is particularly true about books related to ideas such as liberty, freedom, rights of the people, political representation, and peoples' sovereignty, separation of powers and control of political power. At the beginning of the 19th century, those books were considered very dangerous and forbidden in Hispanic America, and their introduction, trafficking and possession were persecuted by the Inquisition Tribunal.

But as always happens with books, and in spite of all prohibitions, they always manage to be available and in the precise hands, as was also the case in such times, despite the Inquisition; being the consequence of such clandestine diffusion, also persecution and punishment. This was the case, for instance, of books and pamphlets related to the 1789 French Declaration of Rights of Man and Citizens. They were of course formally prohibited by the Inquisition Tribunal of Cartagena de Indias,[184] as well as by the Viceroys of Peru, Nueva España and Santa Fe and by the President of the *Audiencia* of Quito. That is why, despite the prohibition and having spread to the

---

182 See Allan R. Brewer-Carías, *Las declaraciones de derechos del pueblo y del hombre de 1811*, Academia de Ciencias Políticas y Sociales, Caracas 2011.

183 See Allan R. Brewer-Carías, *Reflexiones sobre la Revolución Norteamericana (1776), la Revolución Francesa (1789) y la Revolución Hispanoamericana (1810-1830) y sus aportes al constitucionalismo moderno*, Universidad Externado de Colombia, Bogotá 2008, pp. 204 ff; Allan R. Brewer-Carías, "El paralelismo entre el constitucionalismo venezolano y el constitucionalismo de Cádiz (o de cómo el de Cádiz no influyó en el venezolano)," in *Libro Homenaje a Tomás Polanco Alcántara*, Estudios de Derecho Público, Universidad Central de Venezuela, Caracas 2005, pp. 101-189.

184 See P. Grases, *La Conspiración de Gual y España y el Ideario de la Independencia, cit.*, p. 13.

provinces of Venezuela at the end of the 18th century, the General Captain informed the Crown about the fact that "principles of liberty and independence so dangerous to the sovereignty of Spain are beginning to brew in the heads of the Americans."[185]

The text of the French 1789 Declaration of Rights was even published in a clandestine way in the colonies, as was the case of the translation made by Antonio Nariño in Santa Fe de Bogotá in 1792. That was a grave crime to the point that in 1794,[186] it originated a very famous judicial process in which the Inquisition Tribunal condemned Nariño to 10 years in prison in Africa, in addition to the confiscation of all his properties, his perpetual expulsion from the Americas, and the burning, by the hands of the executioner, of the book containing the Rights of Man.[187]

In those same years, the Secretary of the Royal and Supreme Council of Cartagena de Indias also directed a note to the General Captain of Venezuela dated June 7, 1793, asking him to be aware of the intention of the French Government and of some French revolutionaries, as well as some promoters of subversions in the Spanish domains in the new World, that - it was said – "Send there books and documents damaging the purity of the religion, the public peace and the due subordination of the colonies."[188]

But it was a casual fact that occurred in Spain in 1796, which would be the one that was going to have the most important impact in the independence process in the provinces of Venezuela. A conspiracy, called of San Blas, was supposed to take place in Madrid that same year in order to establish a Republic inspired by the French Revolution in substitution of the Monarchy. The conspiration failed, and the conspirators, among them, Juan Bautista Mariano Picornell y Gomilla and Manuel Cortés de Campomares, after being condemned to death, due to the intervention of the French Agent, had their sentence commuted into life imprisonment in the unhealthy dungeons of Puerto Cabello, Portobello and Panama.[189] They were then sent to the Caribbean prisons, being transitorily placed in the prison of La Guaira, the main port of the province of Venezuela.

The conspirators managed to escape the following year, 1797,[190] and began to get in touch with the local elite in the Port, encouraging the conspiracy headed by Manuel Gual and José María España, considered to be the "most serious liberation intent of Hispanic America before the Miranda intent in 1806."[191] The conspiracy

---

185 See in J. F. Blanco y R. Azpúrua, *Documentos para la historia de la vida pública del Libertador, cit.*, Tomo I, p. 177.

186 *Id.*, Tomo I p. 286.

187 *Id.*, Tomo I, pp. 257-259.

188 *Id.*, Tomo I, p. 247.

189 See P. Grases, *La Conspiración de Gual y España.. cit*, pp. 14, 17, 20.

190 See in J.F. Blanco y R. Azpúrua, *Documentos para la historia de la vida pública del Libertador. cit.*, Tomo I, p. 287; P. Grases, *La Conspiración de Gual y España... cit.*, p. 26.

191 P. Grases, *La Conspiración de Gual y España. op. cit.*, p. 27.

also failed,[192] but the product resulting from the intent were a group of papers which were to have enormous importance in the constitutional process of Hispanic America, among them, a book titled *Derechos del Hombre y del Ciudadano con varias máximas Republicanas, y un Discurso Preliminar dirigido a los Americanos,* which of course, was subsequently prohibited by the *Real Audiencia* of Caracas on December 11, 1797. The Tribunal considered that:

> "it had all the intention of corrupting the habits and of making hateful the royal name of his Majesty and of his just government; that for the purpose of corrupting the habits, its authors follow the rules of conduct covered by a multitude of vices, disfigured by a few humanitarian appearances."[193]

The book, probably printed in Guadalupe in 1797[194] contained the translation of the French declaration that preceded the Constitution of 1793,[195] that is, the one of the epoch of the Terror, more violent and openly inviting active revolution.[196]

After the Gual and España Conspiration, and despite its failure and the fierce persecution that followed against all those that had participated in it, the other important event considered as a direct antecedent of the Venezuelan independence was the ashore of the expedition commanded by Francisco de Miranda in the Venezuelan coast (Puerto Cabello y Coro) in 1806, considered to be the most important event regarding the independence that occurred before the abdication of Charles IV and the subsequent abdication of Ferdinand VII in Bayonne in favor of Napoleon.[197] That is why, as mentioned, Miranda has been considered the Precursor of the Independence of the American Columbian Continent, his ideas materialized in the libertarian proclamations he wrote and published in the printing press he bought in New York and that he had in his ship, the Leander, the vessel he contracted in order to lead the invasion of Venezuela, proposing the independence through the formation of a federation of Free Municipal Councils[198] based on some French and North American constitutional principles.

That printing press was going to be, precisely and by chance, the first printing press ever introduced in the Provinces of Venezuela, This occurred two years after

---

192 See in J. F. Blanco y R. Azpúrua, *Documentos para la historia de la vida pública del Libertador. cit.,* Tomo I, p. 332.

193 P. Grases, *La Conspiración de Gual y España..., cit.,* p. 30.

194 Despite that in the front page it appears as published in Madrid, in the printing press of la Verdad, year 1797. See Pedro Grases, "Estudio sobre los 'Derechos del Hombre y del Ciudadano'," in the book *Derechos del Hombre y del Ciudadano* (Estudio Preliminar by Pablo Ruggeri Parra and Estudio histórico-crítico by Pedro Grases), Academia Nacional de la Historia, Caracas 1959, pp. 147, 335.

195 *Id.,* pp. 37 ss.

196 *Id.*

197 See O.C. Stoetzer, *Las Raíces Escolásticas de la Emancipación de la América Española,* Madrid, 1982, p. 252.

198 See Francisco de Miranda, *Textos sobre la Independencia,* Biblioteca de la Academia Nacional de la Historia, Caracas, 1959, pp. 95 ss., y 115 ss.

the failed Miranda invasion, in 1808, when the colonial government of Venezuela decided to authorize its acquisition in Trinidad, where Miranda left it before returning to London, being acquired by Matthew Gallagher,[199] the editor of *Trinidad Weekly Courant*. The printing press was brought to Caracas by its owners along with Francisco Gonzales de Linares who acted on behalf of the Captain General Juan de Casas. The Royal Treasury granted a mortgage loan for the printing operations with the Government as its main customer.

In that way was how printing was introduced in Venezuela, being the *Gazeta de Caracas* the first periodical publication in Caracas, beginning on October 24, 1808.[200] Regarding this printing press, in it the first book edited in Venezuela was published, titled *Resumen de la Historia de Venezuela*) [Summary of the History of Venezuela]; a book of Andrés Bello who was then a very high and distinguished official of the General Captaincy and as mentioned, later played an important role in the editing of the book, *Interesting Official Documents*, in London. Bello himself, as already mentioned, was the first editor of the *Gaceta de Caracas*.

But not only was printing before 1808 a belated matter in the marginal provinces of Venezuela, particularly compared to the introduction of princting press decades before in the main Viceroyalties in America, but since its introduction, it was subjected to strict censure. This was recorded in the same *Preliminary Remarks* preceding our London book, in which references are made to "the public prints...branded with censure and reprobation," and in general, to the fact that in the Colonial provinces:

> "under the most severe threats of punishment, a political inquisition with all its horrors, was established against those who should read, possess, or receive other papers, not only foreign, but even Spanish, that were not out of the Regency's manufacture." [201]

Nonetheless, and despite the prohibition, the French and the American revolutionary ideas extensively spread in Spanish America, thanks to some books that were introduced in a clandestine way, whose content is the only explanation of the basic principles that influenced the constitution making process of 1810-1811 imbued in the *Interested Official Documents* of the Independence published in the London book. Among those books, mention must be made to a few of them referred to the revolution and independence process of the United States of America, that were introduced in Venezuela, due to the work of a group of Venezuelans residing in Philadelphia, who translated and published them, or who served as links for their publication in Venezuela.

---

199 See Tomás Polanco Alcántara, *Miranda*, cit, pp. 208, 227.

200 See "Introducción de la imprenta en Venezuela" in Pedro Grases, *Escritos Selectos*, Biblioteca Ayacucho, Caracas 1988, pp. 97 ss.

201 In the letter Miranda sent to Richard Wellesley Jr.in January 7, 1810, he expresses the same: "There were no printing press in the provinces, and the Spanish government always excluded from the countries all the publications not sent by itself." See in Francisco de Miranda, *América Espera* (Ed. J.L. Salcedo Bastardo), Biblioteca Ayacucho, Caracas 1892, p. 445.

The first book that has to be mentioned is one published in Philadelphia in 1810 by Joseph Manuel Villavicencio, a native of the Province of Caracas, when the revolution was in its first stages in Caracas, containing what can be considered as the first Spanish translation of the Constitution of the United States of America, titled *Constitución de los Estados Unidos de América.*[202] This was, without doubt, the first translation into Spanish of the American Constitution. It was widely distributed in Spanish America despite the ban imposed by the Inquisition to such kind of publications; and was even reprinted in Bogotá and in Cádiz in 1811, during the discussion of the 1812 Cádiz Constitution.

The second book to be mentioned also published in Philadelphia and in Spanish, contained the translation of the most important works of Thomas Paine,[203] which also had extensive diffusion in Spanish America. It contained the text in Spanish of "Common Sense" (Philadelphia, 1776), and the text of two of Paine's "Dissertations on the Principles of Government." It also contained the Spanish version of the Declaration of Independence (July 4, 1776), the Articles of the Confederation (1778), the text of the Constitution of the United States and Perpetual Union (July 8, 1778), and its first twelve Amendments (1791, 1798, 1804); and the text of the Constitutions of Massachusetts (1780), New Jersey (1776), Virginia (1776), and Pennsylvania (1790), and Connecticut.[204] This book, also with the first translation into Spanish of those documents, was the work of another Venezuelan, Manuel García de Sena, and was published with the title: *La Independencia de la Costa Firme justificada por Thomas Paine treinta años ha. Extracto de sus obras* [205] He was the brother of Ramón Garcia de Sena who was very active in the independence process in Venezuela, acting as a military and even as a constituent, in the drafting of the Constitution of the "Sovereign Republic of Barcelona Colombiana, one of the States-

---

202 *Constitución de los Estados Unidos de América. Traducida del inglés al español por don Jph. Manuel Villavicencio*, Filadelfia, Imprenta de Smith y M'Kenzie, 1810.

203 On the significance of Paine's work in the Independence of the United States see, for example, Joseph Lewis, *Thomas Paine. Author of the Declaration of Independence*, Freethought Press, New York 1947.

204 A modern edition of this work is *La Independencia de la Costa Firme, justificada por Thomas Paine treinta años ha.* Translated from English into Spanish by Manuel García de Sena. Foreword by Pedro Grases, Comité de Orígenes de la Emancipación, núm. 5. Instituto Panamericano de Geografía e Historia, Caracas, 1949. In addition, it must be mentioned that the same Manuel García de Sena also published in 1812 -with the same house of T. and J. Palmer in Philadelphia- the Spanish translation of the third edition (1808) of John M'Culloch's book *Concise History of the United States, from the Discovery of America, till 1807*, under the title of *Historia Concisa de los Estados Unidos desde el descubrimiento de la America hasta el año 1807.*

205 The book was published by the press of T. and J. Palmer, 288 pp. A reprint of this work was carried out by the Ministry of Foreign Affairs of Venezuela in 1987, as a Commemorating Edition of the Bicentennial Anniversary of the Constitution of the United States of America, Caracas 1987.

provinces of the new State in Venezuela, of January 12, 1812, which he signed together with Francisco Espejo.[206]

In 1811, therefore, these books, published in Philadelphia in Spanish, were conceived as instruments in order to explain to South Americans the meaning and scope of the American Revolution and its constitutional foundations, being used for the writing of several of the *Interesting Official Documents* of the Independence published in our London book,[207] in which it is possible to find direct influence for instance of Paine's work. The translation of Antonio García de Sena, as he himself explained in the Introduction of his book, was intended to "primarily illustrate his fellow citizens about the legitimacy of the Independence and the benefit that should come from it based on the social, political and economic situation of the United States." That is why, among the first actions that Domingo Monteverde took after occupying Caracas in 1812 was to order the seizure of all copies of that "dangerous" translation of North American revolution materials.

The fact is that despite all the prohibition and persecutions, all these papers had an important impact in Venezuela and generally in Latin America,[208] so at the time of the Independence they were passing from hand to hand, and even part of them were published in the *Gazeta de Caracas,*[209] which since 1810 had resulted to be the most important source of information about the North American constitutional system, and particularly about the functioning of its federal system of government.

On the other hand, and more important, from November 1810 until March 1812, a series of editorials and articles were regularly published in the *Gaceta de Caracas* related to the functioning of the North American constitutional system, precisely during the same months of the constitution-making process in Caracas, influencing in an extremely important way the Venezuelan drafters of the *Interesting Official Documents.*

---

206 See Las Constituciones Provinciales, Academia nacional de la Historia, 1959, p. 249.

207 For instance, in the book, the expression "rights of the people" was used by Paine (for instance "representative system founded upon the rights of the people"), and was reproduced in many of the *Interesting Official Documents.* See in Manuel García de Sena, *La Independencia de Costa Firme justificada por Thomas Paine treinta años ha,* Edición del Ministerio de Relaciones Exteriores, Caracas 1987, pp. 90, 111, 112, 118, 119.

208 See generally, Pedro Grases, *Libros y Libertad,* Caracas 1974; and "Traducción de interés político cultural en la época de la Independencia de Venezuela" en *El Movimiento Emancipador de Hispano América, Actas y Ponencias,* Academia Nacional de la Historia, Caracas 1961, Tomo II, pp. 105 y ss.; Ernesto de la Torre Villas y Jorge Mario Laguardia, *Desarrollo Histórico del Constitucionalismo Hispanoamericano,* UNAM, México 1976, pp. 38–39. See in contrary sense Jaime E. Rodríguez O., "La influencia de la emancipación de Estados Unidos en la independencia de Hispanoamérica,"in *Procesos. Revista Ecuatoriana de Historia,* N° 31, Quito 2010, pp. 25-43; and "Independencia de los Estados Unidos en las independencias hispanoamericanas," in *Revista de Indias,* vol. LXX, N° 250, Madrid 2010, pp. 691-714.

209 Part of the book by Garcia de Serna -including in it the translation of Paine's works – were published the issues of January 14 and 17, 1812. See Pedro Grases "Manual García de Sena y la Independencia de Hispanoamérica" in the edition of García de Sena made by the Ministry of Domestic Affairs, Caracas 1987, p. 39.

Almost all these articles and editorials were published under the name of a certain "William Burke," who at that time had already authored during the previous years, particularly between 1806 and 1808, three books published in London, two of them directly related to South American Independence highlighting the role that Francisco de Miranda needed to play in it. That is why, as it has been said by Mario Rodríquez, the historian and researcher who has most studied this prolific writer, William Burke, and his relation with Miranda:

> "The First Venezuelan Republic, perhaps more that any other Spanish American country had within its reach unquestionably more information on the U.S. model than others in South America, thanks to the presence of "William Burke."[210]

Rodríguez concluded his assertion affirming that "many of Burke's ideas were reflected in the Constitution of December, 1811," his articles in the *Gaceta de Caracas*, being the most important source reflecting the influence of the North American constitutional principles in the new Venezuelan Republic.

But regarding this very distinguished and prolific writer with a unique and extraordinary encyclopedic knowledge, the fact is that eventually he was only known through his writings, being his existence as a real person still a mater of conjecture.

Only one thing is absolutely certain about this extraordinary personage: Between 1806 and 1810 he authored books and articles published in England, including in the *Edinburgh Review*, precisely while Miranda was in London. After Miranda traveled to Venezuela in 1810 and up to 1812, he supposedly also went to Caracas and authored articles and books, but this time in Spanish, including articles related to the Spanish political situation that were all published in the *Gaceta de Caracas*. The other aspect is that after the imprisonment of Miranda and Roscio, in 1812, William Burke just vanished.

All these facts are, without doubt, elements for suspicion. Notwithstanding, Venezuelan historiography explains that William Burke "arrived" in Caracas, supposedly in December 1810, together with Miranda, remaining in Venezuela until the 30th of July 1812,[211] that is, up to the night when Miranda was imprisoned in the port of La Guaira. The truth is that those who actually sailed with Miranda from England to Caracas were two of his most important aides in London, Manuel Cortés Campomares and José María Antepara, and his personal secretary Pedro Antonio Leleux, all remaining with him until his imprisonment on July 30th, 1812.

---

210 See Mario Rodríguez, *"William Burke" and Francisco de Miranda, cit.,* p. 529.

211 In the Venezuelan historiography it is told that Burke, "an Irish publisher" and "friend" of Miranda, had traveled from London to New York and then to Caracas by the end of 1810 "possibly encouraged by fellow countrymen living in London" (See "Nota de la Comisión Editora", William Burke, *Derechos de la América del Sur y México,* Vol. 1, Academia de la Historia, Caracas 1959, p. xi.); that during his stay in Caracas he participated as one of the "important instigators of the moment" (See Elías Pino Iturrieta, *Simón Bolívar,* Colección Biografías de El Nacional N° 100, Editora El Nacional, Caracas, 2009, p. 34) along with other patriots in the process of independence. By the end of the republic, Burke had allegedly fled to Curacao in July 1812 and would have died by the end of that year in Jamaica.

As per William Burke, he has been identified as an Irishmen, and initially, in his book published in London in 1806, the *History of the Campaign of 1805 in Germany, Italy, Tyrol, etc.,*[212] as a "late Army Surgeon." This book is about the Napoleonic wars of that year developed after the reaction of the European Allied against France, whose armies had occupied most of Europe and had threatened to invade England. It contains a detailed account on military policy of the Napoleonic Wars during 1805, and on the reaction of the great European powers against France. The book contained particular references to the battle of Trafalgar held in October 1805 between the combined fleets of France and Spain and the British navy, which would end Napoleon's attempts to invade England. In the book's appendix there were included important documents and treaties signed between the Allied powers as well as various proclamations of Napoleon, and on the cover of the book, as mentioned, Burke was identified as a "Late Army Surgeon." [213]

This book was forwarded that same year, 1806, by another book of the same William Burke that referred to an entirely different subject, also published in London, with the title: *South American Independence: or the Emancipation of South America, the Glory and Interest of England, "by William Burke, the author of the Campaign of 1805,"* J. Ridgway, London 1806.

Despite being quite a different subject, in the front page of the book, the same William Burke appears as its author, although now without any reference to the veterinarian profession of the author, being nonetheless the manifest intention of the editor to establish a clear link between the author of this book with the previous one on the *Campaign of 1805*. The editor's idea was, without doubt, to consolidate a name in the publishing world, using in this case a very well known name like "Burke," but at a time in which it did not actually correspond to any living person in the United Kingdom.[214]

Real persons with that name of William Burke, in effect, can be found in the British Islands before and after the years in which our William Burke wrote his books. It was the case, for instance, a few decades before, of the William Burke

---

212 By *William Burke, Late Army Surgeon, London,* Printed for James Ridgway, N° 170, Opposite Bond Street, Picadilly, 1806. See references in Joseph Sabin, *Bibliotheca Americana. A Dictionary of Books relating to America, from its Discovery to the Present Time* (continued by Wilberforce Eames, and completed by Robert William Glenroie Vail), New York, 1868-1976. In the copy of this book commented by Mario Rodríguez, he noted that in a some sort of advertising, the editor Ridgway also refers to a work by William Burke (*The Armed Briton: or, the Invaders Vanquished. A Play in Four Acts*), and to another work: *The Veterinary Tablet, or, a Concise View of all the Diseases of the Horse; with their Causes, Symptoms, and most approved Modes of Cure, By a Veterinarian Surgeon.* See Mario Rodríguez, *"William Burke" and Miranda, cit.,* pp. 129, 546.

213 See the reference in *Annual Review and History of Literature for 1806*, Arthur Aikin, Ed., Longman etc, Ridgway, London 1807, p. 162.

214 There are no biographical references in the United Kingdom on William Burke who allegedly wrote between 1805 and 1810, for what can be said that there was no such person except in the covers of the books that bear the name.

(1729-1797) who was the co-author with his cousin, Edmund Burke – both Irish - of a book published in London in 1760, entitled: *An Account of the European Settlements in America, in six Parts.*[215] Edmond Burke, on the other hand, was also the very well renowned author of the book: *Reflections on the Revolution in France. And on the Proceeding in Certain Societies in London Relative to That Event in a Letter Intended to Have Been Sent to a Gentleman in Paris,* 1790. By the end of the 18th century, therefore, Burke was a very well established name in the editorial world, of course, those Irish authors not having any relation with our Burke of the beginning of the 19th century.

The other real William Burke (1792-1829), who can be traced in history during those times, younger than our William Burke, acted in quite a different world than books, although also a publicized world, which was the world of crime. Years after the publication of our William Burke's books in London, in effect, another William Burke became notorious as a criminal who along with an accomplice, William Hare (both of them also Irish), began to plunder graves and to trade in human corpses. For such crimes, he was tried and hanged in 1829; and his body was stuffed before 2000 medical students at the University of Edinburgh. His skeleton can still be seen at the Edinburgh University Museum.[216] This Burke, of course, had no relation to our William Burke.

As mentioned, our William Burke was a febrile intellectual and writer, editor and publisher, who, in addition to the two already mentioned books, wrote and published in London in 1807 another book with the title: *Additional Reasons for our Immediately Emancipating Spanish America: deducted from the New and Extraordinary Circumstances of the Present Crisis: and containing valuable information respecting the Important Events, both at Buenos Ayres and Caracas: as well as with respect to the Present Disposition and Views of the Spanish Americans: being intended to Supplement to "South American Independence," by William Burke, Author of that work.*[217] This new book was intended to complement the previous one, but with references to two particular and important events that had occurred in South America between 1806 and 1807, precisely after its appearance. In this book, again, it is noticeable the bond that continues to be develop in the sequence between the author of this work and the authors of the previous work of 1806. In this lat book, it must be mentioned, the *"Letter to the Spanish Americans"* by Juan Pablo Viscardo y Guzmán, which Miranda had published in London in French, on 1799, and in Spanish, in 1801, was also included, in its "Second Edition" Enlarged.[218]

These events that motivated the new book with *Additional Reasons...,* were: first, the expedition organized in 1806 by Francisco de Miranda for the purpose of initiat-

---

215 Published by Rand J. Dodsey, (London 1760)

216 See reference in R Richardson, Death, *Dissection and the Destitute*, Routledge & Kegan Paul, London 1987 and <http://www.sciencemuseum.org.uk/broughttolife/people/burkehare.aspx>.

217 Published by F. Ridgway, London 1807. (Ridgway, London 1808)".

218 Published by F. Ridgway, Ridgway, London 1808, pp. 95-124.

ing the process of independence of Hispanic America that sailed from New York and disembarked in the Province of Venezuela, failing in his attempt; and second, the invasion in 1807 by John Whitelocke, Commander-In-Chief of the British forces in the *Río de la Plata*, of the port of Buenos Aires in 1807, who also failed in his attempt.

In effect, the second part of the book is devoted to analyzing the first of the new events, that is, Francisco de Miranda's expedition the previous year, 1806, that with the understanding of the British authorities and that of the United States authorities - although without their official support- sailed on February 3, 1806 with a group of men from New York to invade the province of Venezuela. Miranda arrived in New York from London in November 1805, where his friend William Steuben Smith helped him mount the expedition, being the President of the United States, Thomas Jefferson, and the Secretary of State, James Madison, duly informed about the project.[219] Nonetheless, after a trial was developed in New York against those who helped Miranda, particularly Smith, Jefferson and Madison argued that it was false that they would have supported the expedition of Miranda.[220]

In any event, the expedition arrived to the port of Jacmel in Haiti, on February 17, 1806 (where the emperor Jean Jacques Dessalines had just been assassinated and where Petion was in the process of consolidating his power in the South of the Island, Miranda came to the islands of Curacao, Aruba and Bonaire. From there, on April 25, he landed in Puerto Cabello failing in his first invasion undertaking. He then put in at the port of Grenada on May 27, where he met with Admiral Alexander Cochrane -commander of the British fleet in the Caribbean- getting his help with boats and supplies. Subsequently, Miranda arrived in Trinidad on June 2, from where on July 23, he sailed to the Vela de Coro where he landed in early August 1806. The expedition found no echo in the population which had already been warned by the colonial authorities, remaining, as its results, the very rich set of papers with the proclamations of independence written by Miranda in Trinidad and Coro, in its capacity as "Commander General of the Colombian Army to the People Residing in the American-Colombian Continent."[221]

On the other hand, the first part of this work was dedicated to analyzing and criticizing the failed British invasion of the city of Buenos Aires in June 1807, with an army of about 10,000 men, after having occupied Montevideo in April of that year. The resistance of the people of Buenos Aires was definitive, beating the British forces and bringing about the capitulation of Whitelocke in humiliating conditions, which was ratified in July 1807. Whitelocke was forced to evacuate the southern border of the Río de la Plata in 48 hours, and to release the city of Montevideo in the two subsequent months. All this occurred on September 1 when Whitelocke left the

---

219 See Miranda's letter to Thomas Jefferson and James Madison dated January 22, 1806 on the secrecy of the expedition, in Francisco de Miranda, *América Espera, cit.* p. 340.

220 See the reference in Tomás Polanco Alcántara, *Miranda, cit.*, p. 194.

221 See Francisco de Miranda, *Textos sobre la Independencia,* Academia Nacional de la Historia, Caracas 1959, pp. 93-99.

estuary along with all his army. Upon his arrival in England in January 1808, Whitelocke was subjected to a martial court that found him guilty of all charges put to him, discharging and declaring him "unfit and unworthy to serve His Majesty in any military class." With these events, as recorded in the book, the British generals and admirals became convinced that South America would never be British.

It was precisely to the analysis of these two important events that this third book of William Burk was dedicated, ending with a criticism of the idea of any attempt to liberate Hispanic America by foreign or British invasion, and promoting the idea of invasion led by Hispanic Americans themselves, promoting the role that Francisco de Miranda needed to have in that process of the independence of South America, even with a direct petition directed to the British government seeking economic support "with precise figures corresponding to the Miranda projects."[222]

For such purpose, the book, after the brief biography of Miranda, goes on directly to make a defense of the Precursor against the slanders that were spread about him about his intentions over the expedition to Venezuela, describing Miranda as the "South America's Washington", and then goes on to make the proposition that Miranda be immediately aided with a military force comprising 6,000 to 8,000 men in order to achieve the independence of its own country, Caracas, and from there the independence of the rest of Spanish America. Miranda, it was argued, could achieve in that way what no British military could claim directly for it would be rejected as it had just been the case in Buenos Aires. In this way, the project of Spanish American independence -the book read- should not be delayed one more day.

Another fact is clear about our William Burke and his authorship of this third book, and it is that by the time it appeared in London, in 1807, Miranda was still in the Caribbean (Barbados) waiting to return to London after his failed invasion of the Province of Caracas. It was, in any case, a publication intended to prepare his return, and so from the recount of his expedition published in Burke's book,[223] it is possible to conclude that it was written by Miranda himself or under his direction. The fact is that the papers related to his expedition used for the book were sent to London by Miranda with his personal representative, Colonel Count Gabriel de Rouvray, who traveled from Barbados with the complete documentation of the expedition in order to seek British support for a new invasion. Rouvray arrived in London in December 1806 and immediately got in contact with two very distinguished London's authors and intellectuals that were the most important friends of Miranda in London, no other that James Mill and Jeremy Bentham.

---

222 See Georges L. Bastin, "Francisco de Miranda, "precursor" de traducciones," in *Boletín de la Academia Nacional de Historia de Venezuela,* N° 354, Caracas 2006, pp. 167-197 and also at <http://www.histal.umontreal.ca/pdfs/FranciscoMirandaPrecursorDeTraducciones.pdf>.

223 Of this undertaking and in addition to the story in Burke's book, there was published in New York a critical book (probably written by one of the Americans involved in the venture): *The History of Don Francisco de Miranda's Attempt to Effect a revolution in South America in a Series of Letters,* Boston 1808, London 1809. See Mario Rodríguez, *"William Burke" and Francisco de Miranda. The Word and the Deed in Spanish America's Emancipation,* University Press of America, Lanham, New York, London 1994, p. 108.

In addition, Miranda must have left them, before his departure for his expedition, important documents related to the Hispanic American independence process, including his own biography that was also published in Burke's book. Leaving James Mill in London as Miranda's representative, Rouvray returned to Barbados in early 1808, with copies of Burke's new book, *Additional Reasons...*, with the recount of the expedition.[224] In it, it was finally argued that if Britain would have given Miranda effective support, his expedition would have not failed; the second half of the text being devoted to promote General Miranda as the most capable person to lead the task of freeing Spanish America with British support.

At that time, James Mill was already a renowned and prominent Scottish philosopher and historian, writer and columnist (1773-1836) and father of John Stuart Mill. He was a prolific writer, his best known works being: *British History of India* (1818), *Elements of Political Economy* (1821), *Essay on Government* (1828) and *Analysis of the Phenomena of the Human Mind* (1829). As an editor and before the publication of these works, he reviewed every imaginable topic and on many occasions he turned to issues relating to Spanish American independence, for example, citing documents of Juan Pablo Viscardo y Guzman. The article *"Pensamientos de un inglés sobre el estado y crisis presente de los asuntos en Sudamérica"* (An Englishman's thoughts over the situation and present crisis of affairs in South America), published in 1810 in *El Colombiano*, which was a newspaper founded and edited by Miranda in London that year, that appeared each fifteen days, between March and May 1810, should correspond to Mill, as evidenced by the references made therein to Mill's works on Spanish America published years before in the *Edinburgh Review* (January and July, 1809). This article was also reproduced in the *Gazeta de Caracas*, January 25, 1811 and was taken by Miranda to Venezuela, along with many others papers, on December 1810.[225] Jeremy Bentham, on his side, was very distinguished lawyer, philosopher and political radical, who from among the universe of matters of their interest, was becoming concerned with the Spanish American affairs. He is primarily known for his moral philosophy, especially his principle of utilitarianism, which evaluates actions based upon their consequences.

It is evident that it was in this alliance between Miranda, Mill and Bentham, where the key factor to identify our prolific writer "William Burke" and his editing venture, can be found, as a pen name or pseudonym, which resulted not only from the editorial design of all his books on the Spanish American independence, but also from the promotion that was made in the books of Francisco de Miranda -including the references to the Napoleonic Wars of 1805 -. All this suggests that the Burke's

---

224 See Mario Rodríguez, *"William Burke" and Francisco de Miranda. The Word and the and the Deed in Spanish America's Emancipation*, University Press of America, Lanham, New York, London 1994, p. 153.

225 See Mario Rodríguez, *"William Burke" and Francisco de Miranda. The Word and the Deed in Spanish America's Emancipation*, University Press of America, Lanham, New York, London 1994, pp. 267-268.

books were of a "collaborative nature,"[226] aldo published with the participation of Francisco de Miranda himself, and of his London friends, Mill and Bentham,[227] who became familiar with the Archives of Miranda. They all were devoted to encourage the process of Spanish American independence, compelling a quick action on the part of England.[228]

James Mill and Jeremy Bentham were so involved in the Spanish American independence process that they had the purpose of accompanying Miranda in his return to Caracas in 1810.[229] In the end, they failed to travel, but their studies, works and papers did effectively travel in the valued Archives of Miranda, of course, altogether with "William Burke," who began to publish his editorials in the *Gaceta de Caracas* even before his supposed "travel" to Caracas. The thruth, in any case, is that the Archive of Miranda travelled three times in the same Royal nay SMM Sap-

---

226 See Eugenia Roldán Vera, *The British Book Trade and Spanish American Independence. Education and Knowledge Transmission in Transcontinental Perspective*, Ashgate Publishing, London 2003, p. 47. Mario Rodriguez is the author that has studied "William Burke" more accurately and comprehensively as the pseudonym under which James Mill and Jeremy Bentham had written several articles on Spanish America. See Mario Rodriguez, *William Burke" and Francisco de Miranda: The World and Deed in Spanish America's Emancipation*, University Press of America, Lanham, New York, London 1994, pp. 123 ss., 509 ss., 519 See also Ivan Jasksic, *Andrés Bello. La pasión por el orden*, Editorial Universitaria, Imagen de Chile, Santiago de Chile 2001, pp. 96, 133.

227 In the group were other supposed friends of Miranda, like Dr. F.S. Constancio, perhaps another penname. Christopher Domínguez Michael says the initials FSM was altogether used by José Francisco Fegorara and Fray Servando de Mier. See in *Vida de Fray Servando*, Ed. Era, México 2004, pp. 394, 447 ss. Mario Rodriguez thought it was a real person guessing that he could have also travelled to Caracas with the Miranda group, where he would have been a stand-in for "William Burke." See Mario Rodriguez, *William Burke" and Francisco de Miranda, cit.* pp. 248, 318, 514, 555.

228 For instance, Georges Bastin, in his "Francisco de Miranda, 'precursor' de traducciones" explains that it is very clear to see Miranda's intervention in the publication of Burke's book: *South American Independence: or, the Emancipation of South America, the Glory and Interest of England*, in 1807, saying also that, as aforementioned, in this document "in its last part he requests the government monetary support including precise numbers corresponding to Miranda's project"; and also that "In 1808, Miranda again prepares much of the other Burke's book titled *Additional Reasons for our immediately emancipating Spanish America...*" made in two editions in London. In the extended second edition, as stated above, Miranda includes his English translation of the *Lettre aux Espagnols Américains* (Letter to the Spanish Americans) by Viscardo y Guzman, as well as five documents with the heading "Cartas y Proclamas del General Miranda" (Letters and Proclamations of General Miranda). Then Miranda and Mill contributing, continued as William Burke, writing articles for the *Annual Register and the Edinburgh Review*. Particularly, on January 1809, James Mill, with the help of Miranda, published an article on "Emancipation of Spanish America" for the *Edinburgh Review*, 1809, N° 13, pp. 277-311. See Georges Bastin, "Francisco de Miranda, 'precursor' de traducciones" in *Boletín de la Academia Nacional de Historia de Venezuela*, N° 354, Caracas 2006, pp. 167-197; and also at <http://www.histal.umontreal.ca/pdfs/FranciscoMirandaPrecursorDeTraducciones.pdf>.

229 See Mario Rodriguez, *William Burke" and Francisco de Miranda, cit.* pp. 242, 315.

phire: in December 1810, from Portsmouth to La Guaira; in July 1812, from La Guaira to Curacao; and in 1814 from Curaçao to Portsmouth; y in al least in one of those occasions, for sure, in the passengers list of the vessel was the name of "William Burke.

The result was that after publishing three books in London between 1806 and 1808, William Burke published in one year and a half (1810-1812) more than eighty editorials in the *Gaceta de Caracas* referring to the all imaginable important matters of those times, including the political situation in Spain, discussions on religious tolerance and mainly, analysis of the government and the Constitution of the United States. No doubt exist in my opinion that all those works were based on papers written by Mill, Bentham and Miranda, in many cases using Miranda's documents contained in his Archives. Also, even Juan German Roscio, himself as editor of the *Gaceta de Caracas*, Francisco Xavier Ustáriz and Miguel José Sanz published some works as Burke's editorials in the *Gaceta*.

Not surprisingly, Augusto Mijares says that Burke's recommendations "immediately bring to mind some of Miranda's projects where the terminology is sometimes followed by Burke."[230]

On the other hand, in the letter from Roscio to Bello of June 9, 1811, Miranda was accused of having excused Burke to the Archbishop in the controversy over the religious matter, stating that the specific letter that caused it had been authored by "Ustáriz, Tovar and Roscio."[231] It must also be mentioned, a supposed "clash between Miranda and Burke" that was mentioned in the letter that Juan German Roscio addressed on June 9, 1811, to Andres Bello (who was in London) and where Roscio exhibited his entire grudge against the Precursor.[232] Indeed, if in that crucial year Roscio was against the positions of Miranda, "Burke" had also to be included because "Burke" was the name by which Roscio, as editor of the *Gaceta de Caracas,* also wrote, at times translating Mill's work, at times writing directly himself.

These editorials of the *Gaceta de Caracas* dated January 11, 15 and 18, 1811 were analyzed by Mario Rodriguez, who concluded that they were written by a Hispanic who clearly was Roscio. The same occurred regarding the essay published in the issue of November 19, 1811, written by Ustáriz, and another essay written by Miguel José Sanz.[233] The name of Burke was also used by Roscio as the subscriber to *La Bagatela*, edited by Antonio Nariño in Santa Fe.[234] On the other hand, some of

---

230 See Augusto Mijares, "Estudio Preliminar," William Burke, *Derechos de la América del Sur y México,* Vol. 1, Academia de la Historia, Caracas 1959, p. 21

231 *Idem,* p. 26

232 A remainder must be made of the fact that five fears earlier, in 1807, Roscio was the Prosecutor against the members of the expedition of Miranda.

233 See Mario Rodriguez, *William Burke" and Francisco de Miranda, cit.* pp. 334, 337, 338, 417, 418.

234 *Idem,* p. 394.

Burke's writings even gave rise to important debates such as the one mentioned on religious tolerance, a matter that has been already treated by Bentham in London.[235]

In the end, seventy of the important set of editorials and articles published by Burke between November 1810 and March 1812 in the *Gaceta*, were collected in a new book of William Burke, the fourth published in six years, this time edited in two volumes in Caracas, titled *Derechos de la America del Sur y Mexico*, [The Rights of South America and Mexico] by *William Burke, el author of "La Independencia del Sur de América, la gloria e interés de Inglaterra," Caracas, printed by Gallagher and Lamb, printers for the Supreme Government, 1811.*[236]

This book, in fact was even published before the new Federal Constitution of December 21, 1811 was sanctioned: the first volume in July 1811, and the second volume in October 1811,[237] the latter even containing some of the texts of the essays that were subsequently to be published in the *Gaceta de Caracas* up to March 20, 1811, when the last article appeared just before the terrible earthquake that occurred in Venezuela (March 26th, 1812). During those months of the publication of the two volumes, undoubtedly, Miranda himself would have participated in their edition, together with his immediate aids, Manuel Cortés de Campomares and José maría Antepara. The first one was one of the conspirators of Madrid's San Blas Conspiration and of the Gual y España Conspiration; and the second, the one that appears publishing papers of Miranda, just before his trip to Caracas in 1810: *South American Emancipation*.

If William Burke had in fact been a real person, he would have been one of the most distinguished writers of his time, which would had been known in the intellectuals circles of London and later of Caracas. But the fact is that nothing is known about this personage whom the Venezuelan historiography identifies only as an Irishmen, a friend of Francisco de Miranda during his last years in London, and who supposedly went to Venezuela, encouraged by Miranda himself, contributing with his writing to the ideas that conformed the constitutional basis of the Venezuelan constitution making process of 1811. In the chronicles of life in Caracas during

---

235 See the text of Burke's article in the *Gaceta de Caracas* N° 20, de 19 de febrero de 1811, in Pedro Grases (Ed.), *Pensamiento Político de la Emancipación Venezolana*, Biblioteca Ayacucho, Caracas 1988, pp. 90-95 ss. On the other hand, it should be mentioned that John Mill specifically addressed the issue of religious tolerance between 1807 and 1809 in collaboration with Jeremy Bentham.

236 See in the edition of the Academy of History, William Burke, *Derechos de la América del Sur y México*, 2 vols, Caracas 1959. Perhaps for that reason, Joseph M. Portillo Valdés observed that "William Burke" would rather have been, at least according to the writings published in Caracas, a "collective pen" used by James Mill, Francisco de Miranda and John German Roscio. See José M. Portillo Valdés, *Crisis Atlántica: Autonomía e Independencia en la crisis de la Monarquía Española*, Marcial Pons 2006, p 272, nota 60. Contra Karen Racine, *Francisco de Miranda: A Transatlantic Life in the Age of Revolution*, SRBooks, Wilmington, 2003, p 318.

237 See Mario Rodriguez, *William Burke" and Francisco de Miranda, cit.* pp. 399, 400, 510, 519.

those days of the independence, nonetheless, he is only mentioned because of his writings and not in any personal character.

The only references that were made about someone with the name of Burk were made after the March 1812 earthquake, by a Scotsman named John Semple, in a letter he wrote to his brother Mathew Semple, mentioned a few "Americans" that had survived the earthquake, among them one named Burke.[238] This "American" Burke would have been the same Burke that in June 1812 Miranda thought of sending on a mission to negotiate military and political support with the United States.[239] It must be mentioned that Augusto Mijares refers to this fact, but in another way, indicating that because a supposed disagreement between Burke (Burke's editorials) and Miranda, he prevented Burke "from leaving the country, even when apparently he had Government submissions for the United States of the North." [240]

In any case, it was through Burke's writings referring to the constitutional system of North America and to the functioning of the federal system of government that these ideas influenced the drafting of the Venezuelan 1811 Federal Constitution and of the other *Interesting Official Documents* contained in the 1812 London book. Among many other elements, this can be corroborated, for instance, in the use of the North American expression "rights of the people" and sovereign "of the people" instead of the French expressions: "rights of man and the citizens" or "sovereignty of the Nation," contained in the declaration of the Rights of the People of July 1, 1811.[241]

VII. FRANCISCO DE MIRANDA, THE LONDON HEADQUARTERS FOR THE INDEPENDENCE OF SOUTH AMERICA EFFORTS AND HIS LAST INTENTS TO ACHIEVE IT

William Burke, or better, the writings of William Burke, and through them the influence of the North American principles of government in the process of independence of South America, undoubtedly was possible because of the presence of Miranda in London at the beginning of the 19th century, which was the most formidable instrument for the establishment of an extended circle comprising all those living or visiting London with interest in such process. It can be said that Miranda, in fact, had contact with persons all over South America, and with all South Americans staying in London. It is worth highlighting his letter of advice to Bernando O'Higgins, the Liberator of Chile, before he left London to return to Santiago, in which he advised him "Not to trust men that had passed 40 years of age, except if you know for sure that they are devoted readers, and particularly of those books that

---

238 See the letter dated April 3, 1811 in *Tres testigos europeos de la Primera República*, Caracas 1934, pp. 86-87

239 See Mario Rodriguez, *William Burke and Francisco de Miranda, cit.* pp. 399, 400, 455, 456, 474, 568, 570

240 See the references in Augusto Mijares, "Estudio Preliminar," William Burke, *Derechos de la América del Sur y México*, Vol. 1, Academia de la Historia, Caracas 1959, pp. 25.

241 See William Burke, *Derechos de la América del Sur y México, cit.*, Tomo I, pp. 113, 118, 119, 120, 123, 127, 141, 157, 162, 182, 202, 205, 241.

had been prohibited by the Inquisition," concluding with his advice "Not to forget the Inquisition, nor its spies, its cassocks, nor its tortures."[242]

Among those relations, were those established with the editing world, the writers and intellectuals, specialized booksellers, printing houses, and the editors of journals related to Spanish American matters. It was due to those relations that the publication of the book en the *Interesting Official Documents* of the Independence was possible, being such book, indirectly, the last editorial venture encouraged by Miranda; a book that as mentioned, he never managed to see, being already imprisoned when it began to be available in London.

While Miranda and his aides, mainly Campomares and Antepara, were in Caracas, the editing process of the book in London resulted in the hands of Andrés Bello, who after arriving with the Venezuelan official Delegation in 1810, never again went back to Caracas. For such task, he had all the needed skills: not only had he been the editor for the *Gaceta de Caracas* from 1808 to 1810, but previously he had had an important governmental experience in Venezuela, as *Oficial Mayor* of the Captaincy General, having been in the months prior to his trip to London, a close collaborator of Juan German Roscio, the Ministry of Foreign Affairs of the Supreme Junta.

Bello was therefore prepared to handle the editing and publication process of such an important testimonial, which he assumed accommodating himself in Miranda's own house, on his capacity as Secretary of the Venezuelan delegation to the British government, a position that allowed him to continue with the contact and relations constructed by Miranda with the Spanish speaking community in London. Among its members, particular reference must be made of José María Blanco y Crespo, better known as Blanco-White, a distinguished Spanish exiled from Seville, editor in 1810 of the newspaper *El Español,* published in Spanish in London by the French bookseller Durlau.[243] Blanco-White was one of the first Europeans to have defended the independence process in Spanish America,[244] and as he was linked to the London publishing world, he must have been, no doubt, the vehicle through which Bello (who had been in close epistolary contact with Roscio) took care of the book's edition[245] using the same French bookseller, Durlau, publisher of the Burke's books, who had its headquarter at Soho Square, London.

From all these facts, it can be said that our *Interesting Official Documents* book, no doubt was the last indirect publishing adventure of Miranda in London, which

---

242   See in Francisco de Miranda, *América Espera, cit.*, pp. 242-244.

243   See *The Life of the Reverend Joseph Blanco White, written by himself with portions of his correspondence*, John Hamilton Thom, London 1845 (Sevilla 1988), p. 22.

244   The Independence Act was published in *El Español*, N° XVI, London, October 30, 1811, p. 44. See the text in Juan Goytisolo, *Blanco White. El Español y la independencia de Hispanoamérica,* Taurus 2010, pp. 197 ss. For this reason, among others, the Regency Council prohibited its difussion in America.

245   This is the same impression of Carlos Pi Sunyer, *Patriotas Americanos en Londres. Miranda, Bello y otras figuras*, Monteavila Editores, Caracas 1978, pp. 217-218.

had begun more than a decade before, in 1794, regarding his French wartime experience,[246] and later, in 1799, upon his arrival in London after having commanded the French Army of the North, with the publication of the letter written in Paris in 1791 by Juan Pablo Viscardo y Guzman Nait, an ex-Jesuit and remarkable intellectual precursor of Spanish American independence, titled *Letter to the Spanish Americans*.[247] The manuscript of this letter with all his papers was left by Viscardo before his death to the American Minister in London, Rufus King, who decided to give them to Miranda. He then, with the help of King, published in London the Viscardo letter in 1799 as a book with the imprint of Philadelphia. The book entitled *Lettre aux espagnols américaines par un de leurs compatriots*,[248] indicated in the "Advertisement" that the author was Viscardo y Guzman. Two years later in 1801, Miranda had the letter translated into Spanish and published it again, this time with London in the imprint, as *Carta dirijida a los españoles americanos por uno de sus compatriotas*.[249] This letter, thanks to the publicity given to it by Miranda, had a huge influence on the independence movement in Spanish America, its contents being reflected, for example, in the very Declaration of Independence and in the Constitution of Venezuela of 1811.[250]

Among the multiple relations and acquaintances Miranda made in London, mention must be made of a French young aid that he meat at the Durlau Bookseller, Pedro Antonio Leleux, who has to become his personal secretary; and of his aid in Caracas, Manuel Cortés Campomanes, who had participated with Picornell y Gomilla in the failed Conspiracy of San Blas in Madrid to change the Monarchy for a republican government (1796). Once detained and condemned, he was sent to prison in the Caribbean dungeon, arriving at the Port of La Guaira. After escaping, he participated in 1797 in the Conspiracy of Gual and España against the colonial govern-

---

246 See Francisco de Miranda, *Correspondence du général Miranda avec le general Doumoriez, les ministres de la guerre, Pache et Beumonville*, Paris 1794. This book was traslated into English and published by Miranda in London in 1976. According to Mario Rodríguez, this publication was motivated by the criticism made against Miranda, considering him an "adventurer" when joining the French Armies, in a book published by Jacques Pierre Brissot de Warville, *Letter to his Constituents*, which was translated by William Burke with the Preface of Edmond Burke, London 1794. See Mario Rodríguez, *"William Burke" and Miranda*, cit, pp. 128, 545-546. As Rodríguez pointed out, this was the only indirect contact of Miranda with the Irish writers who died before the end of the century. *Idem*, p. 128.

247 Miranda would have used only some of the papers because almost all of those which were never in Miranda's files were found in the files of the leading American politician, Rufus King, who had originally received them. See Merle E. Simmons, *Los escritos de Juan Pablo Viscardo y Guzmán. Precursor de la Independencia Hispanoamericana*, Universidad Católica Andrés Bello, Caracas, pp. 15-19.

248 Philadelphie, MDCCXCXIX. The letter was also published in *The Edinburgh Review*. See Tomás Polanco Alcántara, *Miranda, cit.* p. 248.

249 P. Boyle, London 1801.

250 See Georges L. Bastin, "Francisco de Miranda, "precursor" de traducciones," en *Boletín de la Academia Nacional de Historia de Venezuela*, N° 354, Caracas 2006, pp. 167-197, and also at <http://www.histal.umontreal.ca/pdfs/FranciscoMirandaPrecursorDeTraducciones.pdf>.

ment. He got in touch with Miranda in London in 1809,[251] and introduced him to another person that must be mentioned, who also played a special role as an aide of Miranda. It was José María Antepara, who later would edit the important book of and on Miranda titled *South American Emancipation. Documents, Historical and Explanatory Showing the Designs which have been in Progress and the Exertions made by General Miranda for the South American Emancipation, during the last twenty five years.*[252] Both collaborated with Miranda in the editing of the journal *El Colombiano* that he founded and published in London in 1810; and both traveled with Miranda to Caracas in 1810; and both managed to escape from La Guaira the night of July 30, in 1812, on the HRM Sapphire, with Miranda's Archives, while Miranda was imprisoned.[253]

In July 1810, Miranda received the members of the Official Delegation sent to London by the new government of the Province, composed, as already mentioned, by Simón Bolívar and Luis López Mendez and Andrés Bello. Miranda introduced them to the British authorities putting them in contact with the community of intellectuals and British politician friends of Miranda, including Mill and Bentham, as well as with the Hispanics and Americans residing in Great Britain, who disagreed with the Cádiz process in Spain and supported the Spanish American revolution, such as Cortés de Campomares, Antepara and Blanco-White. They all formed the important editorial circle that was used at the time to spread their ideas on the independence of Spanish America. It was during those months, with the aid of Mill and Bentham, and the translations made by Bello, that Miranda prepared all the documents, articles and editorials that a few months later would appear published in the *Gaceta de Caracas* under the name of William Burke.[254]

Nonetheless, the first article of Mill himself and of William Burke was published even before the return of Miranda to Venezuela through Andres Bello who sent them directly to Juan Germán Roscio, the editor of the *Gaceta.*[255]

---

251   See Mario Rodriguez, *William Burke" and Francisco de Miranda, cit.* pp. 248, 555.

252   Edited by R. Juigné, London 1810. See the first Spanish edition in the book: José María Antepara, *Miranda y la emancipación suramericana, Documentos, históricos y explicativos, que muestran los proyectos que están en curso y los esfuerzos hechos por el general Miranda durante los últimos veinticinco años para la consecución de este objetivo* (Carmen Bohórquez, Prólogo; Amelia Hernández y Andrés Cardinale, Traducción y Notas), Biblioteca Ayacucho, Caracas 2009.

253   See Giovanni Meza Dorta, *Miranda y Bolívar, Dos Visiones*, bid & co, editors, 3a ed., Caracas 2011, pp. 24-27.

254   See Mario Rodriguez, *"William Burke" and Francisco de Miranda, cit.* pp. 271, 316, 318, 518, 522. Those documents basically traveled in the archives of Miranda, although some of them must have been sent before by Bello to Roscio, the Editor of the *Gaceta de Caracas.*

255   The first editorial of Burke appeared in the issue of the *Gaceta de Caracas* of November 23, 1810, before the arrival of Miranda, which were sent probably together with some supplies brought in London for the printing press of the *Gaceta*. See Mario Rodriguez, *"William Burke" and Francisco de Miranda, cit.*, pp. 296, 297, 311.

So it was during those same days when the Venezuelan visitors were getting used to life in London, that Miranda himself edited in September 1810, the already mentioned book that appeared under the name of Jose Maria Antepara, titled *South American Emancipation....*[256] For its publishing, he received substantial financial support from some Hispanic American exiles. Noticeable are, for example, the contributions of Mexico's prominent Fagoaga family to the Miranda's publishing activity since the arrival in London, in 1809, of the second Marquis of Apartado, José Francisco Fagoaga y Villaurrutia, his brother Francisco and cousin Wenceslao de Villaurrutia after the autonomy movement led by the City of Mexico Ayuntamiento in 1808. Among the mutual friends of the Fagoaga family and Miranda there was José María Antepara, who was associated with Miranda editorial projects, in books, like the republication of the Viscado y Guzmán letter and in the newspaper *El Colombiano*, which appeared in London every fifteen days, between March and May 1810. In the design and publication of the books with the funding from the Fagoagas, there contributed Manuel Cortés Campomanes, Gould Francis Leckie, James Mill and Joseph Blanco White before the latter founded his own newspaper *El Español*,[257]

Regarding the Antepara's book on *South American Emancipation..*, if it is true that Miranda's name did not appear as its author, the book contained a collection of documents, most of Miranda or about himself, all coming from his precious Archives, including the Letter of Viscardo y Guzman, and James Mill's article on the "Emancipation of South America"[258] in which he made comments to said letter.

This was, therefore, the last of Miranda's direct editorial ventures in London, aiming to pressure the British Government by persuading the public opinion about the need to support Francisco de Miranda in the process of the liberation of Spanish America and the great potential that it meant for long term English prosperity. For this publishing project, Miranda, having received a major funding from the Fagoagas, allowed the name of José María Antepara to appear as the editor of the book, writing its foreword.[259] A copy of the book was received by Miranda once in

---

256 Edited by R. Juigné, London 1810. See the first Spanish edition in the book: José María Antepara, *Miranda y la emancipación suramericana, Documentos, históricos y explicativos, que muestran los proyectos que están en curso y los esfuerzos hechos por el general Miranda durante los últimos veinticinco años para la consecución de este objetivo* (Carmen Bohórquez, Prólogo; Amelia Hernández y Andrés Cardinale, Traducción y Notas), Biblioteca Ayacucho, Caracas 2009.

257 See Salvador Mendez Reyes. v. Salvador Méndez Reyes, "La familia Fagoaga y la Independencia" Ponencia al 49 *Congreso Internacional de Americanistas*, Quito 1997, published at <http://www.naya.org.ar/congresos/contenido/49CAI/Reyes.htmen>.

258 See Salvador Méndez Reyes, "La familia Fagoaga y la Independencia," Ponencia al 49 *Congreso Internacional de Americanistas*, Quito 1997, publicado en <http://www.naya.org.ar/congresos/contenido/49CAI/Reyes.htmen>.

259 See, for instance, the citation to the "Manifiesto de Venezuela" in José Guerra (pseudonym for Brother Servando Teresa de Mier), *Historia de la revolución de Nueva España o antiguamente Anahuac o Verdadero origen y causas con la relación de sus progresos hasta el presenta año 1813*, Guillermo Glindon, Londres 1813, Vol II, p. 241, nota. See the citation in

Caracas, because in October 1810 he travelled to Venezuela, accompanied by his two friends Manuel Cortes de Campomanes and José María Antepara, altogether with his Archives, and no doubt, with the pen of our William Burke.

It was, therefore, in this Spanish American vibrant environment in Britain where the 1810 Venezuelan delegation operated in London. Bolivar only remained in the city a few months returning to Venezuela in December of the same year, 1810. He sailed in the sloop of war, the HRM Sapphire of the Royal Navy, but Miranda had to sail in another vessel (Avon), due to the request of the British authorities, based on political motives, to not to travel with the Venezuelan Official delegation. Nonetheless, his precious Archives of 62 volumes actually sailed in the Sapphire under the custody of his secretary Pedro Antonio Leleux, and of Bolivar,[260] arriving in La Guaira a few days before Miranda's arrival on December 10, 1810.

By the time the travelers returned to Caracas, the Council of Regency in Spain had already, since August 1810, decreed the blockade of the coasts of Venezuela,[261] which was followed by the appointment, in January 1811, of Antonio Ignacio de Cortavarría as Royal Commissioner to "pacify" the Venezuelans. He was the one in charge of organizing the invasion of Venezuela from the colonial headquarters located on the island of Puerto Rico, commanded by Domingo de Monteverde, who in such character landed in Coro the following year, in February 1812, on the same coast where six years earlier Francisco de Miranda had landed for a brief time (1806).

A few months later, on July 25, 1812, as aforementioned, the Capitulation was signed between the two military commanders, which once ignored by Monteverde, provoked the detention of all the so-called "monsters" of America," Roscio and Miranda included. In addition, the persecution of patriots was generalized and the dependencies of the Republic and files were ransacked, its territories occupied by Spanish troops and all its leaders imprisoned or exiled

One month before the Capitulation was signed, on June 26, 1812, Miranda had called an embargo of the port of La Guardia, preventing the free departures of ships, particularly those American ones that had arrived a few weeks earlier with aid for the victims of the March earthquake. He thought that all those ships could be used for a possible political evacuation of men and officers, including those that according to his plans could be headed toward Cartagena de Indias in order to continue

---

Carlos Pi Sunyer. *Patriotas Americanos en Londres (Miranda, Bello y otras figuras),* (Ed. y prólogo de Pedro Grases), Monteávila Editores, Caracas 1978, p. 218.

260 See William Spence Robertson, *Diary of Francisco De Miranda: Tour of the United States 1783-1784,* The Hispanic Society of America, New York, 1928, p. xx.

261 José Blanco White commented on this "stupidity action of the Regency," in an article published in the *Morning Chronicle* of London on September 5, 1810: "Letter of a Cádiz Spaniard to a friend of his in London", which was reproduced by Roscio in the *Gaceta de Caracas,* in the October 30th, 1810 issue. See Mario Rodríguez, *"William Burke" and Francisco de Miranda, cit.* pp. 313-313.

with the independence efforts. After the Capitulation, Miranda arrived at La Guaira on July 30, 1812, lifting the embargo with the clear intention of leaving the country.

Previously, he had instructed his aide and secretary, Pedro Antonio Leleux, to place his archives in a British ship, which he did, consigning them for greater safety to an English merchant named George Robertson of the firm Robertson & Belt, of Curacao;[262] so they were effectively shipped precisely in the same sloop of war, the HRM Sapphire, commanded by the British Captain Henry Haynes, in which coincidentally the same Archives had travelled from London to Caracas in 1810 with all the papers and documents that were later to be published in the *Gaceta de Caracas* under the name of William Burke.

The most interesting fact in all this story is that, as officially reported by Captain Haynes in Curaçao, two days later, on August 1, 1812, in the same HRM Sapphire that sailed from the Port of La Guaira on the 30 of July 1812, among its 37 passengers, in addition to the two main aides of Miranda, Lieutenant General Cortes, without doubt, Cortes de Campomares, identified as a Spanish European, profession "Artillery," and Captain José María Antepara, identified as a South American, profession "Infantry"; there were two persons this time under the name of Burke: one "William Burke," identified as British, profession "Surgeon," "previously in the British Service," and another "Lieutenant Burke," also identified as British, profession "Cavalry," "previously in the British Service."[263]

Who were these Burkes? No doubt that due to the debacle of the night of July 30, 1812, the prohibition issued to foreigners to sail and the imprisonment of many patriots, other persons not listed by Captain Haynes must have been on board, probably covering their real names by using the Burke denomination that nobody was going to question. Perhaps one of them was precisely Pedro Antonio Leleux, the personal secretary and aide of Miranda to whom he charged the task of embarking his archives in a British vessel, which he did in the Sapphire, a fact the Captain Haynes testified.[264] Nonetheless, the name of Leleux, who also escaped that same night from La Guaira,[265] as he reported, was not included in the list made by Captain Haynes in Curacao. Leleux himself, only explained in his letter sent to Chancellor Vanisttart, probably from Curacao dated August 26, 1812, that "he managed to escape and boarded a British ship where he remained hidden in a bunch of straw for

262 See William Spence Robertson, *Diary of Francisco De Miranda: Tour of the United States 1783-1784*, The Hispanic Society of America, New York, 1928, p. xxi.

263 See W.O.1/112- Curacao. 1812. Vol 2nd. Folios 45 and 46 C.O.T Gov'Hodgson. In *Documentos relativos a la Independencia. Copiados y traducidos en el Record Office de Londres por el doctor Carlos Urdaneta Carrillo*. Año de 1811-1812. Fol. 478-479.

264 See Giovanni Meza Dorta, *Miranda y Bolívar, Dos visions*, 3a ed., bid & co. Editor, Caracas 2011, p. 21.

265 See the letter of Leleux to Chancellor Nicholas Vansittart of August 26, 1812, in Giovanni Meza Dorta, *Miranda y Bolívar, Dos visions*, 3a ed., bid & co. Editor, Caracas 2011, Appendix 15, pp. 194-197. See on the testimony of Captain Haynes, in Tomás Polanco Alcántara, *Mianda, cit.*, p. 322.

mules until after having wandered for ten days I arrived in Curacao to the house of Mss Robinson & Belt."[266]

Did he sail in fact in the Sapphire under the name of William Burke, a name that he perfectly knew? Leloux, in addition, knew very well the Sapphire, because he had already sailed in it from London to La Guaira in December 1810, where he arrived precisely with the same archives of Miranda, altogether with José María Antepara and Simón Bolívar.[267]

The fact is that following the debacle of La Guaira and the fall of the First Republic of Venezuela, our prolific writer, William Burke, listed as passenger of the Sapphire, simply disappeared. No other news about him is recorded in history except a reference in Venezuelan Historiography that he died in Jamaica that same year, 1812.

As for the precious Archives of Miranda, they also disappeared and were only found more than a century later in England. The archives were eventually sent from Curaçao to London, in the same HM Shappire, via Jamaica, in 1814 to Lord Bathurst, Secretary of State for War and the Colonies, and remained in his office until he ceased to serve the Crown in 1830 as President of the Privy Council. Since 1830 they were transferred to his personal residence in Cirencester, as his personal property, where they were "discovered" in 1922, precisely by the biographer of Miranda: William Spence Robertson[268]

It was precisely, in the same days of the detention of Miranda in la Guaira, in 1812, that the copies of the book, *Interesting Official Documents,* began to be available in London, even being the subject of quotes and comments,[269] in which the causes of the independence and the construction of a new Republic that already had disappeared, was officially explained. By that time, the provinces of Venezuela were already occupied by the Spanish army, and subjected to the military rule of conquest that was established with profound disdain regarding the constitutional republican framework that had been constructed in the Provinces.

---

266 See Giovanni Meza Dorta, *Miranda y Bolívar, Dos visions*, 3a ed., bid & co. Editor, Caracas 2011, p. 197.

267 See Mario Rodríguez, *"William Burke" and Miranda, cit,* p. 317. Miranda had met Pedro Antonio Leleux in the Durlau Bookseller in Soho Square, London, where among others, Burke's books and the *Interesting Official Documents* were distributed. See Paúl Verna, *Pedro Leleux, el francés edecán secretario y amigo de confianza de Miranda y Bolívar*, Comité Ejecutivo del Bicentenario de Simón Bolívar, Caracas 1982.

268 See William Spence Robertson, *Diary of Francisco De Miranda: Tour of the United States 1783-1784*, The Hispanic Society of America, New York, 1928, p. xxvi.

269 See, for instance, the quotation of the "Manifiesto de Venezuela" in José Guerra (pseudonym for Brother Servando Teresa de Mier), *Historia de la revolución de Nueva España o antiguamente Anahuac o Verdadero origen y causas con la relación de sus progresos hasta el presenta año 1813*, Guillermo Glindon, Londres 1813, Vol II, p. 241, nota. See the citation in Carlos Pi Sunyer. *Patriotas Americanos en Londres (Miranda, Bello y otras figuras),* (Ed. y prólogo de Pedro Grases), Monteávila Editores, Caracas 1978, p.218.

In any case, in contrast with that and all the military regimes that afterward have been installed in Venezuela, the precious book, *Interesting Official Documents relating to the Provinces of Venezuela*, will always remain as the most extraordinary testimony of the first experiment of building a democratic Republic applying the modern principles of constitutionalism derived from the French and American Revolutions. It included, as has been said, the chief documents that supported and validated the independence process of Venezuela which was advanced in the three pivotal years from 1808 to 1811. These documents came to integrate a top political and constitutional collection that reflects all the circumstances and uncertainties of what was the first Spanish American independence movement which was advanced in the seven provinces of the former Captaincy General of Venezuela and which led to the Spanish-American revolution.

The movement, if anything, followed some of the actions and progressions that had been given thirty years ago in the United States and twenty years ago in France. The documents of the book also presented the specificities of the first constituent process that took place in Spanish America after the independence was formally declared, showing thereby the tremendous constitutional effort that was advanced, among others, by prominent jurists who partook in their drafting for the purpose of forming a new federal and republican independent State in the territories of the former Spanish colonies and which new state would be detached from the royal power. These provinces had declared themselves sovereign states, having each adopted its own constitution or form of government (Provincial Constitutions), under the principles of modern constitutionalism, only a few decades after these principles had emerged from the American and French revolutions.[270]

The book, as a whole, was directed to explain to the world, by written evidence, the reasons these former provinces had to declare themselves independent; and particularly, as aforementioned, they were intended for England, where until then and as indicated in the *Preliminary Remarks*:

> "the public prints it has been nevertheless branded with censure and reprobation; they have presented us with nothing but superficial views of disguised facts, often treacherously exaggerated, oftener cloathed in the language of unwarrantable anticipation and unfounded prejudice; nay the causes and circumstances appear rather to have been completely misunderstood."

In the *Preliminary Remarks*, therefore, it was said that Venezuela, with "the resolution of becoming independent," it knew that it would "provoke all the thunder of her enemies" so that with the publication of documents in the book, it was expected that being Britain "a country too liberal, and too enlightened [...] such narrow sentiments" would not exist, having "men, who feel the warm effusions of pleasure, to see advanced the cause of general liberty, and the extension of human happiness."

---

270 See *Las Constituciones Provinciales* (Estudio Preliminar por Ángel Francisco Bice), Biblioteca de la Academia Nacional de la Historia, Caracas 1959; Allan R. Brewer-Carías, *Historia Constitucional de Venezuela*, Tomo I, Editorial Alfa, Caracas 2008, pp. 239 ss.

Therefore, even in the Declaration of Independence, the drafters stated that "before we make use of those Rights, of which we have been deprived by force for more than three centuries, but now restored to us by the political order of human events," Venezuelan proceeded to "to make known to the world the reasons which have emanated from these same occurrences, and which authorise us in the free use we are now about to make of our own Sovereignty."

In doing so, as mentioned, it followed the main principles of modern constitutionalism that were applied for the first time in history after their creation after the American and French revolutions of the 18th century.

Those principles, two hundred years later, still remain today as the basic principles to establish modern democracies, so it is hardly surprising that in the near future they will again be brandished in order to reconstruct the institutions that have been demolished in Venezuela by the authoritarian government that at the beginning of the 21st century, and during the past decade has assaulted its government. Perhaps, among other things, Venezuelans must remember, two hundred years after the publication of the book, the same that the general Congress explained in its *Manifest* to the world of 1811, on the causes that had justified the independence of Venezuela, mentioning the "right of insurrection of the peoples" against despotic governments, departing from the assessment that governments never had, nor can have, any other duration than the utility and felicity of the human race;" and that "that kings are not of any privileged nature, nor of an order superior to other men; that their authority emanates from the will of the people."

Also remembering what was expressed in the *Preliminary remarks* of the book, what is certain is that the "maxim," or "immutable law" attributed to Montesquieu, in the sense "that nations can be saved only by the recovery of their lost principles;" Venezuelans must be conscious that the democratic and constitutionalism principles gathered in the *Interesting Official Documents* of the Independence published in the 1812 London book, now republish in 2012, despite the two hundred years that have past, continue to be the most important inspiration source that we have for the future reestablishment of democracy in the country.

CHAPTER **XXX**

ALEXIS DE TOCQUEVILLE AND SIMON BOLÍVAR. TWO APPROACHES ON THE PRINCIPLES OF MODERN CONSTITUCIONALISM AT THE BEGINNING OF THE NINETEENTH CENTURY

(2012)

This Paper on "Alexis De Tocqueville and Simon Bolívar. Two approaches on the Principles of Modern Constitutionalism (Participation, Representation, Sovereignty of the People, Republicanism, Limited Government, Federalism and the Constitution) at the beginning of the nineteenth century," was written in 2012, on the occasion of the Bicentennial of the collapse of the First Republic in Venezuela after the invasion of the Spanish Army in 1812, in reaction to the declaration of Independence and the constitution of the new State of Venezuela. It was intended to a Lecture programmed to be givern in Washington.

I. COMMENTS ON THE PROCESS OF INDEPENDENCE IN AMERICA

The modern practice of written constitutions in order to organized a State adopted by the people through their representatives and not given by a Monarch, began in the United States of America when the colonies separated from England, declaring themselves independent States (1776), and formulating their constitutions in writing. A Continental Congress in 1776 even invited all the colonies of the Union to draw up their own constitutions, as a political decision of the people.[271]

Nonetheless, the movement towards independence from England began in the United States long before that date when independence was finally declared, having its roots in the independent spirit developed through the colonial assemblies, which had grown in power and influence during the first half of the eighteenth century, by

---

271 See A. C. Mc Laughlin, *A Constitutional History of the United States*, New York 1936, p. 106-109.

resolving many of the colonists' problems at local level.[272] That is why the Declaration and Resolves of the First Continental Congress, 14 October 1774, bearing in mind that "assemblies have been frequently dissolved, contrary to the rights of the people, when they attempted to deliberate on grievances," resolved that "the inhabitants of the English colonies in North America, by the immutable laws of nature, the principles of the English constitution, and the several charters or compacts", had their own rights, among which was:

> "A peaceably right to assemble, to consider their grievances, and petition the king; and that all prosecutions, prohibitory proclamations, and commitments for the same, are illegal."[273]

Therefore, the process of separation of the English colonies in America from the mother country took place on the basis of two fundamental elements: the process towards independence of each one of the colonies, through their own representative governments; and the process towards the unity of the colonies, through the continental congresses. According to what was said by one of its principal protagonists, John Adams, "The Revolution and the Union developed gradually from 1770 to 1776."[274]

During that period, it was initially a process of inter-colonial agreements designed to establish economic boycotts in resistance to the tax pretensions of England. In this context, the first joint meeting of historical and constitutional significance between these colonies was the New York Congress of 1765, which met to demonstrate the colonies' rejection of the Stamp Act passed by the English Parliament on 22 March 1765. This Act placed stamp duties on all legal documents, newspaper pamphlets, college degrees, almanacs, liquor licences and playing cards, and aroused hostility that spread in the colonies.

Besides the social and economic causes of this rejection, the political reaction was based on the cry "no taxation without representation." Thus the 3rd, 4th and 5th rights declared in the Resolutions of the Stamp Act Congress 19 October 1765 stated:

> 3rd That it is inseparably essential to the freedom of a people, and the undoubted rights of Englishmen, that no taxes should be imposed on them, but with their own consent, given personally, or by their representatives.

> 4th. That the people of these colonies are not, and from their local circumstances, cannot be represented in the House of Commons in Great Britain.

---

272 See R.L. Perry, (ed.), *Sources of our Liberties. Documentary Origin of Individual Liberties in the United States Constitution and Rights*, 1952, p. 261

273 *Idem*, p. 287, 288.

274 Quoted by M. García Pelayo, *Derecho constitucional comparado*, Madrid 1957, p. 325.

5th. That the only representatives of the people of these colonies, are persons chosen therein by themselves; and that no taxes ever have been, or can be constitutionally imposed on them, by their respective legislatures.[275]

In this Congress although a "due subordination to that August body, the Parliament of Great Britain", was declared, its representative character was questioned on the grounds that the taxes established in the Stamp Act had not been approved by the Colonial Assemblies. England annulled the Stamp Act, but imposed a series of customs duties on colonial products.

By 1774, it had become clear that the problems of individual colonies were really the problems of them all, and that brought about the need of united action by the Colonies, with the result that Virginia proposed that an annual Congress be held to discuss the joint interests of America. Thus, in 1774 the First Continental Congress met in Philadelphia with representatives from all the colonies, except Georgia.

The main political element discussed in the congress was the authority the colonies should concede to the Parliament, and on what grounds: the law of nature, the British Constitution or the American charters.[276] It was decided that the law of nature should be recognized as one of the foundations of the rights of the colonies, and therefore not only the common law. Thus the Congress declared, as a Right of the inhabitants of the English Colonies in North America, in the same sense of the Resolutions of the Stamp Act Congress:

> That the foundation of English Liberty, and of all free government, is a right in the people to participate in their legislative council; and as the English colonists are not represented, and from their local and other circumstances, cannot properly be represented in the British Parliament, they are entitled to a free and exclusive power of legislation in their several provincial legislatures, where their rights of representation can alone be preserved in all cases of taxation and internal polity, subject only to the negative of their sovereign, in such manner as has been heretofore used and accustomed...[277]

Thus, in these resolutions, loyalty to the king was maintained, but the parliament was denied competence to impose taxes on the colonies.

As a result of this Congress, economic war was declared with the suspension of imports and exports to England. The economic war rapidly became a military one and the Congress met again in Philadelphia and adopted the "Declaration of the Causes and Necessity of Taking up Arms" of 6 July 1775, as a reaction against the "enormous", and "unlimited power" of the Parliament of Great Britain. That is why the American Revolution was, among other factors, a revolution against the sovereignty of the English Parliament.

---

275 See R.L. Perry (ed.), *op. cit.*, p. 270.

276 See Ch. F. Adams (ed.) *The Works of John Adams*, Boston 1850, II, p. 374 quoted by R.L. PERRY, *op. cit.*, p. 275.

277 See R.L. Perry (ed.), *op. cit.*, p. 287.

One year later, the second continental Congress, in its session of 2 July 1776, adopted a proposition whereby the colonies declared themselves free and independent:

> That these United Colonies are, and of right, ought to be, Free and Independent States; that they are absolved from all allegiance to the British Crown, and that all political connexion between them, and the state of Great Britain, is, and ought to be, totally dissolved.[278]

The Congress agreed to draw up a declaration proclaiming to the world the reasons for the separation from its mother country, and on the 4th July, the Declaration of Independence was adopted, in formal ratification of the act already executed.

This document is of universal historical interest; for it was the first time that juridical-political-rationalist legitimacy made its appearance openly in history. There was no longer the recourse to common law, nor to the rights of Englishmen, but exclusively to God and to the laws of nature. There was no longer the recourse to the Bill of Rights, but to self-evident truths, namely:

> That all men are created equal; that they are endowed, by the Creator, with certain unalienable rights; that among these are life, liberty, and the pursuit of happiness. That to secure these rights, Governments are instituted among men, deriving their just powers from the consent of the governed; that whenever any form of government becomes destructive of these ends, it is the right of the people to alter or to abolish it, and to institute a new government, laying its foundation on such principles and organizing the powers in such form, as to them shall most likely effect their safety and happiness.[279]

Consequently, anything, which was not rationally adapted to the objectives established, was unjustified and illegitimate, and, the state was also organized in the most adequate way to achieve the said objectives.

Apart from the importance of this document for the United States, it is undoubtedly also of universal significance: its basic premise, as a syllogism, is constituted by all those acts of the crown which, according to Locke, define tyranny, and the conclusion of the syllogism is obvious: by violating the pact uniting him to his American subjects, the king had lost all claim to their loyalty, and consequently, the colonies became independent states.

Obviously, once the colonies had acquired their independence, they had to regulate their own political organization. Moreover, after the king's proclamation of rebellion on 23 August 1775, the Congress just before the Declaration of Independence urged all colonies to form separate governments for the exercise of all authority. It resolved:

> That it be recommended to the respective assemblies and conventions of the United Colonies, where no government sufficient to the exigencies of their affairs has been hitherto established, to adopt such government as mall, in the opinion of the representatives of the people,

---

[278] *Idem*, p. 317.
[279] *Idem*, p. 319.

best conduce to the happiness and safety of their constituents in particular and America in general.[280]

Thus, the Bill of Rights and the Constitution or Form of Government of Virginia was adopted on 12 June 1776, and the other Constitutions of the States were adopted after the Declaration of Independence until 1787.

These colonial constitutions were of fundamental importance both for constitutional history in general and for the history of the United States itself, since they undoubtedly represented the triumph of the rational normative concept of the constitution, which could already be glimpsed in the Declaration of Independence. Furthermore, there were written systematic and coded constitutions, many of which were preceded by a table of rights inherent in human beings. In accordance with that table of rights the organic part of the constitution was set, adopting, naturally, as a fundamental principle the division of powers, which also made its entry for the first time in constitutional history with the principle of the sovereignty of the law.

Therefore, the rational normative concept of the constitution, with its table of rights, its division of powers, its sovereignty of the law, its distinction between constituent and constituted power, and its division of the constitution into a dogmatic and organic part, comes from America and its colonial constitutions, from where it proceeded to Europe, to the French Declaration of 1789, and through it, to modern constitutional law.

The idea of a Confederation or Union of Colonies was also formulated at the same time as the Declaration of Independence, thereby satisfying the need for a political union mainly derived out of the conduct of the war. Hence the adoption by the Congress, on 15th November 1777, of the "Articles of Confederation" is considered to be the First constitution.[281] It established a confederation and perpetual union between the States, the aim of which was the "common defence, the security of their Liberties and their mutual and general welfare"[282] in a system in which each state retained "its sovereignty, freedom and independence"[283] and any power, jurisdiction and right not expressly delegated to the United States in Congress.

The result was that the sole body of the Confederation was the Congress, in which each state had a vote. Consequently, the Confederation lacked direct taxation power, depended economically on the contributions of the States, had no executive body and only an embryonic form of judicial organization. Despite its weakness, the Confederation succeeded in carrying on the war for 7 years until it won. Following the victory, the precariousness of the Confederation made it necessary to establish a

---

280   *Idem*, p. 318. See A.C. McLaughlin, *op. cit.*, p. 107-108.

281   See R.B. Morris, "Creating and Ratifying the Constitution", *National Forum. Towards the Bicentennial of the Constitution*, fall 1984, p. 9.

282   See A.C. McLaughlin, *op. cit.*, p. 131.

283   *Idem*, p. 137; R.L. Perry, (ed.), *op. cit.*, p. 399.

greater power to achieve national integration and a Federal Convention was called to meet, "for the sole and express purpose of revising the articles of Confederation."[284]

This led in 1787 to the adoption by the Congress of the Constitution of the United States that was the result of a series of general compromises[285] between the political and social components of the independent colonies, of which the following are the most outstanding:

In the first place, the compromise between Federalists and Anti federalists, which provided the Union the necessary competences for its existence, while maintaining the autonomy of the Federated States. From this compromise emerged the form of the Federal state,[286] which appeared for the first time in constitutional history as a political organization of States, through a system of political decentralization or vertical separation of powers. This compromise was one of the main contributions of the North American Constitution to modern constitutional law.

The second great compromise reflected in the constitution was, as a result of a long brewing confrontation, the compromise between large and small States of the Union regarding representation. That is to say, between a Congress in which the States would be represented in proportion to their population and a Congress with a confederate type of representation. The result was a bicameral system in which the House of Representatives was to be made up of a number of deputies proportional to the population of each state, whereas the Senate would comprise two representatives per state, regardless of its size, thus providing equality among the states.[287]

In relation to the latter, the third compromise of the Constitution was that between the North and the South, that is to say, the compromise between free states and pro-slavery states, according to which the slave population was estimated at three fifths in relation to the white population for the purposes of determining the population of each state, both for the appointment of representatives and for tax purposes.

The great slavery issue was also to produce a fourth compromise concerning the question of import and export duties and, therefore, on the import of slaves or its abolition. The middle ground solution led to the adoption of a clause impeding the Congress from making any decision prohibiting slave importation for twenty years, until the year 1808.[288]

The fifth compromise that we can identify in the American Constitution is that between democracy and the interests of the ruling classes, to avoid despotism when voting. Thus, limited mechanisms for voting were established, based on private

---

284 See R.L. Perry (ed.), *op. cit.*, p. 401.

285 See M. García Pelayo, *op. cit.*, p. 336-337.

286 See R.B. Morris, *loc. cit.*, p. 12, 13; M. García Pelayo, *op. cit.*, p. 336; A.C. McLaughling, *op. cit.*, p. 163.

287 See M. García Pelayo, *op. cit.*, p. 336; R.B. Morris, *loc. cit.*, p. 10; A.C. McLaughling, *op. cit.*, p. 179.

288 See R.B. Morris, *loc. cit.*, p. 11; A.C. McLaughling, *op. cit.*, p. 185.

property, as well as a mechanism for direct election of representatives to the House of Representatives as established by each state, and indirect election to the Senate.

The last and final compromise reflected in the constitution was the establishments of a system of separation of powers at federal level, thus, a check and balance system. Therefore, in addition to the legislative body, a strong presidency was provided for, to be occupied by a President elected for four years, by means of a system of indirect suffrage; and a Supreme Court was created, made up of judges elected for life by the two bodies furthest from the masses, the president and the Senate, being granted power to declare the unconstitutionality of acts issued by the other powers against the constitution. Separation of powers and judicial review of the constitutionality of legislative acts are another two main contributions of the American constitution to modern constitutional law.

In addition to these compromises of the constitution of the United States, we must turn our attention to another two main contributions of America to constitutional law: First, constitutionalism itself, in the sense of the adoption of all those compromises of forms of government in a written constitution as fundamental law, and second republicanism, as an ideology of the people against monarchy and hereditary aristocracies,[289] based on political representation.

Eighteenth century Americans decided upon revolution to repudiate royal authority and to erect a republic in its place. Thus, Republicanism and to become republican was what the American Revolution had been about. That is why "the people" who then became the sovereign in constitutional history gave the constitution.

The constitution adopted in 1787, however, was conceived basically as an organic document, regulating the separation of powers within the organs of the new state, both horizontally and vertically among the legislative, the executive and judicial powers and between the states and the United States in accordance with the federal System.

In spite of the colonial antecedents, and of the proposals made in the Convention, it did not contain a Bill of Rights, except the right to representative government. The protests of the opponents of the new Federal system, led particularly by the anti-federalists, during the ratification process, brought about the adoption of the First Ten Amendments to the Constitution, on the 15th December 1791, containing the American Bill of Rights.[290]

II. COMMENTS ON THE PROCESS OF INDEPENDENCE OF HISPANIC AMERICA

Globally, the key political contribution derived from the American Revolution and its constitucionalization process were participation, representation, sovereignty of the people, republicanism, limited government, ederalism and the idea of the

---

289 See G.S. Wood, "The Intelectual Origins of the American Constitution", *National Forum, cit.*, Fall 1984, p. 5.

290 See the text in R.L. Perry (ed.), *op. cit.*, pp. 432-433.

Constitution. All this contributions bear fruits almost immediately in the Spanish Colonies of South America, in particular in the provinces of the General Captaincy of Venezuela.

In effect, the constituent process of the new States in Hispanic America that emerged at the beginning of the 19th century, began with the successful political rebellion occurred in the Province of Caracas on April 19, 1810,[291] when the Metropolitan City Council chaired by the Governor and General Captain, Vicente de Emparan, deposed it as well as all the Spanish authorities. The result was the configuration of a "Supreme Junta to Preserve the Rights of Ferdinand VII," in what can be considered as the first constitutional act of a new government and of the beginning of the legal establishment of a new State in Hispanic America.[292] All this process was provoked as a consequence of the news received from Spain the previous day, on April 18th 1810, regarding the decision taken three months before, on January 30, 1010, by the Central Junta of the Realm about its own dissolution, establishing instead a Regency Council and convening the Cortes; and on the fact that the French invasion of Spain resulted in the occupation of almost all its territory, confining what could be the Supreme Government of Spain to the city of Cadiz. In view of all those facts, the Caracas City Council considered necessary to establish a government to take care of the Provinces of Venezuela in order to assure their status out of the reach of the French Emperor.

Consequently, the City Council of Caracas, against the will of the overthrown Governor and General Captain, assumed the condition of *Junta Suprema de Venezuela Conservadora de los Derechos de Fernando VII*, and as such, the "supreme command" or "supreme authority" of the Province, constituting a "new government". The immediate motivation of this political fact, which was without doubt, the first successful coup d'Etat given in Hispanic America, had been the "completely orphanage" in which the people remained after the abdication of the Kings and after the dissolution of the Supreme Governing Junta of Spain, which replaced the Monarch. The Supreme Junta of Caracas, in order to consolidate its power, repudiated the authority of the regency Council, considering that it "had not been established by the vote of the people of the Province, even after being declared not colonist but part of the Crown of Spain, and as such they have been called to exercise internal sovereignty and to participate in the reform of the Constitution".[293] This was ratified by the Supreme Junta two weeks later, on May 5th 1810, when addressing directly to the Regency Council, questioning its authority and representativeness, as well as the possible representatives that could be elected in America by the City Councils to

---

291 See for example, Daniel Gutiérrez Ardila, *Un Nuevo ReiN° Geografía Política, Pactismo y Diplomacia durante el interregno en Nueva Granada (1808-1816)*, Universidad Externado de Colombia, Bogotá 2010, pp. 157 ss.

292 See in general, Tomás Polanco, "Interpretación jurídica de la Independencia" en *El Movimiento Emancipador de Hispanoamérica, Actas y Ponencias,* Caracas, 1961, Tomo IV, pp. 323 y ss.

293 Véase el texto del Acta del 19-04-1810 en Allan R. Brewer-Carías, *Las Constituciones de Venezuela,* Academia de Ciencias Políticas y Sociales, Caracas 2008, Tomo I, pp. 531-533.

integrate the Cortes, as had been decided in the first convening made for the Cortes, which implied that in Venezuela it was said "in one word, [that] we ignore the new Regency Council." [294]

The revolutionary process of Caracas had a quick expansion effect as a consequence of the immediate divulgation and communication sent to all the other City Councils of the provinces of the general Captaincy of Venezuela, originating the formation of various Juntas in Cumaná (April, 27), Barcelona (April 27), and Margarita (May, 1st), a Superior Government and Conservancy Junta in Barinas (May 5), and a Superior Junta in Guayana (May 11).[295] The result was that two months later, by June 1810, in the former Provinces of the general Captaincy of Venezuela people began to talk officially about the "Confederation of Venezuela,"[296] being at that time the Supreme Junta of Caracas itself integrated by representatives of the provinces of Cumaná, Barcelona y Margarita. Nonetheless, and despite that fact and that the Junta was acting as Supreme Junta of all the Provinces, it needed an official representatives of all the other Juntas, and eventually, the establishment of a "Central Power well constituted." Precisely because, considering that "the moment to organized it" had arrive, it proceeded to convene: "to all classes of free man to the first of the citizens rights, which is to concur with their vote to the delegation of the personal and real rights that originally existed in the common people." It was the call, by the Supreme Junta, of the election and reunion of the representatives that were to conform the "General Junta or Congress of representatives of the provinces of Venezuela", for which purpose an Electoral Regulation was issued on June 11, 1810,[297] in which, it was established that all the Provincial Juntas were to abdicate their powers in the said General Junta, remaining the Supreme Junta only as the Provincial Junta of Caracas (Chapter III, Art. 4). This regulation was without doubt, the first electoral provisions adopted in the Hispanic American World.

On the other hand, in the following months of 1810, other provinces incorporated in the revolutionary movement, so on September 16, the City Council of Merida proclaimed the April 19 Revolution, and constituted itself as a Supreme Junta of Government, to which adhered, on October 14 the Parish of Bailadores; on October 21, the Parrish of San Antonio del Táchira; on October 28, the city of San Cristóbal. In addition, on October 9, 1810, the City Council of Trujillo installed the Patriotic Junta of Trujillo.[298]

---

294 See *Textos Oficiales de la primera República de Venezuela*, Biblioteca de la Academia de Ciencias Políticas y Sociales, Caracas 1982, Tomo I, p. 134.

295 See in Daniel Gutiérrez Ardila, *Un Nuevo Reino… cit.*, p. 211.

296 See the "refutation to the political delirium of Coro, by the Supreme Junta of Caracas,", of June 1st, 1810, in *Textos Oficiales de la Primera República de Venezuela*, Biblioteca de la Academia Nacional de la Historia, Caracas 1959, Tomo I, p. 180.

297 See the text in *Textos Oficiales…, op. cit.*, Tomo II, pp. 61-84; and in Allan R. Brewer-Carías, *Las Constituciones de Venezuela, cit.*, Tomo I, pp. 535-543.

298 See Tulio Febres Cordero (Compilador), *Actas de Independencia. Mérida, Trujillo, Táchira en 1810*, El Lápiz Ed., Mérida 2008.

The election of the representatives to the Congress or General Junta, in which participated only seven of the nine Provinces of the former general captaincy,[299] took place in December 1810, in which a total of 44 representatives were elected as follows: 24 for Caracas, 9 for Barinas, 4 for Cumaná, 3 for Barcelona, 2 for Mérida, one for Trujillo y one for Margarita.[300] The Inauguration of the Congress took place on March 2, 1811, expressly adopting the principle of separation of Powers in order to organize the new government, appointing pending the sanctioning of the new Constitution, a collective Executive Power and a High Court of Justice.

The obsession to legitimize all the authorities that could represent the provinces was so important in Caracas, that when in the city of Cadiz, two American "substitute representatives" were provisionally appointed to the *Cortes* to represent the provinces of Venezuela, contrary to what occurred in many other American Provinces, such appointment was rejected in Venezuela, where a local government already existed that even ignored the Regency Council. That is why, on the occasion of the appointment of the "substitute representatives" for the Province of Caracas (Esteban Palacios y Fermín de Clemente),[301] because they had not being appointed or elected in Venezuela, when they asked the Caracas Junta for instructions, the answer they obtained on February 1811, was that the convening of the *Cortes* in Spain was "as illegal as the Regency Council" and that consequently, "Mss. Palacios and Clemente lacked of power to represent the Provinces of Venezuela," considering and declaring "null and void their acts as representatives." [302]

In any case, since the inauguration of the elected Congress, the need to establish a Confederation of the provinces of Venezuela" began to be discussed, in which the provinces were to preserve their political peculiarities. For such purpose, on march 1811, the Congress appointed a Commission in order to draft the Constitution of the Province of Caracas, which was due to serve as a model for the drafting of the constitutions of the other Provinces of the Confederation, encouraging on April 1811, all the "provincial legislatures," to speed their drafting.[303]

---

299   The provincias of Caracas, Barinas, Cumaná, Barcelona, Mérida, Trujillo and Margarita, participated; and abstained the provinces of Guayana and Maracaibo that remained loyal to the Crown. See José Gil Fortoul, *Historia Constitucional de Venezuela,* Tomo primero, Berlín 1908, p. 223; J. F. Blanco y R. Azpúrua, *Documentos para la historia de la vida pública del Libertador,* Ediciones de la Presidencia de la República, Caracas, 1983, Tomo II, pp. 413 y 489.

300   See C. Parra Pérez, *Historia de la Primera República de Venezuela,* Academia de la Historia, Caracas 1959, Tomo I, p. 477.

301   See J. F. Blanco y R. Azpúrua, *Documentos para la Historia... op. cit.,* Tomo II, pp. 656. See also, Eduardo Roca Roca, *América en el Ordenamiento Jurídico de las Cortes de Cádiz,* Granada, 1986, pp. 22 y 136.

302   See the text in *Gaceta de Caracas,* martes 05-02-1811, Edición Academia Nacional de la Historia, Caracas, 1959, Tomo II, p. 17. See also in, C. Parra Pérez, *Historia de la Primera República ..., op. cit.,* Tomo I, p. 484.

303   See *Libro de Actas del Supremo Congreso de Venezuela 1811-1812,* Biblioteca de la Academia Nacional de la Historia, Caracas, 1959, Tomo II, p. 401.

On July 1st, 1811, the Section of the Province of Caracas for the General Congress, decided to proclaim a "Declaration of the People's' Rights,"[304] which was the first declaration of fundamental rights with constitutional rank in constitutional history after those of the French and North American Revolution. A few days latter, on July 5tf, 1811, the general Congress adopted the "declaration of Independence," being the new Nation named as "American Confederation of Venezuela";[305] and on December 21, 1811, proceeded to sanction the first Constitution of Venezuela and of all the Hispanic American countries, the "Federal Constitution of the Venezuelan States",[306] directly inspire don the principles of the revolutionary constitutionalism of North America and France.

Before the sanction of the Federal Constitution, other Provinces of Venezuela also initiated their own constituent processes,[307] even having sanctioned provincial Constitutiones, as was the case of the *Plan de Gobierno Provisional de la Provincia de Barinas* (March 26, 1811; of the *Constitución Provisional de la Provincia de Mérida* (July 31, 1811); and of the *Plan de Constitución Provisional Gubernativo de la Provincia de Trujillo (September 2, 1811.* [308] Other provinicses enacted Consrtitution in 1812, as was the case of the *Constitución Fundamental de la República de Barcelona Colombiana (January 12, 1812*; and the *Constitución para el gobierno y administración interior de la Provincia de Caracas January* 31,1812.[309]

As can be seen, in Venezuela, under the influence of the North American revolution, the same principles of participation, representation, sovereignty of the People, republicanism, limited government, federalism and the idea of the Constitution were

---

304   See Allan R. Brewer-Carías, *Las Constituciones de Venezuela, op. cit.,* Tomo I, pp. 549-551.

305   See the texto of the sessions of July 5, 1811, in *Libro de Actas... cit.,* pp. 171 a 202. See the declaration of Independence drafted by Juan Germán Roscio, in Pablo Ruggeri Parra, *Historia Política y Constitucional de Venezuela,* Tomo I, apendix, Caracas, 1949, pp. 79 y ss. Also in Francisco González Guinán, *Historia Contemporánea de Venezuela,* Caracas, 1954, Tomo I, pp. 26 y ss.; nd in Allan R. Brewer-Carías, *Las Constituciones de Venezuela, cit.,* Tomo I, pp. 545-548.

306   See the text of the 1811 Constitution, in *La Constitución Federal de Venezuela de 1811 y Documentos afines* (Estudio Preliminar de C. Parra Pérez), Caracas, 1959, pp. 151 y ss., nd in Allan R. Brewer-Carías, *Las Constituciones de Venezuela, cit.,* Tomo I, pp. 553 ss.

307   See in general, Allan R. Brewer-Carías, "Las primeras manifestaciones del constitucionalismo en las tierras americanas: Las Constituciones Provinciales y Nacionales ve Venezuela y la Nueva Granada en 1811-1812 como fórmula de convivencia civilizada," in José Guillermo Vallarta Plata (Coord.), *1812-2012. Constitución de Cádiz. Libertades. Independencia,* Instituto Iberoamericano de Derecho Local y Municipal, Organización Iberoamericana de Cooperación Intermunicipal, Gobierno Municipal, Guadalajara 2012, pp. 297-392.

308   See in general, Carlos Restrepo Piedrahita, *Primeras Constituciones de Colombia y Venezuela 1811–1830,* Universidad Externado de Colombia, Bogotá 1996, pp. 37 y ss.

309   See for instante, on the Constitution of the Province of Caracas, Allan R. Brewer-Carías, *La Constitución de la Provincia de Caracas de 21 de diciembre de 1811,* Academia de Ciencias Políticas y Sociales, Caracas 2012.

also followed,[310] having the same general consequence, which was the constitution building process of new States from what were former colonial provinces, based on constitutional principles radically contrary to the Monarchical ones prevailing in Europe.

III. ALEXIS DE TOCQUEVILLE AND SIMÓN BOLÍVAR ON THE CONSTITUTIONAL PROCESS OF AMERICA

It was regarding these two republican constitutional making processes developed in North America and in South America three decades one after the other, that two very distinguish thinkers of the beginning of the 19th century, directed their attention, although motivated by very different reasons. They were, on the one hand Simón Bolívar, and on the other hand, Alexis de Tocqueville. Almost in a contemporary way, between 1812 and 1830 the first dealt with the constitution making process in Hispanic America, and the second, between 1830 and 1840, analyzed and wrote about the constitution making process in North America.

Alexis de Tocqueville was born in *Verneuil-sur-Seine*, Ile de France on the July 29, 1805 from a royalist and conservative family that suffered assail of the French Revolution during the Terror period. He studied law, and in 1827 he was already acting in the Judiciary, as judge in the Versailles Court. He left the legal profession and accepted a governmental mission together with Gustave de Beaumont, in order to study the United States penitentiary system. He spend two years in his travels through the North American United States, and after his mission he not only wrote the book on *Du système pénitentiaire aux États-Unis et de son application* (1832), but from his observation and study regarding the political and social systems of the United States, he completed his book *De la démocratie en Amérique* (1835-1840), through which he discovered for the Europeans, a political system like the democratic representative republican one, so contrasting with the Monarchical one that prevail in Europe. When he returned to France he devoted himself to the political activity and to the study of the French political process, resulting twenty years later in his incomplete work on the *Ancient Regime and the Revolution* (1856), published three years before his death in Cannes, on April 16, 1859. In a certain way he was the first constitutional law researcher of the modern World, with a unique knowledge of the principles of modern constitutionalism that precisely emerged from the two revolutions that he studied.

By the time when De Tocqueville began his mission in the United States, Simon Bolívar had already died in Santa Marta on December 17, 1830, after resigning to the Presidency of the Republic of Colombia that he hand created between 1819 and 1821. Bolívar was born in Caracas, on July 24 1783, from one of the wealthiest families of the Spanish Colonial system in the Province Caracas, so by when de Tocqueville was born, Bolivar was 22 years old. By that time, he was already a wid-

---

310 See Allan R. Brewer-Carías, *Reflexiones sobre la Revolución Americana (1776), la Revolución Francesa (1789) y la Revolución Hispanoamericana (1810-1830) y sus aportes al constitucionalismo moderno*, 2ª Edición Ampliada, Serie Derecho Administrativo N° 2, Universidad Externado de Colombia, Editorial Jurídica Venezolana, Bogotá 2008.

ower, and was in Paris, in his second visit to Europe in an education and formation travel, in his way to Italy. Bolivar returned to Venezuela in 1806. In contrast with the de Tocqueville activity,

Bolívar was a military and state man, whose actions developed between 1813 and before De Tocqueville initiated his travel to North America. The latter studied as a lawyer and constitutional law expert the two great revolutions of the modern world on the 18th century; Bolivar instead was one of the principal actors of the third revolution of the modern world, the Hispanic American revolution of the beginning of the 19th Century, being one of the most distinguished figures of the American emancipation regarding the Spanish Empire. He not only liberated Venezuela from the military occupation that affected the country since 1812, after the declaration of independence from Spain, for which he was called the Liberator,; but also contributed since 1813 in a decisive way, as a military, to the independence of Colombia, Panamá, Ecuador, Perú and Bolivia. As a politician, between 1813 and 1830, he was Head of State of Venezuela, Colombia, Perú and Bolivia; and as a state man he was the craftsman of the configuration of the states of Venezuela (1819), Colombia (1821) and Bolivia (1826). That is, although he was not actively involved in the constitutional conception of the original Venezuelan State in 1811[311], later on, his intense political and military work was not confined to lead the wars of liberation and independence and to exercise political leadership in the country at a time of total disarray, but he also developed ideas for rebuilding the State[312], adapted to the troubled society that remained in those lands after independence.

These were two persons of the modern World, almost contemporary, whom each ne with their own vision and roll, marked modern constitutionalism in a way that it is interesting to confront: De Tocqueville as a liberal jurist, who expressed the result of his in situ observation of the institution of the United States and of the French revolution and their contribution to modern constitutionalism; and Bolívar, as a state man and military, liberating and conforming the constitutional basis of the new nations emerging in Hispanic America, in a certain way distancing itself from the North American model.

The first one, de Tocqueville, through his books and writings can be considered as the first of the constitutional law thinkers of modern times. He was an exceptional witness to the American and French Revolutions and their constitutional conse-

---

311 Bolivar, after fulfilling his mission in London in 1810, and after returning to Caracas participated in the discussions of the Patriotic Society, being held in parallel to the sessions of the General Congress, in which, on July 3, 1811, on the eve of the Declaration of Independence, he demanded that Congress should "listen to the Patriotic Council, center of light and of all revolutionary interests", calling for the need to declare independence from Spain, saying: "Let us place without fear the cornerstone of South American freedom: to hesitate is to be lost". See Bolivarian Society of Venezuela, Writings of the Liberator, Volume IV, Cuatricentenario de Caracas edition, 1968, p. 81.

312 See the discussion in Allan R. Brewer-Carías. "Ideas centrales sobre la organización del Estado en la obra del Libertador y sus proyecciones contemporáneas", in *Boletín de la Academia de Ciencias Políticas y Sociales* January-June 1984, N° 95-96, p. 137 and ff.

quences being his books authentic masterpieces that are still essential works for understanding the fundamental changes and trends that took place after those events. The second one, Simon Bolívar, can be considered as the most outstanding political leader, ruler and head of State in Latin America, being without doubt the first and more prolific constitutional builder of modern times, after liberating, as a military, almost half of the former Spanish Colonies of South America. The first made an European continental approach to the North American constitutional process, still unknown in that part of the world in the 1830's;[313] and the second, applied many of such principles, in practice, in his constitution building actions, even if he dissented of many of them. In any case, both dealt with the principles of democracy and constitutionalism that had their factual origin in the American Revolution, which radically transformed the constitutional trends of their time, establishing the basis of contemporary constitutional law. Nonetheless, in their analysis of the American political system, although admired by both, they were conscious of being – as de Tocqueville said – very "far from believing that they (the Americans) have found the only form possible for democratic government,"[314] or that the new American Institutions were the only ones, "or the best, that a democratic nation might adopt."[315]

De Tocqueville, for instance, in order to explain to the Europeans what had occurred in North America, began by stressing the situation of the English colonies in the seventeenth century, and particularly that of New England. He sustained that "all the general principles on which modern constitutions rest, principles which most Europeans in the seventeenth century scarcely understood and whose dominance in Great Britain was then far from complete, are recognised and given authority by the laws of New England," mentioning among those principles, "the participation of the people in public affairs, the free voting of taxes, the responsibility of governments officials, individual freedom, and trial by jury." "All these things – he concluded - were established without question and with practical effect."[316] All those things were the key elements that precisely provoked the construction of the federal from of government, which is the most important feature of the North American political system.

That colonial situation previous to the Independence process, which facilitated the constitutional conception of the new Federal State in North America, was also in general terms, although with less freedom and intensity the same in the colonial regime in Hispanic America, where the colonies although more dependent from the Spanish State, had in fact great autonomy in their regular government.

Nonetheless, in December of 1812, only one year after the enactment of the Federal Constitution of the Provinces of Venezuela which followed the trends of the

---

313 See J.P. Mayer, "Foreword", A. De Tocqueville, *Democracy in America* (edited by J.P. Mayer and M. Lerner), London 1968, p. XIII-XXXIII.

314 *Idem*, p. 17.

315 *Ibid*, p. 285.

316 See A. De Tocqueville, *op. cit.*, p. 50.

North American Constitution, and only few month after the fall of the First Vene-zuelan Republic originated by it, Bolivar reacted against the principles of American constitutionalism followed by the Venezuelan constitution making elite of 1811, and wrote in his Manifesto of Cartagena in 1812, that

> "what weakened the Venezuelan government most was the federal form it adopted in keeping with the exaggerated precepts of the rights of man; this form, by authorizing self-government, disrupts social contracts and reduces nations to anarchy. [...] Such was the true state of the Confederation. Each province governed itself independently; and, following this example, each city demanded like powers, based on the practice of the provinces and on the theory that all men and all peoples are entitled to establish arbitrarily the form of government that pleases them. [...] The federal system, although the most perfect and the most capable of providing for human happiness in society, is, nevertheless, the most contrary to the interests of our infant states" [317].

These statements show the very different approach between de Tocqueville and Bolivar in their analysis, based on historical facts, which nonetheless did not prevent them from having common elements of thoughts based on the acceptance of the same "general principles on which modern constitutions rest", as de Tocqueville called them, which since then are the following: First, the notion of constitution itself, as a written document, of permanent value, containing a fundamental or high-er law, which form the basis of the constitutionalization process. Second, the notion of democracy and of the democratic state, in which sovereignty belongs to the peo-ple and not to state organs. Third, the issue of the political territorial organization of the state, as a basic element for its democratization, with references to the Federal form of the state and the development of local government. Fourth, the principle of separation of powers originating the system of check and balance and the different forms of government, in particular, the American presidential system or the Europe-an parliamentary system of government. Fifth, the role of the Judicial power, in par-ticular, of the Supreme Court of Justice and the judicial control of the constitutional-ity of legislation, and Sixth, the adoption of an entrenched constitutional declaration of fundamental rights and liberties.

All these six principles were, and still are, general principles on which modern and contemporary constitutions rested and still rest, which identifies the modern *Etat de droit*. All those principles were analysed, followed or criticized by de Tocqueville and by Bolívar, in relation to the American political systems –North American or South American – which they studied.

IV. CONSTITUTIONALISM AND THE IMPORTANCE OF THE CONSTI-TUTION

The first of the principles of modern constitutionalism derived from the Ameri-can Revolution that after France was followed in Venezuela, is the idea of the Con-stitution, in the sense of the trust place by men in the power of words formally writ-

---

317   See the text in Simón Bolívar, *Escritos Fundamentales,* Caracas, 1982, pp. 61 y 62.

ten down in a superior law to keep a government in order.[318] It is the concept of written constitutions in modern world, which with the exception of Cromwell's *Instrument of Government* 1653, can be considered a North American political invention based on three elementary notions: that of the need for the existence of a greater and higher law placed above government and individuals; that of fundamental rights of individuals, which must be embodied in the Constitution in order to be guaranteed in regard to the state; and that of a charter, where the submission of the state to the law, limiting its powers, and individual rights were to be expressly written, with some sense of permanence.

This practice of written constitutions was precisely initiated in the English colonies in America when they became independent states in 1776, giving rise to the rational-normative concept of the constitution, as a written and systematic document, referring to the political organization of society, establishing the powers of the different state bodies and generally preceded by a list of rights inherent in man. Thus, the general division of the contents of modern constitutions between an organic and a dogmatic part, in which the former comprises the concept of separation of power and supremacy of the law; and the latter, expresses the declaration of fundamental rights. It was subsequent to the Declaration of Rights and the Constitution of Virginia in 1776, that the practice of written constitutions spread to Europe and Latin America.

The basic element in the process of constitutionalization or of constitutionalism is, of course, the concept that the constitution is a supreme and fundamental law, placed above all state powers and individuals. In this respect De Tocqueville when comparing the constitutions of France, England and the United States, pointed out:

> "In France, the Constitution is, or is supposed to be, immutable. No authority can change anything in it; that is the accepted theory.
>
> In England, Parliament has the right to modify the Constitution. In England, therefore, the Constitution can change constantly; or rather it does not exist at all. Parliament being the legislative body is also the constituent one."

American political theories are simpler and more rational -he said-.

> "The American Constitution is not immutable, as in France; it cannot be changed by the ordinary authority of society as in England. It is a thing apart; it represents the will of the whole people and binds the legislators as well as plain citizens, but it can be changed by the will of the people, in accordance with established forms ..."[319]

And he concluded:

---

318 See W.H. Hamilton, "Constitutionalism", *Encyclopaedia of the Social Sciences*, Vol. III, IV, p. 255.

319 See A. De Tocqueville, *op. cit.*, p. 123.

"In America, the Constitution rules both legislators and simple citizens. It is therefore the primary law and cannot be modified by a law. Hence it is right that the courts should obey the Constitution rather than all the laws."[320]

From this came as a consequence, the concepts not only of written constitutions, but also of rigid ones, and above all, the notion of the supremacy of the constitution that by the time de Tocqueville visited the United States, had been developed by Chief Justice Marshall in the famous *Marbury v. Madison* case 1803 decided by the Supreme Court. In relation to this principle of constitutional supremacy, in that case it was stated:

"It is a proposition too plain to be contested, that the Constitution controls any legislative act repugnant to it; or, that the legislature may alter the Constitution by an ordinary act.

Between these alternatives there is no middle ground. The constitution is either a superior paramount law, unchangeable by ordinary means, or it is on a level with ordinary legislative acts, and, like other acts, is alterable when the legislature shall please to alter it."[321]

In the same case, Marshall then concluded with his formidable proposition related to written constitutions:

"Certainly all those who have framed written constitutions contemplate them as forming the fundamental and paramount law of the nation, and consequently, the theory of every such government must be that an act of the legislature, repugnant to the constitution, is void.

This theory is essentially attached to written constitutions, and is, consequently, to be considered by this court as one of the fundamental principles of our society."[322]

Constitutionalism through written, rigid and supreme constitutions is a principle developed as a general trend in modern and contemporary constitutional law, and is followed in almost all countries in the world, except in the United Kingdom and a very few other countries. In any case, it has been the common trend in Latin-American constitutionalism ever since 1811.

As I mentioned, the third republican Constitution of modern world was the Federal Constitution of the provinces of Venezuela of December of 1811, which was intermittently in force during the years that followed after the military invasion of Venezuela by the Spanish Army in 1812, and during the wars for the liberation of the country lead by Simón Bolívar, which began with his invasion of the same territory from Colombia in January 1813, in what was called the "Admirable Campaign." In it, for instance, once the province of Mérida was liberated in May 1813, Bolívar proclaimed for "the establishment of the Venezuelan Constitution that ruled the States before the invasion of the bandits that we have expelled." The following month, from Trujillo, when realizing the social trend of the war he has fighting, on

---

320 *Idem*, p. 124.
321 See *Marbury v. Madison*, 5 U.S. (1 Cranch) 137, 2L, Ed. 60 (1803). See text in R.A. ROSSUM and G. Alan TARR, *American Constitutional Law. Cases and Interpretation*, New York 1983, p. 70.
322 *Idem*, p. 70.

June 15 1813, in his proclamation of the "War to Death," by their former Constitutions and Magistrates"[323]

Nonetheless, that intention last little, not only because the content itself of the Decree of War to Death in which he ordered to execute ("*contad con la muerte*") all those, Spanish or American, that "even being indifferent" do not "actively act for the liberation of Venezuela,"[324] but because his declaration and proclamation of the Martial Law issued in Caracas the following year, on June 17 1814, in which he established "the cessation of all non military authority," with a general order of enlistment, announcing for those who contravene the order that they "shall be condemned as traitors three hours after the crime be demonstrated." From then on, the military law completely ruled the republican side in the Venezuelan territories, a situation that could be added to the one of the "Conquest law" that had been imposed by Monteverde since his occupation of the Venezuelan territories, and violating the Capitulation signed with Miranda, since he received him delivered by his own subordinates. That is why he had explained before the *Audiencia* (High Court) of Caracas on December 30, 2012, that if it was true that Coro, Maracaibo and Guayana, that were the Provinces that remained loyal to the Crown and had not participated in the Federal State of 1811 "deserve been under the protection of the Constitution of the Monarchy," that means the Cádiz 1812 Constitution which he proclaimed in Caracas under military ritual; on the contrary he affirmed that "Caracas and the other provinces that were part of the General Captaincy, must not participate now of its benefits until given proof of their rejection of evil, and under this concept be treated by the conquest law; that is, by the hard rule according to the circumstances. Otherwise all that have been gained will be lost."[325]

It was in that way that all the territories of the Venezuelan State from 1812 to 1819 were subjected to the military law, that is, the martial law or the conquest law, erasing will all that referred to civility, contributing since then, with the development of the resulting militarism.

It was only in 1817 when Bolívar began really to organize the State from a constitutional point of view, enacting Extraordinary decrees regarding the Council of State and the Judiciary, and convening a constituent assembly in order to draft a new Constitution. Angostura, in the province of Guayana was declared as the capital of the Government of Venezuela and temporary residence of its authorities, and among the first decisions Bolivar took, were those tended to establish the basis for the provisional system of government. This was summed up in the Speech to the State Council in Angostura, on 1 November 1817, in which, among other aspects, he said:

---

323 See "Discurso a la Municipalidad de Mérida", May 31,1813, in Hermánn Petzold Pernía," *Bolívar y la ordenación de los Poderes Públicos en los Estados Emancipados*, Caracas 1986, p. 32.

324 See "Decreto de guerra a muerte," June 13, 1813 (facsimilar version), in Hermánn Petzold Pernía," *Bolívar y la ordenación de los Poderes Públicos…, cit*, p. 33

325 See "Representación dirigida a la Regencia el 17 de enero de 1813,", in J.F. Blanco y R. Azpúrua, *Documentos para la historia de la vida pública del Libertador*, Ediciones de la Presidencia de la República, Caracas 1978., Tomo IV, pp. 623–625.

[...] When the people of Venezuela broke the oppressive ties linking it to the Spanish nation, their first objective was to establish a constitution on the basis of modern politics, whose main principles are the separation of powers and the equilibrium of its authorities. So, banning the tyrannical institution of the Spanish monarchy, it adopted the republican system of government, more in line with Justice; and among the republican forms it chose the most liberal of all, the federal government. The vicissitudes of war, which were so contrary to the Venezuelan arms, removed the Republic, and with it, all its institutions".

In that speech, the Liberator argued why war had prevented "giving the government of the Republic the constitutional regularity that the proceedings of Congress had enacted in the first period"; and referring to the third period of the Republic which started in Margarita, after the Expedition of *The Cayos* from Haiti in 1816, he added the following:

"in the island of Margarita the progress of the Republic again took a regular basis, but always with the military character, unfortunately attached to a state of war. The third period of Venezuela had not presented so far, a favorable moment, which could shelter the Constitution from the storms".

Bolivar said in that speech that on May 6, 1816 the Assembly of Margarita had created and named "an executive branch with the title of Supreme Head of Venezuela. Thus, what was only missing was the institution of the legislature and the judiciary", so he added that: "The creation of the State Council should fill the functions of the legislature, corresponding to a High Court the third power of the sovereign body".[326]

Bolívar, in that exceptional document about constitutional organization, also spoke about the regular organization of the free provinces of Venezuela, referring to its various civil and military governors, among them, General Paez in the Provinces of Barinas and Casanare, and Monagas in the Province of Barcelona. Both would exercise the presidency decades later.

The following year in the State Council session of 1 October 1818, Bolívar proposed convening the Congress of Venezuela in order to speed up "the restoration of our republican institutions", and declared "the need and importance of creating a constituent body to give the government a form and character of legality and permanence".[327]

The State Council approved "the Rules and Regulations for convening the second Congress of Venezuela" to be installed in January 1819, which among other tasks would have to "Discuss Government and Constitution". Having had elections during 1818, the Congress of Angostura was installed on February 15, 1819, and on that occasion Bolivar read his beautiful Angostura Speech (*Discurso de Angostura*) explaining the sense and content of the Constitution,[328] in which he shared his ideas

---

326   *Idem,* pp. 173 y 174.

327   See Pedro Grases, "Notas Editorial", in *El Libertador y la Constitución de Angostura de 1819,* Caracas, 1969, p. 7.

328   See the texts in *El Libertador y la Constitución de Angostura,* (ed. Pedro Grases), Publicaciones del Congreso de la República, Caracas, 1969.

about the State and its organization, serving later as the preamble to the Constitution he drafted and submitted to the consideration of the Assembly.[329] The Congress adopted the Constitution of Angostura on 15 of August of 1819, [330] influenced by the principles of modern constitutionalism which had already been incorporated in the Constitution of 1811, and by the Liberator's own ideas.[331]

This 1819 Political Constitution of Venezuela, sanctioned in Angostura, in effect, had as its antecedent, the text of the 1811 Constitution, from which many provisions were taken, and among others, the declaration of rights, the representative democratic principle and the separation of powers; and had the direct influence of Simón Bolívar according to his thoughts expressed in the *Manifiesto de Cartagena* (1812) y en la *Carta de Jamaica* (1815)[332]. Consequently, the 1819 Constitution had an important dissidence in relation to the text of the Constitution of 1811, by establishing, as proposed by Bolivar, a Unitary and Centralistic State abandoning the initial federal formula of 1811. In the new State form, although territorially divided in ten (Barcelona, Barinas, Caracas, Coro, Cumaná, Guayana, Maracaibo, Margarita, Mérida and Trujillo), they were all under the authority of a governor immediately subjected to the President of the Republic, without any provision related to any sort of legislative organ in the provinces.

The constitutional organization of the State in the Angostura Constitution, in any event, was only in force for a few years, not only because the war continued, but because in 1821 Venezuela would disappear as a State and integrated to the Republic of Colombia, as proposed by Bolívar.[333]. For such purpose, a new Constitution was sanctioned in the Congress of Cúcuta in 1821[334], in which, according to the ideas of Bolívar, the process of centralization of the State continued and was accentuated by forming one single State with all the former provinces of Cundinamarca, Venezuela and Ecuador, being named the new territory as the Republic of Colombia, which was divided in three departments (Cundinamarca, Venezuela and Ecuador), each subjected to the political authority of an Intendent, appointed by the President of the Republic with the approval of the Senate.

---

329   See Ángel Francisco Brice, Prologo *Actas del Congreso de Angostura,* Instituto de Derecho Público, Caracas, 1969, pp. 9 ss.

330   See the text in Allan R. Brewer-Carías, *Las Constituciones de Venezuela, cit.,* pp. 351-367.

331   See *El Libertador y la Constitución de Angostura de 1819,* (ed. Pedro Grases), prólogo: Tomás Polanco, Caracas 1970. Se in general, *Los Proyectos Constitucionales de Simón Bolívar, El Libertador 1813–1830,* Caracas 1999.

332   See the Manifiesto de Cartagena (1812) and the Carta de Jamaica (1815) in Simón Bolívar, *Escritos Fundamentales,* Caracas, 1982 y en *Itinerario Documental de Simón Bolívar. Escritos selectos,* Ediciones de la Presidencia de la República, Caracas 1970, pp. 30 y ss. y 115 y ss. See also, Simón Bolívar, *Carta de Jamaica,* Ediciones del Ministerio de Educación, Caracas 1965 y Ediciones de la Presidencia de la República, Caracas 1972.

333   See the Ley Fundamental de la República de Colombia of 1819 and the Ley Fundamental de la Unión de los Pueblos de Colombia de 1821, en Allan R. Brewer-Carías, *Las Constituciones de Venezuela, cit.,* pp. 373-376.

334   See the text in Allan R. Brewer-Carías, *Las Constituciones de Venezuela, cit.,* pp. 379-395.

The constitutional work of Bolivar, embedded in his centralistic conception, later continued, being materialized in the drafting of the Constitution of Bolivia, in the former highlands of Peru, in 1826;[335]; and in 1828 in his draft Constitution for Colombia that was due to be discussed in the Constitutional Convention of Ocaña with representatives of all the provinces. Nonetheless, when he realized that his Constitutional project was not going to be accepted, he boycotted the Convention, and establish by presidential decree the Dictatorship of 1828,[336] through which he governed until his resignation in 1830.

V. DEMOCRACY, REPRESENTATION AND THE PEOPLE'S SOVEREIGNTY

The second of the principles developed in constitutional and political practice in the modern world, influenced by American constitutionalism is that of democracy as republicanism based on the concept of people's sovereignty and representation. With the American Revolution, the traditional monarchical legitimacy of government was definitively substituted. The sovereign was no longer the monarch, but the people, and therefore the practice of democratic government was initiated in the modern world.

This was a fundamental concept in De Tocqueville's work, forming the very title to his book *Democracy in America*, in which he said:

> "Any discussion of the political laws of the United States must always begin with the dogma of the sovereignty of the people."[337]

This principle De Tocqueville considered being "over the whole political system of the Anglo-Americans."[338]

He added:

> "If there is one country in the world where one can hope to appreciate the true value of the dogma of the sovereignty of the people, study its application to the business of society, and judge both its dangers and its advantages: that country is America."[339]

To that end he devoted his book, precisely to study democracy in America.

Of course, democracy developed in America long before independence, and De Tocqueville located its exercise "in the provincial assemblies, especially that of the township" where it "spread secretly"[340] during colonial rule. But once the American Revolution broke out:

---

335 See Simón Bolívar, *Proyecto de Constitución para la República Boliviana,* Lima, 1826, with notes from Antonio José de Sucre, Caracas, 1978.

336 Simón Bolívar, *Proclamas y Discursos del Libertador,* Caracas, 1939, p. 379.

337 See A. De Tocqueville, *op. cit.,* Vol. 1, p. 68.

338 *Ibid,* p. 78.

339 *Ibid,* p. 68.

340 *Ibid,* p. 69.

"The dogma of the sovereignty of the people came out from the township and took possession of the government; every class enlisted in its cause; the war was fought and victory obtained in its name; it became the law of laws."[341]

In accordance with this dogma of the sovereignty of the people, when it prevails in a nation, -he said-, "each individual forms an equal part of that sovereignty and shares equally the government of the state."[342] Thus he asserted that "America is the land of democracy."[343]

The title of the chapter one of the second part of his book said: "Why it can strictly be said that the people govern in the United States," and in its first paragraph De Tocqueville said:

"In America the people appoint both those who make the laws and those who execute them; the people form the jury which punishes breaches of the law. The institutions are democratic not only in principle but also in all their developments; thus the people *directly* nominate their representatives and generally choose them annually so as to hold them more completely dependent. So direction really comes from the people, and though the form of governments is representative, it is clear that the opinions prejudices, interests, and even passions of the people can find no lasting obstacles preventing them from being manifest in the daily conduct of society.[344]

But one of the main aspects to which De Tocqueville referred in relation to democracy, was "the main causes tending to maintain a democratic republic in the United States."[345] He said:

"Three factors seem to contribute more than all others to the maintenance of a democratic republic in the New World.

The first is the federal form adopted by the Americans, which allows the Union to enjoy the power of a greater republic and the security of a small one.

The second are communal institutions which moderate the despotism of the majority and give the people both a taste fox freedom and the skill to be free.

The third is the way judicial power is organized. I have shown -he said- how the courts correct the aberrations of democracy and how, though they can never stop the movements of the majority, they do succeed in checking and directing them."[346]

Thus, he established the relation between democracy and decentralization, and he stated that the problems of the "omnipotence of the majority" and even the "tyranny of the majority"[347] was tempered by the almost non-existence of administrative cen-

---

341 *Ibid*, p. 69.

342 *Ibid*, p. 78-79.

343 *Ibid*, p. 216.

344 *Ibid*, p. 213.

345 Title of Charter IX of 2nd part, *op. cit.*, p. 342.

346 *Idem*, p. 354.

347 *Idem*, p. 304, 309.

tralization in North America,[348] and by the influence of the American legal profession.[349)]

Democracy as a form of government, always attained or maintained, is the second general trend in modern and contemporary constitutionalism, inspired by the American constitutional process, and grounded upon representation and representative governments, elected by the people. Its establishment of course, always imposes the need to reconcile power with liberty, so that the State would be, as it should, the political organization of society that ensured freedom, based on popular sovereignty and in republicanism. Accordingly, the organization of State power had to have popular and democratic support, and could not result from the imposition of one person, discarding any monarchical character of the political system.

That is why, for instance, the establishment of a constitutional order based on popular sovereignty, legitimized through an Assembly or Congress, was a constant in the thought and action of Bolívar particularly during the wars of liberation. Not only was this expressed in his masterful political documents: the Cartagena Manifest (1812), the Jamaica Letter (1815) and the Angostura Address (1819), but was proposed by him repeatedly throughout his life: in 1813, in his submission to the Congress of Bogota after the Admirable Campaign and conquering Caracas[350]; in 1814, in his Address to the Assembly of January 2nd in the Church of San Francisco in Caracas[351]; in 1816, in his Proclamation upon landing in Margarita and initiating the Eastern and Guayana Campaign[352]; in 1817 upon installing the State Council in Angostura[353]; in 1818, in his speech to the session of the Council of State on October 1^{st,} and in his Proclamation to Venezuelans on October 22nd[354]; in 1819, in his Proclamation to the "*Granadinos*" on September 8, after the Battle of Boyacá, when raising the question of the union of Nueva Granada and Venezuela[355]; in 1824, in his Proclamation to the Peruvians on December 25th on the occasion the Battle of Ayacucho[356]; in 1825, in his address to the Constituent Congress of Peru in Lima on February 10[357]; In 1826, in his address to the constituent Congress of Bolivia on May 25[358] in the presentation of the draft constitution for Bolivia[359]; and in his Proclamation to Venezuelans in Maracaibo on December 16, 1826, in which demanded

---

348 *Idem*, p. 323.

349 *Idem*, p. 324.

350 See *Escritos del Libertador, cit.*, Vol. V. p. 5.

351 See *Proclamas y Discursos del Libertador, cit.*, p. 85.

352 *Idem*. p. 146.

353 *Ibídem*. pp. 171 and 172.

354 *Ibídem*. p. 193.

355 *Ibídem*. p. 240.

356 *Ibídem*. pp. 298 y 299.

357 *Ibídem*. pp. 300 y 303.

358 *Ibídem*. pp. 322 y ss.

359 See Simón Bolívar, *Proyecto de Constitución para la República Boliviana*, Lima, 1826, with notes from Antonio José de Sucre, Caracas, 1978.

of them, against separatist tendencies, not to kill the homeland and promised to "call on the people to deliberate" in a Grand National Convention where "the people will freely exercise omnipotence and decree their fundamental laws", concluding: "No one but the majority is sovereign"[360]; in 1828, in his message to the Ocaña Convention on February 29, 1828[361] and in his Address to the Governing Council in Bogota after the dissolution of that Convention[362]; in 1829, in the call he made to the peoples of Colombia for their views on government and the Constitution[363]; and finally, in 1830, in his Address to the Constituent Congress of the Republic of Colombia on January 20[364] and in his Proclamation to the Colombians after leaving office, on January 24, 1830[365].

In all these writings, the Liberator always raised the need for the organization of the State, its Constitution and government, to be the result of a manifestation of popular sovereignty rather than the product of the will of a Supreme Commander. Therefore, in all cases in which he had to take full public power, he always sought legitimacy through consultation with the people and the meeting of a Congress or Assembly.

Specifically, after entering to Caracas in 1813, in his first communication to the Nueva Granada Congress dated August 8, 1813 referred to the liberation of the capital of Venezuela, he expressed:

> "While the Government is being organized legally and permanently, I am exercising the supreme authority, which I will place in the hands of an assembly of notables of this capital, that must be convened to establish a government in accordance to the nature of the circumstances and the instructions I have received from that honorable Congress." [366]

In the Manifesto of the following day, August 9th of 1813, which he addressed to his fellow citizens, he outlined plans for the organization of the State, and insisted in the same idea of legitimizing power:

> "An assembly of notables, of virtuous and wise men, should be solemnly convened to discuss and sanction the nature of government, and about the officials that should be selected to exercise it, in the critical and extraordinary circumstances surrounding the Republic. The Liberator of Venezuela resigns forever, and formally objects, to accept any authority other than to lead our soldiers to the dangers for the salvation of our Fatherland." [367]

This was reaffirmed in another communication to the President of the Nueva Granada Congress in August 14, 1813, in which he insisted in "the convening of a

---

360 *Proclamas y Discursos del Libertador, cit.,* p. 344.

361 *Idem.* p. 370.

362 *Ibídem.* p. 379.

363 See in José Gil Fortoul, *Historia Constitucional de Venezuela,* Berlín 1904, vol. I, p. 468.

364 See *Proclamas y Discursos del Libertador, cit.,* pp. 391 and ff.

365 *Idem.* p. 399.

366 See in *Escritos del Libertador,* Sociedad Bolivariana de Venezuela, Volume V, Caracas, 1969, p. 5.

367 *Idem.,* p. 10.

popular assembly, to determine the nature of government and the constitution of the State", announcing the organization of the Supreme Departments of the Administration[368]. Bolívar undoubtedly had, in 1813, an obsession to reorganize the state and legitimize the supreme power that he had conquered by the force of arms, for which he requested advice about a Provisional Government Plan[369].

The liberation of the Province of Caracas, however, did not mean the liberation of Venezuela. The Spanish army fought back, Caracas was due to be evacuated, and Bolivar went back to Cartagena in September 1814, where, the Nueva Granada Congress appointed him "Captain General of the Armies of the Confederacy." Internal conflicts in Cartagena forced him to resign, leaving for Jamaica in May 1815, where in September 6th, 1815 he wrote the famous Letter from Jamaica (Answer from a South American to a gentleman of this island) [370], where among other things, he outlined his political ideas about the government Venezuela required. In it, among many things, he recognized that political facts developed in Venezuela "proved that the perfectly representatives institutions are not adequate to our current character, uses and lights. As Venezuela has been the American Republic that has more advanced in its political institutions, it has also been the clearest example of inefficiency of the democratic and federal form for our nascent states."[371] He went further to argue that he was not in accordance with the federal system, within the popular and representatives, because being to perfect, imposing political virtues and knowledge quite superior to those existing in the country, and for the same reasons he said he refuses the mixed aristocratic and democratic monarchy, that has been so fortunate in England. Not being possible to attain the most perfect between republics and monarchies, he propose avoid the extreme solutions seeking a middle, suggesting for the first time that the government of the new State "could follow the English example; but with the difference that in lieu of a king, there would be an elective Executive Power, of permanent character (*vitalicio*), and not hereditary if a republic is sought; a legislative chamber or senate hereditary, that in the political storms could be interposed between the popular waves and the government lightings; and a legislative body, of free election; without any other restriction that those of the lower chamber in England."[372]

From Jamaica, the same year 1816 he went on to Haiti where he was hosted by President Alexander Petion; and from there he lead the Expedition of *Los Cayos* to Venezuela, reaching Margarita, where "the independent government of Venezuela" was proclaimed again, ratifying Bolivar, in an Assembly, as the Supreme Head of State and the Armies of Venezuela. There he ratified the need for the installation of

---

368 *Ibídem.* p. 30.

369 See the most remarkable documents in this regard in *Simón Bolívar y la Ordenación del Estado en 1813* (Preliminary studies of Pedro Grases and Tomás Polanco), Caracas, 1979.

370 See in Simón Bolívar, *Escritos Fundamentales, cit.,* pp. 82 and ff.

371 See Carta de Jamaica, in Hermánn Petzold Pernía, *Bolívar y la ordenación de los Poderes Públicos..., cit,,"* p. 57.

372 *Idem* p. 61.

the Congress, expressing in a proclamation to the people of Venezuela, on May 8, 1816, that:

> "Venezuela's Congress will once again be installed wherever and whenever you wish. As independent peoples have given me the honor to be in charge of the supreme authority, I authorize you to name your representatives in Congress with no other official announcement than the present one; entrusting them with the same sovereign powers than in the first period of the Republic."[373]

New conflicts arose between the patriot leaders, being the authority of Bolívar ignored again in the so called Cariaco Congress, which met in May 1817, resulting in the establishment of a federal government and appointing a plural Executive.[374] Bolivar ignored such Congress, gained the freedom of Guayana, and succeeded in successive military operations in obtaining the recognition of his supreme command. In the absence of a Congress he established the Council of State in order to act as legislator (November 17 of 1817), recognizing that once declared the independence the first objective was "to establish a Constitution based on a modern policy, whose basic principles are the division of powers and the equilibrium of authorities. Then, proscribing the tyrannical institution of the Spanish Monarchy, the republican system more conformed with justice was adopted, and among the republican form the most liberal of all was choose, that is the federal one."[375]

The Council of State was charged to prepare the convening of elections for the Congress, which was elected and gathered in Angostura, as a Constituent Assembly. Bolívar submitted to the Congress the draft of a new Constitution to substitute the 1811 Federal Constitution. Nonetheless, in his *Discurso de Angostura* he recognized that "the Republican Government has been, is, and must be the one of Venezuela; it foundations must be the people's sovereignty; the division of powers; civil freedom, proscription of slavery, abolition of the Monarchy and of privileges."[376] Nonetheless, he went again highlighting the virtues of the British Constitution considering it as the model to be followed by all those that want to enjoy the rights of man and the political happiness compatible with our fragile nature." [377] He then eventually propose to organize the legislative power in two Chambers, one elected (representatives) and the other, the Senate, in a quite original way for a republic, as post held for life and also of hereditary character, proposing to integrate such body by "the Liberators of Venezuela" to be elected by the Constituent Assembly, and also by the former Presidents. He considered such hereditary Senate as "the fundamental piece of the Legislative Power, and consequently, of all the Government."[378] The proposal was rejected by the Congress, and also was rejected the other important innovation

---

373 *Proclamas y Discursos del Libertador, cit.*, p. 146.

374 See José Gil Fortoul, *op. cit.,* Vol. I, pp. 246–247.

375 See in Hermánn Petzold Pernía, *Bolívar y la ordenación de los Poderes Públicos..., cit,,"* p. 63.

376 *Idem,* p. 84

377 *Idem,* p. 84

378 *Ibidem,* pp. 86, 96

proposed by Bolívar which was the creation of a Forth branch of Government (besides the Legislative, the Executive and the Judiciary), that he called the "Moral Power,"[379] conducted by an Areopagus integrated by virtuous citizens to be appointed by the Congress for life, with competencies to morally control the actions of citizens and public officials. Those innovations were contrary to the republican and representative democratic principles, having the 1819 Constitution basically followed the general constitutional trends of the 1811 Constitution, except regarding its federal shape, and instead establishing a centralized State with a more strong Executive Power, in a system of Separation of Powers, and with an extended Declaration of Rights and guaranties of Man

The Executive Power was in any case conceived in Bolívar propositions as very strong one, inspired –he said– expressing that "if in a Monarchy it has been necessary to assign it so many competencies, in a republic, they are infinitely more indispensable;" adding that "in the republics the Executive must be the strongest, because everything conspires against it; instead, in the Monarchies the stronger must be the Legislative, because everything conspire in favor of the Monarch."[380]

Despite the rejection of the Bolívar's proposal regarding the "Moral Power," the Congress agreed to incorporate the proposal as an "Appendix" to the constitutional text, reporting that many of its members considered the idea as a "moral inquisition, not less terrible that the religious," very difficult to establish and absolutely impracticable."[381]

The constitutional ideas and proposals of Bolívar were again embodied in the project of Constitution for the new State of Bolivia to be established in the highest territories of Peru (Alto Perú), after attaining independence from the Viceroyalty of la Plata (Buenos Aires); a project that the Constituent Assembly of the country formally requested from Bolívar. Regarding his ideas for such Constitution he announced to the Vice President of Colombia (Santander) in September 1825 that the Constitution for Bolívia was going to have "something of government for life, and something of the freedoms of federalism" recognizing that the proposals were to have friends and enemies,[382] and insisting before Santander that in any case, it was going to be a Constitution much better than the Constitution of Angostura (1819).[383] In another letter to José Antonio Páez, on may 26, 1826 he affirmed that the Bolivian "Constitution is a middle term between federalism and Monarchy,"[384] and on may 30, 1826 in a letter to Santander, he ratified that the project "will put together

---

379 En anexo a la Constitución de 1819, sin embargo, se publicó el Título correspondiente al Poder Moral. Véase en Allan R. Brewer-Carías, *Las Constituciones de Venezuela, cit.,* pp. 367-371.

380 See in Hermánn Petzold Pernía, *Bolívar y la ordenación de los Poderes Públicos..., cit.,* pp. 105, 109

381 *Idem,* p. 131

382 *Ibidem* p. 163

383 *Ibidem,* pp. 164, 1677

384 *Ibidem,* p. 181

the extremes: the federalists will find there desires almost all accomplished, and the aristocrats will find a permanent, solid and strong government; and the democracies will see equality preserved above anything."[385] And in particular, regarding the "federative" ideas, they were just ideas referred not to a single State but to the organization of almost all South America, as a "great federation" to be established between Venezuela, Colombia, Ecuador, Perú and Bolivia, to be ruled by the "Bolivian Constitution" that could serve "for the States in particular and for the federation in general, with the needed variations."[386]

The Bolivian Constitution project was sent by Bolivar to the Congress convened in Chiquisaca, in a letter dated in Lima on may 25, 1826, being the most important innovations it included, the following: first, the organization of the government of the State in to four branches, adding to the traditional Legislative, Executive and Judicial, the "Electoral Power" exercised by the citizens in order to elect the electors; second, the organization of the Legislative Power in three Chambers or bodies: The Tribunes, the Senators and the Censors, the latter being conceived as an Areopagous, with very similar functions as the "Moral Power" he proposed and was rejected for the 1819 Constitution of Angostura; and third, the character for life of the President of the Republic, with the for him right to choose his successor, which Bolivar considered as "the most sublime inspiration of the republican order."[387] The Constitution was sanctioned on November 6, 1826 and Antonio José de Sucre was appointed President for life, although he accepted the post only for two years.

The same Bolivian Constitution was proposed by Bolívar to the electoral constituencies of Peru, being approved, and proposing Bolívar as the President for life. Bolívar was forced to return to Colombia, immersed in a civil war, and the Constitution of Perú was changed two years later, in March 1828.[388] Nonetheless, since August 3, 1826 Bolívar began to propose his Bolivian Constitution to be also approved in Colombia to resolve the political crisis of the country, adding to the figure of the President for life a hereditary Vice-president;[389] begin his friends to promote the idea, considering that "the Bolivian Code, only with slights modifications, seems applicable to all the situations that Colombia could seek."[390] He insisted in considering the Bolivian Constitution as having together "the enchantments of the federa-

385 *Ibidem,* p 181

386 As Bolivar expressed in Letters of May 12, 1826 to Antonio José de Sucre; and ntonio Gutierrez de la Fuente. See, in Hermánn Petzold Pernía, *Bolívar y la ordenación de los Poderes Públicos..., ci.,"* pp. 172, 173

387 *Idem,* p. 197

388 See Polanco, *op. cit.,* 151-152; Hermánn Petzold Pernía, *Bolívar y la ordenación de los Poderes Públicos..., cit,,"* p. 217

389 See Circular Letter August, 3, 1826. See in Hermánn Petzold Pernía, *Bolívar y la ordenación de los Poderes Públicos..., cit,* p. 222.

390 See Letter to Cristobal Mendoza, August 6, 1826, in *Idem* p. 227

tion, the force of centralism, the freedom of the people, the energy of government," not finding another instrument of conciliation that the Bolivian Constitution."[391]

Nonetheless, in the same letter, worried by the political turmoil in Colombia, he expressed with desolation: "I do not believe Colombia could be save neither with the Bolivian Constitution nor with the federation or with the Empire. I am just seen Africa coming to take over America, and all the infernal legions to settle in our country."[392] And finally, although considering the Bolivian Constitution as his "youngest daughter, which I loves with tenderness because being disgraceful,"[393] from Caracas he sharply expressed to Antonio José de Sucre on June 8, 1827: "I don't care about the Bolivian Constitution. If they want to burn it, they are free to do it."[394]

In any case, after his Bolivian Constitution being rejected in Peru, Bolivar returned to Bogotá where he found bitter opposition from those parties seeking a federal government. Regarding his constitutional ideas, on the other hand, since 1826 he faced the opposition of Vice-president Santander, particularly regarding the idea of a President for life. He referred to the idea of "a supreme chief for life and crown," saying to Bolívar: that in such case "I won't be a Colombian, I will sacrifice all my fortune before living in such regime.[395]

In any case, since 1826 he pretended "to devolve to the people its initial sovereignty in order to remake the social pact,"[396] so accordingly, on December 1827 Bolívar once back in Bogotá, he convened a Constitutional Convention in order to change the Angostura Constitution. The Convention was due to meet in Ocaña, in which he thought that "all parties will gather, the people will express their votes and desires with complete freedom, and they will fix in a definitive way their fait."[397]

Nonetheless Bolívar was not very confident in obtaining from the Convention any support to his constitutional ideas. On the contrary, he fears that the federal proposal could prevail. He warned to José Fernández Madrid in December 1827: "If they divide the country, it will be lost, and if they establish week general laws, as are all that comes from very free government, then this extended region will have to suffer the same inconvenient of a country without government, because it is constant that the force of government must be relative to the extension; in one word, Colom-

---

391 See Letter to Santander dated August 8, 1826, in *Idem*, p. 227. In a Letter from Caracas on may 2, 1827 he insisted again in saying that his Bolivian Constitution gathers the liberal Monarchy with the most free Republic. See in *Idem*, p. 239

392 *Idem*.

393 See Letter to Robert Wilson, June 16, 1827, in *Idem*. p. 240.

394 *Idem*, p. 240

395 See Letter of July 6, 1826. See Rafael Arraiz Lucca, *Venezuela: 1728-1830, Guipuzcoana e Independencia*, Ed. Alfa, caracas 2011, p. 187.

396 See Letter to Santander October 14, 1826, in Hermánn Petzold Pernía, *Bolívar y la ordenación de los Poderes Públicos...*, *cit*, pp. 235

397 Letter to José Fernández Madrid, September 27, 1827, in *Idem*, p. 241. He insisted in the same idea in a Letter to Santander from Neiva on November 5, 1826, and in a Proclamation in Bogotá on November 23, 1826. See in *Idem*, pp. 236-238

bia and the whole America are countries lost for this generation."[398] The next month, in January 1828 he was more pessimistic", and said: "I don't see human way to maintain Colombia; the Convention will do nothing, and the result will be the parties, the civil war."[399] In that same line of thought, he warned José Antonio Páez: "we must fortify the government in order for this extended country won't be lost; and if this cannot be achieved, for Colombia would be better to be divided than to subjected to a federation that is destructive and dissolvent of all social principles, of all guaranties," concluding by affirming that "the division is itself the ruin, and the federation, the tomb of Colombia."[400] He was, on these matters, very conclusive. He said: "I have said to friends and enemies that the day in which a federation is establish, the funerals of the Republic will be decreed, to which I will not certainly assist;"[401] and again, expressing his regrets that in the Convention "the general opinion opposes to the constitution and the reform" and that what the representatives wanted was to establish a provisional government" he concluded that in such case he was going to remain in the government "up to the funerals, and if if a government eminently strong is not decreed, I will leave once knowing about the reforms approved."[402]

The Convention was finally installed in Ocaña on April 9 1828, occasion in which a Message written by Bolivar on February 29, 1828 was read. In it, he criticized the functioning of the Government according to the 1821 Constitution, particularly regarding the malfunctioning of the separation of powers mechanism, allowing the encroachment of the balance between the legislative and the Executive, subjecting the latter to the will of the former, and considering the Judiciary as the "weakest branch of the supreme power" proposing the reform of the Constitution in order to establish a strong government.[403] Bolívar did not attend the Convention, and when no agreement could be reached between Bolivarianists and Santanderists that is. Between centralization of federation, the Convention was determined to ratify the 1821 Constitution, but eliminating article 128 regulating the possibility for the President of the Republic to exercise extraordinary powers. In such situation, the Bolivarianist abandoned the Convention, which was then dissolved on June 11, 1828.

In any case, since March 1828, Bolívar began to receive popular support for his constitutional ideas, opposing the federation, expressed through popular assemblies in which he said that "the army and the people are united in order to save the motherhood against the demagogues."[404] In this regards, he wrote to Pedro Briceño Méndez, not only expressing him about the need to establish "a strong and just govern-

---

398   *Idem*, p. 241
399   See Letter to Mariano Montilla, 17 january 1828, in *Idem*, p. 241
400   See Letter to José Antonio Páez, 29-1-1828, in *Idem*, p. 242
401   See Letter to Jose Fernández Madrid, February 14, 1828, in *Idem*, p. 243
402   See Letter to Joaquín Mosquera, 29 February 1828, in *Idem*, p. 243
403   See in *Idem*, pp.. 244-252
404   See Letter of March 24, 1828, in *Idem*, p. 252

ment, provisional or not, because all is provisional in a revolution," but asking him to "say to the federals that if they win, they most not count with motherhood, because the army and the people are resolved to openly oppose them."[405]

As a consequence of the dissolution of the Ocaña Convention, on June 13 1828 a people's assembly in Bogotá, commanded by military officials, decided to ignore the Convention, and to appoint Bolívar as a Dictator, with unlimited power. When he arrived in Bogotá, on June 24, 1828, he expressed at his popular reception that "The national will is the supreme law of governments; submission to the supreme will is the first duty of all citizens, and as such, I declare my submission to it. I will always be a defendant of public freedoms, and being the national will the one that exercises the true sovereignty, it is therefore the only sovereign that I serve as such."[406] The result was that the 1821 Constitution was suspended; Bolivar governed by decrees through which he completely centralized the State, dissolving all the Municipalities and local powers, and on August 27 1828 he enacted an Organic Decree of the Supreme Power, as the "Constitutional law of the State"[407] substituting in a de facto way the 1821 Constitution. Among the justifications of the Decree expressed by the Liberator-President, was the argument that "the national vote had been unanimously expressed in the provinces, through declarations that have reached the Capital, which are the great majority of the nation;" arguing that "after carful and mature deliberation," he decided to take charge "of the Supreme Power of the republic, that I will exercise with the name of Liberator-President, which has been conferred to me by the public laws and the suffrages acts"[408]

The 1829 Organic Decree, as the constitutional law of the State, substituted the 1821 Constitution, and was to be obeyed until a new Congress that was to be elected and convened for January 2, 1830, would adopt a new Constitution for the country.[409] For such purpose, Bolívar in many letters and messages continued to express his ideas for such new Constitution, considering for instance, that "the executive and the legislative of Bolivia will be the models of our new form [of government]; not because it was my own work, but because it conceals many interests."[410] In June 1829 he expressed to Sucre, who was at that time in Bolivia, that the "congress that I have convened will meet and will give a strong government according to the existing public spirit," expressing that "the Executive will be adopted with more strength than yours" but abandoning the idea of a hereditary presidency.[411] He then wrote (what in the manuscript is erased), the following: "Many think on a hereditary gov-

---

405 Letter of March 24, 1828, in *Idem*, p. 253.
406 See in *Idem*, p. 256
407 See in *Idem*, p. 262.
408 See in *Idem*, p. 262
409 See in *Idem*, p. 268
410 See Letter to José María del castillo, June 28, 1829, in *Idem*, p. 270
411 See Letter to Sucre dated 20 and 25 June 1829, in *Idem*, p. 270

ernment, but I oppose it with all my forces, because I don't want to support so enormous weight for all my life in order to transmit it to one of my descendents."[412]

One thing was clear for Bolivar during his final years of dictatorship, and it is that he did not want to continue governing Colombia, and much less when he new that he has been considered as an usurpator and despot, not only by critics in the local parties, but by thinkers he much admired like Benjamin Constant, who had written that he maintained his authority based on "executions and killings."[413] He willingly wanted to leave the Government, but he was aware that his presence as head of State was the only factor that maintained Colombia as one country, including its three departments (Venezuela, Nueva Granada and Ecuador). Regarding this union, he expressed that "Everybody knows that the reunion of Nueva Granada and Venezuela only exists linked to my authority, which can end now and then, when the Providence or man would want;"[414] also recognizing that "Not being able to continue for much time as head of government, after his absence, the country with get divided in the midst of a civil war and of the most awful disorders."[415] That is why, although always defending as a matter of principlei the Union, which was his creation in 1821, he expressed his opinion that eventually, in order to avoid such horrors that were going to happened in the near future, I was "preferable to divide the country legally, in peace and in good harmony."[416] If a peaceful division was not decided by the Congress he expressed, again, that "in such case it was necessary to think in a for life government like the one of Bolivia, with a hereditary Senate as the one I proposed in Guayana. This is all what we can do in order to consult the stability of the government; stability that I consider illusory between Venezuela and Colombia, because in both countries antipathies exists that cannot be overcome."[417]

He then expressed his opinion that "The constituent congress [of 1830] will have to choice one of the only resolutions that remained in the factual situations of the moment: "1. The division of Nueva Granada and Venezuela; 2. The creation of a permanent and strong government. In the first case the division of these two countries must be perfect, just and peaceful. Once it declared, each party will be reorganized in it own way... The other extreme to be adopted by the Congress will be the erection of a for life government, or as they want, but always according to public opinion."[418]

He even proposed as a solution that could be adopted by the Congress in order to maintain the Union, for a president to be appointed, being himself appointed as a

412 See in *Idem*, p. 270.

413 See the referents to the opinion of Constant, expressed in letters to De Pradt, published in *El Correo*, in Bolivars' letters to Rafael Urdaneta, and Robert Wilson dated July 22, 1829, in *Idem*, pp. 275-278

414 See Letter to Daniel F. O'Leary, September 13, 1829, in *Idem*, p. 281

415 See Letter to Estanislao Vergara, June 13, 1829, in *Idem*, p. 272

416 See Letter to Estanislao Vergara, June13, 1829, in *Idem*, p. 272

417 *Idem*. p. 273

418 See Letter to D.F. Oleary, September 1829, in *Idem*, pp. 283-284

generalissimo, in charge of defending and controlling the government and the republic.[419]

No other constitutional ideas were proposed by Bolívar, not even in his Message to the constituent Congress on January 20 1830, in which he resigned to the Presidency of the Republic. He was formally substituted as head of State in May 1830, and decided to abandon America. In the following months Venezuela adopted its own Constitution on September 1830, after the sanctioning of the Constitution of Colombia in April 1830, and its rejection by the Department of Venezuela.

VI. THE VERTICAL DISTRIBUTION OF STATE POWERS: FEDERAL STATE, DECENTRALIZATION AND LOCAL GOVERNMENT

In his study of the American constitution, one of the aspects to which De Tocqueville devoted much of his attention due to its importance to democracy, was that of political decentralization or the vertical distribution of state powers among different political territorial units; the third main feature of modern constitutionalism.

He observed:

> In no country in the world are the pronouncements of the law more categorical than in America, and in no other country is the right to enforce it divided among so many hands.[420]

He stressed that "nothing strikes a European traveller in the United States more than the absence of what we call government or administration .... Functions (are) multiplied... (and) by sharing authority in this way its power becomes, it is true, both less irresistible and less dangerous, but it is far from being destroyed.[421]

He concluded his observation:

> There is nothing centralized or hierarchical, in the constitution of American administrative power, and that is the reason why one is not at all conscious of it. The authority exists but one does not know where to find its representative.[422]

De Tocqueville observed that the distribution of powers in the vertical sense, in North America, was not produced by a process of decentralization but rather of centralization, in the sense that the township, the country and the States, first existed so that "The federal government was the last to take shape in the United States."[423]

In his own words:

> In most European nations political existence started in the higher ranks of society and has been gradually but always incompletely, communicated to the various members of the body social.

---

419 See Letter to Daniel Francisco O'leary, August 21, in *Idem*, p. 279; Letter to José María del Castillo Rada, December 27, 1829, in *Idem*, p. 286.

420 See A. De Tocqueville, *Democracy in America, op. cit*, p. 87.

421 *Idem*, p. 86.

422 *Ibid*, p. 87

423 *Ibid*, p. 72

> Contrariwise, in America one may say that the local community was organized before the county, the county before the States; and the state before the Union.[424]

Referring to New England, he stated that the local communities there had taken complete and definite shape as early as 1650, and he stressed:

> Inside the locality there was a real active life which was completely democratic and republican. The colonies still recognised the mother country's supremacy; legally the state was a monarchy, but each locality was already a lively republic.[425]

Thus, from this historical approach, the importance that De Tocqueville assigned to local government as the source of democracy is classical. His famous words concerning local government are well known and always valid:

> The strength of free peoples resides in the local community. Local institutions are to liberty what primary schools are to society; they put it within the people's reach; they teach people to appreciate its peaceful enjoyment and accustom them to make use of it.[426]

And he added: 'In the townships, ... the people are the source of power, but nowhere else do they exercise their power so directly';[427] that is why, he insisted, local institutions "exercise immense influence over the whole of society",[428] and concluded by saying that "political life was born in the very heart of the townships."[429]

Regarding the federal form of the state, a product of the process of political centralization in a highly decentralized society, De Tocqueville said:

> This constitution, which at first sight one is tempted to confuse with previous federal constitutions, in fact rests on an entirely new theory, a theory that should be hailed as one of the great discoveries of political science in our age.[430]

And in fact, one can say that the federal state came into being in history with the American constitution 1789, and even though the word "federal" or "federation" is not used in the constitution, it was in the United States that this form of political organisation was born.[431]

It did not respond to a previous scheme, but to practical need: the purpose was to seek a formula that made the existence of independent states compatible with a central power with enough attributions to act by itself at federal level.

This new institution, De Tocqueville said, cannot be compared to the confederations that existed in Europe well before the American constitution, mainly because the central power in the American constitution as he observed, "acts without inter-

---

424   *Ibid*, p. 51
425   *Ibid*, p. 51
426   *Ibid*, p. 74
427   *Ibid*, p. 75
428   *Ibid*, p. 75
429   *Ibid*, p. 79
430   *Ibid*, p. 192.
431   See M. García Pelayo, *Derecho constitucional comparado*, Madrid 1957, p. 215, 341.

mediary on the governed, administering and judging them, as do national governments," adding:

> Clearly here we have not a federal government but an incomplete national government. Hence a form of government has been found which is neither precisely national nor federal; but things have halted there, and the new word to express this new thing does not yet exist.[432]

This "new thing" is precisely what in constitutional law is known as federal state, and although De Tocqueville admired its novelty, he also pointed out its defects, and clearly observed that it was not a product for export.

He said,

> The Constitution of the United States is like one of those beautiful creations of human diligence which give their inventors glory and riches but remains sterile in other hands.[433]

In this sense, in his book De Tocqueville referred to the case of Mexico in the 1830's with its imported federal system but his remarks can be applied to all Latin America. Tries Federal organization of the state was, precisely, one of the main features of American constitutionalism that was immediately followed by almost all large Latin-American countries.

In contrast to the centralized states of Europe, and the national concentration of political power, De Tocqueville pointed out that "the most fatal of all defects which I regard as inherent in the federal system is the comparative weakness of the government of the Union", adding that "a divided sovereignty must always be weaker than a complete one."[434]

As we have said, this weakness referred to the federal form of the state, once adopted in the Venezuelan constitution 1811, 6 months after the Declaration of Independence, and which was precisely one of the main causes of the failure of the First Republic the following year. Thus, of Simon Bolivar definitively asserted in a letter to the governor of one of the Venezuelan provinces, (Barinas), on 12 August 1813:

> Never the division of power had established and perpetuated governments; only its concentration had infused respect for a nation.[435]

We mentioned before that Bolivar expressed all his life bitter criticism regarding the federal form of the state and its adoption in Venezuela, and always advocated a concentrated form of state power. In addition, for example, in his famous Manifesto of *Cartagena* of 1812, written the year following the sanctioning of the Constitution and after the failure of the First Republic, he expressed:

> What make the government of Venezuela more weaken was the federal form it adopted, following the exaggerated expression of the rights of man that by allowing them to self-government, braked the social pacts, and leads nations to anarchy. That is the real situation of

---

432 See A De Tocqueville, *op. cit.*, p. 194.

433 *Ibid*, p. 203.

434 *Ibid*, p. 204.

435 See S. Bolívar, *Escritos Fundamentales*, Ed. 1982, p. 63.

the Confederation. Each Province had an independent government; and in accordance with its example, each Township wanted equal powers and adopted the theory that Man and towns the prerogative of establishing, as they liked the government that best suited them... The federal system, if it is true that is the most perfect and oriented to provide human happiness in society, is nevertheless, the most opposed to the interests of our new-born States.[436]

Later, in his address to the Angostura Congress, in 1819, he persisted in the same idea:

The Venezuelans -he said- were not to get the magnificent federal system suddenly after the independence. We were not prepared for so much welfare; the good as well as the evil can kill when it is sudden and excessive. [437]

Finally, one year before his death, in a letter to his former aide-de-camp, Daniel Florencio O'Leary, he definitively qualified the federal system as a

Regularized anarchy, or better still, the law that establishes the implicit duty of disassociation and destruction of the state with all its individuals.[438]

But in spite of Bolivar's remarks and criticism of Federations, in Venezuela's case, since those days of independence and after the 1830 constitution, the form of our state has always been federal, and in the name of federation we had our bloodiest civil war and social revolution in the middle of last century: the Federal War of 1858-1863.

On the other hand, all the largest states of Latin America and of the world today have a federal form, to an extent that the federal system of government covers more than a half of the earth's surface.

Anyway, although De Tocqueville was also a critic of the federal form of state, he conversely praised the beneficial effects of political decentralization and local government. He said:

The partisans of centralization in Europe maintain that the government administers localities better than they can themselves; that may be true when the central government is enlightened and the local authorities are not, when it is active and they lethargic, when it is accustomed to command and they to obey...

But when people are enlightened, awake to their own interests, and used to thinking for themselves, as he had seen in America, he said that he was:

Persuaded that in that case the collective force of the citizens will always be better able to achieve social prosperity than the authority of the government.[439]

He finally declared that:

The political advantages derived by the Americans from a system of decentralization would make me prefer that to the opposite system.[440]

---

436   *Idem*, p. 61-62.
437   *Idem*, p. 140.
438   *Idem*, p. 200, 201.
439   See A. De Tocqueville, *Democracy in America, cit.*, p. 110.

VII. SEPARATION OF POWERS AND PRESIDENTIAL SYSTEM OF GOVERNMENT

In the constitution of the United States of 1787, and previously, in the various constitutions of the former colonies, the fourth principle of modern constitutionalism, the principle of separation of power within the more orthodox doctrine at the time, was formally expressed for the first time.

For instance, the first of those constitutions, the one of Virginia in 1776, stated (Art. III):

> The Legislative, Executive and Judiciary departments, shall be separate and distinct, so that neither exercise the powers properly belonging to the other; nor shall any person exercise the powers of more than one of them at the same time...

The American constitution has no similar norm within its articles, but its main objective was precisely to organize the form of government, within the principles of the separation of powers, but allowing various interferences between them in a check and balance system. Particularly, regulating the powers of the executive in what was a new way, giving rise to presidentialism as opposed to parliamentarism, and to a particular shape of the judiciary, never previously known in constitutional practice.

De Tocqueville referred, in his book, to these two aspects of the principle.

Regarding the executive power, he immediately pointed out that in the United States, "maintenance of the republican form of government required that the representative of executive power should be subject to the national will"; thus, "the president is an elective magistrate... the one and only representative of the executive power of the nation."[441] But, he noted, "in exercising that power he is not completely independent."[442]

That was one of the particular consequences of the check and balance system of separation of powers adopted in the United States, but without making the executive dependent on parliament, as in parliamentary systems of government. That is why when comparing the European parliamentary system with the presidential system of the United States, De Tocqueville referred to the important part that the executive power played in America in contrast with the situation of a constitutional king in Europe.

A constitutional king, he observed, "cannot govern when opinion in the legislative chambers is not in accord with his."[443] In the presidential system, he said, conversely, the sincere aid of Congress to the president "is no doubt useful, but it is not necessary in order that the government should function."[444]

---

440 *Idem*, p. 113, 115.
441 *Idem*, p. 148.
442 *Idem*, p. 149.
443 *Ibid*, p. 155.
444 *Ibid*, p. 156.

The separation of powers and the presidential system of government was followed very closely, sooner or later, in all Latin American republics after Independence or after the monarchical experience that a few countries had.

Thus, one can say that presidentialism is the sign of our constitutional system of government, and to such an extent, that parliamentarism has never developed in Latin America. This is rather a European form of government that Europe never managed to export to Latin America.

VIII. THE ROLE OF THE JUDICIARY

But among the American born constitutional institutions, the one that perhaps has the most distinguished originality is the role assigned to the judicial power in the system of separation of powers. This is true even at the present time, and was so when De Tocqueville visited North America. He devoted a separate chapter of his book to the powers of judges and to its great political importance, beginning with this assertion:

> Confederations have existed in other countries besides America, and there are republics elsewhere than on the shores of the New World; the representative system of government has been adopted in several European States; but so far, I do not think that any other nation in the world has organized judicial power in the same way as the Americans.[445]

Three aspects of the organization and functioning of judicial power can be considered as a fundamental American contribution to constitutional law: the political role of judges; the institution of a Supreme Court; and judicial review of legislation. De Tocqueville noticed all three aspects.

The first thing he observed in the American institutions was the "immense political power"[446] attributed to judges, which he considered "the most important political power in the United States."[447] The reason for this immense power, said De Tocqueville:

> Lies in this one fact: the Americans have given their judges the right to base their decisions on the Constitution rather than on the laws. In other words, they allow them not to apply laws which they consider unconstitutional.[448]

Therefore, "there is hardly a political question in the United States which does not sooner or later turn into a judicial one";[449] thus the fundamental changes in political and social life in the United States that have been led by the Supreme Court decisions in all American history.

---

445 *Ibid*, p. 120.
446 *Ibid*, p. 122, 124.
447 *Ibid*, p. 120.
448 *Ibid*, p. 122.
449 *Ibid*, p. 184.

The second fundamental aspect of the Judiciary in American institutions, De Tocqueville stressed, was the high standing of the Supreme Court among the great authorities in the state. De Tocqueville observed:

> The Supreme Court has been given higher standing than any known tribunal, both by the nature of its rights and by the categories subject to its jurisdiction... a mightier judicial authority has never been constituted in any land.[450]

De Tocqueville explained these powers of the Supreme Court, in which he said, "the peace, prosperity, and very existence of the Union rest continually", by saying the following:

> Without (the judges of the Supreme Court)... the Constitution would be a dead letter; it is to them that the executive appeals to resist the encroachments of the legislative body, the legislature to defend itself against the assaults of the executive, the union to make the states obey it, the states to rebuff the exaggerated pretensions of the Union, public interest against private interest, the spirit of conservation against democratic instability.[451]

Thus, the whole system of check and balance in the separation of powers, in the United States relied and still relies on the Supreme Court, and on the power of judges to control the constitutionality of legislation, precisely, the third main feature of the judiciary in North America.

In effect, in relation to the supremacy of the constitution, De Tocqueville observed that it "touches the very essence of judicial power; it is in a way the natural right of a judge to choose among legal provisions that which binds him most strictly."[452] This led to the control of the constitutionality of law, a creation of American constitutionalism, referred to by De Tocqueville with these simple and logical words:

> If anyone invokes in an American court a law which the judge considers contrary to the Constitution, he can refuse to apply it. That is the only power peculiar to an American judge, but great political influence derives from it.[453]

This was termed as being the "very essence of judicial duty" by John Marshall in the famous *Marbury v. Madison case* (1803), when referring to written constitutions and their fundamental and superior character, in relation to the other laws of society. This duty of the courts to consider void acts of the legislature repugnant to the constitution was described in that famous case with the following logical arguments:

> If an act of the legislature, repugnant to the Constitution, is void, does it, notwithstanding its invalidity, bind the courts, and oblige them to give it effect? Or, in other words, though it be not law, does it constitute a rule as operative as if it was a law? This would be to overthrow in fact what was established in theory, and would seem, at first view, an absurdity too gross to be insisted on. It shall, however, receive a more attentive consideration.

---

450 *Ibid*, p. 184.
451 *Ibid*, p. 185.
452 *Ibid*, p. 123.
453 *Ibid*, p. 124.

Then concluding:

> It is emphatically the province and duty of the judicial department to say what the law is. Those who apply the rule to particular cases must, of necessity, expound and interpret that rule. If two laws conflict with each other, the courts must decide on the operation of each.
>
> So, if a law be in opposition to the Constitution; if both the law and the Constitution apply to a particular case, so that the court must either decide that case conformably to the law, disregarding the Constitution; or conformably to the Constitution, disregarding the law; the court must determine which of these conflicting rules governs the case. This is the very essence of judicial duty.[454]

This judicial duty, discovered by the North Americans, is another of the major contributions of American constitutionalism to contemporary constitutional law, and has been followed and developed all over the world judicial constitutional control, however, is essentially related to the federal form of the state as a mean to control unauthorized invasions and interferences between the decentralized powers of the state. That is why in all the Latin American countries with federal organizations, judicial review of legislation was immediately established under the American influence, a few decades before the first continental ever European experiences in the matter.

Today and ever since the last century, judicial review or control of constitutionality of laws is a general trend of Latin American legal systems, but in a much more original way than the North American system. Various Latin American countries, for instance, as is the case of Venezuela and Colombia since the last century, combine the North American system of judicial review that allows all courts to decide upon the applications of laws on constitutional grounds, with the power of the Supreme Court of Justice to declare a law void with general effects, when considered unconstitutional by means of a popular action granted to all citizens even without particular interest in the matter. This second control is an original Latin American mean of judicial review, developed only with approximate similarities after the twenties and in the forties in some continental European countries.

IX. THE ENTRENCHED DECLARATION OF FUNDAMENTAL RIGHTS AND LIBERTIES

The sixth major contribution of North American constitutionalism to modern constitutional law has been the practice of establishing formal and entrenched declarations of fundamental rights and liberties. As we have said, the first modern declaration of this kind was adopted in the American colonies the same year of the Declaration of Independence, and in this sense the Declaration of Rights of Virginia 1776 is famous.

These declarations of the rights of man were new in history mainly because they were not based on common law or tradition, as the 1689 English Bill of Rights was, but on human nature. They were natural rights of people, declared politically by the new constituent powers of the colonies as a limit on state powers.

---

454 *Marbury v. Madison*, S.U.S. (1 Cranch), 137; 2 L. Ed. 60 (1803).

However, as we have also said, the American constitution, 1787, did not include a bill of rights in its articles, which aroused several objections during the convention. This led to the approval, two years later, of the first ten amendments that the American Bill of Rights contained.

Alexander Hamilton, justifying the absence of a Bill of Rights in the Constitution, said:

> That bill of rights, in the sense and to the extent in which they are contended for, are not only unnecessary in the proposed Constitution, but would even be dangerous. They would contain various exceptions to powers not granted; and, on this very account, would afford a colourable pretext to claim more than were granted.

He finished his argument by asking:

> For why declare that things shall not be done which there is no power to do?[455]

This concept of rights as limitations of state powers was followed in the first ten amendments of the constitution but adding to it the concept of rights as natural rights of man established in the Declaration of Independence 1776. They both influenced all the formal and entrenched declarations of human rights that were adopted later, particularly the French Declaration of Rights of Man and the Citizen, (1789), and through the latter, the Latin American declarations, up to the present, where those declarations have been internationalized.

However, De Tocqueville did not devote particular comments in his book to the declaration of rights, undoubtedly, because by the time he visited America, the French Declaration of 1789 was already famous and unique. Nevertheless, he referred to specific rights, particularly important in North America like equality, freedom of press and political association,[456] and not always with complete acceptance. For instance, referring to freedom of press, he said:

> I admit that I do not feel toward freedom of the press that complete and instantaneous love which one accords to things by their nature supremely good. I love it more from considering the evils it prevents than on account of the good it does.[457]

North American Independence (1776) and the North American constitution (1787) were the immediate results of a great revolution that gave birth to a new state; but at the same time they brought about an authentic revolution in the area of political and constitutional institutions in the world, giving rise to new forms of government and political acts. After the American Revolution, written constitutions, republicanism and sovereignty of the people, federal states, separation of powers in a system of check and balance, presidentialism and judicial review, were all new institutions that spread throughout the world. In the first place, they influenced definitively the shape of Latin American constitutionalism that began to develop twenty years afterwards.

---

455   See A. Hamilton, in *The Federalist* (ed. B.F. Wright), Cambridge, Mass 1961, n° 84, p. 535.
456   See A De Tocqueville, A. De Tocqueville, *op. cit.*, pp. 222, 232.
457   *Idem*, p. 222.

Alexis De Tocqueville was the first European rose in the European continental system of law to study the importance and impact of the American Revolution one hundred and fifty years ago and led the way to major transformations of constitutional institutions in Europe. That is why we consider that we can still say today the same as John Stuart Mill wrote in 1840 about De Tocqueville's Democracy in America, in the sense that it was not only "the first philosophical book ever written on democracy as it manifests itself in modern society", but it was also a book that marked "the beginning of a new era in the scientific study of politics."[458]

Its influence all over the world, therefore, has been outstanding not only because of the book itself, but also because its aim was to study the American institutions that contributed the most to the shaping of modern constitutionalism.[459]

458 See J.S. Mill, *The Edinburgh Review*, October 1840, n° CXLV, p. 3, quoted by J.P. MAYER, "Tocqueville's Democracy in America: Reception and Reputation", in A. DE TOCQUEVILLE, *op. cit.*, Vol. I, p. XIX.

459 See for example, the references to the influence of De Tocquwville book regarding judicial review in México, in R.D. BAKER, *Judicial Review in México. A Study of the Amparo Suit*, Austin 1971, p. 15.

ÍNDICE GENERAL

CHAPTER III

THE 1999 VENEZUELAN CONSTITUTION-MAKING
PROCESS AND THE FRAMING OF AN AUTHORITARIAN
POLITICAL REGIME (2002)

CHAPTER V
GLOBAL VALUES IN THE VENEZUELAN CONSTITUTION: SOME PRIORITIZATIONS AND SEVERAL INCONGRUENCES

CHAPTER VII
THE IMPACT OF THE AUTHORITARIAN GOVERNMENT

CHAPTER VIII

THE CENTRALIZATION OF POWER IN A
"CENTRALIZED FEDERATION" (2004)

CHAPTER IX

CHAPTER X

CHAPTER XI

THE CONSOLIDATION OF AUTHORITARIANISM IN
DEFRAUDATION OF DEMOCRACY (2007)

CHAPTER XIII

THE INTERNATIONAL POLITICAL PERSECUTION OF DISSIDENTS BY THE AUTHORITARIAN GOVERNMENT, AND ITS STOPPAGE THROUGH GLOBAL ADMINISTRATIVE LAW PROCEDURE PROVISIONS (2010)

PART THREE

THE LACK OF INDEPENDENCE OF THE JUDICIARY AND

CHAPTER XIV

DISMANTLING THE RULE OF LAW: THE POLITICAL

CHAPTER XV

OVERVIEW ON THE LACK OF AUTHONOMY AND

CHAPTER XVI

THE CITIZEN'S ACCESS TO CONSTITUTIONAL JURISDICTION:

SPECIAL REFERENCE TO THE VENEZUELAN SYSTEM OF

CHAPTER XVII

THE ILLEGITIMATE JUDICIAL MUTATION OF THE

CHAPTER XVIII

CHAPTER XIX

PART FOUR

THE CONSTITUTIONAL ECONOMIC SYSTEM AND ITS

CHAPTER XX

CHAPTER XXII

THE IMPOSITION OF A SOCIALIST (COMUNIST)
ECONOMIC SYSTEM BY STATUTE, WITHOUT REFORMING
THE CONSTITUTION (2011)

PART FIFTH

CHAPTER XXVIII

THE SITUATION OF THE VENEZUELAN STATE AFTER THE
APRIL 2013 PRESIDENTIAL ELECTIONS: THE CHÁVEZ'S

PART SIXTH

**REFLEXIONS ON THE ORIGINS OF
CONSTITUTIONALISM IN VENEZUELA AT

www.ingramcontent.com/pod-product-compliance
Lightning Source LLC
Chambersburg PA
CBHW052127020426
42334CB00023B/2631